HANDBOOK OF RESEARCH ON THE EDUCATION OF YOUNG CHILDREN

HANDBOOK OF RESEARCH ON THE EDUCATION OF YOUNG CHILDREN

SECOND EDITION

EDITED BY

BERNARD SPODEK
University of Illinois

OLIVIA N. SARACHO
University of Maryland

LEA LAWRENCE ERLBAUM ASSOCIATES, PUBLISHERS
2006 Mahwah, New Jersey   London

Senior Acquisitions Editor:	Naomi Silverman
Assistant Editor:	Erica Kica
Cover Design:	Tomai Maridou
Textbook Production Manager:	Paul Smolenski
Full-Service Compositor:	TechBooks
Text and Cover Printer:	Victor Graphics

This book was typeset in 9/11 pt. ITC Garamond Roman, Bold, and Italic.
The heads were typeset in Novarese, Novarese Medium, and Novarese Bold Italic.

Lawrence Erlbaum Associates, Inc., Publishers
10 Industrial Avenue
Mahwah, New Jersey 07430
www.erlbaum.com

Library of Congress Cataloging-in-Publication Data

Handbook of research on the education of young children / edited by Bernard
  Spodek, Olivia N. Saracho.—2nd ed.
      p.   cm.
  Includes bibliographical references and indexes.
  ISBN 0-8058-4720-0 (casebound : alk. paper)—ISBN 0-8058-4721-9 (pbk. : alk. paper)
    1. Child development.   2. Early childhood education—Curricula.   3. Early childhood education—Research.
  4. Child development—Research.   I. Spodek, Bernard.   II. Saracho, Olivia N.
    LB1119.H25   2006
    372.21′07′2—dc22

                                                            2005019445

Books published by Lawrence Erlbaum Associates are printed on
acid-free paper, and their bindings are chosen for strength and
durability.

Printed in the United States of America
10 9 8 7 6 5 4 3 2

CONTENTS

Part
I

EARLY CHILDHOOD EDUCATION AND CHILD DEVELOPMENT   7

Part
IV

RESEARCH AND EVALUATION STRATEGIES FOR EARLY
CHILDHOOD EDUCATION   441

EDITORIAL ADVISORY BOARD

ADDITIONAL REVIEWERS

Susan Adler, University of Illinois at Urbana-Champaign
Steve Asher, Duke University
Eurydice Bauer, University of Illinois at Urbana-Champaign
Joseph J. Becker, University of Illinois at Chicago
Liora Bresler, University of Illinois at Urbana-Champaign
Patricia Brown, Ball State University
Gail Canella, Arizona State University
Judith Chafel, Indiana University
Joyce Epstein, Johns Hopkins University
Beatrice S. Fenimore, Indiana University of Pennsylvania
Karen Ferdening, University of Illinois at Urban-Champaign
Barbara Finkelstein, University of Maryland
Susan Hendricks, University of Maryland
Susan Holloway, University of California–Berkeley
James Hoot, State University of New York at Buffalo
Fergus Hughes, University of Wisconsin-Green Bay
Mary Jensen, State University of New York-Geneseo
Janice Jipson, National Lewis University
James Johnson, Pennsylvania State University
Robert Kavanaugh, Williams College
Ferre Laevers, Katholic University of Leuven (Brussels)
Glenda MacNaughton, Melbourne University
Marie McCarthy, University of Maryland
Larry Nucci, University of Illinois at Chicago
Stuart Reifel, University of Texas
Karl Rosengren, University of Illinois at Urbana-Champaign
Robert Rueda, University of Southern California
Wendy Schiller, University of South Australia
Jon Shapiro, University of British Columbia
Lee Shumow, Northern Illinios University
X. Christine Wang, State University of New York at Buffalo
Nicola Yelland, Hong Kong Institute of Education

ABOUT THE CONTRIBUTORS

Martha Abbott-Shim, Professor Emeritus, Georgia State University, is Executive Director of Quality Counts, Inc., a non-profit research and evaluation corporation focusing on early childhood education. Her expertise includes assessment of young children and evaluation of early childhood learning environments and teaching practices. She received a M.Ed. in Tests and Measurement from Boston University and Ph.D. in Behavioral Sciences from the University of Michigan. Recent publications include: Abbott-Shim, M., Lambert, R., & McCarty, F. (2003). A comparison of school readiness outcomes for children randomly assigned to a Head Start program and the program's wait list. *Journal of Education for Students Placed at Risk, 8(2),* 191–214.

Jim Anderson is an associate professor in the Department of Language and Literacy Education at the University of British Columbia. He worked for 15 years as a classroom teacher, reading specialist, school principal, language arts consultant, and assistant superintendent of education. His research interests are in early literacy/family literacy. His latest publications include: Anderson, J., Kendrick, M., Rogers, T., & Smythe, S. (Eds.) (in press) *Portraits of literacy across families/communities/schools: Tensions and Intersections* and Anderson, A., Anderson, J. & Shapiro, J. (2004). Mathematical discourse in storybook reading. *Journal for Research in Mathematics Education, 35,* 5–33.

Rebecca K. Andrews is a doctoral student in psychology at Arizona State University. She completed her Bachelor's degree at Colorado State University. Her empirical work focuses on identifying how characteristics of children and adolescents—such as gender, behavioral style, and social-cognitive processes, and their environments, including differing types of relationship histories and relationship processes—are associated with their psychological development and adjustment.

Gina Barclay-McLaughlin is Associate Professor of Urban-Multicultural Teacher Education at the University of Tennessee, Knoxville. She earned a Ph.D. from the University of Michigan in 1995. Her research interests center on child poverty and contexts that influence development and learning. Dr. Barclay-McLaughlin is the author of a chapter in *Coping with Poverty: The Social Contexts of Neighborhood, Work, and Family in the African-American Community* (Danziger & Lin, 2000), in which she introduced the concept of "communal isolation." She is also co-author (with Susan Benner) of "Collaborating to Improve Literacy Outcomes" in *Academic Exchange Quarterly.*

Arthur J. Baroody is a Professor of Curriculum & Instruction at the University of Illinois at Urbana-Champaign. He received his Ph.D. in educational and developmental psychology from Cornell University. He is interested in studying the development of number, counting, and arithmetic concepts and skills by young children and those with learning difficulties. His most recent book is: Baroody, A. J., & Dowker, A. (Eds.) (2003). *The development of arithmetic concepts and skills: Constructing adaptive expertise* (Erlbaum).

Karen Kohn Bradley is Visiting Associate Professor of Dance and Director of Graduate Studies at the University of Maryland, College Park. She is on the Board of the National Dance Education Organization and Chair of the Board of Directors of the Laban/Bartenieff Institute of Movement Studies. Ms. Bradley reviewed the dance studies and wrote the essay on dance for the Arts Education Partnership's *Critical Links: Learning in the Arts and Student Academic and Social Development,* she was a chair of research for the National Dance Education Organization's Research in Dance Education project, and she has written several articles on dance education research.

Jeanne Brooks-Gunn is the Virginia and Leonard Marx Professor of Child Development and Education at Teachers College and the College of Physicians and Surgeons at Columbia University. Dr. Brooks-Gunn earned her Ph.D. in Developmental Psychology in 1975 from the University of Pennsylvania. Her research centers on designing and evaluating interventions and policies to enhance the well-being of children in poverty. She has authored over 400 published articles and 17 books and is the recipient of numerous awards, including the Urie Bronfenbrenner Award for lifetime contribution to developmental psychology in the areas of science and society from the American Psychoogical Association.

Bette Chambers is Vice-President of Development at the Success for All Foundation, where she directs the development of the early childhood, early literacy, evaluation, after-school, and technology programs. Dr. Chambers also directs the research and dissemination of the preschool, kindergarten, and technology programs. She received her B.A. in Early Childhood Education from Concordia University in 1981, and her Ph.D. in Educational Psychology in 1990 from McGill University. Dr. Chambers has authored or co-authored numerous articles, books, and practical guides for teachers, including *Let's Cooperate: Interactive*

Activities for Young Children and *Classroom Connections: Understanding and Using Cooperative Learning.*

Alan Cheung is currently an associate professor in the Department of Educational Policy and Administration at the Hong Kong Institute of Education. He received his Ph.D. in Education from Brigham Young University. Dr. Cheung has authored and co-authored over 40 professional publications, including book chapters, journal articles, technical reports, and creative works. His recent publications include A Synthesis of Research on Language of Reading Instruction for English Language Learners in Review of Educational Research and Effective early reading program for English language learners in Contemporary Perspectives on Early Childhood Education Series. His current research interests are early childhood education, bilingual education, effective reading strategies for English language learners, comprehensive school reform, computer-assisted learning, and private education.

Carl Corter is Director of the Institute of Child Study and Professor of Human Development and Applied Psychology at the Ontario Institute for Studies in Education, University of Toronto. He received his Ph.D. in 1971 from the University of North Carolina at Chapel Hill, in Developmental Psychology. He has led collaborations in teacher education and early childhood education between OISE/UT and the Hong Kong Institute of Education and the Aga Khan University in Pakistan. His research includes studies of kindergarten and early childhood programs as well as parenting and parental involvement in school and other services.

Tanya L. Eckert is an Associate Professor in the Department of Psychology at Syracuse University. She received her doctorate in School Psychology from Lehigh University. Currently, Dr. Eckert is an Associate Editor of *School Psychology Review.* Her research interests include examining factors related to successful school transitions for young children, developing classroom-based interventions to improve children's academic competence, and measuring the social validity of school-based procedures.

Rebecca C. Fauth is a Research Scientist at the National Center for Children and Families at Columbia University's Teachers College. She received her doctorate in Developmental Psychology from Columbia University in 2004. Her primary research interests are contextual influences, neighborhoods in particular, on child and family well-being. Her recent publications include The impacts of neighborhood poverty deconcentration efforts on low-income children and adolescents' well-being. *Children, Youth, and Environments, 14*(1), 1–55. and Short-term effects of moving from public housing in poor to middle-income neighborhoods on low-income, minority adults' outcomes. *Social Science and Medicine, 59*, 2271–2284, with T. Leventhal, & J. Brooks-Gunn,

Barbara H. Fiese is Professor and Chair of Psychology at Syracuse University. She received her doctorate in Clinical and Developmental Psychology from University of Illinois-Chicago. Currently, she is Associate Editor of the *Journal of Pediatric Psychology* and serves on the editorial boards of the *Journal of Family Psychology* and *Family Process.* Her current research

focuses on how family rituals may reduce the risks associated with childhood chronic illness and how representations of family life affect child development.

David L. Gallahue is Professor of Kinesiology and Dean of the School of Health, Physical Education, and Recreation at Indiana University. He received the Ed D degree from Temple University. Dr. Gallahue is active in the study of the motor development and movement skill learning of young children in physical activity and sport settings. He is the author of several textbooks, book chapters, and journal articles. His work has been translated into Spanish, Chinese, Japanese, Portuguese, and Greek. He has been a Visiting Professor, Guest Lecturer, and Keynote Speaker on over 200 occasions at universities and professional conferences in 18 countries.

Dr. Eugene E. García is Vice President for University-School Partnerships and Dean of the College of Education at Arizona State University. He received his Ph.D. in Human Development from the University of Kansas. He served as a Senior Officer in the U.S. Department of Education from 1993–1995. He chairs a National Task Force on Early Education for Hispanics funded by the Foundation for Child Development. His most recent books include, *Hispanic Education in the United States: Raíces y Alas,* and, *Student Cultural Diversity: Understanding and Meeting the Challenge*—both published in 2001. A new book, *Bilingualism and Schooling in the United States,* is in press (Teachers College Press).

Lisa S. Goldstein is an associate professor in the early childhood education program in the Department of Curriculum and Instruction at the University of Texas at Austin, where she also serves as the director of early childhood teacher education. A graduate of the Stanford University School of Education, Lisa is the author of a number of scholarly works focusing on early childhood/elementary teaching practices and on the preparation of early childhood/elementary teachers, including *Teaching with Love: A Feminist Approach to Early Childhood Education, Reclaiming Caring in Teaching and Teacher Education,* and many journal articles.

Susan Grieshaber is an Associate Professor in the School of Early Childhood, Queensland University of Technology, Brisbane, Australia. She completed her PhD at James Cook University of North Queensland and has research interests that include early childhood curriculum, pedagogy, assessment, policy, and families, with a focus on equity and diversity. Recent books include Grieshaber, S. (2004) *Rethinking parent and child conflict,* published by Routledge/Falmer, New York; and Grieshaber, S. & Cannella, G. S. (Eds.) (2001) *Embracing identities in early childhood education: Diversity and possibilities,* published by Teachers College Press, New York.

Dominic Gullo is professor of Elementary and Early Childhood Education at Queens College, City University of New York and a member of the Doctoral Faculty at the City University of New York Graduate Center. He received his doctorate from Indiana University. He taught prekindergarten and kindergarten and in Head Start. He is the author of three books, including *Understanding Assessment and Evaluation in Early Childhood*

Education 2/ed (Teachers College Press) and over 75 research-based publications. His research interests include studying the relative effects and long-range effects of full-day kindergarten and prekindergarten on children's achievement and social adaptation to school routine.

J. Amos Hatch is Professor of Theory and Practice in Teacher Education at the University of Tennessee. He is a qualitative researcher who earned his Ph.D. from the University of Florida. He has published widely in the areas of children's social relationships, teacher philosophies and practices, and teachers' work. He was co-executive editor of *Qualitative Studies in Education* for four years and has written or edited three books on qualitative research, including *Doing Qualitative Research in Education Settings* (SUNY Press, 2002), *Qualitative Research in Early Childhood Settings* (Praeger, 1995), and *Life History and Narrative* (Falmer, 1995).

Sarah L. Herald is a doctoral student in psychology at Arizona State University. She received her bachelor's degree at Slippery Rock University of Pennsylvania. Herald's research interests focus on children's social development. She is particularly interested in identifying how children's behavioral styles, in conjunction with the duration and quality of their peer relationships, impact children's scholastic achievement, engagement, and adjustment.

Susan Hill is employed at the University of South Australia in early childhood education. She completed her doctorate at the University of Illinois at Urbana–Champaign in early childhood education and literacy. She is interested in pedagogy and the organization of the literacy program. She has directed two national longitudinal studies into early literacy development in Australia titled *100 children go to school: Connections between literacy development in the prior to school period and the first year of formal schooling* (1998) and *100 children turn 10: A longitudinal study from the year prior to school to the first four years of school* (2002).

Blythe Hinitz is Professor and Coordinator of Early Childhood Education at The College of New Jersey. Her research interests include history of education; peace, anti-bullying, and human rights education; and social studies. Her most recent books are *History of Early Childhood Education* (with V. Celia Lascarides) (RoutledgeFalmer) and *Teaching Social Studies to the Young Child* (Garland). She is a board member of the World Organization for Early Childhood Education (OMEP)—U.S. National Committee, the National Association of Early Childhood Teacher Educators, and the Eastern Educational Research Association.

Carollee Howes is a Developmental Psychologist in the Department of Education at the University of California at Los Angeles. Her PhD is from Boston University. Dr. Howes conducts research on the development of social relationships with adults and peers. A recent book is *A Matter of Trust*, 2002, Teachers College Press.

Wu-ying Hsieh was an elementary school teacher for 7 years in Taiwan before attending graduate school. She is currently a doctoral candidate in the Department of Special Education at the University of Illinois at Urbana-Champaign, with a focus in early childhood special education (ECSE). Her research interests include ECSE teacher preparation, inclusive education, and early literacy.

Eva Johansson, Ph.D. is associate professor of education in the Department of Childhood Studies, Göteborg University, Sweden. She is engaged in questions on moral learning in early childhood education, including studies on how children experience and develop morality and how teachers approach such issues in their work. Her research also includes studies on quality aspects in preschool and as well as on the relation between play and learning. She has published several books and articles for instance: *Morality in Children's Worlds—Rationality of Thought or Values Emanating from Relations?* (2001), *Morality in Preschool Interaction: Teachers' Strategies for Working with Children's Morality* (2002).

Robert D. Kavanaugh obtained his Ph.D. in psychology at Boston University in 1974. Following a two-year postdoctoral fellowship at the Fels Research Institute, he joined the faculty at Williams College where he is currently Hales Professor of Psychology. Professor Kavanaugh teaches courses on developmental psychology and cognitive development, and is involved in research on the development of pretend play, imagination, and theory of mind.

Gary W. Ladd is Professor of Psychology and of Family and Human Development at Arizona State University. Previously, he was at Purdue University and the University of Illinois at Urbana-Champaign and was a Fellow at the Center for Advanced Studies in the Behavioral Sciences at Stanford University. Ladd was Associate Editor of *Child Development* and the *Journal of Social and Personal Relationships*, and currently is Editor of *Merrill-Palmer Quarterly*. He is widely published in the area of children's social development. As a researcher, Ladd is interested in how socialization experiences with peers, parents, and teachers influence children's early psychological and school adjustment.

Meng-lung Lai is a doctoral student at the University of Illinois at Urbana-Champaign where he received his masters degree. His research interests include early childhood and elementary mathematics education. His recent publication is: Baroody, A., Cibulskis, M., Lai, M., & Li, X. (2004). Comments on the use of learning trajectories in curriculum development and research. *Mathematical Thinking and Learning, 6*(2), 227–260.

Richard G. Lambert is an Associate Professor in the Department of Educational Leadership at the University of North Carolina at Charlotte where he teaches graduate courses in statistics and research methods. He completed his doctorate in research, measurement and statistics at Georgia State University. His research interests include evaluating programs for young children, applied statistics, and teacher stress and coping.

Bernadette Laumann has been a child care teacher, early childhood special education teacher, an early childhood program administrator, and is currently an instructor and doctoral student in the Department of Special Education at the University of Illinois at Urbana-Champaign. Her research interests are in the area of early childhood education and special education teacher preparation especially as it relates to inclusive settings.

Aysegul Metindogan is a doctoral candidate in Child and Family Studies at Syracuse University. Her research interests include social cognition and moral development across cultures.

Kelly S. Mix is an Assistant Professor at Indiana University. She received her Ph.D. in developmental psychology from the University of Chicago. Her research focuses on early number and arithmetic development. She received the Boyd McCandless Award (American Psychological Association) for distinguished contribution to developmental psychology in 2003. Her recent publications include: Mix, K. S., Huttenlocher, J., & Levine, S. C. (2002). *Quantitative development in infancy and early childhood* (Oxford University Press).

Lyndsay Moffatt is a doctoral student at the University of British Columbia. Her research interests include socio-cultural theories of learning and literacy and the sociology of education. Her recent publications include . Mac Kay, R. & L. Moffatt "The Performance of Self in Children's Drawings of Home and School Literacies" in J. Anderson, M. Kendrick, & S. Smythe (eds.) *Portraits of literacy: Critical issues in family, community and school literacies* (Erlbaum) and Moffatt, L. & B. Norton "Popular culture and the reading teacher: A case for a new feminist pedagogy" in *Critical Inquiry in Language Studies: An International Journal.*

Susan Nichols is a researcher at the Centre for Literacy Policy and Learning Cultures at the University of South Australia, where she completed her doctorate, a study of parents' understandings of their children's literacy development. She has contributed to several significant longitudinal ethnographic studies of children's literacy learning across home and school sites and is interested in the interplay of language, culture, gender, age and power relations. She recently edited an issue of the Australian Journal of Language and Literacy on the theme *Questioning Development* and published chapters in *Look again: longitudinal studies of children's literacy learning* (2004) and *Text next: new resources for literacy learning* (2004).

John C. Ozmun is Professor and Chair of the Department of Physical Education at Indiana State University. He received his doctorate from Indiana University with major areas in Motor Development and Adapted Physical Education. Dr. Ozmun is active in the study of early childhood motor development and physical fitness. He is the co-author of *Understanding Motor Development: Infants, Children, Adolescents, Adults*, and has authored or co-authored several book chapters and journal articles. He has made numerous scholarly presentations in the area of early childhood motor development at the national and international levels.

Michaelene M. Ostrosky is an Associate Professor of Early Childhood Special Education at the University of Illinois at Urbana-Champaign. She completed her Ph.D. at Vanderbilt University. Her research interests focus on young children's social-emotional and communication skills, transitions, and personnel preparation. She is committed to translating research into practice, creating the Division for Early Childhood's practitioner

journal, *Young Exceptional Children*. Her publications: include (with Sandall, S. co-editor), *Teaching strategies: What to do to support young children's development*. Sopris West (2001), and (with Turan, Y., Halle, J. W., & DeStefano, L) Acceptability of language interventions: A comparison of preschool and elementary teachers' responses. *Journal of Early Intervention, 26*, 221–233 (2004).

Janette Pelletier is Assistant Professor at the Institute of Child Study and the Department of Human Development and Applied Psychology at the Ontario Institute for Studies in Education, University of Toronto. She is a former kindergarten and primary teacher and received her Ph.D. from the University of Toronto in Applied Psychology with a focus on Early Childhood Education. Research includes: Early Development of Print Understanding, School Readiness for Diverse Families, Family Literacy, Lesson Study Approaches to Reading Comprehension, and Toronto First Duty, an early childhood research and development project combining kindergarten, childcare and parenting services on school sites.

Patricia G. Ramsey is professor of psychology and education at Mount Holyoke College. She is a former preschool and kindergarten teacher and received her Ed.D. from University of Massachusetts at Amherst. She has studied the development of children's attitudes about race and social class and has written articles on this research. She is the author of *Teaching and Learning in a Diverse World: Multicultural Education for Young Children*, 3rd ed. and *Making Friends in School: Promoting Peer Relationships in Early Childhood* (both with Teachers College Press).

Jaipaul L. Roopnarine completed his Ph.D. at the University of Wisconsin. He is Professor of Child Development at Syracuse University. His research interests include father-child relationships across cultures; Caribbean immigrant families and schooling; early childhood education in international perspectives; globalization and childhood; and children's play across cultures. He was Indo-U.S. senior Professor of Psychology at the University of New Delhi, a Visiting scholar at the University of the West Indies in Jamaica. His recent books include *Approaches to Early Childhood Education*, 4th Ed. Merrill/Prentice Hall), *Families in Global Perspective* (Allyn & Bacon), and *Childhood and Adolescence* (Praeger).

Robert Rueda is a professor in the areas of Educational Psychology and Language, Literacy, and Learning at the Rossier School of Education at the University of Southern California. He completed his doctoral work at the University of California at Los Angeles in Educational Psychology and Special Education, and completed a postdoctoral fellowship at the Laboratory of Comparative Human Cognition at the University of California, San Diego. His research has focused on sociocultural issues in learning and motivation, with a focus reading and literacy in English learners, students in at-risk conditions, and students with mild learning handicaps.

Mark A. Runco received his Ph.D. in Cognitive Psychology from the Claremont Graduate School. He is currently Professor of Child and Adolescent Studies at California State University,

Fullerton, and adjunct at the Norwegian School of Economics and Business Administration and the Saybrook Institute. He is Editor of the *Creativity Research Journal* and Fellow and Past President of Division 10 of the American Psychological Association.

Rebecca M. Ryan is a Graduate Research Fellow at the National Center for Children and Families at Columbia University's Teachers College. She received her Masters in Education in Human Development from the Harvard Graduate School of Education in 1998 and is currently a doctoral candidate in Developmental Psychology at Teachers College, Columbia University. Her primary research interests include marriage and father involvement and the impact of these family factors on child well-being. Her recent publications include: Low-income fathers' involvement in their toddlers' lives: Biological fathers from the Early Head Start Research and Evaluation Study. *Fathering, 2004, 2, 5-31.*

Sharon Ryan is assistant professor at Rutgers, the State University of New Jersey. She received her doctorate from Teachers College, Columbia University. Her dissertation used post-structural theory to explore student choice in a kindergarten classroom. Dr. Ryan's research interests are early childhood curriculum and policy, equitable approaches to educating young students, and the use of critical theories for rethinking early childhood practices. She has co-written several articles with Susan Grieshaber exploring the links between postmodernism and early childhood education including "It's more than child development: Critical theories, research, and teaching young children," and "Shifting from developmental to postmodern practices in early childhood teacher education."

Kay Sanders is a doctoral student in the Psychological Studies Program in the Department of Education at the University of California at Los Angeles.

Olivia N. Saracho is Professor of Education in the Department of Curriculum and Instruction at the University of Maryland. Her areas of scholarship include family literacy, cognitive style, teaching, and teacher education in early childhood education. Dr. Saracho was co-editor of the *Yearbook in Early Childhood Education* Series (Teachers College Press). Currently she is coeditor of the *Contemporary Perspectives in Early Childhood Education* series (Information Age Publishers). Dr. Saracho's most recent books are *Contemporary Perspectives on Play in Early Childhood Education, Studying Teachers in Early Childhood Settings* and *Contemporary Perspectives on Language Policy and Literary Instruction in Early Childhood Education*, co-edited with Bernard Spodek (Information Age Publishers).

Jon Shapiro is professor of Language and Literacy Education and Associate Dean in the Faculty of Education at the University of British Columbia. His research interests are in early literacy, affective dimensions of literacy and family literacy. His research has been published in journals in the United States, Canada and Great Britain. He is currently completing two projects examining how parents from different cultural groups mediate print literacy and mathematics with their preschool aged children and the effects of a culturally sensitive family literacy program on parents and their children in inner-city British Columbia schools.

Annette Sibley is President of Quality Assist, Inc. an Atlanta-based educational consulting firm. She completed her doctorate in Early Childhood Education at Georgia State University. She has focused her career on providing technical assistance and consultation based on the formative evaluation of early education settings. Dr. Sibley is particularly interested in translating theory and research into practical solutions that improve early education. She designs and implements innovative solutions and strategies to address the recurring challenges of early education.

Robert Slavin is Director of the Center for Data-Driven Reform in Education at Johns Hopkins University and Chairman of the Success for All Foundation. He received his B.A. in Psychology from Reed College in 1972, and his Ph.D. in Social Relations in 1975 from Johns Hopkins University. Dr. Slavin has authored or co-authored more than 200 articles and 20 books, including *Educational Psychology: Theory into Practice* (Allyn & Bacon, 2003) and *One Million Children: Success for All* (Corwin, 2001). He has received awards from the American Educational Research Association, the Education Commission of the States, and the Council of Chief State School Officers.

Mary Spagnola is a doctoral student in Clinical Psychology at Syracuse University. She is the recipient of a Head Start Dissertation Scholar award. Her research focuses on children's narratives of family life and adjustment of children raised in high-risk conditions.

Bernard Spodek is Professor Emeritus of Early Childhood Education at the University of Illinois. He began in 1952 as an early childhood teacher in the New York City area. He received his doctorate from Teachers College, Columbia University. His research and scholarly interests are in the areas of curriculum, teaching, and teacher education in early childhood education. He was President of the National Association for the Education of Young Children (1976–78) and is currently President of the Pacific Early Childhood Education Research Association. Bernard Spodek was co-editor with Olivia N. Saracho of the *Yearbook in Early Childhood Education* Series (Teachers College Press). They are currently co-editors of the *Contemporary Perspectives in Early Childhood Education* series (Information Age Publishers).

John A. Sutterby obtained a Ph.D. in Curriculum and Instruction from the University of Texas at Austin. He is currently an assistant professor at the University of Texas at Brownsville in early childhood and bilingual education. His research interests include outdoor play environments, children's play in bilingual settings, bilingual teacher preparation and parent involvement. He is a co-author of *The developmental benefits of playgrounds*, with Joe L. Frost, Pei-San Brown and Candra Thornton.

Mary Szegda is a candidate for the Master of Fine Arts degree in Dance at the University of Maryland, College Park. She is also a Registered Dance-Movement Therapist and a licensed massage therapist and is training to be a practitioner of the Feldenkrais™ method.

Christine Marmé Thompson is an Associate Professor in the School of Visual Arts at the Pennsylvania State University, where she is in charge of art education. Professor Thompson earned her Ph.D. in art education at The University of Iowa in 1985, and taught at the University of Illinois at Urbana-Champaign from 1985–2001. Her research focuses on the process of learning to draw in early childhood classrooms, as it is shaped by peers, popular culture, and individual interests. She is the co-editor, with Liora Bresler, of *The Arts in Children's Lives: Context, Culture, and Curriculum* (2002).

Candra D. Thornton is an assistant professor in the early childhood education program in the Department of Curriculum and Teaching at Auburn University. She received her PhD from the University of Texas at Austin. Her research interests include feminist theory, ethical issues of pre-service teachers, and children's play. She is author of "Feminism: Fighting sexist oppression in early childhood education" in the *Early Childhood Education* encyclopedia (New and Cochran, Eds.) and co-author of *The developmental benefits of playgrounds* with Frost, Brown, and Sutterby.

Ann-Marie Wiese is currently a Research Associate with the Teacher Professional Development Program at WestEd. She earned her Ph.D. in Education, specializing in Language, Literacy, and Culture from UC Berkeley. Her research interests include educational policy, bilingual education, and early childhood education as they relate to language minority students. Her most recent publication on two-way immersion programs appears in the international journal *Language and Education, 18*(1). She also has a forthcoming publication in Teachers College Record on the use of ethnographic methods in bilingual educational policy research.

Graham Welch (Ph.D. London) holds the University of London Established Chair of Music Education at the Institute of Education, and is Head of the Institute's School of Arts and Humanities. He is Chair of the Society for Education, Music and Psychology Research (SEMPRE), recent past Co-Chair of the Research Commission of the International Society for Music Education (ISME) and holds Visiting Professorships at the Universities of Sydney, Limerick and Roehampton. Research and publications embrace a variety of aspects of musical development and music education, teacher education, psychology of music, singing and voice science, special education and disability.

HANDBOOK OF RESEARCH ON THE EDUCATION OF YOUNG CHILDREN

INTRODUCTION: A RESEARCHER'S VADE MECUM

Bernard Spodek
University of Illinois

Olivia N. Saracho
University of Maryland

Society has acknowledged the importance of young children's learning. This is evident in the increases in enrollments in early childhood education programs. It is also evident in the increases in early childhood teacher education program at the community college and university level. Parallel to this growth has been the increase in knowledge generating activities in the field, part of which might be attributed to the general knowledge explosion in our society and throughout the world. Evidence of this can be seen in the increase of research activities in the field and the growth of research journals and research associations (Spodek & Saracho, 2003).

This explosion of knowledge and the related increase in research results related to early childhood education that are available requires that this knowledge be more available and readily accessible to the field. This requirement led earlier to the publication of the first edition of the *Handbook of Research on the Education of Young Children* and now to the creation of this second edition. The *Handbook* can be a valuable tool to all who work and study in the field. Thus, the *Handbook* can be referred to as a *vade mecum* (a ceaseless companion) that focuses on important contemporary issues in early childhood education and that provides the information necessary to make judgments about these issues.

KNOWLEDGE OF EARLY CHILDHOOD EDUCATION

Knowledge of the field of early childhood education is of three kinds: theory, research and practice. Although these spheres often seem independent of one another, they are interrelated. The process of knowledge generation is *cyclical*, rather than being deductive (top down) or linear (one step always follows another). The forms all overlap. The process usually begins with a problem or issue that needs to be studied through research; this research is driven by theory and practice. The results also contribute to theory and practice, which then provide directions for future research studies. This cyclical process is presented in Figure 1.1.

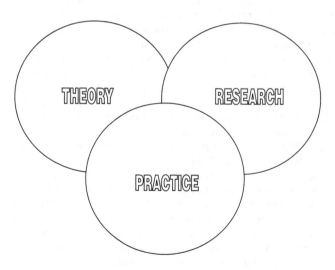

FIGURE 1.1. Interaction process.

This *Handbook* focuses on research conducted over the past decade or so. The decision to focus on the most recent was made so that there would be minimum overlap with the work presented in the first edition of the *Handbook*. The editors recognize that this is a limitation. They also acknowledge, as they have noted elsewhere, that our current research is only possible because of the theoretical work and the research studies that have been done in the past. We very much "stand on the shoulders of giants" (Spodek & Saracho, 2003). However, as a field, we have seen a significant amount of new theory building as well and the development and use of new research paradigms to study early childhood education. These are acknowledged here. Current social and historical circumstances also have aroused a more dynamic focus on the potential practical improving teaching techniques and raising the children's educational and intellectual status. Empirical investigations in these problem areas have contributed to both practical and theoretical underpinnings. By using knowledge generated in the past along with knowledge that is being generated in the contemporary scene, we can best understand early childhood education and serve the teachers and children engaged in it.

HISTORY OF EARLY CHILDHOOD EDUCATION

The field of early childhood education has a history of more than 150 years. The first educational programs in the United States that were specifically designed for young children were *infant schools*. This program was based on the ideas that Robert Owen had developed in Scotland (Owen, 1824). Even before Owen himself came to America, his ideas had crossed the ocean. Infant schools were established in a number of communities in the eastern United States during the first quarter of the 19th century. These programs did not flourish for long. The infant school educated young children separately from their families. The idea of educating young children outside the home was counter to the family ethic of the time (Strickland, 1983).

Later, German immigrants brought the *kindergarten*, created by Freidrich Froebel in Germany, to the United States. The kindergarten slowly expanded in the United States, sponsored by various organizations to serve a number of purposes in addition to educating young children. By the late 19th century, kindergartens began to be incorporated into public school systems (Shapiro, 1983). Today, kindergartens are part of public elementary schools throughout the United States and almost all 5-year-olds go to kindergarten

Other approaches to early childhood education were imported to the United States in the first quarter of the 20th century. The *nursery school*, which originated in England with Margaret Macmillan at the beginning of the 20th century to serve low-income children and their families, was soon established in America. The *Montessori method*, which originated in Italy, was brought to the United States after World War I, although these schools closed during the Great Depression of the 1930s. However, the movement was resurrected in the late 1950s and early 1960s.

The nature of the early childhood programs evolved over the years. Nursery schools and Montessori schools, which were originally designed to serve children of poor families, became programs for more affluent families in America. Kindergarten, which was originally Froebelian, was influenced by American progressive education and reconstructed to become the American kindergarten we can observe today. Even now changes are taking place. Kindergartens, essentially part of the elementary school in America, have been influenced by the program of the primary grades, and at the same time have influenced the program of the primary grade. Today, American kindergartens are more academically oriented, especially since the recent Federal *No Child Left Behind* Act (2001) was passed. In addition to the original Montessori method, a modified method was developed in the United States supported by the American Montessori Society. Similar changes have taken place in other approaches to early childhood education. The changes that have taken place over the years were the result of many influences, but were little influenced by research over the years.

The changes in early childhood programs took place as programs originally developed in other countries were modified to better fit into American society. In addition, as American society has changed, program for young children also have changed. Seldom were early childhood education programs modified by recourse to research, however, until the 1960s.

EARLY CHILDHOOD EDUCATION RESEARCH

Research in early childhood education has had a much shorter history than practice. It seems that research in early childhood education follows practice; a strong foundation of practice was needed before research became established in the field. Until about 50 years ago, the only research on young children was research in child development, even though the field of early childhood education is older than the field of child development. Although universities often established "laboratory nursery schools" on their campuses, these often served to provide "laboratory experiences" for students in child development, home economics and education or to provide research subjects for studies of child development. Seldom were these laboratory nursery schools used to inquire into the nature and consequences of the educational process for young children or as a way of testing new curriculum ideas in early childhood education.

Only in the late 1950s and early 1960s did we see moves toward establishing a research base that was specifically in early childhood education. The impetus came from several major changes: changes in developmental psychology, a concern for America's national defense, and a concern for social justice. For years in America, the maturationist theory of Arnold Gesell and his followers was the accepted theory in child development. This theory posited that most human attributes were determined genetically and were therefore fixed at birth. It was believed that one could thwart developmental attributes by not providing a proper environment, but one could not increase a person's intelligence or modify any other such attribute than make her or him taller. Thus, any attempt to increase the intelligence of individuals or change any other attribute was futile. Academic learning was the domain of the elementary and secondary school. The nursery school and kindergarten were designed to keep children healthy and safe so that their genetic makeup would unfold. Readiness was a naturally occurring maturational process. Real education, it was believed, began in the primary grades, when children were taught to read.

This changed when new English translations of the work of Jean Piaget reached our shore. The arguments regarding the impact of environment were further supported when J. McVicker Hunt, an American psychologist, pulled together a range of studies supporting this notion in a book that had a major impact on psychology and education: *Intelligence and Experience* (1961). Others further argued that preschool experiences could have a greater impact on human development than experiences provided to children later in life (Bloom, 1964). In addition, behavioral psychologists were arguing that environmental conditions could shape human development (Bijou, 1977). It was further found that children growing up in poverty suffered from significant environmental deficiencies that impacted on their learning and development. By offering these children early educational experiences, it was argued, society might be able to ameliorate the consequences of poverty—and ultimately even eliminate poverty.

A second influence was the consequence of the Soviet Union's space efforts. When the Soviets launched orbiting rockets in the 1950s, well before our own space program got underway, there was a concern that we were losing the Cold War and that Soviet technology was overshadowing our own. As a result, there was a press to improve the education of children and youth in our schools. This led to the enactment of the National Defense Education Act, designed to improve public education in America. Teachers were provided with additional education to increase their competence. In addition, a series of curriculum development projects were launched to improve elementary and secondary education. These projects were designed to bring the subject matter of the school more closely in line with the knowledge that scholars in the various fiends were currently developing.

These projects, in science, mathematics, social studies, and language, were focused on the education of children from kindergarten up. Among the products of the curriculum research projects were materials from the *Elementary Science Study* (1970). Three innovative science programs, which were developed and tested as part of the curriculum reform movement, began at the kindergarten level. The first two of these programs used Piagetian theory to justify the design of their activities. The third used a behavioral approach. Each of them ran counter to the uses of kindergarten suggested by the maturationist theorists of child development, who saw kindergarten primarily as either a place for children to adjust to the rigors of the elementary school or a place that supported the development of children's readiness for school learning.

The third influence was the concern for social justice in America. In many ways, early childhood education had been historically linked to a concern for social justice, as the history of the kindergarten movement showed. Kindergartens early on were used as a way to ameliorate the damages to children caused by poverty or to deal with other social ills impacting on children (Shapiro, 1983). This influence was further felt as President Lyndon Johnson established the Head Start program as part of his War on Poverty. Even before the creation of Head Start, a number of research projects, funded by educational foundations, had been developed to test the influence of different curriculums on the development of children from low-income families. These various programs were based on different assumptions about what might be considered an effective early education. (See Spodek, 1973, for a description of these program assumptions.)

These early research projects were the basis later for a major national study of Head Start programs called the Planned Variations project—an attempt to compare the outcomes of different approaches to early education in terms of children's intelligence and school success. These outcomes were to prove which curriculum was most effective for young children. Unfortunately, the evaluation of the outcomes of these various projects were controversial and no "one best system" prevailed. However, the idea that various early educational curriculums can be tested in practice and that various aspects of early childhood education are worthy of study led to a growth in research relating to early education in the United States. In addition, various research studies were undertaken to test the impact of Head Start on children's learning and development. It can be argued that this was the beginning of early childhood educational research in the United States.

CONDITIONS THAT SUPPORT EARLY CHILDHOOD EDUCATION RESEARCH

There are a number of conditions that are necessary for research in a field to flourish. There needs to be a place where research will be nurtured or at least allowed to develop. There needs to be a cadre of well-trained researchers who are knowledgeable of their field. There needs to be financial support for research to be conducted. And there needs to be a way for researchers to share their work—to communicate with one another and with others—practitioners, administrators, and policy makers. These conditions would slowly develop in America.

The majority of research in the United States is conducted in universities. After World War II, many of the state teachers' colleges expanded to become multipurpose colleges and finally full-fledged universities. Thus, a number of venues were created in which research could flourish and there was an increase in the output of research in this era, but not in early childhood education.

However, early childhood education was a small field well into the 1960s. There were no public kindergartens for children in the southeast or the central parts of the United States.

There were few early childhood teacher-training programs in colleges or universities at that time; community colleges were not yet established. Starting in the 1970, there was an expansion of kindergarten education as well as an expansion of the entire field of early childhood education. With that came the establishment and expansion of early childhood education programs in colleges and universities. As that happened, doctoral programs in early childhood education also grew and as did the number of Ph.D.s in early childhood education, trained in research, as one of the requirement of such a program was a dissertation. In addition, most universities require that their faculty engage in research and that the research be published.

Although the production of research in early childhood education increased in the United States, the vehicles for disseminating that research were limited. Over the past years, both American organizations began to sponsor research journals: The *Early Childhood Research Quarterly*, sponsored by the National Association for the Education of Young Children (NAEYC) and published originally by Ablex and currently by Elsevier began publication in 1986. The *Journal of Research in Childhood Education* published by the Association of Childhood Education International (ACEI) began publication at the same time. Additional journals related to research in early childhood education have developed over the year, such as *Early Education and Development* whereas other journals, such as *Early Childhood Education*, have become more scholarly and research-oriented.

There were two other organizations that have served to disseminate research in early childhood education. One of these is the Society for Research in Child Development (SRCD). This organization focuses primarily on child development research and has paid less attention to early childhood education in recent years, both in its journal and in its conference programs. The other organization is the American Educational Research Association (AERA). In addition to sponsoring a number of journals, AERA holds an annual conference. Its divisions and its Special Interest Groups (SIGs) determine the content of that conference. Many early childhood studies are presented in sessions sponsored by divisions B and C (*Curriculum Studies* and *Learning and Instruction*) of the organization. Most important, there are two SIGs that are specifically devoted to early childhood education: the *Early Education and Child Development* SIG and the *Critical Perspectives in Early Childhood Education* SIG. In addition, the conference of the National Association for the Education of Young Children includes a research track. Thus, there have been avenues for the reporting of research and these have increased in the recent past.

The *Handbook of Research in Early Childhood Education* (Spodek, 1982) and the *Handbook of Research on the Education of Young Children* (Spodek, 1993) were developed to bring together in one source the research available at that time in early childhood education. Because the field has changed significantly since 1993, there is a need for an update of these handbooks, as well as one that focuses primarily on studies conducted the last decade of scholarly activity in the field. Hence, the need for this volume.

ORGANIZATION OF THE CURRENT VOLUME

This handbook is organized into four parts: Early Childhood Education and Child Development, Early Childhood Educational Curriculum, Foundations of Early Childhood Educational Policy, and Research and Evaluation Strategies for Early Childhood Education. This is very similar to the sections of the first edition. Although some of the chapters cover the same areas of research and, in a few cases, the authors are the same, all the material in this edition is new. In addition, some areas that were covered in the first edition of the *Handbook* are not covered here, whereas new areas are covered.

In the section on child development and early childhood education, we now have chapters on moral development and on the development of creativity. These are areas of increasing importance in our study of early childhood education.

In the section on curriculum, we have added sections on movement education or dance and on the education of linguistically and culturally diverse children. We have not included chapters on curriculum development, science, social studies, or the use of the electronic media, as there has been relatively little research done in these areas in the last decade.

The section on foundations of policy includes chapters on childhood poverty and the education of bilingual children in addition to areas covered in the first edition. The other chapters also have been reconceptualized.

Our final section on research and evaluation strategies has several chapters on new topics. A chapter on studying history in early childhood education has been included. Additional chapters on postmodern orientations and feminist orientations in early childhood education also have been included as well. These are areas that are receiving and will continue to receive increased attention in our field.

In this edition of the *Handbook*, we included a number of new authors. Among those are scholars in early childhood education and related fields from countries other than the United States, including Australia, Canada, Great Britain, and Sweden. This provides some recognition that the study of early childhood education is not limited to our own country. Rather, it is an international endeavor.

A FINAL NOTE

In the first edition, we ended the introduction with the following paragraph. We believe it is as valid today as it was a decade ago:

A book such as this is often seen as more theoretical than practical. Although research studies educational practice, it seldom leads to the creation of educational practice. Yet research informs practice. By helping practitioners reflect on practice and assess their ideas about their work, the *Handbook* can suggest new visions or early childhood education. In this way it may be among the most practical of educational endeavors (Spodek, 1993, p. 6).

References

Bijou, S. W. (1977). Behavior analysis applied to early childhood education. In B. Spodek & H. J. Walberg (Eds.), *Early childhood education: Issues and insights*. Berkeley, CA: McCutheon.

Elementary Science Study (1970). *The ESS Reader.* Newton, MA: Educational Development Center.

Hunt, J. McV. (1961). *Experience and intelligence.* New York: Roland Press.

No Child Left Behind Act. Conference report to accompany H. R. Rep no. 107–334, 107th Congress, 1st session (2001).

Owen, R. D. (1824). *Outline of the system of education at New Lanark.* Glasgow: Wardlaw and Cunningham.

Shapiro, M. S. (1983). *Child's garden: The kindergarten movement from Froebel to Dewey.* University Park, PA: The Pennsylvania State University Press.

Spodek, B. (1973). *Early childhood education.* Englewood Cliffs, NJ: Prentice Hall.

Spodek, B. (Ed.) (1982). *Handbook of research in early childhood education.* New York: Free Press.

Spodek, B. (Ed.) (1993). *Handbook of research on the education of young children.* New York: Macmillan.

Spodek, B., & Saracho, O. N. (2003). On the shoulders of giants: Exploring the traditions of early childhood education. *Early Childhood Education Journal, 31*(1), 3–10.

Spodek, B., & Saracho, O. N. (2005). Introduction: Early childhood research and practice in international perspective. In B. Spodek & O. N. Saracho (Eds.), *International perspectives in research in early childhood education.* Greenwich, CT: Information Age Publishers.

Strickland, C. E. (1982). Paths not taken. In B. Spodek (Ed.), *Handbook of research in early childhood education*, pp. 321–340. New York: Free Press.

·I·

EARLY CHILDHOOD EDUCATION AND CHILD DEVELOPMENT

COGNITIVE DEVELOPMENT AND THE EDUCATION

OF YOUNG CHILDREN

Kelvin L. Seifert
University of Manitoba

This chapter is about how the cognitive development of young children can be affected by early childhood programs. It therefore does *not* describe everything that psychologists know or believe about cognitive development in young children. Others have already offered general overviews thoroughly and thoughtfully; see, for example, Volume 3 of the *Handbook of Child Psychology* (Mussen, Flavell, & Markman, 1998), or the more British-oriented volume *Childhood Cognitive Development* (Goswami, 2002a). Because I only have one chapter in which to work, I will be more selective about topics, focusing especially on matters central to preschool and primary education. Some readers may therefore find the chapter unbalanced, and may wonder why I have reduced or omitted topics that get more attention in other forums. Or they may wonder, by contrast, whether certain topics described in detail in this chapter really count as "cognitive development," as the topics sometimes get treated as noncognitive elsewhere. As the author, I take responsibility for any of these frustrations. But I will try to persuade how selectivity is not only appropriate but also is the cost of relevance to early childhood education. Not everything that developmental psychologists do, in other words, matters to early childhood teachers.

My guiding principle is that early childhood education is not about young children as such, but about how teachers and children form *relationships* that mutually influence each other and especially children. If I were an early childhood teacher (as, in fact, I once was), I would not be satisfied with simply knowing or observing the behavior of the children in my classroom. I also would want to do something with such knowledge, even if doing something just meant exclaiming how pleased I was with my children's accomplishments. As a teacher, I might often do more than this, of course; I might engage children in further activities that extended their interests, motives, and abilities. But to call myself a teacher of the young, I must *connect* with them somehow, which means interacting, relating, and touching their lives in valuable ways.

Given this perspective—one that focuses directly on the needs of early childhood—certain theories and topics about human change and functioning get "promoted" in value to the exclusion of others. As a rule, theories that highlight social influence or collaborative processes are more useful to teachers of the young than viewpoints that leave human interaction out of the picture. And a number of conventional binary distinctions fade in importance and become useful only if integrated rather than separated. The differences between mind and body, for example, become artificial, as do the differences between thought and feeling, between the individual and the social world, and between observation and intervention (Seifert, 2001). These binaries do not disappear in this chapter, but they will be treated more helpfully, I believe, as mutually dependent concepts, especially in the worlds of young children. Integrating the classic binaries alters how we think of cognition, turning cognitive development into an activity shared with others, and instead of one marked by separation from the social, emotional, or physical (see also Wenger, 2004).

Adopting a relational perspective about cognitive development makes obvious sense for aspects of classroom life that are explicitly social, like the formation of peer relationships or the effect of early attachments on preschoolers' behavior. What may be harder to grasp is that a similarly social or collaborative perspective is both possible and helpful for developmental activities that are less explicitly social—including times, in particular, when children are thinking. We tend to regard cognition as a skill expressed independently—something that is acquired and displayed alone even in the most activity-oriented, developmentally appropriate classroom. But from a broader, adult perspective, truly "independent" thinking is illusory: seen in fuller context, even a child working alone is still a partner with teachers, peers, and (as I will also argue) unseen others in learning and thinking. Teachers therefore need ways to understand and work with children that acknowledge these partnerships fully, even if the partnerships are merely implied. That, at least, is what I will argue below.

I begin the chapter by clarifying some ambiguities in the concepts of *development* and of *cognitive development* in particular. The clarifications will assist in locating the topics described later in the chapter within the larger landscape of developmental theorizing. The topics themselves—pretend play and literacy—definitely do not cover the field of child development as an academic field, but they are arguably the two most central concerns of early childhood educators as professionals: pretend play and literacy. Pretend play is especially important to educators who work with the youngest children and who seek to give them the most developmentally appropriate practice possible. As it turns out, pretend play also clearly supports the claim that cognitive development in early childhood is "really" social. Although the general benefits of play are often noted by early childhood educators, the specific point for this chapter is that the benefits are definitely *not* confined to the social. Because of the focus of the chapter, in fact, I will not in fact focus on its social importance as such, but on how pretend play connects to and stimulates particular cognitive skills in young children. As we will see, the cognitive skills are ones that early childhood teachers value and can encourage deliberately, although not guarantee.

The other area of research discussed, literacy development, is especially important to educators working with "older" young children. Because the research shows the importance of the preschool years for literacy, however, the chapter will focus on emergent literacy during both the preschool and early school-years periods. Although some readers may feel that literacy belongs in a chapter on curriculum studies more than in one about developmental psychology, I will argue the contrary: that literacy both influences and is influenced by cognitive *development* in early childhood. As these comments suggest, however, the term *development* can have several meanings—a problem that can cause confusion when not resolved. Before going on, therefore, the various meanings of development should be clarified.

MULTIPLE MEANINGS OF DEVELOPMENT

When we speak of child development, we usually mean *some* sort of change, but we are often unclear about the sort of change that we mean (Overton, 1998, 2002). At times we point to quantitative *variations* among individuals, including simple comparisons of older and younger children. This is what we are doing when we say that "older children are taller than younger children," or "children gradually acquire larger vocabularies." At other times, we talk about *transformations* within individuals, usually of a qualitative nature. Transformation are what we mean, for example, when we say that "during the preschool years, children become able to tell imaginary stories"—highlighting that they could not do so formerly (Valsiner, 1998).

We also can be unclear about the purpose or function of developmental change in children. In some contexts, we seem focused on the *instrumental* aspects of development—its impact on the rest of us. We study changes in skills, behaviors, or concepts, intending to learn how and why a child begins to fit in socially or remains an outcast, becomes fair-minded or dishonest in dealing with others, or passes academic tests satisfactorily or not. Instrumental effects are what we are talking about when we say, for example, that "developing phonemic decoding skills allows a young child to succeed in first grade." Reading is framed in this sentence as a technical skill, relevant for its contribution to other purposes, especially ones set by adults. In Piagetian terms, instrumental development is mostly accommodation, not assimilation. In other situations, however, we seem focused on how development expresses or enacts the nature or humanity of the child, regardless of effects on others. This is what we mean when we say, "4-year-olds' need for make-believe is so strong that they will use almost anything as a prop." Here we are talking about assimilation, about children being and becoming themselves.

These multiple meanings both confuse and enrich research on child development and the practice of early childhood education. In this chapter, I will therefore try to minimize the confusion and enhance the enrichment by being as explicit as possible about the sorts of development discussed. Doing so will be important because as it happens, most developmental changes—including cognitive ones—are developmental in more than one way. Changes in pretend play, for example, show both individual variation and transformation at some level, and illustrate *both* adjustment to the world *and* the intrinsic humanity of the child. Yet the research on developmental changes does not always remind us of this basic idea, simply because the agendas and purposes of individual studies and research studies tend to be relatively specific. Research on the development of social play, for example, often highlights transformations in the child's nature—although instrumentally oriented studies about the long-term functions of play also exist. Research on literacy is apt to concern itself with individual variations and the child's accommodations to widespread worldly expectations for acquiring literacy. In this chapter, I will not point out such underlying differences in emphasis every time they occur, but I will try to note them when they are important to understanding the significance of research. Hopefully the result will be a more balanced picture of children's cognitive development.

CHILDREN'S PRETEND PLAY AND THINKING

As teachers and parents quickly learn, preschool children engage in a lot of pretend play, at least in middle-class modern societies. Yet even though such play often has a distinctly social flavor, it seems to build distinctly *cognitive* skills, and may thus constitute a bridge between the social world and the more individualistic experience of cognitive skills (Lillard, 2002; Saracho & Spodek, 2003; Sutton-Smith, 1997). Pretense affects thinking in three ways: by teaching how to read others' intentions, by encouraging social referencing, and by creating distinctions between the real and the imaginary. The developmental processes by which these skills evolve and are supported within particular children are not fully clear, but several plausible explanations exist. Although partly speculative, the explanations are useful for early childhood educators, because they suggest ways of planning play in daily practice as well as rationales for justifying play to parents and the public.

Reading Others' Intentions

By definition, pretend play always implies absence. "Cooking" happens without real food present, plastic sand toys are hats, a "pet dog" is led around a room without the real dog present, and so on. To make sense of pretenses, a child needs to supply the missing elements cognitively. He or she must realize that a banana held to the ear is still really a banana, and only a "telephone" because a play actor deems it to be one symbolically. Double meanings abound: what you see is not all of what is offered, intended, or interpreted. Although the double meanings are usually only implied and rarely stated, even very young preschoolers can infer them—a distinctly cognitive achievement. In one study to explore this idea, for example, Tomasello, Striano, and Rochat (1999) observed that when young children were shown a hammering motion *without* a hammer, for example, they often selected a real hammer in response. Even 2-year-olds responded in this way at better than chance rates! When the symbolism is complex or unfamiliar, of course, the intentions of make-believe actors may be misunderstood or lost on the youngest preschoolers. It can be hard to understand what peers are doing when they "play school," for example, if a child is so young that she has had no experience with the typical behaviors of teachers or pupils. But discerning the meaning of more complex pretend play will still be facilitated by its key motivating assumption: that players do mean *something* by their peculiar (in this case school-like) behaviors. Carefully observing players' responses—a form of social referencing, described in the next section—can help to decode ambiguous play.

Social Referencing

Social referencing means observing someone else's responses in order to decide how to respond to an ambiguous situation. We all perform this behavior, whatever our age; it is triggered in adult social gatherings, for example, when someone makes a remark that is not heard clearly or that makes little sense. In order to know how to respond (laugh? frown? ignore it?) puzzled individuals will note how *others* are responding. Not surprisingly, infants and young children engage in social referencing a good deal. In the classic visual cliff experiments, for example, most 1-year-olds avoided crawling across a clear glass drop-off if their mothers showed a negative facial expression. But they were much more likely to take this "chance" if their mothers showed a positive expression (Campos, Hiatt, Ramsay, Henderson, & S vejda, 1978; Mumme, Fernald, & Herrera, 1996).

Similarly, it seems likely that parents and other adults often may assist pretend play by orchestrating play episodes with various smiles, frowns, and directed gaze. Experienced peers also may provide similar social referencing, although not necessarily to the same extent or in the same ways. Whatever the source, social referencing guides a preschooler's efforts to identify the missing referents in pretend play. In pretending to eat a snack, for example, a mother might display more exaggerated smiles or direct her gaze at the child or at particular objects more intently than usual. The behaviors would at least signal that "something is not as it seems," and perhaps also signal "here is how you can choose to feel and respond, in case you are wondering." Such hints indirectly challenge the child to figure out or discern precisely what objects or actions are being played out. In this way the mother's behaviors could create a sort of zone of proximal development (ZPD), in the Vygotskian sense.

Distinguishing Reality and Appearance

Pretend play is like insanity in that players seem to take leave of reality. But unlike the truly insane, pretend players also indicate that they have *not* taken leave of reality by showing somehow that what they are doing is "only" play—only a way of looking at reality, not reality itself. During play, pretense is framed or "quarantined" from reality, not confused with it (Goffman, 1974). In a sense, because pretense is an exploration of what reality *might* be, it constitutes a narratively based form of hypothetical thinking or counterfactual thinking. We usually call such hypothesizing "imagination," and it obviously emerges much earlier than the more expository form of hypothesizing posited by Piaget as a marker of adolescence (Piaget, 1963). Even young children (ages 4 or 5) can reason with counterfactual syllogisms if they are recast as imaginary stories (Goswami, 2002b; Harris, 2000). It is a phenomenon familiar to many early childhood teachers: a formal set of propositions ("All bananas are purple; this is a banana; therefore . . . ") becomes surprisingly manageable if recast in imaginary terms ("Let's pretend that we are all purple bananas . . . "). In this way, therefore, the social activity of pretense lays groundwork for the later development of more solitary forms of cognition, like scientific reasoning and abstract deduction.

In spite of these benefits, there also are times when social play can trigger cognitive confusion instead of clear thinking. Preschool children confuse reality and imagination when, for example, adults deceive them intentionally (Clark, 1995). Santa Claus is a benign example of intentional deception and the resulting confusion, but less happy examples also exist, such as when adults mislead a child about the true severity of a parent's illness or of a parent's misbehavior. Preschool children also can get confused when a play episode is frightening (Bourchier & Davis, 2000): like many older children and adults, preschoolers can "talk themselves into" believing in the scary monsters, ghosts, and such like, even though they themselves have invented the monsters. In these cases a child seems to respond to persisting internal physiological signs of fear (the adrenal rush, etc.) created by his own thinking, and apparently forgets the original source or trigger for the signs, which are the child's own thinking (Harris, 2000). Such self-generated "illogic" is much like the process of negative rumination described in adults by cognitive behavior therapists (Segal, Williams, & Teasdale, 2002), in which mature individuals fail to notice that their own negative thoughts, not anything "real," create anxiety and fear. In either case—whether with child or adult—"as if" thinking remains delayed or impaired.

How Pretend Play Affects Cognitive Development

In early childhood, then, pretend play lies at an intersection of social experience and cognitive development. Developmental psychologists have offered a number of explanations for how the social and cognitive connect through play, many of them based on the "double consciousness" (of reality and its representation) described earlier. In addition to these ideas, developmental explanations have focused on how play both uses and encourages metacognition, how it depends on a Piagetian-style decentration, and on how cognition impacts social-role taking specifically. Studies to assess these explanations have generally provided at least partial support for each of them.

Metacognition. Some developmentalists have proposed that pretend play stimulates the emergence of metacognition, or the ability to think about one's own thinking (Bateson, 1955/1972; Taylor, 1999). The argument can be summarized as follows. First, it seems reasonable that children at play are aware of the fact that they are playing, even if they are initially aware only intuitively or nonverbally. Second, it seems reasonable that time and experience at playing would bring the early intuitive awareness into consciousness. But conscious awareness of pretense amounts to a form of metacognition—of "knowing what you are saying, doing, or thinking" —because it depends on holding both appearance and reality in mind. Perhaps, concludes the argument, the metacognition, which developed from play, also generalizes to other, nonplayful cognitive activities (Sawyer, 1997; Taylor, 1999). Playing with manipulatives, for example, facilitates the early development of numeracy and mathematical skills (Uttal, 2003).

As it happens, research about children's "theory of mind" (for example, false-belief tasks) does find a correlation between certain kinds of pretend play and cognitive skill at understanding the mental states of other people (Wellman, 2002). In this sense, it supports the idea that play promotes metacognitive awareness even beyond the arena of play itself. The kind of pretense that supports awareness of others' mental states, however, is socially oriented—make-believe play *with* other children or adults, as opposed to make-believe play engaged in by one child alone. The metacognitive benefits of solitary play, if any, remain ambiguous. If they do exist, they will be revealed outside the realm of false-belief and theory-of-mind tasks.

Decentration. Another way of describing the cognitive skills needed for pretense is to view it as a type of Piagetian *decentration* (Piaget, 1962), or shift from a single perspective or point to view to coordinated, multiple points of view. The classic Piagetian example of decentration involves showing a child a table

with a model of three mountains on it, and observing whether the child can imagine how the mountains would look from the other side of the table. Basic decentration like this is correlated with skills in pretend play, but—again—only if the play involves other persons (Rubin, Fein, & Vandenberg, 1983; Lillard, 2002). Solitary pretense is *not* related—a finding with implications for early childhood teachers, and therefore one that deserves comment later in this chapter.

The connection between decentration and social play is not surprising, however, given the nature of pretend play and of the concept of decentration. Successful pretense involves imagining how play behaviors look or feel not only to the actor, but also to viewers and fellow actors (Sawyer, 1997). At the simplest level, coordination of viewpoints may involve matters as simple as remembering to face interlocutors or audience members, or remembering to speak lines explicitly (and not just to imagine speaking them). At more complex levels, the coordination with other perspectives becomes a matter of styling your make-believe part so that others will understand and recognize it. Decentration therefore shades into the social role-taking described in the next section.

Social role-taking. Developmental psychologists also have suggested that pretend play promotes cognition by requiring children to "get into" or empathize with the roles that they enact. The empathy both requires and encourages sensitivity to human psychology and feelings, and hence also encourages general reflectiveness, self-awareness, and metacognition about social matters. Research observations on children at play are consistent with this explanation. Studies find, for example, that children engaged in pretend play use more internal state words than usual ("I feel X," "My doll feels Y"), and also find that the internal state words are transferred to situations outside play episodes themselves (Hughes & Dunn, 1997; Howe, Petrakos, & Rinaldi, 1998).Such transfer should not be surprising because pretend play, almost by definition, emphasizes human relationships, the expression of feelings, and the management of conflict. And these topics, in turn, depend on metacognition and decentration of various sorts: a child must know both *that* he is enacting a role and *what* he or she is enacting in order to engage in make-believe successfully. Surrounding the play episodes themselves, furthermore, players may discuss and even dispute the proper enactment of dramatic roles. The disagreements and ensuing negotiations may themselves stimulate decentration and self-awareness both about the social roles and about specific non-social elements of the roles. Put in the constructivist language of Piaget, the disagreements and negotiations stimulate disequilibrium about socially relevant concepts, and prompt a rebalancing of assimilation and accommodation about these concepts.

Using Play to Foster Cognitive Development

Social play. Social play in general, then, it seems that pretend play does bridge the divide between social and cognitive development, and does so primarily when and if it provides *social* experiences. In this sense the research on pretend play confirms

Vygotsky more directly than Piaget: children begin by thinking with others, or at the prompting of others, before they can think in equivalent ways alone (Vygotsky, 1978). Yet Piaget's more individualistic perspective calls attention to the converse possibility: that cognitive skills may also be reflected in or expressed in social arenas, including pretend play. Although there is research evidence for this sort of influence (Piaget, 1945/1951), it is a less useful perspective for teachers, who deal with children primarily in social groups. In typical classrooms of young children, early childhood teachers *assume* the presence of many children and *seek* ways of working with individuals within groups, rather than the other way around. As a teacher, therefore, it seems especially pertinent to know how groups affect areas of individual development, including cognitive development.

The effects of children's play are both variational and transformational, in the sense described at the start of this chapter. Obviously, play contributes to certain kinds of individual variations or differences in cognitive skills: some children become more metacognitive, decentred, and so on than others. But play also transforms each child individually: gradually a child at play becomes self-aware or "metacognitive" in a way that is truly new to that child. The novelty of the change and its cognitive basis may sometimes be overlooked because the developmental transformations may not initially seem like the usual (i.e., nonsocial) expressions of cognition, such as classifying objects or counting objects without assistance. They manifest instead as narrative stories and reenactments, carried out with increasing self-control and finesse as the child develops.

All of which suggests that the social effects on cognition pose special challenges to teachers. Variations among children in the effects of play suggest a need to assist those who are "behind," perhaps by offering greater opportunities to play or by scaffolding and supporting initial play for children unused to sustaining it. At the same time, personal transformations stimulated by play challenge teachers to see clearly where play leads, and to explain its effects convincingly to parents and fellow educators. These other adults may perceive only the immediate, superficial differences between play and "real" (non-make-believe) thinking, and not their long-term developmental connections (Roopnarine, 2003). Early childhood educators face the task of explaining the deeper understanding to others: explaining how play contributes not only to children's current well-being but also to their social and cognitive futures.

The fact that social pretend play seems more consistently beneficial than solitary make-believe suggests that early childhood educators should emphasize social forms of play in their programs: apparently social play is a very developmentally appropriate practice (Bredekamp & Copple, 1997). Although this is not news to teachers and other professionals responsible for young children, it is reassuring nonetheless to find that research supports a teaching practice that already has widespread classroom appeal, at least in early childhood education.

Nonsocial play. In spite of the research summarized here, it would be premature for early childhood teachers to restrict opportunities for *non*social play—such as the "practice play" described in classical Piagetian theory and make-believe play engaged in by children individually. One reason is that supposedly nonsocial play often contains social elements; it only appears to be solitary at the moment when it occurs. A child building a road in a sand box alone, for example, is usually not cut off from the social world unless the child is effectively autistic. In many cases, this sort of solitary, practice-oriented activity is likely either to have grown out of previous activities learned from others, or to be a rehearsal for similar, but very social activities in the future. Viewed in a larger timeframe, nonsocial play often belongs to the social world as much as does social play, and therefore confers many of the same benefits as activities that are more social at the time of their occurrence.

In any case, favoring play activities only for their contributions to other areas of human development is to confuse the instrumental and expressive aspects of play described at the beginning of this chapter. Play, whatever its form, is only partly "for" other purposes; it is always an expression of a human need, at least in modern society. As such, it is valuable even when "useless" for furthering a child's cognitive development (Ariel, 2003; Elkind, 2001). Nonsocial play therefore still deserves educators' support, if only to honor the self-expressive needs of children. To do otherwise turns nonsocial play into a useless educational "frill," and turns social pretense—ironically—into an educational "course requirement" of early childhood.

The final word is not yet in about possible connections between nonsocial play and cognitive development. Piaget's explanation of its functions—that practice and nonsocial play stimulates development of later cognitive operations—has face validity, but research testing the explanation has found many qualifications that limit its generality (Case, 1998). Still, nonsocial play may have instrumental functions, such as fostering particular nonverbal or nonsocial forms of intelligence (Gardner, 1983, 1999), or such as organizing existing ideas or experience, including emotional experience (Erikson, 1977; Chazan, 2002; Ariel, 2003; see also Denham, chap. 5, this volume).

As has been amply demonstrated in the Piagetian literature, small changes in experimental tasks can create large differences in outcomes (Case, 1998). Similarly, context may affect the meaning and impact of children's play: seemingly small changes in the conditions of play may significantly change its meaning to children and its effects on their development. In fact, for those who primarily serve children rather than create developmental research, an obvious limitation of existing research on play is its tendency toward narrow definitions of social context, in spite of the respect often paid, in principle, to contextual influences (Rogoff, 2003; Gauvain, 2001). In general, studies of play tend to take account only of a child's immediate surroundings. If playmates are included, they tend to consist of only one or two parents or immediate relatives, or of a few peers. If interactions are studied, they tend to be dyadic (one-to-one), not group oriented. If the physical setting is noted, it tends to consist of a home living room, an experimental laboratory room, or a classroom. A culture in which children are segregated from the world of adults tends to be selected for study, or even taken for granted. These conceptual starting points reflect cultural assumptions and practices of Western, middle-class society, but they also tend to overlook broader and richer meanings of social context that help in understanding play and its effects on cognition.

In the case of nonsocial play, in particular, an overly narrow definition of "social context" may obscure children's reasons for playing nonsocially—reasons that might paradoxically have *social* origins and consequences if definitions of context were expanded. Suppose, for example, that preschool peer groups sometimes reenact social prejudices of the larger society in spite of teachers' efforts to the contrary. In that case, what looks like certain children may find that social "play" may actually be less playful than it looks, at least for some children (see Cohen, 1994). Or suppose, for another example, that certain children come from communities or cultures that do not segregate children from adult activities as strongly as does white middle-class North America. For these children, the notion of playing *with* others may hold a different meaning than Western-oriented researchers expect. In particular, playing with a single-age peers may seem limiting to them, not freeing or enriching, and the children may consequently rely on same-age peers *less* than usual as models, motivators of action, or confidantes. For early childhood teachers, such possibilities suggest a need for balance and thoughtfulness in providing opportunities for "play" as conventionally understood. No form of play, it seems, may be experienced as equally playful for every child, nor therefore affect cognitive development in the same way (Rogoff, Paradise, Mejia-Arauz, Correa-Chavez, & Angelillo, 2003).

As in other education-related research, the effort of developmental studies to be scientific by focusing observations and conclusions has limited its usefulness to teachers. For the topic of play discussed here, in particular, it is well and good to conclude that social pretend play generally helps children's thinking and that early childhood educators should therefore provide for it. But educators have more precise curriculum needs and more precise hopes for the cognitive development of their children. Most of the time, they seek to encourage not just thinking in general, but particular kinds of thinking skills. Although there is a long list of potentially desirable cognitive skills, the most notable among educators are the skills of literacy—the traditional backbone of the early public schooling. The level and type of literacy expected by educators depends, of course, on the age and maturity of the children that they serve. Teachers working with 5-year-olds will hold different expectations than those serving toddlers, and both will hold different expectations than teachers of 7- or 8-year-olds in the primary grades. Even so, though, those serving the youngest of children will still seek to foster attitudes, skills, and knowledge that will help literacy to emerge. Because of its importance, therefore, the next section therefore looks at literacy development in detail. First it discusses how cognitive development facilitates literacy, and then at how literacy affects children's cognitive development.

THE EMERGENCE OF LITERACY AND COGNITIVE DEVELOPMENT

Literacy and cognition influence each other's development to a significant extent: not only do emerging cognitive skills make initial reading and writing possible, but emerging reading and writing also affect how children organize and experience thinking. The mutual influence is not total, however, nor equivalent to mutual causality. Like other forms of cognition, literacy skills are influenced importantly by social opportunities and human motivations. The next sections explain each of these ideas in turn.

Cognitive Developments That Facilitate Literacy

For most children, literacy begins as a way of representing the world on paper (Olson, 1994). The first signs emerge in the preschool years, and involve treating words or letters as emblems or signs that stand directly for familiar objects, people, or events. A child may "read" the name of her favorite cereal on the cereal box, using some combination of the letters, words, and pictures on the box. In doing so, the child seems to make a fundamental mistake: she assume that text represents or refers to something in the world directly, the same way that oral language represents or refers to the world directly (Adams, Treiman, & Pressley, 1998). On a cereal box, for example, the printed word *Cheerios* is taken to stand for the cereal and/or the box itself, not for the *word* "cheerios." The assumption of direct correspondence is not unreasonable given children's (and adults') experience with oral language, in which a spoken word such as "cheerios" refers to nothing linguistic as such, but to a tangible object or activity. As the child will eventually learn, however, generalizing the function of print from the function of oral language is misleading: print is not, strictly speaking, "about" the world, but "about" a way of representing language.

Evidence for a "correspondence theory of print" can be seen in observations of preschoolers' mistakes when reading. At this age, mistakes tend to honor the context of a textual passage rather than its graphemic details. If an illustration shows a boy walking, for example, along with just one (mysterious) word printed as a caption, a 4-year-old are as likely to "read" (i.e., guess) that the word as *boy*, *go*, *walk*, or *child*. Any of these "readings" may be reasonable given the context or meaning of the text, but graphemically they have little relationship to each other or to clues in the print itslef.

By guessing correctly much of the time, context-oriented reading can sometimes look like the real thing and therefore conceal a child's inability to decode unfamiliar words and sentences. The impression of real reading is especially likely if a preschooler memorizes his or her favorite stories by hearing them read repeatedly. If the child has heard the "Three Bears" ten times, he or she may be able to recite large parts of it verbatim on the eleventh time, much like reciting a poem or singing a song by heart. The result can look like mature reading, but with a difference: on request, the child "read" with eyes closed, a skill that no mature reader ever has (Biemiller, 1979, 1999).

A year or two later, as schooling begins, formal instruction may undermine the child's blithe reliance on context, and instill doubts about its universal appropriateness. Around age 5 or 6 in our society, most children begin realizing that printed text refers *most* directly to something linguistic—to particular words or sentences—and that it refers to the world only *indirectly*, via the particular words inscribed in print. In the short term, this insight can sometimes spoil the fluency (a.k.a. memorization) shown in earlier reading. Now, in first grade, a child may pause longer and hesitate more often, or simply fall silent when faced with what he or she knows is a decoding task to which the child has no sure solution. Sometimes worried parents or teachers may be tempted to interpret the change as regression in reading ability, or as the result of overbearing or poor teaching practices. But a more optimistic interpretation is also possible: silence and hesitation may signify the new, more helpful insight that print *does* represent language rather than the world. The new insight prompts uncertainty about the significance of certain letters, words, or sentences. The child knows that some sort of decoding is necessary, but at first that may be all that the child knows.

Reading skills usually begin developing in earnest sometime during the first year of formal schooling, which happens at about age 6. In spite of the arguments of some whole language theorists, emerging literacy seems to cause children to pay *less* attention to contextual cues (e.g., pictures or associated oral comments), and *more* attention to exactly what is printed on the page (Boran & Comber, 2001; Snowling, 2002). Evidence for this idea again comes from children's misreadings, which imply increasing knowledge of spelling conventions and letter-sound correspondences. In the example described earlier—a captioned picture of a boy walking—the young reader would be more likely to inspect graphemic features of the "mystery" caption than in the past. If he or she noted a "b" at the start of the word, he or she might piece this fact together with prior knowledge of words known to start with this letter. Combining clues from the picture and any mental "files" of words starting with "b," the reader might come up with a correct reading of the word (e.g., *boy*). Even if the child chooses the wrong word, the error is more likely to honor features of the print than at earlier points in reading development: the child might note the word has three letters, for example, and erroneously choose another "b" word with three letters *bag, bad*, big, ...

With most children the overall impression conveyed at this level of development is one of effortful but halting success. When properly understood, effortful reading marks a definite advance over the non responses and "fluent guesswork" that characterized earlier reading. But just as before, the interim achievement is prone to misperception by adults. When observed only casually or occasionally, effortful reading can suggest that formal instruction has spoiled the fun of reading, turned literacy into work, and placed it far behind speaking and listening as a medium for communication and learning. In the short term, in fact, there is some truth in these criticisms, at least for some children. In long-term context, however, the picture gets more complicated. Most children and youth continue learning (i.e., improving) their reading for many years, and most eventually become skillful enough to make reading and writing productive for many purposes (Biemiller, 1999). In spite of the prevalence of reading disabilities among school children and adults, most individuals eventually turn "reading to learn" into "learning to read" by the late elementary years.

Note that this account of reading development is constructivist in the sense that it portrays the child as actively and autonomously choosing among rather general strategies to guide learning. Yet literacy acquisition can be interpreted just as reasonably in terms of information processing (Adams, 2001). From this perspective, the young child does not initially adopt a hypothesis about print that happens to be wrong. Rather, the

child is unable at first to keep two things in mind at once—both the word *and* its meaning. In information processing terms, the young preschooler lacks enough working memory for both parts of this equation, and does not develop a "big" enough memory until the early or mid-elementary years (Case & Okamoto, 1998). In the meantime, the meaning of printed text dominates the child's attention, presumably because meaning has greater immediate utility. In the cereal box example described earlier, for example, the box cover gives many cues and reinforcements for knowing that *cheerios* are inside, but few for knowing how to decode and sound out the letters *c-h-e-e-r-i-o-s*. Eventually, with time and age, the focus on meaning changes as working memory increases in size and speed, and as the social environment begins encouraging simultaneous attention to both print and meaning. Whoever undertakes initial instruction in reading, then, faces the intriguing task of diagnosing and respecting the child's cognitive readiness or lack thereof, while at the same time prompting the child to adopt a new, text-based approach to print. As the next section shows, nudging children toward "higher" states of cognition about print is tricky, because it involves creating phonemic awareness.

A Major Challenge: Phonemic Awareness

Most research suggests that successful early reading, at least in English, is strongly associated with awareness of phonemes (Adams, Treiman, & Pressley, 1998; Adams, 2001). The correlation exists partly because English orthography records or preserves many phonemes in its spelling (or graphemic) conventions, even though English orthography is only mediocre at recording sounds phonetically. (For readers unfamiliar with linguistics, *phonemes* are groups of similar vocal sounds treated as equivalent by native speakers, and *phonetics* refers to individual, acoustically audible sounds themselves.) As a child realizes the connections between orthography and phonemes, he or she can use them to make reasonable guesses about spelling, as well as to do the converse of guessing the pronunciation of unfamiliar words. Orthographic clues (spelling) are not foolproof (we all mispronounce unfamiliar words sometimes), but they are helpful nonetheless.

In spite of the importance of phonemic awareness, however, it is not self-evident how early childhood teachers can help children to develop this skill, because phonemes are by definition not acoustically observable (or audible). Acoustically, normal speech does not pause between or separate most sounds but instead flows continuously. Therefore slowing speech down to aid hearing the individual sounds is not necessarily helpful, since slowing speech alters sounds phonetically, often making them unrecognizable as phonemes (Meyer, 2002). The challenge in any case is not to "hear" specific sounds, but to learn which sounds to treat as equivalent. As already mentioned, phonemes are mental categories or groups of sounds, not single acoustic events. Somehow the child must learn the categories.

Phonemic awareness therefore calls for a form of abstract cognition—the creation and use of mental categories in linguistic contexts. Early childhood teachers therefore have the challenging job of getting children to notice and learn something that neither they nor the teachers can experience directly but can only *infer* from what they hear. On the face of it, this goal would seem to be developmentally *in*appropriate. In spite of this problem, however, good readers somehow figure out phonemic groupings, and do so sooner and more accurately than nonreaders and struggling readers. How do they do it, and why do other children sometimes fail to do it?

Some degree of phonemic awareness must therefore be teachable, or at least learnable, if teachers can just find effective ways of facilitating it. A variety of curricula and programs in fact exist for this purpose, based on various combinations of oral language activities (Adams, 2001; McGee, 2003; Barrett-Pugh & Rohl, 2000; Pressley et al., 1997). For preschool and kindergarten children, phonemic awareness-building includes nursery rhymes, rhymed stories and production, segmentation of sentences into words, clapping or dancing to syllabic rhythms, segmentation and blending of the initial phoneme in short words, and the like. The activities often resemble practices already widely used in early childhood classrooms for other purposes, such as stimulating children's imagination (Bredekamp & Copple, 1997). In one respect, then, the news is good: to support early literacy, early childhood teachers do not have to implement teaching strategies that are in principle unfamiliar or intuitively inappropriate. The bad news, however, is that in preschool classrooms as a whole, reading readiness activities actually only work with about two thirds of all children (Farstrup & Samuels, 2002). The other third arrive in kindergarten, and eventually in first grade, with only poor or mediocre phonemic awareness. This is a rather high "failure" rate for such a crucial skill, and especially for one needed so early in a child's educational career.

Why does teaching phonemic awareness fail with so many children? One reason may simply be the sociological converse of developmental limitations: Because certain children are not yet "ready" to grasp phonemes and meaning simultaneously, the age-graded *curriculum* of schooling is at fault. Too often, perhaps, school curricula expect particular achievements at uniform ages instead of facilitating something more reasonable, namely diversity in children's rates of development. The problem, in other words, is not the child's inability to learn phonemic reading skills, but the schools' insistence on teaching the skills at a certain age.

But even if widespread age-grading is a culprit, phonemic difficulties also may stem from factors that can be remedied by teachers individually and deliberately. One key to successful learning, for example, may be for teachers (and children) to give up the apparently impossible task of sounding words out so as to "hear" them concretely, and instead try associating phonemes with *non*auditory analogs. Some instructional programs have had success at teaching phonemic awareness, for example, not by getting children to listen for phonemes, but by having them physically articulate particular phonemes—to "feel them in the mouth" with tongue, teeth, and the like (Skjelfjord, 1976; Truch, 1991). Other programs have had success by using colored chips to stand for and spell individual phonemes, or even by using letter-like visual symbols for phonemes (Elkonin & Zaporozhets, 1974; Byrne, 1998). Both techniques apparently work because they create concrete, nonauditory referents. In the articulation strategy, the child focuses on the shape of the mouth, the position of the tongue, the timing of voicing, and the

like, that are associated with a phoneme. In the visual chip strategy, the child focuses attention on a permanent visual record of each phoneme available for inspection and reflection, analogous to how printed letters and digraphs function a bit later in childhood, when reading truly begins. In either case, the teaching strategies render phonemes as *objects* of thought, and not merely as the *vehicles* of thought that they were before. This new, metacognitive approach to language initiates an important developmental change relevant to early childhood teachers: the impact not of cognition on reading skills, but of reading skills on cognition.

The Effect of Reading on Children's Cognition

Cognitive development not only influences literacy, but is affected by it in turn. The most important effect is on children's awareness of language: children move from simply *using* language to thinking *about* it. Initial linguistic ability becomes metalinguistic as well (Olson, 2002). The transformation takes many years (actually a lifetime, in fact), as the child continually learns new ways that print corresponds to and maps onto language and speech. From this growing, multifaceted knowledge emerge cognitive distinctions impossible without literacy. Children become aware, for example, that what is said may be different from what is meant, and they begin acquiring vocabulary for "inner" emotions and feelings that previously were expressed or sensed only nonverbally. The next sections explain how these cognitive changes happen.

The preliterate mind. At first—during a child's third and fourth years—print has little distinctive impact on cognition. As explained earlier, children conceptualize print as representations for objects or events, rather than as representations for bits of language. Cognitively, it is therefore just another form of representation, almost equivalent to drawing and make-believe play, which also involve representing objects and events. But note the proviso: writing is *almost* equivalent to other forms of representation but not quite. More on this qualification in a moment.

Evidence that writing represents objects rather than language is plentiful. In early "scribble writing," for example, a child may pluralize words by repeating a scribble instead of by making a different, unique scribble to indicate number. *Duck* may be written as one scribble, but so might the expression *one duck. Two ducks, three ducks*, and *four ducks* may be written as two, three, and four similar scribbles, respectively, even though the number of words in each expression is two and the number of morphemes in each is three (number + /duck/ + /−s/). The number of scribbles in all of these cases corresponds to the *meaning* of the expression, not to the words or morphemes expressing the meaning (Pelletier, 2002).

Research has found an analogous phenomenon not just when young children write, but when they read as well (Kress, 1997). In a proto-typical study of this type (Ferreiro & Teberoksy, 1996), for example, an adult read a card to a young child that contained the expression "three little pigs." The adult then covered up one of the three words and asked the child what the words represented now. Ferreiro and Teberoksy found that children tended to read the revised card as "two little pigs," not as "little pigs" or as "two little." This behavior made sense if children were assuming that each word stood for an object (one pig), and not for a particular word.

Still another piece of evidence that preliterate children reference words to objects and not to language has a touch of irony: young children often find certain expressions impossible to write, in principle. An example was documented by Homer and Olson (1999), who asked preschoolers how to write the expression "no cats." Many children declared that it simply could not be done, apparently because the expression refers to no *objects*, not because the expression contains no *words*. It was as if the children heard the request without its implied quotation marks: they heard a request to draw or represent no cats, rather than to write "no cats."

Finally, and consistent with the other evidence just described, preliterate children often believe that the size of a word is related to the size of the object to which it refers. Thus, when shown the two words *train* and *caterpillar* and asked which word is "train," a preliterate child may point to the longer word (in this case, *caterpillar*) is "train" because trains are longer than caterpillars. For the same reason, *car* and *bicycle* may be confused, or *oven* and *refrigerator*. The phenomenon was originally described in the developmental literature in 1978 as an illustration of Piagetian cognitive development (Sinclair, 1978) but later confirmed in research on emergent literacy (Ferreiro, 1994). (But presumably observant teachers of first-grade noted this phenomenon even earlier than developmental psychologists.)

In spite of these behaviors, however, young children do distinguish between writing and other forms of representation. Preschoolers' drawings look different from their preliterate "scribble-writing," and both of course differ in appearance from their make-believe play (Pelletier, 2002). From the point of view of the child, each activity offers unique constraints and opportunities as a medium of representation, some of which are imposed by adults rather than by the nature of the medium. In the case of reading and writing, the young child also may begin noticing that literate forms of representation are especially privileged. Hopefully, for most children, this insight makes it worth learning to read and write, in spite of the frequent constraints on how it is to be done.

Transitional effects on cognition. By fits and starts—sometime between their fourth and sixth birthdays—most children who receive schooling begin shifting away from the emblematic literacy described earlier, in which print stands directly for meanings instead of for words. Gradually their knowledge of print becomes more phonemically based, both guided by and prompting the hypothesis that printed words represent segments of language, such as syllables, words, and sentences. This new insight takes time to unfold, because it depends on gradually learning many specialized correspondences between letters and sounds, and between letters and words (Snowling, 2002). Meanwhile, children are apt to hang on their earlier, emblematic use of literacy as a default interpretation of print: their writing will mix phonemic knowledge with variations on emblematic scribble-writing.

Precisely how the transition gets started remains an important problem for reading researchers, but one that is only partially understood. One possibility is that children initially use their knowledge of letter names to help in retrieving words from memory (Ehri, 1995). Seeing the letter "b" at the beginning of a word, for example, the child will review various "b-words" that he or she remembers, until a plausible b-word is recalled. This strategy is not exactly phonemic, as the child is using letter names as cues instead of letter sounds. But it does help to establish the principle of print referring not to words but to meanings. For some children, using letter names may be crucial in motivating a search for truly phonemic correspondences between orthography and speech (Pelletier, 2002).

Stages and sequences in the learning of phonemes has been studied extensively, but have yielded only a few reliable generalizations helpful for early childhood teachers. One of the most reliable generalization is that the first phonemes to be learned tend to be initial ones in short, familiar words, such as the /c/ in /cat/ or the /p/ in /pin/, along with their rimes—in these examples, /-at/ and /-in/ (Marsh, Friedman, Welch, & Desberg, 1981; Adams, 2001). Beyond this regularity, developmental patterns become less certain. For purposes of teaching, about all that can be said for sure is that additional sublexical sounds and units—including final phonemes, middle phonemes, and consonant blends—tend to be learned "later." Even though reading curricula often recommend teaching these bits of phonemic awareness in a particular order, research on phonemic awareness has not actually found any particular sequence strongly predictable—or at least not strongly enough to be useful to teachers. Instead, the research tends to show a lot of individuality in the sequence by which children learn specific letter-sound correspondences, and in the strategies that children use to learn them. Within broad, reasonable limits, how children learn specific decodings is somewhat independent of when and what they are taught about the decodings (Thompson & Johnston, 2000).

Given this circumstance, and given the complexity of English orthography, it is not surprising that the transition to full literacy takes several years, if indeed it can ever be said to be complete. In the meantime, children make many errors (miscues) when reading particular words or segments of text. In writing, furthermore, they persist in using an *ad hoc* mixture of emblematic and phonemic strategies, combined with limited but growing knowledge of correct orthographic conventions (Kress, 1996). When asked to write "Mommy has two scissors," for example, a child might combine letters and drawings: "Mom ✂ ✂". Where letters are in fact used to represent words, their spelling is often simplified, as in "I WNT TO S TDAY" for "I went to school today." The details of such simplifications have been studied extensively, both in English and in other languages (Levin, Korat, & Amsterdamer, 1996; Bissex, 1980; Smith, 2003; Turbill, 2003). Overall, graphemic development displays some consistent trends; initial letters tend to be learned before later letters, and consonants tend to be learned before vowels. But like phonemic awareness, a lot of graphemic development is idiosyncratic—or at least enough so that teachers need to keep the individuality of children firmly in mind when teaching reading.

How then are early childhood teachers to make use of the research on early literacy? Various curricula have been proposed to facilitate children's emergent literacy, some of which take into account the individuality of children's strategies (Murphy & Dudley-Marling, 2003; Adams, 2001). Although the details are beyond the scope of this chapter, two general points about these curricula and their associated instruction are worth noting here. The first is that as a group, "good" teaching of emergent literacy tends to use a common, identifiable set of practices. In a survey compiled by Michael Pressley and his colleagues (1997), for example, teachers showed considerable consensus about what constituted effective ways of introducing and developing reading skills. The second is that although the good practices tend to be consistent with research on reading development, they also go beyond the scope of the research to deal with particular methods, styles of teaching, and content. Successful practices include, among other things, a liberal use of "direct" teaching. They also include a focus on skills prerequisite to reading, such as auditory and visual discrimination of shapes and sounds; continual return to key concepts such as *word*; and practice at specific letter-sound associations in both reading and writing, and in context as well as in isolation. In line with the constructivist perspective of most reading research, current "good" practices tend also to include early encouragement for writing, including an emphasis on invented spelling. Cognitively, these practices focus children's attention on how print represents language, and may account for the effect of literacy on cognitive development described next.

The literate mind in early childhood. Once children begin grasping the idea that writing represents language rather than meanings directly, additional beliefs and concepts become both necessary and possible. Children evolve a sort of literate perspective or mind-set, and become increasingly committed to it as time goes on. One part of the perspective is simply that words have fixed meanings—an artifact of the fact that print itself provides a permanent, unchanging record of utterances (Olson, 2002). The idea of fixed meanings in turn creates a distinction between word meaning and speaker meaning—Saussure's *langue* and *parole* (Saussure, 1983). Children begin believing that words can mean something of their own accord, regardless of whatever a speaker may intend when using them. It follows that words can also be *mis*used in two ways: either accidentally or on purpose. Lying—although probably not created by literacy—takes on a new, deeper significance as literacy develops and is extended to the printbased literate "lying" of fiction. More precisely, three new concepts develop and acquire mutually dependent meanings: truth, falsity, and intentions. The latter notion in particular triggers a need for greater attention to inner, psychological states, thus making possible refinements in children's "theory of mind" that develop at about the same age, and that are discussed later (Wellman, 2002; Astington & Pelletier, 1996).

New notions of truth and accuracy therefore make literate accuracy a new issue for young readers, and in more ways than one. Words have to be spelled according to conventions in order to avoid misunderstandings when reading them, and they have to be chosen wisely in order for sentences or paragraphs to make sense. The challenges of spelling and composing in turn make the idea of a dictionary both possible and necessary. Just like adults, early reader/writers begin to find it useful to have a permanent, stable archive of meanings for word meanings and spellings. Disagreements over invented spellings or about how to interpret text can thus be reduced, at least in theory.

But whether it comes from a teacher or a dictionary, authoritative advice about print contributes to an idealization of standards for even the earliest writing, and the idealization has several cognitive effects. One consequence is the new activity of editing, polishing and perfecting of text. Under good conditions, even in early childhood, this activity does achieve its purpose: spelling becomes more canonical and phrasing becomes more grammatical, accurate, and graceful. But editing also has a dark side: if taken too seriously, it can crowd out creativity and expose children to the emotional risks of perfectionism, on the one hand, and of academic apathy, on the other. Because writing can always be improved, even a diligent child may conclude that none of his or her writing will ever be good enough, or that in general, reading and writing may not be worth much effort. These darker possibilities are certainly not news to teachers of the primary grades, but they deserve mention as real developmental effects of literacy for some children (Mather & Goldstein, 2001).

With time, the distinction between print and speech also creates a subtler one, between literal meaning and *in*direct or implied meaning. Sometimes a speaker or author may intend *more* than what he or she actually writes. In addition to stating something outright, a writer also may connote, allude, or hint. The distinction creates a new activity, interpretation. In an early childhood classroom, interpretation of text starts when a teacher asks children comprehension questions about stories that they have read, or invites children to comment on what the stories meant to them personally. Later in life, the possibility and need for interpretation creates literary criticism, whether expressed in informal discussions (for most of us) or as published essays (for a few). But analogs to literary criticism begin in early childhood whenever two or three individuals discuss or comment on a common text (Bruner, 2002; Feldman, 2002).

Distinguishing word meaning from speaker meaning also creates a distinction between exact quotation and paraphrase, and stimulates children to learn that each has distinct social uses. Answering certain questions on a quiz or test, for example, often requires using precise wording—essentially a nearly exact quotation of the teacher or text, even if the teacher does not call it a "quotation." In writing a daily journal, by contrast, a child may be expected to express "original thought," a task that amounts to a lot of unacknowledged paraphrasing by combining words and sentences into familiar, yet novel forms. Each kind of expression—quotation and paraphrasing—is risky outside of its expected context. In writing a personal journal, quoting others' words exactly or even closely may be regarded as "stealing ideas" or as an avoidance of thinking. When taking a test, departing from the expected answers too far risks getting a low mark on the test. So it seems that the twin, mutually dependent notions of plagiarism and academic individuality are born because of literacy.

All in all, as reading and writing become established, the literate mind that emerges becomes consciously psychological.

Distinctions between word meaning and intended meaning, notions of indirect meaning, needs for interpretation: collectively these achievements stimulate and develop a vocabulary of feelings and intentions. In their writing, children gradually realize that written descriptions of human action do not necessarily "speak for themselves" when it comes to the feelings, motives, and intentions motivating them. They sometimes have to be explained in "so many words" (Olson & Kamawar, 2002). Emotional states are often not obvious even when a speaker's words are written down exactly. For example, the written sentence, "John said, 'I love school'" is ambiguous. Was John sarcastic, ashamed of his feeling, proud of it, or what? As children realize that these questions are meaningful and legitimate, they are stimulated to develop concepts that can be used to answer them either in writing or in personal conversations. The concepts name feelings, motives, and other psychological states—or at least point toward them. The stimulus to psychologize begins as soon as young children begin writing—even in making entries, for example, in personal journals in first grade, at a time when recorded writing is likely to be the most abbreviated. In this way, literacy fosters a psychological (i.e., reflective) mindset; it turns thought and feeling, along with language itself, into objects of awareness.

CONCLUSIONS: LEARNING AS DEVELOPMENT, DEVELOPMENT AS LEARNING

Although this chapter has obviously not covered all possible developmental changes about cognition, it has shown some important, direct ways that cognitive development relates to early childhood education and vice versa. The two areas emphasized—play and literacy—constitute priorities for most early childhood programs. Each area of activity gets underway and develops only if certain representational and classification abilities have already become established. Yet play and literacy also *contribute* to these cognitive abilities, taking them to new levels of richness and reflectivity. With time and practice, a child becomes aware of his or her own play, and of how language is used and intended, both orally or in print. The result is not only greater sophistication not only in play and literacy but also transformations in how children think, how they relate socially, and how they direct their own learning. An early childhood teacher who provides opportunities for play and literacy, then, is facilitating these changes. She is helping children to bootstrap learning by development, and development by learning.

Note that the interweaving of learning and development is affects many forms of development, as the forms were discussed at the beginning of this chapter. The changes in play and literacy are not merely variational, even though children do become simply more skilled at these activities—more playful, more literate—during early childhood. The changes are also transformational because they develop qualitatively new cognition as a result of earlier activities: 8-year-olds "know what they are doing" when they read or play with friends, in ways that they did not yet know when they were only three. The developmental changes also are instrumental because improvements in play and literacy contribute directly to children's success in other realms of life, such as schoolwork or making friends. And the changes are expressive because they foster children's self-fulfillment as human beings: skillful playing, reading, and writing allow children to express feelings with more sensitivity and to learn more autonomously than previously. For early childhood teachers, the richness of these developments is a blessing because it offers multiple reasons and avenues for intervening helpfully on behalf of children and their futures. For children themselves, the complexity of their cognitive development is no doubt taken largely for granted, but it is nonetheless a blessing, if only because it makes them so attractiveness and interesting as people.

References

Adams, M. (2001). Alphabetic anxiety and explicit, systematic phonics instruction: a cognitive science perspective. In S. Neuman & D. Dickinson (Eds.), *Handbook of early literacy research*. New York: Guilford Press.

Adams, M., Treiman, R., & Pressley, M. (1998). Reading, writing, and literacy. In P. Mussen, J. Flavell, & E. Markman (Eds.), *Handbook of child psychology, vol. 3: Cognitive development* (pp. 275-355). New York: Wiley.

Ariel, S. (2003). *Children's imaginative play*. Westport, CT: Praeger.

Astington, J., & Pelletier, J. (1996). The language of mind: Its role in teaching and learning. In D. Olson & N. Torrance (Eds.), *The handbook of education and human development* (pp. 593-619). Oxford, UK: Blackwell.

Barrett-Pugh, C., & Rohl, M. (Eds.) (2000). *Literacy learning in the early years*. Buckingham, UK: Open University Press.

Bateson, G. (1955/1972). A theory of play and fantasy. In G. Bateson (Ed.), *Steps to an ecology of mind* (pp. 177-193). New York: Chandler.

Biemiller, A. (1979). Changes in the use of graphic and contextual information as functions of passage difficulty and reading achievement level. *Journal of Reading Behavior*, 11, 307-318.

Biemiller, A. (1999). *Language and reading success*. Cambridge, MA: Brookline Books.

Bissex, G. (1980). *Gnys at work: A child learns to write and read*. Cambridge, MA: Harvard University Press.

Boran, S., & Comber, B. (Eds.). (2001). *Critiquing whole language and classroom inquiry*. Urbana, IL: National Council of Teachers of English.

Bourchier, A., & Davis, A. (2000). The influence of availability and affect on children's pretense. *British Journal of Developmental Psychology, 18*, 137-156.

Bredekamp, S., & Copple, C. (Eds.). (1997). *Developmentally appropriate practice in early childhood programs: Revised edition*. Washington, DC: National Association for the Education of Young Children.

Bruner, J. (2002). Narrative distancing: A foundation for literacy. In J. Brockmeier, M. Wang, & d. Olson (Eds.), *Literacy, narrative, and culture* (pp. 86-96). Richmond, Surrey, UK: Curzon.

Byrne, B. (1998). *The foundation of literacy: The child's acquisition of the alphabetic principle*. Hove, East Sussex, UK: Psychology Press.

Campos, J., Hiatt, S., Ramsay, D., Henderson, C., & Svejda, M. (1978). The emergence of fear on the visual cliff. In M. Lewis & L. Rosenbloom (Eds.), *The development of affect* (pp. 149-182). New York: Plenum.

Case, R. (1998). *The development of conceptual structures*. In W. Damon & R. Siegler (Eds.), *Handbook of Child Psychology, Vol. 2: Cognition* (pp. 745-800). New York: Wiley.

Case, R., & Okamoto, Y. (1998). The role of central conceptual structures in the development of children's thought. *Monographs of the Society for Research in Child Development*, Serial No. 246, 61.

Chall, J. (1967). *Learning to read: The great debate*. New York: McGraw-Hill.

Chazon, S. (2002). *Profiles of play: Assessing and observing structure and process in play therapy*. London: Jessica Kingsley.

Clark, C. (1995). *Flights of fancy, leaps of faith*. Chicago: University of Chicago.

Cohen, E. (1994). *Designing groupwork: Strategies for the heterogeneous classroom* (2nd ed.). New York: Teachers College Press.

Ehri, L. (1995). Phases of development in learning to read words by sight. *Journal of Research in Reading, 18*, 116-125.

Elkind, D. (2001). *The hurried child: Growing up too fast, too soon* (3rd ed.). Cambridge, MA: Perseus Publishers.

Elkonin, D., & Zaporozhets, A. (1974). *The psychology of preschool children*. Cambridge, MA: MIT Press.

Erikson, E. (1977). *Toys and reasons: Stages in the ritualization of experience*. New York: Norton.

Farstrup, A., & J Samuels, J. (Eds.). (2002). *What research has to say about reading instruction*, 3rd edition. Newark, DE: International Reading Association.

Feldman, C. (2002). The construction of mind and self in an interpretive community. In J. Brockmeier, M. Wang, & D. Olson (Eds.), *Literacy, narrative, and culture* (pp. 52-66). Richmond, Surrey, UK: Curzon.

Ferreiro, E. (1994). Literacy development: Construction and reconstruction. In D. Tirosh (Ed.). Implicit and explicit knowledge: An educational approach. *Human Development, 6*, 169-180. Norwood, NJ: Ablex.

Ferreiro, E., & Teberosky, A. (1996). *Literacy before schooling*. Portsmouth, NH: Heinemann.

Gardner, H. (1983). *Frames of mind*. New York: Basic Books.

Gardner, H. (1999). *Intelligence reframed: Multiple intelligences for the 21st century*. New York: Basic Books.

Gauvain, M. (2001). *The social context of cognitive development*. New York: Guilford Press.

Goffman, E. (1974). *Frame analysis: An essay on the organization of experience*. Cambridge, MA: Harvard University Press.

Goswami, U. (2002a). *The Blackwell handbook of childhood cognitive development*. Oxford, UK: Blackwell.

Goswami, U. (2002b). Inductive and deductive reasoning. In U. Goswami (Ed.), *Blackwell handbook of childhood cognitive development* (pp. 282-302). Oxford, UK: Blackwell.

Harris, P. (2000). *The work of the imagination*. Oxford, UK: Blackwell.

Homer, B., & Olson, D. (1999). Literacy and children's conception of words. *Written Language and Literacy, 2*, 113-137.

Howe, N., Petrakos, H., & Rinaldi, C. (1998). "All the sheeps are dead. He murdered them." Sibling pretense, negotiation, internal state language, and relationship quality. *Child Development, 69*, 182-191.

Hughes, C., & Dunn, J. (1997). "Pretend you didn't know": Preschoolers' talk about mental states in pretend play. *Cognitive Development, 12*, 381-403.

Kress, G. (1996). Writing and learning to write. In D. Olson & N. Torrance (Eds.), *Handbook of education and human development* (pp. 225-256). Oxford, UK: Blackwell.

Kress, G. (1997). *Before writing: Rethinking the paths to literacy*. New York: Routledge.

Levin, I., Korat, O., & Amsterdamer, P. (1996). Emergent writing among Israeli kindergartners: Cross-linguistic commonalities and Hebrew-specific issues. In G. Rijlaarsdam, H. van den Bergh, & M. Couzijn (Eds.), *Theories, methods and methodology in writing research* (pp. 398-419). Amsterdam: Amsterdam University Press.

Lillard, A. (2002). Pretend play and cognitive development. In Goswami, U. (Ed.), *Blackwell Handbook of childhood cognitive development* (pp. 188-205). Oxford, UK: Blackwell.

Marsh, G., Friedman, M., Welch, V., & Desberg, P. (1981). A cognitive developmental theory of reading acquisition. *Reading research: Advances in theory and practice* (Vol. 3, pp. 199-223). New York: Academic Press.

Mather, N., & Goldstein, S. (2001). *Learning disabilities and challenging behaviors*. Baltimore, MD: P. H. Brookes.

McGee, L. (2003). Shaking the very foundations of emergent literacy: Book reading versus phonemic awareness. In J. Isenberg & M. Jalongo (Eds.), *Major trends and issues in early childhood education: Challenges, controversies, and insights* (2nd ed., pp. 114-125). New York: Teachers College Press.

Meyer, R. (2002). *Phonics exposed: Understanding and resisting systematic direct intense phonics instruction*. Mahwah, NJ: Erlbaum.

Mumme, D., Fernald., A., & Herrera, C. (1996). Infants' responses to facial and vocal emotional signals in a social referencing paradigm. *Child Development, 67*, 3219-3237.

Murphy, S., & Dudley-Marling, C. (2003). *Literacy through language arts: teaching and learning in context*. Urbana, IL: National Council of Teachers of English.

Mussen, P., Flavell, J., & Markman, A. (Eds.). (1998). *Handbook of Child Psychology, Vol. 3: Cognitive Development*. New York: Wiley.

Olson, D. (1994). *The world on paper: Conceptual and cognitive implications of reading and writing*. Cambridge: Cambridge University Press.

Olson, D. (2002). What writing does to the mind. In E. Amsel & J. Byrnes (Eds.), *Language, literacy, and cognitive development: The development and consequences of symbolic communication* (pp. 153-165). Mahwah, NJ: Erlbaum.

Olson, D., & Kamawar, D. (2002). Writing as a form of quotation. In J. Brockmeier, M. Wang, & D. Olson (Eds.), *Literacy, narrative, and culture* (pp. 187-198). Richmond, Surrey, UK: Curzon Press.

Overton, W. (1998). Developmental psychology: Philosophy, concepts, and methodology. In Mussen, P., Flavell, J., & Markman, A. (Eds.). (1998). *Handbook of Child Psychology, Volume : Theoretical Models of Development* (pp. 107-188). New York: Wiley.

Overton, W. (2002). Development across the life span: Philosophy, concepts, and theory. In R. M. Lerner, M. A. Easterbrooks, & J. Mistry (Eds.), *Comprehensive Handbook of Psychology: Developmental Psychology* (Vol. 6). New York: Wiley.

Pelletier, J. (2002). Young children's "clever misunderstandings" about print. In J. Brockmeier, M. Wang, & D. Olson (Eds.), *Literacy, narrative, and culture* (pp. 245-265). Richmond, Surrey, UK: Curzon.

Piaget, J. (1962). *Plays, dreams, and imitation in childhood*. New York: Norton.

Piaget, J. (1963). *The origins of intelligence in children*. New York: Norton.

Pressley, M., Wharton-Mcdonald, R., Rankin, J., El-Dinary, P., Brown, R., Afflerbach, P., Mistretta, J., & Yokoi, L. (1997). Elementary reading instruction. In G. Phye (Ed.), *Handbook of academic learning: Construction of knowledge* (pp. 151-198). San Diego, CA: Academic Press.

Rogoff, B. (2003). *The cultural nature of human development*. New York: Oxford University Press.

Rogoff, B., Paradise, R., Mejia-Arauz, R., Correa-Chavez, M., & Angelillo, C. (2003). Firsthand learning through intent participation. *Annual Review of Psychology, 54.*

Roopnarine, J. (2003). Play and early development and education: The instantiation of parental belief systems. In O. Saracho & B. Spodek (Eds.), *Contemporary perspectives on play in early childhood education* (pp. 115-132). Greenwich, CT: Information Age Publications.

Rubin, K., Fein, G., & Vandenberg, B. (1983). Play. In Hetherington, E. (Ed.), *Handbook of child psychology: Socialization, personality, and social development.* (4th edition, Vol. 4, pp. 693-774). New York: Wiley.

Saracho, O., & Spodek, B. (Eds.). (2003). *Contemporary perspectives on in early childhood education*. Greenwich, CT: Information Age Publishers.

Saussure, F. (1983). *A course in general linguistics.* (Trans. by R. Harris.). London: Duckworth.s

Sawyer, K. (1997). *Pretend play as improvisation.* Mahwah, NJ: Erlbaum.

Segal, Z., Williams, M., & Teasdale, J. (2002). *Mindfulness-based cognitive therapy for depression.* New York: Guilford Press.

Seifert, K. (2001). Sociable thinking: Cognitive development in early childhood education. In O. Saracho & B. Spodek (Eds.), *Contemporary perspectives on early childhood education* (pp. 15-40). Greenwich, CT: Information Age Publishers.

Sinclair, H. (1978). Conceptualization and awareness in Piaget's theory and its relevance to the child's conception of language. In A. Sinclair, J. Jarvella, & W. Levelt (Eds.), *The child's conception of language* (pp. 191-200). Berlin: Springer-Verlag.

Skjelfjord, D. (1976). Teaching children to segment spoken words as an aid in learning to read. *Journal of Learning Disabilities, 9,* 297-305.

Smith, F. (2003). Myths of writing. In S. Murphy & C. Dudley-Marling (Eds.), *Literacy through language arts: Teaching and learning in context* (pp. 234-243). Urbana, IL: National Council of Teachers of English.

Snowling, M. (2002). Reading development and dyslexia. In U. Goswami (Ed.), *Blackwell handbook of childhood cognitive development* (pp. 394-411). Oxford, UK: Blackwell.

Sutton-Smith, B. (1997). *The ambiguity of play.* Cambridge, MA: Harvard University Press.

Taylor, M. (1999). *Imaginary companions and the children who create them.* Oxford: Oxford University Press.

Thompson, G., & Johnston, R. (2000). Are nonword and other phonological deficits indicative of a failed reading process? *Reading and Writing, 12,* 63-97.

Tomasello, M., Striano, T., & Rochat, P. (1999). Do young children use objects as symbols? *British Journal of Developmental Psychology, 17,* 563-584.

Truch, S. (1991). *The missing parts of whole language.* Calgary, Alberta: Foothills Educational Materials.

Turbill, J. (2003). Developing a spelling conscience. In S. Murphy & C. Dudley-Marling (Eds.), *Literacy through language arts: Teaching and learning in context* (pp. 327-343) Urbana, IL: National Council of Teachers of English.

Uttal, D. (2003). On the relation between play and symbolic thought: the case of mathematics manipulatives. In O. Saracho & B. Spodek (Eds.), *Contemporary perspectives on play in early childhood education* (pp. 97-114). Greenwich, CT: Information Age Publications.

Valsiner, J. (1998). The development of the concept of development: Historical and epistemological perspectives. In Mussen, P., Flavell, J., & Markman, A. (Eds.). (1998). *Handbook of Child Psychology, Vol. 1: Theoretical Models of Human Development* (pp. 189-232). New York: Wiley.

Vygotsky, L. (1978). *Mind in society: The development of higher mental functions.* Cambridge, MA: Harvard University Press.

Wellman, H. (2002). Understanding the psychological world: Developing a theory of mind. In Goswami, U. (Ed.), *Blackwell Handbook of childhood cognitive development* (pp. 167-187). Oxford, UK: Blackwell Publishers.

Wenger, E. (2004). *Communities of practice: Learning, meaning, and identity.* New York: Cambridge University Press.

YOUNG CHILDREN'S PEER RELATIONS
AND SOCIAL COMPETENCE

Gary W. Ladd
Sarah L. Herald
Rebecca K. Andrews
Arizona State University

INTRODUCTION

Western cultural roots, philosophical perspectives, history, and scientific theories have encouraged us to become believers in the critical role of early experience (see Kessen, 1979). Within the modern social sciences, this view has spurred interest in children's early relationships and their potential to affect later growth and development. Much of this interest has been translated into investigations of early caregiving practices, often with the intention of explicating the effects of specific socialization agents and experiences.

Although the domain of parent-child relations has long been a focal point for theory and research on the contributions of early socialization to children's development, it has increasingly been recognized that agemates play a significant role in the socialization of children's competence and adjustment throughout childhood (e.g., see Berndt & Ladd, 1989; Ladd, 1999; 2005). In fact, some have suggested that early childhood may be a sensitive period for social development, and that certain types of peer experiences during this period set the stage for children's later behavior or adjustment. (Bowlby, 1973; Freud & Dann, 1951; Rutter, 1979).

This hypothesis acquires a heightened sense of importance when one considers that parents' use of childcare for young children has increased exponentially in recent years. As Edwards (1992) observed, "The increasing use of preschools, organized playgroups, and child care arrangements has brought the age of access to peer relations down near the beginning of life" (p. 297). Among the middle-class populations of North American, European, and Asian industrialized nations, families have become increasingly isolated within their communities and separate from larger kin networks. Furthermore, parents who value achievement and economic success enroll their children in preschools and day care programs at early ages so they can be exposed to agemates and develop the skills needed for success in grade school (Edwards, 1992).

Given these scientific and secular trends, it has become increasingly important for parents and child-oriented professionals to understand the nature and value of children's early experience with peers. Fortunately, over the past 75 years, researchers have spent considerable time and energy learning about young children's social competencies, the types of peer relationships they form during the early childhood years, and the potential consequences that may accrue from children's participation in these relationships (see Ladd, 2005). The purpose of this chapter is to survey extant findings on the development of young children's peer relations and social competence, and examine the extent to which these factors are linked with current and later indicators of children's health, development, and adjustment.

IDENTIFYING AND DESCRIBING CHILDREN'S
EARLY PEER RELATIONSHIPS

Rudimentary forms of peer sociability emerge during infancy. Typically, infants orient toward peers by 2 months of age, make simple gestures by 3 to 4 months, and direct smiles and vocalizations to peers by 6 months (Vincze, 1971). During the first year, infants engage in sequential actions with peers, and by the second and third years, toddlers begin to engage in more sophisticated forms of "games" and reciprocal play (see Eckerman, Davis, & Didow, 1989; Vandell & Mueller, 1980).

Young children also form relationships with peers. As early as age 2, children prefer certain peers as play partners (Ross & Lollis, 1989; Vandell & Mueller, 1980) and, over time, early playmate preferences and interactions lead to other, more complex forms of relationships. At least three types of peer relations emerge during the preschool years: *friendship, peer group acceptance/rejection,* and *aggressor-victim relations* (i.e., peer victimization). Whereas friendship refers to a voluntary, *dyadic* relationship that often entails a positive affective bond (Berndt, 1996; Buhrmester & Furman, 1986; Howes, 1988), peer group acceptance/rejection is defined as the degree to which an individual child is liked or disliked by the members of his or her social *group* (Asher, Singleton, Tinsley, Hymel, 1979; Bukowski & Hoza, 1989). In contrast, peer victimization describes a type of relationship in which a subset of children are frequently aggressed on by one or more members of their peer group (Perry, Kusel, & Perry, 1988).

Evidence gathered on these relationship distinctions has revealed that children simultaneously participate in different types of peer relations (Ladd, Kochenderfer, & Coleman, 1997). For example, some children who are rejected by their peer group have a friend (Masters & Furman, 1981; Parker & Asher, 1989), and about a third of victimized children are rejected by their peers (Perry, Kusel, & Perry, 1988). In addition, it has been argued that different types of peer relations offer young children varied resources or "provisions" that uniquely contribute to their development (Furman & Robbins, 1985).

It also should be noted that friendship, peer group acceptance/rejection, and victim-aggressor relations are theoretical constructs and that researchers have differing views about how these forms of relationship are best defined and measured. For these reasons, it is essential to consider how researchers have defined and measured friendship, peer status, and victimization at different age levels.

Infants and Toddlers' Friendships

Researchers often document the earliest of friendships with parent- and teacher-report data, or observations of children's social interactions (see Ladd, 1988; Price & Ladd, 1986). Among infants and toddlers, friendship often has been defined in terms of peer familiarity, consistency of interactions between the partners, and/or the mutual display of positive affect, sharing, and play (Howes, 1988, 1996; Vandell & Mueller, 1980). For example, in research conducted by Howes (1983), dyads were considered friends if: (a) at least 50% of their social initiations resulted in social interaction (mutual preference); (b) one or more exchanges of positive affect occurred between partners (mutual enjoyment); and (c) one or more episodes of reciprocal or complementary play occurred between partners (skillful interaction; p. 1042).

In addition, Ross and Lollis (1989) have shown that toddlers' peer relationships are unique, in the sense that both partners tend to adjust the interactions they conduct with each other, and interact in ways that are different from the ways they treat other children. Furthermore, many toddlers' friendships are sustained over time (Vandell & Mueller, 1980; Howes, 1988; Howes & Phillipsen, 1992). Howes (1983) found that 60% of toddler friends sustained their relationship over a period of months, and Howes and Phillipsen (1992) reported that toddlers' friendships, particularly cross-gender friendships, often lasted well into the preschool years.

Preschoolers' and Young Children's Friendships

Investigators have identified preschoolers' friendships using an assortment of criteria including companionship, intimacy, and affection (see Howes, 1996). Companionship has been defined by observing children's preferences for certain peers and the duration of their interactions and proximity with those peers (Berndt, 1989; Howes, 1996). For example, Hayes, Gerschman, and Bolin (1980) considered preschoolers to be "friends" if they spent at least 50% of play time interacting with each other in either parallel or cooperative play. Hinde, Titmus, Easton, and Tamplin (1985) defined "strong associates" as preschoolers who were in each other's company at least 30% of the time sampled. Other investigators have used complementary reciprocal play as a criterion for friendship (Howes, 1996).

Other characteristics also have been used to identify friendships in the preschool years. Positive affect has been emphasized as a defining feature of preschoolers' friendships because it was theorized that children this age have a level of emotional maturity that enables them to form close ties with peers (Howes, 1983, 1988, 1996; Howes & Phillipsen, 1992). Researchers also have considered intimacy as a criterion for defining young children's friendships. Unlike companionship or shared affect, however, intimacy is difficult to document because it must be inferred from children's interactions (Howes, 1996). However, some researchers have proposed that children often express intimacy with friends through self-disclosure and nurturance in fantasy or imaginary play (e.g., Gleason, 2002; Parker & Gottman, 1989).

Because preschoolers are better able to conceptualize, reflect on, and describe their friendships than infants and toddlers, researchers have been able to use children's self reports to assess friendships (Price & Ladd, 1986). Hayes (1978) found that preschool children could name their best friends and articulate reasons for liking them (e.g., common activities, general play). These abilities made it possible to identify preschoolers' mutual friendships on the basis of peers' reciprocated, or mutual friendship nominations (Howes, 1988): friends are peers who mutually nominate each other as a friend or best friend (Masters & Furman, 1981; Howes, 1988).

As with toddlers, another defining feature of friendship during the preschool years is stability. Evidence from several studies suggests that preschoolers' friendships are fairly stable. Using parents' reports, Park and Waters (1989) identified preschoolers who remained best friends for over 7 months, and about half of these children had friendships that lasted as long as 18 months. Gershman and Hayes (1983) found that about two thirds of the preschool friendships they identified were sustained over one school year. Fully 50% to 70% of the reciprocal friendships identified by Howes (1988) were maintained for a year, and approximately 10% of these friendships were maintained for as long as two years (Howes, 1988). Additionally, Ladd (1990) found that many preschoolers maintained their friendships across the transition into kindergarten and throughout the kindergarten school year. These stability estimates were noteworthy because they exceeded the much briefer durations that researchers had anticipated (see Ladd, 1988).

Researchers theorize that one of the factors that most influences the stability of friendships is the initial quality of the friendship (Berndt, Hawkins, & Hoyle, 1986; Bukowski, Hoza, & Boivin, 1993). Accordingly, friendships that have a positive, solid foundation will be more likely to withstand the test of time as compared to friendships based on more negative attributes (e.g., mutual aggression, control).

Preschoolers' and Young Children's Peer Group Relations

The concept of peer acceptance or status has been defined as the degree to which individual children are accepted versus rejected by members of their peer group (Bukowski & Hoza, 1989; Ladd, 1999). Peer acceptance is typically assessed by asking peer group members (e.g., preschool classmates) to rate or nominate persons with whom they most or least like to associate (see Ladd & Coleman, 1993). Sociometric *rating* methods were originally developed in the 1930s (see Moreno, 1932; Koch, 1933) and further revised for preschool children in subsequent years (see McCandless & Marshall, 1957; Asher, Singleton, Tinsley, & Hymel, 1979). Modern methods require children to rate each of their classmates on a scale from one to three by sorting peer's photographs into three categories, each of which is marked so as to signify differing levels of liking. An acceptance score is calculated by averaging and standardizing the ratings children receive from group members. Those who receive higher versus lower scores are deemed more as opposed to less liked (accepted, rejected), respectively.

The peer *nomination* method is most useful when investigators wish to classify children into "peer status" categories. Typically, preschoolers are asked to nominate classmates who "fit" specific criteria, such as someone you most or least like to play with in school (see Asher et al., 1979). In one of the most widely used classification schemes (Coie, Dodge, & Coppotelli, 1982; Coie & Dodge, 1983), the absolute numbers of nominations a child receives for the "liked most" and "liked least" criteria are summed, standardized, and converted into social impact and social preference scores. In turn, preference and impact scores are standardized within age- or grade-level and used to classify children into one of five peer status categories (i.e., popular, average, controversial, neglected, and rejected; Coie et al., 1982). To illustrate, preschoolers who score high on both social impact and social preference are classified as having popular status, whereas those who receive high social impact scores and low social preference scores are considered to have rejected status. Although this classification scheme was originally developed for school-age children, it has commonly been utilized in research with young children (e.g., see Hazen & Black, 1989; Ladd, Price, & Hart, 1988; Mize & Ladd, 1990).

The utility of rating scale versus nomination measures for preschool children is usually dictated by the investigator's objectives (see Asher & Hymel, 1981). Positive nominations measures may be useful for determining the number of peers who consider an individual child as a best friend or a preferred playmate while rating scales can provide an index of a child's overall level of acceptance by peers. Moreover, the use of positive and negative nominations allows researchers to distinguish between children who are *neglected* versus *rejected* by their classmates.

There is some evidence to suggest that teachers represent a reasonable alternative to gathering sociometric nomination and rating data from young children. Wu, Hart, Draper, and Olsen (2001) studied the concordance and reliability of peer and teacher sociometrics for preschool children. Teachers rated each of their preschool pupils on a scale of 1 (very disliked) to 5 (very liked) based on how much they thought other classmates liked to play with each child. Peer and teacher sociometric scores were found to be equally reliable ($r = .79$). Moreover, both informants' perceptions of children's peer group acceptance (i.e., popularity) were moderately similar (although not identical), suggesting that peers and teachers shared a comparable view of children's popularity within the classroom.

There has been some controversy about the utility of rating versus nomination sociometric measures for young children because evidence about the reliabilities of these tools has been inconsistent (Wu et al., 2001). Although superior test-retest reliability has been reported for ratings over nominations (see Asher & Hymel, 1981; Hymel, 1983; e.g., Asher et al., 1979; Wu et al., 2001), it also has been found that nomination scores can be reliable over brief intervals (see Poteat, Ironsmith, & Bullock, 1986). More recently, Wu et al. (2001) reported moderate test-retest correlations for positive and negative peer nominations and a higher stability coefficient for peer ratings. Most likely, further investigation is needed to resolve this debate.

Peer Victimization: Another Aspect of Young Children's Peer Relations

Children who are frequently the recipients of peers' aggressive behaviors have been described as the victims of *peer aggression* or *bullying* (see Graham & Juvonen, 1998; Kochenderfer & Ladd, 1996; Kochenderfer-Ladd & Ladd, 2001; Perry, Kusel, & Perry, 1988). Because exposure to peer abuse during childhood has been linked with young children's adjustment difficulties (see Ladd, Kochenderfer, & Coleman, 1997; Kochenderfer-Ladd & Wardrop, 2001), researchers have attempted to devise reliable ways to identify the victims of peer aggression. Until recently, investigators tended to rely on either self- or peer-report interviews and questionnaires as a means of identifying victimized children. However, because investigators were not consistently utilizing a single data source, controversies arose over the validity of different informants and the generalizability of findings across investigations (see Ladd, 2005).

Recent investigations (see Ladd & Kochenderfer-Ladd, 2002) have shown that, before grade 2, children's self reports of victimization are more reliable than are peer reports. However, by second grade and thereafter, both self- and peer-report measures appeared to produce data that were reliable, increasingly concordant, and valid in the sense that both types of scores were linked with known correlates of peer victimization. Additional results showed that, by second grade and thereafter, a composite measure that included self, peer, and teacher reports of victimization yielded better estimates of children's interpersonal adjustment than did any single-informant measure.

AGENTS AND CONTEXTS THAT FOSTER CHILDREN'S PEER RELATIONS

Evidence from numerous studies suggests that many different types of persons socialize young children's peer relations and social competence in a variety of settings. Included among these agents and contexts are parents and teachers, the family milieu, neighborhoods and community settings, and child care and preschool environments.

Parental Involvement

It has been proposed that the parent-child and child-peer social systems are linked, such that families influence children's peer relationships and vice versa (Ladd, 1992; Parke & Ladd, 1992; Ladd & Pettit, 2002). Some researchers (e.g., Harris, 1995; 1998), however, have challenged these assumptions by arguing that variations in children's behavior and relationships are largely genetically determined and that parents and families have little impact on children's social development (see Harris, 2000; c.f. Vandell, 2000). However, if families do influence some aspects of children's social competence, it becomes important to understand how this might occur, and how such effects might be transmitted.

According to Ladd and Pettit (2002) there are two processes within the family that may socialize children, which they have labeled *indirect* and *direct* influences. Indirect influences represent "aspects of family life that may affect children's social competence, but that do not "... provide the child with any explicit connection to the world of peers" (p. 270). In contrast, direct influences were defined as "parent's efforts to socialize or manage children's social development, especially as it pertains to the peer context" (p. 270). These distinctions are used to organize relevant research on the links between parent's socialization practices and children's peer relationships.

Indirect influences. Parents may, whether they realize it or not, indirectly affect young children's peer relationships or social competence through their everyday interactions and relations with family members. For example, a primary socialization objective for most parents is to create a family environment that is conducive to children's development and harmonious relationships among family members (Ladd, Profilet, & Hart, 1992). However, in reality, there are substantial differences in the quality of family environments and parent-child relations,

and variations in these factors may have consequences for children's peer relations. To illustrate, it has been argued that indirect family processes affect children's peer relations when children transfer behaviors, beliefs, or relationship patterns that they have learned within the family to the peer context.

Attachment. Attachment theory suggests that children obtain emotional resources and internal working models of relationships from the ties they form with parents. It has been hypothesized that, once acquired, children transfer these resources and schema to other, nonparental, relationships such as those formed with peers (Bowlby, 1973; Cummings & Cummings, 2002; Elicker, Englund, & Sroufe, 1992; Sroufe & Fleeson, 1986). Evidence linking children's relationship schema and the quality of their peer relationships has provided some support for this hypothesis (Cassidy, Kirsh, Scolton, & Parke, 1996; Rudolph, Hammen, & Burge, 1995).

It also has been discovered that children who were securely as compared to insecurely attached to their caregivers tended to exhibit higher levels of social competence when interacting with preschool peers (Waters, Wippman, & Sroufe, 1979). Recently, these findings have been augmented by evidence indicating that secure attachment correlated positively with children's participation in friendships and the quality of those relationships (Lieberman, Doyle, & Markiewicz, 1999; Kerns, Klepac, & Cole, 1996). Furthermore, securely attached children tend to have larger support networks (Bost, Vaughn, Washington, Cielinski, & Bradbard, 1998), more positive affect displays, and higher levels of peer acceptance (LaFreniere & Sroufe, 1985).

Whether these attachment findings are indicative of a *substantial* indirect parental influence remains unclear. In a recent meta-analysis of 63 empirical studies, Schneider, Atkinson, and Tardif (2001) found only modest effect sizes, and concluded that the effects attributed to attachment were not particularly strong, and probably only one of many factors that may contribute to children's social competence.

Parent-Child Relationships. In recent years, researchers have placed lesser emphasis on parenting styles (e.g., Baumrind, 1967) and have focused instead on specific features of parent's behaviors, emotions, and interaction styles. Most studied have been dimensions such as parents' emotional and linguistic responsiveness (Black & Logan, 1995; Cassidy, Parke, Bukovsky, & Braungart, 1992), emotional connectedness with the child (Clark & Ladd, 2000), intrusiveness and support (Pettit, Bates, & Dodge, 1997; Pettit, Clawson, Dodge, & Bates, 1996), and synchrony or balance in parent-child relationships (Pettit & Harrist, 1993). Parents' behavior in socialization exchanges with children has also been examined, along with parental engagement, and parental affect. To illustrate, Parke and colleagues (MacDonald & Parke, 1984; Parke, MacDonald, Beitel, & Bhavnagri, 1988; Parke et al., 1989) found that parents' directiveness and verbal engagement during play were associated with children's peer acceptance. Additionally, Pettit, Brown, Mize, and Lindsey (1998) and Lindsey and Mize (2000) found that mothers' play behaviors were more strongly linked with their daughters' social competence, whereas fathers' play behaviors were linked more strongly with their sons' peer competence. Other researchers have shown that when parents act as "playmates" (i.e., "coplayers"), children may have more opportunities to acquire interactional skills that may generalize to play contexts that involve peers (see O'Reilly & Bornstein, 1993). Among the social interactional styles that parents appear to foster when adopting the playmate role are turn-taking, synchronous exchanges, joint determination of the content and direction of play, and matching of affective states (Russell, Pettit, & Mize, 1998).

The role of parent-child emotional connectedness and autonomy support has been examined as well. Clark and Ladd (2000) discovered that parent-child connectedness correlated positively with many features of children's peer relationships, including dimensions such as friendship, friendship quality, and peer group acceptance. Similar constructs, such as parent-child mutuality (i.e., the degree of balance in parents' and children's rates of initiating play and complying to others initiations) have been found to correlate positively with children's peer acceptance (see Ladd & Pettit, 2002).

Researchers have also investigated how negative qualities of the parent-child relationship are related to children's social competence. Eisenberg, Fabes, and Murphy (1996) examined mother's reactions to their children's emotional experiences and found that mothers who minimized their own feelings had children who exhibited lower levels of social competence. Several investigators have found that parental intrusiveness, control, and overprotectiveness increase children's risk for peer problems, including peer victimization (Finnegan, Hodges, & Perry, 1998). To illustrate, one team of investigators found that boys whose parent-child relationships were overly close, or enmeshed, had a greater likelihood of being victimized by their peers (Ladd & Kochenderfer-Ladd, 1998).

Parent's Discipline Styles.
It has been proposed that parent's restrictive and harsh discipline styles may teach (i.e., model) children how to engage in antisocial behaviors and demonstrate that these behaviors are an effective means of achieving one's own ends in peer relationships. Patterson, Reid, and Dishion (1992) found that children who participated in coercive interactions within their families were more likely to use these same behaviors (e.g., aggression and noncompliance) in their interactions with peers. Other studies suggest that both the parent's power-assertive tactics toward their child and the child's aggressiveness toward their parents were associated with children's use of aggression among peers (Dishion, 1990; Hart, Ladd, & Burleson, 1990; MacKinnon-Lewis et al., 1994; Pettit, Bates, & Dodge, 1997).

There is also evidence to suggest that parental discipline that is administered in an unpredictable, overcontrolling, or psychologically manipulative manner interferes with children's social competence. It has been argued that such behaviors undermine children's autonomy and confidence (e.g., shaming and guilt induction), making it more difficult for them to assert themselves or take initiative in peer situations. Extreme forms of psychological or emotional control may make children submissive or fearful of disapproval, making them more vulnerable to peer victimization (Finnegan, 1995; Ladd & Kochenderfer-Ladd, 1998). These disciplinary styles also have been linked with other types of psychological problems in children (e.g., internalizing problems; Barber, 1996).

In sum, research on parental discipline suggests that use of harsh, coercive, or unpredictable parenting styles may put children at a higher risk for peer relationship problems (Harrist, Pettit, Dodge, & Bates, 1994; Nix et al., 1999; Patterson et al., 1992; Pettit, Bates, & Dodge, 1997). A number of researchers have argued that, if parents' disciplinary practices influence children's peer relations, it may be because children have acquired schemas or emotional reactions from these interactions that they eventually transfer or implement within the peer context (Ladd & Pettit, 2002).

The Family Environment.
Stress in the family may negatively impact children's peer relationships by hindering the ability of the family to provide effective parenting, models of socially competent behavior, and appropriate emotional reactions to distress. To illustrate, DeMulder, Denham, Schmidt, and Mitchell (2000) found that family stress was negatively related to children's competence with peers at school (particularly for boys).

Important distinctions have been drawn among various types of family stressors. More than one stressor may operate within the family context, and researchers have found that larger numbers of stressors tend to have cumulative effects on children. Patterson and colleagues (1991, 1992), for example, examined chronic and acute stressors and found that children who were exposed to a greater number of stressors were more likely to exhibit interpersonal difficulties such as peer rejection. Stressors also have been distinguished on the basis of their severity and duration. Chronic stressors refer to experiences that are severe and endure over long periods of time, and acute stressors denote experiences that are intense but brief in duration (see Crnic & Low, 2002; Ladd & Pettit, 2002).

Chronic Stressors.
Both poverty and sustained loss of income have been linked with family dysfunction and children's personal and interpersonal adjustment problems (see Magnuson & Duncan, 2002). For example, Pettit, Bates and Dodge (1997) assessed stress, socioeconomic status (SES), and single-parent status as indexes of adversity as children entered kindergarten and found that all three of these indicators predicted children's future social difficulties. Similarly, extreme forms of poverty (e.g., homelessness) have been linked with childhood anxiety and depression that, in turn, have been shown to predict poor peer relations (see Buckner, Bassuk, Weinreb, & Brooks, 1999; Cole et al., 1998; Harrist et al., 1997).

Acute Stressors.
Among the many acute family stressors that have been studied are divorce and marital problems (see Wilson & Gottman, 2002). Long, Forehand, Fauber, & Brody, (1987) found that adolescents from divorced families reported lower perceived social competence. Other findings suggest that children who have been exposed to conflictual marital relationships tend to be more oppositional in their peer interactions and less successful at forming friendships (Katz & Gottman, 1993).

The evidence reviewed thus far suggests that indirect parental and family processes are associated with children's social competence and success in peer relations. Considered next are parenting practices that are directly linked to the world of peers.

Direct influences. Parents' attempts to manage their children's peer relations can be construed as direct influences (Ladd & Pettit, 2002) because these activities are typically performed with the aim of assisting or preparing children to participate in the peer culture. Examples include parents' attempts to mediate or regulate children's access to particular playmates, and supervise their peer interactions (Ladd & Pettit, 2002).

Parent's Mediation of Children's Peer Contacts and Play Groups.
Parents mediate, or help young children transition from the family to the peer culture by initiating and arranging playdates or other types of peer contacts. Ladd et al. (1988) found that many parents initiate peer contacts for children at very early ages, including the toddler and preschool years. Moreover, it was discovered that in families in which parents initiated larger numbers of playdates, preschoolers tended to develop better peer relations in school (Ladd & Golter, 1988; Ladd & Hart, 1992). However, the extent to which parents use this form of mediation appears to vary with the child's age. Bhavnagri (1987) found that parent-initiated peer contacts were more often utilized for toddlers than for preschool children. It would appear that, as children get older, they become more capable of arranging their own playdates, or need less assistance from parents to accomplish this task.

A study by Ladd and Hart (1992) offered a glimpse into how some families socialized preschoolers to initiate their own playdates. They found that when parents actively scaffolded the child's skill at initiating play dates, their children tended to become more active and competent at self-initiating these activities. Moreover, compared to other preschoolers who had not been socialized this way, these children exhibited greater success in their kindergarten peer relations.

Arrangement of larger, group-oriented peer activities, such as weekly playgroups, is another way that parents may mediate children's early peer relationships. In larger group settings, children may acquire the communicative and leadership skills that are needed for success in school and other group-oriented settings (Ladd et al., 1992). Lieberman (1977) found that children who had participated in playgroups were more responsive to playmates and engaged in more verbal exchanges with peers. In contrast, Ladd, Hart, Wadsworth, and Golter (1988) reported that playgroup experience correlated positively with classroom adjustment for older (ages 41 to 55 months) but not younger preschoolers (ages 23 to 40 months). It would appear that the experiences children have in peer playgroups, which may closely parallel those that occur in childcare and preschool settings, may benefit older more than younger preschoolers.

Parent's Supervision and Monitoring of Children's Peer Interactions and Relations.
Parental *supervision* has been defined as efforts to oversee and regulate children's ongoing interactions, activities, and relationships with peers. Parental *monitoring*, in contrast, has been variously defined as observing or knowing about children's whereabouts (e.g., surveillance), and as acquiring information from children about their social activities (see Ladd & Pettit, 2002; Stattin & Kerr, 2000). In research with young children, investigators have identified three basic types of parental supervision: interactive intervention, directive intervention, and monitoring.

Interactive Intervention. Parents engage in interactive intervention when they supervise children's peer interactions as active participants within the play context. According to Lollis, Ross, and Tate (1992), very young children, or social novices, benefit most from this type of supervision because they require the support of a socially skilled partner to maintain interactions with peers. Consistent with this contention, Bhavnagri and Parke (1991) found that toddlers derived greater benefits from interactive interventions than did preschoolers.

Directive Intervention. This type of supervision tends be reactive rather than proactive, in the sense that parents remain at a distance from children's peer interactions and only intervene to assist with conflicts or other problems that arise in children's play (Lollis et al., 1992). Research shows that directive interventions tend to be used with older preschoolers, and that children who receive this form of supervision exhibit higher levels of peer acceptance in school settings (see Ladd & Pettit, 2002).

Monitoring. Beyond the preschool years, parents rely more on distal forms of supervision to assess children's activities with peers. There is an extensive literature showing that low levels of parental monitoring are associated with social and academic problems in adolescents (Dishion & McMahon, 1998). However, seldom has parental supervision been studied with young children (for an exception, see Ladd & Golter, 1988).

Contextual Antecedents

Peer contexts include settings that bring young children into contact with agemates. Examples include neighborhoods, larger community settings, childcare and preschools, and early school environments.

Neighborhoods. Neighborhoods provide many locations for children to meet and interact with peers (see Bradley, 2002; Leventhal & Brooks-Gunn, 2000). From the perspective of a child, the neighborhood is much more than a geographical location; it is a "social universe" (Medrich, Roizen, Rubin, & Buckley, 1982). Because young children have limited freedom and mobility, their social encounters are dictated partly by the physical and socioeconomic characteristics of neighborhoods (Medrich et al., 1982).

Studies show that friends tend to live near each other (Gallagher, 1958; Segoe, 1939), and that children's contacts with peers are more frequent in neighborhoods that are flat rather than hilly, and that have sidewalks, parks, and playgrounds (Medrich, 1982). In contrast, children have fewer peer contacts in rural and dangerous neighborhoods (see Medrich et al., 1982; Ladd et al., 1992). In some cases, neighborhoods may operate as a protective factor for children. Kupersmidt, Griesler, DeRosier, Patterson, and Davis (1995b) found that low-income children from single parent homes in low-SES neighborhoods tended to engage in higher levels of aggressive behavior than did children with similar backgrounds who resided in middle-SES neighborhoods.

Community settings. Community settings can also serve as contexts for children to meet, interact, and form relationships with peers. Included among these are structured settings (e.g., Brownies, Cub Scouts, and Little League) and unstructured settings (e.g., parks, public libraries, and community pools).

Young children's participation in adult-sponsored, community-based activities appears to vary with age and social class. Older children appear to use unstructured community settings more than younger children, and middle-class children appear to be the primary consumers of organized community activities (Bryant, 1985; O'Donnell & Stueve, 1983). One team of investigators (Ladd & Price, 1987) found that preschool children's experiences in unstructured community settings predicted lower levels of anxiety and school avoidance during their transition to kindergarten.

Child care and preschool programs. One of the priorities advanced by early childhood researchers and educators is understanding the role of childcare in young children's social development. Of particular interest are findings pertaining to the association between children's participation in childcare and changes in their social competence, peer relations, and school readiness. Thus far, evidence reflecting on this aim has been mixed (NICHD, 2003; Prodromidis, Lamb, Sternberg, Hwang, & Broberg, 1995), and there have been controversies about how the effects of childcare should be investigated, and how the resulting evidence should be interpreted. For this reason, a variety of perspectives and findings must be considered.

Evidence Linking Childcare with Children's Behavior Problems and Peer Relations. Members of the National Institutes of Child Health and Human Development (NICHD) Early Child Care Research Network have examined a plethora of childcare variables as correlates and antecedents of children's development. Of principal interest are findings pertaining to the effects of nonmaternal care on children's socioemotional development. One of the Network's findings was that children who spent greater time in childcare exhibited more behavior problems. This finding was corroborated by prior data showing that children's participation in childcare correlated positively with acting out behavior (Youngblade, 2003), and externalizing problems (Egeland & Heister, 1995; Han, Waldfogel, & Brooks-Gunn, 2001).

However, positive links between children's childcare experience and peer relations also have been reported (see Fabes, Hanish, & Martin, 2003; Ladd et al., 1992), and support for this contention has increased in recent years (see Field, Masi, Goldstein, Perry, & Park, 1988; Howes, 1988; Prodromidis, Lamb, Sternberg, Hwang, & Broberg, 1995). For example, Howes (1988) found that, in the context of childcare settings, young children formed friendships at very early ages, and tended to maintain these friendships over considerable periods of time (e.g., up to 2 years). Findings also indicate that the friendships children form in childcare or preschool settings, and the associated interpersonal skills they acquire in these contexts may

function as supports during subsequent developmental transitions, such as entrance into grade school (see Ladd & Price, 1987; Ladd, 1990). Furthermore, when coupled with preventive or compensatory educational programming, childcare has been linked with positive growth in other aspects of children's development. Love et al. (2003), for example, found that children from low-income families who were enrolled in Early Head Start programs displayed reductions in aggressive behavior problems and gains in cognitive, language, and socioemotional development. These results suggest that higher quality childcare environments have the potential not only to improve children's social development but also transmit skills that prepare them for subsequent developmental challenges.

Early school environments and after-school care arrangements. Many young children participate in preschool programs and, by age 5 or 6, nearly all children attend school (Coie et al., 1993). Once in grade school, many children attend after-school programs. In all of these contexts, children are afforded opportunities to meet and form relationships with peers.

Early School Environments. Classrooms provide a context for children's social development, but some educational settings appear better suited to this purpose than others. Kontos, Burchinal, Howes, Wisseh, & Galinsky (2002) found that the provision of creative activities for children (e.g., books, art supplies, creative play, group learning) and teacher involvement (coded as routine, complex, or none) were significant predictors of children's interactions with peers. More specifically, creative activities (e.g., open-ended art projects, fantasy play) and little or no teacher involvement predicted more complex interactions with peers. Other findings have shown that in high-density classrooms (i.e., those with less physical space per child) there is a higher incidence of children's behavior problems (Campbell & Dill, 1985; see Phyfe-Perkins, 1980; Smith & Connolly, 1980). Higher levels of cooperative peer play and positive talk have been documented in classrooms with individual learning centers (Field, Masi, Goldstein, Perry, & Parl, 1988). More fighting and nonsocial play (e.g., parallel play) has been observed in classrooms that contain fewer toys. Some types of play materials, such as Play-doh, sand, water, crayons, or paint appear to elicit primarily nonsocial forms of play (Rubin, 1977; Rubin, Fein, & Vandenberg, 1983).

School playgrounds can be an important context for peer interaction (Hart, 1993; Ladd & Price, 1993). Evidence suggests that outdoor playgrounds stimulate as much or more social play than indoor environments (Frost, 1986; Hart, 1993). There is some evidence to indicate that children develop differing behavioral styles on playgrounds and these propensities may affect the way a child is perceived by their peers. For example, in one study, aggressive children tended to become disliked by peers, whereas cooperative children were favored as play partners (see Ladd, Price, & Hart, 1988; Ladd & Price, 1993).

After-School Care Arrangements. After-school programs are among the fastest growing segments of childcare services (Seligson, Gannett, & Cotlin, 1992). The choices that parents make about after school arrangements may have important implications for the types of social experiences children have with peers. Although research on after-school care is at an early stage, several types of after-school care have been researched including self-care (time spent without adult supervision), mother care (returning home), formal adult-supervised care (after school programs), and other supervised arrangements.

Thus far, investigators have found that whereas children in self-care arrangements often engaged in antisocial behavior, children in formal, adult-supervised care were less prone toward misconduct (Posner & Vandell, 1994). In fact, Posner and Vandell found that children who participated in formal after-school care spent more time in academic and enrichment activities (e.g. art, music, drama) and less time watching television. These children were better adjusted on a number of developmental criteria, including academic achievement and peer relations. Further more corroboration of these findings was obtained by Pettit, Laird, Bates, and Dodge (1997). These investigators studied young school-age children in a variety of after school care arrangements, and found that the amount of time spent without adult supervision, both before and after school, predicted lower levels of peer competence.

In sum, research findings are consistent with the hypothesis that physical and organizational features of classrooms and after school arrangements are associated with children's peer relations and social adjustment.

Culture and cultural differences. In recent years, greater attention has been devoted to ethnic and cultural diversity in children's peer relations. Studies of preschool and grade school children have been conducted both within and across national boundaries.

North American Subcultures.

Descriptive and comparative studies were undertaken to profile the peer relations of majority (typically Euro-American) and minority (typically African-American) children. It was discovered that young children were more likely to form ethnically-diverse friendships and peer-interaction patterns if they attended schools with diverse rather than homogeneous student populations (Howes & Wu, 1990). Studies conducted with African-American children suggested that they tended to have more friendships, as well as more opposite-sex friendships, than did their Euro-American counterparts (Kovacs, Parker, & Hoffman, 1996). Other findings suggested that African-American children were more likely to affiliate with deviant peers in low-income than in higher-income neighborhoods (Ge, Brody, Conger, Simons, & Murry, 2002; Kupersmidt, Griesler, DeRosier, Patternson, & Davis, 1995b), and that middle-income neighborhoods tended to protect single-parent African-American children from engaging in aggressive behavior (Kupersmidt et al., 1995b).

Cross-National Investigations of Children's Peer Relations.

It has become increasingly clear that there are cultural similarities and differences in children's peer relations and in the way social competence is defined. To illustrate, some investigators have found differences across cultures in the way children maintain their friendships and the degree to which they incorporate conflict into these relationships. Studies conducted in Italy and Canada, for example, showed that Italian children were better at maintaining their close relationships with friends and more prone to embrace, and perhaps even enjoy debates and disputes with their friends (Casiglia, LoCoco, & Zappulla, 1998; Corsaro & Rizzo, 1990; Fonzi, Schneider, Tani, & Tomada, 1997; Schneider et al., 1997).

In addition, there is evidence to suggest that the meaning of social competence and social adjustment varies by culture. Researchers working in Sweden, for example, identified two categories of behavior that exemplified social competence: prosocial orientation and social initiative (Rydell, Hagekull, & Bohlin, 1997). The former concept implied that children were generous, altruistic, and helpful toward peers, the latter meant that children were adept at creating peer activities and sociable with playmates. Studies conducted with Chinese children suggested that social competence could be described in much the same way (Chen, Li, Li, Li, & Liu, 2000). However, these parallels do not appear to replicate across all cultures. For example, it appears that North American children are more inclined to think of sociability and leadership as synonymous forms of social competence, whereas children living in southern Italy draw a greater distinction between peers who are outgoing, exuberant, and interested in making friends (sociability) and those who are polite, trustworthy, and good leaders (leadership; Casiglia, Lo Coco, & Zapplulla, 1998). Furthermore, other studies reveal that, among Chinese more than North American children, shy-sensitive behaviors tend to be perceived favorably and correlate positively with peer group acceptance (Chen, Rubin, & Sun, 1992).

Next, another kind of relationship that children form in classrooms—the teacher-child relationship—is considered as a determinant of young children's peer relations and competence.

Teacher-Child Relationships

Compared to evidence assembled on other socializing agents and contexts, far less is known about children's relationships with teachers, and how these relationships are linked with children's social development. Accordingly, investigators have begun to study specific features of the teacher-child relationship, and the association that exists between these features and children's social and scholastic competence (see Birch & Ladd, 1996; Pianta, Hamre, & Stuhlman, 2003).

Features of the teacher-child relationship. It has been theorized that the teacher-child relationship encompasses several important features. Howes and colleagues (e.g., Howes & Hamilton, 1992; 1993; Howes & Matheson, 1992) conceptualized the teacher-child relationship from an attachment perspective, and used this framework to demarcate its features (e.g. secure, avoidant, resistant/ambivalent). Other investigators, such as Lynch & Cicchetti (1992), identified similar features but gave them different labels (e.g., optimal, deprived, disengaged, confused, average). Pianta and colleagues (Pianta & Steinberg, 1992, Pianta, Steinberg, & Rollings, 1995) have drawn on attachment theory and related empirical findings to formulate a model of teacher-child relationship that contains three qualitative features—closeness, conflict, and dependency.

Antecedents of the teacher-child relationship. A key assumption guiding research on the teacher-child relationship is that the child's typical way of interacting or behaving toward others, or their behavioral orientations, affects the relationships they form with teachers. Ladd and colleagues (e.g., Birch & Ladd, 1998; Ladd, Birch, & Buhs, 1999; Ladd & Burgess, 1999) found that the behavioral orientations that predicted children's success or difficulty in peer relationships also forecasted the type of relationships they developed with teachers. To be specific, throughout the early school years, aggressive children were much more likely to develop conflictual rather than close relationships with their teachers. Asocial behavior (moving "away from" others) also was a correlate of children's concurrent and future problems in both relationship domains. Prosocial styles of interacting with peers and teachers were closely tied to children's concurrent closeness with teachers, but not as strong a predictor of future teacher-child relationship quality as were antisocial or asocial behavioral styles.

The teacher-child relationship and children's peer relations and school adjustment. Within early classroom environments, the relationships that children form with teachers have been hypothesized to yield various social "provisions" (i.e., supports, stressors) that may operate as risks or protective factors for children's development (see Birch & Ladd, 1996; Ladd, Kochenderfer, & Coleman, 1997). Evidence gathered in a study conducted by Ladd, Birch, and Buhs (1999) showed that kindergarten children who exhibited higher levels of antisocial behavior not only developed less close and more conflictual relationships with their teachers but also lower levels of peer acceptance and friendships with classroom peers. Subsequently, children who developed these adverse relationships with both teachers and peers manifested lower levels of classroom participation and less favorable achievement trajectories.

Beyond these findings, some corroboration was found for the premise that teacher-child relationships buffer children from maladjustment, especially during periods of challenge or transition. To illustrate, it was discovered that teacher-child closeness at the outset of kindergarten forecasted increases in children's participation in classroom peer activities and in their affection toward school, regardless of their tendency to engage in aggressive behaviors (Ladd & Burgess, 2001; Ladd, Buhs, & Seid, 2001). In sum, closer teacher-child relationships may provide young children with resources (e.g., emotional security, guidance, aid) that facilitate an "approach" orientation (as opposed to an "avoidant" or "resistant" stance) toward the interpersonal and scholastic demands of the classroom and school (Birch & Ladd, 1996; Howes, Matheson, & Hamilton, 1994; Pianta, Steinberg, & Rollins, 1995).

FEATURES AND FUNCTIONS OF CHILDREN'S EARLY PEER RELATIONSHIPS

In addition to describing the types of relationships children have with peers, researchers also have investigated how these relationships are formed, the types of experiences that children have in these relationships, and the possible effects that peer relationships have on children's development. Interest in these processes has been the impetus for a large number of investigations.

Formation of Children's Peer Relationships

Before children can form friendships, become accepted in their peer group, or extricate themselves from aggressor-victim relations, they must first develop the requisite social competencies. For young children, these skills are most likely developed during peer interactions that take place in play dates, neighborhoods, childcare settings, and schools.

Friendship formation. Children are selective about the persons they choose as friends, and their choices are guided by demographic (Hartup, 1983), behavioral (Rubin, Lynch, Coplan, Rose-Krasnor, & Booth, 1994), personal (see Aboud & Mendelson, 1996), or psychological considerations (Epstein, 1989). Children typically befriend others who are similar to themselves in age (Hartup, 1970), sex (Graham & Cohen, 1997; Howes & Phillipsen, 1992; Kupersmidt, DeRosier, & Patterson, 1995a; Masters & Furman, 1981; see Gottman, 1986), and race (Asher, Oden, & Gottman, 1977; Graham & Cohen, 1997; Kupersmidt, DeRosier, & Patterson, 1995a). In addition, children often choose friends that have similar attitudes, beliefs, personalities and interactional styles (Epstein, 1989). Rubin et al. (1994) observed the interactions of unfamiliar preschoolers and found that children tended to associate with peers who engaged in similar play behaviors. Similarly, Poulin et al. (1997) found that third graders tended to be friends with peers who displayed similar behavior patterns including aggression, shyness, leadership, and rough and tumble play.

While most researchers contend that similarity between friends is associated with the formation of the friendship (i.e., selective affiliation; e.g., Poulin et al., 1997; Rubin et al., 1994), current empirical work on determinants of friendship selection has not falsified the theory that similarity develops as a byproduct of the relationship (i.e., mutual socialization; see Aboud & Mendelson, 1996; Hartup, 1996). For example, as dyad members come to know one another, and engage in processes such as self-disclosure, they may begin to adopt some of each other's preferences and behaviors.

Even though research on similarity speaks to the question of how children are attracted to specific peers, it has little to say about the friendship formation process (Parker, 1986). Although there is evidence indicating that children are attracted to peers with whom they share similarities, it is also clear that children do not develop friendships with all of the children to whom they are attracted (Parker, 1986). In fact, it is likely that the friendship formation process is complex. As two children interact and become acquainted and aware of each other's social behaviors, skills, and personalities, their interest in each other may wax and wane (Furman, 1982).

Researchers initially studied the acquaintanceship process by documenting changes in the patterns of interaction among unacquainted children. Both Gottman and Parkhurst (1980) and Furman (1982) proposed unique theories of acquaintanceship involving hierarchical processes or levels of interaction.

According to Gottman and Parkhurst (1980), dyads must successfully progress through eight levels of interaction, ranging from arousing another's interest in an activity to higher-level events such as fantasy play, in order to move beyond simple acquaintanceship and develop qualities such as closeness or intimacy. Based on Furman's (1982) theory of acquaintanceship, children's relationships develop while undergoing four central processes: (a) disclosure of personal information and discovery of similarities, (b) establishment of a common activity, (c) "individualization" of the relationship, and (d) development of an affective bond.

To examine the acquaintanceship process, and gain more insight into how children make friends, Gottman (1983) investigated the role of conversational processes in the formation of preschoolers' friendships. In these studies, Gottman set out to determine whether specific conversational processes would predict the extent to which pairs of unacquainted children "hit it off" and progressed toward friendship. After recording the interactions of many pairs of preschoolers, Gottman (1983) evaluated a small number of salient conversational processes to determine their ability to predict friendship formation. Six conversational elements emerged as important predictors of successful friendship formation: (a) connectedness and clarity of information, (b) information exchange, (c) establishment of common ground, (d) conflict resolution, (e) positive reciprocity, and (f) self-disclosure. Children who were successful at making friends were likely to use information exchange as a safe interaction strategy when conversation went astray, and were able to adeptly escalate and deescalate levels of play as necessary. Moreover, individual children differed in their ability to successfully execute many of these conversational processes. Taken together, these findings suggest that some or all of these six conversational processes are instrumental in the development of children's friendships.

Building on this work, Parker (1986) designed a novel study in which the same six conversational processes identified by Gottman (1983) were manipulated in order to determine whether they were causally related to friendship formation. To accomplish this task, he constructed a "surrogate" preschool child called "Panduit" to act as an experimental confederate. Panduit, a 2-foot-tall green doll, was dressed in silver clothing and contained a hidden electronic receiver/speaker that enabled it to carry on age-appropriate conversations with the preschool subjects. To systematically manipulate the nature of the conversation between the child and Panduit, examples of skilled and unskilled behavior were identified for each of the conversational processes. A female and male assistant were trained to speak as Panduit in a childlike voice while systematically varying the skillfulness of their conversation. Thus, two experimental conditions were created, one in which Panduit was skilled and one in which Panduit was unskilled. It was expected that children who interacted with Panduit in the skilled condition would be more likely that those in the unskilled condition to "hit it off" and progress toward friendship. Results from this study indicated that children who interacted with the skilled Panduit were many times more likely to hit it off than children who were paired with the unskilled Panduit.

The findings from this study, and from Gottman's (1983) longitudinal investigation, illustrated the relative importance of particular conversational processes at different points during the development of friendship. Specifically, as children become acquainted, the clarity and connectedness of communication, information exchange, establishment of common-ground activities, and conflict resolution become increasingly important as determinants of friendship or "hitting it off." Similarly, although self-disclosure processes were of little predictive value during initial encounters, they did forecast progress toward friendship by the second and third sessions. By contrast the predictive power of reciprocity decreased across play sessions. The significance of these findings was further more illustrated by the fact that Gottman (1983) found that these processes could account for more that 80% of the variance in children's progress toward friendship. In sum, these investigators provided considerable insight into the means by which young children form friendships.

Becoming accepted or rejected in peer groups. Joining and becoming an accepted member of a peer group is a social task that nearly all children confront as they venture forth into neighborhoods, day cares, or school systems. To better understand how children approach and successfully join a peer group, which eventually leads to the development of a reputation or status within the group, researchers studied both the processes involved in peer group entry as well as the antecedents of peer group acceptance and rejection. These lines of inquiry required investigators to observe groups of familiar or unfamiliar children as they approached and negotiated social situations in order to better understand how certain positive (i.e., inclusion, acceptance) or negative (i.e. exclusion, rejection) peer group outcomes developed.

Peer Group Entry Research. To ascertain how children approach and successfully join a group of peers engaged in an activity, investigators initially used observational and ethnographic methods in natural settings. For example, as an observer in preschool classrooms, Corsaro (1981) took extensive field notes detailing children's efforts to enter ongoing play groups, and peers' responses to children's entry attempts. Corsaro discovered that peer's initially resisted a child's entry bid around 50% of the time. Because of this high rate of refusal, the investigator examined the tactics that peers used to exclude others from their activities and identified five categories of exclusion strategies (listed in descending order based on percentage of use): claims of ownership, appeals to limitations based on overcrowding, verbal resistance without justification, denial of friendship, and reference to arbitrary rules. Despite the numerous exclusion strategies children faced when trying to join a peer group, Corsaro noted that some children (about 50% of those initially excluded) were able to overcome peers' initial resistance they met and negotiate their way into the group's activity.

Using a more controlled setting, Putallaz and Gottman (1981) extended this line of research by examining how children who were more or less accepted by peers differed in their attempts to enter ongoing peer group activities. Second and third graders who were the most and least accepted by their classmates participated in the study as either an entrant (i.e., the child attempting to enter the group) or as a member of the peer group (dyads were used to represent peer groups). Gaining entry into the dyad's game proved somewhat difficult for all children because the study was designed so that none were able to join the group without some resistance. However, the findings showed that unpopular more than popular children were more likely to have their entry bids ignored or rejected. This likely occurred because the unpopular children tended to use entry bids that drew attention to themselves (i.e., talked about themselves, stated their feelings and opinions) as opposed to acting in ways that were relevant to the peers' ongoing conversation or activity. Thus, Putallaz and Gottman concluded that well-liked children may be better equipped to negotiate entry into peer groups because they are capable of identifying situational norms or expectations and acting accordingly.

To further investigate this hypothesis and correct for previous methodological problems, Putallaz (1983) used two preschool confederates, who were not known by the entrant, to serve as the peer group in the entry situations. The confederates were trained to carry out a scripted conversation while playing different games to ensure that all entrants were exposed to a comparable entry situation. Results corroborated Putallaz and Gottmans's (1981) findings in that children who used entry bids that drew attention to themselves were less likely to gain access to the peer activity. Children in the study who made these self-focused, low relevance entry bids often were not well accepted by their classmates in kindergarten, whereas children who became accepted tended to use more appropriate bids. It was concluded that the relevance of a child's entry bids in relation to peers' activities was an important factor in determining whether the peer group would accept them.

Dodge, Schlundt, Schocken, and Delugach (1983) extended peer group entry research by observing boys of different sociometric statuses as they attempted to enter peer groups in natural and quasiexperimental environments. Analyses revealed that boys' attempts to enter groups were more often successful when they used a particular sequence of entry behaviors. To be specific, successful entrants first gathered information by observing peer's behavior while waiting or hovering on the periphery of their activity. Next, based on information they had gleaned by observing peers and their play, the entrants imitated some of the peer's behaviors. Finally, after completing these steps, the entrants made an effort to join the play by enacting relevant, group-oriented statements or entry behaviors. Results showed that popular and average boys were three times more likely to follow this order of entry behaviors than were rejected or neglected boys. Dodge et al. concluded that children's success at group entry was maximized when they followed this strategy of progressing from lower to higher risk entry behaviors.

In later investigations, researchers investigated how characteristics of both the entrants and the peer group might affect children's success at joining peer groups. Putallaz and Wasserman (1989) observed the entry behaviors of first, third, and fifth grade children in a naturalistic setting and found that children were less likely to approach peer dyads and triads than

individuals or groups composed of four or more peers. They also found that girls' entry bids, as opposed to boys' bids, were more likely to be rejected or ignored by their peers. Zarbatany and colleagues (Borja-Alvarez, Zarbatany, & Pepper, 1991; Zarbatany & Pepper, 1996; Zarbatany, Van Brunschot, Meadows, & Pepper, 1996) found that, when attempting to join peers, girls were less obtrusive and active than boys, and when in the role of a group member or "host," girls admitted more newcomers and were more attentive to entrants than were boys.

Research on the Correlates of Children's Peer Group Status.
In addition to studies of peer group entry, which focused on the behaviors children utilized to access ongoing peer activities, researchers also investigated other factors that were hypothesized to have an effect on children's acceptance by members of their peer groups (e.g., classmates). Early attempts to address this objective were largely correlational in nature. That is, investigators searched for child characteristics that were concurrently associated with peer group acceptance versus rejection. Evidence revealed that that the attractiveness of children's facial appearance was correlated with their peer status (e.g., Vaughn & Langlois, 1983; Young & Cooper, 1944), as were their names, behaviors, and other personal attributes (see Asher, Oden, & Gottman, 1977). Findings from many studies indicated that children who engaged in positive behaviors (e.g., helpfulness, rule following, cooperativeness, prosocial peer interactions) tended to be accepted by peers, whereas children who treated peers negatively (e.g., acted aggressively, were disruptive, violated rules, etc.) tended to be rejected by peers (see Hartup, Glazer, and Charlesworth, 1967; Coie, Dodge, & Kupersmidt, 1990). Other correlates included social cognitions such as the types of goals and strategies that children devised for peer interactions (Asher & Renshaw, 1981; Ladd, & Oden, 1979; Mize & Ladd, 1988; Renshaw & Asher, 1983), and the consequences they expected to result from their goals and strategies (Crick & Ladd, 1990; Perry, Perry, & Rasumssen, 1986).

Later, it was argued that peer-rejected children could be divided into behavioral subtypes based on whether they tended to exhibit aggressive versus withdrawn behavior (see Boivin, Thomassin, & Alain, 1989; French, 1988; Williams & Asher, 1987). Results showed that, in samples of school age children, about 50% of peer-rejected boys acted aggressively toward peers or engaged in other forms of antisocial behaviors (e.g., dishonesty, disruptiveness, noncompliance, impulsiveness). In contrast, only about 13%–20% of peer-rejected boys evidenced shy or withdrawn tendencies (French, 1988; Williams & Asher, 1987). Subtypes of peer-rejected girls, in contrast, were not as easily discerned; attempts to define aggressive and withdrawn subtypes in samples of rejected girls often yielded inconclusive results (French, 1990).

Subsequent studies (Bierman, Smoot, & Aumiller, 1993; Patterson, Kupersmidt, & Griesler, 1990; Volling, Mackinnon-Lewis, Rabiner, & Baradaram, 1993) showed that aggressive-rejected children, when compared with accepted children, were seen as uncooperative, inattentive, poor leaders, lacking a sense of humor, and as having difficulties getting along with adults. Peers tended to see these children as unattractive and scholastically inept. Furthermore, aggressive-rejected children were found to have inflated levels of self-esteem, suggesting that they overestimated their skills and competence. In contrast, withdrawn-rejected children were viewed as more athletically inept than accepted children, and also more unattractive and distressed. Thus, whereas aggressive-rejected boys actively engaged in many forms of misconduct and had fairly serious behavior problems, withdrawn-rejected boys tended to be shy and passive, and often inept in the sense that they were seldom sensitive or prosocial toward others.

Overall, however, investigators attempts to document the concomitants of children's peer group status were of limited value. As Moore (1967) first recognized, correlational data could not help investigators discern whether children's behaviors were a cause or consequence of their peer acceptance or rejection.

Research on the Antecedents of Children's Peer Group Status. In the early 1980s, researchers designed studies that shed greater light on the behavioral antecedents of children's peer status. The most important of these investigations were conducted with school-age boys and were designed as short-term longitudinal studies (see Coie & Kupersmidt, 1983; Dodge, 1983). Dodge (1983) created small playgroups of unacquainted boys and observed their interactions during eight play sessions conducted over a 2-week period. Following the final play session, children completed sociometric interviews, and those who had become popular, average, rejected, or controversial with their play partners were identified. Analyses were then conducted to determine how children behaved before they developed their status or reputations with play partners. Dodge found that different patterns of behavior emerged over time for children in each status group. For example, boys who became well-accepted by their playgroup companions engaged in high rates of social conversation and cooperative play, and seldom acted aggressively. Rejected boys, by contrast, displayed more inappropriate, disruptive behaviors and made more hostile verbalizations than boys who were later identified as average in status. Compared to children in the other status groups, rejected boys also hit peers more often.

Using a similar methodology, Coie and Kupersmidt (1983) identified boys who were classified as popular, average, rejected, or neglected by their peer groups at school, and observed them in either unfamiliar or familiar playgroups over a 6-week period. Four boys, one from each of the four sociometric categories, were assigned to each group. Videotaped observations and sociometric interviews were used to chart the boys' behavior and their evolving peer status in each type of playgroup. Results showed that, in both types of playgroups (i.e., familiar and unfamiliar partners), popular boys rarely engaged in aggressive behavior, often reminded others of the rules, and established group norms. Rejected boys, in contrast, were viewed by playmates as troublemakers (e.g., as persons who start fights) and tended to be more hostile and aggressive in their interactions with peers. In addition, it was discovered that boys who were rejected by their classmates in school quickly formed the same reputations in unfamiliar playgroups. In fact, after only three play sessions, the correlation between children's classroom peer status and the reputations they acquired in their playgroups was as high

in the unfamiliar condition as it was in groups of familiar peers. Based on these findings, it was concluded that rejected peer status could be quite stable because previously rejected boys tend to bring their aversive behaviors with them into new play situations.

Similar findings were reported with samples of preschool children in naturalistic contexts (e.g., classrooms and playgrounds). Ladd, Price and Hart (1988, 1990) found that preschooler's playground behaviors at the outset of school predicted changes in their status among classmates by the middle and end of the school year. Children who played cooperatively became better liked by classmates over time, whereas those who frequently argued with and hit others became disliked and rejected by peers. Similarly, children who utilized prosocial behaviors with a broad range of peers during preschool tended to become better liked and less rejected by new classmates after they entered kindergarten (Ladd & Price, 1987).

As researcher's conceptions of aggression evolved, distinctions were made between different forms of antisocial behavior (e.g., proactive vs. reactive aggression) based on their likely social functions (Dodge & Coie, 1987; Dodge, Coie, Pettit, & Price, 1990). Reactive aggression was defined as aversive behaviors, often elicited by children's emotional or defensive reactions to some form of peer provocation. Conversely, proactive aggressive was defined as behaviors performed to achieve a specific goal, and this behavior was further more differentiated into instrumental aggression, which served the purpose of obtaining external, often object-oriented goals (e.g., hitting to gain access to another's toy) and bullying, which was often used to achieve social domination or control over peers. To better understand how these different forms of aggression affected children's reputations in the peer group, researchers conducted another wave of playgroup studies with children of different ages. For example, Dodge et al. (1990) examined the social interactions of groups of unacquainted first and third grade boys. Results demonstrated that instrumental aggression was associated with peer group rejection at all ages, whereas reactive aggression and bullying were found to be more closely associated with peer group rejection only in older children.

One limitation of this line of research was that investigators tended to focus on forms of aggression that were more characteristic of boys (e.g., physical aggression), and did little to examine the forms of aggression more commonly exhibited by girls (e.g., indirect, social, or relational aggression; see Cairns, Cairns, Neckerman, Ferguson, Gariepy, 1989; Crick & Grotpeter, 1995; Galen & Underwood; 1997; Lagerspetz, Bjorkqvist, & Peltonen, 1988). Because of the tendency to define aggression in ways that were indicative of boys' behaviors, investigators often found that boys were more aggressive than girls (Coie et al., 1982; Coie et al., 1990; French, 1988, 1990). However, these findings were challenged by recent investigators who not only argued that girl's were aggressive but also contended that the forms of aggression exhibited by girls were more subtle and indirect than those used by boys (Cairns et al., 1989; Crick & Grotpeter, 1995; Lagerspetz et al., 1988).

There has been some debate about the definition and measurement of less direct forms of aggression. Scandinavian psychologists used the term *indirect aggression* (Bjorkqvist,

Lagerspetz, & Kaukiainen, 1992; Lagerspetz, Bjorkqvist, & Peltonen, 1988) to refer to subtle and covert aggressive behaviors such as gossiping behind a child's back, telling others not to play with a particular child, and revealing another child's secrets. Alternatively, Crick and colleagues (Crick, 1995, 1996; Crick, Casas, & Mosher, 1997; Crick & Grotpeter, 1995) introduced the term *relational aggression*, which they defined as intentionally manipulating and harming peers' relationships. These investigators found that girls were more likely to engage in relational aggression than boys, and that relational aggression contributed to peer group rejection over and above overt forms of aggression (i.e., proactive and reactive aggression). Additionally, Crick et al. (1997) demonstrated that the link between relationally aggressive behaviors and peer rejection for both boys and girls was apparent as early as the preschool years. In contrast, other investigators proposed the term *social* aggression (Cairns et al., 1989; Galen & Underwood, 1997) to represent indirect forms of aggression that children used to harm others (e.g., damage a peer's self-esteem) or their relationships (e.g., a peer's social reputation). This concept differed somewhat from that postulated by Crick and colleagues (1995, 1996; Crick, Casas, & Mosher, 1997; Crick & Grotpeter, 1995) and the Scandinavian psychologists (Lagerspetz et al., 1988) because it was not measured with items that referred to direct verbal aggression (e.g., "Calls names," Lagerspetz et al., 1988; "Tells friends they will stop liking them unless they do what they say," Crick & Grotpeter, 1995; see Salmivalli, Kaukiainen, & Lagerspetz, 2000), but did include indirect forms of nonverbal aggression (e.g., menacing gestures; rolling one's eyes, etc.).

In addition to early prosocial and antisocial behaviors, other aspects of children's social interactions and skills may play a role in the development of peer status. As is the case with friendship (cf. Gottman, 1983), recent studies suggest that children's communication skills, particularly those contributing to the connectedness and coherence of their discourse with peers, are related to the emergence and maintenance of social status. Hazen and Black (1989) found that well-liked (i.e., high-status) children were more skilled than disliked children at clearly directing verbal and nonverbal communications toward specific peers, and at responding to peers' communications in a contingent and relevant way. High-status children also were more likely to offer a rationale or alternative idea when rejecting peer's initiations.

In a second study, Black and Hazen (1990) identified high and low-status preschoolers and then observed their communications with acquainted and unacquainted peers. With both acquainted and unacquainted peers, low- as compared to high-status children were less likely to respond contingently to other's questions and initiations. They also initiated more irrelevant turns in the conversation. Because disliked children demonstrated these response patterns with acquainted and unacquainted peers, the investigators concluded that communication clarity and connectedness contributes to both the formation and maintenance of peer status (Black & Hazen, 1990).

Pathways to peer victimization. Because it is not ethical to experimentally manipulate the possible causes of peer abuse to determine whether children become victimized, researchers have searched for factors that precede or are associated with peer victimization. Of course, this approach to understanding the processes that lead to victimization is limited because it does not allow researchers to fully discern cause and effect (Perry, Hodges, & Egan, 2001). Thus, caution must be observed when interpreting findings so as not to unfairly blame victims for the maltreatment they experience.

In the last decade or so, the possible determinants of peer victimization that received the most empirical attention were child, interpersonal, and family factors (see Graham & Juvonen, 1998; Perry et al., 2001). Although each of these potential determinants is reviewed separately, it is likely that children's risk for peer victimization is affected by a confluence of child, peer, and family factors (see Perry et al., 2001).

Child Characteristics and Victimization. Data from early studies suggested that victims often were physically weaker than bullies (Olweus, 1978, 1984) and recent findings show that weaker children are at greater risk for increasing or persistent victimization (Egan & Perry, 1998; Hodges & Perry, 1999). There is also evidence to suggest that victimized children fall into at least two behavioral subtypes—*nonaggressive* (i.e., sometimes called "passive") *victims* and *aggressive victims* (cf. also called "provocative" victims; see Olweus, 1978; Schwartz et al., 1997). More research attention has been focused on passive victims than on their aggressive counterparts because more children of the former rather than the latter subtype tend to be identified in research samples (Ladd & Kochenderfer-Ladd, 1998; Kochenderfer-Ladd & Ladd, 2001; Olweus, 1978; Schwartz et al., 1997; Schwartz, Proctor, & Chien, 2001).

It is common for passive victims to display internalizing (inhibiting) emotional reactions or states such as anxiousness, fearfulness, and depression (Gazelle & Ladd, 2003; Harrist et al., 1997; Ladd & Burgess, 1999). In contrast, aggressive victims appear more prone toward externalizing behaviors, restlessness, and negative emotional states (e.g., anger, impulsivity, irritability, dysregulated affect; see Kumpulainen et al., 1998; Perry et al., 1998; Schwartz et al., 1997; Schwartz et al., 2001), as well as retaliatory forms of aggression (i.e., reactive aggression; see Dodge & Coie, 1987). Like passive victims, aggressive victims appear to be at risk for increased victimization over time (Egan & Perry, 1998; Hanish, 1997; Hodges, Boivin, Vitaro, & Bukowski, 1999).

Children who are targeted for peer victimization appear to have thought patterns that differ from nonvictimized children. Like other types of aggressive children, aggressive victims appear to assume that peers harbor hostile intentions toward them (Schwartz et al., 1998, 2001). Reactive-aggressive victims, in particular, have been found to have a tendency to misinterpret peers' motives in ambiguous circumstances as hostile (Schwartz et al., 1998). Low self-regard has been documented in both passive and aggressive victims, with the latter group manifesting the most debilitating self perceptions (Perry et al., 2001).

Peer Relationships and Victimization. Children who fail to develop allies within their peer groups are more likely to become victimized. Children who are rejected, or highly disliked by most members of their peer groups, appear to be most vulnerable to this kind of maltreatment (Gazelle & Ladd, 2002;

Perry et al., 2001) and often are increasingly victimized over time (Hodges & Perry, 1999). In contrast, children who have many reciprocated friendships appear to be less at risk for victimization, even if they possess other risk factors (physical weakness, poor family relationships; Hodges, et al., 1997; Hodges et al., 1999; Schwartz, Dodge, Pettit, & Bates, 2000).

Parenting, Family Socialization, and Victimization.
Qualities of the caregiver-child relationship and caregiver's parenting styles have been linked with children's peer victimization. Investigators have reported that histories of anxious-resistant or anxious-avoidant caregiver attachment antecede preschooler's exposure to peer victimization (Troy and Sroufe, 1987). In studies of passive victims, parent's coercive control and lack of responsiveness correlated positively with girls' status as victims, and maternal overprotectiveness correlated positively with boys' status as victims (Finnegan, 1995; Olweus, 1993). In studies of aggressive boys, abusive family conditions were associated with exposure to peer victimization (Schwartz et al., 1997).

The School Context and Victimization.
Because victimization is particularly likely to happen when adult supervision is minimal, it has been argued that unmonitored school contexts (e.g., school playgrounds, bathrooms, recess periods) may be especially conducive to victimization. At least one researcher (Olweus, 1993) has shown that lower teacher-student ratios during school recess were associated with higher levels of peer victimization.

Features and Processes of Children's Peer Relationships

After identifying the different forms of children's peer relationships (i.e., friendship, peer group acceptance/rejection, victimization), investigators turned their attention toward describing the nature of peer relationships in terms of their underlying features and processes (Ladd, 1999). The impetus for identifying and assessing features of children's peer relationships was to better ascertain how those relationships might expose children to different types of social experiences which in turn, could uniquely contribute to their social, emotional, and cognitive development.

Friendship features and friendship quality.
In research on friendships, researchers have distinguished between the concepts of *friendship features* and *friendship quality* (Berndt, 1996; see Sullivan, 1953). Friendship *features* refer to both positive and negative attributes (e.g., companionship, validation, help, power, conflict) and can be differentiated into relationship processes (i.e., observable behaviors and exchanges among friendship dyads such as play styles, conflict, or cooperation) and relationship provisions (i.e., benefits children gain from their friendships such as self-affirmation, companionship, or security; see Ladd & Kochenderfer, 1996). In contrast, friendship *quality* represents a relationship's worth as estimated from a child's point of view.

Investigators have created several measures of friendship features/quality (for a review, see Furman, 1996), some of which can be used with young children. An examination of the data gathered on friendship features suggests that there is a moderate amount of agreement on the dimensions that children regard as positive and negative aspects of friendship (see Furman, 1996). In a meta-analysis, Newcomb & Bagwell (1995) found that children's interactions in friendships were characterized by more positive behaviors (i.e., smiling, laughing, and sharing) and fewer rivalries. Although the incidence of conflict did not differ between friends and nonfriends, friends were more likely to resolve conflicts via disengagement and negotiation strategies as opposed to power assertion. Additional research suggests that young children are more willing to make sacrifices that benefit a friend rather than an acquaintance (Zarbatany, Van Brunschot, Meadows, & Pepper, 1996), and that preschoolers show greater sympathy toward a distressed friend than toward a distressed acquaintance (Costin & Jones, 1992).

Evidence gathered on the quality of children's friendships tends to show that relationship *satisfaction* is related to the positive or negative features that make up the friendship. Friendships with few negative and many positive features are often perceived to be high in quality (Berndt, 1996). Conversely, low quality friendships tend to be characterized by more negative features such as conflict or power. To illustrate, Ladd et al. (1996) found that kindergarten friends reported greater satisfaction with their friendships if they perceived these relationships to have higher levels of self-affirmation, support, and lower levels of conflict.

Peer group status: characteristics and processes.
Research on peer group dynamics indicates that children's experience in the peer group varies as a function of their peer status (Ladd, 1983). Mize and Ladd (1990) reported that "high status" children were more sociable toward peers than were "low status" children. Masters and Furman (1981) found that young children interacted more positively with liked peers than with disliked peers. In addition, Ladd et al. (1990) found that, as the school year progressed, preschoolers at all levels of social status interacted with popular classmates most often; thus, the popular children appeared to become the focus of the entire peer group's interactions (Ladd et al., 1990). In contrast, it has been shown that peers often abuse and mistreat disliked children (Buhs & Ladd, 2001).

Other data show that once children are rejected by their peer group, they change the nature of their play and contact patterns with peers. Ladd et al. (1990) discovered that, over the course of a school year, popular preschoolers became more selective in their choice of playmates and focused their interactions upon a relatively small number of consistent play partners. In contrast, rejected children maintained an extensive pattern of play contacts, and often "bounced" from one playmate to another. Thus, the patterns of peer contact that emerge after children become rejected appeared to be a consequence of their prior, negative reputations among peers. Once children become disliked, they may be increasingly avoided or excluded by peers, and, thus, forced to search out playmates among a broad range of peers (Buhs & Ladd, 2001; Ladd et al., 1990).

The plight of peer-rejected children is especially problematic in light of the pervasiveness of peer group rejection and the relative stability of peer status classifications over time and across peer groups (Ladd & Price, 1987). To estimate the prevalence of peer group rejection, Ladd, Herald, Slutzky, and Andrews (2004) reported the percentages of children who were identified in large community samples (i.e., $ns > 500$) as belonging to different peer status categories (as indicated by various sociometric classification systems; see Coie & Dodge, 1983; Coie et al., 1982; Asher & Dodge, 1986; Newcomb & Bukowski, 1983). The resulting prevalence estimates implied that approximately 12%–16% of children from normative, community samples were designated as rejected by peers.

The stability of peer group rejection is also important because it has been shown that chronic rather than transient rejection is a more powerful predictor of children's later interpersonal and scholastic adjustment (Ladd & Burgess, 2001; Ladd & Troop-Gordon, 2003). Several investigators have attempted to estimate the stability of children's peer group status. In studies conducted with young children, Howes (1988) reported that 60% of the popular-, 60% of the rejected-, 65% of the average-, 33% of the neglected-, and 80% of the controversial-status preschoolers in her sample were assigned to the same status classifications one year later. Furthermore, Ladd et al. (1987) found that group acceptance scores (i.e., mean sociometric ratings received from all peer group members) were relatively stable from preschool to the beginning of kindergarten ($r = .48$), and from preschool to the end of kindergarten ($r = .47$). Studies conducted with older samples indicate that peer rejection becomes increasingly stable and difficult to change as children get older (Coie & Dodge, 1983; Poteat et al., 1986).

Children's participation in aggressor-victim relations. Findings from recent surveys and epidemiological studies suggest that a substantial number of American children regularly suffer one or more forms of peer abuse, and that this form of victimization is about as prevalent and debilitating as other forms of child maltreatment (e.g., child abuse perpetrated by parents). In one of the initial, broadly-focused surveys conducted in U.S. schools, it was found that as many as 76.8% of middle school and high-school students reported having experienced mild to severe peer abuse at some point in time (Hoover, Oliver, & Hazler, 1992). Recently, more sophisticated surveys conducted in U.S. schools show that peer abuse begins early in children's lives and, for some, may persist over many years (see Kochenderfer-Ladd & Ladd, 2001). To illustrate, it has been shown that a substantial percentage of children (20%–23%) suffer moderate to severe levels of peer abuse soon after they enter kindergarten (see Kochenderfer & Ladd, 1996), and as many as 5% to 10% of these children are chronically abused well into middle childhood (Kochenderfer-Ladd & Wardop, 2001). By the time children reach middle schools and high schools, evidence suggests that the prevalence of peer abuse is somewhat lower (e.g., 5%–13%; Craig, 1997; Nansel et al., 2001). Similarly, recent cross-national surveys suggest that, depending on children's age and nationality, 6% to 22% report moderate to severe levels of peer abuse while in school or traveling to or from school (see Boulton & Underwood, 1992; Boney-McCoy

& Finkelhor, 1995; Kochenderfer & Ladd, 1996; Nansel et al., 2001; Perry et al., 1988). Collectively, these findings show that the probability that children will suffer peer abuse increases as they enter grade school and gradually declines until the mid- to late high school years.

Research on the stability of peer victimization remains at an early stage and most estimations have been derived from either self-report or peer-report victimization measures (see Ladd & Kochenderfer-Ladd, 2002). Estimates based on self-report measures have revealed low to moderate levels of stability over a 5-month period during children's first year in school (.24, kindergarten; Kochenderfer & Ladd, 1996), and somewhat higher stability over a 10-month interval during the later elementary grades (e.g., .34 to .36 for 9- to 12-year-olds; Hawker, 1997). Stability estimates also have been obtained with peer-report measures during both middle and later childhood (e.g., .93 for 9- to 12-year-olds over 3 months, Perry et al., 1988; .30 to .71 for 9- to 12-year-olds for intervals of 10- months to 1 year; Boivin, Hymel, & Bukowski, 1995; Hawker, 1997). Longer-term longitudinal findings reported by Kochenderfer-Ladd and Wardop (2001) suggested that, during the early school years, stable or chronic victimization occurs, but such cases are not highly prevalent. In this study, children were followed from kindergarten through grade 3, and results showed that less than 4% of the sampled children were chronically victimized over a 4-year period.

Contributions of Peer Relationships to Children's Development and Adjustment

The belief that children's development and adjustment are influenced by their peer relationships originated in socialization theories, particularly those that emphasized the importance of agemates in shaping children's development (see Asher & Gottman, 1981; Berndt & Ladd, 1989; Burhmester & Furman, 1986; Hartup, 1970; Sullivan, 1953). In recent years, this question has again become a focal point for research on children's social development (e.g., see Berndt & Ladd, 1989; Parker & Asher, 1987; Harris, 1995; Ladd, 1999).

Investigators who have studied the role of peers in children's development tend to rely on one of two investigative strategies that can be termed *main effects* or *child by environment* models. Main effects models emphasize the contributions of either children's behavioral dispositions or their peer relationships, but not both, as antecedents of their development and adjustment. Child by environment models, in contrast, are based on the premise that both the child's behavioral characteristics and their peer relational environments codetermine children's adjustment (see Coie et al., 1993; Ladd, 2003).

Main effects perspectives. Investigators who have relied on main effects perspectives have studied children's behavioral propensities, particularly aggressive and withdrawn behavioral dispositions, as precursors of child development or adjustment. Other investigators have used this paradigm to explore the possibility that children's participation in poor or dysfunctional peer relationships contributes to their development or adjustment.

Aggressive Behavior as a Predictor of Adjustment. Researchers have found that as early as preschool and kindergarten, some children are more aggressive than others in school settings, and that this behavioral style is a significant predictor of later misconduct, violence, and school adjustment problems (see Coie & Dodge, 1998). For example, Ladd and Burgess (1999) found that aggressive kindergarteners were more likely to have social difficulties with peers and teachers throughout the primary grades.

Investigators also have identified and studied different types of aggression, including those that have been conceptualized as direct aggression (i.e., aggression that is directly expressed towards others; also termed confrontational or overt aggression), and indirect aggression (i.e., aggression manifested indirectly, often termed covert, social, or relational aggression; see Cairns & Cairns, 1994; Crick & Grotpeter, 1995; Galen & Underwood, 1997; Lagerspitz et al., 1988). Current research suggests that both direct and indirect forms of aggression are predictive of children's adjustment problems (Crick, 1996).

Based on these findings, many researchers' have concluded that aggression in childhood is a moderately strong predictor of early and later maladjustment (i.e., poor peer relationships, developing conduct disorders, dropping out of school; see Coie & Dodge, 1998; Parker & Asher, 1987; Parker et al., 1995). There is also considerable evidence to suggest that aggressive preschoolers are at risk for poorer school performance and adjustment (e.g., Ladd & Mars, 1986; Ladd & Price, 1987).

Withdrawn Behavior as a Predictor of Adjustment. Children who interact infrequently with peers can be identified as early as the toddler and preschool years (Rubin, 1985; Rubin, Burgess, & Hastings, 2002). Evidence suggests that these children differ from normative samples in that they tend to make fewer requests of peers, comply more during peer interactions, and are often ignored by peers (Rubin, 1982; Rubin & Borwick, 1984).

Many researchers have attempted to identify different types of withdrawn children and ascertain the level of risk associated with each subtype (e.g., see Harrist et al., 1997; Gazelle & Ladd, 2003). Rubin and colleagues have identified four solitary subtypes (i.e., isolate, solitary-passive, solitary-active, reticent) and differentiated them as follows: isolate preschoolers tend to play alone. Solitary-passive children play alone in a constructive manner, whereas those who are solitary-active engage in repetitive or dramatic play that tends to be disruptive. Lastly, reticent children tend to be wary or seek to maintain distance from peers. Other terms that researchers have used to define solitary children are "passive-anxious," "active-isolated," "withdrawn-depressed," and "unsociable" (see Harris et al., 1997; Ladd & Burgess, 1999) or "asocial-withdrawn" and "aggressive-withdrawn" (see Ladd & Burgess, 1999; Ledingham & Schwartzman, 1984).

Children who manifest a combination of withdrawn behaviors and anxiety (e.g., anxious withdrawal or reticence) appear to be at greater risk for internalizing problems and peer rejection (Coplan et al., 1994; Coplan & Rubin, 1998; Coplan, 2000; Ladd & Troop-Gordon, 2003). Hart et al. (2000) found that reticent solitary behavior was associated with peer rejection as early

as preschool, and Gazelle and Ladd (2003) found that children with stable patterns of anxious-withdrawal during early grade school often were excluded by peers. Moreover, children who were both anxious-withdrawn and excluded were more likely to have elevated trajectories of depression well into middle childhood. In contrast, active isolates or aggressive-withdrawn children appear to be at risk for externalizing problems (Coplan, 2000; Coplan, Gavinsky-Molina, Lagace-Seguin, & Wichmann, 2001; Coplan & Rubin, 1998).

Peer Relationships as a Predictor of Adjustment. Much of the early research on children's peer group relations and their later adjustment was conducted with boys in clinics and child guidance centers (see Parker & Asher, 1987; Kupersmidt, Coie, & Dodge, 1990). Findings from these early, retrospective studies (for a review of design considerations, see Parker & Asher, 1987) suggested that men who were psychologically impaired as adults had histories of poor peer group relations as children (e.g., Frazee, 1953; Roff, 1961, 1963).

Peer Group Acceptance and Rejection. Subsequent longitudinal studies (e.g., DeRosier et al., 1994; Hymel et al., 1990) tended to corroborate earlier evidence by showing that peer group rejection anteceded many different forms of psychological maladjustment (see Ladd, 2003; MacDougall et al., 2001). For example, links were found between peer rejection and loneliness during both early (Cassidy & Asher, 1992) and middle childhood (Asher, Hymel, & Renshaw, 1984; Crick & Ladd, 1993). Peer rejection also anteceded various forms of externalizing problems. Ollendick, Weist, Borden, and Green (1992) followed children who belonged to specific peer status groups (i.e., popular, rejected, average, neglected, and controversial) from ages 9 through 14 and found that rejected children were more likely than popular children to exhibit problems such as misconduct, delinquency, and substance abuse. DeRosier et al. (1994) further revealed that the severity of children's maladjustment increased as a function of how long they had been rejected (i.e., the chronicity of peer rejection).

Among young children, classroom peer acceptance and rejection has been shown to be a significant predictor of school adjustment. Early peer rejection—at school entry—has been shown to predict problems such as negative school attitudes, school avoidance, and underachievement during the first year of schooling (Buhs & Ladd, 2001; Ladd, 1990; Ladd et al., 1999). Later, in the elementary years, peer acceptance has been linked with loneliness (Parker & Asher, 1993), peer interaction difficulties, lower emotional well being, and academic deficits (Ladd et al., 1997; Vandell & Hembree 1994). Evidence from other longitudinal studies suggests that peer rejection predicts absenteeism during the grade school years (e.g., DeRosier et al., 1994; Hymel et al., 1990), and grade retention and adjustment difficulties during the transition to middle school (Coie et al., 1992).

Friendship. Friendships, as well as the quality of children's friendships, have been shown to be important predictors of children's emotional health (Bukowski & Hoza, 1989; Bukowski, Newcomb, & Hartup, 1996; Parker & Asher, 1993), and their adjustment during early and middle childhood (Ladd et al., 1996;

Ladd & Troop, 2003). Children with close friendships view themselves more positively (Berndt & Burgy, 1996; Keefe & Berndt, 1996; Savin-Williams & Berndt, 1990), and children who have one or more close friendships tend to experience greater perceived social support and less loneliness (Ladd et al., 1996; Parker & Asher, 1993). In addition, children who have positive features in their friendships, such as intimacy and support, tend to have higher levels of self esteem (Berndt, 1996).

Although the predictive significance of friendship for children's long-term health has seldom been examined, Bagwell and colleagues (Bagwell, Newcomb, & Bukowski, 1998) identified groups of children who either had friends or were friendless in grade 5, and then assessed their adjustment 12 years later during early adulthood. Results showed that children with friends were better adjusted in grade 5 and as adults in later life on a variety of indicators including trouble with the law, family life, and overall adjustment, as compared to friendless children.

Children's friendships in the classroom have also been linked with indicators of their school adjustment. The presence of pre established friendships in children's kindergarten classrooms (e.g., starting school with a friend established during preschool) was found to predict better adjustment in new classroom environments (Ladd, 1990). Furthermore, as children entered kindergarten, those who formed new friendships tended to develop more favorable perceptions of school and perform better scholastically than those with fewer friends (Ladd, 1990). The processes that typify friends' interactions also have been implicated in children's school adjustment. Young children, especially boys who reported conflict within their friendships, have been shown to have adjustment difficulties, including lower levels of classroom engagement and participation (Ladd et al., 1996). Ladd et al. (1996) also found that when children saw their friendships as offering higher levels of validation (support) and aid (assistance) they tended to perceive classrooms as supportive interpersonal environments.

Peer Victimization. In general, peer victimization has been linked with anxiety (Boulton & Smith, 1994; Crick & Grotpeter, 1996; Slee, 1994, 1995), somatic complaints (i.e., headaches, stomachaches; Williams, Chambers, Logan & Robinson, 1996; Kumpulainen et al., 1998), and depression, loneliness, and suicide (see Hawker & Boulton, 2000). In contrast, aggressive victims are more likely to develop higher levels of externalizing problems such as misconduct and delinquency (Kumpulainen et al., 1998).

Victimized children also have a higher probability of experiencing mild to severe school adjustment problems. Passive victims tend to report moderate to severe levels of anxiety following bouts of bullying at school (Faust & Forehand, 1994; Rigby, 1998, 2001; Schwartz, 2000; Sharp, 1995). Research on school transitions has shown that, following children's entrance into kindergarten, the frequency of children's exposure to peer abuse forecasted significant gains in loneliness and school avoidance over their first year in school (Kochenderfer & Ladd, 1996). Moreover, it was discovered that pronounced or prolonged (e.g., chronic) peer abuse predicted more serious or debilitating forms of school maladjustment (Kochenderfer & Wardrop, 2001). Researchers also have reported that peer

victimization predicts both transient and enduring loneliness in children as early as school entry. Kochenderfer and Ladd (1996) found that the frequency of children's peer victimization experiences as they entered kindergarten forecasted significant gains in loneliness over the remainder of the school year.

Differential Contributions of Peer Relationships to Children's Adjustment. The tendency to study peer relationships individually has been supplemented by investigations in which researchers have examined multiple forms of peer relationship and the relative (differential) "contributions" of these relationships to specific adjustment outcomes (see Ladd, 1989, 1996, 1999; Perry & Weinstein, 1998). Initial efforts to investigate multiple relationship antecedents were focused on friendship and peer acceptance (e.g., see Parker & Asher, 1993; Vandell & Hembree, 1994).

Thus far, most findings suggest that friendship, peer acceptance, and peer victimization make separate contributions to the prediction of both socioemotional adjustment and academic competence (Ladd et al., 1997; Parker & Asher, 1993; Vandell & Hembree, 1994). For young children in particular, it has been shown that friendship, peer acceptance, and peer victimization uniquely predicted changes in kindergartner's school perceptions, avoidance, and performance (Ladd, 1990; Ladd et al., 1997). To be specific, Ladd et al. (1997) examined four forms of peer relationships (i.e., two forms of friendship, peer group acceptance, and peer victimization) as predictors of changes in multiple indices of kindergarten children's school adjustment. Results showed that after adjusting for shared predictive linkages among the four relational predictors, some types of peer relationships better predicted certain adjustment indices than did others. Peer victimization, for example, predicted gains in children's loneliness above and beyond associations that were attributable to the other three forms of peer relationship. In contrast, peer group acceptance uniquely predicted improvements in children's achievement. Such findings are consistent with the hypothesis that the effects of friendship on children's development are unique relative to those conferred by peer acceptance, and that these relationships differ in their adaptive value for specific adjustment outcomes.

Child by environment perspectives. Child by environment models are based on the premise that the precursors of children's adjustment originate not only within the child but also within the child's relational environment. Researchers who have relied on this framework to guide their empirical investigations tend to construe children's behaviors and peer relationships as conjoint rather than separate influences on adjustment.

Research on the Conjoint Influences of Children's Behavior and Peer Relationships. Much of this research has been focused on the contributions of aggression and peer rejection to children's maladjustment (see Ladd, 1999; MacDougall et al., 2001). In a recent review of this literature, MacDougall et al. (2001) concluded that in addition to behavioral risks such as aggression, exposure to relational risks, such as peer group rejection, raised the probability that children would develop internalizing problems (e.g., anxiety, depression, and loneliness; Coie et al., 1995; Lochman & Wayland, 1994; Renshaw & Brown, 1993). Other findings indicated the combinations of aggression and peer rejection were also linked to externalizing behaviors such as misconduct (e.g., Coie et al., 1992; Hymel at el., 1990).

In two short-term longitudinal studies conducted with young children, Ladd, Birch, and Buhs (1999) found that, as children entered kindergarten, their initial behavioral orientations influenced the types of relationships they formed with peers. In particular, young children's use of force or coercive tactics was directly associated with rejection by the peer group. Additional findings showed that, after children were rejected by their classmates, they were less likely to participate in classroom activities, suggesting that this form of relational adversity (e.g., peer rejection) interferes with children's involvement in learning activities and eventually impairs their achievement.

Chronic Behavior and Chronic Peer Relationships as Predictors of Children's Adjustment.

Another line of inquiry has explored how enduring peer adversity (e.g., chronic victimization or peer rejection) or support (e.g., friendship or peer acceptance) combines with children's behavioral styles to affect their later psychological and school adjustment (see Ladd & Burgess, 2001; Ladd & Troop-Gordon, 2003). Ladd and Burgess (2001) used prospective longitudinal assessments to assess children's risk status for aggression and exposure to adverse versus supportive peer relationships as they entered kindergarten (initial behavioral and relational status) and progressed through the primary grades. Results revealed that, after adjusting for children's kindergarten aggression scores, the chronicity of their aggressive risk status across grades predicted changes in a host of school adjustment criteria, including increases in attention problems, thought problems, and behavioral misconduct, and decreases in cooperative classroom participation, and academic achievement. However, it was also discovered that the chronicity of *peer group rejection* predicted many of the same forms of school maladjustment after controlling for children's aggressive histories. Furthermore, social supports such as sustained *peer group acceptance* predicted positive adjustment trajectories, including decreases in children's attention problems and gains in cooperative classroom participation. These findings corroborated the inference that a powerful behavioral risk (aggressiveness) can be exacerbated by chronic relational risks but buffered by stable relational supports, further illustrating the importance of children's peer relationship histories.

In a follow-up prospective longitudinal investigation conducted from kindergarten to grade 4, Ladd and Troop-Gordon (2003) investigated the hypothesis that children who participate in chronic adverse peer relationships have greater exposure to negative relational processes or learning experiences (e.g., sustained peer exclusion, peer abuse, lack of dyadic emotional support), and that the accumulation of such experiences is a more powerful risk factor than are the adversities present in their contemporary peer relationships. Among other findings, results showed that chronic friendlessness, chronic rejection, and chronic victimization were predictive of later forms of

maladjustment, including loneliness and maladaptive behavior. Because these predictive associations were adjusted for children's concurrent peer relationships, the results of this investigation revealed that *chronic* peer relationship adversity, more than the strains of *contemporary* peer relationships, anteceded children's later maladjustment.

INTERVENTION PROGRAMS TARGETING NEGATIVE PEER RELATIONSHIPS

In view of evidence indicating that early exposure to negative peer relationships, particularly peer group rejection, can lead to later maladjustment (e.g., see Kupersmidt, Coie, & Dodge, 1990; Ladd, 2005; MacDougall et al., 2001), researchers have attempted to develop and implement interventions that are designed to improve children's peer relations. Thus far, researchers have tended to devise and evaluate methods for helping children who are rejected by members of their peer group (see Ladd et al., 2004). Much of the theory behind these interventions has been rooted in the hypothesis that rejected children either lack the social skills that promote successful interactions with peers, or engage in an excessive level of antisocial behavior that tends to alienate peers (see Ladd, 1999). As such, most of the interventions that were designed to help peer-rejected children have been based on fundamental social learning principles (i.e., modeling, coaching, and shaping; see Ladd & Mize, 1983) and aimed at reducing children's skill deficits and/or behavioral excesses (see Ladd, 2005). Given the focus of this chapter, only those interventions that were designed to improve young children's peer relationships are reviewed.

Social Skills Training Intervention Programs

Researchers have developed several different types of intervention methods for helping young children learn and apply social skills within peer interactions. The majority of the intervention methods that incorporated social learning principles have been referred to as modeling, coaching, or shaping interventions (see Ladd, Buhs, & Troop, 2002). In modeling interventions, children are encouraged to emulate the behaviors of adults or peers who demonstrate exemplary social skills, as shown in training videos and narratives (see Ladd et al., 2004). Coaching interventions, in contrast, require children to participate in multiple skill training sessions that provide participants with instruction in skilled behaviors, opportunities to practice the skill behaviors, and ongoing feedback about skill usage in real-life peer interactions (see Ladd et al., 1983; 2004; Mize & Ladd, 1990). Interventions that are based on shaping principles present children with rewards after they enact targeted skills, or achieve successive approximations of the targeted skills (see Ladd et al., 1983; 2004).

Modeling interventions (e.g., O'Connor, 1969, 1972) have seldom been proven to have lasting effects on young children's social skills (see Ladd & Mize, 1983). However, there is evidence to suggest that coaching programs do help young children acquire social skills and improve their peer relations (see Mize & Ladd, 1990). Finally, when used in conjunction with other treatment methods (i.e., coaching programs), shaping programs show a modest record of success at promoting proso-cial behaviors, discouraging antisocial behaviors, and enhancing children's peer relationships (e.g., see Bierman, Miller, & Stabb, 1987).

Exemplary interventions. Initially, coaching interventions were designed to improve rejected or low-accepted children's success in peer groups. In these early studies, no attempt was made to distinguish between aggressive-rejected or withdrawn-rejected children, or study the effects of intervention on these subtypes. In one of the first coaching programs, Oden and Asher's (1977) taught low-accepted third and fourth graders in-terpersonal skills related to four specific areas of social interac-tion: communication, cooperation, participation and validation-support. Results showed that children who were coached, un-like those in a control condition, made significant gains in peer acceptance that were maintained over a period of 1 year.

Ladd (1981) investigated the effects of social skills training on unpopular third graders by randomly assigning low-accepted children to one of three conditions: a coaching, a no-treatment control, or an attention-control group. The attention-control group was included in order to rule out the possibility that it was the provision of adult attention and not the skill coaching that led to gains in children's peer acceptance. Whereas coached children exhibited gains in peer group acceptance immediately after the intervention and several weeks later (i.e., in posttest and follow-up assessments), such gains were not evident for children in the two control groups.

In a coaching intervention that was designed for young children, Mize and Ladd (1990) intervened with low-accepted preschool children and coached them on verbal communication skills including leading (e.g., making suggestions about play ac-tivities), asking questions, showing support through positive statements, and making comments during play activities with peers. Results showed that the coached children, unlike con-trols, made gains in their understanding of social interaction principles and classroom peer acceptance after completing the intervention.

After researchers established that there were subtypes of peer group rejection (i.e., aggressive-rejected and withdrawn-rejected children), they began to develop interventions tailored to children's specific behavioral and relational difficulties. For example, Lochman, Coie, Underwood, and Terry (1993) de-veloped a program that was designed to improve aggressive-rejected fourth grader's social problem solving skills, relation-ship formation skills, and control over their anger and aggressive behavior. To test the effectiveness of deficit-specific training, the treatment was given to an aggressive-rejected as well as a nonaggressive-rejected group of children (i.e., children classi-fied as rejected but not aggressive). Analyses revealed that the aggressive rejected children, unlike the controls, exhibited a re-duction in aggressive behavior and peer group rejection over and above that which was exhibited by nonaggressive rejected children.

Preventive Intervention Programs

Instead of targeting only those children who have already developed poor peer relations, there has been a movement toward developing school- or classroom-wide preventive inter-ventions (i.e., universal interventions) that are designed to help all children improve their social skills and peer relationships (see Ladd et al., 2004; Harrist & Bradley, 2003). Although not yet well researched, early evidence suggests that such programs may help children learn pivotal social skills and reduce their chances of developing peer relationship problems.

Harrist and Bradley (2003) conducted a prevention study with young children who were in either treatment or control classrooms. Children in the treatment classrooms listened to a fairy tale (Paley, 1992) that illustrated themes about children's in-clusion or exclusion from peer playgroup activities. On finishing the fairy tale, children participated in discussions and role-plays that elaborated on these same themes. After children completed 8 to 10 intervention sessions, the experimenters introduced a nonexclusion rule (i.e., "you say you can't play") in children's classrooms. Evaluations of this program, which included data from direct observations, teacher reports, child reports, and peer sociometrics, showed that children in the treatment classes liked each other more than did children in the control classes. This effect generalized across all children in the class, not just those who had initially been identified by peers as excluded (i.e., rejected or neglected). Children in the treatment class-rooms also reported higher levels of social dissatisfaction at the end of the school year. Based on these results, the investigators concluded that even though the classwide social intervention improved children's feelings about their classmates, it may have also prompted children to reflect on their own social positions amongst peers question whether they were satisfied with their peer relationships.

SUMMARY AND CONCLUSIONS

Sometime after children have formed their first social relation-ships, typically with adult caregivers, they move beyond this context into the world of peers. Most likely, the peer culture has always been an important force in young children's develop-ment. By nature, peers provide children with experiences that expand their conceptions of the social world and encourage adaptation to this context. Moreover, because peers are simi-lar to children in age and developmental status, but are raised in different families, they offer children a form of companion-ship that cannot be entirely duplicated by parents, teachers, and other adults (Edwards, 1992; Hartup, 1970; Piaget, 1965; Sullivan, 1953).

Modern times have made these speculations into truisms. Secular changes in families, childcare, and schooling have thrust children into the world of peers at earlier and earlier ages. It would no longer be an exaggeration to say that many young children now spend about as much of their time in the company of peers as they do parents (see Ladd & Coleman, 1993).

This review was organized around a number of basic ques-tions that have motivated research on children's peer relations for nearly 75 years (see Ladd, 2005). Chief among these were questions about how children meet peers, form and maintain various types of peer relationships, and are affected by their in-teractions and relationships with agemates. Also considered was the enduring question of whether it is possible to improve children's peer relations (see Chittenden, 1942; Koch, 1935). Other central foci were features of children's lives that may facilitate or inhibit their access to the peer culture, their participation in this context, and their ability to profit from interactions and relationships they have with agemates. In particular, attention was focused on the potential contributions of socialization agents, such as parents and teachers, and contextual factors, including the physical and interpersonal features of neighborhoods, communities, childcare settings, and schools.

Hopefully, the content of this review makes it apparent that much has been learned about each of these questions and issues. But given the substantial corpus of evidence that has been reviewed in this article, what specific inferences and conclusions can be drawn?

Insight Into the Formation of Children's Peer Relationships

First, extant evidence suggests that the processes of relationship formation are complex, and that not all children achieve the same level of success at forming friendships, becoming accepted members of their peer groups, repelling bullies, and so on. Access to agemates does not guarantee that children will develop supportive, high-quality peer relationships. Rather, it appears to be the case that many antecedents, including children's attributes, their social skills, inputs from socializers, and features of their rearing environments play a role in this process.

Fortunately, progress has been made toward mapping some of the factors that may affect children's success at relationship formation. For example, Gottman's (1983) temporal analysis of preschoolers' communications, made it possible to describe a sequence of conversational processes that often led to friendship. Similarly, researchers who investigated the antecedents of peer group entry mapped out a sequence of bids that were associated with children's success at this task. In particular, new discoveries were made about the importance of children's behavior in approaching and negotiating their way into peer group activities. Results showed that children who observed a peer group's activities (i.e., waiting and hovering) and then utilized relevant entry bids (i.e., mimicking, group-oriented statements) were more likely to be granted access to the group than children who used disrupting, self-oriented bids. Investigators were also able to highlight how characteristics of the child (i.e., gender, sociometric status, e.g., Borja-Alvarez et al., 1991; Putallaz & Wasserman, 1989; Zarbatany & Pepper, 1996; Zarbatany et al., 1996), the peer group (i.e., relationship with the entrant, sociometric statuses; e.g., Zarbatany et al., 1996) and the entry situation (i.e., peer group size; Putallaz & Wasserman, 1989) affected the types of entry bids children made and their eventual rate of success at gaining inclusion.

Similarly, by isolating behavior patterns that were differentially linked with emergent peer group status, it was possible for researchers to draw inferences about the likely effects of particular behavioral styles (e.g., aggression vs. prosocial behavior) on the status that children developed in their peer groups. Moreover, we may also infer from these data that there is substantial continuity in children's social status across school settings and peer groups. Clearly, these findings support the conclusion that children's behaviors are partly responsible for the form of status they develop among peers. However, one important qualification should be noted. Wright, Giammarino, and Parad (1986) have argued that the reputational outcomes of specific social behaviors may vary depending on the social context in which they are employed. In fact, these investigators found that aggressive grade-school children tended to be more disliked in peer groups composed of nonaggressive peers, and that withdrawn children tended to be more disliked in groups containing larger numbers of aggressive peers. Perhaps, as these investigators suggest, the effect of children's behavior (or other characteristics) on their peer status is mediated by their similarity to the peer group.

In sum, findings from research with preschool and grade-school samples illustrate the importance of children's behavior (i.e., interaction patterns) as a determinant of their status among peers. One general principle that appeared to cut across all of these findings was that children who succeed in forming peer relationships did so by managing their interactions in ways that nurtured and respected the interests of their play companions.

Unfortunately, past accomplishments have not always fueled future discoveries. For example, despite some fairly dramatic successes (e.g., Black & Hazen, 1990; Coie & Kupersmidt, 1983; Dodge, 1983; Gottman 1983; Parker, 1986) in describing some of the processes that underlie the formation of friendship and peer status, investigations of this type—that is, longitudinal or experimental studies designed to illuminate the antecedents of children's friendships and peer group relations—have not become more prevalent in recent years. This has been the case particularly for research on the antecedents of friendship. As a result, knowledge about other types of behavioral processes that may be important precursors to friendship in young children remains limited. Likewise, it has been rare for researchers to investigate whether some types of interaction processes are more central to friendship formation at different ages, or for children of different genders. As such, there is a compelling need to further explore the interpersonal or behavioral processes that lead to friendships in boys and girls as they progress through the early childhood years (e.g., male and female toddlers, preschoolers, and early grade-schoolers).

The Role of Adult Socialization Agents

Progress also was made toward an understanding of the interconnections between family processes and children's peer relations, and the practices that caregivers use to prepare children for the world of peers. On the one hand, extant evidence indicates that parent-child relations are complex and that many aspects of parenting and family relationships are associated with children's peer competence (Ladd & Pettit, 2002). On the other hand, this realization led researchers to revise existing assumptions, and develop new models for investigating the roles that parents and teachers play in children's social development. Movement in this direction has been accompanied by a conceptual shift away from unidirectional perspectives (i.e., child or parent-effects models) and toward more dyadic and transactional investigative frameworks (see Parker et al., 1995; Ladd & Pettit, 2002). This is reflected in researchers' propensities to develop and utilize dyadic measures of parent-child relations, and work from paradigms in which the direction(s) of effect within parent-child relations are hypothesized to be bidirectional or transactional rather than unidirectional. Among the more noteworthy discoveries were findings showing that children who have experienced secure attachment relations tend to form higher quality friendships, that synchronous and emotionally supportive parent child interactions precede similar forms of competence in children peer interactions, that harsh disciplinary styles antecede children's risk for peer victimization, and that stressful family environments are predictive of children's peer difficulties.

Although it is possible that parents "mindlessly" arrange, supervise, and monitor young children's playdates and peer contacts, it now appears that many parents perform these functions with specific socialization objectives in mind (see Bhavnagri & Parke, 1991; Ladd & Hart, 1992; Lollis et al., 1992). When children are young, it appears that parents act as mediators in order to initiate peer interactions, find playmates for their children, arrange play opportunities, and maintain relationships with specific children (Ladd & Pettit, 2002). As children mature, it appears that parents' supervision of their peer activities changes; results suggest that, as children get older, parents increasingly resort to less direct methods of supervision, and that these adaptations are beneficial for children. Extant evidence is, for example, consistent with the premise that interactive interventions facilitate young children's (e.g., toddlers) peer competence, but that this form of supervision may actually interfere with older children's (preschoolers) ability to develop autonomous and self-regulated play skills. Quite possibly, parents who mediate, supervise, and monitor children's peer interactions play an important role in the socialization of children's social competence. However, because the existing evidence is correlational in nature, it remains to be seen whether direct parental influences are in fact causes or consequences of children's success and competence in peer relations.

Unfortunately, much more remains to be learned about how children's relationships with teachers are associated with their peer relations and social adjustment. Consequently, more investment should be made in this line of investigation within the near future. Thus far, investigators have tended to study two features of the teacher-child relationship—conflict and closeness—and examine how these relationship features are related to children's social participation in classrooms (see Birch & Ladd, 1996). In general, evidence has been consistent with the hypothesis that closeness in the teacher-child relationship, a feature characterized by warmth and open communication, operates as source of emotional support or security that fosters children's participation in classroom activities. Conflictual teacher-child relationships, in contrast, are characterized by discordant, acrimonious, and noncompliant interactions (e.g., causes of anger, resentment, or anxiety), and have been linked with children's classroom disengagement and disruptiveness. Among the more novel contributions of these investigations were findings indicating that even after controlling for the association between kindergartners' peer relations and the quality of their classroom participation, those who formed conflictual teacher-child relationships tended to become less involved in classroom activities (Ladd et al., 1999). Equally important were findings showing that both the features of young children' teacher-child relationships, and their tendencies to engage in risky behaviors (e.g., aggression), predicted early-emerging adjustment (Ladd & Burgess, 2001). Evidence indicated that conflictual teacher-child relationships were linked with increases in maladjustment, regardless of children's propensity to engage in aggression. Thus, conflict in the teacher-child relationship appeared to increase most children's risk for maladjustment. However, for aggressive children, teacher-child conflict appeared to compound (i.e., add to) their adjustment difficulties. In contrast, relational supports such as closeness in the teacher-child relationship predicted decreases in maladjustment independently of aggression, suggesting that this relationship feature reduced maladjustment, regardless of children's risk status for aggression.

The Role of Socialization Contexts

It is also clear that child rearing and socialization contexts, such as neighborhoods, community settings, and schools play an important role in young children's social development. It is within these contexts that young children meet familiar and unfamiliar agemates, and are afforded opportunities to establish and maintain peer relationships. It is also in these contexts that children find opportunities to practice social skills, experience the consequences of peers' reactions, and learn new interpersonal behaviors. Furthermore, it would appear that regular exposure to peers in community settings fosters adaptation to novel situations, such as those encountered during school entrance. These settings may even act as a protective factor for school dropout and behavior problems in later years (Mahoney & Cairns, 1997).

Over the past 25 years, childcare has increasingly become an extension of the family's childrearing practices, and a context that is used to promote the socialization of children. As larger numbers of parents join the workforce, including mothers of young children, the need to understand the potential effects of childcare on children has become a national priority. As has been illustrated, investigative efforts have produced an extensive literature on the correlates of children's childcare experiences. Although the these findings remain controversial, it has not been uncommon for investigators and policy makers to interpret these findings as evidence of childcare's effects on children's social development. Fabes, Hanish, and Martin (2003), for example, have argued that childcare impacts child development because it serves as a setting in which children learn from peers. Childcare is often children's first extended exposure to peers (especially groups of peers) and, thus, it may play a role in facilitating children's relationships with agemates, social competence, adaptation to school, and future adjustment. This interpretation is consistent with the argument that children enrolled in childcare and preschool programs tend to meet a larger number of unfamiliar peers at an earlier age (Belsky, 1984; Rubenstein & Howes, 1983) and, thus, have greater opportunity to practice social skills and make friends (Howes, 1988).

Similarly, it appears that preschool and grade school classrooms may be an important staging area for children's social competence and peer relations. Evidence suggests that schools and the types of peer interactions children encounter in classrooms vary substantially, and some children may profit more than others depending on the types of experiences they have in this context. However, here again, it can be argued that schools and the social milieu of classrooms require children to come into contact with peers, and negotiate interpersonal challenges such as making friends and establishing themselves within fairly large peer groups.

In addition to time in school, there is growing evidence to suggest that the time children spend with peers after school may play a role in shaping their social development. Howes et al. (1987) has suggested that after school programs, when they are supervised and well structured for children's needs, provide a context in which social skills can be practiced and developed. Thus far, however, the weight of the evidence seems to suggest that adult supervised after school activities, rather than informal or nonsupervised care, are positively associated with children's peer competence (Posner & Vandell, 1994). In fact, most of the present findings imply that unsupervised or self-care arrangements are linked with children's developmental difficulties, particularly behavioral and social maladjustment (Pettit, Bates, Dodge, & Meece, 1999). Clearly, investigation and evaluation of after-school childcare and enrichment programs constitutes another priority for future research.

Explicating the Features and Functions of Children's Early Peer Relationships

In general, extant evidence suggests that young children who become accepted by members of their peer groups, form friendships that have positive, supportive features, and avoid becoming victimized by agemates, tend to manifest fewer and less severe psychological and school adjustment problems. These findings corroborate the hypothesis that certain features of childhood peer relationships increase risk or afford protection from different types of short- and long-term adjustment problems. Furthermore, this evidence is consistent with the view that peer relationships are both specialized in the types of resources or constraints they create for children, but also diverse in the sense that some resources may be found in more than one form of relationship.

However, with the advent of research based on child by environment frameworks, it has become clear that conclusions like those listed here may be too general, or lacking in precision. To say that children have peer relational experiences that affect their adjustment ignores the fact that they also have certain behavioral attributes (e.g., behavioral styles) that also may contribute to such outcomes. Moreover, it may also be the case that children's behavioral propensities shape how peers' respond to them and the types of relationships they develop with peers. These relational developments, in turn, might create additional social challenges that require adaptation on the part of the child. Thus, it seems likely that an understanding of children's social

developmental trajectories requires insight into a complex transaction between the nature of the child and the features of the child's peer environment. The discoveries that have been produced by this perspective thus far are limited, but nonetheless represent an advance over what has been learned from previous conceptions, such as main effects models.

At present, research guided by "child by environment" models has produced discoveries that qualify some of the inferences that investigators have drawn from studies based on "main effects" models. These discoveries suggest that, over the course of development, children's behavioral styles and their participation in peer relationships essentially codetermine their success in adapting to life- and school-based challenges. In particular, the evidence reviewed in this chapter lends itself to several preliminary conclusions. First, although it can be said that both children's behavioral dispositions and features of their peer relationships are significant antecedents of their adjustment, there is accumulating evidence to suggest that the predictive power of either factor alone appears to be less than their combined or conjoint contributions. For example, children's early behavioral dispositions, especially those that make children prone toward aggressive interactions, may affect the kind of relational ecology (i.e., form and nature of peer relationships) they develop within classrooms. However, once the child's relational ecology has been established, their ensuing experiences in these relationships (e.g., exclusion from peer group activities, inability to obtain help or support from friends) may have as much or more impact on their school adjustment than does their behavior (e.g., see Ladd et al., 1999). Second, it would appear that along with children's behavioral styles, exposure to enduring relationship adversity (e.g., peer rejection), deprivation (e.g., friendlessness), or support (e.g., peer acceptance) is more closely associated with children's adjustment trajectories than are more transient or proximal experiences within these same relationship domains. In this sense, extant findings not only illustrate the adaptive significance children's peer relationships, but also suggest that children who suffer sustained adversity in their peer relations are likely to have the largest or most severe adjustment problems (e.g., see Ladd & Burgess, 2001; Ladd & Troop-Gordon, 2003). Third, other recent discoveries raise the possibility that enduring peer relationship adversity (e.g., chronic victimization) may worsen children's preexisting behavior problems and, thus, make it even more likely that they will act in ways that alter their development (see Gazelle & Ladd, 2003). Conversely, it also appears that sustained relationship advantages (e.g., a history of peer acceptance) may mitigate children's preexisting behavior problems (e.g., see Ladd & Burgess, 2001).

Intervening on Behalf of Young Children Who Have or Are at Risk for Peer Relationship Difficulties

Finally, the results of experimental prevention and intervention programs provide qualified support for the conclusion that young children can learn social skills that improve peer relationships or prevent relationship difficulties. Particularly promising are results indicating that universal prevention programs can alter the social dynamics of entire classrooms and, therefore, benefit substantial numbers of young children. Equally reassuring are findings showing that some types of intervention programs can effect changes in children's interpersonal skills as well as in their acceptance by classroom peers. Unfortunately, too little has been done to develop and evaluate prevention and intervention programs for young children who are friendless or suffer peer abuse (e.g., bully–victim relations; see Gazelle & Ladd, 2002).

References

Aboud, F. E., & Mendelson, M. J. (1996). Determinants of friendship selection and quality: Developmental perspectives. In W. M. Bukowski, W. M., A. F. Newcomb, & W. W. Hartup (Eds.), *The company they keep: Friendship in childhood and adolescence* (pp. 66–86). New York: Cambridge University Press.

Asher, S. R., & Dodge, K. A. (1986). Identifying children who are rejected by their peers. *Developmental Psychology, 22*, 442–449.

Asher, S. R., & Gottman, J. M. (1981). *The development of children's friendships*. New York: Cambridge University Press.

Asher, S. R., & Hymel, S. (1981). Children's social competence in peer relations: Sociometric and behavioral assessment. In J. D. Wine & M. D. Smye (Eds.), *Social competence*. New York: Guilford Press.

Asher, S. R., Hymel, S., & Renshaw, P. D. (1984). Loneliness in children. *Child Development, 55*, 1456–1464.

Asher, S. R., Oden, S. L., & Gottman, J. M. (1977). Children's friendships in school settings. In L. G. Katz (Ed.), *Current topics in early childhood education* (Vol. 1, pp. 33–61). Norwood, NJ: Ablex.

Asher, S. R., & Renshaw, P. D. (1981). Children without friends: Social knowledge and social skills training. In S. R. Asher & J. M. Gottman (Eds.), *The development of children's friendships* (pp. 273–296). New York: Cambridge University Press.

Asher, S. R., Singleton, L. C., Tinsley, B. R., & Hymel, S. (1979). A reliable sociometric measure for preschool children. *Developmental Psychology, 15*, 443–444.

Austin, S., & Joseph, S. (1996). Assessment of bully/victim problems in 8- to 11-year-olds. *British Journal of Educational Psychology, 66*, 447–456.

Bagwell, C. L., Newcomb, A. F., & Bukowski, W. M. (1998). Early adolescent friendship and peer rejection as predictors of adult adjustment. *Child Development, 69*, 140–153.

Barber, B. K. (1996). Parental psychological control: Revisiting a neglected construct. *Child Development, 67*, 3296–3319.

Baumrind, D. (1967). Childcare practices anteceding three patterns of preschool behavior. *Genetic Psychology Monographs, 75*, 43–88.

Belsky, J. (1984). Two waves of day care research: Developmental effects and conditions of quality. In R. C. Ainslie (Ed.), *The child and the day care setting: Qualitative variations and development* (pp. 37–53). New York: Praeger.

Berndt, T. J. (1989). Contributions of peer relationships to children's development. In T. J. Berndt, & G. W. Ladd (Eds.), *Peer relationships in child development* (pp. 407–416). New York: Wiley.

Berndt, T. J. (1996). Exploring the effects of friendship quality on social development. In W. M. Bukowski, A. F. Newcomb, & W. W. Hartup (Eds.), *The company they keep: Friendship in childhood and adolescence* (pp. 346–365). New York: Cambridge University Press.

Berndt, T. J., & Burgy, L. (1996). Social self-concept. In B. A. Bracken (Ed.), *Handbook of self-concept: Developmental, social, and clinical considerations* (pp. 171–209). New York: Wiley & Sons.

Berndt, T. J., Hawkins, J. A., & Hoyle, S. G. (1986). Changes in friendship during a school year: Effects of children's and adolescent's impressions of friendship and sharing with friends. *Child Development, 57*, 1284–1297.

Berndt, T. J., & Ladd, G. W. (1989). *Peer relationships in child development*. New York: John Wiley & Sons.

Bhavnagri, N. (1987). *Parents as facilitators of preschool children's peer relationships*. Unpublished doctoral dissertation, University of Illinois at Urbana-Champaign.

Bhavnagri, N., & Parke, R. D. (1991). Parents as direct facilitators of children's peer relationships: Effects of age of child and sex of parent. *Journal of Social and Personal Relationships, 8*, 423–440.

Bierman, K. L., Miller, C. L., & Stabb, S. D. (1987). Improving the social behavior and peer acceptance of rejected boys: Effects of social skill training with instructions and prohibitions. *Journal of Consulting and Clinical Psychology, 55*, 194–200.

Bierman, K. L., Smoot, D. L., & Aumiller, K. (1993). Characteristics of aggressive-rejected, aggressive (nonrejected), and rejected (nonaggressive) boys. *Child Development, 64*, 139–151.

Birch, S. H., & Ladd, G. W. (1996). Contributions of teachers and peers to children's early school adjustment. In K. Wentzel & J. Juvonen (Eds.) *Social Motivation: Understanding children's school adjustment* (pp. 199–225). New York: Cambridge University Press.

Birch, S. H., & Ladd, G. W. (1998). Children's interpersonal behaviors and the teacher-child relationship. *Developmental Psychology, 34*, 934–946.

Bjorkqvist, K., Lagerspetz, K., & Kaukiainen, A. (1992) Do girls manipulate and boys fight? Developmental trends regarding direct and indirect aggression. *Aggressive Behavior, 18*, 117–127.

Black, B., & Hazen, N. L. (1990). Social status and patterns of communication in acquainted and unacquainted preschool children. *Developmental Psychology, 26*, 379–387.

Black, B., & Logan, A. (1995). Links between communication patterns in mother-child, father-child, and child-peer interactions and children's social status. *Child Development, 66*, 255–271.

Boivin, M., Hymel, S., & Bukowski, W. M. (1995). The roles of social withdrawal, peer rejection, and victimization by peers in predicting loneliness and depressed mood in childhood. *Development and Psychopathology, 7*, 765–785.

Boivin, M., Thomassin, L., & Alain, M. (1989). Peer rejection and self-perception among early elementary school children: Aggressive-rejectees versus withdrawn rejectees. In B. H. Schneider, G. Attili, J. Nadel, & R. P. Weissberg (Eds.), *Social competence in developmental perspective* (pp. 392–394). Norwell, MA: Kluwer Academic Publishers.

Boney-McCoy, S., & Finkelhor, D. (1995). Special populations: Psychological sequelae of violent victimization in a national youth sample. *Journal of Consulting and Clinical Psychology, 63*, 726–736.

Borja-Alvarez, T., Zarbatany, L., & Pepper, S. (1991). Contributions of male and female guests and hosts to peer group entry. *Child Development, 62*, 1079–1090.

Bost, K. K., Vaughn, B. E., Washington, W. N., Cielinski, K. L., & Bradbard, M. R. (1998). Social competence, social support, and attachment: Demarcation of construct domains, measurement, and paths of influence for preschool children attending Head Start. *Child Development, 69*, 192–218.

Boulton, M. J., & Smith, P. K. (1994). Bully/victim problems in middle-school children: Stability, self-perceived competence, peer perceptions, and peer acceptance. *British Journal of Developmental Psychology, 12*, 315-329.

Boulton, M. J., & Underwood, K. (1992). Bully/victim problems among middle school children. *British Journal of Educational Psychology, 62*, 73-87.

Bowers, L., Smith, P. K., & Binney, V. (1992). Cohesion and power in the families of children involved in bully/victim problems at school. *Journal of Family Therapy, 14*, 371-387.

Bowers, L., Smith, P. K., & Binney, V. (1994). Perceived family relationships of bullies, victims, and bully/victims in middle childhood. *Journal of Social and Personal Relationships, 11*, 215-232.

Bowlby, J. (1973). *Attachment and loss: Vol. 2. Separation.* New York: Basic Books.

Bradley, R. H. (2002). Environment and parenting. In M. H. Bornstein, (Ed.), *Handbook of parenting: Vol. 2. Biology and ecology of parenting* (2nd ed., pp. 281-314). Mahwah, NJ: Lawrence Erlbaum Associates.

Bryant, B. (1985). The neighborhood walk: Sources of support in middle childhood. *Monographs of the Society for Research in Child Development, 50*(3, Serial No. 210).

Buckner, J. C, Bassuk, E. L., Weinreb, L. F., & Brooks, M. G. (1999). Homelessness and its relation to the mental health and behavior of low-income schoolchildren. *Developmental Psychology, 35*, 246-257.

Buhrmester, D., & Furman, W. (1986). The changing functions of friends in childhood: A Neo-Sullivanian perspective. In V. J. Derlega & B. A. Winstead (Eds.), *Friendship and social interaction* (pp. 41-61). New York: Springer-Verlag.

Buhs, E. S., & Ladd, G. W. (2001). Peer rejection as an antecedent of young children's school adjustment: An examination of mediating processes. *Developmental Psychology, 37*, 550-560.

Bukowski, W. M., & Hoza, B. (1989). Popularity and friendship: Issues in theory, measurement and outcome. In T. J. Berndt & G. W. Ladd (Eds.), *Peer relationships in child development* (pp. 13-45). New York: Wiley.

Bukowski, W. M., Hoza, B., & Boivin, M. (1993). Popularity, friendship, and emotional adjustment during early adolescence. *New Directions for Child Development, 60*, 23-37.

Bukowski, W. M., Newcomb, A. F., & Hartup, W. W. (1996). *The company they keep: Friendship in childhood and adolescence.* New York: Cambridge University Press.

Campbell, S. N., & Dill, N. (1985). The impact of changes in spatial density on children's behaviors in a day care setting. In J. L. Frost & S. Sunderlin (Eds.), *When children play* (pp. 255-264). Wheaton, MD: Association for Childhood Education International.

Cairns, R. B., & Cairns, B. D. (1994). *Lifelines and risks: Pathways of youth in our time.* New York: Cambridge University Press.

Cairns, R. B., Cairns, B. D., Neckerman, H. J., Ferguson, L. L., & Gariepy, J. L. (1989). Growth and aggression I: Childhood to early adolescence. *Developmental Psychology, 25*, 320-330.

Casiglia, A. C., Lo Coco, A., and Zapplulla, C. (1998). Aspects of social reputation and peer relationships in Italian children: A cross-cultural perspective. *Developmental Psychology, 34*, 723-730.

Cassidy, J., & Asher, S. R. (1992). Loneliness and peer relations in young children. *Child Development, 63*, 350-365.

Cassidy, J., Kirsh, S. J., Scolton, K. L., & Parke, R. D. (1996). Attachment and representations of peer relationships. *Developmental Psychology, 32*, 892-904.

Cassidy, J., Parke, R. D., Bukovsky, L., & Braungart, J. M. (1992). Family-peer connections: The roles of emotional expressiveness within the family and children's understanding of emotions. *Child Development, 63*, 603-618.

Chen, X., Li, D., Li, Z., Li, B., and Liu, M. (2000). Sociable and prosocial dimensions of social competence in Chinese children: Common and unique contributions to social, academic, and psychological adjustment. *Developmental Psychology, 36*, 302-314.

Chen, X., Rubin, K. H., Sun, Y. (1992). Social reputation and peer relationships in Chinese and Canadian children: a cross-cultural study. *Child Development, 63*, 1336-1343.

Chittenden, G. F. (1942). An experimental study in measuring and modifying assertive behavior in young children. *Monographs of the Society for Research in Child Development*, 7(1, Serial No. 31).

Clark, K. E., & Ladd, G. W. (2000). Connectedness and autonomy support in parent-child relationships: Links to children's socio-emotional orientation and peer relationships. *Developmental Psychology, 36*, 485-498.

Coie, J. D., & Dodge, K. A. (1983). Continuities and changes in children's social status: A five-year longitudinal study. *Merrill-Palmer Quarterly, 29*, 261-282.

Coie, J. D., & Dodge, K. A. (1998). Aggression and antisocial behavior. In W. Damon (Series Ed.) & N. Eisenberg (Vol. Ed.), *Handbook of child psychology: Vol. 3.* (pp. 779-862). New York: John Wiley.

Coie, J. D., Dodge, K. A., & Coppotelli, H. (1982). Dimensions and types of social status: A cross -age perspective. *Developmental Psychology, 18*, 557-570.

Coie, J. D., Dodge, K. A., & Kupersmidt, J. B. (1990). Peer group behavior and social status. In S. R. Asher & J. D. Coie (Eds.), *Peer rejection in childhood* (pp. 17-59). New York: Cambridge University Press.

Coie, J. D., Dodge, K. A., Terry, R., & Wright, V. (1991). The role of aggression in peer relations: An analysis of aggression episodes in boys' play groups. *Child Development, 62*, 812-826.

Coie, J. D., & Kupersmidt, J. B. (1983). A behavioral analysis of emerging social status in boys' groups. *Child Development, 54*, 1400-1416.

Coie, J. D., Lochman, J. E., Terry, R., & Hyman, C. (1992). Predicting early adolescent disorder from childhood aggression and peer rejection. *Journal of Consulting and Clinical Psychology, 60*, 783-792.

Coie, J. D., Terry, R., Lenox, K., Lochman, J., & Hyman, C. (1995). Childhood peer rejection and aggression as predictors of stable patterns of adolescent disorder. *Development and Psychopathology, 7*, 697-713.

Coie, J. D., Watt, N. F., West, S. G., Hawkins, D., Asarnow, J. R., Markman, H. J., et al. (1993). The science of prevention: A conceptual framework and some directions for a national research program. *American Psychologist, 48*, 1013-1022.

Cole, D. A., Peeke, L. G., Martin, J. M., Truglio, R., & Seroczynski, A. D. (1998). A longitudinal look at the relation between depression and anxiety in children. *Journal of Consulting and Clinical Psychology, 66*, 451-460.

Coplan, R. J. (2000). Assessing nonsocial play in early childhood: Conceptual and methodological approaches. In K. Gitlin-Weiner, A. Sandgrund, & C. Schaefer (Eds.), *Play diagnosis and assessment* (2nd ed., pp. 563-598). New York: Wiley.

Coplan, R. J., Gavinski-Molina, M. H., Lagace-Seguin, D. G., & Wichmann, C. (2001). When girls and boys play alone: Nonsocial play and adjustment in kindergarten. *Developmental Psychology, 37*, 464-474.

Coplan, R. J., & Rubin, K. H. (1998). Exploring and assessing nonsocial play in the preschool: The development and validation of the Preschool Play Behavior Scale. *Social Development, 7*, 73-91.

Coplan, R. J., Rubin, K. H., Fox, N. A., Calkins, S. A., & Stewart, S. L. (1994). Being alone, playing alone, and acting alone: Distinguishing among reticence, and passive- and active-solitude in young children. *Child Development, 65*, 129-137.

Corsaro, W. A. (1981). Friendship in the nursery school: Social organization in a peer environment. In S. R. Asher & J. M. Gottman (Eds.), *The development of children's friendships* (pp. 207–241). New York: Cambridge University Press.

Corsaro, W. A., Rizzo, T. A. (1990). *Conflict talk*. Cambridge: Cambridge University Press.

Costin, S. E., & Jones, D. C. (1992). Friendship as a facilitator of emotional responsiveness and prosocial interventions among young children. *Developmental Psychology, 28*, 941–947.

Craig, W. (1997). A comparison among self-, peer-, and teacher-identified victims, bullies, and bully/victims: Are victims an under-identified risk group? In B. Kochenderfer (Chair), *Research on bully/victim problems: Agendas from several cultures.* Symposium conducted at the biennial meeting of the Society for Research in Child Development, Washington DC.

Crick, N. R. (1995). Relational aggression: The role of intent attributions, feelings of distress, and provocation type. *Development and Psychopathology, 7*, 313–322.

Crick, N. R. (1996). The role of overt aggression, relational aggression, and prosocial behavior in the prediction of children's future social adjustment. *Child Development, 67*, 2317–2327.

Crick, N. R., Casas, J. F., & Mosher, M. (1997). Relational and overt aggression in preschool. *Developmental Psychology, 33*, 579–588.

Crick, N. R., & Grotpeter, J. K. (1995). Relational aggression, gender, and social-psychological adjustment. *Child Development, 66*, 710–722.

Crick, N. R., & Grotpeter, J. K. (1996). Children's treatment by peers: Victims of relational and overt aggression. *Development and Psychopathology, 8*, 367–380.

Crick, N. R., & Ladd, G. W. (1990). Children's perceptions of the consequences of aggressive strategies: Do the ends justify being mean? *Developmental Psychology, 26*, 612–620.

Crick, N. R., & Ladd, G. W. (1993). Children's perceptions of their peer experiences: Attributions, social anxiety, and social avoidance. *Developmental Psychology, 29*, 244–254.

Crnic, K. A., & Low, (2002). Everyday stresses and parenting. In M. H. Bornstein (Ed.), *Handbook of parenting: Vol. 5. Practical issues in parenting* (2nd ed., pp. 243–267). Mahwah, NJ: Lawrence Erlbaum Associates.

Cummings, M. E. & Cummings, J. S. (2002). Parenting and attachment. In M. H. Borenstein (Ed.), *Handbook of Parenting: Vol. 5. Practical Issues in parenting* (2nd ed., pp. 35–58). Mahwah, NJ: Lawrence Erlbaum Associates.

DeMulder, E. K., Denham, S., Schmidt, M., & Mitchell, J. (2000). Q-sort assessment of attachment security during the preschool years: Link from home to school. *Developmental Psychology, 36*, 274–282.

DeRosier, M. E., Kupersmidt, J. B., & Patterson, C. J. (1994). Children's academic and behavioral adjustment as a function of the chronicity and proximity of peer rejection. *Child Development, 65*, 1799–1813.

Dishion, T. J. (1990). The family ecology of boys' peer relations in middle childhood. *Child Development, 61*, 874–892.

Dishion, T. J., & McMahon, R. J. (1998). Parental monitoring and the prevention of child and adolescent problem behavior: A conceptual and empirical formulation. *Clinical Child and Family Psychology Review, 1*, 61–75.

Dodge, K. (1983). Behavioral antecedents of peer social status. *Child Development, 54*, 1386–1399.

Dodge, K. A., & Coie, J. D. (1987). Social-information-processing factors in reactive and proactive aggression in children's peer groups. *Journal of Personality and Social Psychology, 53*, 1146–1158.

Dodge, K. A., Coie, J. D., Pettit, G. S., & Price, J. M. (1990). Peer status and aggression in boys' groups: Developmental and contextual analyses. *Child Development, 61*, 1289–1309.

Dodge, K. A., Schlundt, D., Schocken, I., & Delugach, J. (1983). Social competence and children's sociometric status: The role of peer group entry strategies. *Merrill-Palmer Quarterly, 29*, 309–336.

Eckerman, C. O., Davis, C. & Didow, S. (1989). Toddler's emerging ways of achieving social coordination with a peer. *Child Development, 60*, 440–453.

Edwards, C. P. (1992). Cross cultural perspectives on family-peer relations. In R. D. Parke & G. W. Ladd (Eds.), *Family-peer relationships: Modes of linkage* (pp. 285–316). Hillsdale, NJ: Erlbaum.

Egan, S. E., & Perry, D. G. (1998). Does low self-regard invite victimization? *Developmental Psychology, 34*, 299–309.

Egeland, B., & Heister, M. (1995). The long term consequences of infant day care and mother-infant attachment. *Child Development, 66*, 74–85.

Eisenberg, N., Fabes, R. A., & Murphy, B. C. (1996). Parent's reactions to children's negative emotions: Relations to children's social competence and comforting behaviors. *Child Development, 67*, 2227–2247.

Elicker, J., Englund, M., & Sroufe, L. A. (1992). Predicting peer competence and peer relations in childhood from early parent-child relationships. In R. D. Parke & G. W. Ladd (Eds.), *Family-peer relationships: Modes of linkage* (pp. 77–106). Hillsdale, NJ: Lawrence Erlbaum Associates.

Epstein, J. L. (1989). The selection of friends: Changes across the grades and in different school environments. In T. J. Berndt & G. W. Ladd (Eds.), *Peer relationships in child development* (pp. 158–187). Oxford: Wiley & Sons.

Fabes, R. A., Hanish, L. A., Martin, C. L. (2003). Children at play: The role of peers in understanding the effects of child care. *Child Development, 74*, 1039–1043.

Faust, J., & Forehand, R. (1994). Adolescents' physical complaints as a function of anxiety due to familial and peer stress: A causal model. *Journal of Anxiety Disorders, 8*, 139–153.

Field, T., Masi, W., Goldstein, S., Perry, S., & Parl, S. (1988). Infant day care facilitates preschool behavior. *Early Childhood Research Quarterly, 3*, 341–359.

Finnegan, R. A. (1995, March). *Aggression and victimization in the peer group: Links with the mother-child relationship.* Poster presented at the biennial meeting of the Society for Research in Child Development, Indianapolis, IN.

Finnegan, R. A., Hodges, E. V. E., & Perry, D. G. (1998). Victimization by peers: Associations with children's reports of mother-child interaction. *Journal of Personality and Social Psychology, 75*, 1076–1086.

Fonzi, A., Schneider, B. H., Tani, F., Tomada, G. (1997). Predicting children's friendship status from their dyadic interaction in structured situations of potential conflict. *Child Development, 68*, 496–506.

Frazee, H. E. (1953). Children who later become schizophrenic. *Smith College Studies in Social Work, 23*, 125–149.

French, D. C. (1988). Heterogeneity of peer-rejected boys: Aggressive and nonaggressive subtypes. *Child Development, 59*, 976–985.

French, D. C. (1990). Heterogeneity of peer-rejected girls. *Child Development, 61*, 2028–2031.

Freud, A., & Dann, S. (1951). An experiment in group upbringing. In R. Eisler. A. Freud, H, & Hartmann, E. Kris (Eds.), *Psychoanalytic study of the child.* (Vol. 6, pp., 127–168). New York: International University Press.

Frost, J. L. (1986). Children's playgrounds: Research and practice. In G. Fein & M. Rivikin (Eds.), *The young child at play* (pp. 195–211). Washington, DC: National Association for the Education of Young Children.

Furman, W. (1982). Children's friendships. In T. M. Field, A. Huston, H. C. Quay, L. Troll, & G. E. Finley (Eds.), *Review of human development* (pp. 327–339). New York: Wiley.

Furman, W. (1996). The measurement of friendship perceptions. In W. M. Bukowski, A. F. Newcomb, & W. W. Hartup (Eds.), *The company they keep: Friendship in childhood and adolescence* (pp. 41-65). New York: Cambridge University Press.

Furman, W., & Robbins, P. (1985). What's the point? Issues in the selection of treatment objectives. In B. H. Schneider, K. H. Rubin, & J. E. Ledingham (Eds.), *Children's peer relations: Issues in assessment and intervention.* New York: Springer-Verlag.

Galen, B. R., & Underwood, M. K. (1997). A developmental investigation of social aggression among children. *Developmental Psychology, 33,* 589-600.

Gallagher, J. J. (1958). Social status of children related to intelligence, propinquity, and social perception. *Elementary School Journal, 59,* 225-231.

Garmezy, N., Masten, A. S., & Tellegen, A. (1984). The study of stress and competence in children: A building block for developmental psychopathology. *Child Development, 55,* 97-111.

Gazelle, H., & Ladd, G. W. (2003). Anxious solitude and peer exclusion: A diathesis-stress model of internalizing trajectories in childhood. *Child Development, 74,* 257-278.

Ge, X., Brody, G. H., Conger, R. D., Simons, R. L., and Murry, V. M. (2002). Contextual amplification of pubertal transition effects on deviant peer affiliation and externalizing behavior among African-American children. *Developmental Psychology, 38,* 42-54.

Gershman, E. S., & Hayes, D. S. (1983). Differential stability of reciprocal friendships and unilateral relationships among preschool children. *Merrill-Palmer Quarterly, 29,* 169-177.

Gleason, T. R. (2002). Social provisions of real and imaginary relationships in early childhood. *Developmental Psychology, 38,* 979-992.

Goldman, J. A., Corsini, D. A., & DeUrioste, R. (1980). Implications of positive and negative sociometric status for assessing the social competence of young children. *Journal of Applied Developmental Psychology, 1,* 209-220.

Gottman, J. M. (1983). How children become friends. *Monographs of the Society for Research in Child Development, 48*(3, Serial No. 201).

Gottman, J. M. (1986). The world of coordinated play: Same and cross-sex friendship in young children. In J. M. Gottman & J. G. Parker (Eds.), *Conversations of friends* (pp. 197-253). New York: Cambridge.

Gottman, J. M., & Parkhurst, J. T. (1980). A developmental theory of friendship and acquaintanceship processes. In W. A. Collins (Ed.), *Minnesota symposium on child psychology: Vol. 13* (pp. 197-253). Hillsdale, NJ: Erlbaum.

Graham, J. A., & Cohen, R. (1997). Race and sex as factors in children's sociometric ratings and friendship choices. *Social Development, 6,* 355-372.

Graham, S., & Juvonen, J. (1998). Self-blame and peer victimization in middle school: An attributional analysis. *Developmental Psychology, 34,* 587-599.

Han, W., Waldfogel, J., & Brooks-Gunn, J. (2001). The effects of early maternal employment on later cognitive and behavioral outcomes. *Journal of Marriage and the Family, 63,* 336-354.

Hanish, L. D. (1997) *Correlates of peer victimization in urban children: Concurrent and longitudinal analysis.* Unpublished dissertation, University of Illinois at Chicago.

Harris, J. R. (1995). Where is the child's environment? A group socialization theory of development. *Psychological Review, 102,* 458-489.

Harris, J. R. (1998). *The nurture assumption.* New York: Free Press.

Harris, J. R. (2000). Socialization, personality development, and the child's environment: A comment on Vandell (2000). *Developmental Psychology, 36,* 711-723.

Harrist, A. W., & Bradley, K. D. (2003). "You can't say you can't play": Intervening in the process of social exclusion in the kindergarten classroom. *Early Childhood Research Quarterly, 18,* 185-205.

Harrist, A. W., Pettit, G. S., Dodge, K. A., & Bates, J. E. (1994). Dyadic synchrony in mother-child interactions: Relations with children's kindergarten adjustment. *Family Relations, 43,* 417-424.

Harrist, A. W., Zaia, A. F., Bates, J. E., Dodge, K. A., & Pettit, G. S. (1997). Subtypes of social withdrawal in early childhood: Sociometric status and social-cognitive differences across four years. *Child Development, 68,* 278-294.

Hart, C. H. (1993) *Children on playgrounds: Research perspectives and applications.* Albany: State University of New York Press.

Hart, C. H., Ladd, G. W., & Burleson, B. R. (1990). Children's expectations of the outcomes of social strategies: Relations with sociometric status and maternal discipline styles. *Child Development, 61,* 127-137.

Hartup, W. (1970). Peer interaction and social organization. In P. H. Mussen (Ed.), *Carmichael's manual of child psychology, Vol. 2.* (3rd ed., pp. 360-456). New York: Wiley & Sons.

Hartup, W. W. (1983). Peer relations. In P. H. Mussen (Series Ed.) & E. M. Heatherington (Vol. Ed.), *Handbook of child psychology: Vol. 4. Socialization, personality, and social development* (4th ed., pp. 103-196). New York: Wiley.

Hartup, W. W. (1989). Behavioral manifestations of children's friendships. In T. J. Berndt & G. W. Ladd (Eds.), *Peer relationships in child development* (pp. 46-70). New York: Wiley.

Hartup, W. W. (1996). The company they keep: Friendships and their developmental significance. *Child Development, 67,* 1-13.

Hartup, W. W., Glazer, J. A., & Charlesworth, R. (1967). Peer reinforcement and sociometric status. *Child Development, 38,* 1017-1024.

Hawker, D. S. J. (1997). *Socioemotional maladjustment among victims of different forms of peer aggression.* Unpublished dissertation, Keele University, UK.

Hawker, D., & Boulton, M. J. (2000). Twenty years' research on peer victimization and psychosocial maladjustment: A meta-analytic review of cross-sectional studies. *Journal of Child Psychology and Psychiatry and Allied Disciplines, 41,* 441-455.

Hayes, D. (1978). Cognitive bases for liking and disliking among preschool children. *Child Development, 49,* 906-909.

Hayes, D., Gershman, E., & Bolin, T. (1980). Friends and enemies: Cognitive bases for preschool children's unilateral and reciprocal relationships. *Child Development, 51,* 1276-1279.

Hazen, N., & Black, B. (1989). Preschool peer communication skills: The role of social status and interactional context. *Child Development, 60,* 867-876.

Hinde, R. S., Titmus, G., Easton, D., & Tamplin, A. (1985). Incidence of friendship and behavior toward strong associates versus nonassociates in preschoolers. *Child Development, 56,* 234-245.

Hodges, E. V. E., Boivin, M., Vitaro, F., & Bukowski, W. M. (1999). The power of friendship: Protection against an escalating cycle of peer victimization. *Developmental Psychology, 35,* 94-101.

Hodges, E. V. E., Malone, M. J., & Perry, D. G. (1997). Individual risk and social risk as interacting determinants of victimization in the peer group. *Developmental Psychology, 33,* 1032-1039.

Hodges, E. V. E., & Perry, D. G. (1999). Personal and interpersonal antecedents and consequences of victimization by peers. *Journal of Personality and Social Psychology, 76,* 677-685.

Hoover, J. H., Oliver, R. & Hazler, R. J. (1992). Bullying: Perceptions of adolescent victims in midwestern USA. *School Psychology International, 13,* 5-16.

Howes, C. (1983). Patterns of friendship. *Child Development, 54,* 1041-1053.

Howes, C. (1988). Peer interaction of young children. *Monographs of the Society for Research in Child Development, 53*(1, Serial No. 217).

Howes, C. (1996). The earliest friendships. In W. M. Bukowski, A. F. Newcomb, & W. W. Hartup (Eds.), *The company they keep: Friendship in childhood and adolescence* (pp. 66–86). New York: Cambridge University Press.

Howes, C., & Hamilton, C. E. (1992). Children's relationships with caregivers: Mothers and child care teachers. *Child Development, 63*, 859–866.

Howes, C., & Hamilton, C. E. (1993). The changing experience of child care: Changes in teachers and in teacher-child relationships and children's social competence with peers. *Early Childhood Research Quarterly, 8*, 15–32.

Howes, C., Hamilton, C. E., & Matheson, C. C. (1994). Children's relationships with peers: Differential associations with aspects of the teacher-child relationship. *Child Development, 65*, 253–263.

Howes, C., Matheson, C., & Hamilton, C. E. (1994). Maternal, teacher, and child-care history correlates of children's relationships with peers. *Child Development, 65*, 264–273.

Howes, C., & Matheson, C. C. (1992). Sequences in the development of competent play with peers: Social and pretend play. *Developmental Psychology, 28*, 961–974.

Howes, C., Olenick, M., & Der-Kiureghian, T. (1987). After school child care in an elementary school: Social development and continuity and complementarity of programs. *Elementary School Journal, 88*, 93–103.

Howes, C., & Phillipsen, L. C. (1992). Gender and friendship: Relationships within peer groups of young children. *Social Development, 1*, 231–242.

Howes, C. and Wu, F. (1990). Peer interactions and friendships in an ethnically diverse school setting. *Child Development, 61*, 537–541.

Hymel, S. (1983). Preschool children's peer relations: Issues in sociometric assessment. *Merrill-Palmer Quarterly, 29*, 237–260.

Hymel, S., Rubin, K. H., Rowden, L., & LeMare, L. (1990). Children's peer relationships: Longitudinal prediction of internalizing and externalizing problems from middle to late childhood. *Child Development, 61*, 2004–2021.

Isley, S. L., O'Neil, R., Clatfelter, D., & Parke, R. (1999). Parent and child expressed affect and children's social competence: Modeling direct and indirect pathways. *Developmental Psychology, 35*, 547–560.

Katz, L. F., & Gottman, J. M. (1993). Patterns of marital conflict predict children's internalizing and externalizing behaviors. *Developmental Psychology, 29*, 940–950.

Keefe, K., & Berndt, T. J. (1996). Relations of friendship quality to self-esteem in early adolescence. *Journal of Early Adolescence, 16*, 110–129.

Kerns, K. A., Klepac, L., & Cole, A. K. (1996). Peer relationships and preadolescents perceptions of security in the child-mother relationship. *Developmental Psychology, 32*, 457–466.

Kessen, W. (1979). The American child and other cultural inventions. *American Psychologist, 34*, 815–820.

Koch, H. L. (1933). Popularity among preschool children: Some related factors and a technique for its measurement. *Child Development, 4*, 164–175.

Koch, H. L. (1935). The modification of unsocialness in preschool children. *Psychology Bulletin, 32*, 700–01.

Kochenderfer, B. J., & Ladd, G. W. (1996). Peer victimization: Cause or consequence of school maladjustment? *Child Development, 67*, 1305–1317.

Kochenderfer, B. J., & Ladd, G. W. (1997). Victimized children's responses to peers' aggression: Behaviors associated with reduced versus continued victimization. *Development and Psychopathology, 9*, 59–73.

Kochenderfer-Ladd, B. J., & Ladd, G. W. (1998). Linkages between friendship and adjustment during early school transitions. In W. M. Bukowski & A. F. Newcomb (Eds.), *The company they keep: Friendship in childhood and adolescence* (pp. 322–345). New York: Cambridge University Press.

Kochenderfer-Ladd, B. J., & Ladd, G. W. (2001). Variations in peer victimization: Relations to children's maladjustment. In J. Juvonen & S. Graham (Eds.), *Peer harassment in school* (pp. 25–48). New York: Guilford Press.

Kochenderfer-Ladd, B. J., & Wardrop, J. (2001). Chronicity and instability in children's peer victimization experiences as predictors of loneliness and social satisfaction trajectories. *Child Development, 72*, 134–151.

Kontos, S., Burchinal, M., Howes, C., Wisseh, S., & Galinsky, E. (2002). An eco-behavioral approach to examining the contextual effects of early childhood classrooms. *Early Childhood Research Quarterly, 17*, 239–258.

Kovacs, D. M., Parker, J. G., and Hoffman, L. W. (1996). Behavioral, affective and social correlates of involvement in cross-sex friendship in elementary school. *Child Development, 67*, 2269–2286.

Kumpulainen, K., Rasanen, E., Henttonen, I., Almqvist, F., Kresanov, K., Linna, S. L., Moilanen, I., Piha, J., Puura, K., Tamminen, T. (1998). Bullying and psychiatric symptoms among elementary school-age children. *Child Abuse and Neglect, 22*, 705–717.

Kupersmidt, J. B., & Coie, J. D. (1990). Preadolescent peer status, aggression, and school adjustment as predictors of externalizing problems in adolescence. *Child Development, 61*, 1350–1362.

Kupersmidt, J. B., DeRosier, M. E., & Patterson, C. P. (1995a). Similarity as the basis for children's friendships: The roles of sociometric status, aggressive and withdrawn behavior, academic achievement and demographic characteristics. *Journal of Social and Personal Relationships, 12*, 439–452.

Kupersmidt, J. B., Griesler, P. C., DeRosier, M. E., Patternson, C. J., and Davis P. W. (1995b). Childhood aggression and peer relations in the context of family and neighborhood. *Child Development, 66*, 360–375.

Kupersmidt, J. B., Coie, J. D., & Dodge, K. A. (1990). The role of poor peer relationships in the development of disorder. In S. R. Asher & J. D. Coie (Eds.), *Peer rejection in childhood* (pp. 274–305). New York: Cambridge University Press.

Kupersmidt, J. B., Griesler, P. C., DeRosier, M. E., Patterson, C. J., & Davis, P. W. (1995). Childhood aggression and peer relations in the context of family and neighborhood factors. *Child Development, 66*, 360–375.

Ladd, G. W. (1981). Effectiveness of a social learning method for enhancing children's social interaction and peer acceptance. *Child Development, 52*, 171–178.

Ladd, G. W. (1983). Social networks of popular, average, and rejected children in school settings. *Merrill-Palmer Quarterly, 29*, 283–307.

Ladd, G. W. (1988). Friendship patterns and peer status during early and middle childhood. *Journal of Developmental and Behavioral Pediatrics, 9*, 229–238.

Ladd, G. W. (1989). Toward a further understanding of peer relationships and their contributions to child development. In T. J. Berndt & G. W. Ladd (Eds.), *Peer relationships in child development* (pp. 1–15). New York: John Wiley.

Ladd, G. W. (1990). Having friends, keeping friends, making friends, and being liked by peers in the classroom: Predictors of children's early school adjustment? *Child Development, 61*, 1081–1100.

Ladd, G. W. (1992). Themes and theories: Perspectives in process in family-peer relationships. In R. D. Parke & G. W. Ladd (Eds.),

Family-peer relationships: Modes of linkage (pp. 1–34). Hillsdale, NJ: Lawrence Erlbaum Assoiates.

Ladd, G. W. (1996). Shifting ecologies during the 5-7 year period: Predicting children's adjustment to grade school. In A. Sameroff & M. Haith (Eds.) *The Five to Seven Year Shift* (pp. 363–386). Chicago, IL: University of Chicago Press.

Ladd, G. W. (1999). Peer relationships and social competence during early and middle childhood. *Annual Review of Psychology, 50*, 333–359.

Ladd, G. W. (2003). Probing the adaptive significance of children's behavior and relationships in the school context: A child by environment perspective (pp. 43–104). In R. Kail (Ed.), *Advances in child behavior and development*. New York: Wiley.

Ladd, G. W. (2005). *Children's Peer Relationships and Social Competence: A Century of Progress*. New Haven, CT: Yale University Press.

Ladd, G. W., Birch, S. H., & Buhs, E. S. (1999). Children's social and scholastic lives in kindergarten: Related spheres of influence? *Child Development, 70*, 1373–1400.

Ladd, G. W., Buhs, E., & Seid, M. (2000). Children's initial sentiments about kindergarten: Is school liking an antecedent of early classroom participation and achievement? *Merrill-Palmer Quarterly, 46*, 255–279.

Ladd, G. W., Buhs, E. & Troop, W. (2002). Children's interpersonal skills and relationships in school settings: Adaptive significance and implications for school-based prevention and intervention programs. In P. K. Smith & C. H. Hart (Eds.), *Blackwell's handbook of childhood social development* (pp. 394–415). London: Blackwell Publishers.

Ladd, G. W., & Burgess, K. B. (1999). Charting the relationship trajectories of aggressive, withdrawn, and aggressive/withdrawn children during early grade school. *Child Development, 70*, 910–929.

Ladd, G. W., & Burgess, K. B. (2001). Do relational risks and protective factors moderate the linkages between childhood aggression and early psychological and school adjustment? *Child Development, 72*, 1579–1601.

Ladd, G. W., & Coleman, C. C. (1993). Young children's peer relationships: Forms, features, and functions. In B. Spodek (Ed.), *Handbook of research on the education of young children* (pp. 57–76). New York: Macmillan.

Ladd, G. W, & Golter, B. (1988). Parents' management of preschoolers peer relationships: Is it related to children's social competence? *Developmental Psychology, 24*, 109–117.

Ladd, G. W., Hart, C. H. (1992). Creating informal play opportunities: Are parents' and preschoolers' initiations related to children's competence with peers? *Developmental Psychology, 28*, 1179–1187.

Ladd, G. W., Hart, C. H., Wadsworth, E. M., & Golter, B. S. (1988). Preschoolers' peer networks in nonschool settings: Relationship to family characteristics and school adjustment. In S. Salzinger, J. Antrobus, & M. Hammer (Eds.), *Social networks of children, adolescents, and college students* (pp. 61–92). Hillsdale, NJ: Lawrence Erlbaum Associates.

Ladd, G. W., Herald, S. L., Slutzky, C. B., & Andrews, R. K. (2004). Preventive interventions for peer group rejection. In L. Rapp-Paglicci, C. N., Dulmus, & J. S. Wodarski (Eds.), *Handbook of prevention interventions for children and adolescents* (pp. 15–48). New York: Wiley.

Ladd, G. W., & Kochenderfer, B. J. (1996). Linkages between friendship and adjustment during early school transitions. In W. M. Bukowski, A. F. Newcomb, & W. W. Hartup (Eds.), *The company they keep: Friendship in childhood and adolescence* (pp. 322–345). New York: Cambridge University Press.

Ladd, G. W., & Kochenderfer-Ladd, B. J. (1998). Parenting behaviors and the parent-child relationship: Correlates of peer victimization in kindergarten? *Developmental Psychology, 34*, 1450–1458.

Ladd, G. W., & Kochenderfer-Ladd, B. J. (2002). Identifying victims of peer aggression from early to middle childhood: Analysis of cross-informant data for concordance, estimation of relational adjustment, prevalence of victimization, and characteristics of identified victims. *Psychological Assessment, 14*, 74–96.

Ladd, G. W., Kochenderfer, B. J., & Coleman, C. C. (1996). Friendship quality as a predictors of young children's early school adjustment. *Child Development, 67*, 1103–1118.

Ladd, G. W., Kochenderfer, B. J., & Coleman, C. C. (1997). Classroom peer acceptance, friendship, and vicitmization: Distinct relational systems that contribute uniquely to children's school adjustment? *Child Development, 68*, 1181–1197.

Ladd, G. W., & Ladd, B. J. (1998). Parenting behaviors and the parent-child relationship: Correlates of peer victimization in kindergarten? *Developmental Psychology, 34*, 1450–1458.

Ladd, G. W., LeSieur, K. D., & Profilet, S. M. (1993). Direct parental influences of young children's peer relations. In S. Duck (Ed.), *Learning about relationships* (pp. 152–183). London: Sage.

Ladd, G. W., & Mars, K. T. (1986). Reliability and validity of preschooler's perceptions of peer behavior. *Journal of Clinical Child Psychology, 15*, 16–25.

Ladd, G. W., & Mize, J. (1983). A cognitive-social learning model of social-skill training. *Psychological Review, 90*, 127–157.

Ladd, G. W., & Oden, S. L. (1979). The relationship between peer acceptance and children's ideas about helpfulness. *Child Development, 50*, 402–408.

Ladd, G. W. & Pettit, G. S. (2002). Parenting and the development of children's peer relationships. In M. H. Borenstein (ed), *Handbook of Parenting* (2nd ed., Vol. 5, pp. 377–409). Mahwah, NJ: Lawrence Erlbaum Associates.

Ladd, G. W., & Price, J. M. (1987). Predicting children's social and school adjustment following the transition from preschool to kindergarten. *Child Development, 58*, 1168–1189.

Ladd, G. W., & Price, J. M. (1993). Playstyles of peer-accepted and peer-rejected children on the playground. In C. H. Hart (Eds.), *Children on playgrounds: Research perspectives and applications* (pp. 130–183). Albany: State University of New York Press.

Ladd, G. W., Price, J. M., & Hart, C. H. (1988). Predicting children's peer status from their playground behaviors. *Child Development, 59*, 986–992.

Ladd, G. W., Price, J. M., & Hart, C. H. (1990). Preschoolers' behavioral orientations and patterns of peer contact: Predictive of social status? In S. R. Asher & J. D. Coie (Eds.), *Peer rejection in childhood* (pp. 90–118). New York: Cambridge.

Ladd, G. W., Profilet, S., & Hart, C. H. (1992). Parent's management of children's peer relations: Facilitating and supervising children's activities in the peer culture. In R. D. Parke & G. W. Ladd (Eds.), *Family-peer relationships: Modes of Linkage* (pp. 215–254). Hillsdale, NJ: Erlbaum.

Ladd, G. W. & Troop-Gordon, W. P. (2003). The role of chronic peer difficulties in the development of children's psychological adjustment problems. *Child Development, 74*, 1325–1348.

LaFreniere, P. J., & Sroufe, L. A. (1985). Profiles of peer competence in the preschool: Interrelations between measures, influences of social ecology, and relation to attachment history. *Developmental Psychology, 21*, 56–69.

Lagerspetz, K. M. J., Bjorkqvist, K., & Peltonen, T. (1988). Is indirect aggression typical of females? Gender differences in aggressiveness in 11- to 12-year-old children. *Aggressive Behavior, 14*, 403–414.

Ledingham, J. E., & Schwartzman, A. E. (1984). A 3-year follow-up of aggressive and withdrawn behavior in childhood: Preliminary findings. *Journal of Abnormal Child Psychology, 12*, 157–168.

Leventhal, T., & Brooks-Gunn, J. (2000). The neighborhoods they live in: The effects of neighborhood residences on child and adolescent outcomes. *Psychological Bulletin, 126,* 309-337.

Lieberman, A.F. (1977). Preschoolers' competence with peers: Relations with attachment and peer experience. *Child Development, 48,* 1277-1287.

Lieberman, A. F., Doyle, A. B., & Markiewicz, D. (1999). Developmental patterns in security of attachment to mother and father in late childhood and early adolescence: Associations with peer relations. *Child Development, 70,* 202-213.

Lindsey, E. W., & Mize, J. (2000). Parent-child physical and pretence play: Links to children's social competence. *Merrill-Palmer Quarterly, 46,* 565-591.

Lindsey, E. W., Mize, J., & Pettit, G. S. (1997). Differential play patterns of mothers and fathers of sons and daughters: Implications for children's gender role development. *Sex Roles, 37,* 643-661.

Lochman, J. E., Coie, J. D., Underwood, M. K., & Terry, R. (1993). Effectiveness of a social relations intervention program for aggressive and nonaggressive, rejected children. *Journal of Consulting and Clinical Psychology, 61,* 1053-1058.

Lochman, J. E., & Wayland, K. K. (1994). Aggression, social acceptance and race as predictors of negative adolescent outcomes. *Journal of the American Academy of Child and Adolescent Psychiatry, 33,* 1026-1035.

Lollis, S. P., Ross, H. S., & Tate, E. (1992). Parents' regulation of children's peer interactions: Direct influence. In R. D. Parke and G. W. Ladd (Eds.), *Family-peer relationships: Modes of linkage* (pp. 255-294). Hillsdale, NJ: Lawrence Erlbaum Associates.

Long, N., Forehand, R., Fauber, R., & Brody, G. (1987). Self-perceived and independently observed competence of young adolescents as a function of parental martial conflict and recent divorce. *Journal of Abnormal Child Psychology, 15,* 15-27.

Love, J. M., Harrison, L., Sagi-Schwartz, A., van Ijzendoorn, M. H., Ross, C., Ungerer, J. A., Raikes, H., Brady-Smith, C., Boller, K., Constintine, J., Kisker, E. E., Paulsell, D., Chazan-Cohen, R. (2003). Child care quality matters: How conclusions may vary with context. *Child Development, 74,* 1021-1033.

Lynch, M., & Cicchetti, D. (1992). Maltreated children's reports of relatedness to their teachers. In R. C. Pianta (Ed.), *Beyond the parent: The role of other adults in children's lives. New Directions for Child Development: No. 57* (pp. 81-107). San Francisco, CA: Jossey-Bass.

MacDonald, K. B., & Parke, R. D. (1984). Bridging the gap: Parent-child play interaction and interactive competence. *Child Development, 55,* 1265-1277.

MacDougall, P., Hymel, S., Vaillancourt, T., & Mercer, L. (2001). The consequences of childhood peer rejection. In M. R. Leary (Ed.), *Interpersonal rejection* (pp. 213-247). Oxford: Oxford University Press.

MacKinnon-Lewis, C., Volling, B. L., Lamb, M., Dechman, K., Rabiner, D., & Curtner, M. E. (1994). A cross-contextual analysis of boys' social competence: From family to school. *Developmental Psychology, 30,* 325-333.

Magnuson, K., & Duncan, G. (2002). Parents in poverty. In M. H. Bornstein (Ed.), *Handbook of parenting: Vol. 4: Social conditions and applied parenting* (2nd ed., pp. 95-121). Mahwah, NJ: Lawrence Erlbaum Associates.

Mahoney, M. J., & Cairns, R. D (1997). Do extracurricular activities protect against early school dropout? *Developmental Psychology, 33,* 241-253.

Masters, J. C., & Furman, W. (1981). Popularity, individual friendship selection, and specific peer interaction among children. *Developmental Psychology, 17,* 344-350.

McCandless, B. R. & Marshall, H. R. (1957). A picture sociometric technique for preschool children and its relation to teacher judgments of friendship. *Child Development, 28,* 139-147.

Medrich, E. A, Roizen, J., Rubin, V., & Buckley, S. (1982). *The serious business of growing up: A study of children's lives outside of school.* Berkeley: University of California Press.

Mize, J., & Ladd, G. W. (1988). Predicting preschoolers' peer behavior and status from their interpersonal strategies: A comparison of verbal and enactive responses to hypothetical social dilemmas. *Developmental Psychology, 24,* 782-788.

Mize J., & Ladd, G. W. (1990). A cognitive-social learning approach to social skills training with low-status preschool children. *Developmental Psychology, 26,* 388-397.

Moore, S. G. (1967). Correlates of peer acceptance in nursery school children. In W. W. Hartup & N. L. Smothergill (Eds.), *The young child* (pp. 229-247). Washington, DC: National Association for the Education of Young Children.

Moreno, J. L. (1932). *Applications of the group method to classification.* New York: National Committee on Prisons and Prison Labor.

Nansel, T. R., Overpeck, M., Pilla, R. S., Ruan, W. J., Simons-Morton, B., & Scheidt, P. (2001). Bullying behaviors among US youth. *Journal of the American Medical Association, 285,* 2094-2100.

National Institutes of Child Health and Human Development Early Child Care Research Network. (2001). Child care and children's peer interactions at 24 and 26 months: The NICHD Study of Early Child Care. *Child Development, 72,* 1478-1500.

National Institutes of Child Health and Human Development Early Child Care Research Network (2003). Does amount of time spent in child care predict socioemotional adjustment during the transition to kindergarten? *Child Development, 74,* 976-1005.

Newcomb, A. F., & Bagwell, C. L. (1995). Children's friendship relations: A meta-analytic review. *Psychological Bulletin, 117,* 306-347.

Newcomb, A. F., & Bukowski, W. M. (1983). Social impact and social preference as determinants of children's peer group status. *Developmental Psychology, 19,* 856-867.

Nix, R. L., Pinderhughes, E. E., Dodge, K. A., Bates, J. A., Pettit, G. S., & McFadyen-Ketchum, S. (1999). The relation between mothers' hostile attribution tendencies and children's externalizing behavior problems: The mediating role of mothers' harsh disciplinary practices. *Child Development, 70,* 896-909.

O'Connor, R. D. (1969). Modification of social withdrawal through symbolic modeling. *Journal of Applied Behavior Analysis, 2,* 15-22.

O'Connor, R. D. (1972). Relative efficacy of modeling, shaping, and the combined procedures for modification of social withdrawal. *Journal of Abnormal Psychology, 79,* 327-334.

Oden, S., & Asher, S. R. (1977). Coaching children in social skills for friendship making. *Child Development, 48,* 495-506.

O'Donnell, L., & Stueve, A. (1983). Mothers as social agents: Structuring the community activities of school aged children. In H. Z. Lopata & J. H. Pleck (Eds.), *Research in the interweave of social roles: Families and jobs* (pp. 113-129). Greenwich, CT: JAI Press.

Ollendick, T. H., Weist, M. D., Borden, M. G., & Green, R. W. (1992). Sociometric status and academic, behavioral, and psychological adjustment: A five-year longitudinal study. *Journal of Consulting and Clinical Psychology, 60,* 80-87.

Olweus, D. (1977). Aggression and peer acceptance in adolescent boys: Two short term longitudinal studies of ratings. *Child Development, 48,* 1301-1313.

Olweus, D. (1978). *Aggression in the schools: Bullies and whipping boys.* Washington, DC: Hemisphere.

Olweus, D. (1984). Aggressors and their victims: Bullying at school. In N. Frude & H. Gault (Eds.), *Disruptive behavior in schools* (pp. 57-76). New York: Wiley.

Olweus, D. (1993). Bullies on the playground: The role of victimization. In C. H. Hart (Ed.), *Children on playgrounds: Research perspectives and applications* (pp. 85-127). Albany: SUNY Press.

Olweus, D. (1999). In P. K. Smith, Y. Morita, J. Junger-Tas, D. Olweus, R. Catalano, & P. Slee (Eds.), Sweden. *The nature of school bullying: A cross-national perspective* (pp. 7-27). New York: Routledge.

Olweus, D. (2001). Peer victimization: A critical analysis of some important issues. In J. Juvonen and S. Graham (Eds.), *Peer harassment in school* (pp. 3-23). New York: Guilford Press.

O'Neil, R., Welsh, M., Parke, R. D., Wang, S., & Strand, C. (1997). A longitudinal assessment of the academic correlates of early peer acceptance and rejection. *Journal of Clinical Child Psychology, 26,* 290-303.

O'Reilly, A. W., & Bornstein, M. H. (1993). Caregiver-child interaction in play. *New Directions in Child Development, 59,* 55-56.

Paley, V. G. (1992). *You can't say you can't play.* Cambridge, MA: Harvard University Press.

Park, K. A., & Waters, E. (1989). Security of attachment and preschool friendships. *Child Development, 60,* 1076-1081.

Parke, R. D, & Bhavnagri, N. P. (1988). Parents as managers of children's peer relationships. In D. Belle (Ed.), *Children's social networks and social supports* (pp. 241-259). New York: Wiley.

Parke, R. D, & Ladd, G. W. (Eds.). (1992). *Family-peer relationships: Modes of linkage* (pp. 255-294). Hillsdale, NJ: Lawrence Erlbaum Associates.

Parke, R. D., MacDonald, K., Beitel, A., & Bhavnagri, N. (1988). The role of the family in the development of peer relationships. In R. Peters & R. J. McMahon (Eds.), *Social learning systems approaches to marriage and the family* (pp. 17-44). New York: Bruner/Mazel.

Parke, R. D., MacDonald, K., Burks, V. M., Carson, J., Bhavnagri, N., Barth, J. M., & Beitel, A. (1989). Family and peer linkages: In search of linkages. In K. Kreppner & R. M. Lerner (Eds.), *Family systems and life span development* (pp. 65-92). Hillsdale, NJ: Lawrence Erlbaum Associates.

Parker, J. G. (1986). Becoming friends: Conversational skills for friendship formation in young children. In J. M. Gottman & J. G. Parker (Eds.), *Conversations of friends* (pp. 103-138). New York: Cambridge.

Parker, J. G., & Asher, S. R. (1987). Peer relations and later personal adjustment: Are low-accepted children at risk? *Psychological Bulletin, 102,* 357-389.

Parker, J. G., & Asher, S. R. (1989, April). Peer relations and social adjustments: Are friendship and group acceptance distinct domains? In W. Bukowski (Chair), *Properties, processes, and effects of friendship relations during childhood and adolescence.* Symposium conducted at the biennial meeting of the Society for Research on Child Development, Kansas City, KS.

Parker, J. G., & Asher, S. R. (1993). Friendship and friendship quality in middle childhood: Links with peer group acceptance and feelings of loneliness and social dissatisfaction. *Developmental Psychology, 29,* 611-621.

Parker, J. G., & Gottman, J. M. (1989). Social and emotional development in a relational context: Friendship interaction from early childhood to adolescence. In T. J. Berndt & G. W. Ladd (Eds.), *Peer relationships in child development* (pp. 95-131). New York: John Wiley and Sons.

Parker, J. G., Rubin, K. H., Price, J. M., & DeRosier, M. (1995). Peer relationships, child development, and adjustment: A developmental psychopathology perspective. In D. Cicchetti & D. Cohen (Eds.), *Developmental psychopathology: Vol. 2. Risk, disorder and adaptation* (pp. 96-161). New York: Wiley.

Patterson, C. J., Kupersmidt, J. B., & Griesler, P. C. (1990). Children's perception of self and of relationships with others as a function of sociometric status. *Child Development, 61,* 1335-1349.

Patterson, C. J., Vaden, N. A., & Kupersmidt, J. B. (1991). Family background, recent life events, and peer rejection during childhood. *Journal of Social and Personal Relationships, 8,* 347-362.

Patterson, G. R., Reid, J. B., & Dishion, T. J. (1992). *Antisocial boys.* Eugene, OR: Castalia.

Perry, D. G., Hodges, E. V., & Egan, S. (2001). Determinants of chronic victimization by peers: A review and new model of family influence. In J. Juvonen & S. Graham (Eds.), *Peer harassment in school: The plight of the vulnerable and victimized* (pp. 73-104). New York: Guilford Press.

Perry, D. G., Kusel, S. J., & Perry, L. C. (1988). Victims of peer aggression. *Developmental Psychology, 24,* 807-814.

Perry, D. G., Perry, L. C., & Rasumssen, P. (1986). Cognitive social learning mediators of aggression. *Child Development, 57,* 700-711.

Perry, K. E., & Weinstein, R. S. (1998). The social context of early schooling and children's school adjustment. *Educational Psychologist, 33,* 177-194.

Pettit, G. S., Bates, J. E., & Dodge, K. A. (1997). Supportive parenting, ecological context, and children's adjustment: A seven-year longitudinal study. *Child Development, 68,* 908-923.

Pettit, G. S., Bates, J. E., Dodge, K. A., & Meece, D. (1999). The impact of after school peer contact on early adolescent externalizing problems is moderated by parental monitoring, perceived neighborhood safety, and prior adjustment. *Child Development, 70,* 768-778.

Pettit, G. S., Brown, E. G., Mize, J., & Lindsey, E. (1998). Mothers' and father's socializing behaviors in three contexts: Links with children's peer competence. *Merrill-Palmer Quarterly, 44,* 173-193.

Pettit, G. S., Clawson, M., Dodge, K. A., & Bates, J. E. (1996). Stability and change in peer-rejected status: The role of child behavior, parenting, and family ecology. *Merrill-Palmer Quarterly, 42,* 267-294.

Pettit, G. S, & Harrist, A. W. (1993). Children's aggressive and socially unskilled playground behavior with peers: Origins in early family relations. In C. H. Hart (Ed.), *Children on playgrounds: Research perspective and applications* (pp. 240-270). Albany: State University of New York Press.

Pettit, G. S., Laird, R. D., Bates, J. E., & Dodge, K. A. (1997). Patterns of after school care in middle childhood: Risk factors and developmental outcomes. *Merrill-Palmer Quarterly, 43,* 515-538.

Phyfe-Perkins, E. (1980). Children's behavior in preschool settings: A review of research concerning the influence of physical environment. In L. G. Katz (Ed.), *Current topics in early childhood education* (Vol. 3, pp. 91-125), Norwood, NJ: Ablex.

Piaget, J. (1965). *The moral judgment of the child.* New York: Free Press.

Pianta, R. C., Hamre, B., & Stuhlman, M. (2003). Relationships between teachers and children. In W. M. Reynolds & G. E. Miller (Eds.), *Handbook of psychology: Educational psychology* (pp. 199-234). New York: Wiley.

Pianta, R. C., & Steinberg, M. (1992). Teacher-child relationships and the process of adjusting to school. *New Directions for Child Development, 57,* 61-80.

Pianta, R. C., Steinberg, M., & Rollins, K. (1995). The first two years of school: Teacher-child relationships and deflections in children's school adjustment. *Development and Psychopathology, 7,* 295-312.

Posner, J. K., & Vandell, D. L. (1994). Low income children's after school care: Are there beneficial effects of after school programs? *Child Development, 65,* 440-456.

Price, J. M., & Ladd, G. W. (1986). Assessment of children's friendships: Implications for social competence and social adjustment. In R. Prinz

(Ed.), *Advances in behavioral assessment of children and families: Vol. 2* (pp. 121–149). Greenwich, CT: JAI Press.

Poteat, G. M., Ironsmith, M., & Bullock, J. (1986). The classification of preschool children's sociometric status. *Early Childhood Research Quarterly, 1*, 349–360.

Poulin, F., Cillessen, A., Hubbard, J. A., Coie, J. D., Dodge, K. A., & Schwartz, D. (1997). Children's friends and behavioral similarity in two social contexts. *Social Development, 6*, 224–236.

Prodromidis, M., Lamb, M., Sternberg, K., Hwang, C., & Broberg, A. (1995). Aggression and noncompliance among Swedish children in center-based care, family day care, and home care. *International Journal of Behavioral Development, 18*, 43–62.

Putallaz, M. (1983). Predicting children's sociometric status from their behavior. *Child Development, 54*, 1417–1426.

Putallaz, M., & Gottman, J. M. (1981). An interactional model of children's entry into peer groups. *Child Development, 52*, 986–944.

Putallaz, M., & Wasserman, A. (1989). Children's naturalistic entry behavior and sociometric status: A developmental perspective. *Developmental Psychology, 25*, 297–305.

Renshaw, P. D., & Asher, S. R. (1983). Children's goals and strategies for social interaction. *Merrill-Palmer Quarterly, 29*, 353–374.

Renshaw, P. D., & Brown, P. J. (1993). Loneliness in middle childhood: Concurrent and longitudinal predictors. *Child Development, 64*, 1271–1284.

Rigby, K. (1998). The relationship between reported health and involvement in bully/victim problems among male and female secondary schoolchildren. *Journal of Health Psychology, 3*, 465–476.

Rigby, K. (2001). Health consequences of bullying and its prevention in schools. In J. Juvonen & S. Graham (Eds.), *Peer harassment in school: The plight of the vulnerable and victimized.* (pp. 310–331). New York: Guilford Press.

Roff, M. (1961). Childhood social interaction and young adult bad conduct. *Journal of Abnormal Social Psychology, 63*, 333–337.

Roff, M. (1963). Childhood social interactions and young adult psychosis. *Journal of Clinical Psychology, 19*, 152–157.

Ross, H. S., & Lollis, S. P. (1989). A social relations analysis of toddler peer relationships. *Child Development, 60*, 1082–1091.

Rubenstein, J. L., & Howes, C. (1983). Social-emotional development of toddlers in day care: The role of peers and of individual differences. In S. Kilmer (Ed.). *Advances in early education and child care, Vol. 3* (pp. 13–45). Greenwich, CT: JAI Press.

Rubin, K. H. (1977). Play behaviors of young children. *Young children, 32*, 16–24.

Rubin, K. H. (1982). Nonsocial play in preschoolers: Necessary evil? *Child Development, 53*, 651–657.

Rubin, K. H. (1985). Socially withdrawn children: An "at risk" population? In B. Schneider, K. Rubin, & J. Ledingham (Eds.), *Peer relationships and social skills in childhood: Issues in assessment and training* (pp. 125–140). New York: Springer-Verlag.

Rubin, K. H., & Borwick, D. (1984). The communication skills of children who vary with regard to sociability. In H. Sypher & J. Applegate (Eds.), *Social cognition and communication* (pp. 152–170). Hillsdale, NJ: Erlbaum.

Rubin, K. H., Burgess, K. B., & Hastings, P. D. (2002). Stability and social-behavioral consequences of toddlers' inhibited temperament and parenting behaviors. *Child Development, 73*, 483–495.

Rubin, K. H., Chen, X., & Hymel, S. (1993). Socio-emotional characteristics of aggressive and withdrawn children. *Merrill-Palmer Quarterly, 49*, 518–534.

Rubin, K. H., & Clark, M. L. (1983). Preschool teachers' ratings of behavioral problems: Observational, sociometric, and social-cognitive correlates. *Journal of Abnormal Child Psychology, 11*, 273–286.

Rubin, K. H., Fein, G., & Vandenberg, B. (1983). Play. In E. M. Hetherington (Ed) & P. H. Mussen (Series Editor), *Handbook of child psychology: Social development* (pp. 693–774). New York: Wiley.

Rubin, K. H., Lynch, D., Coplan, R., Rose-Krasnor, L., & Booth, C. L. (1994). "Birds of a feather . . .": Behavioral concordances and preferential personal attraction in children. *Child Development, 65*, 1778–1785.

Rudolph, K. D., Hammen, C., & Burge, D. (1995). Cognitive representations of self, family, and peers in school-age children: Links with social competence and sociometric status. *Child Development, 66*, 1385–1402.

Russell, A., Pettit, G. S., & Mize, J. (1998). Horizontal qualities in parent-child relationships: Parallels with and possible consequences for children's peer relationships. *Developmental Review, 18*, 313–352.

Rutter, M. (1979). Maternal deprivation, 1972–1978: New findings, new concepts, new approaches. *Child Development, 50*, 283–305.

Rutter, M. (1990). Commentary: Some focus and process considerations regarding effects of parental depression on children. *Developmental Psychology, 26*, 60–67.

Rydell, A. M., Hagekull, B., and Bohlin, G. (1997). Measurement of two social competence aspects in middle childhood. *Developmental Psychology, 33*, 824–833.

Salmivalli, C., Kaukiainen, A., & Lagerspetz, K. (2000). Aggression and sociometric status among peers: Do gender and type of aggression matter? *Scandinavian Journal of Psychology, 41*, 17–24.

Savin-Williams, R. C., & Berndt, T. J. (1990). Friendship and peer relations. In S. S. Feldman & G. R. Elliott (Eds.), *At the threshold: The developing adolescent* (pp. 277–307). Cambridge, MA: Harvard Press.

Schneider, B. H., Atkinson, L., & Tardif, C. (2001). Child-parent attachment and children's peer relations: A quantitative review. *Developmental Psychology, 37*, 86–100.

Schneider, B. H., Fonzi, A., Tani, F., and Tomada, G. (1997). A cross-cultural exploration of the stability of children's friendships and the predictors of their continuation. *Social Development, 6*, 322–339.

Schwartz, D. (2000). Subtypes of aggressors and victims in children's peer groups. *Journal of Abnormal Child Psychology, 28*, 181–192.

Schwartz, D., Dodge, K. A., & Coie, J. D. (1993). The emergence of chronic peer victimization in boys' play groups. *Child Development, 64*, 1755–1772.

Schwartz, D., Dodge, K. A., Pettit, G. S., & Bates, J. E. (1997). The early socialization of aggressive victims of bullying. *Child Development, 68*, 665–675.

Schwartz, D., Dodge, K. A., Pettit, G. S., & Bates, J. E. (2000). Friendship as a moderating factor in the pathway between early harsh home environment and later victimization in the peer group. *Developmental Psychology, 36*, 646–662.

Schwartz, D., Proctor, L. J., & Chien, H. (2001). The aggressive victim of bullying. In J. Juvonen & S. Graham (Eds.), *Peer harassment in school: The plight of the vulnerable and victimized* (pp. 147–174). New York: Guilford Press.

Schwartz, D., McFadyen-Ketchum, S. A., Dodge, K. A., Pettit, G. S., & Bates, J. E. (1998). Peer group victimization as a predictor of children's behavior problems at home and in school. *Development and Psychopathology, 10*, 87–99.

Schwartz, D., McFadyen-Ketchum, S. A., Dodge, K. A., Pettit, G. S., & Bates, J. E. (1999). Early behavior problems as a predictor of later peer group victimization: Moderators and mediators in the pathways of social risk. *Journal of Abnormal Child Psychology, 27*, 191–201.

Sharp, S. (1995) How much does bullying hurt? The effects of bullying on the personal well being and educational progress of secondary aged students. *Educational and Child Psychology, 12*, 81–88.

Segoe, M. (1939). Factors influencing the selection of associates. *Journal of Educational Research, 27*, 32-40.

Seligson, M., Gannett, E., & Cotlin, L. (1992). Before- and after-school care for elementary school children. In B. Spodek & O. N. Saracho (Eds.), *Issues in child care* (pp. 125-142). New York: Teacher's College Press.

Slee, P. T. (1994). Life in school used to be so good. *Youth Studies Australia, 1*, 20-23.

Slee, P. T. (1995). Bullying: Health concerns of Australian secondary school students. *International Journal of Adolescence and Youth, 5*, 215-224.

Smith, P. K., Bowers, L., Binney, V., & Cowie, H. (1993). Relationships of children involved in bully/victim problems at school. In S. Duck (Ed.), *Learning about relationships. Understanding relationship processes series*: Vol. 2 (pp. 184-204). Newbury Park, CA: Sage Publications.

Smith, P. K., & Connolly, K. J. (1980). *The ecology of preschool behavior.* Cambridge,: Cambridge University Press.

Sroufe, L. A., & Fleeson, J. (1986). Attachment and the construction of relationships. In W. Hartup and Z. Rubin. (Eds.), *Relationships and development* (pp. 57-71). Hillsdale, NJ: Lawrence Erlbaum Associates.

Stattin, H., & Kerr, M. (2000). Parental monitoring: A reinterpretation. *Child Development, 71*, 1072-1085.

Sullivan, H. S. (1953). *The interpersonal theory of psychiatry.* New York: W. W. Norton & Company.

Troy, M., & Sroufe, L. A. (1987). Victimization among preschoolers: Role of attachment relationship history. *Journal of the American Academy of Child and Adolescent Psychiatry, 26*, 166-172.

Vandell, D. L. (2000). Parents, peer groups, and other socializing influences. *Developmental Psychology, 36*, 699-710.

Vandell, D. L., & Hembree, S. E. (1994). Peer social status and friendship: Independent contributors to children's social and academic adjustment. *Merrill-Palmer Quarterly, 40*, 461-477.

Vandell, D. L., & Mueller, E. C. (1980). Peer play and friendships during the first two years. In H. C. Foot, A. J. Chapman, & J. R. Smith (Eds.), *Friendship and social relations in children* (pp. 181-208). Chichester, England: Wiley.

Vaughn, B. E., & Langlois, J. H. (1983). Physical attractiveness as a correlate of peer status and social competence in preschool children. *Developmental Psychology, 19*, 561-567.

Vincze, M. (1971). The social contacts of infants and young children reared together. *Early Child Development and Care, 1*, 99-109.

Volling, B. V., MacKinnon-Lewis, C., Rabiner, D., & Baradaran, L. P. (1993). Children's social competence and sociometric status: Further exploration of aggression, social withdrawal, and peer rejection. *Development and Psychopathology, 5*, 459-483.

Wasik, B. H. (1987). Sociometric measures and peer descriptors of kindergarten children: A study of reliability and validity. *Journal of Clinical Child Psychology, 16*, 218-224.

Waters, E., Wippman, J., & Sroufe, L. A. (1979). Attachment, positive affect, and competence in the peer group: Two studies in construct validation. *Child Development, 50*, 821-829.

Weiss, R. (1974). The provisions of social relationships. In Z. Rubin (Ed.), *Doing unto others* (pp. 17-26). Englewood Cliffs, NJ: Prentice Hall.

Williams, G. & Asher, S. R. (1987, April). *Peer and self-perceptions of peer rejected children: Issues in classification and subgrouping.* Paper presented at the biennial meeting of the Society for Research in Child Development, Baltimore, MD.

Williams, K., Chambers, M., Logan, S., & Robinson, D. (1996). Association of common health symptoms with bullying in primary school children. *British Medical Journal, 313*, 17-19.

Wilson, B. J., & Gottman, J. M. (2002). Marital conflict, repair, and parenting. In M. H. Bornstein (Ed.), *Handbook of parenting: Vol. 4: Social conditions and applied parenting* (2nd ed., pp. 227-258). Mahwah, NJ: Lawrence Erlbaum Associates.

Wright, J. C., Giammarino, M., & Parad, H. W. (1986). Social status in small groups: Individual-group similarity and the social "misfit". *Journal of Personality and Social Psychology, 50*, 523-536.

Wu, X., Hart, C. H., Draper, T. W., & Olsen, J. A. (2001). Peer and teacher sociometrics for preschool children: Cross-informant concordance, temporal stability, and reliability. *Merrill Palmer Quarterly, 47*, 416-443.

Young, L. L., & Cooper, D. H. (1944). Some factors associated with popularity. *Journal of Educational Psychology, 35*, 513-535.

Youngblade, L. M. (2003). Peer and teacher ratings of third and fourth grade children's social behavior as a function of early maternal employment. *Journal of Child Psychology and Psychiatry, 44*, 477-488.

Zarbatany, L., & Pepper, S. (1996). The role of the group in peer group entry. *Social Development, 5*, 251-260.

Zarbatany, L., Van Brunschot, M., Meadows, K., & Pepper, S. (1996). Effects of friendship and gender on peer group entry. *Child Development, 67*, 2287-2300.

· 4 ·

CHILDREN'S MORALITY: PERSPECTIVES AND RESEARCH

Eva Johansson
Göteborg University

This chapter deals with the development of children's morality. The aim is to present different ontological[1] perspectives on morality in research and early childhood education and how these affect research interests as well as educational practices. How is research performed? What questions have been asked and what kind of morality have these questions helped to uncover? What do teachers and researchers regard as an optimal way of teaching morality to children?

If we look at the vast number of international studies, we find three main traditions for moral research: cognitive, emotional, and cultural. However, none of these traditions are internally homogeneous; they emphasize different aspects of children's morality and deal with different research questions. Each defines morality slightly differently by regarding it as something innate, universal, or relative to culture and context. Nevertheless, these traditions have their historical roots and source of inspiration in research by Piaget, Freud, Skinner, and Vygotsky.

Piaget (1960) and Kohlberg (1976) developed the *cognitive* tradition. According to this tradition, a universal morality exists, which is connected to logic and cognition. The child's moral responsibility develops with age and ability to reason. Some researchers within cognitive research have augmented and developed the cognitive tradition as well as expanded the definition of morality. They define morality universally, as a special *domain* concerning questions about other's welfare and take a more cognitive position (cf. Killen & Hart, 1995; Nucci, 1996, 2001; Reed, Turiel, & Brown, 1996; Smetana, 1993; Turiel, 1998; Turiel, Killen, & Helwig, 1987; Turiel & Wainryb, 2000).

The *emotional* tradition stems from Freud's psychoanalytic theory, and is presently represented by Hoffman (1984, 1987, 2000) and Eisenberg and Strayer (1987), among others. Hoffman maintains that empathy is important for moral actions. Empathy involves participating in another person's emotions. The child's empathic emotions develop similar to the ability to understand others as separate human beings. The research on prosocial actions, which means actions to support others (Eisenberg & Fabes 1998; Eisenberg & Mussen, 1997), is linked to the emotional tradition.

The *cultural* tradition is divided into various streams of thought. One part of the cultural tradition emphasizes *culture* as the deciding factor in determining a child's morality; morality is seen as relative to the cultural context (Shweder, Jensen, & Goldsterin, 1995; Shweder, Mahapatra, & Miller, 1987). The cultural *interactive* approach, by contrast, regards the interconnection between individual, contextual, and cultural aspects as the base from which morality develops (cf. Corsaro, 1997; Damon, 1990, 1998; Dunn, 1988; Frønes, 1995; Johansson, 1999; Johansson & Johansson, 2003). The cultural interactive approach also stresses that the child is active in interpreting and giving meaning to the world. Children, individually and with others, give their morality a specific character, shape, and meaning.

Three different traditions, with differing ontological perspectives, have been presented in this introduction. In the following text, research within these three traditions is presented and discussed with regard to research and teaching in early childhood education.

---

[1]Ontology in empirical research consists of philosophical ideas or theories concerning the constitution of the world of investigation and the development of knowledge about this world. The ontology comprises a perspective that guides and shapes the investigation, for example, appropriate methods to use and possible knowledge to reach about the phenomenon in question (Johansson, 2001).

THE COGNITIVE TRADITION

Jean Piaget (1960) and Lawrence Kohlberg (1976, 1978) are the most well-known researchers within the cognitive tradition. They base their theories on the idea that morality and logic are interrelated. According to Piaget and Kohlberg, moral awareness develops gradually through stages parallel to cognitive development. The child's cognitive development determines his or her possible moral awareness. The moral theory behind these researchers' investigations stems from Immanuel Kant's ideas in which rationality and autonomy form a foundation and a purpose for moral development. The cognitive tradition has inspired a number of modern studies about children's morality (cf. Nucci, 1996, 2001; Smetana, 1993; Turiel, 1998; Turiel et al., 1987; Uzgiris, 1996).

Morality Develops Through Stages

Piaget (1960) was mainly concerned with moral judgments. He proposed that morality develops from heteronomy (i.e., dependence on authorities and rules) to autonomy; instead of perceiving norms as unchangeable the child participates in interpreting and creating norms. According to Piaget, morality implies understanding the idea of objective justice and presupposes cooperation and mutual respect. Moral development is divided into stages and becomes more advanced as the intellectual development unfolds.

According to Piaget, there exists in the child two separate moralities. One concerns duty and is related with the moral constraint of the adult. The other is connected to autonomy and mutual cooperation. The young child's capability to be moral is related to the concept of egocentrism; that is, the child's confusion of the ego and the external world. When a child's thinking is freed from the immediate context, from the child's own subjectivity and from the influence of grown-ups and older peers, then the child is able to be moral. Piaget argues that the egocentric child is subject to external constraint but has little capacity for cooperation and objective justice. In order to cooperate, one must be conscious of one's own ego. The subject has to liberate himself or herself from the thoughts and will of others.

> The morality of the autonomous conscience does not tend to subject each personality to rules that have a common content: it simply obliges individuals to place themselves in reciprocal relationship with each other without letting the laws of perspective resultant upon this reciprocity destroy their individual points of view. (Piaget, 1960, p. 404)

For young children this is impossible, as this presupposes logic and intellectual thinking. Piaget argues that to be moral from the perspective of a 6-year-old child is to show obedience and act in conformity with rules imposed by adults. By the age of 8 or later, the child's thinking has developed enough to make him or her able to make autonomous and objective moral judgments. "Logic is the morality of thought just as morality is the logic of action" (Piaget, 1960, p.404). Gradually the child develops a moral sense of cooperation. Now the guiding

principle is solidarity and the primary emphasis is on autonomy of conscience, intentions and responsibility.

The child's view on right and wrong is connected to his or her ability to consider the perspective of others, writes Piaget (1960). The young child considers the results of the acts rather than the motives behind as he or she is unable to think beyond the observable surfaces. Rules are followed literally. When the child's intellectual development has proceeded and the sociocentric thinking improves, the child progressively increases in ability to understand the acts of others.

According to Piaget the child gradually becomes able to discern acts as subjective and embedded with underlying motives and to value behavior on these grounds. Thus, the child has reached an autonomous morality and obedience withdraws in favor of the idea of justice. In this process, intellectual and moral evolution work together. It is a question of "the genetic parallelism existing between the formation of the logical and of the moral consciousness" (Piaget, 1960, p. 407). To achieve this conscious of the functioning of the mind, social life is a necessity, in which the starting point for the good is the initial spontaneous and mutual affections between the child and the parent.

A morality of justice. Piaget (1960) emphasized that young children's morality is guided by adults and characterized by one-sidedness. In the perspective of the child, justice is subordinated to adult authority. The child believes not only in the adult's omniscience, the child also unquestionably believes in the absolute value of the imperatives he or she receives from the adults or other authorities. Nevertheless, Piaget underscored the interaction between contemporaries as highly important for moral development. Moral judgments are, in Piaget's view, fundamentally about relationships and lead toward mutual respect and understanding. Cooperation on equal grounds and justice are the two means and goals in children's moral life.

Kohlberg continued the work of Piaget and developed his theory in relation to moral development in adolescence and adulthood. The moral theory created by Kohlberg (1976) focuses primarily on justice. Moral development proceeds through six stages, all grouped in three levels. The child's moral growth proceeds from an egocentric morality, through conformity with others, to the highest form that is a mature internalized morality. Moral progression starts with the young child's judgments mainly based on obedience and a fear of punishment. Later in adolescence the individual strives to live up to expectations from friends and others. Now judgments are grounded in obligations, conceptions of "good" persons and unchangeable rules. At the last level, the subject has established and internalized universal moral principles such as justice, rights, and respect. The individual has reached an inner and stable morality on which judgments are built. Being criticized from Gilligan (1982) among others, Kohlberg revised his theory and included care as a moral dimension at the highest level (Kohlberg, Levine, & Hewer, 1983).

Research interests—cognition and moral judgement. What questions have been asked and what kind of morality have these questions helped to uncover? The focus of cognitive tradition is on moral judgments and on a child's cognitive ability to reason on given moral dilemmas (i.e., not on moral behavior). These dilemmas are founded on a theory of morality where justice, cooperation and respect are highly valued. The cognitive tradition investigates moral development first and foremost as a psychological phenomenon in human development. The sociability of the subject is emphasized as essential, but the focus of interest is on morality as a cognitive internalized skill.

The methods used are in line with the theory, which means that moral problems are to be reflected upon and solved by the subject. Interviews and dialogues with children and adults on moral issues also serve as a methodological strategy. Morality is perceived as an ability, which gradually becomes more advanced and internalized through interaction with peers and in line with a child's cognitive development. Rationality and logic are cornerstones on which morality rests. Moral autonomy appears, writes Piaget (1960), when the mind regards as necessary an ideal that is independent of all external pressure. A moral individual is assumed to be able to make objective judgments, based on internal autonomy and free from influences of authorities, relations to others, or contextual predicaments.

Of importance for moral development is not only the interaction with equals, primarily peers, but also the subject's continuous endeavor for equilibrium, which is the motor of development. Equilibrium can be seen as a never-ending organizing process of searching for balance between the parts and the whole in the child's construction of knowledge. In peer interaction, for instance, the child's is confronted with the perspective of the other. This leads to an inner conflict, an imbalance between the perspective of the child and that proposed from the other. But this imbalance is solved by the child's constructions, in which the new knowledge is adapted to previous understanding. This dynamic process is working on all levels of development, including the biological, psychological, and social, and in which progression leads from a lower equilibrium to a higher one (Piaget, 1980; see also Chapman, 1988).

The study of morality is, according to Piaget and Kohlberg, based on dilemmas and questions consistent with the theory of morality. The morality in question is objective justice, primarily expressed in language. This presupposes that children are able to reflect on, reason, and express their conceptions in words. The paradox that occurs is that, contrary to the ambitions of the researcher, the child's perspective becomes limited by the theory and research methods to one specific concept (Johansson, 2001). The child's morality is studied and evaluated against a background of a moral theory based on rationality and a specific idea of justice.

Implications for early childhood education. If we look at early childhood education, what is the optimal way of teaching morality from the perspective of the cognitive tradition?

The whole process of teaching is mainly about how to assist the child out of his or her egocentricity and lead him or her towards cooperation (Piaget, 1960). On the one hand, Piaget rejected teachers' attempts to transform the child's mind from the "outside." Instead, he suggested that the adult should become a collaborator. Teaching should be built on the child's free will and the internal drift to reach equilibrium in the process of learning. On the other hand, the adult must not only rely on

the child's biological "nature" alone, writes Piaget (1960). Because all moral and logical norms are the result of cooperation, schools ought to be a place where experiments and reflection are carried out both individually *and* with others.

Of epoch-making importance from the work of Piaget, is the ambition to understand the child's perspective on morality; an approach, which is currently in progress, not only in moral education and research but also in educational research in general. Many researchers claim that teaching ought to build on the child's own unique approaches and understanding of the phenomenon at hand (Bengtsson, 1999; Damon, 1998; DeVries & Zan, 1994; Dunn 1988; Johansson, 1999; Marton & Booth, 1997; Nucci, 2001; Pramling Samuelsson & Asplund, 2003).

A Constructivist Program. In accordance with the research of Piaget, the challenges for the teacher is not only to be sensitive to the child's moral understanding but also to help children expand their ability to reason and reflect on different perspectives of moral issues. From the constructivist program for early childhood education presented below we can learn that a child's freedom to construct a morality based on his or her own judgments is essential.

In line with the cognitive theory, DeVries and Zan (1994) provided a constructivist program for early childhood education. Their work is based on three theoretical assumptions, all derived from the tradition of Piaget. First, moral knowledge is thought to be constructed by the child and undergoes qualitative transformations. Second, socioaffective bonds or lack of bonds motivate social and moral development. Third, equilibration is a process that can be seen in moral development. For example, intrapersonal and interpersonal conflict is crucial in the development of self-regulation in moral development.

According to these researchers, the teacher's responsibility is to stimulate a moral atmosphere in which respect for the child is fundamental and an indispensable aspect of teaching. The teacher's approaches and methods are crucial to support children's moral development, the child must however be left free to construct his or her moral understanding. Rather than implementing moral rules, the teacher ought to help children to develop an autonomous morality based on their inner beliefs about principles for right and wrong. Morality, with respect to DeVries and Zan (1994), is universal and corresponds to the Golden Rule. The teacher's responsibility is to help children to decenter and to recognize other children's feelings.

In this respect, the ideas for the constructivist program also draw on the gradual development of an autonomous self and the awareness of other people's perspectives that children develop (Selman, 1980). This theory by Selman suggests that a child between 3 and 6 years (level 0) is not capable of understanding others as people with feelings of their own. Moreover, the self from this perspective is for the most part heterogeneous and dependent on adults. At the next level (5-9 years, level 1) the child knows that each person has unique experiences, but is, however, incapable of considering more than one perspective at a time. At level 2 (around 7-12 years) the child is able to consider the feelings and thoughts of oneself and others. In adolescence, the individual has gained enough competence and ability where these reciprocal perspectives can be coordinated into a mutual perspective. DeVries and Zan (1994) claim that young children (between 3 and 6 years) have predominantly a moral understanding at level 1, but are occasionally capable of interpersonal understanding at level 2. The authors conclude that a child's level of interpersonal understanding depends more on experience than on age (DeVries & Zan, 1994).

In line with the development of an autonomous morality certain teaching strategies are essential such as, adopting a cooperative attitude, stimulating children's reflection, and encouragement of peer interaction. DeVries and Zan (1994) underscore the teachers' role of providing children with choices to expand their social learning. Moreover, it is of vital importance that teachers learn to recognize the children's negotiation strategies and shared experiences, and also to recognize educational needs based on the children's behavior. The essence of moral development is founded in the child's interests and constructions of thought.

To summarize, this program is based on the cognitive tradition. On the one hand, universal moral stages fill the role of telling something about a child's moral ability or disability. On the other hand, moral stages are employed to facilitate children's moral development and, more specifically, their moral judgment. Central to this work is reflection. A common feature is the idea that morality is universal and gradually develops from heteronomy to autonomy through cooperation between peers and adults as well as through reflections on a higher (next) developmental level. Morality develops within the individual although interaction is considered important for this development. A child's freedom to construct a morality based on his or her own judgments is highlighted. The teacher's responsibility to create a moral atmosphere is fundamental and respect for the child is an indispensable part in this process.

Despite the fact that the effects from the constructivist program have not been studied, the authors attribute its relevance to the work by Kohlberg and Piaget. Embedded in the program is a moral theory that scarcely is made explicit or discussed. The Golden Rule is mentioned as something universal, but this concept is not explicit either in content or meaning. The consequences that follow from the Golden Rule are problematic because the justification of moral acts are based on one's own conception of what is good, and then applying this conception to others. However, what is good for one person is not always beneficial to for the other.

Furthermore, the description of the rationale is very detailed, and the program seems to serve as a manual for ideal moral teaching. The constructivist rationale shows a strong reliance on the suggested methods and their relevance for improving moral development. However, as we will discuss later, research has shown that teachers are confronted with many moral dilemmas when supporting children's moral discoveries; this calls for further investigation.

A common characteristic within the constructivist school is to teach morality from the perspective of the child; this approach is based on respect for the child and his or her intentions. We can also learn that the constructivist program has a focus on the social world of the child, and points to the relation between emotions, cognition, and morality. Indeed, aspects such as peer interaction and cooperation seem to be significant for moral development in schools in general. Peer interaction and cooperation are found within many rationales for early childhood education despite the variations in which morality is defined and expressed in everyday praxis in schools (DeVries & Zan, 1994; Johansson & Johansson, 2003; Solomon, Watson, Battistich, Schaps, & Delucchi, 1996).

Moral Reflection and the Skill to Reason.   Moral judgments dominate the research methods developed by Piaget and Kohlberg and several other researchers (cf. Turiel, 1998, for a review) who have adopted these methods. Indeed, to reflect on moral dilemmas is a strategy that has influenced teachers on different levels of the educational system. For instance, the educational programs within Just-community schools ascribe to the constructivist rationale and are founded on Kohlberg's theory. Moral reflection is central to these programs. The idea is that moral development and learning are supported through moral discussions, rules for democracy and a just community (Kohlberg, 1978; Nucci, 2001; see also Colnerud & Thornberg, 2003).

The effects of the constructivist program have not been studied; however, the results from the scientific evaluation of the Just Community schools indicate that children have developed their skill to reason on moral problems (Garz, 1992; see also Colnerud & Thornberg, 2003). Albeit these positive results we do not know how children in daily life express or experience moral values and norms. Moreover, the relation between what one ought to do, that is, the moral judgment, and the actual consequences of these moral judgments in daily life are not simple. Research indicates that there might be a lot of obstacles on the road between moral ideals and the ideal moral actions. Eisenberg and Fabes (1998, Fabes et al., 1999), for instance, point to a multiple of experiences and interpretations that might influence moral acts. Turiel (1998) claims that various contextual dimensions affect children's moral judgments. Let us consider this problem a bit further.

Johansson and Johansson (2003) analyses tacit processes that are communicated in formalized moral discussions among young schoolchildren in Sweden. The researchers point at some problems of democracy and integrity that occur within these meetings (in Sweden called peer-talks). Peer-talks are intended to function as a forum for the children to express different perspectives, listen to each other, and to make joint decisions on moral issues, but the study also showed that it is necessary to pay attention to the aspects of power that might be hidden in the process. Parallel to the explicit moral issue, positions of power amongst the children were expressed in the peer-talks. Certain children have obtained the power to define the course of events. They talk frequently, give definitions, and provide solutions to moral dilemmas, whereas other children remain quiet and seemed uninterested. The researchers claim that the children learn to master the moral rules of the school for communication in the peer-talks, what to say, how to feel, and the moral solutions that are appropriate (Johansson & Johansson, 2003). This is in line with the conclusions drawn by Roger Säljö (2000) who studies communication processes. He suggests that people in dialogues with others internalize communicative patterns for appropriate interaction, for what to say in a certain context and how to say it. Communication is always a moral and a political matter, writes Säljö. One of the most important means for power is the right to define and describe. The one that gets his or her description accepted has the advantage in the dialogue.

Furthermore, Johansson and Johansson (2003) interpret peer-talks as an arena that visualizes a paradox; the school as a system for discipline as well as for democracy. Two confronting ideals meet. On the one hand, democratic ideals proclaim the individual's liberty to make free choices, children's right to influence, the responsibility of the individual, and the teacher's role as a tutor. On the other hand, we have the implicit authoritarian ideal, which require teachers to keep control and order in class, to maintain rules and be the one to decide.

It seems therefore important to raise questions in regards to power and language since verbal communication plays a main part in the cognitive approaches. Who gets influence over the moral discourse? What about children whose communication strategies and language skills might differ from the official and prescriptive ones? What about values that can not be described in words?

Morality and Cognition.

From the research of Piaget we can conclude that because of egocentrism, young children's moral ability is both limited and different from adults'. However, the paradox is that a child's capacity to be moral is at risk of being underestimated if this capacity is interpreted against a background of a "fully developed" adult morality.

Piaget suggests both the child's social life and affects to be essential and motivational elements in morality, yet the cognitive aspects on morality have been the most salient in his theory. This is understandable because of Piaget's epistemological interests; social and emotional dimensions in moral development have not been in the forefront of his research.

However, a focus mainly on cognition is not sufficient to fully understand children's morality and may also restrict ways of looking at children's morality. Although the subject is supposed to acquire moral autonomy and to be able to make rational and logical moral decisions and to verbalize them, senses and experiences of the body are at risk to be overlooked, as is tacit knowledge not amenable to linguistic formulation (cf. Johansson, 2001; Stern, 1985; Uzgiris, 1996). The moment we limit the focus to cognition we might fail to observe the child's multifaceted social experiences and the importance that these experiences might have for a child's moral learning. Contrarily, recent research has shown that a variety of experiences such as various relations, contextual and cultural interactions, are of essential importance for children's moral life and their perspectives on morality (cf. Corsaro, 1997; Damon, 1990, 1998; Dunn, 1988; Eisenberg & Fabes, 1998; Johansson, 1999; Nucci, 2001; Turiel, 1998).

Piaget's thesis that young children are governed by grown-ups and thus not capable of a self-guided morality has been questioned on empirical grounds. Indeed, many studies have shown that even toddlers, children between 1 and 3 years of age, defend moral values, discern and value moral transgressions different from conventional ones, are aware of moral standards and seem to make moral decisions (cf. Damon, 1990; Dunn,

1988; Eisenberg & Fabes, 1998; Johansson 1999; Smetana, 1993; Turiel, 1998; Young, Fox, & Zahn-Waxler, 1999).

Thus, if morality is strongly associated with cognitive development there might be a risk that the youngest children might be regarded as standing outside of this process. Within a Nordic context, preschool practice and research have traditionally been influenced by psychological developmental theories. This influence has to a large extent lead to an emphasis in early education on the limitations in children's cognitive and moral abilities rather than their capabilities (Dahlberg & Tagucchi, 1994; Nordin-Hultman, 2004; Sommer, 1997). To exemplify, Johansson (2002) studied preschool-teachers' interaction with toddlers in terms of morality. She found that teachers who adopted a cognitive stage theory on children's moral development perceived toddlers to be too young and cognitively immature to understand moral dimensions in daily life. The teachers avoided interfering in moral conflicts between the children, did not take notice, or sometimes prevented children's involvement in others well-being.

Universal Moral Stages.

As we have learned from the constructivist program (DeVries & Zan, 1994), universal moral stages can fulfill the role of telling us something about children's moral ability or inability; however, moral stages also may be employed to facilitate children's moral development. The dominance of universal stages in moral development has begun to be questioned by a number of researchers. Berger and Luckmann (1995; see also Sommer, 1997), for instance, claim that the modern society is so complex and diverse and does not build on a common core of values any longer. From this follows that universal stages are too constricted to explain moral development and learning. To propose universal stages in morality might restrict the discovery of variation between and within stages as well as how contextual and cultural aspects might influence children's perspectives on morality (cf. Eisenberg & Fabes, 1998; Shweder et al., 1987; Turiel, 1998).

Furthermore, Turiel and Wainryb (2000) reject the idea that cultures are commonly defined by shared meanings. Instead, they suggest that conflicts, contradictions and differences in interpretations are a part of every society. Critics of the moral theories developed by Piaget and Kohlberg say that these ideals are a product of a western society and that members of other cultures seldom attain the last stages in Kohlberg's theory (Berk, 2000).

The Domain Specific Theory

Of essential importance from the research of Piaget (1960) are his extensive studies on the child's thinking and how children give meaning to their world. Piaget also highlighted the importance of peer interaction in favor of moral development. Many researchers have been influenced by Piaget's tradition especially when it comes to children's constructions of different phenomena in their world (Turiel & Wainryb, 2000; Uzgiris; 1996).

A significant component within the manifold research made by Killen and Hart (1995), Killen and Nucci (1995), Killen and Smetana (1999), Nucci (1996, 2001), Smetana (1993), Turiel,

(1998), Turiel, Killen, and Helwig (1987) and Turiel and Wainrub (2000), is domain theory. This theory represents a cognitive and interactive tradition in which morality is distinguished from other social domains. The researchers claim that a child's social world can be divided into three domains: the moral, the conventional, and the personal. These three domains appear to be based on qualitatively different experiences, they follow different developmental lines, and give rise to different implications for social interactions.

The moral domain. The moral domain refers to issues of justice, rights, and welfare. Thinking about morality embraces features distinctive from other aspects of thinking about the social world. Morality involves objectives for how to act toward others. Moral transgressions are always about a victim and pertain to physical or psychological harm as well as to questions of fairness and justice. These moral categories and their meanings do not necessarily differ between cultures, albeit different contextual circumstances may influence various interpretations. The idea behind the concept of domains is that culture, as a homogenous surrounding context, is both too global and too limited to explain moral judgments and strategies. Rather, morality is connected to interaction in different contexts within culture, together with individual interpretations and contextual differences in everyday life. Social life is multifaceted. Young children give different situations different meanings and make moral judgments from various experiences in their everyday lives. Interaction with family members, peers and other adults are altogether important issues for moral learning and development (Turiel, 1998; Turiel, Killen, & Helwig, 1987; Turiel, Smetana, & Killen, 1991).

The conventional and the moral domain. The conventional domain are part of constitutive social systems and refer to shared behaviors such as uniformities and rules whose meanings are defined by the social system in which they are embedded. The conventional rules are related to context and may vary by socially constructed meanings (Turiel, 1998).

Smetana (1993) along with Turiel, Killen, and Helwig (1987), Smetana, Killen, and Turiel (1991) studied children's understanding of social rules. These researchers wanted to find out if and how children discriminate between the moral, the conventional and the personal domain. The children, between 2 and 5 years of age, were presented with a series of social acts or infringements in accordance with the distinctions of the domains. The researchers found that even 3-year-old toddlers discriminate between conventional and moral rules even if the distinction between the moral and social conventions became more consistent by about the ages of 4 or 5. Killen and Smetana (1999) have demonstrated that children by 6 or 7 years of age apply distinctions of domains to familiar rather than unfamiliar issues and by 9 or 10 years can apply the distinction between moral and conventional rules to both of these aspects. The younger children judged moral transgressions as more serious and thus deserving more punishment than transgressions of conventional art (cf. Smetana, 1993, 1995; Turiel, 1998; Turiel, Killen, & Helwig, 1987). The researchers conclude that social conventions concern adults' involvement rather than young children. The children were deeply concerned with transgressions of moral rules, but seemed to be somewhat uninvolved with conventional transgressions. The children assessed harming others more to the consequences of acts than conventional transgressions, which in contrast were related to rules. Children, by the end of the third year, judged moral infringements independently of authorities.

Turiel (1998) observed interaction among school children (from first, third, fifth, and seventh grades) and adults in their classroom, during periods of recess, lunchtime, and during transitions from one activity to another. Turiel concludes that social interactions were different for the moral and conventional events. In reaction to moral events children responded with statements about the effects and the unfairness of actions sometimes with physical or verbal revenge. Acts in the moral domain were judged independently of rules, institutional context, or what authority dictated. On the contrary, reactions to the conventional events focused on rules, sanctions, and commands to hinder such behavior.

Eventually, children learn to identify different moral aspects and combine domain components. With increasing age children view mixed transgressions (for instance, is it right or wrong to talk without waiting for one's turn) as wrong even if the teacher changes the rules. This was found by Crane and Tisak (1995) who interviewed preschool children and children from Grade 1 to Grade 3 in school. The younger children believed to a greater extent that transgressions were acceptable if the teacher thought so. Children from Grade 1, along with preschool-children, based their judgments on conventional rules. Combining moral and social rules became more frequent among the elder children.

The researchers conclude that children's judgments and their social experiences are highly multifaceted. The thinking of individuals is flexible and it is not only the family or peers or the culture that bears on children's moral development. Reciprocal interactions include a coordination of emotions, thoughts, and actions and all affect moral development (Turiel & Wainrub, 2000).

The personal domain. Nucci (1996, 2001, also Killen & Nucci, 1995; Killen & Smetana, 1999) explores the idea of "the personal" in childhood. The personal refers to individual preference, privacy, and control over one's body. Personal issues are important prerequisites for a child's growing sense of self-agency and control. The personal domain, writes Nucci (1996), supports the individual's sense of identity as a cultural and as a unique being. The base for the personal is the own body. Moreover, the personal involves the freedom to express oneself, to communicate, and to interact freely. The personal is not a matter of right or wrong, but of preference and choice. Children are active not only in interpreting others' definitions of the personal but also to establish regions for their own personal control and personal choices through a process of interactive negotiation with others (Nucci, 2001).

By 4 years of age, children have rudimentary concepts of personal issues (Nucci & Weber, 1995; see also Killen & Smetana, 1999; Nucci, 1996, 2001). Personal issues concern a basic intuitive moral sense of what is right. This makes restrictions of the personal, from a child's perspective, humiliating and unfair. Definitions of the personal occur within all cultures; however, these definitions might differ with regard to content. Nucci (1996, 2001) regards the personal and the moral as mutually dependent rather than as contrasting pools for development. Indeed, participating in respectful interaction must be based on a feeling for the personal boundaries of others. Moral concepts about freedom are impossible to establish without personal requests of independence, integrity, agency, and individuality, according to Nucci (2001).

Killen and Smetana (1999) explored social interactions regarding personal issues as compared to moral and conventional issues in preschool classrooms. The researchers aimed to shed light on teachers' statements and children's responses to personal events such as personal choice, and to compare them with reactions to moral and conventional events. The study included 347 children and their teachers in 20 preschool and day care classrooms. The children were between 3 and 5 years old.

The results demonstrated that social interactions with respect to personal issues occurred frequently in the preschool classrooms and were more common than moral or conventional events. Responses to moral transgressions by children and teachers focused on the intrinsic consequences of the acts for the other persons' rights and well-being. In addition, teachers responded to conventional transgressions with commands, without information why the acts were wrong, and referred less to the effects of actions for the classroom order. They seemed more geared toward giving the children directives in moral and conventional events than in personal events in the classroom. When classroom activities were less organized and children had more opportunities to interact (for example, during activity time) moral transgressions were more likely to occur, whereas personal events were most frequent during lunch and conventional acts dominated during circle time. Killen and Smetana (1999) emphasize that events referring to the personal domain were actively claimed by the children, which indicates that the personal domain does not primarily consist of issues regulated by teachers. In contrast with the findings of Nucci and Weber (1995), who found that mothers negotiate personal issues with children, the teachers rarely negotiated with children on personal issues in the classroom. With increasing age the children became more autonomous in their judgments and issues like how to dress, what to eat, where to sit and what activity to engage in; these activities within the personal domain were considered to be up to the child's own decision. However, the children did not question the teachers' authority.

Implications for research and education. What will be the consequences in research or teaching if we adopt the domain theory? The domain tradition is concerned with the complexity of the child's various relations and proposes that the social world can be divided into moral, conventional, and personal domains. This encourages research and teaching to strive for complexity in methods as well as in how to interpret children's morality. But when it comes to the moral dimensions the researchers seem primarily interested in the cognitive side of morality, that is, social judgments, albeit the fact that the researchers also emphasize emotions as important for morality. The character of

these studies is mainly of quantitative art in which the majority of investigations have been performed through interviews, although some studies investigate everyday interaction.

The researchers in the domain theory claim that diversity is the base for social judgments, and their moral theory is founded on both universalism and relativism. Nucci writes: "The paradox, then, is that morality is both based on a set of nonrelative universals, and yet ultimately plural in its application" (Nucci, 2001, p. xviii).

The claim that morality is universal, as already discussed, is viewed differently by other researchers, particularly when it comes to definitions of moral and conventional issues. Shweder, Jensen and Goldsterin (1987), for instance, maintain morality to be relative to culture. These researchers propose that events from one perspective could be interpreted as a conventional transgression, but from another perspective similar events might be viewed as a moral transgression. Therefore, to separate moral, conventional, and personal dimensions in children's social life can be a problem. I will come back to this issue.

The connection between the different domains and their affect on children's morality is of interest when researching children's moral judgments within the cognitive tradition. An issue of primary interest is the question of how moral judgments relate to moral behavior, which is a question that calls for further investigation. Nevertheless, as stated earlier, it is necessary to pay attention to the fact that the questions asked and the attained results are at risk of becoming constricted in content, when the focus is limited to the cognitive side of morality.

Moral Education—Moral Atmosphere, Values, and Fostering a Moral Self. If we consider this theory as a basis for early childhood education, what conclusions might follow? What might teachers find of use from the domain theory?

Nucci (2001) suggests three interrelated aspects to be developed in education: establishing a moral atmosphere, integrating education of values into the curriculum, and fostering the moral self.

First of all, Nucci proposes that the teachers should vary their response toward children's behavior in accordance with the different domains. When it comes to moral concerns the teacher may focus on the effects that actions have upon the rights and welfare of persons. The central challenge of moral education in preschool is to help children generate a conception of fairness that requires the reciprocal coordination of two or more points of view. This can be done in the everyday interactions when teachers help children to focus on the effects of their actions and reciprocal implications. Regarding conventional issues the focus ought to be on social organization, social expectations, and rules. The responsibility for establishing a basic framework of conventional rules is mainly on the teacher, but he or she also may engage children in the construction of conventional rules that affect them directly. This may provide children with experiences of the collective and negotiated source of conventional norms.

It is important, according to Nucci (2001), to integrate values into education, as the educative role of the schools is to bring students beyond their own direct encounters with the world. In this respect the construction of a more developed social understanding relies on discussion, claims Nucci, for discussion is the only means we have of allowing one person's ideas to come into direct contact with others. Nucci refers to the difference between the concepts of communicative discourse as compared to the concept of strategic action, developed by Habermas (1971). Thus, the goal of the discussion is the communicative discourse, which means arriving at the best and most compelling position regarding the issue at hand. Strategic action, by contrast, means that the most skilled debater becomes the winner of the discussion. The teacher's responsibility is to be a model for the communicative discourse by showing how to listen to arguments and how to bring the different pieces of a discussion into focus.

To foster the moral self means, according to Nucci (2001), to make a connection between the children's moral affect, their moral understandings and the construction of their personal identity. The foundation for moral identity is formed in early childhood, writes Nucci, but the connection between moral identity and behavior does not have much force until middle childhood and adolescence. Essential in education is to help children construct an orientation of goodwill toward others by creating a warm and positive moral atmosphere based on mutual respect.

Three aspects of the process link the children's conduct to their sense of self. The first is the generation of a worldview, and the placement of self in relation to that view. The second is the construction of self-discipline that enables the child to engage in actions in harmony with his or her moral identity. The third aspect is the assignment of meaning to the components of children's social and personal identities and whether they are "good" or "bad" children (Nucci, 2001).

Moral Awareness. As in the previous discussion based on the theory proposed by Piaget, it is the child's development of moral awareness that is the focus for the type of approach used by teachers; however, an atmosphere of mutual respect and emotional warmth should be at the basis of the teachers' approach. Moral reasoning and judgment occur in conjunction with feelings and emotions, asserts Nucci (2001).

The dilemma for the teacher is to be aware of and minimize the risk of reducing the child 's very existence and learning to one aspect, that is, explicit moral judgments, which gives an advantage to those children that have already discovered how to verbally express meanings. Crucial in this respect is to pay attention to affective climate in the classroom, but also to use various ways to help children develop their ability to reflect on and make different social judgments.

Furthermore, the variety of the social world ought to be on the agenda in education along with the insight that children make different judgments in different contexts in a vast social world. A second dilemma that might occur is how to separate the various social dimensions and to fruitfully make use of them while expanding the child's moral development. Thus, discussions that include variations, conflicts, contradictions, and uncertainties, in which children learn to reflect on moral, conventional, and personal issues, can benefit this process. It is also important for the teacher to consider that different social issues might be embedded in different contexts and to use this knowledge when encouraging a child's moral learning. If moral issues are expressed more frequently in less organized activities while conventional and personal issues seem to come about in circle-time and lunch, what might the educational implications be?

Personal Domain and Morality. Another conclusion is that the boundaries of the personal domain are of importance for morality. This suggests that children should be allowed the freedom to set limits for their personal domain but also to learn about the boundaries and limits of others. This can be associated with a moral issue, such as the value of integrity. This assumption was supported in an investigation on morality among toddlers in a day care setting by Johansson (1999). The results showed that the children in their daily interaction investigated, challenged, and put each other's integrity to the test. Johansson suggests that children in such situations tested the borders for what one could to do to another person. This learning deals with the value of respect for the other's integrity, but it is also about power and powerlessness in defining personal boundaries.

In addition, Nucci (1996, 2001) emphasizes the idea that the personal is necessary for the construction of concepts of rights. Even though the personal and moral belong to different domains, they are interrelated. In the aforementioned Johansson study, the toddlers were deeply concerned with rights. When someone threatened a child's inquiry with things or hindered their shared worlds, this also threatened their very existence, including personal control, freedom, and personal boundaries. Children in the study expressed anger, sadness, and a feeling of being wronged when this happened. This devotion to rights seemed to be a question of the children's lived experiences of what is important in their life-worlds, rather than their being conscious of rights as a concept.

In line with the empirical findings that children and parents refer to the personal domain as a subject's own choice, teachers should give allowance for children to make choices in early education. But, what and whom will set the limitations for children's own choices? Research has shown that opportunities for children to negotiate and make choices in preschool can be rare. Killen and Smetana (1999), for instance, point to the fact that the teachers offered choices to children and at the same time rarely negotiated with the children. Besides, the teachers were equally likely to support as to negate children's choice assertions. Indeed negotiations were rare in the classroom. Johansson and Johansson (2003) found that teachers in early education underscore the child's responsibility and ability to make morally good and rational choices. The children were often encouraged to make choices of their own. But behind these "free" choices often lay the teacher's descriptions of possible alternatives, which in fact restricted the actual alternatives available for the children.

From the perspective of the child, personal issues might likely to be of moral concern, but from the perspective of the adult the experience could be the other way around (also Sweder et al., 1987). Furthermore, conventional acts seem more to be a question for adults rather than a concern of children and such transgressions might also be embedded with moral dimensions. Transgression of a rule, for instance, a general rule in school that prescribes children to organize themselves in a queue is as likely to be referred to (by children and adults) as a moral dimension than to a conventional rule. On one hand the queue-system is about distributive justice, whereas, on the other hand, the queue-system concerns conventional rules for order in school (Johansson & Johansson, 2003; see also Nucci, 2001).

This indicates that the three social dimensions are not easily separated from one another in daily life. As already stated, the teacher has to balance social organizational concerns with classroom order, foster a sense of community and teach young children moral values and conventional rules for the school setting as well as encouraging autonomy and personal decision making. It is easy to seethe complexity in this task.

Conclusions

The cognitive tradition researching young children's morality has developed from the pioneer work of Piaget, in the beginning of the last century, to the manifold studies within the domain theory, which began in the seventies and has continued up to now. Morality is regarded as universal. From the perspective of Piaget morality is about justice and from the domain theory morality is about justice, rights, and welfare. Thus, the concept on morality has been broadened. The domain theory suggests justice, rights, and welfare to be universal moral categories. Their meanings however, do not necessarily differ between cultures, and different contextual circumstances may influence various interpretations. Consequently it is the boundaries of morality the researchers of the domain theory define, rather than outlining a universal moral theory.

As we can learn research interest govern the focus of research and the questions asked for (see also Mauritzson & Säljö, 2001). Research has traditionally focused on moral judgments, but studies have now expanded to include how children judge and justify transgressions within different social areas such as the moral, the conventional, and the personal domains and how these domains are interrelated. The knowledge of the origins of morality has increased from mainly emphasizing changes in development to focus on the complexity of the child's various relations and issues that influence the child's moral judgments. Despite the focus on diversity, research within domain theory has shown similarities in moral reasoning and judgments across cultures.

From the research of Piaget, we have learned that preschool children's moral life is dependent on authorities, but from recent research there is empirical evidence that children both evaluate and question the legitimacy of social rules and authority (cf. Crane & Tisak, 1995). The preschool child is far more skilled on moral issues than Piaget proposed in his theory. We also know that young children generate their initial moral understanding from their experiences in social interaction. However, the connection between moral judgments and moral conduct are questions that remain to be asked and investigated. In this respect, much more knowledge is needed.

The educational approach reliant upon the cognitive tradition has not been systematically evaluated, and studies on teacher's approaches in early childhood education with reference to the different domains needs to be investigated further. The domain theory offers teachers a tool to describe and analyze moral questions in school. Knowing that different social dimensions activate different domains within a child's thinking can be of significant benefit in moral education. This strategy is an inductive method, and by inductive learning the teacher focuses on the consequences of the act, the other's distress together with clarifying how the child's action caused it. Moreover, the teacher ought to make clear the reasons behind moral norms (Hoffman, 2000; Thornberg, 2003). In principal, the domain theory is useful when seeing if and how children separate and judge social domains. However, the primary interest in research does not take into account children's moral actions in everyday settings, or what morality in a broad sense is from a child's perspective.

THE EMOTIONAL TRADITION

Philosophical perspectives within the emotional tradition are disparate, but all agree on the idea that emotions are a determining factor for moral development. A shift in this tradition from focusing inner states such as guilt and anxiety to focus on positive emotions such as altruism, sympathy, and empathy has taken place during the 1970s (Turiel, 1998). In this section, we shall concentrate on the concept of empathy and the research on prosocial actions, or altruistic behavior (Eisenberg & Fabes, 1998; Hoffman, 2000). This research is primarily concerned with motives and inner dispositions for morality.

Empathy

Despite various definitions of empathy the core of empathy can be characterized as an emotional response stemming from— and in congruence with—another's emotional state or situation. Plutchnik (1987), for example, describes empathy as a developmental process in which emotions, either positive or negative, are shared. Fesenbach conceives of empathy as the ability to discriminate and label affective states in others and to assume the others perspective or role while Karniol defines empathy as a way to understand the other's situation and emotions (referred in Eiseenberg & Strayer, 1987). Gilligan and Wiggins (1988) underscore that empathy concerns identifying with the other's emotions, to feel the same as the other. Some researchers stress that a condition for emphatic feelings is the ability to discriminate between one self and others, whereas other researchers do not stress this ability at all (Eisenberg & Strayer, 1987).

Eisenberg and Strayer (1987; Eisenberg & Fabes, 1998), analyze the main outlines of empathy. They suggest that empathy involves sharing the perceived emotion of another—feeling with another. Eisenberg and Strayer underscore that the relation between empathy and moral behavior is neither direct nor inevitable, although many psychologists assume that empathy mediates prosocial behavior. Individuals can, writes Eisenberg and Strayer, emphasize with a variety of emotions but should not always be expected to act in a prosocial manner.

Martin Hoffman (1984, 1987, 2000) has been influential in this field of research. In his theory on the child's empathic development, he defines empathy as an affective response more appropriate to another's situation than one's own. Hoffman regards empathy as a biological disposition of humankind and as a consequence of natural selection. He rejects theories that explain human action in terms of cultural dimensions. In addition, Hoffman pays little or no attention to the impact of interaction or from various contextual issues in his theory of emphatic development. In contrast, the focus is directed toward emotions and cognition within the individual and dimensions of the other's behavior (especially distress from a victim) that might bring forth empathic reactions (2000).

Empathic development. Empathic development, empathic modes, and cognition are integrated, writes Hoffman, and cognition plays a specific role in the development of empathy. The gradual cognitive sense of the other as an individual distinct from oneself is a necessity for empathy. The development of empathy proceeds, according to Hoffman, in four stages in part determined by cognitive capabilities. The simplest form is called *global empathy*, and is characterized by the global unpleasant feelings empathetically aroused in infants witnessing someone in distress. This occurs during the first year when infants entailing a fuse between themselves and others, and acts as though what is happening to the other is also happening to themselves (Hoffman, 2000).

Gradually, a sense of the other as an entity distinct from the self emerges and the child may now be aware of the other's distress, but the other's internal state remains unknown. The child does not distinguish between the other's and one's own internal states. He or she responds to another's distress as if it were his or her own experience. We may now with Hoffman's words talk about *egocentric empathy*. Eventually, the child's concern for his or her own unpleasant feeling shifts toward the other's emotional state. The child is now aware that other people's feelings may differ from one's own and, consequently, the child becomes more responsive to others' emotional cues. This phase is described by Hoffman as *empathy for another's feelings* and begins around ages 2 to 3 years because of the onset of role-taking. When language is acquired the child becomes able to empathize with a range of emotions of more and more refined complexity, for instance, empathizing with another person's self-esteem. The most advanced level is *empathy for another's life condition*. This form of empathy emerges late in childhood when the child has reached a sense of others as continuous persons with their own histories and identities that go beyond the actual situation. At this stage, the child can emphathize with more general life circumstances of others and of groups of people such as poor, oppressed, or handicapped (Hoffman, 1987, 2000).

Empathy and morality. The status of empathy is a moral motive, says Hoffman. In contrast to Eisenberg and Strayer (1987), he states that empathy contributes to morality. This means that empathic affect makes the individual more receptive and motivated to act prosocially and in accordance with moral principals

such as care and justice. The link between empathic distress and caring is direct and obvious, writes Hoffman (2000). He also argues for a link between empathy and justice even if he finds this connection less obvious. Empathy and care proceed in the same direction, they are both directed to others' well-being, says Hoffman. However, the empathic distress that serves as a motive for justice might be about allocating societal resources. When reflecting on motives for distribution of resources one might focus on the implications for oneself or for others, but most likely the two will be combined. Because the empathic emotion concerns the welfare of others, the distress that might occur is a concern for those whose basic needs have been violated (Hoffman, 1987, 2000).

Emotions and Cognition. In Hoffman's terms, a specific set of emotions are connected with morality. He suggests a link between cognition and affects, but his position is that empathic emotions constitute a foundation for, and an expression of morality. Cognition in terms of the child's gradual awareness of the other as a separate being supports the development of empathy.

The role of emotion in moral development has been interpreted differently in research (cf. Arsenio & Lover, 1995; Damon, 1990; Johansson, 2003b; Nucci, 2001; Turiel, 1998). When referring to Piaget (1960), relations and affects are assumed to provide the raw material of moral behavior, whereas it is the cognitive structure that creates opportunities for the individual to reach moral awareness. Affects and cognition are interrelated, but the moral subject is ultimately dependent on cognitive development. With respect to the domain theory, Nucci (2001) rejects a dichotomy between cognition and affects. Contrary he suggests these dimensions accompany one another in the moral process. The child judges the action right or wrong not simply on the basis of what feels right, but on the basis of what the child rationally concludes must be the moral evaluation of the act. Affect is part of adaptive intelligence, but not a substitute for cognitive structure, suggests Nucci (2001). Moreover, Arsenio and Lover (1995) argue that moral principles may originate from the children's emotional experiences, but the child also must then cognitively abstract certain extensions of these principles. Morality is, according to Arsenio and Lover, not the result of unreasoned and unexamined emotions, nor is it a set of rational and impersonal principles. The emergence of morality depends on a variety of abilities, including memories of previous socio-moral encounters and the conclusions drawn from these encounters and their affective experiences, including various social relationships with peers and adults (Arsenio & Lover, 1995).

From these positions we can learn that emotions may be one of several sources of morality. We also can learn that it is inaccurate to make a disjunction between emotions and cognition. Contrary to Hoffman's thesis that a specific sort of emotion leads to morality, the influence of affects on morality is understood in a broad sense as the child's various experiences that may be of relevance for their moral discovery. The researchers do not promote the idea that empathy is the most important emotion, which can be related to morality. A complementary suggestion to this discussion is that emotions—understood in a broad sense—rather than being viewed as moral foundations, might preferably be interpreted as expressions based on *experiences* of a moral value (Johansson, 2003b). From this viewpoint, emotions may therefore manifest moral experiences. Emotions might emerge from some sort of understanding of a situation; a course of events connected with moral values. This does not mean that spontaneous emotions do not exist. But the origin of an emotion might stem from a person's experience, for instance, a violation against—or a defense for—a moral value.

Guilt and moral internalization. What implications from the theory of empathy might be essential when it comes to a child's moral learning?

The foundation for improving children's morality is the internalization of an internal sense of wrongdoing and guilt, writes Hoffman (2000). Empathy-based guilt is an important prosocial motive. In this respect , "discipline encounters" between a child and its parents are of special interest, suggests Hoffman. Discipline encounters begin to occur on a regular basis early in the second year and continue during childhood even though these encounters may take a different shape relevant to the situation and the age of the child. Discipline encounters during early childhood (between 2 and 10 years of age) often regard safety, for instance harming oneself or others. These encounters are characterized by discrepancies between the child's and the parent's perspectives on how to behave concurrent with the parent's attempt to change the child's behavior. The discipline encounters tend to shape an inner conflict between the child's own interests and those of the other. The child can gradually learn to internalize morals and to resolve conflicts. In this process, induction is central.

Induction, in Hoffman's terms, is when parents take the victim's perspectives and show how the child's behavior harms the victim. The parent supports guilt and moral internalization processes by making inferences between the child's egoistic motives, the child's behavior and the harmful consequences for the other, writes Hoffman. Over the years, the child builds up a discipline-encounter schema in which the gradual integration of inductive messages and schemas including norms of concern for others are constructed. Later, argues Hoffman, this norm is activated, for instance by empathic distress, and becomes the motive for prosocial behavior. A moral motive may be internalized when a child feels obligated to abide by its principles without regard to external reward or punishment (Hoffman, 2000).

Implications for research and education. Referring to the tradition of empathy, what questions have been asked and what morality may these questions help to uncover in research and education?

Hoffman defines moral actions in motivational terms. He poses the question: why act morally and answers in terms of feelings that need to be acted on (Turiel, 1998). Hoffman suggests empathy to be a biological ability following a specific developmental line; as this emotional development is thought to be universal. Whereas Piaget and Kohlberg developed stages to describe moral thinking, Hoffman describes changes in the forms that empathy takes, and from which he makes conclusions on

morality. Empathy in Hoffman's position drives not only moral action but also moral judgments and principles (Turiel, 1998).

But the reliability of the stages proposed by Hoffman has been questioned. Turiel (1998), for instance, argues that the most of the sequences are not based on empirical evidence. The idea, according to Turiel, that an infant's mimicry is an evidence of emphatic feelings is not entirely clear and the other stages rely on illustrations with the type of anecdotal examples rather than systematic empirical findings. Eisenberg and Fabes (1998) point to the fact that reactive crying is not found in all infants, nor in all situations.

As mentioned earlier in this discussion, some critics claim that universal stages are both too general and too limited in explaining morality (Sommer, 1997). Eisenberg and Fabes (1998) point to methodological biases when investigating the relation between empathy and prosocial behavior. According to these researchers, the degree of association between measures of empathy-related responding and prosocial behavior seems to vary as a function of the measure of empathy. Recent research suggests that personal distress, an important component in Hoffman's theory, is negatively related to prosocial behavior, whereas sympathy and sometimes empathy (depending on their operationalization) are positively related to prosocial behavior. Eisenberg and Fabes (1998) underscore the importance of identifying situational factors that may influence when and whether empathy is related to prosocial behavior.

Empathy with reference to the very young child is, in line with Hoffman, a reflexive response on other's actions. Therefore, teaching and research do not attach any great importance to questions of culture or context and the influence these may have on children's empathy or morality. Instead of viewing children's interaction and context as a whole, we ought to regard what is happening between young children as *signals* from one (the observer) to another (the victim), as well as, *reactions* that the victim might arouse in the observer. From this more or less behaviorist viewpoint, the child's perspective and discoveries, his or her own ability to reflect, experience and to act intentionally, seem to be of lesser importance for the emergence of morality in the early years.

The Access to a Child's Inner Life. When studying children's empathic ability, the focus of interest is directed toward the child's inner state (also Turiel, 1998). Empathy thus becomes a research and an educational tool, and a way in which we believe children interpret others' feelings. Emotions are given primacy in teaching and research; and it has become essential to understand the individual child's emotions. As a teacher or a researcher, we have to look for the child's expressions of "feeling the same as the other." Embedded in this idea is the belief that a child is capable of experiencing and expressing empathy and that we can fully understand this emotion. Hoffman (2000) regards certain acts to be based on empathy. For instance, a toddler who observes a friend in distress, wrinkles her forehead, gives the friend his dummy, and then goes to her own mother in search of comfort expresses egocentric empathy in Hoffman's terms. But is this the only possible interpretation? It seems a complex task for a researcher and a teacher to define a supportive act as a result of an empathic emotion, feeling the same as the victim, or as a mark of role taking (Damon, 1983; Eisenberg & Fabes, 1998; Johansson, 2003b). Turiel (1998) argues that the distinction between defining an act in terms of motives, or moral judgments is not unambiguous, as the moral judgments one makes may likewise motivate one to act.

The dilemma for the teacher and the researcher is how to get access to a person's inner life and to correctly discern between different emotions. The question is, if it is at all possible (or even necessary), either for the active pedagogue, or the researcher to assert that the observer is experiencing a similar emotional feeling as the one who is affected.

Teachers and Empathy. In early childhood education, the concept of empathy is often used. But is empathy a useful concept in the work with children's morality?

As stated, the concept of empathy and its relation to morality has been questioned (cf. Blum, 1994; Damon, 1983; Gilligan & Wiggins; 1988; Johansson, 2002, 2003b). Damon (1983) proposes that an understanding of others' feelings may likely be used to violate others' feelings. A child's own experiences of violation do not necessarily lead to an understanding of others emotional feelings. Eisenberg and Fabes (1998), show that young children are capable of empathic emotions in response to others distress, but they may also ignore, avoid and at times become aggressive toward the victim. Dunn, Brown and Maguire (1995; see also Dunn, 1987) found that children's reactions to social transgressions are not uniform, and their morality may take various directions according to different relations. With an increasing awareness of standards, toddlers also display teasing of their mothers and siblings, and show a greater interest in what is socially prohibited. The children begin to understand how to manipulate situations and upset others and they may use their knowledge of others feelings to gain their own interest.

According to Brown and Dunn (1996), toddlers' understanding of emotions have been shown to be related to a number of factors, including family discourse about feelings, the quality of family relationships, emotional expressiveness, as well as language ability and social class. Dunn, Brown, Slomkowski, Tesla, and Youngblade (1991) suggest that the understanding of emotions appears earlier in childhood than the ability to understand other minds. Moreover, Youngblade and Dunn (1995; see also Dunn & Hughes, 2001) suggest that early social pretend play is related to the child's developing understanding of others feelings and beliefs. Participation in pretend play, in particular with an older sibling, appears to be connected with later understanding of the situational determinants of others feelings. The intense nature of the sibling relationship combined with the inherent emotionality in pretend play may provide a fertile ground for social understanding (Youngblade & Dunn, 1995). Moreover, in a longitudinal study, Brown and Dunn (1996) found that discussions within the family about reasons behind behavior seemed to influence differences in how well children understood others' experience of conflicting emotions.

Arsenio and Lover (1995; see also Arsenio & Kramer, 1992) investigated what kind of emotions children expect various sociomoral acts to promote and how these expectancies influence children's sociomoral behavior. These researchers support the idea that children remember the emotions that are linked with particular social events and they use these links to anticipate future emotional outcomes and to plan their behavior accordingly. In this process the affective character of the child's relationship is essential. Of special importance is the child's experience of peer-relations. Arsenio and Lover (1995) showed, from their own investigations as well as from other studies, that young children (4, 6, and 8 years old) expected victimizers to feel good, or happy and victims to feel bad, sad, or mad. In several other studies, similar results revealed that the majority of children view the victimizers to feel more positive than victims. According to the children, victimizers gain the desirable outcomes and feel happy, but to be victimized is to loose what is yours and to feel unhappy. Yet, the researchers found a tendency to view victimizers as feeling more mixed or conflicting emotions among the 8-year-old children. This suggests that children between 6 and 8 years old come to see a basic moral conflict, and the positive emotions of victimizers will be modified by the negative emotions of the victims. This transition involving two separate sets of emotional reactions may, according to Arsenio and Lover (1995), be a critical transition in children's moral development.

Johansson (2002) studied how preschool teachers attend to the moral values expressed by the children and the morals that teachers wanted the children to learn. The results showed that some teachers relate morality to children's emotional ability, to their feelings of empathy, guilt and shame. In some situations, teachers tried to make the children refer to their own experiences of hurt feelings, something that is supposed to trigger empathic emotions. However, referring to a similar situation, the children at times seemed to focus mainly on their own experience, rather than empathizing with their friend's feeling of pain.

These studies point to the complexity of how emotions may support, or hinder a child's moral discoveries. The children's emotional state according to transgressions may also be mixed, or vary across situations. We can learn that children's knowledge of the victim's hurt feelings may not always lead to empathy in Hoffman's terms. Research does not provide support for teachers to focus teaching on one specific emotion, such as empathy. Contrarily, such an approach may be both limited and dubious. Instead, the teacher ought to address children's emotions and emotional experiences in a broad sense when endorsing moral education. To analyze and support a moral atmosphere in preschools may be of importance in this respect (DeVries & Zan, 1994; Nucci, 2001), but also to help children discover the moral values that could be hidden behind their friends' emotional expressions in everyday life (Johansson, 1999).

Empathic Guilt—A Bridge to Morality? Hoffman (2000) means that discipline encounters can actualize inner conflicts together with empathic guilt and promote the internalization of morality. There has however, been relatively little research on the role of guilt in prosocial behavior, writes Eisenberg and Mussen (1997), and the issue is difficult to investigate because guilt, like empathy, is an internal response.

The problem is, how we can be sure if the child's emotional experiences are correctly interpreted as empathic guilt. How can we be certain that the child's inner conflicts concern the welfare of others rather than feeling humiliated and misunderstood? Emilia, Garottini, and Venturini (2000), examined 120 Italian children's understanding of sadness, guilt and shame in two separate studies. The children, between 5 and 10 years of age, were interviewed and encouraged to describe events and thoughts that characterized the various emotions. They were asked if and how the presence of a parent might influence the emotion they experienced and how they would cope with the situation. The result showed that all the children knew about the emotions but differed in their depth of understanding according to age. For instance, all the children described guilt as an emotion evoked by transgressing rules including aggression toward peers and disobedience toward adults. Guilt was felt as an awareness of having behaved badly, or (less often) as anticipation of negative consequences that aroused a desire to make amends. This desire was related to age and to the presence of parents, especially among the younger children. For the 5 and 6 year olds the presence of a parent was a necessary condition for guilt. Moreover, the children described shame as a consequence of failure and embarrassing situations. The emotion of shame also was related to a feeling of incompetence and deficiency, which according to the children aroused inaction, crying, and a desire to escape, hide, or search for comfort. The youngest children mentioned negative social events (failure during a performance, being a victim of an attack, and being refused, or scolded), whereas the older children mentioned embarrassing situations (interacting with an unfamiliar person, or someone they were interested in) that might evoke shame (Emilia, Garottini, & Venturini, 2000).

The connection from these emotional states to morality is not clear. The feeling of guilt as a feeling of having behaved badly was connected with the presence of grown-ups and often was followed by a desire to make amends. But how can we determine whether this feeling of behaving badly makes guilt a link to morality instead of a desire to appease grown ups, avoid punishment and, on the whole, escape from an uncomfortable situation? Johansson and Johansson (2003) showed that in order to help children share others feelings the teachers' strategies on the contrary might evoke a sense of humiliation and powerlessness instead of empathy. The teacher's own emotional distress seems to take over and the child's feelings become neglected and oppressed. The paradox is that in his or her ambition to teach a child to empathize with another's distress, to take another person's role and respect other's feelings, the teacher overlooks the emotions and motives that a child might embrace (Johansson & Johansson, 2003).

Hence, to work with discipline encounters in teaching is a complex task that needs to be handled with competence and sensitiveness. If the teacher or parent is not sensitive to the child's perspective and emotional experiences, these situations might work in opposition to the desired moral outcome. The inductive method is reported to be the most successful method of discipline compared to love withdrawal, or assertion of power, according to Turiel (1998); however, Eisenberg and Fabes (1998) emphasize that induction strategies may vary and be associated with different moral orientations. Moreover, the child also may interpret messages conveyed by the adult in various ways.

Hoffman also stresses that being able to take someone else's role is a prerequisite for empathy and morality, but according to Damon (1983, 1990), taking another's role is sometimes an easy and sometimes a manifold and problematic task. There are, argues Damon, many types of perspective taking and the specific nature of the task seem to have a strong influence on how well the child can take another's role. Eisenberg and Fabes (1998) point to the fact that it is generally difficult to identify the processes underlying performance on perspective taking tasks. Therefore additional research methods need to be developed. Nevertheless, research indicates that children with higher perspective-taking skills are somewhat more prosocial, but in many contexts prosocial behavior may be motivated by a number of factors aside from knowledge on another's internal state, according to Eisenberg and Fabes (1998).

Even though emotions such as empathy are part of human reactions, the relation between empathy and morality is not evident and the possibilities to study and work with these issues in education are an ambiguous task. This highlights the need for further investigations on young children's various emotions and their connection to morality. Naturalistic studies may be helpful in this respect. Of special interest is the systematic study of discipline encounters in early childhood education, for instance when it comes to approaches regarding guilt and shame. It may be that guilt and shame often become interrelated in such situations, which points to the need of knowledge on the impact of these emotions in everyday interaction and on their relevance in moral education. Johansson (2002), for instance, concludes that teachers primarily associated feelings of guilt in children to actions of prevention and making children comprehend when they are acting in a morally reprehensible way. In these contexts a behaviorist and moralistic way of acting seemed to be a prominent part of the teachers' strategies. Arsenio and Lover (1995) maintain the importance of investigating the gap between children's conceptions of the positive consequences of victimization for the perpetrator and evidence suggesting that even very young children are sensitive to the pain and loss felt by the victims. Moreover, the correspondence between children's conceptions of moral emotions and their experienced emotions in these contexts need to be investigated further.

Prosocial Behavior

Prosocial behavior is defined as voluntary behavior intended to benefit another person (Eisenberg & Fabes, 1998; Fabes et al., 1999). Much of the research on prosocial behavior emphasizes emotions; particularly empathy and sympathy related emotions that are important for the development of prosocial actions and are therefore associated with the emotional tradition. Most of the studies are concerned with the question of when and at what age the child is able to act prosocially. This research is extensive and this section can only give a brief presentation of the most important work; particularly the investigations by Eisenberg and her colleagues (cf. Eisenberg, 1992, 1995; Eisenberg & Fabes, 1992, 1998; Eisenberg & Mussen, 1997; Eisenberg, Pidada, & Liew, 2001).

Philosophical perspectives. There has been an extensive amount of research on prosocial behavior since the 1970s, but there are relatively few theories pertaining to this tradition compared to other areas (see Eisenberg & Fabes, 1998, for an overview). Philosophical concerns are not salient in this kind of work, writes Eisenberg and Fabes (1998), much because the difficulty to discriminate motives on behavior. The philosophical perspectives on prosocial behavior that can be found often have, according to Eisenberg and Fabes (1998), their roots in different religious traditions, with reference to the need for love, goodness, compassion, and altruism amongst human beings. However, there is a line of demarcation between ideas that claim human nature as basically good and ideas that state that prosocial and moral behavior involves a will and stem from universal principals. Philosophers have debated whether human action can be truly unselfish, or whether selfishness may induce helping; and also whether one should take into account the motives for an action, or the consequences of that action.

The research on prosocial behavior focuses on specific actions and implies an interest in one of two sides of morality, which may be interpreted as the good. However implicit, many investigations define the prosocial act as moral when it is based on an altruistic motive: namely, the ambition to be good toward others. But, prosocial behavior can be performed on various grounds including egoistic and practically oriented concerns. In order to understand morality it is necessary to focus on the broader domain of prosocial behaviors since differentiation between altruistic or egoistic motives is an ambiguous task (Eisenberg & Fabes, 1998).

Biological and contextual influences on prosocial behavior. Many researchers seem to take for granted the idea that human nature is basically good. Eisenberg and Fabes (1992, 1998), for instance, support the idea that humans are biologically equipped to experience empathy and to develop prosocial behaviors, as prosocial behavior is common among all people, even young children. However, these authors also recognize that to understand prosocial behavior requires consideration of mutually interdependent factors including biological influences, earlier environmental influences, as well as, influences from the child's current context.

Research on cultural influences on prosocial development has not been very frequent. Nevertheless, some data exists on processes that point to cultural differences in prosocial behavior, write Eisenberg and Fabes (1998). Because cultures differ in their assessment of different types of prosocial actions, cultural comparisons may be difficult to make. Subcultural variations can have a substantial impact on prosocial values and behavior as well. In spite of this, cultural differences appear to be related to the degree in which prosocial behavior is expressed in everyday life.

On the one hand, some cultures emphasize helpfulness and social responsibilities more than individual rights. This difference in values is reflected in thinking about prosocial behavior. One the other hand, there is an argument for the idea that a personal morality of responsiveness and caring is linked to a strong cultural emphasis on individual rights (Miller & Bersoff, 1992).

Prosocial behavior and empathy. Many of the actual studies on prosocial behavior focus on empathy. However, Eisenberg and Fabes (1998) point at the complexity of this concept. Although there may be evidence for reactive crying among infants, it is unclear whether such crying reflects primitive empathy. Moreover, Zahn-Waxler, Radke-Yarrow, Wagner, and Chapman (1992) found that 1-year-old children tend to respond to others' distress; sometimes with distressed cries and sometimes with a positive affect. There is also evidence, the authors suggest, that prosocial actions not motivated by empathy occur more frequently at the age of 12 months. Prosocial interventions like sharing and helping becomes more evident during the second year. Even though young children do respond with empathy toward others they can also respond to others distress with neglect, avoidance, or aggression.

Toddler's responsiveness to peers is rare, according to Farver and Branstetter (1994). However, Dunn (1988) concludes that 2-year-old children support their mothers in caring for their younger siblings. How the individual child responds to other's distress seems to be influenced by personality, the situation, as well as, experiential factors. For instance, Young, Fox, and Zahn-Waxler, (1999; see also Zahn-Waxler & Hastings, 1999) investigated the role of toddler temperament in the prediction of empathy in 2-year-old children. Infants' temperament was observed for reactivity and affect at 4 months old, and also for inhibition at the age of 2 years. Empathy was measured in toddler's responses to simulations of distress performed by their mothers and simulations performed by adults unfamiliar to the child. Infants manifesting little affect and few reactions showed less empathy toward unfamiliar adults two years later. The researchers concluded that behavioral inhibition of 2-year-old children could be associated with less empathy particularly when the victim was unfamiliar to the child (Young, Fox, & Zahn-Waxler, 1999).

The development of prosocial behavior. Some researchers held the idea that children's helping behavior develops through stages, but, as this review has shown, the relevance of this claim has been questioned on various grounds. Fabes and Eisenberg (unpublished data, referred to in Eisenberg & Fabes, 1998) conducted a meta-analysis of 179 studies with regard to age differences in children's prosocial behavior. Their analyses showed that the magnitude of differences was related not only to the specific age comparison made but also to the way in which prosocial behavior was studied and the type of age-related comparison reported. However, the data supported the conclusion that as the children get older prosocial behavior is generally more likely to occur. Throughout childhood, children develop an increasingly refined understanding of others' emotional states and become more skilled when decoding other people's emotional cues. Such understanding is according to Lourenco (1993), related with prosocial responding. For instance, the ability to evaluate situational factors and behavioral options becomes more complex and accurate by age. Younger children seem to evaluate costs and benefits for themselves more than do older children when deciding whether or not to support others (Lourenco, 1993).

The idea that children's helping behavior develops through stages, as maintained by some researchers, is ambiguous and not always empirically based, notes Eisenberg and Fabes (1998). Initially, helping acts are performed against the chance of getting material rewards; then helping becomes a result of social approval and reciprocity; finally, helping behavior can be expressed as true altruism without self-centered concerns. However, empirical studies have failed to show whether or not these stages actually occur in the proposed order, although an age-related sequence of children's prosocial *reasoning* have been identified, writes the authors. It is however uncertain whether or not sociocognitive processes contribute to the occurrence of prosocial actions (Eisenberg & Fabes, 1998).

Eisenberg, Miller, Shell, McNally, and Shea (1991) found that preschoolers and early elementary schoolchildren primarily use hedonistic justifications in their prosocial reasoning. However, such reasoning decreases later in elementary school and increases slightly in adolescence. Reasoning oriented toward personal needs appears to increase until mid-childhood and then levels off in later childhood. Moreover, children's prosocial reasoning in elementary school reflect a concern for interpersonal relationships and a desire to behave in "good" ways. This way of thinking seems to decline in high school, according to these researchers. In late elementary school children begin to reflect on abstract principles, compassion, perspective taking, consequences of one's behavior on others, and whether or not internalized principles and values are attained.

To some extent, the studies tend to give support for the idea that children's prosocial behavior increases with age. To another extent, findings suggest that age differences related to prosocial behavior are complex and unclear.

Gender and prosocial behavior. The empirical findings lay bare that gender is a complicated issue with no simple connection to prosocial actions. Differences between boys and girls in prosocial behavior vary with the type of prosociocal behavior investigated, with methodological approaches and are, furthermore, related to expectations of gender (Fabes & Eisenberg, unpublished data, referred to in Eisenberg & Fabes, 1998). For instance, the items used for investigating prosocial behavior may sometimes be gender biased. Sex differences were greater (favoring girls) in indexes with attributes such as kindness and considerations than for sharing and helping but were smaller for instrumental helping. Moreover, differences favoring females tended to be greater when using self-reporting methods in data collection, than with observational procedures. This may, suggest Eisenberg and Fabes (1998), reflect people's conceptions on how girls and boys are expected to behave, rather than how they actually behave. Peers, parents, and teachers tend to perceive girls as more prosocial and the reputations for girls prosocial behavior may even be greater than the actual differences. However, it is unclear whether the *degree* of gender differences is because of actual differences or to differences in the way males and females view themselves and desire to be viewed by others.

Nonetheless, these methodological problems and the patterns of girls and boys prosocial behavior may of course differ owing to gender expectations (Gilligan, 1982). For instance,

Walker, Irving, and Berthelsen (2002) investigated gender influences on 179 (91 boys, 88 girls) preschool children's problem-solving strategies. The result indicated that girls' responses were more reflective of successful functioning with peers, than those of boys. Also, the girls' strategies were less likely to involve retaliation, or verbal, or physical aggression. The authors concluded that preschool boys and girls differ in the way they think about and respond to social situations; this fact highlights the impact of gender as a social category (Walker, Irving, & Berthelsen, 2002)

Eisenberg and Fabes (1998) assert that the linear developmental pattern associated with the idea that prosocial behavior increases with age and differs with gender may not hold for children of all ages or for all measures. Developmental changes in prosocial behavior appear sometimes to be influenced by the research methods used. Research should, therefore, strive to expose when and how age-related changes in sociocognitive, emotional, and regulatory capabilities jointly affect prosocial respondses.

Justice and Care—Gender-Biased Orientations?

The connection between gender differences and prosocial behavior is interesting but unclear. Research shows that preconceptions of boys and girls behavior have a great impact on how we conceptualize children's behavior rather than how they actually behave. This does not reduce the role of gender in children's behavior and attitudes. If we look at the moral theory developed by Gilligan and Wiggins (1988; see also Gilligan, 1982) we find two lines in moral development: justice and care. Both lines are, according to these researchers, based on different perspectives on relations.

The basis of morality is the awareness of emotional attachments with other human beings write Gilligan and Wiggins (1988). On the one hand, the child is aware of being unequal and dependent on adults. On the other hand, the child has developed emotional bonds to others. The child discovers different patterns in human interaction through the different ways that people relate to or turn away from each other. These experiences bring about orientations toward different moral concepts such as justice and care. These concepts are organized differently in boys' and girls' development and influence how boys and girls define and solve moral dilemmas respectively. Thence, the orientation of males and females reflect cultural differences and discourses (Gilligan & Wiggins, 1988).

These ideas have been questioned on methodological grounds. Turiel (1998), for instance, claims that the construction of a morality of care was initially not based on extensive research; and the propositions regarding the origins of moral concepts in early relationships such as attachment and inequalities have not been subjected to empirical study. Nonetheless, additional research indicates a tendency for care and justice according to gender, but the patterns are not clear, as these studies also show shifts because of context.

Johansson and Johansson (2003) studied morality among schoolchildren from first to third grades. They found caring behavior among boys as well as girls; however, the children's own descriptions of care sometimes differed. Preconceptions on "how it is" and "how it ought to be" influence not only how the children look on themselves but also their actions. It is easier for girls to be "girlish" and boys to be "boyish"—a fact that can have moral consequences. This means that the good, relational, and caring attributes are ascribed to the world of girls and the rational, logical, and just attributes are allocated to the world of boys (Johansson & Johansson, 2003; see also Walkerdine, 1990).

This knowledge is extremely important for researchers and teachers in early childhood education because it uncovers stereotyped gender roles and expectations on the part of the observer: females are expected to be more empathic and prosocial than are males. These preconceptions play an essential role in how we look on children's behavior. In conclusion, it is essential that researchers and teachers reflect on and analyze the grounds for interpreting children's behavior and intentions.

Prosocial behavior in early education. What is the impact on children's prosocial behavior from school and preschool? The typical classroom environment may not contribute to frequent prosocial interaction among children, propose Eisenberg and Fabes (1998). Findings indicate that spontaneous prosocial actions seem relatively rare in classrooms and preschools; though estimates vary considerably with the operationalization of prosocial behavior. The research has examined differences between home versus group care, but found such differences limited and unclear (Eisenberg & Fabes, 1998). The quality of the caregiving situation at home and in school most likely moderates the degree and type of influence preschools and schools might have on children's prosocial behavior. Emotionally supportive teacher-child relations are associated with children's modeling of prosocial actions and positive interactions among children in elementary school (see also Hastings & Zahn-Waxler, 2000). Children in warm and supportive relationships at home and in school imitate and incorporate prosocial behavior and attitudes. Hägglund and Öhrn (unpublished data) compared the two settings, school and preschool, with regard to the magnitude of prosocial actions that occurred among the children. The results revealed that prosocial actions on the whole were rare in both contexts but tended to be more frequent in preschool. The researchers also found that supportive actions diminished amongst the children when teachers intervened and came to the aid of a child in need. Hägglund and Öhrn concluded that teacher's supportive approaches in contrast to what one should expect, appeared to affect the children's prosocial actions in a negative way. The teachers' intervention gave the implicit message that no further help was needed from the children.

The CDP Program. With inspiration from the research on prosocial behavior, Solomon et al. (1996; Solomon, Watson, & Battistich, 2001; see also Colnerud & Tornberg, 2003) designed a curriculum program: the Child Development Project (CDP), aimed at fostering children's prosocial responding in preschool and school. Prosocial responding was defined as attitudes, motives, and behaviors that reflect a care for others' welfare, needs, and feelings and a willingness to balance one's own needs and desires with those of others.

The program rests on two assumptions: first, that children do possess inner motives to act both prosocially and egoistically;

and, second, that children tend to organize out-groups inaccessible for prosocial norms and values. The CDP program was designed to promote social understanding, highlight prosocial values, and provide helping activities among the children. Children's prosocial behavior was believed to come about through cooperative learning, a child-centered approach built on the child's own resources to learn, to develop self-control, set rules and to solve problems, as well as helping activities. An essential aspect to this work is warm and positive relationships between teachers and children.

The CDP program has been evaluated in two longitudinal studies (Battistich, Solomon, Kim, Watson, & Schaps, 1995; Battistich, Watson, Solomon, Schaps, & Solomon 1991; Solomon, Watson, Delucchi, Schaps, & Battistich, 1988). At first, three schools were involved in the CDP program. These schools including three control schools were tested according to the students' prosocial behavior. The children were followed from preschool through fourth grade. Observations in class and interviews were conducted every school year. Behavior, such as helping, supportiveness, and benevolence, was observed, as was spontaneous helping and caring behavior for others. Moreover, the magnitude of negative actions such as: accusing, commanding, aggressions, criticism, and refusals to help others were observed among the children in both the research and control groups.

The result implicated that students involved in the CDP program generally scored higher on ratings of prosocial behavior compared to control classes. The largest difference between the research group and the control group occurred in spontaneous prosocial actions. However, there tended to be no differences at all between the groups when it came to negative behavior. The impact of the program seemed to be the greatest when first introduced. The interviews showed that the children in the CDP program experienced a greater involvement in shaping of rules and cooperation with others than did children from the control group. The CDP children also seemed aware of the prosocial reasons behind the activities; for instance, the teachers wanted them to learn to cooperate, understand, and appreciate others and become prepared for adult life. Overall, the children in the CDP program seemed to have a community spirit, interpreted by the researchers as an orientation toward others, a tendency to resolve conflicts, express democratic values and social understanding (Solomon et al., 1988; Battistich et al., 1991).

The second longitudinal test on the effects of the CDP was performed during 3 years in 12 CDP schools and 12 control schools (Battistich et al., 1995). As in the previous study, the results showed that the CDP schools had an advantage on prosocial behavior compared to the control groups; however, this advantage was small in some aspects. Nonetheless, the CDP program seemed to have a considerable influence on the students' experience of school as a community and on their motives for acting prosocially. Moreover, the program showed a small but positve effect on the students' justification of democratic values, care for others, and progress in conflict resolutions. As a result, there tended to be a connection between community and the motivation for prosocial actions.

It may be relevant to point to some problems related to the CDP programs and the evaluations of its possible effects. The first studies were carried out in middle-class schools, but the later investigations included children from diverse backgrounds. Apart from this, the teachers seemed to have problems to implementing the program, a situation that may obstruct a correct description of the effects. Furthermore, it may be hard to distinguish to what extent different aspects such as: cooperation, child-centered teaching, highlighting values might impact prosocial behavior (see also Colnerud & Thornberg, 2003). Also it is not evident that prosocial actions are always likely to be good and convenient from a moral perspective. I will come back to this discussion later. However, on the whole, the results from the CDP programs indicate that creating a community atmosphere in the school can be positively connected to student's prosocial attitudes and behavior.

Implications for early childhood education and research. What can we learn from the exposition above that may be relevant to early childhood education? First, the study of prosocial behavior is considerable but diverse. Investigations vary in theoretical approach and methodology. There is a need for further investigation to clarify and develop questions regarding ontology, the relationship between moral theories, the theoretical base, and methodology. In terms of morality, the value of care for others well-being seems central both in research and the CDP program; however, there is little explicit discussion and no core definition on morality or moral theories.

In a sense, research about positively valued behavior is normative rather than explorative. The view on children's morality is restricted to what is reckoned to be good, thereby limiting the knowledge of children's morality. Prescriptive attitudes contribute to a normative tendency in the study of morality. Without minimizing the value of encouraging helping behavior and attitudes among children especially in education; the focus of many studies is nevertheless one-sided and partial to the "good" side of morality. As with the cognitive tradition, morality tends to be measured and defined from a top-down perspective. The researcher defines what is good and desirable attitudes and behaviors; and the ambition is to find out whether or not children possess these abilities.

Second, even though researchers underscore the influences of culture, context, and gender on prosocial behavior, the focus of attention for research is generally on the individual child's emotional and cognitive capacity. Of particular interest are individual abilities and personality traits such as: composure, compliance, and adaptation, which appear to be in the frontline of research. That is to say, morality tends to be comprehended as an innate ability. In contrast to the constructivist rationale (DeVries & Zan, 1994), the CDP program seems to focus more on emotional skills; however, many teaching strategies are similar. These strategies include: cooperation, active participation in the learning process, problem solving, and helpfulness. Additionally, a normative approach in the CDP program is prominent. The good acts are considered to be supportiveness, benevolence, helpfulness and inclusion; and the negative ones are aggression, refusal to help, and being exigent. This implies an unspoken "ideal" of a moral child as an emotionally well-balanced person with a good ability to adapt oneself. But is this ideal possible?

If an ideal of "good behavior" is so strongly related to conformity, then conflicting perspectives and different interpretations of morality might be impeded. Perhaps emotional indignation is an expression for being moral, for instance, defending someone's right or showing courage to stand up for values in conflict with others? It seems important not to overestimate emotional adjustment as "the road" toward morality. Moreover, this idea of emotional self-control seems sometimes close to the edge of moralizing rather than supporting children's moral experiences. What makes an aggressive act negative and not prosocial? It is a risk that teachers interpret aggression as negative and immoral, which, from a child's point of view, might be the opposite, a defense of the good. In such a way, the complexity of children's interactions and morality may be overlooked.

The point here is that how we (researchers and teachers) see and interpret children's behavior determines how we intervene and steer children's moral interaction. Yet, to interpret what is happening is a complex issue, but it is possible to imagine that the actual child's emotional response can be a result of an infringement of rights, which may not appear to us at the first sight. I will come back to this discussion later in the text.

Third, most of the reviewed research puts stress on quantifying and experimental methods rather than observational naturalistic studies. This is in accordance with the main focus of the emotional tradition in which the point of convergence is on abilities and measurements that allow for generalizations to establish stages for the development of prosocial behavior. From this review, we can learn that children by age become better prepared or equipped to act prosocially; their reasoning expands and their ability to consider and reflect upon others needs increase; however, the connection to prosocial behavior is unclear. This is important knowledge, which also can be drawn from the cognitive tradition that stresses cognitive ability as an important condition for morality. In contrast to the cognitive tradition that has tended to point to limitations in toddlers' ability to be moral, prosocial researchers underscore that even very young children posses skill to act prosocially. There is a risk when adopting stages, either for empathy, prosocial or moral development, that the teacher concentrates on the individual child instead of working on the complexity of the group, the school context, and their own teaching strategies. Apart from looking at children's morality as getting more and more advanced with increasing age it is essential to concentrate on various situations that may be critical to help children discover moral values and to practice prosocial actions.

Johansson (2002) show that teachers strive to make preschool children reflect on how to act in order to alter the other's condition in a positive way. The primary focus of adults is to teach children "good behavior." This is often expressed as a notion of restitution, where children are expected to recompensate, pat, and hug their friends (Johansson, 2002). But are these actions good in the perspective of the child who is performing, and the child who is receiving the compensations? From the studies on prosocial behavior in the CDP program it seems unclear whether compensatory behavior supports the understanding of moral values. However, to establish a community atmosphere in school appears to have a bearing on prosocial actions and attitudes.

Noddings (1993) developed a concept of care. Care is a concept related to moral theory and highlights values such as the well-being of others and can therefore contribute to the concept of prosocial behavior. Caring means being personally affected by another's experiences and needs (Noddings, 1993; see also Gilligan & Wiggins, 1988; Hundeide, 2001). Caring is also a mutual process that includes two partakers: one who is providing care and one who is being cared for. Furthermore, caring involves learning, because the competence of the one cared for is supposed to broaden, to reach beyond the actual situation. In terms of learning the responsibility rests on the teacher, being the one who carefully points out the way, whereupon the response from the child is essential for the continuing interaction (Noddings, 1993). From this follows that teachers need to ask themselves: What might improve a child's situation from his or her point of view?

Important issues for teachers and researchers may be to consider what prosocial actions mean from the perspective of a child. What is a realistic expectation for what a child ought to understand about other's emotional experiences? Is there a boundary for showing concern for others? What are the limitations for acting good? In what situations do children need help to react with emotional strength, to say no and object, rather than being composed and complaisant to others? This points to the necessity of reflection over the meanings of moral values from different perspectives.

Conclusions

On the one hand, the focus of interest in this tradition is on emotions, that is, empathy as a biological ability and a prerequisite for morality. On the other hand, the focus is on the "good" behavior, in other words, prosocial actions. Although empathy is emphasized as a moral motive, prosocial actions suggest several other motives for behavior such as altruistic, practical, and egoistic motives. Contrary to the cognitive approach, there is no shared definition of morality in research under the emotional tradition; however, discourse implies a value of care to be central in prosocial behavior, and, in Hoffman's position, justice is added to care. Both the study of empathy and prosocial development struggle with methodology, which indicates a need for further research and for more developed and appropriate methods. Research is often carried out through a top-down perspective; prosocial studies have a normative approach and the study of empathy interprets certain actions as empathic. Thus, both are concerned with the "good," either in behavior or in motives for behavior. Studies investigating culture, context, and gender are rare but can be found in the prosocial research. Most of the studies are carried out through experiments and interviews except for studies on the youngest children, which sometimes are conducted through more naturalistic methods (Eisenberg & Fabes, 1998).

Arsenio and colleagues hold manifold dimensions to be important for morality, this is a fruitful alternative to the tendency in moral research, to dichotomize between emotions and cognition. The relation between emotions and morality is complex; however, emotions in a broad sense may be one of several contributing factors for children's moral discoveries.

CULTURAL TRADITION

The *cultural* tradition is mostly divided and represents perspectives that emphasize both social learning and social constructivism as the basis for morality. Research within this tradition also can be connected with the sociohistorical approach (Vygotsky, 1978), situated learning (Bruner, 1996; Rogoff, 1990), symbolic interactionism (Mead, 1934; Blumer, 1969) critical theory (Habermas, 1971) and phenomenology (Merleau-Ponty, 1962).

The cultural tradition views morality, in a broad sense, as a relational and societal construction. Common to these various positions is the assumption that origins of morality are related to meanings, which are shared and communicated by members, situated in a specific society, in a specific practice, in a certain time, and with a specific history. Children's moral discoveries reflect not only their personal history but also the values, expectations, and forms of the embedded culture. Morality is not caused by some single factor in development, neither is it a product of a sudden shift in cognitive level, but of a continuous, overlapping process of developing functions, experiences and meanings (cf. Nelson, 2003).

Beyond these shared ideas we find two lines. On the one hand, research considers the influence of culture on the child's moral discoveries by combining the *interaction* and connection between individual, contextual, and cultural aspects of moral learning (cf. Corsaro, 1997; Damon, 1990; Dunn, 1988; Johansson, 1999). Although based on somewhat different approaches, these researchers all seem to view morality as a result of concrete social relationships; and that morality plays an essential part in children's lives from the time of their first relationships. Therefore, research is directed toward the child's experiences, meanings, and perspectives on morality in different contexts and social practices.

On the other hand, research concerns how morality is *conveyed to children by culture*. Researchers occasionally stress the overarching culture (often in terms of ethnicity) as the crucial component in determining a child's morality; that is why the child's interpretations are given a more subordinate position in moral learning (Shweder, Mahapatra, & Miller, 1987; Shweder, Much, Mahapatra, & Park, 1997).

The purpose for the following presentation is to introduce certain research within the cultural tradition that may be of interest for moral learning in early education without claiming to be complete. First, the text will focus on the more interactionistic cultural line that puts an emphasis on the child's experiences and perspectives on morality; and, second, the perspective of the overarching culture as the pathway to morality will be discussed.

Interactionistic Cultural Approaches

In this section, we will meet some researchers that strive to understand morality from the child's perspective and the life children live. The approaches differ; however, the researchers all suggest morality to be a result of concrete social relationships and that morality plays a central role in children's lives, and begins with a child's first relationships.

One proposition from research with interactionistic approaches is that a diversity of dimensions is important for children's moral discoveries. Morality is assumed to be a result of intersubjectivity, that is, interactive and communicative relations with others. Thus, the focus changes from looking at a child's cognitive or emotional ability, as in the other traditions, to consideration for complex interactive relations between the child and the world. This does not exclude aspects like emotion, cognition, senses, identity, gender, and such. Children do not simply receive moral knowledge from authorities or society; rather, they construct and reconstruct moral meanings appropriate to their own cultural and social life-worlds.

Children's morality—systems of meaning. Very young children appear to be aware of their social knowledge and they use this in their relationships with others. This is shown by the extensive research of Dunn (1987, 1988; Dunn, Brown, & Marguire, 1995; Dunn & Hughes, 2001), who investigated toddler's emergent social understanding within the family.

In her previous research, Dunn (1987, 1988) declared her interest in the child's lived world. She emphasizes that the young child's social understanding is spontaneous and immediate rather than reflected, and she calls attention to the importance of studying children in various contexts and social activities. To comment on children's expressions without relating them to a connected whole or just observing children in a specific situation without connecting this to the child's life does not provide any sufficient knowledge, says Dunn. The point is not to find out whether children's social knowledge develops earlier than we thought from previous research; rather, the point is to try to understand why and how children develop morality. But a key goal is also to regard the connections between moral understanding, identity, self-interest, and emotional experiences, as well as relations to others. In later research, Dunn and colleagues have mainly focused on the child's understanding of other's feelings rather than questions of morality in a broad sense (cf. Brown & Dunn, 1996; Dunn et al., 1991; Dunn & Hughes, 2001; Youngblade & Dunn, 1995).

Inspired by Herbet Mead (1934) and William James (1961), the research of William Damon focuses on interactive processes that are the basis for children's social life. In his previous work, Damon (1983, 1990) made an effort to understand morality from the young child's perspective. Morality is not a certain set of external standards, which are to be implemented in children's minds by adults, writes Damon (1990). Morality is part of children's lives from the time of their first relationships. Indeed, morality emanates from children's various social experiences with parents and peers in which they are part of from the beginning of life. Children have access to the cultural values and belief system as soon as they start to communicate and can make inferences about their social interaction. This begins in infancy, says Damon.

Damon calls attention to the complex and intertwining processes of moral growth. The access to cultural and moral discourses, according to Damon (1990), enhances the child's sensitivity to moral dilemmas that can arise in social experiences. Out of this rich mix of relationships and cultural values, communicated in interaction with others, grows a childhood

morality with its own vital characteristics. Damon indicates that there is a tendency to look on children's moral concern from the perspective of adults, which by inference can cause the full depth of a child's moral sensibilities to be disregarded. But children have their own life-worlds and they develop their own systems of meaning; to understand these systems we have to come close to and get access to the context of the child's world, concludes Damon (1990).

Morality is not mainly a question of interpreting and reflecting on abstract principals. Rather, morality concerns the ability to discern the complexity of social situations in which values and norms arise and are negotiated, writes Ivar Frønes (1995). Discernment for complex social situations requires a capacity to communicate and be open to various social perspectives. Frønes's reasoning builds mainly on the theory of Habermas (1971), especially the concept of communicative competence. Even though Frønes is critical of this approach to some degree, he uses parts of Habermas's theory to investigate children's socialization and moral learning. Socialization is described by Frønes as the child's gradual development of competence as a person and as an active member in a childhood culture of its own. In this externalization process the child is active, creates meaning, and communicates; as opposed to being a passive object internalizing moral values and culture. With regard to Frønes, communicative competence is central to the child's moral learning. Norms, for instance, must be justified and questioned through critical argumentation. Communicative competence emerges from the child's experiences of interaction with others, especially with peers (Frønes, 1995).

William Corsaro (1987, 1997) investigates the culture of children. His theoretical approach can be described as an interactional and interpretative perspective (cf. Circourel, 1974; Qvortrup, 1993). According to Corsaro (1997) it is necessary to study children's worlds on their own premises rather than taking children's increasing moral development for granted. We need a shift from the traditional conception that children incorporate norms and values, writes Corsaro. Even if we have regarded children as creators of meaning this idea is mainly based on the conception that culture and grownups provide children with guides for moral behavior, ready to use. When children incorporate norms these are supposed to be applicable in various contexts. But general principals and norms are not sufficient in the complexity of everyday life. Instead, principals and norms are given meaning in interactive processes in specific contexts and in concrete situations. From infancy, the child is not only part of its world but also is an active member in creating a social world through interactive and interpretative processes. Gradually the child builds a core of social understanding from which its continuing knowledge of the social worlds is based. Communication is important in this process. According to Corsaro, the child is creating meaning with others and constantly interpreting their surrounding world. In everyday life the child is confronted with problems, questions, and ambiguities that they communicate in other activities and situations, for instance, with peers.

Morality grows out of inseparable relationships between subjects rather than being the result of an autonomous subject's logical reasoning, writes Eva Johansson (1999, 2001, 2002, 2003c).

She investigates morality among children from a phenomenological perspective. The theoretical foundation for the studies is the life-world, mainly as Maurice Merleau-Ponty (1962) discusses it. The life-world is related to a perceiving subject—a subject that experiences, lives, and acts on the world. There is also an intertwined relationship of subject and body; furthermore, the body is central for all our being in the world. Johansson (1999, 2001) concludes that the child's body is not only an object, it is a union of senses, thoughts, emotions, language, and motor actions. The child is in communication with the world and with other people. The child creates meaning and is able to understand other people by their bodily existence in the world. Thus, we can understand that the child experiences and expresses morality through his or her body. At the same time, meanings are conveyed to the child; things and people make references to the use and purpose of various phenomena in the world. Johansson stresses that power is always present in human relations. In every relationship we can choose to act for the good of the other, or we can distance ourselves and act according to our own advantage. We are always locked in this relationship of dependence and responsibility for the other. But the relationship is not built on rationality and logic. It is a concrete intersubjective relationship out of which moral values and norms of behavior emerge.

When interpreting children's morality as a researcher, it is important to take into account the wholeness of the child, including both the physical and mental body as well as the child's experiences and giving meaning (Johansson, 2003a). It is also necessary for the researcher to consider the whole context, where other children as well as the researcher are parts as this has an essential meaning to the child. Finally, the researcher has to be open for the ambiguity and complexity of the life-world.

Morality emerges in interaction with others. The child's moral development emerges in interaction with others, and the child is an active part in this process, writes Dunn (1987, 1988). Moral understanding emanates from the child's self-interest in others' actions. The child is driven by a desire to participate in and to understand others' experiences, rules for interaction, and how to influence others. Emotions, motivation, and affective experiences are crucial dimensions in this process. Dunn proposes that social understanding serves as a tool, which children make use of in their relationships and which is increasingly developed and refined. Social understanding is an instrument that accompanies the child with room to express him or herself, get influence, to cooperate, and to share experiences with others. Cognition and emotion are important aspects in this process as well as context and culture. There is, however, a potential for children to learn about others from strong emotional expressions and in emotional relations between family members, writes Dunn. The sensitivity for others' reactions that a 2-year-old child may embrace is central for identity development and is a result of interactions with others.

In investigating toddlers' social understanding Dunn found that even very young children possess an idea of their own identity and of what it is to be good. The children behaved differently toward different family members and they knew very well how to upset and how to comfort their parents and siblings (Dunn, 1987).

Johansson (1999) investigated young children's experiences of moral values and norms in everyday life within the context of a preschool. The daily interaction of 19 toddlers was video recorded during a period of 7 months. The study showed that morality was an important part of the children's life-worlds. The children defended and valued their own rights and cared for others' well-being. The children also gave power a moral value, for instance: the power to maintain rights and shared worlds. Moreover, power came from the assertion of rights and from the unity of shared worlds. Children in powerful positions also were highly esteemed by the other children. Positions of power were related to age as well as physical and psychological strength. The findings uncovered that conflicts of rights as well as acts that threaten one's own and others' well-being held potential for children's moral learning. A child can learn about morality under certain important conditions, these include: the other's reactions, what the implications and consequences of the acts might be, personal closeness to the other, whether or not the child is the recipient or "victim" of the acts.

Johansson (1999) concludes that morality is not something that first appears in late childhood, nor does morality require logical thinking; instead it is a part of the child's life-world and a part of a child's existence. Values became apparent to the children when they interacted with others, especially when confronted with different values. Furthermore, children's morals and values are not separate from society; children struggle with values regarding existence, ownership, justice, as well as respect for and understanding of others.

Johansson and Johansson (2003) investigated children's and their teacher's conceptions and expressions of values and norms in school. The study was interdisciplinary (education and ethnology) and the theoretical approach used was built on life-world phenomenology (Merleau-Ponty, 1962) and discourse theory (Foucault, 1972). The daily interaction between children and teachers in five classes (preschool and Grades 1 to 3) from four different schools were followed in periods during three semesters. Participants in the study were 10 teachers and 100 children between the ages of 6 and 9 years old. Formal learning situations in class as well as play and other activities, for instance, mealtime, were observed. The teachers and the children were interviewed apart from spontaneous talks in everyday situations.

The results demonstrated that values such as rights, others' well-being, and justice were important for both the children and the teachers, but they interpreted those values somewhat differently. For instance, rights in the context of school seemed very restricted in the perspective of the children; however, the teachers meant that they assigned children rights in school. Power also was present in every moral interaction especially in situations concerning the children's right to or rather lack of integrity. This became apparent in conflicts between teachers and children.

Solidarity was an important moral issue from the children's perspectives; however, teachers were not always aware of these expressions. By contrast to their lack of rights in school, the children developed strategies in which they stood up for and expressed solidarity to their peers and teachers. The children showed concern for each other by seeking help from the teacher, or by expressing support for peers in vulnerable situations. Sometimes children showed support for friends despite the risk of coming into conflict with the opinions of the teachers and the majority of peers; this indicates courage to support friends and defend moral values (Johansson & Johansson, 2003).

Children's friendship—a moral potential. Friendship is one of the child's keenest interests in early childhood, asserts Damon (1983, 1990). The earliest forms of relationship are mainly based on possibilities to play rather than on the choice of a specific friend, but by age the children develop knowledge on how to establish and keep stable and deep relationships. At its best, friendship includes a potential for moral discoveries, suggests Damon. Being friends, the welfare of one party can be seen as synonymous with the welfare of the other. Therefore, friendship motivates children to discover moral values and norms such as care, honesty, solidarity, and reciprocity. Reciprocity is, according to Damon (1990), a basic norm in childhood and in friendship and can be defined as a multifaceted principle of give and take, to mirror and to exchange the other's behavior and actions. Each part in the relationship is free to direct actions and reactions without constraint by the other party. Reciprocity is, writes Damon, fundamental for social relationships and is needed to establish, maintain and repair them. Without reciprocity there can be neither verbal nor nonverbal communication or exchanges of meaning.

One reason for this reciprocity in child-child relations is that children usually perceive each other as equals in status and power, concludes Damon (1990). A sense of equality increases with age. Reciprocity concerns both good and bad, desirable and undesirable behavior; that is, children can comment on a friend's behavior and act in the same way as they have been treated. The children's behavior toward friends can change between friendly play and strong emotional conflicts without influencing the friendship negatively.

From an early age children share experiences and thoughts with peers, which give them various opportunities to discover each other's perspectives, writes Damon (1990, see also Frønes, 1995, Piaget, 1960). Damon is of the understanding that perspective taking is a complicated enterprise rather than a generalized ability. Some situations make taking another's role relatively simple, whereas others pose more complex obstacles in this respect. Children are both social and egocentric; they are aware of others and seek interactive and communicative interactions with them. But, perspective taking is not morally neutral and children can use their insights in another's perspective for good as well as bad purposes. It is this kind of choice between interests that can serve their own or the others' well-being that brings forth the moral dimension of perspective taking acts. Damon concludes that the values that children embrace in their friendships nourish their moral development (Damon, 1983, 1990). This idea is supported by Frønes (1995), who emphasizes that in friendships it is the confrontation with others' perspectives that is essential for children's moral learning. Frønes suggests that exchanging perspectives includes the ability to understand the other as a person rather than just taking another's role. The

children are forced to relate to others' views in their friendships, says Frønes. He also means that conflicts in children's relationships serves them with opportunities to discover variations in perspectives. Gradually the child discovers the other as a person with unique ideas and perspectives. However, children place importance on one another as equals; they are therefore not free from differences of status related to background, gender, or competence (Frønes, 1995). The moral codes for interaction are both changeable and contradictory, as people, situations, and contexts vary. Because friendship is based on equality, definitions of what is right or wrong, good or bad, do not belong to a single person. Therefore, the agreements established between children constantly need to be shaped and reshaped.

Studies clearly reveal that it is important to understand that life in preschool is built upon a feeling of community spirit (Johansson, 1999; Solomon et al., 1996). It is of vital importance for every child in preschool or school to be a part of the common life with peers. To play with friends is essential. The research of Corsaro (1987, 1997) for instance, maintains that being friends is a way for children to solve the problem of becoming a part of others' play. Friendship in preschool serves as a tool for building solidarity, trust, and to safeguard an interactive area.

In her study, Johansson (1999) uncovered that even friendships amongst toddlers are a vital base for morality. In contrast to Damon (1990), Johansson claims that her investigation demonstrates that very young children develop deep and stable relationships. In their friendship, the toddlers could defend a friend's rights, show a concern for their friends' well-being but also could express a strong disappointment when friends let them down or when promises were broken. Johansson takes a somewhat different standpoint than Frønes (1995) and Damon (1990), who suggest that friendship is based on equality. Johansson argues that friendships also include differential and unequal processes and power relations; yet these friendships are embedded in a reciprocal concern for each other's well-being.

Moreover, Johansson and Johansson (2003) suggest that friendship is a moral issue for the children in school. This study revealed that a special care and concern was shown toward friends. The children expressed care for friends through closeness, a friendly tone, and solidarity when needed. The children seemed deeply involved when friends were sad, hurt, or became victims of moral transgressions. Friends also could be given special rights, for instance, permission to play with a new pet. Moreover, the children were keen on sorting things out when something had gone wrong in their relationship. In some situations, the solidarity between friends could be extended to conflicts between groups of children. The collective character of the conflict can strengthen the fellowship community; also, strong feelings emerge in the complex mix of solidarity and power. As with the toddlers in preschool, power between friends was expressed in various ways and could sometimes be concealed behind a caring attitude.

Implications for research. What questions are made in the interactive cultural approaches and what are the possible results? The focus of interest is to understand qualities in children's moral learning and to investigate the child's perspectives on morality. It is suggested that multidimensional interactive processes in children's everyday life form the basis of their moral discoveries. This includes bodily dimensions both of physical and mental character; however, researchers claim these dimensions to be related to the context of children's life-worlds. Children's morality is not supposed to become liberated from the context, from their own subjectivity and personal history, nor from the influence from adults and peers. In the interactive cultural approach communication and giving meaning are assumed to be central to investigations of children's moral life. From this viewpoint, it is crucial to base the study of morality on the child's premises and to gain access into the child's world. The construction of meanings is thought to be a result of *intersubjectivity*. This is quite the reverse to the cognitive perspective that underscores the child's *individual* construction of meanings.

In relation to domain theory we find similarities; for instance, the assumption that manifold dimensions in the child's social life are essential to morality but, contrary to domain theory and the emotional tradition, researchers in the interactive cultural tradition do not focus primarily on moral judgments or empathy. Compared to the tradition investigating prosocial actions, the interactive research is concerned with both sides of morality— good and bad. The studies are mainly of qualitative character, often carried out through naturalistic observations of everyday interaction in different contexts, for instance, at home or in preschool.

The amount of research in the interactive cultural research is small compared to the other traditions, particularly when it comes to phenomenological research. Research that considers the child's bodily being in their life-world is rare. Yet this approach may contribute to a new dimension in moral investigations suitable for the study of morality in early childhood education. There is a need for open-ended studies researching children's perspectives on moral values in day care and school, which include dimensions such as gender, ethnicity, power, integrity, and friendship. It is of great importance to increase knowledge of various educational contexts and discourses and how these contribute to or counteract children's moral understanding.

The Child's Perspective. The ambition to study the child's perspective deserves a critical discussion. A relevant question is how research can get access to children's perspectives. Is this ambition possible?

In society today we see a frequent tendency of referring to children's perspectives in political, practical, and educational contexts, writes Halldén (2003). Research focuses on both children's living conditions and on giving words to the children's voices (Halldén, 2003). Both living conditions and children's voices are covered in this exposition; here we will take a closer look at voicing children's opinions.

There are lots of limitations for a researcher in the study of children's perspectives when claiming to speak in terms of children. First, it is important to note that children's perspectives are manifold simply because the child's worlds are manifold. When investigating children's perspectives, the researchers' responsibility is to develop knowledge about the children's goals, meanings, and experiences of morality in different social and cultural contexts (Damon, 1990; Dunn, 1988; Johansson, 2003a). This demands both mental and physical closeness to children's interaction and their communication. Multiple methods and contrasting interpretations are fundamentally important to provide a just and accurate description. This of course concerns all research, but when we study young children we are confronted with a particular difficulty of interpretation and of inference, says Lamb (1999). It is not just the spoken words that need to be understood, argues Johansson (2003a), but the child's whole being, including his or her personal history and active part in a particular social and cultural world. However, interpretations are always limited as we cannot be the other. The researcher is always part of the world he or she is studying, along with all his or her previous experiences and understandings (Merleau-Ponty, 1962). Piaget (1960) was a pioneer in his desire to understand the child's perspective; however, his theory and methods have been criticized as being based on adult conceptions. There has been a strong tendency in research to look on children's moral concerns from the perspective of adults (Corsaro, 1997; Damon, 1990; Hartman, 1997). As already stated, perspective taking is a multidimensional and difficult task (Damon, 1990); which commands certain skills of the researcher when attempting to study the child's perspective. It is very important that the researcher show respect and consideration to the child's integrity. The child is always in a subordinated position to adults and has few possibilities of either maintaining his or her integrity or to question the researcher's interpretations. As researchers we have the power to define the object studied, to formulate questions and methods. There is, according to Goodnow (1999), a huge gap between approaches that start with a concept and ask how children acquire this, compared to asking what is occurring to children in a specific situation. Even if the researcher defines the moral aspects being investigated, the question of what morality is from the child's perspective must remain open (Johansson, 2001).

Children's conceptions of rights. It has been suggested that education built on children's rights may be among the most useful methods of teaching values (Covell & Howe, 1999, 2001). In a pilot study, Covell and Howe (1999) developed a curriculum based on the United Nations Convention on the Rights of the Child. These researchers claimed that education based on children's rights in school can improve children's reasoning, support teacher and peer relationships, and promote more positive attitudes toward children of ethnic minorities. Furthermore, Covell and Howe (2001) propose that democratic styles of teaching are necessary when working with children's rights. Teachers must, for instance, model the rights children have (see also DeVries & Zan, 1994; Piaget, 1960; Nucci, 2001). The teachers must provide opportunities for debate and exercises in which children are encouraged to interact, to challenge one another's opinions, and to develop their own ideas. When teachers model and teach about rights they are transmitting attitudes and beliefs about the importance of respecting others' rights, which in turn creates a supporting and respectful atmosphere. This effect is contagious; values such as care and others' well-being are nourished in a supporting and respectful atmosphere. Some programs of children's rights have been initiated; however, little

4. CHILDREN'S MORALITY • 77

is known of the impact from these programs. Covell and Howes (2001) claim the education of children's rights to be an effective agent in moral education; yet many questions remain to be answered regarding the effects of this curriculum.

The program presented here takes a departure from rights as developed by the United Nation, but let us here also consider rights from the perspective of the child and teacher in early childhood education.

Johansson (1999) found that toddlers in preschool defended their right to things and to create their own worlds with peers. Sometimes the children also supported and protected each other's rights. Johansson suggests that the idea of having rights may support a more general conception that rights also belong to others. According to Johansson, the right to things and to share worlds with others seems to be of existential importance from a child's perspective. This is a child's way of being and getting to know the world. The exploration of things and sharing of worlds are compulsory activities for children. When children's inquiry about things, or their shared worlds, is threatened or inhibited it also becomes a threat to their very existence. Out of this situation emerges an existential and shared experience of values and rights. This way of describing children's rights is not frequent in any previous research. Contrary, researchers principally describe this phenomenon in terms of children's defense of possessions, ownership, space, or interactive space (Corsaro, 1997; Dunn, 1988; Thorell, 1998). Other studies seldom describe children's commitment to their rights as a moral value. Even though conflicts over toys are well documented in other research, this is mainly discussed as children's capacity to share and as a beginning of their emerging sense of justice, rather than being viewed as rights associated with their moral values (Damon, 1990; Eisenberg & Mussen, 1997).

If we compare this result with how children in school experience rights, we find both similarities and differences (Johansson & Johansson, 2003). On the one hand, the right to things and to share worlds is expressed in children's play. On the other hand the children seemed hardly able to believe that they had any rights at all in school. The children mainly regard rights to be the teacher's territory; however, the teachers seem to be of a contrary opinion. Although the teachers highlighted the children's right to speak, the children referred to their obligation to be quiet. When the teachers emphasized the children's right to be involved in school decisions, the children appeared to conceive themselves as persons with no rights at all in school. Thus, the children seemed to take for granted that, apart from free play, the teacher is responsible for all decisions concerning school (see also Sheridan & Pramling Samuelsson, 2001). However, this did not stop the children from showing disappointments when their voices were not heard, when their ideas were rejected, or when their integrity was challenged by the teachers or by friends (Johansson & Johansson, 2003).

This indicates that children intuitively experience rights, or rather their lack of rights, but they appear to have no verbal expressions for moral values of this kind. Thus, helping children to express and reflect on rights can be an important issue in moral education. When experiencing your own rights, you also can discover the rights of others. In this process, it is crucial to be sensitive to the child's bodily and tacit experiences, as

well as, the child's life-world. Children's moral knowledge is both tacit and verbal; bodily experiences and expressions are as important as words.

The struggle for rights to things also must be related to the position of importance that things have in preschool and school. A basic norm for the children is the principle that the first child to pick up or begin to use each thing has a right to it. Even the youngest children seem to ascribe to this norm. Research also indicates that teachers spontaneously support this norm (Johansson, 1999, 2002). An important question for teachers is not only to consider whether this norm always should be a priority but also to contemplate the kind of morality this norm actually supports.

Implications for early education. Covell and Howe (2001) claim that working with children's rights will give rise to an atmosphere in which other values such as care for others well-being become evident. DeVries and Zan (1994), and Nucci (2001), underscore teacher's responsibility to create a moral atmosphere characterized by warmth and mutual respect. However, research has shown that teachers' strategies sometimes come into in conflict with the values they want children to learn. The approaches and strategies used by teachers include many implicit and explicit moral messages, not always visible to themselves. Moreover, teachers' ambitions for making values apparent to children are not always obvious; the children might not perceive the values being taught as the one's intended. Furthermore, children sometimes create their own interpretations of these values (Colnerud & Thornberg, 2003; Jackson, Boostrom, & Hansen, 1993; Johansson, 2002).

This review has shown that children's morality is complex and includes a spectrum of values including rights, others well-being, justice, and power (Eisenberg & Fabes, 1998; Johansson, 1999; Piaget, 1960; Turiel, 1998). Friendship and reciprocity are from a child's perspective important moral dimensions (Damon, 1990; Frønes, 1995). It is important to bare in mind that the meaning of these values and dimensions from a child's point of view may vary according to interpretation, contexts, and life-worlds, and also may differ compared to the perspective of the adult.

The work with morality is a matter of values. Understanding morality involves learning about values and norms for how to treat others, often by inference. Attention should be directed toward helping children discover the moral values that could be hidden in different interactive processes. Hence, prioritizing one aspect of morality such as rights requires that teachers also increase their sensitivity to the different dimensions of morality in children's lives. The challenge for teachers in moral education is the complexity of approaches and to be able to discern various perspectives of morality in early education. It is crucial to put the focus on moral issues that children communicate and regard as significant, and to become conscious of the moral values teachers want children to learn *and* the moral values that teachers actually use (cf. Goodnow, 1999). This supports the idea expressed by Damon and Gregory (1997) who make a connection between school and the life children live, instead of the ambition to depersonalize and decontextualize in order to teach cognitive skills such as formal reasoning.

Morality Conveyed Through Culture

In this section, we will consider the cultural theory on morality developed by Shweder and colleagues. These researchers are mainly concerned with morality as a result of cultural ideology. Referring to social communication theory, Shweder et al. (1987; see also Shweder et al., 1997) claim that a culture's ideology and worldview have a significant bearing on children's moral understandings. From this viewpoint, it is maintained that social and cultural continuities and practices in which children are indirectly or directly part of have a crucial effect on the their morality. It is proposed that children integrate norms, values, and behavior through imitation, identification, and reinforcement in social and communicative processes.

Culture provides children with a concrete and practical morality, state Shweder et al. (1987). Children discern the moral order as it is communicated and made apparent in everyday practices. By social communication, morally relevant interpretations of events are conveyed to children in the context of routine family life and social practices. Emotional reactions to the child's transgressions in family and everyday life imply moral values as do requests, sanctions, and justifications to maintain social routines. These moral messages are interpreted and reshaped by the child. The point is that the children do not develop morality on their own. Although the child interprets actions, messages, and routines, these are already socially and culturally defined.

Shweder et al. (1987) propose that some (principally Western) cultures embrace an individualistic moral orientation, focusing on rights and autonomy, whereas others possess a collectivist duty-based orientation (mainly non-Western societies), focusing on the interdependent network of relationships between human beings. In recent years, Shweder et al. (1997) developed and augmented these two types of ethics with a third: the ethics of divinity. Although the ethics of autonomy is based on concepts of justice, harm, and rights and the ethics of community is rooted in status, hierarchy, and social order; the ethics of divinity is connected with concepts of sin, sanctity, duty, and natural order. These three ethics, according to these researchers, are all likely to appear in one society, but one often dominates, making the other ethics subordinate and interpreted against the background of this moral mainstream. For instance, in Indian society the ethics of autonomy is subordinate to the ethics of community and the ethics of divinity. This implies that growing up in some cultures may mean a totally different orientation to the moral ideal than in others. In some parts of the world there may be a tendency to universalize one's moral beliefs, whereas in other parts of the world moral maturity means applying one's beliefs flexibly to multiple changing situations.

In contrast to domain theory, which differentiates moral from conventional domains, the social communication theory claims that certain cultures do not view social practices as conventions, but are instead viewed as parts of morality (Shweder et al., 1987). In those cultures, children develop an idea of conventional obligation, which is not separated from the "natural" moral order. Shweder et al. (1987) question the differentiation between moral and conventional events as a universal developmental occurrence, as suggested by domain theory.

Alternatively, these researchers argue that the distinction between morality and convention is culture-specific.

Conclusions

To summarize, culture is seen as a prerequisite for moral development. The idea that culture is the main source of morality refers to theories on socialization. Research is aimed toward the specific moral messages that a child meets in the culture in which the child is supposed to internalize. Moral values and norms are believed to be transmitted to the child through external conditions, institutional acts, traditions, roles, symbols, and symbolic acts. Hence, the child's own creation of meaning is subordinate to culture and less attention is given to children's ability of discerning moral issues in their own terms. In contrast to the interactional approach, the child is supposed to, more or less unconsciously, internalize the surrounding culture, which is already predefined by others.

However, to explain foundations for morality as solely rooted in culture has been questioned as insufficient (cf. Berger & Luckman, 1995; Damon, 1990; Johansson 1999; Turiel, 1998). The concept of an overarching culture is too broad and too abstract to cover and explain the complexity of morality. This position on morality does not explain variations among groups of people, between individuals or within the same person, nor do they explain variations from one situation to another.

According to Turiel (1998), the idea of coherent and integrated cultural patterns in individuals' moral judgments and actions conflicts with the idea of pluralism and that the mind is context-dependent, domain specific, and local. Ethics is suggested by Shweder et al. (1997) either as individualistic, collective, or based on divinity. This presupposes a top down perspective on morality. To refer ethics mainly to three overarching moral orientations sets bounds, which may overlook the possibilities of understanding diversity in morality, and what morality may be in the perspectives of children and to take into account varying features of situations and contexts. According to Turiel (1998), empirical findings demonstrate that individuals' judgments change from context to context, that individual and collective issues coexist, and that personal agency and social solidarity can go together. Research has shown that the child interacts in various contexts with different people, using various strategies and moral ideals, plus the fact that the child makes his or her own inferences of what is good and valuable. This conflicts with the proposals from Shweder et al. (1997).

Interestingly, as we have seen from this exposition, the dialectics concerning universal and pluralistic ideas can be interpreted in various ways. Domain theory, for instance, proposes morals such as justice, rights, and welfare to be universal between cultures, whereas the social communicative position proposes that morals such as individuality, community, or divinity are universal within a culture. Additionally, the interactional cultural position is divided on this issue; however, the emphasis is on pluralism, not only according to culture, history, and time but also to contextual and individual interpretations.

A fruitful position is to be open to the ceaseless dialectic between stability and change, pluralism and universalism, culture and context, the individual and the collective, past and present.

RESEARCH ON CHILDREN'S MORALITY—AN ISSUE OF COMPLEXITY

In this chapter, we have discussed three main traditions of moral research; cognitive, emotional, and cultural. Although none of these traditions are internally homogeneous, they define morality somewhat differently from one another. Each emphasizes different aspects of children's morality and deal with different research questions. All of the traditions mentioned differ in their views regarding morality as innate, universal, or relative to culture and context. Each tradition concerns emotional, cognitive, and cultural issues; however, one of these issues is assumed to have more significance on the impact of children's moral learning. In this overview, we also have encountered different educational programs based on different ideas for how to develop children's moral learning. These ideas guide teachers in their efforts to help children learn moral values. There is reason to believe that teachers in general, more or less consciously, interpret children's morality on the basis of ideas that can be linked to the traditions introduced in this text.

Research and support of children's morality is always a matter of perspectives (Johansson, 2001, 2003b). There is always an ontological basis for a study, a curriculum or teaching strategy, but this ontology is not always discussed or made explicit either by researchers or teachers. Whether made explicit or not, the ontology comprises a perspective that guides and shapes the investigation or the teaching, for example, appropriate methods to use and possible knowledge to reach about the phenomenon in question. The philosophical perspective on morality frames the issues that researchers or teachers find relevant and include, or find irrelevant and exclude in research on children's moral development and learning.

In this overview, discrepancies in methods have been found in whether or not researchers make use of moral judgments or social interaction, apply individual internalization processes, or naturalistic observations to investigate children's morality. There is a difference between research that is interested in generalizing about moral development versus research interested in moral characteristics and processes. The tendency to generalize is found in the cognitive and emotional traditions, whereas the interactive cultural tradition tends to focus on understanding moral qualities, often from the perspective of the child. Furthermore, there is a difference in whether or not the research takes a top-down or a bottom-up approach. On the one hand, researchers strive to learn whether or not children have developed a particular moral trait. This is a top-down approach because the interest is in whether or not children understand certain moral concepts. On the other hand, researchers are seeking to find out how morality might be experienced and expressed from a child's point of view. This bottom-up approach tries to uncover and understand what is happening, in terms

of morality, to children in interaction with others (Dunn, 1987; Goodnow, 1999). The latter approach is often found in the interactive traditions, whereas the first seems more common in the emotional and cultural positions. All these differences mirror the ontological basis for research, the theories of morality proposed by researchers, and how researchers assume knowledge to be gained.

The psychological field dominates the mainstream of studies on children's morality. Only a minority of studies are performed within the context of education. Often, these studies are interested in identifying the effects of a moral program. This means that few studies concerning morality in education and the educational context have been conducted. Many questions on morality related to the discipline of education remain to be answered. The investigations have, with few exceptions from studies among the youngest children, mainly been conducted by quantitative rather than qualitative methods (cf. Colnerud & Thornberg, 2003); despite the fact that aspects such as integration and differentiation are gradually increasing in studies on morality. The majority of investigations have traditionally taken a top-down approach.

If we look at limitations, these mainly concern the inability to fully cover the complexity of morality in children's lives. The cognitive and emotional traditions maintain inner biological abilities as essential for moral development. The cognitive theory assumes young children's moral ability to be restricted and refers the researcher to find moral aspects already defined in the theory. The domain theory highlights the complexity and the diversity of the social world; however, the interest is mainly on moral cognition. The concept of empathy has been questioned to be an insufficient bridge to morality on ontological and empirical grounds. The question on how we (researchers or teachers) can discern and define inner emotional states perceived by the other remains unsolved. The line of research in prosocial actions can be said to be normative as it is primarily concerned with one (the good) side of morality. But morality is concerned with both good and bad. One part of the cultural tradition ties morality to the overarching society, which is supposed to be more or less imposed on children by adults. This appears to disregard the children's ability to interpret and develop a morality on their own terms and with personal characteristics. The interactive cultural position points to the importance of studying morality from the perspective of the active child and taking the context and culture into consideration. Focus is directed on what is occurring between the child and the world, and human qualities are viewed as a complex whole. This raises a dilemma on how to get access to and do full justice to the child's perspective and the complexity of morality. It also can be concluded that all traditions struggle with methodological dilemmas and clinical and experimental methods have predominance.

In spite of this, Eisenberg (1998) points to the fact that research within the field has become more integrated and differentiated. Methods from several disciplines, such as developmental psychology, sociology, and anthropology (note that education is not included here) begin to be more frequent. There is a growing interest in context, which, according to Eisenberg, is reflected in the study of many levels of influence and an increasing knowledge that various social processes are becoming more multifaceted. This overview has shown that there is still much research to do in this respect. Only a minority of studies approach the study of morality in a holistic and broad sense and which take the child's perspectives into account.

From this overview, we have learned that the research problem is complex and refers to a variety of aspects, such as society, culture, development, gender, competence, and construction of meaning in different contexts and situations. Research has tended to divide the child's morality into different aspects, such as cognitive or emotional dimensions. What do we know about the child's moral life if we bring all these dimensions together?

With no ambitions to generalize, there is no doubt that morality is an important dimension in children's lives. Early in life, children show care and concern for others, sense of rights and of justice. Friendship is highly valued as is reciprocity and power. Children differentiate between moral, conventional, and personal issues. However, the boundaries for these domains may be defined differently. Furthermore, children gradually come to understand and relate to others' states of mind and they show a range of supportive acts toward one another. Research indicates that children are of importance for each other's moral understanding. Children teach each other good and bad, right and wrong. We also have learned that children's morality is not separate from society; they struggle with values regarding existence, ownership, justice, respect for and understanding of others. Even if the agreement on this is not at all clear, it has been suggested that children's morality is oriented toward individuality, community or divinity. The child is seen as an interactive agent, a member of culture and society, involved in manifold lifeworld and engaged in various existential periods in life which all may influences his or her morality.

This overview has shown the need for holistic and interactive traditions emphasizing the various influences on morality including the perspectives of children and educators, as well as, context and culture. Research which takes into consideration various social processes in children's moral discoveries can greatly contribute to the knowledge of morality in early childhood education—a field that needs to be studied on its own premises.

References

Arsenio, W., & Kramer, R. (1992). Victimizers and their victims: Children's conceptions of the mixed emotional consequences of victimization. *Child development, 63*, 915-927.

Arsenio, W., & Lover, A. (1995). Conceptions on sociomoral affect: Happy victimizers, mixed emotions, and other expectancies. In M. Killen & D. Hart (Eds.), *Morality in every day life: Developmental perspectives* (pp. 87-128). Cambridge: Cambridge University Press.

Battistich, V., Watson, M., Solomon, D., Schaps, E., & Solomon, J. (1991). The child development project: A comprehensive program for the development of prosocial character. In W. M. Kurtines & J. L. Gewirtz, (Eds.), *Handbook of moral behavior and development, Vol. 3: Application* (pp. 1-34). Hillsdale, NJ: Lawrence Erlbaum Associates.

Battistich, V., Solomon, D., Kim, D., Watson, M., & Schaps, E. (1995). Schools as communities, poverty levels of student populations, and students' attitudes, motives, and performance: A multilevel analysis. *American Educational Research Journal 32*, 627-658.

Battistich, V., Solomon, D., Watson, M., & Schaps, E. (1997). Caring school communities. *Educational Psychologist, 3*, 137-151.

Bengtsson, J. (Ed.) (1999). *Med livsvärlden som grund: Bidrag till utvecklandet av en livsvärldsfenomenologisk ansats i pedagogisk forskning* [The life-world as a base: A phenomenological approach in educational research]. Lund, Sweden: Studentlitteratur.

Berger, P. L., & Luckmann, T. (1995). *Modernity, pluralism and the crisis of meaning: The orientation of modern man*. Gütersloh: Bertelsmann Foundation Publishers.

Berk, L. (2000). *Child development* (5th ed.). Boston, MA: Allyn and Bacon.

Blum, L. A. (1994). *Moral perception and particularity*. Cambridge: Cambridge University Press.

Blumer, H. (1986). *Symbolic interactionism: Perspective and method*. Berkeley, Los Angeles and London: University of California Press.

Brown, J. R., & Dunn, J. (1996). Continuities in emotion: Understanding from three to six years. *Child Development, 67*, 789-802.

Bruner, J. (1996). *The culture of education*. Cambridge, MA: Harvard University Press.

Chapman, M. (1988). *Constructive evolution: Origins and development of Piaget's thought*. Cambridge: Cambridge University Press.

Circourel, A. (1974). *Cognitive Sociology*. New York: Free Press.

Colnerud, G., & Thornberg, R. (2003). *Värdepedagogik i internationell belysning* [The education of values in an international perspective]. Skolverket, Forskning i fokus, 7. Stockholm. Sweden: Fritzes.

Corsaro, W. A. (1987). *Friendship and peer culture in the early years*. Norwood, NJ: Ablex Publishing Corporation.

Corsaro, W. A. (1997). *The sociology of childhood*. Thousand Oaks, CA: Pine Forge Press.

Covell, K., & Howe, B. (1999). The impact of children's rights education: A Canadian study. *International Journal of Children's rights, 7*, 171-183.

Covell, K., & Howe, B. (2001). Moral education through the 3 Rs: Rights, respect, and responsibility. *Journal of Moral Education, 30*(1), 29-41.

Crane, D., & Tisak, M. S. (1995). Does day-care experience affect preschool children's judgements of home and school rules? *Early Education and Development 6*(1), 25-37.

Dahlberg, G., & Lenz Taguchi, H. (1994). *Förskola och skola: Om två skilda traditioner och om visionen om en mötesplats* [Preschool and school: Two different traditions and a vision of a meeting place]. Stockholm, Sweden: HLS Förlag.

Damon, W. (1983). *Social and personality development: Infancy through adolescence*. New York and London: W. W. Norton & Company.

Damon, W. (1990). *The moral child: Nurturing children's natural moral growth*. New York: The Free Press.

Damon, W. (Ed.) (1998). *Handbook of child psychology: Vol. 1-3*. New York: Wiley.

Damon, W., & Gregory, A. (1997). The youth charter: Towards the formation of adolescent moral identity. *Journal of Moral Education, 26*, 117-130.

DeVries, R., & Zan, B. (1994). *Moral classrooms, moral children: Creating a constructivist atmosphere in early education*. New York and London: Teachers College Press.

Dunn, J. (1987). The Beginnings of Moral Understanding: Development in the second year. In J. Kagan & S. Lamb (Eds.), *The emergence of morality in young children* (pp. 91-111). Chicago and London: University of Chicago Press.

Dunn, J. (1988). *The beginnings of social understanding*. Cambridge, MA: Harvard University Press.

Dunn, J., Brown, J. R., & Maguire, M. (1995). The development of children's moral sensibility: Individual differences and emotional understanding. *Developmental Psychology, 31*, 649-659.

Dunn, J., Brown, J., Slomkowski, C., Tesla, C., & Youngblade, L. (1991). Young children's understanding of other people's feelings and beliefs: Individual differences and their antecedents. *Child Development, 62*, 1352-1366.

Dunn, J., & Hughes, C. (2001). "I Got Some Swords and You're dead!": Violent fantasy, antisocial behavior, friendship, and moral sensibility in young children. *Child Development, 72*, 491-505.

Eisenberg, N. (1992). *The caring child*. Cambridge, MA: Harward University Press.

Eisenberg, N. (Ed.) (1995). *Social development*. Thousand Oaks, London, New Delhi: Sage Publications Inc.

Eisenberg. N., & Fabes, R. A. (1992). Emotion, regulation and the development of social competence. In M. S. Clark (Ed.), *Review of personality and social psychology: Emotion and social behavior, 14* (pp. 119-150). Newbury Park, CA: Sage.

Eisenberg, N., & Fabes, R. A. (1998). Prosocial development. In W. Damon (Ed.) & N. Eisenberg (Vol. Ed.), *Handbook of Child Psychology: Vol. 3. Social, emotional and personal development* (pp. 701-776). New York: Wiley.

Eisenberg, N., Miller, P. A., Shell, R., McNally, S., & Shea, C. (1991). Prosocial development in adolescence: A longitudinal study. *Developmental Psychology, 27*, 849-857.

Eisenberg, N. & Mussen, P. H. (1997). *The roots of prosocial behavior in children*. Cambridge: Cambridge University Press.

Eisenberg, N., Pidada, S., & Liew, J. (2001). The relation of regulation and negative emotionality to Indonesian children's social functioning. *Child Development, 72*, 1747-1763.

Eisenberg, N., & Strayer, J. (1987). *Empathy and its development*. Cambridge: Cambridge University Press.

Emilia, A., Garottini, B. C., & Venturini, B. (2000). The understanding of sadness, guilt and shame in 5-, 7-, and 9-year old children. *Genetic, Social & General Psychology Monographs, 126*, 293-329.

Fabes, R. A., Eisenberg, N., Jones, S., Smith, M., Guthrie, I., Poulin, R., et al. (1999). Regulation, emotionality and preschoolers' socially competent peer interactions. *Child Development, 70*, 432-442.

Farver, J A., & Branstetter, W. H. (1994). Preschoolers' prosocial responses to their peers' distress. *Developmental Psychology, 30*, 334-341.

Foucault, M. (1972). *The archaeology of knowledge*. London: Tavistock.

Frønes, I. (1995). *Among peers: On the meaning of peers in the process of socialization*. Oslo, Norway: Universitetsforlaget AS.

Garz, D. (1992). What do the kids say?: Bringing student reactions into the picture. *Moral Education Forum, 17*(2), 1-4.

Gilligan, C. (1982). *In a different voice*. Cambridge, MA: Harvard University Press.

Gilligan, C., & Wiggins, G. (1988). The origins of morality in early childhood relationships. In C. Gilligan, J. V. Ward, & J. McLean Taylor (Eds.) (with B. Bardige), *Mapping the moral domain: A contribution of women's thinking to psychological theory and education* (pp. 111-137). Cambridge, MA: Harvard University Press.

Goodnow, J. (1999). Moral development, issues and approaches. In W. Van Haaften, T. Wren & A. Tellings (Eds.), *Moral sensibilities and education: Vol. 1. The preschool child* (pp. 61-82). Bemmel: Concorde Publishing House.

Habermas, J. (1971). *Towards a rational society*. London: Heineman.

Halldén, G. (2003). Barnperspektiv som ideologiskt och/metodologiskt begrepp [Child perspectives as an ideological or/and a methodological concept]. *Pedagogisk forskning i Sverige, (8)*1-2, 2-23.

Hartman, S. (1997). Barnets rätt att få vara sig själv [The child's right to be itself]. In *Barnets bästa—en antologi*, bilaga till Barnkommitténs huvudbetänkande, SOU 1997:116 (pp. 31-46). Stockholm, Sweden: Fritzes.

Hastings, P., & Zahn-Waxler, C. (2000). The development of concern for others in children with behavior problems. *Developmental Psychology, 36*, 531-546.

Hoffman, M. L. (1984). Empathy, its limitations, and its role in a comprehensive moral theory. In W. M. Kurtines & J. L. Gewirtz (Eds.), *Morality, moral development and moral behavior* (pp. 283-302). Hillsdale, NJ: Erlbaum.

Hoffman, M. L. (1987). The Contribution of empathy to justice and moral judgement. In N. Eisenberg & J. Strayer (Eds.), *Empathy and its development* (pp. 47-80). Cambridge: Cambridge University Press.

Hoffman, M. L. (2000). *Empathy and moral development: Implications for caring and justice*. Cambridge: Cambridge University Press.

Hundeide, K. (2001). *Ledet samspill fra spedbarn til skolealder* [Guided interaction from infancy to school age]. Nesbru, Norway: Vett & Veten.

Hägglund, S., & Öhrn E. (unpublished data). *The marginalisation of "socio-emotional" responsibility in the classroom*. Göteborg, Sweden: University, Department of Education.

Jackson, P. W., Boostrom, R. E., & Hansen, D. T. (1993). *The moral life of schools*. San Francisco: Jossey-Bass Publishers.

James, W. (1982). *Psychology*. New York: Harper Torch Books.

Johansson, E. (1999). *Etik i små barns värld: Om värden och normer bland de yngsta barnen i förskolan* [Ethics in small children's worlds: Values and norms among the youngest children in preschool]. (Goteborg Studies in Educational Sciences, Serial No. 141). Göteborg, Sweden: Acta Universitatis Gothoburgensis.

Johansson, E. (2001). Morality in children's worlds: Rationality of thought or values emanating from relations? *Studies in Philosophy and Education. An International Quarterly, 20*, 345-358.

Johansson, E. (2002). Morality in preschool interaction: Teachers' strategies for working with children's morality. *Early Child Development and Care, 172*, 203-221.

Johansson, E. (2003a). Att närma sig barns perspektiv: Forskares och pedagogers möten med barns perspektiv [Approaching children's perspectives: Research and educational encounters with children's perspectives]. *Pedagogisk forskning i Sverige, 8*(1-2), 46-61.

Johansson, E. (2003b). Barns erfarenhet av andras väl: Att förstå och gripa in i den andres livsvärld [The child's experience of others wellbeing: To understand the other's life-world]. In M. Uljens & J. Bengtsson (Eds.), *Livsvärldsfenomenologi och hermeneutik*, pp. 31-52, (Serial No. 192). Helsingfors, Finland: Helsingfors University, Institution of Education.

Johansson E., & Johansson B. (2003). *Etiska möten i skola: Värdefrågor i samspel mellan yngre barn och deras lärare* [Moral encounters in school: Moral issues in interaction between young children and their teachers]. Stockholm, Sweden: Liber.

Killen, M., & Hart, D. (1995). *Morality in everyday life: Developmental perspectives*. Cambridge, MA: Cambridge University Press.

Killen, M., & Nucci, L. P. (1995). Morality, autonomy and social conflict. In M. Killen & D. Hart (Eds.), *Morality in every day life: Developmental perspectives* (pp. 52-86). Cambridge, MA: Cambridge University Press.

Killen, M., & Smetana, J. G. (1999). Social interactions in preschool classrooms and the development of young children's conceptions of the personal. *Child Development, 70*, 486-501.

Kohlberg, L. (1976). Moral stages and moralization: The cognitive-developmental approach. In T. Lickona (Ed.), *Moral development and behavior: Theory, research, and social issues* (pp. 84-107). New York: Holt, Rinehart and Winston.

Kohlberg, L. (1978). The cognitive-development approach to moral education. In P. Scharf, (Ed.), *Readings in moral education*. Minneapolis: Winston Press.

Kohlberg, L., Levine, C., & Hewer, A. (1983). Moral stages: A current formulation and a response to critics. *Contributions to Human Development 10*, 104-166.

Lamb, S. (1999). The past, present, and future of early moral development. In W. Van Haaften, T. Wren & A. Tellings (Eds.), *Moral sensibilities and education: Vol. 1 The preschool child* (pp. 15-36). Bemmel: Concorde Publishing House.

Lourenco, O. M. (1993). Toward a Piagetanian explanation of the development of prosocial behavior in children: The force of negative thinking. *British Journal of Developmental Psychology, 11*, 91-106.

Mauritzson, U., & Säljö, R. (2001). Adult questions and children's responses: Coordination of perspectives in studies of children's theories of other minds. *Scandinavian Journal of Educational Research, 45*, 213-231.

Marton, F., & Booth, S. (1997). *Learning and awareness*. Inc. Mahwah, NJ: Lawrence Erlbaum Associates.

Mead, J. H. (1934). *Mind, self and society*. Chicago: University of Chicago Press.

Merleau-Ponty, M. (1962). *Phenomenology of perception*. New York, London: Routledge.

Miller, J. G., & Bersoff, D. M. (1992). Culture and moral judgement: How are conflicts between justice and interpersonal responsibilities resolved? *Journal of Personality and Social Psychology, 62*, 541-554.

Nelson, K. (2003). Narrative and self, myth and memory: Emergence of the cultural self. In R. Fivush & Haden, C. (Eds.), *Autobiographical memory and the construction of a narrative self: Developmental and cultural prespectives* (pp. 3-28). Mahwah, NJ: Lawrence Erlbaum Associates, Publishers.

Nordin-Hultman, E. (2004). *Pedagogiska miljöer och barns subjektskapande* [Educational contexts and children's creation of subjectivity]. Stockholm, Sweden: Liber.

Noddings, N. (1993). Caring: A feminist perspective. In K. A. Strike & P. Lance Ternasky (Eds.), *Ethics for professionals in education: Perspectives for preparation and practice* (pp. 43-53). New York and London: Teachers College Press.

Nucci, L. P. (1996). Morality and the personal sphere of actions. In E. S. Reed, E. Turiel, & T. Brown (Eds.) *Values and knowledge* (pp. 41-59). Mahwah, NJ: Lawrence Erlbaum Associates, Inc. Publishers.

Nucci, L. P. (2001). *Education in the moral domain*. Cambridge: Cambridge University Press.

Nucci, L. P., & Weber, E. K. (1995). Social interactions in the home and the development of young children's conceptions of the personal. *Child Development 66*, 1438-1452.

Piaget, J. (1960). *The moral judgement of the child*. London: Routledge and Kegan Paul Ltd.

Piaget, J. (1980). *Adaptation and intelligence*. Chicago: University of Chicago Press.

Plutchnik, R. (1987). Evolutionary bases of empathy. In N. Eisenberg & J. Strayer (Eds.), *Empathy and its development* (pp. 44-46). Cambridge: Cambridge University Press.

Pramling Samuelsson I., & Asplund, M. (2003). *Det lekande lärande barnet* [The playing learning child]. Stockholm, Sweden: Liber.

Qvortrup, J. (1993). Societal position of childhood: The international project: Childhood as a social phenomenon. *Childhood, 1*, 119-124.

Reed, E. S., Turiel, E., & Brown, T. (1996). *Values and knowledge*. Mahwah, NJ: Lawrence Erlbaum Associates.

Rogoff, B. (1990). *Apprenticeship in thinking: Cognitive development in social context*. Oxford: Oxford University Press.

Selman, R. L. (1980). *The growth of interpersonal understanding: Developmental and personal analyses*. New York: Academic Press.

Sheridan, S., & Pramling Samuelsson, I. (2001). Children's conceptions of participation and influence in preschool: A perspective on pedagogical quality. *Contemporary Issues in Early Childhood, 2*(2), 169-194.

Shweder, R. A., Jensen, L. A., & Goldsterin, W. M. (1995). Who sleeps with whom revisited: A method for extracting the moral goods implicit in practice. In J. Goodnow, P. J. Miller, & F. Kessel (Eds.), *Cultural practices as contexts for development: New directions for child development* (pp. 21-39). San Francisco: Jossey-Bass.

Shweder, R. A., Mahapatra, M., & Miller, J. G. (1987). Culture and moral development. In J. Kagan & S. Lamb (Eds.), *The emergence of morality in young children* (pp. 1-83).Chicago and London: University of Chicago Press.

Shweder, R. A., Much, N. C., Mahapatra, M., & Park, L. (1997). The "Big Three" of morality (autonomy, community, divinity) and the "Big Three" explanations of suffering. In A. M. Brant & P. Rozin (Eds.), *Morality and Health* (pp. 119-169). New York: Routledge.

Smetana, J. G. (1993). Understanding of social rules. In M. Bennet (Ed.), *The child as psychologist: An introduction to the development of social cognition* (pp. 111-141). London: Harvester Wheatsheaf.

Smetana, J. G. (1995). Context, conflict and constraint in adolescent-parent authority relationships. In M. Killen & D. Hart (Eds.), *Morality in everyday life: Developmental perspectives* (pp. 225-255). New York: Cambridge University Press.

Smetana, J. G., Killen, M., & Turiel, E. (1991). Children's reasoning about interpersonal and moral conflicts. *Child Development, 62*, 629-644.

Solomon, D., Watson, M., & Battistich, V. A. (2001). Teaching and schooling effects on moral/prosocial development. In V. Richardson (Ed.), *Handbook of research on teaching* (4th ed.). Washington, DC: American Educational Research Association.

Solomon, D., Watson, M., Battistich, V., Schaps, E., & Delucchi, K. (1996). Creating classrooms that students experience as communities. *American Journal of Community Psychology, 2*, 719-748.

Solomon, D., Watson, M., Delucchi, K. L., Schaps, E., & Battistich, V. (1988). Enhancing children's prosocial behavior in the classroom. *American Educational Research Journal, 25*, 527-554.

Sommer, D. (1997). *Barndomspsykologi: Utveckling i en förändrad värld* [The psychology of childhood: Development in a changed world]. Stockholm, Sweden: Runa Förlag.

Stern, D. N. (1985). *The interpersonal world of the infant: A view from psychoanalysis and developmental psychology*. New York: Basic Books.

Säljö, R. (2000). Betecknandets politik: Kommunikation som social handling [The Politics of Defining: Communication as a Social Act]. *Utbildning och Demokrati 9*(2), 49-59.

Thornberg, R. (2003). Att skilja på etik och etikett: Den domänteoretiska forskningen. [To separate between the moral and the conventional: The research of domain theory]. In O. Frank (Ed.), *Liksom värden, typ: Moral och mening med fokus på skolan*. Föreningen lärare i religionskunskap, årsbok 35 (pp. 158-172). Malmö, Sweden: Föreningen lärare i religionskunskap.

Thorell, M. (1998). *Politics and alignments in children's play dialogue: Play arenas and participation*. (Linköping studies in arts and science, Serial No. 173). Linköping, Sweden: Linköping university.

Turiel, E. (1998). The development of morality. In W. Damon (Ed.) & N. Eisenberg (vol. Ed.), *Handbook of child psychology: Vol. 3. Social, emotional and personal development* (pp. 863–932). New York: Wiley.

Turiel, E., Killen, M., & Helwig, C. (1987). Morality: Its structure, functions, and vagaries. In J. Kagan & S. Lamb (Eds.), *The emergence of morality in young children* (pp. 155–243). Chicago and London: University of Chicago Press.

Turiel, E., Smetana, J. G., & Killen, M. (1991). Social contexts in social cognitive development. In J. L. Gewirtz & W. M. Kurtines (Eds.), *Morality, moral development and moral behavior* (pp. 307–372). Hillsdale, NJ: Erlbaum.

Turiel, E., & Wainryb, C. (2000). Social life in cultures: Judgments, conflict, and subversion. *Child Development, 71,* 250–256.

Uzgiris, I. C. (1996). Together and apart: The enactment of values in infancy. In E. S. Reed, E. Turiel, & T. Brown (Eds.), *Values and knowledge* (pp. 17–39). Mahwah, NJ: Lawrence Erlbaum Associates, Inc.

Vygotsky, L. (1978). *Mind in society: The development of higher psychological processes.* Cambridge, MA: Harvard University Press.

Walker, S., Irving, K., & Berthelsen, D. (2002). Gender influences on preschool children's social problem-solving strategies. *The Journal of Genetic Psychology 163,* 197–209.

Walkerdine, V. (1990). *Schoolgirl fictions.* London and New York: Verso.

Young, S. K., Fox, N. A., & Zahn-Waxler, C. (1999). Relations between temperament and empathy in 2-year-olds. *Child Psychology, 35,* 1189–1197.

Youngblade, L. M., & Dunn, J. (1995). Individual differences in young children's pretend play with mother and sibling: Links to relationships and understanding of other people's feelings and beliefs. *Child Development, 66,* 1472–1492.

Zahn-Waxler, C., Radke-Yarrow, M., Wagner, E., & Chapman, M. (1992). Development of concern for others. *Developmental Psychology, 28,* 126–136.

Zahn-Waxler, C., & Hastings, P. D. (1999). Development of empathy: Adaptive and maladaptive patterns. In W. Van Haaften, T. Wren & A. Tellings (Eds.), *Moral sensibilities and education: Vol. 1. The preschool child* (pp. 37–59). Bemmel: Concorde Publishing House.

· 5 ·

THE EMOTIONAL BASIS OF LEARNING AND DEVELOPMENT IN EARLY CHILDHOOD EDUCATION

Susanne A. Denham
George Mason University

Petey runs, darts, and jumps with a ball clenched tightly in his arms. He screams "ok" to an invitation to play, but is unable to restrain his desire to keep the ball and game as his own. He pulls the ball away from another boy, angrily shoving him and screaming insults. In free play, individual, small group, or whole-group activities, he is angry, often out of control, hitting and throwing objects.

Sean, by contrast, speaks hesitantly, often echoing others' communications, as if practicing. He is always the third, fourth, or last, to attempt a task, never asserting ideas or desires. He is quiet, sometimes looking quite sad on the sidelines, seeking the comfort of his thumb. He seems overwhelmed and withdrawn.

Jeremy's behavior paints a different picture: he is a "hurried child" (Elkind, 1982). Although he plays and interacts with peers fairly well, teachers note that he has difficulty permitting other children to lead activities or reject his ideas, and hates to make a mistake. This upsets him very much.

The current educational climate, focusing strongly as it does upon children's cognitive development, promotes early literacy and numeracy. Although these preacademic skills are immensely important, Petey, Sean, and Jeremy are not alone in needing us to focus on other domains of development. Their experiences illustrate that, in order for all young children to learn, and for their development as "whole" persons, emotional and social development require equally careful nurturing. It is more important than ever to reflect upon what we know about children's emotional competence. Young children must learn to send and receive emotional messages, using their knowledge about emotions and their abilities to regulate emotions, so that they may successfully negotiate interpersonal exchanges, form relationships, and maintain curiosity about and enthusiasm for

their world (Halberstadt, Denham, & Dunsmore, 2001; Saarni, 1990). Thus, the main components of emotional competence are the child's expression and experience of emotions, regulation of emotions, and knowledge of emotions. Internal, intrapersonal processes, such as the child's temperament and language abilities, contribute to these components. They are also impacted by other people's modeling of emotional expressiveness, reactions to the child's emotions, and actual discussion and teaching about emotions. Accordingly, the goal of this chapter is to give a view of both the breadth and depth of preschoolers' emotional competence, as well as the contributions made by within-child qualities and the socialization of important others.

Furthermore, emotional competence is crucial not only in its own right but for positive outcomes in both social and academic domains. First, one of young children's most important developmental tasks is achieving sustained positive engagement with peers. The components of emotional competence help to ensure effective, successful social interactions built on specific skills such as listening, cooperating, appropriate help seeking, joining another child or small group, and negotiating. The young child who does succeed at this developmental task is in a good position to continue thriving in a social world: successful, independent interaction with agemates is a crucial predictor of later mental health and well-being, beginning during preschool, continuing during the grade school years when peer reputations solidify, and thereafter (Denham & Holt, 1993; Robins & Rutter, 1990)

Second, emotional competence also supports cognitive development, preacademic achievement, school readiness, and school adjustment, both directly, and indirectly, through its contributions to social competence and self-regulation (Blair, 2002; Carlton & Winsler, 1999; Greenberg & Snell, 1997). Children who enter kindergarten with more positive profiles of emotional competence, as well as well-developed skills of social competence and self regulation, have not only more success in developing positive attitudes about and successful early adjustment to school but also improved grades and achievement (Birch, Ladd, & Blecher-Sass, 1997; Ladd, Birch, & Buhs, 1999; Ladd, Kochenderfer, & Coleman, 1996). In particular, when children enter school with friends, are well liked, are able to make and sustain new friendships, and are able to initiate positive relationships with their teachers, *all of which are supported by emotional competence*, they also feel more positive about school, participate in school more, and achieve more than children who are not described this way. In contrast, children who are victimized by peers or who are angry and aggressive have more school adjustment problems and are at risk for numerous problems, including school difficulties with academic tasks. Later on, they are more likely to drop out and persist in their antisocial behavior, such as delinquency and drug abuse (Gagnon, Craig, Tremblay, Zhou, & Vitaro, 1995; Haapasalo & Tremblay, 1994; Kochenderfer & Ladd, 1996; Raver & Knitzer, 2002). In short, social and emotional factors, such as emotion knowledge, emotion regulatory abilities, social skills, and nonrejected peer status, often uniquely predict academic success, when other pertinent factors, including earlier academic success, are already taken into account (Carlton, 2000; Howes & Smith, 1995; Izard et al., 2001; O'Neil, Welsh, Parke, Wang, & Strand, 1997; Pianta, 1997; Pianta, Steinberg, & Rollins, 1995; Shields et al., 2001).

Because emotional competence is so important—both in its own right and because of its major contribution to social competence and both direct and indirect contributions to school success—the major goals of this chapter are to fully describe: (a) the separate components of emotional competence—emotional expressiveness, emotion knowledge, and emotion regulation; as they develop through the preschool and primary periods; (b) the research knowledge base regarding each of these facets—their manifestations during early childhood, as well as how they relate to successful social development and school success; and (c) the direct and indirect contributions of each aspect of emotional competence, to both social competence and school success. After each of these descriptions, we summarize the promotion of emotional competence by parents, teachers, and others. Finally, the role of early childhood education in addressing each component of emotional competence is considered, along with ideas for future research and applied considerations. First, then, we turn to a more detailed consideration of the general nature and specific manifestations of emotional competence during the early childhood timeframe.

WHAT IS EMOTIONAL COMPETENCE?

The social-emotional skills that preschoolers normally develop are quite impressive. Not everyone looks like Petey, Sean, or Jeremy. Consider the following example:

Four-year-olds Darrell and Jessica are pretending Blue's Clues®. They have drawn a "map" and have pencils and pads ready to "write" the clues, even a magnifying glass. They are having fun!

But then things get complicated, changing fast, as interaction often does. They are trying to decide what to hunt for to bring back to Circle Time. Jessica suddenly decides that she should be Blue, because she is a girl, and that she doesn't want to hunt for clues at the bakery; she wants to go to the music store instead. Darrell shouts, "No way, you have to be Joe!" After a second he added, with a smile, "Anyway, I wanted to do clues for doughnuts—they're your favorite, too!"

At the same time, Jimmy, who had been nearby, runs over and whines that he wants to join in. No way!! Darrell, still concentrating on Jessica's demands, doesn't want Jimmy to join them—he's too much of a baby. Almost simultaneously, Jessica hurts her hand with one of the pencils, and starts to cry. And Tomas, the class bully, approaches, laughing at four-year-olds making believe and crying.

This was much more than a simple playtime. Imagine the skills of emotional competence that are needed to successfully negotiate these interactions! Within a 5-minute play period, a variety of emotional competencies are called for if the social interaction is to proceed successfully. For example, Darrell has to know how to resolve the conflict with Jessica, react to Jimmy without hurting him too much, and "handle" Tomas safely. More generally, Darrell needs to learn how to express his emotions in socially appropriate ways, handle provocation, engage with others positively, and build relationships. Taken together, these abilities are vital for how Darrell gets along with others, understands himself, and feels good in his world, within himself, and with other people.

Many young boys and girls Darrell and Jessica's age are learning to cope with their own emotions and with the many difficulties that arise when dealing with other people. More specifically, emotionally competent young children begin to:

- experience and purposefully express a broad variety of emotions, without incapacitating intensity or duration.
- understand their own and others' emotions
- deal with and regulate their emotions—whenever emotional experience is "too much" or "too little" for themselves, or when its expression is "too much" or "too little" to fit with others' expectations.

These components—experiencing, expressing, understanding, and regulating emotions—form the foundation for the theoretical precepts and empirical findings that will be communicated in this chapter.[1] The first component of emotional competence to be discussed is emotional expressiveness.

EMOTIONAL EXPRESSIVENESS

Many emotion theorists currently take a functionalist view of expressiveness—what, specifically, does the expression of emotions "do for" a child and his/her social group? Most importantly, the expression of emotion signals whether the child or other

---

[1]Attachment relationships with adults—both parents and teachers—are an extremely important foundation for emotional and social competence, but beyond the scope of this chapter.

people need to modify or continue their goal-directed behavior (Campos, Mumme, Kermoian, & Campos, 1994). Hence, such information can shape the child's own behaviors. An example is anger—if a girl experiences anger while playing at the puzzle activity table with another, she may try to avoid the other child the next day, and even tell her mother "I don't want *her* to come to my birthday party." The experience of anger gave her important information that affects her subsequent behavior.

Additionally, emotions are important because they provide social information to other people, and affect others' behaviors. Peers benefit from witnessing other children's expressions of emotion. When the irritated girl's companion witnesses the social signal of her anger, for example, she may know from previous experience whether her most profitable response would be to fight back or to retreat.

In terms of specific expressive skills of emotional competence, young children are learning to use emotional communication to express clear nonverbal messages about a social situation or relationship—for example, stamping feet or giving a hug. They also develop empathic involvement in others' emotions—for example, patting a classmate when she falls down and bangs her knee. Furthermore, they display complex social and self-conscious emotions, such as guilt, pride, shame, and contempt in appropriate contexts.

These emotions need to be expressed in keeping with one's goals, and in accordance with the social context. That is, emotional competence includes expressing emotions in a way that is advantageous to moment-to-moment interaction and relationships over time. This is no small task, because the goals of self and of others must be coordinated. Darrell is well liked by the other children in his kindergarten class, in part, because of his generally pleasant, happy demeanor. When he approaches a group of other children to play, for example, his typical emotional expressiveness is confident, content, and enthusiastic—making it possible for him not only to enjoy playing *Blue's Clues*® today but also to remain friends with Jessica through the second grade.

But exactly what affective message should be sent, for successful interaction? Children slowly learn which expressions of which emotions facilitate specific goals. Jimmy learns that his whiny voice tones, downcast face, and slightly averted body posture are not associated with successful entry into play. Young children also learn that the appropriate affective message is the one that "works" in a particular setting or with a specific playmate. Jimmy may learn that a smile and otherwise calm demeanor is the better key to unlock the door to shared play with Darrell and Jessica; on the other hand, if he needs to defend himself, an angry scowl may get Tomas to back off, at least temporarily.

Children also learn how to send the affective message convincingly. Method, intensity, and timing of an affective message are crucial to its meaning, and eventual success or failure. Darrell has learned that showing slight annoyance for a short while over his disagreement with Jessica is very different than remaining very angry with her for days.

Emotional expressiveness can become even more complex during early childhood. Young children are beginning to realize that a person may feel a certain way "on the inside," but show a different outward demeanor (Denham, 1998). In particular,

they are learning that overt expression of socially disapproved feelings may be controlled, while more socially appropriate emotions are expressed. For example, Darrell at first showed his annoyance about changing the goal of *Blue's Clues*®, but then smiled at Jessica; his charm probably allows him to get his way.

Thus, there are times when real affective messages are not appropriate. Some are relevant to the situation but not the context, and some irrelevant ones need to be masked. For example, disappointment and even rage at being reprimanded by a parent or teacher may be relevant—that is, the adult has indeed blocked the child's goal, as when Darrell's teacher says it is time to clean up and stop playing Blue's Clues®—but such anger with adults is usually imprudent to express. Anxiety when playing a new game is probably irrelevant to the goal of having fun, and needs to be suppressed. So, when real affective messages are inappropriate, "false" messages also must be managed and one must keep in mind the constraints of both self-protective and prosocial display rules. For example, Darrell controlled his feelings of fear when Tomas approached, in favor of showing a neutral expression that masked his internal shakiness; this tactic kept him safer.

Finally, and most difficult, one must consider *unique* characteristics of interaction partners and their interpersonal interchange (Halberstadt, Denham, & Dunsmore, 2001). As he enters the primary grades, Darrell may better understand some ways to maintain peaceful interchanges with Tomas. For example, he may know that Tomas has a lot of bullying bluster, but that unlike other mean kids Darrell knows, he can be diverted by a discussion of his favorite topic, dinosaurs. Darrell knows unique emotional information about Tomas that helps them interact more successfully.

What Are the Implications of Emotional Expressiveness for Getting Along Socially and Academically?

At a simpler, more outcome-oriented, level, emotional expressiveness refers to the individual child's profile of frequency, intensity, or duration of both basic and complex emotions—happiness, sadness, anger, fear, guilt, and empathy, for example. Preschoolers' expression of specific emotions, especially their enduring patterns of expressiveness, relates to their overall success in interacting with peers (i.e., peer status) and to their teachers' evaluation of their friendliness and aggression. *Positive* affect is important in the initiation and regulation of social exchanges; sharing positive affect may facilitate the formation of friendships, and render one more likable (Denham, McKinley, Couchoud, & Holt, 1990; Park, Lay, & Ramsay, 1993; Sroufe, Schork, Motti, Lawroski, & LaFreniere, 1984). Conversely, *negative* affect, especially anger, can be quite problematic in social interaction (Denham, McKinley, et al., 1990; Lemerise & Dodge, 2000; Rubin & Clark, 1983; Rubin & Daniels-Beirness, 1983).

Children who show relatively more happy than angry emotions: (a) are rated higher by teachers on friendliness and assertiveness, and lower on aggressiveness and sadness; (b) respond more prosocially to peers' emotions; and (c) are seen as more likable by their peers (Denham, 1986; Denham, McKinley, et al., 1990; Denham, Renwick, & Holt, 1991; Eisenberg et al.,

1997; Rydell, Berlin, & Bohlin, 2003; Sroufe et al., 1984; Strayer, 1980). Sadness or fear, whether observed in the classroom or in interaction with mother, is related to teacher ratings of withdrawal and internalizing difficulties (Denham, Renwick, & Holt, 1991; Rydell, Berlin, & Bohlin, 2003). Moreover, young children who respond to the emotional expressions of others by sharing positive affect and/or reacting prosocially to others' distress, are more likely to succeed in the peer arena; teachers and peers alike view them as more socially competent than their more antisocial, "mean" counterparts.

Finally, there is evidence (Denham et al., 2001) that emotionally negative preschoolers tend to engage with equally negative playmates, and show increasingly negative evaluations of social competence. Some forms of such emotional negativity can be quite context specific. "Gleeful taunting" may look like positive expressiveness on its surface; when expressed during conflict, however, it is really a form of emotional aggression that predicts negative peer status and teacher ratings more strongly even than anger during conflicts (Miller & Olson, 2000).

In short, young children's own expressed emotions are related to evaluations of their social competence made by important persons in their widening world—happier children fare well, and angrier or sadder children worse. It is easy to envision why children's patterns of emotional expressiveness provide such potent intrapersonal support for, or roadblocks to, interactions with age-mates (Campos & Barrett, 1984). A sad or angry child, with nothing pleasing her, is less able to see, let alone tend to, the emotional needs of others. And it is no wonder when her peers flatly assert, as did one of our 3-year-old research participants, "She hits. She bites. She kicked me this morning. I *don't like* her." Conversely, a happier preschooler is one who can better afford to respond to others.

In terms of the connection between emotional expressivity and academic readiness, school adjustment, or other aspects of cognitive achievement, Blair (2002) notes that young children's emotional expressivity has clear implications for brain developments associated with school success, particularly in those areas of the cortex involved in self-regulated learning. Such emotion-related areas of the brain also are more mature than more cognitive areas and thus are in key position to play a central role in self-regulation (Nelson, 1994).

The rapidity of onset, intensity, and duration of both positive and negative emotions are important to learning and self-regulation. In particular, children who express more positive emotions and moderately intense emotions overall are perceived by their teachers as more teachable, and they achieve more in school (Keogh, 1992; Martin, Drew, Gaddis, & Moseley, 1988; Palinsin, 1986). In fact, those who are less emotionally negative during interactions with the mothers on the first day of kindergarten show better academic performance through eighth grade (Morrison, Rimm-Kauffman, & Pianta, 2003). Positive emotion is conducive to task engagement and persistence, skills that serve the young schoolaged child very well. In contrast, neurological processes associated with expression of negative emotion, particularly fear, interfere with cognition. Although the frequent incidence of intense anger is clearly deleterious to social relationships, its role in self-regulation is as yet less clear.

Emotion expression that is visible to others in the child's milieu exists hand-in-hand with internal emotion experience and its regulation. Because emotional experience assists in organizing and directing cognition (Blair, 2002), it is important for the child to modulate both their experience and expression of emotion in order to interact and to learn. Thus, emotion regulation is the second component of emotional competence to be discussed.

EMOTION REGULATION

Attending school is a particularly important transition that taxes young children's emotion regulatory skills. Play with peers is replete with conflict; unlike adults, preschool- and primary-aged peers are neither skilled at negotiation, nor able to offer assistance in emotion regulation. New cognitive tasks require sustained attention, and the challenges of classroom rules are hard to follow when a child is preoccupied with feelings. At the same time, the social cost of emotional dysregulation is high with both teachers and peers. Initiating, maintaining, and negotiating play, earning acceptance, and succeeding at literacy and numeracy skills, all require young children to "keep the lid on" (Raver, Blackburn, & Bancroft, 1999).

Thus, because of the increasing complexity of young children's emotionality and the demands of their social world—with "so much going on" emotionally—some organized emotional gatekeeper must be cultivated. When the intensity, duration, or other parameters of the experience and expression of emotion are "too much" or "too little" to meet goals and expectations of the child and/or social partners, emotion regulation is needed (Cole, Martin, & Dennis, 2004; Denham, 1998; Saarni, 1999; Thompson, 1994). Candidates for regulation include those emotions that are aversive or distressing and those that are positive but possibly overwhelming, as well as emotions that need to be amplified, for either intra- or interpersonally strategic reasons.

To succeed at emotion regulation, several abilities are key (Halberstadt, Denham, & Dunsmore, 2001). One must experience clear rather than diffused feelings, to know what to regulate. Managing "false" signals is also crucial (e.g., Jimmy had a sudden "tummy rumble" as he neared the others playing *Blue's Clues®*, but ignored it as not pertinent. This did *not* mean he was afraid!). One also can use false self-signals to facilitate communication and achieve a goal. For example, a falling boy feels mad at himself because others are watching, as well as hurt. Maybe he can "use" his anger to motivate a quick, albeit hobbling, recovery. In sum, children learn to retain or enhance those emotions that are relevant and helpful, to attenuate those that are relevant but not helpful, to dampen those that are irrelevant. Moderating emotional intensity when it threatens to overwhelm, enhancing it when necessary to meet a goal, and shifting between emotion states via coping help children to maintain genuine and satisfying relationships with others, pay attention to preacademic tasks, and learn the rules of both social and intellectual experiences in varying settings. For example, Darrell may know that showing too much anger with Jimmy will hurt this boy's feelings but showing too *little* angry bravado with Tomas could make him more of a target. He also may know when a conspiratorial smile may get even this bully on his side.

How Is Emotion Regulation Accomplished?

What do children do to regulate emotions? First, the experience of emotion (i.e., sensory input and physiological arousal) may need to be diminished or modulated. The child may modulate the emotional experience via self-soothing. Or, she may even alter the discrete emotion being expressed; for example, a child feeling anxious during group times in her preschool may smile to convince herself and others that she is happy. Others may avoid situations, or try to change them, to avoid overarousal.

Perceptual and cognitive emotion regulation is also possible: a child may relinquish a goal, choose a substitute goal, or think through new causal attributions, which help her to feel more comfortable in her world. For example, a preschooler who is sad about not going swimming may say to herself, "I didn't want to go anyway." Refocusing attention is a useful perceptual means of regulating emotional experience. When trying to join Jessica and Darrell, Jimmy may focus on the game's "props" rather than the two children whose higher social status makes him uncomfortable. Problem-solving reasoning also can be particularly useful as a regulatory coping strategy. When Darrell becomes irritated with Jessica, he may suggest a compromise that makes them both feel better. Finally, children also *do* things to cope with the experience of emotion—actively fix the problem, look for support from adults, lash out aggressively, or cry even harder to vent emotion or get help (Eisenberg, Fabes, Nyman, Bernzweig, & Pinuelas, 1994).

These emotion regulation strategies are not automatically available, however. Preschoolers often need external support to become skilled at such regulation; caregivers' support allows their strategies to be maximally effective. Parents and teachers assist them in cognitive coping strategies they will eventually use themselves (e.g., purposely redeploying attention). Adults also use emotion language to help children regulate emotion by identifying and construing their feelings (e.g., "this will only hurt a little"), and processing causal associations between events and emotions. They also demonstrate behavioral coping strategies when they problem solve around emotional situations, or structure their child's environment to facilitate regulation (e.g., a mother avoids situations she knows will frighten her daughter, leaving her shaky and less able to process information).

Over time, preschoolers and children in primary grades become more able to make their own independent emotion regulation attempts (Grolnick, Bridges, & Connell, 1996). Their awareness of the need for, and their use of, emotion regulation strategies increase. Increased cognitive ability and control of both attention and emotionality (Lewis, Stanger, & Sullivan, 1989; Lewis, Sullivan, & Vasen, 1987; Shonkoff & Phillips, 2000), assist them in these accomplishments. Over time, they see the connections between their emotion regulation efforts and changes in their feelings, and become more flexible in choosing the optimal ways of coping in specific contexts. Thus, they begin to use very specific coping strategies for regulation— problem solving, support seeking, distancing, internalizing, externalizing, distraction, reframing or redefining the problem, cognitive "blunting," and denial. Many such strategies are indeed quite useful for emotion regulation; they are sequentially associated with decreased anger (Gilliom, Shaw, Beck, Schonberg, & Lukon, 2002). Accordingly, the behavioral disorganization resulting from strong emotion decreases dramatically around the transition to school.

What Are the Implications of Emotion Regulation for Getting Along Socially and Academically?

It is clear that emotion regulation is a crucial ability for managing the demands inherent in interpersonal situations (Parker & Gottman, 1989). When the young child begins to regulate his or her own emotions, he or she begins to show more socially appropriate emotions (Kieras, Tobin, & Graziano, 2003). Furthermore, specific emotion regulation strategies are related to specific social behaviors; for example, reliance on attention-shifting emotion regulation strategies is associated with low externalizing problems and high cooperation, whereas reliance on information gathering strategies is correlated with assertiveness (Gilliom et al., 2002). Not surprisingly, then, emotion regulation is related to having friends in preschool (Walden, Lemerise, & Smith, 1999), as well as to teacher-rated socially appropriate behavior in both preschoolers and primary school children (Eisenberg et al., 1993; Eisenberg et al., 1997, 2001, 2003). In contrast, lack of emotional and behavioral regulation as early as 2 years predicts externalizing problems at 4 years, even with aggressiveness at age 2 controlled (Rubin, Burgess, Dwyer, & Hastings, 2003). Lack of regulation of both exuberant positive emotions and fear, respectively, are related to preschoolers' externalizing and internalizing difficulties (Rydell et al., 2003). In sum, children who regulate emotions capably are seen as functioning well socially by adults and peers, across a range of ages from preschool to the end of grade school. Inability to regulate emotions figures in the trajectory toward behavior difficulties at school entry and thereafter.

As already implied (Kieras et al., 2003), emotion regulation and expressiveness often operate in concert. Children who experience intense negative emotions, *and* are unable to regulate their expressions of such emotion, are especially likely to suffer deficits in their social competence (Contreras, Kerns, Weimer, Gentzler, & Tomich, 2000; Hubbard & Coie, 1994). Specifically, young children who are most emotionally intense, and poorly regulate this intense emotion, show the most difficulty in maintaining positive social behavior and have more troubled relationships with peers (Eisenberg, Fabes, Guthrie et al., 1996; Eisenberg et al., 1995; Eisenberg et al., 1997; Murphy, Shepard, Eisenberg, Fabes, & Guthrie, 1999). In other research (Denham et al., 2003; Denham, Blair, Schmidt, & DeMulder, 2002), kindergarten teachers saw children who had shown much anger, *and* did not regulate it constructively during preschool, as having problems with oppositionality 2 years later, at the end of kindergarten. In contrast, good emotion regulation skills, which caring adults can teach, buffer highly emotionally negative children from peer status problems (Eisenberg, Fabes, Guthrie et al., 1996; Eisenberg et al., 1995; Eisenberg et al., 1997; Murphy et al., 1999).

In terms of the implications of emotion regulation for academic readiness, school adjustment, or other aspects of cognitive achievement, it seems clear that the goals of emotional experience and expression can compete with higher order cognitive processing demands. In particular, when the child regulates emotion in reactive ways, through withdrawal, hypervigilance, or venting, rather than through effortful processes involving higher cognitive abilities like memory, attention, or planning (e.g., problem solving, distraction, reframing the problem), these higher-order cognitive abilities are underused and consequently underdeveloped (Blair, 2002; Shonkoff & Phillips, 2000). Caroline's attention and energy for her entire 3-hour morning in preschool is consumed with fussing about getting her way, her terrible cold, and who gets to play with certain toys; she probably doesn't have the cognitive "space" left over to attend to and process information about the stories, rhymes, and songs her teachers introduce.

The conscious appraisal of emotions is considered by some to be beyond the purview of preschoolers (Blair, 2002). This assertion may be true of young children's abilities to reflect on emotions when experiencing them, although it could be argued that some emotional experiences are not completely subcortically driven, even during this age period (Denham, 1998). Whichever contention is closer to the truth, it is probably indisputable that children are coming to understand much about emotions during early childhood. This knowledge may be most available to them during "cool," nonemotional moments, but forms an important foundation for the development of conscious, "online" emotion appraisal for both self and others. Thus, we now turn to an examination of emotion knowledge during early childhood.

EMOTION KNOWLEDGE

As active participants in the social world, young children continually make attributions about their own and others' behaviors, including emotional ones (Dodge, Pettit, McClaskey, & Brown, 1986; Miller & Aloise, 1989). In fact, emotions, whether one's own or others', are central experiences in the social lives of young children from age 2 onward. In spontaneous conversations they talk about and reflect on their own and others' feelings, and discuss emotions' causes and consequences (Dunn, 1994).

Noticing an emotional signal is the first aspect of emotion knowledge (Halberstadt et al., 2001); this awareness may develop at different rates for different people. In general, however, missing the very existence of emotional information definitely puts one at a disadvantage (e.g., if a boy does not attend to his mother's muted anger after his misbehavior, he may err seriously by laughing at her).

Specific Emotion Knowledge Skills of Early Childhood: Expressions, Situations, Causes, Consequences

Once perceived, affective messages must be interpreted accurately; again, as with all levels of affective information

processing, errors can lead to both intrapersonal and social difficulties. The first and only time that Darrell misattributed Tomas' "big shot" grimace as happiness was also the first and only time that Tomas actually punched him.

After noticing that there is an emotional signal to interpret, children must be able to (a) label emotional expressions both verbally and nonverbally; (b) identify emotion-eliciting situations; and (c) infer the causes of emotion eliciting situations, and the consequences of specific emotions. Thus, preschoolers do become increasingly adept at labeling emotional expressions. Specifically, their abilities to verbally label and nonverbally recognize emotional expressions increase from 2 to 4.5 years of age (Denham & Couchoud, 1990). Emotional situations and attendant facial expressions may be learned together, with the first distinction learned between being happy and not being happy, feeling good versus feeling bad (Bullock & Russell, 1984, 1985). Early recognition of happy expressions and situations is greater than recognition of negative emotions, with understanding anger and fear slowly emerging from the "not happy/sad" emotion category (see also Camras & Allison, 1985; Stifter & Fox, 1987). Early in the preschool period, children's emotion categories are broad, "fuzzy," often including peripheral concepts, especially for negative emotions.

However, simply understanding expressions of emotion is not always definitive. In the overall effort to comprehend one's own or others' emotions, situational cues can be very important, especially when expressions may be masked or dissembled. Understanding the events that can elicit emotion, as well as accompanying expressions, increases preschoolers' flexibility in interpreting emotional signals in their environment. For example, Jessica may note, "When we don't listen, our teacher feels bad," and adjust her behavior, even if her teacher's negative expressions are very muted.

As with expressions, preschoolers initially tend to have a better understanding of happy situations compared to those that evoke negative emotions (Fabes, Eisenberg, Nyman, & Michealieu, 1991). They gradually learn to differentiate among negative emotions; for example, realizing that one feels more sad than angry when getting "time out" from one's preschool teacher. Little by little, children separate angry situations from sad ones (Denham & Couchoud, 1990; Fabes et al., 1991), with fear situations presenting the most difficulty (Brody & Harrison, 1987). They also become increasingly capable of using emotion language to describe emotional situations (Fabes, Eisenberg, McCormick, & Wilson, 1988); for example, reminiscing about family sadness when a pet died.

Young children go even further than recognizing the expressions and eliciting situations for discrete emotions—they make more complex attributions about emotions' causes, and reason more intricately about their consequences for behavior. Using everyday experiences to create theories about the causes of happiness, sadness, and anger, preschoolers, especially those four year olds and older, cite causes for familiar emotions that are similar to ones given by adults (Fabes et al., 1988; Fabes et al., 1991; Strayer, 1986). If asked, Jessica could probably point out that her older brother Brent gets mad because he doesn't want to go to school, but that Daddy is happy to go to work. Preschoolers also ascribe different causes to different emotions, building on early understanding of more general emotional situations to create causal scenarios for specific persons' particular feelings (Denham & Zoller, 1991; Dunn & Hughes, 1998).

Through their increased social sensitivity and experience, older preschoolers also develop strategies for appraising others' emotions when available cues are less salient and consensual. Five-year-olds are more likely than 3- and 4-year-olds to focus their explanations of emotions on personal dispositions as opposed to goal states—"She had a bad day." instead of "She didn't want Billy to play with her." Knowing more abstract causes for emotion, less idiosyncratic than younger preschoolers', can be useful in actual interaction with friends (Fabes et al., 1991).

Sometimes one also must understand the consequences of emotion. Young children do realize the consequences of many emotions; for example, a 3-year-old knows that a parent will comfort her when she is upset. Clearly, knowing why an emotion is expressed (its cause), and its likely aftermath (its consequences in the behavior of self or others), aid a child in regulating behavior and emotions, as well as reacting to others' emotions. In short, discerning consequences of emotion can help a child know what to do when experiencing or witnessing emotion.

Thus, preschoolers learn to distinguish the causes of emotions from their consequences (Denham, 1998; Russell, 1990); for example, fathers "dance" when they're happy, mothers "lay in their bed" when sad, and fathers "give spankings" when angry. What do people do as a consequence of someone else's emotions? Four- and 5-year olds attribute plausible, nonrandom parental reactions to their own emotions (Denham, 1997), such as their parents' matching their own happiness; performing pragmatic action after sadness; punishing anger; and comforting or acting to alleviate the fear-eliciting stimulus. These findings suggest that preschoolers have solid conceptions of the consequences of emotions for both self and others.

Specific Emotion Knowledge Skills of Early Childhood: Complex Causal Parameters

To even more accurately interpret emotional information, information specific to a particular person in a particular situation may be needed. Although this aspect of emotion knowledge is very important, it can be quite difficult to acquire and use. In a series of thought-provoking inquiries, Gnepp described the information needed in deciding what emotion another person is experiencing or will experience in a given situation (Gnepp, 1989; Gnepp & Chilamkurti, 1988; Gnepp & Gould, 1985; Gnepp, McKee, & Domanic, 1987). Important elements of emotional information are whether (a) the situation is equivocal (i.e., could elicit more than one emotion), (b) there are conflicting cues in the person's expressive patterns and the situation, and (c) person-specific information is needed.

Regarding *equivocality*, different people feel different emotions during some emotion-eliciting events. One child is happy to encounter a large, friendly looking dog, panting and "smiling" with mouth open, but another child is terrified. More personal information is needed to know how each person is feeling, and preschoolers are becoming aware of this need. They are beginning to recognize the inherent equivocality of some emotion situations, even if they cannot always identify it spontaneously. Ability to detect and use information about equivocal situations continues developing through early and middle childhood (Gnepp et al., 1987).

Even when a situation is not emotionally equivocal, the person experiencing the event may react *atypically*—there may be a conflict between situational and expressive knowledge. A person may smile when seeing a spider dropping into the room on a strand of web. However, interpreting a reaction as atypical requires a rather sophisticated decision, namely *resolving* conflicting expressive and situational cues to emotions rather than relying on one cue or the other. Young children do not perform such problem solving easily or well; they usually still prefer simple, script-based understanding emotion.

Over time, however, older preschoolers do begin to weight expressive and situational sources of emotional information strategically, much as they come to utilize multiple sources of information in nonsocial cognitive tasks (Hoffner & Badzinski, 1989; Wiggers & Van Lieshout, 1985). One of their means of resolving conflicting emotion cues is attributing an idiosyncratic perspective—"She is smiling because she likes shots." Such attribution of idiosyncrasy may be a precursor of understanding the psychological causes of atypical reactions to emotion-eliciting situations (Gnepp, 1989), an ability fully attained only during gradeschool.

If using complex information to attribute emotions to others is so difficult, what types of personal information are preschoolers able to use successfully in interpreting atypical emotions? First, they can use *unique normative information*, such as, "Sarah lives in Green Valley, where all people are friendly with tigers and play games with them all the time" (Gnepp, Klayman, & Trabasso, 1982). When asked how Sarah would feel, preschoolers used unique information about liking tigers to modify their responses to a normally unequivocal situation. Preschoolers are also becoming aware that cultural categories such as age and gender moderate emotions experienced in differing situations. For example, a boy might not be overjoyed to receive a doll as a gift.

Second, information about *personality characteristics* that are stable across time and situations can be especially useful. But in Gnepp's studies, only children six years old and older used such information to answer questions about feelings in situations that normally could be considered unequivocal (e.g., "How would a clownish person feel if he wore one black shoe and one white to school, and everybody laughed?") (Gnepp & Chilamkurti, 1988).

Third, other *person-specific information* is sometimes needed. Gnepp and colleagues (1982) provided stories in which characters' behavioral dispositions modified normally strong emotion-event associations. "Mark eats grass whenever he can. It's dinner time and Mother says they're having grass for dinner. How will Mark feel?" Four- and 5-year-olds were able to utilize such information, with responses reflecting the unique perspective of the character in the story.

Specific Emotion Knowledge Skills of Early Childhood: Dissemblance, Display Rule Usage, and Mixed Emotions

It is tricky to interpret true *or* false emotional signals from others while interacting with them. One must be able to ignore false affective messages if ignoring benefits one's goals, or to accept them as real if that is advantageous. One must also: (a) pick up real, relevant, helpful messages; (b) ignore real but irrelevant messages; and (c) somehow deal with real and relevant but not helpful messages. For example, perhaps Kristen's physiognomy, especially her droopy eyebrows and down-turned lips, looks rather sad naturally; her playmates need to know this and not try to comfort her, or worse yet, avoid her. Darrell needs to ignore Tomas's low level glares as he makes an effort to play with him.

Before to understanding the actual display rules that people use for minimizing, or substituting one emotion for another, and when they use them, young children understand the effort to completely hide, or mask, emotion. Masking emotions can be advantageous to young children as soon as they realize that they can pose expression voluntarily. Knowing when and when not to show emotions is immeasurably valuable in maintaining social relations. Such dissemblance does not require knowledge of display rules that are normative to a family or culture, but merely the need to send a signal that differs from the emotion felt. Knowledge of dissemblance continues to develop through gradeschool (Gross & Harris, 1988).

Understanding of specific cultural or personal display rules, whether prosocial or self-protective, appears rudimentary during early childhood (e.g., Gnepp & Hess, 1986), even though children already modify expressiveness to fit such rules. Despite this assertion, close to half the preschool children in Gnepp and Hess' (1986) study cited at least verbal, if not emotional, rules for regulating emotion (i.e., verbal masking: "I don't care that I lost this silly contest"). Even more important, investigators using more developmentally appropriate methodological simplifications have found that even young children may begin to understand display rules as they begin to use them (Banerjee, 1997; Josephs, 1994; Rozek, 1987), perhaps beginning with emotions subject to early socialization pressure, such as anger (Feito, 1997).

For older children and adults, it is not uncommon to experience "mixed emotions," as when Darrell's older sister is somewhat amused at her younger brother's antics, but mostly annoyed when he tries to leap over her backpack but lands on it, breaking the earphones inside. Gradeschoolers are generally considered to show the first "true" understanding of simultaneous and ambivalent emotions (Harter & Whitesell, 1989). But because young children's expressiveness is becoming more intricate as they leave the preschool period, they may begin to experience simultaneous emotions and ambivalence themselves, and thus begin to understand them. The findings for one key set of more recent studies shows that procedural improvements preserve Harter's sequence but accelerate it (Wintre, Polivy, & Murray, 1990; Wintre & Vallance, 1994). Again, asking questions via more age-appropriate methodology has revealed that preschoolers have more knowledge about mixed emotions than previously assumed (Donaldson & Westerman, 1986; Kestenbaum & Gelman, 1995; Peng, Johnson, Pollock, Glasspool, & Harris, 1992). However, as with other complex aspects of emotion knowledge, young children can recognize and explain conflicting emotions before they can spontaneously talk about them (Gordis, Rosen, & Grand, 1989).

Specific Emotion Knowledge Skills of Early Childhood: Complex Emotions

Another big accomplishment in the domain of emotion knowledge is understanding the more complex emotions, particularly sociomoral emotions such as guilt and shame, and also such self-referent and social emotions as pride, embarrassment, and empathy. For example, English, Dutch, and Nepali 5- to 14-year-olds extended their causal understanding of emotions to social emotions such as pride, worry, and jealousy, complex emotions that cannot be linked with a discrete facial expression (Harris, Olthof, Meerum Terwogt, & Hardman, 1987).

Because young children and their peers are beginning to express complex emotions, they have some understanding of them, but it is still quite limited, and the development of such understanding proceeds quite slowly. Even older preschoolers are unable to cite pride, guilt, or shame in success, failure, and transgression experiences—pride at a gymnastic feat or resisting temptation, or guilt for stealing a few coins out of a parent's wallet—until at least age 6 (Arsenio & Lover, 1995; Berti, Garattoni, & Venturini, 2000; Harter & Whitesell, 1989; Nunner-Winkler & Sodian, 1988). They are more likely to report simpler, noncomplex emotions.

In summary, young children acquire much emotion knowledge to assist them in social interactions with family and peers. However, it is equally clear that many of the finer nuances of emotion knowledge are either just emerging for them as they enter elementary school, or not yet within their repertoire at all.

What Are the Implications of Emotion Knowledge for Getting Along Socially and Academically?

Because personal experiences and social interactions or relationships are guided, even defined, by emotional transactions (Arsenio & Lemerise, 2001; Denham, 1998; Halberstadt et al., 2001; Saarni, 1999), understanding of emotions figures prominently in personal and social success. Specifically, succeeding at a crucial development task of the early childhood period, moving into the world of peers (Gottman & Mettetal, 1986; Parker & Gottman, 1989), calls for emotion knowledge. For example, if a preschooler sees one peer bickering with another, and correctly deduces that the peer suddenly experiences sadness or fear, rather than intensified anger, she may comfort her friend rather than retreat or enter the fray. The youngster who understands emotions of others also should interact more successfully when a friend gets angry with him or her, and can be more empathic with a peer gets hurt on the playground. Talk about one's own emotions can aid in negotiating disputes with friends. Darrell knows that it can be helpful to tell Jessica, "Hey, I was Blue® first. Don't be so mean and make me mad."

In these ways, emotion knowledge supports young children's attempts to deal with and communicate about the emotions experienced by themselves and others, and allows them to se-lectively attend to other aspects of social experiences (Denham, 1998). Accordingly, children who understand emotions are more prosocially responsive to their peers, and rated as more socially competent by teachers and peers alike (Denham, 1986; Denham & Couchoud, 1991; Denham et al., 1990; Roberts & Strayer, 1996; Smith, 2001; Strayer, 1980).

More specifically, dyad members' emotion situation knowl-edge and child-friend emotion conversation are involved in con-flict resolution, positive play, cooperative shared pretend, and successful communication (Brown, Donelan-McCall, & Dunn, 1996; Brown & Dunn, 1991; Dunn, Brown, & Maguire, 1995; Dunn & Cutting, 1999; Dunn & Herrera, 1997). Preschoolers' understanding of emotion expressions and situations are also related to use of reasoned argument with, and caregiving of, siblings (Dunn, Slomkowski, Donelan, & Herrera, 1995; Garner, Jones, & Miner, 1994). As well, preschoolers' spontaneous use of emotion language is related to higher quality peer interac-tions and greater peer acceptance (Fabes, Eisenberg, Hanish, & Spinrad, 2001; Garner & Estep, 2001). Furthermore, young chil-dren's understanding of emotion situations is *negatively* related to nonconstructive anger during peer play (Garner & Estep, 2001). Finally, understanding mixed emotions in kindergarten is associated with understanding friends, as well as expecting teachers to react benignly to one's mistakes (Cutting & Dunn, 2002; Dunn, Cutting, & Fisher, 2002).

More recent research with slightly older children (Dodge, Laird, Lochman, Zelli, & Conduct Problems Prevention Research Group, 2002; Mostow, Izard, Fine, & Trentacosta, 2002) has shown that emotion knowledge contributes to social problem solving and/or skilled social behavior, which then predicts later social competence, particularly sociometric status with peers. These new reports are exciting, in that they add longitudinal and school success elements to the current arguments, and show more about *how* emotion knowledge can augment chil-dren's performance with peers (i.e., via reasoning about social encounters and choice of positive social behaviors).

Lack of Emotion Knowledge and Unsuccessful Social Interaction

In contrast, preschoolers with identified aggression and op-positionality or peer problems have been found to show spe-cific deficits in understanding emotion expressions and sit-uations, both concurrently and predictively (Denham et al., 2003; Denham, Blair et al., 2002; Denham, Caverly et al., 2002; Hughes, Dunn, & White, 1998). Furthermore, low-income, pre-dominantly African-American, first graders' difficulties in un-derstanding emotional expressions also were related to their problems with peers and social withdrawal, even when preschool verbal ability and self control measures were already accounted (Izard et al., 2001; Schultz, Izard, Ackerman, & Youngstrom, 2001; Smith, 2001).[2]

Difficulties in 3-year-old emotion understanding also pre-dicted inability to attribute mixed feelings to victimizers in

kindergarten (Dunn, Brown et al., 1995). Children with such difficulties may have more trouble understanding that victim-izing another can yield both happiness (at one's power) and sadness (at the victim's distress).

Arsenio, Cooperman, and Lover (2000) have extended these general lines of inquiry. In their study, aggression mediated the association between lack of emotion expression and situation understanding and lower levels of peer acceptance; that is, de-velopmental delays in emotion knowledge predicted aggression, which was associated with peers' dislike. Emotion knowledge deficits' relation to aggressive behavior explained their relation to lower peer status. Although these results were contempo-raneous, the patterns of association suggest that lack of emo-tion knowledge is associated with impairment in behavioral responses to playmates, and that these impaired behavioral re-sponses are seen as unlikable by these same playmates.

Other research examines, in more detail, the implications of specific errors in emotion understanding made by young chil-dren, which may be pivotally related to risk for aggression prob-lems, such as the hostile attribution bias (Dodge & Somberg, 1987). For example, Barth and Bastiani (1997) uncovered a sub-tle relation that may underlie aggressive children's social diffi-culties: preschoolers' mistaken perceptions (overattributions) of peers' expressions as angry—a recognition bias similar to the hostile attribution bias of later years were associated with nega-tive social behavior. Errors in emotion understanding, especially such overattribution of anger, are also concurrently related to preschool aggression and peer rejection (Denham et al., 1990; Schultz, Izard, & Ackerman, 2000; Spence, 1987).

In sum, these patterns of results suggest that deficits in early childhood emotion knowledge are related to children's social and behavior problems preceding, and extending into, the pri-mary grades. Boosting such emotion knowledge, and doing so before school entry, thus increases in importance. In the future, ascertaining these early social cognitive difficulties could make it easier to intervene with children before their difficulties with aggression become entrenched.

Finally, the interrelationships of all aspects of emotional com-petence must again be underscored (Halberstadt et al., 2001). As Dodge (1989) notes, emotion knowledge undoubtedly plays an important role in children's expressive patterns and their abil-ity to regulate emotion; when a child knows, for example, that her playmate is delighted to have heaved the tricycle upright at last, she no longer is distressed herself, trying to figure out what to do with an angry friend. She can focus her attention on other aspects of the situation. Thus, because of the intricate in-terworkings of emotion knowledge, emotional expressiveness, and emotion regulation, it is no surprise that *both* deficits in emotion knowledge *and* underregulated expression of anger at age 3 to 4 predicted difficulties with teachers and peers 2 years later, in kindergarten (Denham, Caverly et al., 2002). More evi-dence is needed about the ways in which emotion knowledge and regulation work together during this age range, so that early childhood educators can refine social-emotional programming.

In terms of the contribution of emotion knowledge to school readiness and academic success, fewer research reports are

---

[2]It should be noted, however, that much still needs to be learned about the ways in which young children's language abilities work together with emotional and social competence to support or hinder early school success (Hyson, 2002).

available, but they are emerging. Recent studies have shown that emotion knowledge at the beginning of the Head Start year uniquely predicted, as did emotion regulation, year-end school adjustment (i.e., behavioral regulation, preacademic ability, compliance/participation, forming relationships, Shields et al., 2001). Furthermore, emotion knowledge during the preschool years contributes to the prediction of later academic competence even after controlling for the effects of verbal ability and emotional (Izard, 2002; Izard et al., 2001). In addition to the direct effects of emotion knowledge on academic outcomes, it also plays the role of mediator. In a longitudinal study of Head Start children, emotion knowledge in preschool mediated the effect of verbal ability on academic competence in third grade; that is, children with higher verbal ability in Head Start had greater emotion knowledge, which predicted third grade academic competence (Izard, 2002). More research in this area is sorely needed.

WHAT FUELS THE DEVELOPMENT OF EMOTIONAL COMPETENCE?

Both intrapersonal and interpersonal factors impact the developing competencies described here. First, intrapersonal contributors no doubt are important; abilities and attributes of the children themselves can either promote or hinder emotional competence. For example, some children are blessed with cognitive and language skills that allow them to better understand their social world, including the emotions within it, as well as to better communicate their own feelings, wishes, desires, and goals for social interactions and relationships (Cutting & Dunn, 1999). A preschooler who can reason more flexibly can probably also more readily perceive how another person might emotionally react to a situation in a different manner than he himself would; for example some people really are fearful of swimming pools, even though they delight *me*. In a similar manner, children with greater verbal abilities can ask more pointed questions about their own and others' emotions (e.g., "why is he crying?"), and understand the answers to these questions, giving them a special advantage in understanding and dealing with emotions. A preschooler with more advanced expressive language also can describe his/her own emotions more pointedly—"I don't *want* to go to bed! I am *mad*!"—which not only allows him/her to get their emotional point across but also allows for others to communicate with them.

Similarly, children with different emotional dispositions (i.e., different temperaments) are particularly well- or ill-equipped to demonstrate emotional competence. An especially emotionally negative child, for example, will probably find she has a greater need for emotion regulation, even though it is at the same time harder for her to do so. Such a double bind taxes her abilities "unhook" from an intense emotional experience (see, e.g., Eisenberg et al., 1993; Eisenberg et al., 1994; Eisenberg et al., 1997). Conversely, a child whose temperament predisposes him to flexibly focus attention on a comforting action, object, or thought, and shift attention from a distressing situation, is better able to regulate emotions, even intense ones.

SOCIALIZATION OF EMOTIONAL COMPETENCE

So, children come to their preschool years with particular intrapersonal factors well in place. These intrapersonal factors are either foundations of or roadblocks to emotional and social competence. Caring adults are faced with such children on a daily basis. What differences do our efforts make? How do we foster these emotional and social competencies that stand children in such good stead as they move into their school years?

Much of the individual variation in the components of children's emotional competence derives from experiences within the family and preschool classroom (Denham, 1998; Hyson, 1994). Important adults—and children—in each child's life have crucial roles in the development of emotional competence.

Socialization of emotions is ubiquitous in children's everyday contact with parents, teachers, caregivers, and peers. All the people with whom children interact exhibit a variety of emotions, which the children observe. Furthermore, children's emotions often require some kind of reaction from their social partners, and intentionally teaching about the world of emotions is considered by some adults to be an important area of teaching (Dix, 1991; Eisenberg & Fabes, 1994; Eisenberg, Fabes, & Murphy, 1996; Eisenberg et al., 1994; Eisenberg et al., 1999; Gottman, Katz, & Hooven, 1997). These three mechanisms describe socialization of emotion: modeling emotional expressiveness, reactions to children's emotions, and teaching about emotion (Denham, 1998; Denham, Grant, & Hamada, 2002; Eisenberg, Cumberland, & Spinrad, 1998; Halberstadt, 1991; Tomkins, 1991). Each of these mechanisms can influence children's emotional expression, understanding, and regulation, as well as social functioning.

Most of the extant research on the socialization of emotional and social competence involves young children and their parents. Of course, parents are not the only socializers of emotional competence. Others, including preschool teachers and day care caregivers, as well as siblings and peers, are important from the preschool years on. In the following, results regarding young children's interactions with their parents are most often reported, because by far the most research exists on these socializers. However, it is likely that many of the influences identified likely hold true for other adults in preschoolers' lives, as well. Where there is specific information on teachers, siblings, and peers, it is highlighted.

Modeling of Emotional Expressiveness

Children observe the ever-present emotions of adults, and incorporate this learning into their expressive behavior, often via affective contagion. They also vicariously learn *how* to exhibit emotional expressions, and *which* to express *when* and in what context (e.g., Denham, 1989; Denham & Grout, 1993; Denham, Mitchell-Copeland, Strandberg, Auerbach, & Blair, 1997).

Parents' emotional displays also foster their children's emotion knowledge, by telling children about the emotional significance of differing events, which behaviors accompany differing emotions, and others' likely reactions. By modeling various emotions, moderately expressive parents give children information about the nature of happiness, sadness, anger, and fear—their expression, likely eliciting situations, and more personalized causes. Thus, adults' emotional expressiveness is associated with children's understanding of emotions as well as their expressive patterns (Denham & Couchoud, 1990; Denham & Grout, 1993; Denham et al., 1997; Denham, Zoller, & Couchoud, 1994; Liew et al., 2003).

A mostly positive emotional climate makes emotions more accessible to children, in terms of their own emotion regulation, emotion knowledge, and concomitant positive social behavior. Thus, when children have experience with clear but not overpowering parental emotions, they also may have more experience with empathic involvement with others' emotions (Denham & Grout, 1992, 1993; Denham et al., 1991; Denham, Renwick-DeBardi, & Hewes, 1994; Denham, Zoller et al., 1994; Gottman & Mettetal, 1986; Liew et al., 2003; Parke, Cassidy, Burks, Carson, & Boyum, 1992). Both middle- and low-income preschoolers' emotion regulation is facilitated by their mothers' appropriate expressiveness (Garner et al., 1994). Conversely, children whose mothers self-report more frequent anger and tension also are less prosocial, and less well liked than children of more positive mothers (Eisenberg et al., 2001; Eisenberg et al., 2003; Garner & Spears, 2000). Emotionally negative preschool classroom environments are also related to aggressive, disruptive peer behavior in second grade, especially for boys (Howes, 2000).

Hence, clear and mostly positive emotional environments are associated with positive outcomes in young children's emotional expressiveness, emotion knowledge, emotion regulation, and positive social behavior. Much less research has clearly targeted the expressive modeling of teachers, however, despite the existence of observational ratings that can be used to capture the emotional environment in early childhood classrooms (Arnett, 1989; Harms & Clifford, 1980). Denham, Grant, and Hamada (2002) have, however, found evidence that the socialization of emotion of both preschool teachers and mothers is important for the development of children's emotion regulation; maternal expressiveness and teachers' attitudes about teaching young children about emotion, the last component of emotion socialization, were the most important predictors of emotion regulation.

Conversely, parental expressiveness can make it more difficult for young children to address issues of emotion altogether. In particular, exposure to negative emotions expressed by adults in their lives can be problematic for young children. Although exposure to *well-modulated* negative emotion can be positively related to understanding of emotion, parents' frequent and intense negative emotions may disturb children, as well as discourage self-reflection, so that little is learned about emotions, other than how to express negativity (Denham, 1998). It is easy to imagine the confusion and pain of children relentlessly exposed to parents' negative emotions; in the aftermath of such confusion and pain, children whose mothers self-report more frequent anger and tension also are more angry themselves, less prosocial, and less well liked than children of more positive mothers. As well, the trajectory from age 2 aggressiveness to age 4 externalizing problems is clearest for toddlers who experience high levels of maternal negative expressiveness (Rubin et al., 2003); thus, it may be that exposure to higher levels of parental

negativity overarouses the young child who cannot yet regulate emotions well, and represents a hostile-aggressive template for children to follow in their reactions to people and events. At the same time, parents whose expressiveness is quite limited impart little information about emotions.

In sum, with regard to modeling, exposure to parents' and others' broad but not overly negative emotions helps children learn about emotions and come to express similar profiles. In particular, whether in families or classrooms, adult negative emotion is deleterious to young children's emotion knowledge, profiles of expressiveness, emotion regulation, and social competence.

Contingent Reactions to Children's Emotions

Adults' contingent reactions to children's behaviors and emotional displays are also linked to young children's emotional competence. Contingent reactions include behavioral and emotional encouragement or discouragement of specific behaviors and emotions (Tomkins, 1991). More specifically, adults may punish children's experiences and expressions of emotions, or show a dismissive attitude toward the world of emotions, by ignoring the child's emotions in a well-meant effort to "make it better" (Denham, Renwick-DeBardi, & Hewes, 1994; Denham, Zoller, & Couchoud, 1994). In emotion-evoking contexts, children who experience such adult reactions have more to be upset about—not only their emotion's elicitor but also adults' reactions (Eisenberg et al., 1998, 1999).

Positive reactions, such as tolerance or comfort, convey a very different message: that emotions are manageable, even useful (Gottman et al., 1997). Parents who are good "emotion coaches," at least in the United States, accept children's experiences of emotion and their expression of emotions that do not harm others; they empathize with and validate emotions. Emotional moments are seen as opportunities for intimacy (Denham & Kochanoff, 2003; Eisenberg & Fabes, 1994; Eisenberg, Fabes, & Murphy, 1996). As children develop their own effective emotion regulatory abilities, parents decrease the frequency, intensity, and nature of their reactions, in part because they are transferring responsibility for regulation from caregiver to child (Grolnick, Kurowski, McMenamy, Rivkin, & Bridges, 1998).

Little or no research has been conducted on how peers socialize each others' emotions. However, Sorber (2001) did examine how kindergarten and third graders indicated that they would react to specific peer emotions via a computer story game. Happy characters were given the most approval, with angry characters given the least approval; acceptance of the various emotions (i.e., happy, sad, angry, and scared) was not based on gender stereotypes.

Thus, there is much more research on the ways in which parents respond to young children's emotions, as compared to the reactions of teachers, siblings, and agemates. The clearest take-home message is that adults' and older siblings' optimal emotional and behavioral responses to children's emotions are associated with young children's own emotional expressiveness, emotion knowledge, and empathic reactions to peers' and others' emotions (Denham & Kochanoff, 2003; Fabes, Leonard,

Kupanoff, & Martin, 2001; Fabes, Poulin, Eisenberg, & Madden-Derdich, 2003; Strandberg-Sawyer et al., 2003; Zahn-Waxler, Radke-Yarrow, & King, 1979). For example, when mothers show benevolent patterns of reactions to children's negative emotions, children show less egoistic distress and more sympathetic concern to the distress of others. They have warm, empathic, nurturant guides to follow in responding to others' distress (Denham, 1993; Denham & Grout, 1993). However, much more research is needed in this area, especially to elucidate the central prediction of links between parental reactions to children's emotions and children's patterns of emotional expressiveness, and of socializers other than parents.

Teaching About Emotions

This last aspect of emotion socialization is the most direct. What parents and other adults say, or intentionally attempt to convey through other means, may impact their children's emotion knowledge. In its simplest form, coaching consists of verbally explaining an emotion and its relation to an observed event or expression. It also may include directing the child's attention to salient emotional cues, helping children understand and manage their own responses, and segmenting social interactions into manageable emotional components (Denham & Auerbach, 1995).

Teachers' and parents' tendencies to discuss emotions, if nested within a warm relationship, assist the child in acquiring emotional competence. The central aspect of this teaching is providing reasons for emotional events in the child's life, including correction of their mistaken behaviors. Such strategies coach children to perceive the social consequences of their digressions (e.g., "Johnny will be mad at you and not want to play with you again, if you keep taking away his toys") and to empathize or consider another's viewpoint (e.g., "That hurt Toby's feelings—look, he feels sad").

Adults who are aware of emotions, especially negative ones, and talk about them in a differentiated manner (e.g., clarifying, explaining, pointing out the child's responsibility for others' feelings when necessary, but not "preaching") assist their children in expressing experiencing, identifying, and regulating their own emotions (Gottman, Katz, & Hooven, 1997). Again, dismissing adults may want to be helpful, but refrain from talking too much about children's emotions. Alternatively, poor coaches may actively punish children for showing or querying about emotions.

Accordingly, conversations about feelings are an important context for coaching children about emotions and how to express and regulate them (Bretherton et al., 1986; Brown & Dunn, 1992). Discussing emotions provides children with reflective distance from feeling states themselves, and space in which to interpret and evaluate their feelings and to reflect upon causes and consequences (Denham, Cook, & Zoller, 1992; Denham & Grout, 1992; Eisenberg et al., 1998; Gottman et al., 1997; Zahn-Waxler et al., 1979). Verbal give-and-take about emotional experience within the scaffolded context of chatting with a parent or teacher helps the young child to formulate a coherent body of knowledge about emotional expressions, situations, and causes (Denham, Zoller et al., 1994; Dunn, Brown, & Beardsall, 1991; Dunn, Slomkowski et al., 1995). There is evidence that such associations between mothers' emotion language and preschoolers' emotion knowledge are often independent of the child's linguistic ability.

Children of such emotion-coaching parents and teachers gradually formulate a coherent body of knowledge about emotions (Denham, Renwick-DeBardi, & Hewas, 1994; Dunn, Brown, Slomkowski, Tesla, & Youngblade, 1991). When parents discuss and explain their own and others' emotions, their children are more capable of empathic involvement with peers (Denham & Grout, 1992; Denham, Renwick-DeBardi, & Hewas, 1994; Denham, Zoller, & Couchoud, 1994). The general trend of these findings also hold true for low-income, minority mothers and their children (Garner, Jones, Gaddy, & Rennie, 1997).

In one study of children in child care transitions (Dunn, 1994), preschoolers remembered both sadness and fear during these times, as well as the support given them by teachers and friends, to help them feel better. So it is clear that young children absorb not only the content, but also the form and quality, of nonparental adults' emotion coaching; how can this content, form, and quality be characterized? Two recent investigations (Ahn, 2003; Reimer, 1996) revealed that teachers of toddlers and preschoolers also socialize children's emotions differently based age, tailoring their reactions to children's emotions, and their teaching about emotions, to the developmental level of the children. In Ahn's study, toddler teachers used physical comfort and distraction in response to children's negative emotions more often than did preschool teachers, who relied more on verbal explanations. Preschool teachers helped children infer the causes of their negative emotions, and taught them constructive ways of expressing negative emotion more frequently than did toddler teachers. Teachers of older children were also less likely to match the positive or encourage positive emotion, and more likely to discourage such displays. Finally, this study demonstrated that teachers did not validate children's negative emotion very often—one of the major tenets of emotion coaching.

Reimer (1996) also found that teachers respond to about half of preschool children's emotions, most often in service of socializing emotion regulation; verbal references to children's emotions constituted about one half of their responses. These teacher verbalizations referred to causes and consequences of the child's emotion, which emotions were appropriate, and how to express emotions under various circumstances. Overall, these recent studies suggest that, to promote emotional competence, teacher/caregiver training should focus on validating children's emotions, while at the same time creating and sustaining adult-child emotion conversations.

Summary: How Adults Socialize Emotional Competence

In sum, there is a growing body of knowledge regarding the contributions of adults to young children's emotional and social competence. These elements will be useful in building adult roles in any successful social-emotional programming for young children. Although cultural values and variations crucially require our attention because we must honor the unique perspectives of both adults and children, several principles seem to hold true across groups. A generally positive picture emerges of "emotion coaching." Its elements will be useful not only in parenting but also in building any successful social-emotional programming for young children. In terms of promoting emotional and social competence, teacher/caregiver training should include a focus on ways to assist early childhood educators in becoming good emotion coaches.

APPLICATION TO THE EARLY CHILDHOOD CLASSROOM

The material covered in this chapter shows that *emotions matter* (Raver, 2002)—there is a clear association between emotional and social competence, and between emotional competence and school success. The development of emotional competence improves children's abilities to cope with stressful situations, leads to improved brain development, and plays an integral role in learning through its role in focusing attention and persistence (Blair, 2002). At the same time, the development of social competence enables children to form positive relationships and refrain from problem behavior. These competencies are inextricably intertwined, forming an important foundation for academic success: Social competence and executive control are strongly influenced by a child's emotional competence (especially emotion regulation); in turn, each plays a powerful role in adjustment and success in school (Hawkins, Smith, & Catalano, 2004).

For all children, especially those at greatest risk—because of poverty, community violence, family stress and discord, un- or underemployment, maltreatment, pace of life, and family life changes, including those consonant with new welfare-to-work policies—the learning of emotional and social competence should not be left to chance (Peth-Pierce, 2000; Pianta & Nimetz, 1992). As detailed in this chapter, young children with deficits in emotional and social competence may learn to act in increasingly antisocial ways, and become less accepted by both peers and teachers. They participate less, and do worse in school, and are considered hard to teach, provided with less instruction and positive feedback, even in preschool. Even the cognitive competencies of those whose behavior is perceived as negative are less likely to be recognized than those of their more socially skilled agemates. As a final snub, peers don't want to work with such children—gradually, the emotionally and socially *in*competent children come to avoid school altogether (Raver & Knitzer, 2002).

Preschool and kindergarten teachers, as well as day care providers, concur with these views, reporting that difficult behavior resulting from emotional and social competence deficits is their single greatest challenge (Arnold, McWilliams, & Arnold, 1998; Rimm-Kaufman, Pianta, & Cox, 2000). There has, in fact,

been a call for primary and secondary prevention programs targeted at preschoolers' emotional and social competence needs (Knitzer, 1993), to ensure their smooth transition to kindergarten and early school success, so they not fall behind from the start. Attention to these areas during early childhood, as crucial for later well-being, mental health, and even learning and academic success, has blossomed in recent years (Huffman, Mehlinger, & Kerivan, 2000; Peth-Pierce, 2000; Raver & Knitzer, 2002). More and more evidence-based prevention and intervention programming is being tested and promoted in early childhood education (Denham & Burton, 1996, 2003; Domitrovich, Cortes, & Greenberg, 2002; Frey, Hirschstein, & Guzzo, 2000; Izard, 2002; Izard & Bear, 2001; Webster-Stratton & Taylor, 2001). A detailed review of such programming and extant early childhood assessment tools for emotional and social competence can be found in Denham and Burton (2003; see also Joseph & Strain, 2003).

However, although early childhood educators may recognize the need to bolster students' social-emotional development, their concern has historically often been implicit, rather than made explicit through specific interventions (Denham, Lydick, Mitchell-Copeland, & Sawyer, 1996). At the same time, the public is demanding ever-greater accountability for students' academic achievement, with increasing emphasis on test scores and related standards. Early childhood educators often experience so much pressure to meet various standards that they do not have the time or energy to devote to anything else. In addition, many educators are uncertain about how to address SEL issues most effectively (Zins, Weissberg, Wang, & Walberg, 2004). Thus, because of the crucial nature of early childhood social and emotional competence, and the considerable risk associated with their absence, early childhood educators need support so that they may give more widespread attention to promoting emotional and social competence in early childhood programming. Two specific sources of support already exist: (1) the early childhood special education interventions literature (e.g., McEvoy & Yoder, 1993, although much material in this area refers to solely social, rather than emotional, competence); and (2) the Head Start Center for Social-Emotional Foundations to Early Learning (http://www.csefel.uiuc.edu), which has a variety of information on teaching social-emotional skills.

There also are clearly identified means for early childhood educators to promote emotional competence (Hyson, 2002), which fit well with the material conveyed in this chapter:

- modeling genuine, appropriate emotional responses
- helping children to understand emotions of themselves and others
- supporting children's regulation of emotions
- recognizing and honoring children's expressive styles while promoting appropriate expressiveness
- giving children many opportunities to experience the joys and to overcome the frustrations of new learning opportunities[3]

---

[3]Hyson calls this task "uniting children's learning with positive emotions" (p. 77)—such experiences help children become able to tackle hard work, persist at tasks, and seek out challenges.

Teachers seem to quickly recognize the emotional competence needs of children in their care, when they are brought to their attention. Although some early childhood educators retain their original notions that emotions are not the province of their work (Hyson & Lee, 1996), for many it is like turning on a faucet of understanding. The appropriate handling of emotions in the classroom becomes one of great concern to them when emotional competence is highlighted for them, commensurate with their concerns about children's behavior.

As noted by Hyson and Molinaro (2001), early childhood teachers and caregivers, in general, believe that children need physical affection and emotional closeness from teachers, that they learn about emotions from seeing how adults behave, and that children learn from adults how to express feelings acceptably. However, early childhood educators do vary in their beliefs about their role in the development young children's emotional competence—on whether it is their role to teach about emotions at all, the importance of modeling emotional expressiveness and talking about children's feelings, and whether such young children learn about controlling emotions. These differences in beliefs are often associated with teacher training, culture, teachers' own relationship styles. Thus, it seems clear, along with the other research needs already mentioned in this chapter, that more research is needed on the following:

- how teachers' beliefs about emotions change across time, and why
- how classroom practices vary with teachers' emotion-related beliefs
- what kind of preservice and inservice experiences help teachers to cultivate positive attitudes toward emotion coaching, as

well as provide them with the evidence-based tools to foster children's social and emotional development

As well, there are several higher-order needs that early childhood educators and applied developmental psychologists may help to meet (Hyson, 2002):

- to increase policy makers' awareness of research linking emotional competence and later social and academic success
- to advocate for resources for emotional competence and social competence-focused assessment and programming
- to see that early childhood standards, curricula, and assessment tools incorporate developmentally appropriate attention to emotional competence
- to evaluate extant emotional competence programming for (a) treatment fidelity, (b) treatment generalization, (c) treatment maintenance, (d) social validity of outcomes, (e) acceptability of interventions, (f) replication across investigators, (g) replication across clinical groups, (h) evidence across ethnic/racially diverse groups, and (i) evidence for replication across settings (Joseph & Strain, 2003). Moving toward evidence-based programming helps to ensure that our efforts in this area will be efficacious

Working together, we can make sure that Darrell continues from his early excellent footing in emotional and social competence, to successfully meet the challenges of learning to read, write, calculate, problem solve, and sustain more complex relationships with others. We can help Jimmy, Tomas, and even Jessica to find better ways to interact so that their well-regulated behaviors support their social, emotional, and academic pursuits throughout their lives.

References

Ahn, H. J. (2003). *Teacher's role in the socialization of emotion in three child care centers*. Paper presented at the Society for Research in Child Development, Tampa, FL.

Arnett, J. (1989). Issues and obstacles in the training of caregivers. In J. S. Lande, S. A. Scarr & N. Gunzenhauser (Eds.), *Caring for children* (pp. 241–255). Hillsdale, NJ: Lawrence Erlbaum.

Arnold, D. H., McWilliams, L., & Arnold, E. H. (1998). Teacher discipline and child misbehavior in day care: Untangling causality with correlational data. *Developmental Psychology, 34*, 276–287.

Arsenio, W., Cooperman, S., & Lover, A. (2000). Affective predictors of preschoolers' aggression and peer acceptance; Direct and indirect effects. *Developmental Psychology, 36*, 438–448.

Arsenio, W., & Lemerise, E. A. (2001). Varieties of childhood bullying: Values, emotion processes and social competence. *Social Development, 10*, 57–74.

Arsenio, W., & Lover, A. (1995). Children's conceptions of sociomoral affect: Happy victimizers, mixed emotions and other expectancies. In M. K. D. Hart (Ed.), *Morality in everyday life Developmental perspectives* (pp. 87–128). Cambridge: Cambridge University Press.

Banerjee, M. (1997). Hidden emotions: Preschoolers' knowledge of appearance-reality and emotion display rules. *Social Development, 15*, 107–132.

Barth, J. M., & Bastiani, A. (1997). A longitudinal study of emotional recognition and preschool children's social behavior. *Merrill-Palmer Quarterly, 43*, 107–128.

Berti, A. E., Garattoni, C., & Venturini, B. A. (2000). The understanding of sadness, guilt, and shame in 5-, 7-, and 9-year-old children. *Genetic, Social, and General Psychology Monographs, 126*, 293–318.

Birch, S. H., Ladd, G. W., & Blecher-Sass, H. (1997). The teacher-child relationship and children's early school adjustment: Good-byes can build trust. *Journal of School Psychology, 35*, 61–79.

Blair, C. (2002). School Readiness: Integrating Cognition and Emotion in a Neurobiological Conceptualization of Children's Functioning at School Entry. *American Psychologist, 57*, 111–127.

Bretherton, I, Fritz, J, Zahn-Waxler, C, et al. (1986). Learning to talk about emotions: A functionalist perspective. *Child Development, 56*, 529–548.

Brody, L. R., & Harrison, R. H. (1987). Developmental changes in children's abilities to match and label emotionally laden situations. *Motivation and Emotion, 11*, 347–365.

Brown, J. R., Donelan-McCall, N., & Dunn, J. (1996). Why talk about mental states? The significance of children's conversations with friends, siblings, and mothers. *Child Development, 67*, 836–849.

Brown, J. R., & Dunn, J. (1991). "You can cry, mum": The social and developmental implications of talk about internal states. *British Journal of Developmental Psychology, 9*, 237-256.

Brown, J. R., & Dunn, J. (1992). Talk with your mother or your sibling? Developmental changes in early family conversations about feelings. *Child Development, 63*, 336-349.

Bullock, M., & Russell, J. A. (1984). Preschool children's interpretations of facial expressions of emotion. *International Journal of Behavioral Development, 7*, 193-214.

Bullock, M., & Russell, J. A. (1985). Further evidence on preschoolers' interpretation of facial expressions. *International Journal of Behavioral Development, 8*, 15-38.

Campos, J. J., & Barrett, K. C. (1984). Toward a new understanding of emotions and their development. In C. E. Izard, J. Kagan & R. B. Zajonc (Eds.), *Emotions, cognition, & behavior* (pp. 229-263). New York: Cambridge University Press.

Campos, J. J., Mumme, D. L., Kermoian, R., & Campos, R. G. (1994). A functionalist perspective on the nature of emotion. *Monographs of the Society for Research in Child Development, 59*(2-3), 284-303.

Camras, L. A., & Allison, K. A. (1985). Children's understanding of emotional facial expressions and verbal labels. *Journal of Nonverbal Behavior, 9*, 84-94.

Carlton, M. P. (2000). Motivation and school readiness in kindergarten children. *Dissertation Abstracts International Section A Human and Social Sciences, 60*(11-A), 3899.

Carlton, M. P., & Winsler, A. (1999). School readiness: The need for a paradigm shift. *School Psychology Review, 28*, 338-352.

Cole, P. M., Martin, S. E., & Dennis, T. A. (2004). Emotion regulation as a scientific construct: methodological challenges and directions for child development research. *Child Development, 75*, 317-333.

Contreras, J. M., Kerns, K., Weimer, B. L., Gentzler, A. L., & Tomich, P. L. (2000). Emotion regulation as a mediator of associations between mother-child attachment and peer relationships in middle childhood. *Journal of Family Psychology, 14*, 111-124.

Cutting, A. L., & Dunn, J. (1999). Theory of mind, emotion understanding, language, and family background: Individual differences and interrelations. *Child Development, 70*, 853-865.

Cutting, A. L., & Dunn, J. (2002). The cost of understanding other people: Social cognition predicts young children's sensitivity to criticism. *Journal of Child Psychiatry and Psychology and Allied Disciplines*, 849-860.

Denham, S. A. (1986). Social cognition, social behavior, and emotion in preschoolers: Contextual validation. *Child Development, 57*, 194-201.

Denham, S. A. (1989). Maternal affect and toddlers' social-emotional competence. *American Journal of Orthopsychiatry, 59*, 368-376.

Denham, S. A. (1993). Maternal emotional responsiveness and toddlers' social-emotional functioning. *Journal of Child Psychology and Psychiatry, 34*, 715-728.

Denham, S. A. (1997). "When I have a bad dream, Mommy holds me": Preschoolers' consequential thinking about emotions and social competence. *International Journal of Behavioral Development, 20*, 301-319.

Denham, S. A. (1998). *Emotional development in young children.* New York: Guilford.

Denham, S. A., & Auerbach, S. (1995). Mother-child dialogue about emotions. *Genetic, Social, and General Psychology Monographs, 121*, 311-338.

Denham, S. A., Blair, K. A., DeMulder, E., Levitas, J., Sawyer, K. S., Auerbach-Major, S. T., & Queenan, P. (2003). Preschoolers' emotional competence: Pathway to mental health? *Child Development, 74*, 238-256.

Denham, S. A., Blair, K. A., Schmidt, M. S., & DeMulder, E. (2002). Compromised emotional competence: Seeds of violence sown early? *American Journal of Orthopsychiatry, 72*, 70-82.

Denham, S. A., & Burton, R. (1996). A social-emotional intervention for at-risk 4-year-olds. *Journal of School Psychology, 34*, 225-245.

Denham, S. A., & Burton, R. (2003). *Social and emotional prevention and intervention programming for preschoolers.* New York: Kluwer-Plenum.

Denham, S. A., Caverly, S., Schmidt, M., Blair, K., DeMulder, E., Caal, S., Hamada, H., & Mason, T. (2002). Preschool understanding of emotions: Contributions to classroom anger and aggression. *Journal of Child Psychology and Psychiatry, 43*, 901-916.

Denham, S. A., Cook, M. C., & Zoller, D. (1992). Baby looks very sad: Discussions about emotions between mother and preschooler. *British Journal of Developmental Psychology, 10*, 301-315.

Denham, S. A., & Couchoud, E. A. (1990). Young preschoolers' understanding of emotion. *Child Study Journal, 20*, 171-192.

Denham, S. A., & Couchoud, E. A. (1991). Social-emotional predictors of preschoolers' responses to an adult's negative emotions. *Journal of Child Psychology and Psychiatry, 32*, 595-608.

Denham, S. A., Grant, S., & Hamada, H. A. (2002, June). *"I have two 1st teachers": Mother and teacher socialization of preschoolers' emotional and social competence.* Paper presented at the Paper in symposium submitted to 7th Head Start Research Conference, Washington, DC.

Denham, S. A., & Grout, L. (1992). Mothers' emotional expressiveness and coping: Topography and relations with preschoolers' social-emotional competence. *Genetic, Social, and General Psychology Monographs, 118*, 75-101.

Denham, S. A., & Grout, L. (1993). Socialization of emotion: Pathway to preschoolers' affect regulation. *Journal of Nonverbal Behavior, 17*, 215-227.

Denham, S. A., & Holt, R. W. (1993). Preschoolers' likability as cause or consequence of their social behavior. *Developmental Psychology, 29*, 271-275.

Denham, S. A., & Kochanoff, A. T. (2003). Parental contributions to preschoolers' understanding of emotion. *Marriage & Family Review, 34*(3/4), 311-345.

Denham, S. A., Lydick, S., Mitchell-Copeland, J., & Sawyer, K. (1996). Social-emotional assessment for atypical infants and preschoolers. In M. Lewis & M. E. Sullivan (Eds.), *Emotional development in atypical children* (pp. 227-271). Hillsdale, NJ: Erlbaum.

Denham, S. A., Mason, T., Caverly, S., Schmidt, M., Hackney, R., Caswell, C., & DeMulder, E. (2001). Preschoolers at play: Co-socializers of emotional and social competence. *International Journal of Behavioral Development, 25*, 290-301.

Denham, S. A., McKinley, M., Couchoud, E. A., & Holt, R. (1990). Emotional and behavioral predictors of peer status in young preschoolers. *Child Development, 61*, 1145-1152.

Denham, S. A., Mitchell-Copeland, J., Strandberg, K., Auerbach, S., & Blair, K. (1997). Parental contributions to preschoolers' emotional competence: Direct and indirect effects. *Motivation and Emotion, 27*, 65-86.

Denham, S. A., Renwick, S., & Holt, R. (1991). Working and playing together: Prediction of preschool social-emotional competence from mother-child interaction. *Child Development, 62*, 242-249.

Denham, S. A., Renwick-DeBardi, S., & Hewes, S. (1994). Affective communication between mothers and preschoolers: Relations with social-emotional competence. *Merrill-Palmer Quarterly, 40*, 488-508.

Denham, S. A., & Zoller, D. (1991). "When my hamster died, I cried": Preschoolers' attributions of the causes of emotions. *Journal of Genetic Psychology, 152*, 371-373.

Denham, S. A., Zoller, D., & Couchoud, E. A. (1994). Socialization of preschoolers' understanding of emotion. *Developmental Psychology, 30,* 928-936.

Dix, T. (1991). The affective organization of parenting: Adaptive and maladaptative processes. *Psychological Bulletin, 110,* 3-25.

Dodge, K. A., Laird, R., Lochman, J. E., Zelli, A., & Conduct Problems Prevention Research Group. (2002). Multidimensional latent-construct analysis of children's social information processing patters: Correlations with aggressive behavior problems. *Psychological Assessment, 14,* 60-73.

Dodge, K. A., Pettit, G., McClaskey, C. L., & Brown, M. M. (1986). Social competence in children. *Monographs of the Society for Research in Child Development, 51* (b), 1-85.

Dodge, K. A., & Somberg, D. R. (1987). Hostile attribution biases among aggressive boys are exacerbated among conditions of threat to the self. *Child Development, 58,* 213-224.

Domitrovich, C. E., Cortes, R., & Greenberg, M. (2002, 2002, June). *Preschool PATHS: Promoting social and emotional competence in young children.* Paper presented at the 6th National Head Start Research Conference, Washington, DC.

Donaldson, S. K., & Westerman, M. A. (1986). Development of children's understanding of ambivalence and causal theories of emotions. *Developmental Psychology, 22,* 655-662.

Dunn, J. (1994). Understanding others and the social world: Current issues in developmental research and their relation to preschool experiences and practice. *Journal of Applied Developmental Psychology, 15,* 571-583.

Dunn, J., Brown, J. R., & Beardsall, L. A. (1991). Family talk about emotions, and children's later understanding of others' emotions. *Developmental Psychology, 27,* 448-455.

Dunn, J., Brown, J. R., & Maguire, M. (1995). The development of children's moral sensibility: Individual differences and emotion understanding. *Developmental Psychology, 31,* 649-659.

Dunn, J., Brown, J. R., Slomkowski, C., Tesla, C., & Youngblade, L. (1991). Young children's understanding of other people's feelings and beliefs: Individual differences and their antecedents. *Child Development, 62,* 1352-1366.

Dunn, J., & Cutting, A. L. (1999). Understanding others, and individual differences in friendship interactions in young children. *Social Development, 8,* 201-219.

Dunn, J., Cutting, A. L., & Fisher, N. (2002). Old friends, new friends: Predictors of children's perspective on their friends at school. *Child Development, 73*(2), 621-635.

Dunn, J., & Herrera, C. (1997). Conflict resolution with friends, siblings, and mothers: A developmental perspective. *Aggressive Behavior, 23,* 343-357.

Dunn, J., & Hughes, C. (1998). Young children's understanding of emotions within close relationships. *Cognition & Emotion, 12,* 171-190.

Dunn, J., Slomkowski, C., Donelan, N., & Herrera, C. (1995). Conflict, understanding, and relationships: Developments and differences in the preschool years. *Early Education and Development, 6,* 303-316.

Eisenberg, N., Cumberland, A., & Spinrad, T. L. (1998). Parental socialization of emotion. *Psychological Inquiry, 9,* 241-273.

Eisenberg, N., & Fabes, R. A. (1994). Mothers' reactions to children's negative emotions: Relations to children's temperament and anger behavior. *Merrill-Palmer Quarterly, 40,* 138-156.

Eisenberg, N., Fabes, R. A., Bernzweig, J., Karbon, M., Poulin, R., & Hanish, L. (1993). The relations of emotionality and regulation to preschoolers' social skills and sociometric status. *Child Development, 64,* 1418-1438.

Eisenberg, N., Fabes, R. A., Guthrie, I. K., Murphy, B. C., Maszk, P., Holmgren, R., et al. (1996). The relations of regulation and emotionality to problem behavior in elementary school children. *Development & Psychopathology, 8,* 141-162.

Eisenberg, N., Fabes, R. A., Murphy, B., Maszk, P., Smith, M., & Karbon, M. (1995). The role of emotionality and regulation in children's social functioning: A longitudinal study. *Child Development, 66,* 1360-1384.

Eisenberg, N., Fabes, R. A., & Murphy, B. C. (1996). Parents' reactions to children's negative emotions: Relations to children's social competence and comforting behavior. *Child Development, 67*(5), 2227-2247.

Eisenberg, N., Fabes, R. A., Nyman, M., Bernzweig, J., & Pinuelas, A. (1994). The relation of emotionality and regulation to preschoolers' anger-related reactions. *Child Development, 65,* 1352-1366.

Eisenberg, N., Fabes, R. A., Shepard, S. A., Guthrie, I., Murphy, B. C., & Reiser, M. (1999). Parental reactions to children's negative emotions: Longitudinal relations to quality of children's social functioning. *Child Development, 70,* 513-534.

Eisenberg, N., Fabes, R. A., Shepard, S. A., Murphy, B. C., Guthrie, I. K., Jones, S., Friedman, J., Poulin, R., & Maszk, P. (1997). Contemporaneous and longitudinal prediction of children's social functioning from regulation and emotionality. *Child Development, 68,* 642-664.

Eisenberg, N., Gershoff, E. T., Fabes, R. A., Shepard, S. A., Cumberland, A., Losoya, S., Guthrie, I. K., & Murphy, B. C. (2001). Mothers' emotional expressivity and children's behavior problems and social competence: Mediation through children's regulation. *Developmental Psychology, 37,* 475-490.

Eisenberg, N., Valiente, C., Morris, A. S., Fabes, R. A., Cumberland, A., Reiser, M., Gershoff, E. T., Shepard, S. A., & Losoya, S. (2003). Longitudinal relations among parental emotional expressivity, children's regulation, and quality of socioemotional function. *Developmental Psychology, 39*(1), 3-19.

Elkind, D. (1982). The hurried child. *Instructor, 91*(5), 40-43.

Fabes, R. A., Eisenberg, N., Hanish, L. D., & Spinrad, T. L. (2001). Preschoolers' spontaneous emotion vocabulary: Relations to likeability. *Early Education and Development, 12*(1), 11-28.

Fabes, R. A., Eisenberg, N., McCormick, S. E., & Wilson, M. S. (1988). Preschoolers' attributions of the situational determinants of others' naturally occurring emotions. *Developmental Psychology, 24,* 376-385.

Fabes, R. A., Eisenberg, N., Nyman, M., & Michealieu, Q. (1991). Young children's appraisal of others spontaneous emotional reactions. *Developmental Psychology, 27,* 858-866.

Fabes, R. A., Leonard, S. A., Kupanoff, K., & Martin, C. L. (2001). Parental coping with children's negative emotions: Relations with children's emotional and social responding. *Child Development, 72*(3), 907-920.

Fabes, R. A., Poulin, R. E., Eisenberg, N., & Madden-Derdich, D. A. (2003). The Coping with Children's Negative Emotions Scale (CC-NES): Psychometric properties and relations with children's emotional competence. *Marriage & Family Review, 34*(3/4), 285-310.

Feito, J. A. (1997). Children's beliefs about the social consequences of emotional expression. *Dissertation Abstracts International, 59*(03B), 1411.

Frey, K. S., Hirschstein, M. K., & Guzzo, B. A. (2000). Second Step: Preventing aggression by promoting social competence. *Journal of Emotional and Behavioral Disorders, 8,* 102-112.

Gagnon, C., Craig, W. M., Tremblay, R. E., Zhou, R. M., & Vitaro, F. A. (1995). Kindergarten predictors of boys' stable behavior problems at the end of elementary school. *Journal of Abnormal Child Psychology, 23,* 751-766.

Garner, P. W., & Estep, K. M. (2001). Emotional competence, emotion socialization, and young children's peer-related social competence. *Early Education and Development, 12,* 29-48.

Garner, P. W., Jones, D. C., Gaddy, G., & Rennie, K. (1997). Low income mothers' conversations about emotions and their children's emotional competence. *Social Development, 6*, 37–52.

Garner, P. W., Jones, D. C., & Miner, J. L. (1994). Social competence among low-income preschoolers: Emotion socialization practices and social cognitive correlates. *Child Development, 65*, 622–637.

Garner, P. W., & Spears, F. M. (2000). Emotion regulation in low-income preschoolers. *Social Development, 9*, 246–264.

Gilliom, M., Shaw, D. S., Beck, J. E., Schonberg, M. A., & Lukon, J. L. (2002). Anger regulation in disadvantaged preschool boys: Strategies, antecedents, and the development of self-control. *Developmental Psychology, 38(2)*, 222–235.

Gnepp, J. (1989). Personalized inferences of emotions and appraisals: Component processes and correlates. *Developmental Psychology, 25*, 277–288.

Gnepp, J., & Chilamkurti, C. (1988). Children's use of personality attributions to predict other people's emotional and behavioral reactions. *Child Development, 59*, 743–754.

Gnepp, J., & Gould, M. E. (1985). The development of personalized inferences: Understanding other people's emotional reactions in light of their prior experiences. *Child Development, 56*, 1455–1464.

Gnepp, J., Klayman, J., & Trabasso, T. (1982). A hierarchy of information sources for inferring emotional reactions. *Journal of Experimental Child Psychology, 33*, 111–123.

Gnepp, J., McKee, E., & Domanic, J. A. (1987). Children's use of situational information to infer emotion: Understanding emotionally equivocal situations. *Developmental Psychology, 23*, 114–123.

Gordis, F., Rosen, A. B., & Grand, S. (1989, April). *Young children's understanding of simultaneous conflicting emotions.* Paper presented at the Biennial Meetings of the Society for Research in Child Development, Kansas City, MO.

Gottman, J. M., Katz, L. F., & Hooven, C. (1997). *Meta-emotion: How families communicate emotionally.* Mahwah, NJ: Erlbaum.

Gottman, J. M., & Mettetal, G. (1986). Speculations about social and affective development of friendship and acquaintanceship through adolescence. In J. M. Gottman & J. Parker (Eds.), *Conversations of friends Speculations on affective development* (pp. 192–237). New York: Cambridge University Press.

Greenberg, M. T., & Snell, J. L. (1997). Brain Development and Emotional Development: The Role of Teaching in Organizing the Frontal Lobe. In P. Salovey & D. J. Sluyter (Eds.), *Emotional development and emotional intelligence* (pp. 93–119). New York: Basic Books.

Grolnick, W. S., Bridges, L. J., & Connell, J. P. (1996). Emotion regulation in two-year-olds: Strategies and emotional expression in four contexts. *Child Development, 67*, 928–941.

Grolnick, W. S., Kurowski, C. O., McMenamy, J. M., Rivkin, I., & Bridges, L. J. (1998). Mothers' strategies for regulating their toddlers' distress. *Infant Behavior & Development, 21*, 437–450.

Gross, D., & Harris, P. (1988). Understanding false beliefs about emotion. *International Journal of Behavioral Development, 11*, 475–488.

Haapasalo, J., & Tremblay, R. E. (1994). Physically aggressive boys from ages 6 to 12: Family background, parenting behavior, and prediction of delinquency. *Journal of Consulting and Clinical Psychology, 62*, 1044–1052.

Halberstadt, A. G. (1991). Socialization of expressiveness: Family influences in particular and a model in general. In R. S. Feldman & S. Rimé (Eds.), *Fundamentals of emotional expressiveness* (pp. 106–162.). Cambridge: Cambridge University Press.

Halberstadt, A. G., Denham, S. A., & Dunsmore, J. (2001). Affective social competence. *Social Development, 10*, 79–119.

Harms, T., & Clifford, R. M. (1980). *Early Childhood Environmental Rating Scale.* New York: Teachers College Press.

Harris, P. L., Olthof, T., Meerum Terwogt, M., & Hardman, C. E. (1987). Children's knowledge of the situations that provoke emotion. *International Journal of Behavioral Development, 10*, 319–343.

Harter, S., & Whitesell, N. R. (1989). Developmental changes in children's understanding of single, multiple, and blended emotion concepts. In P. Harris & C. Saarni (Eds.), *Children's understanding of emotion* (pp. 81–116). Cambridge: Cambridge University Press.

Hawkins, J. D., Smith, B. H., & Catalano, R. F. (2004). Social development and social and emotional learning: The Seattle Social Development Project. In J. E. Zins, R. P. Weissberg, M. C. Wang & H. J. Walberg (Eds.), *Building school success on social and emotional learning: what does the research say?* New York: Teachers College Press.

Hoffner, C., & Badzinski, D. M. (1989). Children's integration of facial and situations cues to emotion. *Child Development, 60*, 415–422.

Howes, C. (2000). Social-emotional classroom climate in child care child-teacher relationships and children's second grade peer relations. *Social Development, 9*, 191–204.

Howes, C., & Smith, E. W. (1995). Relations among child care quality, teacher behavior, children's play activities, emotional security, and cognitive activity in child care. *Early Childhood Research Quarterly, 10*, 381–404.

Hubbard, J. A., & Coie, J. D. (1994). Emotional correlates of social competence in children's peer relationships. *Merrill-Palmer Quarterly, 40*, 1–20.

Huffman, L. C., Mehlinger, S. L., & Kerivan, A. S. (2000). Risk factors for academic and behavioral problems at the beginning of school. *Off to a good start: Research on the risk factors for early school problems and selected federal policies affecting children's social and emotional development and their readiness for school.* Chapel Hill: University of North Carolina FPG Child Development Center.

Hughes, C., Dunn, J., & White, A. (1998). Trick or treat? Uneven understanding of mind and emotion and executive dysfunction in "hard-to-manage" preschoolers. *Journal of Child Psychology & Psychiatry & Allied Disciplines, 39*, 981–994.

Hyson, M. (2002). Emotional development and school readiness. Professional development. *Young Children, 57(6)*, 76–78.

Hyson, M. C. (1994). *The emotional development of young children: Building an emotion-centered curriculum.* New York: Teachers College Press.

Hyson, M. C., & Lee, K.-M. (1996). Assessing early childhood teachers' beliefs about emotions: Content, contexts, and implications for practice. *Early Education and Development, 7*, 59–78.

Hyson, M. C., & Molinaro, J. (2001). Learning through feeling: Children's development, teachers' beliefs and relationships, and classroom practices. In S. L. Golbeck (Ed.), *Psychological perspectives on early childhood education: Reframing dilemmas in research and practice The Rutgers invitational symposium on education series* (pp. 107–130). Mahwah, NJ: Lawrence Erlbaum Associates, Publishers.

Izard, C. E. (2002). Emotion knowledge and emotion utilization facilitate school readiness. *SRCD Social Policy Report, XVI(3)*, 8.

Izard, C. E. (2002). Translating emotion theory and research into preventive interventions. *Psychological Bulletin, 128*, 796–824.

Izard, C. E., & Bear, G. (2001). *Head Start/ECAP emotions curriculum.* Newark: University of Delaware Instructional Resources Center.

Izard, C. E., Fine, S., Schultz, D., Mostow, A., Ackerman, B., & Youngstrom, E. (2001). Emotions knowledge as a predictor of social behavior and academic competence in children at risk. *Psychological Science, 12*, 18–23.

Joseph, G. E., & Strain, P. S. (2003). Comprehensive Evidence-Based Social-Emotional Curricula for Young Children: An Analysis of Efficacious Adoption Potential. *Topics in Early Childhood Special Education, 23(2)*, 65–76.

Josephs, I. (1994). Display rule behavior and understanding in preschool children. *Journal of Nonverbal Behavior, 18*, 301-326.

Keogh, B. K. (1992). Temperament and teachers' views of teachability. In W. Carey & S. McDevitt (Eds.), *Prevention and early intervention: Individual differences as risk factors for the mental health of children* (pp. 246-254). New York: Bruner/Mazel.

Kestenbaum, R., & Gelman, S. (1995). Preschool children's identification and understanding of mixed emotions. *Cognitive Development, 10*, 443-458.

Kieras, J. C., Tobin, R. M., & Graziano, W. G. (2003, April). *Effortful Control & Emotional Responses to Undesirable Gifts.* Paper presented at the Society for Research in Child Development, Tampa, FL.

Knitzer, J. (1993). Children's mental health policy: Challenging the future. *Journal of Emotional and Behavioral Disorders, 1*, 8-16.

Kochenderfer, B. J., & Ladd, G. W. (1996). Peer victimization: Cause or consequence of school maladjustment? *Child Development, 67*, 1305-1317.

Ladd, G. W., Birch, S. H., & Buhs, E. S. (1999). Children's social and scholastic lives in kindergarten: Related spheres of influence? *Child Development, 70*, 1373-1400.

Ladd, G. W., Kochenderfer, B. J., & Coleman, C. C. (1996). Friendship quality as a predictor of young children's early school adjustment. *Child Development, 67*, 1103-1118.

Lemerise, E. A., & Dodge, K. A. (2000). The development of anger and hostile interactions. In M. L. J. M. Haviland-Jones (Ed.), *Handbook of emotions* (2 ed., pp. 594-606). New York.: Guilford Press.

Lewis, M., Stanger, C., & Sullivan, M. E. (1989). Deception in three-year-olds. *Developmental Psychology, 25*, 439-443.

Lewis, M., Sullivan, M. E., & Vasen, A. (1987). Making faces: Age and emotion differences in the posing of emotional expression. *Developmental Psychology, 23*, 690-697.

Liew, J., Eisenberg, N., Losoya, S. H., Fabes, R. A., Guthrie, I. K., & Murphy, B. C. (2003). Children's Physiological Indices of Empathy and Their Socioemotional Adjustment: Does Caregivers' Expressivity Matter? *Journal of Family Psychology, 17*(4), 584-597.

Martin, R. P., Drew, D., Gaddis, L. R., & Moseley, M. (1988). Prediction of elementary school achievement from preschool temperament: Three studies. *School Psychology Review, 17*, 125-137.

McEvoy, M. A., & Yoder, P. (1993). *Interventions to promote social skills and emotional development: DEC recommended Practices.* In *DEC recommended practices: Indicators of quality in programs for infants and young children with special needs and their families.* Reston, VA: Council for Exceptional Children.

Miller, A. L., & Olson, S. L. (2000). Emotional expressiveness during peer conflicts: A predictor of social maladjustment among high-risk preschoolers. *Journal of Abnormal Child Psychology, 28*(4), 339-352.

Miller, P. H., & Aloise, P. A. (1989). Young children's understanding of the psychological causes of behavior: A review. *Child Development, 60*, 257-285.

Morrison, E. F., Rimm-Kauffman, S., & Pianta, R. C. (2003). A longitudinal study of mother-child interaction at school entry and social and academic outcomes in middle school. *Journal of School Psychology, 41*, 185-200.

Mostow, A. J., Izard, C. E., Fine, S., & Trentacosta, R. (2002). Modeling emotional, cognitive, and behavioral predictors of peer acceptance. *Child Development, 73*, 1775-1787.

Murphy, B. C., Shepard, S., Eisenberg, N., Fabes, R. A., & Guthrie, I. K. (1999). Contemporaneous and longitudinal relations of dispositional sympathy to emotionality, regulation, and social functioning. *Journal of Early Adolescence, 19*, 66-97.

Nelson, C. A. (1994). Neural bases of infant temperament. In J. Bates & T. E. Wachs (Eds.), *Temperament: Individual differences at the interface of biology and behavior* (pp. 47-82). Washington, DC: American Psychological Association.

Nunner-Winkler, G., & Sodian, B. (1988). Children's understanding of moral emotions. *Child Development, 59*, 1323-1338.

O'Neil, R., Welsh, M., Parke, R. D., Wang, S., & Strand, C. (1997). A longitudinal assessment of the academic correlates of early peer acceptance and rejection. *Journal of Clinical Child Psychology, 26*, 290-303.

Palinsin, H. A. (1986). Preschool temperament and performance on achievement tests. *Developmental Psychology, 22*, 766-770.

Park, K. A., Lay, K., & Ramsay, L. (1993). Individual differences and developmental changes in preschoolers' friendships. *Developmental Psychology, 29*, 264-270.

Parke, R. D., Cassidy, J., Burks, V. M., Carson, J. L., & Boyum, L. (1992). Familial contribution to peer competence among young children: The role of interactive and affective processes. In R. D. P. G. W. Ladd (Ed.), *Family-peer relationships Modes of linkage* (pp. 107-134). Hillsdale, NJ: Erlbaum.

Parker, J. G., & Gottman, J. M. (1989). Social and emotional development in a relational context: Friendship interaction from early childhood to adolescence. In T. J. Berndt & G. W. Ladd (Eds.), *Peer relationships in child development* (pp. 95-131). New York: John WIley.

Peng, M., Johnson, C. N., Pollock, J., Glasspool, R., & Harris, P. L. (1992). Training young children to acknowledge mixed emotions. *Cognition and Emotion, 6*, 387-401.

Peth-Pierce, R. (2000). *A good beginning: Sending America's children to school with the social and emotional competence they need to succeed.* Chapel Hill, NC: The Child Mental Health Foundations and Agencies Network.

Pianta, R. C. (1997). Adult-child relationship processes and early schooling. *Early Education and Development, 8*, 11-26.

Pianta, R. C., & Nimetz, S. L. (1992). Development of young children in stressful contexts: Theory, assessment, and prevention. In M. Gettinger, S. N. Elliott & T. R. Kratochwill (Eds.), *Preschool and early childhood treatment directions* (pp. 151-185). Hillsdale, NJ: Lawrence Erlbaum.

Pianta, R. C., Steinberg, M., & Rollins, K. (1995). The first two years of school: Teacher-child relationships and deflections in children's classroom adjustment. *Development & Psychopathology, 7*, 295-312.

Raver, C. C. (2002). Emotions matter: Making the case for the role of young children's emotional development for early school readiness. *SRCD Social Policy Report, XVI*(3), 3-18.

Raver, C. C., Blackburn, E. K., & Bancroft, M. (1999). Relations between effective emotional self-regulation, attentional control, and low-income preschoolers' social competence with peers. *Early Education and Development, 10*, 333-350.

Raver, C. C., & Knitzer, J. (2002). *Ready to enter: What research tells policymakers about strategies to promote social and emotional school readiness among three- and four-year-olds.* New York: National Center for Children in Poverty.

Reimer, K. J. (1996). Emotion socialization and children's emotional expressiveness in the preschool context (emotional expression). *Dissertation Abstracts International, 57*(07A), 0010.

Rimm-Kaufman, S. E., Pianta, R. C., & Cox, M. J. (2000). Teachers' judgements of problems in the transition to kindergarten. *Early Childhood Research Quarterly, 15*, 147-166.

Roberts, W. R., & Strayer, J. A. (1996). Empathy, emotional expressiveness, and prosocial behavior. *Child Development, 67*, 449-470.

Robins, L. N., & Rutter, M. (1990). *Straight and devious pathways from childhood to adulthood.* Cambridge: Cambridge University Press.

Rozek, M. K. (1987). Preschoolers' understanding of display rules for emotional expression. *Dissertation Abstracts International, 47*(12B), 5076.

Rubin, K. H., Burgess, K. B., Dwyer, K. M., & Hastings, P. (2003). Predicting preschoolers' externalizing behaviors from toddler temperament, conflict, and maternal negativity. *Developmental Psychology, 39*, 164-176.

Rubin, K. H., & Clark, M. L. (1983). Preschool teachers' ratings of behavioral problems: Observational, sociometric, and social-cognitive correlates. *Journal of Abnormal Child Psychology, 11*, 273-286.

Rubin, K. H., & Daniels-Beirness, T. (1983). Concurrent and predictive correlates of sociometric status in kindergarten and grade 1 children. *Merrill-Palmer Quarterly, 29*, 337-352.

Russell, J. A. (1990). The preschooler's understanding of the causes and consequences of emotion. *Child Development, 61*, 1872-1881.

Rydell, A.-M., Berlin, L., & Bohlin, G. (2003). Emotionality, emotion regulation, and adaptation among 5- to 8-year-old children. *Emotion, 3*(1), 30-47.

Saarni, C. (1990). Emotional competence. In R. Thompson (Ed.), *Nebraska symposium Socioemotional development* (pp. 115-161). Lincoln: University of Nebraska Press.

Saarni, C. (1999). *Children's emotional competence.* New York: Guilford Press.

Schultz, D., Izard, C. E., & Ackerman, B. P. (2000). Children's anger attribution bias: Relations to family environment and social adjustment. *Social Development, 9*, 284-301.

Schultz, D., Izard, C. E., Ackerman, B. P., & Youngstrom, E. A. (2001). Emotion knowledge in economically disadvantaged children: Self-regulatory antecedents and relations to social difficulties and withdrawal. *Development & Psychopathology, 13*, 53-67.

Shields, A., Dickstein, S., Seifer, R., Giusti, L., Magee, K. D., & Spritz, B. (2001). Emotional competence and early school adjustment: A study of preschoolers at risk. *Early Education & Development, 12*(1), 73-96.

Shonkoff, J. P., & Phillips, D. A. (2000). *From Neurons to Neighborhoods: The Science of Early Childhood Development.* Washington, DC: National Academy Press.

Smith, M. (2001). Social and emotional competencies: Contributions to young African-American children's peer acceptance. *Early Education and Development, 12*(1), 49-72.

Sorber, A. V. (2001). The role of peer socialization in the development of emotion display rules: Effects of age, gender, and emotion. *Dissertation Abstracts International, 62*(02B), 1119.

Spence, S. H. (1987). The relation between social cognitive skills and peer sociometric status. *British Journal of Developmental Psychology, 5*, 347-356.

Sroufe, L. A., Schork, E., Motti, F., Lawroski, N., & LaFreniere, P. (1984). The role of affect in social competence. In C. E. Izard, J. Kagan & R. B. Zajonc (Eds.), *Emotions, cognition, & behavior* (pp. 289-319). Cambridge: Cambridge University Press.

Stifter, C., & Fox, N. (1987). Preschoolers' ability to identify and label emotions. *Journal of Nonverbal Behavior, 10*, 255-266.

Strandberg-Sawyer, K., Denham, S. A., DeMulder, E., Blair, K., Auerbach-Major, S., & Levitas, J. (2003). The contribution of older siblings' reactions to emotions to preschoolers' emotional and social competence. *Marriage & Family Review, 34*(3/4), 183-212.

Strayer, J. (1980). A naturalistic study of empathic behaviors and their relation to affective states and perspective-taking skills in preschool children. *Child Development, 51*, 815-822.

Strayer, J. (1986). Children's attributions regarding the situational determinants of emotion in self and others. *Developmental Psychology, 22*, 649-654.

Thompson, R. A. (1994). Emotion regulation: A theme in search of definition. *In N. A. Fox (Ed.), The development of emotion regulation: Biological and behavioral considerations. Monographs of the Society for Research in Child Development*, Serial No. 240, 259 (242-243), 225-252.

Tomkins, S. (1991). *The negative affects: Anger and fear* (Vol. II). New York: Springer Publishing Co.

Walden, T., Lemerise, E. A., & Smith, M. C. (1999). Friendship and popularity in preschool classrooms. *Early Education and Development, 10*, 351-371.

Webster-Stratton, C., & Taylor, T. (2001). Nipping early risk factors in the bud: Preventing substance abuse, delinquency, and violence in adolescence through interventions targeted at young children (0-8 years). *Prevention Science, 2*, 165-192.

Wiggers, M., & Van Lieshout, C. F. (1985). Development of recognition of emotions: Children's reliance on situational and facial expressive cues. *Developmental Psychology, 21*, 338-349.

Wintre, M., Polivy, J., & Murray, M. A. (1990). Self-predictions of emotional response patterns: Age, sex, and situational determinants. *Child Development, 61*, 1124-1133.

Wintre, M., & Vallance, D. D. (1994). A developmental sequence in the comprehension of emotions: Multiple emotions, intensity and valence. *Developmental Psychology, 30*, 509-514.

Zahn-Waxler, C., Radke-Yarrow, M., & King, R. A. (1979). Child rearing and children's prosocial initiations toward victims of distress. *Child Development, 50*, 319-330.

Zins, J., Weissberg, R. P., Wang, M. C., & Walberg, H. J. (Eds.). (2004). *Building academic success on social and emotional learning : what does the research say?* New York: Teachers College Press.

·6·

MOTOR DEVELOPMENT IN YOUNG CHILDREN

David L. Gallahue
Indiana University

John C. Ozmun
Indiana State University

In its simplest form, the term *development* refers to change in function over time. As such, development encompasses all change throughout the life span in the cognitive, affective, and motor domains of human behavior. Understanding the motor development of young children is of keen interest to parents and educators, as well as scholars, physicians, and therapists.

Motor development may be defined as adaptive change toward competence in motor behavior across the life span. As such, motor development is studied both as a product and as a process. Knowledge of the *products* (i.e., the outcomes) and the *processes* (i.e., the underlying mechanisms) of changes in motor behavior over time provide us with information that is vital to understanding the individual particularly during a time of rapid developmental change—the period of early childhood.

In terms of "product," understanding the motor development of young children provides us with descriptive profiles of developmental change in the motor behavior of normally developing children, thereby providing us with information about the "what" of motor development, namely: (a) What are the typical phases and stages of motor development during childhood? (b) What are the approximate age-periods associated with typical markers of motor behavior in young children? and (c) What do we know about predictable patterns of change in motor behavior that are typically seen in normally developing children as compared to those who may be either developmentally delayed, or developmentally advanced? In short, descriptive views of motor development equip us with a better understanding, in general terms, of what lies ahead in terms of anticipated change. Historically, descriptive profiles of developmental change have yielded rather specific "appropriate" age-markers for a desired behavior. Caution needs to be exercised in placing emphasis on these markers beyond what they may reveal in general terms. For

example, although the developmental *sequence* for acquisition of rudimentary and fundamental movement skills is highly similar in normally developing children, *the rate* of development is highly variable and context specific. Children raised in different ecological and cultural settings may be significantly ahead or behind their age-mates in terms of movement skill acquisition and physical development. So, too, are children with various developmental disabilities, or who have been exposed to certain kinds of gross and fine motor activities such as skateboarding or violin playing not generally available to others.

In terms of "process," understanding the motor development of young children helps us address the mechanisms that underlie developmental change. As such we gain information about the "how" and "why" of development, namely: (a) How does change occur as it does? (b) Why is developmental change a nonlinear, self-organizing dynamic process? and (c) How do heredity and the environment interact with the requirements of the motor task as one strives for greater motor control and movement competence? In short, better understanding the mechanisms that underlie motor development provide us with specific explanations of why change occurs as it does in young children.

Although our focus is on the motor development of children during the early childhood period, it is important to note that change in movement skill acquisition is a progressive process resulting in measurable products and that it begins during the prenatal period and extends throughout life. Although we can depict motor development hierarchically in a phase-stage sequence, as in Table 6.1, it is important to emphasize that the age sequence of movement skill acquisition becomes increasingly variable as one advances from phase to phase namely the *reflexive movement phase* of early infancy to the *rudimentary movement phase* of infancy and toddler hood, the *fundamental*

TABLE 6.1. Gallahue's Phases of Motor Development (2006)

Movement Phase	Typical Age Period of Development	Movement Characteristics of Phases
Reflexive	In utero to 4 month 4 months to 1 year	Information encoding stage Information decoding stage
Rudimentary	Birth to 1 year 1–2 years	Precontrol stage Reflex inhibition stage
Fundamental	2–3 years 4–5 years 6–7 years	Initial stage Elementary stage Mature stage
Specialized	7–10 years 11–13 years 14 years and beyond	Transition stage Application stage Lifelong utilization stage

movement phase of early childhood, and finally to the *specialized movement phase* of later childhood and beyond (Gallahue & Ozmun, 2006). As movement skills become increasingly complex, they become differentially influenced by the specific requirements of the movement task itself, the biology of the individual and the specific conditions of the learning environment. As such, the notion that there is a maturationally determined universal unfolding of fundamental movement skills is not supported by fact (Haywood & Getchell, 2005).

The *reflexive movement phase* typically extends from the fourth or fifth month of the prenatal period well into the first year of postnatal life. Primitive reflexes such as the Moro reflex, asymmetrical tonic neck reflex, and Babinski reflex, as well as postural reflexes such as the body righting reflex, crawling reflex, and primary stepping reflex appear, and are inhibited on a universally predictable schedule in normally developing infants.

During the *rudimentary movement phase* typical of infancy, a variety of movement patterns are established that involve control of the head, neck, and trunk (body stability), controlled reaching, grasping and releasing (object manipulation), and proficiency in creeping and crawling (purposeful locomotion). Although the sequence of acquisition of these rudimentary movement tasks tends to follow a sequential progression from simple to more complex, the rate of their acquisition may vary by a matter of several months among infants who are developing normally.

On the average, normally developing children are generally seen as being at the *fundamental movement phase* of motor development during the preschool and primary school years. This is the period of time during which young children experiment and explore their movement potential in a variety of movement tasks that form the building blocks for the more complex movement skills at the fifth and final phase. During this phase, there is marked variability in the rate of movement skill acquisition ranging from a few months to several years. Later in this chapter, we will focus our discussion on the fundamental movement phase of motor development.

At the *specialized movement skill phase* more complex movement skills are refined and mastered. Variability in the rate and extent of skill acquisition is determined by a wide variety of environmental as well as biological factors. For example, learning how to play the game of basketball, tennis, or golf with sufficient skill to be able to participate at a recreational

or competitive level will vary widely among individuals due to the extent to which they have been exposed to these activities, received quality instruction, and have among other things the physical, psychological and perceptual attributes necessary for success.

This chapter focuses on two aspects of motor behavior that are studied in the context of developmental change during childhood, namely: (a) Acquisition of Fundamental Movement Skills and (b) Children's Physical Activity and Physical Fitness. What the available research tells us about each of these aspects of motor behavior during childhood is presented along with syntheses of findings in table form.

ACQUISITION OF FUNDAMENTAL MOVEMENT SKILLS

As children approach their second birthdays, marked changes can be observed in how they relate to their surroundings. By the end of the second year, most children have mastered the rudimentary movement abilities of infancy. These movement abilities form the basis on which children develop and refine the fundamental movement skills of early childhood and the specialized movement skills of later childhood and beyond. Young children are no longer immobilized by their basic inability to move about freely or by the confines of their crib or playpen. They are now able to explore the movement potential of their bodies as they move through space (*locomotion*). They no longer have to maintain a relentless struggle against the force of gravity but are gaining increased control over their musculature in opposition to gravity (*stability*). They no longer have to be content with the crude and ineffective reaching, grasping, and releasing of objects characteristic of infancy but are rapidly developing the ability to make controlled and precise contact with objects in their environment (*object manipulation*).

Young children are involved in the process of developing and refining their movement skills in a wide variety of fundamental stability, locomotor, and manipulative movements (Gabbard, 2003; Gallahue & Ozmun, 2006; Haywood & Getchell, 2005; Payne & Isaacs, 2005). This means that they should be involved in a series of coordinated and individually appropriate experiences designed to enhance knowledge of their body and its potential for movement. Development of fundamental, or basic, movement skills is basic to the motor development of young children. By engaging in a wide assortment of movement experiences in active play settings, of both a gross motor and fine motor variety, children have a wealth of information on which to base their perceptions of themselves and the world (Gallahue & Cleland, 2003; National Association for Sport and Physical Education, 2000, 2003, 2004a,b).

Fundamental movement skill development is not specifically concerned with developing high degrees of skill in a limited number of movement situations but, rather, with developing acceptable levels of proficiency and efficient body mechanics in a wide variety of movement patterns. As such a fundamental movement only involves the basic elements of a particular movement task. It does not include such things as the individual's style or personal peculiarities in performance. It does not emphasize the combining of a variety of fundamental movements into more complex skills such as the layup shot in basketball or a floor exercise routine in gymnastics. Each fundamental movement skill is first considered in relative isolation from others, and then as skill develops linked with others in a variety of combinations. The locomotor movements of running, jumping, and leaping, or the manipulative movements of throwing, catching, kicking, and trapping, are examples of fundamental movement skills first mastered separately by the child. These basic skills are then gradually combined and enhanced in a variety of ways to become more complex and specialized movement skills that are used in daily living, recreational, and sport activities (Roberton, 2004; Rose, 1997; Seefeldt & Haubenstricker, 1982; Walkley, Holland, Treloar, & Probyn-Smith 1993; Wickstrom, 1983).

The basic elements of fundamental movements have been found to be essentially the same for normally developing children. In the 1960s and 1970s, several scales appeared in the North American literature that illustrated a relationship between chronological age and motor performance. Although several decades have elapsed since these studies, they remain as classics in providing us with broad descriptive profiles of age-related changes in fundamental movement skill acquisition. They are not, however, sensitive to ecological differences that may be expressed in varying cultures, racial and ethnic groups, and socioeconomic strata.

Johnson (1962), using a large sample of U.S. boys and girls from Grades 1 through 6, found that the mean scores on a variety of motor performance items showed a definite upward trend until the fifth grade. Cratty and Martin (1969) presented age-related sequences of acquisition for a variety of locomotor, manipulative, and perceptual abilities of 365 U.S. children ranging in age from 4 to 12 years. Williams's (1970) summary of the movement abilities of North American children between 3 and 6 years old revealed more advanced forms of movement with increases in age. Sinclair (1973) studied the motor development of 2- to 6-year-old children in the United States. The results of her longitudinal film analysis of 25 movement tasks, at 6-month intervals, lent further support to the hypothesis that movement skill acquisition is age-related during the early childhood years. Tables 6.2A–C provide a visual representation of the emergence sequence and approximate age-range for several fundamental stability, locomotor, and manipulative skills, respectively.

These early normative studies of motor development are interesting in that they provide valuable descriptive insights about performance variables throwing for distance ("how far,"), running for speed ("how fast"), and performing a number of repetitions ("how many"). They fail, however, to provide information about qualitative change that occurs as the child progresses toward a more mature form. As a result, a number of investigators, all using film and computer techniques to analyze the intraskill aspects of a variety of fundamental movement patterns, began to collect data leading to a stage concept of motor development during early childhood (Knudson & Morrison, 1997; Miller, 2001). As reported in Gabbard (2003), O'Connor (2000), and Payne and Isaacs (2005) several researchers conducted important investigations into the intraskill sequences of a variety of

fundamental movement tasks. Out of these investigations have come three popular methods of charting the stage classification of children in observational settings. The systems originally devised by Roberton (1978a,b), McClengahan and Gallahue (1978), and Seefeldt and Haubenstricker (1976) set the stage for the use of observational assessment as a reliable method for screening the development of fundamental movement skills for instructional purposes. The Roberton method expands stage theory to an analysis of the separate components of movement within a given pattern and is commonly referred to as the *segmental assessment approach* (also known as the component approach). The Seefeldt method assigns an overall stage classification (stage 1 through stage 5) and is referred to as a *total body assessment approach* (also known as the total body configuration approach).

In their book *Developmental Physical Education for All Children* (2003) Gallahue and Cleland offer a practical, easy-to-use, and reliable system for classifying individuals at the "initial," "elementary," "mature," or "sport skill" stages along with a wide variety of developmentally appropriate movement experiences for each stage in 23 fundamental movement skills. This method encourages use of both the total body assessment and segmental analysis approaches to informally assess fundamental movement pattern development for instructional purposes. First, the examiner observes the movement task using a total body assessment approach. This provides a general picture of the stage at which the individual, group, or class is performing a specific fundamental movement skill. If the movement is observed to be at the mature or sport skill stage, further diagnostic observational assessment is not necessary. If, however, the fundamental movement skill is observed to be at the initial or elementary stage in a general sense, then further assessment is warranted. At this time, a segmental assessment is conducted to specifically identify those body parts that are lagging behind. This method recognizes the differential rates of development within fundamental movement patterns as well as the need for an easy-to-apply practical tool for daily teaching situations.

Development Differences

When observing fundamental movement skills whether using a segmental assessment approach, a total body assessment approach or a combination of the two, it soon becomes apparent that there are between-child differences, between-pattern differences, and within-pattern differences (Gallahue & Ozmun, 2006). A movement "pattern" differs from a movement "skill" in terms of emphasis. That is, a pattern of movement is focused simply on the underlying biomechanics or process for the action, whereas a movement skill is focused more closely on the results, or product, of the action.

Between-child differences highlight the principle of individuality in all learning. The sequence of progression through the initial, elementary, and mature stages is generally the same for most children. The rate, however, may vary considerably, depending on a combination of both environmental and biological factors (Malina, Bouchard, & Bar-Or, 2004). Whether a child reaches the mature stage depends primarily on the ecological

TABLE 6.2A. Sequence of Emergence of Selected Fundamental Stability Skills

Movement Pattern	Selected Abilities	Approximate Age Range of Onset
Dynamic Balance		
Dynamic balance involves maintaining one's equilibrium as the center of gravity shifts	Walks 1-inch (2.5 cm) straight line	2–4 years
	Walks 1-inch (2.5 cm) circular line	3–5 years
	Stands on low balance beam	2–3 years
	Walks on 4-inch (10 cm) wide beam for a short distance	2–4 years
	Walks on same beam, alternating feet	3–5 years
	Walks on 2- or 3-inch (5.1 or 7.6 cm) beam	3–5 years
	Performs basic forward roll	2–5 years
	Performs mature forward roll*	5–7 years
Static Balance		
Static balance involves maintaining one's equilibrium while the center of gravity remains stationary	Pulls to a standing position	7–10 months
	Stands without handholds	9–11 months
	Stands alone	10–12 months
	Balances on one foot 3–5 seconds	3–5 years
	Supports body in basic 3-point inverted positions	4–6 years
Axial Movements		
Axial movements are static postures that involve bending, stretching, twisting, turning, and the like	Axial movement abilities begin to develop early in infancy and are progressively refined to a point where they are included in the emerging manipulative patterns of throwing, catching, kicking, striking, trapping, and other activities	2 months–6 years

*The child has developmental "potential" to be at the mature stage. Attainment will depend on factors within the task, individual, and environment.
Used with permission: Gallahue, D. L. & Ozmun, J. C. (2006). *Understanding motor development: Infants, children, adolescents, and adults.* Boston: McGraw-Hill. p. 189.

TABLE 6.2B. Sequence of Emergence of Selected Fundamental Locomotor Skills

Movement Pattern	Selected Abilities	Approximate Age Range of Onset
Walking		
Walking involves placing one foot in front of the other while maintaining contact with the supporting surface	Rudimentary upright unaided gait	9–15 months
	Walks sideways	13–16 months
	Walks backward	14–17 months
	Walks upstairs with help	18–20 months
	Walks upstairs alone—follow step	20–24 months
	Walks downstairs alone—follow step	22–25 months
Running		
Running involves a brief period of no contact with the supporting surface	Hurried walk (maintains contact)	14–18 months
	First true run (nonsupport phase)	2–3 years
	Efficient and refined run	4–5 years
	Speed of run increases, mature run*	4–6 years
Jumping		
Jumping takes three forms:	Steps down from low objects	14–18 months
(1) jumping for distance;	Jumps down from object with one-foot lead	18–24 months
(2) jumping for height; and	Jumps off floor with both feet	24–28 months
(3) Jumping from a height.	Jumps for distance (about 3 ft/1 m)	4–5 years
It involves a one- or two-foot takeoff with a landing on both feet	Jumps for height (about 1 ft/30 cm)	4–5 years
	Mature jumping pattern*	5–6 years
Hopping		
Hopping involves a one-foot takeoff with a landing on the same foot	Hops up to 3 times on preferred foot	2–3 years
	Hops from 4 to 6 times on same foot	3–4 years
	Hops from 8 to 10 times on same foot	4–5 years
	Hops distance of 50 feet (15 m) in about 11 seconds	4–5 years
	Hops skillfully with rhythmical alteration, mature pattern*	5–6 years
Galloping		
The gallop combines a walk and a leap with the same foot leading throughout	Basic but inefficient gallop	3–5 years
	Gallops skillfully, mature pattern*	5–6 years
Skipping		
Skipping combines a step and a hop in rhythmic alteration	One-footed skip	3–4 years
	Skillful skipping (about 20%)	5–6 years
	Skillful skipping for most*	5–7 years

*The child has developmental "potential" to be at the mature stage. Attainment will depend on factors within the task, individual, and environment.
Used with permission: Gallahue, D. L. & Ozmun, J. C. (2006). *Understanding motor development: Infants, children, adolescents, and adults.* Boston: McGraw-Hill. p. 190.

TABLE 6.2C. Sequence of Emergence of Selected Fundamental Manipulative Skills

Movement Pattern	Selected Abilities	Approximate Age Range of Onset
Reach, Grasp, Release		
Reaching, grasping, and releasing involve making successful contact with an object, retaining it in one's grasp, and releasing it at will	Primitive reaching behaviors	2–4 months
	Corralling of objects	2–4 months
	Palmer grasp	3–5 months
	Pincer grasp	8–10 months
	Controlled grasp	12–14 months
	Controlled release	14–18 months
Throwing		
Throwing involves imparting force to an object in the general direction of intent	Body faces target, feet remain stationary, ball thrown with forearm extension only	2–3 years
	Same as above but with body rotation added	3½–5 years
	Steps forward with leg on same side as the throwing arm	4–5 years
	Boys exhibit more mature patterns than girls	5 years and over
	Mature throwing pattern*	4–6 years
Catching		
Catching involves receiving force from an object with the hands, moving from large to progressively smaller balls	Chases ball; does not respond to aerial ball	18–24 months
	Responds to aerial ball with delayed arm movements	2–3 years
	Needs to be told how to position arms	2–3 years
	Basket catch using the body	2–5 years
	Fear reaction (turns head away)	3–5 years
	Catches using the hands only with a small ball	3–5 years
	Mature catching pattern*	5–6 years
Kicking		
Kicking involves imparting force to an object with the foot	Pushes against ball; does not actually kick it	14–18 months
	Kicks with leg straight and little body movement (kicks *at* the ball)	18–36 months
	Flexes lower leg on backward lift	3–4 years
	Greater backward and forward swing with definite arm opposition	4–5 years
	Mature pattern (kicks *through* the ball)*	5–6 years
Striking		
Striking involves sudden contact to objects in an over arm, sidearm, or underhand pattern	Faces object and swings in a vertical plane	2–3 years
	Swings in a horizontal plane and stands to the side of the object	4–5 years
	Rotates the trunk and hips and shifts body weight forward	4–6 years
	Mature horizontal pattern with stationary ball*	5–7 years

*The child has developmental "potential" to be at the mature stage. Attainment will depend on factors within the task, individual, and environment.
Used with permission: Gallahue, D. L. & Ozmun, J. C. (2006). *Understanding motor development: Infants, children, adolescents, adults.* Boston: McGraw-Hill. p. 191.

context of the environment including factors such as instruction, encouragement and opportunities for practice, and biological factors such as perceptual-motor maturity and various anatomical and physiological considerations.

Between-pattern differences are seen in all children. A child may be at the initial stage in some movement tasks, the elementary stage in others, and the mature stage in still others. Children do not progress evenly in the development of their fundamental movement skills. Play opportunities and instructional experiences will greatly influence the rate of development of fundamental locomotor, manipulative, and stability skills (Thelan, 1995).

Within-pattern differences are an interesting and often curious phenomenon (Roberton, 1978a; 1982, 2004). Within a given movement pattern, a child may exhibit a combination of initial, elementary, and mature elements. For example, in the throw, the arm action may be at the elementary stage while the leg action is at the mature stage and the trunk action at the initial stage. Developmental differences within movement patterns are common and usually the result of one or more of the following: (a) incomplete modeling of the movements of others, (b) initial success with the inappropriate action, (c) failure to require an all-out effort, (d) inappropriate or restricted learning opportunities, or (e) incomplete perceptual-motor integration. Children exhibiting within-pattern differences should be assessed using the segmental analysis approach (Roberton, 1982). This will permit the observer to accurately determine the stage of development of each body segment. With this knowledge, appropriate intervention strategies can be mapped out.

In summary, the period of early childhood is a time for the development and mastery of a variety of basic movement skills. Although most normally developing children have the potential to be at the mature stage in most fundamental skills, it is critically important that they have ample opportunities for practice and quality instruction in a caring and nurturing environment. As such a developmentally based physical education program should be a central component of their early childhood education. Children who are skillful movers have the basic building blocks necessary for an active way of life that maximizes their individual potential in terms of physical fitness and regular participation in physical activity (Gallahue, 1982; Gallahue & Cleland 2003;).

YOUNG CHILDREN'S PHYSICAL ACTIVITY AND PHYSICAL FITNESS

Malina, Bouchard, and Bar-Or, experts in the area of developmental physical activity and fitness, note that: "Physical activity is a behavior that occurs in a variety of forms and contexts, including free play, house chores, exercise, school physical education, and organized sport" (2004, p.6). As such, *physical activity* may be defined as any form of bodily movement that results in increased energy expenditure. *Physical fitness*, by contrast, is a aspect of physical activity that refers specifically to the several health-related components of fitness (namely, aerobic endurance, muscular strength and endurance, joint flexibility, and body composition, or body fatness), and its performance-related components (namely, balance, speed, agility, power, and coordination)

For years, noted professionals have reported that children do have sufficient levels of physical activity in their daily routine to promote increased levels of physical fitness (Kuntzleman & Reiff, 1992; Updyke, 1992; Baranowski & Simons-Morton, 1990; Schlicker, Borra, & Regan, 1994; Dietz, 2004; Morrow, 2004; McKenzie, 2004). Moreover, the National Children and Youth Fitness Study (Ross & Gilbert, 1985) revealed that more than one third of the children and youth tested were not sufficiently active in their daily lives for aerobic benefit. A more recent survey (National Center for Health Statistics, 2001) clearly revealed that children in the United States are heavier and fatter than their counterparts of just 20 years ago. Based on their research, Sable and colleagues (2002) suggest that a decrease in the level of physical activity tends to follow rather than precede the development of obesity in children.

It has been assumed, often erroneously, that children are naturally active and get plenty of vigorous physical activity as a normal part of their daily routines. However, apartment living, city dwelling, and the ubiquitous television set and computer have created sedentary lifestyles for many children (DuRant, Baranowski, Johnson, & Thompson, 1994). Bar-Or and Malina (1995), however, dispute this contention. Based on their review of the literature they concluded that "children may be more active than the health surveys have indicated or than they are perceived to be" (p. 87).

Children's level of physical activity, that is the amount of energy expended during a given period of time, is studied in both laboratory and field settings using doubly labeled water, accelerometry, parent-reported physical activity diaries, and parent-reported physical activity assessments (O'Connor et al., 2003). For years, researchers have used a variety of techniques to measure physical activity. Doubly labeled water is an expensive but highly accurate technique and the acknowledged

"gold standard" for measuring physical activity. This technique involves ingesting a stable isotope and measuring its rate of secretion through the urine. Because of its expense and the very nature of the assessment measure itself, studies using doubly labeled water with young children are still rare.

Two less direct, but frequently used field techniques are parent-reported physical activity diaries and parent-reported physical activity assessments of children's physical activity. In the diary technique an exhaustive record of physical activity is recorded by an adult, usually for three full days. The parent-reported assessment of physical activity is a forced choice subjective view of the activity level of one's child. Although valid instruments with adolescents and adults, they are not recommended for research purposes with children under age 10 because of the inability of most boy and girls under this age to cognitively recall, in detail, their physical activity.

Heart rate monitors also have been used extensively to measure daily physical activity. Once again, validity is doubtful, especially with children, because heart rates below 120 beats per minute are not valid predictors of exercise intensity (Rowlands, Eston, & Ingledew, 1997), and other factors, such as emotions can elevate the heart rate. Direct observation of physical activity, although valid for use with children, is unrealistic because of the time required in collecting sufficient information for each child.

As a result, accelerometers have emerged as a preferred means of assessing children's physical activity because it is a valid and economical. An accelerometer is an electromechanical device worn by the subject that detects and records motion in a single plane or multiple planes over a specified period of time. In a study by Ott, Pate, Trost, Ward, and Saunder (2000), 28 children 9 to 11 years of age wore accelerometers while engaged in a variety of physical activities. The results of this study revealed that average heart rates did not differ significantly between girls and boys for seven of the eight activities (video game play, throw and catch, walking, bench stepping, basketball, aerobic dance, and running) measured. Hop-scotch was the lone exception.

Although there are few valid and reliable gold standards for assessing physical fitness, experts working with young children have a fertile area for the study of physical fitness and physical activity. Largely because of advances in technology, carefully controlled studies and innovative research designs are beginning to yield new information about the physical activity and fitness of young children (Bar-Or & Malina, 1995; Baranowski & Simons-Morton, 1990; Dietz, 1995). With this in mind we now turn to a discussion about what we know about the health-related and performance-related aspects of children's physical fitness. The information that follows is based on information gleaned from laboratory, field, and clinical settings.

Health-Related Fitness

Extensive studies in the area of physical fitness have been conducted over the past several years, and we are gradually piecing together what is known about children's physical fitness. The components of health-related fitness are associated with health

TABLE 6.3. Common Measures of Children's Health-Related Fitness and a Synthesis of Findings

Health-Related Fitness Components	Common Tests	Specific Aspect Measured	Synthesis of Findings
Cardiovascular endurance	Step test Distance run Treadmill stress test Bicycle ergometer Heart rate monitor Accelerometer	Physical work capacity Aerobic endurance Max VO$_2$ Max VO$_2$ Heart rate Heart rate	VO$_2$ max estimates are tenuous with young children. Children can achieve maximum VO$_2$ values at or above adults when corrected for body weight. Maximal heart rates decrease with age. Trend for improved VO$_2$ max values in both boys and girls with age.
Muscular strength	Hand dynamometer Back and leg dynamometer Cable tensiometer	Isometric grip strength Isometric back and leg strength Isometric joint strength	Annual increase for boys from age 7 on. Girls tend to level off after age 12. Boys slow prior to puberty, then gain rapidly throughout adolescence.
Muscular endurance	Push-ups Sit-ups Flexed arm hang Pull-ups	Isotonic upper body endurance Isotonic abdominal endurance Isometric upper body endurance Isotonic upper body endurance	Similar abilities throughout childhood slightly in favor of boys on most items. Lull in performance prior to age 12. Large increases in boys from 12 to 16, then a leveling off.
Joint Flexibility	Bend and reach Sit and reach	Hip joint flexibility Hip joint flexibility	Flexibility is joint specific. Girls tend to be more flexible than boys at all ages. Flexibility decreases with reduced activity levels.
Body Composition	Hydrostatic weighing Skin fold calipers Body mass index Electrical impedance	Percent body fat Estimate of percent body fat Estimate of percent body fat Estimate of percent body fat	Children at all ages have higher percentages of fat than their age-mates of 10–20 years ago. Active children are leaner than obese children at all ages. Obese children are less active than non-obese children.

Used with permission: Gallahue, D. L. & Ozmun, J. C. (2006). *Understanding motor development: Infants, children, adolescents, and adults.* Boston: McGraw-Hill. p. 253.

outcomes that can be modified through physical activity (Pate & Shephard, 1989). A review of the literature on fitness, however, reveals a marked lack of information on children less than 6 years of age. The reasons for this are many. Most tests of physical fitness require the individual to go "all out" and perform at his or her maximum. Anyone familiar with young children will recognize the difficulty of this situation. The problems lie in: (a) being able to sufficiently motivate the youngster for maximal performance, (b) accurately determining whether a maximum effort has been achieved, and (c) overcoming the fears of anxious parents.

Aerobic endurance, muscular strength and endurance, joint flexibility, and body composition are the components of health-related fitness. Each is discussed briefly in the following paragraphs and summarized in Table 6.3.

Aerobic endurance. Aerobic endurance is an aspect of muscular endurance, specific to the heart, lungs, and vascular system. *Aerobic endurance* refers to the ability to perform numerous repetitions of a strenuous activity requiring considerable use of the circulatory and respiratory system. Maximal oxygen consumption (VO$_2$ max) refers to the largest quantity of oxygen an individual can consume during physical work while breathing air at sea level. It is a measure of one's maximum ability to transmit oxygen to the tissues of the body. An increase in one's aerobic capacity is an excellent indicator of a higher energy output. It is generally considered that up to a 20% improvement in the VO$_2$ max of an aerobically untrained individual is possible, because one's genetic inheritance plays a crucial role in the capacity to

consume oxygen (Rowland, 1996). Maximal oxygen consumption tends to improve as a function of age until about 18 to 20 in males but tends to level off at about 14 in females (Armstrong & Welsman, 2000). Improvement thereafter is primarily a function of training. Because of size differences, females possess about 75% of the capacity of males to consume oxygen. More specifically, when comparing females and males at various age levels boys' values are about 12% higher than girls at age 10 (Malina, Bouchard, & Bar-Or, 2004). The differences between males and females prior to puberty are largely unexplored. Oxygen consumption in children under 8 has been investigated by relatively few researchers, and the results have often been conflicting because of the questionable reliability and reproducibility of VO$_2$ max measures with this young age group. However, attempts are being made to develop and establish clinical guidelines for measuring aerobic factors with pediatric populations.

Over the years several laboratory studies have been conducted with children to determine their VO$_2$ max values. Pate and Blair (1978) in their review of two decades of studies concluded that values ranging from 45 to 55 ml of oxygen per kg of body weight (ml.kg) had been consistently reported in the United States. A review of 29 longitudinal studies, Krahenbuhl, Skinner and Kohrt (1985) found similar mean values. Armstrong and Welsman (2000) noted that VO$_2$ max relative to weight remains stable for males 8 to 18 years at about 48 to 50 ml.kg but declined for females from 45 to 35 ml.kg as they advanced in years. A minimum VO$_2$ max threshold value of 42 is generally recommended for adults, and according to Simons-Morton and colleagues (1987), in their review of children and fitness, "it appears that most children are well above this level" (p. 297).

Heart rate responses to exercise are sometimes used as crude measures of cardiovascular endurance in young children because of the difficulty in gathering accurate VO_2 max data. Normal resting heart rates steadily decline during the early childhood years. The resting heart rate of a 1-year old, on average, is about 100 beats per minute. A 6-year-old has about 80 beats per minute, and a 10-year-old, on average, has a resting heart rate of about 70 beats per minute. Sex differences are insignificant until around age 10 when girls resting heart rates are reported to be about three to five beats faster than boys (Malina, Bouchard, & Bar-Or, 2004).

Mrzena and Macuek (1978) in what should be considered a pioneering experiment because of its methodology, tested children 3 to 5 years old on the treadmill. Each subject was required to walk or run for 5 min at a level grade with the treadmill set at three different speeds (3, 4, and 5 km/h). The highest heart rates were recorded at 142 beats per min. Another group performed the treadmill task at 4 km/h, whereas the grade was increased to 5° to 10° to 15°. This group produced heart rates averaging 162 beats per min. Investigators noted that when the treadmill speed was increased to 6 km/h and the inclination to 20°, "the children were not able to increase the step frequency and lost their balance" (p. 31). The average maximum aerobic capacity of preschool children is certainly greater than the scores obtained in this experiment, but maturity of movement as well as the psychological and emotional state of the young child determines the degree of cooperation and effort during testing.

In an investigation by Parizkova (1977), heart rates of 160 beats per min were recorded in a bench-stepping task with 3-year-old children. The children had considerable difficulty maintaining the cadence of 30 steps per min on the low bench without the investigator's assistance. The children in this investigation also had difficulty maintaining the task even though normal play heart rates of young children often exceed 200 beats per min. Cumming and Hantiuk (1980) reported that normal maximal heart rates for children range from 180 to 234 beats per min. This investigation again reminds us of the extreme difficulty in achieving a maximal effort for a sustained period with young children.

A meta-analysis of the effects of aerobic training on children was completed by Payne and Morrow (1993). Their investigation, which included 30 studies that the met inclusion criteria, revealed that:

In the most rigorously controlled studies (pre/post test), subjects improved less than 2 ml.kg-1.min-1. When contrasting studies with "sufficient" and "insufficient" training protocols, significance was not achieved. These findings indicate that many current practices concerning children's fitness should be viewed with skepticism (p. 3).

Many leading professionals and national professional associations endorse the practice of increasing the amount of a child's vigorous physical activity as a means of enhancing aerobic endurance. To date, however, the data do not conclusively support this hypothesis. Training protocols that produce significant training effects in young children should be studied, and the specific attributes of those being trained must be identified.

Muscular strength and endurance. *Muscular strength* is the maximum force a muscle or group of muscles can exert against a resistance (Gaul, 1996). In its purest sense, it is the ability to exert one maximum effort. *Muscular endurance* is the ability of a muscle or a group of muscles to perform work repeatedly against moderate resistance. Muscular endurance is similar to muscular strength in the activities performed but it differs in emphasis. Strength-building activities require overloading the muscles to a greater extent than endurance activities. Endurance-building activities require less of an overload on the muscle but more repetitions. Therefore, endurance may be thought of as the ability to continue in strength performance (Blimkie & Bar-Or, 1995). Children engaged in daily active play are enhancing their leg strength and endurance by running and bicycling. Their arm strength and endurance is developed through such activities as lifting, carrying objects, handling tools, and swinging on the monkey bars.

In laboratory situations strength is commonly measured by using a dynamometer or tensiometer. These devices are highly reliable when used by trained personnel. Dynamometers are calibrated devices designed to measure grip strength, leg strength, and back strength. Tensiometers are more versatile than dynamometers in that they permit measurement of many different muscle groups (Gaul, 1996). Near linear increases in strength have been reported from early childhood until the onset of puberty (Blimkie & Sale, 1998). These yearly increases are most closely associated with size increases and improvement in fundamental movement skills. In boys from age 6 onto the onset of puberty (generally around age 12) there is a gradual linear increase in strength, with dramatic acceleration to age 17 and beyond.

Historically, in girls, we have seen linear strength increases until about age 15, followed by a pronounced plateau and regression in the late teens and beyond. However, the impact of Title IX Federal Legislation which has opened the doors of opportunity for girls and women in sport and physical activity in the United States very well might be a significant factor in girls and women in this country being stronger longer than their counterparts of only 10 to 20 years ago.

Although information is limited on young children, Beunen and Thomis (2000) reported that from 3 to 6 years of age there are minimal sex differences and that strength gradually increases from year to year. Armstrong and Welsman (1997) and Blimke and Sale (1998), however, reported sex-related differences in favor of boys as young as 3 years of age. Furthermore, Oja and Jurimae (1998) using a large sample of young Estonian children also found significant sex-related differences in grip strength favoring boys.

Relatively few longitudinal investigations have been conducted on the development of strength in children at all ages. However, the available information indicates consistency in the development of strength in children over time. Strength has been shown to increase more rapidly than muscle size during childhood (Beunen & Thomis, 2000). This is probably because of the improved skill and coordination with which maximal contractions may be performed. This indicates the interrelationship between strength, coordination, and motor performance in children.

Although strength is a relatively stable quality throughout childhood, predicting strength levels at later years from measures taken in childhood has met with little success. The "strong" child at age 8, for example, will not necessarily make the greatest gains in strength from childhood through adolescence. Neither will the "weak" child necessarily make the least gains in strength from childhood through adolescence. Rapid change in body size, positively correlated with strength, and individual variability of growth patterns, plus the fact that many individuals actively train in order to gain strength, make prediction a precarious venture.

With proper supervision, strength training can benefit prepubescent children in strength enhancement, injury reduction, and improved performance (Payne, Morrow, Johnson, & Dalton, 1997; Rowland, 1996). However, strength training is different from weight lifting. Strength training involves the use of progressive resistance techniques using the body, weights, or machines to improve one's ability to exert or resist a force. Weight lifting is a sport in which one attempts to lift the maximum number of pounds possible. Weight lifting is not recommended for prepubescent children (American Academy of Pediatrics, 2001). A primary cause of epiphyseal damage in children engaged in weight lifting and chronic stress activities is improper training techniques. In addition, some equipment may be unsuitable with or without proper technique. Most machine-type resistance equipment is made to adult body proportions, with little or no consideration given to youth proportions. Epiphyseal growth plate injuries due to overuse have also been reported in children participating in certain sports. Chronic hip and knee injuries, neck and back injuries, and shoulder and elbow injuries are the all-too-common result of training for distance running, gymnastics, and competitive swimming, respectively. Each of these training activities, if carried to excess have the potential for causing overuse injuries in the prepubescent athlete. Overuse injuries are also beginning to be reported in sports such as soccer as playing seasons continue to increase in length.

Protein synthesis in muscle tissue involves the complex interaction of many anabolic hormones (muscle-enhancing) and catabolic hormones (muscle-destroying). One of the most important anabolic hormones is growth hormone (GH), found in prepubescent children. According to Bernuth (1985), "Exercise has been found to be the most potent stimulus for GH release in children" (p. 100). It seems, therefore, that children have at least some of the hormones necessary for muscle hypertrophy. Most studies examining prepubescent weight training, however, have found no evidence of muscle hypertrophy following a training program (Blimkie, Ramsay, Sale, MacDougall, Smith, & Garner, 1989; Ozmun, Mikesky, & Surburg, 1994).

Prepubescent children can increase their strength through resistance training due to enhanced stimulation of the central nervous system beyond that which would occur with normal growth and maturation. The term neuromuscular adaptation is used for changes that result from training. When the body is subjected over time to significant amounts of anatomical or physiological stress, the natural reaction is to adapt to the new conditions. It has been demonstrated that a short-term weight-training program results in neuromuscular adaptations

with prepubescent participants (Blimkie, et al., 1989; Ozmun, Mikesky, & Surburg, 1994; Blimkie & Sale, 1998). There are, however, special considerations for the preadolescent involved in a strength-training program.

The possibility that weight training harms the still-growing epiphyseal growth plates in young bones is a concern. Indeed, these cartilaginous structures, by their soft and spongy nature, are susceptible to injury, especially from excessive weight-bearing, shearing forces, and chronic stress. The potential vulnerability of the growth plates through excessive stress must be minimized. A high correlation exists between damage to these areas and children involved in weight lifting (Gumbs, 1982; Blimke & Sale, 1998).

Joint flexibility. Joint flexibility is the ability of the various joints of the body to move through their full range of motion. There are two types of flexibility: static and dynamic. Static flexibility is the range of motion achieved by a slow and steady stretch to the limits of the joints involved. Dynamic flexibility is the range of motion achieved when rapidly moving a body part to its limits (Brodie & Royce, 1998).

Besides strength and endurance training, another key health-related fitness component considered essential to injury prevention is joint flexibility. Improving the range of motion about the various joints of the body plays an important role in enhancing movement performance. Historically, it was believed that any type of weight training would decrease an individual's flexibility by not allowing the muscle to work through the full range of motion. The isokinetic weight-training equipment of today is designed to solve this problem. With the principle of variable resistance, an intricate system of cams and pulleys compensates for the inherent weak areas in a joint's range of motion. Flexibility can be maintained or even augmented with proper technique and certain types of weight-training equipment.

Flexibility is joint specific and can be improved with practice. Dynamic flexibility in the shoulder, knee, and thigh joints tends to decrease with age among sedentary children. Brodie and Royce (1998) reviewed the research on flexibility and concluded that girls are significantly more flexible than boys during early childhood and beyond. They further noted that age alone is the strongest single predictor of joint flexibility, and that flexibility begins to decrease as early as age 10 in boys and age 12 in girls. The time and rate of decrease is, of course, also related to changing physical activity patterns over time.

The National Children and Youth Fitness Study II (AAHPERD, 1987) tested thousands of children 6 to 9 years of age for flexibility. A sit-and-reach test was used as a measure of joint flexibility in the lower back and hip area. Mean scores clearly favored the girls. They tended to be slightly more flexible than boys at all ages. Girls showed little improvement with age, but neither did they regress. The boys, however, were on the average slightly less flexible at age 9 than they were at age 6.

Micheli and Micheli (1985) reported less flexibility in males and females during the prepubescent growth spurt. The reason is that bone growth precedes muscle and tendon growth. As a result, musculotendinous units tighten. It is essential for the prepubescent athlete to engage in a good stretching program along with any form of strength or endurance training to help counter the tendency for reduced flexibility. Overuse injuries such as "swimmer's shoulder" are related to a lack of flexibility. Do not assume that endurance activities such as running and swimming promote flexibility. The young performer must be encouraged to engage in a proper stretching program before and after any endurance workout to minimize the possibility of injury to the area around the joints.

Body composition (body fatness). Body composition, or body fatness as it is sometimes called, is defined as the proportion of lean body mass to fat body mass. Relative fatness can be determined through a variety of means. Hydrostatic weighing (i.e., underwater weighing) techniques, although the most accurate, are seldom used in studying body composition of young children. Instead, skinfold calipers are the preferred field method, even though the accuracy of measurement is questionable because of the increased possibility of measurement error (Lohman, 1994; Rowland, 1996). Measurement sites include the triceps, subscapular region, and the medial portion of the calf.

National surveys of body fatness have shown that children of all ages are fatter than they were 20 years ago (American Obesity Association, 2002; Dietz, 1995; National Center for Health Statistics, 2001). This trend toward increased fatness of American youth reflects dramatic changes in physical activity patterns and nutritional habits (American Heart Association, 2004; National Center for Education in Maternal Child and Health, 2002; National Association for Sport and Physical Education, 2004).

With regard to body composition and physical activity patterns, Parizkova (1972, 1973, & 1977) and Parizkova and Hills (1998) demonstrated repeatedly that young athletes are less fat than their more sedentary-age mates. Conversely, physical activity has been repeatedly documented that obese children are significantly less active than their lean peers (Bandini, 1987; Romanella, Wakat, Lloyd, & Kelly, 1990; Rowland, 1991; Sable, et al., 2002). Moreover, among youth, physical activity is inversely associated with obesity and a variety of cardiovascular risk factors (Sallis, & Patrick 1994; Sallis, Prochaska, & Taylor, 2000), as well as Type II diabetes (Goran, 2001), and social discrimination (Wabitsch, 2000). Convincing evidence suggests that patterns of physical activity established early in life may persist into childhood and beyond (Telama, Tang, Laakso, & Vilkari, 1997)

Rickard, Gallahue, Gruen, Tridle, Bewley, and Steele (1995a) found that a multicomponent intervention program with obese children that used a play approach with young children could serve as a valuable means of reducing health risks associated with obesity. Parents, classroom teachers, health workers, and teachers working as a team can play important roles in reversing the trend toward increased body fatness in children (Dietz & Robinson, 1993). Cross-sectional studies tend to indicate that in young children percent body fat and body weight are negatively associated with participation in physical activities (Sable, et al., 2002; National Center for Education in Maternal Child and Health, 2002a & 2002b).

Motor Fitness

Although the research literature is replete with information dealing with the motor fitness and performance levels of adolescents and adults, comparatively little is known about young children (Blair, 1995). Studies on the specific factors that make up children's motor fitness indicate that a well-defined structure is present during early childhood but that these factors may differ somewhat from those of older age groups (Seefeldt, 1980) and those with disabilities (O'Brien & Hayes, 1995). There is a statistically determined structure of motor abilities in children generally consisting of four or five items depending on the age level investigated (Hands & Larkin, 2001).

Movement control factors of balance (both static and dynamic balance) and coordination (both gross motor and fine motor coordination), coupled with the force production factors of speed, agility, and power, tend to emerge as the components that most influence motor performance (Hands, 1998; Ulrich, 2000).

The movement control factors (balance and coordination) are of particular importance during early childhood when young children are enhancing their fundamental movement skills (Gallahue & Ozmun, 2006). The force production factors (speed, agility, and power) become more important after children have gained control of their fundamental movements and pass into the specialized movement skill phase of later childhood and beyond.

Fjortoft (2000) studying 5- to 6-year-olds found differences in motor fitness to be dependent mainly on age and to a lesser extent on sex. Differences in height and weight at these ages do not seem to correlate with measures of motor fitness.

As with the components of health-related fitness, one's motor fitness is intricately interrelated with movement skill acquisition. One depends in large part on the other. Without adequate motor fitness, a child's level of skill acquisition will be limited, and without adequate skill acquisition, the level of motor fitness attainment will be impeded. The components of motor fitness are discussed here and synthesized in Table 6.4.

Coordination. Coordination is the ability to integrate separate motor systems with varying sensory modalities into efficient patterns of movement in both time and space (Thelan, 1989; Miller, 2001). The more complex the movement tasks, the greater the level of coordination necessary for efficient performance (Broderick & Newell, 1999). Coordination is linked to the motor fitness components of balance, speed, and agility, but does not appear to be closely aligned with strength and endurance (Hands, 1998). Coordinated behavior requires the child to quickly and accurately perform specific movements in a series. Movement must be synchronous, rhythmical, and properly sequenced to be coordinated (Hands, 1998; Thelan, 1989).

Eye-hand and eye-foot coordination are characterized by integrating visual information with limb action. Movements must be visually controlled and precise to project, make contact with,

TABLE 6.4. Common Measures of Children's Motor Fitness and A Synthesis of Findings

Motor Fitness Components	Common Tests	Specific Aspect Measured	Synthesis of Findings
Coordination	Cable jump	Gross body coordination	Year-by-year improvement with age in gross body coordination. Boys superior from age 6 on in eye-hand and eye-foot coordination.
	Hopping for accuracy	Gross body coordination	
	Skipping	Gross body coordination	
	Ball dribble	Eye-hand coordination	
	Foot dribble	Eye-foot coordination	
Balance	Beam walk	Dynamic balance	Year-by-year improvement with age Girls often outperform boys, especially in dynamic balance activities, until about age 8. Abilities similar thereafter.
	Stick balance	Static balance	
	One-foot stand	Static balance	
	Flamingo stand	Static balance	
Speed	20-yard dash	Running speed	Year-by-year improvement with age Boys and girls similar until age 6 or 7, at which time boys make more rapid improvements. Boy's superior to girls at all ages.
	30-yard dash	Running speed	
Agility	Shuttle run	Running agility	Year-by-year improvement with age Girls begin to level off after age 13. Boys continue to make improvements.
	Side straddle	Lateral agility	
Power	Vertical jump	Leg strength and speed	Year-by-year improvement with age Boys outperform girls at all age levels.
	Standing long jump	Leg strength and speed	
	Distance throw	Upper-arm strength and speed	
	Velocity throw	Upper-arm strength and speed	

Used with permission: Gallahue, D. L. & Ozmun, J. C. (2006). *Understanding motor development: Infants, children, adolescents, adults.* Boston: McGraw-Hill. p. 255.

or receive an external object (Thelan, 1989). Bouncing, catching, throwing, kicking, and trapping all require considerable amounts of visual input integrated with motor output to achieve efficient coordinated movement. The developmental progression for acquiring both fine and gross motor coordination takes several years to complete (Getchell & Whitall, 2003, 2004).

Gross body coordination in children involves moving the body rapidly while performing various fundamental movement skills. Measures such as the shuttle run, 30-yd dash, various hopping and skipping tests, and the standing long jump require high levels of gross body coordination. Gross body coordination and eye-hand and eye-foot coordination appear to improve with age in a roughly linear fashion. Also, boys tend to exhibit better coordination than girls throughout childhood (Frederick, 1977; Van Slooten, 1973). This conclusion, however, has been challenged as being culturally biased (Sovik & Maeland, 1986) and task specific (Getchell, Forrester, & Whitall, 2001). Getchell and Whitall (2003) tested 4-, 6-, 8-, and 10-year-olds on their ability to perform simultaneous upper and lower body extremity rhythmic clapping when walking and when galloping. They found a clear indication of coordinated action improving with age as indicated by less variability in performance and noted that "the manner in which the limbs coupled changed developmentally" (p.138).

Balance. Balance is the ability to maintain the equilibrium of one's body when it is placed in various positions. Balance is often defined as static or dynamic. Static balance refers to the ability of the body to maintain equilibrium in a stationary position. Dynamic balance refers to the ability to maintain equilibrium when moving from point to point. Balance is basic to all movement and is influenced by visual, tactile-kinesthetic, and vestibular stimulation.

Vision plays an important role in balance with young children. Cratty and Martin (1969) found that boys and girls age 6 and under could not balance on one foot with their eyes closed. By age 7, however, they were able to maintain balance with their eyes closed, and balancing ability continued to improve with age. Use of the eyes enables the child to focus on a reference point to maintain balance. The eyes also enable the young child to visually monitor the body during a static or dynamic balance task.

Balance is profoundly influenced by the vestibular apparatus. The fluid contained in the semicircular canals and the otolith plays a key role in helping an individual maintain equilibrium. The receptors in the semicircular canal respond to changes in angular acceleration (dynamic and rotational balance), whereas the otolith receptors respond to linear accelerations (static balance). The movements of macula (hairs) in either the otolith or the semicircular canals trigger nerve impulses by changing the electrical potential of adjoining nerve cells. Movement of the body and gravity are sensed by these vestibular receptors to keep the individual aware of both static and dynamic postural changes and changes in acceleration. The vestibular apparatus coordinates with the visual, tactile, and kinesthetic systems in governing balance. It appears that vestibular development of balance occurs early in life and that the vestibular apparatus is structurally complete at birth. However, the body musculature and the other sensory modalities involved in maintaining balance must mature and be integrated with vestibular clues to be of any use to the child in maintaining either static or dynamic balance.

Balancing on one foot, standing on a balance board, and performing a stick balance are common means for assessing static balance. Research on the static balance of children shows a linear trend toward improved performance from ages 2 through

12 (DeOreo, 1971; Keogh, 1965; Van Slooten, 1973). Before age 2 children generally are not able to perform a one-foot static balance task, probably because of their still-developing abilities to maintain a controlled upright posture. DeOreo (1980) indicated that clear-cut boy-girl differences are not as apparent in static balance performance tasks as they are with other motor performance tasks. Girls tend to be more proficient than boys until about age 7 or 8, whereupon the boys catch up. Both sexes level off in performance around age 8, before a surge in abilities from age 9 to age 12.

Balance beam walking tests are used most often as measures of dynamic balance in children. The available literature on dynamic balance indicates a trend similar to that for static balance. Girls are often more proficient than boys until age 8 or 9, whereupon they perform at similar levels. Both slow in their progress around age 9, before making rapid gains to age 12 (DeOreo, 1971; Frederick, 1977).

Speed. Speed is the ability to cover a short distance in as brief a time as possible. Speed is influenced by reaction time (the amount of elapsed time from the signal "go" to the first movements of the body) as well as movement time (the time elapsed from the initial movement to completion of the activity). Reaction time depends on the speed with which the initial stimulus is processed through the afferent and efferent neural pathways and is integrated with the initial response pattern. Reaction time improves in children as they get older.

Cratty (1979) reported that the information available on simple reaction time indicates that it is about twice as long in 5-year-olds as it is in adults for an identical task and that there is rapid improvement from age 3 to age 5. These developmental differences are probably because of neurological maturation, variations in the information-processing capabilities of children and adults, as well as to environmental and task consideration. Speed of movement in children is most generally measured through various tests of running speed. Frederick (1977), who tested the running speeds of five groups of children 3 to 5 years of age on the 20-yd dash, found linear improvement with age but no gender differences. In a study of the running speed of elementary school children, Keogh (1965) found that boys and girls are similar in running speed at ages 6 and 7, but boys were superior from ages 8 to 12. Both boys and girls improve with age at a rate of about 1 ft per second per year from ages 6 to 11 (Cratty, 1979). Keogh (1965) also found similar improvements and boy-girl differences in the 50-ft hop for speed, although girls tended to perform better than boys on hopping and jumping tasks requiring greater precision and accuracy of movement.

Fifty-yard sprint run scores are recorded as part of the Amateur Athletic Union (AAU) Physical Fitness Program (1993). These data are viewed as highly representative of the running speed of children and adolescents because of the large sample size, geographical distribution, and randomization techniques used. Both boys and girls are reported to make annual incremental improvements with males slightly outperforming females at all ages. Similarity in performance on the sprint run does not appear to carry over into the adolescent years. Males continue to make dramatic improvements throughout the teen years,

whereas females tend to regress slightly after age 14. Both factors are associated with pubescent male strength increases, limb length increases and body fat decreases, and female body fat increases.

Speed of movement generally improves until about age 13 in both boys and girls. After this, however, girls tend to level off and even regress, whereas boys tend to continue improving throughout the adolescent years. The movement speed of both boys and girls may be encouraged during childhood and beyond through vigorous physical activity that incorporates short bursts of speed (Lee & Coladarci, 2004). .

Agility. Agility is the ability to change the direction of the body rapidly and accurately. With agility, one can make quick and accurate shifts in body position during movement. Over the years, an assortment of agility runs have been used as indirect measures of agility which makes it difficult to compare studies. More recently, scores from the 30-ft shuttle run have been used as a measure of agility. Annual incremental improvements are seen throughout childhood with an edge given to boys at all ages (AAU, 1993).

Power. Power is the ability to perform a maximum effort in as short a period as possible. Power is sometimes referred to as "explosive strength" and represents the product of force divided by time. This combination of strength and speed is exhibited in children's activities that require jumping, striking, throwing for distance, and other maximum efforts. The speed of contraction of the muscles involved, as well as the strength and coordinated use of these muscles, determine the degree of power of the individual. It is difficult, if not impossible, to obtain a pure measure of this component because power involves a combination of motor abilities. The often-used throwing and jumping measures give only an indirect indication of power because of the skill required for both of these tasks. Jurimae and Jurimae (2000) reported significant sex-differences favoring 6-year-old boys in the standing long jump. Frederick (1977) found significant yearly increments in vertical jump, standing long jump, and distance throwing tasks for children ages 3 through 5. Boys outperformed girls on all measures at all age levels. The same results were found by Keogh (1965) for boys and girls from 6 to 12 years of age and by Van Slooten (1973) for children 6 to 9 years of age on the throw for distance, but with gender differences magnified beyond age 7. Luedke's (1980) review of the literature on throwing supports these results.

Linear improvements and differences between boys and girls have been demonstrated in the standing long jump from age 3 through 5 (Frederick, 1977), from age 6 through 12 (Keogh, 1965), and from age 10 through 17 (Ross & Gilbert, 1985), and from 11 to 13 (Lee & Coladarci, 2004). Differences in throwing velocity based on age and gender also have been shown in samples of children from age 6 to 14 years old (Glassow & Kruse, 1960; Luedke, 1980). However, differences from age to age and between sexes are closely related to yearly strength and speed of movement increments as well as to the varying sociocultural influences on boys and girls. Branta, Haubenstricker and Seefeldt

(1984) summarized a 16-year mixed-longitudinal study of children 5–10 years of age and found age-related improvement in measures of leg power such as the standing long jump, vertical jump, and 30-yd dash.

SUMMARY

Never before has the physical education profession been so strategically positioned and so vitally needed to make a difference in the lives of children in terms of promoting increased levels of physical activity. *Physical Activity and Health: a Report of the Surgeon General* (USDHHS, 1996), and the more recent Surgeon General's *Call to Action to Prevent and Decrease Overweight and Obesity* (USDHHS, 2001), two important publications from the Centers for Disease Control and Prevention entitled *Guidelines for School and Community Programs to Promote Lifelong Physical Activity among Young people* (CDC 1997) and *Increasing Physical Activity: A Report on Recommendations of the Task Force on Community Prevention Services* (CDC 2001), along with *Bright Futures in Practice: Physical Activity* (Patrick et al., 2001), and *Healthy People 2010* (USDHHS, 2000) all represent important efforts by the U.S. government that clearly point to the need for increased physical activity and quality physical education programs for all. Similar initiatives are being undertaken by countries around the world that equal or surpass what is being done in the United States. Unfortunately, however, no large-scale studies exist with young children that demonstrate the efficacy of physical education programs that emphasize increasing physical activity. Although a number of studies have been conducted with elementary school-aged children that have yielded varying degrees of success (Stone, McKenzie, Welk, & Booth, 1998; Wallhead & Buckworth, 2004), none have looked at younger populations. There is a clear need to examine the effects of physical activity programs on preschool and primary grade children not only in terms of improved physical fitness but also in terms of fundamental movement skill acquisition (O'Connor, 2000). The acquisition of fundamental stability, locomotor and manipulative skills provides children with the tools for an active way of life. These basic skills form the building blocks for the more complex specialized movement skills used in sport and recreational and daily living activities of ones culture. Fundamental movement skill development is too important to be left to chance if we are truly concerned about increasing young children's level of physical activity.

References

Amateur Athletic Union. (1993). *The Chrysler Fund-Amateur Athletic Union Physical Fitness Program.* Bloomington, IN: Poplars Building.

American Academy of Pediatrics. (2001). Strength training by children and adolescents. *Pediatrics, 107,* 1470–1472.

American Heart Association. (2004). *Exercise (physical activity) and children.* Retrieved April 29, 2005, from http://www.americanheart.org/presenter.jhtml?identifer=4596

American Obesity Association. (2002). *Childhood obesity.* Retrieved April 29, 2005, from http://www.obesity.org/subs/childhood/

Armstrong, N., & Welsman, J. (1997). *Young people and physical activity.* London: Oxford University Press.

Armstrong, N., & Welsman, J. (2000). Development of aerobic fitness during childhood and adolescence. *Pediatric Exercise Science, 12,* 128–149.

Bai, D. L., & Bertenthal, B. I. (1992). Locomotor status and the development of spatial search skills. *Child Development,* 63, 215–226.

Bandini, L. G. (1987). *Energy expenditure in obese and nonobese adolescents.* Unpublished doctoral dissertation, Massachusetts Institute of Technology.

Baranowski, T., & Simons-Morton, B. G. (1990). Dietary and physical activity assessment in school-aged children: Measurement issues. *Journal of School Health, 61,* 195–197.

Bar-Or, O., & Malina, R. M. (1995). Activity, fitness, and health of children and adolescents. In L. W. Y. Cheung, & J. B. Richmond (Eds.), *Child Health, Nutrition, and Physical Activity* (pp. 79–112). Champaign, IL: Human Kinetics.

Bernuth, G. A. (1985). Age, exercise, and the endocrine system. In K. Fotherby & S. B. Pal (Eds.), *Exercise endocrinology.* New York: Walter de Gruyter.

Beunen, G., & Thomis, M. (2000). Muscular strength development in children and adolescents. *Pediatric Exercise Science, 12,* 174–197.

Blair, S. N. (1995). Youth fitness: directions for future research. In L. W. Y. Cheung, & J. B. Richmond (Eds.), *Child health, nutrition, and physical activity* (pp. 147–152). Champaign, IL: Human Kinetics.

Blimkie, C. J. R., & Bar-Or, O. (1995). *New horizons in pediatric exercise science.* Champaign, IL: Human Kinetics.

Blimkie, C. J. R., Ramsay, J., Sale, D., MacDougall, D., Smith, K., & Garner, S. (1989). Effects of 10 weeks of resistance training on strength development in prepubertal boys. In S. Oseid & K. H. Carlsen (Eds.), *International series on sport sciences: Children and exercise XIII.* Champaign, IL: Human Kinetics.

Blimkie, C. J. R., & Sale, D. G. (1998). Strength development and trainability during childhood. In E. Van Praagh (Ed.), *Pediatric anaerobic performance* (pp. 193–224). Champaign, IL: Human Kinetics.

Branta, C., Haubenstricker, J., & Seefeldt, V. (1984). Age changes in motor skills during childhood and adolescence. *Exercise and Sport Science Review, 12,* 467–520.

Broderick, M., & Newell, K. (1999). Coordination patterns in ball bouncing as a function of skill. *Journal of Motor Behavior 31,* 165–175.

Brodie, D. A., & Royce, J. (1998). Developing flexibility during childhood and adolescence. In E. Van Praagh (Ed.), *Pediatric anaerobic performance* (pp. 65–93). Champaign, IL: Human Kinetics.

Centers for Disease Control and Prevention. (1997). Guidelines for School and Community Programs to Promote Lifelong Physical Activity Among Young People. *MMWR, 46,* No. RR-6.

Cratty, B. J. (1979). *Perceptual and motor development in infants and children.* Englewood Cliffs, NJ: Prentice Hall.

Cratty, B. J., & Martin, M. (1969). *Perceptual-motor efficiency in children.* Philadelphia: Lea & Febiger.

Cumming, G. R., & Hantiuk, A. (1980). Establishing of normal values for exercise capacity in a hospital clinic. In K. Berg & B. Erickson (Eds.), *Children and exercise IX.* Baltimore, MD: Academic Press.

DeOreo, K. L. (1971). *Dynamic and Static Balance in Preschool Children*. Unpublished doctoral dissertation, University of Illinois.

DeOreo, K. L. (1980). Performance of fundamental motor tasks. In C. B. Corbin (Ed.), *A textbook of motor development*. Dubuque, IA: Wm. C. Brown.

Dietz, W. H. (1995). Childhood obesity. In L. W. Y. Cheung, & J. B. Richmond (Eds.). *Child health, nutrition, and physical activity* (pp. 155–178). Champaign, IL: Human Kinetics.

Dietz, W. H. (April, 2004). *Physical Activity and Obesity—What We Know and What We Can Do*. 2004 R. Tait McKenzie Lecture. Annual Convention of the American Alliance for Health, Physical Education, Recreation and Dance, New Orleans.

Dietz, W. H., & Robinson, T. N. (1993). Assessment and treatment of childhood obesity. *Pediatric Review, 14,* 337–343.

DuRant, R. H., Baranowski, T., Johnson, M., & Thompson, W. O. (1994). The relationship among television watching, physical activity, and body composition of young children. *Pediatrics, 94,* 449–455.

Fjortoft, I. (2000). Motor fitness in pre-primary school children: The Eurofit motor fitness test explored on 5- to 7-year-old children. *Pediatric Exercise Science, 12,* 424–436.

Frederick, S. D. (1977). *Performance of selected motor tasks by three, four, and five year old children*. Unpublished doctoral dissertation, Indiana University.

Gabbard, C. (2003). *Lifelong motor development*. Boston: Addison-Wesley.

Gallahue, D. L. (1982). *Developmental movement experiences for young children*. New York: Wiley.

Gallahue, D. L., & Cleland, F. (2003). *Developmental physical education for all children* (4th ed.). Champaign, IL: Human Kinetics.

Gallahue, D. L., & Ozmun, J. C. (2006). *Understanding motor development: Infants, children, adolescent and adults* (6th ed.). Boston: McGraw-Hill.

Gaul, C. A. (1996). Muscular strength and endurance. In D. Docherty (Ed.), *Measurement in pediatric exercise science* (pp. 225–258). Champaign, IL: Human Kinetics.

Getchell, N., Forrester, L., & Whitall, J. (2001). Individual differences and similarities in the stability, timing, consistency, and natural frequency of rhythmic coordinated actions. *Research Quarterly for Exercise and Sport, 72,* 13–21.

Getchell, N., & Whitall, J. (2004). Transitions to and from asymmetrical gait patterns. *Journal of Motor Behavior, 36,* 13–27.

Getchell, N., & Whitall, J. (2003). How do children coordinate simultaneous upper and lower extremity tasks? The development of dual motor task coordination. *Journal of Experimental Child Psychology, 85,* 120–140.

Glassow, R. L., & Kruse, P. (1960). Motor performance of girls age 6–14 years. *Research Quarterly, 31,* 426–431.

Goran, M. I. (2001). Metabolic precursors and effects of obesity in children: A decade of progress, 1990-1999. *American Journal of Clinical Nutrition, 73,* 158–171.

Gumbs, V. L. (1982). Bilateral distal radius and ulnar fractures in adolescent weight lifters. *The American Journal of Sports Medicine, 10,* 375–379.

Hands, B. (1998). *Employing the Rasch model to measure motor ability in young children*. Unpublished doctoral thesis, University of Western Australia.

Hands, B., & Larkin, D. (2001). Using the Rasch measurement model to investigate the construct of motor ability in young children. *Journal of Applied Measurement 2,* 101–120.

Haywood, K. M., & Getchell, N. (2005). *Life span motor development*. Champaign, IL: Human Kinetics.

Johnson, R. (1962). Measurement of achievement in fundamental skills of elementary school children. *Research Quarterly, 33,* 94–103.

Jurimae, T., & Jurimae, J. (2000). *Growth, physical activity, and motor development in prepubertal children*. Boca Raton, FL: CRC Press.

Keogh, J. F. (1965). *Motor performance of elementary school children*. Los Angeles: University of California, Physical Education Department.

Knudson, D. V., & Morrison, C. S. (1997). *Qualitative analysis of human movement*. Champaign, IL: Human Kinetics.

Krahenbuhl, G. S., Skinner, J. S., & Kohrt, W. M. (1985). Developmental aspects of maximal aerobic power in children. In R. L. Terjung (Ed.), *Exercise science and sport research*. New York: Macmillan.

Kuntzleman, C. T., & Reiff, G. G. (1992). The decline in American children's fitness levels. *Research Quarterly for Exercise and Sport, 63,* 107–111.

Lee, J., & Coladarci, T. (2004). Growth rates in running speed and vertical jumping in boys and girls ages 11-13. *Perceptual and Motor Skills, 99,* 225–234.

Lohman, T. G. (1994). *Advances in body composition assessment*. Champaign, IL: Human Kinetics.

Luedke, G. C. (1980). *Range of motion as the focus of teaching the overhand throwing pattern to children*. Unpublished doctoral dissertation, Indiana University.

Malina, R. M., Bouchard, C., & Bar-Or, O. (2004). *Growth, maturation and physical activity*. Champaign, IL: Human Kinetics.

McClenaghan, B. A., & Gallahue, D. L. (1978). *Fundamental movement: Observation and assessment*. Philadelphia: W. B. Saunders.

McKenzie, T. L. (2004, April). *Environment, Youth and Physical Activity*. 13th Annual Raymond A. Weiss Lecture. Annual Convention of the American Alliance for Health, Physical Education, Recreation and Dance. New Orleans.

Micheli, L. J., & Micheli, E. R. (1985). Children's running: Special risks? *Annals of Sports Medicine, 2,* 61–63.

Miller, J. A. (2001). *The product and process performance of the two handed sidearm strike for primary school-aged children; The interrelationship of coordination, age, and gender*. Unpublished doctoral thesis, University of New England, NSW, Australia.

Morrow, J. R. (2004, April). *Are American children and youth fit? It's time we learned*. 25th Anniversary Charles H. McCloy Lecture. Annual Convention of the American Alliance for Health, Education, Recreation and Dance. New Orleans.

Mrzena, B., & Macuek, M. (1978). Uses of treadmill and working capacity assessment in preschool children. In J. Borms & M. Hebbelinck (Eds.), *Medicine and sports series, Vol. II. Pediatric work physiology*. Basel, Belgium: S. Karger.

National Association for Sport and Physical Education. (2000). *Appropriate practices in movement programs for young children*. Reston, VA: NASPE.

National Association for Sport and Physical Education. (2003). *Your active child*. Reston, VA: NASPE.

National Association for Sport and Physical Education. (2004a). *Physical activity for children: A statement of guidelines*. Reston, VA: NASPE.

National Association for Sport and Physical Education (2004b). *Kids in Action*. Accessed April 29, 2005, at http://www.aahperd.org/naspe/pdf_files/brochure.pdf

National Center for Education in Maternal and Child Health. (2002a). *Bright futures in practice: Nutrition*. Washington, DC: NCEMCH.

National Center for Education in Maternal and Child Health. (2002b). *Bright futures in practice: Physical activity*. Washington, DC: NCEMCH

National Center for Health Statistics. (2001). *Prevalence of Overweight among Children and Adolescents*. Accessed April 14, 2005, at www.cdc.gov/nchs/products/pubs/pubd/hestats/overweight99.htm

AAHPERD. (1987). National Children and Youth Fitness Study II. *Journal of Physical Education, Recreation and Dance, 58*(9), 49-96.

Oja, L., & Jurimae, T. (1998). Relationship between physical activity, motor ability, and anthropometric variables in 6-year-old Estonian children. In J. Parizkova & A. P. Hills (Eds.), *Physical fitness and nutrition during growth* (pp. 68-78). Basel, Belgium: Karger.

O'Brien, C., & Hayes, A. (1995). *Normal and impaired motor development*. London: Chapman and Hall.

O'Connor, J. (2000). *An investigation into the hierarchical nature of fundamental movement skill development*. Unpublished doctoral thesis, Royal Melbourne Institute of Technology, Australia.

O'Connor, J., Ball, E. J., Steinbeck, K. S. Davies, P. S. W. Wishart, C., Gaskin, K. J., & Baur, L. A. (2003). Measuring physical activity in children: A comparison of four different methods. *Pediatric Exercise Science, 15*, 202-215.

Ott, A. E., Pate, R. R., Trost, S. G., Ward, D. S., & Saunder, S. R. (2000). The use of uniaxial and triaxial accelerometers to measure children's "free play" physical activity. *Pediatric Exercise Science, 12,* 360-370.

Ozmun, J. C., Mikesky, A. E., & Surburg, P. R. (1994). Neuromuscular adaptations following prepubescent strength training. *Medicine and Science in Sports and Exercise, 26,* 510-514.

Parizkova, J. (1972). Somatic development and body composition changes in adolescent boys differing in physical activity and fitness: A longitudinal study. *Anthropologie, 70,* 3-36.

Parizkova, J. (1973). Body composition and exercise during growth and development. In G. L. Rarick (Ed.), *Physical activity: Human development*. New York: Academic Press.

Parizkova, J. (1977). *Body fat and physical fitness*. The Hague, Netherlands: Martinus Nayhoff B. V. Medical Division.

Parizkova, J., & Hills, A. P. (1998). *Physical fitness and nutrition during growth*. Basel, Belgium: Karger.

Pate, R. R., & Blair, S. N. (1978). Exercise and the prevention of atherosclerosis: Pediatric implications. In W. Strong (Ed.), *Pediatric aspects of atherosclerosis*. New York: Grune and Stratton.

Pate, R., & Shephard, R. J. (1989). Characteristics of physical fitness in youth. In C. Gisolfi, & D. Lamb (Eds.), *Perspectives in exercise science and sports medicine: Youth exercise and sport* (pp. 1-46). Indianapolis, IN: Benchmark Press.

Patrick, K., Spear, B., Holt, K., & Sofka, D. (2001). *Bright futures in practice: Physical activity*. USDHHS, Washington, DC: National Center for Education in Maternal and Child Health.

Payne, V. G. & Isaacs, L. D. (2005). *Human motor development: A lifespan approach*. Boston: McGraw-Hill.

Payne, V. G., & Morrow, J. R. (1993). Exercise and VO2 Max in children: A meta-analysis. *Research Quarterly for Exercise and Sport, 64,* 305-313.

Payne, V. G., Morrow, J. R., Johnson, L., & Dalton, S. N. (1997). Resistance training in children and youth: A meta analysis. *Research Quarterly for Exercise and Sport, 68,* 80-88.

Peterson, K. L., et al. (1974, April). *Factor analyses of motor performance for kindergarten, first and second grade children: A tentative solution*. Paper presented at the annual convention of the AAHPERD, Anaheim, CA.

Rickard, K. A., Gallahue, D. L., Gruen, G. E., Tridle, M., Bewley, N., & Steele, K. (1995). The play approach in the context of families and schools: An alternative paradigm for nutrition and fitness education for the 21st century. *Journal of the American Dietetic Association, 95,* 1121-1126.

Rickard, K., Gallahue, D. L. Bewley, N., & Tridle, M. (1995). The play approach to learning: An alternative paradigm for healthy eating and active play. *Pediatric Basics, 76,* 2-7.

Roberton, M. A. (1978a). Stability of stage categorization in motor development. In D. M. Landers & R. W. Christina (Eds.), *Psychology in motor behavior and sport-1977*. Champaign, IL: Human Kinetics.

Roberton, M. A. (1978b). Stages in motor development. In M. V. Ridenour (Ed.), *Motor development: Issues and applications*. Princeton, NJ: Princeton Book Company.

Roberton, M. A. (1982). Describing "stages" within and across motor tasks. In J. A. S. Kelso & J. E. Clark (Eds.), *The development of movement control and co-ordination* (pp. 294-307). New York: Wiley.

Roberton, M. A. (2004, April). *Research on the Development of the Overarm Throw: Are There Hints for How to Teach the Throw?* 2004 Research Consortium Scholar Lecturer of the American Alliance for Health, Physical Education, Recreation and Dance. New Orleans.

Romanella, N. E., Wakat, D. K., Loyd, B. H., & Kelly, L. F. (1990). Physical activity and attitudes in lean and obese children and their mothers. *International Journal of Obesity, 15,* 407-414.

Rose, D. J. (1997). *A multilevel approach to the study of motor control and learning*. Boston: Alyn and Bacon.

Ross, J. G., & Gilbert, G. G. (1985). The national children and youth fitness study: A summary of findings. *Journal of Physical Education, Recreation and Dance, 56*(1), 45-50.

Rowland, T. W. (1991). Effects of obesity on aerobic fitness in adolescent females. *American Journal of Diseases of Children, 145,* 764-768.

Rowland, T. W. (1996). *Developmental exercise physiology*. Champaign, IL: Human Kinetics.

Rowlands, A. V., Eston, R. G., & Ingledew, D. K. (1997). Measurement of physical activity in children with particular reference to the use of heart rate and pedometry. *Sports Medicine, 24,* 258-272.

Sable, A. D., Weyer, C., Harper, I., Lindsey, R. S. Ravussin, E., & Tatarani, P.A. (2002). Assessing risk factors for obesity between childhood and adolescence. *Pediatrics, 110,* 307-314.

Sallis, J. F. & Patrick, K. (1994). Physical activity guidelines for adolescents: Consensus statement. *Pediatric Exercise Science, 6,* 302-314.

Sallis, J. F., Prochaska, J. J., & Taylor, W. C. (2000). A review of correlates of physical activity of children and adolescents. *Medicine and Science in Sports and Exercise, 32,* 963-975.

Schlicker, S. A., Borra, S. T., & Regan, C. (1994). The weight and fitness status of United States children. *Nutrition Reviews, 52,* 11-17.

Seefeldt, V., & Haubenstricker, J. (1976). *Developmental sequences of fundamental motor skills*. Unpublished research, Michigan State University.

Seefeldt, V., & Haubenstricker, J. (1982). Patterns, phases, or stages: An analytic model for the study of developmental movement. In J. A. S. Kelso & J. E. Clark (Eds.), *The development of movement control and co-ordination* (pp. 309-318). New York: Wiley.

Seefeldt, V. (1980). Physical fitness guidelines for preschool children. In *Proceedings of the National Conference on Physical Activity and Sports for All*. Washington, DC: President's Council on Physical Fitness and Sports, pp. 5-19.

Simons-Morton, B. G. et al. (1987). Children and fitness: A public health perspective. *Research Quarterly for Exercise and Sport, 58,* 295-303.

Sinclair, C. (1973). *Movement of the young child*. Columbus, OH: Merrill.

Sovik, N., & Maeland, A. (1986). Children with motor problems (clumsy children). *Scandinavian Journal of Education, 30,* 39-53.

Stone, E. J., McKenzie, T. L., Welk, G. J., & Booth, M. L. (1998). Effects of physical activity interventions in youth: Review and synthesis. *American Journal of preventative Medicine, 15,* 298-315.

Telama, R., Yang, X., Laakso, L., & Vilkari, J. (1997). Physical activity in childhood and adolescence as predictor of physical activity in young adulthood. *American Journal of Preventative Medicine, 13,* 317-323.

Thelan, E. (1989). Evolving and dissolving synergies in the development of leg coordination. In S. A. Wallace (Ed.), *Perspectives on the coordination of movement* (pp. 259-281). North Holland, Amsterdam: Elsevier Science Publishers.

Thelen, E. (1995). Motor development: A new synthesis. *American Psychologist, 50,* 79-95.

Ulrich, D. (2000). *Test of gross motor development-2.* Austin, TX: Pro-Ed.

Updyke, W. (1992). In search of relevant and credible physical fitness standards for children. *Research Quarterly for Exercise and Sport, 63,* 112-119.

U.S. Department of Health and Human Services. (1996). *Physical activity and health: A report of the Surgeon General.* Atlanta, GA: Center for Disease Control and Prevention.

U.S. Department of Health and Human Services. (2001). *The Surgeon General's call to action to prevent and decrease overweight and obesity.* Rockville, MD: U.S. Department of Health and Human Services, Public Health Services, Public Health Service, Office of the Surgeon General.

Van Slooten, P. H. (1973). *Performance of selected motor-coordination tasks by young boys and girls in six socioeconomic groups.* Unpublished doctoral dissertation, Indiana University.

Wabitisch, M. (2000). Overweight and obesity in European children and adolescents: Causes and consequences, treatment and prevention. *European Journal of Pediatrics, 159* (S1), S5-S-7.

Walkley, J., Holland, B., Treloar, R., & Probyn-Smith, H. (1993). Fundamental motor skill proficiency in children. *The ACHPER National Journal (spring),* 11-14.

Wallhead, T. L., & Buckworth, J. (2004). The role of physical education in the promotion of youth physical activity. *Quest, 56,* 285-301.

Wickstrom, R. (1983). *Fundamental motor patterns.* Philadelphia: Lea & Febiger.

Williams, H. (1970). *A study of perceptual-motor characteristics of children in kindergarten through sixth grade.* Unpublished paper, University of Toledo.

Williams, H. (1983). *Perceptual and motor development.* Englewood Cliffs, NJ: Prentice Hall.

·7·

THE DEVELOPMENT OF CHILDREN'S CREATIVITY

Mark A. Runco
California State University, Fullerton
The Norwegian School of Economics and Business Administered

Creativity is very important for children and for development. It is, however, easy to misunderstand. It is unlike the creativity of adults, and not easy to study scientifically. The creativity of adults often leads to some product—a work of art, a solution to a problem, a new way of accomplishing something. Children's creativity, by contrast, may not produce a tangible product or result. It may take the form of imaginative play, self-expression, or a new understanding of the world. We can compare the art work of Lichtenstein with that of Warhol, but we cannot rely on norms to understand the creativity of children.

Creativity is critical to children's development in much the same way that variation is vital for societal progress and biological evolution. Children are creative when they pretend, for example, and when they express themselves in an uninhibited fashion. Play and the construction of meaning (which is necessary for self-expression) provide children a grasp of what is possible. Because children do pretend and do express themselves in an uninhibited fashion, the range of possibilities is enormous. They can think about, explore, and act on both the realistic and the imaginary. In that sense, children have larger repertoires than adults. Children are more playful and less inhibited; they have fewer routines, make fewer assumptions, and are often more spontaneous than adults. Each of these allows children to think broadly, divergently, and imaginatively. As they grow older, however, they are socialized, which simply put means that they are taught which ideas and behaviors are appropriate, and which are not appropriate. In this light, imaginative play and creative thinking provide the variations, and socialization is a kind of selection.

If children do not fully utilize their imagination, explore possibilities, try new things, consider new actions, invent understandings, and experiment, they will not be able to discover who they are, what they are capable of, and what is acceptable in their family, school, peer-group, and culture. Parents and teachers should therefore both support children's imaginative play and experimentation, but also provide feedback, structure, and appropriate values. Parenting (and teaching, for that matter) is very much a matter of balance (Runco & Gaynor, 1993). If such balanced experiences are available to children, they can develop mature forms of creative talent, and perhaps become productive adults. At the very least children will maintain the capacity to express themselves with only optimal and healthful levels of inhibition. The child will also, through creative self-expression, recognize his or her own uniqueness. The range of options mentioned above will provide the creative child with possible solutions to problems, so he or she is likely to be good at solving problems, both those presented in school and those encountered in the natural environment (Runco, 2003). The creative child will even be in position to avoid psychological disturbance and even illness. (Many disorders are tied to the lack of self-expression [Pennebaker, 1998].) Children who receive balanced experiences, with opportunities to explore and experiment, as well as mature feedback, will be able to cope with and adapt to our ever-changing world. Creativity is an important part of development, and if encouraged, children will fulfill their potentials and may contribute in a meaningful fashion to society.

This chapter reviews the research on children's creativity. It identifies influences on children's creativity and defines it in a manner that allows adults to recognize it. The chapter first reviews two concepts (i.e., *stages* and *domains*) that describe the how creative children may differ from one another. The creativity of preschool children is, for instance, different from that of schoolaged children, which in turn differs from that of adolescents and adults. *Domains of creative performance* are explored next, for it is impossible to understand creativity without putting it into context. This is especially true on the individual level: a child who has creative potential in the musical domain may be quite dissimilar to the child who has creative potential in the mathematical, verbal, athletic, or some other domains.[1] These two concepts—stages and domains—are described first because very little about creativity applies across the board; most everything else about creativity must be qualified by taking stage and domain into account. The remainder of this chapter explores "most everything else," but in particular examines influences on creative potential and its fulfillment. Family and cultural context are, for instance, discussed in this chapter, for each is a significant influence on creativity and its development. The *implicit theories* held by parents and teachers are described after cultural context, and research on creativity and play, art, and divergent thinking reviewed. Because it deemphasizes products and achievements, the theory of *personal creativity* is very useful when thinking about the creativity of children and is therefore described in some details. This chapter concludes with a brief elaboration of the concept of optimization. As we will see, that is the most general practical principle: Creativity flourishes when developmental experiences and conditions are optimal.

STAGES

Creative talents and potentials express themselves in different ways at different ages. Evidence suggest that there are stages, for example, and that the creativity of a preschool child differs from that of a schoolaged child or an adolescent. The most famous stage is probably that which occurs in the fourth grade. Perhaps I should say the most *infamous* stage occurs during the fourth grade, for a number of investigations have identified a fourth grade *slump* in original thinking (Raina, 1980; Runco, 1999; Torrance, 1968). There are various explanations for this, and indications that it is not only found in the United States (Raina, 1984). One explanation emphasizes the environment. By the fourth grade, children have experienced several years of formal education, for instance, and have been expected to raise hands before speaking, sit in rows, and follow a precise daily schedule. This structure may be internalized such that, by the fourth grade, there is a loss of initiative and original thought. Yet it seems that at least some of the slump is maturational and tied to biological changes. The nervous system may become increasingly sensitive to conventions at this stage, and of course conventional behavior is unlikely to be original. An increase in conventionality will led directly to a decrease in originality. This perspective is consistent with reports of a literal stage in language (Gardner, 1982), a conventional stage of moral reasoning (Kohlberg, 1987), and the tendency of children to adhere in a rigid fashion to rules when playing games (Runco & Charles, 1997). Smith and Carlsson (1985) suggested that there is a second slump (the first being the fourth grade) in preadolescence.

Conventionality is apparently quite relevant to children's artistic endeavors. Rosenblatt and Winner (1988), for instance, found that professional artists prefer the art work of preschool children over that of older children, the reason being that the former were more spontaneous and self-expressive than the latter. Preschool children were described as *preconventional* because they did not produce art that was a clear representation of reality—a kind of conventional thinking—but instead drew from their own preferences and uninhibited feelings. The older children in this research (those in the middle- and latter-grades of elementary school) had apparently entered the conventional stage and tried to produce art that was representational and realistic; the result being that their art was commonplace and judged to be uncreative.

The idea of preconventional artwork suggests that preschool-aged children can be creative. Their creativity is, however, different from that of older children, adolescents, and adults. Preschool children do not produce works of art or solutions to problems that help and assist other people; their creativity is typically authentic self-expression. This self-expression is typically original—after all, it is preconventional—and fitting, at least given the child's own situation. What is most important is that even the things they do are not intended for wide audiences, young children do things that satisfy the two requirements of creativity: originality and usefulness. This is probably the most apparent in studies of young children's play. Schmukler (1985), for instance, emphasized children's play and imagination as bases for later creative skill. As she put it:

Play [is] an activity which is not obviously goal-directed, such as recreating and acting out what the child has observed. Imaginative play refers to the introduction by the child of settings, times, and characters which are not immediately present in the environment and, since it makes something out of nothing, can be seen as creative expression with important developmental implications. (p. 75)

Russ (1994), Ayman-Nolley (1992), and Smolucha (1992a, b), and Singer and Singer (in press) also tie the play of young children to creative potentials. Daugherty (1993) agreed that young children have creative potentials, but she felt these potentials were expressed in private speech. Matuga (2004) also saw creativity in the private speech of young children, as well as in their drawings.

Piaget's (1962) description of imaginative play as assimilatory implies a strong connection to creative potentials, and he too saw a kind of peak in imaginative behavior in preschool children. He described the imaginative play of young children as highly assimilatory, meaning that children's thinking tendencies allowed them to interpret objective experience in a personal and subjective fashion. No wonder children can play about super heroes, believing themselves to be Superman, Spiderman, or some other ultrastrong being, even though they are in actuality small and physically immature. They do not look like Superheroes, but that does not keep them from creating imaginary worlds were they are Superheroes.

---

[1]There is an interesting issue here, regarding domains of performance. Essentially the issue is, how many domains? On the one hand, it is useful to have a long list. With a longer list of domains, we are the most likely to recognize any one child's talents. On the other hand, too long a list and we sacrifice the concept of *talent* and idea of *giftedness*. As Runco (1994) asked, "Is every child gifted?" That may not sound so bad, but then again giftedness becomes a meaningless category if every child has talent; and every child will have talent of some sort, if the list is long enough.

There is controversy. Dudek (1974), for instance, raised the possibility that children are not really creative. She described their original insights and behavior as accidental rather than creative. She felt that children sometimes do not know what is the correct or conventional thing to say or way to behave, and as a consequence they do the wrong thing. This surprises adults who explain the mistakes as creative rather than accidental. Runco and Charles (1997) argued for the other extreme perspective and went so far as to suggest that young children are more creative than individuals at any other age. They described children as extremely playful and unfamiliar with routines. Children also do not make many, if any, assumptions, and they are not inhibited by social conventions. All of this may give them an edge and allow them to think and behavior in a spontaneous and original fashion.

Runco and Charles (1997) additionally suggested that the fourth grade slump is only a potential loss and need not occur, if parents and educators provide the opportunities, models, and reinforcement for continued self-expression and original behavior. At present, many children tend to slump, and the slump has been reported again and again for at least 30 years (when Torrance, 1968, first identified it), but this does not indicate how things should or must be. Indeed, the fourth grade slump is far from universal. Torrance found approximately 50–60% of the children in his sample experienced it. The best way to view stages is as age-bounded potentials (Runco & Charles, 1998). Usually potentials imply the possibility of growth (Cohen, 1989; Kohlberg, 1987; Piaget, 1976) but apparently children also have the potential to experience possibility a slump or two at particular ages. These drops may not occur; they are just possibilities, or potential slumps. In this light, they might be avoided. Just as experiences are necessary for an individual to fulfil his or her potential, so too can a slump probably be avoided with the right experiences. Suggestions for avoiding slumps and enhancing creativity are discussed later.

Before leaving the topic of preconventional thinking, something should be said about creative morality. This is germane in part because the original conception of conventional thinking developing in stages (i.e., preconventional, conventional, and postconventional) was an attempt at describing moral reasoning (Kohlberg, 1987). Rosenblatt and Winner (1988) later used the same stages to describe the development of artistic skills, and Runco and Charles (1997) even later applied it to divergent thinking. There is, however, an intriguing and important connection between creativity and morality, and indeed, a number of attempts have been made to encourage investments specifically in this area (Gruber, 1993, 1997; Runco, 1993). Gruber (1997) pointed specifically to the need to develop *creative altruism*. In his words:

The term "altruism" implies some unsolved problem in the disposition of human resources: it also implies that there may be something that ought to be done, which if done will eliminate the discrepancy between the actual and desired state of affairs. . . . The self-chosen task of the creative altruist, to work to bring such a change about, necessarily involves an exchange with others. In this exchange, there is a donor with available assets and a recipient with an unmet need. No matter how such exchanges begin, in the ideal case the long range outcome will be to reduce or eliminate the discrepancy. Moreover, appropriate planning and action will require cooperation among all the participants that is, both the donors and recipients. Only through such cooperation can the desired change be brought about; indeed, such cooperation is not only part of the solution process but often part of the goal. (Gruber, 1997, p. 466)

The need for creative morality and altruism is especially pressing now, with evolution occurring at such a rapid pace and ethical dilemmae being so numerous (McLaren, 1993). Everyone studying creative morality seems to feel that the solution is to encourage empathy, altruism, and integrity in the schools—along with creative thinking. Haste (1993) detailed an educational program that would be of great value along these lines.

The connection between moral reasoning and creativity was explored by Runco (1993), who used the stages of conventional thought, mentioned earlier, and by Gruber (1993, 1997). Runco concluded that parents and teachers need to target postconventional thought, for here the individual takes morals, laws, rules, traditional, and conventions into account, but he or she thinks for him- or herself. Gruber (1997) focused on the

awareness of the possibility of something new, followed by the patient evolution of the understanding of the problem. Both [creativity and moral reasoning] require the translation of the inner life of desire and fantasy into forms of action in and upon the world. Both require prolonged, intentional search for adequate and harmonious solutions. Both require sensitivity to the impact of the innovation on some prospective audience or recipients. Especially in creative altruism, this takes the form of empathic awareness of the needs and feelings of the other. (p. 466)

DOMAIN DIFFERENCES

Domain differences have long been recognized in studies of creativity, although early on (e.g., Patrick, 1935, 1937; MacKinnon, 1960) the focus was on creative adults with special skills in poetry, music, architecture, and so on. Many fascinating differences were uncovered by the IPAR research group in Berkeley, when creativity research was first becoming unambiguously scientific (Barron, 1972; Helson, 1960; MacKinnon, 1983). In 1983 Gardner identified seven clear-cut domains of talent and supported their independence with cognitive, psychometric, developmental, and neuropsychological evidence. The first seven domains were verbal-symbolic, mathematical-logical, musical, spatial, bodily-kinesthetic, intrapersonal, and interpersonal. Later he used the same criteria for domains and added "the naturalist." Gardner argued that each of these domains depended on particular core characteristics (e.g., symbols for the verbal domain), and on the nervous system. For Gardner, the domain-specific talents of prodigies and gifted children also depends on idiosyncratic developmental experiences.

This particular claim about idiosyncratic developmental experiences has been compellingly supported by the longitudinal work of Albert (1980, 1990). Longitudinal studies, such as Albert's, are extremely useful for understanding development because they allow researchers to actually observe changed that occur as individuals age (also see Helson, 1999; Subotnik, 1999; Plucker, 1999). Albert began his study 30 years ago with two groups of children, one exceptionally gifted in the sense of a high IQ score (all above 155), and one equally exceptionally gifted but with talents specifically in mathematics. His premise was that there are differences in the developmental backgrounds of individuals in different domains, and differences at different levels of talent. Albert's interest in developmental background led him to collect a huge amount of data from the families of the exceptionally gifted children and their families. Various developmental experiences have been related to the creative talents of the children involved in the longitudinal research: Level of independence, for example, was associated with creative potential (Albert & Runco, 1985), as was achievement motivation that does not lead to conformity (Runco & Albert, in press). As Gardner (1983) predicted, particular developmental experiences characterized children with talents in different domains. Albert and Runco found, for instance, that boys with exceptional talents in the mathematical domain had fathers who were more stereotypically masculine than other fathers.

Empirical demonstrations of domain differences have also been presented by Milgram (1990), Runco (1986), and Wallach and Wing (1969). Very significantly, Wallach and Wing not only discovered that original and creative thinking were predictive of achievement in specific extracurricular domains (e.g., leadership, art, music, mathematics); they also demonstrated that GPA and school performances were of limited validity. GPA and traditional intelligence was related only to academic achievements, while creative thinking seemed to contribute to performance in the natural environment. Along the same lines, Milgram (1990) proposed that extracurricular (leisure-time) activities are important to consider because they reflect what an child is actually motivated to do. In school, the child may be responding to incentives and grades, but what happens when those are not available? The child may not behave in the same fashion. But if a child chooses to do something during his or her leisure time (e.g., write a poem), it is much more likely that this child will pursue that domain and continue working within it. This emphasis on leisure-time activities can be used when there is a need to identify gifted and talented children—it allows reliable assessment (Milgram, 1990). It is also justified by the research showing that creative work is often intrinsically motivated (Amabile, 1990; Eisenberger, 2002; MacKinnon, 1965). Renzulli (1978) proposed that intrinsic motivation ("task commitment"), creative potentials, and traditional intelligence each be used to identify gifted children.

Most definitions of giftedness include IQ or general intellectual ability. The alternative is to recognize specific domains of talent, which may be extricable from general ability. The recognition of domains would seem to be justified by cultural differences and by the biases and sometimes questionable validity of IQ tests (Gardner, 1983). For the present purposes, what may be most important is that it is feasible to define giftedness such that creativity is a prerequisite. This is precisely what Renzulli (1978) suggested. The curvilinear relationship between traditional intelligence and creativity test scores (Guilford, 1968; Runco & Albert, 1986), however, suggests that some creative children may have only a moderate level of tested intelligence. It may be

best to recognize different kinds of giftedness, both in terms of the various domains but also in terms of creative talents. A child may be creatively gifted, for example, with exceptional creative potential but only moderate levels of traditional intelligence, or academically gifted, with high levels of traditional intelligence but unexceptional creative talents. Such specificity in definitions would allow parents and teachers to best understand each individual child.

It is possible that other domains of creative performance exist, in addition to those proposed by Gardner (1983). Some of these may be subdomains, however, for someone who has a talent for poetry may not do much journalism or prose. It is one thing to write music, but something else to perform it. Of special importance is the idea that there is a domain which has been called "everyday creativity" (Runco & Richards, 1997). The basic idea here is that individuals may not be interested or talented in music, mathematics, the language arts, or any widely recognized domain, but that individual may be highly creative in the natural (everyday) environment. He or she may be creative when solving problems involving friends, pets, allowances, homework, or attire. Admittedly, the everyday domain of creative talent has not yet been verified with the same criteria and rigor used by Gardner (1983).

FAMILY BACKGROUND

The family thus plays a critical role in the development of children's creativity. Actually, it plays various critical roles. Parents are models for their children, for example, and provide *resources*, *values*, and *opportunities*. Discipline styles also may have some impact. The idea of balance, introduced earlier, may apply to discipline: It is likely that some autonomy is beneficial for children and allows them to learn to think for themselves; yet too much freedom and they may not learn to focus on a task until it is completed or put enough effort into traditional skills as they should. A bit more will be said below about autonomy. Turning to resources, creative children frequently have had *diverse experiences* (Schaefer, 1960). Experience very clearly plays a role in insightful problem solving (Epstein, 1990), and insight is just as clearly frequently tied to creative thinking (Ward & Smith, in press). Sadly, resources may be influenced by socioeconomic status and the like, meaning that certain children have advantages and others disadvantages which are germane to creative potential.

In her discussion of "facilitating family environments," Schmukler (1985) emphasized children's play and imagination as bases for creative skill. She also suggested that a child's opportunities for play, and thus the development of creativity, are determined by the parents, and often mostly by the mother. This view is consistent with the ideas mentioned above, from Ayman-Nolley (1992) and Smolucha (1992). They too emphasized social interactions and play as influences on creative potentials.

Less intentional family influence is exerted by so-called *family structure*. This includes "sibsize" (number of siblings), age gap (interval between two siblings), and birth order (or ordinal position). Sibsize is very strongly related to traditional intelligence (Zajonc & Markus, 1975), but it is an inversely relationship: Larger families tend to have children with lower Scholastic Aptitude Test (SAT) scores. Zajonc's explanation for this focuses on the intellectual climate of the home. Apparently, when there are few children, that climate can be quite stimulating intellectually. When there are more children, the climate of the home is not as likely to be intellectually stimulating. Very importantly, one small study suggests that what held true for SAT does not hold true for creative potential. Runco and Bahleda (1986) reported that larger families tended to have children with higher scores on a battery of divergent thinking tests. These tap a child's potential for solving problems in an original fashion (and are described in more detail later in this chapter). Perhaps large families provide children with more autonomy, which in turn allows them to develop independent and original thought. Recall here that autonomy and independence have been tied to creative potential in developmental, personality, and cognitive research (Albert & Runco, 1989). Family size was, however, related to creative potential in one relatively small investigation (with 240 children) and replications are certainly warranted.

Birth order and age gap are at least as important a variable as sibsize. Sulloway (1996), for instance, found that middle children are "born to rebel." Apparently, many older children develop a need for achievement in traditional areas (like education), and although they may do well in school or other similar areas, their achievement motives take them only to conventional areas and thinking styles. Middle children tend to seek unique family niches and thereby avoid conflicts with the older, more mature sibling. If the older sibling tends to a conventional direction, the middle child goes in the opposite directly, namely, the unconventional one. Such unconventional behavior is easily tied to original thought; and Sulloway's data confirm that many rebels in the arts and sciences have indeed been middle children. A child's tendency toward unconventional thought and action might be mitigated by a large age gap. If the older sibling is much older, there is no need to work to find a unique niche. Age itself provides uniqueness. Hence with large gaps, there is less diversity and less likelihood of the middle child being unconventional.

Aside from family planning, studies of family structure may not sound like they are very useful. There are, however, a number of things parents can actually control. Runco (1990) suggested that families need to provide three things: *Opportunities* to practice creative thinking, *models* of creativity, and an *appreciation* of creative efforts. Clearly, parents who model and value creativity are more likely than other parents to raise creative children. Models may be the parents or siblings, or they may be *remote models* (i.e., creative people in books or in the media). The appreciation may take the form of rewards and reinforcers (Epstein, 1990), yet care must be taken here. This is because rewards and the like can actually undermine the intrinsic motivation that tends to support creative efforts. This is the *overjustification effect* (Amabile, 1990). If an individual enjoys something, but then receives rewards for doing it, he or she may forget that the task was at one point intrinsically interesting.

The independence and autonomy, mentioned earlier, should be explored further. It makes good theoretical sense that these would be related to creative potential; originality assumes a kind of independence. It assumes an independence from conventional ways of thinking, and independence from norms and sometimes expectations. Albert and Runco (1989) found support for the relationship between parental independence and creative thinking in three samples of children. One was nongifted, and the other two exceptionally gifted. The mothers of the children with exceptionally high IQs (all in excess of 150) reported the highest levels of independence, meaning that they allowed their children to do more things on their own at younger ages. The ratings of independence from the children (i.e., their expectations about what they could do on their own) and those from the mothers were both significantly correlated with divergent thinking test scores. This indicates that the children's expectations about autonomy, and the mothers' allowing independence in the home, were both predictive of the children's capacity for original thought. Weisberg and Springer (1961) also offered support for the relationship between creative potential and independence in the home.

It is possible that the relationship of independence and children's divergent thinking reflects *practice*, which is one reason children need opportunities to think for themselves, in an original fashion. If children have numerous opportunities to solve problems on their own—opportunities to work independently and autonomously—they will be able to practice the requisite skills. The relationship between parental independence and divergent thinking could also reflect family values. These are communicated to children in various ways (e.g., parents' own actions suggest what they value), and families that value independent thinking will probably communicate in many ways the idea that autonomy is a respectable capacity. The same thing can be said about creativity per se; it is probably directly related to family values (Cheung, Lau, Chan, & Wu, 2003; Kwang, 2001; Runco, 2001). This takes us to cultural context, for many family values are determined by culture.

CULTURAL CONTEXT

Children's creativity depends a great deal on the family, and on the educational system, but it also depends on the wider cultural context. This was implied by the earlier discussion of domain differences. Certain domains are recognized in any one particular culture, and other domains ignored. Each culture defines the talents that will be encouraged. This is, of course, another way of describing the values found withing a given culture, and those values in turn define what is appropriate and what is not. Earlier I referred to this as socialization. Domains in which a child expresses an interest may be judged as appropriate or inappropriate, as will particular behaviors and even ideas. This process is analogous to *sex-typing*, in which cultural values proscribe what boys and girls are expected to do—and what they are not supposed to do.

Cultural values are communicated to children within the family and, later, the school system, but they are also communicated via the media and other informal experiences. Most experimental research of the impact of the media on children's creativity has focused on the media themselves, not on the values broadcast by the media. TV, for example, may provide too much information to children (pictures, sounds, and so on) and not allow them to use their imaginations (Meline, 1978; Pezdek & Runco, 1984). Additionally, the models available on TV programming is often quite stereotyped, and this in turn leaves little room for the individuality that is more conducive to creative behavior.

Sex typing is a good example of the socialization processes because it is both clearly related to culture and to creative potentials. Although the data are not overwhelming in this regard, by and large children and adolescents who exhibit high levels of *psychological androgeny* tend to perform in the most creative fashion (Baer, in press; Harrington, et al., 1991). Androgeneous individuals have access to both stereotypically masculine and stereotypically feminine behaviors. They do not conform to expectations about sex roles and make choices based on what is expected of them based on their being a boy or a girl, but instead think for themselves and react in a spontaneous and personally meaningful fashion. Because they do not conform to stereotypes, they have a wide range of options available to them when solving problems. An androgenous boy will not think only of stereotypically masculine solutions to a problem, for example, and a girl will not think merely of stereotypically feminine solutions. Each will consider appropriate solutions regardless (or at least deemphasizing) stereotypes. It is really just another example of the unconventional capacities of creative persons, though it is also useful to view it from the other direction of effect as well, namely, with androgeny as an influence on creative potential. Interestingly, androgenous individuals also tend to be psychologically healthy.

Much has been made of differences between Eastern and Western cultural values (e.g., Kwang, 2001; Runco, 2001), although of course this is a generalization. Not all Eastern cultures are identical, nor are Western cultures all the same. There is much variation and differences within each. Definitions of appropriateness may differ among the 50 U.S. states, to mention one example that is close to home, and of course most cultures are diverse with regard to socioeconomics, religion, and dialects. Yet there are commonalities. The most recognized and relevant include an appreciation of harmony and collaboration, in the East, and independence and competition in the West.

IMMEDIATE CONTEXT

Contextual influences on creativity may be immediate and local. This was implied by the discussion of the family above, with resources and so on potentially influencing creativity and its development. Parallel influences may be exerted by the school environment (Dudek, Strobel, and Runco, 1994; Wallach & Kogan, 1965). Wallach and Kogan, for instance, found that a *permissive school environment* allowed children to think divergently and creatively. A testlike environment, in contrast, seemed to inhibit creative thinking. Indeed, when school children were given divergent thinking exercises in the testlike environment, only children who had done well on traditional academic tests performed at high levels. But when the same exercises were administered in the permissive environment (i.e., children were told that the exercises were games, not tests, that spelling did not matter, and that no grades would be given), many children who did not do well on traditional academic tests performed at very high levels.

These children had outstanding creative potential which would have been overlooked if they had received either (a) tests of academic aptitude or (b) tests of creative potential administered in a structured environment. Dudek et al. (1993) also found the classroom and school environments to be significantly related to performance on tests of creative potential.

The physical environment may have some influence on creativity. Much has been made of this in the organizational literature and in the research on the creativity of adults (Mace et al., 2003; McCoy, 2000), but no doubt many of the factors they identify could also influence children's creativity. McCoy suggested that five situational factors are related to creative performances: color (few cool colors), view of the natural environment, complexity of visual detail, natural materials (and few artificial ones).

Importantly, all levels of context, from cultural to the more specific immediate environment, include people. The home environment, for example, is often defined by parents, and the school environment is defined by educators. One way of examining this kind of influence is to study *implicit theories*. These are the assumptions and expectations held by people. They are implicit in the sense that they may not be articulated nor tested. In fact, it may be easiest to explain implicit theories by contrasting them with explicit theories. These are held by scientists and researchers. They are explicit in the sense that they are articulated and tested. Scientists may have a theory of creativity, but they must explore it and share it with colleagues; and to be scientific, they must extract hypotheses, make these known, and test them. Importantly, the implicit theories of various groups, including parents, teachers, children, artists, and scientists, seem to differ from each other.

Johnson et al. (2003) recently examined the implicit theories of parents and teachers in India and the United States. Interestingly, Johnson et al. obtained ratings of creativity, taking both indicative and contraindicative traits into account, and ratings of social desirability. The last of these was examined because frequently profiles of "the ideal child" (Singh, 1980; Torrance, 1971) emphasize conformity, punctuality, consideration, and other traits that have little to do with original or creative behavior. Johnson et al. (2003) confirmed that the parents and teachers in India and the United States recognized both indicative and contraindicative aspects of creativity. There were, then, traits that they felt supported creative efforts, and traits that inhibited it. In that light, the implicit theories of the parents and teachers were consistent with explicit theories of creativity. Most parents and teachers in Johnson et al.'s study (2003) gave high social desirability ratings to the traits that were associated with creative talent. This was not true of all creative traits, but it was true of most of them. The adults in India differed from the adults in the United States in ratings of various "intellectual" and "attitudinal" traits but, surprisingly, there were negligible differences between the parents and teachers. This was a surprise because earlier work had found parents to value the intellectual aspects of creativity, and teachers to value the more social aspects (Runco, 1984, 1989). In another investigation Proctor (in press) described the "traits often exhibited by creative students and noted in the literature . . . are: asking 'what if?' questions; being full of ideas; possessing high verbal fluency; being constructive and building and rebuilding; coping with several ideas at once; becoming irritated and bored by the routine and obvious; going beyond assigned tasks; enjoying telling about own discoveries or inventions; finding different ways of doing things; and finally, not minding if others think he or she is "a little different." Here again there is some overlap with explicit theories of children's creativity, especially in the unconventional behaviors suggested by "not minding what others think."

In many ways the implicit theories of parents and teachers are more important than explicit theories. This is because the former lead directly to expectations, and expectations in turn lead directly to action. If a teacher expects creative children to be a trouble-making nonconformist, for example, that teacher will expect a creative child to disrupt the classroom. Expectations are powerful influences on development (Rosenthal, 1991). The example just given may not sit well, for it suggests that creative children are nonconformists, but research does suggest that what teachers think of "an ideal student" is very different from the traits usually associated with creative children. Ideal students are polite, punctual, and conventional. Creative children ask questions, follow their own interests, and can be unconventional.

To make matters more difficult for adults, creative children tend to think in an idiosyncratic fashion. As a matter of fact, all creative thinking (that of children or adults) may be difficult to follow. Creative insights are new and original, and thus by definition different and surprising. This tendency is compounded when we take a child's stage of development into account. As Elkind (1981) put it, children are "cognitive aliens." They all think differently from the way adults think. Practically speaking, then, a child may have a remarkably creative idea for a project or assignment, but as he or she is a cognitive alien, and because the insight is original, an educator may not grasp its significance or creativity. The educator may not even see its relevance. If educators are not careful, and open to surprises, they will overlook creative thinking by children. They certainly can't reward creative thinking if they can't recognize it.

Evidence suggests that both parents and teachers have difficulty recognizing creative ideas (Runco, Luptak, & Nobel, 1989; Westby, 1993). This evidence is based on judgments by parents and teachers when they were asked to rate the originality or creativity of ideas actually generated by children who were given open-ended *divergent thinking* exercises. The children might have been asked to "name all of the things you can think of that move on wheels," for example, or "list as many uses as you can for a brick." Such exercises allow children to think for themselves and to generate original ideas (Guilford, 1968; Runco, 1999; Torrance, 1968). The thinking that is captured by these exercises is predictive of creative activity and accomplishment in the natural environment (Milgram, 1990; Runco, 1990; Runco, Plucker, & Lim, 2001–2002) and, very significantly, is independent of the kind of *convergent thinking* that is required

by IQ tests and most traditional academic exercises and tests (Guilford, 1968; Runco & Albert, 1986). In other words, this kind of original thinking will not be found if educators rely on traditional examinations. Fortunately, many such exercises are available (Scott et al., 2004), and many programs have been designed specifically to encourage divergent thinking.

Divergent thinking tests are probably the most commonly used measure of the potential for creative thought. They by no means guarantee actual performance: They are estimates of potential. They are highly reliable, with moderate predictions to creative activity in the natural environment (Runco, 1986; Runco et al., 2003; Torrance, 1981). Of course, divergent thinking is related in different ways to creative activities in various domains. Other useful measures have been developed, some of the most impressive focus on performance in the natural environment rather than performance on a paper-and-pencil test (Milgram, 1990). Portfolios also have been used as indicators of creative potential, but there is a discrepancy between research and practice. Hunsaker and Callahan (1995) studied the creativity measurement instruments that were used by 418 school districts as part of their identification procedures for gifted students. Their results indicated that districts often selected instruments for assessing creativity without first paying careful attention to the definition of the construct

PERSONAL CREATIVITY

Earlier in this chapter, I pointed out that children's creativity is unlike that of adults. In fact, the stages mentioned twice in this chapter suggest that creativity takes one form early in life, another form a bit later, and so on throughout life.[2] Adult creativity is usually defined in terms of actual performance. Adults invent things, solve problems, and produce art and innovations. This facilitates the study of adult creativity because there are products which can be counted, monitored, studied. We can be objective, and therefore scientific, about creative products. Children do not create these kinds of things. If they do produce something, it is unlikely to be original by adult norms. It is likely to be original only by the child's own standards. It is still original and useful—that is how creativity is usually defined—but not by adult norms.

It is useful to look to children's divergent thinking, as suggested earlier, but creativity is not merely a result of cognitive skill. This is probably why predictions of actual creative performance from divergent thinking are only moderate (Plucker, 1999; Runco, 1999). They only take cognitive skills into account. Creativity is more than cognition. The intrinsic and extrinsic theories reviewed earlier included intrinsic motivation, openness, curiosity, and autonomy, just to mention a few extracognitive tendencies that often play a role in children's creative efforts.

[2]It may be relevant for adults working with children to recognize one tendency of adulthood, namely to become less flexible (Chown, 1961; Rubenson & Runco, 1995). This not only influences our own creative behavior, but since we are models for children, it can influence theirs as well. Perhaps most notable is that our tendency to rely more on routines and assumptions can make us rigid, in the sense that we do not consider new ideas. This is a huge problem when working with children, for it means that we will have difficulty recognizing their original thinking if it is contrary to what we expected or have grown accustomed to.

This takes us back to the topic noted briefly early in this chapter, namely, concerning the possibility of protecting children from slumps and allowing them to maintain high levels of self-expression and creativity. Amabile (1990) suggested that children can be "immunized" such that they will stick with their intrinsic interests. This immunization involves role-playing and discussion of video models. Many other educational programs focus on tactics which facilitate creative thinking and creative problems solving. Some tactics are easy to communicate to children. Harrington (1975), for example, demonstrated that originality can be enhanced if students are told to "be creative," and various investigations have used this idea with schoolaged children. The key idea is to be explicit about how the children can find creative ideas. Not surprisingly, this technique is called "explicit instructions." With young children, in early elementary school, it may be best to be concrete and suggest that they "give ideas that no one else will think of." That provides children with a technique that allows them to find original ideas, and it communicates the notion that being different can be a good thing. Runco (1986) and Milgram (1976) found various explicit instructions to be very effective, even in third and fourth grade school children (also see Smith, Hoever, & Michaels, 1990).

Elsewhere I suggested that the most important thing parents and teachers can do is allow a child to develop *ego strength* (Runco, 1996, 2003). This is a bit like self-confidence. It allows the child to stand up to pressures to conform and to believe in his or her own thinking and ideas. Very likely the fourth grade slump in creativity occurs because children become very sensitive to peer pressure and conventions at about that age. They may still have original ideas, but they may not be willing to share and explore them. They will share and explore them if they are confident and have developed optimal ego strength. They will even think before conforming to conventional expectations.

Ego strength is also not sufficient. In the theory of *personal creativity*, children also must have the potential to construct original interpretations of experience. This, however, is probably a nearly universal talent. It parallels what Piaget (1976) said about assimilation and is involved in every adaptation a child makes. In that light adults probably don't need to do much for this aspect of creativity. Instead, they need to insure that children have ego strength—and discretion.

If a child lacks discretion, but has the ability to produce original ideas and the ego strength to believe in them, he or she may go too far. The child may rely entirely on original ideas and pay no attention to the curriculum or to standard knowledge. Discretion will allow the child to recognize when to be original, and when to conform. If he or she is working on an art project, very likely there is room for originality. If he or she is asked who invented the light bulb, it would be best to give the conventional answer rather than making one up. Many schools encourage students to "make good choices," and that applies to creative talents.

CONCLUSIONS

Children's creativity is related to individual skills and talents, including ego-strength and divergent thinking skills. It is also related to various extrapersonal influences—the family, school, and culture each play a role in the fulfillment of creative potential. These extrapersonal influences may be interpersonal (e.g., parents and teachers), or they may involve the physical environment. Creative potentials seem to vary in different stages, and there are clear differences between various domains of activity. Admittedly, the generality and specificity of creative skills is a matter of ongoing debate (Baer, 1991).

Throughout this chapter, I suggested that children's creative potentials are related to autonomy (and postconventionality or independence of thought) and self-expression. Autonomy is a part of divergent thinking, for example, because the original ideas that are recorded with divergent thinking exercises and tests require an independence of thought. Original ideas are unique or at least unusual, and they are found by thinking for one's self. Self-expression is also a reflection of autonomy, and it is by definition manifest. This is in turn important, because children are often not creative in the sense of being productive, and looking to their original and meaningful self-expressions may give us a behavioral indicator of talent. Note the implied definition of children's creativity: it is behavior which is original, spontaneous, and self-expressive. It may not result in a tangible product but is instead manifested in a process, again, the process of original self-expression. Definitions of creativity that focus on adults always include value, fit or appropriateness, as well as originality (Runco, 1988; Runco & Charles, 1993), and this makes sense because original things can be worthless! A highly bizarre invention may be original, but useless, and is thus just novel but not creative. A definition of children's creativity must accept self-expression instead of normative appropriateness. Children are not creative in the same fashion as adults. They behave in a creative fashion, but they do not produce things that will sell or attract wide attention. They may act in a creative fashion, play in a creative fashion, and behave in a creative fashion, but they do no produce creative products.

Obviously there are implications for adults who work with (or simply parent and raise) children. Self-expression is easy to identify and easy to encourage. It is also important that individuals who have the opportunity to express themselves tend to maintain psychological health. Admittedly, some creative adults have had psychological problems (most common is probably a mood or affective disorder; Richards, 1990), but many creative persons are remarkably healthy. Indeed, creativity is sometimes a part of the highest level of psychological health, namely self-actualization (Maslow, 1968; Rogers, 1961; Runco et al., 1991). Creative self-expression also may lead to physical health (Eisenman, 1998; Pennebaker, 1998). We should not worry that helping our children to be creative will lead them to ill health or disturbance. More likely, creative talents will work to a child's advantage on both behavioral and psychological levels.

Recall also the idea introduced early in this chapter about balance. The optimization implied by balance is also germane to health, divergent thinking, ego strength, and conventionality. Indeed, optimization and balance may apply very generally to all kinds of creativity (Runco & Gaynor, 1993). Simply put, if the child is capable of creative and original behavior but balances this with the capacity for conventional actions, he or she is likely to be adaptive and healthy. Ill health is often a lack of balance and adaptability, or a lack of discretion that leads the individual to be original when he or she should conform. Applied to divergent thinking, optimization would allow children to find original ideas and solutions, but also to think convergently when taking a multiple choice test or when working in an area when they should focus on what adults have deemed to be correct. Ego strength may help children "just say no," but children also should be open minded and listen to what others have to say. It may be good to be unconventional some of the time, for the sake of originality, but much of the time it is good to consider conventional wisdom and conventional rules. Children should be capable of balance such that they can fit in and support peer group and family, but they should maintain the potential for creative thought as well.

References

Albert, R. S. (1980). Family position and the attainment of eminence: A study of special family positions and special family experiences. *Gifted Child Quarterly, 24,* 87–95.

Albert, R. S. (1990). In M. A. Runco & R. S. Albert (Eds.). *Theories of creativity.* Newbury Park, CA: Sage.

Albert, R. S., & Runco, M. A. (1989). Independence and cognitive ability in gifted and exceptionally gifted boys. *Journal of Youth and Adolescence, 18,* 221–230.

Amabile, T. M. (1990). Within you, without you: Towards a social psychology of creativity, and beyond. In M. A. Runco & R. S. Albert (Eds.), *Theories of creativity.* Newbury Park, CA: Sage.

Ayman-Nolley, S. (1992). Vygotsky's perspective on the development of imagination and creativity. *Creativity Research Journal, 5,* 101–109.

Baer, J. (1991). Generality of creativity across performance domains. *Creativity Research Journal, 4,* 23–40.

Baer J. (in press). Sex differences. In M. A. Runco (Ed.), *Creativity research handbook* (Vol. 3). Cresskill, NJ: Hampton Press.

Barron, F. (1969). *Creative person and creative process.* New York: Holt, Rinehart & Winston.

Barron, F. (1972). *Artists in the making.* New York: Seminar Press.

Cheung, P. C., Lau, S., Chan, D. W., & Wu, W. Y. (2003). Creative Potential of School Children in Hong Kong: Norms of the Wallach-Kogan Creativity Tests and Their Implications. *Creativity Research Journal, 16,* 69–78.

Chown, S. M. (1961). Age and the rigidities. *Journal of Gerontology, 16,* 353–362.

Cohen, L. M. (1989). A continuum of adaptive creative behaviors. *Creativity Research Journal, 2,* 169–183.

Daugherty, M. (1993). Creativity and private speech: Developmental trends. *Creativity Research Journal, 6,* 287–296.

Dudek, S. Z. (1974). Creativity in young children: Attitude or ability? *Journal of Creative Behavior, 8,* 282–292.

Dudek, S. Z., Strobel, M., & Runco, M. A. (1994). Cumulative and proximal influences of the social environment on creative potential. *Journal of Genetic Psychology, 154,* 487–499.

Eisenberger, R., & Shanock, L. (2003). Rewards, intrinsic motivation, and creativity: A case study of conceptual and methodological isolation. *Creativity Research Journal, 15,* 121–130.

Eisenman, R. (1998). In M. A. Runco & R. Richards (Eds.), *Eminent creativity, everyday creativity, and health.* Norwood, NJ: Albex.

Elkind, D. (1981). *The hurried child.* Cambridge, MA: Persus Publishing.

Epstein R. (1990). Generativity theory as a theory of creativity. In M. A. Runco & R. S. Albert (Eds.), *Theories of creativity.* Newbury Park, CA: Sage.

Gardner, H. (1982). *Art, mind, and brain: A cognitive approach to creativity.* New York: Basic Books.

Gardner, H. (1983). *Frames of mind.* New York: Basic Books.

Gardner, K., & Moran, J. D. (1990). Family adaptability, cohesion, and creativity. *Creativity Research Journal, 3,* 281–286.

Gaynor, J. L., & Runco, M. A. (1992). Family size, birth order, age-interval, and the creativity of children. *Journal of Creative Behavior, 26,* 108–118.

Gruber, H. E. (1993). Creativity in the moral domain: Ought implies can implies create. *Creativity Research Journal, 6,* 3–15.

Gruber, H. E. (1997). Creative altruism, cooperation, and world peace. In M. A. Runco & R. Richards (Eds.), *Eminent creativity, everyday creativity, and health* (pp. 463–479). Greenwich, CT: Ablex.

Guilford, J. P. (1968). *Creativity, intelligence, and their educational implications.* San Diego, CA: Robert Knapp/EDITS.

Harrington, D. M. (1975). Effects of explicit instructions to be creative on the psychological meaning of divergent test scores. *Journal of Personality, 43,* 434–454.

Helson, R. (1990). Creativity in women: Outer and inner views over time. In M. A. Runco & R. S. Albert (Eds.), *Theories of creativity* (pp. 190–212). Newbury Park, CA: Sage.

Helson, R. (1999). A Longitudinal Study of Creative Personality in Women. *Creativity Research Journal, 12.*

Hunsaker, S. L., & Callahan, C. M. (1995). Creativity and giftedness: Published instrument uses and abuses. *Gifted Child Quarterly, 39,* 110–114.

Johnson, D., Runco, M. A., & Raina, M. K. (2003). Parents' and teachers' implicit theories of children's creativity: A cross-cultural perspective. *Creativity Research Journal, 14,* 427–438.

Kohlberg, L. (1987). The development of moral judgment and moral action. In L. Kohlberg (Ed.), *Child psychology and childhood education: A cognitive developmental view* (pp. 259–328). New York: Longman.

Kwang, N. (2001). *Why Asians are less creative Than Westerners.* Singapore: Prentice-Hall.

Mace, M.-A., & Ward, T. (2000–2001). Modeling the Creative Process: A Grounded Theory Analysis of Creativity in the Domain of Art Making. *Creativity Research Journal, 14.*

MacKinnon, D. (1983). The highly effective individual. In R. S. Albert (Ed.), *Genius and eminence: A social psychology of creativity and exceptional achievement* (pp. 114–127). Oxford: Pergamon. (Original work published 1960).

Maslow, A. H. (1968). *Toward a psychology of being* (2nd ed.). New York: Van Nostrand Reinhold.

Matuga, J. M. (2004). Situated Creative Activity: The Drawings and Private Speech of Young Children. *Creativity Research Journal, 16, 2–3,* 267–281.

McCoy, J., & Evans, G. W. (2000–2001). The Potential Role of the Physical Environment in Fostering Creativity. *Creativity Research Journal, 14.*

McLaren, R. (1993). The dark side of creativity. *Creativity Research Journal, 6,* 137–144.

Meline, C. W. (1976). Does the medium matter? *Journal of Communication, 26,* 81–89.

Milgram, R. M. (1990). Creativity: An idea whose time has come and gone? In M. A. Runco & R. S. Albert (Eds.), *Theories of creativity* (pp. 215-233). Newbury Park, CA: Sage.

Milgram, R. M., & Milgram, N. (1976). Creative thinking and creative performance in Israeli students. *Journal of Educational Psychology, 68*, 255-258.

Patrick, C. (1935). Creative thought in poets. *Archives of Psychology, 26*, 1-74.

Patrick, C. (1937). Creative thought in artists. *Journal of Psychology, 4*, 35-73.

Pennebaker, J. W., Kiecolt-Glaser, J. K., & Glaser, R. (1997). Disclosure of trauma and immune functioning: Health implications for psychotherapy. In M. A. Runco & R. Richards (Eds.), *Eminent creativity, everyday creativity, and health* (pp. 287-302). Norwood, NJ: Ablex.

Pennebaker, W. (1998). In M. A. Runco & R. Richards (Eds.), *Eminent creativity, everyday creativity, and health*. Norwood, NJ: Albex.

Piaget, J. (1962). *Play, dreams and imitation in childhood*. New York: Basic Books.

Piaget, J. (1970). Piaget's theory. In P. H. Mussen (Ed.), *Carmichael's handbook of child psychology* (3rd ed., pp. 703-732). New York: Wiley.

Piaget, J. (1976). *To understand is to invent*. New York: Penguin.

Plucker, J. (1999). Is the Proof Really in the Pudding? Reanalyses of Torrance's Longitudinal Data. *Creativity Research Journal, 12*.

Raina, M. K. (1975). Parental perception about ideal child. *Journal of Marriage and the Family, 37*, 229-232.

Raina, T. N., & Raina, M. K. (1971). Perception of teacher-educators in India about the ideal pupil. *Journal of Educational Research, 64*, 303-306.

Raina, M .K. (1984). *Social and cultural change and changes in creative functioning in children*. New Delhi: National Council of Educational Research and Training.

Renzulli, J. (1978). What makes giftedness? Re-examining a defintion. *Phi Delta Kappan, 60*, 180-184.

Richards, R. (1990). Everyday creativity, eminent creativity, and health: Afterview for CRJ issues on creativity and health. *Creativity Research Journal, 3*, 300-326.

Rogers, C. R. (1961). *On becoming a person*. Boston, MA: Houghton Mifflin.

Rosenblatt, E., & Winner, E. (1988). The art of children's drawings. *Journal of Aesthetic Education, 22*, 3-15.

Rosenthal, R. (1991). Teacher expectancy effects: A brief update 25 years after the Pygmalion experiment. *Journal of Research in Education, 1*, 3-12.

Rubenson, D. L., & Runco, M. A. (1995). The psychoeconomic view of creative work in groups and organizations. *Creativity and Innovation Management, 4*, 232-241.

Runco, M. A. (1984). Teachers' judgments of creativity and social validation of divergent thinking tests. *Perceptual and Motor Skills, 59*, 711-717.

Runco, M. A. (1986). Divergent thinking and creative performance in gifted and nongifted children. *Educational and Psychological Measurement, 46*, 375-384.

Runco, M. A. (1988). Creativity research: Originality, utility, and integration. *Creativity Research Journal, 1*, 1-7.

Runco, M. A. (1989). Parents' and teachers' ratings of the creativity of children. *Journal of Social Behavior and Personality, 4*, 73-83.

Runco, M. A., & Albert, R. S. (1986). The threshold hypothesis regarding creativity and intelligence: An empirical test with gifted and nongifted children. *Creative Child and Adult Quarterly, 11*, 212-218.

Runco, M. A. (1990). Implicit theories and creative ideation. In M. A. Runco & R. S. Albert (Eds.), *Theories of creativity* (pp. 234-252). Newbury Park, CA: Sage Publications.

Runco, M. A. (1993). Moral creativity: Intentional and unconventional. *Creativity Research Journal, 6*, 17-28.

Runco, M. A. (1996). Personal creativity: Definition and developmental issues. *New Directions for Child Development*, No. 72 (Summer), pp. 3-30.

Runco, M. A. (1999). Divergent thinking. In M. A. Runco & Steven Pritzker (Eds.), *Encyclopedia of creativity* (pp. 577-582). San Diego, CA: Academic Press.

Runco, M. A. (2001). The intersection of creativity and culture: Foreword. In N. A. Kwang, *Why Asians are less creative than Westerners*. Singapore: Prentice-Hall.

Runco, M. A. (2003). Education for creative potential. *Scandinavian Journal of Education, 47*, 317-324.

Runco, M. A., & Albert, R. S. Parents' personality and the creative potential of exceptionally gifted boys. *Creativity Research Journal*.

Runco, M. A., & Bahleda, M. D. (1986). Implicit theories of artistic, scientific, and everyday creativity. *Journal of Creative Behavior, 20*, 93-98.

Runco, M. A., & Charles, R. (1993). Judgments of originality and appropriateness as predictors of creativity. *Personality and Individual Differences, 15*, 537-546.

Runco, M. A., & Charles, R. (1997). Developmental trends in creativity. In M. A. Runco (Ed.), *Creativity research handbook* (vol. 1, pp. 113-150). Cresskill, NJ: Hampton.

Runco, M. A., Ebersole, P., & Mraz, W. (1991). Self-actualization and creativity. *Journal of Social Behavior and Personality, 6*, 161-167.

Runco, M. A., Plucker, J. A., & Lim, W. (2000-2001). Development and psychometric integrity of a measure of ideational behavior. *Creativity Research Journal, 13*, 393-400.

Runco, M. A., & Gaynor J. L. R. (1993). Creativity as optimal development. In J. Brzezinski, S. DiNuovo, T. Marek, & T. Maruszewski (Eds.), *Creativity and consciousness: Philosophical and psychological dimensions* (pp. 395-412). Amsterdam/Atlanta: Rodopi.

Runco, M. A., Noble, E. P., & Luptak, Y. (1990). Agreement between mothers and sons on ratings of creative activity. *Educational and Psychological Measurement, 50*, 673-680.

Runco, M. A., & Pezdek, K. (1984). The effect of radio and television on children's creativity. *Human Communications Research, 11*, 109-120.

Runco, M. A., & Richards, R. (Eds.). (1998). *Eminent creativity, everyday creativity, and health*. Norwood, NJ: Ablex.

Runco, M. A., Johnson, D. J., & Bear, P. K. (1993). Parents' and teachers' implicit theories of children's creativity. *Child Study Journal, 23*, 91-113.

Russ, S., Robins, A. L., & Christiano, B. A. (1999). Pretend Play: Longitudinal Prediction of Creativity and Affect in Fantasy of Children. *Creativity Research Journal, 12*.

Schaefer, C., & Anastasi, A. (1968). A biographical inventory for identifying creativity in adolescent boys. *Journal of Applied Psychology, 54*, 42-48.

Scott, G., Leritz, L., & Mumford, M. D. (2004). Effectiveness of creativity training: A quantitative review. *Creativity Research Journal, 16*, 361-388.

Schmukler, D. (1985). Foundations of creativity: The facilitating environment. In J. Freeman (Ed.), *The psychology of gifted children* (pp. 75-91). New York: Wiley.

Singer, J. (2003). *Creativity research handbook* (vol. 3). Cresskill, NJ: Hampton Press.

Singer, J., & Singer, D. (in press). In M. A. Runco (Ed.), *Creativity research handbook* (vol. 3). Cresskill, NJ: Hampton Press.

Singh, R. P. (1987). Parental perception about creative children. *Creative Child and Adult Quarterly, 12*, 39-42.

Smith, K. L. R., Michael, W. B., & Hocevar, D. (1990). Performance on creativity measures with examination-taking instructions intended to induce high or low levels of test anxiety. *Creativity Research Journal, 3*, 265-280.

Smith, G. J. W., & Carlsson, I. (1985). Creativity in middle and late school years. *International Journal of Behavioral Development, 8*, 329-343.

Smolucha, F. (1992a). A reconstruction of Vygotsky's theory of creativity. *Creativity Research Journal, 5*, 49-67.

Smolucha, F. (1992b). The relevance of Vygotsky's theory of creative imagination for contemporary research on play. *Creativity Research Journal, 5*, 69-76.

Sternberg, R. J. (1985). Implicit theories of intelligence, creativity, and wisdom. *Journal of Personality and Social Psychology, 49*, 607-627.

Subotnik, R., Steiner, C., & Chakraborty, B. (1999). Procrastination Revisited: The Constructive Use of Delayed Response. *Creativity Research Journal, 12*.

Sulloway, F. 1996. *Born to Rebel.* New York: Pantheon.

Torrance, E. P. (1963). The creative personality and the ideal pupil. *Teachers College Record, 65*, 220-227.

Torrance, E. P. (1968). A longitudinal examination of the fourth-grade slump in creativity. *Gifted Child Quarterly, 12*, 195-199.

Torrance, E. P. (1981). Non-test ways of identifying the creatively gifted. In J. C. Gowan, J. Khatena, & E. P. Torrance (Eds.), *Creativity: Its educational implications* (2nd ed., pp. 165-170). Dubuque, IA: Kendall/Hunt.

Wallach, M. A., & Kogan, N. (1965). *Modes of thinking in young children.* New York: Holt, Rinehart & Winston.

Wallach, M. A., & Wing, C. (1969). *The talented student.* New York: Holt, Rinehart & Winston.

Ward. T., & Smith, S. (in press). Insight. In M. A. Runco (Ed.), *Creativity Research handbook* (Vol. 3). Cresskill, NJ: Hampton Press.

Weisberg, P.A., & Springer, K. J. (1961). Environmental factors in creative functioning. *Archives of General Psychiatry, 5*, 64-74.

Westby, E. L., & Dawson, V. L. (1995). Creativity: Asset or burden in the classroom? *Creativity Research Journal, 8*, 1-10.

Zajonc, R. B., & Markus, G. B. (1975). Birth order and intellectual development. *Psychological Review, 82*, 74-88.

EARLY CHILDHOOD
EDUCATIONAL CURRICULUM

·8·

RECONCEPTUALIZING LANGUAGE EDUCATION IN EARLY CHILDHOOD: SOCIO-CULTURAL PERSPECTIVES

Jim Anderson
Lyndsay Moffatt
Jon Shapiro
University of British Columbia

The past 10 years or so have seen a continuing shift or reconceptualization in terms of how early childhood researchers and educators view learning and language development. This reconceptualization—in other words, different ways of thinking about these issues—can be seen in the kinds of questions researchers ask, the sites at which they investigate, and the methods they use in their investigations. It also can be seen in the kinds of interventions educators recommend for children considered to be at risk or language delayed. In previous decades, research concerning children's language learning tended to focus on issues of individual's cognition and to rely on standardized tests to help assess children's language proficiency. Interventions for children considered to be language delayed tended to reflect a behaviorist and subskills orientation. In contrast, research conducted in the past decade or so suggests that issues of sociocultural context may be much more significant than was previously thought. In other words, current research has begun to focus on how sociocultural issues such as bilingualism, ethnicity, and socioeconomic class affect children's language acquisition. From a sociocultural perspective, the importance ascribed to language and literacy, the manner in which language and literacy learning is mediated, and the uses and functions of language and literacy vary considerably across social and cultural groups (e.g., Clay, 1993). This research has led to further questions about how best to assess and facilitate children's language learning.

Whereas some researchers using cognitive/developmental models of children's language acquisition, continue to use standardized tests to measure children's language competence, and continue to promote standardized strategies of intervention for diverse groups of children, many researchers using sociocultural theories of learning and language acquisition have begun to raise questions about such assessments and programs. Evidence concerning children's language acquisition accumulated over the last 10 years has led many researchers to ask fundamentally different questions and to explore some remarkably new territory. For example, recent research has begun to ask questions about the ways in which certain early language assessment tools may be culturally biased and how students' familial and peer interactions may contribute to children's language development. Similarly, educators and researchers approaching the study of children's language learning from a sociocultural perspective have begun to ask questions about how some interventions may be appropriate for diverse groups of learners, whereas others may not. In the following pages, we will explore some of the most recent developments in early childhood language education research.

CHANGING PERSPECTIVES: THE SOCIOCULTURAL CONTEXT

Kramsch (2002) suggests that researchers interested in language acquisition from the end of 1960s to the end of the 1970s tended to be informed by a psycholinguistic perspective. They were apt to use a conception of "learner as computer" as they attempted to map out how learners transformed language *input* into language *output*. In contrast, from the late 1970s through the 1980s into the 1990s (and continuing into the 21st century), researchers working from a language socialization perspective have been more likely to see learners as apprentices who learn through active participation in a variety of language communities. Throughout the past 10 years, researchers concerned with children's language acquisition have increasingly turned their focus from how individual children develop language skills toward the contexts and conditions in which children acquire language. In particular, researchers have begun to ask how social interaction and sociocultural contexts affect language use and development.[1]

This shift in the kinds of questions being asked has also affected the kinds of places that researchers have chosen to investigate and the methods they choose to collect data. For example, while earlier studies tended to take place in laboratories in (ostensibly) controlled conditions and relied heavily on quantitative research methods, more recent studies have examined children's language development in more naturalistic settings such as in homes, day cares, preschools, and primary classrooms using a variety of qualitative and quantitative methods. This research reflects what Gee (1989) refers to as the "social turn" or the burgeoning interest among researchers and theorists in the social nature of language, literacy, and indeed of learning

In asking these kinds of questions and in exploring language development in a variety of contexts using diverse methods, researchers interested in early language acquisition have begun to document how sociocultural context plays a significant role in the ways in which children acquire language skills. This evidence and the popularization of the work of key theorists such as Bakhtin (1986), Bourdieu (1990), and Vygotsky (1978) also have had a significant impact on the way that early childhood researchers now conceptualize learning. Although previously researchers and theorists tended to see learning as linked to individual children's mental strategies, or characteristics, more recent conceptualizations of learning have stressed the importance of children's social relations and social positions or their "interactional circumstances" (McDermott, 1993). Although some researchers continue to describe students' relationships to language learning that focus on individual personality traits, others have begun to see language acquisition as embedded in sociocultural interactions. In other words, these theorists have argued that what people learn and how much they learn depends less on their supposedly innate capabilities and more on who they interact with or the kinds of "discourses" (Gee, 1989) to which they are exposed. Thus, although some researchers choose to examine the role of individual characteristics such as motivation in language and literacy learning (Pintrich, 2003; Watkins & Coffey, 2004), others have begun to examine the role of social relations and power dynamics in early childhood language/literacy acquisition. As noted by Toohey (2000), until recently, relatively little research on children's language acquisition has "considered how social relations among learners, or among learners and those who judge their performances, might affect judgements of cognition, social adjustment or learning styles" (p. 7).

In the following pages we will explore some of the current shifts in thinking about early childhood language acquisition and we will highlight some directions for future research. The following three questions provide a framework for the organization of this chapter:

How can we best understand children's language development?
How can educators assess language competence?
How can educators support children's language learning?

UNDERSTANDING LANGUAGE DEVELOPMENT

Recent studies of young children's language development reveal that there are enormous variations in terms of the kinds of talk that children are exposed to and produce (Hart & Risley, 1995). For example, in a recent large-scale longitudinal study of a heterogeneous group of preschool children, Snow, Tabors, and Dickinson (2001) found considerable variation in terms of the kinds of language that children from different families are exposed to. In examining 74 preschool children (36 males and 38 females) from diverse backgrounds (47 Caucasian, 16 African-American, 6 Latino, and 5 biracial children) Snow, Tabors, and Dickinson (2001) found that while all of the children spoke English at home, there were vast differences in the kinds and amounts of talk that they heard and participated in. Data collection for this study began when the children were 3 years old and involved a home visit in which mothers were interviewed as to their "life circumstances and the types of activities they participated in." The children were then audiorecorded as they shared books with their mother, told a story about a recent event, and played with toys. A family mealtime also was taperecorded after the completion of a home visit. These home visits were repeated when the children were 4 and 5 years old and the same data collection procedures were used. At age 5, the children completed a range of measures typically used to assess language and literacy development in kindergarten, including concepts of print and story, letter recognition, and receptive vocabulary. Snow, Tabors, and Dickinson found that there was considerable variation in the discourse practices found in the children's homes. A particularly striking example was the wide variation in terms of the amount of parent and child "nonimmediate" talk during the storybook reading sessions. DeTemple (2001) notes that nonimmediate talk "refers to information that is not immediately visible in the illustrations or the text, it typically involves longer utterances and more explicit, complex language than does labelling or the yes-no questioning that constitutes much of immediate talk" (DeTemple, 2001, p. 39). During the storybook reading, the amount of "nonimmediate talk" typically ranged between 43 and 60% of the parent-child interactions (depending on the book). However, in some of the families, this kind of talk accounted for only 11 to 18% of the parent-child interactions (again depending on the book). In other words, some

---

[1]Readers interested in reading further about sociocultural theories of learning should consult: B. Rogoff (2003), *The cultural nature of human development. (New York: Oxford University Press).*

families consistently engaged in much less nonimmediate talk than did others. This form of talk is thought to contribute to children's language development as well as to their general cognitive development. As noted by DeTemple (2001), children in families where there is less nonimmediate talk tend to perform less well on language and literacy measures that are often used in kindergarten.

Katz (2001) found similar patterns of variation in terms of parent-child talk during play. She explained that as children interact with each other and with significant others in this context, they engage in labeling, develop procedural skills as they organize a series of play events in sequence, and negotiate through conversation. Play also involves "pretend talk," which is a form of "nonimmediate talk," and therefore extended discourse. Katz reported that there was considerable variation across parent-child dyads as to the amount of pretend and nonpretend talk. Furthermore, there was more pretend talk when children were 4 than 3, but pretend talk again decreased when children were 5. Katz concluded, "skill with the extended discourse of pretend talk in the preschool years is related to the language and literacy skills that are important for kindergarten" (p. 71). It should be pointed out that Katz offered the following caveat about this finding:

We also recognize that different cultural beliefs regarding language, pretending and play may lead to different parenting practices in these areas (Goncu, 1999). In some cultures, for instance, the inventiveness of pretend talk may seem to be an affront to truthfulness, rather than a confirmation of imagination (Heath, 1983). In addition, although playing with children is a valued activity among many European American middle-income families, some culture groups in the United States may not agree. (p. 71)

Somewhat surprisingly, though, Katz proceeded to offer suggestions for parents that appear to represent a middle-class, Eurocentric orientation.

Variation across families also has been found in the other contexts. For example, Beals (2001) analyzed family talk at mealtime and found that some families engaged in extensive mealtime discussions while others did not. It has been theorized that several benefits accrue from mealtime talk including, exposure to and participation in narratives as stories are told, using exploratory talk, and vocabulary development. Interestingly, the researchers concluded that children benefit from mealtime talk through exposure to it and they need not actually be engaging in the conversation. Beals (2001) found that the amount of narrative and exploratory talk children were exposed to at mealtime was positively related to later achievement in language and literacy. It is important at this point to note that these studies do not suggest there is only one way for children to learn to speak or to become literate, but that some family practices may translate into children performing better on standardized measures of language and literacy achievement. What these studies do highlight is the wide variation in terms of language experiences that young children bring to preschool and primary classrooms.

Building on the notion that children acquire some level of the meanings of a new word through even a single exposure to it, Tabors, Beals, and Weizman (2001) examined the frequency in which families used "rare words" in toy play, at mealtime, and in storybook reading. They concluded that all three contexts provided an opportunity for children to acquire new words. Four ways of helping children associate meaning with new words were identified: using the *physical context* by referring to an action or object; using *prior knowledge* by calling on previous experiences; using the *social context* by referring to social norms; and using a verbal explanation to provide *semantic support* (Tabors, Beals, & Weizman, 2001, p. 105). But, again, they found that families varied in terms of children's exposure to new or rare words. Once again, they also found that children's exposure to new words was positively related to later measures of language knowledge.

Dickinson (2001a) argued that book reading is potentially a rich site for language leaning in preschool classrooms as children are exposed to different language structures and to new words and concepts. Interestingly, despite the importance that the teachers in the study ascribed to book reading, they spent relatively little time sharing books with children. Indeed, Dickinson observed that children spent more time in transition as they cleaned up or moved from one area to the next than they did in shared book reading. As well, whereas some teachers made storybook reading interactive by encouraging discussion and questioning, others provided relatively few such opportunities.

Dickinson (2001b) also examined the influence of the preschool classroom on children's language and literacy development. Teachers varied in the amount of support they provided for children's language development. Several teacher and classroom variables were identified as contributing to children's language development including the provision of a well-defined, well-equipped writing area. As well, teachers in classrooms with a lower teacher-student ratio tended to provide more opportunity for children to engage in discussion. Furthermore, better-educated teachers tended to support children's language development across contexts more so than did less well-educated teachers. These findings clearly point to the need to allocate adequate resources to early childhood education in the form of well-equipped classrooms, adequate staffing levels and properly trained, well-paid teachers. However, as Dickinson soberly reminds us, "Our society has yet to recognize and appropriately reward pre-school teachers" (p. 286).

In an attempt to compare children's language development in different childcare contexts, the National Institute of Child Health and Human Development Early Child Care Research Network conducted a large-scale study that measured the language development of children who had been cared for almost exclusively by their mothers and the language development of children who had experienced different types of childcare. The sample consisted of 1,364 families selected when their children were 1 month old. Families were from cities in various areas across the United States and the sample was representative of the general population in terms of education level, ethnicity, income, and marital status. The children were assessed at 15, 24, and 36 months using various instruments including the *MacArthur Communicative Development Inventory* and the *Reynel Development Language Scales*. As well, observations occurred at home and at the childcare centres using instruments such as the *Home Observation for Measurement of the Environment* and *the Observational Record of the Care giving Environment*. Results indicated that "[f]or the most part, children in full time maternal care had scores similar to those of children in child care" (National Institute of Child Health and Human Development Early Child Care Research Network, 2000, p. 974). Furthermore, the total number of hours children spent in childcare did not predict measures of children's language development. These findings clearly contradict conservative voices (e.g., Lewin, 2002) in the media and elsewhere that promulgate the notion that children's development suffers when they are in daycares and not at home being cared for by mothers. However, the quality of childcare did predict children's language development indicating the importance of providing high quality childcare to optimize children's cognitive and linguistic development.

Much of the current research on children's language acquisition has tended to focus almost exclusively on the role that adults play in supporting children's language development. However, Gregory (2001) has critiqued this narrowness of vision and called into question the common concept of scaffolding popularized by Bruner (1986) and others. Gregory suggests that the construct of scaffolding implies an unequal relationship between the child and significant others which may or may not hold true. In an ethnographic study with eight Bangladeshi and eight Anglo families in a socially and economically disadvantaged area of London, Gregory documented how siblings supported each other's language and literacy learning through play routines at home. Gregory argued that the learning that occurs in these interactions goes beyond traditional notions of scaffolding and collaborative learning. Instead, she described these interactions "as a synergy, a unique reciprocity whereby siblings act as adjuvants in each other's learning . . ." (p. 309). Gregory's work clearly demonstrates how young children can support each other, particularly when learning a second language.

Similarly, Long (1998) documented her daughter's learning Icelandic over an 8-month period. Long's study helps to demonstrate the importance of peers in supporting a young child's second language learning. Long maintains that "the acquisition of a new language and the process of becoming literate in that language . . . [are] interwoven in the process of learning to get along [with one's peers]" (Long, 1998, p. 9). In examining her daughter's experiences, Long argued that children's out of school play may be the most supportive context for language learning. In contrast, Long found that learning Icelandic in school was more gradual and involved less experimentation and more hesitancy (p. 28). Long also found that although language learning with peers revolved around play and involved experimentation, at times, the children also used direct teaching, a finding consistent with Gregory's research. In concluding, Long proposed that the support offered by her daughter's peers in helping her acquire a second language closely resembled the way that caregivers support young children's language acquisition. Furthermore, she posited, her daughter's language learning was an embodiment of Cole's (1996) notion of prolepsis, "a form of support that occurs as more experienced cultural members represent/project in language and behaviour, the newcomer's potential future" (Long, 1998, p. 10).

Parke, Drury, Kenner, and Robertson (2002) noting the dearth of research documenting young children's simultaneous acquisition of English and a low-status mother tongue, described four qualitative research studies conducted in an inner-city area of England involving children, age 4 through 7, whose first languages were Pahari, Gujarati, or Urdu. The specific contexts of each of the studies were as follows: talking at home, writing in a nursery school, retelling English texts, and participating in a school assembly (Parke, Drury, Kenner, & Robertson, 2002, p. 199). In the first study, the children appropriated the routines and discourse patterns from their nursery school into their play as they practiced English at home. The children also demonstrated that they were adept code switchers, reverting to Pahari to keep siblings engaged or to insure that they clearly understood instructions. In the second study, analysis of a 4-year-old child's writing in the nursery school revealed that her writing was a hybrid text that incorporated orthographic features of English and Gujarati. Gregory (2003) maintains that as educators, we must come to understand the importance of this hybridity in recognizing

. . . the syncretism taking place as children blend new and old practices. Nobody—and certainly not young children—is fixed in any particular way of learning. As we traced the learning of siblings together, we noticed how crucially they have been blending strategies from home, from their community language classes, and from their English schools to produce a new type of literacy learning.

In the third study, three children (ages 5:6, 6:3, and 6:8) retold in English and in their first language (Pahari or Urdu), a text that had been read to them in English. Although the children heard the text in English only, their retellings in their first language revealed that they comprehended the text fully and accurately whereas their retellings in English were less detailed, less coherent and less accurate (p. 214). In the final study, the author examined the effects of introducing culturally relevant practice in a school assembly. In reviewing the changes in the children's behavior, the author contrasted a group of primary children's disengagement—indeed disruptive behavior—during a regular school assembly with their concentration and attention when a language support teacher explained an upcoming Muslim religious festival. The change in the children's engagement when the discursive and textual practices from their own community was brought to the fore is described thus:

After some clearly signalled rituals such as covering her head, she [the support teacher] explains in both Pahari and English that she is about to read one small fraction of the Qu'ran in preparation for Eid. Then she proceeds to read. The children fall silent. Fifteen minutes later, the whole school is still able to concentrate and listen including that very disruptive year 2 class. (Parke, Drury, Kenner, & Robertson, 2002, p. 215)

In a recent study, Bauer (2000) documented the biliteracy and bilingual development of her daughter, Elena. In this longitudinal case study, she traced her daughter's emerging language and literacy development commencing when the child turned two. Data collection included ". . . field notes, journals, audio and videotaped observations of Elena's participation in literacy routines" (p. 109), with a particular focus on the child's code switching during shared reading. Bauer found that code switching was reduced in highly patterned texts, that the child's code switching was influenced by the child's view of the task, and code switching that occurred during the discussions of the text resembled that which occurred in talk outside of literacy events. As Bauer (2002) indicates, there will be considerable variation in children's language and literacy learning across contexts, an important point that educators and researchers need always consider.

These studies exemplify some of the most recent research on early childhood language acquisition and use. They draw our attention to the vast differences in terms of the kinds of language that children are exposed to and to the significant role that family, peers and community play in language learning. In particular, it is important to note the role that play and culturally relevant practices may have in encouraging children's language development.

Children's Written Language: Sociocultural Perspectives

The idea that socialcultural context affects learning also has had an impact on research in the teaching and learning of young children's written language. In particular, recently researchers have shown considerable interest in young children's emerging knowledge of genre (or different forms of communication) as well as on the importance of families and communities in children's written language learning (e.g., Chapman, 1994; Dyson, 1999; Woolman-Bonnila, 2001). Research in the 1980s and early 1990s tended to focus on children's personal writing and issues of process writing. However, research conducted in the late 1990s and into the 21st century has begun to examine how young children learn to incorporate the content and style of different genres into their writing.

Proponents of genre pedagogy (e.g., Cope & Kalantzis, 1993) initially advocated the explicit teaching of the textual features of various genres (Haneda & Wells, 2000). However, as Chapman (1999) points out, genres are now thought of not as rules for producing particular models of writing but as "cultural resources upon which writers draw" (p. 469). She quoted Bazerman thus:

Genres are not just forms. Genres are forms of life, ways of being. They are frames for social action. They are environments for learning. They are locations within which meaning is constructed. Genres shape the thoughts we form and the communications by which we interact. Genres are the familiar places we go to create intelligible communicative action with each other and the guideposts we use to explore the unfamiliar. (Bazerman, 1997, p. 19)

Wollman-Bonilla (2001) documented families' contributions to children's writing development through an analysis of Family Message Journals. Informed by the work of Bakahtin (1986) and Vygotsky (1978), Wollman-Bonilla framed her study from the perspective that, in addition to the need to acquire "... graphophonic knowledge and be able to present that knowledge on paper, they [children] must also be able to appropriate the forms and purposes for communication valued in their culture"

(p. 168). Wollman-Bonilla analyzed the message journals of four children representing a range of literacy abilities and sociocultural backgrounds. All of the children attended the same first grade classroom located in a middle-class neighborhood in the eastern United States. Analayzing parents' written responses to their children's journals, Wollman-Bonilla found that parents provided instructional support for their children by asking questions, by acknowledging the impact of the writing on the family such as when the children made requests, and by acknowledging their children's learning. Parents in their replies also modeled the following genres, in order of frequency: informational text, jokes and riddles, narrative, moral lessons, and poetic texts. Interestingly, when interviewed, the families did not see themselves as teaching writing and, indeed, the families could not describe how they were supporting their children's writing.

Chapman (1994) examined the writing development of 6 Grade 1 children (three boys and three girls) representing different developmental levels from an urban school in British Columbia. Focusing especially on their emerging knowledge of genre, Chapman collected writing samples produced during Writer's Workshop from the beginning, midpoint, and end of the school year. These samples were then analyzed for their uses of genre and for complexity. Chapman identified 15 different genres in children's writing including, records, narratives, lists, labels, notes, letters and written dialogue. She concluded, "... genres emerged both in terms of quantity, that is, increasing repertoires, and [in terms of] quality" (p. 370). She also found that children's other forms of communicating such as talking, drawing, and reading were interwoven with and supported their writing. Significantly, although there was evidence of a developmental trajectory as children's writing moved from relatively simple to more complex forms, Chapman concluded that growth in the children's writing was uneven and irregular (p. 371). In this way, Chapman's findings cast doubt on theories of children's uniform, lockstep writing development.

Over the last decade or so, Anne Dyson has been one of the leading researchers in terms of young children's written language. Her research shows that children appropriate what she terms "cultural texts" for their writing. Dyson (1999) maintained that "we are all textual borrowers" as we "... learn our words from particular people in particular places and then we recontextualize them" (p. 369). Working in a first grade classroom in which children represented a variety of socioeconomic classes, Dyson documented children's participation in a writer's workshop and other school activities during the school year. Focusing on six African-American children (two boys and four girls), Dyson found that children consistently incorporated knowledge from their own social worlds learned through popular media into their writing. Dyson's essential position is that schools must permit children to talk and write about that which they know, including popular culture. Although many teachers attempt to curb or ignore references to popular culture in school writing activities, Dyson argues, "By ignoring children's media use, schools collaborate in solidifying and perpetuating societal divisions in cultural art forms and in children's orientations to each other and to school itself" (Dyson, 2000, p. 356).

Haneda and Wells (2000) documented the writing that occurred in classrooms where teachers attempted to create "communities of inquiry." Central assumptions in such class-rooms were: (1) writing is a means to construct knowledge, (2) writing must be functional and purposeful, and (3) a range of modes of inquiry and means of representing knowledge need to be valued and encouraged. For example, they showed how a teacher in a Grade 1 classroom used "post-it notes" to record information and then used a web to arrange and organize the information. They pointed out, ". . . one of the key character-istics of a knowledge-building community is purposeful and thoughtful use of language both oral and written as children actively engage in interactive/collaborative activities that in-volve . . . literate thinking" (pp. 449–450). They concluded that the students in these classrooms demonstrated a level of interest and involvement that would not have occurred had the students not been involved in collaborative reading, writing, listening, speaking, and representing.

To conclude this section, several points bear reiteration. First, oral and written language learning occurs in different so-cial contexts and is affected by the amount and kinds of sup-port that children are provided. Second, high quality childcare appears to have a positive effect on children's language develop-ment. Given the relationship between early language develop-ment and later cognitive skills, this effect will likely have further positive effects across the lifespan. Third, although caregivers are obviously important in children's language development, the important roles of siblings, peers, and popular culture are also beginning to be documented and recognized. In the light of these recent developments in early childhood language edu-cation research, a number of issues have come to the fore. In particular, as we begin to recognize the importance of social context to learning and to realize how remarkably diverse chil-dren's preschool language experiences are, it becomes more and more difficult to delineate "normal" from "abnormal" develop-ment. In this way, issues of language assessment have become much more complicated. In the following section we address some of the most recent developments within the field of early childhood language assessment.

ASSESSING LANGUAGE LEARNING

One of the most important shifts in recent research concern-ing the assessment of young children's language learning has been in educators' and researchers' understanding of how dif-ficult it is to gauge children's language abilities. In particular, researchers and theorists have argued that there are severe lim-itations to using norm—referenced standardized language tests to assess what children know about language, how children acquire language, or the functions and purposes of language in their daily lives. Consequently, educators, parents, and re-searchers have begun to advocate for alternative methods of assessing children's language learning. Although there may be some situations in which standardized language tests are use-ful (e.g., as baseline data; in large-scale assessment), much of the current literature reveals the limitations of these assessment tools, especially when they are used to make judgements and decisions about individual children in isolation from more eco-logically valid data. In the following section, we explore some of these limitations and some alternative methods for gauging children's language abilities.

The Limits of Standardized Language Tests

Although standardized testing is experiencing a considerable re-naissance throughout the postindustrial world, there is little to suggest that such tests actively contribute to students' learning or that they help educators to create more effective curricula. In contrast, there is much evidence to suggest that standardized tests are fairly imprecise tools for assessing students' language and literacy skills. Furthermore, there is also evidence that the use of standardized tests may have a negative impact on chil-dren's education (MacNeil, 2000; Reay & Wiliam, 1999).

One of the main reasons why standardized tests offer lim-ited information about young children's language abilities stems from the complexity of language itself. As Dockrell (2001) noted, the variability of normal patterns of language develop-ment and the difficulty of distinguishing between enduring problems and transient ones make it difficult to draw useful conclusions about young children's language abilities from their scores on standardized language assessments. These complex-ities are also compounded by how children acquire language and by the diversity of dialect and language experiences in the current multicultural, multilingual, and globalized world. If, as it appears, what children learn is greatly determined by the en-vironment they are born into, then it is important to ask what standardized language tests are actually assessing (Gee, 2003; Gipps, 1995; Lave & Wenger, 1991; McDermott, 1993). Do they evaluate young children's ability to use language and whether they need remedial attention or do they merely help to describe how children use language in their communities in compari-son with mainstream or hegemonic sociocultural groups? Socio-cultural perspectives of language learning suggest that standard-ized tests can only accomplish the latter. From this view, typi-cal standardized tests are of limited use as tools for evaluating whether a child needs extra language support as they can only help to describe current language compared with the popula-tion for which the tests were normed. In this way, standardized tests cannot chart "normal" development." In other words, as soon as we begin to question ideas of "normal development" and to understand that normativity is highly dependant on so-ciocultural context, then standardized tests (and tests that are created without due attention to sociocultural context) become questionable in terms of their validity.

Unfortunately, some educators argue that the use of standard-ized tests is not only of limited value for assessing young chil-dren's language abilities but also that widespread use of them may reinforce racist and classist ideas of children's language skills (Diniz, 1999; Mehan, 1992). Recent work points to the cultural bias implicit in standardized language tests (Campbell & Dollaghan, 1997; Craig & Washington, 2002; Restrepo & Silverman, 2001). Researchers who have examined the valid-ity of such tests have noted that, ironically, many tend both to overrefer and to underrefer children from marginalized commu-nities for remediation (Laing, 2003; Laing & Kamhi, 2003; Pena, Iglesias, & Lidz, 2001).

On one level, overreferral may not seem problematic. Many educators may feel that it is better to overrefer than to underrefer when children's learning is at stake. However, it is important to recognize the impact that such overreferral can have on individual children and their families, as well as on teachers' conceptions of various communities. For example, in the past 25 years, it has been found that, in the United States, African-American children, Hispanic children, children from linguistic minorities, and children from lower socioeconomic classes tend to be identified as needing language intervention at a much higher rate than children from white, Anglophone, middle-class families. Campbell and Dollaghan (1997) and Laing and Kamhi (2003), among others, have suggested that these differences in levels of identification have more to do with which community has created the tests and what the test makers think of as "normal" language use, than they have to do with children's actual language abilities or capacity for learning language or for becoming literate. Cross, De Vaney, and Jones (2001) and Feiler and Webster (1999) argue that the uncritical acceptance of standardized tests perpetuate racist and classist conceptions of children from certain communities as deficient and of others (usually children from white, Anglo, middle-class communities) as normative or advanced (Cross, De Vaney, & Jones, 2001; Feiler & Webster, 1999).

In an examination of issues of equity in assessment, Murphy (1995) argued that the validity of an assessment task relies on the assessor and the student sharing the same understanding of the task. Yet, recent research suggests that assessment tasks are often interpreted very differently by students from different sociocultural groups and that student responses are often interpreted differently by assessors from different sociocultural groups (Cross et al., 2001; Heath, 1986b; Pena, 1997). Heath (1986a) and Pena (1997) argue that the manner in which much testing is conducted, in which typically an educator or researcher takes a child aside and then proceeds to ask him or her to label decontextualized pictures or to answer "known-information" questions, reflects a particular cultural bias. Ethnographic and sociolinguistic research demonstrates that some cultures are more likely than others to engage in these kinds of interactions and routines with children outside of testing situations. Indeed, differences in cultural questioning practices may result in children from different cultural groups having varied answers to the same assessment task. As noted by Pena (1997), "rehearsing facts particularly in the contexts of a question-answer routine between adult and child is not emphasized in the same manner or frequency across cultural/linguistic groups." Thus, when asked to name pictures of objects that the adult examiner presumably knows, a child from a sociocultural group that does not engage in known-information question routines may provide a description instead of the one word answer considered to be "correct." For example, when presented with a picture of a pumpkin, the child may exclaim "Halloween!" or when presented with a picture of an umbrella she/he may say "you use it when it is raining" (Pena, 1997), answers that may be considered "incorrect" by the marking scheme of the assessment. In this way, perceived problems in vocabulary acquisition may have more to do with children's experiences with language and their culturally based expectations about how language is used than with their actual language abilities.

Researchers also have found that examiners bring cultural expectations to the assessment task. Cross, Devaney, and Jones (2001) found that preservice teachers held more favourable attitudes toward speakers from cultural groups similar to their own. In an examination of 111 preservice teachers at a small college in the United States, Cross, Devaney, and Jones found that future educators were willing to make a range of judgments about readers' intelligence, friendliness, consideration, education, trustworthiness, ambition, honesty, and social status based solely on the readers' dialects. After listening to short taped passages read with a range of local dialects, preservice teachers were asked to rate the readers on the above list of personality characteristics. Results indicated that white respondents had more favorable impressions of white readers and black respondents had more favorable impressions of black readers. We imagine that such judgments would likely play out when these educators began teaching and assessing students' performances.

Similarly, in a study of teachers' ratings of the future academic competence of 105 poor and working-class kindergarten students, Hauser-Cram, Sirin, and Stipek (2003) found that teachers rated students as less likely to succeed when they perceived a value difference between themselves and their students' families regardless of their students' actual competencies. The results of these studies suggest that perhaps preservice and practising teachers could benefit from intensive discussions of the origins and legitimacy of different dialects, the value of diversity and the consequences of linguistic judgments and assessments in the classroom. As the work of Cross, Devaney, and Jones (2001) and Hauser-Cram, Sirin, and Stipek (2003) exemplifies, valid interpretation of assessment outcomes relies on the assessor having an understanding of cultural, linguistic, dialectal, and socioeconomic differences. This understanding is particularly important when educators and researchers attempt to assess the language skills of students who come from sociocultural, socioeconomic, linguistic, or dialect backgrounds different from their own (Delpit, 1995; Feiler & Webster, 1999; Murphy, 1995). Given that minority and English language learners comprise the majority of many urban schools, whereas 90% of teachers in the United States are Euro-American, these issues will likely remain at the forefront of attempts to create equitable and effective schools in the coming decades (National Education Association [NEA], 1997).

Finally, research into what students think about the experience of being tested using standardized assessments reveals that the experience is often a confusing and uncomfortable one that can have a negative impact on their ideas about school and about themselves as learners. To date, few studies have examined the impact of testing on young children. However, recent research with primary aged children suggests that standardized assessments provoke significant anxiety and may lead to children's negative constructions of themselves as learners. As noted by Reay and Wiliam (1999), children often believe tests can reveal something intrinsic about their abilities and that the process of being tested provides a definitive statement about them as learners. Preschool children may be less aware than older children of the role of testing in society. However, many young children are surprisingly astute about this aspect of assessment and the resultant anxiety about their abilities and self-worth could conceivably have deleterious effects.

As standardized language tests offer limited information, frequently reflect and reinforce racist and classist ideas of children's language abilities, and may have a negative impact on what children feel about schooling, there is good reason to question the efficacy of using such tests with young children. However, there is also a need to be able to identify students who appear to be experiencing some form of language delay so that we may offer them extra assistance. In this way, educators and researchers have begun to develop alternative ways of assessing students' language abilities.

Alternative Modes of Assessment

Although there have been some attempts to modify standardized tests to accommodate different communities' language use, practitioners, parents, and educators also have advocated using other methods to assess whether children need additional language support (Laing, 2003). One of the most straightforward ways that early childhood educators can assess whether a child needs language support is to maintain open communication with the child's primary caregivers. Researchers have found that parents or primary caregivers are as reliable as standardized tests in terms of recognizing whether a child is struggling and needs extra language assistance or whether she/he is developing "normally" (Boone & Crais, 1999; Laing, Law, Levin, & Logan, 2002).

Plainly, encouraging and maintaining open communication with parents and primary caregivers requires active work on the part of the educator and how the educator attempts to build this rapport is significant. In particular, it is important to remember that some parents may have had negative experiences in schools themselves and that they may need a variety of positive interactions with an educator before they feel comfortable discussing their child's needs (Brink, 2002). In this way, the educator may need to think about how to create informal and formal opportunities for positive interaction with a child's primary caregivers and she/he may have to make repeated attempts at dialogue. However, as these efforts will likely assist in building a positive rapport with the child's parents/caregivers, they also may translate into making the preschool, day care, and primary classroom a more productive learning environment for the child. In this way, the educator will not only be more capable of assessing whether a child needs additional language support, but she/he also may be providing a better learning community.

Some researchers advocate involving parents and primary caregivers in the assessment of children's language abilities by asking these adults to complete a questionnaire about their child's language use (Marchman & Martinez-Sussmann, 2002). Some of the available questionnaires have been translated into a variety of languages making them more appropriate for multilingual and multicultural communities. However, as these questionnaires require a certain level of literacy on the part of the adult, they may not be appropriate for all parents/caregivers. In addition, because questionnaires often ask parents both to observe and interpret their children's language use, it may be necessary to set aside time to train parents/caregivers in order to insure reliable and valid information (Dockrell, 2001). Finally, it is important to recognize that like checklists and standardized assessments, in some ways, parent questionnaires can only offer limited insight into what a child knows about language and what she/he can do with it. For example, they cannot give us much insight into how a child approaches a task or which element of a task she/he finds difficult. Following research using some of the most popular parent questionnaires, including the *Mac Arthur Communicative Development Inventories,* Feldman and colleagues (2000) argue that educators and researchers should exercise caution when using such questionnaires to identify children at risk or to compare children from different sociodemographic contexts. Pena, Quinn and Iglesias (1992) caution that even attempts to make such questionnaires or tests reflect the local community may be problematic as the target population may contain wide variability in terms of language use.

As language learning is more complicated than merely acquiring new grammatical structures and learning new vocabulary, other methods of assessment also have been advocated in an attempt to capture what children actually know about language and whether they are suffering from language impairment. Researchers such as Schoenbrot, Kumin, and Sloan (1997) have advocated using narrative assessments to help evaluate young children's language abilities. In these assessments, the educator/researcher elicits a narrative from a child by asking him/her particular questions. Narrative assessments have been seen as more useful than standardized tests as narratives contain more elaborated speech than typical labeling tasks. However, once again, issues of sociocultural context and bias present themselves, as children from different sociocultural groups often experience different forms of narrative socialization (Delpit, 1995; Gutierrez-Clellen, Pena, & Quinn, 1995; Minami, 1996, 2001). In other words, there is no universal logic to storytelling. Different sociocultural groups tell stories in different ways.

In an attempt to address some of the problems with current standardized language assessments, Dickinson, McCabe, and Sprague (2003) developed the Teacher Rating of Oral Language and Literacy instrument. This assessment tool is designed so that teachers are able to describe what children actually do based on their observations of and interactions with them on a daily basis. As well, teachers are encouraged to consider sociocultural differences in children's language use when using the instrument. Moreover, the developers recognize that parents have insights into their children's language and literacy abilities that teachers do not have and they describe ways of including parents in describing children's language and literacy development.

Finally, the persistent difficulty of creating an unbiased language assessment has led some researchers to experiment with process oriented or dynamic assessments and processing-dependent, as contrasted with knowledge-dependent, measures (Laing & Kamhi, 2003; Pena et al., 2001; Pena, Quinn, & Iglesias, 1992). When using process oriented or dynamic assessments, educators/researchers begin with a pretest to assess certain aspects of a child's language use and then spend time teaching the skill or vocabulary that they are attempting to assess. Following this mini-lesson, the child is then assessed again. In this way, dynamic assessment can help educators/researchers see how a child incorporates new knowledge into his/her language use. Studies that have examined the reliability of dynamic assessments suggest that such process oriented evaluations can help to differentiate effectively between language differences and language disorders (Pena, Iglesias, & Lidz, 2001; Pena, Quinn, & Iglesias, 1992). Experiments using "processing-dependent" measures or measures that place more emphasis on processing abilities than on prior knowledge, also have had similar results (Campbell & Dollaghan, 1997; Laing & Kamhi, 2003). For example, Campbell and Dollaghan (1997) conducted a comparison of minority and majority children's knowledge-dependent and process-dependent language tests. They found that the minority children faired less well than majority children on the knowledge-dependent tests but fared equally well on the processing-dependent tests. Given the need to make distinctions between children who suffer from language impairments and those who do not, and the complexity of doing so, process oriented or dynamic assessments and process dependent measures may be the most potentially useful forms of assessment for educators/researchers attempting to gauge young children's language abilities.

FACILITATING LANGUAGE LEARNING

In the last decade, research into how best to facilitate young children's language learning have tended to cluster around two kinds of interventions: storybook reading and phonemic awareness. Additional research has begun to investigate the impacts of bilingual or multilingual education and family literacy programs. In the following section, we examine the results of some of the current research in these areas.

Storybook Reading

In the decade since the last handbook was published, there has been what might described as an explosion of interest into the effects of storybook reading on language development. Although a few studies concerning the effects of storybook reading were reported prior to the 1990s, this number pales in comparison with the number of studies conducted within the last decade. However, the efficacy of this kind of intervention continues to be debated.

Two major meta-analyses have been conducted on the effects of storybook reading. Scarborough and Dobrich (1994) and Bus, vanIJzendoorn, and Pellegrini (1995) agreed that storybook reading accounted for only 8% of the variance in children's later language performance. However, these reports differed significantly in their views of the importance of their findings. Bus et al. concluded that storybook reading is a "necessary preparation" (p. 17) for language and literacy learning, whereas Scarborough and Dobrich postulated that these findings might indicate an overemphasis on storybook reading as an intervention strategy. Furthermore, Scarborough and Dobrich suggested that focusing

on storybook reading may even be counterproductive in some cases. Regardless of these contradictory views, there appears to be a consistent interest in the effects of storybook reading on children's language development.

As we have postulated elsewhere (Shapiro, Anderson & Anderson, 2002), the current importance that is afforded to storybook reading had its genesis the foundational research of Clark (1976) and Durkin (1966). Both researchers reported that a common feature of young, precocious readers was that a significant other had read to them. Despite the fact that researchers (e.g., Bissex, 1980; Taylor, 1983) later demonstrated that children engage in a wide range of literacy activities as they become literate, storybook reading has come to be regarded as central to language and literacy development. Indeed, for many teachers, parents, and researchers, storybook reading has become "the way" into literacy and hence it has been afforded a central place in early childhood and primary grade classrooms (Anderson, Anderson, Lynch, & Shapiro, 2003).

Research that demonstrates that parents have diverse ways of interacting with their children (Hart, 2000) both in terms of what they talk about and how much time they spend with their children. Recent studies also have indicated that there can be wide differences in the ways parents or primary caregivers (DeTemple & Tabors, 1995; Shapiro, Anderson, & Anderson, 1997) and teachers (Dickinson & Smith, 1994) read storybooks to children. DeTemple and Tabors, working with low-income mothers of preschool children, found three distinct styles of readers: "straight readers" or those who read the text to their children with virtually no interaction related to the book; "standard interactive readers" or those who stopped to engage their children in conversation about the story and; "nonreaders" or those who only spoke about the illustrations. Similarly, in a study with a small group of middle-class mothers and their children, Shapiro, Anderson, and Anderson (1997) discovered a large range in the types of comments mothers used to call their children's attention to print and to illustrations. This study also found diversity in terms of the mothers' comments and questions.

In their study of preschool teachers and low-income children, Dickinson and Smith (1994) coded book reading episodes as falling into three main categories: (1) "co-constructive," in which the teachers' talk was analytic in nature, clarifying, extending, and amplifying the text; (2) "didactic-interactional," in which there was little talk before or after the book was read but the teacher asked recall questions or the children repeated phrases of text; and (3) "performance-oriented," in which the small amount of talk that occurred during reading was analytical and in which, after reading, teachers commented and asked questions about characters, analyzed vocabulary, and attempted to make personal connections for the students. Because of this diversity and likely range of effects on language, these differences in storybook reading techniques have become the focus of recent investigations.

For example, over the last decade, or so, Monique Senechal and her colleagues in Canada and Grover Whitehurst and his coinvestigators in the United States have conducted a number of studies on the impact of storybook reading on language growth. In 1993, Senechal and Cornell reported on a study investigating whether young children learned new vocabulary from a single storybook reading and on the impact of different parental book reading behaviors. Eighty 4-year-olds and 80 5-year-olds from middle-class backgrounds were read a storybook with 10 target words unfamiliar to them. The story contained an episode that was repeated 25 times, thereby allowing for the insertion of the target words. The study included four different story conditions. In the first condition, named "questioning," the children were asked simple "what" and "where" questions after target words were read. The children were then asked to label the target items and if they were not correct, the examiner labeled and pointed to the target word. In the second condition, known as "recasting" the examiner read the sentence and then reread (or recast) the sentence but used a synonym for the target word. In the third condition, "word repetition," the examiner simply reread the sentence with the target word. In the final condition, "verbatim reading," the children simply listened to the story. The children were tested for acquisition of the target words immediately after reading and again 1 week later with a test similar to that of the *Peabody Picture Vocabulary Test-Revised* (Dunn & Dunn, 1981) in which the examiner stated a word and the child pointed to one picture out of an array of four. Children also were asked to label illustrations of the target words as way to measure their expressive vocabulary. Results indicated that children in all conditions made gains in receptive vocabulary both in the immediate and delayed recall formats with the 5-year-olds making greater gains. There were no gains in expressive vocabulary. Senechal and Cornell concluded that a single reading of a storybook can influence receptive vocabulary learning but also noted that the active condition, where children participated in the storybook reading, showed no greater gains than the other conditions. Interestingly, the view persists that children's participation in the storybook reading results in greater learning. (e.g., Whitehurst et al., 1994).

In a 1995 study, Senechal, Thomas, Monker and Lawson attempted to determine whether children with greater word knowledge, as determined by their performance on the *PPVT-R* (Dunn & Dunn, 1981), learned more novel words when listening to storybooks than did children with less vocabulary knowledge. The sample of 4-year-olds was also middle-class and spoke English in their homes. Two storybooks, again containing repetitive episodes, were used and once again target words were introduced. However, in this study, there were only two conditions, a listening condition in which children heard each story twice, and the same labeling condition as the 1993 study. Results indicated a significant effect for the labeling conditions for both receptive and expressive vocabularies. In other words, children with greater word knowledge produced more new words than those with lesser word knowledge. This finding parallels the phenomenon of the Matthew effect in reading (i.e., good readers read more and become better readers; poor readers read less and fall further behind) that Stanovich (1986) described.

As part of the Senechal et al. study, parents also were asked to estimate how often they read to their children on a weekly basis. Correlations between home reading frequency and word knowledge were significant. Frequency was seen to account for 23% of the variance in *PPVT-R* scores. The researchers concluded that having children practice retrieval (i.e., labeling) during book reading had positive effects on vocabulary growth and that frequent book reading at home also contributed to vocabulary development.

In a follow-up experiment, Senechal et al. attempted to do a finer analysis of retrieval by modifying the listening condition through the addition of repetitive sentences containing target words and also by adding a pointing condition where children were asked to point to illustrations depicting the target words. Only 10 target words were used with a different group of 48 4-year-olds, again classified as having high or low word knowledge. For receptive vocabulary, active responding was again significant when compared to just listening and there were no differences between the pointing and labeling conditions. For expressive vocabulary, the children in the active conditions again performed better but there were no differences between the two active participation groups. Once again, frequency of home book reading appeared to be related to *PPVT-R* scores and accounted for 9% of the variance. These two experiments provide support for the notion that regardless of their level of word knowledge, children can benefit from active involvement in shared book reading and that the frequency of home book reading also can make modest contributions to vocabulary development.

This latter finding is consistent with those of the two meta-analyses referred to previously. Senechal and colleagues postulated that the relatively low contribution of frequency of home reading to vocabulary growth might be because of the different ways home reading has been investigated. In 1996, Senechal, LeFevre, Hudson, and Lawson designed two experiments to explore this variable. They constructed surveys that measured parents and children's knowledge of storybooks through recognition of titles and used this measure as a proxy for frequency of reading. Their hypothesis was that parents who read more and children who were read to more often would both have a better knowledge of children's literature.

The first experiment involved 119 4-year-old middle-class children and their parents, the majority of whom spoke English only. The children were administered the *PPVT-R* as a measure of receptive vocabulary. The parents were given a checklist of titles of children's books and one of authors of children's books. At the same time, they also were asked to estimate their frequency of storybook reading, the number of children's books in the home, and frequency of their child's library visits. Regression analyses indicated that storybook exposure, as measured by the checklists, predicted variance in children's *PPVT-R* scores. The second experiment utilized children's knowledge of storybooks to predict both receptive and expressive vocabularies. Forty-five 4-year-old children were administered the *PPVT-R* and the *Expressive One-Word Picture Vocabulary Test—Revised* or *EOWPVT-R* (Gardner, 1990). Parents once again responded to checklists to assess their knowledge of titles and authors. The children also were administered a book exposure measure consisting of illustrations from the books used in the parental checklist. Children were asked if they recognized each of the illustrations, and if they could identify the name of the story and tell something about the story. Findings again indicated significant correlations between all measures of story knowledge (both parents and children) with the vocabulary measures and the regression analysis confirmed the findings for receptive vocabulary and expressive vocabulary. The children's book identification task (titles) accounted for a fairly large portion of variance in the *PPVT-R* (16%) and the *EOWPVT* (34%). The researchers concluded that storybook exposure does indeed have an influence on vocabulary development. Finally, Senechal (1997) examined the effects on vocabulary growth of different styles of storybook reading. With a sample of 30 3-year-old and 30 4-year-old middle-class children, she investigated the impact of three styles of storybook reading: a one-time reading of the book, a repeated reading condition, and a questioning condition in which the examiner asked "what" or "where" questions about particular target words in the narrative (note: the book and procedure in the latter condition were identical to that in the Senechal and Cornell 1993 study). Children were pretested and posttested using measures of receptive and expressive vocabulary. Both measures used the target words, with the receptive test modeled on the PPVT and the expressive test requiring children to label the target words depicted in the storybook. There was a significant effect of reading condition on receptive vocabulary with a single reading being the least effective. Answering questions did have an impact on receptive vocabulary acquisition. For expressive vocabulary, age and reading condition were factors with 4-year-olds producing more of the target words and repeated reading and questioning having positive effects. Interestingly, asking labeling questions had a greater impact on expressive vocabulary indicating that different styles of book reading have a differential impact on vocabulary growth.

Throughout the 1990s, Whitehurst and his colleagues have followed up on his earlier work that investigated the effects of parental storybook reading as an intervention strategy that provided more verbal engagement with children (e.g., Whitehurst et al., 1988). The program, known as "dialogic reading," was based on the belief that practice with feedback and scaffolded interaction would accelerate young children's language development. In this program, parents were trained to model specific behaviors, ask questions, provide feedback, and to encourage the child to attempt to tell the story.

In 1994, Arnold, Lonigan, Whitehurst, and Epstein reported on a study designed to see if short-term training program utilizing videotape could also impact language development. Sixty-four middle-to-upper-class children ranging from 2 to 3 years of age and their mothers participated in the study. Three reading conditions were implemented: a control condition, a group that received dialogic reading training directly from graduate assistants, and a group of mothers who received their training through an instructional videotape. Children were assessed using standardized receptive and expressive vocabulary measures before to and 4 weeks after intervention. At the posttest, expressive vocabulary was assessed using the verbal expression subtest of the *ITPA* (Kirk, McCarthy & Kirk, 1968). Posttest analyses revealed significant differences on all measures. Children of parents in the videotrained group outperformed the children from the control group on both measures of expressive language but not on the test of receptive language whereas the direct training group only outperformed the control group on the ITPA subtest. When comparing the video and direct training groups, it was found that the children in the former group scored significantly

higher on the expressive and receptive vocabulary tests. The researchers concluded that dialogic reading intervention can significantly impact children's language abilities and that training in this method can be cost-effective by using video.

The majority of the work described thus far was conducted with middle- to upper-class children and their parents. Somewhat ironically, at the same time, the focus of educators' attention was on children from impoverished backgrounds where there was some evidence that there were fewer books and less storybook reading occurring in their homes (Neuman & Celano, 2001). Indeed, Adams (1990) estimated that children from poor and working class homes enter first grade having had an average of 25 hrs of one-to-one book reading experiences, whereas middle-class children would have somewhere between 1,000 to 1,700 hrs of such experience (p. 85).

Up to the early 1990s, the only trial of dialogic reading with lower income children had occurred in Mexico (Valdez-Menchaca & Whitehurst, 1992) but the results of this study, which indicated growth in mean length of utterance and complex sentence production, were not generalizable because of some of the procedures used in the study. Whitehurst and his colleagues extended their trials of dialogic reading to a low-income group in a study they reported in 1994. Seventy 3-year-old children who had less than half the book reading experiences as that reported for middle-class children participated. The children entered the study scoring below average on standardized measures of vocabulary and expressive language.

Three treatment conditions were used over a 6-week period. The children were then tested again. A follow-up assessment was conducted 6 months later. In one condition, *school reading*, the teacher or a teacher's aide was trained in dialogic reading using the previously designed videotape training. The reading sessions were to occur daily in groups no larger than 5 children. In the second condition, school *plus home reading* a parent/primary caretaker of each child also was trained to read at home in dialogic reading procedures using the same training as the teachers. Finally, the third condition was a control wherein this group of children was given daily small group play periods instead of the dialogic reading sessions. The books used in the first two conditions were not available to the children in the control condition. Once again, the *PPVT-R*, the *EOWPVT-R*, and the expressive subtest of the *ITPA* were used as pre and post tests. In addition, the researchers created their own measure of expressive vocabulary similar in format to the *EOWPVT-R* but that targeted novel vocabulary from the treatment books.

The researchers found considerable variability in the degree to which teachers and parents adhered to the scheduled reading or play periods. The dialogic reading also was not continued beyond the 6-week intervention period in the schools. On the receptive measure, the *PPVT-R*, there were no apparent differences between the groups who experienced the different conditions. However, because of the variability in terms of how the teachers adhered to the conditions and the playtime, there appeared to be a marginal interaction between center and condition. In terms of the *EOWPVT-R*, the children in both reading conditions, as one would expect, scored higher than the control group with the *school plus home* also differing from the *school only* group. On the follow-up assessment, there appeared to be no differences between the reading groups. For the researchers-designed expressive test, differences between the pre- and posttests were the same for the children in the reading conditions. Both groups doubled the number of words they could identify. No differences were found at the follow-up and no differences were found for the *ITPA*.

In a follow-up study with children from low-income homes, Lonigan and Whitehurst (1998) added a *home-only* dialogic reading treatment to the conditions reported above. Ninety-one 3-year-old and 4-year-old children from English-speaking homes participated. Once again, the intervention period was 6 weeks in duration and the adults received training in dialogic reading via videotape. The *PPVT-R*, the *EOWPVT-R*, and the verbal expression subtest of the *ITPA* were used and a subset of children's verbal productions (i.e., mean length of utterance, semantic diversity) during a reading interaction was analyzed. Analyses revealed significant treatment effects for the *EOWPVT* and *ITPA* subtest but not for the *PPVT-R* and there were care centre/treatment interactions. In centers where there was good compliance in delivering the treatment, none of the treatment groups differed from each other on the EOWPVT but both scored higher than the control group and the *school plus home* group had the best results. In low compliance centers, there were no differences between the treatment groups and the control group but the *school plus home* group scored higher than the other treatment groups. Interestingly, in the low compliance centers, the *school-only* treatment group performed worse than the control group.

For verbal productions in high compliance centers, significant effects of the treatments were seen in mean length of utterance, total number of words produced, semantic diversity for an unfamiliar book and a familiar book (one used during the intervention). However, there appeared to be no significant differences between the treatments. Lonigan and Whitehurst concluded that consistent with the results in middle-class samples, brief training in dialogic reading using a cost-effective video methodology can produce gains in vocabulary in low-income children. Looking at the resulting moderate to high effect sizes, they assert that some forms of storybook reading are useful in enriching children's language development. In this way, their findings contradict the less robust findings reported in the Bus et al. (1995) and Scarborough and Dobrich (1994) meta-analyses. Similar results have been found in studies of children classified as being language delayed. As Crain-Thoreson and Dale (1999) reported, children classified as language delayed appear to benefit from dialogic reading sessions with only slight modifications to the dialogic reading procedure (Crain-Thoreson & Dale, 1999).

Phonemic Awareness

In addition to the abundance of research on the effects of storybook reading to children's language development, in the last decade considerable attention also has focused on young children's development of phonemic awareness. Some researchers (e.g., Adams, 1990) postulate that phonemic awareness is a necessary skill in order for children to learn to read and write, whereas others argue that phonemic awareness is a result

of becoming literate, not a prerequisite to it (e.g., Scholes, 1997). Many educators assume a less polemical position and believe that some level of phonemic awareness is facilitative of children's literacy development. Assuming such a position, Regush, Anderson, and Lee (2002) reported on an action research project in which the first author implemented a 6-week long, play-based, phonemic awareness program in a kindergarten classroom in a suburban middle class area of Vancouver, Canada. Pre- and postmeasures showed significant gains in children's phonemic awareness over the 6 weeks. A control group of children of similar ability and demographics who were taught by the same teacher using essentially the same curriculum and instruction as in the intervention class but without the play based phonemic awareness instruction did not make similar gains. The authors concluded that this play-based program of about 18 hours duration not only enhanced children's phonemic awareness but also led to an increase in children's inclusion of literacy materials and events in their play routines as observations of a subset of the children revealed. The results of this study suggest that helping children acquire phonemic awareness can be achieved in a relatively short time span in a manner that fits with a play-based curriculum favored by many early childhood educators and primary-grade teachers.

Although results of the storybook reading interventions described above are somewhat encouraging and reflect a growing focus on this language event, there is still a lack of consistency in results (Karweit & Wasik, 1996). Furthermore, the results of the studies reviewed in this chapter raise some interesting questions, as well as some concerns. For example, in the series of studies by Senechal and colleagues, gains were found in receptive vocabulary, usually related to the style of reading that the adult enacted. Yet, in the Whitehurst studies of dialogic reading, the primary area of improvement or growth was in the area of expressive language. If the dialogic reading style also encourages the adult to engage the child it is difficult to understand the origins of these differences. It is possible that they are due to the fact that there were fewer constraints on the adult reader in the dialogic reading research. As noted earlier, the individual studies reported a great deal of variability in adherence to the program, whereas the Senechal studies experimentally controlled this dimension. If it is difficult to control the formats of story reading intervention with teachers and with parents and thus have a degree of confidence in the fidelity (and hence the generalizability) of the results, the promotion of storybook reading as *the* method of facilitating language development becomes questionable. Whether storybook reading is as useful as it at first seems becomes even more important when we examine the research that indicates differential effects for questioning or labeling or commenting during book reading (Kertoy, 1994; Hockenberger, Goldstein, & Haas, 1999; Justice, 2002). Furthermore, some research suggests that teaching ways of intervention through storybook reading may be confusing to both parents and teachers and attempts to teach these "unnatural" acts (van Tuijl, Leseman, & Ripens, 2001) with different cultural groups run the danger of alienating the individuals whom we wish to encourage to read to their children (Janes & Kermani, 2001).

It is also important to recognise that training parents to use a particular styles or methods (e.g., dialogic reading) essentially involves privileging a particular discourse style often linked to middle-class, Eurocentric culture, over all others. Although schools also tend to privilege these particular discursive practices, there are plainly ethical dilemmas when we attempt to train parents from outside the mainstream cultural group to read in particular ways as in effect we are negating their current literacy/oral practices. As we have pointed out elsewhere (Anderson, Anderson, Lynch, & Shapiro, 2003), for some time, early childhood educators and researchers have recognized that storybook reading to young children is nonexistent in some cultures that nevertheless produce a literate citizenry. Furthermore, some cultural groups find dialogic storybook reading troubling. For example, Janes and Kermani (2001) described an intervention program that centred on training immigrant parents from Central America and Mexico to read to their children in an interactive or dialogic manner. They found that storybook reading became an unpleasant and tense time for the parents and children involved. In recognition of the participants' discomfort, the researchers resolved to reframe the intervention program and encouraged the parents to read in any manner that felt natural to them. They then found that although the parents adopted a didactic style when they shared the books with their children, storybook reading became an enjoyable and engaging event for the participants. Given these concerns and the somewhat mixed results of research studies designed to measure the impact of storybook reading on children's language (and literacy) development, we wonder why so much importance is ascribed to the phenomenon.

Finally, as mentioned elsewhere in this chapter, in reviewing these studies it appears important to raise questions about the ways in which we choose to measure language growth. Standardized measures have tended to be reified in the conduct of much of the current research on storybook reading. Sometimes we elect to use these measures because they are convenient, as well as because the use of researcher-constructed instruments, although more ecologically valid, make it difficult to replicate or to build on previous studies. However, in conducting research it is important that we ensure that these measures are acceptable for use with the populations we study. This is true not only in terms of what and how they measure the targeted skills but also whether they are still considered valid. In reviewing the literature, it is not unusual to find old editions of tests still being used rather than new or revised ones. We run a danger in interpreting our findings when we use measures that have had serious questions raised about their validity rather than the revised versions that have attempted to rectify the shortcomings. We need to raise questions about why a 30-year-old measure would be used to evaluate children's progress, when other options exist. As producers and consumers of research, we continually need to ask, "What does the information revealed by the instruments used tell us about the language capabilities of the children with whom we work?"

Bilingual and Multilingual Education

Although research concerning the effects of bilingual or multilingual education on children's language development has not experienced the depth of discussion that storybook reading or phonemic awareness have in early childhood language research, there is substantial evidence that children's language and literacy learning are enhanced if they learn to read and write initially in their first language (e.g., Bialystok, 1997; Gunderson, 2004; Snow, Burns, & Griffin, 1998).

Cummins (2002) described three examples of programs that are built on current knowledge of language learning and pedagogy: Richmond Road School in Auckland, New Zealand; Oyster Bilingual School in Washington, DC; and the Foyer Model of Trilingual/Bicultural Education in Belgium, Brussels. In all three programs, children are taught in their first language and a second (or in the case of the Foyer Model, a second and a third) language simultaneously. The cultures of the different groups are also an integral part of curriculum and the pedagogy. In all cases, children are highly successful academically, they acquire an appreciation of diversity, and they develop an awareness of their own cultural and linguistic identities.

Family Literacy Programs

In recognizing the importance of families and communities in children's language and literacy acquisition, a number of researchers and educators have attempted to create programs that tap into families as a resource for encouraging children's language development. For example, Anderson, Smythe, Shapiro, and Morrison (2003) describe a culturally responsive family literacy program (Parents As Literacy Supporters, or PALS) developed by the first and last authors. The program is designed for 4- and 5-year-old children and their caregivers. Unlike many family literacy programs, parents and teachers were involved in its conceptualization and development. As well, parents are invited to work with their children in the classroom (or daycare), helping to develop positive home-school relationships. Furthermore, whereas storybook reading is valued within PALS, a variety of other language and literacy activities such as storytelling, riddles, raps and rhymes, drawing, and early writing, and attending to environmental print are also promoted. According to Anderson, Smythe, and Shapiro (2005), parents report increased awareness of the multiple ways that they can support their children's literacy development, whereas teachers demonstrate greater sensitivity to the cultural and social diversity of the families with whom they work and insights as to how they can work with parents in supporting their children's literacy development in respectful ways.

CONCLUSION

In spite of the numerous advances in our understanding of language development over the last several decades, many practices still reflect outmoded conceptions of language and language development. For example, as Wong-Fillmore (1996) points out, powerful lobby groups such as the "English movement" push for, and effect, "English-only" policies in schools in the United States, despite evidence that children's language and literacy learning are enhanced if they learn to read and write initially in their first language (Dicker, 2000; Gunderson, 2004). Furthermore, large-scale initiatives such as the American educational policy known as *No Child Left Behind* (United States Department of Education, 2002), with its very heavy emphasis on accountability as determined by standardized tests, reveal a lack of understanding of current theories and research concerning language development and diversity.

We believe that an overarching principle guiding research in early childhood language education should be the recognition of the increasingly global and diverse nature of society (Martinez-Roldan & Malve, 2004). For example, in Vancouver, British Columbia, the city in which we work, more than 50% of children speak a language other than English at home, more than 150 language groups are represented in the schoolaged population and in some early childhood classrooms, children speak more than a dozen different languages. As Luke (2003) reminds us, we have a moral and ethical obligation to pay attention to the realities of an increasingly global and diverse community.

In terms of future research, we see the need for a number of different foci. First, more research with different social and cultural groups is needed. Many new immigrants come from societies where conceptions of childhood and of language and literacy development differ in radical and fundamental ways from the mainstream North American views (e.g., Canella & Virru, 2002). It is important that researchers document the literacy practices of children and families from different backgrounds so that early childhood educators can support and build on

these. In light of the increasing linguistic diversity of North American society, more research is needed in terms of young children's early biliteracy and bilingual development. And finally, the emerging research on the role of popular culture (e.g., Dyson, 1999; Marsh, 2000) and technology (e.g., Labbo & Kuhn, 2000) in children's language and literacy development needs to be continued.

Furthermore, new programs, curricula and assessments will need to be developed to match the ever-changing demographics of contemporary schools. Educators and researchers will need to develop new and innovative ways in which to assess what children know about language and how it is used that recognize the diversity of their students/subjects. Given that parents are often the most reliable sources of information on their children's development, and families are highly significant in terms of children's language and literacy development, educators may find themselves developing new language and literacy assessments and programs that focus on families and communities. In doing so they may help to transform schools, day cares, and preschools from isolated institutions into vibrant and evolving centers of community (e.g., Moll, 1992) input and learning.

ACKNOWLEDGMENT

We are thankful to the three anonymous reviewers for their helpful comments and suggestions on an earlier draft of this chapter.

References

Adams, M. (1990). *Thinking and learning about print*. Cambridge, MA: MIT Press.

Anderson, J., Smythe, S., & Shapiro, J. (2005). Working with families, communities and schools: A critical case study. In J. Anderson, M. Kendrick, T. Rogers & S. Smythe (Eds.), *Portraits of literacy across families, communities and schools: Intersections and tensions* (pp. 63–85). Mahwah, NJ: Lawrence Erlbaum Associates

Anderson, J., Anderson, A., Lynch, J., & Shapiro, J. (2003). Storybook reading in a multicultural society: Critical perspectives. In A. van Kleeck, S. A. Stahl, & E. Bauer (Ed.), *On Reading Books to Children: Parents and Teachers* (pp. 203–230). Mahwah, NJ: Erlbaum.

Anderson, J., Smythe, S., Shapiro, J., & Morrison, F. (2003). Issues in family literacy programmes in inner city communities. In G. Shiel and U. Dhalaigh (Eds.), *Other ways of seeing: Diversity in language and literacy: Proceedings of the 12th European conference on reading* (pp. 119–124). Dublin, Ireland: Reading Association of Ireland.

Arnold, D., & Lonigan, C. (1994). Accelerating language development through picture book reading: Replication and extension to a videotape training format. *Journal of Educational Psychology, 86*, 235–243.

Bakhtin, M. (1986). *Speech genres and other late essays*. Austin: University of Texas Press.

Bauer, E. B. (2000). Code-switching during shared reading and independent reading: Lessons learned from a preschooler. *Research in the Teaching of English, 35*, 1010–130.

Bauer, E. B., Hall, J. K. & Kruth, K. (2002). The pragmatics role of code-switching in play context. *International Journal of Bilingualism, 6*, 52–79.

Bazerman, C. (1997). The life of genre, the life in the classroom. In H. Ostrom (Ed.), *Genres and writing: Issues, arguments alternatives* (pp. 19–26). Portsmouth, NH: Heinemann.

Beals, D. (2001). Eating and reading: Links between family conversation with preschoolers and later language and literacy. In D. Dickinson & P. Tabors (Eds.), *Beginning literacy with language* (pp. 75–92). Toronto: Paul H. Brookes Publishing Company.

Bialystok, E. (1997). Effects of bilingualism and biliteracy on children's emerging concepts of print. *Developmental Psychology, 33*, 429–440.

Bissex, G. (1980). *Gyns at wrk: A child learns to write and read*. Cambridge, MA: Harvard University Press.

Boone, H., & Crais, E. (1999). Strategies for achieving family-driven assessment and intervention planning. *Young Exceptional Children, 3*, 2–11.

Bourdieu, P. (1990). *Reproduction in education, society and culture*. London: Sage.

Brink, M. (2002). Involving parents in early childhood assessment: Perspectives from an early childhood interventions instructor. *Early Childhood Education Journal, 29*, 251–257.

Bruner, J. (1986). *Actual minds, possible worlds*. Cambridge, MA: Harvard University Press.

Bus, A., Van Ijezendorn, M., & Pellegrini, A. D. (1995). Joint book reading makes for success in learning to read: A meta-analysis on intergenerational transmission of literacy. *Review of Educational Research, 65,* 1-21.

Campbell, T., & Dollaghan, C. (1997). Reducing bias in language assessment: Processing-dependent measures. *Journal of Speech, Language and Hearing Research, 40,* 519-525.

Canella, G., & Virru, R. (2002). Euro-American constructions of education of children (and adults) around the world: A postcolonial critique. In J. Kincheloe (Ed.), *Kidworld: Childhood studies, global perspectives and education* (pp. 197-211). New York: Peter Lang.

Chapman, M. (1994). The emergence of genres: Some findings from an examination of first grade writing. *Written Communication, 11,* 348-380.

Chapman, M. (1999). Situated, social, active: Rewriting genre in the elementary classroom. *Written Communication, 16,* 469-490.

Clark, M. (1976). *Young fluent readers: What can they teach us?* London: Heinemann.

Clay, M. (1993). Always a learner: A fable. *Reading Today, 3,* 10.

Cole, M. (1996). *Cultural Psychology: A Once and Future Discipline.* Cambridge, MA: Harvard University Press.

Cope, B., & Kalantzis, M. (Eds.). (1993). *The powers of literacy: a genre approach to teaching writing.* Pittsburgh: University of Pittsburgh Press.

Craig, H., & Washington, J. (2002). Oral language expectations for African American preschoolers and kindergarteners. *American Journal of Speech-Language Pathology, 11,* 59-70.

Crain-Thoreson, C., & Dale, P. (1999). Enhancing linguistic performance: Parents and teachers as book reading partners for children with language delays. *Topics in Early Childhood Special Education, 19,* 28-40.

Cross, J., De Vaney, T., & Jones, G. (2001). Pre-service teacher attitudes toward differing dialects. *Linguistics and Education, 12,* 211-227.

Cummins, J. (2002). Rights and responsibilities of educators of bilingual/bicultural children. In L. D. Soto (Ed.), *Making a difference in the lives of bilingual/bicultural children* (pp. 195-210). New York: Peter Lang.

DeTemple, J. (2001). Parents and children reading books together. In D. Dickinson & P. Tabors (Eds.), *Beginning literacy with language* (pp. 31-52). Toronto: Paul H. Brookes Publishing Company.

DeTemple, J., & Tabors, P. (1995). Styles of interaction during a book reading task: Implications for literacy intervention with low-income families. In C. Kizner (Ed.), *Perspectives on literacy research and practice: 44th Yearbook of the National Reading Conference* (pp. 265-271). Chicago: IL: National Reading Conference.

Delpit, L. (1995). *Other people's children: Cultural conflict in the classroom.* New York: The New Press.

Dickinson, D. (2001a). Book reading in preschool classrooms. In D. Dickinson & P. Tabors (Eds.), *Beginning literacy with language* (pp. 175-204). Toronto: Paul H. Brookes Publishing Company.

Dickinson, D. (2001b). Putting the pieces together: Impact of preschool on children's language and literacy development in kindergarten. In D. Dickinson & P. Tabors (Eds.), *Beginning literacy with language.* Toronto: Paul H. Brookes Publishing Company.

Dickinson, D., McCabe, A., & Sprague, K. (2003). Teacher rating of oral language and literacy: Individualizing early literacy instruction with a standards based instrument. *The Reading Teacher, 56,* 554-564.

Dickinson, D., & Smith, M. (1994). Long term effects of preschool teachers' book readings on low-income children's vocabulary and story comprehension. *Reading Research Quarterly, 29,* 105-122.

Dicker, S. (2000). Official English and bilingual education: The controversy over language pluralism in U.S. society. In J. Hall & W. Eggington (Eds.), *The sociopolitics of English Langaue Teaching* (pp. 45-67). North York, ON: Multilingual Matters.

Diniz, F. (1999). Race and special education needs in the 1990's. *British Journal of Special Education, 26,* 213-218.

Dockrell, J. (2001). Assessing language skills in preschool children. *Child Psychology & Psychiatry Review, 6,* 74-85.

Dunn, L., & Dunn, L. (1981). *Peabody Picture Vocabulary Test (Revised).* Circle Pines, MN: American Guidance Services.

Durkin, D. (1966). *Children who read early.* New York: Teachers College Press.

Dyson, A. H. (1999). Coach Bombay's kids learn to write: Children's appropriation of media material for school literacy. *Research in the Teaching of English, 33,* 366-402.

Dyson, A. H. (2000). On reframing children's words: The perils, promises and pleasures of writing children. *Research in the Teaching of English, 34,* 352-367.

Feiler, A., & Webster, A. (1999). Teacher predictions of young children's literacy success or failure. *Assessment in Education, 6,* 341-356.

Feldman, H., Dollaghan, C., Campbell, T., Kurs-Lasky, M., Janosky, J. & Paradise, J. (2000). Measurent properties of the *MacArthur Communicative Development Inventories* at ages one and two years. *Child Development, 71,* 310-322.

Gardner, M. (1981). *Expressive One-Word Picture Vocabulary Test.* Novato, CA: Academic Therapy Publications.

Gee, J. (2003). Opportunity to learn: A language-based perspective on assessment. *Assessment in Education, 10,* 27-46.

Gee, J. P. (1989). What is literacy? *Journal of Education, 171,* 18-25.

Gipps, C. (1995). What do we mean by equity in relation to assessment? *Assessment in Education, 2,* 271-280.

Goncu, A. (1999). *Children's engagement in the world: Sociocultural perspectives.* New York: Cambridge University Press.

Gregory, E. (2003). Getting to know strangers: A socio-cultural approach to reading, language and literacy. *Reading Online, 7,* 3. Retrieved September 10, 2003, from http://www.readingonline. org/international/inter_index.asp?HREF=/international/edinburgh/ gregory/

Gregory, E. (2001). Sisters and brothers as language and literacy teachers: Synergy between siblings playing and working together. *Journal of Early Childhood Literacy, 1,* 301-322.

Gunderson, L. (2004). The language, literacy, achievement and social consequences of English-only programs for immigrant students. *53rd Yearbook of the National Reading Conference* (pp. 1-27). Oak Creek, WI: National Reading Conference.

Gutierrez-Clellen, V., Pena, E., & Quinn, R. (1995). Accomodating cultural differences in narrative style: A multicultural perspective. *Topics in Language Disorders, 15,* 54-67.

Haneda, M., & Wells, G. (2000). Writing in Knowledge-Building Communities. *Research in the Teaching of English, 34,* 430-457.

Hart, B. (2000). A natural history of early language experience. *Topics in Early Childhood Special Education, 20,* 28-32.

Hart, B., & Risley, T. R. (1995). *Meaningful differences in the everyday experiences of young American children.* Baltimore, MD: Paul H. Brooks.

Hauser-Cram, P., Sirin, S., & Stipek, D. (2003). When teachers' and parents' values differ: Ratings of academic competence in children from low income families. *Journal of Educational Psychology, 95,* 813-820.

Heath, S. (1983). *Ways with words: Language, life and work in communities and classrooms.* New York: Cambridge University Press.

Heath, S. (1986a). *Sociocultural contexts of language development.* Los Angeles: California State University.

Heath, S. (1986b). Sociocultural Contexts of Language Development. In S. Heath (Ed.), *Beyond language.* Los Angeles: CA: State University, Evaluation, Dissemination and Assessment Center.

Hockenberger, E., Goldstein, H., & Haas, L. (1999). Effects of commenting during joint book reading by mothers with low SES. *Topics in Early Childhood Special Education, 19*, 15-28.

Janes, H., & Kermani, H. (2001). Caregivers story reading to young children in family literacy programs: Pleasure or punishment? *Journal of Adolescent and Adult Literacy, 44*, 458-446.

Justice, L. (2002). Word exposure conditions and preschoolers novel word learning during shared storybook reading. *Reading Psychology, 23*, 87-106.

Karweit, N., & Wasik, B. (1996). The effects of story reading programs on literacy and language development of disadvantaged preschoolers. *Journal of Education for Students Placed at Risk, 1*, 319-348.

Katz, J. (2001). Playing at home: The talk of pretend play. In D. Dickinson & P. Tabors (Eds.), *Beginning literacy with language* (pp. 53-74). Toronto: Paul H. Brookes.

Kertoy, M. (1994). Adult interactive strategies and spontaneous comments of preschoolers during joint storybook readings. *Journal of Research in Childhood Education, 9*, 58-67.

Kirk, S., McCarthy, J., & Kirk, W. (1968). *Illinois Test of Psycholinguistic Abilities*. Urbana: University of Illinois Press.

Kramsch, C. (2002). Introduction: "How can we tell the dancer from the dance" In C. Kramsch (Ed.). *Language acquisition and socialization: Ecological perspectives*. London: Continuum.

Labbo, L., & Kuhn, M. (2000). Weaving chains of cognition and affect: A young child's understanding of CD-ROM talking books. *Journal of Literacy Research, 32*, 79-92.

Laing, G., Law, J., Levin, A., & Logan, S. (2002). Evaluation of a structured test and a parent led method for screening for speech and language problems: Prospective population based study. *British Medical Journal, 325*, 1152.

Laing, S. (2003). Assessment of phonology in preschool African American vernacular English speakers using an alternate response mode. *American Journal of Speech-Language Pathology, 12*, 273-281.

Laing, S., & Kamhi, A. (2003). Alternative assessment of language and literacy in culturally diverse populations. *Language, Speech and Hearing Services in Schools, 34*, 44-55.

Lave, J., & Wenger, E. (1991). *Situated learning: Legitimate peripheral participation*. Cambridge: Cambridge University Press.

Lewin, T. (2002, July 17). Study links working mothers to slower learning. *The New York Times*, p. A14.

Long, S. (1998). Learning to get along: Language acquisition and literacy development in a new cultural setting. *Research in the Teaching of English, 33*, 8-47.

Lonigan, C., & Whitehurst, G. (1998). Reflective efficacy of parent and teacher involvement in a shared-reading intervention for preschool children from low-income backgrounds. *Early Childhood Research Quarterly, 13*, 263-290.

Luke, A. (2003). Literacy education for a new ethics of global community. *Language Arts, 81*, 20-22.

MacNeil, L. (2000). *Contradictions of school reform: Educational costs of standardized testing*. New York: Routledge.

Marchman, V., & Martinez-Sussmann, C. (2002). Concurrent validity of caregiver/parent report measures of language for children who are learning both English and Spanish. *Journal of Speech, Language and Hearing Research, 45*, 983-997.

Marsh, J. (2000). "But I want to fly too!" Girls and superhero play in the infant classroom. *Gender and Education, 12*, 209-220.

Martinez-Roldan, C., & Malve, G. (2004). Language ideologies mediating literacy and identity in bilingual contexts. *Journal of Early Childhood Literacy, 4*, 155-180.

McDermott, R. (1993). The acquisition of a child by a learning disability. In S. Chaiklin (Ed.), *Understanding Practice: Perspectives on Activity and Context* (pp. 269-305). Cambridge: Cambridge University Press.

Mehan, H. (1992). Understanding inequality in schools: The contribution of interpretive studies. *Sociology of Education, 65*, 1-20.

Minami, M. (1996). Japanese preschool children's narrative development. *First Language, 16*, 339-363.

Minami, M. (2001). Maternal styles of narrative elicitation and the development of children's narrative skill: A study on parental scaffolding. *Narrative Inquiry, 11*, 155-180.

Moll, L. (1992). Bilingual classroom studies and community analysis: Some recent trends. *Educational Researcher, 21*, 20-24.

Murphy, P. (1995). Sources of inequity: Understanding students' responses to assessment. *Assessment in Education: Principles, Policy & Practice, 2*, 249-271.

National Institute of Child Health and Human Development Early Child Care Research Network. (2000). The relation of child care to cognitive and language development. *Child Development, 71*, 960-980.

National Education Association. (1997). *Status of the American public school teacher*. Washington, DC: NEA.

Neuman, S., & Celano, D. (2001). Access to print in low-income and middle-income communities. *Reading Research Quarterly, 36*, 8-27.

Parke, T., Drury, R., Kenner, C., & Robertson, L. (2002). Revealing invisible worlds: Connecting the mainstream with bilingual children's home and community learning. *Journal of Early Childhood Literacy, 2*, 195-220.

Pena, E. (1997). Task familiarity: Effects on the test performance of Puerto Rican and African American children. *Language, Speech and Hearing Services in Schools, 28*, 323-332.

Pena, E., Iglesias, A., & Lidz, C. (2001). Reducing test bias through dynamic assessment of children's word learning ability. *American Journal of Speech-Language Pathology, 10*, 138-153.

Pena, E., Quinn, R., & Iglesias, A. (1992). The application of dynamic methods to language assessment: A non-biased approach. *The Journal of Special Education, 26*, 269-280.

Pintrich, P. (2003). A motivational science perspective on the role of student motivation in learning and teaching contexts. *Journal of Educational Psychology, 95*, 667-686.

Reay, D., & Wiliam, D. (1999). 'I'll be a Nothing': Structure, agency and the construction of identity through assessment. *British Educational Research Journal, 25*, 343-354.

Regush, N., Anderson, J., & Lee, E. (2002). Using play to support the development of kindergarten children's phonemic awareness. In P. Linder, M. B. Sampson, J. Duggan & B. Brancatto. (Eds.), *Celebrating the faces of literacy* (pp. 234-246). Commerce, TX: College Reading Association.

Restrepo, M. A., & Silverman, S. (2001). Validity of the Spanish preschool language scale 3 for use with bilingual children. *American Journal of Speech-Language Pathology, 10*, 382-393.

Scarborough, H., & Dobrich, W. (1994). On the efficacy of reading to preschoolers. *Developmental Review, 14*, 245-302.

Scholes, R. (1997, March). *The case against phonemic awareness*. Paper presented at the Annual Meeting of the Society for the Scientific Study of Reading. Chicago, Illinois.

Schoenbrot, L., Kumin, L., & Sloan, J. (1997). Learning disabilities existing concomitantly with communication disorder. *Journal of Learning Disabilities, 30*, 264-281.

Senechal, M. (1997). The differential effect of storybook reading on preschoolers' acquisition of expressive and receptive vocabulary. *Journal of Child Language, 24*, 123-138.

Senechal, M., & Cornell, E. (1993). Vocabulary acquisition through shared reading experiences. *Reading Research Quarterly, 28*, 360-374.

Senechal, M., Le Fevre, J., Hudson, E., & Lawson, E. (1996). Knowledge of storybooks as a predictor of young children's vocabulary. *Journal of Educational Psychology, 88,* 520–536.

Senechal, M., Thomas, E., Monker, J., & Lawson, E. (1995). Individual differences in 4 year old children's acquisition of vocabulary during storybook reading. *Journal of Educational Psychology, 87,* 218–229.

Shapiro, J., Anderson, J., & Anderson, A. (1997). Diversity in parental storybook reading. *Early Childhood Development and Care, 127,* 47–59.

Shapiro, J., Anderson, J., & Anderson, A. (2002). Storybook reading: What we know and what we should consider. In O. Saracho & B. Spodek (Eds.), *Contemporary perspectives in early literacy.* Greenwich, CT: Information Age Publishing.

Snow, C., Tabors, P., & Dickinson, D. (2001). Language development in preschool years. In D. Dickinson & P. Tabors (Eds.), *Beginning literacy with language* (pp. 1–26). Toronto: Paul H. Brookes Publishing Company.

Snow, C., Burns, M., & Griffin, P. (1998). *Preventing reading difficulties in young children.* Washington, DC: National Academy Press.

Stanovich, K. (1986). Matthew effects in reading: Some consequences of individual differences in the acquisition of literacy. *Reading Research Quarterly, 21,* 360–407.

Tabors, P., Beals, D., & Weizman, Z. (2001). 'You know what oxygen is?': Learning new words at home. In D. Dickinson & P. Tabors (Ed.), *Beginning literacy with language.* Toronto: Paul H. Brookes Publishing Company.

Taylor, D. (1983). *Family literacy: Young children learning to read and write.* Exeter, NH: Heinemann.

Toohey, K. (2000). *Learning English at School: Identity, Social Relations and Classroom Practice.* Clevedon: Multilingual Matters.

United States Department of Education. (2002). Retrieved August 1, 2003, from *No Child Left Behind.* http://www.ed.gov/nclb/landing.jhtml

Valdez-Menchaca, M., & Whitehurst, G. (1992). Accelerating language development through picture book reading: A systematic extension to Mexican daycare. *Developmental Psychology, 24,* 1106–1114.

van Tuijl, C., Leseman, P., & Rispens, J. (2001). Efficacy of an intensive home based educational intervention programme for 4–6 year old ethnic minority children in the Netherlands. *International Journal of Behavioral Development, 25,* 148–159.

Vygotsky, L. (1978). *Mind in society: The development of higher psychological processes.* Cambridge, MA: Harvard University Press.

Watkins, M., & Coffey, D. (2004). Reading motivation: Multidimensional and indeterminate. *Journal of Educational Psychology, 96,* 110–118.

Whitehurst, G., Arnold, D., Epstien, J., Angell, A., Smith, M., & Fischel, J. (1994). A picture book reading intervention in daycare and home for children from low-income families. *Developmental Psychology, 30,* 679–689.

Whitehurst, G., Falco, F., Lonigan, C., Fischel, J., De Baryshe, B., Valdez-Menchaca, M., & Caufield, M. (1988). Accelerating language development through picture book reading. *Developmental Psychology, 24,* 552–559.

Wollman-Bonilla, J. (2001). Family involvement in early writing instruction. *Journal of Early Childhood Literacy, 1,* 167–192.

Wong-Fillmore, L. (1996). What happens when languages are lost? An essay on language assimilation and cultural identity. In D. Slobin, J. Gevhart, A. Kyratizis, & J. Guo (Eds.), *Social interaction, social context ad language: Essays in honor of Susan Ervin-Tripp* (pp. 435–444). Mahwah, NJ: Lawrence Erlbaum.

· 9 ·

EMERGENT LITERACY: SYMBOLS AT WORK

Susan E. Hill
Sue Nichols
University of South Australia

Emergent literacy is a passionately contested field of study. Like the concepts of literacy and literacy learning more broadly, emergent literacy can be differently inflected, depending on the theoretical perspective which is prevailing. Lively debates over the past decades, between proponents of these theoretical perspectives, prevent the field from achieving a single dominant view. Much is at stake in definitions of emergent literacy, from the design of early childhood curriculum to the early identification and support of children at risk of falling behind in literacy acquisition. Therefore, it is important to acknowledge and consider these different theoretical perspectives and their implications. In this chapter, we begin by identifying several perspectives each of which offer a different view on the concept of emergent literacy. In doing this we have extended on the review of research by Yaden, Rowe, and MacGillivray (2000), who focused on the "unconventionality of children's early literacy behaviours in informal settings at home and at school prior to beginning formal instruction" (p. 426). We put particular emphasis in this chapter on a new entrant to the field, the semiotic perspective, which we believe holds considerable promise to enrich theorizations of emergent literacy.

It is also important to be aware that, from its inception, research exploring the concept of "emergent literacy" has also employed a range of methodological approaches, which also influence what can be known. There have been case studies of individual children's language and literacy development (Bissex, 1980); studies of preschoolers' home and community literacy environments (Taylor, 1983; Teale, 1986); and print awareness studies in which researchers presented students with common labels, signs, and logos from their everyday environments in varying degrees of contextualisation (Teale, 1986). Researchers in the field of emergent literacy have always been creative in identifying and exploring new developments in literacy practices. So it is that as historical conditions change, new issues, topics, and approaches emerge. More recently, studies are

investigating the impact of information and communication technologies (ICT) on early literacy acquisition and using ICT to develop research methodologies for exploring these phenomena. In turn, the definition of emergent literacy is changing to take into account new forms of literacy practice. This is a key point to which we will return throughout this review.

EMERGENT LITERACY: CHANGING THEORETICAL PERSPECTIVES

There is a broad spectrum of theoretical stances about children learning to be literate from maturationist, connectionist, developmentalist, constructivist, and critical views (Crawford, 1995; Hill, Comber, Louden, Rivalland, & Reid, 1998). Current perspectives on early literacy embody a diverse range of theories and practices and have at their core different values and beliefs about the nature of literacy, the process of literacy learning, how children are viewed and different futures for young children's education. These theoretical orientations may be viewed on a historical continuum. What has been termed the emergent literacy perspective occupies a position historically between developmentalist and critical perspectives. However, because of the additive nature of educational knowledge (old theories are rarely completely discarded as new entrants arrive) currently many theories seeking to explain children's acquisition of literacy simultaneously contest the field of knowledge. The work of Crawford (1995) is useful in summarizing these separate positions and we refer to her work later.

From a maturationist perspective, all children pass through a series of invariant stages that cannot be hurried. Maturation occurs as a result of a biological process of neural ripening, a little like ripening fruit or a blossoming. In the allied developmental readiness view, the key idea is that children must be *ready* before they can learn how to read. However, rather than letting nature take its course, nurturing takes precedence. In this view children's readiness for reading can be influenced by prereading activities.

From the connectionist perspective, priority is placed on learning the code as a means to fluent reading and increased comprehension. This approach is closely linked to the developmental readiness perspective where knowledge is based on elements or pieces that are then put together or connected to make a whole. Adams (1990) in the book *Beginning to read* notes the benefits of over-learning letter forms, grapheme-phoneme associations, and spelling patterns. Prereading and reading readiness are concepts consistent with this perspective. However, connectionist theory may be criticized for its lack of attention to writing as a way in to reading. Both Strickland and Cullinan (1990) point out that the concepts of "prereaders" and "reading readiness" are not sufficiently broad enough to take account of literacy development as being on a continuum of ever increasing competence. In addition, the notion of precompetence is discussed by Freebody (1995) as a narrow adult construction of childhood. To do well in learning literacy, a child must quickly discover what the adult's theories of precompetence are and then the child must use the behavior appropriate or displays of being a successful beginning reader and writer.

In the emergent perspective, literacy learning is not viewed as the acquisition of a series of reading skills but, rather, as a dynamic, ongoing process that begins long before children begin formalized schooling (Teale & Sulzby, 1986). The process of oral language is provided as a model for the development of print related literacy. Teachers immerse children in a print rich environment with real books and encourage writing original texts. Children develop as readers and writers through immersion in print rich environments and from experiences with print that encourage engagement, experimentation and risk-taking. Invented spellings and approximations are accepted as part of the learner's ongoing process of making sense and gaining control over literacy. Developmentally appropriate practices guide both the curriculum and the structure of class activities. Formal direct instruction, particularly the teaching of isolated skills and worksheets, are seen as inappropriate for young children.

Defining the boundaries of the emergent stage, McGee and Purcell-Gates (1997) limit the period of emergent literacy from birth to when literacy independence at a conventional level is in evidence. They suggest that there are two time periods (0–5 and 5–independence). The sociocultural context for the first period is the home/community and perhaps preschool and religious school and for the second period the formal school instructional context and the home/community. The transition from home to school settings is a central issue. Continuity between these settings is seen as the ideal situation, as Teale (1995) writes, "[E]mergent literacy stresses continuities between emergent and conventional reading, between the concerns and issues traditionally associated with early childhood educators and those associated with reading teachers, and between the home and school environments" (p. 124).

This stress on continuity, though, arises from observations of the differences between home and school settings, particularly in terms of the different relationships between the child and significant adults. Whether formal educational settings should

become more like homes in order to ease children's transition to school literacy or whether parents should be assisted to introduce school literacy into the home is a perennial debate in the field. Regardless of the preferred approach, it is taken as axiomatic that all children benefit from such continuities. Like maturationist readiness and connectionist theories, the emergent literacy perspective draws on developmental principles that reinforce the belief that generic patterns of literacy learning can be expected from all children regardless of their sociocultural experiences. If there is a deviation from the series of cognitive developmental stages, this may be seen as a deficit.

The social constructivist perspective views children as competent and capable users of oral and written language and argues that formal literacy education should build on these competencies (Crawford, 1995). Children purposefully learn and make sense of the complex semiotic signs and symbols of their culture. This meaning making or sense making process in the young child is no different from the processes engaged in by older children and adults. From the social constructivist perspective, the early literacy curriculum builds on the cultural and social language and literacy experiences children have before formal schooling. From the social constructivist perspective, reading and writing activities of even very young children are reflective of their culture and are characterized by both purposefulness and intentionally. The differences between the processes of young readers and more proficient language users is a matter of sophistication, practice and experience, not a particular stage of psychological development. However, although social constructivism highlights enacted social relationships, Dyson (1995) points out that it does not necessarily reveal the hierarchical nature of those relationships.

Critical perspectives acknowledge that the power bases within different sociopolitical contexts are not equal ones and are concerned with change and social action (Gee 2002; Siegal & Fernandez, 2000; Luke, Comber, & O'Brien, 1994). This view contends that social practices are set up to meet the interests and help maintain the privileged positions of those within the dominant culture. Critical perspectives claim that the interests of the dominant culture are accepted more readily and have more influence than any minority interests that may seek to disrupt the existing hierarchical power relationships. However the complexity of the sociocultural world and the struggle within and between groups entails more than a simple model of social transmission. Gee (2002) writes of the importance of teachers finding associational "bridges" between a child's primary Discourse and the school-based language and literacy practices if schools are to resonate with the child's experiences of the world and initial sense of self. A child's primary Discourse with a big "D" is similar to an "identity kit" and includes "ways of talking, listening writing, reading, acting, interacting, feeling, believing, valuing, and feeling (and using various objects, symbols, images, tools, and technologies) in the service of enacting meaningful socially situated identities and activities" (Gee, 2002, p. 35). Working from a critical perspective, Luke and colleagues (1994) describe ways teachers use community texts, for example, Mother's Day catalogues, to develop emergent literacy and to analyse ways the portrayal of mothers in advertising campaigns.

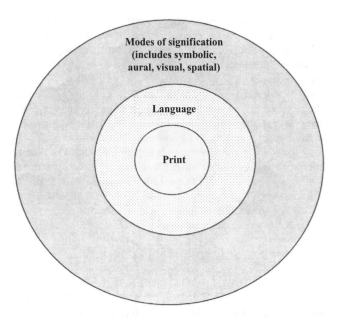

FIGURE 9.1. A semiotic model of literacy (Nichols, 2000).

The semiotic perspective can be summed up by the statement "text is more than language" (Kress, 1999, p. 468). In the same way that we can ask how individuals and groups use print to make meanings, we can ask how meanings are made and goals accomplished using other "semiotic resources" such as oral language, visual imagery, numerical symbols, and music (Lemke, 1990). We concur with Kress's (1997) and the New London Group's (1996) prediction that children will be increasingly exposed to communication tools and situations that are multimodal rather than exclusively linguistic. As Labbo (1996) suggests, at the onset of the 21st century young children are increasingly making meaning by drawing on multiple sign systems and multimedia symbol systems and these electronic symbol making systems may be best understood from a semiotic perspective.

The semiotic approach does not replace older definitions of literacy. Rather, it is inclusive of, and adds to, both the traditional print-oriented and the more recent language-oriented communications model. Figure 9.1 illustrates this: The inner circle represents the traditional print-oriented definition of literacy. Here there is an emphasis on encoding and decoding print. The middle circle of Figure 9.1 represents a language-oriented definition of literacy, which includes print but extends the range of representational resources to include oral language. In the outer circle, literacy encompasses print and language plus a broader range of representational resources, or modalities. For example in multimedia, print is combined with sound, movement, and visual imagery to create complex texts that require the "reader" to process in multiple modes simultaneously.

The semiotic perspective aligns readily with a social constructivist perspective. From both perspectives, to be a social being is to be continually producing and interpreting meanings co-constructively with other social beings. One's meaning-making resources include all the constructive and interpretive practices that one knows how to participate in at any particular time, and the materials and tools that are used in these practices. According to this view, with which we concur, literacy is not a technical skill that can or should be isolated from its semiotic and social context.

These theoretical positions explain the diversity of emergent literacy research and in particular why some studies focus closely on the alphabetic principle and phonemic awareness and others on sociocontextual environment for learning literacy in homes and preschools. Worthwhile contributions have been made in many dimensions over the last decade. In order to build a comprehensive picture of young children's emergence into literacy in these complex times it is necessary to draw from this wide range of perspectives and approaches. In the review that follows, we have divided the studies under thematic headings: emergent writing; electronic literacies; literate language; emergent literacy for bilingual children; book reading; phonemic awareness and early intervention. In so doing, we aim to provide a sense of the richness of this complex field and to make room for some new perspectives and debates.

EMERGENT WRITING

The comment is frequently made that writing has received less attention in early literacy research than has reading (Nixon & Topping, 2001). A strong body of work has, however, been building over the last 10 years, informed by sociocultural and semiotic theories that support a view of writing as a meaning making practice undertaken in specific social contexts. For the purpose of this chapter, we will concentrate on studies of early writing that focus on the significance of social context and on the place of writing within a complex repertoire of representational practices. This includes studies of the mark-making that is one of the first indicators of very young children's understanding of symbolic significance. Studies of early writing are contributing much to our understanding of the complex interrelationships between different representational practices and their contexts.

These interrelationships have been explored in range of studies. Lancaster (2001) uses video to look closely at a 2-year-old child making a Mother's Day card with her father. She identifies the following meaning-making practices used by young Anna in this collaborative text production: oral language, gesture, gaze, and symbol-making. For instance, the drawing of a zigzag mark, the finger pointing to the mark, the vocalizing "at's cat" [That's a cat] and the gaze toward her father all coordinate to signify 'I have represented a cat with this mark. Please show that you recognise my meaning-making' (p. 141).

At the other end of what is often considered the "emergent literacy" phase, Dyson (2001) focuses on a 6-year-old children undertaking a classroom task, that of writing a factual report. Here also, the semiotic and sociocultural perspective enables a rich description of the complex relationships of meaning-making involved in the production of a specific text, in this case a written report on the topic "Space." Dyson describes one child, Noah, in the process of producing the text "Space Case says there was a space ship." (Space Case is a television adventure). The production of this text involves the coordination of writing, drawing, oral language, and symbolic sounds. Noah begins by vocalising each word in the text as he writes it. However, halfway through the word "there," he stops writing and begins drawing a space ship. At the same time, he begins to narrate a scene from a space adventure in a dramatic voice complete with sound effects. Noah's meaning-making, his complete text, is multimodal and dynamic. It does not reside only in the piece of paper that holds his marks.

Manipulation of objects, collaborative talk, and symbol production are interrelated elements in children's collaborative play as analyzed by Van Oers and Wardekker (1999). In the context of a junior school in the Netherlands, children aged between 4 and 6, play in the "shoe shop" area where they are provided with real shoes and blank, unlabeled boxes. The impetus to produce symbols comes about when the children realize that it is impossible to tell what kind of shoes are in the boxes without opening the lids. They discuss how to mark the boxes and eventually come up with the symbols M (mama shoes), P (papa shoes), and K (*kinderen*—Dutch for children). The shoes being sorted into their appropriately labeled boxes, the children then collaboratively produce a graphic representation of the piles of boxes, again using their symbols M, P, and K. The actual written linguistic text here is limited to three letters and, from one perspective, tells us little about the children's competence. However, the production of linguistic symbols needs to be seen in the context of the full semiotic activity. Labeling objects (the shoe boxes) is integrally related to the organizational task of sorting them into meaningful categories, and of making a visible recording of this organizational pattern.

Young children use a wide variety of materials in their representational practices, not all of them conventional literacy materials such as paper and pencil. Pahl (2002, p. 146) uses the term "artefactual" to designate the practice of making texts out of objects. One example, from her ethnographic study of three boys at home and school, is of Fatih making a map out of beads on the carpet at home. This study brings to light the ephemeral and often invisible emergent literacy practices, which are embedded in children's and families' activities. A few minutes before Fatih has made the bead-map, he had been praying with the beads, according to his family's religious practice and shortly after its production, the map was cleared away to make room for other activities. Pahl calls these ephemeral products "momentary texts" (p. 160). This concept of the momentary text is particularly useful in thinking about literacy in the context of new technologies that enable children to rapidly create, destroy, and transform textual products.

Rich descriptions such as those discussed here have been a hallmark of early literacy research for decades. However, they are assuming a different kind of significance in relation to current debates about the meaning of literacy, and of literacy acquisition, not just for young children but for all social actors. In the past, young children's use of a combination of linguistic and non-linguistic resources for making meaning has been understood as a characteristic of an emergent stage before the achievement of literate competence. This view rested on a definition of literate competence as competence in the consumption and production of print (reading and writing).

Current redefinitions of what it means to be fully literate in these technologised times are changing the way we understand these descriptions of early writing and mark-making (Kress, Lankshear, & Knobel, 2003; New London Group, 1996). The ability to simultaneously coordinate multiple linguistic and non-linguistic elements is now understood as a quality of literate competence in all social actors. The meaning of "emergent literacy" is changing with the acknowledgment that what the child is "emerging" into is a complex world of signification.

Not all early writing research is inclusive of such a full semiotic range as the studies above. Many studies, however, situate writing within a broader communicative framework that encompasses both written and oral language. In the next section, we discuss studies which investigate the relationship between oral and written language and between the ways in which both are acquired.

ELECTRONIC LITERACIES

Much of the research into emergent literacy is print-based or "book-centric" (Yaden, Rowe, & MacGillivray, 2000) and includes knowledge of the alphabetic principle, phonological awareness, and print awareness, book handling, writing, and talking about texts (Clay, 1993). New forms of literacy multi-literacies (New London Group, 1996) expand reading, writing, speaking, and listening to include multimedia symbol forms. Computers are "symbol machines" (Labbo & Kuhn, 1998) that allow children to negotiate a complex interplay of multiple sign systems (e.g., video clips, music, sound effects, icons, virtually rendered paint strokes, text in print-based documents), multiple modalities (e.g., linguistic, auditory, visual, artistic), and recursive communicative and cognitive processes (e.g., real time and virtual conversations, cutting/pasting text, manipulating graphics, importing photographs). With these new technologies it becomes imperative for us to grapple with the impact electronic literacies have on learning and instruction. It has been suggested that the supportive auditory narrations, word pronunciations, text reading, visual animations, demonstrations, and prompts enable young children to be able to read at or above their reading instructional level (McKenna, 1998).

Research into electronic literacies is sparse. In Neuman and Dickinson's (2002) review of early literacy research of the 30 articles there were no review articles on technology and the changing nature of early literacy. The various strands of early literacy development included print-based spelling, writing, and reading. In a review of research into reading (Barr et al., 2000) of 47 chapters on various aspects of literacy research, only two general articles connected literacy and technology and neither of these dealt specifically with emergent early childhood education.

In Lankshear and Knobel's (2003) review of literacy and technologies in the early years of school, they note 554 articles from 9 different journals in which only a fraction of these articles relate to early childhood, new technologies and literacy. In these research articles, there was an over whelming emphasis on using technology to promote abilities to handle conventional alphabetic print texts rather than to generate multimodal texts and to understand principles of multimodal meanings.

Of the small number of research studies into new technologies and literacy, Hutinger and colleagues (1997) report on an early childhood emergent literacy project that took place in 16 preschool classes involving preschoolers with mild to moderate disabilities working with graphics and story making software. The study reports significant gains in communication and other emergent literacy behaviours as well as enhanced interpersonal interactions amongst learners. Another study into the use of electronic books Labbo and Kuhn (2000) focuses specifically on kindergarteners and used the distinction between "considerate" (multimedia effects that are integral to and coherent to the story) and "inconsiderate" (incongruent or incidental effects) CD-ROM stories. They found that considerate CD-ROMs supported the child's understanding and retelling and enlisted meaning making responses. Inconsiderate CD-ROMs impeded cohesive retellings and fostered passive viewing. The best CD-ROMs, according to a study of 60 electronic books by Jong and Buss (2003), combine multimedia and interactive additional that support aspects of literacy. They suggest that multimedia options open up an interactive vista that can support children's literacy development in a digital world and provide them with stories that may be beyond their reading level.

Research into emergent electronic literacies is important because technological change is increasingly defining the nature of literacy. Leu (2000) writes that reading and writing ability will become even more important in the future because of the increasing need for acquiring and communicating information rapidly in a world of global competition and information economies. In an age in which speed of information is central to success, reading proficiency will be even more critical to our children's futures. In addition, there are an ever increasing variety of meanings inherent in multiple media forms in which messages will increasingly appear (Labbo, 1996).

Children absorb the semiotics of signs, symbols, prints, number, illustrations, and diagrams around them. Kress's (1997) detailed observations at home of his young children's journey toward literacy includes descriptions of their dramatic play with household objects, playing out stories with small toys, making collages, drawing, and cutting out as well as beginning to write and show interest in print. The children had the ability to flick from one mode of representation to another as they engaged in meaning making.

The visual aspects of literacy are a fertile ground for further research. In a longitudinal study of children drawing in the home, preschool, and school, Anning (2003) writes that our construct of the development of literacy is associated with a narrow version of literacies confined to aspects of learning to decode and encode print. The communication systems such as television, videos, computer games, and the Internet are increasingly characterized by multimodality and multiliteracy. Much of children's spontaneous play based behaviors, and related graphic representations before school reflect the multimodality of the communication systems. Rather than ignoring this, schools can build on young children's flexible approaches to combining speech action, drawing, and sound in activities.

LITERATE LANGUAGE

The group of studies to be discussed here (Cox, Fang, & Otto, 1997; Jones, 2002; Jones, 2003; Pellegrini & Jones, 1996; Pellegrini, Galda, Flor, Bartini, & Charak, 1997) all use the concept of "literate language" or "literate register" to indicate language that is characterized by a range of features: consciousness of audience beyond the immediate participants, abstraction, and commentary on the process of text production or metalinguistic language. Cox and colleagues (1997) refer to texts produced in the literate register as "written-for-others" text though it is also possible for speech to be "literate" in this way (Farr, 1993). Jones defines "literate language" as "a highly decontextualised oral register that is realised on the expression of meaning through choice of words" (2003, p. 166). Literate language then is often distinguished from other kinds of language registers by its distanced and mediated relationship to context. Whether this distinction holds in children's actual experience of acquiring and using literacy is one question we will be addressing through surveying the research literature. Putting that question aside, it is clear that the development of literate language is integrally related to the development of writing.

In a series of studies, beginning before the 10-year scope of this review, Pellegrini and Jones have worked separately and together to investigate literate language in young children in educational settings from preschool to junior primary (Jones, 2002; 2003, Jones & Pellegrini, 1996; Pellegrini et al., 1997; Pellegrini, Galda, Shockley, & Stahl, 1994). Foundational concepts of their work are: from Vygotsky, that cognition develops within social relations and proceeds from external speech-with-others to internalized dialogue-with-self; and from Piaget, that disequilibrium or cognitive conflict is a key driver in children's learning. On this basis, they have hypothesized that literate language must occur in social interaction before the child internalizes an understanding of literacy as decontextualized writing-for-others. They also have argued that peer interaction should produce the element of conflict needed to prompt children to reassess their understandings of literacy and trial new strategies. To test these hypotheses, they have designed studies in which children write with different kinds of partners (friends and nonfriends) on different kinds of writing tasks (individual and collaborative, traditional, and computer-mediated). They also have considered out-of-school factors in the development of children's literate language and literacy, such as their social networks and their opportunities to participate in literacy events.

Taken as a body of work, these studies reinforce the complex contribution of both oral and written communication to the development of competence in the literate register. At the same time, the different ways in which "literate language" is identified, measured, and analyzed across these studies raise questions about its definition and identification particularly at the emergent stage.

In one study, 64 kindergarten-age children were observed in literacy events in friend and nonfriend dyads in kindergarten settings (Pellegrini et al., 1997). The children's talk was recorded and analyzed for indicators of literate language, emotional language, conflicts, and resolutions. In this study, literate language was identified through the use of linguistic terms (e.g., talk, read, write) and cognitive terms (e.g., think, know, make sense). The researchers found that talk between friends contained more literate language as well as resolutions and emotional terms. Where conflicts were resolved, this correlated with emotional language and literate language in both groups. Shy children responded differently with friends, participating in more conflicts and resolutions. The researchers recommend that young children be placed with friends for literacy activities to stimulate conflict that is constructive but not threatening. This enables children to develop the decentered perspective that is associated with literate language.

In another study that focused on young children's interaction during collaborative writing, literate language was conceptualized as a combination of oral and written practices (Jones & Pellegrini, 1996). Children's peer talk during was analyzed for their use of metacognitive language. Their written texts were analyzed to see how effectively they used the literate register, as identified by measures of cohesion, lexical density, and narrative structure. Children's cognitive decentering also was assessed separately from their talk and writing, using a test of perspective-taking in which they were asked to take the perspective of various characters in a story. This was done in order to investigate correlations between cognitive decentering, metacognitive talk, and writing in the literate register. Additionally, comparisons were made between conventional and computer mediated collaborative writing. The most important finding from our perspective was that metacognitive talk and writing in the literate register were strongly correlated. Interestingly, the mode of writing made significant differences to children's use of metacognitive talk and to many writing measures including grammatical cohesion and lexical density. On all these measures, scores were higher in computer mediated than conventional collaborative writing. So writing collaboratively using a multimodal childfriendly program prompted young children to verbalise their thinking and to produce more literate texts.

Peer interaction during writing was also the subject of three studies by Jones (2000, 2002, 2003). It is the most recent of these studies that we discuss here (Jones, 2003). The researcher chose to avoid conventional pen-and-paper writing and focus solely on computer-mediated collaborative writing, having determined previously (Jones & Pellegrini, 1996) that the latter enabled young children to produce more metacognitive talk and literate texts. As with previous studies, children's talk was recorded and analyzed for literate language, metacognitive language, conflict, and resolution. Metacognitive language was further defined as "self-regulation" and the category of "social regulation" was added, indicated by talk features such as advice giving and correcting.

In this study, Jones was particularly interested in the order in which these talk categories appeared within a literacy event. Patterns of sequencing did yield significant findings, though these depended on the unit of analysis (i.e., two-part sequences of

longer ones). A recurring pattern over longer stretches of talk was a sequence of social regulation followed by metacognitive talk, followed in turn by literate language, reading aloud and further metacogitive talk. However, this study did not investigate whether such sequences were correlated with the development of a more literate register in the children's written products.

A somewhat different approach to researching young children's literate language was taken by Cox and colleagues (1997). A challenge facing literacy researchers in the early years is that children's competence in writing has not developed to the stage that allows them to demonstrate literate language to any significant extent. As we have seen, this can be in part overcome through use of computer mediated writing. In this case, to overcome children's lack of competence with written production, the researchers elicited oral narratives from 4- and 5-year-old children, by asking them to tell a story about something that had happened to them. Then, they asked each child to dictate the previously told story to a researcher who would write it down so that it could be read to others. Thus, the told-to-a-specific-other text was transformed into a written-for-others text. Both the oral narrative and the dictated written narrative were analysed for indicators of the literate register as indicated by cohesion, specificity, elaboration, and booklike language. Additionally, the children's ability to dictate a literate text was correlated with their emergent reading scores, with their preschool settings and with demographic factors.

Two main findings were advanced. First, young children can demonstrate an understanding of the literate register even before they have developed competence in writing. They are able to adjust their text production to suit the different relationships between text producer and audience characteristic of oral and written language. In other words, they can produce both more and less decontextualized texts. Second, their ability to do so correlates with exposure to book-reading experiences, either at home or in their preschool settings. Unfortunately for the low SES children, their neighborhood preschool did not offer such experiences. This, the researchers argued, accounted for their lower scores in the literate register.

EMERGENT LITERACY FOR BILINGUAL CHILDREN

We have argued that literacy, even when print-language-based, requires the mastery of multiple modes of representation and practices of communication. The picture becomes even more complex when we consider the multiple languages that are available within our communities. In countries with one official language, to be literate is understood in relation to that dominant language. Families with a different first language (L1) take on the official language as their second (L2). Entry into the school system is often the point at which immersion in the L2 begins. So at the same time these "minority" children are encountering school literacy, many of them they are acquiring a second language and moving from a monolinguality in L1 to bilinguality. Thus, we can speak of "emergent bilingualism" as well as "emergent literacy" (Volk, 1997). Because exposure to L2 often comes later than L1, this also effectively lengthens the period of "emergence." We will be referring to English as the official language (and L2 for minority language speakers). However, the same issues are experienced in countries with other official languages, such as Germany.

When considering the emergence of literacy in situations in which more than one language is in use, it is useful to distinguish between different features of language. Some language features are specific to a particular language or group of languages, so in order to become fully competent in these languages one must acquire knowledge of and facility with these features. We present an example later in this section relating to acquisition of written Chinese. Other language features may cross linguistic boundaries. The concept of language register is useful here. Following Halliday, we define a language register as a "configuration of semantic resources that the member of a culture typically associates with a situation type" (1994, p. 26). What we have referred to as literate language is a register that can be expressed not only in English but in many languages.

A study of bilingual children's story retelling illustrates this point (Parke, Drury, Kenner, & Robertson, 2002). This study focused on three bilingual children aged between 5 and 7 whose L1 was either Pahari or Urdu and whose verbal competence in English was limited. The children were asked to listen to a story read to them in English and then to retell this story, first in English and then in their mother tongues. Their L1 retellings displayed significantly greater faithfulness to the original in language and narrative detail, were more coherent and also more fluently delivered. Parke et al. (2002) notes that the children had "succeeded in internalizing the text-type" through listening to the original story. We would add that these children may well have brought to the task understandings of narrative structure acquired in home L1 contexts (for instance through an oral folktale tradition) which their L2 competence did not yet enable them to display. Whatever the explanation, young bilingual children's competence in the literate language register may well exceed their competence in English.

Another important language register that children acquire at school is the pedagogic register, that is, the pattern of language used in interactions around teaching and learning. For bilingual children, this represents an additional challenge at a time when they are just beginning to build L2 competence. As with literate language, children's understanding of pedagogic registers may not be visible, because of their reticence in using their L2. This is demonstrated in a case study by Drury (reported in Parke et al., 2002). Samia, a 4-year-old girl whose first language is Pahari, attends a nursery school where there is a settled routine to facilitate children's learning. Every session, each child selects and plans an activity, indicating this by registering their name on a white board. After carrying out the activity, they report on their learning to the whole group. The pedagogic register here is characterized by self-regulatory and explanatory language on the part of children and facilitative language on the part of adults. Samia is observed to carry out the planing and the activities competently though with minimal interaction with peers or adults. At reporting time, she is extremely reticent, having only her limited L2 available for communication with the whole group.

At home, however, Samia plays "nursery school" with her little brother. Here, she takes on the teacher's facilitative language and encourages her sibling to participate in the role of nursery student (that is, to take on what is her own role in real life). The play activity is conducted bilingually, as Samia switches between English and Pahari. What is interesting is her choice of language for different play elements. All the game activities and talk is conducted in English, whereas Samia's instructions as to how to play the game are given in Pahari. For instance, in the role of teacher, she says in English "you want paper" and "choose colour" when in the role of play fellow and sibling she says in Pahari (given here in English translation) "give it to big sister" (Parke et al., 2002, p. 204). From this we can see that Samia's understanding of the pedagogic register of her educational setting, and even her competence in L2 code, exceeds what is visible to her teachers.

The role of community language schools in developing young children's L1 literacy is another interesting topic in the research literature. Observing in these schools, researchers can learn much about how literacy emerges in languages other than English. In one interesting study, the researchers observed young children from three different L1 backgrounds (Arabic, Spanish, and Chinese) in home, school, and community settings (Kenner & Kress, 2003). They also set up a series of peer-teaching activities in which each child taught an English-speaking, monolingual partner some of the basics of writing in the focus child's first language. In this way, they were able to discover children's understanding of pedagogic registers in literacy teaching and learning, as well as their competence in written language production.

One case focused on Selina, a Chinese-background girl who attended a community school each Saturday morning. At this school, she learned to write characters by building up a sequence of strokes. Each page of her books was ruled into a grid and each character was written in the center of a grid square. The learning routine consisted of teacher modeling with minimal explanation followed by sustained, silent writing of many repetitions of a single character. The researchers note that many Western teachers "would not expect a five-year-old to be capable of such physical control over the act of writing" (Kenner & Kress, 2003, p. 186). Selina demonstrated her understanding of the pedagogic register of her L1 teaching when she acted as peer teacher. She demonstrated how to write the character and instructed her peer to "do it like this one." However, when her peer was unable to reproduce the character with sufficient accuracy, Selina showed that she had also grasped the pedagogic register of her mainstream educational setting. She increased her verbal feedback and suggested to her peer "pretend you're in Year 1 in Chinese school."

Kenner and Kress's study (2003) also takes a semiotic perspective to emergent literacy, arguing that different language codes have different semiotic properties. The spatial arrangement of symbols on the field of the page is completely different in Arabic, for instance, than in English. Different perceptual and physical competencies are involved in producing and interpreting texts written using different language systems. Rather than seeing this as confusing and disadvantageous, they claim that new literacies require a broader repertoire of representational practices: therefore bi- and multilingual children should be better positioned for a multiliterate future. This can only be the case, however, if their competencies are made visible within the mainstream and if the complexities of their double emergence into L1 and L2 literacy are understood.

BOOK READING

The ways emergent readers develop has been the focus of a large body of research for more than a decade (Sulzby, 1985; Elster, 1994). Sulzby's (1985) research is seminal because it described emergent reading behaviors that developed from preschool picture-governed reading to print-governed reading. This research showed the development of 11 specific categories of emergent reading behaviors from non-narrative to narrative language, from an oral-like to a written-like narrative register, and from picture-dominated to print-dominated reading.

Further studies of book reading have explored textual features that influence emergent reading. Young children were found to read narrative and expository texts differently (Pappas, 1993). There is evidence that emergent readers do control a repertoire of registers and they can apply them to different text genres. Duke and Kays (1998) report on a study in which the teacher read aloud information books to children age 4 and 5 years of age for 3 months. After three months of reading information books aloud the students made substantial gains in their knowledge of several key features of information book language. When the children were asked to pretend-read an unfamiliar wordless information book, they used the appropriate information book language. These read aloud sessions of information books also led to high levels of engagement, great enjoyment, and spontaneous interactions with the text.

Duke's (2000) research into the types of books provided in first grade revealed a scarcity of information texts and a predominance of narrative in classroom libraries, on classroom walls, and in classroom written language activities. Duke notes that findings are a cause for concern both because of the missed opportunity to prepare young children for information reading and writing they will encounter in later schooling and life, and for the missed opportunity to use informational text to motivate more students' interest in literacy in their present lives. Of particular concern is the fact that information texts were particularly scarce in the classrooms in low socioeconomic settings. Students with less socioeconomic capital were offered fewer opportunities to develop this important form of semiotic capital—the ability to read and write information texts. How children read various genre was further explored by Donovan and Smolkin (2002), who found that although teachers in the past have provided beginning readers with a diet of narrative texts, recent research and teacher observations have raised questions about this long-held practice.

Several studies highlight the importance of other modes of meaning-making associated with book reading. Elster (1994) found that emergent readings of preschoolers were a sequence of reading and talk episodes in which a combination of reading and talk strategies were used. The children combined visual cues from pictures; they drew on their memories, experiences, and knowledge base and on the social interactions with a listener long before beginning to attend to print. The features of the book being read, including the salience of the illustrations, predictable language patterns, and changing print formats, influenced the strategies used by the emergent readers. The adult listeners were used as resource as the preschool children moved from dialogue to monologue and from nonnarrative to narrative language.

Elster (1994) pointed out that emergent readers use multiple sources of information concurrently: pictures, print, social interaction, memory of teacher-led discussions, attention to text language, and understanding of oral and written language conventions. Elster found through microanalysis of children's reading and talk about particular books that these different sources of information were chosen and combined situationally by readers in response to the book, the child's memory, and social interaction.

It would appear from research on emergent book reading that children use dialogue about the book, the genre, and features of the book and their familiarity with written and spoken language register to create meaning from texts.

PHONOLOGICAL AWARENESS

In the past decade, phonological awareness has taken a central position no doubt influenced by the important work by Adams (1990). Adams reviewed over 20 years of basic and applied research in beginning reading and claimed that through all the studies reviewed the two best predictors of reading achievement in first grade, were letter knowledge and phonological awareness.

Phonological awareness can be defined as the ability to reflect on units of spoken language smaller than the syllable (Stahl, 2002). It may include blending, segmentation, deletion and word-to-word matching (Stahl, 2002; Adams, 1990). There are two important aspects of phonological awareness. First, it involves spoken not written language. This makes it different from phonics. Second, it involves awareness of phonemes or onsets and rimes (Treiman, 1992). These units are not acoustically transparent and must be analysed to be perceived (Stahl, 2002).

The issue of instruction in the area of phonological awareness often falls into two camps, (1) direct instruction, an explicit approach to teaching phonemic awareness, and (2) fostering insights into all forms of emergent literacy knowledge. However, Richgels (1995) states that this is not an either-or argument as emergent literacy behaviors develop in an array of areas: meaning-making, forms, meaning-form links, and functions of written language. Fostering insights into all these areas is an important consideration when planning the best instructions for readers and writers, including the best mix of incidental and direct instruction.

Stahl (2002) also suggests that phonological awareness rather than a precursor to reading may be intricately involved in early reading acquisition. Along these lines Morris, Bloodgood, Lomax, & Perney, 2003) explored the relationship between phonemic awareness and other emergent reading behaviors. The authors tested a hypothesis about the growth of word knowledge in kindergarten/first grade readers. It was predicted that (a) phoneme awareness develops in phases and (b) concept of word in text (ability to finger point read) interacts with phoneme awareness in the development of early reading skills. Their longitudinal study demonstrated relationship between phoneme awareness and concept of word in text. The notion of finger pointing where the reader struggles to match spoken word with written word is very easily taken for granted.

Ehri (1995) provided a comprehensive description of how word knowledge develops in the beginning reader and proposed four phases of word recognition development. In the *prealphabetic* phase, which is similar to the logographic phase, children remember how to read words by connecting salient visual cues in the word (e.g., the tail at the end of the word "big") with the word's pronunciation and meaning. The child's ability to commit new words to memory via idiosyncratic cues is taxed when visually similar words are confronted in a text (eg will, wall, leg, big, hug).

In the next *partial alphabetic* phase, beginners commit printed word to memory by forming connections between one or more letters and the corresponding sounds detected in the word's pronunciation. For example, a child may remember the word "back" by connecting the beginning and end letters (/b/ and /k/). To enter this partial alphabet stage, children must know some letter-sound correspondences and be able to segment either initial or initial and final sounds in words.

In the *full alphabetic* phase, readers have formed complete connections between letters seen in the written word and phonemes detected in the word's pronunciation. In the final *consolidated alphabetic* phase, the beginning reader starts to notice multiletter sequences that are common to many words he or she has stored in memory (e.g., "ight" in light, night, bright). This chunking strategy is helpful for reading longer multisyllabic words.

A common theme in developmental formulations is the progressive unfolding of phonemic awareness in reading acquisition. At first, beginning readers can only attend to the initial sound in a spoken word cup /k/ /-//-/. Later they can attend to the initial and ending sounds /k/ /-/ /p/ and finally to each sound in a word /k/ /u/ /p/.

If phonological awareness and learning to read are a two-way reciprocal relationship what is it about reading that enhances phonological awareness? Few researchers have tackled this question and those that have suggest that phonemic awareness is enhanced by beginning readers developing a concept of word in text, which is an awareness that spoken words match to printed words in the reading of a text (Clay, 1991). Clay suggested that in order to read simple texts the child must "break up his produced speech into word units; locate the visual patterns [in text]; move in the correct direction; and coordinate the timing of his pointing and looking with his uttering" (p. 162). This suggests that the seemingly simple act of finger pointing and matching spoken words to written words is closely related to the development of phonemic awareness.

Following the line of research into the importance of phonological awareness to emergent literacy development, Hecht and Close (2002) found that phonemic awareness influenced growth in invented spelling in emergent literacy. The authors write that the effects were bidirectional in that development in invented spelling also had an effect on phonemic awareness. The authors suggest that interventions designed to improve phonemic awareness should combine explicit training in the sound structure of oral language with considerable emphasis on early spelling skills.

The research into phonological awareness often seeks the predictive relationship between approaches to instruction in of phonological awareness and later literacy success. However, much of the research in this area highlights the idea that phonological awareness, rather than a precursor to reading and writing may be intricately and reciprocally involved in early literacy acquisition.

EMERGENT LITERACY AND EARLY INTERVENTION

Research studies into emergent literacy before school and at school entry are important because of emergent literacy's predictive association with later school success. There are strong arguments that intervention is more successful earlier rather than later (McNaughton, 2002) because inappropriate learning strategies may not have yet taken hold and it is best to nip in the bud low achievement in literacy and associated school failure before it becomes entrenched. Questions of what type of early intervention, how early should intervention occur, and the effects of different forms of early intervention are the focus of much of the research.

The potentially best time for early intervention is considered in a comprehensive review of the research into the effectiveness of interventions for young children who are at risk of having problems learning to read (Snow, Burns, & Griffin, 1998). Snow et al. (1998) found that the assessment of children's literacy early in preschool predicted later reading achievement nearly as well as similar assessments conducted in kindergarten. The authors suggest that a focus on preschool literacy behaviors holds great potential for those interested in designing instructional and assessment programs aimed at preventing reading difficulty in learning to read.

The importance of the preschool for early literacy intervention was the subject for a substantial review of the research into preschool literacy education by Barnett (2002). He writes that the research into preschool early intervention programs falls into two streams. One stream concerns the effects of early education on children from a variety of backgrounds and the other stream is the effects of intervention programs specifically designed to serve children from low-income backgrounds. Interventions may produces short-term and long-term effects however, overall, preschool education in a variety of forms, improves general cognitive abilities during early childhood and long-term increases in reading achievement. Programs provided in the preschool resulted in immediate higher gains for disadvantaged children on tests of academic abilities. Some types of intervention programs were more successful than others. Further research into the effectiveness of home-based programs, programs for parents, and programs in full day child-care is required.

The curriculum provided in the various early intervention programs is also contested among researchers. In a review of emergent literacy intervention programs Yaden, Rowe, and MacGillivray (2000) found evidence contrary to the current controversial stance that kindergarten children designated at risk or primary-grade children identified as having reading difficulties need structured phonics activities and phonemic awareness training (Foorman, Francis, Fletcher, Schatschneider, & Mehta, 1998). Yaden, Rowe, and MacGillivray (2000a) found positive results from holistic emergent literacy programs in which children engaged with events such as storybook reading and play. The features shared by all these emergent literacy programs included (a) drawing children in as socially competent partners, (b) allowing them to experiment without duress, (c) providing them with a variety of adult- and peer-mediated dialogue about literature and ways to read and write, and (d) creating any number of opportunities for them to practice their unconventional yet emerging skills.

The effect of intervention programs for children with special needs was explored by O'Connor (2000). In this skills-based intervention, the first layer included attention to sounds in spoken words, letter names, and sounds and developing speaking, listening vocabularies, phonological skills, and letter knowledge in mid-kindergarten; phonological skills and word reading in early first grade; and phonological decoding and spelling toward the end of first grade. The findings were sobering as the children with disabilities and several others who were at risk lost ground when the reading instruction retreated to the status quo and the authors commented that short-term interventions did not significantly decrease the proportion of children identified for special education.

Reporting on a 4-year longitudinal intervention program in homes, communities, and childcare settings for children with English as a Second Language (ESL) Yaden, Tam, Madrigal, Brassell, Massa, Altamirano, and Armendariz (2000) discuss children's substantial increase in early language awareness from Spanish to English. The study began with providing Spanish-speaking 4-year-olds with a variety of reading and writing activities within childcare settings, homes, and communities. The results showed that children gained in book handling awareness, letter and word concepts, and understandings of print directionality during an emergent literacy intervention before their kindergarten year. In addition as a result of the intervention program many of the families established read-aloud routines at home.

In a preschool early intervention program involving over 2,000 preschool children, the teachers were asked to report on the early literacy behaviors that they thought predicted later success in reading in first grade or over (Sayeski, Burgess, Pianta, & Lloyd, 2001). The preschool teachers' predictions of preschoolers' later success in reading at the end of first grade were associated with a number of variables such as "understanding a story that is read aloud" and "predicting story events." The authors comment that the teachers may consider language and skills at the semantic and syntactic level more important than skills at the phonological level. The authors also stated that perhaps the preschool teachers were unaware of the literature

(Adams, 1990; Ehri, 1997) indicating that facility with phonology and letters is crucial to early reading success.

Critics of early intervention (Luke & Luke, 2001) portray these programs as an industry of inoculation against later literacy failure. This criticism has been countered by McNaughton (2002) who comments on the importance of early intervention at an early age because children are possibly less damaged by having successive years of school failure. Age is also a crucial concern, but not because of literacy readiness. Age is an index for the processes taking place associated with time and school. The earlier the age (the closer to the beginning of school for example) the less "damage" has been done. It is at this point that the default conditions of differential instruction described so powerfully in the ubiquitous "Matthew effect" begin to bite (Stanovich, 1986). The later the age, the more developmental ground an intervention has to cover to overcome gaps that have been created in classrooms (McNaughton, 2002). The age for intervention is also important for children for whom school creates significant disjunctions with family and community literacy practices. This is because the instruction in mainstream classes is usually a set of processes that makes it difficult for children who are not familiar with mainstream practices to engage.

In response to debates about the curriculum content and processes of early intervention programs (McNaughton, 2002) comments that families may prefer early intervention programs to focus on access to and control over conventional print-based literacies. Without print-based literacies, families find it difficult to access other forms of literacy through tertiary and other institutions that control the forms of knowledge that in turn function as gatekeepers to occupations and incomes. Interestingly, the research into emergent literacy intervention points to the importance of developing a rich and a varied array of emergent literacy behaviors from book handling, drawing, developing literate spoken and written language, peer and adult interaction to stimulate language, writing, and phonological awareness, and this suggests for some out-of-the-ordinary-children a narrowly focused one-off-intervention is not sufficient.

SUMMARY

Emergent literacy research continues to be a highly contested area with a range of theoretical positions and related research methodologies. This review of the research suggests several areas that require further research.

Much research into emergent literacy has been of a predictive nature to find discrete elements of literacy, which may be a precursor or predictor for future development. The research in this review points, however, to the many reciprocal and intricately related aspects of emergent literacy. Book reading, writing, phonological awareness, literate language, and new electronic literacies all appear to complement and enhance the growth of each other. Future research may focus on the reciprocal nature of emergent literacy learning and how the different aspects of emergent literacy inform each other in a dynamic way rather than occurring in any one narrow, linear lockstep concept of development.

We believe that much is to be gained by defining literacy more broadly from a semiotic position to include linguistic and nonlinguistic forms of communication. Literacy is changing and children are increasingly exposed to communication tools and situations that are multimodal rather than exclusively linguistic. More research is required into children's knowledge of these multimodal electronic literacies, and to do this it is necessary to broaden the base of what we know about emergent literacy to understand how children are making meaning with these new forms.

Similarly, although emergent reading is currently of great importance, the interrelated communication tools of writing, drawing, talk, and gesture should not be ignored as all feed into and support each other in a dynamic process. We echo the call by Yaden and colleagues (2000) for emergent literacy researchers to consider the bigger picture, the epistemological parameters of their work. What counts as knowledge in emergent literacy? Where is knowledge located? How is knowledge attained?

References

Adams, M. (1990). *Beginning to read: Thinking and learning about print.* Cambridge, MA: Massachusetts Institute of Technology.

Anning, A. (2003). Pathways to the Graphicity Club: The crossroad of home and preschool. *Journal of Early Childhood Literacy, 3*(1), 5–35.

Barnett, W. S. (2002). Preschool education for economically disadvantaged children: Effects on reading achievement and related outcomes. In S. Neuman & D. Dickinson (Eds.), *Handbook of Early Literacy Research* (pp. 421–444). New York: The Guilford Press.

Barr, R., Kamil, M., Mosenthal, P., & Pearson, P. D. (Eds.). (2000). *The Handbook of Reading Research.* Mahwah, NJ: Lawrence Erlbaum Associates.

Bissex, G. (1980). *GYNS AT WRK: A child learns to read and write.* Cambridge, MA: Harvard University Press.

Brooker, L. (2002). Five on the first of December! What can we learn from case studies of early childhood literacy? *Journal of Early Childhood Literacy, 2*(3), 291–313.

Clay, M. (1991). *Becoming literate: The construction of inner control.* Auckland, NZ: Heinemann Education.

Clay, M. (1993). *An observation survey: Of early literacy achievement.* Auckland, New Zealand: Heinemann.

Cox, B. E., Fang, Z., & Otto, B. W. (1997). Preschoolers' developing ownership of the literate register. *Reading Research Quarterly, 32*(1), 34–53.

Crawford, P. (1995). Early literacy: Emerging perspectives. *Journal of Research in Childhood Education, 10*(1), 71–86.

Donovan, C., & Smolkin, L. (2002). Children's genre knowledge: An examination of K-5 students' performance on multiple tasks providing differing levels of scaffolding. *Reading Research Quarterly, 37*(94), 428–465.

Duke, N. (2000). 3.6 minutes per day: The scarcity of information texts in first grade. *Reading Research Quarterly, 35*(2), 202–224.

Duke, N. K., & Kays, J. (1998). Can I say once upon a time?: Kindergarten children developing knowledge of information book language. *Early Childhood Research Quarterly, 3*(2), 295–318.

Dyson, A. H. (2001). Where are the childhoods in childhood literacy? An exploration in outer (school) space. *Journal of Early Childhood Literacy, 1*(1), 9–39.

Dyson, Haas, A. (1995). Writing children: Reinventing the development of childhood literacy. *Written Communication, 12*(10), pp. 4–46.

Ehri, L. (1995). Phases of development in learning to read words by sight. *Journal of Research in Reading, 18*, 116–125.

Elster, C. (1994). Patterns within preschoolers' emergent readings. *Reading Research Quarterly, 29*(4), 402–418.

Farr, M. (1993). Essayist literacy and other verbal performances. *Written Communication, 10*(1), 4–38.

Foorman, B. R., Francis, D. J., Fletcher, J. M., Schatschneider, C., & Mehta, P. (1998). The role of instruction in learning to read: Preventing reading failure in at-risk children. *Journal of Educational Psychology, 90*, 37–55.

Freebody, P. (1995). Identity and precompetence in early childhood: The case of school-literacy learning. *Australian Journal of Early Childhood, 20*(1), 17–22.

Freebody, P., & Luke, A. (1990). Literacies' programs: debates and demands in cultural context. *Prospect, 5*(3), 7–16.

Gee, J. (2002). A sociocultural perspective on early literacy development. In S. Neuman & D. Dickinson (Eds.), *Handbook of Early Literacy Research* (pp. 40–42). New York: Guildford Press.

Halliday, M. (1994). Language as social semiotic. In J. Maybin (Ed.), *Language and Literacy in Social Practice* (pp. 11–22). Clevedon: Multilingual Matters.

Hill, S., Comber, B., Louden, W., Rivalland, J., & Reid, J. (1998). *100 Children go to School: Connections and disconnections in literacy development in the year prior to school and the first year of school.* Canberra: Department for Education, Employment, Training and Youth Affairs.

Hecht, S., & Close, L. (2002). Emergent literacy skills and training time uniquely predict variability in responses to phonemic awareness in training in disadvantaged kindergarteners. *Journal of Experimental Child Psychology, 82*, 93–115.

Hutinger, P., Bell, C., Beard, M., Bond, J., Johanson, J., & Terry, C. (1997). *Final Report: The Early Childhood Emergent Literacy Technology Research Study.* Macomb, IL: Western Illinois University. (ERIC Document Reproduction Service No. ED 418545)

Jones, I. (2002). Social relationships, peer collaboration and children's oral language. *Educational Psychology, 22*(1), 63–73.

Jones, I. (2003). Collaborative writing and children's use of literate language: A sequential analysis of social interaction. *Journal of Early Childhood Literacy, 3*(2), 165–178.

Jones, I., & Pellegrini, A. D. (1996). The effects of social relationships, writing media, and microgenetic development on first-grade students' written narratives. *American Educational Research Journal, 33*(3), 691–718.

Jong, M., & Bus, A. (2003). How well suited are electronic books to supporting literacy? *Journal of Early Childhood Literacy, 2*(3), 147–164.

Kantor, R., Miller, S., & Fernie, D. (1992). Diverse paths to literacy in a preschool classroom: A sociocultural perspective. *Reading Research Quarterly, 27*(3), 185–201.

Kress, G. (1999). Genre and the changing contexts for English language arts. *Language Arts, 76,*(6), 461–469.

Kenner, C., & Kress, G. (2003). The multisemiotic resources of biliterate children. *Journal of Early Childhood, 3*(2), 179–202.

Kress, G., Lankshear, C., & Knobel, M. (2003). New technologies in early childhood literacy research: A review of research. *Journal of Early Childhood Literacy, 3*(1), 59–82.

Labbo, L. (1996). A semiotic analysis of young children's symbol making in a classroom computer center. *Reading Research Quarterly, 31*(4), 356–385.

Labbo, L., & Kuhn, M. (1998). Computers and emergent literacy: An examination of young children's computer-generated communicative symbol making. In D. Reinking, L. Labbo, M. McKenna & Kieffer, R. (Eds.), *Literacy for the 21st century: Technological transformations in a post-typographic world* (pp. 79–91). Mahwah, NJ: Lawrence Erlbaum Associates.

Labbo, L., & Kuhn, M. (2000). Weaving chains of affect and cognition: A young child's understanding of CD-ROM talking books. *Journal of Literacy Research, 32*(2), 187–210.

Lancaster, L. (2001). Staring at the page: The functions of gaze in a young child's interpretation of symbolic forms. *Journal of Early Childhood Literacy, 1*(2), 131–152.

Lankshear, C., & Knobel, M. (2003). New technologies in early childhood literacy research: A review of research. *Journal of Early Childhood Literacy, 3*(1), 59–82.

Lave, J., & Wenger, E. (1991). *Situated learning: Legitimate peripheral participation.* Cambridge: Cambridge University Press.

Lemke, J. (1990). *Talking science: Language, learning and values.* Norwood, NJ: Ablex Publishing Corporation.

Lemke, J. (1998). Metamedia literacy: Transforming meanings and media. In D. Reinking, L. Labbo, M. McKenna & Keiffer, R. (Eds.), *Handbook of literacy and technology: Transformations in a post-typographic world* (pp. 283–301). Mahwah, NJ: Lawrence Erlbaum Associates.

Leu, D. (2000). Literacy and technology: Deictic consequences for literacy education in an information age. In M. Kamil, P. Mosenthal, P. D. Pearson & R. Barr, (Eds.), *Handbook of Reading Research Volume 3* (pp. 745–772). Mahwah, NJ: Lawrence Erlbaum Associates.

Luke, A., Comber, B., & O'Brien, J. (1994). Making community texts objects of study. *The Australian Journal of Language and Literacy, 17*(2), 139–149.

McGee, L., & Purcell-Gates, V. (1997). Conversations: So what's going on in research in emergent literacy? *Reading Research Quarterly, 32*(3), 310–319.

McKenna, M. C. (1998). Electronic texts and the transformation of beginning reading. In D. Reinking, M. McKenna, L. Labbo, & R. Kieffer (Eds.), *Handbook of literacy and technology: Transformations in a post-typographic world.* Mahwah, NJ: Lawrence Erlbaum Associates.

McNaughton, S. (2002). On making early interventions problematic: A comment on Luke and Luke (2001). *Journal of Early Childhood Literacy, 2*(1), 97–103.

Morris, D., Bloodgood, J., Lomax, R., & Perney, J. (2003). Developmental steps in learning to read: A longitudinal study in kindergarten and first grade. *Reading Research Quarterly, 38*(3), 302–328.

New London Group (1996). A pedagogy of multiliteracies, *Harvard Educational Review, 60*(1), 66–92.

Neuman, S., & Dickinson, D. (Eds.). (2002). *Handbook of Early Literacy Research.* New York: Guildford Press.

Nichols S., & Broadhurst, D. (2002). Literacy as a site of child development: Research agendas and classroom practice. In S. Hill, B. Comber, W. Louden, J. Rivalland, & Reid, J. (Eds.), *100 Children Turn 10: A longitudinal study of literacy development from the year prior to school to the first four years of school.* Canberra: Department for Education, Employment, Training and Youth Affairs.

Nixon, J. G., & Topping, J. (2001). Emergent writing: The impact of structured peer interaction. *Educational Psychology, 21*(1), 41–56.

O'Connor, R. (2000). Increasing the intensity of intervention in kindergarten and first grade. *Learning Disabilities Research & Practice, 15*(1), 43–54.

Pahl, K. (2002). Ephemera, mess and miscellaneous piles: Texts and practices in families. *Journal of Early Childhood Literacy, 2*(2), 145–166.

Parke, T., Drury, R., Kenner, C., & Robertson, L. H. (2002). Revealing invisible worlds: Connecting the mainstream with bilingual children's home and community learning. *Journal of Early Childhood Literacy, 2*(2), 195–220.

Pellegrini, A. D., Galda, L., Shockley, B., & Stahl, S. (1994). *The Nexus of Social and Literacy Experiences at Home and School: Implications for First-Grade Oral Language and Literacy.* U.S. Office of Educational Research and Instruction: National Reading Research Centre. (Reading Research Report No. 21).

Pellegrini, A. D., Galda, L., Flor, D., Bartini, M., & Charak, D. (1997). Close relationships, individual differences, and early literacy learning. *Journal of Environmental Child Psychology, 67*, 409–422.

Reinking, D., McKenna, M., Labbo, L., & Kieffer, R. (Eds.). (1998). *Handbook of literacy and technology: Transformations in a post-typographic world.* Mahwah, NJ: Lawrence Erlbaum Associates.

Richgels, D. (1995). Invented spelling ability and printed word learning in kindergarten. *Reading Research Quarterly, 30*(1), 96–109.

Sayeski, K., Burgess, K., Pianta, R., & Lloyd, J. (2001). *Literacy behaviours of preschool children participating in an early intervention program.* Ann Arbor: University of Michigan, Center for the Improvement of Early Reading Achievement. (CIERA report #2-014)

Sarama, J., & Clements, D. H. (2002). Learning and teaching with computers in early childhood education. In O. N. Saracho & B. Spodek (Eds.), *Contemporary Perspectives in Early Childhood Education.* Greenwich, CT: Information Age Publishing.

Siegal, M., & Fernandez, (2000). Critical approaches. In M. Kamil, P. Mosenthal, P. Pearson & R. Barr (Eds.), *Handbook of Reading Research. Volume 3* (pp. 141–151). Mahwah, NJ: Lawrence Erlbaum Associates.

Stahl, S. (2002). Teaching phonics and phonological awareness. In S. Neuman & D. Dickinson (Eds.), *Handbook of Early Literacy Research* (pp. 333–348). New York: The Guilford Press.

Stanovich, K. (1986). Matthew effects in reading: Some consequences of individual differences in the acquisition of literacy. *Reading Research Quarterly, 21*, 360–407.

Snow, C. (1983). Literacy and language: Relationships during the preschool years. *Harvard Educational Review, 53*(2), 165–189.

Snow, C., Burns, S., & Griffin, P. (1998). *Preventing reading difficulties in young children.* Washington, National Academy Press.

Strickland, D., & Cullinan, B. (1990). Afterword. In Adams, M. *Beginning to read: Thinking and learning about print.* Cambridge, MA: Massachusetts Institute of Technology.

Sulzby E. (1985). Children's emergent reading of favourite story books: A developmental study. *Reading Research Quarterly, 20*, 458–479.

Teale, W. (1986). Home background and young children's literacy development. In William H. Teale and Elizabeth Sulzby (Eds.), *Emergent literacy: Writing and reading.* Norwood, New Jersey. Ablex Publishing Corporation.

Teale, W. (1995). Young children and reading: Trends across the twentieth century. *Journal of Education, 177*(3), 95–127.

Teale, W., & Sulzby, E. (1986). *Emergent literacy: Writing and reading.* Norwood, NJ: Ablex Publishing Corporation.

Taylor, D. (1983). *Family literacy: Young children learning to read and write.* Exeter, NH: Heinemann.

Van Oers, B., & Wardekker, W. (1999). On becoming an authentic learner: Semiotic activity in the early grades. *Journal of Curriculum Studies, 31*(2), 229-249.

Volk, D. (1997). Questions in lessons: Activity settings in the homes and school of two Puerto Rican kindergartners. *Anthropology and Education Quarterly, 28*(1), 22-49.

Yaden, D., Rowe, D., & MacGillivray, L. (2000). Emergent literacy: A matter (Polyphony) of perspectives. In R. Barr, M. Kamil, P. Mosenthal & D. Pearson (Eds.), *The Handbook of Reading Research, Volume 3* (pp. 425-455). Mahwah, NJ: Lawrence Erlbaum Associates.

Yaden, D., Tam, A., Madrigal, P., Brassell, D., Massa, J., Altamirano, L. S., & Armendariz, J. (2000). Early literacy for inner-city children: The effects of reading and writing interventions in English and Spanish during the preschool years. *The Reading Teacher, 54*(2), 186-188.

·10·

THE LITERACY EDUCATION OF LINGUISTICALLY AND CULTURALLY DIVERSE YOUNG CHILDREN: AN OVERVIEW OF OUTCOMES, ASSESSMENT, AND LARGE-SCALE INTERVENTIONS

Robert Rueda
David B. Yaden, Jr.
University of Southern California

INTRODUCTION

Approximately a decade ago, in the precursor to this volume, a review of educational issues with linguistically and culturally diverse children (Garcia, 1993) began with the significant demographic changes that were taking place at the time. A decade later, it seems just as critical to consider continued demographic change as a foundation for the chapter, as these changes have not only continued but increased. Further more, these changes have served to both test the limits of traditional educational and psychological theories and to have caused reconsideration of accepted traditional educational practice. In the short span of a decade, early childhood education also has become more salient in policy terms, and a strong academic focus with concomitant accountability concerns have changed the nature of service delivery for early childhood education.

In this chapter, we focus on studies with children primarily under the age of 5; but we have included some studies of kindergarten and first-grade as the outcomes from those grades are often reported in large-scale, national investigations of young children's literacy development after preschool (U.S. Department of Education, 1998, 2001; Zill & West, 2000). For studies related to the literacy development of older, linguistically, and culturally diverse children, please refer to such sources as Garcia (2000), Jiménez (2004), and Goldenberg (2004). Similarly, we highlight

literacy development specifically as opposed to the broader topics of bilingualism and types of instructional programs. These issues are covered in recent, integrative reviews by Tabors and Snow (2004) and Hudelson, Poyner, and Wolfe (2003).

In the remainder of this chapter, we first describe the population changes that have occurred in the last decade, and discuss the current educational policy context that forms the backdrop for current early childhood education concerns. As this chapter will suggest, reading and literacy have become a key focus of research, policy, and practice. Given this emphasis, the chapter will then focus more specifically on the issue of reading and literacy with particular attention to linguistically and culturally diverse children. We highlight three areas because of their salience in the current educational arena: early literacy and biliteracy development, assessment, and large-scale interventions for language-minority students. We conclude the chapter with suggestions for areas needing continued development.

Why a Focus on Literacy?

Literacy development in young children has become a major national policy concern and a major focus of educational reformers. What are the reasons for this focus? How is it manifested? And what are the consequences for early childhood education and diverse learners in particular?

A major impetus for the current focus on literacy is the ever increasing demand from a technological society such as the United States for more complex literate abilities in both work and school settings (Bronfenbrenner, McClelland, Wethington, Moen, & Ceci, 1996). However, there are additional circumstances that have been key in redirecting educational efforts and concerns toward academic as well as the socioemotional needs of children prior to their entrance into formal schooling. In their report entitled *Eager to Learn: Educating our Preschoolers* (Bowman, Donovan, & Burns, 2001), the National Research Council-appointed Committee on Early Childhood Pedagogy mentions three of these trends in particular: (a) the huge influx of women into the labor force, which has created a pressing demand for quality childcare; (b) increased agreement between educators and parents that young children need early and enriching educational experiences; and (c) the growing evidence from research that young children are readily capable of learning from these early experiences and, more important, that this early start has a direct, and positive relationship with later school achievement and social benefit (pp. 1–2).

As a result of these larger, macro waves of changing sociopolitical attitudes and the emerging consensus of science that both cognitive and affective processes of mental and linguistic development are dramatically effected by experiences during the preschool years, other government-sponsored panels have been appointed to probe more deeply into research emanating from biology and the neurosciences (see Shonkoff & Phillips, 2000), children learning English as a second language (August & Hakuta, 1997), learning theory (Bransford, Brown, & Cocking, 1999), and investigations into the causes of reading difficulty (Snow, Burns, & Griffin, 1998). Taken together, the findings from these expert synthesis panels, as they pertain to children, point to the fact that all cognitive and affective learning processes are highly complex interactions between both inherited and environmental factors as well as being selectively affected by variations in childrearing practices, socioeconomic circumstances, family structures, adult-child interactions, educational environments, and other contextual and developmental factors (Shonkoff & Phillips, 2000). Additionally, these research syntheses dispel the notion that there are optimal, educational situations that work for all children at all times but, rather, there are differentiated learning situations that work for certain children under specific circumstances—and even these selected, "optimal" conditions are balanced precariously by the numbers of "risk" or "compensatory" factors in a child's life.

From our perspective as authors of this chapter focused on early literacy, the volume *Preventing Reading Difficulties in Young Children* has had arguably the greatest impact on recent literacy research, policy and practice, providing a powerful impetus for other major research syntheses on literacy instruction (see also the Final Report of the National Reading Panel, 2000) as well as sweeping legislative mandates for the nation's schools regarding reading pedagogy, professional development, school choice and accountability as embodied in the No Child Left Behind Act of 2001 (U.S. Department of Education, 2001). After an extensive investigation into several literatures pertaining to normal and delayed reading development, groups identified at-risk for reading failure, and instructional methodologies,

both developmental and correctional, Snow, Burns, and Griffin (1998) summarized the committee's findings by the following sobering statements:

- large numbers of schoolage children, including children from all social classes, have significant difficulties in learning to read
- failure to learn to read adequately for continued school success is much more likely among poor children, among nonwhite children, and among non-native speakers of English
- increasing numbers of children in public schools are learning disabled, with most of the children identified as such because of difficulties in learning to read.

In order to address this growing problem of more children encountering reading difficulties, new competitive grant programs have been initiated by various government agencies responsible for the education and well-being of young children. In addition to the U.S. Department of Education's Reading First program authorized at $900 million in 2002 to help states and districts set up "scientific, research-based" reading programs for children in grades K-3 (with priority given to high-poverty areas), the Head Start Bureau, for example, as a part of its 1998 reauthorization, launched its Family Literacy Initiative and has committed 80 million dollars to the further education of Head Start teachers and the improvement of literacy instruction (U.S. Department of Health and Human Services, 2001). Grants also were awarded to university researchers to establish Head Start Quality Research Centers to improved academic outcomes for children as well as to support teacher training, curriculum development, and assessment practices. Additionally, 17 universities are funded to be involved in the Early Head Start Research and Evaluation Project, which will track cohorts of Head Start Children from birth until they enter kindergarten (U.S. Department of Health and Human Services, 2000.)

Similarly, the Even Start Family Literacy Program, the U.S. Department of Education's family literacy program directed at the nation's most needy families, will distribute 250 million dollars in fiscal year 2002–2003 to approximately 1,000 local projects in every state, with one of its major goals being to promote literacy-based programs between parents and their children (U.S. Department of Education, 2003). Although Even Start grantees are encouraged to continue to balance the four central components of the program (early childhood education, adult literacy, adult basic education, and parenting education), past evaluations of the literacy outcomes for children have led to a renewed emphasis on literacy instruction because children served by Even Start have not done better than control groups in randomized experiments (St. Pierre, Ricciuti, Tao, Creps, Kumagawa, & Ross, 2001).

As is evident in this description of new funding streams and programs, all aspects of literacy, including its early foundation before formal schooling have become highly salient topics. Intense federal attention to this area has resulted in new encompassing legislation that makes new demands on states and increases the emphasis on accountability demonstrated through high stakes measures, which some scholars see as highly problematic when administered to young children (see Dickinson,

2003; Meisels, 1999). We will return to these issues later, as the consequences of these developments are highly significant for students from diverse backgrounds.

In the next section, we provide a look at the characteristics of students and their families, as they form an important backdrop for the current discussion.

The National Demographic Context

In general, the country has become more diverse over the last century. In 2000, an estimated 10.4% of the U.S. population was foreign-born, up from 7.9% in 1990, with Mexico accounting for more than one quarter of the foreign born population (Schmidley, 2000). Overall, according to the latest figures, whites comprise 68.8% of the population, blacks 12.6%, Hispanics 12.5%, with Asians, Pacific Islanders and Native Americans comprising 6.3% (U.S. Census Bureau, 2000).

Not surprisingly, this diversity has spilled over into public schools, although disproportionately in some states. Data from 2001–2002 indicate that there were 47,687,871 students in elementary and secondary schools combined, of whom 18,815,623 (39.46%) were minority.[1] In geographical terms, 62.5% were in large and midsize cities, 35.9% were in urban fringes of large cities, and 20.8% were in small towns or rural settings (U.S. Dept. of Education, 2002). In terms of racial/ethnic breakdowns, White, non-Hispanic students make up the majority (61.2%) followed by black students (17.2%) and Latino students (16.3%), with Asian/Pacific Islander students making up 4.1% of the public school population, and American Indian/Alaska Native students comprising 1.2% (Young, 2002). However, in six states (California, Hawaii, Louisiana, Mississippi, New Mexico, and Texas) as well as the District of Columbia, 50% or more of the students were non-white. Black, non-Hispanic students made up more than 50% of all students in the District of Columbia and Mississippi while New Mexico reported 50.2% of its students as Hispanic, and Hawaii reported 72.3% of its student body as Asian/Pacific Islander (Young, 2002).

An interesting dimension to the demographic changes that have occurred over the past 10 years is the marked increase in the Latino[2] population. In the period from 1990 to 2000, the Latino population increased by 58% (by 12.9 million people), to about 35 million total, such that about one in eight Americans are of Latino descent, making this group the largest "minority" group in the United States (U.S. Census Bureau, 2000). Most of the Latino population was born in the United States (60.9%) (U.S. Census Bureau, 2000). Given that the Latino population is projected to account for 51% of the country's population growth in the next five decades (National Center for Educational Statistics, 2003), by 2050, Latinos will represent about one

fourth of the total U.S. population, more than three times their current number.

It is important to note that the Latino population is made up of several subgroups, as this fact has important implications for generalizing results of research, which will be discussed later. In 2000, 58.5% of the Latino population was Mexican, followed by Puerto Ricans (9.6%), Cubans (3.5%), Central Americans (4.8%), South Americans (3.8%), Dominican's (2.2%), Spaniards (0.3%), and Other (17.3%) (National Council of La Raza, 2001; US Census Bureau, 2000). In addition, the population is relatively young—the median age of Latinos in the United States is 26.6 years, younger than the median age for any other racial or ethnic group. Moreover, the number of Hispanic children as a proportion of all children has been increasing faster than for white and black children (Llagas & Snyder, 2003).

The Current Educational Context for Young Children

Although the preceding data give a picture of the broader population, Table 10.1 provides a useful profile of some of the key demographic characteristics related to participation in early childhood education programs. There are some interesting disparities in terms of who is enrolled in programs by ethnicity. For example, in 2001 59% of white students, 63.7% of black students, and 39.8% of Latino students, ages 3–5, were enrolled. The lower, overall number of 3- to 5-year-old children Latino children can be attributed to the fact that Latino parents as a group delay enrolling their preschoolers in center-based programs until ages 4 and 5 as statistics for 1999 indicate for enrolled 3-year-olds only with Hispanics at 26%, whites at 47% and blacks at 60% (Llagas & Snyder, 2003, p. 22). By age 5, however, there are no statistically significant differences in enrollment by ethnicity. Whether or not this difference between 2 years of preschool versus 3 years has an impact on Latino children's overall lower literacy scores at the beginning of kindergarten remains to be tested.

Risk factors and poverty. Regardless of ethnicity, a substantial number (46.7%) of all enrollees were below the poverty line. These overall figures mask important group differences, however; 46.1% of white students, 60.1% of black students, and 36.2% of Hispanic students were below the poverty line in 2001. Given the focus on early literacy and schooling, information on poverty and other childhood risk factors is important as both mediate many outcomes of interest.

With respect to poverty,[3] the rates between American Indian and Alaska Natives, Blacks and Latinos are similar and are notably higher than that of whites (9.7%) or Asians and Pacific Islanders (10.7%). A 3-year average of poverty rates from 1999 to 2001

---

[1] Minority includes all groups except white, not Hispanic. Community types classify the location of a school relative to populous areas. Percentages are based on schools reporting. U.S. totals include the 50 states and the District of Columbia.

[2] The terms "Hispanic" and "Latino" are used interchangeably by the U.S. Census Bureau to identify persons of Mexican, Puerto Rican, Cuban, Central and South American, Dominican, Spanish, and other Hispanic descent. They may be of any race. In practice, there is significant contention about the appropriate term, both in the research and popular press (Fears, 2003).

[3] To define poverty, the U.S. Census Bureau utilizes a set of money income thresholds that vary by family size and composition. A family, along with each individual in it, is considered poor if the family's total income is less than that family's threshold. The poverty thresholds do not vary geographically and are updated annually for inflation using the Consumer Price Index (U.S. Department of Commerce, 2000).

TABLE 10.1. Enrollment in Early Childhood Education Programs: Percentage of Children Ages 3–5 Who Were Enrolled in Center-Based Early Childhood Care and Education Programs

Characterstic	1991	1993	1995	1996	1999	2001
Total*	52.8	52.7	55.1	55.0	59.7	56.4
Age						
3	42.3	40.4	40.7	42.1	45.7	43.0
4	60.4	62.2	64.7	63.2	69.6	66.2
5	63.9	65.7	74.5	72.8	76.5	72.8
Sex						
Male	52.4	52.5	55.0	55.0	60.8	53.6
Female	53.2	52.9	55.2	54.9	58.6	59.2
Race/ethnicity						
White	54.0	53.5	56.9	57.1	60.0	59.0
Black	58.3	57.3	59.5	64.7	73.2	63.7
Hispanic	38.8	42.8	37.4	39.4	44.2	39.8
Poverty status						
Below poverty	44.2	43.3	45.1	43.8	51.4	46.7
At or above poverty	55.7	56.0	58.8	59.1	62.3	59.1
Power status and race/ethnicity						
Below poverty						
White	41.0	39.6	43.4	39.4	43.2	46.1
Black	55.4	53.2	54.9	60.9	72.2	60.1
Hispanic	34.4	37.2	30.1	32.5	41.2	36.2
At or above poverty						
White	56.4	56.0	59.6	60.3	62.6	60.8
Black	61.8	62.6	66.1	69.0	74.1	66.2
Hispanic	42.2	48.1	43.8	45.1	46.8	42.4
Family Type						
Two parents	53.7	52.1	54.9	53.8	58.8	56.5
One or no parent	49.7	54.2	55.6	57.9	61.9	56.1
Mother's education						
Less than high school	31.5	33.1	34.8	37.3	40.3	38.3
High school diploma or equivalent	45.8	43.2	47.6	49.0	51.7	47.1
Some college, including vocational/technical	60.2	60.3	56.8	57.8	62.9	62.0
Bachelor's degree or higher	71.9	73.4	74.5	73.0	73.9	69.5
Mother's employment status						
Worked 35 hours or more per week	59.3	61.3	60.2	63.1	64.8	62.9
Worked less than 35 hours per week	58.0	56.7	62.1	64.4	64.0	61.4
Looking for work	43.2	48.1	51.8	46.9	54.6	46.9
Not in labor force	45.3	44.2	46.5	43.1	52.2	46.8

*Children from racial/ethnic groups other than White, Black, and Hispanic are included in the totals but not shown separately.

Note. Estimates are based on children who had not entered kindergarten. Center-based programs include day care centers, Head Start, preschool, nursery school, prekindergarten, and other early childhood programs. Children without mothers in the home are not included in estimates concerning mother's education or mother's employment status.

Source. U.S. Department of Education, NCES. National Household Education Surveys Program (NHES), "Parent Interview" survey, various years. Retrieved from http://nces.ed.gov/programs/coe/2002/section1/tables/t01_1.asp

indicated that the poverty rate for all other groups was more than twice as high with Hispanics at 21.9%, blacks at 22.9%, and American Indian and Alaska Natives at 24.5% (U.S. Census Bureau, 2001).

As suggested earlier, many of the risk factors just described are related to various indicators of importance in early childhood development. The following section provides an overview of some of these relationships.

Risk factors and literacy development. As noted earlier in this chapter, failure to learn to read adequately for continued school success is much more likely among poor children, among nonwhite children, and among non-native speakers of

English (Snow, Burns, & Griffin, 1998). There are several studies that suggest an association between poor educational outcomes and several family-related factors such as parents who have not completed high school (Bianchi & McArthur, 1993; West & Brick, 1991; Zill, 1996a), low SES (Zill, Collins, West, & Germino-Hansken, 1995), living in a single-parent family (Dawson, 1991; Entwisle & Alexander, 1995; McLanahan & Sandefur, 1994; Zill, 1996b), and coming from a home where English is not the native language (Bianchi & McArthur, 1993; Kao, 1999; Rumberger & Larson, 1998).

Although inequities in schooling plays a critical role (Kozol, 1991), recent data from the U.S. Department of Education's Early Childhood Longitudinal Study, Kindergarten Class of 1998–1999 (ECLS-K) provides additional evidence for the importance of

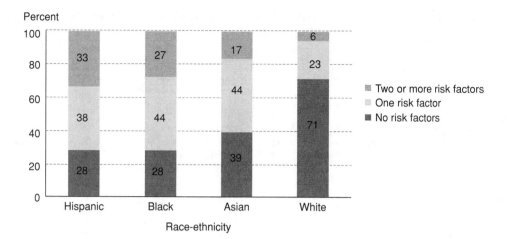

FIGURE 10.1. Percentage distribution of first-time kindergartners, by number of risk factors and race-ethnicity: Fall 1998.
Note: Percentages may not add to 100 due to rounding.
Source: U.S. Department of Education, NCES. Early Childhood Longitudinal Study, "Kindergarten Class of 1998–99," Fall 1998. Retrieved from http://nces.ed.gov/programs/coe/2000/essay/e03f.asp on August 1, 2003.

other factors as well. This study is important because, unlike much earlier research, it is based on a national sample and uses direct assessment rather than secondhand reports, although unfortunately students not proficient in English were excluded from portions of the data collection. Nevertheless, the overall findings are instructive with respect to risk factors and their impact on various outcomes.

The specific risk factors considered by ECLS-K were (a) a mother with less than a high school education, (b) a family receiving food stamps or welfare, (c) a single-parent household, and (d) parents whose primary language is other than English. The data indicate that among first-time kindergartners, 23% come from a single-parent family, 18% have received welfare or food stamps, 14% have mothers with less than high school education, and 9% have parents who do not speak English. Of the entire sample, 31% had at least one risk factor, and another 16% had two or more (U.S. Dept of Education, NCES, 2001).

These risk factors are not distributed equally among all groups. Figure 10.1 shows the distribution of risk factors for first time kindergartners by race-ethnicity. Although 71% of whites have no risk factors, only 28% of Hispanics and blacks respectively have none (U.S. Department of Education, NCES, 2001). Importantly, there are some data that suggest a relationship between risk factors and indicators of opportunity to learn and later achievement. For example, Table 10.2 indicates that mothers' education level is related to reading and mathematics scores in both kindergarten and first grade with mothers having less than a high school education also having children who make less academic gain. In addition, Fig. 10.2 suggests that there is a relationship of specific reading skills and number of family risk factors. Forty-four percent of students in the multiple-risk group could identify letters of the alphabet, compared with 57% of those in the single-risk group and 75% of those in the

no-risk group. Also, children from families with multiple-risk factors were roughly one third as likely to be able to associate letters with sounds at the ends of words as children from families with none of the four risk factors. Children from families with one risk factor were half as likely to do so. Twenty-two percent of the no-risk group, 11% of the single-risk group, and 6% of the multiple-risk group were at this third proficiency level in reading.

Previous studies have suggested that these risk factors are cumulative such that children with multiple risk characteristics are more likely to be educationally disadvantaged or have difficulty in school (Pallas, Natriello, & McDill, 1989). Similarly, in the ELCS study, children with one risk factor are twice as likely to have reading scores that fall in the lowest 25% of the overall skill distribution as children no risk factors. Thirty-three percent of the single-risk group was in the lowest fourth of the distribution. Also, children with two or more risk factors are about three times as likely as those with no risk factors to score in the bottom quartile in reading. Finally, children with one risk factor are half as likely to achieve reading scores that are in the highest 25% of the skill distribution as those with no risk factors (16 vs. 33%). Those with multiple risks are one third as likely to be in the top quartile (U.S. Department of Education, NCES, 2001, p. 20). Children from family settings where multiple risk factors are present seem to have especially difficult problems with achievement in areas such as vocabulary (Nord, Zill, Prince, Clarke, & Ventura, 1994), verbal IQ (Sameroff, Seifer, Barocas, Zax, & Greenspan, 1987), and grade repetition or school suspension (Nord, et al., 1994).

The final pattern of note in the ELCS-K data is the distribution of at-risk factors by geographic location. Given the strong interest in urban school settings, it is noteworthy that the proportion of kindergartners who come from at-risk families changes

TABLE 10.2. Children's Reading and Mathematics Scale Scores From Kindergarten Through First Grade, by Mother's Education: 1998–2000

Mother's Education	Kindergarton			1st Grade			Total gain[2]
	Fall	Spring	Gain[1]	Fall	Spring	Gain[1]	
			Reading				
Total	23	33	10	38	57	19	34
Less than high school	18	27	9	32	48	16	30
High school diploma or equivalent	20	31	11	36	55	19	35
Some college, including vocational/technical	23	33	10	39	58	19	35
Bachelor's degree or higher	27	37	10	43	63	20	36
			Mathematics				
Total	20	28	8	34	44	10	24
Less than high school	16	23	7	28	39	11	23
High school diploma or equivalent	18	27	9	31	42	11	24
Some college, including vocational/technical	20	29	9	34	45	11	25
Bachelor's degree or higher	24	33	9	39	48	9	24

[1] Gain is calculated as the difference from fall to spring for kindergarten and first grade, respectively.

[2] Total gain is calculated as the difference in scale score from fall kindergarten to spring first grade.

Note. Estimates based on children assessed in English in fall and spring of kindergarten and first grade (excludes approximately 19% of Asian and 31% of Hispanic children). Esimates based on children who entered kindergarten for the first time in fall 1998 and were promoted to first grade in fall 1999. The reading scale score ranged from 0 to 72, and the mathematics score from 0 to 64. See Supplemental Note 3 for more information on the Early Childhood Longitudinal Study, Kindergarten Class of 1998–99 (ECLS-K).

Source. U.S. Department of Education, NCES, Early Childhood Longitudinal Study, Kindergarten Class of 1998–99 (ECLS-K), Longitudinal Kindergarten-First Grade Data files, fall 1998 through spring 2000, previously unpublished tabulation (March 2001).

Retrieved from http://nces.ed.gov/programs/coe/2003/section2/tables/t09_1.asp

dramatically from urban to suburban and rural America and across different racial-ethnic groups. In cities with populations above 250,000, nearly two thirds of entering kindergartners have one or more risk factors, and 26 percent have multiple risk factors. In contrast, in the suburbs of large cities and in small towns, the situation is almost reversed. In those communities, nearly two thirds of kindergartners have none of the four risk factors, and about 1 in 10 have two or more. Rural areas and midsize cities and their suburbs are similar to the national averages in the frequency of risk factors (U.S. Department of Education, NCES, 2001).

Although these data are troublesome, it is useful to be cautious about the interpretation of these data. Although children with one or more risk factors may lag behind other students *as a group*, it does not mean that every individual student will experience problems. These data are descriptive and correlational in nature, and caution should be exercised in creating rigid profiles and stereotypes of children from certain racial, ethnic, or socioeconomic groups. What should be noted from these data is that there is significant intercorrelation among the variables involved, and significant variation in the experiences, skills, and knowledge of students as they enter kindergarten. Attention to these individual differences is critical given the variation noted.

In the remainder of the chapter, we turn attention to three selected areas that we deem critical in considering the issue of reading/literacy development for young children, with special attention to students from diverse backgrounds. These include early literacy/biliteracy development, assessment, and large-scale interventions. Because of space limitations, we provide a brief rather than an exhaustive overview, to give the reader a sense of the current work. We conclude with an analysis of the existing literature and with recommendations for future work.

EARLY LITERACY AND BILITERACY DEVELOPMENT

Early childhood, especially kindergarten and first grade, represents a critical time of rapid growth and learning for children that forms the foundation for later academic work and lifelong pursuits. This realization, in part, has helped fuel the current focus on reading and literacy. During the last five to seven years in particular, integrative reviews (Garcia, 2000; National Reading Panel, 2000; Snow, Burns, & Griffin, 1998; Sulzby & Teale, 2003; Whitehurst & Lonigan, 1998; Yaden, Rowe, & MacGillivray, 2000), meta-analyses (Bus, van Izjendoorn & Pelligrino, 1995; Scarborough & Dobrich, 1994), and evaluations commissioned by the federal government related to beginning reading and the education of young children (e.g., U.S. Department of Education, National Center for the Education Statistics [NCES], 2001), have substantiated the importance of frequent early literacy experiences during the preschool years as the initial foundation on which the beginnings of conventional reading and writing are built.

One of the key findings from the research on literacy interventions involving parental reading components with many implications for linguistically and culturally diverse children is the consistent pattern of short- and some long-term gains (e.g., Goldenberg, Reese, & Gallimore, 1992; Phillips, Norris, & Mason, 1996; Bus, van Izjendoorn, & Pellegrini, 1995). At the same time, research has suggested that there may be significant differences in the home and community literacy environments of children from diverse backgrounds in terms of language, SES, or cultural background. Several studies (e.g., Baker et al., 1996; Delgado-Gaitan, 1990, 1996; Heath, 1983; Purcell-Gates, 1995,

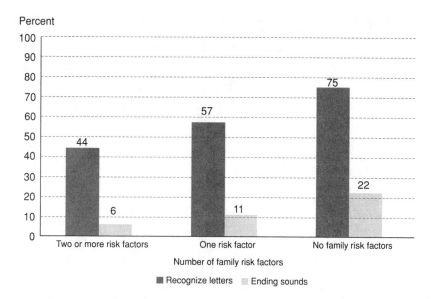

FIGURE 10.2. Percentage of first-time kindergartners with specific reading skills, by number of family risk factors: Fall 1998.
Note: Based on those assessed in English. Excludes 19 percent of Asian and 30 percent of Hispanic children. Detail may not add to 100 due to rounding.
Source: U.S. Department of Education, NCES. Early Childhood Longitudinal Study, "Kindergarten Class of 1998–99," Fall 1998.
Retrieved from http://nces.ed.gov/programs/coe/2000/essay/e03f.asp

1996; Taylor & Dorsey-Gaines, 1988; Teale, 1986, 1987) have shown that literacy interactions of considerable variety occur even within low-income families. Duke and Purcell-Gates (2003) recently reported on the genres or types of text encountered by a group of 4- to 6-year-old children of low (SES) backgrounds at home and a group of first-grade children of low SES backgrounds at school. Some genres were found in only one or the other setting, some were found in both. The authors suggest that knowledge about genres young children encounter at home and at school offers opportunities to bridge home and school literacies and enhance children's literacy development.

The Early Childhood Longitudinal Study

One weakness of much of the research on early childhood is that it has tended to rely on second hand reports of parents or caretakers about what children of varying backgrounds know and can do (Zill, Collins, West, & Germino-Hausken, 1995). More recent research has made available data based on direct assessments of children with the launching of the U.S. Department of Education's Early Childhood Longitudinal Study in the fall of 1998. This large-scale study assesses the knowledge, skills, health, and behavior of a large and nationally representative sample of American kindergartners (approximately 19,000 children from a national probability sample of kindergartners attending 940 public and private schools). Additional data has been gathered about the children, their families, and their schools through interviews and questionnaires with parents, teachers and school administrators, and archival school records data. The participants in the study will be followed through the fifth grade (West, Denton, & Germino-Hausken, 2000; West, Denton, & Reaney, 2001; Zill & West, 2000).

This study has produced very useful data on what children can do upon entering kindergarten. Sixty-six percent of the sample already knew the letters of the alphabet, 30% knew the letter-sound relationship at the beginning of words, and 17% knew the letter-sound relationship at the end of words. However, only 3% could read sight words and only 1% could read words in context (U.S. Department of Education, NCES, 2003).

There were important between-group differences, however, as white children scored higher than black and Latino children on these reading skills (West, Denton, & Germino-Hausken, 2000). In addition, children with higher maternal education levels scored higher, as did children from higher SES groups (Denton & West, 2000; West, Denton, & Germino Hausken, 2000, also see Table 10.2). Table 10.3 illustrates differences in the frequency of occurrence of early markers of home literacy such as race/ethnicity, mother's home language, mother's education, mother's employment status, number of parents in the household, and SES. As one example, being read to at home has been shown to be important precursor for later school reading and literacy achievement (Buss, van Izjendoorn, & Pelligrini,

TABLE 10.3. Percentage of Children Ages 3–5 Not Yet Enrolled in Kindergarten Who Participated in Home Literacy Activities With a Family Member Three or More Times in the Week Before the Survey, by Selected Child and Family Characteristics: 1993 and 2001

Child and Family Characterstic	Read to[1]		Told a Story		Taught Letters, Words, or Numbers		Taught Songs or Music	
	1993	2001	1993	2001	1993	2001	1993	2001
Total	78.3	84.1	43.0	54.3	57.7	74.2	41.0	54.1
Age								
3	79.4	83.6	46.4	54.5	57.2	71.2	45.0	59.9
4	77.8	85.2	41.2	54.6	58.1	77.1	38.9	51.7
5	75.9	81.5	35.8	52.0	57.9	74.6	33.1	40.6
Sex								
Male	77.4	82.1	42.6	59.2	57.7	72.8	38.3	51.4
Female	79.2	86.1	43.4	55.4	57.7	75.7	43.8	56.9
Race/ethnicity[2]								
Asian/Pacific Islander	68.8	87.4	52.1	98.1	61.8	77.9	35.9	50.4
Black	65.9	76.7	39.0	51.2	62.7	77.5	48.9	53.9
White	84.8	89.4	44.3	57.9	57.2	74.8	40.2	53.4
Other[3]	75.9	86.5	48.1	61.8	56.0	78.4	31.3	57.9
Hispanic	58.2	70.7	37.7	42.3	53.9	68.2	38.7	56.6
Mother's home language[4]								
English	81.4	67.7	43.7	56.3	58.4	76.0	42.0	55.2
Not English	42.1	59.4	35.7	34.2	51.9	62.1	32.6	50.0
Mother's education								
Less than high school	59.7	69.0	36.6	43.2	56.4	66.6	39.8	54.4
High school diploma or equivalent	75.7	80.8	41.2	53.0	56.4	73.1	41.3	54.6
Some college, including vocational/technical	83.3	85.6	45.1	53.5	60.4	76.0	42.4	55.3
Bachelor's degree	90.0	93.0	47.9	57.9	56.6	75.8	38.5	51.6
Graduate/professional degree	89.9	96.0	49.6	67.2	59.5	80.0	49.8	56.8
Mother's employment status								
Employed Full time or part time	79.3	85.6	43.6	59.8	56.5	73.5	41.2	54.6
35 hours or more per week	77.9	83.5	42.7	51.3	55.7	73.1	41.9	52.5
Less than 35 hours per week	81.5	89.4	45.0	58.6	57.7	74.2	40.2	58.5
Looking for work	70.9	76.5	42.9	55.9	65.8	72.8	49.2	40.1
Not in labor force	78.9	83.1	42.5	54.3	58.3	75.8	40.0	56.1
Family type								
Two-parent household	81.1	86.7	43.8	55.3	57.1	74.5	39.9	54.1
Home or one-parent household	70.8	76.9	40.7	91.3	59.1	73.5	43.9	54.2
Poverty status								
Below poverty threshold (poor)	67.9	73.7	39.1	90.7	59.6	72.4	45.2	97.0
At or above poverty threshold (nonpoor)	82.1	87.1	44.3	55.3	57.0	74.7	39.5	53.3
Between 100 and 200 percent of poverty threshold	75.5	80.8	42.5	54.4	58.1	72.1	39.4	53.0
Above 200 percent of poverty threshold	86.8	90.1	45.6	55.8	56.2	76.0	39.5	53.4
Number of children								
1	80.9	84.3	45.9	52.7	65.0	77.1	44.0	54.6
2–3	78.7	84.6	43.1	94.1	55.8	73.6	39.7	52.9
4 or more	72.4	81.8	38.3	56.9	56.8	73.4	43.3	59.1

[1] In 1993, respondents were asked about reading frequency in one of the two versions of the survey questionnaire. The percentages presented in the table are for all of the respondents who answered three or more times on either version of the questionnaire.

[2] Black includes African American, Pacific Islander includes Native Hawaiian, and Hispanic includes Latino. Race categories exclude Hispanic origin unless specified.

[3] Other includes American Indian and Alaska Native.

[4] Children without mothers (birth, adoptive, step, or foster) residing in the household are not included in estimates dealing with mother's education, mother's language at home, or mother's employment status. Excludes 86 children in 1993 and 65 children in 2001 when there was no mother (birth, adoptive, step, or foster) residing in their household and the survey respondent on the telephone was not a female.

Source. U.S. Department of Education, NCES, School Readiness and Early Childhood Education Program Participation Surveys of the National Household Education Surveys Program (SR-NHES:1993 and ECPP-NHES:2001).

Retrieved from http://nces.ed.gov/programs/coe/2003/section6/tables/t37_1.asp

1995; Yaden, Rowe, & MacGillivray, 2000). Data in Table 10.3 indicate that 87.4% of Asian and 89.4% of white students were read to at home, whereas 76.7% of black and 70.7% of Latino students were read to. Mother's home language also was strongly related to this variable. In addition, 87.7% of the students whose mother spoke English were read to, but only 59.4% of those whose mothers were non-English speaking were read to. Although these data are reason for concern with those who are interested in children from linguistically diverse backgrounds, there are some indications that emergent literacy can be fostered with the right types of programs that provide optimal learning conditions and build upon existing practices and values (Madrigal, Cubillas, Yaden, Tam, & Brassell, 1999; Valero, 2002; Yaden & Brassell, 2003; Yaden, Madrigal & Tam, 2003).

The National Reading Panel Report

In terms of national policy, the recent National Reading Panel Report is especially influential, because it has been drawn on heavily for educational policy at the federal level that in turn has impacted states to a significant degree. Among the most attended to findings were those involving the importance of phonemic awareness and systematic instruction of phonics. Although other findings in areas such as comprehension and guided reading also were addressed, these have been far less influential.

There are some criticisms of both the panel's findings as well as how it has been used for policy purposes. Pressley (2002), for example has argued that the panel intentionally limited both the methodological and conceptual scope of the report. In terms of methodology, the report considered only studies employing true experiments (studies involving random assignment of participants to instructional conditions, with the instructional conditions then compared using formal statistical procedures). Conceptually, the panel focused only on the following reading instruction topics—alphabetics (phonemic awareness and phonics instruction), fluency, comprehension (vocabulary instruction, text comprehension, teacher preparation and comprehension strategies instruction), teacher education and reading instruction, and computer technology and reading instruction. Pressley (2002) pointed out some areas that could have been addressed but were not: instruction at home, television, community resources, whole language instruction, language of instruction, and school reform movements. These areas may be particularly critical for diverse learners, and the lack of attention to these factors may have had an especially significant impact on their short- and long-term literacy acquisition.

Despite this growing database on the acquisition of early literacy, there is some reason for concern with respect to linguistically and culturally diverse children. As Whitehurst and Lonigan (1998) point out, much of the emergent literacy research has been compiled from children whose first language is English, although many more reports of studies with Spanish-speaking populations, in particular, have been appearing during the last decade (see Delgado-Gaitan, 1996; Flores, 1990; Goldenberg, Reese, & Gallimore, 1992; Lesar, Espinosa, & Diaz, 1997; Madrigal, Cubillas, Yaden, Tam, & Brassell, 1999; Valdez-Menchaca & Whitehurst, 1992; Weber & Longhi-Chirlin, 2001; Yaden, 2000;

Yaden et al., 2000, for some representative examples). In addition, there is growing evidence (e.g., Goldenberg et al., 1992; Madrigal et al., 1999) that classic emergent literacy activities such as storybook reading are perceived, and, more important, conducted differently in the homes of many students from diverse backgrounds than they are in other settings where the families are English-speaking and more of middle income. Thus, before widespread implementation of emergent literacy programs can be seen as providing for culturally and linguistically diverse learners the foundation for academic learning it has proven to be for other populations, it becomes critically important to understand the family context (values, beliefs, daily routine) in which these students are raised and into which traditional emergent literacy activities may be imported in order to gauge the impact that these possible "transformations" of early literacy activities have on future reading achievement. What is needed to advance understanding, therefore, is specific research into both formal and infomal indices of early literacy growth (in various language and cultural settings), the specific linguistic and discourse features of target populations, and the relationship of these variables to a broad range of reading and literacy outcomes.

Fortunately, there is a effort underway to address some of the shortcomings of the National Reading Panel. SRI International and the Center for Applied Linguistics have been contracted by the Institute of Education Sciences (U.S. Department of Education) to conduct a comprehensive, evidence-based review of the research literature on the development of literacy among language minority children and youth. This 24-month study complements the scope of the study conducted by the National Reading Panel (which specifically excluded literacy development among language minority students). It is organized along similar lines but will include quantitative experimental studies, quantitative nonexperimental studies, and qualitative studies. The panel's work also includes specific attention to the issues of culture and context that were not included in the National Reading Panel's work.

ISSUES IN THE ASSESSMENT OF YOUNG, ENGLISH LANGUAGE LEARNERS' LANGUAGE AND LITERACY PERFORMANCE

As mentioned earlier, with the increased federal emphasis on early childhood education, the assessment of young children in general and, in particular, young English language learners has become one of the issues at the forefront of educational concern (Meisels, 1994; Meisels & Piker, 2001). Recently, for example, Dickinson (2002, 2003) has suggested that many of the current assessments used to assess the quality of classroom and literacy activities are not designed to measure specific academic abilities such as literacy and have not kept up with recent research on early literacy assessment. Responding to a critique by Lambert (2003) regarding his [Dickinson's] earlier evaluation (Dickinson, 2002) of the uses of currently available assessments, Dickinson (2003) raises the following questions:

Can we honestly say that researchers with deep content knowledge in literacy, language, mathematics, science, self-regulation, and social and emotional development have carefully reviewed such tools and found that they capture those activities that one would expect would lead to optimal child outcomes? Or are they simply the best available tools? (p. 27)

From our perspective, the answers to the above questions are "no"—they haven't been reviewed adequately to establish strong construct validity and "yes"—many instruments are used, not because they are appropriate but, rather, because they are available. We discuss some of these instruments in the following sections.

Issues in Assessing Language Proficiency

According to the most recent *Survey of the States' Limited English Proficient Students and Available Educational Programs and Services 2000–01* (Kindler, 2002), the tests used most often to identify children as English language learners are ranked as follows (see Table 10.4). Because a critique of several aspects of the above measures has been made recently by Yaden, Rueda, Tsai and Esquinca (2004), only a brief summary will be provided here. First of all, the most commonly used language proficiency tests listed in Table 10.4 are designed for school-aged children, not preschoolers. Thus, oftentimes preschool children are taking tests that are designed for older children. Second, with the exception of tests such as the *LAS-Oral* and the *Woodcock-Munoz*, which take into account students' knowledge of language pragmatics, most other measures areare based on the assumption that language proficiency can be measured accurately by only sampling discrete aspects such as phonology, syntax, morphology, and lexicon and do not consider aspects of language that are integral to academic success, such as pragmatic competence (Cummins, 2000). Third, scholarly reviews of the above tests have pointed out widespread item validity problems (Haber, 1985; Carpenter, 1994; Hedberg, 1995; Kao, 1998), low interrater reliability (Crocker, 1998), and, in the case of language minorities, nonrepresentative norming samples (Chesterfield, 1985; Haber, 1985; Shellenberger, 1985; Lopez, 2001).

TABLE 10.4. Rankings of Language Tests Used to Identify Children as English Language Learners

Language Proficiency Test	No. of SEAS Reporting	% of SEAS Reporting
	51	94
Language Assessment Scales (LAS)	46	85%
IDEA Language Proficiency Tests (IPT)	38	70%
Woodcock-Muñoz Language Survey	28	52%
Language Assessment Battery	13	24%
Basic Inventory of Natural Languages (BINL)	6	11%
Maculaitis Assessment (MAC)	6	11%
Secondary Level English Proficiency (SLEP)	6	11%
Woodcock Language Proficiency Battery	6	11%

Note. Adapted from Kindler (2002), Table 2. "Methods and Top Tests Used to Identify LEP Students, 2000–2001." *Survey of the States' Limited English Proficient Students and Available Educational Programs and Services*. Washington, DC: National Clearinghouse for English Language Acquisition & Language Instruction Educational Programs.

Finally, state educational agencies frequently report that achievement tests such as the *Stanford Achievement Test and Iowa Tests of Basic Skills (ITBS)*, not language proficiency tests, are commonly used to both identify and reclassify students as non-limited English proficiency students.

In summary, the findings described have serious implications for English language learners. If academic programs rely primarily on achievement tests to place ELLs in bilingual services, to reclassify them within a particular bilingual program, and to allow them to exit the same bilingual services, then such tests are not being used properly. In addition, even the most frequently used language proficiency tests have serious validity and reliability issues of which test consumers should be aware. Furthermore, most tests focus only on discrete aspects of language that are quantifiable, and these are not the only aspects of language competence that a language learner must master.

Language Assessment of Young, English Language Learners

Most important, very young English language learners require assessments that are especially designed for them, in other words, that are developmentally appropriate and have been field-tested with representative populations (Meisels, 1994). In addition, any one measure should not be used as the sole determiner for screening, reclassification and program exit (transition) decisions. These types of decisions must be based on triangulation of instruments—in a portfolio-type fashion. Finally, assessments must take into consideration the child's linguistic background (such as sociolinguistic variety), and be constructed to allow children to demonstrate what they can do in actual language settings.

Issues in Assessing Early Literacy

Reminiscent of problems with assessments designed to measure oral language proficiency, literacy assessments for young, second-language learners raise similar issues. In the first place, reading and writing assessments in languages other than English are very sparse. For example, in his review of some 79 commonly used reading readiness instruments, Meisels (1999) found only four that were available in Spanish. In addition, although there have been a few normed measures developed to assess early concepts about print (Clay, 2002; Downing, Sheaffer, & Ayers, 1993; Reid, Hresko, & Hammill, 2001) and phoneme awareness (Yopp, 1988), almost none exist for the assessment of early comprehension abilities in prereaders that , in turn, provide the bases for the development of later reading comprehension of narrative or expository material in school. Until recently, only Sulzby's emergent reading classifications scheme (1985; Kaderavek & Sulzby, 1999) provided any systematic way of assessing children's beginning understandings of the form and functions underlying written texts. More commonly, researchers are usually forced to design their own measures if trying to understand very young children's interpretations of stories or other types of comprehending tasks (e.g., see van den Broek, 1999).

TABLE 10.5. Levels and Characteristics of Sulzby's Emergent Reading Classification Scheme

	Stage	Characteristics
Picture Governed	Labeling and commenting	• Each page is treated as a separate unit • Child either names or describes person/animal on each page or comments on it
	Following the action	• Each page is treated as a separate unit • Child describes the action on each page
	Dialogic storytelling	• Child begins to make links between pages. • Overall, the listener can perceive a story, although it is disjointed • Storytelling is dialogic, propelled by prompts from adult.
	Monologic storytelling	• Child bridges plot between pages. • Tends to take the form of a monologue.
Print Governed	Reading and Storytelling mixes	• Fluctuations between speech appropriate for an oral context and speech appropriate for a written context
	Reading similar-to-original story	• Child sounds like a reader while still looking at pictures as though reading from them • Child uses reading-like intonation patterns
	Text governed reading	• Child attempts to render a verbatim reading of the print.

However, during the funding period (1997–2002) of the Center for the Improvement of Early Reading Achievement (CIERA), several researchers have developed instruments that can be given in children's home languages in addition to indexing early comprehending ability. Four of these instruments are briefly described here.

The narrative comprehension of picture books (NC). Developed by Paris and Paris (2001), this assessment is one of the first measures of children's narrative competence, which not only can be used with a variety of children's books but also provides scoring rubrics as well as evidence of reliability and validity studies. Designed for children 4 through 8 years of age and to be administered in 15 min, the task itself consists of three parts: (a) a *Picture Walk* in which children are encouraged to look through a wordless picture book and make statements about what they are thinking about the pictures or story; (b) a *Retelling,* which is elicited from the child, following the Picture Walk; and (c) *Prompted Comprehension,* which entails the child and examiner going back through the book with the latter asking a series of questions aimed at tapping the child's understanding of explicit information, the elements of story structure and inferences about "characters' feelings, dialogue, causal inferences, predictions and themes" (p. 7).

To date, the *NC* test has been administered to approximately 250 African-American, Asian, and Caucasian children, pre-K through Grade 2, and has further been shown to be correlated with components of both the Qualitative Reading Inventory-II (Leslie & Caldwell, 1995) and the Michigan Literacy Progress Profile (Michigan Department of Early Literacy Committee, 1998). In terms of an early comprehension measure, this is the first of its kind to have developed a systematic, direct measure of narrative understanding in prereaders with a standardized scoring system that can be used across a wide variety of children's books by either teachers or researchers.

Sulzby classification scheme for emergent storybook reading. Although Sulzby first described this scheme in 1985 (see also Kaderavek & Sulzby, 1999), it has been revised and adapted from purely a research instrument to an assessment which can be given and scored easily by practitioners in the classroom. In this task, children are asked to choose and "read" a favorite storybook to the examiner. Children's attempts at reading are categorized along a 7-level scale ranging from emergent reading attempts "governed by pictures" to attempts "governed by print" and eventually to correct or nearly correct readings. These categories are briefly described in Table 10.5.

This has been used with children in a variety of settings and languages (e.g., Bus, et al., 2001; Kaderavek & Sulzby, 1999), and it is still the only measure available to early literacy researchers that provides an index in the early stages of children's acquisition of the register of written language, or their understanding that books use different syntax, vocabulary, and text structure than oral language. This is an important understanding, as children develop the notion and vocabulary of "academic" language.

Teacher rating of oral language and literacy (TROLL). The *TROLL* battery has been developed by David Dickinson (Dickinson, McCabe, & Sprague, 2001) and is comprised of three subscales: (a) language use, (b) reading, and (c) writing. This Lickert-style rating tool has been designed for early childhood teachers to, first of all, assess children's conversational ability with adults and peers, propensity to use rhyme, use new and varied vocabulary and to demonstrate curiosity. The second subscale is aimed at indexing the child's attentiveness in group storybook reading, independent book behavior, and ability to recognize a few sight words as well as understanding of stories that are read aloud. Finally, the writing subscale is meant to provide information on the child's development toward using conventional graphic forms, ability to write his/her name or other's names and some simple words and whether or not the child attempts to produce larger segments of text (songs, poems, etc.).

According to its authors, the TROLL requires no special training, can be administered quickly (5–10 min) and correlates highly with both the *Peabody Picture Vocabulary Test* and other measures of phonemic awareness (Dickinson & Chaney, 1997). Finally, Dickinson, McCabe, & Sprague (2001) points out that in addition to its being a useful tool for teachers as well as parents to track the progress of an individual child's literacy progress, it also can be used for larger program evaluation.

Adult/child interactive reading inventory (ACIRI). In a slightly different vein, the *ACIRI* "is an observational tool for assessing joint reading behaviors of both adults and children" (DeBruin-Parecki, 1999). As with the practice of assessing early comprehension as mentioned earlier, where as several systems of adult-child storybook reading analysis have been used over the years in individual studies (Snow & Nino, 1986; Pappas, 1993, Yaden, Smolkin, & Conlon, 1989; Yaden, Smolkin, & MacGillivray, 1993), the *ACIRI* provides a more systematic observational scheme, which can be scored easily either during or after viewing adult-child storybook reading behavior.

The observational instrument consists of a list of storybook reading behaviors arranged in two columns (Adult Behavior; Child Behavior) and divided into three general areas: (a) Enhancing Attention to Text, (b) Promoting Interactive Reading and Supporting Comprehension, and (c) Using Literacy Strategies. Four behaviors are listed under each area and rated 0–3, depending on the frequency of which they are observed. For example, when observing adult behavior in the "Using Literacy Strategies" category, the observer rates on the 4-point scale whether the reader (a) identifies visual cues related to story reading (i.e., pictures, repetitive words), (b) solicits predictions, (c) asks child to recall information from the story, and (d) elaborates on child's ideas. Similarly, the complimentary child behaviors that can be rated simultaneously are (a) child responds to parent on identifies visual cues related to the story, (b) child is able to guess what will happen next based on picture cues, (c) child is able to recall information from story, and (d) child spontaneously offers ideas about story (DeBruin-Parecki, 1999, p. 24). DeBruin-Parecki (1999) has recommended that the actual scoring be done after the examiner or teacher leaves the home and that the numerical scores should be used for program evaluation purposes only and not as a means of evaluating individual parents.

These four measures offer the teacher and researcher new tools to look at children's language and literacy development in the preschool. Previously, we have had strong measures of children's knowledge of print concepts (e.g., Clay, 2002); these new measures should be able to provide a richer view of children's narrative development and have the advantage of being given in any language.

SYSTEMATIC INTERVENTIONS AT THE NATIONAL, STATE AND LOCAL LEVELS

As pointed out by Shonkoff and Phillips (2000), editors of *Neurons to Neighborhoods: The Science of Early Childhood Development*, the "generic" question of "whether or not we can intervene successfully in young children's lives has been answered in the affirmative and should be put to rest" (p. 10). Model programs such as the Perry Preschool Program (Schweinhart & Weikart, 1993), the Carolina Abecedarian Project (Campbell & Ramey, 1994), Project Care (Wasik, Ramey, Bryant, &

Sparling, 1990), as well as several others (see Bowman, Donovan, and Burns, 2001, pp. 134–135) have demonstrated long-term gains on several cognitive and socioemotional outcomes. However, despite a strong, professional consensus on the philosophical foundations of successful interventions (e.g., individualization, adequate resources, sufficient time, intensity and duration, family-centered, see Shonkoff & Phillips, 2000, Chapter 13, for other criteria), data from large-scale, public programs are much more inconsistent, especially when linguistically diverse children are involved.

Because it is these types of programs that are designed to reach the largest numbers of children and potentially should have the broadest impact on improving cognitive and social outcomes for the children and families to whom these programs are developed to serve, in the following section we will focus on a select group of programs which have been implemented at three different levels—national, state, and large urban municipal—as to their efficacy with linguistically diverse children of color. Although it has been pointed by two of the most recent national panels (Shonkoff & Phillips, 2000; Bowman, Donovan, & Burns, 2001) that the emphasis of past intervention efforts has been overbalanced on cognitive outcomes, we will keep with our focus on literacy since the latter ability, perhaps more than ever, has become the driving force for research funding at all of these aforementioned levels.

National Efforts

***Evaluation of* Head Start.** At the beginning of 1997, the Administration for Children and Families launched the Family and Childhood Experiences Survey (FACES) to assess the effectiveness of Head Start, the nation' oldest, largest (serving nearly 800,000 children) and most costly of early childhood education programs supported by the U.S. Department of Education. For this study, 3,200 children from 40 programs nationwide were randomly selected in order to assess whether or not children served by the program made gains in kindergarten and first grade on both cognitive as well behavioral measures. As a part of this first data collection period, 120 families also were selected for case study follow-up involving more detailed parent, teacher interviews and classroom observation. Further more in the year 2000, a second cohort of 2,800 children from 43 programs were randomly selected as well with the additional goal of studying more specifically the relationships between both classroom and family characteristics on the children's outcome measures. Both the Third and Fourth Progress Reports (U.S. Department of Health & Human Services 2001, 2003) are discussed below after a brief overview of selected population characteristics.

***Characteristics of children in* Head Start.** According to enrollment records for all 3- and 4-year-old children, percentages by ethnicity for the three largest groups are relatively equal with white children comprising 30.7%, black children comprising 28.8%, followed by Hispanics at 27%. Native American, Asian/Pacific Islander, and others of multiple ethnicities constitute 11.9%. However, these current percentages mask the fact that Hispanic children's enrollment in Head Start increased by 51% in the last decade as compared to increases of only 3.1% for white children and 8.5% for Black children (U.S. Department of Health and Human Services, 2002, p. 152). And unlike the general Latino population for whom over half (57%) report that English is spoken at home (NCES, 2003), Head Start families indicate that Spanish is spoken in 90.4% of the cases (U.S. Department of Health and Human Services, 2002, p. 156). Thus, given that Head Start's curriculum is delivered primarily in English, their challenge of educating linguistically diverse children is enlarged considerably. In addition, given that 83% of Head Start's total population of children has between 1–4 risk factors (U.S. Department of Health and Human Services, 2002, p. 155) the full extent of the education problem is truly daunting.

Evaluation of literacy outcomes for language-minority children in **Head Start.** As might be expected, all 4-year-old children who entered Head Start both in the fall of 1997 and fall of 2000 were considerably below grade level in vocabulary, emergent reading, writing ability, and letter identification, as much as two thirds to a full standard deviation below national norms (U.S. Department of Health and Human Services, 2001). Although the actual sample of Spanish children tested was much less than their representative percentage of enrollment (e.g., only 114 children were assessed in both data collection periods of academic year 1997–1998 in Spanish), their performance lags not only behind the U.S. population of preschoolers but also considerably behind other English-speaking Head Start enrollees. For example, in the spring of 1998, significant differences existed between the Spanish-speaking Head Start children and their English-language peers in vocabulary, math, and letter-word identification (U.S. Department of Health and Human Services, 2001, p. 24). Only in writing ability did the two groups perform similarly (figures in standard scores with a mean of 100: Spanish children = 85.9; English-speaking = 88.1).

In the FACES 2000 sample of Spanish-speaking children, the overall results did not show significant improvement. Although this group of children made greater gains over the course of the year in English-language speaking abilities, their vocabulary scores were still one and a third standard deviations below other language-majority, Head Start children (U.S. Department of Health and Human Services, 2003, p. 21). Similarly, language-minority children's performance on letter recognition remained approximately two thirds of a standard deviation below national norms (U.S. Department of Health and Human Services, 2003, p. 23). Because the assessment team tested administered additional language measures in Spanish during the spring of 2001, an encouraging finding was that children's gains in Spanish vocabulary and Spanish letter identification was equal to their gains in English, signifying a growing bilingualism. However, despite an increase in overall abilities from the 1997–1998 cohort of language-minority students, the most recent cohort of Spanish-dominant children had not made any significant gains against the abilities of their English-speaking peers nationwide.

Evaluation of **Even Start.** Started some 25 years later than Head Start, the Even Start Family Literacy Program was initially funded in 1989 with a broad focus on family literacy and children, birth to 7-years-old, and, typically, serves families with both incomes and education lower than other programs such as Head Start (St. Pierre et al., 2003, p. 4). Focusing on a wider range of children and services for families, the primary components of the Even Start program include adult basic education, parenting education, early childhood education services and interactive parent/child literacy activities. Initially funded directly by the U.S. Department of Education, since 1992 most Even Start programs are state-administered with the exception of Native American and migratory worker programs (U.S. Department of Education, Program Resource Manual, 2003). Even Start grantees typically include a consortium of local education agencies (LEAs), medical and social service organizations that are coordinated by a local director whose primary job is to see that all of the providers are delivering the services as promised in the funded proposal. Smaller in scope than Head Start, Even Start programs served an estimated 50,000 families in 2002–2003.

Characteristics of children in **Even Start.** Similar to the increase in Latino families in Head Start, the numbers of Hispanic children have doubled since the beginning of the program, so that by 2003–2003 Even Start's proportion of Hispanic families was nearly 50% This increase was, in turn, offset by the decrease in both white children (from 40% to 30%) and black families (from 26% to 20%). Unlike the increase in Asian and Pacific Islanders in the Head Start program, this population in Even Start has decreased in proportion from 8% to 3%. Not surprisingly, the greater proportion in non-English speaking parents and children also has impacted program delivery as some 75% of newly enrolled parents report having difficulty reading, speaking, and writing English (St. Pierre et al., 2001). Even Start officials have, however, recently stressed the importance of delivering the program in the primary language, particularly as it relates to literacy activities involving 3- to 5-year-olds, the largest age group of children served.

Regarding the literacy levels of the children on entry, parents reported that few of the children under 3 knew any letters of the alphabet. However, parents also indicated that preschool-aged children were more likely to know some of the letters (75%) and that the schoolaged children knew most, if not all of the letters of the English alphabet. Although lower than other studies have reported, 25% of Even Start parents report reading to their children daily and another 25% indicate that they read at least three times a week (St. Pierre et al., 2001, p. 3). Interestingly, Even Start parents reported that 53% of their toddlers were observed *reading* and that 92% of the preschoolers were engaged in pretend reading as well. Parents also reported that similar percentages of their toddlers and preschoolers to be involved in a variety of writing activities, either in English or the primary language (St. Pierre et al., 2001).

Evaluation of literacy outcomes for language minority children in **Even Start.** Unlike the FACES Study, Even Start's Third National Evaluation included a control group of families randomly selected from each of the 18 projects participating in the impact study. The sample from which the findings are drawn include 309 Even Start families and 154 families assigned to the control group. As pointed out by the evaluation team, whereas the actual sample is overrepresented by Hispanic families and language-minority children, the findings provide important information about this ever-growing segment of families served by Even Start.

Key findings include that Even Start children did not perform better on literacy and language development measures than control group families, about one third of whom had received some type of early childhood or adult education services (St. Pierre et al., 2003, p. 3). In addition, whereas Even Start children gained as much as Head Start children on vocabulary measures, their overall scores remained very much below national norms in several areas such as vocabulary (6th percentile), sound blending (24th percentile), letter-word identification (23rd percentile), and dictation (14th percentile).

Interestingly, the children's literacy and language scores were higher when compared to their peers than scores for their parents against other parents on similar measures as the average Even Start parent scored at the 5th percentile on letter-word identification, the 2nd percentile on passage comprehension, the 14th percentile on word attack, and the 1st percentile on reading vocabulary (St. Pierre et al., pp. 166–167).

When Even Start children and their parents were compared to other Even Start participants who did not received a similar proportion of services in adult or childhood education, the group of families and children who had received services did not improve significantly. Similarly, the evaluation did not show that increased hours spent in adult education or parenting education improved scores on any of the parent assessments. When parents self-reported, however, they did indicate an increase in literacy-related behaviors for their children as well as positive changes in their own participation with their children in book-related activities. As the evaluation team pointed out, though, it was difficult to tease out which changes can be attributed to actual program impacts as opposed to parental motivation or simple maturational processes of the children.

State Efforts at Universal Preschool

Responding to mandates on the federal level as indicated earlier in this chapter regarding the importance of early literacy experiences for young children, over half of the states in the nation have large-scale publicly-financed preschool programs of various types (Demanding results, 1999). For the most part, these programs have been aimed at children of poverty, culturally-diverse and language-minority children identified as those most likely to have academic difficulties in school. Two states that have managed on-going evaluations of these programs are Virginia and Michigan. These particular states have been chosen, not so much as exemplars of programs but, rather, because they have recent evaluations available to the public, the designs of which have been planned and carried out by professional evaluators, and findings reported for either substantial numbers of English language learners or children of color.

Evaluation of the Virginia Preschool Initiative

The Virginia Preschool Initiative (created in 1997), evaluated with support from the Center for the Improvement of Early Reading Achievement (CIERA) and the Virginia Department of Education, reported both literacy outcomes and teacher self-reports for 2,759 children (63.8 % African American, 27.6 % white, 3.5% Hispanic, 5% Other) deemed "at risk" according to criteria developed by the Virginia Department of Education (Sayeski, Burgess, Pianta & Lloyd, 2001). As a part of the evaluation, 240 teachers (two thirds of the preschool teacher population in VPI) evaluated children's growth from fall to spring with an instrument adapted from the *Early Childhood Literacy Scale* (Meisels, Nicholson, & Atkins-Burnett, 1997).

Although children made significant gains during the year on all of the 14 items assessing early literacy behaviors (e.g., understanding concepts about print, ability to rhyme, letter knowledge, phonological awareness, early writing, understanding stories read aloud), the researchers found that one third of the preschoolers were still not able to recognize beginning word sounds, 54% could not write any words from memory, and 46% were not understanding conventions of print or beginning to exhibit any early writing ability (Sayeski, Burgess, Pianta, & Lloyd, 2001, p. 8).

Interestingly, the study found that although many of children did not demonstrate knowledge of the common, discrete skills shown to predict later reading behavior (e.g., letter identification, rhyming and phonological sensitivity), teachers rated over half of the children as making substantial progress more general language and literacy areas such as using complex sentence structure, making predictions, understanding and interpreting stories read aloud, and choosing reading as an independent activity (p. 13). In fact, when teachers themselves were asked to choose what factor they thought was most important in predicting later reading success, they overwhelmingly picked "understands and interprets story read to him or her" (p. 10).

Although these teachers' insights contrast with the current emphasis on phonological awareness and its importance as a predictor of future reading success (e.g., Stanovich, 2000, found that phonological awareness was a stronger predictor in his study than either IQ or language measures), we suspect that the storybook reading stressed by the teachers in the Virginia study may lead to growth in some areas, possibly vocabulary, but not in others, such as written word knowledge (see the papers in van Kleeck, Stahl, & Bauer, 2003). This hypothesis, however, cannot be verified without further longitudinal study into the primary grades.

Evaluation of the Michigan School Readiness Program

The Michigan School Readiness Program (MSRP) is unusual in that it was instituted in 1985, although the following figures represent the first evaluation of the program since that time. Serving some 20,000 preschool children across the state each year, the longitudinal evaluation was carried out by researchers from the High Scope Educational Research Foundation (Xiang,

et al., 2000) and includes three general groups of children identified at the beginning of kindergarten in two cohorts (beginning
in 1995–1996 and 1996–1997) who have been followed for 3
years. The groups include children who (a) participated in the
preschool program in either of the years mentioned earlier; and
(b) children who did not have any systematic, preschool experiences, but whose household income as reported by parents
would have qualified them to participate in the program; and
(c) a group of children participating in Head Start. Thus, the final sample was comprised of 565 MSRP children across 11 sites,
478 control group (no preschool) children, and 209 Head Start
participants for a total sample of 1,252.

Interestingly, the evaluation team did not collect information on ethnicity or percentage of different language speakers,
although in 1998, 10.5% of parents self-reported information
regarding limited English proficiency (Xiang et al., 2000). In
general, however, participants in programs in urban areas such
as Detroit are predominantly African American, whereas in suburban areas they tend to be mostly white. The smaller group of
language minority children includes many from the Middle Eastern countries as well as of Hispanic origin (L. J. Schweinhart,
personal communication, September 17, 2003).

Unlike the evaluation reports previously discussed, however,
findings from the Michigan evaluation show distinct, significant differences between MSRP children and the comparison
groups. For example, on the *Child Observation Record* (COR),
which measures subscales such as initiative, social relations, creative representation, music and movement, language and literacy, logic and mathematics, the MSRP participants scored significantly better ($p < .05$) on all scales except logic and math. And,
importantly, these results take into consideration several factors
known to correlate highly with both social and academic outcome measures for children such as mother's education, single
parent, teen parents, low family income, unemployed adults in
the household, limited English-speaking and other well-known
risk factors as indices for each of these were used as covariates
in the calculation of gains.

As in other studies, the MSRP evaluation found that the number of risk factors also correlated negatively with child outcomes
in the kindergarten year. However, despite the fact that the
MSRP children averaged over four risk factors per child, the
program children showed academic gains in literacy and social
skills both at the end of kindergarten and on several other indicators such as lower grade retention and school readiness through
second grade (Xiang et al., 2000). As the evaluators noted, however, these positive differences were not uniform over all the
sites, and necessitate a more in-depth examination of both risk
and program factors and how these influence achievement for
individual children.

Local Program Efforts

As noted earlier, early experiences with books, print environments, and literate adults are significant factors in later school
achievement. It is also clear that the types of literacy experiences and print-related materials may not be the same for all
students. As described previously, there is good evidence that

both the type and amount may vary substantially by not only by
SES, but by racial, ethnic, and linguistic backgrounds (Duke &
Purcell-Gates, 2003; Gee, 1989; Heath, 1983) and even type of
preschool program (McGill-Franzen, Lanford, & Adams, 2002).
This is not to say that the early literacy experiences or environments of these students are impoverished, but it is also true
that they may not easily map onto what schools require or expect. However, there is evidence that it is possible to improve
academic success with targeted programs (Pressley, 1998). For
example, Elley (1997) showed that vocabulary knowledge was
developed incidentally from listening to stories in school, even
when there were no explanations from the teacher.

Other investigators have been able achieve positive results
with related approaches targeted at developing early conventional literacy skills. Neuman (1999) increased emergent literacy
scores by employing a small amount of teacher training combined with book floods with low-income students in a day care
setting. Purcell-Gates, McIntyre, and Freppon (1995) reported
that kindergartens that were rich in storybook language facilitated development of the written language register even with
low SES children without extensive joint reading experience at
home. Other studies with different populations and approaches
(e.g., Whitehurst et al., 1998, using shared or "dialogic" reading around picture books with Head Start children; Wasik &
Bond, 2001, using concrete representations of targeted vocabulary, book exposures, and open-ended discussions in preschool
classrooms; McGill-Franzen, Allington, Yokoi, & Brooks, 1999,
focusing on teachers' talk before, during, and after book reading with urban kindergarten students) have shown equally important results. Yaden, Madrigal, and Tam (2003) have shown
impressive results with a book loan program designed for immigrant Latino students and their families. Not only did the program increase the use of conventional print materials, but it
also impacted parent-child interactions around books and attitudes toward literacy. In short, although many children from
diverse socioeconomic, ethnic, racial, and language groups may
not come to school with literacy experiences and print environments that look like those found in most schools, there is good
evidence that strategically designed and implemented programs
can ensure later school success.

CONCLUSIONS

Several trends are apparent in the review of the early childhood
area, especially with respect to students from diverse cultural
and linguistic backgrounds. For example, continuing an already
existing pattern, diversity among the population of the country is increasing, and continues to be related to achievement
differences. Risk factors, which characterize many students of
diverse backgrounds in urban school settings, continue to show
a strong relationship to later school success. At the same time,
researchers have begun to caution that there is a great deal of
heterogeneity both within groups, and at the individual level.
Broad generalizations about subgroups in the population based
on language, culture, SES, and related factors needs to be carefully qualified and trustworthy to the extent that it is empirically
verified.

Another trend that is evident is the strong national, state, and local focus on education in general, and early childhood literacy in particular. Recognition of the importance of this developmental period and of the importance of literacy for later school achievement has helped to sustain this focus. The various research syntheses and reports described in this chapter have been valuable but at times have neglected the specific issues related to specific factors such as ethnicity, race, language, and culture. Although many of the large-scale early childhood intervention programs have included and targeted diverse learners, the results have been less successful than smaller-scale locally implemented programs. This raises the issue of whether attempts at large-scale interventions that can be packaged and transported are equally successful with all groups in all contexts, or whether attention to local contextual variables specific to individual communities and populations need to be accounted for. It may be that general principles might hold across contexts, but that program implementation might need to incorporate sensitivity to the specific context under consideration. The issue might not be so much, "What works"? as "What works best, with what groups, in which context, using which specific methods"? It appears that as noted earlier, recent research syntheses dispel the notion that there are optimal, educational situations which work for all children at all times but, rather, there are differentiated learning situations which work for certain children under specific circumstances

A related issue has to do with how the results of intervention efforts are assessed. There are significant problems in the area of assessment when learners are very young, are not English speakers, or come from backgrounds that may not provide experiences and background knowledge that are tapped by existing assessments. Important program effects may be overlooked, whereas at the same time accurate developmental information needed for program implementation may be inaccurate or invalid. There is significant work that remains to be done in the area of assessment development.

Although the current investment in early childhood research and education is commendable, it needs to reflect the changing population. Not only should it reflect the variation introduced by differences in ethnicity, race, culture, SES, and other sociocultural variables, it also should address the variation introduced by the specific local communities and contexts when programs are implemented. Although there are advantages to developing and implementing programs that can be easily packaged and scaled up, there may be a price in terms of impact that will favor some groups and some settings more than others.

References

August, D., & Hakuta, K. (Eds.). (1997). *Improving schooling for language-minority children: A research agenda.* Washington, DC: National Academy Press.

Baker, L, Allen, J.,Schokley, B., Pelligrini, A. D., Galda, L, & Stahl, S. (1996). Connecting school and home: Constructing partnerships to foster reading development. In L. Baker, P. Afflerbach, & D. Reinking (Eds.), *Developing engaged readers in school and home communities* (pp. 21–41). Mahwah, NJ: Lawrence Erlbaum Associates, Inc.

Bianchi, S., and McArthur, E. (1993). Characteristics of children who are "behind" in school. Paper presented at the Annual Meeting of the American Statistical Association, San Francisco, CA.

Bowman, B. T., Donovan, M. S., & Burns, M. (Eds.). (2001). *Eager to learn: Educating our preschoolers.* Washington, DC: National Academy Press.

Bransford, J. D., Brown, A. L., & Cocking, R. R. (1999). *How people learn: Brain, mind, experience, and school.* Washington, DC: National Academy Press.

Bronfenbrenner, U. P., McClelland, E., Wethington, E., Moen, P., & Ceci, S. J. (1996). *The state of Americans.* New York: Free Press.

Bus, A. G., van Ijzendoorn, M. H., & Pellegrini, A. D. (1995). Joint book reading makes for success in learning to read: A meta-analysis on intergenerational transmission of literacy. *Review of Educational Research, 65,* 1–21.

Carpenter, C. D. (1994). Review of *Language Assessment Scales, Reading and Writing Supplement to the eleventh mental measurements yearbook.* Lincoln: University of Nebraska Press.

Chesterfield, K. B. (1985). Review of *Language Assessment Battery. The Ninth Mental Measurements Yearbook* (Vol. I). Lincoln: University of Nebraska Press.

Clay, M. M. (2002). *An observation survey of early literacy achievement* (2nd ed.). Portsmouth, NH: Heinemann Education.

Clark, C., O'Brien, R., & D'Elio, M. A. (2003). *Head Start FACES 2000: A whole-child perspective on program performance: Fourth progress report.* Washington, DC: U.S. Department of Health & Human Services, Administration for Children and Families, Child Outcomes Research and Evaluation and the Head Start Bureau.

Clay, M. M. (2002). *An observation survey of early literacy achievement* (2nd ed.) Portsmouth, NH: Heinemann.

Crocker, L. (1998). Review of the *Woodcock-Muñoz Language Survey. The Thirteenth Mental Measurements Yearbook.* Lincoln: University of Nebraska Press.

Cummins, J. (2000). *Language, power, and pedagogy: Bilingual children in the crossfire.* Clevedon, UK: Multilingual Matters Ltd.

Dawson, D. (1991). "Family structure and children's health and well-being: Data from the 1988 National Health Interview Survey on Child Health." *Journal of Marriage and the Family, 53,* 573–584.

DeBruin-Parecki, A. (1999). *Assessing adult/child storybook reading practices* (Tech. Rep. No. #2-004). Ann Arbor: University of Michigan, Center for the Improvement of Early Reading Achievement.

Demanding results (1999, January 11). Quality counts 1999: Rewarding results, punishing failure. *Education Week, 18,* p. 5.

Delgado-Gaitan, C. (1990). *Literacy for empowerment: The role of parents in children's education.* New York: Falmer Press.

Delgado-Gaitan, C. (1996). Parenting in two generations of Mexican American families. *International Journal of Behavioral Development, 16*(3), 409–427.

Denton, K., & West, J. (2002). *Children's reading and mathematics achievement in kindergarten and first grade.* (NCES 2002-125). U.S. Department of Education, NCES. Washington, DC: U.S. Government Printing Office.

Dickinson, D. K. (2002). Shifting images of developmentally appropriate practice as seen through different lenses. *Educational Researcher, 31,* 26–32.

Dickinson, D. K. (2003). Are measures of "global quality" sufficient? *Educational Researcher, 32,* 27-28.

Dickinson, D. K., & Chaney, C. (1997). *Profile of early literacy development.* Newton, MA: Education Development Center.

Dickinson, D. K., McCabe, A., & Sprague, K. (2001). *Teacher Rating of Oral Language and Literacy (TROLL): A research-based tool* (Tech. Rep. No. #3-016). Ann Arbor: University of Michigan, Center for the Improvement of Early Reading Achievement.

Downing, J., Schaefer, B., Ayres, J. D. (1993). *LARR test of emergent literacy.* Windsor, Berkshire, UK: NFER-Nelson Publishing Company Ltd.

Duke, N. K., & Purcell-Gates, V. (2003). Genres at home and at school: Bridging the known to the new. *Reading Teacher, 57*(1), 30-37.

Elley, W. (1997). *In praise of incidental learning* (CELA Rep. No. 10002). Albany: University at Albany, State University of New York.

Entwisle, D. R., and Alexander, K. L. 1995. "A parent's economic shadow: Family structure versus family resources as influences on early school achievement." *Journal of Marriage and the Family, 57,* 399-409.

Fears, D. (2003, August 25). Latinos or Hispanics? A debate about identity. *Washington Post,* p. A01.

Federal Interagency Forum on Child and Family Statistics. (2002). *America's children: Key national indicators of well-being, 2002).* Washington, DC: US Government Printing Office.

Flores, B. (1990). *Children's sociopsychogenesis of literacy and biliteracy.* Proceedings of the Research Symposium on Limited English Proficient Students' Issues (1st, Washington, DC, September 10-12, 1990). (ERIC Document Reproduction Service No. ED341268)

Garcia, E. E. (1993). The education of linguistically and culturally diverse children. In B. Spodek (Ed.), *Handbook on the education of young children* (pp. 372-384). New York: Macmillan.

Garcia, G. E. (2000). Bilingual children's reading. In M. L. Kamil, P. B. Mosenthal, P. D. Pearson, & R. Barr (Eds.), *Handbook of reading research,* (Vol. III), (pp. 813-834). Mahwah, NJ: Lawrence Erlbaum Associates, Inc.

Gee, J. P. (1989). Literacy, discourse, and linguistics: Essays by James Paul Gee [Special Issue]. *Journal of Education, 171*(1).

Goldenberg, C. (2004). Literacy for all children in the increasingly diverse schools of the United States. In R. B. Ruddell & N. J. Unrau (Eds.), *Theoretical models and processes of reading* (5th ed., pp. 1636-1666). Newark, DE: International Reading Association.

Goldenberg, C., Reese, L., & Gallimore, R. (1992). Effects of literacy materials from school on Latino children's home experiences and early reading achievement. *American Journal of Education, 100,* 497-536.

Haber, L. (1985). Review of *Language Assessment Scales. The Ninth Mental Measurements Yearbook Volume I.* Lincoln: University of Nebraska Press.

Heath, S. B. (1983). *Ways with words: Language, life, and work in communities and classrooms.* Cambridge: Cambridge University Press.

Hedberg, N. L. (1995). Review of *Language Assessment Scales—Oral. The Twelfth Mental Measurements Yearbook.* Lincoln: University of Nebraska Press.

Hudelson, S., Poynor, L., & Wolfe, P. (2003). Teaching bilingual and ESL children and adolescents. In J. Flood, D. Lapp, J. R. Squire, & J. M. Jensen (Eds.), *Handbook of research on teaching the English Language Arts* (2nd ed., pp. 421-434). Mahwah, NJ: Erlbaum.

Jiménez, R. (2004). Literacy and the identity development of Latina/o students. In R. B. Ruddell & N. J. Unrau (Eds.), *Theoretical models and processes of reading* (5th ed., pp. 201-239). Newark, DE: International Reading Association.

Kaderavek, J. N., & Sulzby, E. (1999). *Issues in emergent literacy for children with language impairments* (Tech. Rep. #2-002). Ann

Arbor: University of Michigan, Center for the Improvement of Early Reading Achievement.

Kao, C. (1998). Review of the *Woodcock-Mu noz Language Survey. The Thirteenth Mental Measurements yearbook.* Lincoln: University of Nebraska Press.

Kao, G. 1999. Psychological well-being and educational achievement among immigrant youth. In D. J. Heinadez (Ed.), *Children of immigrants: Health, adjustment, and public assistance* (pp. 410-477). Washington, DC: National Academy Press.

Kindler, A. (2002). *Survey of states' limited English proficiency students and available educational programs and services: 2000-2001 summary report.* Washington, DC: National Clearinghouse for English Language Acquisition and Language Instruction Educational Programs.

Kozol, J. (1991). *Savage inequalities: Children in America's schools.* New York: Crown.

Lambert, R. G. (2003). Considering purpose and intended use when making evaluations of assessments: A response to Dickinson. *Educational Researcher, 32,* 23-26.

Leslie, L., & Caldwell, J. (1995). *The qualitative reading inventory.* Glenview, IL: Scott Foresman.

Lesar, S., Espinosa, L., & Diaz, R. (1997). Maternal teaching behaviors of preschool children in Hispanic families: Does a home intervention program make a difference? *Journal of Research in Childhood Education, 11,* 163-171.

Llagas, C., & Snyder, T. D. (2003). *Status and trends in the education of Hispanics.* Washington, DC: US Department of Education, National Center for Education Statistics.

Lopez, E. A. (2001). Review of the *IDEA Oral Language Proficiency Test. The Fourteenth Mental Measurements Yearbook.* Lincoln: University of Nebraska Press.

Madrigal, P., Cubillas, C., Yaden, D., Tam, A., & Brassell, D. (1999). *Creating a book loan program for inner-city Latino parents* (CIERA Tech. Rep. No. 2-003). Ann Arbor: University of Michigan School of Education, Center for the Improvement of Early Reading Achievement.

McGill-Franzen, A., Lanford, C., & Adams, E. (2002). Learning to be literate: A comparison of five urban early childhood programs. *Journal of Educational Psychology, 94*(3), 443-464.

McGill-Franzen, A., Allington, R. L., Yokoi, L., & Brooks, G. (1999). Putting books in the room seems necessary but not sufficient. *Journal of Educational Research, 93,* 67-74.

McLanahan, S. S., & Sandefur, G. (1994). *Growing up with a single parent: What hurts, what helps?* Cambridge, MA: Harvard University Press.

Meisels, S. J. (1994). Designing meaningful measurements for early childhood. In B. L. Mallory & R. S. New (Eds.), *Diversity and developmentally appropriate practices: Challenges for early childhood education* (pp. 202-222). New York: Teachers College Press.

Meisels, S. J. (1999). Assessing readiness. In R. C. Pianta & M. J. Cox (Eds.), *The transition to kindergarten* (pp. 39-66). Baltimore, MD: Paul Brookes Publishing Co.

Meisels, S. J., & Piker, R. (2001). *An analysis of early literacy assessments used for instruction* (CIERA Rep. No. #2-013). Ann Arbor: University of Michigan, Center for the Improvement of Early Reading Achievement.

Michigan Department of Early Literacy Committee (1998). *Michigan Literacy Progress Profile.* Lansing, MI: Department of Education.

National Council of La Raza. (2001). *Beyond the census: Hispanics and an American agenda.* Washington, DC: National Council of La Raza.

National Reading Panel (2000). *Teaching children to read: An evidence-based assessment of the scientific research literature on reading and its implications for reading instruction: Reports of the subgroups.* Washington, DC: National Institute of Child Health and Development.

Neuman, S. B. (1999). Books made a difference: A study of access to literacy. *Reading Research Quarterly, 34,* 286–311.

Nord, C. W., Zill, N., Prince, C., Clarke, S., & Ventura, S. (1994). Developing an index of educational risk from health and social characteristics known at birth. *Bulletin of the New York Academy of Medicine, 71*(2), 167–87.

O'Brien, R. W., D'Elio, M. A., Vaden-Kiernan, M., Magee, C., Younoszai, T., Keane, M. J., Connell, D C, & Hailey, L. (2002). *A descriptive study of Head Start families: FACES Technical Reports, Parts I and II.* Washington, D C: U.S. Department of Health & Human Services, Administration on Children, Youth & Families, Commissioner's Office of Research & Evaluation and the Head Start Bureau.

Pallas, A., Natriello, G., & McDill, E. (1989). The changing nature of the disadvantaged population: Current dimensions and future trends. *Educational Researcher, 18,* 16–22.

Pappas, C. C. (1993). Is narrative primary? Some insights from kindergartners pretend readings of stories and information books. *Journal of Reading Behavior, 25,* 97–129.

Paris, A. H., & Paris, S. G. (2001). *Children's comprehension of narrative picture books* (Tech. Rep. No. #3-012). Ann Arbor: University of Michigan, Center for the Improvement of Early Reading Achievement.

Phillips, L. M., Norris, S. P., & Mason, J. M. (1996). Longitudinal effects of early literacy concepts on reading achievement: A kindergarten intervention and five-year follow up. *Journal of Literacy Research, 28*(1), 173–195.

Pressley, M. (2002). Effective beginning reading instruction. *Journal of Literacy Research, 34*(2), 165–188.

Purcell–Gates, V. (1995). *Other people's words: The cycle of low literacy.* Cambridge, MA: Harvard University Press.

Purcell-Gates, V. (1996). Stories, coupons, and the *TV Guide*: Relationships between home literacy experiences and emergent literacy knowledge. *Reading Research Quarterly, 31*(4), 406–428.

Purcell-Gates, V., McIntyre, E., & Freppon, P. (1995). Learning written storybook language in school. *American Educational Research Journal, 32,* 659–685.

Reid, D. K., Hresko, W. P., Hammill, D. D. (2001). *Test of early reading ability* (3rd ed.). Austin, TX: Pro-Ed., Inc.

Rumberger, R. W., & Larson, K. A. (1998). Toward explaining differences in educational achievement among Mexican American language-minority students. *Sociology of Education, 71,* 69–93.

Sameroff, A., Seifer, R., Barocas, R., Zax, M., & Greenspan, S. (1987). Intelligence quotient scores of 4-year-old children: Socioenvironmental risk factors. *Pediatrics, 79,* 343–350.

Sayeski, K. L., Burgess, K. A., Pianta, R. C., & Lloyd, J. W. (2001). Literacy behaviors of preschool children participating in an early intervention program (CIERA Tech. Rep. No. #2-014). Ann Arbor: University of Michigan, School of Education.

Scarborough, H. S., & Dobrich, W. (1994). On the efficacy of reading to preschoolers. *Developmental Review 14*(3), 245–302.

Schmidley, A. D. (2000). US Census Bureau, Current population reports, Series P23-206, *Profile of the foreign born population in the United States: 2000.* Washington, DC: US Government Printing Office.

Schweinhart, L., & Weikart, D. P. (1993). Success by empowerment: The High/Scope Perry Preschool study through age 27. *Young Children, 49,* 54–58.

Shellenberger, S. (1985). Review of *Bilingual Syntax Measure II. The Ninth Mental Measurements Yearbook Volume I.* Lincoln: University of Nebraska Press.

Shonkoff, J. P., & Phillips, D. A. (2000). (Eds.). *From neurons to neighborhoods: The science of early childhood development.* Washington, DC: National Academy Press.

Snow, C. E., & Ninio, A. (1986). The contracts of literacy: What children learn from learning to read books. In W. H. Teale & E. Sulzby (Eds.), *Emergent literacy: Writing and reading* (pp. 116–138). Norwood, NJ: Ablex Publishing Corporation.

Snow, C. E., Burns, M. S., & Griffin, P. (1998). *Preventing reading difficulties in young children.* Washington, DC: National Academy Press.

St. Pierre, R., Ricciuti, A., Tao, F, Creps, C., Kumagawa, T., & Ross, W. (2001). *Executive summary: Third national Even Start evaluation: Description of projects and participants.* Washington, DC: U.S. Department of Education, Office of the Under Secretary, Planning and Evaluation Service, Elementary and Secondary Division.

St. Pierre, R., Ricciuti, A, Tao, F., Creps, Kumagawa, T., & Ross, W. (2001). *Executive summary: Third Even Start evaluation: Description of projects and participants.* U.S. Department of Education, Office of the Under Secretary, Planning and Evaluation Service, Elementary and Secondary Division. [see p. 47]

Sulzby, E. (1985). Children's emergent reading of favorite storybooks: A developmental study. *Reading Research Quarterly, 20,* 458–481.

Sulzby, E., & Teale, B. H. (2003). The development of the young child and the emergence of literacy. *Handbook of research on teaching the English language arts* (2nd ed., pp. 300–314). Mahwah, NJ: Lawrence Erlbaum Associates.

Tabors, P., & Snow, C. E. (2002). Young bilingual children and early literacy development. In S. B. Neuman & D. Dickinson (Eds.), *Handbook of Early Literacy Research* (pp. 159–178). New York: The Guilford Press.

Taylor, D., & Dorsey-Gaines, C. (1988). *Growing up literate: Learning from inner-city families.* Portsmouth, NH: Heinemann.

Teale, W. H. (1986). Home background and young children's literacy development. In W. H. Teale & E. Sulzby (Eds.), *Emergent literacy: Writing and reading* (pp. 173–206). Norwood, NJ: Ablex.

Teale, W. H. (1987). Emergent literacy: Reading and writing development in early childhood. In J. E. Readence, R. S Baldwin, J. P. Konopak, & H. Newton (Eds.), *Research in literacy: Merging—perspective: Thirty-sixth Yearbook of the National Reading Conference* (pp. 45–74). Rochester, NY: National Reading Conference.

U.S. Census Bureau. (2000, March). *Current population survey, the Hispanic population in the United States.* Washington, DC: U.S. Government Printing Office.

U.S. Census Bureau. (2001). Number of poor and poverty rate by race and Hispanic origin: 2001. Retrieved August 1, 2003, from http://www.census.gov/hhes/poverty/poverty01/table2.pdf

U.S. Department of Health and Human Services (2000). *Leading the way: characteristics and early experiences of selected Early Head Start programs* (Executive Summary). (Publication No. 0439.00). Retrieved May 5, 2005 from Head Start Information & Publication Center, Catalog of Head Start Materials. Access: http://www.acf.hhs.gov/programs/opre/ehs/ehsresrch/reports/imp acts_exesum/impacts_exesum_title.html

U.S. Department of Health & Human Services (2001). *Head Start FACES: Longitudinal findings on program performance—Third Progress Report.* Retrieved May 5, 2005, from Head Start Information & Publication Center, Catalog of Head Start Materials. Access: http://www.acf.hhs.gov/programs/core/pubs_report/faces/meas_99_intro.html

U.S. Department of Commerce, Bureau of the Census. (2000). *Household relationship and living arrangements of children under 18 years, by age, sex, race, Hispanic origin, and metropolitan residence.* Washington, DC: U.S. Bureau of the Census.

U.S. Department of Commerce, Bureau of the Census. (2000). *Poverty in the United States: 2000*. Washington, D. C.: U.S Bureau of the Census.

U.S. Department of Education (2001). *PL 107-110: No Child Left Behind Act of 200*. Retrieved on August 5, 2003, from http://www.ed.gov/legislation/ESEA02/

U.S. Department of Health and Human Services (2001). *Promoting family literacy through Headstart* (Publication No. 0041.00). Retrieved May 5, 2005, from Head Start Information & Publication Center, Catalog of Head Start Materials. Access. http://www.bmcc.edu/Headstart/Literacy/

U.S. Department of Education, National Center for Education Statistics, (2002). Common Core of Data (CCD), "Public Elementary/Secondary School Universe Survey," 2001-02, and "State Non-fiscal Survey of Public Elementary/Secondary Education," 2001-02. Retrieved August 1, 2003, from http://nces.ed.gov/pubs2003/overview03/table_11.asp#f1

U.S. Department of Education, National Center for Education Statistics, (1998). *Kindergarten Class of 1998-99*. Washington, DC: US Government Printing Office.

U.S. Department of Education, National Center for Education Statistics. (2001). *Entering kindergarten: A portrait of American children when they begin school: Findings from The Condition of Education 2000*. Nicholas Zill and Jerry West, NCES. 2001-035 Washington, DC: U.S. Government Printing Office.

U.S. Department of Health & Human Services (2002). *A descriptive study of Head Start families: FACES Technical Report I*, Retrieved from Office of Planning, Research & Evaluation website. Access: http://www.acf.hhs.gov/programs/opre/hs/faces/reports/technical_report/technicalreport.pdf

U.S. Department of Education, National Center for Education Statistics, (2003). *The condition of education, 2003—Special analysis, reading—Young children's achievement and classroom experiences*. NCES 2003-067 Washington, DC: U.S. Government Printing Office.

U.S. Department of Health & Human Services (2003). *A whole child perspective on program performance: Fourth progress report—Fourth Progress Report*. Retrieved from Office of Planning, Research & Evaluation website. Access: http://www.acf.hhs.gov/programs/opre/hs/faces/reports/faces004thprogress.pdf

U.S. Department of Education. (2003). *Program Resource Manual: Even Start Family Literacy*. Washington, DC.: Planning and Evaluation Service, Elementary and Secondary Division.

Valdez-Menchaca, M. C., & Whitehurst, G. J. (1992). Accelerating language development through picturebook reading: A systematic extension to Mexican day care. *Developmental Psychology, 28,* 1106-1114.

Valero, A. (2002). Emergent literacy development among Latino students in a rural preschool classroom. *Dissertation Abstracts International, 63*(12A), p. 4217.

van den Broek, P. (1999). The role of television viewing in the development of reading comprehension. Retrieved May 6, 2005, from: CIERA Archive Web site:

van Kleeck, A., Stahl, S. A., Bauer, E. B. (Eds.). (2003). *On reading books to children: Parents and teachers*. Mahwah, NJ: Lawrence Erlbaum.

Wasik, B. A., & Bond, M. A. (2001). Beyond the pages of a book: Interactive book reading and language development in preschool classrooms. *Journal of Educational Psychology, 93,* 243-250.

Weber, R. M. & Longhi-Chirlin, T. (2001). Beginning in English: The growth of linguistic and literate abilities in Spanish-speaking first graders. *Reading Research and Instruction, 41,* 19-50.

West, J., & Brick, J. M. (1991 August). *The national household education survey: A look at young children at risk*. Proceedings of the Social Statistics Section, Meetings of the American Statistical Association, Anaheim, CA.

West, J., Denton, K., & Germino-Hausken, E. (2000). *America's Kindergartners* (NCES 2000-070). U.S. Department of Education, NCES, Washington, DC: U.S. Government Printing Office.

West, J., Denton, K., & Reaney, L. M. (2001). *The Kindergarten Year*. (NCES. 2001-023). U.S. Department of Education, NCES Washington, DC: U.S. Government Printing Office.

Whitehurst, G. J., Falco, F., Lonigan, C. J., Fischel, J. E., DeBaryshe, B. D., Valdez-Menchaca, M. C., & Caufield, M. (1998). Accelerating language development through picture-book reading. *Developmental Psychology, 24,* 555-558.

Whitehurst, G. J., & Lonigan, C. J. (1998). Child development and emergent literacy. *Child Development, 69,* 848-872.

Yaden, D. B. (2001). An emergent literacy preschool intervention with inner-city children. In F. Lamb-Parker, J. Hagen, & Ruth Robinson (Eds.), *Head Start's Fifth National Conference, Developmental and contextual transitions of Children and Families: Implications for Research Policy and Practice* (pp. 339-344). New York: Columbia University's Mailman School of Public Health, Heilbrunn Center for Population and Family Health and the Society for Research in Child Development.

Yaden, D. B., & Brassell, D. (2002). Enhancing early literacy with Spanish-speaking preschoolers in the inner city: Overcoming the odds. In C. Roller (Ed.), *Comprehensive reading instruction across the grade levels* (pp. 20-39). Newark, NJ: International Reading Association.

Yaden, D., Madrigal, P., & Tam, A. (2003). Access to books and beyond: Creating and learning from a book lending program for Latino families in the inner city. In G. G. Garcia (Ed.), *English learners: Reading the highest level of English literacy* (pp. 357-386). Newark, DE: International Reading Association.

Yaden, D. H., Rowe, D. W., & McGillivray, L. (2000). Emergent literacy: a matter (polyphony) of perspectives. In M. Kamil, P. B. Mosenthal, P. D. Pearson, & R. Barr (Eds.), *Handbook of reading research, Vol. III*. Mahwah, N.J: Lawrence Erlbaum Associates, Inc.

Yaden, D. B., Jr., Smolkin, L., & Conlon, A. (1989). Preschoolers' questions about pictures, print convention, and story text during reading aloud at home. *Reading Research Quarterly, 24,* 188-214.

Yaden, D. B., Jr., Smolkin, L, & MacGillivray, L. (1993). A psychogenetic perspective on children's understanding about letter associations during alphabet book readings. *Journal of Reading Behavior, 25,* 43-68.

Yaden, D. B., Tam, A., Madrigal, P., Brassell, D., Massa, J., Altamirano, L. S., & Armendariz, J. (2000). Early literacy for inner-city children: The effects of reading and writing interventions in English and Spanish during the preschool years. *The Reading Teacher, 54*(2), 186-189.

Young, B. A. (2002). *Public school student, staff, and graduate counts by state: School year 2000-01*. NCES 2002-348. Washington, DC: National Center for Education Statistics, U.S. Department of Education.

Xiang, Z., Schweinhart, L. J., Hohmann, C., Smith, C., Storer, E., & Oden, S. (2000). *Points of light: Third year report of the Michigan School Readiness evaluation*. Ypsilanti, MI: High/Scope Educational Research Foundation.

Zill, N. (1996a). Family change and student achievement: What we have learned, what it means for schools. In A. Booth & J. P. Dunn (Eds), *Family-school links: How do they affect educational outcomes?* Hillsdale, NJ: Lawrence Erlbaum Associates.

Zill, N. (1996b). Parental schooling and children's health. *Public Health Reports* 111, 34-43.

Zill, N., & West, J. (2000). *Entering Kindergarten.* NCES 2001–035. U.S. Department of Education, NCES. Washington, DC: U.S. Government Printing Office.

Zill, N., Collins, M., West, J., and Germino-Hausken, E. (1995). *Approaching kindergarten: A look at preschoolers in the United States.* NCES 95–280. Washington, DC: U.S. Department of Education, NCES.)

Zill, N., Resnick, G., Kim, K., McKey, R. H., Clark, C., Pai-Samant, S., Connell, D., Vaden-Kiernan, M., O'Brien, R., & D'Elio, M. A. (2001). *Head Start FACES: Longitudinal findings on program performance: Third progress report.* Washington, DC: U.S. Department of Health & Human Services, Administration on Children, Youth & Families, Commissioner's Office of Research & Evaluation and the Head Start Bureau.

·11·

THE DEVELOPMENT OF YOUNG CHILDREN'S EARLY NUMBER AND OPERATION SENSE AND ITS IMPLICATIONS FOR EARLY CHILDHOOD EDUCATION[1]

Arthur J. Baroody
Meng-lung Lai
University of Illinois at Urbana-Champaign

Kelly S. Mix
Michigan State University

Survey responses such as "I don't do mathematics" and "Young children shouldn't do mathematics... it's not appropriate" indicate that many early childhood teachers feel uncomfortable about teaching mathematics (Copley, 2004a, p. 403). Indeed, early childhood educators have long viewed young children and mathematics education like water and oil, as things that do not mix. As a result, they have tended to focus on literacy and to overlook numeracy. Balfanz (1999) observed that this has not always been the case. Indeed, "some of the founding figures of early childhood education, like Fredrick Froebel and Maria Montessori,... advanced the notion that young children are capable of complex mathematical thought and enjoy using mathematics to explore and understand the world around them" (p. 3). Based on their careful observations of children in natural settings, both Froebel and Montessori incorporated rich mathematical experiences into their early childhood programs. However, between 1820 and 1920, the influence of such pedagogues was contested by social theorists, including leading psychologists and educators of the era, and was then eclipsed by them (see Balfanz, 1999, for a detailed account).

In recent years, though, attitudes toward teaching mathematics to young children, including preschoolers, again has changed dramatically. For example, the National Council of Teachers of Mathematics (NCTM, 2000) concluded that "the foundation for children's mathematical development is established in the earliest years" (p. 73), and, along with the National Association for the Education of Young Children (NAEYC), now takes the position that "high-quality, developmentally

[1]This chapter is based, in part, on a keynote address given by the first author at the Lesley University Early Childhood Institute, November 17, 2003. Support for the preparation of this chapter was provided, in part, by a grant from the National Science Foundation (BCS-0111829), Department of Education (R305K050082), and the Spencer Foundation (200400033). The opinions expressed are solely those of the authors and do not necessarily reflect the position, policy, or endorsement of the National Science Foundation, Department of Education, or the Spencer Foundation. We thank Dr. Herbert P. Ginsburg and another anonymous reviewer for their most helpful comments on an earlier draft of this chapter.

appropriate mathematics education for children 3-6 is vital" (Clements, Copple, & Hyson, 2002, p. 1; see also http://www. naeyc.org/resources/position).

In Part I of this chapter, we discuss key reasons for this renewed and intense national interest in early childhood mathematics education. This includes summarizing the findings of recent research that have helped propel the mathematics education of young children into the spotlight. In Part II, we discuss what recent research on number and operation sense suggests about the nature of early childhood mathematics education. Number and operation sense are an intuitive feel for how numbers are related and behave. It stems from well-interconnected knowledge about numbers and how they operate or interact.

A CASE FOR EARLY CHILDHOOD MATHEMATICS EDUCATION

In our increasingly technology- and information-based society, *mathematical proficiency* has become as important a gatekeeper as literacy. Despite the often-heated debate about reforming mathematics instruction, sometimes dubbed the "math wars" (see Baroody, 2004b, and Ralston, 2004, for analyses), there is considerable agreement that the aim of mathematics instruction from preschool to college should be mathematical proficiency (Kilpatrick, Swafford, & Findell, 2001). Such proficiency entails *conceptual understanding, computational fluency, strategic mathematical thinking*, and a *productive disposition*. Conceptual understanding can be thought of as a web of connections (e.g., Ginsburg, 1977; Hiebert & Carpenter, 1992). Unlike rote knowledge that can be applied only to familiar tasks (*routine expertise*), meaningful knowledge (*adaptive expertise*) can be flexibly adapted and appropriately applied to learning new concepts or skills or to solving novel problems (Hatano, 1988, 2003; cf. Wertheimer, 1945). In a real sense, then, conceptual understanding is a key basis for the other aspects of mathematical proficiency (Baroody, 2003). Computational fluency involves using basic skills appropriately and flexibly, as well as efficiently (i.e., quickly and accurately). Conceptual understanding can aid appropriate and efficient use of skills and is probably critical to their flexible use. Strategic mathematical thinking includes creative problem solving and adaptive reasoning, both of which are facilitated by a rich web of interconnected knowledge.[2] A productive disposition includes interest and the confidence to solve challenging problems, both of which are more likely if mathematics makes sense to a child. Furthermore, there is considerable agreement these aspects of mathematical proficiency should be fostered in an *intertwined manner* (Kilpatrick et al., 2001).

However, it has long been clear that our public schools, particularly many inner-city and rural schools, do not adequately foster mathematical proficiency, especially among children at risk for school failure (e.g., those from low-income families and those with learning difficulties), and that serious reform is necessary (e.g., Carnegie Forum on Education and the Economy, 1986; McNight et al., 1987; National Commission on Excellence in Education, 1983). Indeed, international studies indicate U.S. students' mathematical achievement lags significantly behind as early as first grade (e.g., Stigler, Lee, & Stevenson, 1990). Concern about the quality of mathematics instruction, economic competitiveness, and equity (e.g., equal opportunity to develop mathematical proficiency and to obtain good jobs) has led, for instance, the NCTM (1989, 2000) and the National Research Council (Kilpatrick et al., 2001) to advocate fostering the mathematical proficiency of *all* children (e.g., Baroody, 2004d; Fuson, 2004; Tate, 1997; Thornton & Bley, 1994).

How, though, are concerns about mathematical proficiency and equity related to early childhood education? Consider three important and interrelated findings from recent research (for detailed reviews, see, e.g., Clements, Sarama, & DiBiase, 2004; Ginsburg, Klein, & Starkey, 1998):

1. Preschoolers can develop a wealth of *informal* mathematical knowledge. (Informal knowledge is gleaned from everyday activities in what are not normally considered instructional settings—such as home, playground, grocery store, shopping mall, family car, or park—[Gelman & Massey, 1987; Ginsburg, 1977; Ginsburg, Cannon, Eisenband, & Pappas, 2006; Pound, 1999]. Such knowledge is usually represented nonverbally or verbally and often learned incidentally. In contrast, formal mathematical knowledge is school taught, largely represented in written form, and frequently the result of deliberate efforts by teachers and students. The distinction between informal and formal knowledge should be thought of as a continuum and, thus, in some cases can be quite fuzzy. Nevertheless, there is now widespread use of the term *informal knowledge* in the U.S. and elsewhere. For instance, within the Directorate for Education and Human Resources, the National Science Foundation has a unit called the *Elementary, Secondary, and Informal Sciences Division*, which includes in its mission promoting the infrastructure and resources needed to improve pre-K science, technology, engineering, and mathematics education.)

2. This informal knowledge is a critical basis for understanding formal mathematics, successfully mastering and retaining basic skills, devising and applying effective problem-solving and reasoning strategies, and developing a productive disposition.

---

[2]*Strategic mathematical thinking* encompasses two aspects of mathematical proficiency identified by Kilpatrick et al. (2001), namely strategic competence and adaptive reasoning. We will not distinguish between these two competencies and will use the more general term *strategic mathematical thinking* for two reasons. One is that the two components are intricately interrelated. For example, logical reasoning is a key strategy for solving problems. Another reason is that mathematical thinking involves an exploratory side as well as the logical side (Clements & Battista, 1992). In *Adding It Up* (Kilpatrick et al., 2001), the importance of deductive reasoning is correctly emphasized. Indeed, adaptive reasoning is defined in terms of this type of reasoning. However, little mention is made of other key types of mathematical reasoning—those that comprise the exploratory side of mathematics, namely intuitive and inductive reasoning. Strategic mathematical thinking is a broad term that encompasses all types of mathematical reasoning, as well as other processes such as problem solving, conjecturing, and justifying.

3. Within as well as across areas of knowledge, preschoolers' informal knowledge can differ significantly among and within social classes, medical conditions, and other categories.

These findings and their implications for early childhood mathematics instruction are discussed in turn.

Finding 1: Preschoolers' Surprising Informal Knowledge

Over the course of the twentieth century, psychologists came to dramatically different conclusions about the nature of young children's mathematical competence and its basis. After reviewing these two changes in the conventional wisdom regarding children's mathematical knowledge, we draw some theoretical conclusions and discuss their educational implications.

Changes in the conventional wisdom regarding the nature of preschoolers' informal knowledge. Like a pendulum, the conventional wisdom about young children's number and arithmetic competence has swung from extremely pessimistic to extremely optimistic and then back toward the middle.

Early Pessimistic Views. For most of the century, psychologists held a pessimistic view and focused on what children *can't do.* This view reinforced the rationale for narrow and limited mathematics instruction in early childhood. For example, William James (1890) described an infant's perception of the world as a "great, blooming, buzzing confusion." Geary (1996) facetiously observed that such a description better characterizes the parents of newborns than the newborns themselves.

Edward L. Thorndike (1922) further concluded that young children were so mathematically inept that "little is gained by [doing] arithmetic before grade 2, though there are many arithmetic facts that can [be memorized by rote] in grade 1" (p. 198). He epitomized the social theorists' assumption that "young children started school with no prior mathematical knowledge or experience and that limited instruction" on the first 10 numbers, simple addition and subtraction, and recognition of basic shapes was sufficient for the early grades (Balfanz, 1999, p. 8). Given this perspective, it made little sense to emphasize mathematics in kindergarten and even less sense to do so in the preschool years. A minimalist mathematics curriculum is still evident and even predominant today in preschools and kindergartens (Balfanz, 1999; see also Copley, 2004a; Ginsburg, Inoue, & Seo, 1999; Hunting & Kamii, 2002).

Thorndike's (1922) work influenced early childhood mathematics instruction in another powerful way. Advocates of his associative-learning theory essentially concluded that early number and arithmetic knowledge should be learned by rote. Direct instruction and repetitive practice continue to this day to be the instructional mainstay of many parents and early childhood teachers (Ginsburg et al., 1998).

Interestingly, Thorndike's (1922) views also contributed indirectly to narrowing and limiting mathematics instruction in early childhood settings. As Copeley's (2004a) quotes at the beginning of the chapter illustrate, many social theorists and early childhood educators believed that organized mathematics instruction in early childhood was not only unnecessary but inappropriate or even harmful. That is, many feared that the direct instruction and drill advocated by Thorndike as necessary to learn basic number and arithmetic competencies would, for example, stifle creativity and interest in learning in preschoolers (and older children). Thus, social theorists recommended postponing mathematics instruction until after the beginning of formal schooling. That is, they provided early childhood educators, many of whom felt uncomfortable about mathematics (Coates & Thompson, 1999; Patton & Kokoski, 1996), a noble excuse for avoiding the topic for the most part or altogether.

Piaget's (e.g., 1965) work had several different effects. On the one hand, it helped focus attention on young children's informal knowledge. His theory underscored the key point that mathematical thinking and knowledge do not simply blossom in the school age children as a result of formal instruction (see, e.g., Ginsburg, 1977). Their genesis begins in the preschool years, indeed in infancy, with informal experiences. Piaget's (1964) mutually dependent principles of assimilation and accommodation imply that cognitive development is a gradual building or constructive process and that preschool experiences are an essential basis for understanding school taught mathematics.[3] Furthermore, the primitive reasoning of young children paves the way for more sophisticated reasoning that emerges in late childhood and adolescence.

At the height of Piaget's influence in the 1960s and 1970s, his focus on preschoolers' informal knowledge created interest in preschool mathematics education. These educational efforts focused on fostering children's logical reasoning ability, as this was thought to be the basis for constructing an understanding of number and arithmetic (see, e.g., Furth & Wachs, 1974; Gibb, & Castaneda, 1975; Maffel & Buckley, 1980; Sharp, 1969).

On the other hand, Piaget's work had the effect of limiting expectations about what young children can learn and be taught. His views (Piaget, 1965) about the abilities and capacities of young children were relatively pessimistic. For instance, he believed that preschoolers are *pre*operational thinkers, incapable of logical and systematic thinking or constructing abstract concepts (e.g., a true concept of number or understanding of arithmetic). He ridiculed attempts to accelerate the development of logical operations or concepts by means of training as the "American question" (e.g., Elkind, 1988; Hall, 1970; Philips, 1969). Piagetians argued that teaching number and arithmetic concepts before the concrete operational stage did not make

---

[3]Assimilation is the process of interpreting new information in terms of existing knowledge. Piaget (1964) considered it, not associative learning, the primary fact of mental life. For example, prior existing knowledge is probably the best predictor of whether a child will understand new content. The process of assimilation necessarily entails its complementary process accommodation. Because new information does not exactly fit existing schemata, assimilation requires these existing mental structures to change to accommodate the new information and reality. The process of accommodation enables children to construct more accurate knowledge of the world as opposed to an idiosyncratic view of it.

TABLE 11.1. Principles Underlying (Non-verbal or Verbal) Object Counting (Gelman & Gallistel, 1978)

Stable-Order Principle: Tags (nonverbal symbols or number words) must always be used in the same order when enumerating collections.
One-to-One Principle: One and only one tag must be assigned each item in a collection.
Abstraction Principle: For enumeration purposes, a collection can be composed of unlike objects.
Cardinality Principle: The last tag used in the enumeration process has special significance because, it not only labels the last item, it represents the total.
Order-Irrelevance Principle: The order in which the items of a collection are enumerated does not matter because it does not affect the cardinal value of the collection.

sense and that premature instruction was worse than no teaching at all (e.g., Hall; May & Kundert, 1997). To this day, some constructivists argue that an abstract or genuine understanding of number does not develop until children are at least 4 years of age or even older (Bermejo, 1996; Copeland, 1979; Kamii, 1985; Munn, 1998; Steffe, Cobb, & von Glasersfeld, 1988).

The Shift to a Highly Optimistic View. In the last quarter of the 20th century, psychologists adopted a highly optimistic view and focused on what children *can do* (Gelman, 1979). After establishing that posttoddlers develop a variety of mathematical competencies (see, e.g., Gelman & Gallistel, 1978; Ginsburg, 1977; Hughes, 1986; Schaeffer, Eggleston, & Scott, 1974; Wagner & Walters, 1982), researchers turned their attention to even younger preschoolers. For example, Wynn (1998) noted that "findings over the past 20 years have shown infants are sensitive to number" (p. 5). Specifically, she argued they are born with an ability to recognize and distinguish among *oneness*, *twoness*, and *threeness* and can even reason about or operate on very small numbers (e.g., recognize that one object added to another makes two and that two objects minus one is one)—all before they develop verbal-based counting competencies. Indeed, some nativists (e.g., Gelman & Meck, 1992) have argued that children are innately endowed with counting principles (see Table 11.1)—principles that allow infants to nonverbally count (using nonverbal tags or representations) and

toddlers to quickly learn number words and how to use them to count collections.

The Recent Shift to Middle Ground Views. Some research over the last 10 years indicates that nativists such as Wynn (1992a, 1998) may be too optimistic and that a more balanced view of children's informal mathematical knowledge is needed (Baroody, Benson, & Lai, 2003; Haith & Benson, 1998; Leslie, 1999; Mix, Huttenlocher, & Levine, 2002a, b; Wakeley, Rivera, & Langer, 2000a, b; Simon, 1997).

Consider, for example, the work of Janellen Huttenlocher and colleagues (e.g., Huttenlocher, Jordan, & Levine, 1994) regarding preschoolers' nonverbal addition and subtraction ability (see Figure 11.1). These researchers found that:

- Children between 2.5 and 3 years of age were successful in mentally determining sums and differences with the "intuitive numbers" (collections of one to three or possibly four items) only about 25% of the time.
- A majority of children did not succeed on even the simplest trials (1 + 1 and 2 + 1) of the nonverbal addition and subtraction task until 3 years of age.

Huttenlocher et al. concluded that, if 1.5 to 3 year olds typically cannot perform simple arithmetic operations, it is not likely infants can do so.

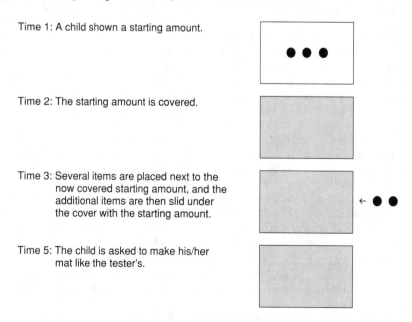

Time 1: A child shown a starting amount.

Time 2: The starting amount is covered.

Time 3: Several items are placed next to the now covered starting amount, and the additional items are then slid under the cover with the starting amount.

Time 5: The child is asked to make his/her mat like the tester's.

FIGURE 11.1. Nonverbal addition (and subtraction) task.

Two influential middle ground models are the *mental models view* (e.g., Huttenlocher et al., 1994; Mix et al., 2002a) and the *progressive abstraction view* (Resnick, 1992, 1994). Each of these models focuses on a key but different aspect of number and arithmetic development.

According to the mental models view, *how* children represent number evolves.

- **Pretransition 1: Inexact Perception-Based Representation.** Children initially represent all quantities *nonverbally* and *inexactly* using one or more perceptual cues such as area, contour length (total perimeter), density, and length (Mix et al., 2002a, b). For example, infants may represent two squares, each with sides 2 in long and a total perimeter of 16 in, as different from three squares with sides of 2 in each and a total perimeter of 24 in or two squares each with sides of 4 in and a total perimeter of 32 in.

- **Transition 1: Exact Nonverbal Representation.** Children next develop the ability to mentally represent the intuitive numbers nonverbally and *exactly* (Transition 1). Three factors may account for this transition. First, the evolution of object individuation (perceiving objects as discrete, permanent, and distinct) provides a basis for precounters to construct an understanding of one-to-one correspondence, which, in turn, provides a basis for identifying and representing collections and the groundwork for an informal understanding of numerical equivalence and number (e.g., Mix et al., 2002a). (Note that this view is consistent with Piaget's, 1965, hypothesis that one-to-one correspondence is a foundational concept of number, but unlike Piaget, an understanding of one-to-one— at least with small numbers—is seen as evolving well before 7 years of age, the onset of concrete operational thought.) Second, between 2.5 and 3.5 years of age, children begin developing the ability for symbolic representation (e.g., Huttenlocher, Jordan, & Levine, 1994). Third, another important step toward understanding number is recognizing that—like color (Sandhofer & Smith, 1999), size, and weight—it is an important basis for categorizing and, thus, identifying and comparing things (Mix et al., 2002a).

- **Transition 2: Number-Word Representation.** Transition 1 and the development of counting permit the *exact verbally based* representation of any number (Mix et al., 2002a).

Because children can represent and operate on exact but nonverbal representations of number (Transition 1) before they can do so with exact and verbal representations, they are able to solve nonverbal addition and subtraction problems (again see Figure 11.1) before they can solve verbal versions of the same problems (word problems) or correctly respond to verbal presented expressions such as, "How much is two and two?" (Levine, Jordan, & Huttenlocher, 1992).

According to the progressive abstraction view (Resnick, 1992, 1994), *what* children represent also evolves. In this view, concepts and reasoning move from concrete (context-specific) to abstract (general; cf. Baroody, Wilkins, & Tiilikainen, 2003; Benson & Baroody, 2002).

- *Protoquantitative (context-specific, qualitative) reasoning.* Initially, children reason about non-quantified amounts in a

global way. For example, a child knows that adding an item to a collection "makes it larger."

- *Context-specific quantitative reasoning.* With the acquisition of counting (or other processes for representing collections exactly), children can reason about specific quantities in a particular and meaningful context. For instance, given two cookies and then offered one more, a child might count his new total and discover that one cookie added to two cookies always makes three cookies altogether.

- *Numerical reasoning.* This involves reasoning about (verbal) numbers without reference to a particular and meaningful context. In effect, numbers are now treated as nouns instead of as adjectives as in the previous level. For example, a child might discover or reason that two and one more is the next number after two in the counting sequence, namely *three*.

- *Abstract reasoning.* Children eventually recognize general principles that apply to any context or number. For instance, preschoolers typically discover the following general rule for adding one: The sum of any number (*n*) and 1 more is the number after *n* in the counting sequence.

Resnick's last three levels are essentially a restatement of Colburn's (1828) view:

The idea of number is first acquired by observing sensible objects. Having observed that this quality is common to all things with which we are acquainted, we obtain an abstract idea of number. We first make calculations about sensible objects; and we soon discover the same calculations will apply to things very dissimilar; and finally that they can be made without reference to any particular thing. Hence from particulars we establish general principles, which serve as the basis of our reasonings, and enable us to proceed, step by step, from the most simple to the most complex operations. (p. 4)

Changes in the conventional wisdom regarding the basis of preschoolers' informal knowledge of number and arithmetic. Like a pendulum, the conventional wisdom about the role of language in number development has also shifted back and forth over the last 100 years or so (see Mix, Sandhofer, & Baroody, 2005, for a detailed discussion).

The First Shift. Dewey (1898) and Thorndike (1922) concluded that children's initial training in mathematics should focus on counting. Russell (1917) set the tone for the rest of the twentieth century by denouncing this informal approach and arguing that *initial* mathematical training should focus on developing children's logical thinking about classes. Subsequently, nativists, Piagetians, and the previously mentioned middle-ground theorists (Huttenlocher and Resnick) all agreed on one point, namely, that language development does not play a role (directly or otherwise) in children's initial construction of an inexact number concept. All but perhaps Resnick (1992) would further agree that it is not essential for the *initial* construction of exact representations also.

Piaget (1965), for example, dismissed verbal and object counting as skills learned by rote, skills that had no impact on constructing a number concept. He argued that the construction of a number concept depended on the development and synthesis of the logical thinking abilities necessary for classifying and ordering (e.g., Gibb & Castaneda, 1975). More recently, early verbal counting (specifically the numbers from 1 to 12 or so in English) was considered merely a singsong (Ginsburg, 1977) or a meaningless string of sounds (e.g., Fuson, 1988). Clearly, children's initial uses of number words are non-functional (Baroody, 1987; Mix et al., 2002a). However, this perspective has obscured the roles even nonfunctional number words may play in constructing a number concept.

The Second Shift. Although nativists (e.g., Gelman, 1991; Wynn, 1998), Piagetians (e.g., Beilin, 1975; Beilin & Kagan, 1969), and proponents of the mental models view (e.g., Huttenlocher et al., 1994; Mix et al., 2002a) would agree that language is important in transcending the limits of early number or quasi-number representation and extending a concept of number, these theorists did not feature language playing a role in the initial formation of a concept of cardinal number (Benson & Baroody, 2003). Since the turn of the 21st century, some researchers have proposed that learning the number words is key to constructing such a concept (Baroody, Benson, & Lai, 2003; Benson & Baroody, 2002; Mix et al., 2005; Sandhofer & Mix, 2003; Spelke 2003a, 2003b; Van de Walle, Carey, & Prevor, 2000). For example, Spelke has argued that this learning is what prompts the transition from a relatively concrete (perception-based) quasi-numerical representation of the intuitive numbers to a relatively abstract (numerical) representation and the transition from an inexact to an exact representation of larger numbers. That is, number-word learning helps explain why ("how") children's representation of number changes and "what" changes.

More specifically, in her *core knowledge view*, Spelke (2003a, b) proposed that infants are born with specialized, task-specific cognitive systems, which form the core of advanced cognitive abilities. She further proposed that infants use two distinct and initially uncoordinated core systems to represent and operate on (e.g., compare, add, subtract) the intuitive numbers and larger numbers, namely object individuation and number sense, respectively (cf. Spelke & Tsivkin, 2001).

According to Spelke (2003a, b), infants use an object-individuation system to represent exactly the intuitive numbers but treat the items of such collections as distinct or unconnected entities. This representation enables infants to recognize that adding an item to another results in an item and another item, which makes it appear they understand "one and one is two," or removing an item from an item and another item results in a single item, which makes it appear they understand "two take away one is one." However, it does not permit them to view collections of one to about three items as a set—as a group whose cardinal (numerical) value can be compared to the cardinal value of other sets. That is, contrary to the nativist's view, it does not guarantee that preverbal children recognize that single entities share the commonality of *oneness*, that pairs of items share the commonality of *twoness*, and that triplets share the commonality of *threeness*. In brief, basic perception-based processes may enable preverbal children to behave in ways that create the *appearance* of understanding number and arithmetic but without real understanding of these concepts (see also Van de Walle et al., 2000).

Spelke (2003a, b) further suggested that infants use a number-sense system to represent inexactly (approximately) larger collection. This enables them to treat larger collections as an approximate set and make numerical comparisons across sets. However, because infants fail to represent these collections as persisting, distinct items, they are incapable of adding one to or subtracting one from such collections.

According to the core knowledge view (Spelke, 2003a, b), then, infants represent small collections as individual items but not as sets and large numbers as sets but not as individual items. A number concept, though, requires representing collections as *sets of individuals*—simultaneously recognizing the whole and its constitute parts (Piaget, 2001; von Glasersfeld, 1982).

What then enables children to integrate the object individuation and number sense core systems and thus, treat collections of any size as sets of individuals? Spelke (2003a, b) argued that the learning of the first few number words prompts the formation of a numerical concept. Likewise, Van de Walle et al. (2000) have suggested that number words provide a vehicle for abstracting the intuitive numbers. The word "two," for instance, may enable children to construct a notion of "twoness" that applies to various pairs of items despite apparent or physical differences (see also Baroody, Benson, & Lai, 2003; Benson & Baroody, 2002, 2003; Mix et al., 2002a). Support for the proposition that language plays a role in constructing a number concept comes from the growing evidence that words facilitate the formulation of other function-based or kind concepts by infants and toddlers (Balaban & Waxman, 1997; Dueker & Needham, 2003; Fulkerson & Mansfield-Koren, 2003; Sandhofer & Smith, 1999; Waxman & Markow, 1995; Xu, 1998, cited in Van de Walle et al., 2000).

Theoretical conclusions. The mental models, progressive abstraction, and core knowledge views have not as yet been thoroughly tested, are not entirely consistent with each other and the existing data, and are by themselves incomplete descriptions of early number arithmetic development. An integrated view (Baroody, Benson, & Lai, 2003) is an effort to combine the best features of these views and to provide a more complete developmental account. In this view, infants may indeed form inexact and then exact nonverbal representations of one or two things and even discriminate among small collections under some circumstances, but they probably do not have a concept of oneness or twoness. That is, they can apprehend the equivalence of such collections without representing their cardinal values (Leslie, 1999). Number symbols (usually number words but possibly written numbers) serve as the catalyst for a number concept, which includes understanding equivalence based on cardinal values (Benson & Baroody, 2002).

Figure 11.2 (pp. 193–195) illustrates a hypothetical developmental trajectory for key aspects of early number and arithmetic development suggested by the integrated view. Note that the foundation for the depicted developmental hierarchy is (usually) verbal number recognition (reliably and discriminately recognizing and verbally labeling a collection). Specifically, verbal number recognition provides a basis for constructing cardinality concepts (see footnote a in Figure 11.2) and discovering all or at

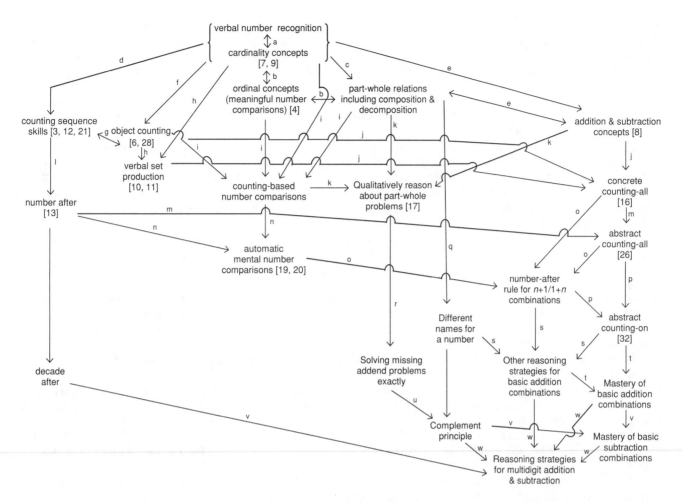

FIGURE 11.2. A hypothetical learning trajectory for some key number and arithmetic skills.

Note. The arrows in the figure above and footnotes below indicate developmental relations. The numbers within the brackets indicate the TEMA-3 (Ginsburg & Baroody, 2003) test items that gauge a particular competence. In conjunction with this test, this figure can be used as a diagnostic tool to identify a deficiency in informal or formal knowledge and its developmental prerequisites, which can then be assessed and, if necessary, remedied.

[a] By seeing different examples of a number labeled with a unique number word and nonexamples labeled with other number words, children can achieve reliable verbal number recognition (VNR) and the construction of cardinality concepts. That is, they can abstract oneness, twoness, and, in time, threeness and fourness—view collections of items as both parts or individual items and as a whole or a set (Rosu & Baroody, 2004) and equivalent collections as the same amount despite the physical differences of the items within or across collections (Baroody, Benson, & Lai, 2003; Benson & Baroody, 2002).

[b] Meaningful VNR enables a child to directly see that a collection of two is more than one and three is more than two. This is aided by the ability to see two as one and one and three as two and one. VNR, then, can underlie children's recognition that the number words represent ordinal relations (e.g., a collection of three is not merely different than one involving two items but is [one] more than it).

[c] Conceptually based VNR enables a child to decompose a whole into its parts—to literally see collections of two as one and one and collections of three as two and one or even one, one, and one (Rosu & Baroody, 2004).

[d] By using VNR, for example, to recognize a collection of one as "one," adding an item and using VNR to recognize the new collection as "two," adding yet another item and using VNR to recognize this even larger collection as "three," children could effectively re-discover the conventional order of the first few number words ("one, two, three") that start the counting sequence (Rosu & Baroody, 2004). That is, VNR applied to successively larger collections may help children discover what Gelman & Gallistel (1978) called the *stable order principle*.

[e] Experiences composing and decomposing small, easily quantified collections may be the basis for constructing an informal concept of addition and subtraction. For example, meaningful VNR enables children to directly see that one item added to another results in two and that one item removed from two leaves one. Once children can reliably recognize three, they can do the same for two and one or three take away two. Such composing and decomposing processes foster an understanding of part-whole relations and vice versa.

Figure 2. Continued.

[f] VNR linked to cardinality concepts help children understand the whys and the hows of verbal one-to-one counting (object counting). By observing others use number words to count small collections easily quantified by VNR, children can discover that object counting is another process for labeling a collection with a number word and the following how-to-count principles:

- By observing adults enumerate small collections easily recognized by VNR, children may be more likely to abstract the one-to-one principle—to understand why an adult labels each item with a single number word (otherwise the outcome is different than the cardinal value as determined by VNR).
- By observing others model object counting with collections easily enumerated by VNR, children can discover the cardinality principle—that the last number word used in the counting process represents the total (Baroody et al., 2004). With a collection of three, for example, a child who can recognize the collection as "three" can understand why others emphasize or repeat the last number word used in the object counting process.
- By observing adults count heterogeneous collections and labeling them with the cardinal value that can also be "seen" (determined) by VNR, children can discover the abstraction principle.
- By observing adults or themselves count small numerically identifiable collections in different directions or arrangements and arrive at the same number word each time, children may also induce the order-irrelevance principle (Baroody, 1987; Piaget, 1964).

Once children understand the purpose of object counting, VNR can serve to check and correct counting efforts with small collections (e.g., it can focus attention on labeling each item with one and only one number word so that the outcome matches the results of VNR). Meaningful counting can motivate the learning of object counting subskills (e.g., learning how to better keep track of counted and uncounted items).

[g] Meaningful object counting can also fuel the drive to master more of the counting sequence. In turn, this mastery is a prerequisite for enumerating larger and larger collections.

[h] Meaningful VNR provides a basis for verbally producing small collections (e.g., responding to a request "Give me two blocks" by putting out two blocks from a pile of blocks). This, in turn, may help a child understand how counting may be useful in verbally producing collections. Specifically, by putting out three items in response to a give-me-n request, and then counting the collection to check their effort, children may recognize the cardinal-count concept—that the requested n the last number word when counting out a collection and that the counting-out process should stop. Alternatively, VNR may—in a similar manner—help children make sense of adult demonstrations of the counting-out procedure.

[i] Meaningful VNR of small collections, particularly in order of size, plus the insight that numbers have an ordinal meaning and part-whole relations can lead to the discovery that the number word further along in the counting sequence represents the larger collection (e.g., Schaeffer et al., 1974).

[j] A concept of addition as increasing the size of a collection (and indirectly part-whole relations including composition and decomposition and ordinal concepts) provide the conceptual basis for inventing counting-based addition strategies. Because the most basic of these strategies (concrete counting-all) entails representing each addend with items and then counting all the items put out to determine the total, verbal set production and enumeration skills are necessary prerequisites for this strategy.

[k] An understanding of part-whole relations (e.g., composition and decomposition) and addition and subtraction and skill at mentally comparing numbers can enable children to reason qualitatively about missing-addend problems. Consider, for example, the problem: *Susan had three cookies, then her mom gave her some more, now she has five cookies. How many cookies did mom give her?* Effective qualitative reasoning would entail recognizing that the answer had to be a number smaller than five (Sophian & Vong, 1995; Sophian & McCorgray, 1994).

[l] In time children's increasing familiarity with the counting sequence enables them to specify the number after another without verbally counting from one.

[m] Children, at some point, realize that they can count or represent *both* addends at the same time they count to determine the sum (Fuson, 1988, 1992). This insight might be prompted by children's use of concrete counting all to compute the sums of $n + 1$ items and the discovery that the answer to such items is the number-after after n. For instance, while solving a problem involving "three and one more," a child might represent each addend with a finger pattern, count all the fingers extended ("1, 2, 3, 4"), and realize that the sum *four* is just one count beyond *three*. This discovery could lead children to eschew counting out objects to represent each addend of a $n + 1$ problem or expression in favor of verbally counting up to the cardinal value of n and then verbally counting once more to determine the sum. Children might then further reason that problems or expressions involving $n + 2$, $n + 3$, and so forth could, in principle, be solved in a similar manner—via an abstract counting-all strategy.

Figure 2. Continued.

[n]Once children recognize that the counting sequence can be used to compare numbers and they master the number-after skill, they can efficiently compare neighboring numbers as well as those further apart in the counting sequence.

[o]Children may first memorize by rote a few $n + 1$ combinations. However, once they recognize that such combinations are related to their existing counting knowledge—specifically their (already efficient) number-after knowledge—they do not have to repeatedly practice the remaining $n + 1$ combination to produce them. That is, they discover the *number-after rule* for such combinations: "the sum of $n + 1$ is the number n in the counting sequence." This reasoning process can be applied efficiently to any $n + 1$ combination for which a child knows the counting sequence, even those a child has not previously practiced (Baroody, 1988, 1992a). Regarding link v, this can include large combinations such as $1,000,128 + 1$. (Note that the application of the number-after rule with multi-digit numbers builds on previously learned and possibly automatic *rules* for generating the counting sequence.) In time, the number-after rule for $n + 1$ combinations becomes automatic and can be applied quickly, efficiently, and without thought.

[p]Research has found that both typically developing children and those with learning difficulties discovered the "number-after rule for $n + 1$ combinations" (the sum of $n + 1$ is the number after n in the counting sequence) just before inventing the general counting-on strategy. This insight into the connection between adding one and extant counting knowledge appears to have served as a scaffold for generalized counting-on (e.g., if $7 + 1$ is the number after 7, then $7 + 2$ must be two numbers after 7: "8, 9"; Baroody, 1995, 1996b; Bråten, 1996). Experiences concretely and mentally composing and decomposing increasingly large numbers may facilitate this discovery.

[q]A part–whole concept and experience with composition and decomposition may underlie an understanding of "number families" or the different-names-for-a-number concept (a number can be represented in various ways because a whole can be composed or decomposed in various ways) and is one key link between number and arithmetic. The number represented by 5 can also be represented by, for example, $0 + 5, 1 + 4, 2 + 3, 3 + 2, 4 + 1, 5 + 0, 6 - 1, 7 - 2$ (as well as |||||, ₦₦, V, *five*, and ∴ •.).

[r]In time children use their conceptual understanding of part-whole relations, including composition and composition and qualitative reasoning about such situations, to construct strategies for determining missing addends exactly.

[s]Meaningfully learning the basic addition combinations entails constructing concepts and discovering patterns or relations. For example, children who construct the "big ideas" of composition and decomposition are more likely to exhibit adaptive expertise, to translate addition combinations (particularly larger ones) into easier or known expressions, and invent such reasoning strategies as the "doubles plus or minus one" (e.g., $7 + 8 = 7 + [7 + 1] = [7 + 7] + 1 = 14 + 1$) or "make a ten" (e.g., $9 + 7 = 9 + [1 + 6] = [9 + 1] + 6 = 10 + 6 = 16$).

[t]Research further indicates that fluency with basic number combinations may involve flexible use of a variety of efficient strategies (LeFevre, Smith-Chant, Hiscock, Daley, & Morris, 2003). With practice, many of the reasoning strategies children devise may become semiautomatic or automatic. Recent evidence further indicates that the mental representation of basic number-combination knowledge of mental-arithmetic experts is a web of richly interconnected ideas. For example, evidence indicates that understanding of commutativity not only enables children to learn all basic multiplication combinations by practicing only half of them (Baroody, 1999c) but also enables them to store both combinations as a single representation in long-term memory (Butterworth, Marschesini, & Girelli, 2003; Rickard & Bourne, 1996; Rickard, Healey, & Bourne, 1994; Sokol, McCloskey, Cohen, & Aliminosa, 1991). This view is further supported by the observation that the calculation prowess of arithmetic savants does not stem from a rich store of isolated facts but from a rich number sense (Heavey, 2003). In brief, the counting and reasoning phases may be essential for laying the conceptual groundwork and providing at least some the strategies for fluency with the basic combinations (the mastery phase).

[u]Children who construct the "big ideas" of composition and decomposition are also more likely to notice that addition and subtraction are related (Whole – Part 1 = Part 2 ⟷ Part 1 + Part 2 = Whole)—a relation that is otherwise not salient to young children—and to invent the "missing-addend" reasoning strategy for subtraction (e.g., for $9 - 4 = ?: 4 + ? = 9, 4 + 5 = 9; ? = 5$; Baroody, 1985, 1999a; Baroody, Ginsburg, & Waxman, 1983; Canobi, 2004; Fuson, 1988, 1992; Putnam, deBettencourt, & Leinhardt, 1990).

[v]As children practice the "missing-addend" reasoning strategy for subtraction , this reasoning strategy can become increasingly automatic.

[w]As with the single-digit arithmetic), children invent increasingly sophisticated mental-computation procedures (Cobb & Wheatley, 1988; Kamii, 1989) and fluency entails flexibly drawing on a variety of strategies. As with single-digit addition and subtraction, they discover patterns and relations that allow them to devise rules or reasoning strategies, which can become automatic. For example, children discover that adding single-digit numbers and 10 results in an analogous teen (e.g., $7 + 10$ or $10 + 7 \rightarrow$ *seven + teen*). This may become embodied as the general (algebraic) "teen rule": $n + 10$ to $n +$ *teen*. Children also discover relations that allow them to exploit their existing knowledge. Some discover, for instance, that adding $40 + 30$ can be thought of as four 10s and three 10s and related to $4 + 3 = 7$ for a sum of seven 10s or 70. These discoveries are far more likely if children are accustomed to thinking in terms of the big ideas of composition and decomposition.

least some of the counting principles described in Table 11.1 (see footnotes d and f in Figure 11.2). It is also hypothesized to be the developmental basis for other key number and arithmetic concepts (again see Figure 11.2, particularly footnotes b, c, and e).

As Table 11.2 illustrates, the integrated view represents a middle ground between the highly optimistic view of nativists, who argue that a number concept and the counting principles are innate, and the highly pessimistic view of (early) Piagetians, who argued that a number concept develops independently of language, including the (rote) skills of verbal and object counting. This view represents, then, represents a moderate position in the concepts-before-skills versus skills-before-concepts debate (Baroody, 2004c).

Educational implications of research finding 1

Mathematical Learning Begins Early, Very Early.
Because of the earlier conventional wisdom about mathematical development (e.g., the pessimistic views of James, 1890; Thorndike, 1922; Piaget, 1965), early childhood educators have, since the beginning of the twentieth century, generally not appreciated preschoolers' significant potential for informal mathematical knowledge and thinking. As a result, instruction in this area has typically been overlooked. Number and arithmetic instruction, if implemented at all, often focused on learning by rote the counting sequence, reading and writing numerals, and perhaps, single-digit number combinations such as "two and two makes four."

Although children may not be born with innate knowledge of number and arithmetic, as nativists contend, a concept of number and arithmetic begins to emerge in toddlers and is more robust than earlier scholars (e.g., James, 1890; Thorndike, 1922; and Piaget, 1965) suggested. Two key implications for childhood educators follow from existing research:

- Number and arithmetic concepts may not be naturally given but require nurturing.
- This nurturing can begin early, indeed, as early as toddlerhood (Baroody, 2000; Baroody & Benson, 2001; Clements et al., 2002). For example, toddlers and somewhat older children can be engaged in one-to-one correspondence activities such as completing shape or knob puzzles or retrieving a cookie for each of several children, classification activities such as sorting objects into egg cartons by rows, equivalence activities such as determining whether there are the same number of spoons as bowls or whether two people have fair shares of candies, ordering activities such as gauging whether a 2-year-old or a 3-year-old is older, and addition or subtraction activities such as gauging a child's age at their next birthday or how many candies will be left if one is eaten.

Learning Number Words May Help Toddlers Construct an Understanding of Number.
Learning number words may help toddlers to abstract oneness, twoness, and threeness.

- Toddlers may benefit from seeing a variety of both examples and *nonexamples* of the intuitive numbers. For instance, by seeing ••, △△, and ▫□ (examples of pairs) all labeled "two," young children may recognize that the appearance of the items in the collections is not important (e.g., shape and color are irrelevant to number). Furthermore, seeing •,•••, △, △△△, ▫□, and ▫□ (nonexamples of pairs) labeled as "not two" or as a number word other than "two" may help them define the boundaries of the concept of "two" and more accurately or selectively apply this number word.

- Learning to recognize regular number patterns (e.g., immediately seeing that the •• array on a die, a triangular array such as •••, and letter-shaped arrays such as •• and ••• as "three") may speed the process of abstracting the intuitive numbers and constructing an understanding of composition and decomposition. This stands in contrast to Piaget's (1965) dismissal of number-pattern recognition as a skill learned by rote and unimportant to number-concept development. (Note, though, that pattern recognition should be done as a component of the previous point. Otherwise, children may equate a number word with a particular pattern, not the general numerosity it represents.)

- Although helping children to discern other conceptual categories such as the colors can lay the foundation for discovering that numbers are a useful means of categorizing or classifying things, there is little evidence that logical training is necessary for developing a concept of number or at least certain types of number concepts (e.g., Baroody, 1987; Clements & Callahan, 1983).

- There is considerable evidence that counting experiences are related to the richness of a number sense and play a key role in extending children's understanding of number beyond the intuitive numbers (e.g., Baroody, 1987, 1992b; Fuson, 1988, 1992; Gelman & Gallistel, 1978). Indeed, research suggests that practice on meaningful counting activities leads to improved performance on logical tasks as well as number tasks (Payne & Huinker, 1993).

Finding 2: Informal Knowledge as a Critical Basis for Success With Formal Mathematics

Figure 11.2 illustrates the cumulative nature of mathematical development—how the earliest informal knowledge provides the basis for other informal competencies, which in turn ultimately provide the bases for formal competencies.

Research

Informal Knowledge as a Foundation for School Learning.
A now large body of research indicates that the quality and quantity of children's informal experiences and knowledge is a key foundation for mathematical achievement in school (see reviews by, e.g., Dowker, 1998; Ginsburg et al., 1998; Kilpatrick et al., 2001). Blevins-Knabe and Musun-Miller (1996), for instance, found that the frequency with which parents engaged their children in number-related activities in the home was correlated to numerical knowledge as measured by an achievement test, namely, the *Test of Early Mathematics, Second Edition* (*TEMA-2*, Ginsburg & Baroody, 1990). Longitudinal

TABLE 11.2. Three Views of the Developmental Relations Among Number Recognition, Number Words, a Number Concept, and Object Counting

Immediate number recognition, sometimes called *subitizing*, entails quickly recognizing the number of items in a collection without object counting. Although sometimes viewed as a single process, it probably involves a number of skills, including nonverbal number recognition (e.g., equating ••• with $\stackrel{\circ}{\circ}\circ$) and efficient verbal number recognition (e.g., immediately recognizing or labeling ••• or •ː• as "three"). The latter encompasses recognizing regular patterns (e.g., equating a triangular array such as •ːˑ with "three") or decomposing collections into smaller recognizable collections and either using addition or multiplication to determine the total (e.g., viewing •ˑ • •ˑ as 2 and 3 = 5 or viewing ⁞⁞⁞⁞ as 3 groups of 4 or 12). Whether nonverbal number recognition, verbal number recognition, or object counting indicate a conceptual understanding of number is matter of considerable debate. Proponents of the Piagetian or extremely pessimistic view imply a skills-before-concepts (skills-first) view, whereas nativist or proponents of the extremely optimistic view advocate a concepts-first view. The Integrated View is consistent with intermediate perspectives, namely the iterative view and the simultaneous view.

Skills-First View: The Simultaneous Use of Meaningless Number Recognition, Number Words, and Object Counting Lead to a Number Concept

In the skills-first view, number (and arithmetic) skills are learned by rote memorization through imitation, practice, and reinforcement. The result is that skill learning is piecemeal. Through applying their skills, children discover number (and arithmetic) regularities view and concepts.

Specifically, von Glasersfeld (1982) argued that the early reciting of number words is a meaningless skill. He also hypothesized that the skill of verbal number recognition is initially a perceptual skill that does not imply an understanding of number, because children view collections as perceptual configurations—as a set or whole, not as a set of individual items or units. He further argued that object counting is also initially a skill learned by rote. Although the object counting process forces children to treat counted objects as individual items (units), they do not conceptually understand that counting is a tool for determining the total number of units (the cardinal value of the collection or the whole). Thus, the initial use of number words, verbal number recognition, and object counting do not entail viewing collection in terms of a true number concept—as *a set of individual items*. All three skills do not start to become meaningful until children use them in conjunction. By counting a collection they also can immediately recognize and verbally label, children realize that the former results in the total and that the perceptual configuration of latter is comprised of units. In brief, the simultaneous application of meaningless verbal-number-recognition and object-counting skills leads to a number concept and the meaningful use of these skills.

Concepts-First View: An Innate Number Concept Underlies Meaningful Use or Learning of Number Recognition, Number Words, and Object Counting

In the concepts-first view, children's conceptual understanding enables them to devise meaningful procedures or skills. As indicated earlier, according to nativists' accounts (e.g., Gelman & Gallistel, 1978), children have an innate and nonverbal understanding of number and counting principles, and this prior understanding underlies infants' ability to nonverbally subitize the number of items in small collections and toddlers' capacity to rapidly learn number words and object counting procedures.

Iterative or Simultaneous View: Meaningful Number Recognition and Number Word Use Coevolve and Underlie the Meaningful Learning of Object Counting

According to the iterative view, conceptual knowledge can lead to the invention of procedural knowledge, the application of which can lead to a conceptual advance, which in turn can lead to more sophisticated procedural knowledge, and so forth (Baroody, 1992b; Baroody & Ginsburg, 1986; Fuson, 1988; Rittle-Johnson & Siegler, 1998). Alternatively, a skill can be learned by rote and its application can lead to the discovery of a concept. This understanding can lead to a procedural advance and reflection of its application can lead to a deeper understanding and so forth. In some cases, concept and skill coevolve (the simultaneous view; Rittle-Johnson & Siegler).

Children's initial use of the first few number words may well be meaningless as von Glasersfeld (1982) suggested. However, the use of these words in conjunction with seeing examples and nonexamples of each can imbue them with meaning (Baroody, Cibulskis, Lai, & Li, 2004). As children hone the skill of verbal number recognition, they construct a cardinal concept of one, two, three, and four—abstracting oneness, twoness, threeness, and fourness (Baroody, Benson, & Lai, 2003; Benson & Baroody, 2002). In this view, then, children's initial procedural knowledge (the verbal number recognition skill) and conceptual knowledge (cardinal concepts of one to about three or four) develop simultaneously.

Moreover, this coevolution of number skill and concept may also enable children to see two as one and one and three as two and one or as one and one and one—as a collections composed of units or a whole composed of individual parts (Freeman, 1912). For example, in the case of Alice (Rosu & Baroody, 2005), a 2-year-old saw a collection of one and labeled it as "one." After seeing an item added to the initial collection, she commented, "Another one" and used visual number recognition to label the collection "two." (The child had not yet learned to count even small collections and, indeed, did not consistently generate the first few number words in the standard order.) After yet another item was added, the girl commented, "Another one" and again used verbal number recognition to label the collection "three." Apparently, she treated the three objects as a collection of units—as a whole composed of individual parts.

The coevolution of verbal number recognition skill and conceptual knowledge of the intuitive numbers' cardinality can also serve as the foundation for meaningful enumeration. Once children can reliably and meaningful recognize and label small collections, the use of this conceptually based verbal number recognition skill in conjunction with seeing enumeration modeled by others can enable children to understand the why and the how of the latter. Specifically, meaningful verbal number recognition can enable children to discern the purpose of object counting (its another way of determining the total number of items of a collection or its cardinal value) and the rationale for counting procedures (e.g., why others emphasize or repeat the last number word used in the counting process because it represents the total number of items or cardinal value of the collection; see footnote f in Figure 11.2 for further discussion).

research indicates that preschool mathematical performance or achievement is predicative of mathematical achievement in school (e.g., Jimerson, Egeland, & Teo, 1999; Shaw, Nelsen, & Shen, 2001; Stevenson & Newman, 1986; Young-Loveridge, 1989). Furthermore, the quality of child care is at least modestly predictive of long-term mathematical achievement (Broberg, Wessels, Lamb, & Hwang, 1997; Peisner-Feinberg et al., 2001; Roth, Carter, Ariet, Resnick, & Crans, 2000).

However, citing Clements (1984) as an exception, Arnold, Fisher, Doctoroff, and Dobbs (2002) concluded that there is little experimental evidence documenting a causal connection between early (preschool) knowledge and mathematical performance in school. Moreover, the vast majority of existing empirical work focuses on post-Transition 2 developments, such as the relation between informal counting skills (e.g., verbal- or object-counting proficiency) and informal arithmetic skills (e.g., devising counting- or reasoning-based strategies to add or subtract), formal number skills (e.g., recognizing numerals), or arithmetic competencies (e.g., mastery of basic number combinations). (For a detailed discussion, see, e.g., Baroody, 1987, 2004a; Baroody & Tiilikainen, 2003; Bideaud, Meljac, & Fischer, 1992; Clements & Sarama, in press; Cowan, 2003; Fuson, 1988, 1992; Ginsburg, 1977; Ginsburg & Baroody, 2003; Hughes, 1986; Kilpatrick et al., 2001; Mix et al., 2002a; Nunes & Bryant, 1996; Pound, 1999; Verschaeffel, Greer, & DeCorte, in press). Put differently, although there is substantial evidence for relations such as g to i and k to w in Figure 11.2, there is currently little or no evidence for the relations between nonverbal skills or verbal number recognition and other informal concepts or skills (e.g., relations a to f in Figure 11.2) and their long-term impact on school achievement.[4] Although intuitively it makes sense that non-verbal skills or verbal number recognition would be indirectly or directly associated with later school success, clearly research is needed to determine whether this is so.

Knowledge Gaps: A Key Source of Learning Difficulties.
Ginsburg (1977) noted that a key source of learning difficulties is a gap between a child's existing knowledge and instruction. For primary-level children, in particular, existing knowledge consists largely of their informal mathematical knowledge. Gaps can occur for essentially two reasons:

1. *Unconnected Formal Instruction.* A gap can occur because formal instruction does not build on a child's informal mathematical knowledge or strengths. This makes it difficult, if not impossible, to understand school instruction. The consequences can be routine expertise (Hatano, 1988, 2003) at best and learning difficulties and math anxiety at worse. Not surprisingly, mathematical learning difficulties and underachievement are often the result of an increasing gap between children's informal knowledge and the symbolic (written) procedures and

formulas formally taught in school (Ginsburg, 1977; Griffin, Case, & Capodilupo, 1995).

2. *Spotty or Inadequate Informal Knowledge.* A gap can also occur when a child does not have well-developed informal knowledge. Inadequate informal knowledge can greatly delay or hamper the learning of school mathematics in at least two ways (e.g., Allardice & Ginsburg, 1983; Baroody, 1987, 1996a, 1999b; Baroody with Coslick, 1998; Donlan, 2003; Ginsburg, 1977; Ginsburg & Baroody, 2003; Jordan, Hanich, & Urberti, 2003; New, 1998): (a) If a teacher attempts to relate formal instruction to common everyday experiences, a child without such experiences will not have a basis for meaningfully assimilating the school instruction. (b) Inadequate informal knowledge can also prevent children from inventing informal problem-solving strategies or interfere with their efficient execution or effective application. For instance, Donlan (2003) observed it is widely assumed that the development of arithmetic skills and the learning of number combinations, in particular, depend primarily on counting skill[s] (e.g., Fuson, 1988; Ginsburg, 1977)" (p. 342).

Case study evidence (e.g., Baroody, 1987; Dowker, 1998; Ginsburg, 1977) and a growing amount of longitudinal research (Oakes, 1990b; Roth et al., 2000; Shaw et al., 2001) indicate that inadequate informal mathematical knowledge is detrimental to school mathematics achievement. For example, Baroody (1984) found that improficiency with counting backward, which depends on learning the forward sequence and number-before relations, can seriously interfere with children's ability to informally determine differences or solve subtraction problems. This is because they often use a counting-down procedure to model subtraction situations, a complex procedure that requires counting backward efficiently (e.g., for $9 - 7$, "*Eight* is one taken away, *seven* is two, *six* is three, *five* is four, *four* is five, *three* is six, and *two* is seven taken away—so the answer is two"). Inefficient, particularly inaccurate, informal (counting-based) arithmetic procedures, in turn, make it less likely that children will discover the patterns and relations necessary to invent more sophisticated reasoning strategies (e.g., "$9 - 7 = ?$ can be thought of as $7 + ? = 9$" or $10 - 7$ is 3 and 9 is one less than 10, so $9 - 7$ is 2"; Baroody, in press; Dowker, 1998) or to memorize arithmetic facts accurately (e.g., Donlan, 2003).

Analogously, Donlan (2003), citing his own and Fazio's (1994, 1996, 1999) longitudinal research, noted that children with specific language impairments often "show substantial deficits in counting procedures" (p. 355). These and short-term memory deficits "may combine to limit strategy development in simple arithmetic" (p. 355), the cumulative effect of which can seriously restrict conceptual development.

In this same vein, Mazzocco and Myers (2003) found that, although no single criterion or combination of criteria in

---

[4]Research in this area has just begun, and the little that is available is often ambiguous. Hannula and Lehlinea (2004, in press), for instance, found remarkable individual differences among 3- to 7-year-olds in their use of object counting and possibly verbal number recognition in the service of solving a nonverbal problem (imitating a tester who put out, e.g., 2, 2, and 1 items successively). They equated performance on this task with a tendency to attend to numerical information (SFON for Spontaneous Focusing On Numerosity) and concluded conceptual and procedural advances in object counting facilitated SFON, which in turn prompted a greater tendency to apply and thus practice object counting, further promoting SFON, and so on. Although this conclusion makes intuitive sense, unfortunately the correlational analysis used did not permit a causal analysis.

kindergarten consistently predicted which children would be categorized as having a mathematical learning disability in Grades 2 or 3, a score of less than the tenth percentile on the *TEMA-2* (Ginsburg & Baroody, 1990) was the most consistent criteria. They attributed this result to the fact that the *TEMA-2* assessed a wide range of informal, as well as formal, concepts and skills. Mazzocco, Myers, and Thompson (2003) subsequently found that a battery of four tests administered to preschoolers was predictive of which children would be designated "learning disabled" in second grade. Interestingly, a composite of three informal items (cardinality, comparisons of one-digit numbers, and mentally adding one-digit numbers) and one formal item (reading numerals) from the *TEMA-2* were nearly as predictive as the entire battery (Mazzocco & Thompson, in press).

Educational implications of research finding 2. There have been numerous efforts to survey the specific number and arithmetic competencies of children entering first grade (Brownell, 1941; Buckingham & MacLatchy, 1930; Callahan & Clements, 1984; Ginsburg & Baroody, 1983, 1990, 2003) and kindergarten (e.g., Bjonerud, 1960; Reaney & West, 2003; Rea & Reys, 1971; Reys & Rea, 1970; see Kraner, 1977, for a review). There have even been a number of efforts, particularly in recent years, to survey such knowledge among preschoolers (Ginsburg & Baroody; McLaughlin, 1935; again see Kraner for a review). Perhaps the most notable is the national effort by the National Center for Education Statistics to track development from birth through first grade (http://nces.ed.gov/ecls).

Despite these survey efforts and the extensive research literature on preschoolers' number and arithmetic development (see, e.g., Baroody, 1987, 2004a; Baroody & Wilkins, 1999; Bideaud, Maljac, & Fischer, 1992; Clements et al., 2004; Frye, Braisby, Lowe, Maroudas, & Nicholls, J. 1989; Fuson, 1988, 1992; Gelman, 1998; Gelman & Gallistel, 1978; Ginsburg, 1977; Ginsburg, Inoue, & Seo, 1999; Ginsburg et al., 1998; Hall, 1891; Mix et al., 2002a; Rittle-Johnson, & Siegler, 1998; Sophian, 1995, 1998; Sophian, Harley, & Martin, 1995; Wynn, 1990, 1992b), preschool and elementary-level educators have, in the past, overlooked the importance of informal mathematical knowledge. Typically, the result has been that informal strengths and weakness have not been assessed and deficiencies in informal knowledge have not been remedied (Baroody & Ginsburg, 1991; Ginsburg & Baroody, 2003).

With the trend toward reform-based or Standards-based instruction, ensuring that students have solid informal knowledge is more important than ever. This is because such instruction—unlike traditional instruction—focuses on achieving all aspects of mathematical proficiency, and—unlike meaningless skill learning—conceptual understanding, appropriate and flexible application of skills, and autonomous strategic mathematical thinking depend on accessing ample prior knowledge. This may help to explain why research (e.g., Boaler, 1998; Fuson, Carroll, & Drueck, 2000; Lubienski, 2000; Sowder, Philipp, Armstrong, & Schapelle, 1998; Woodward & Baxter, 1997) often finds that Standards-based curricula help to promote the conceptual understanding, mastery of basic skills, and problem-solving ability of high and average achievers but not low

achievers, who typically have serious gaps in their informal knowledge. In brief, two key implications follow:

1. Formal mathematical instruction, including the mastery of basic skills (e.g., reading and writing of numerals and fluency with single-digit number combinations), should build on children's informal mathematical knowledge.
2. Gaps in informal knowledge need to be identified and filled early (during the preschool years or the first years of school).

If school instruction does not build on children's informal knowledge, it will probably not make sense and thus, will make learning mathematics unduly difficult and the achievement of all aspects of mathematical proficiency unlikely (Baroody with Coslick, 1998). This is particularly true if gaps in informal knowledge are not filled early because the result all too often is that children become victims of a spiral of frustration, failure, and despair (Ginsburg & Baroody, 2003).

Finding 3: Individual Differences in Informal Knowledge

The research on individual difference is summarized first (see also Dowker, 1998). The debate about the source of most of these individual differences is then addressed.

Research on individual differences. Significant individual differences in verbal and written number and arithmetic skills are already evident when children enter kindergarten or first grade (Baroody, 1987; Klein & Starkey, 2004; Starkey & Klein, 2000; Wright, 1991). For example, Canobi (2004) found individual differences in conceptual knowledge of part-whole relations and problem-solving ability among 6- and 7-year-olds and that differences in the former had a significant impact on the latter. As differences in part-whole knowledge were independent of grade, Canobi concluded that these differences were due to variation in concept development during the preschool years.

Furthermore, children with low skills at the onset of school tend to remain relatively low achievers throughout their formal education, and many develop math anxiety, do not pursue more advanced courses in mathematics, or otherwise disengage from mathematics (Wright, 1994).

Recently, research has focused on individual differences in nonverbal number and arithmetic skills. The results regarding individual differences among preschool children in this area have not been entirely consistent. On the one hand, Jordan and colleagues (Jordan, Huttenlocher, & Levine, 1992, 1994; Jordan, Levine, & Huttenlocher, 1994), for example, have found that children from low-income families were as successful at nonverbal arithmetic but *not* as successful at verbal arithmetic (word problems) as were children from middle-income families (Jordan, Hanich, & Uberti, 2003).

Jordan et al. (2003) concluded that social class differences are not apparent with nonverbal mathematical competencies because such skills do no require social support, but differences do appear with verbal number and arithmetic skills because these competencies do require social mediation. In effect, the former could be considered akin to cognitive universals. It would follow, then, that individual differences would be significantly less evident for nonverbal than for verbal number and arithmetic skills, even among children from low-income families.

On the other hand, other researchers (e.g., Baroody, Benson, & Lai, 2003; Klein & Starkey, 2004; Starkey & Klein, 2000) have found individual differences among 2- to 4-year-olds on precounting number tasks. For instance, Starkey and Cooper (1995) found that 2-year-olds differed significantly in their ability to nonverbally subitize (recognize) collections of one to four items. Evidence suggests that nonverbal number skills with larger intuitive numbers (three and four) may depend on verbal number recognition (Benson & Baroody, 2003). Analogously, Mix (1999) found that, with collections no larger than four, preschoolers were unsuccessful on all but the simplest equivalence tasks (e.g., simultaneously presented collections of the same kind of item). She concluded that a verbal represented aided or was critical to success on more advanced equivalence tasks (e.g., simultaneous homogeneous collections of dissimilar objects such as four blocks and four balls, simultaneous heterogeneous collections, or collections presented successively). These results suggest that facility with nonverbal number skills, with larger intuitive numbers at least, may depend on verbal number skills and, thus, social mediation.

In brief, important individual differences may occur with verbal number and arithmetic competencies and at least some nonverbal skills. Further research is needed to determine what role number words play in number and arithmetic development, particularly with the intuitive numbers, and whether delays or difficulties in verbal number recognition have a domino effect that ultimately has an adverse impact on formal achievement.

The primary cause of individual differences in nonverbal and verbal mathematical competencies among preschoolers. Undoubtedly, some individual differences are due to genetic or acquired organic impairment. See, for example, Delazer (2003) and Macaruso and Sokol (1998) for a review of the effects of brain injuries on mathematical competencies, Baroody (1999b) for the effects of mental retardation, Donlan (1998, 2003) for a review of the effects of specific language deficits, and Nunes and Moreno (1998) for reviews of the effects of hearing impairments. However, most individual differences are probably due to the lack of opportunity. Support for this conjecture comes from two sources of group differences, research on the effects of (a) social class and (b) culture.

The Effects of Poverty. Although research does not consistently find social class differences (even within the same study) some trends are evident. Overall, research indicates that socioeconomic status (SES) is a key factor in school success.

For example, middle-class children outperform children from low-income families on at least some number and arithmetic tasks (e.g., Denton & West, 2002; Griffin & Case, 1997; Griffin, Case, & Siegler, 1994; Kirk, Hunt, & Volknar, 1975; Starkey & Klein, 2000; Starkey, Klein, & Wakeley, 2004; but cf. Seo & Ginsburg, 2004; see Arnold & Doctoroff, 2003, Kilpatrick et al., 2001, and Secada, 1992, for reviews). "Students reporting higher levels of parental education tend to have higher average scores on [National Assessment of Educational Progress] assessments" (Kilpatrick et al., 2001, p. 143).

A spiral of failure or "poor math trajectories in low-SES children begins very early" (Arnold & Doctoroff, 2003). Indeed, poverty is associated with cognitive, achievement, and behavior differences among preschoolers (e.g., Duncan & Brooks-Gunn, 2000). Low social or economic status can adversely affect early informal knowledge (Case, 1975; Entwisle & Alexander, 1990, 1996; Shaw et al., 2001). Students identified as having lower SES enter school with lower achievement levels in mathematics than middle- or high-SES students (see reviews by Arnold & Doctoroff, 2003, Kilpatrick et al., 2001, and Secada, 1992). More specifically, many children from low income families have relatively few productive informal experiences and, as a result, enter kindergarten with significantly less number and arithmetic knowledge (Denton & West, 2002; Griffin, Case, & Siegler, 1994; Hughes, 1986; Jordan, Huttenlocher, & Levine, 1994, Klein & Starkey, 1995; Saxe, Guberman, & Gearhart, 1987). For example, Ginsburg and Russell (1981) found that although children from low-income families had a number of informal strengths, they were significantly less likely to informally solve arithmetic word problems.

Poverty itself, of course, does not cause learning difficulties. A chief candidate for the intervening or linking variable between them is family process (Brooks-Gunn, 2003). For example, often because of their own academic difficulties, parents in low-income families provide less support for academic learning in the form of monitoring, scaffolding, and expectations (Brooks-Gunn, Klebanov, & Liaw, 1995; Campbell & Mandel, 1990; Entwisle & Alexander, 1996; Halle, Kurtz-Costes, & Mahoney, 1997; Jimerson et al., 1999; Klein & Starkey, 1995). For example, middle-class parents tend to provide a broader range of activities and more complex tasks and did so more often than working-class parents (Saxe et al., 1987; Starkey et al., 1999).[5] In brief, the behavior and beliefs of many low SES parents make it less likely their children will achieve the four aspects of mathematical proficiency. This is not to say there are not important exceptions. For instance, Moll, Amanti, Neff, and Gonzalez (1992) discussed the funds of knowledge available in low SES Latino homes. See Lubienski (2003) for a balanced and thoughtful analysis of both the positive and negative effects of social class on learning, including the role structural inequities may play.

---

[5]There continues to be considerable debate about the relative contributions of genetics and environment. Some have argued that innate endowment significantly influences the level of intelligence, and the latter, in turn, affects SES and the inadequate or otherwise ineffective parent stimulation for learning informal mathematics. Although there may be an element of truth in this argument, particularly for extreme cases, it seems at least plausible that most social class variation in the quantity and quality of parental stimulation stems from environmental factors. For example, Benigno and Ellis (2004) found that middle-class parents were more likely to use games as an opportunity to teach number skills if they were playing with only a preschooler than if they were playing with a preschooler and an older sibling. It is not clear why this is the case, but many people who have raised children might attribute at least some of the drop off in attentiveness to fatigue. This sibling-fatigue factor may be even more pronounced in families with low income because such families often have more children than in middle-class families.

Another chief candidate for a linking variable between social class and low achievement is that the quality of schools serving low SES children is generally inferior to that of schools serving higher SES children. Poverty is significantly associated with academic failure in first grade and becomes more so with time (Griffin et al., 1995; McLoyd, 1998; Pagani, Boulerice, & Tremblay, 1997), a result that suggests public education is not helping or even failing disadvantaged children (Brooks-Gunn, 2003).

Indeed, the curricula of elementary schools serving high-poverty communities tend to focus on routine expertise (mastery of basic facts and other skills by rote), whereas those serving affluent are more likely to focus on adaptive expertise and strategic mathematic thinking (Anyon, 1980, 1981; Matti & Weiss, 1999; Means & Knapp, 1991; Oakes, 1990a). Given their traditional instruction (and parents' views on teaching and learning), it is not surprising that low SES students tend to feel comfortable with direct instruction and drill and uncomfortable with problem- or inquiry-based instruction—that they hold beliefs that can interfere with achieving all aspects of mathematical proficiency (Lubienski, 2000, 2002).

The teachers of low SES students may focus on fostering routine expertise because fostering all aspects of mathematical proficiency requires highly qualified teachers and schools serving minority and low-income children are less likely to have such a faculty than schools serving more affluent children (Darling-Hammond, 2000; Ferguson, 1991, 1998; Greenwald, Hedges, & Laine, 1996; Wright, Horn, & Sanders, 1997). This, in turn, is due at least in part to inferior working conditions (e.g., larger class size and less teacher autonomy), conditions that work against recruiting and retaining highly qualified teachers (Darling-Hammond, 1997; Gilford & Tenebaum, 1995; Ingersoll, 1999). Another reason for inferior curricula and instruction is that schools serving low-income or minority students have fewer technology resources than more affluent schools (Educational Testing Service Policy Information Report, 1997).

Cross-Cultural Evidence. The superior mathematical performance of Asian schoolchildren has been well documented (see, e.g., McKnight et al., 1987; Miura & Okamoto, 2003; Song & Ginsburg, 1987; Stevenson, Lee, & Stigler, 1986; Stevenson & Stigler, 1992; Stigler, Lee, Lucker, & Stevenson, 1982; Takeuchi & Scott, 1992; Towse & Saxton, 1998). As Ginsburg, Choi, Lopez, Netley, and Chao-Yuan (1997) noted, one hypothesis about the source of this discrepancy "is that Asian children enter school with superior informal mathematical abilities in such areas as counting, concrete and mental arithmetic, and concepts of more and less. This informal knowledge might provide Asian children with a superior foundation for learning what is later taught ... in school" (p. 166; cf. Starkey et al., 1999).

However, the relatively little cross-cultural research on preschoolers' informal mathematical knowledge has yielded mixed results. Consistent with the hypothesis just discussed, Geary, Bow-Thomas, Fan, and Siegler (1993) found that even before formal instruction, Chinese children outperformed American children in mental addition. Inconsistent with the hypothesis, Baroody and Lai (2003) did not find a significant difference between U.S. and Taiwanese 4- to 6-year-olds'

informal understanding of the addition-subtraction inverse principle (e.g., adding two items to a collection can be undone by taking away two other items).

Similarly, Song and Ginsburg (1987) found that, on a variety of competencies measured by a standard test of early mathematical ability (Ginsburg & Baroody, 1983), U.S. 4- and 5-year-olds significantly outperformed their Korean counterparts. However, these results are not conclusive because the test was developed for U.S. children and may not have been entirely appropriate for Korean children (Ginsburg et al., 1997). Using a more sensitive instrument, Ginsburg et al. found that Chinese, Japanese, and Korean preschoolers exhibited a small but consistent advantage over U.S. preschoolers.

Both Miura (1987; Miura, Kim, Chang, & Okamoto, 1988; Miura & Okamoto, 1989) and Miller (1996; Miller, Smith, Zhu, & Zhang, 1995; Miller & Stigler, 1987) have noted that the highly regular nature of Asian (Chinese, Japanese, and Korean) counting sequences facilitates the learning of this sequence and grouping-by-ten concepts and that the somewhat irregular nature of the English counting sequence interferes with mastering these competencies (see Miura & Okamoto, 2003, for a review). However, Towse and Saxton (1998) observed that an association between differences in language and differences in performance on a conceptual (grouping-by-ten) task does not rule out alternative explanations or demonstrate a direct causal relation. They argued that differences in the nature or amount of parent-child interactions or preschool experience may be more important than differences in the orderliness of counting sequences. For example, parents in Asian countries value education and mathematics more than U.S. parents, and this may translate into more informal instruction in the home. (Tudge and Doucet, 2004, found that U.S. parents engaged their 3-year-olds in mathematically related activities infrequently, regardless of ethnicity or social class.) Asian countries have well-organized and extensive preschools (Towse & Saxton, 1998). In both informal home settings and more formal preschool settings, Asian cultures may put more emphasis on key concepts such as composition (composing a whole from its parts, perhaps in different ways) and decomposition (decomposing a whole into its constitute parts, perhaps in different ways) by, for instance, making available an abacus, which can highlight that $1 + 4$, $2 + 3$, $3 + 2$, or $4 + 1$ are all ways of making five.

Interestingly, though, Miller (e.g., 1996) found the advantage of a regular counting sequence did not carry over to understanding counting principles or applying object-counting skills, such as understanding the cardinality principle. Case's (Case, Griffin, McKeough, & Okamoto, 1991; Case & Okamoto, 1996; Griffin & Case, 1995b) results were analogous to Miller's. They tested 4-, 6-, 8-, and 10-year-old children from high, medium, and low social classes from the United States, Canada, Japan, and China over a 6-year span. In the domain of number, Case and Okamoto (1996) found, for instance, large and consistent differences favoring the Japanese in particular numerical skills and concepts (e.g., number knowledge and computational skill) but not in central numerical structures (general concepts). They concluded that high parental expectations and involvement and language structure may help Japanese children perform better in the particular numerical skills. However, although specific instructional opportunities differ widely across the two groups, more general educational opportunities do not. The everyday lives of children in both cultures provide ample opportunity to encounter quantitative problems in such domains as number and arithmetic and to construct central structures or general concepts in these domains. Whether this is true of only a few (those assessed by extant research), many, most, or all central concepts (e.g., composition and decomposition), however, is currently unclear.

Educational implications. In the past, early childhood and primary-level educators largely underestimated either the serious individual differences among children's informal knowledge or the need for targeted opportunities to close gaps in this knowledge. These oversights are embodied in the traditional policies or practices for enrolling children at risk or with a developmental delay in kindergarten. One practice is to provide no intervention before kindergarten and, if children fail to prosper in kindergarten, have them repeat this grade (i.e., provide the same experiences again a year later). The second practice is to delay the start of kindergarten by a year. In effect, both traditional practices are based on the assumption that some children just take longer to develop and simply postponing the start of formal mathematics (and reading) instruction (entry into first grade) will be sufficient.

However, research indicates that "time alone may not serve to improve academic achievement" of children at risk or developmentally delayed (Reaney & West, 2003). Put differently, the historical practices of delaying the start of the first year of kindergarten, repeating kindergarten, or transition classes are not effective (May & Kundert, 1997). Other research on individual differences and related factors have created enormous interest in early childhood mathematics instruction for a number of interrelated reasons:

- The evidence that opportunity is a key factor in individual differences underscores the need and even the civil right for equitable education (Miller, 1995; Moses, 2001; Oakes, 1990a; Schoenfeld, 2002).
- Children from low-income families or minority groups are particularly likely to lack the opportunities to develop robust informal mathematical knowledge, a disadvantage that is further compounded by poor formal instruction. Therefore, such children are especially prone to be caught in a spiral of failure and, thus, are more often excluded from professional and technology-related jobs, jobs that require a high degree of mathematical proficiency.
- An increasing number of families, both parents work (Hoffman, 1989) and, thus, an increasing number of preschoolers are enrolled in preschools or other early care (U.S. Department of Education, 2000).
- In part because of the research and reform effort discussed earlier, the mathematics goals and curricula for preschool, kindergarten, and later primary grades have become more demanding (Karweit, 1994).
- Gaps in mathematical achievement stem from structural factors such as poverty and other inequities (Oakes, Joseph, & Muir, 2004). Furthermore, the number of preschoolers living

in poverty—including ESL children—and, thus, at risk for school failure is increasing (McLoyd, 1998).
- Current preschool learning environments typically do "not provide focused, systematic support for young children's mathematics development" (Starkey et al., 2004, p. 101). This is particularly critical for children from low-income families or otherwise at risk (see bullets 2 to 4, above).
- Although not conclusive (Karweit, 1994), some evidence indicates that early childhood intervention is an important investment for later school success (e.g., Campbell, Pungello, Miller-Johnson, Burchinal, & Ramey, 2001; Frank Porter Graham Child Development Center, 1999; National Institute of Child Health and Human Development, 1998; Reynolds & Temple, 1998; Schweinhart, Barnes, & Weikart, 1993; Weikart & Schweinhart, 1992; Weikart, 1998; Weikart & Schweinhart, 1997; Zigler & Styfco, 1998; but cf. Gray, Ramsey, & Klaus, 1983).

Ensuring that all students have solid foundational knowledge, then, seems to be an essential first step for achieving *equity* (e.g., NCTM, 1989, 2000; Kilpatrick et al., 2001). Early intervention is now viewed as one key step toward ensuring a level playing field. This is particularly true when intervention builds on the informal strengths that at-risk children do have and target specific gaps in their informal knowledge (Clements & Sarama, 2003; Ginsburg & Baroody, 1990, 2003).

Unfortunately, relatively few intervention studies have to date focused on mathematical knowledge. Of those that have, fewer yet have focused on the effects of long-term intervention or the long-term effects of intervention of any kind. For example, Arnold et al. (2002) examined the effects of intervention lasting 6 weeks on participants immediately after the end of intervention. Several long-term early interventions have had a positive impact on the children at risk for academic failure at least in the short term (Kim, Charmaraman, Klein, & Starkey, 2000; Klein & Starkey, 2004; Sarama, 2004; Sophian, 2004; Starkey & Klein, 2000).

Another limitation of existing research is that the dependent measures involved global assessment such as standard mathematics achievement scores (e.g., Arnold et al., 2002). For example, Dev, Doyle, and Valente (2002) found that after 2 years of intervention, children at risk for reading and mathematics difficulties showed improvement on the WRAT-III and were no longer in need of special education services at the end of second grade. A number of recent efforts (e.g., Starkey et al., 2004) have entailed examining mathematical performance in some detail (i.e., include training and testing of, e.g., matching and comparing, sorting, patterning, sequencing, and numbers). However, even this level of specificity is relatively general and not sufficient to detail conceptual and procedural learning trajectories. For instance, number entails a variety of specific concepts and skills, such as object counting (counting a collection to determine its cardinal value) and verbal production (counting out a requested number of items as in "Give me three blocks").

One notable early intervention effort parallels the *Reading Recovery* program. The *Math Recovery* program (Wright, Martland, & Stafford, 2000; Wright, Martland, Stafford, & Stanger,

2002) builds on constructivist theory (e.g., Cobb & Wheatley, 1988; Steffe & Cobb, 1988) and involves individual instruction by specially trained teachers for 30 min a day, 4 days a week for 12 to 20 weeks. Informal number, counting, and arithmetic competencies are evaluated and intervention entails challenging children to use increasingly sophisticated strategies in these areas. The aim of the program is to help children at risk match the informal competencies of their more advantaged peers. Efforts to evaluate this program have only recently begun.

THE NATURE OF EARLY CHILDHOOD MATHEMATICS EDUCATION

Early in the 20th century, John Dewey experimented with reforming instruction. His "Progressive Education Movement" was largely a reaction to traditional instruction and, thus, in many ways a direct opposite of it. In place of direct instruction by a teacher, for example, children were encouraged to explore their world unencumbered by adult intervention. Disappointed by the results of his early experiment with educational reform, Dewey (1963) summarized the lessons learned in *Experience and Education.* These lessons are still valuable today as early childhood educators consider how to improve preschool intervention and revise primary-level instruction. In effect, Dewey laid out three criteria for successfully changing instruction.

1. **Methods: *How* to teach.** New teaching methods cannot be substituted for traditional methods merely because they are different from the latter. *New teaching approaches, methods, or tools must have their own theoretical, empirical,* and *practical justification.*
2. **Goals: *What* to Teach.** Instruction cannot simply consist of a hodgepodge of activities without clear educational purposes. *Teachers must strive to provide educative experiences* (experiences that lead to worthwhile learning or a basis for later learning; see also Sophian, 2004), not *miseducative experiences* (activities for the sake of activity and that may actually impede development). In a similar vein, Lilian Katz cautioned that "just because [children] can, does not mean they *should*!" For example, "little children can learn to do formal sums but that does not mean they should—or that it would be in their long-term interests to do so.... They may be learning that mathematics is boring" (Pound, 1999, p. 35).
3. **Timing: *When* to Teach.** Educative experiences result "from an interaction of external factors, such as the nature of the subject matter and teaching practices, and internal factors, such as a child's [developmental readiness] and interests" (Baroody, 1987, p. 37). Teachers, then, must ensure that external and internal factors mesh. Dewey's principle of interaction bears on the issues of how, what, and when to teach. In regard to the latter, teachers need to consider the developmental readiness when deciding to introduce a topic, using, for instance, children's questions as a guide.

In this part of the chapter, we review some of the relevant research on each of the three issues discussed above and discuss its educational implications.

Research Implications Regarding How to Teach Mathematics

In general, we have found that the younger the child, the less willing he or she was to answer thoughtfully, or at all, as a task moved from one initiated by the participant to one imposed by an adult (Baroody, 2001, 2002; Benson & Baroody, 2002). Consider the case of Nathaniel (2.8 years; Baroody, Benson, & Lai, 2003). Adult-initiated testing indicated he had little nonverbal or verbal number knowledge. He did not, for example, respond correctly to a matching or a nonverbal production task involving one to four items. (The former required creating a collection equivalent to a visible collection; the latter task involved doing the same for a previously seen but hidden collection.) He also refused to play a game that entailed determining the cardinal value of small collections. However, as the tester was cleaning up, Nathaniel asked for a soldier, and she allowed him to keep one until the next session. As tester was leaving, he became upset and said, "I want two soldiers." He went into her bag and grabbed another soldier and said, "Aha! I got two!" He apparently recognized that the one soldier in his hand was not enough (not "two"); he also appeared to know that he needed another soldier to have two soldiers. In brief, the adult-initiated testing did not accurately reflect his knowledge, which was exhibited in self-initiated activities (see also Mix, 2002). (Parenthetically, it seems plausible that low SES children may be even less accepting of adult-imposed tasks and that traditional research on the effects of social class underestimate the mathematical—and other intellectual—competencies of these children; H. P. Ginsburg, personal communication, March 1, 2004.)

How can such results be reconciled with Dewey's (1963) guidelines? Listed below is a continuum of types of teaching or testing tasks and approaches to teaching or testing (Baroody, 2001):

- Traditional direct instruction and drill/Adult-imposed task— Directed response (e.g., a direct question or work sheet)
- Guided discovery learning/ Adult-initiated task—Invited response (e.g., a project or math game)
- Flexible guided discovery learning/Child-initiated task— Guided response (e.g., building on a child's question)
- Unguided discovery learning/Child-initiated task—Unguided response (e.g., free play)

As the case of Nathaniel illustrates, our research indicates that an overly direct approach risks not engaging children and may not be effective, particularly with younger children. Dewey's experience indicated that unguided discovery approach risks not providing educative experiences. Early childhood educators face a balancing act—that is, an approach that is neither too direct nor too hands off. The two middle courses listed here, then, seem to be the most promising. See, for example, Clements et al. (2004), Ginsburg et al. (in press), and Pound (1999), for general instructional guidelines and examples of developmentally appropriate preschool curricula. See Zur and Gelman (2004) for an excellent example of how careful observations by teachers can lead to a developmentally appropriate and interesting educational (computational estimation) game. See Benigno and Ellis (2004) for an interesting analysis of how parents can take advantage of a game as an opportunity to teach basic number skills.

Consider, for example, the role of manipulatives. On the one hand, research suggests that direct instruction with manipulatives is not likely to provide an educative experience for young children. That is, simply demonstrating concrete models for children and then requiring them to imitate such manipulative-based procedures may not promote conceptual learning (e.g., Baroody 1989c; Clements & McMillen, 1996; Fuson & Burghardt, 2003; Miura & Okamoto, 2003; Resnick, 1982; Seo & Ginsburg, 2003; cf. Sophian, 2004). It is difficult, if not impossible, to impose understanding. On the other hand, the presence of manipulatives alone in a free play context does not guarantee an educative experience either. That is, simply providing manipulatives without a purpose, direction, guidance, or feedback may not promote conceptual understanding, computational fluency, or strategic mathematical thinking. Manipulatives may be most useful when children have a purpose of their own or an adult creates one and when children reflect on their use or peers or adults cause them to do so. Meaningful use of manipulatives also entails children relating (assimilating) this experience to their existing knowledge. This may be more likely to happen if students are asked to use what they know to devise their own solutions (guided or flexibly guided discovery) than if they are shown how to use manipulatives (direct instruction). (See Balfanz, 1999, for a thoughtful discussion of how Froebel and Montessori artfully used manipulatives to guide discovery of mathematical ideas.)

Our conclusions are consistent with those of the NAEYC and the NCTM. Clements et al. (2002), for example, noted that it is doubtful that incidental experiences or learning will promote educative experiences. They concluded that existing evidence indicates young children are ready for organized, sequenced experiences embedded in specific activities (e.g., reading children's literature, music or art activities), play (e.g., math games or physical activities), projects, or a careful combination of approaches.

Not coincidentally, a number of scholars (e.g., Bredekamp & Copple, 1997) now consider the Vygotskian, rather than the Piagetian, perspective "the central theoretical grounding within the field of early childhood education" (Winsler, 2003, p. 254).[6] Vygotsky (1962) differed with Piaget (e.g., 1965) in key ways, including:

- a focus on sociocultural factors as well as cognitive factors;
- a central role for teachers as well as for peers and individual reflection;
- a key role for language in shaping learning and thought.

These key interrelated differences parallel three important Vygotskian concepts now commonly cited in developmental and early childhood literature:

- The *zone of proximal development* is the domain-specific—or even activity-specific—competence a child can exhibit with careful and minimal assistance. This zone exists between the zone of competence (what a child can do independently) and the zone of incompetence (what a child cannot learn even with help). See Ginsburg et al. (2006) for an interesting and informative discussion of teaching experiments that use problem-solving situations "under adult guidance or in collaboration with more capable peers" (Vygotsky, 1986, p. 86) to take advantage of young children's zone of potential development.

- *Scaffolding* refers to the (minimal or indirect) support a teacher, parent, or others can provide (e.g., asking the child a question or creating cognitive conflict, instead of telling him or her what to do). It entails using an engaging activity to assess a child's zone of proximal development and, ideally, carefully decreasing guidance to keep the child in this zone.

- Gradual *internalization* of cultural tools. For instance, thought is viewed as self-directing language that has become subvocal. (See Chapter 4 of Vygotsky, 1978, 1987, for a detailed discussion of the transformations that occur, the interaction between rational and cultural lines of development, and how his views on the topic differ from the behaviorist views of Watson, 1930).

The key implication of Vygotsky's (1962, 1978) theory for the topic under discussion is his central thesis that "early number understanding emerges first in social interaction with more capable partners and only gradually becomes internalized" (Benigno & Ellis, 2004, p. 6). Put differently, whereas a Piagetian approach is generally consistent with an unguided discovery learning approach, a Vygotskian approach is more consistent with a guided discovery or flexible guided discovery learning approach. Winsler (2003) noted there has been an explosion of Vygotskian-based educational research in recent years. In the area of mathematics, he cited, for example, Berenson (1997); Bussi and Bartolini (1998); De Abreu (2000); Jones and Thornton (1993); Lerman (1996, 2001); Saxe, Dawson, Fall, and Howard (1996); Saxe and Guberman (1998); and Waschesio (1998). For a comprehensive survey of Vygotsky's thinking regarding developmental and educational psychology, see Langford (2004).

Note that effectively implementing guided discovery learning has important implications for class size. Such instruction is difficult to implement with 15 or more students. Even preschool teachers with small class sizes need to consider how to involve curriculum supervisors/specialists, parents, preservice teachers, older children, peers, and volunteers trained to perform

---

[6]The influence of Vygotsky on educational practice is a worldwide phenomenon. For example, educators from both mainland China and Taiwan have concluded that traditional curricula are not effective in promoting all aspects of mathematical proficiency (e.g., Chang, 1999; Huang, 1988) and that reform based on Vygotsky's views (e.g., child-centered but adult guided instruction) is needed (Chung, 2000). In China, the reform movement began in the early 1990s under the name of "Quality Education" (Zhou, 1995). In Taiwan, the reform movement likewise began in the early 1990s (e.g., Government Information Office, 2003).

TABLE 11.3. Four Levels of Number Goals (Based on a Portion of Table 1.1 in Clements, et al., 2004)

Topic	2–4 years	4–5 years
Counting Counting can be used to find out *how many* in a collection. (Level 1)		
b. Another key element of object-counting readiness is learning standard sequences of number words. (Level 2)	←——————————— Verbally count by ones (Level 3) from · · · ——————————→ 1 to 10 (Level 4)	1 to 30 (Level 4)
c. Object counting involves creating a one-to-one correspondence between a number word in a verbal counting sequence and each item of a collection, using some action indicating each action as you say a number word. (Level 2)	←——————— Count the items in a collection and know the last counting word tells "how many" (Level 3)————————→ 1 to 4 items (Level 4)	1 to 10 items (Level 4)
	←——————— Count out (produce) a collection of a specified size (Level 3)————————→ 1 to 4 items (Level 4)	1 to 10 items (Level 4)
d. Number patterns can facilitate determining the number of items in a collection or representing it. (Level 2)	←——— Verbally subitize (quickly "see" and label with a number; Level 3) · · ·———→ collections of 1 to 3 (Level 4)	collections of 1 to 5 (Level 4)

specific instructional duties (e.g., reading a story to a group of children or helping a small group undertakes an investigation). They need to consider other ways of multiplying effort such as engaging children with educative computer programs, audio-visual work station (e.g., an instructional station with a story, questions, instruction, etc. on a video- or audiotape, CD, or DVD), educational television programs, and educative activities, projects, or play stations.

Research Implications Regarding What to Teach

Our discussion of what to teach will focus on (a) levels of developmentally appropriate goals, (b) the need for integrated instruction (instruction that encompasses several or many goals), and (c) the need for teachers to focus on big ideas (major goals), rather than specific facts or procedures.

Topic 1: Levels of developmentally appropriate goals. Early childhood educators need clear-cut goals ranging from global aims ("really big ideas") to specific objectives (Baroody, 2004d). For example, see in Clements (2004) the Developmental Guidelines for Number and Operations (his Table 1.1) and in Baroody (2004a), A Sample of Possible Early Childhood Number and Operations Goals (his Table 7.1). A portion of the former, which illustrates three levels of goals, is shown in Table 11.3.

It makes sense for pre- and in-service teacher education to begin with the most general goals. These broad aims can help teachers focus on what is most important to accomplish, are less overwhelming to learn than are more detailed goals, can help them see connections between diverse examples or topics, and can bolster confidence that they can be effective mathematics teachers. Once broad aims are grasped, teachers may feel a need and thus welcome increasingly specific goals and information about how to achieve them. In effect, levels of goals are consistent with the view that worthwhile learning is an active and gradual building process, which can be facilitated by big ideas

that enable the learner to see connections or relations with a minimum of guidance (Baroody et al., 2004).

Topic 2: Integrated instruction. A detailed list of specific competencies (e.g., as those in Table 11.3) is not intended as a laundry list of skills that a teacher focuses on one at a time. It is intended to guide curriculum developers, curriculum coordinators, and teachers for what might be developmentally appropriate for a particular age range. The activities used to engage children in learning or practicing even specific competencies should provide *rich, integrated* experiences (e.g., projects, games, real problems) that promote the development of several competencies simultaneously (see, e.g., Figure 11.3).

Topic 3: Focusing on big ideas. Teachers should focus on helping students discover and understand *big ideas*— overarching concepts that connect numerous topics and applications (Baroody et al., 2004). For example, the really big idea of equally dividing up a whole (*equal partitioning*) and its informal analogy of fair sharing underlies such diverse concepts as division, fractions, measurement, averages (the mean), and the unit principle (e.g., $5 = 1 + 1 + 1 + 1 + 1$). For instance, 12 ÷ 3 can be informally viewed as sharing 12 items among three people and 2/3 can be done so as the size of each person's share of two cookies are shared fairly among three people (see Baroody, 2004a, for a detailed discussion).

As Paulos (1991) advised, *"stress a few basic principles and [leave] most of the details to [the student]"* (p. 7). If students understand the big ideas, most will be able to rediscover or reinvent the principles, properties, and procedures central to elementary arithmetic, including the commutative principle of addition, reasoning strategies for using known number combinations to logically determine unknown sums or differences, and renaming procedures. Understanding big ideas can help students understand the rationale for specific methods (e.g., procedures and formulas), adapt them to meet the challenge of new problems or tasks ("adaptive expertise"), and see how various concepts and procedures are related. This can help students

Animal Spots (Wynroth, 1986)

Animal Spots requires players to throw a die with 0 to 5 dots to determine how many pegs ("spots") they can take for their leopard or giraffe (an animal figure cut out of wood with holes drilled for pegs). (The game also can be played with 0- to 10-dot die or cards.) The first child to fill his or her animal with spots is the winner. Playing *Animal Spots* entails oral counting, enumeration, the cardinality principle, and production of sets. To ensure accurate set production, have children count their pegs into a dish before placing them in their animal. By learning the rules of a game, a child learns a key mathematical concept such as equivalence ("same number as"). Thus, games are used to teach concepts as well as practice skills.

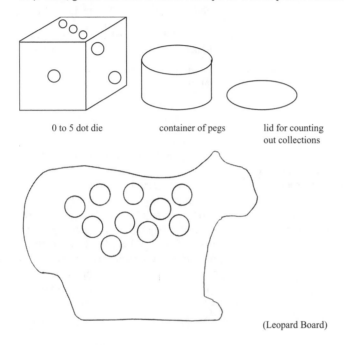

0 to 5 dot die   container of pegs   lid for counting out collections

(Leopard Board)

FIGURE 11.3. Animal spots (Wynroth, 1986).

see that mathematics is a system of knowledge. This in turn can make learning diverse ideas and procedures much easier. An example of a really big idea (composition and decomposition) is described in Table 11.4 and instructional games useful in fostering reflection on this big idea are illustrated in Figure 11.4.

Research Implications for When to Teach

Our discussion of when to teach will focus on (a) hypothetical learning trajectories, which provide a guide for constructing hierarchies of developmentally appropriate instruction, and (b) the issue of developmental readiness.

Topic 1: Hypothetical learning trajectories (HLTs). Efforts to define instructional sequences or potential developmental paths are not new, but recent efforts to detail HLTs (originally proposed by Simon, 1995) represent a significant improvement in such efforts (Baroody et al., 2004; Clements & Sarama, 2004; Gravemeijer, 2004). In the past, instructional sequences or learning hierarchies focused on skill hierarchies (e.g., Gagné

& Briggs, 1974) or relatively simple ladder-like sequences of concepts and skills (e.g., Baroody, 1989a; Griffin et al., 1994; Ginsburg & Baroody, 1983, 1990, 2003). Unlike many previous efforts to define learning sequences, HLTs entail a combination of all of the following: (a) goals for meaningful student learning, (b) tasks geared to achieve this learning, and (c) hypotheses about the process of student learning (local learning theories). Specifically, HLTs are based on constructivist research of how children actively build conceptual understanding; entail systematic development of curriculum, instructional activities, and assessment tools; and are based on domain- or even task-specific theory that can entail multiple hypothetical developmental paths or web-like mental structures (Battista, 2004; Lesh & Yoon, 2004).

HLT then can serve as a uniting force for developing and implementing standards (goals), curriculum or instructional activities, teaching strategies, assessment, and teacher training (Clements et al., 2002). Furthermore, HLTs serve to focus educators' attention on teaching students rather than merely implementing a curriculum. That is, successful teachers focus on student learning—children's progress through a conceptually

TABLE 11.4. An Example of a Big Idea: Composition and Decomposition

A fundamental idea underlying various aspects or topics of mathematics is that a *quantity or whole can consist of parts and be broken apart (decomposed) into them and that the parts can be combined (composed) to form the whole:*

- **Other names for a number** (e.g., different parts can compose to make the same whole, such as $1 + 7$, $2 + 6$, $3 + 5$, and $4 + 4 = 8$... and a whole can be decomposed in constitute parts in different ways, such as $8 = 1 + 7, 2 + 6, 3 + 5, 4 + 4...$)
- **invention of reasoning strategies and mastery of larger addition combinations** (e.g., $7 + 8 = 7 + [7 + 1] = [7 + 7] + 1 = 14 + 1 = 15$ or $7 + 8 = 7 - [-2] + [8 + 2] = 5 + 10 = 15$)
- **part-whole number relations** (e.g., one of two or more parts is smaller than its whole and conversely a whole is larger than any one of its multiple parts)
- **missing-addend** (part) problems (e.g., in the problem below or in the equation $4 + ? = 6$, the missing part must be smaller than the whole 6 and when added to 4 equals 6)

Georgia had 4 dresses. Her mother bought her some more. Georgia found 6 dresses hanging in closet. How many new dresses did Georgia's mom buy?

- **invention of reasoning strategies and mastery of subtraction combinations** (e.g., for $6 - 4 = ?$, the whole 6 minus the part 4 is equal to the other part, which when added to 4 makes 6; i.e., $6 - 4 = ?$ is related to the missing-addend expression $4 + ? = 6$ and, because $4 + 2 = 6$, the unknown part is 2)
- **renaming (carrying and borrowing) procedures** (e.g., for $37 + 28$, a child must be able to recognize that the sum of the ones digits 15 can be decompose into a 10 and a 5 and that this 10 must be added to the three 10s and two 10s shown in the 10s place)
- **geometry** (e.g., a square can be decompose into two [right, isosceles] triangles and vice versa).

based trajectory—not on progressing through a curriculum (Fuson et al., 2000).[7]

When recommendations for instructional activities and local learning theories (e.g., hypotheses about common misconceptions or other learning difficulties, how students might make connections or construct understanding, and what questions might naturally arise) are coupled with the developmental trajectories outlined in Figure 11.2, this hierarchical sequence can serve as a HLT. For sources of instructional guidelines, activities, and local learning theories regarding the components of this hierarchical sequence, see Baroody (1987, 1989a), Baroody with Coslick (1998), Clements et al. (2004), Copley (1999, 2000, 2004b), Fromboluti and Rinck (1999), and Ginsburg and Baroody (2003; particularly Table 1.1, Chapter 6 in the *Examiner's Manual,* and the *Assessment Probes and Instructional Activities Manual*).

As an example of a research-based HLT, consider initial number instruction. Mothers reported that the most common number activity in which they engaged their preschoolers, particularly 3.5- to 4.5-year-olds, was verbal and object counting (Blevins-Knabe & Musun-Miller, 1996). Our own case study work indicates that many parents begin number instruction with counting objects (Baroody et al., 2004). This appears to be confusing to children—a miseducative experience—because number words are used in two different ways:

- During the counting process, they are used as *ordinal* terms (to specify the order of the items).
- At the end of the counting process, the last number word used also has a *cardinal* meaning, namely, it specifies the cardinal value of the collection (the total number of items in the collection).

Understanding the second point above (the *cardinality principle*) is fundamental to meaningful object counting or functional enumeration. Children's confusion about this switch in number meaning (the absence of a cardinality principle) can be manifested by, for example, recounting a collection when asked, "How many?" (cf. Fluck, 1995; Fluck & Henderson, 1996). Our observations indicate parents' efforts to impose counting on children often leads to learning the object counting process by rote and its nonfunctional, mechanical, or error-prone application (Baroody et al., 2004).

A more optimal instructional route suggested by research is to first encourage *verbal number recognition* of small collections (Baroody et al., 2004). For example, by initially

---

[7]An argument against using HLTs is that such an approach draws heavily on imperfect research and does not take into account what Vygotsky (1978) called children's zone of proximal development. Therefore, basing trajectories on such research can be dangerously restrictive. Even among proponents of HLTs, there are serious disagreements (see, e.g., Clements & Sarama, 2004). For example, Lesh and Yoon (2004) worried that linear (ladderlike) sequences and even multiple-path (branching-tree) trajectories (a) suggest a one correct instructional-path approach, (b) imply stable stages of understanding across different but applicable tasks, and (c) do not adequately represent rich (weblike) learning situations.

However, proponents of HLT recognize that the research basis for a HLT is imperfect (and will always be incomplete to some degree). HLTs are tentative local theories or conjectures, which is precisely why they are called *hypothetical* learning trajectories. A key aspect of an HLT approach is its cyclical nature: Construct an HLT based on the best theory and research available, mathematical history, mathematical needs, and so forth. Develop instructional activities to promote each component of the HLT. Test the HLT by trying out the instructional activities; adjust the HLT and instructional activities accordingly; and so on. Note that this try and adjust process would take into account children's zone of proximal development. Furthermore, Lesh and Yoon's (2004) concerns are not an entirely fair of most HLT efforts (see Baroody et al., 2004, for a detailed discussion).

The Number Goal Game

Two to six children can play this game. A large center card (square) is placed in the middle with a number such as 13 printed on it. Each player draws six small squares numbered 1 to 10 from a pile of squares all facing down. The players turn up their squares. On his or her turn, a player may compose two or more squares to a sum equal to the number in the center.

If a player had squares 2, 3, 5, 5, 5 and 8, she could combine 5 and 8 and 3, 5, and 5 to make 13. As each solution would be worth 1 point, the player would get two points for the round. If the player had chosen to combine 2 + 3 + 8, no other possible combinations of 13 would be left, and the player would have scored only 1 point for the round.

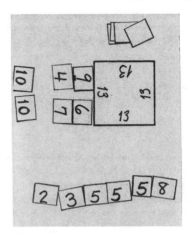

An alternative way of playing (scoring) the game is to award points for both the number of parts used to compose the target number (e.g., the play 3 + 5 + 5 and 5 + 8 would be scored as 5 points, whereas the play 2 + 3 + 8 would be scored as 3 points).

Number Goal—Tic Tac Toe (or Three in a Row)

This game is similar to the *Number Goal Game.* Two children can play this game. Each player draws six small squares numbered 1 to 10 from a pile of squares all facing down. The players turn up their squares. On his or her turn, a player may compose two or more squares to create a sum equal to one of the numbers in the 3 x 3 grid. If a player can do this, s/he places her/his marker on the sum in the 3 x 3 grid, discards the squares used, and draws replacement squares. The goal is the same as *Tic-Tac-Toe*-that is, to get three in a row.

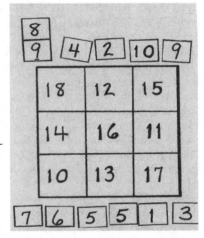

Using Egyptian Hieroglyphics to Underscore Decomposition and Base Ten/Place-Value Ideas (Based on Investigation 6.1 in Baroody with Coslick, 1998)

$|= 1$ ⬛ $= 10$ ⬛ $= 100$

Challenge student to find how many ways the digits 1, 2, and 5 can be combined to form a three-digit numeral. Ask them if 153, 215, 251, 512, and 521 represent the same number as 125 (Whitin & Wilde, 1992). Repeat the challenge with Egyptian hieroglyphics. Discuss the similarities and differences between our Arabic numerals and Egyptian hieroglyphics.)

FIGURE 11.4. Examples of a composition-decomposition activity.

labeling various examples of single instances "one" and various examples of pairs "two" and larger collections (nonexamples) as "not one" or "not two," children can abstract a concept of oneness and twoness. Once this is achieved, a child can in a similar way be helped to abstract threeness and then fourness.

With this basis, counting instruction should make more sense to young children. If a parent models counting a collection of three items, for example, it is far more likely a child will understand the switch in how the last number word is used. Specifically, when the parent models "One, two, three, see three, " or "One, two, t-h-r-e-e," the child who has already used verbal number recognition to see that there are three things in the collection may better understand why their parent repeated or emphasized the word "three" and, thus, more likely to abstract the cardinality principle. Is this *the best* way to help children understand? Perhaps, perhaps not, but it seems to be a more effective path than what many parents and preschool teachers currently use.

Topic 2: Developmental readiness: Estimation and zones of comfort. Our discussion of developmental readiness will focus on the overlooked topic of estimation, a key component of number sense. When (and also how) estimation should be introduced remains unclear. Some researchers have argued that, given the relative difficulty of the topic, it makes sense to postpone its instruction until formal schooling begins (Brade, 2003), perhaps even until second grade (Fuson & Hall, 1983). Others have argued that such instruction needs to begin early before schooling creates the mistaken belief that only exact answers are desirable and to help children construct effective estimation strategies (Baroody with Coslick, 1998; Baroody & Gatzke, 1991). Because estimation is a key component of number sense, it is important to address whether such instruction is appropriate for preschoolers or kindergartners.

Another reason we focus on estimation is a key issue that arises from research on the topic, namely that there are zones of comfort and engagement ranging from interested involvement to disinterested disengagement. This issue is akin to Piaget's moderate novelty principle and has broad implications for planning and implementing any preschool mathematics instruction.

Research Evidence. Both numerical estimation (gauging the approximate size of a collection) and computational estimation (gauging the approximate outcome of an operation) are, at heart, problem-solving activities requiring thoughtful analysis and flexibility (Markovits & Sowder, 1994; Siegel, Goldsmith, & Madson, 1982). Unfortunately, many school age students do not appreciate the value of estimation and respond inflexibly and poorly on estimation tasks (Carpenter, Coburn, Reys, & Wilson, 1976; Kouba, Carpenter, & Swafford, 1989).

How estimation competence and difficulties emerge remains unclear. Relatively little research that has been done on the topic of numerical and computational estimation (Carter, 1986; Fuson & Hall, 1983) and, with few exceptions (e.g., Baroody, 1989b, 1992a; Barth et al., in press; Condry, Gramzow, & Clayton, 2003; La Mont, Barth, & Spelke, 2003; Sowder & Wheeler, 1989), research on the latter has focused on children over 10 years of age (Brade, 2003; Dowker, 2003). Almost no research has examined

the emergence of numerical or computational estimation among children at risk for or with learning difficulties (but see, Baroody, 1988).

Zones of Comfort. Dowker (1997, 2003) identified the following three levels of mental-computation and estimation competence among elementary school children, which can also be applied to gauging number.

1. *The zone of competence* (familiarity and comfort) in which they can determine the exact answer by computation or recall—or, in the case a collection, can visually recognize and accurately specify ("subitize") the cardinal value of the collection.
2. *The zone of proximal competence* (moderate familiarity and comfort) in which they can effectively use existing knowledge to estimate the answer—or, in the case a collection, can reasonably approximate the cardinal value of the collection.
3. *The zone of incompetence* (unfamiliarity and discomfort) in which they "meltdown" (e.g., refuse to respond or resort to a wild guess).

Research on Preschoolers' Zones of Comfort. When designing the tasks for our ongoing work with young preschoolers, we purposely limit the trials to one to four items for two reasons:

1. We wanted to avoid overwhelming our young participants— that is, avoid possible meltdowns.
2. If children could reliably use the number words "one" and "two" or even just "one," it seemed plausible that "three" and "four" would be within their zone of proximal competence. This would seem particularly true if nativists are correct that children so young can form a nonverbal but relatively exact cardinal representation of collections of one to about three items (e.g., Starkey & Cooper, 1995; Wynn, 1992a, 1998).

Surprisingly, though, across a variety of tasks but particularly when required to form and use a mental representation, many children seemed to perceive collections of four and even three items as overwhelmingly large numbers and melted down (Baroody, Benson, & Lai, 2003). The size of the collection that caused a meltdown not only varied among children but varied for a particular child depending on the task complexity or demands.

Consider, for example, the case of Sarah (almost 3 years old). In session 1 with a matching game, she correctly created equivalent collections for visible collections of one, two, and three. However, asked to do so for four items, Sarah put out three items, shook her head to indicate that they were not the same, but said that she couldn't make them the same. In session 2 a week later, she again responded correctly to the matching trials involving one, two, or three items. With four items, Sarah became visibly upset, put out three items, but seemed to be uncertain of her answer. In the *Hiding Game* (nonverbal production of a single collection administered during session 2), she likewise responded correctly to trials involving one, two, or three items. When presented the trial with four items, Sarah started crying. In sessions 3 and 4, 1 and 2 weeks later, respectively, she likewise cried when a task became too challenging on the *Fast Hiding Game* (nonverbal subitizing in which the model collection was displayed for < 2s) trial involving four. These results indicated that one to three was in her zone of competence and that four was in her zone of incompetence—whether the model collection remained visible or not—whether forming a mental representation for a single collection was not or was required.

On more challenging tasks involving the mental representation of two collections, Sarah's zone of incompetence expanded. In session 1 with the *Double Hiding Game* (nonverbal production of two collections), she successfully created equivalent collections for two previously viewed but hidden collections of one item each (the 1 & 1 trial). However, when administered the 3 & 2 trial, the child said, "I can't do it." When subsequently given the 2 & 4, trial, she started crying. In session 2, Sarah again responded correctly to the 1 & 1 trial. With the 2 & 3 trial, the girl ran away and said she didn't want to play again. In sessions 3 and 4, Sarah became tearful on the *Super Hiding Game* (nonverbal addition and subtraction) trials involving $3 - 2$, $1 + 2$, and $3 + 1$. Comparable to Leslie's (1999) results with 12-month-old infants, these results indicate that Sarah could simultaneously form a mental representation of two collections of a single item each (zone of competence) but not of two larger collections (zone of incompetence). Whether she would have responded correctly, melted down, or given an approximate answer (zone of partial competence) for 1 & 2, 2 & 1, 2 & 2 is not known. In brief, these results indicate that with cognitively more demanding tasks (i.e. tasks that required mentally representing two collections and, thus, a greater load on working memory than those involving a single collection), Sarah's zone of competence shrank even further below four.

Hadley, a 3-year-old, similarly was able to nonverbally produce two items but melted down with four. After viewing four items for 3 seconds and seeing them hidden, she responded, "I don't know what that number is, Can I count it?" Encouraged by the tester to put out what she thought, Hadley requested a second look so that she could count the collection. Again encouraged by the tester to put out what she thought, the girl simply grabbed all the available chips.

Research on Preschoolers' Estimation.
Our pilot work with 3-year-olds indicates that more developmentally advanced children spontaneously invent decomposition strategies to gauge either exactly or inexactly collections of three to six items. For example, Bruce decomposed a collection of three items into two and one and a collection of four into two and two and quickly determined the total of each. Four-year-olds in a preschool program for at-risk children were able to indicate the size of a collection within ±25% of its actual cardinality about 75% of the time with briefly viewed (< 2 s) collections of three to five items (Baroody, Eiland, Lai, & Li in preparation). However, reasonable estimates for collections of 7 to 11 fell to about 45%.

A number of children in the previously mentioned estimation study tried to count collections before they were hidden. Although some then gave as their estimate the last number used

in the enumeration process, some gave a number one or more after the last counting number used. Whether they counted the visible collection or not, a few children verbally counted when asked for an estimate. Although this appeared to be a haphazard process for a few, some tailored the length of their count to the relative size of the collection.

Children 8 years old or younger sometimes use a moderately sophisticated benchmark strategy (i.e., compared a collection to a mental representation of a well known number such as 10; Fuson & Hall, 1983; Siegel et al., 1982). Baroody and Gatzke (1991) found that potentially gifted kindergartners seem to use such a strategy effectively with collections less than 10 (with a benchmark of 5), but most had difficulty with larger collections and benchmarks. Brade (2003) replicated these results with typical kindergartners and first graders. Moreover, she found that computer-based estimation instruction from the *Building Blocks* curriculum twice weekly over a period of about 4 weeks did not significantly improve her participants' estimation skill. One possible reason for this is that the intervention was inadequate (e.g., too brief) to help participants construct the big ideas of composition and decomposition or use them to construct more sophisticated estimation strategies, such as decomposing a collection into more or less equal size and subitizeable parts (Siegel et al., 1982). Clearly, much more research is needed to address these issues.

Pedagogical Implications.
The research just discussed has six instructional implications. The first below is general to all mathematics instruction; the remaining implications are specific to estimation instruction.

- *Instruction (and testing) should be sensitive to a children's developmental level in general and their individual zones of competence, partial competence, or incompetence in particular.* In order to ensure that external factors mesh with internal ones so as to promote meaningful learning (Dewey, 1963), preschool teachers should be aware that what constitutes an overwhelmingly large number varies from child to child and that this key internal factor can involve very small numbers and may be narrow (exceeded quickly).

- *Estimation experiences probably can begin during the preschool years if done in a developmentally appropriate manner.*

- *Consistent with the first two points, estimation instruction should begin with numbers just beyond children's zone of competence.* For 3-year-olds, this may be collections as small as about four items. For 4- and 5-year-olds, this may involve collections in the range of 5 to 10 items.

- Instruction that underscores the purposes of estimation and the gradual development of big ideas that underlie strategies for gauging exactly or approximately the size of small or larger collections, such as composition and decomposition, may be helpful. Such big ideas and the sophisticated estimation strategies that build on them arise from number sense and cannot quickly be imposed.

- Children should be encouraged to devise and share informal strategies for quickly recognizing intuitive numbers (e.g., decomposing three into two and one) and encouraged to apply them to increasingly larger collections, whether done so exactly or inexactly. Informal estimation strategies, such as stating a number beyond the last number reached during an aborted enumeration attempt and tailoring a verbal count response to the relative size of a collection, can be encouraged by prompting children to share their estimation strategy and encouraging students to evaluate whether it makes sense. The same can also be done with nonproductive strategies (e.g., citing the last number word generated in an aborted enumeration effort or haphazardly guessing). Strategies, particularly nonproductive ones, could be modeled by a teacher using a muppet such as Count Count or Cookie Monster, and students could be encouraged to help it by evaluating its strategy.

- Help older preschoolers construct a benchmark (mental image) of five; help kindergartners construct a mental image of 10.

CONCLUSIONS

As a society, we can no longer afford to overlook early childhood mathematics education. Given the wealth of informal mathematical knowledge preschoolers seem able to construct and its probable importance for later success with formal mathematics, it is important that all children be given the opportunity to develop mathematical proficiency before formal schooling. Given the evidence of significant individual and group differences in informal knowledge, it is imperative that children at risk for academic failure (e.g., those from low-income, uneducated, non-English-speaking, or single-parent families) be provided early and high quality intervention. In most cases, such intervention alone will not be sufficient to ensure success later during the school years (e.g., Zigler, 2003), but it may be an initial necessary ingredient for achieving equity.

Efforts are already under way to develop effective preschool interventions. Service organizations (e.g., NYAEC and NCTM), state and federal governments (e.g., the National Science Foundation and National Institutes of Health), and private foundations and industry (ExxonMobil Foundation) are supporting the development of appropriate goals or standards (see Clements et al., 2004) and coherent, research-based, and effective curricula and instructional materials such as *Big Math for Little Kids* (Balfanz, Ginsburg, & Greenes, 2003; Ginsburg, Greenes, & Balfanz, 2003; Greenes, Ginsburg, & Balfanz, 2004), *Building Blocks* (Clements & Sarama, 2003, 2004; Sarama & Clements, 2002, 2003), *Everyday Mathematics* (Carroll & Issacs, 2003; SRA/McGraw Hill, 2003), and *Number Worlds* (Griffin, 2000, 2004; Griffin & Case, 1995a, 1996; Griffin et al., 1995), and *Round the Rug Math: Adventures in Problem Solving* (Casey, Kersh, & Young, 2004). The NCTM and NYAEC jointly or separately have published several resources for pre-school educators detailing units, lessons, or activities for promoting specific goals (Copley, 1999, 2000, 2004b). A number of resources detail mathematical games appropriate for early childhood instruction, including Baroody (1987, 1989a), *Early Childhood Games*

Kit (Everyday Mathematics, 2003), Kamii (1985), and Wynroth (1986). Tools for assessing specific informal concepts and skills, such as the *TEMA-3* (e.g., Ginsburg & Baroody, 2003) are also now available.

Given that kindergarten sets the stage for formal mathematics instruction and success, another positive step would be a consistent nationwide policy regarding kindergarten (Vecchiotti, 2003). Currently there are no general standards for mandatory kindergarten attendance, the age of entry, and appropriate curriculum and instructional methods or screening and assessment practices.

The success of early intervention efforts, however, ultimately depends on preschool and kindergarten teachers who are highly knowledgeable about mathematics (including the relevant big ideas), children's learning of it, and techniques for effectively fostering such learning (Baroody, 2004d). The knowledgeable teacher can, for example, see teaching opportunities in everyday routines, unexpected events, children's questions, and play time and take advantage of them to artfully guide learning (Baroody with Coslick, 1998; Bruner, Jolly, & Sylva, 1976; Guha, 2002; Seo & Ginsburg, 2004). However, this more sophisticated type of teaching will require seriously upgrading the pre- and in-service preparation of preschool teachers (Hyson, 2001; Kersaint & Chappell, 2001; Sarama & DiBiase, 2004). This preparation should include integrated mathematical content, developmental, and pedagogical instruction that focus on understanding and how to foster developmentally appropriate big ideas.

A general trend in the research on mathematical development provides an important lesson for the mathematics instruction of preschoolers or kindergartners pre- or in-service teachers, and all students in between. Many researchers have remarked on the stark contrast between preschoolers' surprising mathematical competence and schoolchildren's disturbing mathematical incompetence. Nativists have argued that this paradox is evidence for "privileged domains," knowledge with an innate basis that unfolds readily in the preschool years, and nonprivileged domains, knowledge not supported by an innate endowment and that must be learned with relative difficulty in school. An alternative and perhaps more plausible explanation is that preschoolers' surprising competence with number and simple arithmetic is due to their opportunities to gradually develop adaptive expertise in a supportive, rather than a directive, environment (Baroody & Tiilikainen, 2003). Put differently, the purposeful, meaningful, and inquiry-based of preschoolers' informal learning environment enables them to construct conceptual understanding, meaningful computational procedures, informed strategic thinking, and a productive disposition (i.e., all aspects of mathematical proficiency). Schoolchildren's disturbing incompetence is due to the lack of such opportunities. In other words, the approach and focus of formal schooling, namely highly directive instruction with the aim of fostering routine expertise, ensures the lack of mathematical proficiency. As we prepare preschoolers, kindergartners, and their teachers, it is well worth keeping in mind the results of this natural experiment—that formal instruction might better imitate children's informal preschool learning environment than vice versa.

References

Allardice, B. S., & Ginsburg, H. P. (1983). Children's learning problems in mathematics. In H. P. Ginsburg (Ed.), *The development of mathematical thinking* (pp. 319–349). New York: Academic Press.

Anyon, J. (1980). Social class and the hidden curriculum of work. *Journal of Education, 162*(1), 67–92.

Anyon, J. (1981). Social class and school knowledge. *Curriculum Inquiry, 11,* 3–42.

Arnold, D. H., & Doctoroff, G. L. (2003). The early education of socioeconomically disadvantaged children. *Annual Review of Psychology, 54,* 517–545.

Arnold, D. H., Fisher, P. H., Doctoroff, G. L. & Dobbs, J. (2002). Accelerating math development in HeadStart classrooms. *Journal of Educational Psychology, 94,* 762–770.

Balaban, M. T., & Waxman, S. R. (1997). Do words facilitate object categorization in 9-month-old infants? *Journal of Experimental Child Psychology, 64,* 3–26.

Balfanz, R. (1999). Why do we teach young children so little mathematics? Some historical considerations. In J. V. Copley (Ed.), *Mathematics in the early years* (pp. 3–10). Reston, VA: National Council of Teachers of Mathematics, and Washington, DC: National Association for the Education of Young Children.

Balfanz, R., Ginsburg, H. P., & Greenes, C. (2003). The Big Math for Little Kids early childhood mathematics program. *Teaching Children Mathematics, 9,* 264–268.

Baroody, A. J. (1984). Children's difficulties in subtraction: Some causes and questions. *Journal for Research in Mathematics Education, 15*(3), 203–213.

Baroody, A. J. (1985). Mastery of the basic number combinations: Internalization of relationships or facts? *Journal of Research in Mathematics Education, 16,* 83–98.

Baroody, A. J. (1987). *Children's mathematical thinking: A developmental framework for preschool, primary, and special education teachers.* New York: Teacher's College Press.

Baroody, A. J. (1988). Mental-addition development of children classified as mentally handicapped. *Educational Studies in Mathematics, 19,* 369–388.

Baroody, A. J. (1989a). *A guide to teaching mathematics in the primary grades.* Boston: Allyn & Bacon.

Baroody, A. J. (1989b). Kindergartners' mental addition with single-digit combinations. *Journal for Research in Mathematics Education, 20,* 159–172.

Baroody, A. J. (1989c). One point of view: Manipulatives don't come with guarantees. *Arithmetic Teacher, 37*(2), 4–5.

Baroody, A. J. (1992a). *The development of kindergartners' mental-addition strategies. Learning and Individual Differences, 4,* 215–235.

Baroody, A. J. (1992b). The development of preschoolers' counting skills and principles. In J. Bideaud, C. Meljac, & J. P. Fischer (Eds.), *Pathways to number* (pp. 99–126). Hillsdale, NJ: Erlbaum.

Baroody, A. J. (1995). The role of the number-after rule in the invention of computational short cuts. *Cognition and Instruction, 13,* 189–219.

Baroody, A. J. (1996a). An investigative approach to teaching children labeled learning disabled. In D. K. Reid, W. P. Hresko, & H. L. Swanson (Eds.), *Cognitive approaches to learning disabilities* (3rd ed.; pp. 545–615). Austin, TX: Pro-Ed.

Baroody, A. J. (1996b). Self-invented addition strategies by children classified as mentally handicapped. *American Journal on Mental Retardation, 101*(1), 72–89.

Baroody, A. J. (1999a). Children's relational knowledge of addition and subtraction. *Cognition and Instruction, 17,* 137–175.

Baroody, A. J. (1999b). The development of basic counting, number, and arithmetic knowledge among children classified as mentally retarded. In L. M. Glidden (Ed.), *International review of research in mental retardation, Vol. 22* (pp. 51–103). New York: Academic Press.

Baroody, A. J. (1999c). The roles of estimation and the commutativity principle in the development of third-graders' mental multiplication. *Journal of Experimental Psychology, 74,* 153–193.

Baroody, A. J. (2000). Does mathematics instruction for 3- to 5-year olds really make sense? *Young Children, 55*(4), 61–67.

Baroody, A. J. (2001, April). *Number and operations instruction in early childhood.* Discussant's comments on the symposium "Research-based standards for pre-K–2 Mathematics: Findings from the National Conference" at the Research Pre-session of the annual meeting of the National Council of Teachers of Mathematics, Orlando.

Baroody, A. J. (2002, May). *The developmental foundations of number and operation sense.* Poster presented at the EHR/REC (NSF) Principal Investigators' Meeting ("Learning and Education: Building Knowledge, Understanding Its Implications"), Arlington, VA.

Baroody, A. J. (2003). The development of adaptive expertise and flexibility: The integration of conceptual and procedural knowledge. In A. J. Baroody and A. Dowker (Eds.), *The development of arithmetic concepts and skills: Constructing adaptive expertise* (pp. 1–34). Mahwah, NJ: Erlbaum.

Baroody, A. J. (2004a). The developmental bases for early childhood number and operations. In D. Clements, J. Sarama, & A. M. DiBiase (Eds.), *Engaging young children in mathematics: Standards for early childhood mathematics education* (pp. 173–219). Mahwah, NJ: Erlbaum.

Baroody, A. J. (2004b). A perspective on school mathematics reform. A review of Standards-Based School Mathematics Curricula: What are they? What do students learning? *American Journal of Psychology, 117,* 443–478.

Baroody, A. J. (2004c, April). *The relation between conceptual and procedural knowledge: Past, present, and future.* Paper for a symposium ("Finding Balance: Re-visiting the Relations Between Conceptual and Procedural Knowledge") presented at the annual meeting of American Educational Research Association, San Diego, CA.

Baroody, A. J. (2004d). The role of psychological research in the development of early childhood mathematics standards. In D. Clements, J. Sarama, & A. M. DiBiase (Eds.), *Engaging young children in mathematics Standards for early childhood mathematics education* (pp. 149–172). Mahwah, NJ: Elrbaum.

Baroody, A. J. (in press). Why children have difficulties have mastering the basic number facts and how to help them. *Teaching Children Mathematics.*

Baroody, A. J., & Benson. A. (2001). Early number instruction. *Teaching Children Mathematics, 8,* 154–158.

Baroody, A. J., Benson, A. P., & Lai, M. L. (2003, April). *Early number and arithmetic sense: A summary of three studies.* Paper presented at the annual meeting of the Society for Research in Child Development, Tampa, FL.

Baroody, A. J., Cibulsksis, M., Lai, M., & Li, X. (2004). Comments on the use of learning trajectories in curriculum development and research. *Mathematical Thinking and Learning, 6,* 227–260.

Baroody, A. J., with Coslick, R. T. (1998). *Fostering children's mathematical power: An investigative approach to K-8 mathematics instruction*. Mahwah, NJ: Erlbaum.

Baroody, A. J., Eiland, M., Lai, M.-L., & Li, X. (in preparation). *Number estimation by 4-year-olds*.

Baroody, A. J., & Gatzke, M. S. (1991). The estimation of set size by potentially gifted kindergarten-age children. *Journal for Research in Mathematics Education, 22*(1), 59-68.

Baroody, A. J., & Ginsburg, H. P. (1986). The relationship between initial meaningful and mechanical knowledge of arithmetic. In J. Hiebert (Ed.), *Conceptual and procedural knowledge: The case of mathematics* (pp. 75-112). Hillsdale, NJ: Lawrence Erlbaum Associates.

Baroody, A. J., & Ginsburg, H. P. (1991). A cognitive approach to assessing the mathematical difficulties of children labeled learning disabled. In H. L. Swanson (Ed.), *Handbook on the assessment of learning disabilities: Theory, research and practice* (pp. 177-227). Austin, TX: Pro-Ed.

Baroody, A. J., Ginsburg, H. P., & Waxman, B. (1983). Children's use of mathematical structure. *Journal for Research in Mathematics Education, 14*, 156-168.

Baroody, A. J. & Lai, M. L. (2003, April). *Preschoolers' understanding of the addition-subtraction inverse principle*. Paper presented at the annual meeting of the Society for Research in Child Development, Tampa, FL.

Baroody, A. J., & Tiilikainen, S. H. (2003). Two perspectives on addition development. In A. J. Baroody & A. Dowker (Eds.), *The development of arithmetic concepts and skills: Constructing adaptive expertise* (pp. 75-125). Mahwah, NJ: Erlbaum.

Baroody, A. J., & Wilkins, J. L. M. (1999). The development of informal counting, number, and arithmetic skills and concepts. In J. Copley (Ed.), *Mathematics in the early years, birth to five* (pp. 48-65). Reston, VA: National Council of Teachers of Mathematics.

Baroody, A. J., Wilkins, J. L. M., & Tiilikainen, S. (2003). The development of children's understanding of additive commutativity: From protoquantitative concept to general concept? In A. J. Baroody & A. Dowker (Eds.), *The development of arithmetic concepts and skills: Constructing adaptive expertise* (pp. 127-160). Mahwah, NJ: Erlbaum.

Barth, H., La Mont, K., Lipton, J., Dehaene, S., Kanwisher, N., & Spelke, E. (in press). Non-symbolic arithmetic in adults and young children. *Cognition*.

Battista, M. T. (2004). Applying cognition-based assessment to elementary school students' development of understanding of area and volume measurement. *Mathematical Thinking and Learning, 6*, 185-204.

Beilin, H. (1975). *Studies in the cognitive basis of language development*. New York: Academic Press.

Beilin, H., & Kagan, J. (1969). Pluralization rules and the conceptualization of number. *Developmental Psychology, 1*, 697-706.

Benigno, J. P., & Ellis, S. Two is greater than three: Effects of older siblings on parental support of preschoolers' counting in middle-class families. *Early Childhood Research Quarterly, 19*, 4-20.

Benson, A. P., & Baroody, A. J. (2002, April). *The case of Blake: Number-word and number development*. Paper presented at the annual meeting of the American Educational Research Association, New Orleans.

Benson, A. P., & Baroody, A. J. (2003, April). *Where does non-verbal production fit in the emergence of children's mental models?* Paper presented at the annual meeting of the Society for Research in Child Development, Tampa, FL.

Berenson, S. B. (1997). Language, diversity, and assessment in mathematics learning. *Focus on Learning Problems in Mathematics, 19*(4), 1-10.

Bermejo, V. (1996). Cardinality development and counting. *Developmental Psychology, 32*, 263-268.

Bideaud, J., Meljac, C., & Fischer, J. P. (Eds.). (1992). *Pathways to number*. Hillsdale, NJ: Erlbaum.

Bjonerud, C. (1960). Arithmetic concepts possessed by the preschool child. *The Arithmetic Teacher, 7*, 347-350.

Blevins-Knabe, B., & Musen-Miller, L. (1996). Number use at home by children and their parents and its relationship to early mathematical performance. *Early Development and Parenting, 5*, 35-45.

Boaler, J. (1998). Open and closed mathematics: Student experiences and understandings. *Journal for Research in Mathematics Education, 29*, 41-62.

Brade, G. A. (2003). *The effect of a computer activity on young children's development on numerosity estimation skills*. Unpublished doctoral dissertation, State University of New York at Buffalo.

Bråten, I. (1996). *Cognitive strategies in mathematics. Report No. 10, 1996*. Oslo, Norway: Institute for Educational Research, University of Oslo.

Bredekamp, S., & Copple, C. (1997). *Developmentally appropriate practice in early childhood programs*. Washington, DC: National Association for the Education of Young Children.

Broberg, A. G., Wessels, H., Lamb, M. E., & Hwang, C. P. (1997). Effects of day care on the development of cognitive abilities in 8-year-olds: A longitudinal study. *Developmental Psychology, 33*, 62-69.

Brooks-Gunn, J. (2003). Do you believe in magic?: What can we expect from early childhood intervention programs? *Social Policy Report 17*(1), 3, 4, 6, 7, 9, 11.

Brooks-Gunn, J. Klebanov, P. K., & Liaw, F. (1995). The learning, physical, and emotional environment in the home in the context of poverty: The Infant Health and Development Program. *Children and Youth Services Review, 17*, 251-276.

Brownell, W. A. (1941). *Arithmetic in grades I and II: A critical summary of new and previously reported research*. Durham, NC: Duke University Press.

Bruner, J. S., Jolly, A., & Sylva, K. (1976). *Play: Its role in development and evolution*. New York: Basic.

Buckingham, B. R., & MacLatchy, J. (1930). The number abilities of children when they enter grade one. *Yearbook of the National Society for the Study of Education: Report of the Society's Committee on Arithmetic, 29*, 473-524.

Bussi, M., & Bartolini, G. (1998). Joint activity in mathematics classroom: A Vygotskian analysis. In F. Seeger, J. Voigt, & U. Waschescio (Eds.), *The culture of the mathematics classroom* (pp. 13-49). New York: Cambridge University Press.

Butterworth, B., Marschesini, N., & Girelli, L. (2003). Basic multiplication combinations: Passing storage or dynamic reorganization. In A. J. Baroody & A. Dowker (Eds.), *The development of arithmetic concepts and skills: Constructing adaptive expertise* (pp. 189-202). Mahwah, NJ: Lawrence Erlbaum Associates.

Callahan, L. G., & Clements, D. H. (1984). Sex differences in rote counting ability on entry to first grade: Some observations. *Journal for Research in Mathematics Education, 15*, 378-382.

Campbell, F. A., Pungello, E. P., Miller-Johnson,, S., Burchinal, M., & Ramey, C. T. (2001). The development of cognitive and academic activities: Growth curves from an early childhood educational experiment. *Developmental Psychology, 37*, 231-242.

Campbell, J. R., & Mandel, F. (1990). Connecting math achievement to parental influences. *Contemporary Educational Psychology, 15*, 64-74.

Canobi, K. H. (2004). Individual differences in children's addition and subtraction knowledge. *Cognitive Development, 19*, 81-94.

Carnegie Forum on Education and the Economy. (1986). *A nation prepared: Teachers for the 21st century*. New York: Carnegie Corporation.

Carpenter, T. P., Coburn, T. G., Reys, R. E., & Wilson, J. W. (1976). Notes from national assessment: Estimation. *Arithmetic Teacher, 23*(4), 297–302.

Carroll, W. M., & Issacs, A. (2003). Achievement of students using the University of Chicago School Mathematics Project's Everyday Mathematics. In S. L. Senk, & D. R. Thompson, (Eds.) (2003). *Standards-based school mathematics curricula: What are they? What do students learn?* (pp. 79–108). Mahwah, NJ: Erlbaum

Carter, H. (1986). Linking estimation to psychological variables in the early years. In H. L. Schoen and M. J. Zweng (Eds.), *Estimation and mental computation* (pp. 74–81). Reston, VA: National Council of Teachers of Mathematics.

Case, R. (1975). Social class differences in the intellectual development: A Neo-Piagetian investigation. *Canadian Journal of Behavioral Sciences/Revue Canadienne des sciences du Comportement, 7*, 244–262.

Case, R., Griffin, S., McKeough, A., Okamoto, Y. (1991). Parallels in the development of children's social, numerical, and spatial thought. In R. Case (Ed.), *The mind's staircase: Exploring the conceptual underpinnings of children's thought and knowledge* (pp. 269–284). Hillsdale, NJ: Lawrence Erlbaum Associates.

Case, R., & Okamoto, Y. (1996). The role of central conceptual structures in the development of children's thought. *Monographs of the Society for Research in Child Development, 61* (1–2, Serial No. 246).

Casey, B., Kersh, J., & Young, J. M. (2004). Storytelling sagas: An effective medium for teaching early childhood mathematics. *Early Childhood Research Quarterly, 19*, 167–172.

Chang, C. K. (1999). Learning constructivist teaching by doing: A course for in-service teachers. *Proceedings of the 1999 International Conference on Mathematics Teacher Education* (274–287). Department of Mathematics National Taiwan Normal University, Taipei, Taiwan.

Chung, J. (2000). School-based teacher improvement as an effective support for mathematical curriculum reform. *Mathematics, Science and Technology Education (Taiwan), 10*(2), 71–89.

Clements, D. H. (1984). Training effects on the development and generalization of Piagetian logical operations and knowledge of number. *Journal of Educational Psychology, 76*, 766–776.

Clements, D. H. (2004). Major themes and recommendations. In D. H. Clements, J. Sarama & A.-M. DiBiase (Eds.), *Engaging young children in mathematics: Standards for early childhood mathematics education* (pp. 7–72). Mahwah, NJ: Erlbaum.

Clements, D. H., & Battista, M. T. (1992). Geometry and spatial reasoning. In D. A. Grouws (Ed.), *Handbook of research on mathematics teaching and learning* (pp. 420–464). New York: Macmillan.

Clements, D. H., & Callahan, L. G. (1983). Number or prenumber foundational experiences for young children: Must we choose? *Arithmetic Teacher, 31*(3), 34–37.

Clements, D. H., Copple, C., & Hyson, M. (Eds.) (2002). Early childhood mathematics: Promoting good beginnings. *A joint position statement of the National Association for the Education of Young Children (NAEYC) and the National Council for Teachers of Mathematics (rev. ed.)*. Washington, DC: National Association for the Education of Young Children/National Council for Teachers of Mathematics.

Clements, D. H., & McMillen, S. (1996). Rethinking "concrete" manipulatives. *Teaching Children Mathematics, 2*, 270–279.

Clements, D. H., & Sarama, J. (2003). *DLM Early Childhood Express Math Resource Guide*. Columbus, OH: SRA/McGraw-Hill.

Clements, D. H., & Sarama, J. (Guest Eds.). (2004). Special issue: Hypothetical learning trajectories in mathematics education. *Mathematical Thinking and Learning, 6*.

Clements, D. H., & Sarama, J. (in press). Early childhood mathematics learning. In F. Lester (Ed.), *Second handbook of research on mathematics teaching and learning*. Greenwich, CT: Information Age Publishers.

Clements, D., Sarama, J., & DiBiase, A. M. (Eds.). (2004). *Engaging young children in mathematics: Standards for early childhood mathematics education*. Mahwah, NJ: Erlbaum.

Coates, G. D. & Thompson, V. (1999). Involving parents of four- and five-year-olds in their children's mathematics education: The FAMILY MATH experience. In J. V. Copley (Ed.), *Mathematics in the early years* (pp. 205–214). Reston, VA: National Council of Teachers of Mathematics.

Cobb, P., & Wheatley, G. (1988). Children's initial understanding of ten. *Focus on Learning Problems in Mathematics, 10*(3), 1–28.

Colburn, W. (1828). *Intellectual arithmetic upon the inductive method of instruction*. Boston: Hilliard, Gray, Little, & Wilkins.

Condry, K. Gramzow, E., & Cayton, G. (2003, April). *Three-year-old children's counting: Inferences about addition and subtraction*. Poster presented at the annual meeting of the Society for Research in Child Development, Tampa, FL.

Copeland, R. W. (1979). *How children learn mathematics*. New York: Macmillan.

Copley, J. (Ed.). (1999). *Mathematics in the early years, birth to five*. Reston, VA: National Council of Teachers of Mathematics, and Washington, DC: National Association for the Education of Young Children.

Copley, J. (Ed.). (2000). *The young child and mathematics*. Washington, DC: National Association for the Education of Young Children, and Reston, VA: National Council of Teachers of Mathematics.

Copley, J. (2004a). The early childhood collaborative: A professional development model to communicate and implement the standards. In D. Clements, J. Sarama, & A. M. DiBiase (Eds.), *Engaging young children in mathematics: Standards for early childhood mathematics education* (pp. 401–414). Mahwah, NJ: Erlbaum.

Copley, J. (Ed.). (2004b). *Showcasing mathematics for the young child: Activities for three-, four-, and five-year-olds*. Reston, VA: National Council of Teachers of Mathematics.

Cowan, R. (2003). Does it all add up? Changes in children's knowledge of addition combinations, strategies, and principles. In A. J. Baroody and A. Dowker (Eds.), *The development of arithmetic concepts and skills: Constructing adaptive expertise* (pp. 35–74). Mahwah, NJ: Erlbaum.

Darling-Hammond, L. (1997). *The right to learn: A blueprint for creation schools that work*. San Francisco: Jossey-Bass.

Darling-Hammond, L. (2000). Teacher quality and student achievement: A review of state policy evidence. *Education Policy Analysis Archives*. Retrieved May 1, 2004 from http://epaa.asu.edu/epaa/v8n1.

De Abreu, G. (2000). Relationships between macro and micro sociocultural contexts: Implications for the study of interactions in the mathematics classroom. *Educational Studies in Mathematics, 41*(1), 1–29.

Delazer, M. (2003). Neuropsychological findings on conceptual knowledge of arithmetic. A. J. Baroody & A. Dower (Eds.), *The development of arithmetic concepts and skills: Constructing adaptive expertise* (pp. 385–407) Mahwah, NJ: Erlbaum.

Denton, K., & West, J. (2002). *Children's reading and mathematics achievement in kindergarten and first grade*. Washington, DC: National Center for Educational Statistics

Dev, P., Doyle, B. A., & Valente, B. (2002). Labels needn't stick: "At-risk" first graders rescued with appropriate intervention. *Journal of Education for Students Placed at Risk, 7*, 327–332.

Dewey, J. (1898). Some remarks on the psychology of number. *Pedagogical Seminary, 5*, 416–434.

Dewey, J. (1963). *Experience and Education*. New York: Collier.

Donlan, C. (1998). Number without language? Studies of children with specific language impairments. In C. Donlan (Ed.), *Development of mathematical skills* (pp. 225–254). Hove, England: Psychology Press.

Donlan, C. (2003). Numeracy development in children with specific language impairments: The interaction of conceptual and procedural knowledge. In A. J. Baroody & A. Dowker (Eds.), *The development of arithmetic concepts and skills: Constructing adaptive expertise* (pp. 337–358). Mahwah, NJ: Erlbaum.

Dowker, A. D. (1997). Young children's addition estimates. *Mathematical Cognition, 3*, 141–154.

Dowker, A. D. (1998). Individual differences in normal arithmetical development. In C. Donlan (Ed.), *The development of mathematical skills* (pp. 275–302). Hove, England: Psychology Press.

Dowker, A. D. (2003). Young children's estimates for addition: The zone of partial knowledge and understanding. In A. J. Baroody & A. Dowker (Eds.), *The development of arithmetic concepts and skills: Constructing adaptive expertise* (pp. 35–74). Mahwah, NJ: Elrbaum.

Dueker, G., & Needham, A. (2003, April). *Labeling facilitates 5-month-olds' infants' category formation*. Poster presented at the annual meeting of the Society for Research in Child Development, Tampa, FL.

Duncan, G. J., & Brooks-Gunn, J. (2000). Family poverty, welfare reform and child development. *Child Development, 71*, 188–196.

Educational Testing Service Policy Information Report. (1997). *Computers and Classrooms: The status of technology in the U.S.* Princeton, NJ: Author.

Elkind, D. (1988). Acceleration. *Young Children, 43*(4), 2.

Entwisle, D. R., & Alexander, K. L. (1990). Beginning school math competence: Minority and majority comparisons. *Child Development, 61*, 454–471.

Entwisle, D. R., & Alexander, K. L. (1996). Family type and children's growth in reading and math other the primary grades. *Journal of Marriage and the Family, 58*, 341–355.

Everyday Mathematics. (2003). *Games Kit: Early Childhood* (ISB 0-07-572761-7). DeSoto, TX: SRA/McGraw-Hill.

Fazio, B. (1994). The counting abilities of children with specific language impairments: A comparison of oral and gestural tasks. *Journal of Speech and Hearing Disorders, 37*, 358–368.

Fazio, B. (1996). Mathematical abilities of children with specific language impairment: A follow-up study. *Journal of Speech and Hearing Research, 39*, 839–849.

Fazio, B. (1999). Arithmetic calculation, short term memory and language performance of children with specific language impairment: A five year follow-up. *Journal of Speech, Language, and Hearing Research, 42*, 420–431

Ferguson, R. F. (1991). Paying for public education: New evidence on how and why money matters. *Harvard Journal of Legislation, 28*, 465–498.

Ferguson, R. F. (1998). Can school narrows the Black-White test score gap? In C. Jencks and M. Phillips (Eds.), *The Black-White Test Score Gap* (pp. 318–374). Washington, DC: Brookings Institution.

Fluck, M. (1995). Counting on the right number: Maternal support for the development of cardinality. *Irish Journal of Psychology, 16*(2), 133–149.

Fluck, M., & Henderson, L. (1996). Counting and cardinality in English nursery pupils. *British Journal of Educational Psychology, 66*, 501–517.

Frank Porter Graham Child Development Center (1999). *Early Learning, later success: The Abecedarian study, executive summary*. Chapel Hill: University of North Carolina Press.

Freeman, F. N. (1912). Grouped objects as a concrete basis for the number idea. *Elementary School Teacher, 8*, 306–314.

Fromboluti, C. S., & Rinck, N. (1999). *Early childhood, where learning begins, mathematics: Mathematical activities for parents and their 2- to 5-year-old children*. Jessup, MD: U.S. Department of Education.

Frye, D., Braisby, N., Lowe, J., Maroudas, C. & Nicholls, J. (1989). Young children's understanding of counting and cardinality. *Child Development, 60*, 1158–1171.

Fulkerson, A. L., & Mansfield-Koren, M. (2003, April). *Verbal labeling facilitates 12-month-olds'formation of novel categories in a modified word extension task*. Poster presented at the annual meeting of the Society for Research in Child Development, Tampa, FL.

Furth, H. G., & Wachs, H. (1974). *Thinking goes to school: Piaget's theory in practice*. New York: Oxford University Press.

Fuson, K. C. (1988). *Children's counting and concepts of number*. New York: Springer-Verlag.

Fuson, K. C. (1992). Research on whole number addition and subtraction. In D. Grouws (Ed.), *Handbook of research on mathematics teaching and learning* (pp. 243–275). New York: Macmillan.

Fuson, K. C. (2004). Pre-K to Grade 2 goals and standards: Achieving 21st Century Mastery for all. In D. Clements, J. Sarama, & A. M. DiBiase (Eds.), *Engaging young children in mathematics: Standards for early childhood mathematics education* (pp. 105–148). Mahwah, NJ: Erlbaum.

Fuson, K. C., & Burghardt, B. H. (2003). Multidigit addition and subtraction methods invented in small groups and teacher support of problem solving and reflection. In A. J. Baroody & A. Dowker (Eds.), *The development of arithmetic concepts and skills: Constructing adaptive expertise* (pp. 267–304). Mahwah, NJ: Erlbaum.

Fuson, K., Carroll, W., & Drueck, J. (2000). Achievement results for second and third graders using the Standards-based curriculum *Everyday Mathematics*. *Journal for Research in Mathematics Education, 31*, 277–295.

Fuson, K. C., & Hall, J. W. (1983). The acquisition of early number word meanings: A conceptual analysis and review. In H. P. Ginsburg (Ed.), *The development of mathematical thinking* (pp. 49–107). New York: Academic Press.

Gagné, R. M., & Briggs, L. J. (1974). *Principles of Instructional Design*. New York: Holt, Rinehart & Winston.

Geary, D. C. (1996). *Children's mathematical development: Research and practical applications*. Washington, DC: American Psychological Association. (Originally published 1994)

Geary, D. C., Bow-Thomas, C. C., Fan, L., & Siegler, R. S. (1993). Even before formal instruction, Chinese children outperform American children in mental addition. *Cognitive Development, 8*, 517–529.

Gelman, R. (1979). Preschool thought. *American Psychologist, 34*, 900–905.

Gelman, R. (1991). Epigenetic foundations of knowledge structures: Initial and transcendant constructions. In S. Carey & R. Gelman (Eds.), *The epigenesis of mind: Essays on biology and cognition. Hillsdale, NJ: Erlbaum* (pp. 293–322).

Gelman, R. (1998). Domain specificity in cognitive development: Universals and non-universals. In M. Sabourin, F. Craik, & M. Robert

(Eds.), *Advances in psychological science: Vol. 2. Biological and cognitive aspects* (pp. 557-579). Hove, England: Psychology Press.

Gelman, R., & Gallistel, C. R. (1978). *The child's understanding of number*. Cambridge, MA: Harvard University Press.

Gelman, R., & Massey, C. (1987). The cultural unconscious as contributor to supporting environments for cognitive development: Commentary on social processes in early number development. *Monographs of the Society for Research in Child Development, 52*(2, Serial No. 216).

Gelman, R., & Meck, E. (1992). Early principles aid initial but not later conceptions of number. In J. Bideaud, C. Meljac, & J. P. Fischer (Eds.), *Pathways to number* (pp. 171-189). Hillsdale, NJ: Erlbaum Associates.

Gibb, E. G., & Castaneda, A. M. (1975). Experience for young children. In J. N. Payne (Ed.), *Mathematics learning in early childhood* (37th Yearbook, pp. 96-124). Reston, VA: National Council of Teachers of Mathematics.

Gilford, D. M., & Tenebaum, E. (Eds.). (1995). *Precollege science and mathematics teachers: Monitoring supply, demand, and quality*. Washington, DC: National Academy Press.

Ginsburg, H. P. (1977). *Children's arithmetic*. New York: D. Van Nostrand. (Republished in 1989 by Pro-Ed of Austin, TX, as *Children's arithmetic: How they learn it and how you teach it*.)

Ginsburg, H. P., & Baroody A. J. (1983). *The test of early mathematics ability*. Austin, TX: Pro-Ed.

Ginsburg, H. P., & Baroody, A. J. (1990). *Test of early mathematics ability* (2nd ed.) (TEMA-2). Austin, TX: Pro-Ed.

Ginsburg, H. P., & Baroody, A. J. (2003). *Test of early mathematics ability* (3rd ed.) (TEMA-3). Austin, TX: Pro-Ed.

Ginsburg, H. P., Cannon, J., Eisenband, J., & Pappas, S. (2006). Mathematical thinking and learning. In K. McCartney & D. Phillips (Eds.), *The handbook of early child development*. Malden, MA: Blackwell Publishing.

Ginsburg, H. P., Choi, Y. E., Lopez, L. S., Netley, R., & Chi, C.-Y. (1997). Happy birthday to you: The early mathematical thinking of Asian, South American, and U.S. children. In T. Nunes & P. Bryant (Eds.), *Learning and teaching mathematics: An international perspective* (pp. 163-207). East Sussex, England: Psychology Press.

Ginsburg, H. P., Greenes, C., & Balfanz, R. (2003). Big math for little kids. Parsippany, NJ: Dale Seymour Publications.

Ginsburg, H. P., Inoue, N., & Seo, K.-H. (1999). Young children doing mathematics: Observations of everyday activities. In J. V. Copley (Ed.), *Mathematics in the early years* (pp. 88-99). Reston, VA: National Council of Teachers of Mathematics.

Ginsburg, H. P., Klein, A., & Starkey, P. (1998). The development of children's mathematical knowledge: Connecting research with practice. In I. E. Sigel & K. A. Renninger (Eds.), *Handbook of child psychology: Vol. 4. Child psychology in practice* (5th Ed., pp. 401-476). New York: Wiley & Sons.

Ginsburg, H. P., & Russell, R. L. (1981). Social class and racial influences on early mathematical thinking. *Monographs of the Society for Research in Child Development, 46*, 16 (Serial No. 193).

Government Information Office (2003). *Republic of China (Taiwan) Yearbook 2003: Education*. Retrieved 12/19/2003 from http://www.gio.gov.tw/taiwan-website/5-gp/yearbook/chpt18.htm

Gravemeijer, K. (2004). Local instructional theories as support for reform. *Mathematical Thinking and Learning, 6*, 105-128.

Gray, S. W., Ramsey, B. K., & Klaus, R. A. (1983). The early Training Project 1962-1980. In Consortium for Longitudinal Studies (Ed.), *As the twig bends... Lasting effects of preschool programs*. Hillsdale, NJ: Erlbaum.

Greenes, C., Ginsburg, H. P., & Balfanz, R. (2004). Big math for little kids. *Early Childhood Research Quarterly, 19*, 159-166.

Greenwald, R., Hedges, L. V., & Laine, R. D. (1996). The effects of school resources on student achievement. *Review of Educational Research, 66*(3), 361-396.

Griffin, S., & Case, R. (1995a). *Number worlds: Kindergarten level*. Durham, NH: Number World Alliance.

Griffin, S., & Case, R. (1995b). Evaluating the breadth and depth of training effects when central conceptual structures are taught. *Society for Research in Child Development Monographs, 59*, 90-113.

Griffin, S., & Case, R. (1997). Re-thinking the primary school math curriculum: An approach based on cognitive science. *Issues in Education, 3*(1), 1-49.

Griffin, S., Case, R., & Capodilupo, A. (1995). Teaching for understanding: The importance of the central conceptual structure in the elementary mathematics curriculum. In A. McKeough, J. Lupart. & A. Marini (Eds.), *Teaching for transfer* (pp. 123-151). Mahwah, NJ: Erlbaum.

Griffin, S., Case, R., & Siegler, R. (1994). Rightstart: Providing the central conceptual prerequisites for first formal learning of arithmetic to students at risk for school failure. In K. McGilly (Ed.), *Classroom lessons: Integrating cognitive theory and classroom practice*. Cambridge, MA: The MIT Press.

Guha, S. (2002). Integrating mathematics for young children through play. *Young Children, 57*(3), 90-92.

Haith, M. H., & Benson, J. B. (1998). Infant cognition. In D. Kuhn & R. Siegler (Eds.), *Handbook of Child Psychology: Vol. 2 Cognition, perception and language* (5th ed., pp. 199-254). New York: John Wiley & Sons.

Hall, E. (1970). A Conversation with Jean Piaget and Barbel Inhelder. *Psychology Today, 3*, 25-26.

Hall, G. S. (1891). The content of children's minds on entering school. *Pedagogical Seminary, 1*, 139-173.

Halle, T. G., Kurtz-Costes, B., & Mahoney, J. L. (1997). Family influences on school achievement in low-income African American children. *Journal of Educational Psychology, 89*, 527-537.

Hannula, M. M., & Lehtinen, E. (2004). *Relationships between spontaneous focusing on numerosity and early mathematical skills*. Paper presented at the annual meeting of the American Educational Research Association. San Diego, CA.

Hannula, M. M., & Lehtinen, E. (in press). Spontaneous focusing on numerosity and mathematical skills of young children. *Learning and Instruction*.

Hatano, G. (1988). Social and motivational bases for mathematical understanding. In G. B. Saxe & M. Gearhart (Eds.), *Children's mathematics* (pp. 55-70). San Francisco: Jossey-Bass.

Hatano, G. (2003). Forward. In A. J. Baroody & A. Dowker (Eds.), *The development of arithmetic concepts and skills: Constructing adaptive expertise* (pp. xi-xiii). Mahwah, NJ: Erlbaum.

Heavey, L. (2003). Arithmetical savants. In A. J. Baroody & A. Dowker (Eds.), *The development of arithmetic concepts and skills: Constructing adaptive expertise* (pp. 409-433). Mahwah, NJ: Erlbaum.

Hiebert, J., & Carpenter, T. P. (1992). Learning and teaching with understanding. In D. Grouws (Ed.), *Handbook of research on mathematics teaching and learning* (pp. 65-97). New York: Macmillan.

Hoffman, L. W. (1989). Effects of maternal employment in the two-parent family. *American Psychologists, 44*, 283-292.

Huang, K. (1988). *Instruction Principle*. Taipei: National Taiwan Normal University Press.

Hughes, M. (1986). *Children and number: Difficulties in learning mathematics*. New York: Basil Blackwell.

Hunting, R. P., & Kamii, C. K. (2002). Fostering the mathematical thinking of young children, Pre-K-2. In Cockburn, A. D., Nardi, E. (Eds.) *Proceedings of the 26th conference of the International Group for the Psychology of Mathematics Education—North American Chapter* (pp. 163–167). Athens, GA.

Huttenlocher, J., Jordan, N. C., & Levine, S. C. (1994). A mental model for early arithmetic. *Journal of Experimental Psychology: General, 123*, 284–296.

Hyson, M. (2001). Better futures for young children, better preparation for their teachers: Challenges emerging from national reports. *Young Children, 56*(1), 60–62.

Ingersoll, R. M. (1999). The problem of underqualified teachers in American secondary schools. *Educational Researcher, 28*(20), 26–37.

James, W. (1890). *Principles of psychology*. New York: Holt.

Jimerson, S., Egeland, B., & Teo, A. (1999). A longitudinal study of achievement trajectories: Factors associated with change. *Journal of Educational Psychology, 91*, 116–126.

Jones, G. A., & Thornton, C. A. (1993). Vygotsky revisited: Nurturing young children's understanding of number. *Focus on Learning Problems in Mathematics, 15*, 18–28.

Jordan, N. C., Hanich, L. B., & Uberti, H. Z. (2003). Mathematical thinking and learning difficulties. In A. J. Baroody & A. Dowker (Eds.), *The development of arithmetic concepts and skills: Constructing adaptive expertise* (pp. 359–383). Mahwah, NJ: Erlbaum.

Jordan, N. C., Huttenlocher, J., & Levine, S. C. (1992). Differential calculation abilities in young children from middle-and low-income families. *Developmental Psychology, 28*, 644–653.

Jordan, N. C., Huttenlocher, J., & Levine, S. C. (1994). Assessing early arithmetic abilities: Effects of verbal and nonverbal response types on the calculation performance of middle- and low-income children. *Learning and Individual Differences, 6*, 413–432.

Jordan, N. C., Levine, S. C., & Huttenlocher, J. (1994). Development of calculation abilities in middle- and low-income children after formal instruction in school. *Journal of Applied Developmental Psychology, 15*, 223–240.

Kamii, C. (1985). *Young children reinvent arithmetic: Implication of Piaget's theory*. New York: Teachers College Press.

Kamii, C. (1989). *Young children continue to reinvent arithmetic—2nd grade*. New York: Teachers College Press.

Karweit, N. L. (1994). Can preschool alone prevent early learning failure? In R. E. Slavin, N. L. Karweit, & B. A. Wasik (Eds.), *Preventing early school failure: Research, policy, and practice* (pp. 58–77, ch. 3). Boston: Allyn and Bacon.

Kersaint, G., & Chappell, M. F. (2001). Helping teachers promote problem solving with young at-risk children. *Early Childhood Education Journal, 29*, 57–63.

Kilpatrick, J., Swafford, J., & Findell, B. (Eds.) (2001). *Adding it up: Helping children learn mathematics*. Washington, DC: National Academy Press.

Kim, S., Charmaraman, L., Klein, A., & Starkey, P. (June, 2000). *Supporting the development of informal mathematics knowledge in young children*. San Francisco, CA: Presentation at the Fifth Annual Head Start National Research Conference.

Kirk, G. E., Hunt, J. M., & Volkmar, F. (1975). Social class and preschool language skills: Cognitive and semantic mastery of number. *Genetic Psychology Monographs, 92*, 131–153.

Klein, A., & Starkey, P. (1995, March). Preparing for the transition to school mathematics: The Head Start family math project. In P. Starkey (Chair), *School readiness and early achievement of impoverished children*. Symposium conducted at the meeting of the Society for Research in Child Development, Indianapolis, IN.

Klein, A., & Starkey, P. (2004). Fostering preschool children's mathematical knowledge: Findings from the Berkeley Math Readiness Project. In D. H. Clements, J. Sarama, & A.-M. DiBiase (Eds.), *Engaging young children in mathematics: Standards for early childhood mathematics education* (pp. 343–360) Mahwah, NJ: Erlbaum.

Kouba, V. L., Carpenter, T. P., & Swafford, J. O. (1989). Numbers and operations. In M. M. Lindquist (Ed.), *Results from the Fourth Mathematics Assessment of the National Assessment of Educational Progress* (pp. 64–93). Reston, VA: National Council of Teachers of Mathematics.

Kraner, R. E. (1977). The acquisition age of quantitative concepts of children from three to six years old. *Journal of Experimental Education, 46*(2), 52–59.

Langford, P. (2004). *Vygotsky's developmental and educational psychology*. Hove, England: Psychology Press.

La Mont, K. A., Barth, H., & Spelke, E. S. (2003, April). *Can representations of large, approximate numerosities support addition in preschool children?* Poster presented at the annual meeting of the Society for Research in Child Development, Tampa, FL.

LeFevre, J. A., Smith-Chant, B. L., Hiscock, K., Daley, K. E., & Morris, J. (2003). Young adults' strategic choices in simple arithmetic: Implications for the development of mathematical representations. In A. J. Baroody & A. Dowker (Eds.), *The development of arithmetic concepts and skills: Constructing adaptive expertise* (pp. 203–228). Mahwah, NJ: Lawrence Erlbaum Associates.

Lerman, S. (1996). Intersubjectivity in mathematics learning: A challenge to the radical constructivist paradigm? *Journal for Research in Mathematics, 27*, 133–150.

Lerman, S. (2001). Cultural, discursive psychology: A sociocultural approach to studying the teaching and learning of mathematics. *Educational Studies in Mathematics, 46*, 87–113.

Lesh, R., & Yoon, C. (2004). Evolving communities of mind—Where development involves several interacting and simultaneously developing strands. *Mathematical Thinking and Learning, 6*, 205–226.

Leslie, A. M. (1999, April). *The attentional index as object representation: A new approach to the object concept and numerosity*. Paper presented at the biennial meeting of the Society for Research in Child Development, Albuquerque, NM.

Levine, S. C., Jordan, N. C., & Huttenlocher, J. (1992). Development of calculation abilities in young children. *Journal of Experimental Child Psychology, 53*, 72–103.

Lubienski, S. T. (2000). Problem solving as a means toward "mathematics for all": An exploratory look through a class lens. *Journal for Research in Mathematics Education, 31*, 454–482.

Lubienski, S. T. (2002). A closer look at black-white mathematics gaps: Intersections of race and SES in NAEP achievement and instructional practices data. *Journal of Negro Education, 71*, 269–287.

Lubienski, S. T. (2003). Celebrating diversity or denying disparities: A critical assessment. *Educational Researcher, 32*(8), 30–38.

Maffel. A. C., & Buckley, P. (1980). *Teaching pre-school math: Foundations and activities*. New York: Human Sciences Press.

Macaruso, P., & Sokol, S. M. (1998). Cognitive neuropsychology and developmental dyscalculia. In C. Donlan (Ed.), *The development of mathematical skills* (pp. 201–225). Hove, England: Psychology Press.

Markovits, Z., & Sowder, J. (1994). Developing number sense: An intervention study in Grade 7. *Journal for Research in Mathematics Education, 25*, 4–29.

Matti, M. C. & Weiss, I. R. (with Boyd, S. L., Boyd, S. E., Kroll, J. L., Montgomery, D. L., et al.). (1994). *Science and mathematics education: Briefing book volume IV*. Chapel Hill, NC: Horizon Research.

May, D. C., & Kundert, D. K. (1997). School readiness practices and children at-risk: Examining the issues. *Psychology in the Schools, 34*(2), 73–84.

Mazzocco, M. M., & Myers, G. F. (2003). Complexities in identifying and defining mathematics learning disability in the primary school-age years. *Annal of Dyslexia, 53*, 218–253.

Mazzocco, M. M. M., Myers, G. F., & Thompson, R. (2003, April). *Early predictors of risk for poor math achievement.* Poster presented at the biennial meeting of the Society for Research in Child Development, Tampa, FL.

Mazzocco, M. M. M., & Thompson, R E. (in press). Kindergarten predicators of math learning disability. *Learning Disabilities Research and Practice.*

McLoyd, V. C. (1998). Socio-economic disadvantage and child development. *American Psychologist, 53,* 185-204.

McLaughlin, K. L. (1935). Number ability of preschool children. *Childhood Education, 11,* 348-353.

McKnight, C. C., Crosswhite, F. J., Dossey, J. A., Kifer, E., Swafford, J. O., Travers, K. J., & Cooney, T. J. (1987). *The underachieving curriculum: Assessing U.S. school mathematics from an international perspective.* Champaign, IL. Stipes.

Means, B., & Knapp, M. S. (1991). Cognitive approaches to teaching advanced skills to educationally disadvantaged students. *Phi Delta Kappan,* December, 282-289.

Miller, K . F. (1996). Origins of quantitative competence. In R. Gelman & T. K. Au (Eds.), *Perceptual and cognitive development* (pp. 213-241). San Diego, CA: Academic Press.

Miller, K. F., Smith, C. M., Zhu, J., & Zhang, H. (1995). Preschool origins of cross-national differences in mathematical competence: The role of number-naming systems. *Psychological Science, 6,* 56-60.

Miller, K. F., & Stigler, J. W. (1987). Counting in Chinese: Cultural variation in a cognitive skill. *Cognitive Development, 2,* 279-305.

Miller, S. (1995). *An American imperative: Accelerating minority educational advancement.* New Haven: CT University Press.

Miura, I. (1987). Mathematics achievement as a function of language. *Journal of Educational Psychology, 79,* 79-82.

Miura, I. T., Kim, C. C., Chang, C.-M., & Okamoto, Y. (1988). Effects of language characteristics on children's cognitive representation of number: Cross-national comparisons. *Child Development, 59,* 1445-1450.

Miura, I. T., & Okamoto, Y. (1989). Comparisons of U.S. and Japanese first graders' cognitive representation of number and understanding of place value. *Journal of Educational Psychology, 81,* 109-113.

Miura, I. T., & Okamoto, Y. (2003). Language supports for mathematics understanding and performance. In A. J. Baroody & A. Dowker (Eds.), *The development of arithmetic concepts and skills: Constructing adaptive expertise* (pp. 229-242). Mahwah, NJ: Erlbaum.

Mix, K. S. (1999). Preschoolers' recognition of numerical equivalence: Sequential sets. *Journal of Experimental Child Psychology, 74,* 309-332.

Mix, K. S. (2002). The construction of number concepts. *Cognitive Development, 17 (Special Issue: Constructivism Today, J. Langer & E. Turiel, Eds.),* 1345-1363.

Mix, K. S., Huttenlocher, J., & Levine, S. C. (2002a). *Math without words: Quantitative development in infancy and early childhood.* New York: Oxford University Press.

Mix, K. S., Huttenlocher, J., & Levine, S. C. (2002b). Multiple cues for quantification in infancy: Is number one of them? *Psychological Bulletin, 128,* 278-294.

Mix, K. S., Sandhofer, C. M., & Baroody, A. J. (in press). Number words and number concepts: The interplay of verbal and nonverbal processes in early quantitative development. R. Kail (Ed.), *Advances in child development and behavior, Vol. 33.* New York: Academic Press.

Moll, L. C., Amanti, C., Neff, D., & Gonzalez, N. (1992). Funds of knowledge for teaching: Using a qualitative approach to connect homes and classrooms. *Theory into Practice, 31,* 132-141.

Moses, R. P. (2001). *Radical equations: Math literacy and civil rights.* Boston: Beacon Press.

Munn, P. (1998) Number symbols and symbolic function in preschoolers. In C. Donlan (Ed.), *The development of mathematical skills* (pp. 47-71). Hove, England: Psychology Press.

National Commission on Excellence in Education. (1983). *A nation at risk.* Washington, DC: U.S. Government Printing Office.

National Council of Teachers of Mathematics (1989). *Principles and standards for school mathematics: Standards 1989.* Reston, VA: Author.

National Council of Teachers of Mathematics (2000). *Principles and standards for school mathematics: Standards 2000.* Reston, VA: Author.

National Institute of Child Health and Human Development. (1998). *The NIHCD study of early child care.* Washington, DC: National Institutes on Health, NIH Pub. 98-4318.

New, R. S. (1998). Playing fair and square: Issues of equity I preschool mathematics, science, and technology (138-156). *Dialogue on Early childhood Science, Mathematics, and Technology Education.* Washington, DC: American Association for the Advancement of Science.

Nunes, T., & Bryant, P. (1996). *Children doing mathematics.* Cambridge, MA: Blackwell.

Nunes, T., & Moreno, C. (1998). Is hearing impairment a cause of difficulties in learning mathematics? In C. Donlan (Ed.), *Development of mathematical skills* (pp. 227-254). Hove, England: Psychology Press.

Oakes, J. (1990a). *Multiplying inequalities: the effects of race, social class, and tracking on opportunities to learn mathematics and science.* Santa Monica, CA: Rand Corporation.

Oakes, J. (1990b). Opportunities, achievement, and choice: Women and minority students in science and mathematics. In C. B. Cazden (Ed.), *Review of research in education, 16* (pp. 153-222). Washington, DC: American Educational Research Association.

Oakes, J., Joseph, R., & Muir, K. (2004). Access and achievement in mathematics and science: Inequalities that endure and change. In J. A. Banks & C. M. Banks, (Eds.), Handbook of Research on Multicultural Education, San Francisco: Jossey Bass.

Pagani, L. S., Boulerice, B., & Tremblay, R. E. (1997). The influence of poverty on children's classroom placement and behavior problems. In G. J. Duncan & J. Brooks-Gunn (Eds.), *Consequences of growing up poor* (pp. 311-339). New York: Sage.

Patton, M. M., & Kokoski, T. M. (1996). How good is your early childhood science, mathematics, and technology program? Strategies for extending your curriculum. *Young Children, 51*(5), 38-44.

Paulos, J. A. (1991). *Beyond numeracy: Ruminations of a numbers man.* New York: Alfred A. Knopf.

Payne, J. N., & Huinker, D. M. (1993). Early number and numeration. In R. J. Jensen (Ed.), *Research ideas for the classroom: Early childhood mathematics* (pp. 43-71). Reston, VA: National Council of Teachers of Mathematics

Peisner-Feinberg, E. S., Burchinal, M. R., Clifford, R. M., Culkins, M. L., Howes, C., Kagan, S. L., & Yazejian, N. (2001). The relation of preschool child-care quality to children's cognitive and social developmental trajectories through second grade. *Child Development, 72,* 1534-1553.

Piaget, J. (1964). Development and learning. In R. E. Ripple & V. N. Rockcastle (Eds.), *Piaget rediscovered* (pp. 7-20). Ithaca, NY: Cornell University

Piaget, J. (1965). *The child's conception of number.* New York: Norton.

Piaget, J. (2001) *Studies in reflective abstraction.* Philadelphia: Taylor and Francis.

Philips Jr., J. L. (1969). *The origins of intellect: Piaget's theory.* San Francisco: W. H. Freeman.

Pound, L. (1999). *Supporting mathematical development in the early years*. Philadelphia: Open Press.

Putnam, R. T., deBettencourt, L. U., & Leinhardt, G. (1990). Understanding of derived fact strategies in addition and subtraction. *Cognition and Instruction, 7*, 245-285.

Ralston, A. (2004). Research mathematicians and mathematics education: A critique. *Notices of the AMS, 51*, 403-411.

Rea, R. E., & Reys, R. E. (1971). Competencies of entering kindergarteners in geometry, number, money, and measurement. *School Science and Mathematics, 71*, 389-402.

Reaney, L. M., & West, J. (2003, April). *Examining the impact of kindergarten enrollment decisions on first grade reading and mathematics achievement*. Poster presented at the biennial meeting of the Society for Research in Child Development, Tampa, FL.

Resnick, L. B. (1982). Syntax and semantics in learning to subtract. In T. P. Carpenter, J. M. Moser, & T A. Romberg (Eds.), *Addition and subtraction: A cognitive perspective* (pp. 136-155). Hillsdale, NJ: Erlbaum.

Resnick, L. B. (1992). From protoquantities to operators: Building mathematical competence on a foundation of everyday knowledge. In G. Leinhardt, R. Putnam, & R. A. Hattrup (Eds.), *Analysis of arithmetic for mathematics teaching* (pp. 373-425). Hillsdale, NJ: Erlbaum.

Resnick, L. B. (1994). Situated rationalism: Biological and social preparation for learning. In L. A. Hirschfield & S. A. Gelman (Eds.), *Mapping the mind. Domain-specificity in cognition and culture* (pp. 474-493). Cambridge: Cambridge University Press.

Reynolds, A. J., & Temple, J. A. (1998). Extended early childhood intervention and school achievement: Age thirteen findings from the Chicago Longitudinal Study. *Child Development, 69*, 231-246.

Reys, R. E., & Rea, R. E. (1970). The comprehensive mathematics inventory: An experimental instrument for assessing the mathematical competencies of children entering school. *Journal for Research in Mathematics Education, 1*, 180-186.

Rickard, T. C., & Bourne, L. E., Jr. (1996). Some tests of an identical elements model of basic arithmetic skills. *Journal of Experimental Psychology: Learning, Memory, and Cognition, 22*, 1281-1295.

Rickard, T. C., Healy, A. F., & Bourne, L. E., Jr. (1994). On the cognitive structure of basic arithmetic skills. Operation, order, and symbol transfer effects. *Journal of Experimental Psychology: Learning, Memory, and Cognition, 20*, 1139-1153.

Rittle-Johnson, B., & Siegler, R. S. (1998). The relationship between conceptual and procedural knowledge in learning mathematics: A review. In C. Donlan (Ed.), *The development of mathematical skills* (pp. 75-110). Hove, England: Psychology Press.

Rosu, L., & Baroody, A. J. (2005). *The case of Alice: Early number word and number development*. Unpublished manuscript. University of Illinois at Urbana-Champaign.

Roth, J., Carter, R., Ariet, M., Resnick, M. B., & Crans, G. (2000, April). Comparing fourth-grade math and reading achievement of children who did and did not participate in Florida's statewide prekindergarten early intervention program. Paper presented at the annual meeting of the American Educational Research Association, New Orleans, LA.

Russell, B. (1917). *Introduction to mathematical philosophy*. London: George, Allen, Unwin.

Sandhofer, C. & Mix, K. S. (April, 2003). Number language and number concepts: Evidence from a long-range microgenetic study. Paper presented at the biennial meeting of the Society for Research in Child Development, Tampa.

Sandhofer, C. M., & Smith, L. B. (1999). Learning color words involves learning a system of mappings. *Developmental Psychology, 35*, 668-679.

Sarama, J. (2004). Technology in early childhood mathematics: Building Blocks as an innovative technology-based curriculum. In D. H. Clements, J. Sarama & A.-M. DiBiase (Eds.), *Engaging young children in mathematics: Standards for early childhood mathematics education* (pp. 361-375). Mahwah, NJ: Erlbaum.

Sarama, J., & Clements, D. H. (2002). Building Blocks for young children's mathematical development. *Journal of Educational Computing Research, 27*(1&2), 93-110.

Sarama, J. & Clements, D. H. (2003). Building blocks of early childhood mathematics. *Teaching Children Mathematics, 9*, 480-484.

Sarama, J., & Clements, D. H. (2004). Building blocks for early childhood mathematics. *Early Childhood Research Quarterly, 19*, 181-189.

Sarama, J., & DiBiase, A.-M. (2004). The professional development challenge in preschool mathematics. In D. H. Clements, J. Sarama & A.-M. DiBiase (Eds.), *Engaging young children in mathematics: Standards for early childhood mathematics education* (pp. 415-446). Mahwah, NJ: Erlbaum.

Saxe, G. B., Dawson, V., Fall, R., & Howard, S. (1996). Cultural and children's mathematical thinking. In R. Sternberg & T. Ben-zeev (Eds.), *The nature of mathematical thinking* (pp. 119-144). Hillsdale, NJ: Erlbaum.

Saxe, G. B., & Guberman, S. R. (1998). Studying mathematics learning in collective activity. *Learning and Instruction, 8*, 489-501.

Saxe, G. B., Guberman, S., & Gearhart, M. (1987). Social processes in early number development. *Monographs of the Society for Research in Child Development, 52* (Serial No. 2).

Schaeffer, B., Eggleston, V. H., & Scott, J. L. (1974). Number development in young children. *Cognitive Psychology, 6*, 357-379.

Schoenfeld, A. H. (2002). Making mathematics work for all children: Issues of standards, testing, and equity. *Educational Researcher, 31*, 13-25.

Schweinhart, L. J., Barnes, H. V., & Weikart, D. P. (1993). *Significant Benefits: The High/Scope Perry Preschool Study Through Age 27*. Monographs of the High/Scope Educational Research Foundation, Number 10. Ypsilanti, MI: High/Scope Press.

Secada, W. G. (1992). Race, ethnicity, social class, language, and achievement in mathematics. In D. A. Grouws (Ed.), *Handbook of Research on Mathematics Teaching and Learning* (pp. 623-660). New York: Macmillan.

Seo, K., & Ginsburg, H. P. (2003). "You've got to carefully read the math sentence . . . ":Classroom context and children's interpretations of the equals sign. In A. J. Baroody & A. Dowker (Eds.), *The development of arithmetic concepts and skills: Constructing adaptive expertise* (pp. 161-187). Mahwah, NJ: Erlbaum.

Seo, K., & Ginsburg, H. P. (2004). What is developmentally appropriate in early childhood mathematics education? Lessons from new research. In D. H. Clements, J. Sarama, & A.-M. DiBiase (Eds.), *Engaging young children in mathematics: Standards for early childhood mathematics education* (pp. 91-104). Mahwah, NJ: Erlbaum.

Sharp, E. (1969). *Thinking is child's play*. New York: E. P. Dutton.

Shaw, K., Nelsen, E., & Shen, Y. L. (2001, April). *Preschool development and subsequent school achievement among Spanish-speaking children from low-income families*. Paper presented at the annual meeting of the American Educational Research Association, Seattle, WA.

Siegel, A., Goldsmith, L., & Madison, C. (1982). Skill and estimation problems of extent and numerosity. *Journal for Research in Mathematics Education, 13*, 211-232.

Simon, M. A. (1995). Reconstructing mathematics pedagogy from a constructivist perspective. *Journal for Research in Mathematics Education, 26*, 114-145.

Simon, T. J. (1997). Reconceptualizing the origins of numerical knowledge: A "nonnumerical" account. *Cognitive Development, 12*, 349-372.

Sokol, S. M., McCloskey, M., Cohen, N. J., & Aliminosa, D. (1991). Cognitive representations and processes in arithmetic: Inferences from the performance of brain-damaged subjects. *Journal of Experimental Psychology: Learning, Memory, and Cognition, 17*, 355-376.

Song, M., & Ginsburg, H. P. (1987). The development of informal and formal mathematics thinking in Korean and U.S. children. *Child Development, 58*, 1286-1296.

Sophian, C. (1995). Representation and reasoning in early numerical development: Counting, conservation, and comparisons between sets. *Child Development, 66*, 559-577.

Sophian, C. (1998). A developmental perspective on children's counting. In C. Donlan (Ed.), *The development of mathematical skills* (pp. 27-46). Hove, England: Psychology Press.

Sophian, C. (2004). Mathematics for the future: Developing a Head Start curriculum to support mathematics learning. *Early Childhood Research Quarterly, 19*, 59-81.

Sophian, C., Harley, H., & Martin, C. S. M. (1995). Relational and representational aspects of early number development. *Cognition and Instruction, 13*, 253-268.

Sophian, C., & McCorgray, P. (1994). Part-whole knowledge and early arithmetic problem-solving. *Cognition and Instruction, 12*, 3-33.

Sophian, C., & Vong, K. I. (1995). The parts and wholes of arithmetic story problems: Developing knowledge in the preschool years. *Cognition and Instruction, 13*, 469-477.

Sowder, J., Philipp, R., Armstrong, B., & Schappelle, B. (1998). *Middle-grade teachers' mathematical knowledge and its relationship to instruction.* Albany, NY: SUNY.

Sowder, J. T., & Wheeler, M. M. (1989). The development of concepts and strategies use in computational estimation. *Journal for Research in Mathematics Education, 20*, 130-146.

Spelke, E. (2003a, April). *What makes humans smart?* Invited address presented at the biennial meeting of the Society for Research in Child Development, Tampa, FL.

Spelke, E. (2003b). What makes us smart? Core knowledge and natural language. In D. Genter & S. Goldin-Meadow (Eds.), *Language in mind.* Cambridge, MA: MIT Press.

Spelke, E. S., & Tsivkin, S. (2001). Language and number: A bilingual training study. *Cognition, 78*, 45-88.

SRA/McGraw-Hill. (2003). *Everyday Mathematics Games Kit—Early childhood.* DeSoto, TX: Author.

Starkey, P., & Cooper, R. G. (1995). The development of subitizing in young children. *British Journal of Developmental Psychology, 13*, 399-420.

Starkey, P., & Klein, A. (2000). Fostering parental support for children's mathematical development: An intervention with Head Start families. *Early Education and Development, 11*, 659-680.

Starkey, P., Klein, A., Chang, I., Qi, D., Lijuan, P., & Yang, Z. (1999, April). *Environmental supports for young children's mathematical development in China and the United States.* Paper presented at the biennial meeting of the Society for Research in Child Development, Albuquerque, NM.

Starkey, P., Klein, A., & Wakeley, A. (2004). Enhancing young children's mathematical knowledge through a pre-kindergarten mathematics intervention. *Early Childhood Research Quarterly, 19*, 99-120.

Steffe, L. P., & Cobb, P. (1988). *Construction of arithmetic meanings and strategies.* New York: Springer-Verlag.

Steffe, L. P., Cobb, P., & von Glasersfeld, E. (1988). *Construction of arithmetical meanings and procedures.* New York: Springer-Verlag.

Stevenson, H. W., Lee, S. Y., & Stigler, J. W. (1986). Mathematics achievement of Chinese, Japanese, and American children. *Science, 231*, 693-699.

Stevenson, H. W., & Newman, R. S. (1986). Long-term prediction of achievement and attitudes in mathematics and reading. *Child Development, 57*, 646-659.

Stevenson, H. W., & Stigler, J. W. (1992).*The learning gap.* New York: Summit.

Stigler, J. W., Lee, S. Y., Lucker, G. W., & Stevenson, H. W. (1982). Curriculum and achievement in mathematics: A study of elementary school children in Japan, Taiwan, and the United States. *Journal of Educational Psychology, 74*, 315-322.

Stigler, J. W., Lee, S. Y., & Stevenson, H. W. (1990). *Mathematical knowledge of Japanese, Chinese, and American elementary school children.* Reston, VA: National Council of Teachers of Mathematics.

Takeuchi, M., & Scott, R. (1992). Cognitive profiles of Japanese and Canadian kindergarten and first grade children. *The Journal of Social Psychology, 132*,505-512.

Tate, W. F. (1997). Race-ethnicity, SES, gender, and language proficiency in mathematics achievement: An update. *Journal for Research in Mathematics Education, 28*, 652-679.

Thorndike, E. L. (1922). *The psychology of arithmetic.* New York: Macmillan.

Thornton, C. A., & Bley, N. S. (Eds.). (1994). *Windows of opportunity: Mathematics for students with special needs.* Reston, VA: National Council of Teachers of Mathematics.

Towse, J., & Saxton, M. (1998). Mathematics across national boundaries: Cultural and linguistic perspectives on numerical competence. In C. Donlan (Ed.), *The development of mathematical skills* (pp. 129-150). Hove, England: Psychology Press.

Tudge, J. R. H., & Doucet, F. (2004). Early mathematical experiences: Observing young black and white children's everyday activities. *Early Childhood Research Quarterly, 19*, 21-39.

U.S. Department of Education, N.C.E.S. (2000). *The condition of education 2000.* Washington, DC: U.S. Government Printing Office.

Van de Walle, G. A. Carey, S., & Prevor, M. (2000). Bases for object individuation in infancy: Evidence from manual search. *Journal of Cognition & Development, 1*(3), 249-280.

Vecchiotti, S. (2003). Kindergarten: An overlooked educational policy priority. *Social Policy Report, 17*(2), 1, 3-14, 16-19.

Verschaeffel, L., Greer, B., & DeCorte, E. (in press). Whole number concepts and operations. In F. Lester (Ed.). *Second handbook of research on mathematics teaching and learning.* Greenwich, CT: Information Age Publishers.

von Glasersfeld, E. (1982). Subitizing: The role of figural patterns in the development of numerical concepts. *Archives de Psychologie, 50*, 191-218.

Vygotsky, L. S. (1962). *Thought and language* (E. Hanfmann & G. Vakar, Eds. & Trans.). Cambridge, MA: MIT Press.

Vygotsky, L. S. (1978). *Mind in Society.* Cambridge, MA: Harvard University Press.

Vygotsky, L. S. (1986). *Thought and language* (A. Kozulin, Trans.). Cambridge, MA: The MIT Press.

Vygotsky, L. S. (1987).Thinking and speech. In R. W. Rieber & A. S. Carton (Eds.), *The collected works of L. S. Vygotsky (Vol. 1): Problems of general psychology*, (N. Minick, Trans., pp. 112-220). New York: Plenum Press.

Wagner, S., & Walters, J. (1982). A longitudinal analysis of early number concepts: From numbers to number. In G. Forman (Ed.), *Action and thought* (pp. 137-161). New York: Academic Press.

Wakeley, A., Rivera, S., & Langer, J. (2000a). Can young infants add and subtract? *Child Development, 71*, 1525-1534.

Wakeley, A., Rivera, S., & Langer, J. (2000b). Not proved: Reply to Wynn. *Child Development, 71*, 1537-1539.

Waschescio, U. (1998). The missing link: Social and cultural aspects in social constructivist theories. In F. Seeger, J. Voigt, & U. Waschescio (Eds.), *The culture of the mathematics classroom* (pp. 221-241). New York: Cambridge University Press.

Watson, J. B. (1930). *Behaviorism*. Chicago: University of Chicago Press.

Waxman, S. R., & Markow, D. B. (1995). Words as invitations to form categories: Evidence from 12- to 13-month-old infants. *Cognitive Psychology, 29*, 257-302.

Weikart, D. P. (1998). Changing early childhood development through educational intervention. *Preventive Medicine: An International Devoted to Practice & Theory, 27*, 233-237.

Weikart, D. P., & Schweinhart, L. J. (1992). High/Scope Preschool Program outcomes. In J. McCord & R. E. Tremblay (Eds.), *Preventing antisocial behavior: Interventions from birth through adolescence* (pp. 67-86). New York: Guilford Press.

Weikart, D. P., & Schweinhart, L. J. (1997). High/Scope Perry Preschool Program. In G. W. Albee & T. P. Gullota (Eds.) *Primary preventions works. Issues in children's and families' lives, Vol.6* (pp, 146-166). Thousand Oaks, CA: Sage Publications.

Wertheimer, M. (1959). *Productive thinking*. New York: Harper & Row. (Originally published 1945)

Whitin, D. J., & Wilde, S. (1992). *Read any good math lately: Children's books for mathematical learning*. K-6. Portsmouth, NH: Heinemann.

Winsler, A. (2003). Introduction to the special issue: Vygotskian perspectives in early childhood education. *Early Education and Development, 14*, 253-269.

Woodward, J., & Baxter, J. (1997). The effects of an innovative approach to mathematics on academically low achieving students in inclusive settings. *Exceptional Children, 63*, 373-388.

Wright, R. J. (1991). What number knowledge is possessed by children entering the kindergarten year of school? *The Mathematics Education Research Journal, 3*(1), 1-16.

Wright, R. J. (1994). A study of the numerical development of 5-year-olds and 6-year-olds. *Educational Studies in Mathematics, 26*, 25-44.

Wright, R. J., Martland, J., & Stafford, A. (2000). *Early numeracy: Assessment for teaching and intervention*. London: Paul Chapman Publications/Sage.

Wright, R. J., Martland, J., Stafford, A., & Stanger, G. (2002). *Teaching Number: Advancing skills and strategies*. London: Paul Chapman Publications/Sage.

Wright, S. P., Horn, S. P., & Sanders, W. L. (1997). Teacher and classroom content effects on student achievement: Implications for teacher evaluation. *Journal of Personnel Evaluation, 11*, 57-67.

Wynn, K. (1990). Children's understanding of counting. *Cognition, 36*, 155-193.

Wynn, K. (1992a). Addition and subtraction by human infants. *Nature, 358*, 749-750.

Wynn, K. (1992b). Children's acquisition of the number words and the counting system. *Cognitive Psychology, 20*, 220-251.

Wynn, K. (1998). Numerical competence in infants. In C. Donlan (Ed.), *Development of mathematical skills* (pp. 1-25) Hove, England: Psychology Press.

Wynroth, L. (1986). *Wynroth math program—The natural numbers sequence*. Ithaca, NY: Wynroth Math Program. (Originally published 1975)

Young-Loveridge, J. M. (1989). The relationship between children's home experiences and their mathematical skills on entry to school. *Early Child Development and Care, 43*, 43-59.

Zhou, Y. (1995). *Quality education and reforms in primary math education*. *HuBei Education*, Issues 1 and 2.

Zigler, E. (2003). Forty years of believing in magic is enough. *Social Policy Report, 17*(1), 10.

Zigler, E., & Styfco, S. J. (1998). Applying the findings of development psychology to improve early childhood intervention. In S. G. Paris & H. M. Wellman (Eds.), *Global prospects for education: Development, culture, and schooling* (pp. 345-365). Washington, DC: American Psychological Association.

Zur, O., & Gelman, R. (2004). Young children can add and subtract by predicting and checking. *Early Childhood Research Quarterly, 19*, 121-137.

REPOSITIONING THE VISUAL ARTS IN EARLY CHILDHOOD EDUCATION: A DECADE OF RECONSIDERATION

Christine Marmé Thompson
The Pennsylvania State University

Five minutes remained before class was scheduled to begin, but Ming-Jen had already arrived at his Saturday morning art class. The opening routine was familiar, and he moved through it without hesitation, retrieving his name tag and his sketchbook from the counter just inside the door, locating a carpet square close to a container brimming with markers, and settling on the floor to draw. He selected a spot close to a favorite student teacher, a young man seated in the midst of carpet squares, markers, and children, ready to watch and to respond to the children and their drawings. The atmosphere was industrious as children trailed in sleepily or bounded through the door with great exuberance, and, having been greeted by teachers and friends, settling quickly to their work.

Ming-Jen's first drawing of the morning, his warm up, stood out among his more typical renditions of exotic creatures and landscapes. He drew a flower, a center surrounded by petals, each outlined and filled with a different markered color, placed symmetrically around the central perimeter. As unremarkable as it may be for a young child to draw a flower, there was something unusual about the way that this drawing was constructed. Like many of Ming-Jen's drawings—and unlike those of many young children who compose their drawings part-by-contiguous-part until objects are completed or spaces filled—this one was composed deliberately in such a way that room was reserved for parts not yet drawn, negative spaces left between stem and center to be filled later with petals.

As soon as this drawing was finished, Ming-Jen turned to a fresh page in his sketchbook, taking a moment to smooth the pages with the side of his hand. Grabbing a blue marker from the bin beside him, he drew a scalloped line across the two page spread open before him. Just above this line in the middle of the left-hand page, he added a curving triangular shape. The student teacher just behind Ming-Jen noticed what he had done and intoned, "Uh oh." Another child, sprawled on the floor 3 ft away, declared, "A shark's fin," in recognition of Ming-Jen's plan, executed silently with a faint smile on his lips. Clearly aware that he had attracted a growing and attentive audience, Ming-Jen drew the sweep of a whale's tail emerging from the waterline. A child looking on observed, "Well, he draws a lot," as if to reassure his companion that there *was* an explanation for the remarkable ability Ming-Jen was demonstrating before their eyes. Ming-Jen continued to add details beneath the waterline, and the student teacher next to him remarked, very quietly, "That's a wonderful picture." A small grin played with Ming-Jen's lips, but he drew on without comment, conscious of the spectators huddled around him, willing to keep them guessing as the drawing continued to materialize on the page. "Are you gonna color it?" one of the children asked, noticing that the scene so far had been drawn in a single color, with one marker flowing continuously across the page, describing one object, then another. "What's that?" Yujie inquired as Ming-Jen began a large form that straddled the central spiral bisecting his drawing surface. "A big starfish," she suggested, "or an octopus?" Again Ming-Jen failed to respond, drawing on with the undivided attention of three onlookers focused on him. Finally, the page filled with flotsam and jetsam, his performance completed, Ming-Jen leaned back against the knee of the student teacher behind him, and shared a satisfied smile with the group.

In many respects, this was a small and ordinary incident of classroom life, readily recognizable as the type of fleeting interaction that occurs at drawing tables or art centers, as children gather to admire the skillful performance of one of their peers. And yet accounts of children drawing in the social space of early childhood classrooms are still relatively rare. Once, and not so very long ago, researchers concerned with children's art would have focused their attention exclusively on Ming-Jen himself, the solitary artist in dialogue with his work (Dyson, 1989). The presence of others, their comments and questions, their critical or appreciative responses, would have been reduced to background noise or erased entirely from an account of this drawing being made (Atkinson, 2002; Matthews, 1999). As Pearson (2001) suggests, the act of drawing might have passed without remark, in favor of an analysis of the drawing itself, for children's artworks have often been granted greater significance than the work that produced them. Even when advice to teachers continued to insist upon the primacy of process over product, researchers focused attention exclusively on the residue of that process.

In the decade just past, art educators concerned with the education of young children have devoted considerable energy to the serious critique of the research and theory on which practice in early childhood art has been based. Stimulated by a renewed sense of responsibility for early childhood education, and more direct involvement with young children and their teachers, art educators in museums, schools, and universities have joined in questioning many of their shared assumptions about young children and their encounters with art. This reconceptualization draws on sources previously overlooked or lightly used in the past, when developmental psychology structured thinking about young children and their art and child-centered approaches to early art education were widely accepted as exemplary practice. As recently as 1993, Jeffers reported that the art educators she surveyed emphasized developmental issues in the methods classes they offered to university students majoring in early childhood and elementary education, identifying development as one of three major concerns addressed in such courses. This finding was somewhat surprising, in an era in which a discipline-based approach to art education prevailed, and, to an extent all but unprecedented in the history of North American art education, developmental issues vanished from ongoing conversations within and beyond that field.

This discipline-based perspective has evolved in the past decade, expanding toward a focus on visual culture, broadly defined (e.g., Duncum, 2003), but leaving in its wake an enduring commitment among art educators to the study of images and objects in their aesthetic, critical, historical, social and political contexts. There has also been a marked resurgence of interest in the art experience of contemporary children and adolescents, and in the development of curricular theory and instructional approaches that are responsive to that experience.

Jeffer's (1993) reading of the content of preservice education of teachers suggests that there has been an arrhythmia in the field, a lack of syncopation between what beginning teachers are taught, and what researchers and theorists recommend. The developmental stage theories that served as the foundation of early art education throughout much of the 20th century are undeniably appealing to prospective teachers, providing a measure of predictability in a curricular area which many classroom teachers approach with considerable uncertainty and apprehension. Developmental stages supply a structure that is comprehensible and comprehensive, an approach to early art education that can be reproduced in any classroom, if children's experiences with art are structured in a particular way that accords well with the child-centered traditions of early childhood practice. At the same time, researchers and theorists who focus on early art education have begun to question the "hegemony of developmental psychology on our understanding of children" (Tarr, 2003, p. 7) and the traditional structure of universal stages with their tendency to "decontextualize child and children" (Tarr, 2003, p. 7).

Art education research, necessarily interdisciplinary in focus, has become increasingly attuned to larger cultural issues. A pervasive reconceptualization of the "image of the child" (Malaguzzi, 1995) can be seen in the emergence of the new sociology of childhood (James, Jenks, & Prout, 1998) and studies of children's culture (Jenkins, 1998), and exemplified in the practice of preschool education in Reggio Emilia. The most dramatic changes that have occurred in research on early childhood art and art education in the past decade involve changes of perspective or theoretical orientation. As our understanding of young children and of the content and contexts of art education have continued to evolve, different forms and different emphases have emerged as priorities in art education research.

Art education's relationship to early childhood practice is historically close and often beset by difficulty. Art educators seldom teach young children directly, although the establishment of preschool programs in public schools, and the interest in the role of the *atelierista* (Vecchi, 1998) has changed this situation to some extent, in some communities. Indeed, many of the art educators who have worked most closely with young children, and who have written about those experiences, entered early childhood classrooms as researchers, often simultaneously working with those who are actually doing the teaching (for example, Tarr, 1995; Taunton & Colbert, 2000; Thompson, 1999, 2002, 2003; Thompson & Bales, 1991). Art education in early childhood classrooms depends primarily on early childhood specialists (Baker, 1994), who sometimes rely on advice provided by art educators through publication or teaching. This means, among many other things, that art educators are often outside observers in the early childhood settings where their research takes place, and seldom in a position to submit their ideas directly to the test of practice. This may account for a tendency, apparent in research on children's art from the beginning of its history, to wrap descriptions of child art in prescriptions for practice, to offer educational advice extrapolated from psychological study (for example, Kellogg, 1970; Luquet, 1927/2001). This advice was frequently motivated by a desire to preserve children's art in the most unadulterated state possible. Fortunately, this tendency seems to be muted as researchers enter classrooms with the intention of viewing children's art-making and response as "social practice" (Pearson, 2001) in action, and confront the urgency of formulating advice for teachers that is sound, practical, and clearly articulated.

As Wilson (1997) points out,

Child "art" is a product of the modernist era. To the modernist art educator and psychologist, artistic development was essentially a natural unfolding process that led to individual expression. This belief was not unlike the preferred modernist view of the artist as an individual with the obligation, perhaps the moral imperative, to develop a unique style of expression unconstrained by artistic convention. (p. 82)

But, Wilson continues, child art, like all art, is an "open concept" (Weitz, 1959, pp. 145-156), defined and redefined in response to changing conditions: "objects and events become child art when they are so interpreted" (Wilson, 1997, p. 81). The boundaries of art continually expand, as new media, new experiences, and new understandings become available. The emergence of photography projects for children (Ewald & Lightfoot, 2001) and video as a medium for telling stories in the classroom (Grace & Tobin, 2002) are recent examples of approaches to art making that fundamentally alter the circumstances in which children experience themselves as artists. Wilson acknowledges that understanding child art inevitably requires interpretation, and that this phenomenon, historically and persistently of interest to so many different constituencies, cannot help but mean different things to different people: "When individuals with different sets of interests and values interpret children's objects differently, those objects are transformed into very different things, things that are sometimes works of art and sometimes not" (Wilson, 1997, p. 82). The world of art, the world of education, and the world of the child provide distinct perspectives on the same phenomenon, and each perspective, on its own, may well conceal as much as it reveals.

The attitudes we hold toward children's art and art experience are inevitably conditioned by prevailing cultural beliefs about art and childhood (Korzenik, 1981; Leeds, 1989; Wilson, 1997), beliefs that are shaped by things seen and discussions heard through the media, in our daily conversations with colleagues and service station attendants and our children's teachers, or in the more rarified conversations that occur in the "official" art worlds of galleries, museums, and critical reviews, and the equally heady realms of educational research and theory. At one time, in the middle of the twentieth century, the lush easel paintings produced by preschool children were prized, both by artists who saw in them an enviable freedom of gesture and a complete indifference to the task of representing tangible objects and scenes, and by psychologists and educators who saw them as evidence of a healthy confidence and exuberant well-being. More recently, interest in the narrative dimensions of children's art emerged among artists and critics, coinciding with increased attention among educators to the role of drawing in the "prehistory" of writing (Vygotsky, 1962) and in the process of meaning making in which young children are constantly engaged (Wilson & Wilson, 1982). These values, absorbed from our culture in the process of living, affect the kinds of experience teachers provide for children, and the interests researchers bring to the classrooms where these experiences are pursued. Neither childhood nor art are simple or static concepts: Neither is amenable to stable or enduring definition in a manner that

will stand the test of time or transfer, in tact, from one context to another. In the early years of the 21st century, the primary focus of research in early art education, defined in the broadest possible terms, is the process through which children learn to represent and to read the world by means of visual images. As it has been throughout its history, early childhood art remains an object of scholarly attention for psychologists, art educators and early childhood specialists, artists and art historians, and an immediate practical interest for parents and teachers. These multiple perspectives, diverse as they often are, converge in three broad, overlapping categories—development, context, and curriculum (Bresler & Thompson, 2002)—that provide organization to the remainder of this discussion.

DEVELOPMENT: QUESTIONING TRADITIONAL VIEWS

"Can we think beyond the developmental stages in art that we have taken for granted for so long and that have implicitly limited the possibilities of experiences and materials that we have offered children?" (Tarr, 2003, p. 8)

Although the developmentalist perspective has been subjected to repeated challenges over the past 20 years (Wilson & Wilson, 1982; Wolf & Perry, 1988), the basic description of evolutionary patterns in children's drawings formulated in the first half of the 20th century retains a powerful presence in early childhood education. Textbooks published within the past decade for teachers who are preparing to work with young children continue to feature stages of artistic development originally described by Viktor Lowenfeld in the 1940s (Edwards, 1997; Schirrmacher, 1993), by Rhoda Kellogg in the 1960s (Schirrmacher, 1993), occasionally supplemented, though not supplanted, by more current research (Jalongo & Stamp, 1997). In many cases, these texts reflect the continuing influence of Piaget on thinking in the field (Atkinson, 2002), even as the recommendations for teaching that they offer suggest the need for adult structure (often overt structure) in art programs for young children. A more Vygotskian perspective is apparent in a text published recently by Althouse, Johnson and Mitchell (2003), who recognize the essential role that adults play in initiating, scaffolding, and responding to young children's earliest encounters with art.

Cognitive psychologists continue to undertake studies related to children's art experiences, operating within an established consensus regarding the nature of age-related changes in children's drawings (for example, Cox, 1992; Freeman & Cox, 1985; Lange-Kuettner & Thomas, 1995; Thomas & Silk, 1990). Reith (1997) observes persistent interest among his colleagues in children's passage from "intellectual" to "visual realism" (Luquet, 1927). He notes that psychologists are particularly interested in the phenomena that seem to occur after age 5, when children display more concern with the inclusion of relevant details in their drawings, and, at 8 or 9, when children seem to develop a more acute (and critical) sense of what might be seen from a particular view point (see also Korzenik, 1973-1974). The ongoing debate, Reith notes, concerns the explanations for these phenomena. Some psychologists stress the role of "knowledge about objects" (Reith, 1997, p. 61): "Drawings are believed to reflect the subject's mental representations and conceptual knowledge about the objects they draw. Drawings become more accurate and detailed as children's mental models of the world become more extensive and differentiated" (p. 61). As Reith points out, this belief about the relationship between drawing and cognition is firmly established, having served as the basis for the Draw-a-Man Test (Goodenough, 1926; Harris, 1963). Recent research tends to stress the negative impact of knowledge on drawing (Cox, 1989; Freeman & Janikoun, 1972), the extent to which what children *know* about an object prevents them from drawing what they *see*. A classic example of this tendency is seen when young children include details of an object that are hidden from their view, choosing to depict the canonical view in preference to one that is more accurate to the model, but less informative about the characteristic features of the object as the child knows them. Presented with the challenge of drawing a mug with its handle turned away from their view, for example, young children often include the unseen handle in the interest of clearly depicting a mug which, distinct from a drinking glass, depends upon this appendage (Cox, 1992).

Some psychologists who concentrate on this area of research challenge the proposition that the major questions surrounding child art have been satisfactorily answered. Golomb (1997) suggests that, "Despite much productive research in the domain of drawing, no clear consensus has been reached regarding the course of development, the nature of the progression, the validity of a stage conception, and the goals or end-states of graphic development" (p. 131). The possibility of continual generation of fresh perspectives on child art is seen in John Matthew's (1999) reconsiderations of scribbling, in which he links early forms of motor behavior that are first mastered and then continued as playful manipulations, with markers in hand, but also in play with scarves and blocks and toy trucks and action figures. At the same time, Matthews raises objections to the widely held assumption that scribbles are "prerepresentational" traces of motor activity caught on paper—gestural, pleasurable, non-referential. Matthews stresses the basis of these early marks in children's effort to produce meaning:

During the phase when infants are supposed to be mindlessly scribbling, they imbue their marking actions with profound expressive and representational intention. . . . For many children, these drawings are products of a systematic investigation, rather than haphazard actions, of the expressive and representational potential of visual media. (p. 19)

Matthews continues, contributing to the critique of the ways in which representation is defined in discussions of child art: "Early drawings lack meaning only if one assumes that drawing is necessarily the depiction of objects" (p. 20). He contends that children are also interested in the expression of movement and emotion:

In the hands of a 1- or 2-year-old, drawing and painting become sensitive media, responsive to even minute fluctuations in the child's own feelings and in the ambient emotional temperature. When representational values appear in children's drawing these are unrecognizable to those who assume that visual representation is about recognizable pictures of recognizable things. Some early paintings and drawings are not pictures of things, but they are representations in a fuller sense, in that they record the child's process of attention to objects and events. (Matthews, 1999, pp. 20–21)

As Egan (1988, 1999; Egan & Ling, 2002) suggests, many "taken-for-granted truisms about children's thinking and learning" (1999, p. 86) continue to permeate educational thought, persisting, implicit and unquestioned, both in everyday discussions and teaching practice, and in research. Egan points, instead, to those things that young children do well, in some cases, more spontaneously and fluidly than they will at other periods of their lives, including the contemplation of philosophical questions (Matthews, 1980) and participation in the arts. Egan's recognition of the rich resources for thought and action young children demonstrate in artistic pursuits supports Howard Gardner's (1980) description of the late preschool years as a "golden age," a time in which children demonstrate intellectual and imaginative versatility. Egan and Ling conclude, "The basics of our cultural lives are the arts" (2002, p. 100), effectively inverting the fundamental teleologies underlying traditional understandings of what children are developing from, and toward.

In the past decade, participating in a more general critique of the developmentalist perspective, researchers have raised the possibility that the conceptualization of human development that guides much educational discourse may begin with a fundamental misunderstanding that is particularly detrimental to consideration of children's art or symbolic behaviors. As Gallas (1994) frames the question:

What if we were to assume that children came to school more, rather than less, able to communicate their thinking about the world? Why not assume that when the child enters school, he or she presents us with an enormous number of innate tools for acquiring knowledge and, rather than considering them to be "constraints" as Gardner (1991) suggests, consider them to be assets? (p. xv)

For much of the 20th century, a model of "natural development" prevailed in discussions of child art, describing an innate and universal process with children "located in one of several stages, which are internally consistent, formally logical and intellectually revealing" (Freedman, 1997, p. 95). These stages of artistic development, as outlined by Luquet (1927; Costall, 2001), Lowenfeld (1957) and others, were supported by psychobiological explanations. Based upon the "presupposition of innate ability" (Atkinson, 2002, p. 7), stage theory encouraged the belief that artistic competence unfolds predictably from within the individual child, given the most minimal encouragement. Landmarks along the path of artistic development were labelled differently and sometimes described in terms that varied, if only slightly, from one researcher to the next. Puzzling detours and derailments of the process in its later stages were noted. However, the journey's destination remained constant: Children were developing toward the capacity to draw realistically, to capture visual likeness on the drawing page, to create convincing two-dimensional versions of a three-dimensional world.

Two assumptions underlying the traditional model of artistic development have come into question since the 1980s.

Doubts initially raised by Wilson and Wilson (1982), Wolf and Perry (1988), and others about two elements of developmental theory—(1) the idea that representational accuracy is the sole or universal endpoint of the process of artistic development, and (2) the belief that benign neglect was the most favorable ground in which this process would unfold—have been confirmed by subsequent research.

Questioning the Standard of Realism

Although few researchers in art education overtly acknowledge their debt to Piaget, the research and theory of artistic development, from Lowenfeld to the present day, has emerged in dialogue with Piagetian assumptions (Atkinson, 2002). Piaget rarely wrote directly about artistic development. In his occasional statements on the matter, Piaget admitted how puzzling he found children's drawings, in their defiance of the expected trajectory of skills developing toward increased refinement in middle childhood, and in their deviations from realistic representation.

The aspects of child art that provoked Piaget continue to puzzle researchers, leading to questions concerning both the validity of the original developmental descriptions, and their continued viability in contemporary culture (see, e.g., Kindler & Darras, 1997; Thompson, 2003; Walsh, 2002; Wilson, 1997; Wilson & Wilson, 1977, 1982; Wolf & Perry, 1988). These critiques frequently penetrate to the most basic assumptions of developmental theory. Kindler and Darras (1997), for example, point out that stage theories of artistic development define art too narrowly, focusing primarily on children's drawings, and excluding or ignoring large swaths of behavior that are considered artistic in contemporary practice, including many of the art works that children make for their own purposes and pleasure. They argue that stage theories of artistic development are too linear and monofocal to account for the multiple symbolic languages that children accumulate as they grow. They suggest instead that it is the distinctive "repertoires" (Wolf & Perry, 1988) that children acquire that allow them to choose between different styles of drawing as the occasion warrants (Bremmer & Moore, 1984; Kindler, 1999).

Particularly problematic is the traditional emphasis on realistic representation as the single, desirable end-point of artistic development (Golomb, 2002). This assumption is questionable from the standpoint of both Western and world art where expression and narrative frequently surpass realistic rendering as the primary concerns of visual representation. As psychologist Claire Golomb (1992) remarks, in elevating photorealistic likeness to the pinnacle of artistic achievement, "we mistake a style valued by our culture for an intrinsic phase of human development" (p. 46).

Golomb (1997) suggests that young children fare badly in the face of "a hypothesized standard of realism," when their efforts to represent some aspect of their experience in the world, presumably intended to be realistic, are, almost inevitably, "declared . . . deficient" (p. 131). When research begins with this perspective on the nature of representation, deviations from reality are seen as evidence of conceptual immaturity. Golomb

suggests that this notion has been adopted rather uncritically by Piagetians, neo-Piagetians, and the British school of researchers (i.e., Cox, 1992; Freeman, 1980; Freeman & Cox, 1985) who examine task demands and production deficits in children's drawings.

Yet these researchers have continued to examine issues of graphic representation in ways that acknowledge the complexity of factors contributing to that process. For example, Cox (1992, 1993, 1997; Freeman & Cox, 1985) offers a variation of the "production deficit hypothesis" (Golomb, 2002, p. 13) originally proposed by Freeman (1980; Freeman & Cox, 1985), a theory that looks to children's inexperience in drawing, rather than their conceptual deficits, to explain the problems they encounter when they attempt to compose a drawing. Attempting to explain why children's drawings of the same object may vary according to the task proposed to them, the intentions the child brings to the task, and the child's engagement in the process, Cox suggests that the child's internal mental model mediates between immediate perception, prior knowledge of the object, and the drawing currently appearing on the page. This conclusion is compatible with a theory of drawing developed by Wilson and Wilson (1977), which substitutes the notion that children develop and choose among multiple "drawing programs" for Lowenfeld's proposal that young children slowly develop and gradually modify schemas for each of the objects they draw and for the arrangement of those objects within the space of a drawing (Freedman, 1997, p. 101). Whereas Wilson and Wilson recognize the importance of small incremental changes in children's drawings, and the potential of simultaneously developing drawing programs, repertoires and end-points (Wolf & Perry, 1988), however, Cox continues to regard the realistic vantage of the "view-centered" representation as the more advanced, and hence desirable, destination for children's drawing (Cooke, Griffin, & Cox, 1998).

Matthews (1999) raises the question, "What does it mean to talk about 'the way things really look'? What is the true shape of a cat or a cloud?" (p. 5). Influenced by the theoretical perspective of Rudolph Arnheim, Golomb offers a perspective on children's artistic experience as a gradual process of differentiation, in which structures acquire greater fluidity, complexity and detail as the intentions children bring to drawings change and the range of graphic strategies at their disposal expands. She adopts an inclusive definition of representation in order to acknowledge the centrality and the difficulty of the task children undertake in drawing and other symbolic activities: "Representation is a constructive mental activity; it is not a literal or exact imitation or copy of the object, although the perceiver may, at times, find a resemblance striking or even deceptive. Representation in this sense is a major biological, psychological, and cultural achievement" (Golomb, 2002, p. 5).

Atkinson (2002) ponders the extent to which the "natural attitude" (p. 34) toward representation is perpetuated and enforced through teaching practice at all educational levels. As he notes, this presumption creates a self-fulfilling prophecy in art education: "in valuing particular traditions of practice it attempts to reproduce them and thus perpetuate a particular cultural hegemony towards practice and understanding in art education" (p. 35).

Clearly there has been a significant period of unrest in terms of understanding children's artistic development. There seems to be an increasing allegiance to a "sociological perspective on development" (Freedman, 1997). There is an interest in retaining the sense that children's actions have "an internal structure and systematicity" (Matthews, 1999, p. 6), while acknowledging those factors in each child's environment and experience that may alter that internal structure and modify its systems of operation in ways that distinguish the artistry of a particular child (Thompson, 1999).

Sociocultural Perspectives: Development as Learning

Despite the caution they introduce about reliance on traditional stage theories of development, Kindler and Darras (1997) remark that existing descriptions of the earliest stages of children's art-making, particularly the prerepresentational phase typically referred to as the "scribbling stage," seem to be relatively reliable. They note that stage theories tend to become increasingly unstable as children reach the middle school years and descend into the trough of the U-curve described by Gardner (1982) and others (Davis, 1997). At the same time, there is growing evidence that preschool art, even in these earliest moments, is culturally conditioned and socially influenced (Alland, 1983; Matthews, 1999). The most basic configurations of marks made on paper often reflect the prevailing aesthetic of a child's cultural surround. As Kindler and Darras (1997) observe, this recognition of the malleability of the artistic process renders reliance on stage theories problematic, since, "Stage theories are founded on a culture-free assumption and either neglect to consider the implications of the cultural and social context, or view any extraneous influences as detrimental to the natural, biologically defined process of development" (p. 19). The significance of sociocultural factors, recognized by many researchers engaged in crosscultural study of children's drawings early in the twentieth century (cf. Paget, 1932, for example), was downplayed by researchers intent on emphasizing the universality of child art (Kellogg, 1970; Golomb, 1992). However, as Kindler and Darras point out, those who are reluctant to admit exceptions to the rules of a universal language of child art are forced to minimize and discount obvious cultural and individual differences in children's drawings: "Even if one is willing to regard cultural and social factors as simply contributing to the variability within the general rule (Golomb, 1992), this variability needs to be acknowledged and addressed" (Kindler & Darras, 1997, p. 19). In a manner congruent with a more general post-Piagetian perspective (Inagaki, 1992), the existence and significance of these individual and cultural variations are increasingly recognized and addressed in art education research (Kindler, 1994; Thompson & Bales, 1991; Wilson & Wilson, 1977, 1982, 1984, 1985).

Interest in social, cultural, and individual variations on the themes of artistic development has existed from the beginning of the study of child art. In the introduction to his recent translation of Luquet's *Le Dessin Enfantin* (1927), Costall (2001) emphasizes Luquet's recognition that children make choices in the act of drawing: "The young child chooses intellectual realism. . . . Intellectual realism is not something the child 'undergoes' as a preliminary to visual realism. It reflects a 'reasonable' commitment to an alternative *ideal* of what a drawing should be" (pp. xvii–xviii), and persists as "a serious and enduring option" (p. xix) for image making throughout life. Following what Costall (2001) describes as an initial "frenzy for amassing vast collections of drawings, usually with the help of school teachers, but [with] the researchers seldom [having] anything to do with the children themselves" (pp. vii–viii), the study of child art has gravitated toward studies that are smaller in scale, often taking the form of longitudinal case studies, or, more recently, observations of classrooms and children working within them. There has been substantial interest at certain historical moments in children's responses to works of art and other visual phenomena, topics that have also been studied both through formal experimentation and informal methods of observation. Although traditional experimental designs are still employed, particularly in psychological approaches to the study of child art, qualitative approaches to research in early childhood art education have become increasingly prevalent.

Reconsidering the Art in Artistic Development

Zurmuehlen and Kantner (1995) demonstrate the ways in which general tendencies appear and are embodied in the work of individual children, sharing a more nuanced view of the process through which children acquire the rudiments of artistic practice. The authors illustrate the centrality of narrative in young children's art making, and the importance of repetition and "boundedness" in the transition from "doing" to "making," from exploratory play with materials and forms to intentional exploration of form and creation of meaning. In doing so, they emphasize the continuities of thought and practice that unite young children with mature artists, extending a strand of thought that envisions artistic development as a cumulative process rather than a series of radical reorganizations and displacements of the old by the new (Arnheim, 1969; Beittel, 1973; Gardner, 1973, 1980, 1982; Read, 1945; Schaefer-Simmern, 1948; Wilson & Wilson, 1982; Winner, 1982; Wolf & Perry, 1988).

Researchers involved with Harvard's Project Zero, for example, point to the similarities between the works of young children and mature artists. Gardner (1980) refers to the ages between 5 and 7 as "the golden age of drawing," and the research team has devoted considerable attention to the apparent demise of artistry in middle to late childhood and its unreliable resurgence in adolescence. Even admitting clear differences between artists and children (Davis, 1997), the continuity of artistic practice has been an assumption of Project Zero since its inception in 1967, a basic premise of the "Symbol Systems Approach" (Davis, 1997, p. 46), grounded in the aesthetic theories of Nelson Goodman and Rudolph Arnheim, and the psychological work of Jean Piaget. Interested in young children's ready use of metaphor in words and images, Project Zero applied the same aesthetic criteria to the work of children and professional artists, investigating, for example, the existence of "repleteness" or exploitation of the potential of the medium, in the work of both groups. They began, too, with the belief that the production and the perception of images are equally important in the construction of symbolic meaning. As Davis (1997) explains, "Through internal symbols or representations, the individual child or producer of art constructs a world view. Through external symbols or representations, the individual shares a world view. This happens when that construction of meaning is recognized or reconstructed by a receptive, equally active meaning-maker, the perceiver of art" (p. 48).

Among the most consistent findings of the research conducted by Project Zero is that the perception of the "aesthetic properties" in works of art seems to improve just as the ability to create aesthetically balanced and expressive images seems to decline, in middle childhood. Preschoolers' drawings are most likely to rival the expressiveness of adult art. As children approach middle childhood, the "flavorfulness" (Davis, 1997, p. 48) or visual richness of their art works appears to wane. Project Zero researchers attribute this phenomenon to the quest for photographic realism in drawing that children undertake between ages of 8–11.

Davis (1997) reports a recent study involving a large and varied sample: 20 5-year-olds, 20 8-year-olds, 20 11-year-olds, 20 14-year-olds who considered themselves to be artists, 20 14-year-olds who did not think of themselves in this way, 20 nonartist adults, and 20 professional artists. She asked each participant to draw the emotional states, "happy," "sad," and "angry," in any way they pleased The 420 drawings produced in response were judged on the following criteria: overall expression, balance, use of line and composition as appropriate to the emotion expressed. Davis found that it was the 5-year-olds and the 14-year-old artists whose works were judged to be closest to the work of professional artists: These groups of very young children and very highly motivated adolescents formed "the two high ends of the 'U'" (Davis, 1997, p. 53), both approximating the level of artistic accomplishment recognized as exemplary in contemporary American culture.

Artists were among the first groups to evince a interest in the aesthetic qualities and inventiveness of young children's images, as the 19th century turned to the twentieth. Recent work by art historian Jonathon Fineberg (1997; 1998) documents the extent and longevity of this interest, and raises provocative questions about the cultural status of children's art, and the values it is assigned in differing historical periods.

Golomb (1974, 1997, 2002; Golomb & McCormick, 1995) has been persistent in her efforts to expand research attention to aspects of child art beyond drawings, traditionally the data of choice, as they are profusely available, easily stored and manipulated, and subject to comparison with many previous studies. Golomb's interest in doing so is not merely to acknowledge alternate media and forms of children's artistic practice, but to question basic assumptions about the stagelike progression of artistic development and the nature of the relationship between children's internal images and the representations they produce in clay, paint, or marker. Golomb's research in this area operationalizes a theoretical insight articulated, on separate occasions, by Arnheim (1954/1974) and Forman (1994), and embodied in the pedagogical strategies practiced in the preschools of Reggio Emilia (Reggio Children & Project Zero, 2001): that is, the concept that each medium presents its own characteristic strengths and weaknesses, its own "affordances" (Forman,

1994, p. 42) that allow children to learn certain things about a topic that would be less readily evident in the terms of another medium.

Golomb and McCormick (1995) asked 109 children between the ages of 4 and 13 to model a series of eight objects in clay. These objects—a cup, a table, a man, a woman, a person bending down, a dog, a cow, and a turtle—were selected to vary in complexity, symmetry and the technical difficulty of balancing a figure. Golomb and McCormick found that most children created three-dimensional forms in response to the tasks that were relatively simple in structure, symmetrical and balanced, especially in response to their request to model the cup and the table. Golomb (1997) noted that the work of the youngest participants in this study revealed "unsuspected competence:" "Children seem to approach modeling with an incipiently three-dimensional conception that becomes gradually refined and differentiated, provided the child is exposed to this medium and experiments with various tasks and possibilities" (p. 139). The children encountered the same problems that more mature people with little experience working with clay encounter, "how to create a satisfying representation in a medium that puts a premium on balance, uprightness, and the modeling of multiple sides, all of which require great skill and patience" (Golomb, 1997, p. 140). For Golomb and others, this observation raises the question of whether principles governing child art might apply equally to beginners in a particular medium, regardless of age.

This, and other studies undertaken by Golomb and her associates, was designed to shed light on artistic development, highlighting the difference between constraints in children's approach to art making that are specific to art media with which they may have limited experience, and those constraints imposed by conceptual immaturity. As Golomb (2002) frames the question underlying these investigations, "Does a uniform concept override the properties of the medium, or does it respond selectively to its possibilities and constraints?" (p. 51). Extending a program of research that has been ongoing since the early 1970s, Golomb's recent research converges in a powerful critique of the conceptual deficit theory so often used to explain the apparent anomalies in child art. In a recently published study by Gallo, Golomb and Barroso (2003), for example, 45 children, ages 5, 7, and 9, were presented with three themes, and asked to represent each in three ways: in a drawing, with precut shapes on felt board, and a wooden board with pieces provided. The researchers constructed these tasks to explore the conceptual deficit theory, particularly as expressed by Piaget and as countered by Arnheim. Although Arnheim would predict change in the ways children represent an idea in each of the media provided, Piaget would predict uniformity, due to the dominance of a single mental model guiding the child's decisions. In this study, as well, researchers found significant effects for age and medium, and ample support for Arnheim's theory that representational concepts are formed in response to the provisions of a particular medium. Children's work with felt board and three-dimensional wooden pieces demonstrated more sophisticated spatial understanding than was apparent in their drawings. The 5-year-olds were exceptionally enthusiastic about the opportunity to work out their concepts in three-dimensional media. The striking contrast the research team detected between two- and three-dimensional solutions suggests that children may achieve more sophisticated visual and conceptual solutions in response to "revisable tasks" (p. 20), in clay, collage, or construction, than they can produce in their capacity as "novices learning to draw" (Freeman, 1980).

An ambitious proposal formulated by Kindler and Darras (1997) strives to circumvent some of the difficulties inherent in traditional stage theories. They present this proposal as one which preserves the continuity of artistic practice from child-hood through maturity, and respects the varieties of uses to which visual imagery may be put. Theirs is

an attempt to conceptualize the development of pictorial representation in a way that does not rely on any particular definition of art . . . [but] embraces a diversity of pictorial manifestations without implying value judgments on the artistic merit of any of them, allows for consideration of sociocultural variables, and is concerned with the process from its onset in early childhood and on through the adult years. (p. 19)

Kindler and Darras offer a semiotic model, based on the belief that all art is potentially communicative of "thoughts, ideas, emotions, values, states, understandings, or realities" (p. 19), which may be presented through the use of icons, indexes and symbols that constitute signs. Drawing upon the semiotic theory formulated by Peirce (1931–1935) and Vygotsky's perspective on development as a socially-mediated process, their model describes artistic development in terms of three segments and five types of "iconicity," none of which are outgrown and discarded, all of which, once recognized, may be chosen as strategies at any time in life.

This emphasis on the way drawings function for children is equally central to the poststructuralist view of drawing practice offered by Atkinson (2002) who suggests:

Drawing is a semiotic practice and when viewed as such this calls into question conventional understandings of visual representation as an attempt to represent or reproduce views of a prior reality. If drawing is concerned with signification rather than a conventional mimetic idea of representation, then any direct relation between representation and reality is fractured . . . as a semiotic practice, a drawing qua signifier relates not to a fixed external referent in the world which exists prior to the drawing, but to other signifiers which consist of other images and discourses in which we understand visual structures. (p. 15)

CONTEXT

"In the context of childhood education the post-modern experience of being a kid represents a cultural earthquake" (Kincheloe, 1998, p. 172).

Much of the impetus for these changes in thinking about early art education derive from the unavoidable recognition of changes in the circumstances of young children's lives, which has, in many and complex ways, brought the education of young children back into the realm of art educators' responsibility. As increasing numbers of young children began to spend their days in the company of unrelated adults and peers, in preschools and day care settings, the opportunities for art educators and

researchers to work directly with young children or with their teachers multiplied rapidly. As a direct result, researchers concerned with early childhood art have begun to look at children in context, learning to draw and to make sense of images in classrooms and neighborhoods, with the help of other children and teachers as well as parents. The domesticated childhood, and the solitude of early artistic ventures, that were assumed in earlier studies, can no longer be considered the norm for young children in North America.

Young children's formal introductions to the art experience frequently occur in contexts that are structured, social and school-like, making early art education an issue of equal importance to teachers and to parents. As art educators' contact with young children has increased, it has also become apparent that even the youngest among them bring prior aesthetic experiences and values to school, preferences developed through interactions with friends and family, established attachments to certain images and objects, and constant exposure to visual culture, including "art for children" (Bresler, 2002; Walsh, 2002).

With this recognition of the fluidity of demographic and sociological patterns has come an understanding that contemporary children and circumstances "no longer fit the existing explanations" (Graue & Walsh, 1998, p. 33). James, Jenks, and Prout (1998) note that the conceptions of childhood that inform educational thought and practice are subject to rapid and radical change within a culture, as they are to marked variations between cultures. Many of the assumptions we hold dear about young children, the conventional wisdom we exchange in daily conversations and professional discourse, do not withstand close scrutiny, as Jenkins observes: "Our grown-up fantasies of childhood as a simple space crumble when we recognize the complexity of forces shaping our children's lives and defining who they will be, how they will behave, and how they will understand their place in the world" (p. 4). As Duncum (2002) suggests, "children never were what they were" (p. 97). And child art, like childhood itself, is, was, and always will be an interpreted phenomenon, a construction of adult understanding. Recognizing this, we are obliged to become conscious of the interests that accompany us when we watch children making art, and to attempt to look more closely both at the child and the context in which he or she works: "If we are to understand child art we must look at what the child has represented and expressed, the conditions under which child art is made, and ourselves and others in the act of studying it" (Wilson, 1997, p. 83).

Among the most dramatic effects of this attention to the contexts of early art experience has been the recognition that much that was accepted as established knowledge about child art may no longer pertain to children's art when it is understood as a "social practice" (Pearson, 2001, p. 348). Previous research concentrated primarily on analysis of the products or "artifactual residue" of the art making process, and often involved experimental procedures, designed quite deliberately to require children to grapple with problems that they would not attempt in their spontaneous drawings (e.g., Freeman & Janikoun, 1972; Willats, 1977). Matthews (1999) points out that, "Studies of children's art and drawing based solely upon experimental data always distort descriptions of development" (p. 3) for this reason.

Matthew's own research relies heavily on naturalistic observational work, both with his own children at home and in classrooms in London and Singapore. He notes, however, that some experimental studies are useful in illuminating issues that are difficult to observe in naturalistic settings. Costall (2001) indicates that Luquet, working early in the 20th century, shared this conviction that direct observation was a far more appropriate and informative method for the study of children's art than formal experimentation.

Pearson, among others (Leeds, 1986; Thompson & Bales, 1991; Thompson, 1997), argues that children's reasons for making art can and should be distinguished from the products of that activity. Pearson acknowledges that the collection and analysis of children's drawings is an engrossing pursuit, that children's works, treated as archeological artifacts, can and do yield intriguing information. Not only does analysis of drawings inform us about the construction of visual images, but, approached from a more postmodern perspective (for example, Gamradt & Staples, 1994), it also promises insight into children's interests and concerns. As Pearson points out, however, children's drawings have typically been used in attempts to understand something that is not "children drawing," whether that is the nature of their experience at school or at home, or the ways in which they conceptualize and represent hierarchies of value or relationships among objects arrayed in space. Pearson's critique articulates a shift in thinking more profound, even, than the movement toward direct observation of drawing events, a trend that recognizes the thick layers of information that become available when researchers witness a drawing being made and the contextual influences that are enfolded in the final product. He points toward a movement beyond the consideration of children's drawings as developmental evidence, toward research that attempts to document the child's lived experience of making images, often within the mediated social space of a classroom or peer culture. The timeworn adage that advises teachers of young children to focus on the art process, rather than the product, applies to this more contextualized approach to research, with the qualification that the products of children's activity are frequently important as the documentation and embodiment of that process.

Pearson suggests further that traditional research, by insisting that drawing is a universal activity among young children, has failed to recognize the indisputable fact that some children, and many adults, do not draw. Pearson suggests that the reasons children choose to draw, or not to draw, are complex and heavily reliant on context:

Whatever value drawing has for children is bound to the context in which it takes place, and as the context shifts so does the value. This is why drawing can be play activity, narrative activity, a measured strategy for social approval, or the equally measured pursuit of the inductively grasped competence appropriate to given representation systems. Drawing is also a strategy for coping with boredom, with isolation. It can be a retreat from violent social relations. It can be the means for pursuing a passionate interest in horses or trains which at the same time achieves some or all of the above ends. (pp. 357–358)

Pearson suggests that research on children drawing should move away from examinations of the documents that result from that process toward the individual and situational factors that prompt children to make the choice to engage in that activity in the first place. Walsh (2002) cautions that children are unable to create "artistic selves" in the absence of opportunity, the availability of materials and models and the time to explore them, and the encouragement to do so. Pearson suggests that, when these conditions are in place, we may learn a great deal about the nature of art experience and its role in "good human functioning" (Arnheim, 1997, p. 11) by studying those children who do not take advantage of these opportunities as closely as those who do.

The concept that there are "varieties of visual experience" (Feldman, 1992) in which children participate is by no means new. Lark-Horovitz, Lewis, and Luca (1973) articulated subtle but significant differences in the content, form, and agency involved in spontaneous, voluntary, directed, and copied or to-be-completed works 30 years ago, and discussions of the characteristics and relative merits of school art and spontaneous children's art that begin with Wilson (1974) and Efland (1976, 1983) continue today (Anderson & Milbrandt, 1998; Bresler, 1992, 1994, 2002; Hamblen, 2002). Contemporary research concentrates both on children's "directed" work, made in response to an adult request, usually with a topic specified, and their independent or "voluntary" drawings (Thompson, 1997). Research has identified clear differences between "spontaneous and scaffolded" (Boyatzis, 2000, p. 15) drawings, leading Boyatzis to recommend that both the actual developmental level demonstrated in "spontaneous" drawings and the proximal developmental level attained in drawings made with instruction should be considered in evaluations of a child's developmental level: "perhaps artistic skill level ought to be conceived not only in terms of either the modal (functional) drawing level or the highest (optimal) level. Rather artistic skill may be better conceptualized as that range of symbolic flexibility between the two" (p. 15).

Several researchers are particularly concerned with children's choices, both habitual and occasional, and the manner in which choices of subject matter serve both as social and cultural capital, and in determining the trajectory of individual development. As Thunder-McGuire (1994) suggests, "Our preoccupation has been with individual works or performative acts, rather than a body of work" . . . but different perspectives open when we consider the child's "sustained 'artistic serial'" (p. 51). The range of children's accomplishments and the idiosyncrasy and cultural specificity of the changes that occur in children's drawings have become significant preoccupations for researchers.

Drawing Together: Social Context and Child Art

"Researchers who study children's graphic symbolism stress the interaction between children and their own products. . . . In centers and classrooms, though, the dialogue between children and their papers can include other people, as children's skills as collaborative storytellers and players infuse their drawings" (Dyson, 1990, p. 54).

As early as 1979, Cocking and Copple noted that the "exposure to others" that occurs as children draw together expands children's conceptions of what is possible in drawing. For many years, partially because of the limited opportunities available to art educators to study children in groups, the implications of this observation remained unexplored. Still operating under the deeply engrained cultural wisdom that defines artistic practice in general, and early artistic practice in particular, as highly individualized, unpredictable, and immune to influence, researchers frequently treated as extraneous any interactions that did occur in the classrooms they were studying. "Many accounts of the development of children's drawing seem to assume that some of the children's actions ... are simply irrelevant to drawing proper" (Matthews, 1999, p. 5). Now, as Boyatzis and Watson (2000) suggest, there is a growing tendency to see "social and symbolic processes" (p. 1) entwined in early artistic experiences.

There has been a movement toward adoption of a Vygotskian perspective in both art education practice and research in recent years, supplanting more clearly Piagetian approaches used in earlier research (Newton & Kantner, 1997; Thompson & Bales, 1991) and teaching. As Atkinson (2002) points out, a still more radical poststructural perspective views both the nature and culture positions as discourses which create particular versions of the child: "From a post-structural perspective, the Piagetian or Vygotskian child is not to be viewed as a natural or social entity but as an ideological product of particular discourses in which the child is constructed accordingly" (p. 6). No matter what its prospects for longevity of influence may be, the Vygotskian perspective has been especially fruitful for art education research, particularly in regard to the attention it has drawn to peer learning as an almost inevitable, and desirable, fixture of classrooms in which children make art together (Zurmuehlen, 1990). Boyatzis and Albertini (2000) believe that peer influence reaches its maximum strength in middle childhood, when gender segregation, conformity, and criticality reach their peaks. However, the effects they describe are by no means absent from early childhood classrooms:

Peer influence could occur through various means. Children's actual drawings—their themes, details, colors, or technical qualities—could function as models, offering children opportunities for observational learning. Observational learning has been posited as a crucial mechanism in children's learning in peer and collaborative contexts (for example, Botvin and Murray, 1975, Gauvain and Rogoff, 1989). Such learning would occur to the extent that children actually look at their peers' art, perhaps due to peers showing and displaying their work to others. In their conversations, children could share ideas and make explicit comparisons between each others' drawings and drawing techniques. Such exchanges would include many ability comparisons that could trigger artistic changes in children, particularly motivating then to improve their drawings to bring them more in line with local norms of style (that is, the themes, technical qualities, and meanings in their peers' drawings). (p. 33)

Many young children are inclined to accompany their actions with running commentaries that may be taken as conversational overtures, even when they are not intentionally addressed to another person (Thompson, 2002; Thompson & Bales, 1991). When children draw in the presence of peers, such private speech is frequently mistaken as a form of address that elicits an answer from another child. Many of the resulting comments, which may or may not evolve into conversations, tend to be evaluative, with one child offering an (often unsolicited) evaluation of the other's work or of the thought that is impelling that work forward. Cunningham (1997) observed that 7-year-olds tend to offer positive comments in situations such as this, and these unsolicited evaluations often lead to revisions. Teachers may be squeamish about the sometimes brutal honesty of the critical comments children exchange. Boyatzis and Albertini (2000) suggest that there is more good than harm to be found in such exchanges which they consider a primary benefit of children drawing together in the social space of the classroom:

This image of artistic development as socially embedded is consistent with a Vygotskian model of development rather than one that characterizes the child as a solitary graphic problem solver. . . . Children surely draw alone, make stylistic choices independently, and undergo endogenous symbolic development. But our observations . . . point toward the value of conceptualizing children's drawing and artistic development as occurring within sociocognitive contexts that may function as a zone of proximal development in which the interpsychological is internalized. . . . Surely children often draw alone, but even then they may benefit from hearing the internalized questions, evaluations, and suggestions of peers echoing from actual dyadic and group interaction. (pp. 45–46)

In line with contemporary reassessments of the developmental process in early art education, unprecedented attention has been paid to the necessity of adults and peers in structuring and supporting the process of learning to create and to respond to visual forms (Kindler, 1995; Thompson, 1995, 1997; Zurmuehlen, 1990). In spite of this increased attention to the desirable influence of teachers and peers in the emergence of early childhood art, few studies have focused on the role of parents as children's first art teachers. Exceptions are found in recent studies by Braswell (2002) and Yamagata (1997). Yamagata studied two parent-child dyads, drawing together at home, at one month intervals between the child's 24th and 30th months. He found that more representational drawings were produced in collaborative episodes than when they child drew alone or simply alongside the mother. He further noted that the intention to represent may emerge before the child develops the production skills needed to do so. Although mothers initially suggested more subjects for drawing more frequently than the children, the children took over this role as time passed. Braswell (2001) found similar patterns of guided participation and gradual exchange of roles in his study in which parents were asked to solicit both voluntary drawings and copies of complex forms from their young children.

Responding to Works of Art

Following a period of intense research activity on the issue of young children's responses to works of art (Kerlavage, 1995), relatively little research has been conducted on this issue in the past decade. A number of important theoretical and pedagogical texts have been published, though few of these explicitly address the aesthetic learning in young children (Danko McGhee, 2000, provides a notable exception), reflecting a movement away from assumptions grounded in formalist aesthetics and toward attention to more experiential, phenomenological, and cultural issues and methods of inquiry. The reciprocity between making and responding to images and objects created by others is by now firmly established as a principle of early art education, with aesthetic response, and historical and critical study of imagery, acknowledged as links to other areas of study within the curriculum. This dual interest in making and responding to works of art (and other elements of visual culture) has been a central tenet in the research on symbolic development conducted under the auspices of Harvard's Project Zero since the 1980s. A similar understanding was expressed in Parson's (1988) identification of what he considered to be two primary issues in child art: (1) the significance of sociocultural influences on the process and content of art making; and (2) an interest in understanding of art in general and of particular works.

Cross-Cultural Research: Questioning the Universality of Child Art

The long-established tradition of crosscultural research in the study of children's art originated, and survived for many years, in an attempt to garner evidence of the universality of the impulse to make art, and of children's art as universal language, a political position adopted by many artists, philosophers, and educators following the World Wars (see, for example, Kellogg, 1970). Many early investigations, including the drawings collected by Harris (1963) in his refinement of the Draw-a-Man Test (Goodenough, 1926), were interpreted as support for the existence of a universal developmental process, stressing persistent structural similarities but not absolute likeness in drawings produced in distinct cultural environments. Earlier crosscultural studies, many conducted by anthropologists such as Paget (1932), acknowledged local traditions within familiar characteristics, but emphasized the ubiquity of familiar graphic models and sequences. Golomb (2002) notes that, despite documentation of local variations across and even within cultures, "the dominant impression is of a universal graphic language clearly recognizable to the student of child art, a language whose basic grammar allows for variations on a common underlying structure" (p. 87). These commitments have sometimes proven difficult to forsake (Golomb, 1992; Kindler, 1997), but an awareness of the cultural specificity of educational supports and children's responses to them is strongly emphasized in recent research.

Golomb (2002) observes that recent cross-cultural studies vary radically in methodology, but often solicit drawings that are restricted to a single theme or a single trial. Most such studies are administered in group settings without attention to peer influence or the effects of prior instruction. (Andersson, 1995; Court, 1994; Martlew & Connelly, 1996). In many cases, the studies are implicitly crosscultural, insofar as the researchers enter a culture not their own, and inevitably interpret what they find there on the basis of what is known about child art, knowledge derived largely from studies in the West.

Most cross-cultural research focuses on art-making, and drawing continues to predominate, despite observations by researchers such as Fortes (1981) who noted that Tallensi children's favorite pastime was modeling small animals and figures to use as toys, and commented in passing on the strong three-dimensional understanding children displayed, even in the absence of relevant models in their culture. Newton and Kantner (1997) review crosscultural studies in aesthetic response, describing studies (primarily from the 1970s and 1980s) that investigated children's perception of imagery from the perspectives of various research paradigms.

In the past decade, Kindler, Darras, and Kuo (2000) undertook an ambitious crosscultural study of "the ways in which cultural contexts shape formation of knowledge about art in the early years" (p. 44). Choosing to focus on issues more inclusive than those tackled in many earlier studies of aesthetic response, this multilayered study examines children's conceptions of art, how the term "art" is interpreted and understood by children in a variety of cultural contexts. The researchers share an interest in issues of globalization, and the effects of heritage and enculturation in the formation of social knowledge.

In structured interviews with 70 4- and 5-year-old children in Canada, France, and Taiwan, Kindler, Darras, and Kuo (2000) posed questions regarding the nature of art. They were particularly interested in speaking with diasporic or "transplanted" children in each culture: French Canadian and Chinese Canadian children. They asked three questions of each child interviewed: What is art? Does art have to be beautiful? Can nature make art or does art have to be made by a person? (p. 46). The results of these interviews confirm that understandings of art do not seem to be readily transplanted from one culture to another. Some traditional views of art and beauty seemed to be more persistent than others, and time spent in the new culture seemed to influence children's responses, as did the degree of assimilation cultivated by members of their community. The authors offer this study as confirmation of the fact that even very young children hold some preconceptions about art related to cultural and familial values. They recommend caution in assuming the "direct portability of cultural beliefs" (p. 52) in the design of multicultural art education, and emphasize the importance of considering both original and transplanted cultures as contexts.

In an earlier study, Kindler and Darras (1995) interviewed 80 children, ages 3 to 5, in Canada and France to explore their conceptions of the nature of drawing competencies and the ways in which they are achieved. The series of structured interviews they conducted confirmed the authors' prediction that children as young as 3 hold and can express beliefs about their own drawing ability and that of others, and that even very young children take note of the values enacted by those around them. Some differences in age and culture were detected: All Canadian kindergartners, for example, indicated that they were capable of drawing whatever they desired, whereas only 80% of their French peers expressed similarly unbridled confidence. More than half the children felt that all people know how to draw, and that generally drawing improves with age, though they acknowledged the importance of practice and teaching, and the role of significant others in support of drawing skills. Interestingly, children themselves did not experience the process of learning to draw as a natural unfolding: "the majority of children recognized the importance of socially mediated learning, valued imitative activities as a learning strategy, and did not regard development of drawing skills as a private process of biologically determined unfolding.... When asked how they learned how to draw, 69% of the French children and 40% of the Canadians reported that they learned from others" (Kindler & Darras, 1995, p. 92). Although few children thought of drawing as "an autonomous discovery" (Kindler & Darras, 1995, p. 92), this belief was somewhat more prevalent among Canadian children.

Asked the question, "Why do people draw?," half of the preschool subjects could not answer, and older children found the question more readily addressed in terms of personal enjoyment, a response offered by 60% of the children. As to the purposes of drawing, 64% of French children, and 40% of Canadian kindergartners and 30% of the Canadian preschoolers, mentioned decoration or embellishment as primary purposes, with the production of gifts and surprises as a close second. Kindler and Darras observe, "The association between the giving and the beauty seems to be mediated very early to young children through routines that they observe in their immediate environment. Children's pictorial productions are judged by their parents and other family members as beautiful and consequently become desirable gifts" (p. 95). Finally, when asked whether it is important to learn how to draw, 80% of Canadian children and only 46% of French children responded affirmatively. These percentages parallel the responses to the question of whether children see their parents draw, an event that is witnessed with far greater frequency by Canadian children than by their French counterparts.

Chen (2001) studied Taiwanese young children and adolescents, comparing their responses to those obtained by Freeman and Sanger (1995) who constructed a "net of intentional relations" involving the Artist, Beholder, Picture, and World. Freeman and Sanger employed a questionnaire to measure the aesthetic understandings of 352 rural school children in the United Kingdom, the youngest in Grade 3. Replicating this study in Taiwan, Chen found that, contrary to Freeman and Sanger's findings, young children in Taiwan tend to merge the roles of artist and beholder, assuming that they could infer intention from the works themselves, and that artists always work with beholders in mind.

Working within a research paradigm demonstrated by British psychologists including Norman Freeman and Maureen Cox, Chun-Min Su (1995) studied American and Chinese children's ability to produce drawings of partially occluded figures, using a robber and policeman format to measure young children's ability to create the illusion of one-thing-hiding-behind-another when a meaningful motivation for doing so is presented. Su found, among other things, that Chinese children were more likely than American children to erase their drawings and to emit other evidence of dissatisfaction with their response to the problem presented. She attributed this result, in part, to the demands of learning Chinese characters with the precision required to successfully write their own names.

Cox, Perara and Fan (1999) compared drawings by 952 children between the ages of 6 and 13 in the United Kingdom and China. The researchers failed to detect any consistent cultural differences in the quality of the drawings, expect for those produced by the 240 children in Beijing who attended weekend art school. These children's drawings were rated consistently higher by expert judges on criteria of style, composition, color, and depth. The authors invoked the results of this study in support of arguments for more structured and formal teaching in art. Educators in the West were first alerted to the exceptionally high and consistent aesthetic achievement of Chinese children's art in an article published by Ellen Winner (1989) and several exhibitions of art by Chinese children organized in England. The authors acknowledge the possibility that the quality of children's work may be attributed to the high status of art in Chinese culture, but they speculate that the way in which art is taught to children is equally significant. According to Winner (1989), Chinese art education at the elementary level focuses on technique and skill-building, with attention paid to copying schema from blackboards, a practice antithetical to most (if not all) of the strictures that have surrounded art teaching in the West since at least mid-20th century. In this study, children were all assigned the same topic, a scene described by the examiner, in order to compare children in three groups: in ordinary schools in the United Kingdom and in China and among children who chose to attend special art school. The resulting drawings were rated on a 5-point scale by two art advisers from the United Kingdom and one Chinese researcher familiar with children's drawings. Observation and videotapes of classrooms made during the collection of drawings suggest that Chinese art instruction is not as rigid or unidimensional as it is often characterized to be, nor are British instructions as laissez-faire as expected. But children's drawings displayed differences in style that made it easy for independent judges to guess the country of origin for each drawing.

In his recent work, Wilson (1997, 2002) examines the Japanese phenomenon of *manga*, both as a prime example of the collusion between children and commercial interests in the creation of national identity, and as a significant aspect of the process of learning to draw in a culture in which attractive and attainable graphic models are abundant—a process all children enact as they master the tools and symbols systems their particular culture provides (Vygotsky, 1978).

Gender as Social Mediation

Examinations of the influence of gender on the subject matter and style of children's drawings also boast a long tradition in visual arts research. Recent concern with the perpetuation of gender stereotypes through teaching (Collins & Sandell, 1996) and of the effects of gendered choices on children's drawings (Thompson, 1999; Tuman, 1999, 2000) represent recent trends in this inquiry.

In 1997, Duncum considered the subjects children choose to draw in their unsolicited drawings, a topic that has attracted sporadic bursts of attention throughout the history of study of child art, beginning with Maitland's study of "what children draw to please themselves," published in 1895. Reviewing this literature, Duncum identified a striking consistency in the findings on thematic and subject matter preferences and gender differences: From the earliest studies (e.g., Ballard, 1913;

Maitland, 1895; Munro, Lark-Horovitz, & Barnhart, 1942) to the most recent (Robertson, 1989; Thompson, 1999; Tuman, 1999, 2000), strong gender differences have been apparent. Girls tend to concentrate on scenes of ordinary life and autobiographical experience, whereas boys gravitate, quickly and noticeably, toward fantasy, historical fiction, combat and strong action. Flannery and Watson (1995) found more aggressive themes in boys' drawings, and "argue that boys' drawing content reflects a socialized interest in fantasy and violence that extends beyond their everyday life experience, whereas girls' drawing content appears to be more realistic and tranquil and to relate to their everyday experience" (Tuman, 1999, p. 41).

Although exceptions certainly exist, these patterns appear to be remarkably robust, particularly among prolific "drawers" who tend to specialize in particular subjects or themes, most of which conform to gendered stereotypes. Duncum (1997) suggests that these motives are so firmly established that, "Boys and girls may draw what appears to be the same subject matter for a very different reason or purpose due to their gender socialization" (p. 111). As Tuman (2000) notes, "We have come to understand that the drawings of boys and girls reveal unique reflections of society through visual narratives of the world of personal experience" (p. 17).

While the conventional wisdom in art education once assumed that gender differences did not appear in children's drawings until they reached school age, Boyatzis and Albertini (2000) suggest that these distinctions are apparent long before clearly identifiable subject matter appears: "Gender differences in art emerge even earlier, in the preschool years, as boys' scribbles are rated as more masculine and girls' scribbles as more feminine by judges who are ignorant of the children's genders" (p. 31; see also Alland, 1983).

Other differences have been noted in more overtly representational drawings, in addition to the subject matter itself. There is growing evidence that the intentions children bring to their drawings, the subject matter they choose to practice and perfect, may influence the style of their work as profoundly as it determines the substance, as first suggested by Feinburg (1979) in her study of children's drawings of fighting and helping. As Tuman (1999) remarks, "Favored engendered content domains may foster favored tendencies in characteristics" (p. 41). Tuman expressed concern, however, that erroneous assertions have been made about the relative abilities of boys and girls through inadequate consideration of the themes children of each gender choose to draw. For example, Kerschensteiner (1905) concluded that boys' drawing ability surpassed that of girls on a measure of spatial relationships, but failed to take into account the relatively spacious subject matter that boys prefer and even require in order to stage the actions they tend to depict. Goodenough (1926) concluded that girls were superior to boys in their drawings of detailed human figures, a finding reaffirmed by later investigations in America, England, and Denmark (Cox, 1993; Harris, 1963; Koppitz, 1968; Mortensen, 1991), without probing deeply into the possible reasons for this phenomenon. Recent studies tend to turn away from questions of superiority or inferiority to examine more subtle issues of style and substance, manifesting particular interest in subject matter preferences.

In a study of 300 elementary students, in Grades 1 through 5, Tuman (1999) investigated whether "gender differences in subject preference also call into play the manipulation of formal elements, which together with gendered context form a gender-related style" (p. 42). The children, primarily white and middle- to upper-middle-class, listened to a narrative motivation designed to elicit stereotypical attitudes toward gender. The children were then asked to illustrate what they liked best in the story and to write a brief descriptive title for their finished art work. Tuman randomly selected 250 drawings for analysis in order to insure an equal number of boys and girls in the final sample. Tuman (1999) found that, "when presented with masculine and feminine content themes, boys and girls rarely incorporate subject matter choices outside predicted gendered content domains in their drawing" (p. 52). Her study did not replicate Kerschensteiner's findings of male superiority in spatial representation, but did raise concerns about the limitations imposed on the representational possibilities children of either gender are apt to explore, if they are allowed to persist in drawing within the stereotypical range. Tuman suggests that this may be particularly detrimental to girls, a concern shared by Thompson (1999) in her reflection on the choices of subject matter made by preschool and kindergarten children drawing in sketchbooks over a period of 12 years. The potential consequences of these choices for drawing development may well be profound, for the relative advantages of focusing upon imaginative scenarios that are continually evolving and available instead of relying on personal experience to provide fodder for representation seem as evident as they are problematic (see, for example, Egan, 1988; Helm & Katz, 2001; Katz, 1998).

CURRICULUM

It would not be surprising to find that neither the operational curriculum nor instructional practices in early childhood art education have kept pace with the recommendations drawn from research and theory in recent years. What research would now suggest departs abruptly from the traditional wisdom long accepted as appropriate art education practice in early childhood settings. Art experiences are cherished by elementary and early childhood teachers as the last bastion of creative freedom in the schools (Bresler, 2002), a freedom threatened by art educators' recent insistence that art is a process which must be structured and scaffolded if it is to satisfy children's expectations, much less fulfill its educational potential.

Katz (1998) remarked that one of the lessons she had learned from her many visits to the preschools of Reggio Emilia was that young children can use graphic languages—drawing, painting, collage, construction—"to record their ideas, observations, memories, and so forth ... to explore understandings, to reconstruct previous ones, and to co-construct revisited understandings of the topics investigated" (p. 20). This understanding of "art as epistemology" (Gallas, 1994, p. 130), as a way of "enabling children to know what they know," allows us to recognize and employ art in the classroom as a "method for examining his[her] world as well as his[her] means of externalizing what he[she] was learning for others to share" (Gallas,

1994, p. 135). This interest in "drawing to learn" (Anning, 1999, p. 166), widespread in British schools and preschools, disrupts many strongly held beliefs about the young child as natural artist, and the role of the teacher in preserving that artistry untarnished by adult manipulation. It suggests not only that topics for drawings and painting can be assigned, but that experiences with art materials can, and perhaps should, be structured with both expressive and communicative purposes in mind. This approach to art as a symbolic language, the subject of considerable discussion in the waning decades of the last century, emphasizes the possibility of teachers helping children to develop facility in "the hundred languages" (Malaguzzi, 1998, p. 3) available to them, to master an expanded range of the tools and symbol systems (Vygotsky, 1978) that are used in their culture.

Equally as influential as the accumulating consensus of research and theory in affecting this radical shift in thinking about the nature of curriculum and instruction in early childhood art has been the example of Reggio Emilia. Although serious and sustained research on the theory and practice of art education in the preschools of Reggio Emilia is accumulating slowly, the work routinely produced by the children who benefit from that practice demonstrates unequivocally the possibility of exceptional sophistication in teaching and learning, and the range of artistic expression that is possible for young children who are encouraged to explore challenging content through visual forms.

The influence of Reggio Emilia is extensive, the questions it raises for early art education, profound and challenging. Pitri (2003) observed a university-based preschool in order to document the conceptual problem solving that occurred during art activities. She found that some conceptual problems were teacher-generated, in situations in which the teacher asked children to plan and to make choices. Child-generated conceptual problems emerged in response to interpersonal or practical challenges, for example, in attempts to join an ongoing activity or negotiations about the sharing of art materials. Other problems were more substantive, "caused by children's representational or expressive challenges" (p. 20). Drawing on previous research on the definition of problems during art activities, Pitri concluded that, "Problem finding is related to being receptive to ideas and responding to changes in the environment" (p. 21). She noted that this approach is exemplified in the practice of Reggio Emilia.

Tarr (2003) sees in the "image of the child" maintained in the theory and practice of Reggio Emilia an opportunity to question the image that guides curriculum development and instructional practice in North American early art education:

What images of children do we hold when we plan curriculum that follows accepted practices of studio, criticism and art history? Do we plan a different delivery system where children individually recreate the art culture(s) they are in? When they have a discussion about a work of art, are they consuming culture or actively constructing understanding about the work that is unique to each child and to each group? Do we celebrate this construction, or do we try to replace it with cultural replication? (p. 10)

This discussion occurs, however, within earshot of continuing debates regarding the relative merits of "unfolding or teaching" (Gardner, 1976) in early art education. While this debate may no longer rest upon the question of whether adults should influence child art, as it once did, differences of opinion remain in regard to the nature and extent of that influence. Even this is a dramatic departure from the emphasis on "spontaneous self-instruction" (Froebel, in Kellogg, 1970, p. 62) that long characterized understandings of "best practices" in early art education.

Kindler (1995) states, "Adult intervention may not only be useful, but essential to children's artistic learning" (p. 11), and others readily agree (Boyatzis, 2000; Chapman, 1978; Davis & Gardner, 1993; Golomb, 1992; Reggio Children & Project Zero, 2001). Even researchers long associated with traditional interpretations of the developmental process now advocate a more contextual approach to the understanding of art experience in childhood (Boyatzis, 2000).

Zimmerman and Zimmerman (2000, p. 87) point out that young children rely upon adults to make encounters with art possible, at the most basic level in which materials and occasions to use and discuss them are provided. As Daniel Walsh (2002) points out, children may never discover their "artistic selves" if they have no opportunity to do so, just as children growing up on the plains may not discover their propensities for water sports or marine biology. He argues that the possibility of developing "artistic selves" exists only in contexts which permit or encourage exploration of media and ideas, and that this possibility should be made available to all children. "The goal is not a society of artists, any more than a society of athletes or physicists, but a society of people with many well developed selves, one or more of which is artistic" (Walsh, 2002, p. 108).

Hamblen (2002) recognizes clear differences among the knowledge, values, and attitudes that are promoted in each context in which children encounter art. "School art" (Anderson & Milbrandt, 1998; Bresler, 1994, 1999, 2002; Efland, 1973, 1976; Greenberg, 1996; Smith, 1995) occupies ground distinct from the professional practices of artists and from the spontaneous art work of children and adults. Hamblen suggests that the informal learning that is characteristic of local contexts and traditional cultures typifies good early childhood practice, in that it is exploratory, concrete, experiential, and situated. She challenges art educators to preserve this approach to art making at all levels, valuing local contexts of art making even more than the professional art worlds as models for the majority of students.

With this recognition of the importance of adult influence and the scaffolding of early artistic learning has come a conviction that direct instruction of young children is not only possible but desirable, as an element within a curriculum that is constructed to preserve independent exploration. This balance between teacher direction and children's agency, between "voluntary" and "directed" work (Lark-Horovitz, Lewis, & Luca, 1973) has been achieved in a number of programs and projects documented in recent literature (Grace & Tobin, 2002; Tarr, 2003), most notably in the educational programs originating in Reggio Emilia. And yet the concept remains controversial, both among teachers for whom the concept of directing young children's work with art materials defies the doctrine they were taught and have come to accept, and among researchers, whose recommendations for teaching are more often appended as opinions than offered as corollaries of research (e.g., Matthews, 1999; Winner, 1989).

Several authors have pointed to the dangers inherent in these recommendations that teachers' involvement in early artistic learning increase. The difficulty of preserving children's choices, of reserving a space for the expression of ideas and experiences that matter most deeply to children, must be acknowledged (Tobin, 1995; Thompson, 2003). Writing about primary art education in the United Kingdom, Anning (1999) comments:

Though the technicalities and styles of learning how to draw are left to serendipity, the content of drawings in schools is clearly prescribed by teachers.Children learn that their drawings in schools must reflect teachers' views of "childhood innocence"—nothing violent or unseemly—safe and sanitized portraits of "people who help us" or observational drawings of pot plants or stuffed animals in glass cases borrowed from museums (Anning, 1995, 1997). In most primary classroom settings, as the children grapple with the conventions of "school art," their unofficial drawing about what really interests them goes underground. (p. 170)

The conflict of values that underlies the situation Anning describes has to do with teachers' understanding of art and of children, as well as their sense of what may be appropriate (or comfortable) to discuss in an educational context. It also suggests that, after decades of insisting on its disciplinary status, art remains on the margins of educational thought and practice, conceived as something other than the sturdy fabric of education, a decorative element that may enhance the garment but is in no way essential to its function. Although researchers involved with child art have long insisted that art is far more tightly interwoven in the fabric of human learning than contemporary Western culture tends to admit, the complex sociocultural and historical reasons for the peripheral position of art in North American schools and preschools remain to be fully explicated, widely understood, and revised in action.

Egan and Ling (2002) draw on Vygotsky to formulate an argument for the centrality of art education in early childhood learning. Its current marginalization, they suggest, is based upon acceptance of "a set of basic educational ideas that are mistaken" (p. 93), those ideas about young children that are so often taken for granted in casual conversation, including the presumption that children are egocentric and easily distracted. They point to the ways in which these shared understandings pervade research and pedagogy, as well, citing in particular the tenacity of the belief that intellectual development follows a path much like biological development, climbing continually onward toward greater complexity and facility. Continued reliance on these unquestioned assumptions results in "a devaluation of both the preschool child's state of knowing and the cognitive area of artistic expression" (Davis, 1997, p. 54). Egan and Ling propose instead that some important intellectual capacities reach their peak in the early years of life and decline thereafter, a possibility recognized by Piaget and others who have speculated on U-shaped developmental trajectories in children's drawing. Identifying those things that young children do more easily than they will at any other time in their lives, Egan and Ling refer specifically to the ability to think imaginatively.

Arnheim (1997) suggests that, "Child art, then, profits from being recognized as an inseparable aspect of good human

functioning. No society can afford to ignore the fact that the capacity for behaving artistically is inherent in every human being and cannot be neglected without detriment to the individual and to society as a whole" (p. 11). There is a growing recognition of the arts as intrinsically interdisciplinary. Goldberg (1997) suggests the limitations of an art-for-arts-sake model, which emphasizes the disciplinary integrity of the subject at the expense of severing its ties to other aspects of children's learning: "Students can learn about the arts, learn with the arts, and learn through the arts. The most familiar, most common, and least integrated experience students have with the arts is learning about them" (p. ix). Gallas (1994) suggests three ways to move the arts to a central position in the curriculum, by considering them as (1) methodologies for acquiring knowledge; (2) subjects of study; and (3) an array of expressive opportunities for communicating with others. She demonstrates these possibilities ably in her accounts of learning in her classrooms. Davis, Soeap, Maira, Remba, and Putnoi (1993) note the need for more research documenting what many of those working in the schools observe on a daily basis, the positive impact of art learning on children's school experience: "the power of arts production to provide students with positive habits of learning from the realization of cultural roots and individual potential to the discipline of seeing a project through from beginning to end" (Davis, 1997, p. 54).

As Tarr (2003) acknowledges, these concepts regarding the depth of learning made possible when art is perceived as a form of inquiry are exemplified in the schools of Reggio Emilia:

Experiences in visual expression are not add-ons or isolated activities but are a form of inquiry or way to investigate a theory, idea, or a problem, a way of clarifying understanding, the communication of an idea.... Reggio educators present provocations to children that ask them to see situations from multiple perspectives, through the experiences they set up, and through the use of interpersonal encounters that challenge and support acceptance of diversity, flexibility, and creativity.... They provide situations where children translate ideas developed in one media to another, which helps clarify children's thinking about aspects of the problem not encountered in previous experience (pp. 10–11).

CONCLUSION: UNANSWERED QUESTIONS AND EMERGING ISSUES

As this selective review of recent research in art education suggests, perennial questions remain unresolved, as new issues emerge. As in the past, these concerns reflect changes in art worlds and cultural life, as well as shifting perspectives on childhood and education.

One such issue, still largely unexamined in the research literature (but see Matthews, 1999; Matthews & Jessel, 1993a, 1993b), is the future of drawing in an age of electronic media. As Atkinson (2002) poses the question, "The contemporary explosion of new forms of visual expression and visual production in a variety of media almost begs the question how is it possible to understand or theorise art practice today, what does this term mean?" (p. 13).

The problem Atkinson identifies has been considered also by teachers working in Reggio Emilia, where drawing to learn (and learning to draw) are integral to educational practice. As Vecchi (2001) notes:

In comparison to the past, a great many images are available to children today, many of which come from TV—images that are beautiful or ugly, inventions that are intelligent, standard, or stereotyped. Having exposure to many images does not necessarily mean having the ability to draw better. Perhaps there is a greater distance between mental images and the level of graphic ability linked to biological age; children seem to find it harder than they did in the past to accept a graphic result so far removed from the representations of reality that they see and that contribute to constructing their imagery of the world. Equally, children find it hard to accept that better representational skills, and consequently greater satisfaction with their products, are gained by drawing more and accepting that they have to put themselves to the test again and again when drawing the same subject. (pp. 188—189)

Future research in early childhood art must address these issues of the nature of drawing and its evolution in an age in which imagery is arguably more ubiquitous and insistent than ever before, when the benefits of graphic representation as a means of inquiry have been documented and widely acknowledged. As Golomb (1992) observes, "Clearly, drawings can provide multiple sources of satisfaction that are at once of an emotional, cognitive, and aesthetic order" (p. 162). It is possible to argue that the use of drawings, and sculpture and photography and other forms of graphic representation, should become central to North American educational practice, as means for "symbolic representation of thinking" (Gallas, 1994, p. xvi). It is necessary to recognize the fundamental restructuring of educational thought and practice that this attention to multiple languages for learning would entail. Carefully interpreted research documenting such theories in practice in preschools and elementary schools is necessary to support that proposition.

Closely related to this concern is the question of how early childhood education will, or should, be affected by the movement in art education toward the study of visual culture. In much the same way that young children were neither seen nor heard in discussions of the discipline-based proposals of the 1980s and 'nineties, early childhood education has been represented in ongoing discussions of visual culture primarily in the form of theory and proposals for practice. In research conducted thus far, the entry of popular media culture into the classroom has been a dominant concern. Thompson (2003) traces changes in the subject matter of children's voluntary drawings as they are increasingly influenced by visual culture—especially media and peer culture—producing idiosyncratic developmental trajectories quite different from those that describe the kinds of drawings we recognize as child art classics. Grace and Tobin (2002) describe a classroom video production, in which the unofficial interests of children shift to center stage, and document the choices children make as they begin to consider the sensibilities of their audience. As Dyson (1997) comments, children's autonomously chosen story lines may be "culturally unsettling" (p. 3) to the adults with whom they work.

At the end of this decade devoted to reconsideration and reconceptualization of the assumptions that have guided educators and researchers concerned with art experience in the early childhood years, the time for focused research activity, addressing issues of development, context, and curriculum, has arrived. There is a clear consensus in this large and loosely organized field that traditional answers no longer tell us much about contemporary childhood, that art itself has changed in ways that must be reflected, even in the preschool classroom. There is a need for increasingly situated studies of children making art and interpreting visual images in the company of other children and adults, in the contexts where significant learning about art occurs, in classrooms and community-based programs, families, and neighborhoods.

References

Alland, A., Jr. (1983). *Playing with form: Children draw in six cultures.* New York: Columbia University Press.

Althouse, R., Johnson, M. H., & Mitchell, S. T. (2003). *The colors of learning: Integrating the visual arts into the early childhood curriculum.* New York and Washington, DC: Teachers College Press & National Association for the Education of Young Children.

Anderson, T., & Milbrandt, M. (1998). Authentic instruction in art: Why and how to dump the school art style. *Visual Arts Research, 24*(1), 13–20.

Andersson, S. B. (1995). Local conventions in children's drawings: A comparative study in three cultures. *Journal of Multicultural and Crosscultural Research in Art Education, 13*, 101–111.

Anning, A. (1999). Learning to draw and drawing to learn. *Journal of Art and Design Education, 18*(2), 163–172.

Arnheim, R. (1969). *Visual thinking.* Berkeley: University of California Press.

Arnheim, R. (1954/1974). *Art and visual perception.* Berkeley: University of California Press.

Arnheim, R. (1997). A look at a century of growth. In A. M. Kindler (Ed.), *Child development in art* (pp. 9–16). Reston, VA: National Art Education Association.

Atkinson, D. (2002). *Art in education: Identity and practice.* Boston: Kluwer Academic Press.

Baker, D. (1994). Toward a sensible art education: Inquiring into the role of visual arts in early childhood education. *Visual Arts Research, 20*(2), 92–104.

Ballard, P. B. (1913). What children like to draw. *Journal of Experimental Pedagogy and Training College Record, 2*, 127–129.

Beittel, K. R. (1973). *Alternatives for art education research.* Dubuque, IA: Wm. C. Brown.

Boyatzis, C. J. (2000). The artistic evolution of Mommy: A longitudinal case study of symbolic and social processes. In C. Boyatzis & M. W. Watson (Eds.), *Symbolic and social constraints on the development of children's artistic style* (pp. 5–30). San Francisco: Jossey-Bass.

Boyatzis, C. J., & Albertini, G. (2000). A naturalistic observation of children drawing: Peer collaboration processes and influences in child art. In C. Boyatzis & M. W. Watson (Eds.), *Symbolic and social constraints on the development of children's artistic style* (pp. 31-48). San Francisco: Jossey-Bass.

Boyatzis, C., & Watson, M. W. (Eds.) (2002), *Symbolic and social constraints on the development of children's artistic style*. San Francisco: Jossey-Bass.

Braswell, G. (2001). Collaborative drawing during early mother-child interactions. *Visual Arts Research, 27*(2), 27-39.

Bremner, J. G., & Moore, S. (1984). Prior visual inspection and object naming: Two factors that enhance hidden feature inclusion in young children's drawings, *British Journal of Developmental Psychology, 2*, 371-376.

Bresler, L. (1992). Visual art in the primary grades: A portrait and analysis. *Early Childhood Research Quarterly,* 7, 397-414.

Bresler, L. (1994). Imitative, complementary and expansive: Three roles of visual arts curricula. *Studies in Art Education, 35*(2), 90-104.

Bresler, L. (1999). The hybridization and homogenization of school art: Institutional contexts for elementary art students. *Visual Arts Research, 25*(2), 25-37.

Bresler, L. (2002). School art as a hybrid genre: Institutional contexts for art curriculum. In L. Bresler & C. M. Thompson (Eds.), *The arts in children's lives: Context, culture, and curriculum* (pp. 169-183). Boston: Kluwer Academic Press.

Bresler, L., & Thompson, C. M. (Eds.) (2002). *The arts in children's lives: Context, culture, and curriculum.* Boston: Kluwer Academic Press.

Chapman, L. (1978). *Approaches to art in education.* New York: Harcourt Brace Jovanovich.

Chen, J. C.-H. (2001). Aesthetic thinking of young children and adolescents. *Visual Arts Research, 27*(2), 47-56.

Cocking, R. R., & Copple, C. E. (1979). Change through exposure to others: A study of children's verbalizations as they draw. In M. K. Poulsen & G. I. Lubin (Eds.), *Piagetian theory and its implications for the helping professions (Proceedings, Eighth Interdisciplinary Conference, Vol. II)* (pp. 124-132). University Park: University of Southern California Press.

Collins, G., & Sandell, R. (1996). *Gender issues in art education: Content, context, and strategies.* Reston, VA: National Art Education Association.

Cooke, G., Griffin, D., & Cox, M. (1998). *Teaching young children to draw.* Bristol, PA: Falmer Press.

Costall, A. (2001). Introduction. In G.-H. Luquet, *Children's drawings (Le dessin enfantin)* (Trans., with introduction, by A. Costall, pp. vii-xxiv). New York: Free Association Books.

Court, E. (1994). Researching social influences in the drawings of rural Kenyan children. In D. Thistlewood, S. Paine, & E. Court (Eds.), *Drawing, art, and development* (pp. 219-260). London: Longmans.

Cox, M. (1992). *Children's drawings.* New York: Penguin Books.

Cox, M. (1993). *Children's drawings of the human figure.* Hove, UK: Lawrence Erlbaum.

Cox, M. (1997). *Drawings of people by the under-fives.* London, UK: Falmer.

Cox, M. (1989). Knowledge and appearance in children's pictorial representation. *Educational Psychology, 9*, 15-25.

Cox, M., Perera, J., & Fan, X. (1999). Children's drawing in the UK and China. *Journal of Art & Design Education, 18*(2), 173-181.

Cunningham, A. (1997). Criteria and processes used by seven-year-old children in appraising art work of their peers. *Visual Arts Research, 23*(1), 41-48.

Danko-McGhee, K. (2000). *The aesthetic preferences of young children.* Lewistin, NY: E. Mellen Press.

Davis, J. (1997). The "U" and the wheel of "C:" Development and devaluation of graphic symbolization and the cognitive approach at Harvard Project Zero. In A. M. Kindler (ed.), *Child development in art* (pp. 45-58). Reston, VA: National Art Education Association.

Davis, J., & Gardner, H. (1993). The arts and early childhood education: A cognitive developmental portrait of the young child as artist. In B. Spodek (Ed.), *Handbook of research in early childhood education* (2nd ed.). New York: Macmillan.

Davis, J., Soeap, E., Maira, S., Remba, N., Putnoi, D., Gardner, H., & Gonzalez-Pose, P. (1993). *Safe havens: Portraits of educational effectiveness in community art centers that focus on education.* Cambridge, MA: Project Co-Arts, Harvard Project Zero.

Duncum, P. (1984). How 35 children born between 1724 and 1900 learned to draw. *Studies in Art Education, 26*(2), 93-102.

Duncum, P. (1997). Subjects and themes in children's unsolicited drawings and gender socialization. In A. M. Kindler (Ed.), *Child development in art* (pp. 107-114). Reston, VA: National Art Education Association.

Duncum, P. (2002). Children never were what they were: Perspectives on childhood. In Y. Gaudelius & P. Speiers (Eds.), *Contemporary issues in art education* (pp. 97-106). Upper Saddle River, NJ: Prentice Hall.

Duncum, P. (2003). Theorising everyday aesthetic experience with contemporary visual culture. *Visual Arts Research, 28*(2), 4-15.

Dyson, A. H. (1989). *Multiple worlds of child writers: Friends learning to write.* New York: Teachers College Press.

Dyson, A. H. (1990). Symbol makers, symbol weavers: How children link play, pictures, and print. *Young Children, 42*(2), 50-57.

Dyson, A. H. (1997). *Writing superheroes: Contemporary childhood, popular culture, and classroom literacy.* New York: Teachers College Press.

Edwards, L. C. (1997). *The creative arts: A process approach for teachers and children* (2nd ed.). Upper Saddle River, NJ: Prentice Hall.

Efland, A. D. (1976). School art style: A functional analysis. *Studies in Art Education, 17*(2), 37-44.

Efland, A. D. (1983). School art and its social origin. *Studies in Art Education, 24*, 49-57.

Egan, K. (1988). *Primary understanding: Education in early childhood.* New York: Routledge.

Egan, K. (1999). *Children's minds, talking rabbits, and clockwork oranges*: Essays on education. New York: Teachers College Press.

Egan, K., & Ling, M. (2002). We begin as poets: Conceptual tools and the arts in early childhood. In L. Bresler & C. M. Thompson (Eds.), *The arts in children's lives: Context, culture, and curriculum* (pp. 93-100). Boston: Kluwer Academic Press.

Ewald, W., & Lightfoot, A. (2001). *I wanna take me a picture: Teaching photography and writing to children.* Boston: Beacon Press.

Feinburg, S. (1979). The significance of what boys and girls choose to draw: Explorations of fighting and helping. In J. Loeb (Ed.), *Feminist collage: Educating women in the visual arts* (pp. 107-122). New York: Teachers College Press.

Feldman, E. B. (1992). *Varieties of visual experience.* Englewood Cliffs, NJ: Prentice Hall.

Fineberg, J. (1997). *The innocent eye: Children's art and the modern artist.* Princeton, NJ: Princeton University Press.

Fineberg, J. (1998) (Ed.), *Discovering child art: Essays on child art, primitivism, and modernism.* Princeton, NJ: Princeton University Press.

Flannery, K., & Watson, M. (1995). Sex differences and gender-role differences in children's drawings. *Studies in Art Education, 36*(2), 114-122.

Forman, G. (1994). Different media, different languages. In L. G. Katz & B. Cesarone (Eds.), *Reflections on the Reggio Emilia approach* (pp. 41-54). Urbana, IL: ERIC.

Fortes, M. (1981). Tallensi children's drawings. In B. Loyd & J. Gay (eds.), *Universals of human thought* (pp. 46-70). Cambridge, UK: Cambridge University Press.

Freeman, N. H. (1980). *Strategies of representation in young children*. London: Academic Press.

Freeman, N. H., & Cox, M. (1985). *Visual order*. London: Academic Press.

Freeman, N. H., & Janikoun, R. (1972). Intellectual realism in children's drawings of a familiar object with distinctive features. *Child Development, 43*, 1116-1121.

Freeman, N. H., & Sanger, D. (1995). Commonsense aesthetics of rural children. *Visual Arts Research, 21*(2), 1-10.

Freedman, K. (1997). Artistic development and curriculum: Sociocultural learning considerations. In A. M. Kindler (Ed.), *Child development in art* (pp. 95-106). Reston, VA: National Art Education Association.

Gallas, K. (1994). *The languages of learning*. New York: Teachers College Press.

Gallo, F., Golomb, C., & Barroso, A. (2003). Compositional strategies in drawing: The effects of two- and three-dimensional media. *Visual Arts Research, 28*(1), 2-23.

Gamradt, J., & Staples, C. (1994). My school and me: Children's drawings in postmodern educational research and evaluation. *Visual Arts Research, 20*(1), 36-49.

Gardner, H. (1973). *The arts and human development*. New York: John Wiley & Sons.

Gardner, H. (1976). Unfolding or teaching? On the optimal training of artistic skills. In E. W. Eisner (Ed.), *The arts, human development, and education* (pp. 5-18). Berkeley: McCutchan.

Gardner, H. (1980). *Artful scribbles: The significance of children's drawings*. New York: Basic Books.

Gardner, H. (1982). *Art, mind, and brain*. New York: Basic Books.

Goldberg, M. (1997). *Arts and learning*. New York: Longman.

Golomb, C. (1974). *Young children's sculpture and drawing: A study in representational development*. Cambridge, MA: Harvard University Press.

Golomb, C. (1992). *The child's creation of a pictorial world*. Berkeley: University of California Press.

Golomb, C. (1997). Representational concepts in clay: The development of sculpture. In A. M. Kindler (Ed.), *Child development in art* (pp. 131-141). Reston, VA: National Art Education Association.

Golomb, C. (2002). *Child art in context: A cultural and comparative perspective*. Washington, DC: American Psychological Association.

Golomb, C., & McCormick, M. (1995). Sculpture: The development of three-dimensional representation in clay. *Visual Arts Research, 21*(1), 35-50.

Goodenough, F. L. (1926). *Measurement of intelligence by drawing*. New York: Harcourt, Brace, and World.

Grace, D. J., & Tobin, J. (2002). Pleasure, creativity, and the carnivalesque in children's video production. In L. Bresler & C. M. Thompson (Eds.), *The arts in children's lives: Context, culture, and curriculum* (pp. 195-214). Boston: Kluwer Academic Press.

Graue, M. E., & Walsh, D. J. (1998). *Studying children in context: Theories, methods and ethics*. Thousand Oaks, CA: Sage Publications.

Greenberg, P. (1996). Time, money, and the new art education versus art and irrelevance. *Studies in Art Education, 37*(2), 115-116.

Hamblen, K. (2002). Children's contextual art knowledge: Local art and school art context comparisons. In L. Bresler & C. M. Thompson (Eds.), *The arts in children's lives: Context, culture, and curriculum* (pp. 15-27). Boston: Kluwer Academic Press.

Harris, D. B. (1963). *Children's drawings as measures of intellectual maturity*. New York: Harcourt, Brace, and World.

Helm, J. H., & Katz, L. (2001). *Young investigators: The project approach in the early years*. New York: Teachers College Press.

Inagaki, K. (1992). Piagetian and post-Piagetian conceptions of development and their implications for science education in early childhood. *Early Childhood Research Quarterly, 7*, 115-133.

Jalongo, M. R., & Stamp, L. N. (1997). *The arts in children's lives: Aesthetic education in early childhood*. Needham Heights, MA: Allyn & Bacon.

James, A., Jenks, C. & Prout, A. (1998). *Theorizing childhood*. New York: Teachers College Press.

Jeffers, C. (1993). A survey of instructors of art methods classes for preservice elementary teachers. *Studies in Art Education, 34*(4), 233-243.

Jenkins, H. (1998) (Ed.). *The children's culture reader*. New York: New York University Press.

Katz, L. G. (1998). What can we learn from Reggio Emilia? In C. Edwards, L. Gandini, & G. Forman (Eds.), *The hundred languages of children: The Reggio Emilia approach—advanced reflections* (2nd ed.). (pp. 27-45). Westport, CT: Ablex Publishing.

Kellogg, R. (1970). *Analyzing children's art*. Palo Alto, CA: Mayfield Publishing Co.

Kerlavage, M. (1995). A bunch of naked ladies and a tiger: Children's responses to adult works of art. In C. M. Thompson (Ed.), *The visual arts and early childhood learning* (pp. 56-62). Reston, VA: National Art Education Association.

Kerschensteiner, G. (1905). *Die Entwicklung der Zeichnerischen Begabung*. [The development of drawing talent]. Munich: Carl Greber.

Kincheloe, J. (1998). The new childhood: Home alone as a way of life. In H. Jenkins (Ed.), *The children's culture reader* (pp. 159-177). New York: New York University Press.

Kindler, A. M. (1994). Artistic learning in early childhood: A study of social interactions. *Canadian Review of Art Education, 21*(2), 91-106.

Kindler, A. M. (1995). Significance of adult input in early artistic development. In C. M. Thompson (Ed.), *The visual arts and early childhood learning* (pp. 10-14). Reston, VA: National Art Education Association.

Kindler, A. M. (1999). "From endpoints to repertoires": A challenge to art education, *Studies in Art Education, 40*(4), 330-349.

Kindler, A. M., & Darras, B. (1997). Map of artistic development. In A. M. Kindler (Ed.), *Child development in art* (pp. 17-44). Reston, VA: National Art Education Association.

Kindler, A. M., & Darras, B., (1995). Young children's understanding of the nature and acquisition of drawing skills: A crosscultural study. *Journal of Multicultural and Crosscultural Research in Art Education, 13*, 85-100.

Kindler, A., Darras, B., & Kuo, A. (2000). When a culture takes a trip: Evidence of heritage and enculturation in early conceptions of art. *Journal of Art & Design Education, 19*(1), 44-53.

Koppitz, E. (1968). *Psychological evaluation of children's human figure drawings*. New York: Grune & Stratton.

Korzenik, D. (1973-74). Role-taking and children's drawings. *Studies in Art Education, 15*(3), 17-24.

Korzenik, D. (1981, September). Is children's work art? Some historical views, *Art Education*, 20-24.

Lange-Kuettner, C., & Thomas, G. V. (1995). *Drawing and looking*. New York: Harvester Wheatsheaf.

Lark-Horovitz, B., Lewis, H., & Luca, M. (1973). *Understanding children's art for better teaching* (2nd ed.). Columbus, OH: Charles E. Merrill.

Leeds, J. A. (1986). Teaching and the reasons for making art. *Art Education, 39*(7), 17-21.

Leeds, J. A. (1989). The history of attitudes toward child art. *Studies in Art Education, 30*(2), 93-103.

Lowenfeld, V. (1957). *Creative and mental growth* (3rd ed.). New York: Macmillan.

Luquet, G.-H. (1927/2001). *Children's drawings* (Trans., with intro, by A. Costall). London: Free Association Books.

Maitland, L. M. (1895). What children draw to please themselves. *The Inland Educator, i*, 77-81.

Malaguzzi, L. (1995, May). Your image of the child: Where teaching begins. *Child Care Information Exchange*, no. 96, 52-61.

Malaguzzi, L. (1998). No way. The hundred is there. In C. Edwards, L. Gandini, & G. Forman (Eds.), *The hundred languages of children: The Reggio Emilia approach—advanced reflections* (p. 3). Westport, CT: Ablex Publishing.

Martlew, M., & Connolly, K. J. (1996). Human figure drawings by schooled and unschooled children in Papua New Guinea. *Child Development, 67*, 2743-2762.

Matthews, G. (1980). *Philosophy and the young child*. Cambridge, MA: Harvard University Press.

Matthews, J. (1999). *The art of childhood and adolescence: The construction of meaning*. Philadelphia: Falmer Press.

Matthews, J., & Jessels, J. (1993). Very young children use electronic paint: The beginnings of drawing with traditional media and computer paintbox, *Visual Arts Research, 19*(1), 47-62.

Mortenson, K. (1991). *Form and content in children's human figure drawings: Development, sex differences, and body experiences*. New York: New York University Press.

Munro, T., Lark-Horovitz, B., & Barnhart, E. N. (1942). Children's art abilities: Studies at the Cleveland Museum of Art. *Journal of Experimental Education, 11*(2), 97-155.

Newton, C., & Kantner, L. (1997). Cross-cultural research in aesthetic development: A review. In A. M. Kindler (Ed.), *Child development in art* (pp. 165-182). Reston, VA: National Art Education Association.

Paget, G. W. (1932). Some drawings of men and women made by children of certain non-European races. *Journal of the Royal Anthropological Institute, 62*, 127-144.

Parsons, M. (1988). *How we understand art: A cognitive account of aesthetic development*. New York: Cambridge University Press.

Pearson, P. (2001). Towards a theory of children's drawing as social practice. *Studies in Art Education, 42*(4), 348-365.

Pitri, E. (2003). Conceptual problem solving during artistic representation. *Art Education, 56*(4), 19-23.

Read, H. (1945). *Education through art*. New York: Pantheon.

Reggio Children & Project Zero (2001). *Making learning visible: Children as individual and group learners*. Reggio Emilia, Italy: Reggio Children.

Reith, E. (1997). Drawing development: The child's understanding of the dual reality of pictorial representations. In A. M. Kindler (Ed.), *Child development in art* (pp. 59-80). Reston, VA: National Art Education Association.

Robertson, A. (1987). Development of Bruce's spontaneous drawings from six to sixteen. *Studies in Art Education, 29*(1), 37-51.

Schaefer-Simmern, H. (1948). *The unfolding of artistic activity*. Berkeley: University of California Press.

Schirrmacher, R. (1993). *Art and creative development for young children* (3rd ed.). Albany, NY: Delmar Publishers.

Smith, P. (1995). Commentary: Art and irrelevance. *Studies in Art Education, 36*(2), 123-125.

Su, C.-M. (1995). A cross-cultural study of partial occlusion in children's drawings. In C. M. Thompson (Ed.), *The visual arts and early childhood learning* (pp. 91-94). Reston, VA: National Art Education Association.

Tarr, P. (1995). Preschool children's socialization through art experiences. In C. M. Thompson (Ed.), *The visual arts and early childhood learning* (pp. 23-27). Reston, VA: National Art Education Association.

Tarr, P. (2003). Reflections on the image of the child: Reproducer or creator of culture. *Art Education, 56*(4), 6-11.

Taunton, M., & Colbert, C. (2000). Art in the early childhood classroom: Authentic experiences and extended dialogues. In N. J. Yelland (Ed.), *Promoting meaningful learning: Innovations in educating early childhood professionals* (pp. 67-76). Washington, DC: National Association for the Education of Young Children.

Thomas, G. V., & Silk, A. M. J. (1990). *An introduction to the psychology of children's drawings*. New York: New York University Press.

Thompson, C. M. (1997). Transforming curriculum in the visual arts. In S. Bredekamp & T. Rosegrant (Eds.), *Reaching potentials: Transforming early childhood curriculum and assessment* (pp. 81-98). Washington, DC: National Association for the Education of Young Children.

Thompson, C. M. (1999). Action, autobiography, and aesthetics in young children's self-initiated drawings. *Journal of Art & Design Education, 18*(2), 155-161.

Thompson, C. M. (2002). Drawing together: Peer influence in preschool-kindergarten art classes. In L. Bresler & C. M. Thompson (Eds.), *The arts in children's lives: Context, culture, and curriculum* (pp. 129-138). Boston: Kluwer Academic Press.

Thompson, C. M. (2003). Kinderculture in the art classroom: Early childhood art and the mediation of culture. *Studies in Art Education, 44*(2), 135-146.

Thompson, C., & Bales. S. (1991). "Michael doesn't like my dinosaurs:" Conversations in a preschool art class. *Studies in Art Education, 33*(1), 43-55.

Thunder-McGuire, S. (1994). An inner critic in children's artists' bookmaking. *Visual Arts Research, 20*(2), 51-61.

Tobin, J. (1995, May). The irony of self-expression. *American Journal of Education, 103*, 233-258.

Tuman, D. (1999). Gender style as form and content: An examination of gender stereotypes in the subject preference of children's drawing. *Studies in Art Education, 41*(1), 40-60.

Tuman, D. (2000). Defining differences: A historical overview of the research regarding the difference between the drawings of boys and girls. *The Journal of Gender Issues in Art and Education, 1*, 17-30.

Vecchi, V. (1998). The role of the atelierista: An interview with Lella Gandini. In C. Edwards, L. Gandini, & G. Forman (Eds.), *The hundred languages of children: The Reggio Emilia approach—advanced reflections* (2nd ed., pp. 139-148). Westport, CT: Ablex Publishing.

Vecchi, V. (2001). The curiosity to understand. In Reggio Children & Project Zero (eds.), *Making learning visible: Children as individual and group learners* (pp. 158-212). Reggio Emilia, Italy: Reggio Children.

Vygotsky, L. S. (1962). *Thought and language* (Trans. & Ed., E. Hanfmann & G. Vakar). Cambridge, MA: Harvard University Press.

Vygotsky, L. S. (1978). *Mind in society*. Cambridge, MA: Harvard University Press.

Walsh, D. (2002). Constructing an artistic self: A cultural perspective. In L. Bresler & C. M. Thompson (Eds.), *The arts in children's lives: Context, culture, and curriculum* (pp. 101-111). Boston: Kluwer Academic Press.

Weitz, M. (1959). The role of theory in aesthetics. In M. Weitz (Ed.), *Problems in aesthetics: An introductory book of readings* (pp. 145-159). New York: Macmillan.

Willats, J. (1977). How children learn to draw realistic pictures. *Quarterly Journal of Experimental Psychology, 29*, 367-382.

Wilson, B. (1974). The superheroes of J. C. Holz. *Art Education, 27*(8), 2–9.

Wilson, B. (1997). Child art, multiple interpretations, and conflicts of interest. In A. M. Kindler (Ed.), *Child development in art* (pp. 81–94). Reston, VA: National Art Education Association.

Wilson, B. (2002). Becoming Japanese: Manga, children's drawings, and the construction of national character. In L. Bresler & C. M. Thompson (Eds.), *The arts in children's lives: Context, culture, and curriculum* (pp. 43–56). Boston: Kluwer Academic Press.

Wilson, B., & Wilson, M. (1977). An iconoclastic view of the imagery sources in the drawings of young people. *Art Education,* 5–11.

Wilson, B., & Wilson, M. (1982). *Teaching children to draw: A guide for parents and teachers*. Englewood Cliffs, NJ: Prentice Hall.

Wilson, B., & Wilson, M. (1984). Children's drawings in Egypt: Cultural style acquisition as graphic development. *Visual Arts Research, 10*(1), 13–26.

Wilson, B., & Wilson, M. (1985). The artistic tower of Babel: Inextricable links between culture and graphic development. *Visual Arts Research, 11*(1), 90–104.

Winner, E. (1982). *Invented worlds*. Cambridge, MA: Harvard University Press.

Winner, E. (1989). How can Chinese children draw so well? *Journal of Aesthetic Education, 23*(1), 41–63.

Wolf, D. P., & Perry, M. D. (1988). From endpoint to repertoires: Some new conclusions about drawing development. *Journal of Aesthetic Education, 22*(1), 17–34.

Yamagata, K. (1997). Representational activity during mother-child interaction: The scribbling stage of drawing. *British Journal of Development, 15*, 355–366.

Zimmerman, E., & Zimmerman, L. (2000). Art education and early childhood education: The young child as creator and meaning maker within a community context. *Young Children,* 87–92.

Zurmuehlen, M. (1990). *Studio art: Praxis, symbol, presence*. Reston, VA: National Art Education Association.

Zurmuehlen, M. & Kantner, L. (1995). The narrative quality of young children's art. In C. M. Thompson (Ed.), *The visual arts and early childhood learning* (pp. 6–9). Reston, VA: National Art Education Association.

·13·

THE DANCE OF LEARNING

Karen Bradley
With Mary Szegda
University of Maryland, College Park

In the life of a young child, every day is a new journey. The vehicle for the journey is movement. From the early morning bounce or slide out of bed, until the last crawl or rollover at night, every child negotiates his/her way along a pathway of body actions in space and time, with an ever-increasing and specific array of expressive and functional actions.

Movement may, in fact be considered the primary intelligence. It certainly precedes both vocal and verbal language development and informs visual-spatial, auditory and other sensory development. A child's evolving sense of self and the nature of the world of objects (also called "learning") are based on the feedback loop of reflexive, responsive, volitional, interactive, and expressive actions.

In this sense, the entire learning process may be seen as a form of "dancing"—as a conscious choosing to explore and interact with data that is based in rhythmic and spatial sequences of movements. Reflexive movement, which takes place in a lower aspect of the brain, provides information to the emotional and cognitive processing areas of the brain. The brain depends on the motor cortex and spinal column to provide information about sensations and interactions with the world outside the skin. It is this dance of inner and outer experiences, lower and higher processing centers, and functional and expressive actions that is the material of learning.

As the child develops, rhythm organizes and delineates the temporal aspects of expression and reception. From pat-a-cake to double-Dutch, from marching games to rap for kids, repetitive ever-more complex rhythmic structures bring children away from the passive entertainment world of the television and electronic games. Rhythm activates, focuses, and organizes them socially and interactively.

Ancient representations of children in art and other descriptions show clapping games and circle dances. As early as 1929, articles were written on how to use rhythms to help children organize for learning. Gerhardt (1973) describes rhythm as a "dynamic time-of-thought-and time-of action relationship"

(p. 51). Benari (1995) writes about the relationship of rhythmic awareness to breathing rhythms.

In many schools around the United States, dance education classes are called rhythms. Somehow, it seems, the expressive resultant phenomenon of temporally organized movement is valued, even as the art form of dance is not. In urban streets, in suburban basements, outside shopping malls, on playgrounds, wherever children gather; there are rhythmic games and boom box music. Children, it appears, understand how to reference the need for organization and expression.

Bradley's evidence of the power of rhythm came in her son's fourth grade class. She was in the classroom for the day at the behest of the teacher, who was struggling with the group. The school was new, the children previously unknown to each other and the atmosphere was chaotic most of the time. The day she was there was also the day of the Stanford-9 (United States achievement tests administered annually in many public schools) tests. All of the adults were in despair over the picture of such disorganized bodies (children) sitting at desks for 2 hours answering questions.

They began with growing and shrinking movements, based on breath rhythms and with the support of John Coltrane's version of "My Favorite Things," surely one of the most lush pieces of music ever recorded. The students responded to the syncopated waltz rhythms immediately. Bradley and the students rolled down the spine and up the spine, stretched in all directions, and just got down with the music. After 20 minutes, the fourth graders sat at their desks, picked up their pencils and began the test. One could have heard a pin drop.

Mastery of rhythm supports the kind of thinking/action interaction that reveals the complex nature of active learning. Therefore, the games of children worldwide make sense both as community building and as a set point for learning readiness. Warming up for learning, as in Bradley's son's class, makes much more sense than the usual lesson warmup activity of answering questions from a book, or doing a sheet of math problems.

The development of the child can be thought of as both a continuing refinement of skills through practice and a construction of the nature of self and reality through interactions with the world of objects/people. If both of these processes are interactive and inform each other, it is but a small step to see how critical both functional and expressive movement are to the development of the cognitive, social and kinesthetic life of the child.

Mihaly Csikszentmihaly (1990), in his book *Flow: The psychology of optimal experience*, addresses the feedback loop of active learning in regard to movement:

Flow activities . . . have rules that require the learning of skills, they set up goals, they provide feedback, they make control possible. . . . Because of the way they are constructed, they help participants and spectators achieve an ordered state of mind that is . . . enjoyable. (p. 72)

Thus moving, however it forms and allows for encounters, is *a priori* to knowing. We do not know and then move, we move in order to know.

COMPONENTS OF MOVEMENT

Rhythm underlies one aspect of movement, the "how" or qualitative aspect of moving. Children move in space, using body parts and organizing them, with qualities such as degrees of attention, degrees of strength or resistance, degrees of hastening or lingering, and degrees of flowing through or holding back. These qualities modify actions of the body in space, and have been named Effort by the movement theorist Rudolf Laban (1879–1958).

Laban organized the analysis of movement into the components of Body (*what* is moving), Space (*where* it is moving), and Effort (*how* it is moving). Another category has been added to the systematic analysis of human movement (called Laban Movement Analysis, or LMA): Shape (*how* the body adjusts its shape in relationship to an external factor—such as an object or another person) (See Figure 13.1).

Laban's work found favor with physical educators and dance educators in Britain during and immediately following World War II. Through the vocabulary that developed from Laban's theoretical framework, teachers encouraged children to discover how they could make up their own movement sentences: phrases of body parts moving in space, with rhythm and qualities, and in relationship to outside factors such as objects, partners, groups or the space itself. As James Davidson (2001) wrote in the obituary of John Hodgson, a theatre professor and Laban archivist:

Laban is movement's greatest map-maker. . . . Hodgson compares him to Stravinsky, Picasso, and Stanislavsky, and it wouldn't surprise me if he turned out to be more significant than all of these. (*The Daily Telegraph*, London, July 21, 2001)

Marion North (1975) developed Laban's work further, utilizing the framework and map to observe children. In her studies that she compiled in her book, *Personality assessment through*

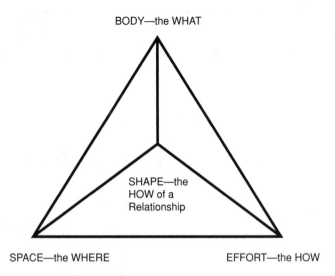

FIGURE 13.1. Laban movement analysis

movement, she focused on the *Effort* components primarily; but she also made the point that it is the whole movement event that must be observed first. (North, 1975, p. vi). North (1975) provides a clear overview of the Laban "map" for movement, and a number of examples of her own use of the vocabulary in assessing children from a movement analysis. Chapter 6 in her book is a comparative analysis of deaf children from the Laban *Effort* framework, classroom teachers' reports, and a personality test developed by a psychologist called the "B scale." There is a high correlation between the movement analysis and the classroom teachers' reports; the B scale identifies specific deficits in the child's makeup. What becomes apparent in her book is that there is a tremendous amount of information about how a child succeeds in a movement profile, whereas there is not much directive information in most personality tests. Both prescriptive and positive reinforcement responses are much more challenging in the case in which such tests are the only source of diagnostic information.

Through the systematic observation of and exposure to movement experiences and movement interactions, children construct their own maps of the world of objects and beliefs. What is revealed when children create their own "dances" or phrases of expressive movement? We can see the very act of learning unfolding. We can see patterns of interaction with the fabric of the emerging self, and with the social/interpersonal field of possibilities. We also see applications of prior knowledge as the dancers make random movements meaningful.

Children's Learning Through Movement

In asking the question, "How exactly do children learn to move?" Children give rise to movement, voice, and mind from the simple and usually unconscious act of breathing. When the infant gasps, cries, coos, or sleeps, the body response to the rhythm and quality of the breath results in both voicing and movement. The infant begins to differentiate the variety of felt experiences from the response from the world to those expressions.

Adults reflect, reinforce, and extend the undifferentiated expressions of infants by mirroring, bridging, accommodating, feeding, talking, singing, rocking, and playing with infants. It is in these interactions that the child begins to map his/her sense of the world of objects and the place of the self within that world.

Antonio Damasio (1999) wrote about how the self becomes conscious of itself. He describes two players, the organism and the object, in terms of the relationship between them. That relationship is a two-way street in which knowledge is constructed via the dynamic exchange between an organism and an object. The object in the relationship is causing a change in the organism (p. 133).

From such constructions of reality come beliefs, including beliefs about the nature of one's self. The child comes to see herself as competent, or clumsy, or delicate, or strong, depending, in part, on the responses of and interactions with the powerful adults in her life. Whether or not this becomes a process of closing doors and narrowing beliefs, or becomes an expansive process, in which options and choices are exercised actively, depends on the range of explorations allowed. The feedback given plays a role too; what is rewarded and what is extinguished over time comes to define a child's inward moral compass as well as a sense of safety and intactness.

The Kestenberg Movement Profile

The work of Judith Kestenberg, a protégé of Laban and Anna Freud's, looks at how parent and infant interactions support and shape the development of the primary relationship on both the expressive and the social sides. The Kestenberg Movement Profile (KMP) allows the trained observer to note patterns of expressive and relational behavior through the degree of attunement in two categories.

The baby, Kestenberg proposed, enters the world with two primary regulatory systems that operate in the form of tension-flow and shape-flow. Tension-flow reflects the elasticity of effortful movement and affect-related expressivity. Shape-flow is the other side of tension-flow, and reflects the changing relational experience; how the organism relates to the structures around them (Sossin, 2002).

An integral aspect within the KMP is attunement. Attunement occurs when two individuals share a common experience. It is essential in relational development and can occur on many levels. Tension-flow attunement is particularly powerful when engaging an infant in interaction. Rhythms shared lead to a sense of connection or synchrony. Synchrony is a phenomenon of groups that can build group cohesion and trust. In environments in which two people attune, or "sync up," communication and understanding become more likely.

Trust develops from patterns of mutual relatedness identifiable through shape-flow rhythms. A bonding process can happen as the result of attunement with *in utero* shape-flow patterns. Because the shape-flow mode of self-attunement flows on breath rhythms, adults can, naturally or through training, attune breathing patterns to those of children and build up an atmosphere of mutuality and trust over time. The conscious attuning process is a technique used in Kestenberg work both with infants in-utero and as a therapeutic technique with infants and young children.

Sossin (2002) notes the KMP system is complex. Robert Prince (2002) describes Kestenberg's extensive psychodynamic training and favorable predictions of broad KMP applications made by respected peers of Dr. Kestenberg at the time of the development of the system. However, few educators or researchers are aware of the KMP.

Interrater reliability of the KMP is moderately high (Koch, 1997) to moderately low for a few aspects of the system. The fact that novice raters were more inconsistent than experienced raters places the KMP in a similar category to the Laban Movement Analysis system, in which the building of consensus over time is a significant part of the training, and a factor in the degree of interrater reliability.

Research that has been completed using the KMP includes infant sleep pattern analysis (Lotan & Yirmiya, 2002), and as an assessment tool for identifying neglected children (Leirvag, 2001). In the Lotan and Yirmiya (2002) study, 30 toddlers were videotaped as they fell asleep. Using the Kestenberg Movement Profile, researchers determined that low intensity babies (babies whose movements were less "loaded"—i.e., expressed fewer qualities at the same time—expressively and who fall more toward the free flow side of the spectrum) fell asleep more quickly than high intensity babies and that the presence and length of presence of the parents in the room made a difference as well. Parents who spent more time in the room tended to have babies who kicked more, banged, and strained more (description of high intensity movement preferences), whereas parents who spent less time in the room tended to have lower intensity babies. The movement variables were superior predictors of falling asleep time.

The implications of the research demonstrate that the KMP, and movement analysis in general, are important tools for unpacking behavior. Without the specificity and observability of such systems of analysis, parents may only speculate about the importance of their role in the development of the child.

Effort and Shape

The Kestenberg work looks at developmental stages in object relations and expressive movement threads. Laban Movement Analysis takes the analysis to the next stages developmentally.

Effort is the category describing the qualitative expressive modifiers of action or the "how" of movement. As a child's personality develops, observable patterns of expressivity appear. One child may be "mild-mannered," whereas another is "intense." One is "strong-willed," another "light-hearted." The expressive components appear in recurring phrases of movement behavior that formulate a baseline. Children (as well as adults) are not limited to these characteristics. Everyone has a range. But certain patterns appear in specific contexts, and loved ones recognize the individual's patterns easily.

Effort observation is one way to track change and growth in a child's expressive range. A great deal of creative movement curricula that is utilized in schools includes development of a greater range of expressive actions, or a broadened palette of choices for personal expression.

Joan Russell (1965) describes *Effort* as "the attitude of the mover to the motion factors of weight, space, time, and flow" (p. 22). Sue Stinson (1988) uses the terms space, time, and energy to describe the expressive possibilities in creative movement. Her definition of these qualities is "factors that modify basic action" (p. 21). Whatever the specific definitions are of each factor, however, the changes in expressivity over time or in the moment are observable, and can be tracked.

Why is it desirable to develop the expressive range of children in movement? For one thing, exploration of a range of material is helpful in developing a sense of mastery. Such explorations allow children to understand that they have options. They can make choices about how they present themselves and can develop a degree of complexity of personality that is comfortable. Children who have an expressive range can accommodate to tasks more readily. It helps to have access to both quick and sustained time effort in most athletic endeavors, for example.

Children also can learn to observe the unique patterns in others and to appreciate the subtly different ways each of us negotiates our way through interactions, tasks, and creative endeavors. And a range of expressive choices supports innovative thinking; trying a new idea just a little differently. The child can appreciate that another route may produce a new, and perhaps better, destination.

Shape changes are modes of relating. Although some children prefer to attend to self and will rock themselves to sleep and have lots of self-care taking skills, others will relate to objects and loved ones through a bridging across the space and defining a boundary (a me-you relationship). Still others prefer to hug, mold, and shape around the "other" (an "us" relationship). Most children go through all three phases and utilize each as appropriate. But they have preferred modes that are a kind of default pattern; something to fall back on and rely on.

In movement learning situations, it is not common to find such different ways of relating to others addressed. Most of the literature describes shape as the making of a static shape, holding a position, much like a statue or sculpture. The term "Sculpture" is, in fact, a fairly common creative movement activity. Benzwie (1987) devotes 21 pages of her book to "Sculpting" activities, all of which direct children to be frozen, or still, or to hold a shape. But frozen shapes do not reveal a degree of relationship. It is only in the changing movement relationship that the preferred mode is revealed.

Consider the handshake and how much is conveyed within such a simple, and often unconscious ritual. When one first encounters a friend, the mode of the handshake can tell a great deal about the relative status of the two participants, the mood of each, or the degree of intimacy between the two. If the clasp includes both self-care (shape-flow, as above in the KMP section) and shaping, the degree of intimacy is revealed and reinforced by the abilities of each to open up to his/her own flow of communication and to share equally in the encounter.

So, too, children, interact with each other, recapitulating the relationship patterns they have developed with their parents and siblings. Children take care of themselves, connect to others, and share hugs based on many contextual cues, and on habit. Movement activities can reveal those patterns, but also can teach children to explore other choices as well. Mirroring games, Follow-the-Leader type games, and Contact Improvisation (where children can use a finger to follow a contact point through shared space and time with a partner), all lead to increased *Shape* choices.

Shape can be thought of as the container for *Effort*, just as the relationship of the child to others can be thought of as the container for the development of the self and one's personality. In movement terms, children adjust and accommodate to other movers and, within those adjustments, express who they are.

Space as Organizing

Rhythm is not the only organizer for movement. Children also organize by orienting in *space*.

The newborn's . . . sense of space . . . is restricted to proprioceptive body experiences. . . . As the human being moves in a spatial surrounding, he gains awareness of the all-encompassing quality of that space. Sounds, smells and sights exist in space relative to the front-back, top-bottom, and left-right of the body. (Gerhardt, 1973, pp. 14–15)

Spatial differentiation is driven, of course, by gravity. If we did not have the pull toward the center of the earth, our movement and our construction of reality would be quite different, even with the same body part relationships. A great deal of early spatial orientation is built upon the establishment of equilibrium against and within the force of gravity.

Establishing a midline of the body, in which the differentiation of right and left halves is key, is essential to any number of cognitive skills, not the least of which is reading. In American and other Western cultures, reading goes from left to right, crossing the midline of the body as the eyes track the letters and words. With children who have difficulty tracking, often we can see a lack of midline organization. In one unpublished study completed by Bradley (1984), five dyslexic children were exposed to a set of whole body experiences (Bartenieff Fundamentals™) and Laban space exercises. Visual tracking across a midline improved significantly for those children who had had difficulty with it in the beginning.

From the midline and the subsequent patterns of laterality and verticality, children can develop a sense of the sagittal dimension, or front-back. The sagittal dimension seems to allow for a sense of moving forward/moving back, both metaphorically and physically. One of the children in the above study (Bradley, 1984), expressed his own dilemma with the sagittal dimension:

Mark came into the room today and seemed sad. "What's going on," I asked? "It's my birthday," he answered. I looked at him. In my own experience, birthdays are not sad events. But I realized this child had a very difficult time not only tracking across the midline, but in moving forward in space as well. He was not timid or shy, but expressed himself most often from where he was at the moment. "It's scary to CHANGE, isn't it?" He looked at me, relieved. "Yes," he whispered.

We decided to do some movement in the sagittal dimension, first tiptoeing forward and back, like we were sneaking up on somebody, and then, eventually, after many such explorations, we were able to stride confidently into the future. (p. 15)

Rich vocabulary, such as laterality, verticality, directionality, pathways, reach space, and trace forms are all skills for mapping one's way through the world. The more options children have, the better the choices they can make. By the same token, simple experiences such as the defining of one's kinesphere (or personal space) can help children find a sense of "place" or home base.

It is the interaction of the bodily experiences connecting to the space at hand and modified by shape and effort qualities that provide the basis of what Howard Gardner (1983) calls "bodily-kinesthetic intelligence." Yet, Gardner (1983) does not acknowledge that this intelligence is the first intelligence; the one from which all of the others learn.

As the dance/movement therapist and movement analyst, Suzi Tortora (2003) states:

My approach in working with such populations is to regard the child's nonverbal behaviors as a form of communication portraying their experiences and sense of self. Specifically, I respond to the child's particular movement expressions as he or she interacts within the surrounding spatial environment. It is this interaction between self and spatial environment, observable in these personal characteristic movement patterns, which display how the child is relating, adapting and responding to their environment. In this way the child becomes the catalyst of the therapeutic intervention. (p. 3)

CREATIVE MOVEMENT

Once the child has established a sense of control and choices within the body-space continuum, the possibility for true invention begins. Child's play is so often grounded in movement play: pretending to be a cloud, or a princess, an animal, or a cowboy. The child adjusts his/her patterns to portray a role. Imagination, the inner construct of a reality wished for rather than directly experienced, comes from such explorations. And imagination may be the fast track to both empowerment and choices.

Creative movement is a divergent process. There are no right answers and the goals include a deepening of metaphoric and an enrichment of abstract material. As the child's imagination grows, the range of options also grows. We think of the child who daydreams as "not living up to her potential," but, in fact, she may override her limits.

Gunilla Lindqvist (2001) addressed the relationship between play and dance in her study. She analyzed the dance experiences in five Swedish towns of children 6 to 8 years old. Lindqvist delineated two principles of early dance education; one based on the divergent approaches of Laban and the other a more imitative approach. Most of the Swedish students had positive responses to the first approach and saw the experience as play. A typical lesson includes "circle time, warming up, practicing basic

movements, steps and formations, improvisation, and reverance" (p. 47).

She goes on to cite Laban's concerns that literary approaches to dance should be used sparingly for young children; that the movement itself is enough of a stimulus to help them make their own dances and tell their own "stories." Lindqvist comes down firmly on the side of explorations and play as a source for dance in the early grades.

Movement is more than daydreaming, however. It is *in vivo* practice. The adage "If I can imagine it, I can achieve it" may inspire, but for the child who no idea how to bridge between the worlds of hopes and realities, movement experiences can make the connection. Theory can become practice.

Park (1997), White (1992), and Corso (1997) have all researched the role of race, body-level organization and learning preferences. Park found that Asian-American students in Los Angeles have a preference for kinesthetic learning. White found that African-American students had preferences for auditory, tactile, and kinesthetic learning. These same students demonstrated a greater degree of success in field-dependent (relational) learning situations.

Corso (1997) completed a small study (28 students over 5 years) in which she correlated body organization (specifically, midline organizational abilities) with learning styles. Using writing and drawing activities, the 28 children's reading difficulties were revealed. Although this study is not a dance study per se, the indications that reading difficulties may correlate with midline organizational difficulties is worth exploring, and, potentially, remediating through movement

The relationships of young children to the world around them are full of magic. Sue Stinson (1988) has written extensively on the process of movement exploration. She points out:

... pre-school children think in concrete rather than abstract terms. For example, I might teach a class based on a theme of thunderstorms. With preschoolers I have no desire to teach the scientific explanation of thunderstorms; I prefer my own preschooler's explanation of the big black dragons in the sky that roar and breathe fire. I ask for and listen to their explanations and stories. However, merely directing children to 'pretend to be a thundercloud or a big black dragon" yields little depth of movement . . . abstract movement concepts . . . "translate" the phenomenon into rich movement experiences. (p. 28)

Mastery over the realms of the imaginative and objective worlds gives children agency. From such an empowered stance, children find it easy to create whole pieces, stories, skits, drawings. Instead of becoming passive recipients of information, they are constructing knowledge, making art, and sharing their tales.

DANCING CHILDREN

Learning through dance is not the same thing as learning to dance. Every dance teacher has heard the story of Shirley Temple or Savion Glover, child prodigies who had full careers before the ages of 5 and 10, respectively. But the specificity of tap dancing, informed by the predilections of two talented children is not for every child. Yet, most young children love to dance, or at the very least relate to the role of the "dancer."

When Bradley's son was around 5, she signed him up for a dance class that was advertised as appropriate for boys and girls. He went to the first class and there was only one other boy there, who would not move. So the son sat with the other boy. The next week they returned, the son opened the door and quickly shut it again. He said, "I can't go in there. It's too pink!" And indeed it was. Every girl—and there were only girls in the room—was covered in pink, from the hair ribbons, through the tutus, and into beribboned pink slippers. They wanted to be dancers. Bradley's son just wanted to dance.

The act of dancing will continue to be overwritten by the role of the dancer. Until we can, as a culture, transcend the role for the act, in Western education cultures, dancing will continue to be associated with gender. This is not as it should be, nor is it that way in other cultures. The act of dancing should not be precluded from any group or category of child. The functions of dance include technique (the execution of dance phrases), the style or form (ballet, modern, hip-hop, tap, etc.), choreography (or dance-making), and performance. Every child can benefit from any experiences within the field of dance, but to experience improvisation/creative movement, choreography, technique, and informal performance provides great benefits.

Still, there are questions that need to be raised about very young children studying technique, a particular dance form, or performing. Conventional wisdom holds that it is very difficult for the young child to maintain the level of motor control, nuanced expression, and sequences of steps or movements that are required for particular forms or styles. For the same reason that young children do not start training seriously for a competitive sport, the 2- to 5-year-old needs exploratory and self-directed experiences first.

The dance recital in which costumed, madeup little girls twirl and glide and forget their steps is a well-known scenario. When a young child performs for family and friends, unconditional approval should ensue. Adding strangers, unreasonable expectations, flashbulbs and video cameras has undone more than one budding ballerina.

Dance classes for 2- to 5-year-olds can and should be observed by parents, however. Such opportunities for feedback and audience can help a child learn in the moment, refining skills in the heightened context of demonstrating learning. Audience is a form of witnessing and giving approval, and a way of encouraging a child to learn more.

There are actually no studies of which the authors are aware that unpack the role of dance technique, style or performance on the young child, including from other parts of the world. The "evidence" cited herein is anecdotal and part of an oral tradition within the field of dance education.

in fact, the first intelligence—the one from which the other areas derive.

The primacy of the bodily-kinesthetic intelligence extends beyond the years of infancy. In the Chicago schools, the Whirlwind Basic Reading Through Dance program has amassed an impressive array of statistics that indicate support for such a notion (McMahon, Rose, & Parks, 2003). The program addresses basic reading skills, especially phoneme segmentation, rhythmic phrasing, and letter shapes.

In the study (McMahon, Rose, & Parks, 2003) of 721 Chicago first graders, significant gains were found for the experimental group. The numbers were impressive, in part because the control group actually tested higher on the pretest. The students in the Whirlwind program advanced beyond them.

There are few studies with the scope and rigor of the Whirlwind study. But anecdotal evidence and descriptive studies for the learning of math concepts, geography, science facts and processes, and other aspects of literacy through dance/movement do exist. The work of Anne Green Gilbert (personal communication, 2004) in the Seattle public schools has been lauded over the years, but not analyzed statistically. However, in 1977–1978, Gilbert (2004) did conduct a preliminary examination of 325 K-Sixth grade students who had been involved with her *Dance and the Three R's* programs. In a comparison of the 325 students with the test scores on the Metropolitan Achievement Tests that year, the students in her program averaged 13% higher than the rest of the District.

In the summary of the Whirlwind study, McMahon, Rose, and Parks (2003) conclude that "if reading instruction can focus more on visual and kinesthetic images and less on text-based information, children may be more likely to retain and recall the information they learn" (p.107).

The same is likely to hold true for concepts in math, science, social studies, and languages. Research needs to be done before we can know for certain, but the vast amount of evidence indicates that such an approach is likely to yield rich results.

In math, for example, computation is easily physicalized and externalized. So is calculation. Rhythm is metrical and can be divided into "sets" or phrases and quantified. Therefore, the oft-observed but never proven "Mozart Effect" (several researchers in the United States have claimed that listening to Mozart's music can increase intelligence, but the research is suspect; a quick Web search can reveal both the claims and the disputing of the claims), may in fact be a phenomenon in which the complex rhythmic structures of Mozart's music affect the kinesthetic responses in the body in an organizing way. If that is so, the example of the students in Bradley's (1984) son's fourth grade class moving to Coltrane may be a similar phenomenon.

COGNITIVE SKILLS: READING AND MATH, PROBLEM-SOLVING

The construction of knowledge through movement is not a new discovery. An old Chinese saying says: "I hear and I forget, I see and I remember, I do and I understand." Howard Gardner (1983) identified eight "intelligences." The bodily-kinesthetic is,

EARLY CHILDHOOD STANDARDS

The National Dance Education Organization (2003) asked several members to develop *Standards for Dance in Early Childhood*. A guide for teachers, parents, and caregivers of young children, the standards are divided into outcomes for infants, 2-year-olds, 3-year-olds, 4-year-olds, and 5-year-olds.

The structure of the standards is based on four categories that "provide a balance between creative freedom, that enhances individual expression and growth, and disciplined concentration that develops the proficient artist or capable, realistic adult." (National Dance Education Organization, 2003, p. 3). The categories: Creating, Performing, Responding, and Inter-Connecting, include Content Standards that remain constant across age groups and Achievement Standards that build on prior knowledge and increase in sophistication with each age group.

The standards are not designed to be a stand-alone curriculum for dance with young children but can provide guidelines for what might be included in a rich program. Assessment rubrics are also included, so that the child's progress can be tracked. Although the notion of developing standards for young children may seem strange to educators from other, less-competitive cultures, for Americans, defining dance education is not simple, as the authors have attempted to demonstrate. Definitions and expectations are often based on culture and what the media has popularized. In a culture where even small children watch videos and cable television programs in which sexualized movement is common, movements are shortened and edited into fractured moments, and the all-pink ballet class is universal, clarifying appropriate material for the population of young children is a challenge. The standards help parents and early childhood educators understand a full range of components and experiences that are useful and appropriate.

RECOMMENDATIONS FOR FUTURE RESEARCH

For very young children, comparisons of teacher-centered ("follow me") versus child-centered (exploratory) approaches need to be done, especially as the two approaches affect the development of expressive choices and range. One finds assumptions the one approach is superior and the other inferior throughout the field of dance education practice. But one finds very little, if any, research comparing the two approaches in actual effects.

Unpacking the learning process in dance and movement is actually not difficult, because dance is a visual art form; the child's development of and within the material can be observed. With the vocabulary referred to above (Laban, Kestenberg, etc.), visible movement changes can be noted and learning patterns acknowledged. Such analysis requires time and expertise, but every dance and movement teacher already engages in such assessments informally, at least.

Next steps must include a concerted effort on the part of the dance education field to produce such research, but first, the administrators of educational institutions, policy groups and legislative offices must understand the need for such studies. Funding, coordination, and resources are needed in order for such research to be meaningful and robust. The fact that serious examination of the process has not been sought after, encouraged, or rewarded is regrettable, because so much of the learning process that is cognition is rendered visible as children move and solve challenges. With the emphasis on text-based testing in order to know if children are learning, the pressure on young children to produce language and text is extraordinary.

The quantitative research that has been done with young children requires the child to be able to complete some sort of pre- and posttest, usually text-based. Efforts are made to prove that the dependent variable is affected by the exposure to the independent variable. In the case of the Whirlwind study (McMahon, Rose, & Parks, 2003), the independent variables (physicalizing letter shapes, moving sounds, blending sounds temporally and spatially) were designed to reflect and inform reading skills. The transfer was reinforced overtly. In the case of a dance program in which the independent variables are neither so well delineated nor directly reinforced, any pre- or posttesting will be unlikely to reveal any effects. But that does mean there are no effects. The effects simply may not be on the dependent variable being tested.

There are other ways to unpack the dance learning process, including interviews, art-based responses such as collages and drawings, and scored rubrics. Interviews require, but may not account for, sophisticated verbal skills. Art-based responses require fine motor and visual-conceptual skills. Scored rubrics require the sophisticated eye of an observer, or observers, but, at least what is being observed is movement itself, not an application of movement to another response mode.

The challenge of assessment of learning in the arts, and in particular, dance is often presented as a negative; that is, as an area so subjective that appropriate assessment tools cannot be developed. That perception is accurate if text-based approaches and causal results are required in order for the type of learning that dance offers to be considered valid. However, if the teacher's eye is trained to see and track visible movement changes, learning can become transparent.

All around the world, dance teachers observe the style and details of how and how much their students are learning. Because dance is both preverbal and reflective of inner processes, all that is really necessary to assess its effects is an insightful observer. With appropriate support, analysis of content and process, comparisons with results and outcomes, dance education can take its rightful place as a potent, rich modality for young children to find their creative, interactive, rich, way into the world.

SUMMARY

This chapter unpacks the dance learning process, describing the components of a dance curriculum that includes creative exploration, dance-making, technical training in various styles and forms of dance, and appropriate performing activities for the young child. Several key areas of analysis of learning in and through dance activities are examined and explanations of Laban Movement Analysis (LMA) and the Kestenberg Movement Profile (KMP) are provided. Applications of LMA and the KMP in literature were also addressed. The existing published research in early childhood dance education was reviewed, and recommendations were made for how dance educators ought to proceed to address the lack of robust studies in the field. In the end, the authors hope to have provided both an overview of the field today and a sense of direction for where early childhood dance education needs to go next.

References

Benari, N. (1995). *Inner rhythm*. Chur, Switzerland: Harwood Academic.

Benzwie, T. (1987). *A moving experience: Dance for lovers of children and the child within*. Tucson, AZ: Zephyr Press.

Bradley, K. (1984). *LMA and learning-disabled students*. Unpublished certificate project, Laban/Bartenieff Institute of Movement Studies, New York.

Corso, M. (1997). *Children who desperately want to read but are not working at grade level: using movement patterns as "windows" to discover why*. Paper presented at the Annual International Conference of the Association for Children's Education, Portland, Oregon. (ERIC Document Reproduction Service No. ED402549)

Corso, M. (1999a). *Children who desperately want to read but are not working at grade level: Part II: the transverse midline*. (ERIC Document Reproduction Service No. ED432733)

Corso, M. (1999b). *Children who desperately want to read but are not working at grade level: Part III: the frontal midline*. (ERIC Document Reproduction Service No. ED432751)

Corso, M. (1999c). *Children who desperately want to read but are not working at grade level: Part IV: crossing all midlines automatically*. (ERIC Document Reproduction Service No. ED432752)

Csikszentmihaly, M. (1990). *Flow: The psychology of optimal experience*. New York: Harper Collins.

Damasio, A. (1999). *The feeling of what happens: Body and emotion in the making of consciousness*. New York: Harcourt.

Gardner, H. (1983) *Frames of mind: The theory of multiple intelligences*. New York: Basic Books.

Gerhardt, L. (1973). *Moving and knowing: The young child orients himself in space*. Englewood Cliffs, NJ: Prentice Hall.

Gilbert, A. G. (1976). *Teaching the three r's through movement experience*. Minneapolis, MN: Burgess Publishing.

Koch, S. (1997). *The Kestenberg Movement Profile*. Unpublished master's thesis, Allegheny University of Health Sciences, Philadelphia, PA.

Leirvag, L. M. (2001). *A proposed dance-movement therapy assessment to identify child neglect*. Unpublished master's thesis, Hahnemann University, Philadelphia, PA. Retrieved September 15, 2003, from http://www.livdans.org/livmarie.doc

Lindqvist, G. (2001). The relationship between play and dance. *Research in Dance Education, 2*(1), 41-52.

Lotan, N., & Yirmiya, N. (2002). Body movement, presence of parents, and the process of falling asleep in toddlers. *International Journal of Behavioral Development, 26*(1), 81-88

McMahon, S.D., Rose, D. S., & Parks, M. (2003). Basic reading through dance, *Evaluation Review, 27*(1/2), 104-125.

National Dance Education Organization. (2003). *Standards for dance in early childhood*. Bethesda, MD: National Dance Education Organization.

North, M. (1975). *Personality assessment through movement*. Boston, MA: Plays, Inc.

Park, C. C. (1997a). Learning style preferences of Asian-American (Chinese, Filipino, Korean, and Vietnamese) students in secondary schools. *Equity and Excellence in Education, 30*(2), 68-77.

Park, C. C. (1997b). Learning style preferences of Korean-, Mexican-, Armenian- American and Anglo students in secondary schools. *Research brief, National Association of Secondary School Principals Bulletin, 81* (585), 103-11.

Park, C. C. (1997c). Learning style preferences of Southeast Asian students. *Urban Education, 35*(3), 245-68.

Prince, R. (2002). *Toward understanding mutuality*. American Psychological Association. website: Prevention, Infant Therapy and the Treatment of Adults section. Retrieved January 5, 2004, from http:/www.section five.org/kestenberg.htm

Russell, J. (1965). *Creative Dance in the Primary School*. London: MacDonald and Evans.

Sossin, M. (2002). Toward understanding mutuality. American Psychological Association website: *Prevention, Infant Therapy and the Treatment of Adults Section*. Retrieved January 5, 2004, from http:/www.sectionfive.org/kescomment.htm,

Stinson, S. (1986) Preschool dance curriculum: the process. *Journal Of Physical Education, Recreation, and Dance, 57*, 27-28.

Stinson, S. (1988) *Dance for young children: Finding the magic in movement*. Reston, VA: American Alliance for Health, Physical Education, Recreation, and Dance.

Tortora, S. (2003). *Developmental difficulties and trauma*. Retrieved June 15, 2004, from http://suzitortora.org/pg3.htm

White, S. E. (1992). *Factors that contribute to learning differences among African American and Caucasian students*. (ERIC Document Reproductive Services No. ED374177)

·14·

THE MUSICAL DEVELOPMENT AND EDUCATION
OF YOUNG CHILDREN

Graham F. Welch
Institute of Education, University of London

INTRODUCTION

There is now considerable research evidence that an essential feature of the human species is to find subjective meaning and pleasure in the patterned organisation of sound and silence that we label as *music*. As humans, we are capable of exhibiting a wide range of musical behaviors, whether as producers or receivers (cf. Zatorre & Peretz, 2001; BERA Music Education Review Group, 2001; Welch, 2001; Peretz & Zatorre, 2003; Welch & Adams, 2003). Musicality is not an option; it is part of our human design (e.g., Koelsch, Gunter, Friederici, & Schröger, 2000), given normal neuropsychobiological functioning. As humans, we make sense of the sounds that we label as *music* through a hierarchy of increasing complexity and specificity, namely, through the perception and conception of *psycho-acoustic features* (such as pitch, loudness, duration, timbre), *structures* (the detection/construction of patterns, regularities), *syntactic and communicative elements* (the potential for musical sounds to be characterised by a grammatical function within the musical context: music as a form of language), and *semiotics* (the meanings that we attribute to particular musical experiences) (Spender, 1987; Welch, 1998, 2002). Increasing experience and familiarity with examples from the dominant musical genres, allied to maturational processes (see later), allow us to progress through this hierarchy in our dealings with our musical worlds. In addition, music also has strong *emotional* associations (Adachi & Trehub, 1998; Juslin & Laukka, 2001, 2003), with evidence that differing personality types may be attracted to music of varying genres (Kemp, 1996).

Nevertheless, musical behaviors do not occur in a vacuum. They are the product of a complex interaction between biological, developmental, and environmental factors over time. Furthermore, the nature of this interaction is not uniform across the species because of relative differences and biases arising from the interface and shaping of our basic neuropsychobiology by experience, sociocultural imperatives, and maturational processes (Altenmüller, 2004). As a result, *particular* musical behaviors may be more or less developed. Consequently, we are likely to exhibit a musical profile that is both relatively *unique* and peculiar to the individual, while having some commonality with others of a similar sociocultural background, age and experience. Although individual differences in musical behavior are normal, there is also research evidence to suggest a generic musical potential that may be realized in relatively common musical behaviors for many children at particular ages and phases of musical development, subject to experience and behavioral context (Welch, 2002).

Following general trends in developmental psychology and early childhood studies (cf. Bennett, 1999; Nadel & Butterworth, 1999; Anning, 2000; David, Goouch, Powell, & Abbott, 2003; BERA Early Years Special Interest Group, 2003), recent music research studies have sought increased ecological validity through the observation of musical behaviors in naturalistic settings. Researchers have used focused observation of contextualized self-initiated musical behaviors, as well as social music play between infants and their peers and caregivers, in order to generate critical insights into children's basic musicality, particularly in a nurturing setting (cf. Whiteman, 2001; Barrett, 2003a; Young, 1999, 2004; Tafuri & Villa, 2002a). Such studies are in contrast to much of the earlier research literature (cf. Young, 2000) that was frequently characterized by an underlying *deficit-model* of musical behavior in which the developing child was seen as being somehow an inadequate or incomplete version of the musically competent adult. Musical behavior was often described in terms of what the child could *not* (yet) do musically in terms

251

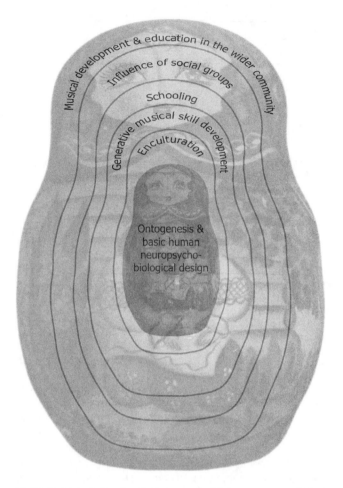

FIGURE 14.1. A *Russian Dolls*-type model for conceptualizing the literature on the nature of the influences in early childhood musical development.

of conventional music theory, usually within a Western cultural high art tradition. Although it is still possible to compare the changing complexity of musical competences over developmental time (such as by charting differences in creative instrumental music-making or in singing) and in particular experimental contexts (a continuing U.S. research bias), there has been a marked shift in several of the latest research studies toward locating such enquiries within a more contemporary mainstream view of early childhood (e.g., Mang, 2002; Young, 2002; Barrett, 2000, 2003b). This view acknowledges the contested conceptualization of *knowing* and *learning*, such as in the contrasts between behaviorist/empiricist, cognitive/rationalist, and situative/pragmatist-sociohistoric perspectives (see BERA EY SIG, 2003 for a review) and that *early childhood* is a relative concept that is subject to social and cultural construction (James, Jenks, & Prout, 1998; Gammage, 1999).

The narrative that follows explores the nature of musical development from prebirth into childhood and its links to education. Its perspective accords with current philosophical views on the first years of life in which infants are seen as being designed to "learn from, with and about, firstly the people and

cultural environment about them, followed by the material environment," where play is perceived to foster cognitive development and where young children "make sense and transform knowledge, experiences and events through imaginative and creative activity" (David et al., 2003, p. 112).

A *Russian Dolls* type model (Fig. 14.1, cf. Hargreaves & North, 1997; BERA, 2001; Welch & Hallam, 2004) has been adopted to conceptualize and make sense of key sources within the early childhood music literature and as a way of illustrating the discrete, yet integrated, nature of the various influences that shape musical development. The model is designed to indicate that musical behavior is a product of each learner's basic neuropsychobiological design (Greenough & Juraska, 1986—being related to the hard-wired integration of nervous, psychological, and biological processes) that has its function shaped by musical enculturation and through the acquisition and development of generative (creative) musical skills (cf. Sloboda, 1988). Both enculturated behavior and skill development arise from interactions within particular sociocultural environments that arise from membership of social groups (such as family, peers, gender, social class, age, ethnicity, musical genre) and the effects of education (formal and informal) within a wider (musical) community, which provide encounters with a diversity of musical forms and processes.

THE ONTOGENESIS OF MUSICAL BEHAVIORS IN THE FIRST YEAR OF LIFE: BASIC HUMAN NEUROPSYCHOBIOLOGICAL DESIGN

Musical development begins prebirth with the development of the auditory system. Normally, hearing is functioning in the final trimester of pregnancy (Lecanuet, 1996). The womb is a relatively quiet environment and the developing fetus reacts reliably to external sounds (Shahidullah & Hepper, 1994), including music, and particularly to the pitch contours of the mother's voice in speech and singing.

These fetal auditory experiences lead to *recognition responses* in the neonate who demonstrate sensitivities to their own mother's voice (Thurman & Grambsch, 2000) and to the musical features of melodic contour and rhythmic patterning within the soundscape of the maternal culture (Trehub, 2003a), including the music that the mother listened to during pregnancy (Woodward, Fresen, Harrison, & Coley 1996). The perceptual salience of maternal pitch contour (Trehub, 1987) is also shown in the reported ability of infants aged 3 to 4 months to imitate an exaggerated prosodic pitch contour presented by their mothers (Masataka, 1992), as well as an ability to imitate basic vowels at the same age after only 15 min laboratory exposure (Kuhl & Meltzoff, 1996). Similarly, 6-month-old infants demonstrate increased amounts of sustained attention when viewing videorecordings of their mothers' singing as compared with viewing recordings of them speaking (Trehub, 2001).

At a neurological level, sound from the human voice is processed bilaterally and simultaneously in several different areas of the brain (Belin, Zatorre, Lafaille, Ahad, & Pike, 2000). Linguistic features (semantic and phonetic elements) are biased toward the left hemisphere (Kuhl, Tsao, Zhang, & De Boer, 2001), whereas prosodic elements (patterns of stress and intonation—the melodies of speech) are processed more in the right hemisphere (Zatorre, Evans, Meyer, & Gjedde, 1992; Van Lancker, 1997; Brust, 2001). As sound passes from the ear to brain it undergoes a variety of filtering processes that are designed initially to identify sonic patterns, the location of the sound source and whether there is a need for selective attention amongst a group of sounds (Altenmüller, 2004). A *modular* neurological perspective on music processing (Peretz & Coltheart, 2003) suggests that the acoustic analyses of temporal organisation (rhythmic and related motoric patterns) are differentiated from the analyses of pitch organization. The latter embraces a theorized linear processing hierarchy in which melodic contour is analyzed first, then musical intervals and finally tonal encoding. This pitch processing hierarchy accords with the research literature on young children's singing development in which vocal pitch accuracy of melodic contour often precedes competency in matching a song's constituent pitch intervals and overall tonality (Welch, Sergeant, & White, 1997—and see the section on *enculturation* later). Similarly, 5-month-old infants have been found to be sensitive to the sequential structure of melodies (Chang & Trehub, 1977).

Music, like language, is widely distributed neurologically with significant cross-hemispheric processing (Schuppert, Münte, Weiringa, & Altenmüller, 2000; Fuster, 2003). Nevertheless, the brain's functional asymmetry allows different features of musical sound to be processed in a manner that is both biased toward particular cortical structures, while also being networked to others, depending on the focus of the listener and their musical experience. For example, in relatively musically *naïve* (untrained) listeners, there is likely to be preferential activity being evidenced in regions of the left hemisphere in the perception of simple rhythmic patterns, but a shift occurs toward certain regions of the right hemisphere for more complex patterns (Altenmüller, 2004). In contrast, pitch and melody processing tend to have a right hemisphere bias in musically naïve listeners, but trained and professional musicians show increased activity in the left hemisphere when focusing on pitch discrimination and chords.

Similarly, in certain musical cultures, there are some individuals who are able to identify, or produce a specific pitch by musical name without any objective reference tone, termed *Absolute Pitch* (AP) ability (Ward, 1999). Neurologically, this ability has been related to a specialised neural network for the retrieval and manipulation of verbal-tonal associations (Zatorre, Perry, Beckett, Westbury, & Evans 1998). Although this is considered to be a rare musical behavior, with estimates ranging between 1 in 1,500 to 1 in 10,000 in the general population (Levitin, 1994), there is evidence that AP is culturally determined. In Greece, for example, there is virtually no reference, nor official recognition of its existence in contemporary Greek musical culture and the term does not have a Greek language equivalent, whereas, in Japan, AP is regarded as an important musical behavior and there are several specialist schools that offer courses in its development for young musicians. Furthermore, a series of

studies of musical memory in young children has revealed that 7- and 10-month-old infants are capable of exhibiting the equivalent of both AP and relative pitch (RP) behaviors, depending on the nature of the musical task and previous listening experience (Saffran & Griepentrog, 2001; Saffran, 2003). If the musical material was familiar to them, the infants were capable of recognizing musical transpositions (exhibiting RP behavior), but small changes within relatively unfamiliar music were perceived differently (suggesting that an underlying AP behavior was employed).

There is a growing literature on music and the brain (e.g., see Zatorre & Peretz, 2001: Peretz & Zatorre, 2003; Altenmüller, 2004, for reviews). Neural areas and networks have been identified in the perception of tonal structures (Janata, Birk, Van Thorn, Leman, Tillmann, & Bharucha, 2002), features of musical *syntax* (Maess, Koelsch, Gunter, & Friederici, 2001; Patel, 2003), relative and *absolute* pitch processing (Zatorre et al., 1998), harmony (Parsons, 2003), and temporal processing (Samson, Ehrlé, & Baulac, 2001). Researchers have identified that practice produces change in the motor cortex (Pascuel-Leone, 2001) and that specific neural circuits are activated to link the perception of musical dissonance with the emotional systems (either in the paralimbic structures or more frontal areas) (Blood, Zatorre, Bermudez, & Evans, 1999; Blood & Zatorre, 2001).

At the moment (and probably for the foreseeable future), the neurological literature concerning music is dominated by data from studies that have employed adult participants, either as in clinical studies (such as in the understanding of brain trauma), or as basic neurological research. Relatively little is known directly (with the possible exception of the inferences within the Saffran studies—see earlier) about underlying brain function in relation to musical behaviors in infancy. However, the application of research into brain development (e.g., Brothers, 1997) has led the U.K. early childhood education community to conclude that, in general, the structure of the young brain is organized, reorganized, and changed in infant learning (BERA EY SIG, 2003). There is no reason to expect that infant learning in music should be any different, particularly as there is considerable research on developmental changes in musical behavior (cf. Altenmüller, Parlitz, & Gruhn, 1997; Altenmüller, Gruhn, Parlitz, & Liebert, 2000; see the section on enculturation and generic skill development later).

The latest neurospsychobiological research suggests that there is interplay between early vocal development, emotional state, and the processing of musical features. This begins pre-birth in the dual exposure of the developing fetus to the mother's voiced sounds (speaking and singing) concomitantly with the emotional correlates of such maternal sounds. The mother's emotional state when vocalizing is encoded hormonally in the maternal bloodstream that is interfaced with the fetal bloodstream (Seckl, 1998). The likely outcome is that the fetus perceives the prosodic/melodic contours of the mother's voice from soundwaves transversing through the amniotic fluid while also experiencing a related (filtered) neuroendocrine change (Thurman & Grambsch, 2000; Keverne, Nevison, & Martel, 1997; Uvnäs-Moberg, 1997). It is argued, therefore, that the child is likely to enter the world with an emotional *biasing* toward certain sounds, linked to the infant's earliest acoustic and affective experiences of the maternal vocal pitch contour (see Welch, 2005, for a more detailed review). During the first year of life and subsequently, preschool children continue to be able to perceive strong emotional qualities in their soundworlds of speech and music (Nawrot, 2003).

ENCULTURATION INTO THE DOMINANT MUSICAL CULTURE AND GENERATIVE SKILL DEVELOPMENT

The newborn enters the world capable of perceiving tiny differences in voiced sound (Eimas, Siqueland, Jusczyk, & Vigorito, 1971; Aslin & Smith, 1988). Infants are *universalists* (Trehub, 2003b) in the sense that they are perceptually equipped at birth to make sense of the musics and languages of any culture. This predisposition leads developmentally to the discrimination of vowel categories and consonantal contrasts in the native language by the end of the first year (Kuhl, Williams, Lacerda, Stevens, & Lindblom,1992; Vihman, 1996; Nazzi, Bertoncini, & Mehler, 1998). During these initial 12 months of life, it is the prosodic (pitch and rhythm) features of *infant-directed speech* (also known as *motherese* or *parentese*: Werker & McLeod, 1989) that dominate early communication from parent/caregiver to child (Fernald & Kuhl, 1987; Papousek [H], 1996). The prosodic envelopes that define spoken phrases are thought to be essential perceptual building blocks in the infant's developing comprehension of language (Jusczyk et al., 1992).

The mother's infant-focused utterances also are typified by having a regulation of pulse, vocal quality and narrative form. These are theorized collectively as a *communicative musicality* (Malloch, 1999) that engages with an *intrinsic motive pulse*, being an innate ability to sense rhythmic time and temporal variation in the human voice (Trevarthen, 1999, 2002; Nazzi et al., 1998). The expressive prosodic contours, pitch glides and prevalence of basic harmonic intervals (3rds, 4ths, 5ths, octaves) of *infant-directed speech* (Fernald, 1992; Papousek [H], 1996) occur alongside the mother's *infant-directed singing* (Trehub, 2001), a special limited repertoire of lullaby and play songs that is characterized by structural simplicity, repetiveness, higher than usual pitches (somewhat nearer the infant's own vocal pitch levels), slower tempi, and a more emotive voice quality. Maternal singing also works at an emotional level to moderate infant arousal (Shenfield, Trehub, & Nakata, 2003).

The power of enculturation in the development of early singing behaviors is emerging in data from an ongoing longitudinal Italian study of mothers and their babies (Tafuri & Villa, 2002a, b; Tafuri, 2003). In the opening phase of the project, the participant mothers were encouraged to attend special music classes during pregnancy and to keep daily diaries of their singing behaviors both during pregnancy and subsequently. Subsequently, by the age of 2 to 3 years, a significant majority (78%) of the infants whose mothers had continued to participate in the *inCanto* project were singing songs imitatively in tune with their mothers (Tafuri & Villa, 2002b). This level of pitch competency is higher than that reported in the general population at

that age (Jorquera, Balboni, Bella, Ferioli, & Minichiello, 2000; Dowling, 1999; Welch, 2000a), but, in line with other studies that have focused on the importance of maternal/parental singing in fostering musical competencies (e.g., Kirkpatrick, 1962; Berger & Cooper, 2003). In contrast to the high levels of pitch accuracy in their imitative singing, the same Italian 2- to 3-year-olds' improvised singing in play contexts was judged to be less pitch-accurate (Tafuri, 2003). This is an example how musical behavior is often context-sensitive, particularly for young children.

Further evidence of enculturation may be found in recent comparative intercultural studies of maternal language and infant singing behaviours (Mang, 2001; 2002). Longitudinal data from Hong Kong indicate that Chinese-speaking children aged between 2 to 5 years use similar pitch centers in conversational speech and in singing their *favorite* songs, whereas English-speaking children in Hong Kong of the same ages develop increasingly distinct pitch centers, with their speech averaging a tone lower than their singing. Enculturation is implicated in the singing behaviors of both language groups. In general, as young children mature, the underlying anatomical and physiological structures change and increase in size, resulting in a gradual lowering of vocal pitch across the preschool years (Titze, 1994; see Welch & Howard, 2002, for a review). So it is to be expected that all Hong Kong children would develop lower speaking voices by the age of 5, irrespective of ethnicity. But also, because of their early years' exposure to different vocal pitch centers in listening to adult conversational speech, as well as *infant-directed singing* and *infant-directed speech* (in ascending order of musical pitch center: Trehub, 2001, 2003), the young English-speaking children's customary singing and speech behaviors would be likely to become increasingly differentiated. However, their Chinese-speaking peers would have been exposed to a different maternal culture in which there is a very close correspondence between the linguistic pitch of their tonally based language and the melodic pitch of traditional Chinese songs. Enculturation would thus shape their singing and speaking toward similar pitch centers.

Other studies in Hong Kong indicate that there is a positive interrelationship for Cantonese-speaking children between their pitch accuracy in singing and their growing mastery of language (Chen-Hafteck, 1996, 1998). There also is evidence that Hong Kong children with a year's formal classical musical training on an instrument have better verbal memory than either those without such training or those who discontinued lessons after 3 months (Ho, Cheung, & Chan, 2003). A similar verbal memory advantage for musicians has been reported in a Canadian study of young adults (Kilgour, Jakobson, & Cuddy, 2000). The underlying reasons are unclear, but it may be that the neurological pattern-detecting mechanisms required for advanced musical study, in making sense of the *language* of music, are also required in verbal memory tasks. In any case, it is further evidence of a symbiotic link between music and language.

There is also a symbiotic relationship between enculturation and generative (creative) skill development. This is strongly evidenced and exemplified in the development of vocal behaviors. Parents and caregivers interact with infants through infant-directed speech and infant-directed singing to facilitate a growing sophistication in the infants' vocalization, with spontaneous singing being relatively indiscriminable from the precursors of early speech (Papousek [M.], 1996). Infants make preverbal sounds that progress from crying and noncrying vegetative sounds (birth to 1 month) to prolonged *euphonic cooing* with melodic modulation (2 to 3 months), exploratory vocal play (4 to 6 months), repetitive babbling (7 to 11 months), *variegated babbling* and early words (9 to 13 months), to a *one-word* stage (12 to 18 months). The latter stages are characterized by the use of *protowords* to name persons, objects, and events in the infant's microenvironment (H. Papousek, 1996, p. 45).

Concomitantly, longitudinal data suggest that spontaneous singing during the early years is characterized principally by the control of melodic-rhythmic contour patterns (Dowling, 1988; Sundin, 1997). Between the ages of 1 to 2 years, for example, a typical infant song consists of repetition of one brief melodic phrase at different pitch centers. In contrast, by the age of 3 years, characteristically three different phrases are evidenced with both variation and repetition and one phrase singing is rare (Dowling, 1988). More recent case study research with 2- to 3-year-olds in a free-play day care setting (Young, 2002) suggests that young children's spontaneous singing embraces a wide range of musical behaviors, namely, *free-flow vocalizing* (a wordless vocal creation often associated with solitary play with no defined overall musical shape), *chanting* (often short, repeated phrases), *reworking of known songs* (the utilization of enculturated song fragments), *movement vocalizing* (either of self or objects), singing for *animation* (associated with dramatic play), and the imitation of actual sounds (defined as *comic-strip types noises*, usually associated with object play). Comparative case study data of adjacent age groups (Young, 2002) indicates that, in the same day care setting, younger children (1 to 2 years) sang less in free-play contexts, whereas 3- to 4-year-olds spent more time interacting with peers, with more speaking rather than singing behaviors in evidence. It may be that the age of 2 years is particularly a time for a wide variety of spontaneous singing to be exhibited, depending on the opportunities afforded by the local context.

PHASES OF MUSICAL DEVELOPMENT IN THE EARLY YEARS

The emergence of research data to suggest that musical behaviors normally change over time has led several researchers to characterize preschool musical development in terms of distinct *phases* in which certain behaviors predominate for a time before being replaced by others, usually perceived as being more complex or sophisticated. Hargreaves (1996), for example, identifies two *phases* of early musical development across four areas of musical behavior (singing, musical representation, melodic perception, and composition). His *sensorimotor* phase (using the Piagetian label) embraces the first 2 years of life and refers to the developing infant's preoccupation with the practice and development of physical skills and coordinations. Children in

this developmental phase will produce musical scribbles on paper that are seen as *action equivalents* of the timing of sound patterns that they are hearing, but with the scribbled outcomes bearing little or no resemblance to the actual sounds. It is suggested that their creative musical behaviors are focused on the sensations afforded by the sound making tools that they have to hand. Singing behaviors are likely to be limited to musical babbling or vocal play (Dowling, 1999; akin to the *free-flow vocalizing* identified by Young, 2002, in slightly older children) and imitation of single melodic phrases (Dowling, 1988). Although infants also have auditory perceptual abilities that are capable of making extremely fine discriminations in pitch, timing, and timbre, it is melodic contour that is a dominant feature in music perception (Dowling, 1999; Trehub, 2003; Peretz & Coltheart, 2003). Infants, like adults, notice and can remember small changes in melodic contour.

The next phase identified by Hargreaves (1996) covers the ages 3 to 5 and is termed *figural*. This label is used to convey the young child's developing ability to symbolize objects, people, and situations that are not physically present. The term *figural* implies a facility to depict an outline (such as in drawings of musical structure), while not yet being able necessarily to portray accurately all the detail (cf. Bamberger, 1991). Young children in this phase of development will be more likely to produce their own relatively idiosyncratic musical notation which will have a greater correspondence to musical sound and structure than previously, but that may not be metrically accurate or completely unambiguous.

A more elaborate framing of early musical behaviors derives from longitudinal data concerning 1- and 2-year-olds with distinct phases in musical behaviour emerging over time (Gruhn, 2002), although with no necessary correspondence between chronological and developmental age. Infants in this study were observed to move from a general awareness of their musical surroundings to having a specific *attentional* focus, often to a person singing. This was followed by an *imitative* phase that progressed from being relatively uncoordinated to coordinated in which there was observable intentionality to imitate accurately the musical model provided by the adult/teacher. Finally, there was evidence of an *elaboration* of musical understanding in improvised vocal activities (song singing and chanting).

Another recent model of enculturated musical development has been proposed by Lamont (1998a, 1998b) in relation to children's understanding of musical pitch, based on a large sample of children and adolescents aged 6 to 16. She outlines a hierarchy of five different ways of understanding: primitive capacities (the neurological bases of musical understanding), a *listening grammar* that is based on fundamental features of the musical system, then *figural* understandings based on shapes and outlines through musical experiences at home and at school, followed by *formal* and *metacognitive* modes of representation that are based on abstract properties and relationships within particular musical genres. Notwithstanding the age ranges of the participants, the initial phases of the model compliment those reported by other researchers in relation to early childhood (cf. Hargreaves, 1996; Swanwick & Tillman, 1986; Gruhn, 2002; Welch, 2002) and neurological processing (Peretz & Coltheart, 2003).

In general, phased-based models of musical development tend to suggest that four or five distinctive phases are evidenced, but that there can be considerable differences in behavior between individuals, depending on maturation, experience, task, and context.

In addition to such generic phase-based models of musical development, several other researchers have tended to focus on generative (creative) skill development in relation to *specific* areas of musical behavior, such as composing and improvising, the notating of musical sounds and singing. Although each of these musical behaviors normally has clear distinguishing features in older children and adults, there can be considerable interpretation required when observing and categorizing the often overlapping behaviours of infants and young children. (This has led some researchers, for example, to use terms that are more descriptive, such as *spontaneous vocalization* [Young, 2002] and *invented songs* [Sundin, 1997].)

Composing and Improvising

One of the more influential theories to emerge in recent years concerning developmental processes suggests that four distinct phases of musical understanding are evidenced in children's *composing* from the ages of 3 to 15 years (Swanwick & Tillman, 1986). The developmental phases are seen as being based on a shift in children's prime focus from musical *materials* to musical *expression*, then *form* and, subsequently, symbolic *value*. The model makes use of a broad-based definition of composing that embraces the "briefest utterances as well as more sustained and rehearsed invention" (Swanwick, 1991, p. 23) and draws on concepts drawn from Piaget (1951) and the Manhattanville Music Curriculum Project (Thomas, 1970). The original data set suggests that young children up to the age of 3 have an initial interest in the *sensory* aspects of sounds, such as timbre and dynamic levels, with sound organization being spontaneous and unstructured. Children then enter a more *manipulative* phase where the interest is in handling instruments and other sound sources and in controlling the sounds intentionally. Music making for 4- and 5-year-olds is more affected by the instruments' physical structure and layout (and also by the children's existing movement vocabulary—Young, 2003). Musical thinking develops further through an *imitation* phase (ages 5 to 8) that embraces a gradual establishment of dominant musical conventions, such as phrasing, *glissandi*, metrical organization, *ostinati* and the general patterning of sounds. Compositions draw on other musical experiences, such as singing and listening.

The original London-based study was followed up in Cyprus (Swanwick, 1991). This provided further evidence for the particular conceptual framing of the developmental phases and also of possible enculturation effects. Compared to the English children, the Cypriot participants appeared to be less developmentally *advanced* in their compositions with increasing age. Although there was no difference between participants by country at ages 4 and 5, at the ages of 7 and 8 a greater percentage of the English children were perceived to be at the *imitation* phase and were making more use of general musical conventions. Subsequent research in Brazil (Hentschke & Oliviera,

1999) produced further support for the model and also for the effects of enculturation. Over a 3-year period, differences in aspects of development were noted between children related to the type of school (private and state) and region. Brazilian children in private school settings often were seen as being more developmentally advanced, a possible effect of better economic, social, and educational variables in their upbringing.

A less-elaborated model of compositional development has been proposed by Kratus (1989, 1994) in which the main compositional processes are termed *exploration, development*, and *repetition. Exploration* is defined as the unfolding of new ideas, with *development* being their revision and *repetition* their review. Younger children are perceived as being more biased toward exploration, often because the composing context is more *free-play*, self-directed and less structured. In contrast, older children make greater use of musical development and repetition and draw on their growing familiarity with a performance and listening repertoire (Eastlund Gromko, 2003).

This simple conceptual framework for understanding the development of composing skills has been extended subsequently and applied to musical *improvisation*. This is defined as "purposeful, non-random movements to create musical sounds over time . . . which form the resultant musical product" (Kratus, 1995, p. 27). Improvisation is distinguished from composition in that the musical products (outcomes) are not open to revision, unlike in composition. A seven-phase developmental model has been proposed that has correspondences to Swanwick and Tillman's (1986) model of composing. The opening phases of the developmental sequence embrace *exploration*, followed by improvisation that is *process-oriented* (linked to Swanwick and Tillman's *manipulative* phase) and then *product-oriented*. A related study of melodic improvisation in 6- to 8-year-olds (Brophy, 2002) offers support for Kratus's conceptualization. The study's youngest children's improvisations were seen as *process-oriented* because they employed repeated rhythmic and melodic patterns with little evidence of larger structures such as phrase organization or musical motif development.

However, there is evidence that younger children are indeed capable of relatively sophisticated compositional and improvisational behaviors when working in a musical context in which they are able to use a familiar instrument, their voice, in a familiar genre, song (Davies, 1986, 1992, 1994; Barrett, 1998). Five- to seven-year-old children's invented songs often demonstrate a close correspondence between playing with words and melody, evidence of two- and four-bar phrases, clear beginnings and ends to their songs, patterns of alternation and repetition and also musical transformation. In this context, children are able to demonstrate both that they have absorbed dominant musical forms from their cultural environment and also that they are able to play and explore with these to create their own musical products.

The Notating of Musical Sounds

Within the growing literature on children's musical development, there has been increasing interest in children's *phonographic behavior*, defined as children's invented notations in response to musical stimuli (Elkoshi, 2002). The interest has arisen, at least initially, because children's notations have been seen as a *window* into the operation and development of the musical mind. Nevertheless, in the same way that print and talk may be seen as complimentary, but different, aspects of linguistic competency, so reading musical notation and making musical sounds are related, but also distinct forms of musical behavior. Enculturation brings children into contact with many different orthographies, but proficiency in the handling of such symbols, whether related to sounds or words, appears to be closely related to actual experience. Children learn that print is a translation of speech and that there are cultural conventions to be mastered (Ehri, 1992; Adams, 1994). Similarly, children are able to understand that, in music, sound can relate to symbol. However, any perceived ambiguity in children's early music notation is not necessarily a weakness to be addressed by education, not least because designed imprecision in notation is also a characteristic of many contemporary mature musical genres from across the musical spectrum (including Western classical and traditional musics). Conventional musical notation can only ever be an approximation to the intended or actual musical outcome. This essential difference between the symbolization of sounds and words is crucial because it means that young children's invented notations can be celebrated in their own right without necessarily viewing them as somehow limited or deficient transitions toward a convention. The individual makes sense of their auditory experience by seeking order and pattern (see *structures* earlier), which may be recorded as symbols. These then have the potential for translation back into sound, for musical meaning to be constructed by the original notator or by others. In terms of musical experience (and also as a pedagogic strategy), the sound comes before the sign (McPherson & Gabrielsson, 2002).

Children use a range of strategies when notating their musical experiences, such as drawing the source of the sound (the musical *instrument*), depicting strong perceptual features (such as rhythm or melodic change), different sized shapes (to indicate changes in intensity or rhythm), and using abstract symbols (such as a cross or circle) (Bamberger, 1991, Domer & Gromko, 1996, Poorman, 1996, Smith, Cuddy, & Upitis, 1994, Young & Glover, 1998, Barrett, 1998, 1999, 2003a). Visually, there is often a sense of pattern and grouping, related to *units of perception*, such as musical motifs, figures and phrases (Bamberger, 1991, 1996). Young children are able to represent sound as symbols through drawing (Bamberger, 1991; Welch, 1991) and also in the manipulation of shaped, textured, or colored materials (Walker, 1985; Poorman, 1996).

There appears to be a difference between young children's notation that is text-based (as in song) compared with that which is more instrumentally focused (Barrett, 1997; 1999). With singing tasks, the words of the songs often appear to be the dominant perceptual feature underlying the invented notation (see also *singing* later), with some children even stating that they are unable to notate a song that they have just sung because "I don't know my letters yet" (Barrett, 1998). However, these same children are quite capable of notating the musical features of their compositions when the focus is purely instrumental.

Developmentally, the two earliest generic phases (*sensorimotor* and *figural*—see Hargreaves, 1996, earlier) are evidenced in changes in young children's notational outputs. The earliest *scribbling* phase (under 2 years) is characterized by *action equivalents* in which the young child makes marks on paper, which correspond to their physical actions and that may match the timing of heard sounds (Goodnow, 1971; Barrett, 2003a), but otherwise no obvious graphic-sonic relationship is evident. The *figural* phase (Bamberger, 1991) derives its label from the correspondence between the child's notation and a particularly dominant feature of the perceived sound, such as duration or melodic shape. Initially (2 to 5 years), the invented notation signifies a single musical dimension and then (5 to 8 years) several dimensions at once (cf. Hargreaves, 1996; Durrant & Welch, 1995). These phases in notational development have a correspondence with those mentioned earlier for composition, with notational *scribbles* being associated with sensory impressions and *figural* notations embracing development across the *manipulative* and the *imitative* phases.

In common with other musical abilities, notational behavior is both task-specific and susceptible to adult intervention and training. Preschoolers invented notations, for example, showed qualitative changes after 12 weeks of music instruction, particularly for those children who were already more experienced musically (Domer & Gromko, 1996). At the end of the training period, fewer of the children's melodic representations of stimulus songs were at the *scribble* stage, and more were interpreted as either *enactive* (being accurate representations of the continuous pulse of the whole song), or as *melodic* (being systematic and relatively accurate visual representations of the song's actual melodic contour).

Singing

The interaction between enculturation and generative (creative) skill development is powerfully evidenced in changes to singing behaviors through childhood and beyond. Maternal vocal behaviors (speaking and singing—see *ontogenesis* and *enculturation* sections earlier) are central to the earliest musical experiences from prebirth onward. Concomitantly, the newborn's plastic neuropsychobiological facility to perceive the dominant acoustic features of any language and music are shaped by exposure to the dominant sound cultures of the maternal community across the first 12 months of life (H. Papousek, 1996; M. Papousek, 1996; Vihman, 1996; Meltzoff, 2002; Trehub, 2003b; see Welch, 2005, for a review).

The foundations for singing development are established during infancy because of the physical and structural interrelatedness between early infant vocalisation (Tafuri & Villa, 2002), infant-directed speech (Kuhl & Meltzoff, 1996), and infant-directed singing (Trehub, 2001), alongside the existence (and persistence) of songs designed for an infant audience within the maternal culture (Unyk, Trehub, Trainor, & Schellenberg, 1992). (The combination of these four elements is an example of how the *layers* in the suggested Russian Dolls model interact–see Fig. 14.1.) Infant vocal behaviors are constrained by the limited structures and behavioral possibilities of the developing vocal system (cf. Kent & Vorperian, 1995). The first vocalizations are related to the communication of an affective state, whether discomfort and distress (crying), or the subsequent sounds of comfort and eustress. The predisposition to generate vocal sounds that have quasi-melodic features first emerges around the age of 2 to 4 months (Stark, Bernstein, & Demorest, 1993), with increasing evidence of control during the 3 months that follow (Vihman, 1996). These prelinguistic infant vocalizations are characterized by the voluntary modulation and management of pitch that emulates the predominant prosodic characteristics of the mother tongue (Flax, Lahey, Harris, & Boothoyd, 1991), while also exploring rhythmic syllabic sequences with superimposed melodies and short musical patterns (M. Papousek, 1996).

Melodic shape and pattern are central to perception and neurological processing (Peretz & Coltheart, 2003) and are key features of early musical experience and development. Melody is also strongly evidenced in data from longitudinal studies of singing development (Davidson, 1994; Dowling, 1999; Welch, 2000a). Children begin to sing spontaneously around the age of 9 months to a year, often over a wide pitch range, but also including "patterns of vowel sounds sung on locally stable pitches" (Dowling, 1999, p. 611). Over the next 12 months, singing become characterized by the repetition of brief phrases and melodic contours at different pitch levels. Rhythmic patterns tend to be coherent and linked to speech patterns.

A hierarchy of musical competencies is evidenced, with increasing mastery of rhythmic patterns and melodic shapes emerging, prior to the accurate sung reproduction of constituent interval relationships, tonality, and key stability within a conventional musical genre. The powerful influence of language and words in singing development is indicated by differences in singing behaviours between individuals. Some children are able to master the musical conventions of song singing relatively easily and subsequently to enter school as competent *in-tune* singers. Others of the same age appear to have their perception and production continuing to be dominated by rhythmic and speech patterns within a limited pitch range (see also Davidson, 1994, later). Nevertheless, many (if not all) of the latter will become competent singers before the age of 11, particularly if they have musical experiences that are matched to their developmental needs (Welch, 2000a).

A developmental, phase-based model of singing has been proposed, drawing on a diverse range of research evidence (Welch, 1986, 1998, 2002; and see Davidson, 1994, and Dowling, 1999, for detailed case studies of individual children):

• *Phase 1* The song text appears to be the initial centre of interest rather than the melody, singing often is described as *chant-like*, employing a restricted pitch range and elements of melodic phrases. In infant vocal pitch exploration and first songs, descending patterns predominate.
• *Phase 2* There is a growing awareness that vocal pitch can be a conscious process and that changes in vocal pitch are controllable. Sung melodic outline begins to follow the general (macro) contours of the target melody or key constituent phrases. Tonality is essentially phrase based. Self-invented and

schematic songs *borrow* elements from the child's musical culture. The vocal pitch range used in *song* singing expands.
• *Phase 3* Melodic shapes and intervals are mostly accurate, but some changes in tonality may occur, perhaps linked to inappropriate singing register usage. Overall, however, the number of different reference pitches is much reduced.
• *Phase 4* There are no significant melodic or pitch errors in relation to relatively simple songs from the singer's musical culture.

Evidence from studies of Ghanaian (Addo, 1995, 1998), Cantonese (Chen-Hafteck, 1996, 1998) and Zimbabwean [Shona] (Kreutzer, 2001) children's native singing offer a melodic contour-driven model of being *in-tune* rather than the customary Western intervallic/scalic version. Each of these three cultures has a pitch-based language in which grammatical meaning is accessed in the rise and fall of the individual spoken tones. There is a close association between speech and singing contours. Vocal pitch accuracy relates to the correspondence between the macro- and micro-contours of the song and the vocal behavior of the developing singer. In these cultures, children are sensitive to and able to assimilate the tone language and its influences on the melody.

There are several possible explanations for differences in the singing competencies of individual children. One 5-year longitudinal study (Davidson, 1994), for example, examined nine firstborn children's singing from the age of 1 year onward. Analysis of the children's vocal products led the researchers to suggest that the basis of tonal knowledge and mastery (as evidenced in young children's singing) is the development of song *contour schemes*. *Contour* refers to the figurative shape of the melody and *schemes* refers to differing levels of mental organization. The underlying theory is that children's knowledge of tonal relationships is expressed through their song performance. This may be the case, but, as with the commentary on notation (see earlier), individual musical understanding of tonal structures may be complimentary to vocal behaviors, but each could also be relatively discrete. Contour schemes are characterized by a single framing interval (initially a 3rd, then a 4th, 5th, and 6th), which marks the developing pitch boundaries of the contour of the infant's song repertoire (Davidson, 1994, p. 118). Mastery development is demonstrated by the child's increasing ability to *fill in* accurately the constituent musical intervals within each pitch boundary.

Another longitudinal study (Welch, Sergeant, & White, 1996, 1997, 1998) focused on nearly 200 children's singing during their first 3 years of statutory schooling in London (ages 5 to 7) and compliments data from the Harvard Project Zero (Davidson, 1994). In general, at each successive age group, the young children were much more accurate in reproducing the deconstructed *elements* of songs (simple contours, single pitches, and pitch patterns) in comparison to their ability to reproduce the totality of these when they were combined with the song text. Conversely (but in line with the developmental models), they simultaneously demonstrated a remarkable facility to learn and reproduce the words of the target songs (see Fig. 14.2).

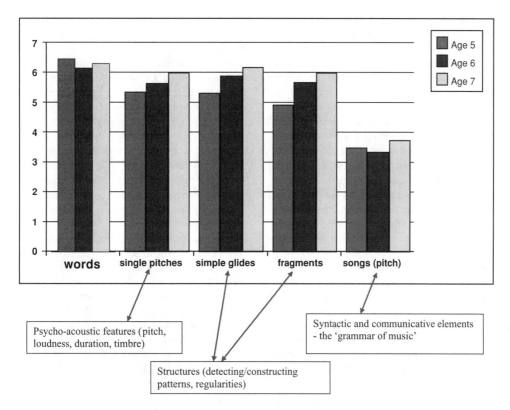

FIGURE 14.2. Three-year longitudinal data ($n = 184$ children), using a 7-point rating scale by a panel of judges, of 5-, 6-, and 7-year-old children's developing abilities to sing (a) the elements of songs (words, single pitches, simple glides, fragments) and (b) all of these in combination as complete *songs* (Welch et al., 1996, 1997, 1998).

These findings are in line with those elsewhere in the literature and also correspond to the perceptual hierarchy of increasing complexity by which sounds are perceived and conceived, namely that the ability to make sense of *psycho-acoustic features* (such as pitch, loudness, duration, timbre) and *structures* (the detection/construction of patterns, regularities) precedes that for music's *syntactic and communicative elements* (the grammar of music) (see Fig. 14.2 and the Introduction earlier).

Children's developing abilities in relation to songs from the maternal culture can impact on the formation of their musical identities. Their identity as a *musician* is often defined in relation to singing competency and this relates to (a) the nature of the match between their phase of singing development and nature of the singing task and (b) to comments from listeners about their singing. Given that the various longitudinal research studies support a phase-based model of development, if the singing task is appropriately matched to the individual's phase of development, then the infant/young child will demonstrate *competency*. However, if there is a mismatch, the child will usually appear less than competent. For example, they will produce the singing behaviour that is characteristic of their phase of development (such as being able to produce a melodic outline that is relatively accurate, but without overall key stability), whereas the target song may require a more advanced set

of behaviors (usually reproductive accuracy in all features)—a common event in the classroom that uses songs from the dominant culture to mark events in the school year, such as the seasons and religious festivals. In such cases of mismatch, there may be extreme disapproval about their singing, usually from a significant person in their life, such as parent, teacher, or peer (Welch, 2001). The outcome of this disapproval is often a negative attitude, both toward the act of singing and themselves as *singers*. A sense of musical *disability* can remain within them into adulthood (Lidman-Magnussen, 1994; Knight, 1999). Nevertheless, even for *nonsinging* adults, there is evidence that their *interrupted* singing development can be kick-started and that singing competency be gained in an appropriately nurturing environment (Richards & Durrant, 2003).

THE INFLUENCE OF SOCIAL GROUPS

Every young child is also a member simultaneously of several social groups and each of these has an influence on individual musical behaviour and development (O'Neill & Green, 2001). For example, in general, children from economically advantaged groups are more likely to be enculturated into *classical (high-art)* music and to experience instrumental playing in the home.

Conversely, children who have never had the opportunity to play a musical instrument are far more likely to endorse a fixed view of musical ability (O'Neill, 2002).

Two particular forms of social grouping concerning the *family* and *gender* are offered as exemplars below of how group membership can affect the musical behaviors of young children.

The *family* can have a key role in the shaping of musical behavior, such as through the provision of an environment in which the acquisition of musical skills is valued. This often derives from the parent's positive memories of the special place that music had in their own childhood. There is a sense in which they feel that they have a duty to pass on an engagement with music to the next generation (Borthwick & Davidson, 2002). Within two-child families in which the parents have positive memories of music in their own childhood, it is often their first-born child for whom there is the greatest expectation of high musical competency.

A U.S. Web-based survey of parent-infant musical relationships (Johnson-Green & Custodero, 2002) suggests that there are regular and systematic opportunities for musical communication in parental daily routines, such as feeding, changing, bathtime, traveling in the car, and bedtime. Survey respondents indicate that parent's musical choices are based on the preferences and reactions of the infants and toddlers in their care. There often is continuity of musical choice, with a specific song being associated with a specific routine.

The vast majority of parents of 4- to 6-month-olds in the U.S. survey reported that they regularly sang and played music to their young children (classical 46% of parents, rock 45%, children's song and lullabies 37%) (Custodero & Johnson-Green, 2003). Musically experienced parents were more likely to play and sing music for their infants. The playing of classical music to their infants was associated with them having played an instrument or having taken lessons. Data analyses suggest that there is also a strong correlation between singing as a parent and being sung to by a parent, especially mothers.

Parents can have a significant role in infants' musical play (Berger & Cooper, 2003). The researchers identified three major types of adult involvement. Negative effects were observed in *unfinished play* and *extinguishing play*. These were contexts in which adult intervention (conscious or inadvertent) leads to an inappropriate interruption in the young child's musical explorations. In contrast, *enhancing play* was characterized by an adult willingness to participate in child-led activities, by an explicit acceptance and valuing of all of the child's musical behaviors, and by the provision of adequate time and musical tools. Similarly, evidence from Argentina suggests that a sustained period of musical activities designed for small groups of 3-year-olds with their parents both promotes musical development and also has positive benefits on the quality of parent-child communication and understanding (Grätzer, 1999).

In general, positive engagement in musical activities by the family, such as playing, singing, listening, discussing, or attending musical events, can support the musical development of children (Gembris & Davidson, 2002). This also applies to children with disabilities. For example, a recent international survey of visually disabled children with septo-optic dysplasia indicates that music is highly valued by their parents because of its positive emotional and communicative significance in their lives, often from a very young age (Ockelford, Pring, Welch, & Treffert, 2005).

Another important social grouping effect is evidenced in studies of *gender* and musical behavior. Much of the research has focused on late childhood and adolescence, exploring such issues as children and adolescent's gender stereotyping of musical instruments and musical styles, gendered practices in performance and composition and influences on musical identity (cf. see O'Neill, 1997; Green, 1997; O'Neill & Green, 2001; Dibben, 2002, for reviews).

For young children, gender effects may be implicated in the large number of research reports concerning differences between girls and boys in their developing singing competencies (cf. Welch, 2000a; Trollinger, 2003). Girls tend to be reported as more developmentally advanced as a group in their song singing compared to boys of the same age. However, when the focus is on children' vocal ability to imitate non-text musical items (as in Fig. 14.2), there are no differences between the sexes. It is only in song-singing that a sex difference is evidenced. Furthermore, in one longitudinal study, this difference emerged during the first 3 years of schooling. Although girls and boys in the study were approximately equal in their song singing ability at age 5, there was a significant difference in favor of girls by age 7 (Welch, 2000a; Welch et al., 1997).

Such sex differences could stem from the interface of enculturation with psychobiological maturation processes that then become magnified by cultural experiences in the shaping of a developing musical identity. For example, mothers are highly implicated in early musical development (Trehub, 2002), particularly in relation to their singing (see the section on *enculturation* earlier). Also, concerning language development, girls tend to produce language earlier than boys (Karmiloff & Karmiloff-Smith, 2001). So it may be that song singing (a facility to combine words and music) is a musical behavior that is more strongly identified with females, not least because the vast majority of preschool and early years teachers are women, and that the emerging musical identities of young boys includes the avoidance of behaviors that appear to be *feminine* (O'Neill, 1997; Dibben, 2002). Support for such an interpretation may be found in studies of the gender stereotyping for musical instruments, such as drums, guitar, and trumpet being perceived as *masculine* and flute, piano, and violin as *feminine* (O'Neill, 1997). Five-year-olds do not exhibit this behaviour, whereas it is more strongly evidenced in 10-year-olds, adolescents, and adults, indicating the emergence of gender effects with age. Young children also are reported as being more willing to listen to different musical styles compared to older children and adolescents (Hargreaves and North, 1999; Karper, 2001), while also being idiosyncratic in their listening behaviours (Sims & Cassidy, 1997; Sims, 2001).

The act of singing conveys information about age, gender, culture, and social group membership. Several studies have demonstrated that listeners are able to identify and label certain features of both the singer (as a *child*) and the singing (as *childlike*) (cf. Sergeant, Sjölander, & Welch, 2005; Welch & Howard, 2002). Often there is an accurate correspondence between the listener assessment and the acoustic item, but this is not always the case because of the variables involved, both in relation to the listener and to the singer.

SCHOOLING AND MUSICAL DEVELOPMENT

There is evidence that making special provision for music-making in preschool classrooms can facilitate musical development. Provision may relate to the organisation of the physical environment, such as through the designation of a free-play *music corner* (Fash, 1990; Gluschankof, 2002) and often with the adult acting as an *audience* for the child musician (Young, 1995, 1999; Barrett, 2003a, 2003b), and through specially designed interventions (Suthers, 1996; Gruhn, 2002). The music corner is seen as both legitimating musical behavior while also enabling the young children to be more in control, to have agency in their development. At the same time, any adult present is likely to act as an audience (whether intentional or not) to interact, provide support (or not) and comment on the children's activities (Berger & Cooper, 2003).

A longitudinal German study of 1- and 2-year-olds compared the musical behaviors and development of a group of children with their parents in a special weekly music program to an equivalent *control* group in a day care setting (Gruhn, 2002). After 40 weeks, there were marked differences between the two groups (notwithstanding individual differences), with higher ratings for the special program infants in the quality of their physical movements to music and in their imitation of rhythmic patterns.

Other evidence of structured education and enculturation in musical development is provided by research that focused on an analysis of children's response to changes in musical mode (major/minor) (Costa-Giomi, 1996). Although a brief training period had little effect on preschoolers' (age 4) perception of musical mode, by contrast, an identical training permitted kindergarten children (age 5) to perceive mode changes. Furthermore, following such training, 5-year-olds were also able both to identify *major* and *minor* tonalities and to use correctly the appropriate verbal label.

The effects of schooling on young children's musical behaviour and development also are evidenced in a comparative analysis of different schools in the longitudinal study on singing reported above (Welch, 2000b). Developmental progress in singing appeared to be linked to the school ethos. For example, notwithstanding economic disadvantages and a lack of musical resources, if there was a clear expectation in the school that all young children could and should sing and that singing development should be a musical priority, all children improved significantly over a 3-year period. In contrast, where there appeared to be a more *laissez-faire* attitude to singing, irrespective of the resourcing levels, development was less marked and some children were rated as less competent at age 7 than at age 5.

This emphasis on the effects of an underlying belief system on young children's musical development is a common theme in the research literature, including that relating to the role of the adult in an educational setting (Young, 2000). As mentioned in the introduction to this chapter, when young children are provided with a resource-rich and supportive environment for idiosyncratic music making and exploration, or where the adult takes a facilitating and interactive role (Adachi, 1994; Barrett, 2003a; Tafuri, 2003), the research evidence suggests that they are more likely to flourish and develop a wider range and depth of musical skills.

MUSICAL DEVELOPMENT AND EDUCATION IN THE WIDER COMMUNITY

Several impacts of the available musical cultures within the wider community have already been discussed in relation to enculturation and generative skill development and the effects of group membership. The musical behaviors of adult caregivers and preschool educators are socially and culturally located and thus impact on the ways that they interact with infants and young children. Both adults and children share similar sound worlds. At the same time, there is also diversity as children become exposed to a variety of different musical styles and genres as they progress from being *lap babies* to *knee children* to *yard children* (Whiting & Edwards, 1988). There are likely to be widespread musical encounters through children's media, such as in the worlds of animation and music, including *Barney the Dinosaur* and *Bob the Builder*, and in the sound effects incorporated into modern picture books and toys. Musical exposure to other (or identical) musical genres will occur when traveling, depending on the carer's choice of in-car entertainment. For example, a recent study of musical provision for children in the special education sector in England revealed that one of the prime sources of musical experience was the journey to and from school (Welch, Ockelford, & Zimmerman, 2001).

Ethnicity is also a factor. Across U.K.-Asian communities, for example, over 40 different musical genres are performed, with considerable stylistic differences between popular genres, such as *bhangra* and *filmi* music, and the more traditional musics (Farrell, Welch, & Bhowmick, 2000/2001). One outcome of exposure to such communities in that, when at play, ethnicity is evidenced in the children's manner of singing, with Euro-American and Asian children likely to sing pitched melodies, whereas African-American children perform more nonpitched rhythmic chants (cf. Campbell, 2002). Similarly, ethnicity is evidenced in singing development, such as in the Cantonese, Ghanaian, and Zimbabwean studies mentioned earlier.

SUMMARY

Overall, it is clear from the research literature that infancy and early childhood are critical periods for the development of musical abilities and the formation of musical identity. The young child is capable of a wide range of musical behaviors in relation to the dominant musical culture. These behaviors evolve and change over time in response to maturational processes and experience, including interaction with caregivers and opportunities to experience different musics from the wider community.

Across the research literature, there are a number of key messages for education and community policy makers, early childhood educators, parents, and other caregivers:

• Assuming normal development, all children are musical and capable of a diverse range of musical behaviours.
• Musical development can be fostered by an appropriate range of experiences throughout the early years of childhood.
• The first year of life is characterized by socialization into the dominant musical culture(s). The broader the range of experiences, the greater the likelihood that musical skill development will be enhanced.
• Caregivers, especially mothers, are critical agents in their children's musical socialisation and development. But both parents can make significant contributions to their children's singing development.
• Early experience of singing is linked to the development of musical competencies.
• Encouraging participation in musical activities can have nonmusical benefits, such as in the development of verbal memory, motor control, emotional awareness, and communication skills.
• Teachers of young children should look out for, encourage, and celebrate a diversity of different singing behaviors from the age of 2 years onward.
• Children progress through a variety of phases in their musical development. Adults need to be sensitive to the musical behaviors that characterize such phases and open to the possibility of growth. Rich musical experience can foster progression through these phases and may accelerate development.
• Young children should be provided with opportunities to compose and improvise, such as in invented songs and exploratory play with simple musical instruments. These experiences can also provide the basis for the development of early, preschool musical symbolization and notation. Teachers should remember that the sound should precede the sign.
• Young children are likely to demonstrate good singing skills if they have been sung to since birth. If singing skill needs to be developed, teachers should focus on mastery of the different elements (melodic contour, pitch patterns, rhythmic patterns, text) before the combination of these into the whole song.
• Early inappropriate disapproval of current singing abilities can lead to lifelong negative self-labeling of perceived musical disability.
• Girls often appear to develop musical skills earlier than boys. Parents and teachers need to be proactive in seeking opportunities to foster young boys' musical development and to counter any suggestion that certain musical behaviors are feminine.
• Policy makers for schools and the wider community should encourage parental participation with their children in early musical activities. In particular, early childhood settings and schools should have clear policies to promote a wide range of developmental phase-sensitive musical activities.

The challenge for the early years music teacher is to celebrate the child's developing musical competencies and to provide a nurturing framework for musical activity, especially creative musical activity, that enables the child to draw on, share and extend their existing musical knowledge (see Welch & Adams, 2003). Such a framework should include sufficient opportunities and time to make music, with lots of sound making materials and simple instruments, to create, review, polish, and perform, using notation as appropriate. An engagement with music is literally our birthright.

References

Adachi, M. (1994). The role of the adult in the child's early musical socialisation: A Vygotskian perspective. *The Quarterly Journal of Music Teaching and Learning, V*(3), 26–35.

Adachi, M., & Trehub, S. (1998). Children's expression of emotion in song. *Psychology of Music, 26*(2), 133–153.

Adams, M. J. (1994). *Beginning to read: Thinking and learning about print*. Cambridge, MA: MIT Press.

Addo, A. (1995). *Ghanaian children's music cultures: A video ethnography of selected singing games*. Unpublished Ph.D. thesis, University of British Columbia, Canada.

Addo, A. (1998). Melody, Language and the development of singing in the curriculum. *British Journal of Music Education, 15*(2), 139–148.

Altenmüller, E. (2004). Music in your head. *Scientific American, 14*(1), 24–31.

Altenmüller, E., Parlitz, D., & Gruhn, W. (1997). Music learning produces changes in brain activation patterns: a longitudinal DC-EEG study. *International Journal of Arts Medicine, 35*, 28–33.

Altenmüller, E., Gruhn, W., Parlitz, D., & Liebert, G. (2000). The impact of music education on brain networks. Evidence from EEG studies. *International Journal for Music Education, 35*, 47–53.

Anning, A. (2000). *The influence of socio-cultural context on young children's meaning making through mark-making, drawing, modeling and playing with objects*. Working Paper 2.2. Leeds: The Center for Research Family, Kinship and Childhood, University of Leeds.

Aslin, R. N., & Smith, L. B. (1988). Perceptual development. In M. R. Rozenzweig & L. W. Porter (Eds.), *Annual Review of Psychology, 39*, 435–473.

Bamberger, J. (1991). *The mind behind the musical ear: how children develop musical intelligence*. Cambridge MA: Harvard University Press.

Bamberger, J. (1996). Turning music theory on its ear. Do we hear what we see, do we see what we say? *International Journal of Computers and Mathematical Learning, 1*(1), 48–74.

Barrett, M. (1997). Invented notations: A view of young children's musical thinking. *Research Studies in Music Education, 8*, 2–14.

Barrett, M. (1998). Researching children's compositional processes and products: Connections to music education practice? In B. Sundin, G. McPherson, & G. Folkestad (Eds.), *Children Composing* (pp. 10–34). Malmö: Malmö Academy of Music.

Barrett, M. (1999). Modal dissonance: An analysis of children's invented notations of known songs, original songs, and instrumental compositions. *Bulletin of the Council for Research in Music Education, 141,* 14–22.

Barrett, M. (2000). Windows, mirrors and reflections: A case study of adult constructions of children's musical thinking. *Bulletin of the Council for Research in Music Education, 145,* 43–61.

Barrett, M. (2003a). Musical children, musical lives, musical worlds. In S. Wright (Ed.), *Children, meaning-making and the arts* (pp. 63–89). New South Wales: Pearson Education.

Barrett, M. (2003b). Freedoms and constraints: Constructing musical worlds through the dialogue of composition. In M. Hickey (Ed.), *Composition in the schools: A new horizon for music education* (pp. 3–27). Reston, VA: MENC.

Belin, P., Zatorre, R. J., Lafaille, P., Ahad, P., & Pike, B. (2000). Voice-selective areas in the human auditory cortex. *Nature, 403,* 309–312.

Bennett, M. (1999). (Ed.), *Developmental psychology: Achievements and prospects.* London: Taylor and Francis/Psychology Press.

BERA [British Educational Research Association] Music Education Review Group. (2001). *Mapping music education research in the UK.* Southwell, UK: British Educational Research Association.

BERA [British Educational Research Association] Early Years Special Interest Group. (2003). *Early years research: Pedagogy, curriculum and adult roles, training and professionalism.* Southwell, UK: British Educational Research Association.

Berger, A. A., & Cooper, S. (2003). Musical play: A case study of preschool children and parents. *Journal of Research in Music Education, 51*(2), 151–165.

Blood, A. J., Zatorre, R., Bermudez, P., & Evans, A. (1999). Emotional responses to pleasant and unpleasant music correlate with activity in paralimbic brain regions. *Nature Neuroscience, 2*(4), 382–387.

Blood, A. J., & Zatorre, R. J. (2001). Intensely pleasurable responses to music correlate with activity in brain regions implicated in reward and emotion. *Proceedings of the New York Academic of Sciences, 98,* 11818–11823.

Borthwick, S. J., & Davidson, J. W. (2002). Developing a child's identity as a musician: a family *script* perspective. In R. A. R. MacDonald, D. J. Hargreaves, & D. Miell (Eds.), *Musical Identities* (pp. 60–78). Oxford: Oxford University Press.

Brophy, T. S. (2002). The melodic improvisations of children aged 6–12: A developmental perspective. *Music Education Research, 4*(1), 73–92.

Brothers, L. (1997). *Friday's footprint: How society shapes the human mind.* Oxford: Oxford University Press.

Brust, J. C. M. (2001). Music and the Neurologist: A Historical Perspective. In R. J. Zatorre & I. Peretz (Eds.), *The biological foundations of music* (vol. 930, pp. 143–152). New York: Annals of the New York Academy of Sciences.

Campbell, P. S. (2002). The musical cultures of children. In L. Bresler & C. Marme Thompson (Eds.), *The arts in children's lives: Context, culture and curriculum* (pp. 57–69). Dordrecht: Kluwer Academic Publishers.

Chang, H. W., & Trehub, S. E. (1977). Auditory processing of relational information by young infants. *Journal of Experimental Child Psychology, 24,* 324–331.

Chen-Haftek, L. (1996). *Effects of the pitch relationship between text and melody in Cantonese songs on young children's singing.* Unpublished Ph.D. thesis, University of Reading, UK.

Chen-Haftek, L. (1998). Pitch abilities in music and language of Cantonese-speaking children. *International Journal of Music Education, 31*(1), 14–24.

Costa-Giomi, E. (1996). Mode discrimination abilities of preschool children. *Psychology of Music, 24*(2), 184–198.

Custodero, L. A., & Johnson-Green, E. A. (2003). Passing the cultural torch: Musical experience and musical parenting of infants. *Journal of Research in Music Education, 51*(2), 102–114.

David, T., Goouch, K., Powell, S., & Abbott, L. (2003). *Birth to three matters: A review of the literature.* London: Department for Education and Skills.

Davidson, L. (1994). Songsinging by young and old: A developmental approach to music. In R. Aiello with J. Slobod (Eds.), *Musical Perceptions* (pp. 99–130). New York: Oxford University Press.

Davies, C. (1986). Say it till a song comes: reflections on songs invented by children 3–13. *British Journal of Music Education, 3*(3), 279–293.

Davies, C. (1992). Listen to my song: a study of songs invented by children aged 5 to 7 years. *British Journal of Music Education, 9*(1), 19–48.

Davies, C. (1994). The listening teacher: An approach to the collection and study of invented songs of children aged 5 to 7. In H. Lees (Ed.), *Musical connections: Tradition and change* (pp. 120–127). Auckland, NZ: International Society for Music Education.

Dibben, N. (2002). Gender identity and music. In R. MacDonald, D. J. Hargreaves, & D. Miell (Eds.), *Musical identities* (pp. 117–133). Oxford: Oxford University Press.

Domer, J., & Eastland Gromko, J. (1996). Qualitative changes in preschoolers' invented notations following music instruction. *Contributions to Music Education, 23,* 62–78.

Dowling, W. J. (1988). Tonal structure and children's early learning of music. In. J. Sloboda (Ed.), *Generative processes in music* (pp. 113–128). Oxford: Oxford University Press.

Dowling, W. J. (1999). The development of music perception and cognition. In D. Deutsch (Ed.), *The Psychology of Music* 2nd ed., (pp. 603–625). London: Academic Press.

Durrant, C., & Welch, G.F. (1995). *Making sense of music.* London: Cassell.

Eastlund Gromko, J. (2003). Children composing: Inviting the artful narrative. In M. Hickey (Ed.), *Composition in the schools: A new horizon for music education* (pp. 69–90). Reston, VA: MENC.

Ehri, L. C. (1992). Reconceptualising the development of sight word reading and its relationship to recoding. In P. Gough, L. C. Ehri, & R. Trieman (Eds.), *Reading acquisition* (pp. 383–417) Hillsdale, New Jersey: Lawrence Erlbaum Associates.

Eimas, P. D., Siqueland, E. R., Jusczyk, P. W., & Vigorito, J. (1971). Speech perception in infants. *Science, 171,* 303–306.

Elkoshi, R. (2002). An investigation into children's responses through drawing, to short musical fragments and complete compositions. *Music Education Research, 4*(2), 199–211.

Farrell, G., Welch, G., & Bhowmick, J. (2000/2001). South Asian music and music education in Britain. *Bulletin of the Council for Research in Music Education, 147,* 51–60.

Fash, L. (1990). Changing perceptions of music with Reception children. *British Journal of Music Education, 7*(1), 43–65.

Fernald, A. (1992). Meaningful melodies in mothers' speech to infants. In H. Papousek, U. Jurgens, & M. Papousek (Eds.), *Nonverbal vocal communication: comparative and developmental approaches* (pp. 262–282). Cambridge: Cambridge University Press.

Fernald, A., & Kuhl, P. K. (1987). Acoustic determinants of infant preference for motherese speech. *Infant Behaviour and Development, 10,* 279–293.

Flax, J., Lahey, M., Harris, K., & Boothoyd, A. (1991). Relations between prosodic variables and communicative functions. *Journal of Child Language, 18,* 3–19.

Fuster, J. M. (2003). *Cortex and mind*. Oxford: Oxford University Press.

Gammage, P. (1999). The once and future child. *European Early Childhood Educational Research Journal, 7*(2), 103–117.

Gembris, H., & Davidson, J. W. (2002). Environmental Influences. In R. Parncutt & G. E. McPherson (Eds.), *The science and psychology of music performance* (pp. 17–30). Oxford: Oxford University Press.

Gluschankof, C. (2002). The local musical style of kindergarten children: A description and analysis of its natural variables. *Music Education Research, 4*(1), 37–49.

Goodnow, J. (1971). Auditory-visual matching: Modality problem or translation problem?. *Child Development, 42,* 1187–1210.

Grätzer, D. P. de (1999). Can music help to improve parent-child communication? Learning music with parents—an Argentine experience. *International Journal of Music Education, 34,* 47–56.

Green. L. (1997). *Music, gender, education*. Cambridge: Cambridge University Press.

Greenough, W. T., & Juraska, J. M. (1986). *Developmental neuropsychobiology*. Orlando, FL: Academic Press.

Gruhn, W. (2002). Phases and stages in early music learning: A longitudinal study on the development of young children's musical potential. *Music Education Research, 4*(1), 51–71.

Hargreaves, D. J. (1996). The development of artistic and musical competence. In I. Deliege, & J. Sloboda (Eds.), *Musical beginnings* (pp. 145–170). Oxford: Oxford University Press.

Hargreaves, D. J., & North, A. C. (1997). *The social psychology of music*. Oxford: Oxford University Press.

Hargreaves, D. J., & North, A. C. (1999). Developing concepts of musical style. *Musicae Scientiae, 3,* 193–216.

Hentschke, L., & Oliviera, A. (1999). Music curriculum development and evaluation based on Swanwick's theory. *International Journal of Music Education, 34,* 14–29.

Ho, Y-C., Cheung, M-C., & Chan, A. S. (2003). Music training improves verbal but not visual memory: Cross-sectional and longitudinal explorations in children. *Neuropsychology, 17*(3), 439–450.

James, A., Jenks, C., & Prout, A. (1998). *Theorising childhood*. Cambridge, UK: Polity Press.

Janata, P., Birk, J. L., Van Thorn, J. D., Leman, M., Tillmann, B., & Bharucha, J. J. (2002). The cortical topography of tonal structures underlying Western music. *Science, 298,* 2167–2170.

Johnson-Green, E., & Custodero, L. (2002). The toddler top 40: Musical preferences of babies, toddlers and their parents. *Zero to Three.* [September] 47–48.

Jorquera, M. C. J., Balboni, A., Bella, C., Ferioli, S., & Minichiello, A. (2000). Influenza del compito vocale e del genere sulla capacità di intonare in bambini di 6-7 anni, In J. Tafuri (Ed.), *La ricerca per la didattica musicale* (pp. 165–171). Atti del Convegno SIEM, 2000, *Quaderni della SIEM, 16*.

Jusczyk, P. W., Kemler Nelson, D. G., Hirsh-Pasek, K., Kennedy, L., Woodward, A., & Piwoz, J. (1992). Perception of acoustic correlates of major phrasal units by young infants. *Cognitive Psychology, 24,* 252–293.

Juslin, P. N., & Laukka, P. (2001). Impact of intended emotion intensity on cue utilisation and decoding accuracy in vocal expression of emotion. *Emotion, 1*(4), 381–412.

Juslin, P. N., & Laukka, P. (2003). Communication of emotions in vocal expression and music performance: Different channels, same code? *Psychological Bulletin, 129*(5), 770–814.

Karmiloff, K., & Karmiloff-Smith, A. (2001). *Pathways to language*. Cambridge, MA: Harvard University Press.

Karper, K. (2001). The effects of repeated exposure and instructional activities on the least preferred of four culturally diverse musical styles with kindergarten and pre-k children. *Bulletin of the Council for Research in Music Education, 151,* 41–50.

Kemp, A. E. (1996). *The musical temperament*. Oxford: Oxford University Press.

Kent, R. D. & Vorperian, H. K. (1995). Development of the craniofacial-oral-laryngeal anatomy: A review. *Journal of Medical Speech-Language Pathology, 3*(3), 145–190.

Keverne, E. B., Nevison, C. M., & Martel, F. L. (1997). Early learning and the social bond. In C. S. Carter, I. I. Lederhendler, & B. Kirkpatrick (Eds.), *The Integrative Neurobiology of Affiliation* (Vol. 807, pp. 329–339). New York: Annals of the New York Academy of Sciences.

Kilgour, A. R., Jakobson, L. S., & Cuddy, L. L. (2000). Music training and rate of presentation as mediator of text and song recall. *Memory and Cognition, 28,* 700–710.

Kirkpatrick, W. C. (1962). The relationship between singing ability of pre-kindergarten children and their home environments. *Dis. Abs. 23*(3), 886.

Koelsch, S., Gunter, T., Friederici, A. D., & Schröger, E. (2000). Brain indices of music processing: "Nonmusicians" are musical. *Journal of Cognitive Neuroscience, 12*(3), 520–541.

Knight, S. (1999). Exploring a cultural myth: what adult non-singers may reveal about the nature of singing. In B. A. Roberts, & A. Rose (Eds.), *The phenomenon of singing II.* (pp. 144–154). St. John's, Newfoundland: Memorial University Press.

Kratus, J. (1989). A time analysis of the compositional processes used by children ages 7 to 11. *Journal of Research in Music Education, 37,* 5–20.

Kratus, J. (1994). The ways children compose. In H. Lees (Ed.), *Musical connections: Tradition and change* (pp. 128–141). Auckland, NZ: ISME.

Kratus, J. (1995). A developmental approach to teaching music improvisation. *International Journal of Music Education, 26,* 27–38.

Kreutzer, N. J. (2001). Song acquisition among Rural Shona-speaking Zimbabwean children from birth to 7 years. *Journal of Research in Music Education, 49*(3), 198–211.

Kuhl, P. K., & Meltzoff, A. N. (1996). Infant vocalisations in response to speech: Vocal imitation and developmental change. *Journal of the Acoustical Society of America, 100,* 2425–2438.

Kuhl, P. K., Tsao, F-M., Liu, H.-M., Zhang, Y., & De Boer, B. (2001). Language/culture/mind/brain: Progress at the margins between disciplines. In A. R. Damasio, A. Harrington, J. Kagan, B. S. McEwen, H. Moss, & R. Shaikh (Eds.), *Unity of Knowledge: The Convergence of Natural and Human Science* (Vol. 935, pp. 136–174). New York: Annals of the New York Academy of Sciences.

Kuhl, P. K., Williams, K. A., Lacerda, F., Stevens, K. N., & Lindblom, B. (1992). Linguistic experience alters phonetic perception in infants by 6 months of age. *Science, 255,* 606–608.

Lamont, A. (1998a). Music, education, and the development of pitch perception: The role of context, age and musical experience. *Psychology of Music, 26*(1), 7–25.

Lamont, A. (1998b). *The development of cognitive representation of musical pitch*. Unpublished Ph.D. thesis, University of Cambridge.

Lecanuet, J.-P. (1996). Prenatal auditory experience. In I. Deliege & J. Sloboda (Eds.), *Musical beginnings* (pp. 3–34). Oxford: Oxford University Press.

Levitin, D. (1994). Absolute memory for musical pitch: evidence from the production of learned melodies. *Perception and Psychophysics 56,* 414–423.

Lidman-Magnussen, B. (1994). *Inhibited singing development*. Unpublished dissertation. Stockholm: Royal Academy of Music.

Malloch, S. N. (1999). Mothers and infants and communicative musicality. *Musicae Scientiae* [Special Issue], pp. 29–57.

Maess, B., Koelsch, S., Gunter, T. C., & Friederici, A. D. (2001). Musical syntax is processed in Broca's area: an MEG study. *Nature Neuroscience, 4*(5), 540-545.

Mang, E. (2001). A cross-language comparison of preschool children's vocal fundamental frequency in speech and song production. *Research Studies in Music Education, 16,* 4-14.

Mang, E. (2002). An investigation of vocal pitch behaviors of Hong Kong children. *Bulletin of the Council for Research in Music Education, 153/4,* 128-134.

Masataka, N. (1992). Pitch characteristics of Japanese maternal speech to infants. *Journal of Child Language, 19,* 213-223.

McPherson, G. E., & Gabrielsson, A. (2002). From sound to sign. In R. Parncutt & G. E. McPherson (Eds.), *The science and psychology of music performance* (pp. 99-115). Oxford: Oxford University Press.

Meltzoff, A. N. (2002). Elements of a developmental theory of imitation. In A. N. Meltzoff and W. Prinz (Eds.), *The imitative mind* (pp. 19-41). Cambridge, UK: Cambridge University Press.

Nadel, J., & Butterworth, G. (1999). *Imitation in infancy.* Cambridge: Cambridge University Press.

Nawrot, E. S. (2003). The perception of emotional expression in music: evidence from infants, children and adults. *Psychology of Music, 31*(1), 75-92.

Nazzi, T., Bertoncini, J., & Mehler, J. (1998). Language discrimination by newborns: towards an understanding of the role of rhythm. *Journal of Experimental Psychology: Human Perception and Performance, 24,* 756-766.

Ockelford, A., Pring, L., Welch, G. F., & Treffert, D. (2005). *Focus on Music: Exploring the musical interests and abilities of blind and partially-sighted children with septo-optic dysplasia.* London: Institute of Education/Royal National Institute of the Blind.

O'Neill, S. (1997). Gender and music. In D. J. Hargreaves & A. C. North (Eds.), *The Social psychology of music* (pp. 46-63). Oxford: Oxford University Press.

O'Neill, S. (2002). The self-identity of young musicians. In R. MacDonald, D. J. Hargreaves, & D. Miell (Eds.), *Musical identities* (pp. 79-96). Oxford: Oxford University Press.

O'Neill, S., & Green, L. (2001). Social groups and learning in music education. In British Educational Research Association [BERA] Music Education Review Group, *Mapping Music Education Research in the UK* (pp. 26-31). Southwell, UK: British Educational Research Association.

Papousek, H. (1996). Musicality in infancy research: Biological and cultural origins of early musicality. In I. Deliege & J. Sloboda (Eds.), *Musical beginnings* (pp. 37-55). Oxford: Oxford University Press.

Papousek, M. (1996). Intuitive parenting: A hidden source of musical stimulation in infancy. In I. Deliege & J. Sloboda (Eds.), *Musical beginnings* (pp. 88-112). Oxford: Oxford University Press.

Parsons, L. M. (2003). Exploring the functional neuroanatomy of music performance, perception, and comprehension. In I. Peretz & R. Zatorre (Eds.), *The cognitive neuroscience of music* (pp. 247-268). Oxford: Oxford University Press.

Pascuel-Leone, A. (2001). The brain that plays music and is changed by it. In R. J. Zatorre & I. Peretz (Eds.), *The biological foundations of music* (Vol. 930, pp. 315-329). New York: Annals of the New York Academy of Sciences.

Patel, A. D. (2003). Language, music, syntax and the brain. *Nature Neuroscience, 6*(7), 674-681.

Peretz, I., & Coltheart, M. (2003). Modularity and music processing. *Nature Neuroscience, 6*(7), 688-691.

Peretz, I., & Zatorre, R. (Eds.). (2003). *The cognitive neuroscience of music.* Oxford: Oxford University Press.

Piaget, J. (1951). *Play, dreams and imitation in childhood.* London: Routledge and Kegan Paul.

Poorman, A. Smith (1996). The emergence of symbol use: Prekindergarten children's representations of musical sound. *Contributions to Music Education, 23,* 31-45.

Richards, H., & Durrant, C. (2003). To sing or not to sing: A study on the development of "non-singers" in choral activity. *Research Studies in Music Education, 20,* 78-89.

Saffran, J. (2003). Mechanisms of musical memory in infancy. In I. Peretz & R. Zatorre (Eds.), *The cognitive neuroscience of music* (pp. 32-41). Oxford: Oxford University Press.

Saffran, J. R., & Griepentrog, G. J. (2001). Absolute pitch in infant auditory learning: Evidence for developmental reorganisation. *Developmental Psychology, 37,* 74-85.

Samson, S., Ehrlé, N., & Baulac, M. (2001). Cerebral substrate for musical temporal processes. In R. J. Zatorre & I. Peretz (Eds.), *The biological foundations of music* (Vol. 930, pp. 166-178). New York: Annals of the New York Academy of Sciences.

Schuppert, M., Münte, T. F., Weiringa, B. M., & Altenmüller, E. (2000). Receptive amusia: Evidence for cross-hemispheric neural networks underlying musical processing strategies. *Brain, 123,* 546-559.

Seckl, J. R. (1998). Physiologic programming of the fetus. *Clinical Perinatology, 25*(4), 939-962.

Sergeant, D. C., Sjölander, P., & Welch, G. F. (2005). Listeners' identification of gender differences in children's singing. *Research Studies in Music Education, 25.*

Shahidullah, S., & Hepper, P. G. (1994). Frequency discrimination by the fetus. *Early Human Development, 36,* 13-26.

Shenfield, T., Trehub, S. E., & Nakata, T. (2003). Maternal singing modulates infant arousal. *Psychology of Music, 31*(4), 365-375.

Sims, W. L. (2001). Characteristics of preschool children's individual music listening during free choice time. *Bulletin of the Council for Research in Music Education, 149,* 53-63.

Sims, W. L., & Cassidy, J. W. (1997). Verbal and operant responses of young children to vocal versus instrumental song performances. *Journal of Research in Music Education, 45*(2), 234-244.

Sloboda, J. (Ed.). (1988). *Generative processes in music.* Oxford: Oxford University Press.

Smith, K. C., Cuddy, L. L., & Upitis, R. (1994). Figural and metric understanding of rhythm. *Psychology of Music, 22*(2), 117-135.

Spender, N. (1987). Psychology of music. In R. L. Gregory (Ed.), *The Oxford companion to the mind* (pp. 499-505). Oxford: Oxford University Press.

Stark, R. E., Bernstein, L. E., & Demorest, M. E. (1993). Vocal communication in the first 18 months of life. *Journal of Speech and Hearing Research, 36,* 548-558.

Sundin, B. (1997). Musical creativity in childhood—a research project in retrospect. *Research Studies in Music Education, 9,* 48-57.

Suthers, L. (1996, July). *Using puppetry to help toddlers find their singing voices.* Paper presented at the 7th International Seminar of the ISME Early Childhood Commission, Winchester, UK.

Swanwick, K. (1991). Further research on the musical development sequence. *Psychology of Music, 19*(1), 22-32.

Swanwick, K., & Tillman, J. (1986). The sequence of musical development. *British Journal of Music Education, 3*(3), 305-339.

Tafuri, J. (2003, September). Melodic structures in spontaneous songs of children aged 2-3. In R. Kopiez, A. C. Lehmann, I. Wolther, & C. Wolf (Eds.), *Proceedings.* 5th Triennial ESCOM Conference, Hannover.

Tafuri, J., & Villa, D. (2002a). Musical elements in the vocalizations of infants aged 2 to 8 months. *British Journal of Music Education, 19*(1), 73-88.

Tafuri, J., & Villa, D. (2002b, October). *Singing a song: Melodic accuracy in children aged 2-3.* Paper presented at the Neurosciences and Music Conference, Venice.

Thomas, R. (1970). *MMCP synthesis: A structure for music education.* New York: Media Materials Inc. Bardonia.

Thurman, L., & Grambsch, E. (2000). Foundations for human self-expression during prenate, infant, and early childhood development. In L. Thurman & G. Welch (Eds.), *Bodymind and voice: Foundations of voice education*, Revised Edition (pp. 660–695). Iowa: National Center for Voice and Speech.

Thurman, L., & Welch, G. F. (Eds.). (2000). *Bodymind and voice: Foundations of voice education.* Rev. ed., Iowa: National Center for Voice and Speech.

Titze, I. (1994). *Principles of voice production.* Englewood Cliffs, NJ: Prentice Hall.

Trehub, S. E. (1987). Infants' perception of musical patterns. *Perception and Psychophysics, 41,* 635–641.

Trehub, S. E. (2001). Musical predispositions in infancy. In R. J. Zatorre & I. Peretz (Eds.), *The biological foundations of music* (Vol. 930, pp. 1–16). New York: Annals of the New York Academy of Sciences.

Trehub, S. E. (2002). Mothers are musical mentors. *Zero to Three.* [September] 19–22.

Trehub, S. E. (2003a). Musical predispositions in infancy: An update. In I. Peretz & R. Zatorre (Eds.), *The cognitive neuroscience of music* (pp. 3–20). Oxford: Oxford University Press.

Trehub, S. E. (2003b). The developmental origins of musicality. *Nature Neuroscience, 6*(7), 669–673.

Trevarthen, C. (1999). Musicality and the intrinsic motive pulse: evidence from human psychobiology and infant communication. *Musicae Scientiae, Special Issue,* 155–215.

Trevarthen, C. (2002). Origins of musical identity: Evidence from infancy for musical social awareness. In R. A. R. MacDonald, D. Hargreaves, & D. Miell (Eds.), *Musical Identities* (pp. 21–38). Oxford: Oxford University Press.

Trollinger, V. L. (2003). Relationships between pitch-matching accuracy, speech fundamental frequency, speech range, age and gender in American English-speaking preschool children. *Journal of Research in Music Education, 51*(1), 78–94.

Unyk, A. M., Trehub, S. E., Trainor, L. J., & Schellenberg, E. G. (1992). Lullabies and simplicity: A cross-cultural perspective. *Psychology of Music, 20*(1), 15–28.

Uvnäs-Moberg, K. (1997). Physiological and endocrine effects of social contact. In C. S. Carter, I. I. Lederhendler & B. Kirkpatrick (Eds.), *The integrative neurobiology of affiliation* (Vol. 807, pp. 146–163). New York: Annals of the New York Academy of Sciences.

Van Lancker, D. (1997). Rags to riches: Our increasing appreciation of cognitive and communicative abilities of the human right cerebral hemisphere. *Brain and Language, 57*(1), 1–11.

Vihman, M. M. (1996). *Phonological development.* Oxford: Blackwell.

Walker, A. R. (1985). Mental imagery and musical concepts: Some evidence from the congenitally blind. *Bulletin of the Council for Research in Music Education, 85,* 229–237.

Ward, W. D. (1999). Absolute pitch. In D. Deutsch (Ed.), *The Psychology of Music* (2nd Ed., pp. 265–298). London: Academic Press.

Welch, G. F. (1986). A developmental view of children's singing. *British Journal of Music Education, 3*(3), 295–303.

Welch, G. F. (1991). Visual metaphors for sound: a study of mental imagery, language and pitch perception in the congenitally blind. *Canadian Journal of Research in Music Education. 33,* 215–222.

Welch, G. F. (1998). Early childhood musical development. *Research Studies in Music Education, 11,* 27–41

Welch, G. F. (2000a). The developing voice. In L. Thurman & G. F. Welch (Eds.), *Bodymind and voice: Foundations of voice education* (Rev. ed., pp. 704–717). Iowa: National Center for Voice and Speech.

Welch, G. F. (2000b). Singing development in early childhood: the effects of culture and education on the realisation of potential. In P. J. White (Ed.), *Child voice* (pp. 27–44). Stockholm: Royal Institute of Technology.

Welch, G. F. (2001). *The misunderstanding of music.* London: Institute of Education.

Welch, G. F. (2002). Early childhood musical development. In L. Bresler & C. Marme Thompson (Eds.), *The arts in children's lives: Context, culture and curriculum* (pp. 113–128). Dordrecht: Kluwer Academic Publishers.

Welch, G. F. (2005). Singing as communication. In D. Miell, R. MacDonald, & D. Hargreaves (Eds.), *Musical Communication* (pp. 239–259). New York: Oxford University Press.

Welch, G. F., & Adams, P. (2003). *How is music learning celebrated and developed?* Southwell, UK: British Educational Research Association. [see http://www.bera.ac.uk/publications/pureviews.php for downloadable electronic version]

Welch, G. F., & Hallam, S. (Eds.). (2004). Mapping music education research: International perspectives. [Special Issue]. *Psychology of Music, 32*(2).

Welch, G. F., & Howard, D. (2002). Gendered voice in the cathedral choir. *Psychology of Music, 30*(1), 102–120.

Welch, G. F., Ockelford, A., & Zimmerman, S-A. (2001). *The provision of music in special education (PROMISE).* London: University of London Institute of Education/Royal National Institute of the Blind.

Welch, G. F., Sergeant, D. C., & White, P. (1996). The singing competences of five-year-old developing singers. *Bulletin of the Council for Research in Music Education, 127,* 155–162.

Welch, G. F., Sergeant, D. C., & White, P. (1997). Age, sex and vocal task as factors in singing "in-tune" during the first years of schooling. *Bulletin of the Council for Research in Music Education, 133,* 153–160.

Welch, G. F., Sergeant, D. C., & White, P. (1998). The role of linguistic dominance in the acquisition of song. *Research Studies in Music Education, 10,* 67–74.

Werker, J. F., & McLeod, P. J. (1989). Infant preferences for both male and female infant-directed talk: A developmental study of attentional and affective responsiveness. *Canadian Journal of Psychology, 43,* 230–246.

Whiteman, P. (2001). *How the bananas got their pyjamas: A study of the metamorphosis of preschoolers' spontaneous singing as viewed through Vygotsky's Zone of Proximal Development.* Unpublished Ph.D. thesis, University of New South Wales, Australia.

Whiting, B. B., & Edwards, C. P. (1988). *Children in different worlds.* Cambridge, MA: Harvard University Press.

Woodward, S. C., Fresen, J., Harrison, V. C., & Coley, N. (1996, July). *The birth of musical language.* Paper presented at the 7th International Seminar of the ISME Early Childhood Commission, Winchester, UK.

Young, S. (1995). Listening to the music of early childhood. *British Journal of Music Education, 12*(1), 51–58.

Young, S. (1999). Just making a noise? Reconceptualising the music-making of three- and four-year-olds in a nursery context. *Early Childhood Connections: Journal of Music and Movement-based Learning, 5*(1), 14–22.

Young, S. (2000). *Young children's spontaneous instrumental music-making in nursery settings.* Unpublished Ph.D. thesis, University of Surrey Roehampton.

Young, S. (2002). Young children's spontaneous vocalisations in free play: Observations of two- to three-year-olds in a day care setting.

Bulletin of the Council for Research in Music Education, 152, 43–53.

Young, S. Time-space structuring in spontaneous play on educational percussion instruments among three- and four-year-olds. *British Journal of Music Education, 20*(1), 45–59.

Young, S. (2004). The interpersonal dimension: A potential source of musical creativity for young children? *Musicae Scientiae: Journal of the European Society of the Cognitive Sciences of Music, VIII–1.*

Young, S., & Glover, J. (1998). *Music in the early years.* London: Falmer Press.

Zatorre, R. J., Evans, A. C., Meyer, E., & Gjedde, A. (1992). Lateralisation of phonetic and pitch discrimination in speech processing. *Science, 256*(5058), 846–849.

Zatorre, R. J., & Peretz, I. (Eds.). (2001). *The biological foundations of music* (Vol. 930). New York: Annals of the New York Academy of Sciences.

Zatorre, R. J., Perry, D. W., Beckett, C. A., Westbury, C. T., & Evans, A. C. (1998). Functional anatomy of musical processing in listeners with absolute pitch and relative pitch. *Proceedings of the National Academy of Sciences, 95,* 3172–3177.

·15·

PRETEND PLAY

Robert D. Kavanaugh
Williams College

The study of pretend play has a long history in psychology. As early as the 1920s, scholarly treatises on child development included the topic of pretend play, although typically without empirical support (Fein, 1981). Following this initial interest, pretend play remained dormant in the psychological literature until roughly 1950, when personality theorists, eager to test elements of psychoanalytic theory as they applied to children (e.g., sibling rivalry, aggression), revived research on pretend play (Fein, 1981). Interest in the emotional and clinical features of play continues today (cf. Slade & Wolf, 1994), including the psychoanalytic hypothesis that play may reveal unconscious motives kept from awareness to protect the child from feelings of anxiety (Scarlett, 1994).

For many developmental psychologists, however, research on pretense has roots that lead inexorably to the publication of Piaget's (1946/1962) seminal work, *Play, Dreams, and Imitation*. In that book, Piaget identified the early exemplars of pretend actions, often drawing on observations of his own children at play. He also established an important theoretical link between pretense and the child's developing symbol systems (e.g., language). Piaget focused on the pretend actions children produced during solitary or isolate play. Embedded in that choice were two key decisions: (a) to look at the production of pretend actions as opposed to the comprehension of the pretend actions of others, and (b) to examine pretense during solitary play as opposed to pretense that unfolds in social situations, that is, play with one or more partners. Both decisions had an enormous impact on the field. Indeed, the influence of Piaget's work is almost impossible to overstate even more than 50 years after the publication of *Play, Dreams, and Imitation*. Piaget's insights set the stage for subsequent research on children's production of pretend actions (e.g., Nicolich, 1977), established a link between pretend play and the child's developing language (e.g., McCune, 1995), and prefigured the potential importance of pretense for more advanced forms of cognition (Leslie, 1987; Harris, 2000).

In this chapter, I review research on the development of children's capacity for pretense, concentrating on the preschool years (prior to age 6 years) when children are known to be deeply involved in pretending. My goal is to consider the critical features of pretense, to assess the relationship between involvement in pretense during the toddler period and the later understanding of mental states, and to review the personal and educational implications of pretend play. I begin with a brief overview of the database of empirical studies of pretend play.

IDENTIFYING PRETEND PLAY

Although there is no single definition of pretense, there is considerable agreement that pretend actions are nonliteral and simulative (Fein, 1981). They involve projecting an idea (e.g., serving tea) on to an actual situation (e.g., play partner's empty cup) (Lillard, 2001b). Pretenders engage in "acting as if" (Fein, 1981; Leslie, 1987), or what Garvey (1977) referred to as the "voluntary transformation of the here and now, the you and me" (p. 82).

Because pretend actions involve deliberate distortions, pretenders must know the difference between the actual state of affairs and the nonactual situations they are enacting (Lillard, 2001a). In this respect, Leslie (1987) noted an important distinction between "acting as if" and "acting in error." I am pretending when I act as if a long and narrow piece of clay is a snake. I may pretend that my "snake" is slithering along the ground, or preparing to pounce on unsuspecting prey, but I remain cognizant that what I have in my hand is actually a piece of clay. The situation is quite different, however, if unexpectedly I come on this same piece of clay and momentarily withdraw in fear believing that I have encountered an actual snake. Clearly, only the first instance qualifies as pretense. It involves what McCune-Nicolich (1981) called "double knowledge"—knowledge of both the real and imagined properties of objects. In sum, there is reasonable consensus about what pretenders know and do as well as what constitutes a pretend act. A pretender is someone who understands the reality of a current situation, has an idea about a different reality, and then deliberately creates the counterfactual situation. Pretend acts are nonliteral and transformative. They constitute involvement in a projected reality as distinct from an actual situation.

Consensus on a conceptual definition, of course, is only part of the task that researchers face. There is the additional problem of identifying the appropriate operational criteria for studying pretense, a problem that is particularly challenging when observing young children at play. A good deal of research on pretend play involves children under the age of 2 years. Before age 2, actions that we might characterize as pretend typically come from behaviors that are part of the child's everyday repertoire. For example, during the course of playing with objects, a child might "sip" from an empty cup, or push a toy car along the floor while saying "brrrmm." If we adopt a skeptical attitude (Huttenlocher & Higgins, 1978), how certain can we be that these are genuine pretend actions? Several researchers have warned that often these simple behaviors are "functional" rather than pretend acts (Leslie, 1987; Ungerer & Sigman, 1981). In pushing a toy car across the floor, for example, the child may demonstrate knowledge of the conventional use of a car but not be engaged in a transformative act of pretense.

Leslie (1987) argued that three types of action distinguish genuine pretend acts from functional play: object substitutions, attribution of make-believe properties, and imaginary objects. As the term implies, pretend play with object substitution involves using one object as a pretend surrogate for another (e.g., child enacts "washing" by using a round block as though it were a bar of soap). Attribution of make-believe properties involves play in which the child imagines something nonexistent in her immediate surrounds (e.g., child uses a cloth to wipe pretend "dirt" from the floor). Imaginary object play involves make-believe actions that the child depicts or mimes (e.g., child uses hands to simulate the action of eating with a spoon). In effect, Leslie's (1987) adopted a "conservative" approach to classifying actions as pretend. By his argument, a child who pushes a toy car across a floor, even with accompanying sound effects, may still be engaged in functional play. This child has not demonstrated unequivocally that she possesses what Lillard (2001a) called the idea of pretending—a mental representation that guides imagined actions.

One advantage of Leslie's (1987) criteria is that they provide a way distinguish to clearly between functional or conventional object play and pretend play with objects. Other researchers also have felt compelled to distinguish between these two types of play, although their criteria are not identical to Leslie's. For example, McCune (1995) identified five levels of play that range from presymbolic (functional) to advanced symbolic (pretend). Similarly, Bornstein and his colleagues differentiated "exploratory" from "symbolic play." The former generally included the functional use of objects, whereas the latter consisted of actions that met some although not all of Leslie's conditions for pretense (Bornstein, Haynes, O'Reilly, & Painter, 1996).

Although different investigators have used somewhat varying operational criteria to identify pretend acts there is general agreement that pretend play must be distinguished from functional or sensorimotor actions as well as reasonable consensus on how to make such a distinction. Even Piaget (1946/1962), who eschewed formal criteria to identify pretend actions, nonetheless recognized the importance of noting context (e.g., "sleeping" during day time play) as well as telltale actions, such as smiling or laughing, that signaled the child's involvement in the simulated behaviors he referred to as pretense.

CULTURAL VARIATIONS IN PRETEND PLAY

Pretend play begins early in life. Simple but easily recognizable pretend actions appear regularly in 12- to 15-month-olds (Piaget, 1946/1962; Nicolich, 1977; Haight & Miller, 1992, 1993), and have been observed among children living in many different cultures. The early and widespread appearance of pretend actions, even in cultures in which pretend play is not actively encouraged, suggests that the capacity for pretense may be innate (Lillard, 2002). Harris (2000) has speculated about an evolutionary basis for pretense by remarking on the possible fusion of language and imagination at some point in our history. The interlocking of language and imagination could lead to the development of a mind that can reason about possible as well as actual situations, an enormous adaptive advantage for *Homo sapiens* (Harris, 2000).

Although the innateness position is intriguing, the findings from research on pretend play in communities worldwide lend support to a cultural argument as well. Indeed, the two positions are not in opposition. Evolution may provide the biological "push" whereas cultural influences contribute to the shape and form of expressions of pretense and imagination that emerge in a particular community. This argument has merit particularly if we find, as noted later, that cultures differ in the degree to which they encourage and reward pretend play, sanction the involvement of parents and siblings in pretense, and utilize pretend play and imagination in the instruction of the young.

Cross-cultural research has revealed differences in the frequency of children's pretend play (Farver, 1993; Göncü, Tuermer, Jain, & Johnson, 1999), the make-believe themes that children enact (Farver, 1999; Haight, Wang, Fung, Williams, & Mintz, 1999), and the degree and type of parental involvement in children's pretense (Haight, Wang, Fung, Williams, & Mintz, 1999; Gaskins, 1996; Taylor & Carlson, 2000). For example, Göncü and his colleagues found that American and Turkish toddlers (1- to 2-year-olds) engaged in more pretend play with their caregivers than did Indian and Guatemalan toddlers, and that pretend play themes in the two non-Western communities (Turkey, India) differed notably from the play themes often observed in research on Western communities (Göncü, Tuermer, Jain, & Johnson, 1999). Similarly, Korean children's pretend play tended to center on family themes (Farver, 1999), whereas fantasy themes predominate in American children's pretense (Haight et al., 1999).

Differences in the frequency and type of pretend play appear to have a direct relationship to parental and community values. In their interactions with children, parents may encourage certain types of pretend play or discourage pretending altogether.

Haight and her colleagues found that although both American and Chinese (Taiwanese) parents initiated pretend play episodes with their children, American parents tended to involve the children in fantasy themes, whereas Chinese parents used pretend play to teach children about proper conduct (Haight et al., 1999). Gaskins (1996) reported that in the Mayan culture she observed adults viewed participation in children's pretend play as neither particularly appropriate nor central to children's development. In the United States, the Mennonites hold strong negative opinions about pretend play, viewing it largely as wasteful of children's time and, consequently, offering little encouragement to children to engage in pretend activities (Taylor & Carlson, 2000).

Cultural differences are worth emphasizing not only because they broaden our view of the different contexts in which pretend play unfolds but also because they highlight the limitations in generalizing from the existing database, much of which consists disproportionately of studies of North American and European children, primarily Caucasian, engaged in play with their mothers, either at home or in laboratory playroom settings. It also is worth noting that studies of the pretend actions that children produce, in contrast to research on children's understanding of other people's pretend actions, dominate the existing database. The importance of this latter point is that with increasing frequency investigators have focused on children's involvement in shared pretense, that is, pretend play in which two or more play partners construct joint themes. Clearly, the *sine qua non* of shared pretending is the ability to understand the pretend overtures of a play partner and to respond to those overtures in collaborative fashion. This makes both producing pretend actions *and* understanding the make-believe overtures of others an important part of the child's overall capacity for pretense.

GENERATING PRETEND ACTIONS

Pretend play begins during the early part of the second year often with brief "self-referenced" actions. Piaget's observations of his own children provide some of the classic examples of self-referenced pretend acts. For example, Piaget (1946/1962) made the following observation of his daughter, Jacqueline, at 15 months (p. 96):

J. saw a cloth whose fringed edges vaguely recalled those of a pillow; she seized it, held a fold of it in her right hand, sucked the thumb of the same hand, and lay down on her side, laughing hard. She kept her eyes open, but blinked them from time to time as if she were alluding to closed eyes. (p. 96)

Subsequent research confirmed Piaget's observations that these simple acts of pretense begin somewhere around 12 to 15 months (Nicholich, 1977). By 18 to 24 months, two important changes occur among the populations where pretend play is valued and encouraged. One is a striking increase in the frequency of pretend play; the other is a lessening of solitary pretend play with a concomitant increase in pretending that is more social in nature. By age 2 years, pretend play often involves interactions with play partners, usually familiar adults or siblings/peers, as

well as "replica" objects, such as dolls and toy animals. The pretend acts of 2-year-olds tend to be oriented toward others, for example, a child "pours" tea for her mother or "feeds" a doll make-believe cereal from an empty bowl (Fein, 1981).

Children whose pretend play involves replica objects typically show a further transition toward the middle of the third year (around age $2^1/_2$ years) when they begin to ascribe make-believe intentions to these objects. For example, a child might pretend that a baby doll placed on a bed is "sleeping" or that a mother doll is "scolding" a "naughty" baby. This type of attribution of an imagined animate state to an inanimate object has been called "passive" agency to distinguish it from "active" or independent agency in which children pretend that replica toys can carry out their own make-believe actions, for example, the child uses a mother doll to pretend to give juice to a baby doll (Bretherton, O'Connell, Shore, & Bates, 1984; Fenson, 1984; Watson & Fischer, 1977; Wolf, Rygh, & Altshuler, 1984). Once children begin to incorporate independent agency into their pretend play the scenarios they create become increasingly complex. By age 4, investigators have observed children assigning make-believe thoughts and feelings to dolls, stuffed animals, and other replica objects, for example, a child proclaims that a doll feels "sad" or is "hurt" (Wolf et al., 1984). By age 3, and even earlier among siblings and convivial peers (Dunn & Dale, 1984), children also engage in pretend play by acting out complementary roles (e.g., doctor-patient or bus driver-passenger). Role-play is a highly intricate form of social interaction that may well have implications for mental state awareness, as I note later in this chapter. However, because role-play involves understanding the pretend intention of others I turn first to the question of how children accomplish that skill.

UNDERSTANDING PRETEND ACTIONS

Although we often think of pretense as performative or enacted, it is not solely about the behaviors that children (or adults) produce. Pretense can also refer to the ability to comprehend the make-believe actions of others. Furthermore, as noted earlier, comprehension is a crucial component of joint or shared pretend play. Children engage in shared pretend play with primary caregivers, siblings and peers beginning as early as 2 years (DeLoache & Plaetzer, 1985; Dunn & Dale 1984; Haight & Miller, 1993; Howes, Unger, & Seidner, 1989; Kavanaugh, Whittington, & Cerbone, 1983; Miller & Garvey, 1984). Typically, researchers observe a dyad consisting of a young child and a more experienced play partner, with the data collection taking place in the child's home or in a laboratory playroom, often with a standard set of toys provided by the investigator. The make-believe scenarios that arise from these settings frequently involve domestic themes that parallel the child's real-world experiences. In the North American and European samples that dominate the literature, themes of eating, drinking, cleaning, and vehicle use (e.g., flying in a plane) are common. A make-believe tea party is an illustration of a fairly common pretend theme. For example, a parent might pick up an empty teapot, pretend to "pour" tea into a cup, and then hand the empty cup to the child. Such an action highlights the crucial component of pretense comprehension.

The burden of the dialogue of make-believe now shifts to the child. Failure to comprehend the parent's pretend action may disrupt or even terminate an emerging shared pretend theme.

The largest number of studies of shared pretend play involve toddlers (2-year-olds) and their mothers. Researchers have noted that in the course of playing with their children mothers employ a number of specific "strategies" that assist and support child involvement in shared pretend themes. These include prompts and explicit directions (Miller & Garvey, 1984; Haight & Miller, 1993), descriptions of the child's pretense (Kavanaugh et al., 1983), demonstrations and descriptions of their own pretend gestures and actions (O'Connell & Bretherton, 1984; Kavanaugh & Harris, 1991), as well as supportive commentary and "how to" suggestions and expansions on child pretend utterances (Kavanaugh et al., 1983; Haight & Miller, 1993).

To evaluate the efficacy of shared pretend play with mothers, investigators have contrasted the level of pretense children achieve during joint play with their mothers with the levels they attain when playing alone. These studies have shown consistently that maternal involvement typically increases the duration (Slade, 1987; Fiese, 1990; Haight & Miller, 1992), complexity (Slade, 1987), and diversity (O'Connell & Bretherton, 1984) of children's pretend play. On rare occasions, however, mothers' intrusive questions or mistimed directions have been found to interfere with or derail children's pretend themes (Fiese, 1990).

What do we know of children's ability to participate in shared pretense? To illustrate what is involved for the young child, I return to the tea party scenario, a familiar staple of mother-child pretend play in North American samples. A common variant of this scenario has the mother "making" and "pouring" make-believe tea from an empty tea pot into the child's empty tea cup. To make sense of this situation, the child must first recognize the mother's implied stipulation—this is pretense. The mother may assist the child by commenting on her own pretend actions (e.g., "I'm making some tea for us") or by making a request of the child ("Would you like some tea?"). The child must accept the mother's *de facto* invitation to engage in pretense and then substitute an imagined alternative—mother is "pouring" make-believe tea into a cup—for the child's everyday understanding that when someone lifts and tips a tea pot over a container real liquid will flow into the container (Harris & Kavanaugh, 1993). In this example, the child might continue the make-believe theme by holding out a cup so that the parent can "pour" the imaginary tea, or the child might answer the parent's question ("Would you like some tea?") in a manner that implies an understanding of the pretend theme ("Want tea").

It is easy to underestimate the social-cognitive demands that these seemingly simple scenarios place on young children. In naturalistic studies, children under 2 years frequently make no response to their mother's pretend overtures, thereby requiring the mother either to repeat the overture or to change to a different play theme (Kavanaugh et al, 1983). Admittedly, no response is ambiguous—perhaps the child is disinterested in the mother's play theme—but there is additional evidence that points to potential pretense-reality confusions when children are engaged in play with adults. Lillard (2002) reported signs of confusion when children observed their mothers pretending to eat a snack. Even more strikingly, DeLoache and Plaetzer (1985) found that roughly 25% of the child participants in a mother-child tea party episode showed some form of the pretend-reality confusion as demonstrated vividly by a 30-month-old who appeared to search for real liquid after his mother told him to wipe up the "tea" that had "spilled" from his overturned empty tea cup.

A different approach to the study of young children's understanding of pretend episodes involves constructing experimental analogues of mother-child play. Studies such as these require children to demonstrate pretense comprehension by completing a make-believe episode initiated by an experimenter. For example, an experimenter might pretend to pour make-believe tea over the head of one of two identical toy pigs and then ask a child to use a nearby cloth to "dry" the pig that is all "wet" (Harris & Kavanaugh, 1993, Experiment 5). By age $2^1/_2$, children begin to do quite well on this task but children under 2 years (mean age of 20 months) perform rather poorly, that is, they "dry" the wrong pig, "dry" both pigs, or make no response at all. A number of variations on this design, some more taxing than others, have revealed that between ages 2 and 3 years children make substantial gains in their ability to understand the pretend actions of others. They are able to watch a pretend action (e.g., experimenter makes pig "muddy" by rolling it across brown paper) and then to point to a picture that correctly depicts the make-believe outcome (e.g., picture of a pig with brown spots on it) (Kavanaugh & Harris, 1994), to describe the experimenter's pretend actions by using nonliteral language (e.g., the child says the pig rolled across the brown paper "is all muddy") (Harris & Kavanaugh, 1993, Experiments 6 & 7), and even to make complex deductions about a series of pretend actions, such as understanding that a previously full bowl of cereal is now "empty" after an experimenter pretends to "eat" all the cereal in the bowl (Walker-Andrews & Harris, 1993).

In sum, children make important strides in understanding other people's pretend intentions and actions during the first 3 years. Pretense comprehension is clearly a crucial component of engaging with others in jointly constructed play scenarios. However, beyond the enjoyment children find in shared pretense, is there any particular cognitive or social value to this type of play? One possibility is that shared pretend play, and in particular a version of it known as role-play, might encourage children to reflect on their own thoughts as well as the thoughts of their play partner. Role-play deserves special consideration because of its potential link to important gains in understanding the mental states of others (Harris, 2000).

ROLE-PLAY

Role-play is about acting or more specifically impersonating. Typically, it is the province of 3- to 5-year-olds but has been observed in 2-year-olds as well (Dunn, 1991; First, 1994). Role-play episodes involve two or more people enacting complementary roles, such as mother and baby, driver and passenger, or doctor and patient. Children may discuss or negotiate beforehand who will play which role, and turn taking (switching roles) is also common. Children also may supplement their actions with intonations (e.g., high pitched voice of mother speaking to baby) and gestures (e.g., cradling baby) that befit the character they are impersonating. The apparent ease with which preschool children engage in role-play should not lead us to underestimate its complexity. Effective role-play places nontrivial social-cognitive demands on the child that involve an understanding of mutuality and reciprocity. For a role-play episode to unfold fully and richly, the two players must be like-minded in purpose and complementary in words and actions. As Harris (2000) notes, in role-play children do not follow a prescribed script by simply mimicking what they have observed others do. Rather, they create their own dramas and then update and edit the actions and words of their characters as the episode unfolds.

Before turning to the question of how role-play may influence children's understanding of other people's cognitions and emotions, I should note the argument that having an imaginary companions is a form of role-play (Harris, 2000). In classic form, an imaginary companion is an invisible character, often named and embued with highly specific personal characteristics, whom children become intensely involved with for a substantial period of time (Svendsen, 1934). In addition to the invisible form, recent studies have revealed two other types of imaginary companion (Gleason, Sebanc, & Hartup, 2000; Taylor, 1999; Carlson & Taylor, in press). One type involves projecting the identity of an imaginary companion onto a favored doll, who then is invested with the same personal characteristics of the classic invisible companions. The other type is found among children, primarily boys, who spend long periods of time acting as if they were a particular character (e.g., wearing clothing that identifies the character, insisting on being called by the name of the character).

Children who develop imaginary companions are involved in sustained episodes of role play (Harris, 2000). They become deeply involved with the personal characteristics of their imaginary companions and their make-believe lives. Indeed involvement with imaginary companions is so intense that at one time they were viewed as a possible sign of emotional disturbance in children (Svendsen, 1934). However, more recent research has revealed that although some children with emotional problems do have imaginary companions many normally developing children also create imaginary friends. In fact, depending on the defining criteria, somewhere between 50 and 65% of normally developing children have imaginary companions for a substantial period of their childhood years (Taylor, 1999). Moreover, there are many positive correlates of having an imaginary companion including greater social skills as well as the ability to better understand the thought and beliefs of others (Taylor & Carlson, 1997).

MENTAL STATES

One of the accomplishments of the early childhood years is an understanding that unobserved mental states—thoughts, beliefs, and desires—are what motivate people to behave the way they do. Adults recognize that mental states form the unseen foundation of everyday behavior. People do not behave mindlessly. They act in particular ways because of the thoughts they entertain, the beliefs they hold, or the outcomes they desire. Understanding the role of mental states in everyday life, often

referred to as a theory of mind, is a developmental phenomenon that unfolds gradually. During the preschool years, children make substantial progress in understanding that people have mental states, that mental states motivate people to act the way they do, and that different people may hold contradictory mental states (Perner, 1991).

Children's progress in understanding mental states is apparent in their everyday conversations (Bartsch & Wellman, 1995) as well as in their response to structured assessments known as false belief tasks. A false belief task requires children to distinguish between their beliefs and the beliefs of others. In a well known version, a child is introduced to two dolls and shown a small diorama, in which an experimenter enacts a brief scenario. For example, a piece of candy belonging to one of the dolls is placed in a drawer. After that doll departs the scene (so that it can no longer witness what takes place), a second doll moves the candy from the drawer to a cupboard. The experimenter then returns the first doll to the scene and asks the child where that doll will search for the candy. To answer the question correctly, the child must understand that the first doll now holds a mistaken belief about the location of the candy. Crucially, children must distinguish between what they know to be true (candy is now in the cupboard) and what the unknowing first doll believes to be true (candy is in the drawer where it was left). Children's performance on false belief tasks improves considerably between the ages of 3 and 5, with a notable improvement typically occurring sometime after age 4 (Wellman, Cross, & Watson, 2001).

A question of interest to many investigators is what factors influence the development of mental states, in particular children's understanding of false beliefs. One possibility is that children's experience with siblings, particularly older siblings, has a positive effect on their ability to understand mental states. Support for this hypothesis comes from research showing a positive relationship between number of siblings and performance on false belief tasks (Perner, Ruffman, and Leekam, 1994). Subsequent research qualified this result by noting that it is children with older siblings who have the greatest advantage on false beliefs tasks (Ruffman, Perner, Naito, Parkin, & Clements, 1998; Youngblade & Dunn, 1995). However, there is also evidence that time spent with adults leads to improved performance on false belief tasks (Lewis, Freeman, Kryiakidou, Maridaki-Kassotaki, & Berridge, 1996). It is possible, then, that different types of social-interaction, rather than experience with particular people, aids children's understanding of false belief (Wellman, 2002). Consistent with this interpretation are the results of Dunn and her colleagues who found that children who participate more in family discussions about emotions demonstrate a precocious understanding of mental states (Dunn, Brown, & Beardsall, 1991), and that children's tendency to talk about emotions at age 3 was associated with their ability to take another person's perspective some 4 years later.

ROLE-PLAY AND MENTAL STATES

Taken as a whole, the research above suggests that children profit both socially and intellectually from discussions of thoughts and feelings. These discussions appear to alert children to the possibility that mental states underlie overt behavior and, importantly, to the further possibility that other people may hold beliefs that differ from their own. To the extent that this is true, the social interactions inherent in role-play—negotiating roles, taking turns with different roles, and responding to the dialogue of the partner—become an excellent candidate for mental state development. In fact, a number of investigators have found a positive relationship between role play and comprehension of the mental states of others (Astington & Jenkins 1995; Connoly & Doyle, 1984; Lalonde & Chandler, 1995; Schwebel, Rosen, & Singer, 1999; Taylor & Carlson, 1997; Youngblade & Dunn, 1995).

In an early study supporting such a relationship, Connolly and Doyle (1984) found that among a group of young children observed in a day care setting those who engaged in more complex joint pretend play more accurately identified the emotions of others in an independent assessment of role taking ability. Subsequent investigations have both corroborated and strengthened this finding by adding important details. Youngblade and Dunn (1995) observed the same children at two ages during the preschool period, 33 and 40 months. At 33 months the authors observed children interacting at home with their mothers and older siblings, and noted their involvement in pretend play, and then at 40 months they assessed children's understanding of false belief. Only one pretend play measure, role enactment, correlated significantly with children's subsequent performance on false belief tasks. In two other studies, investigators have observed a positive association between having an imaginary companion and better performance on theory of mind tasks (Lalonde & Chandler, 1995; Taylor & Carslon, 1997). For example, Taylor and Carlson (1997) interviewed children between $3^1/_2$ and $4^1/_2$ to identify those who had an imaginary companion of either the classical (invisible) type or of the impersonator variety. Compared to children who did not have an imaginary companion, those who had companions were better able to distinguish between their beliefs and the beliefs of others.

Several investigations have strengthened the role-play–mental-state development connection further by noting the highly specific nature of the relationship, and by controlling for possible confounding variables such as verbal fluency and social skills. In two different studies, among a variety of measures of children's involvement in pretense only role-play was related to success on theory of mind tasks (Astington & Jenkins 1995; Schwebel, Rosen, & Singer, 1999). In one instance, investigators observed children playing in small groups and noted that discussions about make-believe games (e.g., who would be involved in the play) showed no relationship to performance on false belief tasks whereas actual engagement in role-play did show a positive relationship (Astington & Jenkins, 1995). In the other, researchers found that role-play, but not solitary pretend play, bore a strong relationship to 3- to 5-year old's performance on theory of mind tasks Schwebel et al (1999). Importantly, in both studies the role play-false belief relationship held even after controlling for age and verbal abilities. Likewise, Lalonde and Chandler (1995) reported that another potential confounding variable, good social skills (e.g., playing well with others),

showed no relationship to performance on a variety of false belief measures

Among the reasons that role-play might assist children in the appreciation of the inner world of mental states, particularly the thoughts and feelings of others, two possibilities stand out. One is that role-play is an exercise in perspective taking. By definition, role-play forces children to appreciate what someone else is doing. The effective role-player takes account of the actions of the partner and responds appropriately. Without an understanding of the play partner's view of the world the role play episodes cease to be productive. Even more fundamentally, however, it is possible to view role play as a process of simulation by which children imagine themselves in a particular situation, assume the cognitive-emotional states of the characters they are portraying, and then act accordingly (Harris, 2000). The act of imagining the world as another person sees it would be a profoundly important step in children's understanding of the role of thoughts, beliefs, and emotions in everyday life.

IMPLICATIONS AND CONCLUSIONS

In considering the educational implications of research on pretend play, two distinct areas of inquiry are worth considering. The more obvious of these is early childhood education. There has been great deal of interest among early childhood educators in play generally conceived, and pretend play more specifically, often referencing Vygotsky's notion of advances in social/intellectual development through interactions with others (e.g., zone of proximal development). However, although less obvious, and certainly not as well studied, it is also possible to consider the long-term implications of involvement in pretend play and the life of the imagination more broadly.

Pretend Play and Literacy

One area of interest for early childhood educators is the intersection of pretend play and language and literacy skills. Pretend play is a classic example of going beyond the immediate situation to what Garvey called the "voluntary transformation of the here and now, the you and me" (1977, p. 82). Although language is not required to produce pretend actions (e.g., consider the child who picks up a banana and silently "plays it" as though it were a saxophone), over time children rely on language to enrich their make-believe play, particularly shared play with parents, sibling/peers, and teachers.

What are the specific language and literary skills associated with pretend play? First, as Roskos and Newman (1998) note, there is evidence that the symbolic transformations involved in early pretend play (e.g., at age 3 years) correlate positively with the later development of children's reading and writing. As with all correlational data, causal interpretations are not possible. Still, an approximate 2-year cross-time relationship between pretend play and language and reading abilities establishes the hypothesis that the symbolic transformations involved in early pretending may contribute meaningfully to children's literary development. Indeed, research on centers found in preschool and day care settings confirms that children who are involved with activities that emphasize literacy routines make important advances in understanding printed materials (Neuman & Roskos, 1992).

Second, among a wide range of childhood activities and experiences, pretend play is a likely candidate to enhance children's narrative skills. As noted earlier, preschool children often develop themes, characters, and structured scenarios during shared pretend play. In the view of several authors, there is an implicit narrative structure to the pretend play of young children that bears a striking relationship to their storytelling and story comprehension skill (Eckler & Weininger, 1989; Guttman & Fredickson, 1985; Kavanaugh & Engel, 1998; Sachs, Goldman, & Chaille, 1985). Eckler and Weininger (1989), for example, noted that the pretend play of roughly three quarters of their sample of 4- to 8-year old children conformed to a story grammar analysis that included an initiating event, a desired goal for a protagonist, and an outcome resolution.

There is evidence, then, that (a) the skills involved in early pretend play are associated with the later development of the building blocks of literacy—reading and writing and (b) that pretend play provides children with the opportunity to create sequences and scenarios that parallel the plot planning and story grammar crucial to the full blown narrative skills that emerge during the elementary years. In short, pretend play appears to offer an early opportunity to gain mastery of the roles, scripts, and layered scenarios—effectively to learn to use the tools—associated with narrative development and literacy more broadly

Pretend Play and Social-Cognitive Development

There is both theoretical and empirical support for the claim that pretend play is important to children's social-cognitive development. At the theoretical level, shared pretend play conforms to Vygotsky's emphasis on the importance of collaborative constructions in advancing children's learning and provides one example of the "zone of proximal development" (Vygotsky, 1978). Research with preschoolers also has shown that pretend play is an excellent forum to practice communicative intent both by making known your own intentions and by understanding/responding to the intention of others (Göncü, 1993).

One way to evaluate the role of pretend play in children's social-cognitive development is to consider training studies designed to boost children's perspective taking and problem solving skills. There is a well-established literature on this question dating back to Smilansky's (1968) work with economically disadvantaged Israeli preschool children. Smilansky (1968) found that infrequent and poorer quality sociodramatic (role) play was common among these children, but that they could be trained to engage in robust role-play. Smilansky's (1968) research inspired a number of subsequent studies that demonstrated that training in sociodramatic (Rosen, 1974; Burns & Brainerd, 1979) and fantasy play (e.g., children encouraged to dramatize folk tales such as "Little Red Riding Hood") (Saltz & Johnson, 1974) led to improvements on intelligence, problem solving, and affective perspective taking tasks.

Pretend Play and Adult Development

The actor Michael J. Fox once responded to a question about how he practiced his craft by noting that it was easy—quite similar, he observed, to playing cowboys and Indians when he was 4 years old. No doubt he spoke lightheartedly, yet Fox's succinct answer is still intriguing. Could there be a relationship between children's engagement in pretense, particularly shared pretending that incorporates role-play, and adult involvement in the arts? Put somewhat differently, beyond the early childhood years what is the fate of pretend play?

One possibility is that pretend play declines in middle childhood, as Piaget believed, or even disappears altogether. However, an opposing view is that pretend play may go underground during the school years but emerges again in adulthood as the basis for the appreciation of art and literature (Currie, 1990; Walton, 1990). This developmental perspective on pretense has strong theoretical support. For example, in his philosophical analysis of the arts, Currie (1990) noted parallels between engagement in childhood make-believe and the appreciation of fiction in adulthood. Both the reader of fiction and the participant in pretend games become involved, albeit temporarily, with what Currie called "fictional truths." Indeed, the parallel was so apparent to Currie (1990) that he contended that the reader of fiction "is invited by the author to engage in a game of make-believe" (p. 70). Likewise, Walton (1990) saw continuity between participation in childhood make-believe activities and adult appreciation of the visual arts. In Walton's (1990) view, paintings are really elaborate props that invite viewers to embrace the depicted scene and to imagine their own involvement with what the artist has portrayed.

Harris (2000) extended this line of argument even further by reviewing studies of text processing which demonstrate that adult readers become absorbed in a text to the point of literally adopting the viewpoint of a protagonist. He argued that the text processing literature demonstrates convincingly that readers place themselves along side the protagonist as the narrative unfolds (Harris, 2000). The upshot is a mental process that allows readers to respond quickly and accurately to questions about what the protagonist sees or experiences from his or her perspective. Rall and Harris (2000), investigating whether young children engage in a similar mental process, found that 3- and 4-year-olds's recall of the key verb of a familiar vignette was more accurate when they responded to questions that were consistent with a protagonist's viewpoint than when they answered questions at odds with that viewpoint. Together with the research on adults, the Rall and Harris (2000) findings suggest that beginning in childhood people are able to use their imagination to view the world from the perspective of others.

What conclusions can we draw from the theoretical and empirical work on pretend play and the appreciation of art and literature? Perhaps the firmest conclusion is that childhood involvement in pretend play is not a developmental cul-de-sac. The capacity for pretending, particularly shared pretend play, appears to assist children in developing an understanding of the mental states—the thoughts, beliefs, and emotions—of other people. Games of make-believe, particularly those that involve role-play, invite children to engage in turn-taking, to plan and negotiate roles, and to create dramatic scripts around those roles. Role-play is a mutually constructed activity that calls for an understanding of different viewpoints and one that that may be related to children's perspective taking and understanding of mental states. Beyond the early childhood years, the parallel between games of make-believe and an abiding appreciation of fiction seems particularly striking and, as noted earlier, draws empirical support from the childhood and adult literatures on text processing.

Nevertheless, it is important to note that as yet we cannot draw causal connections between pretend play and higher mental processes. The studies supporting a pretend play–theory of mind connection, for example, are correlational in nature and so prevent us from determining unequivocally the direction of the relationship. Although involvement in pretense may dispose children to understand the mental states of others, it is not unreasonable to assume the opposite trajectory, namely that a precocious capacity to understand others causes children to be involved in shared pretend play (Lillard, 2001b). Furthermore, as with any correlational relationship it is possible that some underlying variable is the governing principle linking role-play and theory of mind rather than that one causes the other. Perhaps either by virtue of cognitive style and/or personal disposition, some children are more likely than others both to engage frequently in role-play and to perform well on theory of mind tasks (Lillard, 2002). For example, children with a strong interest in people or with an inclination to create stories involving people—children whom Wolf and Gardner (1979) called dramatists—might come to better understand thoughts and motives of others (Lillard, 2002).

At the moment, then, what we have is a strong suggestion, though not conclusive proof, that deep involvement with particular expressions of make-believe may lead to an earlier advancement in understanding mental states, particularly the thoughts and beliefs of others, and may even prime the child for an appreciation of reading. Although this suggestion must take the form of a working hypothesis some implications still follow. There appears to be good reason to encourage shared pretend play among young children. Because many children engage quite readily in shared pretense, encouragement is quite simple and straight forward. It amounts to offering children opportunities for shared pretense, and role-play in particular, by providing space, provisioning play areas with age-appropriate props, and allowing time for unstructured activities. Other expressions of role enactment, such as imaginary companions, develop spontaneously and cannot be encouraged *per se* but neither should they be discouraged. The bottom line, from both a cognitive and social viewpoint, is that within the reasonable limits that most normally developing children impose make-believe play has no known downside and, at least in some forms, has the upside potential of improving perspective taking and deepening children's involvement with reading and literature.

References

Astington, J. W., & Jenkins, J. M. (1995). Theory of mind development and social understanding. *Cognition and Emotion, 9*, 151-165.

Bartsch, K., & Wellman, H. M. (1995). *Children's talk about the mind.* New York: Oxford.

Bornstein, M., Haynes, O. M., O'Reilly, A., & Painter, K. (1996). Solitary and collaborative pretense play in early childhood: Sources of individual variation in the development of representational competence. *Child Development, 67*, 2910-2929.

Bretherton, I., O'Connell, B., Shore, C., & Bates, E. (1984). The effect of contextual variation in symbolic play: Development from 20 to 28 months. In I. Bretherton (Ed.), *Symbolic play: The development of social understanding* (pp. 271-298). New York: Academic Press.

Burns, S. M., & Brainerd, C. J. (1979). Effects of constructive and dramatic play on perspective taking in very young children. *Developmental Psychology, 15*, 512-521.

Carlson, S. M., & Taylor, M. (in press). Imaginary companions and impersonated characters: Sex differences in children's fantasy play. *Merrill-Palmer Quarterly.*

Connoly, J. A., & Doyle, A. (1984). Relation of social fantasy to social competence. *Developmental Psychology, 20*, 797-806.

Currie, G. (1990). *The nature of fiction.* Cambridge, UK: Cambridge University Press.

DeLoache, J. S., & Plaetzner, B. (1985, April). *Tea for two: Joint mother-child pretend play.* Paper presented at the biennial meetings of the Society for Research in Child Development, Toronto.

Dunn, J. (1991). Understanding others: Evidence from naturalistic studies of children. In A. Whiten (Ed.), *Natural theories of mind: Evolution, development and simulation of everyday mindreading* (pp. 51-61). Oxford: Blackwell.

Dunn, J., Brown, J., & Beardsall, L. (1991). Family talk about feeling states and children's later understanding of others' emotions. *Developmental Psychology, 27*, 448-455.

Dunn, J., & Dale, N. (1984). I a Daddy: 2-year-olds' collaboration in joint pretend with sibling and with mother. In I. Bretherton (Ed.), *Symbolic play: The development of social understanding.* (pp. 131-158). New York: Academic Press.

Eckler, J. A., & Weininger, O. (1989). Structural parallels between pretend play and narratives. *Developmental Psychology, 25*, 736-743.

Farver, J. M. (1993). Cultural differences in scaffolding pretend play: A comparison of American and Mexican-American mother-child and sibling-child dyads. In K. MacDonald (Ed.), *Parent-child play: Descriptions and implications* (pp. 349-366). Albany: SUNY Press.

Farver, J. M. (1999). Activity setting analysis: A model for reexamining the role of culture in development. In A. Goncu (Ed.), *Children's engagement in the world: A sociocultural perspective* (pp. 99-127). Cambridge, UK: Cambridge University Press.

Fein, G. G. (1981). Pretend play: An integrative review. *Child Development, 52*, 1095-1118.

Fiese, B. H. (1990). Playful relationships: A contextual analysis of mother-child interaction and symbolic play. *Child Development, 61*, 1648-1656.

First, E. (1994). The leaving game, or I'll play you and you play me: The emergence of dramatic role play in 2-year-olds. In A. Slade and D. P. Wolf (Eds.), *Children at play: Clinical and developmental approaches to meaning and representation* (pp. 48-61). New York: Oxford University Press.

Fenson, L. (1984). Developmental trends for action and speech in pretend play. In I. Bretherton (Ed.), *Symbolic play: The development of social understanding* (pp. 249-270). New York: Academic Press.

Garvey, C. (1977). *Play*. Cambridge, MA: Harvard University Press.

Gaskins, S. (1996). How Mayan parental theories come into play. In S. Harkness & C. Super (Eds.), *Parents' cultural belief systems* (pp. 345-363). New York: Guilford.

Gleason, T. R., Sebanc, A. M., & Hartup, W. W. (2000). Imaginary companions of preschool children. *Developmental Psychology, 36,* 419-428.

Göncü, A. (1993). Development of intersubjectivity in the dyadic play of preschoolers. *Early Childhood Research Quarterly, 8,* 99-116.

Göncü, A., Tuermer, U., Jain, J., & Johnson, D. (1999). Children's play as cultural activity. In A. Goncu (Ed.), *Children's engagement in the world: A sociocultural perspective* (pp. 173-202). Cambridge: Cambridge University Press.

Guttman, M., & Fredericksen, C. H. (1985). Preschool children's narratives: Linking story comprehension, production, and play discourse. In L. Galda & A. Pellegrini (Eds.), *Play, language, and stories: The development of children's literate behavior* (pp. 99-128). Norwood, N.J.: Ablex.

Haight, W. L., & Miller, P. J. (1992). The development of everyday pretend play: A longitudinal study of mothers' participation. *Merrill-Palmer Quarterly, 38,* 331-349.

Haight, W. L., & Miller, P. J. (1993). *Pretending at home: Early development in a sociocultural context.* Albany: SUNY Press.

Haight, W. L., Wang, X.-l, Fung H., Williams, K., & Mintz, J. (1999). Universal, developmental, and variable aspects of young children's play: A cross-cultural comparison of pretending at home. *Child Development, 70,* 1477-1488.

Harris, P. L. (2000). *The work of the imagination.* Oxford: Blackwell.

Harris, P. L., & Kavanaugh, R. D. (1993). Young children's understanding of pretense. *Monographs of the Society for Research in Child Development, 58* (1, Serial No. 231).

Howes, C., Ungerer, O., & Seider, L. B. (1989). Social pretend play in toddlers: Parallels with social play and with solitary pretend. *Child Development, 60,* 77-84.

Huttenlocher, J., & Higgins, E. T. (1978). Issues in the study of symbolic development. In W. Collins (Ed.), *Minnesota Symposium on Child Development* (Vol. 11, pp. 98-140). Hillsdale, NJ: Erlbaum.

Kavanaugh, R. D., & Engel, S. (1998). The development of pretense and narrative in early childhood. In O. N. Saracho & S. Spodek (Eds.), *Multiple perspectives on play in early childhood education* (pp. 80-99). Albany: SUNY Press.

Kavanaugh, R. D., & Harris, P. L. (1991, September). *Comprehension and production of pretend language by two-year-olds.* Paper presented at the annual meeting of the Developmental Section, British Psychological Society, Cambridge, UK.

Kavanaugh, R. D., & Harris, P. L. (1994). Imagining the outcome of pretend transformations: Assessing the competence of normal children and children with autism. *Developmental Psychology, 30,* 847-854.

Kavanaugh, R. D., Whittington, S., & Cerbone, M. J. (1983). Mothers' use of fantasy in speech to young children. *Journal of Child Language, 10,* 45-55.

Lalonde, C. E., & Chandler, M. J. (1995). False belief understanding goes to school: On the social-emotional consequences of coming early or late to a first theory of mind. *Cognition and Emotion, 9,* 167-185.

Leslie, A. M. (1987). Pretense and representation. The origins of 'theory of mind'. *Psychological Review, 94,* 412-426.

Lewis, C., Freeman, H. Kyriakidou, C. Maridaki-Kassotaki, K. M., & Berridge, D. M. (1996). Social influences on false belief access: Specific sibling influences or general apprenticeship? *Child Development, 67,* 2930-2947.

Lillard, A. S. (2001a). Pretend play as Twin Earth. *Developmental Review, 21,* 495-531.

Lillard, A. S. (2001b). Pretending, understanding pretense, and understanding minds. In s. Reifel (Ed.), *Play and cultural studies* (Vol. 3). Westport, CT: Ablex.

Lillard, A. S. (2002). Pretend play and cognitive development. In U. Goswami (Ed.), *Blackwell Handbook of Childhood Cognitive Development* (pp. 188-205). Oxford: Blackwell.

McCune, L. (1995). A normative study of representational play at the transition to language. *Developmental Psychology, 31,* 198-206.

McCune-Nicolich, L. (1981). Toward symbolic functioning: Structure of early pretend games and parallels with language. *Child Development, 52,* 785-797.

Miller, P., & Garvey, C. (1984). Mother-baby role play: Its origins in social support. In I. Bretherton (Ed.), *Symbolic play: The development of social understanding* (pp. 101-130). New York: Academic Press.

Neuman, S. B., & Roskos, K. (1992). Literacy objects as cultural tools: Effects on children's literacy behaviors in play. *Reading Research Quarterly, 27,* 202-225.

Nicolich, L. (1977). Beyond sensorimotor intelligence: Assessment of symbolic maturity through analysis of pretend play. *Merrill-Palmer Quarterly, 23,* 89-99.

O'Connell, B., & Bretherton, I. (1984). Toddler's play, alone and with mother: The role of maternal guidance. In I. Bretherton (Ed.), *Symbolic play: The development of social understanding* (pp. 337-368). New York: Academic Press.

Piaget, J. (1946/1962). *Play, dreams and imitation in childhood.* New York: Norton. (Originally published 1946)

Perner, J. (1991). *Understanding the representational mind.* Cambridge, MA: MIT Press.

Perner, J., Ruffman, T. & Leekam, S. R. (1994). Theory of mind is contagious: You catch it from your sibs. *Child Development, 65,* 1228-1238.

Rall, J., & Harris, P. L. (2000). In Cinderella's slippers? Story comprehension from the protagonist's point of view. *Developmental Psychology, 36,* 202-208.

Rosen, C. E. (1974). The effects of sociodramatic play on problem-solving behavior among culturally disadvantaged preschool children. *Child Development, 45,* 920-927.

Roskos, K., & Neuman, S. B. (1998). Play as an opportunity for literacy. In O. N. Saracho & S. Spodek (Eds), *Multiple perspectives on play in early childhood education* (pp. 100-115). Albany: SUNY Press.

Ruffman, T., Perner, J., Naito, M., Parkin, L., & Clements, W. (1998). Older (but not younger) siblings facilitate false belief understanding. *Developmental Psychology, 34,* 161-174.

Sachs, J., Goldman, J., & Chaille, C. (1985). Narratives in preschoolers' sociodramatic play. In L. Galda & A. Pellegrini (Eds.), *Play, language, and stories: The development of children's literate behavior* (pp. 45-62). Norwood, NJ: Ablex.

Saltz, E., & Johnson, J. (1974). Training for thematic-fantasy play in culturally disadvantage children: Preliminary results. *Child Development, 66,* 623-63.

Scarlett, G. W. (1994). Play, cure, and development: A developmental perspective on the psychoanalytic treatment of young children. In A. Slade and D. P. Wolf (Eds.), *Children at play: Clinical and developmental approaches to meaning and representation* (pp. 48-61). New York: Oxford University Press.

Schwebel, D. C., Rosen, C. S., & Singer, J. L. (1999). Preschoolers' pretend play and theory of mind: The role of jointly constructed pretense. *British Journal of Psychology, 17,* 333-348.

Slade, A., & Wolf, D. P. (Eds.). (1994). *Children at play: Clinical and developmental approaches to meaning and representation* (pp. 48-61). New York: Oxford University Press.

Slade, A. (1987). A longitudinal study of maternal involvement and symbolic play during the toddler period. *Child Development, 58*, 367–375.

Smilansky, S. (1968). *The effects of sociodramatic play on disadvantaged preschool children*. New York: Wiley.

Svendsen, M. (1934). Children's imaginary companions. *Archives of Neurology and Psychiatry, 2*, 985–989.

Taylor, M. (1999). *Imaginary companions and the children who create them*. New York: Oxford.

Taylor, M., & Carlson, S. M. (1997). The relation between individual differences in fantasy and theory of mind. *Child Development, 68*, 436–455.

Taylor, M., & Carlson, S. M. (2000). The influence of religious beliefs on parental attitudes about children's fantasy behavior. In K. Rosengren, C. Johnson, & P. Harris (Eds.), *Imagining the impossible: The development of magical, scientific, and religious thinking in contemporary society* (pp. 247–268). Cambridge: Cambridge University Press.

Ungerer, J. A., & Sigman, M. (1981). Symbolic play and language comprehension in autistic children. *Journal of the American Academy of Child Psychiatry, 20*, 318–337.

Vygotsky, L. S. (1978). The role of play in development. In M. Cole, V. JohnSteiner, S. Scribner, & E. Suberman (Eds.), *Mind in society* (pp. 92–104). Cambridge, MA: Harvard University Press.

Walker-Andrews, A., & Harris, P. (1993). Young children's comprehension of pretend causal sequences. *Developmental Psychology, 29*, 915–921.

Walker-Andrews, A., & Kahana-Kalman, R. (1999). The understanding of pretence across the second year of life. *British Journal of Developmental Psychology, 17*, 523–536.

Walton, K. L. (1990). *Mimesis as make-believe*. Cambridge, MA: Harvard University Press.

Watson, M. W., & Fischer, K. W. (1977). A developmental sequence of agent use in late infancy. *Child Development, 48*, 828–836.

Wellman, H. M. (2002). Understanding the psychological world: Developing a theory of mind. In U. Goswami (Ed.), *Blackwell Handbook of Childhood Cognitive Development* (pp. 167–187). Oxford: Blackwell.

Wellman, H. M., Cross, D. & Watson, J. (2001). A meta-analysis of false belief reasoning: The truth about false belief. *Child Development, 72*, 655–684.

Wolf, D., & Garner, H. (1979). Style and sequence in early symbolic play. In N. R. Smith & M. B. Franklin (Eds.), *Symbolic functioning in children* (pp. 117–138).

Wolf, D. P., Rygh, J., & Altshuler, J. (1984). Agency and experience: Actions and states in play narratives. In I. Bretherton, *Symbolic play: The development of social understanding* (pp. 195–217). New York: Academic Press.

Youngblade, L. M., & Dunn, J. (1995). Individual differences in young children's pretend play with mother and sibling: Links to relationships and understanding of other people's feelings and beliefs. *Child Development, 66*, 1472–1492.

Zukow, P. (1989). Siblings as effective socializing agents: Evidence from central Mexico. In P. Zukow (Ed.), *Sibling interaction across cultures: Theoretical and methodological issues* (pp. 79–105). New York: Springer-Verlag.

· 16 ·

EARLY CHILDHOOD MULTICULTURAL EDUCATION

Patricia G. Ramsey
Mount Holyoke College

Multicultural education has been a significant force for school reform over the past three decades, giving rise to new educational theories and research at all educational levels. During this period, it has profoundly influenced early childhood curriculum and practice. The first part of this chapter is a review the history and current trends of the multicultural movement in the United States. The second part will focus on developmental and educational research that is most germane to early childhood multicultural education.

HISTORY AND TRENDS OF MULTICULTURAL EDUCATION

The forces that formed and continue to influence multicultural education reflect the sociopolitical history of the United States and the disparate histories of native people and immigrants (Ramsey & Williams, 2003). The history of each group is complex and fraught with hardships and losses (Takaki, 1993), but some groups—namely, immigrants from Britain and other northwestern European countries—have economically and politically dominated the United States for the past three and one-half centuries. Many immigrants from other parts of Europe initially suffered discrimination but, through intermarriage and educational and occupational achievement, their descendents became fully assimilated into the Anglo-dominated society, although some retain symbolic ethnic identities (Alba, 1990). People emigrating from Asia, by contrast, were the targets of more intransigent discrimination and rigid immigration restrictions (e.g., Chinese workers could not bring their families), and their descendents are still seen as outsiders in many settings. Others who came by force (enslaved African Americans) or were conquered (Native Americans, Mexican Americans) have suffered extreme discrimination and have been denied equal access to education and employment. Not surprisingly, they have been less successful at entering the educational and occupational mainstream, even

after legal restraints were lifted during the 1950s and 1960s. The lines of assimilation and advantage follow a clear pattern; people who look most similar to the early settlers from Northwestern Europe enjoy the benefits of a system of racial privilege, whereas those who look the most different are excluded and disadvantaged (Tatum, 1992).

The inequities and conflicts that have characterized the social and political responses to racial, ethnic, and cultural diversity have permeated the educational system. According to Tyack (1995), over the past century, educational strategies have included *discriminating* against particular groups, relegating them to no or very poor schools; *separating* children into classes to fit their perceived or actual needs (e.g., special education and vocational programs); pressuring children and families to *assimilate* into mainstream society; *desegregating* schools to secure full educational rights for all children; *ignoring* differences (i.e., the "color-blind" approach); *compensating* for presumed academic deficits (e.g., Head Start programs for poor children); *celebrating* differences by honoring contributions of diverse groups; and *preserving* cultural and linguistic differences (e.g., bilingual education, Afrocentric curriculum). During the 19th and early 20th centuries, educators were concerned primarily with "Americanizing" immigrants from non-English speaking European countries. After World War II, however, the focus shifted to addressing the long-term discrimination suffered by African Americans, culminating in the *Brown v. Topeka, Kansas, Board of Education* and the civil rights legislation that *legally* ended segregation in the schools and racial discrimination in all institutions and the War on Poverty designed to end economic disparities.

Multicultural education grew out of several of these reforms, and, in particular the disillusionment with programs initiated in the 1950s and 1960s. Because of lengthy court battles, white flight, and unequal funding, school desegregation had failed to provide widespread equal educational opportunities and true racial integration. Likewise, many communities and organizations openly practiced racist policies. War on Poverty programs such as Head Start and Job Corps were underfunded and had not fulfilled their promise of equalizing academic access and success. Critics have pointed out that many reforms and programs in the 1960s failed because they did not address the dynamics of power and oppression that caused discrimination and poverty in the first place (Giroux & McLaren, 1994; Fennimore, 2000).

Spearheaded by several African-American scholars, notably James Banks, Geneva Gay, and Carl Grant, the multicultural movement first became a force in education during the 1970s. Philosophically it reflected the work of early African American scholars such as W.E.B. Du Bois (1896/1973, 1899/1973) and Carter Woodson (1921, 1933, 1935) that exposed the myths of equality that prevailed in the white version of the history of the United States (Banks, 1996). Multiculturalism also embodied "cultural pluralism," a model in which specific groups maintain their unique cultures that in turn enhance the whole society (Hunter, 1973). The purpose of multicultural education was to increase individual awareness and respect for people of all races and cultural backgrounds; to help all individuals develop positive racial and ethnic identities; to ensure that all children had access to high quality education; and to challenge social and economic injustices.

During the 1980s, many curriculum designers and writers developed and advocated a wide range of multicultural practices. The different approaches and the political messages that they embody were articulated by Sleeter and Grant in 1987 and more fully developed by their book *Turning on Learning* (Grant & Sleeter) in 1989 and further refined in 1999. Their typology of multicultural education included the following approaches.

• *Education of culturally different children* involves adapting existing programs to bridge cultural discontinuities between home and school. This approach is geared to facilitating the academic success of children of recent immigrants and other groups whose cultures do not fit with the individualistic, competitive orientation of most public schools. However, it does not address the discrimination and economic inequities that also profoundly affect children's lives in schools.
• *Single group studies* grew out of the Ethnic Studies movement and focus on the literature, art, history, and culture of specific ethnic and national groups. This approach provides information about marginalized groups that is often missing from mainstream education texts and courses, and, thereby, potentially supports the development of positive ethnic identities for children of groups that are underrepresented in the typical curriculum. By providing a fuller picture of the history and arts in this country, this approach also can enrich the education of all children. Unfortunately, in practice, information about particular groups is often presented in isolation and frequently only to members of that group so that children do not learn about similarities and differences across groups and their shared experiences of suffering and resisting discrimination.
• *Human relations* approach seeks to enhance positive intergroup relationships and to reduce prejudice by encouraging students to recognize and challenge their biases and to learn how to communicate and work with people from a wide range of cultural and racial groups. This approach frequently involves group discussions, role-plays, and cooperative projects. It has been effective in fostering intergroup connections, but, by focusing on identifying and changing individual attitudes and relationships, it glosses over the effects of institutional racism and other biases.
• *Multicultural education* emphasizes the positive, adaptive value of cultural pluralism and encourages children to be competent in more than one cultural system. It typically involves using images, books, and toys (e.g., plastic foods, cooking utensils, dolls) that represent a wide range of cultural and racial groups. The underlying premise is that exposing children to a wide range of values and life styles will help them appreciate and respect their own and other groups. In practice, this approach has often been limited to providing materials with little discussion about the values underlying specific cultural artifacts and mores. Moreover, teachers often emphasize traditional cultural elements (holidays, costumes, traditional foods, music, and dance) and portray groups as exotically different, unwittingly reinforcing rather than challenging stereotypes.
• *Education that is multicultural and social reconstructionist* takes a more critical perspective about institutional and national inequities and focuses on the need for profound social, economic, political, and educational changes to create a truly equitable society. This approach consists of many elements of the four approaches described above but goes beyond appreciating and respecting other individuals and groups and emphasizes the power differentials among groups and ways to challenge them. It tackles the deep issues that underlie discrimination and inequities and therefore is at the heart of multiculturalism. Unfortunately, this approach is rarely fully implemented in classrooms because teacher education programs do not provide students with backgrounds in politics, economics, sociology, and social justice movements to prepare them to engage in this work in their classrooms. Moreover, many school administrators are reluctant to "rock the boat," and teachers are often discouraged from engaging their students in critical analyses and social justice work.

The Anti-Bias Curriculum, written by Louise Derman-Sparks and associates and published in 1989, was one of the earliest examples applying the social reconstructionist approach in early childhood classrooms. Using activities and stories, this book has helped teachers to foster the development of children's ethnic identities and their interpersonal and intergroup respect and relationships and to see and challenge the bias in their classrooms and communities. It continues to be widely used in early childhood classrooms and is reflected in the National Association for the Education of Young Children (NAEYC) accreditation standards. However, as I will discuss in the third section of this chapter, teachers often have difficulty implementing the critical thinking and social activism aspect of this curriculum.

In the 1970s and 1980s, multicultural education focused primarily on race, ethnicity, and culture. Because these terms are ambiguous and have different meaning, I will clarify how they are used in this chapter. *Race* popularly refers to biological traits that distinguish populations that have originated from different regions. During the 16th century, the English developed the notion of the "savage other" when they conquered the Irish. They brought this belief with them to North America, which they used to justify the genocide of Native Americans and the enslavement of Africans in the 17th and 18th centuries (Smedley, 1993). The Framers of the Constitution, in turn, created elaborate and contradictory ideologies in order to permit slavery in a new society predicated on individual liberty and rights.

Three broad racial groups have been commonly identified—Caucasoid, Negroid, and Mongoloid. In the 19th and early 20th centuries, many scientists "discovered" more elaborate racial categories that "proved" the superiority of people from northwestern Europe (Brown 2002). This work provided a justification for oppression and genocide of many groups, even within the Caucasoid "race" (e.g., discrimination against Italians, and Jews). With recent genetic research and the human genome project in particular, we now know that there is more *intra*-race than *inter*-race genetic variability (Quintana, 1998) and that there are no valid biological bases for distinguishing racial groups. Moreover, many families are multiracial, making racial classifications even more questionable and irrelevant. Racial categories, however, continue to be defined by social, economic, and political forces (Omi & Winant, 1986) and, in turn, influence the social status and life prospects of families and children, who are racially privileged or disadvantaged. Even today, some scientists (e.g., *The Bell Curve* by Hernstein and Murray, 1994) misrepresent findings or disconnect them from their social, political, and economic contexts in order to "prove" the genetic basis of racial superiority and inferiority.

Ethnicity refers to "primarily sociological or anthropological characteristics, such as customs, religious practices, and language usage of a group of people with a shared ancestry or origin" (Quintana, 1998, p. 28). For a variety of reasons, such as their recent arrival, discrimination practiced by the larger society, or by their own choice, ethnic groups remain an identifiable group within the larger cultural environment. In addition to sharing common cultural roots, members of ethnic groups often have similar physical characteristics, live in concentrated groups, and occupy the same socioeconomic status. Ethnicity, like race, implies a degree of social isolation from the mainstream.

Virtually every person has been socialized by a *culture* and in many cases by more than one (e.g., national origin, gender, religion, occupation, leisure activities). Culture "imposes order and meaning on our experiences. It allows us to predict how others will behave in certain situations" (Gollnick & Chinn, 1998, p. 4). At the same time, cultures themselves are dynamic and constantly evolving as groups interact and mutually influence each other. Moreover, the salience of particular cultures in individuals' lives also shifts across contexts and with developmental and historical changes.

From its inception in the 1970s, multicultural education has undergone several changes. In *Multicultural Research: A Reflective Engagement with Race, Class, Gender and Sexual Orientation* (Grant, 1999), a number of prominent scholars in the field write about the evolution of their thinking about multicultural education. These accounts illustrate the wide range of ideas and experiences underlying the commitment to multicultural education and influencing its recent development and provide a rich resource for readers wishing to know more about the history and trends of multicultural education. There are too many ideas, critiques, and directions to include all of them in this chapter. However, the following trends appear to be most profoundly influencing on the shape of multicultural education at the beginning of the 21st century.

First, the scope of multicultural education has broadened since the 1970s. As multicultural theorists recognized and analyzed the power differentials underlying race and culture, they began to focus more on social class and economic discrimination. Then, as gender disparities in school performance became the focus of feminist critics, multiculturalists realized that gender was also a source of inequity and needed to be included in multicultural curricula. During the 1970s, people with disabilities and their families had begun to protest their educational and occupational marginalization. With changing legislation, culminating with the passage of the Americans with Disabilities Education Act in 1990, more and more children with disabilities were "included" in regular classrooms, and disability issues were woven into multicultural curricula. More recently, wider recognition of the hate crimes targeting gay men and lesbian women has led to sexual orientation becoming a theme in multicultural education, an addition that has caused controversy both within and outside the field. Currently, some writers (e.g., Grunewald, 2003; Ramsey, 2004; Running-Grass, 1994) are examining how inequities and the exploitation of certain groups are linked to the destruction of the natural environment. The ecojustice movement has highlighted the disproportionate amount of environmental degradation in poor communities and countries (i.e., the practice of locating high pollution factories and practicing destructive agricultural practices in locations where residents have little political clout). Related to these connections are concerns about how hyperconsumption (e.g., the media-inspired competition to purchase the latest toys and clothes) may undermine interpersonal and intergroup relationships (e.g., Giroux, 1999; Ramsey, 2004; West, 1993).

Second, multicultural education has been profoundly changed by the explicit incorporation of critical pedagogy, which focuses on recognizing and challenging injustices. From the beginning, multicultural education had a critical stance and a liberatory potential (Apple, 1977; Gay, 1983). However, many of the multicultural programs and guides published in the 1970s and 1980s focused on celebrating cultural differences (e.g., foods, costumes, and dances) and fostering intergroup connections, while glossing over or ignoring the inequities of power and economics that defined people's lives. One critic described these common multicultural practices as "tourist curricula" (Derman-Sparks et al., 1989). Inspired by the Latin American liberation movements and, in particular, by the work of Paulo Freire (1970), critical pedagogy became the centerpiece of a number of multicultural programs. In 1992 Sonia Nieto first published *Affirming Diversity*, which placed critical pedagogy at the center of multicultural teaching and demonstrated how critical multicultural education can be implemented in schools.

Two edited volumes that were published in the 1990s, *Empowerment through Multicultural Education* (Sleeter, 1991) and *Multicultural Education, Critical Pedagogy and the Politics of Difference* (Sleeter & McLaren, 1995b) contain essays that further elaborate how multicultural education and critical pedagogy mutually enhance each other. Writing from a critical multicultural perspective, McLaren (2000), and Sleeter (1996) argue that multiculturalism is a political movement that is centered on the complexities and conflicts inherent in all people's experiences, with a primary goal of liberating people from oppression by challenging the societal, economic, political structures that maintain these inequities. Sleeter argues that teachers need to work as allies with parents and other members of their communities in order to pressure schools and communities to serve children better and to teach their students to think and act politically and to advocate for themselves and other marginalized people.

A third trend in multicultural education that appeared in the late 1990s was the critically analysis of the identities and assumptions of white people. Because multicultural education grew out of the frustration about educational inequities experienced by African Americans and other marginalized groups, it initially focused on making classrooms more responsive to the needs and interests of children of color and recent immigrants. As they worked with teachers in many capacities, multicultural educators began to realize that many white teachers either overtly or covertly resisted examining their own biases and the extent to which they personally benefited from their racial privilege (e.g., Sleeter, 1992). They concluded that tacit acceptance of the status quo prevented white teachers from truly understanding and embracing multicultural perspectives and goals. Spearheaded by Peggy McIntosh (1995), a number of authors (e.g., Frankenberg, 1993; Howard, 1999; Sleeter, 1994) have analyzed how white people—often unconsciously—exercise their unearned racial privileges and how that interferes with learning to teach from a multicultural perspective.

Finally, as multicultural education has become more widely implemented and has taken a more critical stance toward societal inequities, it has become the source of a great deal of controversy and the target of criticism from both the left and the right (see Nieto, 1995; Sleeter, 1995, for more detailed analyses). Conservatives (e.g., Bloom, 1987; D'Souza, 1991; Hirsch, 1987; Schlesinger, 1992) argue that multicultural education is divisive because it focuses on the cultures, values, and histories of particular ethnic and racial groups instead of on the traditional European intellectual roots. They also claim that it sentimentalizes and glorifies cultures outside of the mainstream European American canon and leads to shoddy scholarship and weak academic programs that pander to members of particular groups. Finally, by focusing on systemic inequities, multiculturalism undermines the principle that all individuals in the United States have an equal chance to succeed and that their level of success depends solely on individual effort and talents. Nieto (1995) notes that many teachers, even those who are sympathetic to the goals of multicultural education, echo the conservative criticism that multicultural programs fail to address issues of academic rigor, accountability, and equity. Olneck (2000) echoes these sentiments, "Multiculturalists have

to publicly identify their enterprise with standards and academic excellence. . . . They must also insist on inclusion in the state mechanisms formulating and implementing those efforts [to improve the quality of education]" (p. 337).

Critics from the left have criticized multicultural education for attending to superficial issues related to diversity and avoiding the hard issues, such as exploitation, oppression and structural inequalities in the system (Giroux, 1992; Mattai, 1992; McCarthy, 1990a, b; McLaren, 1997; Olneck, 1990). They argue that many programs practice cultural pluralism, yet leave hierarchical and discriminatory structures and practices unchallenged and avoid divisive subjects such as racism and social class differences. A second criticism is that multicultural reforms have usually consisted of a few add-on activities and have failed to transform schools, leaving the status quo and "White Studies" virtually intact.

In summary, multicultural education has been through many changes and controversies in the past three decades (see Ramsey & Williams, 2003, and Tyack, 1995, for more in-depth analyses of this history). During this time, a number of multicultural approaches and materials have been developed. Some address the educational needs of students who experience cultural gaps between home and school or are the targets of the discrimination; others focus on learning about and respecting other individuals and groups; and still others engage students in challenging the inequities of our society. Despite the many changes and diverse approaches, the basic goals of equalizing educational opportunities and creating a diverse and truly equitable society have remained constant. During this time, many early childhood researchers and practitioners have investigated developmental issues related to multicultural education and have proposed and implemented programs to encourage children to develop an antibias worldview, as is illustrated in the following sections of this chapter.

RESEARCH RELATED TO EARLY CHILDHOOD MULTICULTURAL EDUCATION

Three research questions are most germane to the multicultural education for young children: (1) How do racial, cultural, socioeconomic, gender, and ability differences, divisions, and inequities affect the quality of children's lives and their future prospects? (2) How do children develop their cognitions, attitudes, identities, and behaviors related to these dimensions? (3) How is multicultural education implemented in early childhood classrooms and how do these efforts affect children's ideas, feelings, and behaviors? Over several decades, many researchers have explored the first two questions, so this review will summarize these findings. Unfortunately, very few studies have been done on the actual implementation and effects of multicultural curriculum in early childhood classrooms so these studies will be described in more detail.

Before beginning this review, I want to note the biases and limits of the research and theories that will be included. Most studies about the effects of different social and economic circumstances on development and about children's developing attitudes have been done by researchers trained in traditional child development theories and methodologies that are derived from the work of early psychologists who by large were European or North American men (e.g., Erikson, Freud, Piaget, Hall, Skinner). Developmental theorists and researchers traditionally ignored the context of children's lives and assumed that developmental goals, stages, and phases class are universal—the same for all children in all situations (see Garcia Coll et al., 1996, for a more extensive critique). The developmental "norms" that emerged from this earlier work were based on European and European American middle-class families. As a result, children from other backgrounds are often judged "deficient" because their developmental profiles do not match the norms established by this small and relatively privileged segment of the world's population.

In response to concerns about this limited perspective, researchers have raised the question of which aspects of development are universal, which ones are individual, and which ones are environmental. Bowman and Stott (1994) point out that, except in conditions of extreme sensory and social deprivation, all children regardless of background and child rearing goals establish mutually satisfying social relationships and ways of organizing and integrating their perceptions and categorizing new information. They also learn how to speak and perhaps to write a particular language and how to think, imagine, and create. Individual physical differences such as sensitivity to pain, distractibility, timing of onset of puberty, and body build play formative roles in children's development. However, Bowman and Stott assert that all developmental phases and individual traits become meaningful *only* in the context of the child's social life. Children learn how to express their emerging needs and skills in ways that fit the resources, values, and expectations of their group, which in turn is influenced by the larger social and economic context.

Over the past two decades, researchers have begun to question assumptions that all children should optimally follow the same developmental path. The 1980s and 1990s saw the publication of several books and research reviews that interpreted minority children's development and behaviors within their own contexts and represented a shift away from earlier work that measured them with the norms, paradigms and methods based on studies of white children (e.g., Spencer, Brookins, & Allen, 1985; the *Child Development Special Issue on Minority Children*; Gibbs, Huang, & Associates, 1989); McAdoo, 1993). Also many researchers are beginning to use qualitative methods such as case studies and ethnographies, which capture the contexts and nuances of children's development.

Garcia Coll et al. (1996) argue that researchers and educators need to analyze children's development within the larger context of social stratification that includes racism, prejudice, discrimination, oppression, and segregation and the local expressions of social stratification such as quality of schools, access to health care, and resources available in neighborhoods. Although Garcia Coll et al. do not dispute the deleterious effects of social, political, and economic disadvantage, they caution against pathologizing groups of people and point out that communities, families, and individuals develop adaptive cultures, competencies and strategies to overcome and resist the effects

of discrimination. In a similar vein, Swadener and Lubeck (1995) cogently argue against the "at-risk" analysis of poor families and families of color.

In short, developmental theories and research can contribute to our understanding of children's lives and thinking, but we must read them critically, apply them cautiously, and work to create more inclusive and critical theories and research methods.

Societal Divisions and Children's Development

Everyone in the United States lives in multiple worlds including work, home, community, school, and social and religious groups. Individuals also have a number of identities and behavioral repertoires that shift among contexts. However, some children and families experience more discontinuities between school and home than others. These gaps are exacerbated when children are targets of negative stereotypes and assumptions. Moreover, resources among groups vary enormously; whereas some parents are able to provide their children with an abundance of material goods and opportunities, others struggle to raise theirs in extreme financial and material deprivation.

In this section and the following one, I have divided the research review by specific social divisions, namely, race, economics, culture, gender, and ability differences. Organizing the material this way facilitates focusing on specific issues, but it erroneously implies that these dimensions are separate. In fact, they are constantly interacting and mutually influencing each other. For example, race and social class are highly correlated, and cultural attitudes profoundly influence responses to gender and ability differences.

Race. As discussed previously, racial categories do not reflect actual genetic differences, yet they continue to function as social and political constructs that influence children's life prospects and their relationships with others. Moreover, even though overt and legally sanctioned racist practices have declined, the more subtle forms of contemporary racism are deeply imbedded in our society and resistant to change (Devine, Plant, & Blair 2001). Decades of research have shown the deleterious effects of racism on families and children's lives (e.g., Cose, 1993; Feagin & Sikes, 1994; Gibbs, Huang, & Associates, 1989). Many families face a constant and debilitating confrontation with racism and prejudice that has been described as "mundane extreme environmental stress" (Peters, 1985). West (1993) describes the psychological costs of discrimination as "the lived experience of coping with a life of horrifying meaninglessness, hopelessness, and . . . lovelessness . . . a numbing detachment from others and a self-destructive disposition toward the world" (p. 14).

Children of color including those who have multiracial backgrounds often have to overcome the negative stereotypes of their groups and alienation from the social mainstream in order to form positive identities (Cross, 1991; Root, 1996; Spencer & Markstrom-Adams, 1990). School experiences often contribute to these difficulties because children of color, especially African Americans and Latinos, are disproportionately represented in special education classes, lower tracked ability groups, and disciplinary actions. In contrast, whiteness is the "invisible norm" that sets the standards for everyone else's experience (Levine, 1994; McLaren, 1994; Sleeter, 1994). Whites disproportionately occupy high status positions in schools and workplaces yet rarely "see" the privileges that they enjoy on a day-to-day basis (Howard, 1999; McIntosh, 1995).

Economic disparities. Socioeconomic status is "an encompassing structure . . . it relates to virtually every aspect of human psychological development and across a considerable period of time" (Gottfried et al., 2003, p. 204) and inevitably has a profound effect on children's lives. Despite our egalitarian principles, the United States has been moving *away from*, not toward, more equitable distribution of wealth, especially during the last two and a half decades (Huston, 1991 ; Lott, 2002; McLoyd, 1998a; T. Thompson & Hupp, 1992). Between 1979 and 1997, the after-tax income of the poorest 20% declined from $10,900 to $10,800, whereas the incomes of the top 1% rose from $263, 700 to $677,900 (Lott, 2002). Over 16% of all children under the age of 6 in the United States are living below the national poverty level (Children's Defence Fund, 2003).

Analysts attribute this trend to the decline of well-paid semiskilled and low-skilled jobs; cutbacks in federal programs that supported poor families before the 1980s; welfare "reform" that further eliminated these supports in the 1990s; deregulation and tax cuts that favor the wealthy and penalize poor and working-class families; and the increasing numbers of female-headed households. These economic shifts have had a devastating effect on poor, working-class, and many middle-class families. These inequities also intersect with race, gender, and age. Disproportionately high numbers of families of color, female-headed households, children, and elderly people fall below the poverty line (Children's Defense Fund, 2003).

Being poor in and of itself does not necessarily impair development (Thompson, 1992). Many families face the daunting challenges of poverty with fortitude and resolve and protect their children from its most deleterious effects. However, common consequences of growing up in poverty—malnutrition, inadequate health care, exposure to violence, toxins, and diseases, homelessness, unsafe living conditions, neighborhood disorder, frequent moves, and poor educational facilities—do pose enormous risks for children (Brooks-Gunn, Duncan, & Maritato, 1997; McLoyd & Ceballo, 1998; Jackson, Brooks-Gunn, Huang, Glassman, 2000; Kohen, Brooks-Gunn, Levanthal, & Hertzman, 2002; Lott, 2002; McLoyd, 1998b; Stronge, 1992). Economic stress sometimes causes parental depression and family tensions, which can spill over into conflicts with children (Conger, Ge, Elder, Lorenz, & Simons, 1994) and in turn make children more vulnerable to depression, low self-confidence, poor peer relationships, and conduct disorders (McLoyd & Wilson, 1992; Yeung et al., 2002).

Contrary to our ethic of equal opportunity, institutions and beliefs in our society often aggravate these difficulties. Despite the heterogeneity of children in all social class groups, teachers and administrators often classify children by their socioeconomic backgrounds and form their expectations accordingly (Bigelow, 1995; Gollnick & Chinn, 1998; McLoyd, 1998a; Polakow, 1993; Rist, 1970). Poor people are also socially stigmatized and often blamed for their plight. Nonpoor people distance themselves from poor families with "exclusion, separation, devaluing, and discounting. . . poor people tend to seen as other and lesser in values, character, motivation, and potential" (Lott, 2002, p. 108).

Cultural differences. Cultural values and traditions influence childrearing goals, strategies, and outcomes such as level of independence (e.g., Gonzalez-Ramos, Zayas, Cohen, 1998); discipline practices (e.g., Kobayashi-Winata & Power, 1989); play styles (e.g., Farver, Kim, & Lee, 1995; Farver & Shin, 1997; Roopnarine, Lasker, Sacks, & Stores, 1998; Whiting & Edwards, 1988; Whiting & Whiting, 1975); sleeping patterns (Lebra, 1994); family responsibilities (Whiting & Edwards, 1988); and emotional expression (Farver, Wells-Nystrom, Frosch, Wimbarti, & Hoppe-Graff, 1997).

Many children and their families feel culturally alienated from schools. They may have recently immigrated to this country or perhaps have moved to a new region, or are the only member of their particular group in the school. The following discussion focuses primarily on the experiences of recent immigrants, but many of their dilemmas are relevant to families who feel culturally disconnected from schools for other reasons.

Children of recent immigrants suffer from the dislocation and confusion that inevitably accompanies leaving the familiar and coping with a whole new language and school structure (Igoa, 1995). Learning a new language is an enormous challenge for children and adults alike and can delay children's academic progress and integration into the social world. Different uses of language and views of what information is important and how it should be conveyed is another source of discomfort for children (Delpit, 1995; Phillips, 1994).

Since the early 1970s, bilingual education programs have been available in some schools to ease these transitions by helping children maintain both of their languages and cultures and by making schools more hospitable for parents. In the 1990s, however, bilingual education was the target of a great deal of political opposition (for more details, see Crawford, 1999; Minami & Ovando, 1995; Moran & Hakuta, 1995). As a result, bilingual programs in some states have been curtailed or virtually eliminated.

Immigrant parents often have difficulty providing their children with support because they themselves are going through the same transition and are exhausted and confused (Vasquez, Pease-Alvarez, and Shannon, 1994). Also, children usually learn the new language and customs more rapidly than their parents and may start refusing to speak their home language. This communication gap means that parents cannot teach their values, beliefs, and wisdom; to their children and families become less intimate (Wong-Filmore, 1991). Moreover, because language and culture are inextricably bound (Nieto, 2004), the loss of language also diminishes children's knowledge of their culture.

Gender and sexual orientation. Gender differentiation and roles emerge in almost all societies (Liben & Bigler, 2002; Whiting & Edwards, 1988) and are usually associated with inequities. In the United States, despite a great deal of legal and attitudinal change, girls and boys are still not treated equally in schools (see Sadker & Sadker, 1995). Girls are often overlooked by teachers and not encouraged to excel, particularly in math and science and in physically challenging activities. They do, however, learn to be nurturing and emotionally expressive and often are skilled at maintaining personal relationships. Boys, by contrast, are encouraged to be aggressive, to excel, to take physical risks, and to hide their emotions. They are both the best students and the worst troublemakers (Sadker & Sadker, 1995). Several recent books attest to the toll that the emotionally limited roles of traditional masculinity take on boys (e.g., Garbarino, 1999; Kindlon & Thompson, 1999; Kivel, 1999; Pollack, 1998). Thus, although girls have been more materially shortchanged in schools and workplaces, both sexes suffer from the effects of rigid gender-role expectations.

Gender roles are resistant to change and are recreated with each generation. One reason for this intransigence is the prevalent use of gender in our society to divide and differentiate people (Bem, 1981, 1983; Liben & Bigler, 2002). This pattern is exacerbated by consumerist pressures that reinforce gender-specific fantasies (e.g., Barbie dolls, action figures) (Hughes & MacNaughton, 2001).

Related to gender roles is the discrimination faced by people of different sexual orientations and gender identities. In contrast to their careful avoidance of public racist and sexist comments, many religious, political, and community leaders vociferously denounce gay, lesbian, bisexual, and transgendered individuals and seek to exclude them from equal protection under the law. Ironically, their arguments that are usually based on religious or moral beliefs create and condone a climate of hatred in which homophobic insults and violence occur with frequency and impunity.

In the United States, different sexual orientations are now more openly acknowledged than they were two or three decades ago. A number of networks and publications for and by gay and lesbian people currently exist in different occupations (Casper, Cuffaro, Schultz, Silin, & Wickens, 1996). Still, in most schools, sexual orientation is rarely mentioned and often actively evaded (Alvarado, Derman-Sparks, & Ramsey, 1999). Not only are teachers uncomfortable with this issue themselves, but they also worry about the reaction of parents, principals, and community members. Given the vitriolic response to even token efforts to incorporate these issues into classrooms (Casper & Schultz, 1999), these concerns are justified.

Gay and lesbian parents face particular dilemmas about disclosing their family relationships to their children's teachers and parents of their classmates. Unlike race and gender, sexual orientation is not obvious at first sight, so gay and lesbian parents usually have the option of not revealing the nature of their family relationships. At the same time, *not* disclosing exacts a high price because they must always be on their guard and cannot engage openly with teachers and other parents (Casper & Schultz, 1999).

Abilities/disabilities. Children also are affected by where they fit on the abilities/disabilities continua. In the United States, the approach to disabilities has changed over the past 30 years. Until the 1970s, children with clearly identified disabilities (e.g., cerebral palsy, Down syndrome) were usually placed in special classrooms and isolated from their "typical" peers. Children with milder or less identifiable disabilities, such as cognitive delays or attention deficit disorder, often remained undiagnosed and struggled to keep up in regular classrooms. After the 1970s, and particularly since the passage of PL 94-142 and PL 99-457, the principle of offering children services in the "least restricted environment" has guided efforts to insure that "all children, no matter how diverse their needs, should expect to be served in the regular education setting that they would attend at any specific age" (Sheridan, Foley, & Radlinski, 1995, p. 42).

Effective inclusion of children with disabilities requires a multifaceted approach including close coordination among parents, teachers, and specialists; careful scheduling of transportation, tutoring, and medications; and creative adaptations of curriculum, classroom routines, and the physical environment. A full consideration of all of these aspects is beyond the scope of this chapter. A number of resources (e.g., Kemple, 2004; Kostelnick, Onaga, Rohde, & Whiren, 2002; Odom, 2002; Sheridan, Foley, & Radlinski, 1995) describe strategies and examples of successful inclusive classrooms.

Despite legal and educational reforms, children with disabilities are often socially and academically isolated from their peers (Diamond, Le Furgy, & Blass, 1993; Nabors, 1995; Pearl, Farmer, Van Acker, Rodkin, Bost, Coe, & Henley, 1998; Sheridan, Foley, & Radlinski, 1995). Odom and his colleagues (2002) did an extensive study of children's social inclusion in 16 preschool programs. They found that across all of them, one third of the children with disabilities were rejected by their peers. These children tended to be aggressive, disruptive, withdrawn, lacking in communication skills, or often engaged in conflicts with peers and adults (Odom, Zerchr, Marquart, Li, Sandall, & Wolfberg, 2002). Thus, children with behavioral and emotional disabilities are particularly likely to be rejected by peers (Pearl et al., 1998). Unfortunately some children with disabilities become more isolated during the school year (Diamond et al., 1993; Guralnick, Connor, Hammond, Gottman, & Kinnish, 1996; Guralnick & Groom, 1987), demonstrating that merely having contact with each other does not break down the barriers between children with and without disabilities. Our concept of education, which embodies a narrow definition of academic success (e.g., literacy and math but not the arts), makes it hard for children with different aptitudes and learning styles to feel and be viewed as competent. The current accountability movement with its stress on testing specific information and skills further thwarts teachers' efforts to nurture a wide range of learning styles and interests.

Social isolation, however, is not inevitable and may be overreported. Odom and his colleagues (2002) also found that one third of the children with disabilities were accepted by their peers. Even children who may be quite distant from the social mainstream often have one friend who serves as a social buffer and provides companionship (Juvonen & Bear, 1992).

Despite many challenges, integrating children with disabilities into regular classrooms clearly has advantages. Many studies show that both children with and without disabilities thrive socially and academically in inclusive settings (Diamond & Innes, 2001; Odom, 2002).

In summary, children's development, educational success, and future prospects are influenced by the discrimination and privilege that are associated with race, social class, culture, gender, sexual orientation, and abilities/disabilities. As long as these patterns of advantage and disadvantage remain deeply imbedded in our society, efforts to create equity in schools will have a limited effect. Thus, as early childhood educators, we need to actively participate in movements for social and economic justice for all families.

Children's Responses to Differences

Early childhood multicultural education presents teachers with the challenge of how to engage young children in exploring issues of diversity and inequality in meaningful, authentic and hopeful ways. To support these efforts, this review summarizes past and current research on children's understandings and feelings related to race, culture, social class, gender, and disabilities.

Race. Although the concept of "race" is murky and contradictory, it is a prominent category in our society, and children quickly learn to group people by racial characteristics. Over the past seven decades, researchers have attempted to learn how children view racial differences, using a wide variety of methods. Despite numerous studies, our knowledge about children's reactions to racial differences is still incomplete and fragmented. Most research in the United States has compared European-American and African-American children's responses to same and cross-race dolls, pictures, and classmates. Only recently have researchers begun to include broader populations and a wider variety of methods.

During the 1940s and 1950s, a number of studies of children's racial awareness and attitudes appeared to demonstrate that segregation and discrimination had a negative effect on African-American children's identity and self-concept development (e.g., Clark & Clark, 1947; Goodman, 1952). These studies were incorporated into arguments for integrating public schools in the 1954 *Brown v. Board of Education* Supreme Court decision. Subsequently, a number of researchers studied the social dynamics of desegregated schools and the conditions that either fostered or undermined positive cross-race relationships (e.g., Patchen, 1982; Schofield, 1989; Singleton & Asher, 1977; Slavin, 1980). The growing recognition that desegregation did not necessarily lead to successful integration or reduction in prejudice contributed to the shift toward multicultural education and gave rise to research on the complexities of racial awareness and attitudes.

Children's responses to racial differences involve a complicated set of cognitive, affective, and behavioral dimensions (Garcia Coll & Garcia, 1995; Katz, 1976, 1982; Sigelman & Singleton, 1986). In terms of *cognition*, infants have been observed to consistently react to racial differences by 6 months (Katz & Kofkin, 1997). By ages 3–4, most children have a rudimentary concept of race (Katz, 1976) and can easily identify, match, and label people by racial group (e.g., Clark & Clark, 1947; Goodman, 1952; Porter, 1971, Ramsey 1991b; Ramsey & Myers, 1990). During their elementary school years, children elaborate their concepts of race as they begin to associate social information with the physical attributes that they see (Katz,

1976). As this shift occurs, they rely less on color cues and begin to grasp the social connotations of racial distinctions (Alejandro-Wright, 1985). The onset and accuracy of racial awareness appears to be related to amount of contact with people from different racial groups (Katz, 1976; Ramsey, 1991b; Ramsey & Myers, 1990). Children growing up in multiracial environments generally learn racial labels and distinctions sooner than those in monoracial settings.

Children's understanding of racial differences changes as they get older, as illustrated in their questions about race, which shift from questions about physical attributes to ones about the social significance of racial distinctions (Derman-Sparks, Higa, & Sparks, 1980). Their explanations of racial differences reflect their changing understanding of the physical environment (Clark, Dembo, & Hocevar, 1980; Ramsey, 1986b) and shift from attributing racial differences to supernatural causes to understanding that racial characteristics are inherited from one's biological family. A number of studies have found that children do not understand that race is an irrevocable characteristic until after they have acquired gender permanence (usually between ages 4 and 6), the realization that the physical characteristics of gender are not going to change, despite hair cuts and dress changes (Katz, 1976, 1982; Ramsey, 1987; see Ocampo, Bernal, & Knight, 1993 for a review). However, after conducting a set of studies in which preschoolers accurately predicted the race of older children and adults based on their parentage and their characteristics as babies and young children, Hirschfield (1995) concluded that preschoolers *do* understand that race is an inherited and unchangeable characteristic and have formed elaborated views of race based on popular images. These findings diverge from earlier ones and raise some provocative questions about the nature of children's racial cognitions, how they may be changing, and the effects of different research methodologies.

In the 1990s researchers (e.g., Bigler & Liben, 1993; Hirschfield, 1994, 1995; Ramsey & Myers, 1990, Ramsey, 1991a) turned their attention to the processes underlying children's racial cognitions. The two Ramsey studies demonstrated that the salience of race varies across situation (e.g., whether a child is sorting pictures of other children or identifying who she is) and across communities with different racial compositions. Bigler and Liben focused on individual differences and found that children who tended to use more rigid classification systems for nonsocial information held stronger stereotyped images of both African and European Americans and had more difficulty recalling counterstereotyped information than their peers who used more flexible and multidimensional classifications.

Affective reactions are incorporated into a child's rudimentary awareness of race, but how they change over time is the source of some debate. Based on earlier studies, researchers concluded that attitudes become more consolidated and elaborated with age (Goodman, 1952; Katz, 1976; Milner, 1983; Porter, 1971). Later studies (e.g., Black-Gutman & Hickson, 1996; Hirschfield, 1994) also concluded that racial prejudice increases with age. However, other reviews and studies (Aboud, 1988; Aboud & Amato, 2001; Doyle & Aboud, 1993; Garcia Coll & Garcia, 1995) suggest that racial prejudice decreases with age as children develop their abilities to empathize with others, recognize different perspectives, and differentiate among individuals in less familiar groups.

These contradictory findings suggest that environmental factors may play a role in children's reactions to race. However, identifying variables that contribute to the formation of racial and ethnic attitudes has been difficult and also has revealed disparate trends. Some researchers have focused on personality traits (e.g., Allport, 1954), and others on situational factors, such as heterogeneity and degree of upward mobility (Rotheram & Phinney, 1987), and attitudes in the local community. Attending monoracial schools appear to be related to higher levels of cross-race distrust and aversion (Holmes, 1997); whereas attending multiracial schools may help children develop more cross-race trust and acceptance (Rotenberg & Cerda, 1994), especially when racial proportions are fairly equal (Kistner, Metzler, Gatlin, & Risi, 1993). Interestingly, Aboud and Doyle (1996) did not find strong relationships between children's racial attitudes and those expressed by their parents and friends. However, parents' unconscious racial views (e.g., choosing to live in an all-white neighborhood) may influence their children more than the "beliefs" that they explicitly express on a questionnaire or in an interview. Children also absorb attitudes from printed and electronic media, which often reflect prevailing stereotypes (Cortes, 2000; Milner, 1983).

Across all ages and three decades of research, white children tend to show stronger same-race preferences than their African-American classmates do (Fox & Jordan, 1973; Newman, Liss, & Sherman, 1983; Ramsey & Myers, 1990; Rosenfield & Stephan, 1981; Stabler, Zeig, & Johnson, 1982; Van Ausdale & Feagin, 2001) and these differences increase with age (Aboud & Amato, 2001). Conversely, Black children's patterns are more variable and reflect greater cross-race acceptance (Graham & Cohen, 1997; Hallinan & Teixeira, 1987; Ramsey & Myers, 1990). The pervasiveness of pro-white bias in our society also influences African-American children's *intra* racial attitudes. Averhart and Bigler (1997) found that African-American children showed a positive bias toward photographs of African-Americans with lighter skin tones over those with darker skin tones when choosing potential teachers, neighbors, and playmates.

There have been relatively few studies of children's actual *cross-racial behavior*, and the findings are mixed. Porter (1971), Singleton and Asher (1977), and Urberg and Kaplan (1989) observed few signs of cross-race avoidance or antagonism in preschool children's play partners. However, in other studies (Finkelstein & Haskins, 1983; Fishbein & Imai, 1993; Ramsey & Myers, 1990; Van Ausdale & Feagin, 2001), preschool and kindergarten children, especially white children, played more with their own race peers. During the elementary years, racial cleavage often increases as children absorb more of the prevailing social attitudes, and the awareness of "us" versus "them" becomes more established (Farmer & Farmer, 1996; Katz, 1976). This trend continues, and studies of racially mixed middle schools and high schools show how vehemently and explicitly many (not all) youth avoid and discourage others' cross-race contacts (Patchen, 1982; Perry, 2002; Schofield, 1989; Ulichny, 1994).

Children's attitudes and behaviors toward racially different peers are complex and contradictory as illustrated in two ethnographic studies done in England (Troyna & Hatcher, 1992; Wright (1992). For example, in their study of 8- to 10-year-old children in predominately white schools in Britain, Troyna and Hatcher found that White children often advocated racial equality but, in the next breath, blurt out racist ideologies and epithets.

Economic disparities. Understanding social class differences involves learning about a number of different concepts, such as the role of money, the status of occupations, availability of jobs, and inherited wealth. Most preschool children have little awareness of the mechanics of the economic system (Berti, Bombi, & Lis, 1982). Even at ages 6 and 7, children's view of economics consists of visible monetary transactions (Furth, 1980; Jahoda, 1979). Harrah and Friedman (1990) asked children about money, salaries, prices, and taxes and found that 8-year-olds had only a fragmentary and rudimentary understanding of the economic system; 11-year-olds had more knowledge; but only the 14-year-olds had a grasp of the overall system of the economy and how all the pieces fit together. Thus, most studies of children's understanding of economics and social class have focused on children over the age of 8 (Furnham & Stacey, 1991). However, well before they understand the system, children absorb economically related attitudes. Based on a cross-age and cross-social class study of children's economic beliefs, Dittmar and Van Duuren (1993) concluded that "cognitive and linguistic abilities clearly affect the complexity of information and processes that children can comprehend and communicate, but the content of their economic beliefs and values is shaped by the dominant, socially shared meaning systems in their environment and culture" (p. 60). For these reasons measuring young children's understanding of social class is complicated because common indices of wealth, such as education and occupational prestige, may not be visible and meaningful to them. However, more concrete clues including differences in clothing, homes, and, particularly, possessions are potentially salient to them.

Leahy (1983), who conducted a major research project (720 subjects, ages 6-adolescence, in the United States) on children's views of social class, suggests that after the preschool period, children's understanding of social class goes through three stages. Early elementary school children are likely to both describe and explain poverty and wealth in observable concrete terms, such as numbers of possessions and type of residence. When they are around 10 years of age, children begin to refer to people's psychological traits, such as motivation (e.g., willingness to work), in their explanations for the unequal distribution of resources. Finally, adolescents are capable of seeing the role of the social and economic structure in the unequal distribution of wealth, although very few participants in the study offered these explanations. As children get older, they also make the connection between having a job and getting money and learn more about the status and financial benefits associated with specific occupations (Furnham & Stacey, 1991). Although children are not able to grasp the causes of wealth and poverty until adolescence, economic status is often internalized into children's career aspirations at an early age (DeLone, 1979).

As children learn about the sources of economic disparity, they appear to absorb the prevailing attitudes about the value of wealth. Even preschoolers assume that rich people are happier and more likeable than poor people (Naimark, 1983; Ramsey 1991b). In one study, only a few young children tried to answer questions about whether or not it was fair that some people had more money than others, but those who did said that it was not fair (Ramsey, 1991b). Another group of young children suggested that the rich should share with poor people (Furby, 1979). Leahy (1983) and Furby (1979) found that elementary school children also advocate equalizing resources, but older children and adolescents were more likely to justify inequalities by claiming that poor people get what they deserve (Leahy, 1990). Taken together these findings illustrate how children in our society are developing their understanding of the economic system in the context of one of the intransigent contradictions of our society: the ideal of democratic equality versus the emphasis on economic competitiveness and individualism that inevitably results in some people being disadvantaged (Chafel, 1997). According to Furnham and Stacey (1991), children come to believe the notion that unequal distribution of wealth is justified and even desirable because these values are prevalent in all institutions and the media, are reflected in parents' financial anxieties or aspirations for upward mobility, and are unchallenged by alternative visions of how society could be organized.

There is little formal research about the effects of growing up in a consumerist society where children are bombarded by advertisements (Burnett & Sisson, 1995). However, psychologists have expressed concern that children are learning to relate to physical objects, especially toys in terms of *getting* and *having* instead of using and *enjoying* them; and learning to identify and judge themselves and others in terms of possessions (Kline, 1993). Moreover, research studies have shown that affluent children tend to be less happy and more at risk for drug and alcohol abuse than their less affluent peers (Csikszentmihalyi, 1999; Csikszentmihalyi & Schneider, 2000; Luthar & Becker, 2002), suggesting that beyond a certain point consumption does not bring contentment to children but instead stimulates new desires.

Cultural differences. Very few researchers have examined children's understanding of culture, in part because it is difficult to design appropriate measures. As early studies suggest (Lambert & Klineberg, 1967; Piaget & Weil, 1951), most young children do not grasp the relationships between nations, national origin, and traditions and do not have a concept of "culture." At the same time, when confronted with practical manifestations of cultural diversity, they respond appropriately. For example, bilingual children quickly switch languages when they play with friends from different language groups (Orellana, 1994). Moreover, preschoolers notice language differences and often associate them with racially different people and unfamiliar clothing and dwellings, although they do not necessarily have an accurate understanding of the sources and connections among these differences (Hirschfield & Gelman, 1997).

Quintana (1998) developed a model of the levels in ethnic perspective taking ability that synthesizes a number of cognitive and affective trends found in the research on children's responses to race and culture. His four-level model and is based on Selman's (1980) theory of social perspective taking and provides a framework for future research studies. At Level 0 (ages 3–6),

children are making affective distinctions between races based on the prevailing pro-white anti-black bias in society. These evaluations do not appear to be related to parents' explicit attitudes (as described earlier) and seem to be immune to parents' direct ethnic socialization when it contradicts the prevailing social attitudes. Because of their level of cognitive development, young children often exaggerate the intergroup differences and minimize the intragroup ones (Aboud, 1988; Aboud & Amato, 2001; Katz, 1976) and have difficulty seeing that people can be simultaneously the same and different. As a result, young children often make statements that echo prevailing stereotypes but do not necessarily reflect their feelings for children they actually know from other groups. At Level 1 (ages 6–10 years), children shift from relying on visible racial cues and begin to understand the more cultural aspects of ethnicity such as language, food, and ancestry. At this age, they have a fairly literal view of ethnicity (e.g., "I am Mexican American because I eat American food and Mexican food" (Quintana, p. 35). Racial and ethnic bias potentially declines during this period as children become more aware of others' perspectives and can see cross-group similarities and within group differences as found by Doyle and Aboud (1993). Children at Level 2 (ages 10–14) are becoming aware of the subtle and social aspects associated with race and ethnicity such as segregation, discrimination, and differences in wealth and may feel more mistrustful of individuals from other ethnic groups. Finally, adolescents at Level 3 develop an active ethnic-group consciousness, which shapes their group loyalty and motivates them to learn more about their own ethnic group(s) and to express their ethnic identity and stereotypes about other groups.

Gender differences. As children grow up, they construct their gender identities and concepts from overt and covert messages in their environment. Many studies have shown that during preschool, children in the United States learn stereotypic beliefs and attitudes about gender-roles that affect a wide range of behaviors, psychological constructs and aspirations including peer interactions, memory skills, self-identity, self-esteem, and social, educational, and vocational goals (Bigler, 1997). A full discussion of these implications is beyond the scope of this chapter, but two that are particularly germane to multicultural education are gender stereotypes and gender segregation.

A number of researchers have proposed that *gender stereotypes* are developed and maintained by children's gender schema, theories about the characteristics of males and females that influence how children interpret information (Bem, 1981, 1983; Martin & Halverson, 1981). These schema are complex and often contradictory. Liben and Bigler (2002) found that many children had different gender expectations for themselves than they did for others (e.g., a girl might think that both boys and girls could do carpentry, but she would not endorse that for herself). However, once they are established, gender stereotypes are self-perpetuating, and children often deny information that challenges them. Gender and racial stereotype cognitions are similar in some respects. First, children's sex-typed stereotypes increase during the preschool years, peak in early elementary school, and then decline during the middle-elementary school years (Signorella, Bigler, & Liben, 1993). Bigler (1997) speculates that this decrease in stereotyping may be linked to cognitive development, in particular to the ability to make multiple classifications and to comprehend gender constancy. Second, as with racial stereotypes, children who use more flexible classification schemes for nonsocial information are less likely to express gender stereotypes and can remember counter stereotypic information better than their peers who are more rigid classifiers (Bigler & Liben, 1992).

Children clearly prefer same-sex peers—all of their hypothetical and actual playmate choices demonstrate this over and over (Bigler, 1995). *Gender segregation* begins before preschool and becomes increasingly entrenched during the early childhood years (Ramsey, 1995). This division continues to increase during the elementary years and is reaffirmed by children's engagement in "borderwork" between the two groups (e.g., giving cooties to each other), and invasions in which one group disrupts the play of the other (Thorne, 1986). Children with cross-gender friends or those who prefer crossgender roles and activities (e.g., girls who like science and particularly boys who enjoy dressing up and playing with dolls) are often rejected and ridiculed by both children and adults, especially as they enter elementary school (e.g., MacNaughton, 2000; Sadker & Sadker, 1995). Thus, as children spend more time in gender-typed activities and segregated playgroups, they form gender-segregated groups that have their own cultures and rules, and the divisions become self-perpetuating and almost insurmountable (Maccoby, 1998).

Because children readily divide themselves by gender, teachers, often unintentionally, support and reinforce this segregation by using gender as a way of organizing their classes (e.g., seating, work groups) (Thorne, 1986). In a comparative study, Bigler (1995) found that, in elementary classrooms explicitly organized by gender (such as boys' and girls' teams and lines), children developed more gender stereotyped views of occupations and more rigid assumptions about the homogeneity of males and females than did their peers in classrooms in which gender differences were not emphasized.

Breaking down the gender divide and, in particular, equalizing power between the two groups is difficult and requires active interventions (MacNaughton, 2000). Even when teachers do implement strategies to reduce gender segregation, they are not always successful. In a number of studies, children initially responded positively to rewards, praise, or new activities and played with more cross-sex peers. However, after the interventions were over, they reverted back to their same-sex classmates (e.g., Maccoby, 1986; Serbin, Tonick, & Sternglanz, 1977; Swadener & Johnson, 1989).

Sexual orientation. Because of the controversial nature of this topic, it is virtually impossible to conduct research studies on children's awareness of sexual orientation and related attitudes. Thus, we have little formal research in this area. We do know, however, from informal observations children frequently use homophobic insults (which they may not even understand) to enforce gender-role conformity. Casper and Schultz (1999) did one of the very few studies on children's ideas about sexual orientations when they conducted extensive observations in early childhood classrooms that contained a number of children from openly gay- and lesbian-headed families. Their findings may not generalize to more heterosexist environments, but they do

give us an idea of the questions and concerns children would express if they were encouraged.

Casper and Schultz found that most of the children's questions and comments focused on whether or not someone needed to have had both a mother and a father to be born and on who could make up a family. They also noted that children were most likely to bring up questions about family composition and alternative methods of reproduction when they had ample time to develop their fantasy play and toys that gave them the latitude to play out different family constellations (e.g., multiple adult puppets of both genders).

Older children, when encouraged, are able to express and explore their explicit feelings about sexual orientation as is illustrated in Chasnoff and Cohen's (1996) videotape entitled *It's Elementary: Talking about Gay Issues in School.* This video of conversations between middle school teachers and their students shows children working through their initial anxieties and stereotypes about gay/lesbian people to recognizing that these views are unfounded, unjust, and harmful.

Abilities and disabilities. In the past two decades, a number of studies have contributed to our knowledge about children's awareness and attitudes related to disabilities (see Diamond & Innes, 2001, for a comprehensive review). Children's awareness and understanding vary across type of disability (Conant & Budoff, 1983; Diamond, 1993; Diamond & Hestenes, 1996). They usually learn about orthopedic and sensory disabilities during their early childhood years because they are more visible and concrete (DeGrella & Green, 1984; Diamond & Hestenes, 1996). Many young children have misconceptions about the causes of disabilities. They often explain disabilities by the equipment that children use (Diamond & Innes, 2001) (e.g., "he can't walk because he has a wheel chair"), immaturity (e.g., "She hasn't learned to talk yet."), or some kind of illness, injury or other trauma (e.g.," He had a really bad earache and now can't hear.") (Diamond, 1993; Diamond & Hestenes, 1996; Sigelman, 1991).

Children's attitudes toward people with disabilities shift during their preschool and elementary school years. Preschoolers often state that they could be friends with peers with disabilities (Diamond & Hestenes, 1996). However, as they get older and more concerned about how their skills compare with others', children tend to develop more biases against persons with disabilities (DeGrella & Green, 1984; Goodman, 1989). Moreover, during the elementary school years, mutual friendships between peers with and without disabilities tend to shift to lopsided care taking relationships (Grenot-Scheyer, Staub, Peck, & Schwartz, 1998; Salisbury & Palombar, 1998).

Children's attitudes vary across type of disability. As mentioned before, children are most likely to reject peers with emotional and cognitive disabilities. Likewise, impulsive behavior is often interpreted as misbehavior (Kostelnick et al., 2002). Because children do not usually understand the parameters of cognitive and language disabilities (Nabors & Keyes, 1995), they tend to make more generalized negative assumptions about peers with cognitive and language delays than they do about peers with physical disabilities (Diamond, 1994). Children are also more accepting toward peers who have disabilities that are clearly no fault of their own (e.g., blindness) than they are toward peers perceived as having more responsibility for their disability (e.g., obesity; poor impulse control) (Diamond & Innes, 2001).

Despite their misconceptions and biases, children without disabilities benefit from being in integrated classrooms. They become more sensitive to other people and more accepting of differences (Diamond, Hestenes, Carpenter, & Innes, 1997; Favazza & Odom, 1997). They also potentially learn to see how they are similar to people with disabilities and to see their strengths and avoid pitying them and trying to do things *for* them rather than *with* them (Kostelnik et al., 2002; Palmer, 2001; Salisbury & Palombar, 1998).

In summary, children are learning about racial, socioeconomic, cultural, gender, sexual orientation, and ability differences from a myriad of interactions, experiences, and sources throughout their childhood. They do not fully understand the causes and implications of these variations until they reach adolescence or adulthood. However, throughout their childhoods, they absorb prevailing views and draw conclusions that affect their perceptions and feelings about themselves and other individuals and groups. We cannot assume that the developmental trends described in this review apply to all children, but they do provide starting points for exploring how children's cognitions, attitudes, and behavior are developing and how they are shaped by particular contexts and experiences. Likewise, these research findings give us some parameters to consider when developing multicultural early childhood curriculum. However, we must keep in mind that our information is incomplete as many groups have been underrepresented in the research, particularly children from multiethnic or multiracial backgrounds. Moreover, we must always keep in mind that children develop unique views that reflect their individual predispositions and the influence of families, peers, community values, and the media.

Research on the Implementation and Effects of Early Childhood Multicultural Programs

During the 1980s and 1990s, the demographics of the United States changed with the influx of many new immigrants, and school districts throughout the United States adopted policies to include multicultural content in the K–8 curriculum. Many created positions such as multicultural coordinators to support these efforts (Meinert & Winsberry, 1998). Washburn (1996) found that 46% of the 713 school districts that were surveyed had multicultural programs. Most of these targeted all students (not just minority students). About half of them used an ethnic studies approach in social studies classes; 30% had antiracist programs explicitly dealing with bias; and 10% were oriented toward fostering intergroup relationships (human relations approach).

Most multicultural texts include suggestions for program or curriculum evaluation. However, very little formal research on the implementation or impact of particular multicultural programs has been done. Grant and Tate (1995) pointed out that "From the 1960s to the early 1990s was a period when multicultural theorists devoted much, if not most, of their attention to preparing essays and writing books defining and describing multicultural education, and declaring and celebrating it as a field of scholarship. As we head into the 21st century . . . scholarship in the area of multicultural education research must take center stage" (p. 161). Aboud and Levy (2000), speaking as psychologists, echo these views. "The challenge for future researchers is to evaluate rigorously the many [multicultural] interventions currently used in education settings, while continuing to examine in more controlled settings the mechanisms underlying prejudice reduction" (p. 289).

Grant and Tate (1995) note several barriers to doing multicultural education research: (1) As a group, education faculty lack the experience, ethnic diversity, and epistemological backgrounds to deal with the complexities of multicultural research and to prepare graduate students to do it. (2) The pervasive Eurocentrism and belief in the United States as a meritocratic society limit researchers' abilities to honestly and critically examine power relationships among racial, ethnic, economic, gender and ability groups. (3) The lack of funding for multicultural education research has resulted in few graduate students being trained to do the long-term and multifaceted evaluations that would capture the complexity of multicultural education. Sleeter and Grant (1999) also point out that because multicultural education practitioioners have never received much federal funding, they have not been required to conduct evaluations and so this expertise was not developed.

The broad goals and complexities of multicultural education give rise to the question of what kind of research is appropriate and meaningful. Grant and Tate (1995) make a distinction between "research on multicultural education" and "multicultural education research." The former reflects traditional educational research in which the effects of a particular curriculum are assessed by "objective" pre- and posttests or observations. The authors are critical of this orientation because it evaluates multicultural programs and materials for their effectiveness in helping children assimilate into schools but not to question the status quo of schools and society. "Multicultural education research," by contrast, is oriented toward studying justice and power relationships in schools from a number of perspectives. Its underlying premise is that race, class, gender, sexual orientation, and abilities/disabilities influence the relationship between knowledge and power. The primary goal is to apply this information to achieve equity, human dignity, and pluralism rather than assimilation. (See Grant, 1992 for more discussions about the possibilities and challenges to doing multicultural research.)

Unfortunately, very few studies exist that fit either of Grant's and Tate's definitions. Because of the complexities of conducting multicultural research and the lack of funding for implementing and evaluating programs, we have very few systematic studies of the effects of multicultural programs at any grade level and almost none in early childhood settings. Most of the early childhood multicultural studies are either controlled lab-based psychological studies or case studies of particular classrooms. Some of the latter are teachers' accounts of work in their own classrooms, which raises the question of researcher bias (Grant & Tate, 1995). However, several contain detailed information about children's responses to specific activities and provide useful feedback about the effects of specific approaches.

The perspectives and goals of the programs analyzed in these studies represent the approaches delineated by Sleeter and Grant (1987, 1999) (with the exception of single group studies). Therefore the following review is organized by those categories.

Education for the culturally different. One of the most carefully documented programs for adapting teaching practices to accommodate the needs and learning styles of children from different cultures is the KEEP project (the Kamehameha Elementary Education Project) (Tharp & Gallimore, 1988). Classroom practices in some of the elementary schools in a native Hawaiian community were adapted to be more compatible with the children's culture (e.g., cooperative mixed-sex peer learning centers). At the end of the study, the KEEP schools' children were academically ahead of the children who attended the regular public schools. When the study was expanded to include children on the Navajo reservation, the researchers learned that cultural compatibility varied in subtle ways across groups. The cooperative group structure that worked in the Hawaiian schools did not work in the Navajo schools until the teachers had the children work in same-sex pairs, which was a better fit with the social patterns in Navajo homes and communities.

Igoa (1995) used observations and interviews to document how specific techniques helped immigrant children in her classrooms adjust to life and schools in the United States. She helped the children to make filmstrips to express and share the pain of dislocation from their native lands and the difficulties of adjusting to a new country. To ease this transition, Igoa also encouraged children to create their own places in the classroom by bringing in pictures and artifacts from their homeland.

Human relations approach. Starting in the 1970s, a number of researchers have studied the effects of strategies designed to reduce prejudice and to facilitate intergroup relationships. In a chapter in the first edition of *Handbook of Research on the Education of Young Children*, Banks (1993) concluded that three methods had the most promise to change (particularly white) young children's own-race preferences: reinforcement of positive feelings about the color black; perceptual training to learn how to differentiate faces of members of less familiar groups; and cooperative learning in mixed ethnic/racial groups. Based on two decades of research, Johnson and Johnson (2000) likewise found that cooperative groups, constructive conflict, and civic values (shared commitment to the common good) were effective tools for reducing prejudice and discrimination. In another review of the effects of cooperative learning on cross-group relationships, Slavin (1995) stated that, when the conditions of role equality (as defined by Allport, 1954) have been met, strong interracial friendships often form. This intervention has a ripple effect because cross-ethnic connections outside of the groups increase as friends of members of an interracial group get to know each other.

However, to facilitate cross-ethnic relationships, cooperative activities need to be structured to insure that all members contribute in positive ways and that their roles do not simply recreate the patterns of domination that occur in the larger society (Hertz-Lazarowitz & Miller, 1992). Cohen and Lotan (1995)

directly addressed this issue by training teachers in a 2-week workshop to identify children who were low status (ignored or rejected by their peers) for any reason (e.g., disabilities, limited English proficiency, lack of social skills) and to enhance their status by designing curriculum that used a variety of abilities and drawing attention to low-status children's particular skills while working in cooperative groups. In their study of 13 classrooms (Grades 2–6), Cohen and Lotan (1995) found that, when teachers used these techniques, low-status children increased their rate of participation in heterogeneous cooperative groups.

Most research studies of cooperative activities have been done with older children, but one early childhood project (Anicich & Kirk, 1996) has been reported. Teachers in a multiracial kindergarten with nine severely handicapped children initiated a series of cooperative activities culminating in a collaborative Culture Quilt—comprised of squares made by each child. The authors did not systematically observe the children before and after the projects, but their anecdotal evidence that suggests these activities did help children to connect across race and ability lines.

Swadener (1988) observed teachers and children in two day care centers and concluded that both the formal and informal curricula supported the development of flexible gender roles and the children's appreciation of individual differences and acceptance of their peers with disabilities (both centers had a number of children with disabilities). Observations showed that cross-ability interactions increased during the year, indicating that multicultural strategies can counteract the previously described tendency for children with and without disabilities to become more distant over the course of the year (Diamond et al., 1993; Guralnick, Connor, Hammond, Gottman, & Kinnish, 1996; Guralnick & Groom, 1987). Moreover, Swadener saw children frequently challenging each other's gender stereotypes and negotiating flexible gender roles in their dramatic play. Despite their success in socially integrating children with special needs and fostering flexible gender roles, the teachers did not address racial or cultural differences or oppression or inequality. When asked why, the teachers reported that did not have the background, time, or resources to do the research and curriculum development to bring less familiar material and/or social issues into the classroom in pedagically effective ways.

Aboud (1993) studied the effects of a cognitively oriented curriculum called *More Than Meets the Eye* that is designed to reduce individual prejudice and heighten children's ability to differentiate among members of different groups. Pre- and posttests measured changes in fifth grade children's ability to differentiate members of other racial groups and their preferences for different racial groups and same- and cross-ethnic classmates. When compared to a control group, the children who participated in the curriculum significantly improved their abilities to differentiate members of other racial groups and slightly increased their cross-race preferences. Children of color in the experimental group, but not in the control group, expressed more positive feelings about their own group. In another study focusing on cognitive strategies, Bigler, Jones, and Lobliner (1997) found that children who learned to make flexible and multiple categories for both social and nonsocial items improved their recall for counterstereotyped racial images.

Aboud and Doyle (1996a) found that prejudice could be mitigated with conversations among peers. High-prejudice and low-prejudice (determined by responses to the Multiresponse Racial Attitude Measure) 8–11 year old children were paired to talk about the racial evaluations they each had made on MRA pretest. In the postdiscussion assessment, high-prejudice children expressed less prejudice than they did before; the low-prejudice children's views remained unchanged. In another study using conversation as the intervention (Reeder, Douzenis, & Bergin, 1997), five second-grade students whom teachers had identified as highly prejudiced, participated in counselor-led discussions about racial similarities and differences and social skills. Based on classroom observations and pre- and posttests using the Racial Relations Survey, Reeder et al. reported that, after the discussions, the children felt more comfortable with different race classmates and were less likely to make racially prejudiced comments.

Wasson-Ellam and Li (1999) studied the effects of different strategies in a combined multiethnic Grade 2–3 in Canada. They found that efforts to enhance children's ethnic identities were often overwhelmed by peer pressures to fit images of white consumerist culture. They did, however, describe several interesting conversations about cultural backgrounds that were initiated by reading "culturally conscious books . . . that aim to open children's minds and hearts so that they learn to understand and value both themselves and others' perspectives" (p. 30). The authors felt that the teacher's efforts to use collaborative groups and curriculum that reflected the children's backgrounds created a strong sense of community among the children (although they did not systematically measure these effects).

Affectively oriented interventions have focused on role-playing and empathy often based on the well-known "Blue Eyes, Brown Eyes" demonstration (Elliot, 1971). In a meta-analysis of 26 studies using role-playing and antiracist teaching (with a range of subjects from young children to college students) that were conducted between 1966 and 1987, McGregor (1993) concluded that, when used together, these methods can mitigate racist attitudes, especially in younger students. However, most of these studies were short-term interventions done by individual teachers or trainers, rather than long-term changes in school systems. Despite considerable publicity about Elliot's work and the encouraging outcome of the original demonstration, the intensive role-playing (where children enact the roles of dominant/subordinate groups over a period of time) has not been systematically replicated and evaluated with other groups of children in recent years (Aboud & Levy, 2000). The stringent federal regulations that now govern research with children might preclude this kind of project, as it does cause considerable distress.

Over the past two decades, a number of studies have examined efforts to increase the social integration of children with disabilities in regular classrooms. Although not formally labeled as "multicultural research," these interventions and assessments add to our understanding of factors that promote the interpersonal connections among people who are often isolated from each other (i.e., the human relations approach). A recurrent theme is that adults play crucial roles in the social inclusion of children with disabilities (Bronson, Hauser-Cram,

& Warfield, 1997; Gonsier-Gerdin, 1995; Kostelnick, Onaga, Rohde, & Whiren, 2002; Odom, Jenkins, Speltz, DeKlyen, 1982; Odom et al., 1996; Putnam, Markovchick, Johnson & Johnson, 1996; Sheridan et al., 1995; Stevens & Slavin, 1995; Swadener & Johnson, 1989). First, when adults obviously enjoy interacting with children with disabilities and support interactions between them and their peers, the children with disabilities are more a part of the classroom social life. Second, adults can facilitate cross-ability relationships by closely monitoring the level of social integration and providing activities and instructions to enhance social skills and positive peer interactions. Third, activities and classrooms that are structured around cooperative learning are more conducive to social integration than competitive ones. Fourth, children should be identified by everyone including themselves as a full member of the group and an integral part of all activities; disruptions for special services should be minimized.

Multicultural education. Since the inception of multicultural education, many multicultural books, posters, toys, art materials, and props have been created to incorporate diverse cultures into classrooms. In the 1970s and 1980s, many teachers relied heavily on these materials to convey multicultural principles, a practice that has been criticized because it portrays cultures in superficial ways and avoids difficult issues related to inequities (e.g., Derman-Sparks et al., 1989). Aboud and Levy (2000) reviewed several studies done in the 1970s that revealed that simply exposing children books and televised images about other groups did not change their views. They concluded that to be effective in reducing prejudice, teachers should not simply provide materials but also need to discuss and model alternative attitudes.

Day (1995) reached a similar conclusion after observing British preschool children's reactions to multicultural materials—props and clothing representing different cultural groups—that were introduced into the classroom. Although the children played enthusiastically with the new items, they appeared to be mostly attracted by the novelty of the materials and did not connect them with different cultures. The author noted that the materials themselves had some limitations (e.g., dolls in national costumes, which portrayed groups as exotically different). Also most of the items were oriented toward domestic play (e.g., cooking materials and clothing) and therefore appealed primarily to the girls. Based on her observations of the teachers and children in the classroom, Day concluded that rather than rely on materials to teach multiculturalism, the government should provide training to teachers to help them work effectively with children from different backgrounds and address issues related to diversity.

Lee and Lee (2001) implemented a kindergarten curriculum using dolls representing different racial and cultural groups that came with traditional costumes, contemporary (Western) clothing, and accessories that could be used to represent specific disabilities (e.g., wheelchair, seeing-eye dog). The authors also had the children cut out photographs in the *National Geographic* of people who looked different from them and they would not expect to see in their neighborhoods. The authors report that children mostly attended to differences in clothing and jewelry, rather than to other dimensions such as occupation, race, and household composition. This finding is not surprising given that young children usually notice concrete elements and are constantly exposed to clothing commercials in our fashion-oriented society. The dolls with their different clothing and equipment have the potential to be an effective way of talking to children about diversity, but, as described in the article, this curriculum had a number of shortcomings. In particular, by using *National Geographic* and making assumptions about which people children would and would not see in their communities, the teacher (probably unintentionally) conveyed the message that unfamiliar people are exotic "others" who are distant and different from the children in the class.

Neubert and Jones (1998) insightfully analyze the challenges and benefits of incorporating culturally relevant curriculum by describing the reactions when several teachers at Pacific Oaks School introduced *el Dia de los Muertos*. This Mexican holiday falls at the same time as Halloween and has somewhat parallel themes. However, rather than emphasizing scary images, celebrants acknowledge the reality of death and welcome back the souls of family members and friends who have died by creating altars and serving food. The teachers felt that this celebration was a way of honoring the traditions of the Mexican families at the school and in the surrounding community and also a vehicle for talking openly about death in a hopeful and loving way, rather than as a scary topic to be avoided. Many parents enthusiastically supported this activity, but a few parents were uncomfortable because they felt that the images of skulls and skeletons associated with *el Dia de los Muertos* were too scary or sacrilegious. The authors also found that the youngest children also came away from the holiday activities with misperceptions about death. However, they concluded that despite conflicts and misunderstandings, the curriculum had helped adults and children to grow and stretch their thinking beyond their familiar comfortable assumptions and to practice their conflict resolution skills. "Good curriculum is significant; it raises issues to be grappled with by adults and children alike" (p. 19).

Social reconstructionism. A couple of studies show how parent empowerment and social reconstructionism can be used to make schools more culturally compatible for children. Delgado-Gaitan and Trveba (1991) followed 20 Mexican-American families for 3 years and described how power relationships can change. The parents initially felt intimidated by the schools, but after forming a group and beginning to participate in the schools, they began to press teachers and administrators to make the classrooms more culturally compatible for their children. At the end of the study, they were collaborating with the teachers as equals and had effected many changes in the schools. Another investigation documents how Mexican-American parents used local elections to gain power. As they organized and gained more voter strength, parents became members of the school board and were in positions to influence the schools to be more culturally accessible to their children (Trueba, Rodriguez, Zou, & Cintron, 1993).

Levine (1993) documents how a kindergarten–first grade teacher was able to blend culturally relevant, human relations and social reconstructionist approaches in her classroom. The

observations capture the subtle ways that the teacher was able to create a safe space for all children in the classroom to express and compare their perspectives and to challenge the "authority" of the written word and social conventions. Although this study shows children's responses to specific activities and teacher conversations, it does not measure children's changes during the year, so we do not know whether or how these strategies influenced children's ideas and feelings over the long term.

De Marquez (2002) describes some effects of multicultural teaching in her kindergarten classroom. Although she does not describe her full program, she does report that teaching all the children some words from the different language groups in the classroom helped children to form cross-group friendships. She also describes discussion groups in which the children raised and challenged each other about social justice issues, demonstrating that, under the right conditions, young children can understand and discuss complex concerns.

Marsh (1992) documented her efforts to implement the antibias curriculum (Derman-Sparks et al., 1989) in a racially mixed kindergarten in the Midwest. She describes the organization of the year and the major themes that she addressed including topics such as immigration, conflict resolution, cooperation, and peace, Native Americans, and friends from around the world. According to excerpts from the children's conversations and Marsh's own journal, some of the children became more aware of injustices and began to take actions (e.g., protesting the lack of African American crossing guards, organizing a peace march). This kind of observational study is valuable because it shows how children actually respond to specific multicultural/antibias activities. Unfortunately, Marsh did not systematically measure children's ideas and feelings before and after the curriculum, so we do not know if the curriculum had an impact on all the children or only a few and if it had a cumulative effect on children's attitudes.

Lakey (1997) describes some of the challenges that arose when teachers and parents implemented antibias perspectives in a parent cooperative preschool. The parents had fully supported this approach until the teachers decided to provide images and books that portrayed different family orientations, particularly those with gay or lesbian parents. When the teachers told the parents that they were going to read the book *Daddy's Roommate*, a number of parents were very upset and boycotted the school that day, and one parent even withdrew her child. Lakey describes several emotional meetings and then how a resolution was finally reached. A committee of parents and teachers met several times and developed several curriculum possibilities that addressed issues of sexual orientation using different terms and images. The parents then voted on which approach they found most comfortable, and, eventually a compromise was reached. This account illustrates how easily conflicts and misunderstandings can occur around the emotionally charged topics that are part of multicultural education, the importance of working closely with parents, and the growth that occurs when groups openly discuss issues.

Goodman (1992) describes how the goals of critical democracy can be implemented in an elementary school. Using excerpts from field notes of interactions between staff and among staff and students, he shows how tensions between individual freedom and community needs emerge and ways they can be resolved that support power sharing and critical thought among all children and adults in the school. This account offers a hopeful message that teachers and children can create democratic communities that are both idealistic and functional. One limitation of the study is that the school is a small independent school, which raises the question of how well these strategies would work in other sites, especially large public schools.

In sum, a number researchers and teachers have studied different aspects of multicultural education, primarily using small-scale interventions or classroom case studies. These reports have demonstrated that various strategies can work to change children's thinking and behavior in the short run. However, we have no studies have compared the outcomes of different approaches to multicultural education nor any that have examined long-term effects on children's thinking and behavior. Thus, we cannot conclude that any particular approach is optimal. Moreover, no one has tackled the question of whether multicultural education can have an effect on larger societal and economic inequities.

These deficiencies are not surprising; the task of analyzing power relationships in schools and classrooms and assessing the effects of multicultural curricula and teaching practices is daunting. No one study can possibly capture all the aspects of pedagogical innovations. Furthermore, what works in one setting may not work in another one; so the context of each study is critical. Authentic multicultural education research also requires close collaboration among schools, communities, and universities. To capture the subtle, day-to-day contradictory and elusive power relationships at a school, administrators, teachers, children, and parents all must be actively involved in the research. This research agenda requires a well-funded comprehensive program and researchers and teachers who are highly trained in multicultural education. As new generations of students experience multicultural education at all levels (from preschool through graduate school) and enter the field, they will hopefully be able to develop the knowledge base and skills to explore the implementation and effects of multicultural education in more depth.

CONCLUSION

Multicultural Education grew out of several political movements and the disillusionment with many of the reforms of the 1950s and 1960s. For the past 30 years, it has been shaped and honed by the changing political landscape and by the expanding awareness of the multiple dimensions of oppression and inequity. Overall, the scope of multicultural education has become broader, and it has shifted from a focus on changing individual attitudes and celebrating diversity to a more hard-hitting critical analysis of systemic inequities.

The field of multicultural education has both used and inspired considerable psychological and educational research. From the 1950s to the present time, we have gathered a great deal of information about how children develop in different contexts and how they learn about the divisions and inequities

of their social and economic worlds. This research has shown clearly that development is an interaction between individual traits and contexts that include race, economics, culture, gender, and abilities/disabilities. Discrimination and privilege, and poverty and affluence profoundly influence the well being of children and their current and future prospects. Whereas multicultural education can help teachers to create more accessible and supportive classrooms for all children, it cannot erase the effects of social and economic disadvantages that many families suffer. One clear implication is that any teacher, administrator, family member, or policy maker who wants to embrace multiculturalism needs to be actively involved with organizations that are pressing for social, political, educational, and economic equity.

The research also shows us that, despite many popular myths, even very young children are aware of race, social class, culture, gender, and abilities/disabilities. In fact, children often express views that uncannily reflect prevailing social attitudes that many adults would like to deny. Thus, we must move beyond our own discomfort with difficult issues and our faith in the "colorblindness" of children and honestly and supportively help them explore their assumptions and curiosities about the multiple aspects of their worlds. Young children also have strong sense of fairness, which makes them natural social activists, and we need to find ways for them to feel that they can have an impact on their world—whether it is making up classroom rules or protesting a stereotyped book.

One limitation with the current developmental research is that most studies are limited by the questions and methods that derive from theories and methods of traditional child development research, which tend to view people in linear and single-dimensioned ways. Moreover, many studies compare all children to a white middle-class norm and often conclude that children of color or poverty are deficient in some ways. We need to keep raising questions and developing new modes of inquiry to gain a fuller and more balanced understanding of how children develop and learn within different social contexts.

In contrast to the child development research, we have very little information about what actually occurs in classrooms where multicultural early childhood education is practiced and how these efforts affect children. The information we do have suggests that the implementation of multicultural goals is uneven and fragmented, with very few programs combining more than one approach. The studies that were reviewed in this chapter suggest that some multicultural strategies, particularly those oriented toward educating the culturally different, enhancing human relations, and social reconstructivism, have potential to affect the thinking, behavior, and school success of young children. However, the information is skimpy and hard to generalize to other situations. We have almost no studies that look at the effectiveness of these strategies over time and no way of comparing them with each other. Some of the most interesting information come from case studies of individual classrooms. They contain many compelling examples of children's reactions to activities and suggest that multicultural activities can engage children and help them to challenge assumptions and learn new ways of seeing the world. However, these findings are limited because much of the data is anecdotal and may be biased.

To address of the limitations of both developmental and classroom research, we need programs that combine quantitative and qualitative methods and engage participation from many communities. Not only would these studies provide a fuller picture of the overall impact and more finely grained effects of multicultural programs, but they also have the potential to advance our knowledge of how children experience and learn about the contradictions and inequities in our society.

References

Aboud, F. E. (1988). *Children and prejudice*. New York: Basil Blackwell.

Aboud, F. E., & Amato, M. (2001). Developmental and socialization influences on intergroup bias. In R. Brown & S. L. Gaerther (Eds.), *Blackwell handbook of social psychology: Intergroup processes* (pp. 65-85). Oxford, UK: Blackwell Publishers.

Aboud, F. E., & Doyle, A. B. (1996). Does talk of race foster prejudice or tolerance in children? *Canadian Journal of Behavioural Science, 28*(3), 161-170.

Aboud, F. E., & Fenwick, V. (1999). Exploring and evaluating school-based interventions to reduce prejudice. *Journal of Social Issues, 55*(4), 767-786.

Aboud, F. E. & Levy, S. R. (2000). Interventions to reduce prejudice and discrimination in children and adolescents. In S. Oskamp (Ed.), *Reducing prejudice and discrimination*. Mahwah, NJ: Earlbaum.

Alba, R. D. (1990). *Ethnic identity: The transformation of white America*. New Haven, CT: Yale University Press.

Alejandro-Wright, M. N. (1985). The child's conception of racial classification: A socio-cognitive developmental model. In M. B. Spencer, G. K. Brookins, & W. R. Allen (Eds.), *Beginnings: The social and affective development of black children* (pp. 185-200). Hillsdale, NJ: Lawrence Erlbaum.

Allport, G. W. (1954). *The nature of prejudice*. Reading, MA: Addison-Wesley.

Alvarado, C., Derman-Sparks, L., & Ramsey, P. G. (1999). *In our own way: How anti-bias work shapes our lives*. St. Paul, MN: Redleaf Press.

Averhart, C. J., & Bigler, R. S. (1997). Shades of meaning: Skin tone, racial attitudes, and constructive memory in African American children. *Journal of Experimental Child Psychology, 67*, 363-388.

Banks, J. A. (1993). Multicultural education for young children: Racial and ethnic attitudes and their modification. In B. Spodek & O. Saracho (Eds.), *Handbook of Research on the Education of Young Children*, pp. 236-250. Hillsdale, NJ:

Banks, J. A. (1996). The African American roots of multicultural education. In J. A. Banks (Eds.), *Multicultural education: Transformative knowledge and action* (pp. 30-45). New York: Teachers College Press.

Bem, S. L. (1981). Gender schema theory: A cognitive account of sex typing. *Psychological Review, 88*, 354-364.

Bem, S. L. (1983). Gender schema theory and its implications for child development: Raising gender-aschematic children in a gender-schematic society. *Journal of Women in Culture and Society, 8*, 597-616.

Berti, A. E., Bombi, A. S., & Lis, A. (1982). The child's conception about means of production and their owners. *European Journal of Social Psychology, 12*, 221-239.

Bigelow, B. (1995). Dumb kids, smart kids, and social class. *Rethinking Schools, 10*(2), 12-13.

Bigler, R. S. (1995). The role of classification skill in moderating environmental influences on children's gender stereotyping: A study of the functional use of gender in the classroom. *Child Development, 66*, 1072-1087.

Bigler, R. S., Jones, L. C., & Lobliner, D. B. (1997). Social categorization and the formation of intergroup attitudes in children. *Child Development, 68*(3), 530-543.

Bigler, R. S. (1997). Conceptual and methodological issues in the measurement of children's sex-typing. *Psychology of Women Quarterly, 21*, 53-69.

Bigler, R. S., & Liben, L. S. (1992). Cognitive mechanisms in children's gender stereotyping: Theoretical and educational implications of a cognitive-based intervention. *Child Development, 63*, 1351-1363.

Bigler, R. S., & Liben, L. S. (1993). A cognitive-developmental approach to racial stereotyping and reconstructive memory in Euro-American children. *Child Development, 64*, 1507-1518.

Black-Gutman, D., & Hickson, F. (1996). The relationship between racial attitudes and social-cognitive development in children: An Australian study. *Developmental Psychology, 32*(3), 448-456.

Bloom, A. C. (1987). *The closing of the American mind*. New York: Simon & Schuster.

Bowman, B. T., & Stott, F. M. (1994). Understanding development in a cultural context. In B. L. Mallory & R. S. New (Eds.), *Diversity and developmentally appropriate practices: Challenges for early childhood education* (pp. 119-133). New York: Teachers College Press.

Bronson, M. B., Hauser-Cram, P., & Warfield, M. E. (1997). Classrooms matter: Relations between the classroom environment and the social and mastery behavior of five year old children with disabilities. *Jounral of Applied Developmental Psychology, 18*, 331-348.

Brooks-Gunn, J., Duncan, G. J., & Maritato, N. (1997). Poor families, poor outcomes: The well-being of children and youth. In G. J. Duncan & J. Brooks-Gunn (Eds.), *Consequences of growing up poor* (pp. 1-17). New York: Russell Sage.

Brown, C. S. (2002). *Refusing racism: White Allies and the struggle for civil rights*. New York: Teachers College Press.

Burnett, M. N., & Sisson, K. (1995). Doll studies revisited: A question of validity. *Journal of Black Psychology, 21*(1), 19-29.

Casper, V., Cuffaro, H. K., Schultz, S., Silin, J. G., & Wickens, E. (1996). Toward a most thorough understanding of the world: Sexual orientation and early childhood education. *Harvard Educational Review, 66*(2), 271-293.

Casper, B., & Schultz, S. B. (1999). *Gay parents, straight schools: Building communication and trust*. New York: Teachers College Press.

Chafel, J. A. (1997). Children's views of poverty: A review of research and implications for teaching. *The Educational Forum, 61*, 360-371.

Chasnoff, D., & Cohen, H. (1996). *It's elementary: Talking about gay issues in school* [videotape]. San Francisco, CA: Women's Educational Media.

Children's Defense Fund. (2003). 2002 Facts on Child Poverty in America. www.children'sdefense,org/familyincome/childpoverty/basicfacts.asp

Clark, K. B., & Clark, M. P. (1947). Racial identification and preference in Negro children. In T. M. Newcomb & E. L. Hartley (Eds.), *Readings in social psychology* (pp. 169-178). New York: Holt, Rinehart & Winston.

Clark, A., Hocevar, D., & Dembo, M. H. (1980). The role of cognitive development in children's explanations and preferences for skin color. *Developmental Psychology, 16*, 332-339.

Cohen, E. G., & Lotan, R. A. (1995). Producing equal-status interaction in the heterogeneous classroom. *American Educational Research Journal, 32*, 99-120.

Conant, S., & Budoff, M. (1983). Patterns of awareness in children's understanding of disabilities. *Mental Retardation, 21*(3), 119-125.

Conger, R. D., Ge, X., Elder, G. H., Lorenz, F. O., & Simons, R. L. (1994). Economic stress, coercive family process, and developmental problems of adolescents. *Child Development, 65*, 541-561.

Cortes, C. E. (2000). *The children are watching: How the media teach about diversity*. New York: Teachers College Press.

Cose, E. (1993). *The rage of a privileged class*. New York: HarperPerennial.

Cross, W. E. (1991). *Shades of black*. Philadelphia: Temple University Press.

Crawford, J. (1999). *Bilingual education: History, politics, theory, and practice* (4th ed.). Los Angeles, CA: Bilingual Education Services.

Csikszentmihalyi, M. (1999). If we are so rich, why aren't we happy? *American Psychologist, 54*, 821-827.

Csikszentmihalyi, M., & Schneider, B. (2000). *Becoming adults: How teenagers prepare for the world of work*. New York: Basic Books.

Day, J. A. E. (1995). Multicultural resources in preschool provision—an observational study. *Early Child Development and Care, 110*, 47-68.

DeGrella, L. H., & Green, V. P. (1984). Young children's attitudes toward orthopedic and sensory disabilities. *Education of the Visually Handicapped, 16*(1), 3-11.

de Marquez, T. M. (2002). Stories from a multicultural classroom. *Multicultural Education, 9*, 19-20.

Delgado-Gaitan, C., & Trueba, H. (1991). *Crossing cultural borders*. New York: Falmer.

DeLone, R. H. (1979). *Small futures: Children, inequality, and the limits of liberal reform*. New York: Harcourt Brace Jovanovich.

Delpit, L. (1995). *Other people's children: Cultural conflict in the classroom*. New York: New Press.

Derman-Sparks, L., & A. B. C. Task Force. (1989). *Anti-bias curriculum: Tools for empowering young children*. Washington, DC: National Association for the Education of Young Children.

Derman-Sparks, L., Higa, C. T., & Sparks, B. (1980). Children, race and racism: How race awareness develops. *Interracial Books for Children Bulletin, 11*, 3-9.

Derman-Sparks, L. & Phillips, C. B. (1997). *Teaching/learning antiracism: A developmental approach*. New York: Teachers College Press.

Dubois, W. E. B. (1973a). *The Philadelphia Negro: A socil study*. Milkwood, NY: Kraus-Thompson. (Original work published 1899)

Dubois, W. E. B. (1973b). *The suppression of the African slave trade to the United States of America 1638-1870*. Milkwood, NY: Kraus-Thompson. (Original work published 1896)

Devine, P. G., Plant, E. A., & Buswell, B. N. (2000). Breaking the prejudice habit: Progress and obstacles. In S. Okamp (Ed.), *Reducing prejudice and discrimination* (pp. 185-208). Mahwah, NJ: Lawrence Erlbaum Associates.

Diamond, K. E. (1993). Preschool children's concepts of disability in their peers. *Early Education and Development, 4*(2), 123-129.

Diamond, K. E. (1994). Evaluating preschool children's sensitivity to developmental differences in their peers. *Topics in Early Childhood Special Education, 14*(1), 49-62.

Diamond, K. E., & Hestenes, L. L. (1996). Preschool children's conceptions of disabilities: The salience of disability in children's ideas about others. *Topics in Early Childhood Special Education, 16*, 458-475.

Diamond, K. E., Hestenes, L. L., Carpenter, E. S., & Innes, F. K. (1997). Relationships between enrollment in an inclusive class and preschool children's ideas about people with disabilities. *Topics in Early Childhood Special Education, 17*(4), 520-536.

Diamond, K. E., & Innes, F. K. (2001). The origins of young children's attitudes toward peers with disabilities. In M. J. Guralnick (Ed.), *Early childhood inclusion: Focus on change* (pp. 159-178). Baltimore, MD: Paul H. Brooks.

Diamond, K., Le Furgy, W., & Blass, S. (1993). Attitudes of preschool children toward their peers with disabilities: A year-long investigation in integrated classrooms. *Journal of Genetic Psychology, 154*, 215-221.

Dittmar, H., & Van Duuren, M. (1993). Human nature beliefs and perceptions of the economic world. *The Journal of Foundation of Organizational Research*, Spring, 49-62.

Doyle, A., & Aboud, F. E. (1993). Social and cognitive determinants of prejudice in children. In K. A. McLeod (Ed.), *Multicultural education: The state of the art* (pp. 28033). Toronto, Ontario, Canada: University of Toronto Press.

D' Souza, D. (1991). *Illiberal education: The politics of race and sex on campus*. New York: The Free Press.

Farmer, T. W., & Farmer, E. M. Z. (1996). Social relationships of students with exceptionalities in mainstream classrooms: Social networks and homophily. *Exceptional Children, 62*(5), 431-450.

Farver, J. M., Kim, Y. K., & Lee, Y. (1995). Cultural differences in Korean-and Anglo-American preschoolers' social interaction and play behaviors. *Child Development, 66*, 1088-1099.

Farver, J. M., Welles-Nystrom, B., Frosch, D. L., Wimbarti, S., & Hoppe-Graff, S. (1997). Toy stories: Aggression in children's narratives in the United States, Sweden, Germany, and Indonesia. *Journal of Cross-Cultural Psychology, 28*(4), 393-420.

Farver, J. M., & Shin, Y. L. (1997). Social pretend play in Korean- and Anglo-American preschoolers. *Child Development, 68*(3), 544-556.

Favazza, P., & Odom, S. L. (1997). Promoting positive attitudes of kindergarten-age children toward people with disabilities. *Exceptional Children, 63*, 405-418.

Feagin, J. R., & Sikes, M. P. (1994). *Living with racism: The Black middle-class experience*. Boston: Beacon.

Fennimore, B. S. (2000). *Talk matters: Refocusing the language of public schooling*. New York: Teachers College Press.

Finkelstein, N. W., & Haskins, R. (1983). Kindergarten children prefer same-color peers. *Child Development, 54*, 502-508.

Fishbein, H. D., & Imai, S. (1993). Preschoolers select playmates on the basis of gender and race. *Journal of Applied Developmental Psychology, 14*, 303-316

Fox, D. J., & Jordan, V. B. (1973). Racial preference and identification of Black, American Chinese, and White children. *Genetic Psychology Monographs, 88*, 229-286.

Frankenberg, R. (1993). *White women, race matters: The social construction of whiteness*. Minneapolis: University of Minnesota Press.

Freire, P. (1970). *Pedagogy of the oppressed*. New York: Seabury.

Furby, L. (1979). Inequalities in personal possessions: Explanations for and judgements about unequal distribution. *Human Development, 22*, 180-202.

Furnham, A., & Stacey, B. (1991). *Young people's understanding of society*. New York: Routledge.

Furth, H. G. (1980). *The world of grown-ups: Children's conceptions of society*. New York: Elsevier.

Garbarino, J. (1999). *Lost boys: Why our sons turn violent and how we can save them*. New York: Free Press.

Garcia Coll, C., Lamberty, C., Jenkins, R., McAdoo, H. P., Crnic, K., Wasik, B. H., & Vazquez Garcia, H. (1996). An integrative model for the study of developmental competencies in minority children. *Child Development, 67,* 1891-1914.

Gay, G. (1983). Multiethnic education: Historical developments and future prospects. *Phi Delta Kappan, 64,* 560-563.

Gibbs, J. T., Huang, L. N., & Associates. (1989). *Children of color: Psychological interventions with minority youths.* San Francisco: Jossey-Bass.

Giroux, H. A. (1992). Post-colonial ruptures and democratics possibilities: Multiculturalism as anti-racist pedagogy. *Critical Critique, 21,* 5-40.

Giroux, H. A. (1999). *The mouse that roared: Disney and the end of innocence.* Lanham, MD: Rowman & Littlefield.

Giroux, H. A., & McLaren, P. (1994). *Between borders: pedagogy and the politics of cultural studies.* New York: Routledge.

Gollnick, D. M., & Chinn, P. C. (1998). *Multicultural education in a pluralistic society* (5th Edition). Columbus, OH: Merrill.

Gonsier-Gerdin, J. (1995, March–April). *An ethnographic case study of children's social relationships in a full inclusion elementary school.* Poster presented at the biennial meeting of the Society for Research in Child Development, Indianapolis.

Gonzalez-Ramos, G., Zayas, L. H., & Cohen, E. V. (1998). Child-rearing values of low-income, urban Puerto Rican Mothers of preschool children. *Developmental Psychology, 29*(4), 377-382.

Goodman, J. (1992). *Elementary schooling for critical democracy.* Albany: State University of New York Press.

Goodman, J. E. (1989). Does retardation mean dumb? Children's perceptions of the nature, cause, and course of mental retardation. *The Journal of Special Education, 23,* 313-329.

Goodman, M. (1952). *Race awareness in young children.* Cambridge, MA: Addison-Wesley.

Gottfried, A. W., Gottfried, A. E., Bathurst, K., Guerin, D. W., Parramore, M. M. (2003). Socioeconomic status in children's development and family environment: Infancy through adolescence. In M. Bornstein (Ed.), *Socioeconomic status, parenting, and child development* (pp. 189-207). Mahwah, NJ: Lawrence Erlbaum Associates.

Graham, J. A., & Cohen, R. (1997). Race and sex as factors in children's sociometric ratings and friendship choices. *Social Development, 6*(3), 355-372.

Grant, C. A. (Ed.) (1992). *Research and multicultural education: From the margins to the mainstream.* Washington, DC: Falmer Press.

Grant, C. A. (1999). *Multicultural research: A reflective engagement with race, class, gender, and sexual orientation.* London: Falmer.

Grant, C. A., & Sleeter, C. E. (1989). *Turning on learning: Five approaches for multicultural teaching plans for race, class, gender, and disability.* Columbus, OH: Merrill.

Grant, C. A., & Tate, W. F. (1995). Multicultural education through the lens of the multicultural education research literature. In J. A. Banks & C. A. M. Banks (Eds.), *Handbook of research on multicultural education* (pp. 145-166). New York: Macmillan.

Grenot-Scheyer, M., Staub, D., Peck, C. A., & Schwartz, I. S. (1998). Reciprocity and friendships: Listening to the voices of children and youth with and without disabilities. In L. H. Meyer, H-S. Park, M. Grenot-Scheyer, I. S. Schwarz, & B. Harry (Eds.), *Making friends: The influences of culture and development* (pp. 149-167). Baltimore, MD: Paul Brooks.

Gruenewald, D. A. (2003). The best of both worlds: A critical pedagogy of place. *Educational Researcher, 32,*(4), 3-12.

Guralnick, M. J., Connor, R. T., Hammond, M. A., Gottman, J. M., & Kinnish, K. (1996). The peer relations of preschool children with communication disorders. *Child Development, 67,* 471-489.

Guralnick, M. J., & Groom, J. M. (1987). The peer relations of mildly delayed and nonhandicapped preschool children in mainstreamed playgroups. *Child Development, 58,* 1556-1572.

Hallinan, M. T., & Teixeira, R. A. (1987). Opportunities and constraints: Black-White differences in the formation of interracial friendships. *Child Development, 58,* 1358-1371.

Harrah, J., & Friedman, M. (1990). Economic socialization in children in a midwestern American community. *Journal of Economic Psychology, 11,* 495-513.

Hernstein, R. J., & Murray, C. (1994). *The bell curve: Intelligence and class structure in American life.* New York: Free Press.

Hertz-Lazarowitz, R., & Miller, N. (Eds.). (1992). *Interaction in cooperative groups.* Cambridge: Cambridge University Press.

Hirsch, E. D., Jr. (1987). *Cultural literacy: What every American needs to know.* New York: Houghton-Mifflin.

Hirschfield, L. A. (1994). On acquiring social categories: Cognitive development and anthropological wisdom. *Man, 23,* 611-638.

Hirschfield, L. A. (1995). Do children have a theory of race? *Cognition, 54,* 209-252.

Hischfield, L. A., & Gelman, S. A. (1997). What young children think about the relationship between language variation and social difference. *Cognitive Development, 12,* 213-238.

Holmes, R. M. (1997). Children's use of social distance: The effects of race and gender. *Child Study Journal, 27*(2), 129-144.

Howard, G. (1999). *We cannot teach what we do not know: White teachers, multiracial schools* New York: Teachers College Press.

Hughes, P. & MacNaughton, G. (2001). Fractured or manufactured: Gendered identities and culture in the early years. In S. Grieshaber & G. S. Cannella (Eds.), *Embracing identities in early childhood education: Diversity and possibilities* (pp. 114-130). New York: Teachers College Press.

Hunter, W. A. (1973). Cultural pluralism: The whole is greater than the sum of its parts. *Journal of Teacher Education, 24*(4), 262.

Huston, A. C. (1991). Children in poverty: Developmental and policy issues. In A. C. Huston (Ed.), *Children in poverty: Child development and public policy* (pp. 1-22). Cambridge: Cambridge University Press.

Igoa, C. (1995). *The inner world of the immigrant child.* New York: St. Martin's Press.

Jahoda, G. (1979). Construction of economic reality by some Glaswegian children. *European Journal of Social Psychology, 9,* 115-127.

Johnson, D. W., & Johnson, R. T. (2000). The three Cs of reducing prejudice and discrimination. In S. Okamp (Ed.), *Reducing prejudice and discrimination* (pp. 239-268). Mahwah, NJ: Lawrence Erlbaum Associates.

Juvonen, J., & Bear, G. (1992). Social adjustment of children with and without learning disabilities in integrated classrooms. *Journal of Educational Psychology, 84,* 322-330.

Katz, P. A. (1976). The acquisition of racial attitudes in children. In P. A. Katz (Ed.), *Towards the elimination of racism* (pp. 125-154). New York: Pergamon.

Katz, P. A. (1982). Development of children's racial awareness and intergroup attitudes. In L. G. Katz (Ed.), *Current topics in early childhood education* (pp. 17-54). Norwood, NJ: Ablex.

Katz, P. A., & Kofkin, J. A. (1997). Race, gender, and young children. In S. Luthar, J. Burack, D. Cicchetti, & J. Weisz (Eds.), *Developmental perspectives on risk and pathology* (pp. 51-74). New York: Cambridge University Press.

Kemple, K. M. (2004). *Let's be friends: Peer competence and social inclusion in early childhood programs.* New York: Teachers College Press.

Kindlon, D., & Thompson, M. (1999). *Raising Cain: Protecting the emotional lives of boys*. New York: Ballantine Books.

Kirk, R., & Anicich, M. (1996). Dropping the barriers in kindergarten: Cultural awareness in education. *Journal of Instructional Psychology, 23*(4), 312-314.

Kistner, J., Metzler, A., Gatlin, D., & Risi, S. (1993). Classroom racial proportions and children's peer relations: Race and gender effects. *Journal of Educational Psychology, 85*(3), 446-452.

Kivel, P. (1999). *Boys will be men: Raising our sons for courage, caring, and community*. Gabriola Island, BC: New Society Publishers.

Kline, S. (1993). *Out of the garden: Toys and children's culture in the age of TV Marketing*. London, UK: Verso.

Kobayashi-Winata, H., & Power, T. G. (1989). Child rearing and compliance: Japanese and American families in Houston. *Journal of Cross-Cultural Psychology, 20*(4), 333-356.

Kohen, D. E., Brooks-Gunn, J., Leventhal, T., & Hertzman, C. (2002). Neighborhood income and physical and social disorders in Canada: Associations with young children's competencies. *Child Development, 73*(6), 1844-1860.

Kostelnik, M. J., Onaga, E., Rohde, B., Whiren, A. (2002). *Children with special needs: Lessons for early childhood professionals*. New York: Teachers College Press.

Lakey, J. (1997). Teachers and parents define diversity in an Oregon preschool cooperative—democracy at work. *Young Children, 52*(4), 20-28.

Lambert, W. E., & Klineberg, O. (1967). *Children's views of foreign peoples*. New York: Appleton-Century-Crofts.

Leahy, R. (1983). The development of the conception of social class. In R. Leahy (Ed.), *The child's construction of inequality* (pp. 79-107). New York: Academic Press.

Leahy, R. (1990). The development of concepts of economic and social inequality. *New Directions for Child Development, 46*, 107-120.

Lebra, T. S. (1994). Mother and child in Japanese socialization: A Japan-U.S. comparison. In P. M. Greenfield & R. R. Cocking (Eds.), *Cross-cultural roots of minority child development* (pp. 259-274). Hillsdale, NJ: Erlbaum.

Lee, C. E., & Lee, D. (2001). Kindergarten geography: Teaching diversity to young people. *Journal of Geography, 100*, 152-157.

Levine, L. (1993). "Who says?" Learning to value diversity in school. In F. Pignatelli & S. W. Pflaum (Eds.), *Celebrating diverse voices: Progressive education and equity*. Newbury Park, CA: Corwin Press.

Levine, J. (1994, March/April). White like me: When privilege is written on your skin. *Ms.*, pp. 22-24.

Liben, L. S., & Bigler, R. S. (2002). The developmental course of gender differentiation: Conceptualizing, measuring, and evaluating constructs and pathways. *Monographs of the Society for Research in Child Development, 67*(2, Serial No. 269).

Lott, B. (2002). Cognitive and behavioral distancing from the poor. *American Psychologist, 57*(2), 100-110.

Luthar, S. S., & Becker, B. E. (2002). Privileged but pressured? A study of affluent youth. *Child Development, 73*, 1593-1610.

MacAdoo, H. P. (1993). *Family ethnicity: Strength in diversity*. Beverly Hills, CA: Sage Publications.

Maccoby, E. E. (1986). Social groupings in childhood: Their relationship to prosocial and antisocial behavior in boys and girls. In D. Olewus, J. Block, & M. Radke-Yarrow (Eds.), *Development of antisocial and prosocial behavior* (pp. 263-284). New York: Academic Press.

Maccoby, E. E. (1998). *The two sexes: Growing up apart: Coming together*. Cambridge, MA: Harvard University Press.

MacNaughton, G. (2000). *Rethinking gender in early childhood education*. Thousand Oaks, CA: Sage Publications.

Marsh, M. M. (1992). Implementing antibias curriculum in the kindergarten classroom. In S. Kessler & B. B. Swadener (Eds.), *Reconceptualizing the early childhood curriculum: Beginning the dialogue* (pp. 267-288). New York: Teachers College Press.

Martin, C. L., & Halverson, C. (1981). A schematic processing model of sex typing and stereotyping in children. *Child Development, 52*, 1119-1134.

Mattai, P. R. (1992). Rethinking multicultural education: Has it lost its focus or is it being misused? *Journal of Negro Education, 61*(1), 65-77.

McCarthy, C. (1990a). *Race and curriculum*. London: The Falmer Press.

McCarthy, C. (1990b). Race and education in the United States: The multicultural solution. *Interchange, 21*(3), 45-55.

McGregor, J. (1993). Effectiveness of role playing and antiracist teaching in reducing student prejudice. *Journal of Education Research, 86*, 215-226.

McIntosh, P. (1995). White privilege and male privilege: A personal account of coming to see correspondences through work in women's studies. In M. L. Anderson & P. H. Collins (Eds.), *Race, class, and gender: An anthologys* (pp. 76-87). Belmont, CA: Wadsworth.

McLaren, P. (1994). White terror and oppositional agency: Towards a critical multiculturalism. In D. T. Goldbert (Ed.), *Multiculturalism: A critical reader* (pp. 45-74). Cambridge, MA: Blackwell.

McLaren, P. (1997). *Revolutionary Multiculturalism: Pedagogies of dissent for the new millenium*. Boulder, CO: Westview Press.

McLaren, P. (2000). White terror and oppostional agancy: Towards a critical multiculturalism. In E. M. Duarte & S. Smith (Eds.), *Foundational Perspectives in Multicultural Education* (pp. 213-241). New York: Longman.

McLoyd, V. C. (1998). Changing demographics in the American population: Implications for research on minority children and adolescents. In V. C. Mcloyd & L. Steinberg (Eds.), *Studying minority adolescents: Conceptual, methodological, and theoretical issues* (pp. 3-28). Mahwah, NJ: Lawrence Erlbaum Associates.

McLoyd, V. C., & Wilson, L. (1992). The strain of living poor: Parenting, social support, and child mental health. In A. C. Huston (Ed.), *Children in poverty: Child development and public policy* (pp. 105-135). New York: Cambridge University Press.

McLoyd V. C., & Ceballo, R. (1998). Conceptualizing and assessing the economic context: Issues in the study of race and child development. In V. C. McLoyd & L. Steinberg (Eds.), *Studying minority adolescents: Conceptual, methodological, and theoretical issues* (pp. 251-278). Mahwah, NJ: Lawrence Erlbaum Associates.

Minami, M., & Ovando, C. J. (1995). Language issues in multicultural contexts. In J. A. Banks & C. A. M. Banks (Eds.), *Handbook of research on multicultural education* (pp. 427-444). New York: Simon & Schuster Macmillan.

Meinert, R., & Winberry, S. (1998). The multicultural debate and the K through 8 curriculum. *Early Child Development and Care, 147*, 5-15.

Milner, D. (1983). *Children and race*. Beverly Hills, CA: Sage Publications.

Moran, C. E., & Hakuta, K. (1995). Bilingual education: Broadening research perspectives. In J. A. Banks & C. A. M. Banks (Eds.), Handbook of research on multicultural education (pp. 445-462). New York: Macmillan.

Nabors, L. (1995, March). *Attitudes, friendship ratings, and behaviors for typically developing preschoolers interacting with peers with disabilities*. Paper presented at the biennial meeting of the Society for Research in Child Development, Indianapolis.

Nabors, L., & Keyes, L. (1995). Preschoolers' reasons for accepting peers with and without disabilities. *Journal of Developmental and Physical Disabilities, 7*(4), 335-355.

Naimark, H. (1983). *Children's understanding of social class differences*. Paper presented at the biennial meeting of the Society for Research in Child Development, Detroit, MI.

Neubert, K. & Jones, E. (1998). Creating culturally relevant holiday curriculum: A negotiation. *Young Children, 53*(5), 14–19.

Newman, M. A., Liss, M. B., & Sherman, F. (1983). Ethnic awareness in children: Not a unitary concept. *The Journal of Genetic Psychology, 143*, 103–112.

Nieto, S. (1995). From brown heroes and holidays to assimilationist agendas: reconsidering the critiques of multicultural education. In C. E. Sleeter & P. L. McLaren (Eds.), *Multicultural education, critical pedagogy, and the politics of difference* (pp. 191–220). Albany: State University of New York Press.

Nieto, S. (1992). *Affirming diversity: The sociopolitical context of multicultural education* New York: Longman.

Nieto, S. (2004). *Affirming diversity: The sociopolitical context of multicultural education* (4th ed.). New York: Longman.

Ocampo, K. A., Bernal, M. E., & Knight, G. P. (1993). Gender, race, and ethnicity: The sequencing of social constancies. In M. E. Bernal & G. P. Knight (Eds.), *Ethnic identity: Formation and transmission among Hispanics and other minorities* (pp. 11–30). Albany: State University of New York Press.

Odom, S. L. (2002). *Widening the circle: Including children with disabilities in preschool programs*. New York: Teachers College Press.

Odom, S. L., Jenkins, J. R., Speltz, M. L., & DeKlyen, M. (1982). Promoting social interaction of young children at risk for learning disabilities. *Learning Disability Quarterly, 5*, 379–387.

Odom, S. L., Peck, C. A., Hanson, M., Beckman, P. J., Kaiser, A. P., Lieber, J., Brown, W. H., Horn, E. M., & Schwartz, I. S. (1996). Inclusion at the preshool level: An ecological systems analysis. *Social Policy Report of the Society for Research in Child Development, 10*(2/3), 18–30.

Odom, S. L., Zercher, C., Marquart, J., Li, S., Sandall, S. R., & Wolfberg, P. (2002). Social relationships of children with disabilities and their peers in inclusive classrooms. In S. L. Odom (Ed.), *Widening the circle: Including children with disabilities in preschool programs* pp. 61–80). New York: Teachers College Press.

Olneck, M. (1990). Symbolism and ideology in intercultural and multicultural education. *American Journal of Education, 98*(2), 147–174.

Omi, M., & Winant, H. (1986). *Racial formation in the United States*. New York: Routledge & Kegan Paul.

Orellana, M. F. (1994). Appropriating the voice of the superheroes: Three preschoolers' bilingual language uses in play. *Early Childhood Research Quarterly, 9*, 171–193.

Palmer, A. (2001). Responding to special needs. In E. Dau (Ed.), *The anti-bias approach in early childhood* (2nd Ed., pp. 83–94). Frenchs Forest, New South Whales, Australia: Pearson Education Australia.

Patchen, M. (1982). *Black–White contact in schools: Its social and academic effects*. West Lafayette, IN: Purdue University Press.

Pearl, R., Farmer, T. W., Van Acker, R., Rodkin, P. C., Bost, K. K., Coe, M., & Henley, W. (1998). The social integration of students with mild disabilities in general education classrooms: Peer group membership and peer-assessed social behavior. *The Elementary School Journal, 99*(2), 167–185.

Peters, M. F. (1985). Racial socialization of young Black children. In H. P. McAdoo & J. L. McAdoo (Eds.), *Black children: Social, educational, and parental environment* (pp. 159–173). Newbury Park, CA: Sage.

Phillips, C. B. (1994). The movement of African-American children through sociocultural contexts: A case of conflict resolution. In B. L. Mallory & R. S. New (Eds.), *Diversity and developmentally appropriate practice* (pp. 137–154). New York: Teachers College Press.

Piaget, J., & Weil, A. M. (1951). The development in children of the idea of the homeland and of relations to other countries. *International Social Science Journal, 3*, 561–578.

Pollack, W. (1998). *Real boys: Rescuing our sons from the myths of boyhood*. New York: Random House.

Polakow, V. (1993). *Lives on the edge*. Chicago: University of Chicago Press.

Porter, J. D. (1971). *Black child, White child: The development of racial attitudes*. Cambridge, MA: Harvard University Press.

Putnam, J., Markovchick, K., Johnson D. W., & Johnson, R. T. (1996). Cooperative learning and peer acceptance of students with learning disabilities. *Journal of Social Psychology, 136*, 741–752.

Quintana, S. M. (1998). Children's developmental understanding of ethnicity and race. *Applied and Preventive Psychology, 7*, 27–45.

Ramsey, P. G. (1986b). Racial and cultural categories. In C. P. Edwards with P. G. Ramsey, *Promoting social and moral development in young children: Creative approaches for the classroom* (pp. 78–101). New York: Teachers College Press.

Ramsey, P. G. (1987). Young children's thinking about ethnic differences. In J. Phinney & M. Rotheram (Eds.), *Children's ethnic socialization: Pluralism and development* (pp. 56–72). Beverly Hills, CA: Sage.

Ramsey, P. G. (1991a). *Making friends in school: Promoting peer relationships in early childhood*. New York: Teachers College Press.

Ramsey, P. G. (1991b). The salience of race in young children growing up in an all-White community. *Journal of Educational Psychology, 83*, 28–34.

Ramsey, P. G. (1995). Changing social dynamics of early childhood classrooms. *Child Development, 66*, 764–773.

Ramsay, P. G. (2004). *Teaching and learning in diverse world: Multicultural education for young children* (3rd ed.) New York: Teachers college Press.

Ramsey, P. G., & Myers, L. C. (1990). Salience of race in young children's cognitive, affective and behavioral responses to social environments. *Journal of Applied Developmental Psychology, 11*, 49–67.

Ramsey, P. G., & Williams, L. R. with Vold, E. B. (2003). *Multicultural education: A Source book* (2nd ed.). New York: RoutledgeFalmer.

Reeder, J., Douzenis, C., & Bergin, J. J. (1997). The effects of small group counseling on the racial attitudes of second grade students. *Professional School Counseling, 1*(2), 15–18.

Rist, R. C. (1970). Student social class and teacher expectations: The self-fulfilling prophecy in ghetto education. *Harvard Educational Review, 40*, 411–451.

Root, M. (1996). *The multiracial exeperience: Racial borders as the new frontier*. Thousand Oaks, CA: Sage.

Roopnarine, J. L., Lasker, J., Sacks, M., & Stores, M. (1998). The cultural contexts of children's play. In O. Saracho & B. Spodek (Eds.), *Play in Early Childhood* (pp. 194–219). Albany: State University of New York Press.

Rosenfield, D., & Stephan, W. G. (1981). Intergroup relations among children. In S. S. Brehm, S. M. Kassin, & F. X. Gibbons (Eds.), *Developmental social psychology* (pp. 271–297). New York: Oxford University Press.

Rotenberg, K. J., & Cerda, C. (1994). Racially based trust expectancies of Native American and Caucasian children. *The Journal of Social Psychology, 134*(5), 621–631.

Rotheram, M. J., & Phinney, J. (1987). Introduction: Definitions and perspectives in the study of children's ethnic socialization. In J. Phinney & M. J. Rotheram (Eds.), *Children's ethnic socialization: Pluralism and development* (pp. 10–28). Beverly Hills, CA: Sage.

Running-Grass. (1994). Towards a multicultural environmental education. *Multicultural Education, 2*(1), 4–6.

Sadker, M., & Sadker, D. (1995). *Failing at fairness: How our schools cheat girls*. New York: Simon & Schuster.

Salisbury, C. L., & Palombar, M. M. (1998). In L. H. Meyer, H-S. Park, M. Grenot-Scheyer, I. S. Schwarz, & B. Harry (Eds.), *Making friends: The influences of culture and development* (pp. 81-104). Baltimore, MD: Paul Brooks Publishing.

Schlesinger, A. M., Jr. (1992). *The disuniting of America*. New York: Norton.

Schofield, J. W. (1989). *Black and White in school: Trust, tension, or tolerance*. New York: Teachers College Press.

Selman, R. L. (1980). *The growth of interpersonal understanding: Developmental and clinical analyses*. San Diego, CA: Academic Press.

Serbin, L. A., Tonick, I. J., & Sternglanz, S. H. (1977). Shaping cooperative cross-sex play. *Child Development, 48*, 924-929.

Sheridan, M. K., Foley, G. M., & Radlinski, S. H. (1995). *Using the supportive play model: Individualized intervention in early childhood practice*. New York: Teachers College Press.

Sigelman, C. K. (1991). The effect of causal information on peer perceptions of children with physical problems. *Journal of Applied Developmental Psychology, 12*, 237-253.

Singleton, L. C., & Asher, S. R. (1977). Peer preferences and social interaction among third-grade children in an integrated school district. *Journal of Educational Psychology, 69*, 330-336.

Sigelman, C. K., & Singleton, L. C. (1986). Stigmatization in childhood: A survey of developmental trends and issues. In G. Becker, L. M. Colema, & S. Ainley (Eds.), *The dilemma of difference: A multidisciplinary view of stigma* (pp. 185-208). New York: Plenum.

Signorella, M. L., Bigler, R. S., & Liben, L. S. (1993). Developmental differences in children's gender schemata about others: A meta-analytic review. *Developmental Review, 13*, 147-183.

Slavin, R. E. (1980). Cooperative learning. *Review of Educational Research, 50*, 315-342.

Slavin, R. E. (1995). Cooperative learning and intergroup relations. In J. A. Banks & C. A. M. Banks (Eds.), *Handbook of research on multicultural education* (pp. 628-634). New York: Macmillan.

Sleeter, C. E. (Ed.). (1991). *Empowerment through multicultural education*. Albany: State University of New York Press.

Sleeter, C. E. (1992). *Keepers of the American Dream*. London: The Falmer Press.

Sleeter, C. E. (1994). White racism. *Multicultural Education, 1*, 5-8, 39.

Sleeter, C. E. (1995). An analysis of the critiques of multicultural education. In J. A. Banks & C. A. McGee Banks (Eds.), *Handbook of research on multicultural education* (pp. 81-94). New York: Macmillan.

Sleeter, C. (1996). *Multicultural education as social activism*. Albany: SUNY Press.

Sleeter, C. E., & Grant, C. A. (1987). An analysis of multicultural education in the United States. *Harvard Educational Review, 57*, 421-444.

Sleeter, C. E., & Grant, C. A. (1999). *Making choices for multicultural education: Five approaches to race, class, and gender* (3rd ed.). Upper Saddle River, NJ: Merrill-Prentice Hall.

Sleeter, C. E., & McLaren, P. L. (1995b). *Multicultural Education, critical pedagogy, and the politics of difference*. Albany: State University of New York Press.

Smedly, A. (1993). *Race in North America: Origin and evolution of a world view*. Boulder CO: Westview.

Spencer, M. B., Brookins, G. K., & Allen, W. R. (1985). *Beginnings; The social and affective development of black children*. Hillsdale, NJ: Lawrence Erlbaum.

Spencer, M. B., & Markstrom-Adams, C. (1990). Identity processes among racial and ethnic minority children in America. *Child Development, 61*, 290-310.

Stabler, J. R., Zeig, J. A., & Johnson, E. E. (1982). Perceptions of racially related stimuli by young children. *Perceptual and Motor Skills, 54*(1), 71-77.

Stevens, R. J., & Slavin, R. E. (1995). The cooperative elementary school: Effects on students' achievement, attitudes, and social relations. *American Educational Research Journal, 32*(2), 321-351.

Stronge, J. H. (Ed.). (1992). *Educating homeless children and adolescents: Evaluating policy and practice*. Newbury Park, CA: Sage.

Swadener, E. B. (1988). Implementation of education that is multicultural in early childhood settings: A case study of two day care programs. *Urban Review, 20*(1), 8-27.

Swadener, E. B., & Johnson, J. E. (1989). Play in diverse social contexts: Parent and teacher roles. In M. N. Block & A. D. Pellegrini (Eds.), *The ecological context of children's play* (pp. 214-244). Norwood, NJ: Ablex.

Swadener, B. B., & Lubeck, S. (1995). *Children and families "at promise"*. Albany: State University of New York Press.

Takaki, R. (1993). *A different mirror: A history of multicultural America*. Boston, MA: Little, Brown.

Tatum, B. D. (1992). Talking about race, learning about racism: The application of racial identity development theory in the classroom. *Harvard Educational Review, 62*(1), 1-24.

Tharp, R. G., & Gallimore, R. (1988). *Rousing minds to life: Teaching, learning, and schooling in social context*. Cambridge: Cambridge University Press.

Thompson, T. (1992). For the sake of our children: Poverty and disabilities. In T. Thompson & S. C. Hupp (Eds.), *Saving children at risk: Poverty and disabilities* (pp. 3-10). Newbury Park, CA: Sage.

Thompson, T., & Hupp, S. C. (Eds.). (1992). *Saving children at risk: Poverty and disabilities*. Newbury Park, CA: Sage.

Thorne, B. (1986). Girls and boys together . . . but mostly apart: Gender arrangements in elementary schools. In W. W. Hartup & Z. Rubin (Eds.), *Relationships and development* (pp. 167-184). Hillsdale, NJ: Lawrence Erlbaum Associates.

Troyna, B., & Hatcher, R. (1992). *Racism in children's lives: A study of a mainly white primary school*. London: Routledge.

Trueba, H.T., Rodriguez, C., Zou, Y., & Cintorn, J. (1993). *Heading multicultural America: Mexican immigrants rise to power in rural California*. New York: Falmer.

Tyack, D. (1995). Schooling and social diversity: Historical reflections. In In W. D. Hawley & A. W. Jackson (Eds.), *Toward a common destiny: Improving Race and Ethnic Relations in America* (pp. 3-38). San Francisco: Jossey-Bass.

Ulichny, P. (1994, April). *Cultures in conflict*. Paper presented at the annual meeting of the American Educational Research Association, New Orleans, LA.

Urberg, K. A., & Kaplan, M. G. (1989). An observational study of race-, age-, and sex-heterogeneous interaction in preschoolers. Journal of *Applied Developmental Psychology, 10*, 299-311.

Van Ausdale, D., & Feagin, J. R. (2001). *The first R: How children learn race and racism*. Lanham, MD: Rowman & Littlefield.

Vasquez, O. A., Pease-Alvarez, L., & Shannon, S. M. (1994). *Pushing boundaries: Language and culture in a Mexican community*. Cambridge: Cambridge University Press.

Washburn, D. E. (1996). *Multicultural education in the United States*. Philadelphia: Inquiry International.

Wasson-Ellam, L., & Li, G. (1999). Identity-weaving in the places and spaces of a cross-cultural classroom. *Canadian Children, 24*(2), 23-34.

West, C. (1993). *Race matters*. Boston: Beacon.

Whiting, B. B., & Whiting, J. W. M. (1975). *Children of six cultures: A psychocultural analysis*. Cambridge, MA: Harvard University Press.

Whiting, B. B., & Edwards, C. P. (1988). *Children of different worlds: The formation of social behavior*. Cambridge, MA: Harvard University Press.

Wright, C. (1992). *Race relations in the primary school*. London: David Fulton Publishers.

Wong-Filmore, L. (1991). When learning a second language means losing the first. *Early Childhood Research Quarterly, 6*(3), 323–346.

Woodson, C. G. (1921). *The history of the Negro church*. Washington, DC.: The Associated Publishers.

Woodson, C. G. (1933). *The mis-education of the Negro*. Washington, DC.: The Associated Publishers.

Woodson, C. G. (1935). *The story of the Negro retold*. Washington, DC: The Associated Publishers.

Yeung, W. J., Linver, M. R., Brooks-Gunn, J. (2002). How money matters for young children's development: Parental investment and family processes. *Child Development, 73*(6), 1861–1879.

Part
·III·

FOUNDATIONS OF EARLY CHILDHOOD EDUCATIONAL POLICY

·17·

CREATING PLAY ENVIRONMENTS FOR EARLY CHILDHOOD: INDOORS AND OUT

John A. Sutterby
University of Texas at Brownsville

Joe Frost
University of Texas at Austin

CHANGING PLAY ENVIRONMENTS

Play environments have undergone significant changes over the last decade. Evaluating play environment research requires an evaluation of the factors that are taken into consideration when creating the play environment. According to a cultural-ecological model, children's play and play environments are influenced by a combination of distal factors like societal influences, opportunities to play and play settings and proximal factors like social networks and relationships (Whiting, 1980). For the purposes of this chapter, play environments, including materials, equipment and settings, are the physical elements of play along with the general societal rules that impact when and how play environments are created, used, or limited. An understanding of the physical elements and the societal aspects that impact play can give a clearer picture of the state of knowledge about play and play environments.

Societal trends affecting the field of education are having a great impact on the development of play environments. The view of the role of play and its importance for the development of children has changed recently. Understanding societal trends helps educators and advocates recognize the ways that play environments are changing and adapting. The first trend affecting play environments is the increasing knowledge about brain development and growth and how environments impact this growth. The second major trend that has impacted play environments is the growing standardization of outdoor play

environments. The third major trend is the increasing emphasis on accountability. The accountability movement has impacted play environments as schools have eliminated recess and forced indoor play environments into increasing academic programs (Frost, Wortham, & Reifel, 2001; Schultz, 1998).

Technology and Learning Research

The explosive growth in technology for monitoring brain activity has led to increased interest in the activities and environments that influence brain growth and development. This interest has resulted in the development of a large number of play materials intended to promote brain development (Klugar & Park, 2001) Growing lack of opportunities to play or play deprivation is also a major factor affecting children, which also impacts children's brain development (Frost & Jacobs, 1995; Frost, Wortham, & Reifel, 2005).

Government Regulations

The regulatory environment that emphasizes promoting safety and avoiding litigation by schools and cities has resulted in the development of standardized play equipment in schools and parks. Safety regulations and standardization of play environments have influenced the elimination of playground equipment in many instances, as schools do not have the funds to upgrade unsafe equipment (Pellegrini, 1995; Frost, Wortham, & Reifel, 2005).

Testing and the Accountability Movement

The accountability movement has had a major impact on play and play environments over the last 10 years, culminating in the passage of the No Child Left Behind Act of 2002. The movement emphasizes standards and ways of measuring those standards and raising test scores. Schools emphasize the "basics" and seek to eliminate the so-called frills of physical education, recess, and the arts—subjects readily tested over areas that are not commonly tested. Consequently, schools under pressure to raise test scores focus on academic development and deemphasize play activities like recess (Schultz, 1998). Play and play environments in the era of accountability must promise measurable positive effects on test scores, otherwise they are replaced with academically focused programs.

PLAY IN DIFFERENT CONTEXTS

One area of play environment research in which we can see the interplay of proximal and distal factors is in the different contexts where play occurs and how culture influences children's play activities. The environment for play differs depending on the cultural values of a society. Children from different sociocultural contexts may have different expectations for play in their play environments. The locations or activity settings for play and the materials, available for play also differ depending on the sociocultural context (Farver, 1999). In addition, the meanings associated with different materials can change over time. The ideals of play environments are often based on Western societies with available time, materials, and space for play. Play contexts outside of Western societies often differ as these societies have different perspectives on the meaning of play, appropriate environments for play, and the use of materials for play (Roopnarine, Johnson, & Hooper, 1994).

Play in Western Societies

Children in Western societies typically engage in extended amounts of solitary play with an emphasis on imaginary play with toys and other play materials, resulting in the development of novel play activities (Sutton-Smith, 1999; Tudge, Lee, & Putnam, 1998). Home play in the United States involves the use of replica toys such as toy cars and dolls. Bedrooms for American children are used as storerooms for play materials while play tends to occur in communal rooms like living rooms, playrooms, and kitchens. Pretend play between adults and children is common as adults highly value the symbolic actions of children (Haight & Miller, 1993). Families influence play directly and indirectly—directly by elaborating on children's expressions and promoting pretend play, and indirectly by arranging the home environment and purchasing toys (Haight, 1998).

Views of play environments in the United States are often based on suburban middle-class European-American norms. Subgroups from different cultural, racial, ethnic, and regional areas may have different conceptions of play and play environments. In culturally continuous contexts children play in play environments that are relatively unchanged from those of their parents and grandparents, whereas in culturally discontinuous contexts such as migrant, immigrant, and refugee families, children play in ways and places that are substantially different and changing (Slaughter & Dombroski, 1989).

In an ethnographic study of differences between culturally bounded views of play in home and school contexts for a group of Latino children, Woods (1996) found that a mismatch existed between play in a Head Start program and children's home play. Unlike suburban home contexts, in which children are expected to engage in solitary play with objects, the children in Woods' study were expected to play together in common areas of the home. Special areas were not designated for play as common areas, with adults looking on, served as play environments for children. The Head Start pattern of activity specific centers conflicted with children's views that dramatic play occurs in all areas. Limitations on the number of children in a center also conflicted with their desire to play in large social groups.

A cross-cultural study of children's play in Korea and the United States revealed similarities and differences in the play behaviors of children. Differences exist in the types of play, the role of parents, and gender play. Academic play is more common in Korean society than in the United States, whereas children from the United States are more likely to engage in pretend play. Children from middle-class communities from both societies were more likely to engage in academic play than children from working-class backgrounds. U.S. children are more likely to initiate play and lessons. Mothers in Korea are more likely to participate in play but most frequently take the role of a passive observer (Tudge, Lee, & Putnam, 1998).

One significant impact on the cultural environment of children's play in Western societies is the increasing influence of the media on children's play, play things, and play environments. The direct marketing of toys to children through toy-based programs took off in the 1980s with the development of a toy line based on the program *He Man and the Masters of the Universe* (Kline, 1995; Cross, 1997). Currently licensed toy lines are frequently codesigned with a television program (Kline, 1993, 1995). According to Kline (1995), television and play dominate children's after school lives. He found a relationship between the toys children possessed and the television shows they watched. When asked to draw pictures of themselves playing, 68% of children drew themselves playing with licensed product toys.

Licensed toys can be controversial for they can represent violent images or commercialized images. Barbie dolls and other licensed toys are criticized for their images of women, the emphasis on products and shopping, and, particulars in one case, in which a talking Barbie doll said, "Math class is tough" (Cross, 1997; Steinberg, 1997). MacNaughton (1996), by contrast, views Barbie and other toys such as Power Rangers as having less of an influence on children than typically suggested. Toys are seen as representations of culture rather than controlling culture and the conceptions that children have about violence and gender roles.

Commercialization of toys is seen in the different ways that marketers of toys conduct their advertising. Marketing for children involves creating toy-based television shows and managed fads in which toys come with a toy line of accessories. Marketing to adults targets traditional values and focuses on nostalgia for toys from adult's youth. For example, American Girl dolls have historical backgrounds as well as storybooks to go with the dolls and their outfits, whereas movies such as *Toy Story* include toys such as Mr. Potato Head, cowboys, and space toys to appeal to adults nostalgic for toys from their youth (Cross, 1997).

Play in Non-Western Societies

Play activities in non-Western societies often emphasize group integration and interdependent activities. Play in interdependent cultures emphasizes traditions rather than novelty, and in subsistence cultures, play is limited to imitation of adult activities and scripted roles that are repeated. International studies of children's play environments have examined how different cultures treat play and play environments (Sutton-Smith, 1999; Tudge, Lee, & Putnam, 1998).

Fasoli (1999) describes an attempt to create a play group in Northern Australia with a Western conception of play based on toys, centers, books, and art materials. Several attempts to engage the Aboriginal mothers and their children in play with these objects were unsuccessful. One informant suggested a different activity, which involved hunting and cooking turtles from a nearby reservoir, which the Aboriginal mothers and their children engaged in with great enjoyment. This event brought eager participation from all of the members of the aboriginal group. After this experience, the organizers of the playgroup changed their approach and began to engage in a number of outdoor activities involved in food gathering. This activity challenged the authors' original conception of what constitutes beneficial play involving toys and other materials.

The environment for play in many non-Western societies differs in that the spaces and materials for play are based on the natural world rather than manufactured equipment. Play in Polynesia does not involve providing special areas for play because children use the surf, boats, and trees for play places. Group play is defined by having all the members of the group doing the same activities at the same time, usually involving found and natural objects. As all of the children engage in the same activities at the same time there is little negotiation of game plans (Martini, 1994).

The meaning associated with the materials for play can also differ depending on the sociocultural context. Yup'ik Eskimo girls engage in play with materials involving the creation of stories in mud using a knife. During this play, called story knifing, young girls travel to areas away from adults to tell stories using symbols carved in soft patches of mud with knives. Story knifing can use traditional folk stories, everyday happenings, or non-Eskimo stories, all serving as ways for girls to socialize and develop culture (deMarrais, Nelson, & Baker, 1994).

The research discussed earlier signals the complexities of play from a cultural perspective. The ecological context of play is influenced by the materials available for play, the social interactions that occur during play, and the attitudes that society has towards play. The cultural context for play can also be influenced by media as licensed products influence children's play environments. The ecology of play can be continuous or discontinuous as children bring different experiences to play environments which may or may not meet their expectations. The following section focuses primarily on indoor play environments in Western settings, examining the materials available for play, how materials influence children's play, and the arrangement of play spaces for children.

INDOOR PLAY ENVIRONMENTS

Play Materials

The most significant proximal factor for play environments are the materials that children use during play. Play material researchers over the past decade have investigated how the types of materials included in play environments influence the nature and types of children's play. Selecting play materials for use in the classroom is one of the most important tasks of teachers. They make decisions on play materials based on the goals of the program, the types of play to be encouraged, and the interests of the children. In addition, teachers must take into consideration practical considerations such as messiness of the materials, the time it takes to clean up the materials, and the costs of the materials.

Philosophically, materials come from different traditions or lenses. Didactic programs emphasize materials that are closed ended and focused on specific academic learning (Frost, Wortham, & Reifel, 2005). Cognitive constructivist programs emphasize experiences with open-ended materials such as blocks, dramatic play, and sand, which offer children many opportunities to imagine and problem solve, rather than relying on adult-directed activities (Grossman, 2004; Van Hoorn, Nourot, Scales, & Alward, 2003). Vygotsky (1978) describes play materials as "pivots" as they help children to separate themselves from concrete reality and to separate the object from the meaning of the object. Socioemotional programs emphasize materials that encourage recreating emotional experiences, or creativity. Flexible materials such as sand, water, and art materials are important elements for expression of emotions (Frost, Wortham, & Reifel, 2005). The effects of play materials on children's play have been widely researched. Some of the most frequently studied areas include language, cognition, socialization, and emotional responses to materials.

Play Materials and Language

Play materials influence the types of language produced by children and their interactions. Toys create a context for the use of language during play (Pellegrini & Jones, 1994). This context can facilitate storytelling, initiation of topics, interactions between peers and improvisation. Typical materials used in investigations include dramatic play props, sand and water areas, games, art materials, and outdoor play settings.

Play materials support storytelling. In one study, 26 4-year-old middle-class children were given two sets of toys, one a family set of dolls and, in another, an alligator and spool were added. The presence of the alligator encouraged more stories based on villainy, whereas the family set encouraged longer stories. The psychological attributes of the toys, helplessness in the case of the baby and villainy in the case of the alligator, facilitated the storytelling (Fein, 1995).

Play materials can impact topic initiation in play. Burroughs and Murray (1992) established three conditions for play, a Play-doh area, a farm toy area, and a hand puppet area. All three areas elicited equal amounts of language utterances; however, children initiated more topics in the hand puppet area. The open-ended nature of the puppets allowed children more topic flexibility, whereas the farm set limited the possible topics to "farming." The Play-doh and farm toy areas elicited greater topic maintenance. The Play-doh area required extended periods of construction, which limited the possible topics of conversation, whereas the farm toy limited the possible number of themes, influencing children to stay on the same topic.

Play materials also can support language interactions. An ethnographic study of a bilingual play setting found that some settings facilitated interactions between peers who did not share a language. Settings that facilitated language play included card games. The children playing the games could participate because they knew all of the rules and the play was not improvisational. By following the rules, the game continued even though not all peers shared the same language. Block and dramatic play areas discouraged cross-linguistic play interactions because the improvisational nature of the play in these areas required players to share a certain level of common language in order to maintain the play frame. Other settings for play did not encourage language interactions because these settings encouraged functional play. Settings such as sand and water play and outdoor play (chasing, running, tricycling) areas did not require high amounts of language, as children were able to engage in these activities without shared language (Sutterby, 2002).

When used by same language peers, the sand area is one of the most improvisational in that it encourages indirect performance play. The presence of small replica figures in the sand area encouraged a variety of play topics based on indirect performance play, which Sawyer identifies as the most sophisticated level of play interaction. Similar to the puppets, replica toys help children imagine a variety of scenarios to engage in (Sawyer, 1997).

Drawing activities also have been studied in their relation to language play. In a study of children's drawing behaviors, Escobedo (1998) found that children used language in construction play when drawing as they named objects and drew objects in order to transform objects into symbols. Children also used language for imaginative play when drawing and invented worlds related to their drawings. In addition, children used language in collaborative play when drawing as they created shared dramas around their drawings.

Play Materials and Cognition

Several researchers over the past decade have explored the relationship between the environment and brain activity. The Mozart effect, for example, was supposed to increase children's spatial relations through listening to music (Rauscher, Shaw & Ky, 1993). Brain research took on a significant role during the 1990s and parents and professionals learned how important early play experiences were for brain development (Burghardt, 2004). This led to the development of play materials that were designed to stimulate children's mental growth.

Store shelves groan with new products purported to stimulate babies' brains in ways harried parents don't have time for. There are baby Mozart tapes said to enhance spatial reasoning and perhaps musical and artistic abilities too. There are black, white and red picture books, said to sharpen visual acuity. There are bilingual products said to train baby brains so they will be more receptive to multiple languages. . . . Parents who don't avail themselves of these products do so at their children's peril: the brain, they are told, has very limited windows for learning certain skills. Let them close, and kids may be set back forever. (Kluger & Park, 2001, p. 50)

Many parents were tempted by music and educational toys that would ostensibly stimulate brain growth and give children an educational advantage. In reality, brain research has not yet reached a level of sophistication to recommend many widely recommended practices (McKelvie & Low, 2002).

Although a specific link between brain development and materials has not been found, play materials can have an effect on children's cognition in the ways they approach problem-solving tasks (Bedrova & Leong, 2004). Play materials have been studied in relation to a wide range of factors including play object realism, the development of cognitive skills, and academic.

Sociodramatic play is often viewed as the most cognitively sophisticated level of play. Play materials can improve cognition by encouraging sociodramatic play over functional or practice play (Smilansky & Sheftaya, 1990). Trawick-Smith (1993) found that the effect of level of realism of a toy on sociodramatic play depended on the age of the child. Realistic toy props encouraged increased dramatic play for 2 to 3-year-olds. Four-year-olds preferred a blend of realistic and nonrealistic props, whereas 5 to 6-year-olds engaged in more dramatic play with nonrealistic props.

Realism of play material also can elicit the development of play themes. In a comparison of low realism and high realism props, children engaged in equal amounts of group dramatic play under the two different conditions. However, the low realism props elicited more types of play themes and more types of roles and unintended use of play materials (Hogan & Howe, 2001). Open-ended play materials also encourage the development of ideational fluency, in that children are able to create more ideas and more varied ideas when playing with open-ended materials such as art materials and sculpting clay (Fisher, 1992).

The relationship between play materials and academic development has been questioned by Uttal et al. (1998). These researchers suggest that the development of the understanding of symbols and how materials can represent other concepts like mathematical concepts may not be readily apparent to the child. "Play certainly is vital to cognitive development. However, just because children have played with an object does not mean that they have learned from the experience. In fact . . . play can be counterproductive when the object is intended to serve as a symbol" (p. 76). Children may be attending to the meaning of the math manipulative as a representation of a toy and not to the object representing a fraction or counting aid.

Finally, Rost, and Hanses (1994), found that the toys possessed and used by gifted children did not differ from toys used by children of average intelligence, indicating that the presence of materials and their use had little effect on their levels of intelligence. The type and amount of play materials available depended on socioeconomic status, suggesting that the amount and type of toys available is a sign of social status for parents rather than an indication of giftedness.

Play Materials and Socioemotional Development

Social and emotional development are closely related and discussed collectively here. The theoretical foundations for socioemotional development through play are long-standing and strong. Although focus primarily on cognitive development, Piaget's (1962) cognitive-developmental theory held that play has a fundamental role in the child's social-cognitive development. Erikson's psychosocial theory (1950) concluded that make-believe play permits children to learn about their social world and to try out new social skills. Vygotsky's (1966) sociocultural theory held that make-believe play is vital for the acquisition of social and cognitive competence.

Perhaps the largest body of research on emotional development and play materials has been conducted by scholars in play therapy. Play therapy is "...the systematic use of a theoretical model to establish an interpersonal process wherein trained play therapists use the therapeutic powers of play to help clients prevent or resolve psychosocial difficulties and achieve optimal growth and development" (Board of Directors of the Association for Play Therapy, 1997, p. 14). However, with respect to emotional and social development, the emphasis here is that play has *natural* therapeutic powers that are utilized and focused for success in play therapy.

Nondirective play therapy has grown significantly over the last 50 years since Virgina Axline (1969) extended Carl Rogers's (1951) concepts of nondirective therapy to children's play. Play therapy is based on two principles; first, play helps children reduce anxiety after a stressful event and, second, children include elements of past stressful or traumatic events in play (Power, 2000). Solitary object play has been found to reduce stress more than peer play (Barnett, 1984). Play is the child's natural medium for self-expression, experimentation, and learning. The child can readily relate to toys and play out concerns with them because she feels at home in a play setting. Play allows a cathartic release of feelings and frustrations (Frost, Wortham, & Reifel, 2005). Stressful experiences appear in children's play, although there may be a delay between the event and the appearance of the play episode (Watson, 1994).

Play materials and the play space are very important for play therapy. Play places and play materials "should communicate a message of 'Be yourself in playing rather than a message of 'Be careful'" (Landreth, 1991, p. 115). Play materials for therapeutic purposes take many forms, including dramatic play materials,

toy guns, musical instruments, and materials for pounding. The materials for play therapy should be open-ended and encourage creative expression and emotional expression. In addition, materials should be of sturdy construction to allow for active use.

Play therapy as currently practiced takes many forms including structured, nondirective, filial, relationship, psychoanalytical, and child-centered. Each form has adherents and to some degree, specific audiences. Materials for play therapy commonly include puppets, sand, water, mud, clay, costumes, blocks, and art materials. The contexts include playrooms, hospitals, schools, psychiatric settings, university laboratories, and even homes (Frost, Wortham, & Reifel, 2005). However, play is naturally therapeutic and, for most children, does not require specific adult contrived techniques to be beneficial for emotional development.

Conclusions from extensive play therapy research, summarized in Frost, Wortham, and Reifel (2005), include primarily positive outcomes for overall functioning, personality, social and emotional adjustment, self-concept, healing, self-control, relief from phobias, coping with death, progress in reading, intelligence, academic performance, recovery from child abuse, creativity, and recovery from sexual abuse.

The type of play materials available to children can effect children's social interactions. Foundational research by Parten (1933) and Rubin (1977) found that children engage in different levels of social play with different types of play materials. Materials such as dramatic play props, dolls, dress-up clothes, vehicles, and blocks encourage more group and dramatic play, whereas puzzles, beads, art, Play-doh, sand, and water encourage more solitary or functional play.

The type of toy also affects the level of social interactions that occur when children play. Children who played with representational toys participated in social play in 61% of play intervals and parallel play in 36%, whereas children who played with transforming toys, which changed from a car to a robot, participated in social play in 32% and parallel play in 66% of play intervals. Children playing with transformational toys were more focused on the toy as they manipulated the object to create the transformation, whereas the children playing with the representational objects were more likely to be engaged with a play partner (Bagley & Chaille, 1996).

Play Environments and Curriculum

The National Association for the Education of Young Children advocates for play as a foundation of early education programs. Designing appropriate environments which encourage play are an important part of the role of the teacher as decision maker (Bredekamp & Copple, 1997). The Association for Childhood Education International (Isenberg & Quisenberry, 2003) released a position paper strongly endorsing play environments and play opportunities for children. According to ACEI, children need indoor and outdoor environments that are stimulating, safe, and accessible for children with disabilities. Although the rhetoric of child advocates emphasizes the importance of play for young children, the actual practices of teachers in the field vary widely and are often contradictory (DeVries, 2001).

Play can fulfill many roles in the classroom. Play in classrooms can take a peripheral role in comparison to classroom work, often left for the end of the class day as a reward for academic work. Play can be disguised as academic exercises, in which materials encourage the development of academic content such as letter matching and color identification. By contrast, play may be viewed primarily for social and emotional development, in which children have free choices but are not challenged to extend their thinking. Finally, play can be integrated with settings and opportunities for social and emotional development as well as moral and intellectual development. In this type of play environment, children engage in group games, math, and spatial reasoning, and literacy activities as they participate in pretend and construction play (DeVries, 2001).

Play Materials and Academic Development

The development of play materials to be used in schools for academic purposes has a long history. Froebel's Gifts and Occupations were the first extensive materials developed for use in schools. These materials were used in kindergartens throughout Europe in the late 19th and early 20th centuries and influenced 20th century artistic styles and architecture (Brosterman, 1997). Froebel's philosophy and materials also were very influential in early American kindergartens and remain influential to this day.

Play-based programs traditionally emphasized the importance of social and emotional development for early childhood. More recently, programs have integrated academic activities into the selection of play materials. One area of academic development receiving extensive discussion is literacy (Neuman & Roskos, 1992; Roskos & Neuman, 1998). These authors recommend the inclusion of literacy materials including writing materials, paper, notepads, and books in all areas of the classroom. The inclusion of these materials in the play centers increased the number of literacy behaviors of the children when playing.

Learning math skills through play is a widely encouraged activity (Kieff & Casbergue, 2000; Van Hoorn et al., 1999). Using math manipulatives as play materials is very common in many early childhood classrooms. Play with Unit Blocks for example has been related to the development of mathematical skills such as one to one correspondence, counting, spatial relationships, conservation of area and volume, and measurement (Leeb-Lundberg, 1984; Reifel & Yeatman, 1991). Some research indicates that using manipulatives may not help children's development of math concepts. According to Ball (1992), math manipulatives do not help children understand math concepts that they do not already understand. Playing with the material may encourage children to view the material as a representation of a toy rather than as a representation of a math concept.

Play materials are frequently designed with academic goals in mind rather than general play value. Marketers of play materials often focus on their educational value encouraging a belief that they are of greater value than materials created by children (Cross, 1997). However, the marketing of toys for educational purposes may create difficulties for toy manufacturers. "By attaching the label 'educational toys' to a specific segment of its production, the toy industry created a dilemma for itself, because if the other toys produced were not educational, what were they?" (Almqvist, 1994, p. 51).

Adults typically view toys as educational if they fall under two categories. First, if they reinforce some specific skill such as reading, mathematics, or knowledge, or second if they develop creative abilities such as art materials, open-ended play props, collections, or hobby and craft materials (Cross, 1997). Parental choices often differ from children's choices of play materials especially when parents with middle-class values look for toys to advance their children's abilities in order to give them academic advantages. When selecting toys as gifts, middle-class parents often select academically focused materials, such as books, crafts, and construction toys over toys that have licenses from controversial media including wrestling and violent movies (Sutterby, Brown, Thornton, & Therrell, 2002).

Play Spaces

Arrangement of space. The arrangement of the environment and the type of play space has an impact on the ways that children engage in play. Trawick-Smith (1992) suggests that play environments have a logical arrangement of space, modified open plan design and stimulus shelters. Logical arrangement of space involves placing centers with similar levels of noisiness and activity together, such as the dramatic play center and the block center. Less active centers such as library centers should be placed away from more active areas to allow children to become deeply involved in reading. Modified open-plan design is defined as having defined spaces for particular play activities like dramatic play, art, and block play. Areas for centers are defined by using low shelves on two or three sides. The low shelves increase children's persistence in play and double children's engagement in play tasks (Moore, 1987; Trawick-Smith & Landry-Fitzsimmons, 1992). Stimulus shelters are places for children to escape from active and noisy classrooms and give children a sense of comfort and security (Frost, Wortham, & Reifel, 2005).

Teachers preparing play environments also need to consider how to include children with disabilities. Children with disabilities are often limited in their play due to access issues. The classroom environment should be arranged so that children can access as much as possible without assistance (Bishop, 2004). Support for the child can include environmental supports, modifications in activities or materials, and modifications in arrangement of the environment. Each child will require individualized modifications and supports. "The critical steps are to observe the child's play and match the level of support to the child's need" (Sandall, 2004, p. 44).

Arranging for accessibility sometimes involves the use of assistive technology. The use of positioning equipment like Rifton chairs, prone standers, corner seats, and Zippie wheelchairs, is one way to improve children's access to play and communication. Positioning equipment allows children to be more independent since they can play without caregiver support. The use of positioning equipment improved the play of children with disabilities, allowing them to engage in increased communication, and to have more opportunities to engage in solitary play (O'Brien et al., 1998).

The materials included in the classroom can have an impact on children with disabilities. An analysis of the sensory elements of a play environment can enhance the play experiences of children with disabilities (Bishop, 2004). Blind children prefer noise making objects and musical instruments or objects more often than sighted children. They tend to play less with dramatic play props, construction toys, painting and craft materials (Troster & Brambring, 1994).

Alternative spaces for play. A variety of play environments are being designed for children that are outside of the classroom. As children are less likely to be allowed to play outdoors unsupervised, more controlled places for play are being designed to meet the needs of parents and teachers concerned about the children's safety. Areas such as children's museums have been developed as play environments outside the home and the classroom. Children's museums, hospitals, and pay-for-play arcades are growing in popularity as play spaces outside of schools (Frost, Wortham, & Reifel, 2001).

Children's museums are places where adults and children engage in play activities in an indoor environment designed for play. These environments allow children and adults to explore materials, explore concepts, and engage in pretend play. They encourage interactions between adults and children. Shine and Acosta (1999, 2000) found play activities to be brief, sporadic, and noncontingent in the museum's shopping play area. The prepared environment for play led parents to view play as a learning experience with the parent's role as a guide and framer for the play. In addition, parents took on traditional roles and participated in scripts. Children spent time pretending in solitary play, exploring materials, and looking for inventive uses for the materials but they resisted parent attempts to frame play for educational purposes, which usually disrupted the play

Hospitals often cause stress and fear in children. Hospital workers are trained to use play to help children deal with the stress of hospital procedures. Typically, play therapy in the hospital involves a play room and a nondirective play therapist who must consider factors such as the medical condition of the child and the limitations of the play room when preparing for play. Children are often interested in playing with toys that represent doctors' instruments and bags along with dolls or puppets which allow them to play out hospital themes (James, 1997). Such play helps children heal both physically and mentally.

Theme parks and pay-for-play arcades, and video and computer games are becoming increasingly popular. Advances in technology are allowing more engagement of the player with the game. Technology play can benefit children's academic and problem solving abilities; however, it also results in increased sedentary, passive play activities, and substitute for free, spontaneous play (Frost, Wortham, & Reifel, 2005).

As discussed earlier, developing indoor play spaces involves investigating the materials and arrangement of space and the influence of teachers on the language, cognitive, social, and emotional development of children. In addition, making decisions about play spaces involves the development of a play-based curriculum in order to meet the expectations of increased emphasis on standards and academic content. Indoor play spaces are more controlled play environments, which lead to more adult-child interaction, but that may be too academically focused.

OUTDOOR PLAY SPACES

Changing Environments for Outdoor Play

Outdoor environments for play have undergone great change over the last 10 years. They are increasingly standardized and regulated, whereas unregulated areas for children's play such as open lots and alleys are disappearing or declared off limits. Increased automobile traffic has limited children's play in streets and alleys and has limited their ability to reach organized play spaces. Increased emphasis on academics is reducing the amount of time children have for play, and growing risk of crime, pollution, and effects of the sun have resulted in children being shifted from outdoor to indoor play (Rivkin, 1995).

Outdoor play environments encourage different types of play than indoor play environments. Outdoor play spaces allow for a greater range of movement, and noisier and messier play than is typically allowed in indoor play spaces (Frost, Wortham, & Reifel, 2005). Creating "ideal" outdoor environments involves developing a space, which takes into consideration the many ways that children play outside.

Frost (1992) describes the development of play spaces that allow for children's active play, dramatic play, and functional play as well as quiet areas for introspection. Outdoor play can involve both exploration of manufactured equipment and natural materials. The development of ideal play spaces is a mythical concept in that cultural, safety, and economic concerns impact the types of play environments that can be created. Elements that can lead to varied types of play as well as integration of different ability levels of children include designing for a variety of play types, designing for increased physical activity, designing for safety, and designing for accessibility. Elements to include in the play environment include amount of space available, playground equipment, loose parts, nature, gardens, and stimulus shelters.

Valuing Children's Outdoor Play

Children engage in many types of play activities in outdoor play environments. One of the most important differences between outdoor and indoor play environments is the decreased amount of adult control over outdoor activities. Adults and children have very different views of "appropriate" outdoor environments. Adults are usually concerned with cost, maintenance, and safety, which are of little concern to children (Hendricks, 2001). Adults may be concerned about misuse of playground equipment. However, misuse of playground equipment may be an inappropriate or misguided adult concept. In reality, children explore playground equipment in many ways that are typically labeled "misuse" by adults. Children see play environments as places to explore and challenge, whereas adults may have certain ideas about how playground equipment is to be used (Thompson, 1988).

Outdoor play can have important social and emotional benefits. Sobel (1993) believes that outdoor play spaces for older children should be away from adult viewing. He describes the development and purposes of outdoor clubhouses for both boys and girls and their role in development. The importance of these out of the way play places, built in remote locations out of natural and discarded building materials, appears to be based on the child's need for privacy and escape. The development of these places begins around age 7 and increases as children enter middle childhood around age 11–12. Sobel suggests that personal spaces and the development of a sense of space are important for children's psychological development.

Outdoor play also can be important for cognitive and academic development. Recess is an important component of school programs related to outdoor play. Children became less attentive to school work when recess was delayed (Pellegrini, Huberty, & Jones, 1995). Another study found that children's increased participation in physical activity did not reduce their levels of academic achievement (Sallis et al., 1999). Children who have the opportunity to engage in recess breaks during school are less fidgety in the classroom (Jarrett et al., 1998). Children who engage in more object play on the playground have significantly higher scores on the Georgia Criterion Reference Test (GCRT). In addition, interactions with peers are significantly related to GCRT scores, whereas interactions primarily with adults led to lower scores, on the GCRT (Pellegrini, 1995).

Designing for Variety of Play Types

Children do not play in the same ways in all play environments. Elements that impact play in outdoor environments include quality of the environment, time for play, playmates available, and the personality of the child. As children play differently depending on these factors, play spaces should be unique. Different play structures and materials should be available at different play sites. One exception to what Hendricks calls the non-repeat rule are swings, which she suggests should be available at all play locations (Hendricks, 2001).

Stine (1997) examines designing play spaces from the perspective of the experiences they encourage rather than the equipment that is present. Basic design elements for outdoor spaces should include dichotomous relationships of different sensory, cognitive, and social experiences:

Accessible	Inaccessible
Active	Passive
Challenge/Risk	Repetition/Security
Hard	Soft
Natural	People-Built
Open	Closed
Permanence	Change
Private	Public
Simple	Complex

Creating outdoor environments requires looking at the entire space. Cognitive aspects of the outdoor environment include the complexity and variety of the play space, the problem-solving opportunities, and potential for choice. Social aspects include opportunities for interaction, isolation, and accessibility (Stine, 1997).

Designing for Physical Activity

The number of obese children has more than doubled over the past 20 years to reach 25% of children and is now a major health concern (Gabbard, 2000). Children are not participating in sufficient levels of physical activity and are engaging in increasing hours of sedentary behavior including television viewing and video game playing (Bar-Or, 2000); in addition, schools are limiting recess and requiring more hours of sedentary behavior in schools and more homework, which leads to sedentary activities at home (Sallis et al., 1999).

Equipment and physical activity. In a comparison of children's play during free play on two different playgrounds, traditional fixed equipment, and fixed equipment enhanced with additional loose parts such as construction and dramatic play materials, Barbour (1999) found that children on the enhanced playground engaged in a greater variety of play activities including enhanced construction and dramatic play. In addition, children with high levels of physical competence were more likely to initiate active physical play, whereas children with low levels of physical competence were less likely to initiate play based on physical skills. Social status was related to physical competence in that children with high levels of physical competence were able to engage in more types of activities as well as being able to engage with a greater variety of peers. Low physical competence children were more likely to be rejected by peers on the enhanced playground and were more likely to engage in solitary activities.

The role of the play environment for increasing physical activity is a recent research focus. Children who played in a colorful indoor play environment consisting of tubes, slides and other climbing structures maintained a heart rate of 158 beats per minute, about 20 beats per minute higher than children who played on a typical outdoor playground, and about 10 beats per minute higher than the heart rate of 147–149, which indicates moderate to vigorous physical activity (Centers for Disease Control & Prevention, 1997; Whitehurst, Groo, & Brown, 1996).

Adding elements to the environment can affect children's physical activity levels. Children who played on a playground with playground markings of pirate ships, geometric shapes and giant snakes added to a playground with brightly colored paint had heart rates seven beats per minute higher than control group children who played on an unmarked playground (Stratton, Marsh, & Moores, 2000). A comparison of children's physical activity between an environment with playground equipment and an environment without playground equipment found that children's heart rates were raised to 152.7 in the playground equipment condition, 6.9 beats per minute higher than the playground without equipment (Sutterby, Brown, & Thornton, 2004).

Access to outdoor play. The opportunities for outdoor play also can have an impact on how much physical activity children engage in. Access to areas for recreational activities after school is related to children's physical activity levels (Epstein et al., 2001). Children who participate in physical education programs or have access to community recreation areas are more likely to be physically active. In addition, living in a high crime area was likely to reduce opportunities for physical activity. Low-income children were less likely to have access to physical education and community recreation centers and are more likely to live in high crime areas (Gordan-Larsen, McMurray, & Popkin, 2000).

Opportunities to participate in physical activity at school also are impacting children's physical activity. Recess is an important time for children to engage in social and physical play; however, because of increased emphasis on academics, recess is slowly being eliminated from the school day. The amount of time allowed for recess has declined greatly since the 1970s and has been eliminated by about 40% of schools in the United States (Kieff & Chaille, 2001). In addition, children who have opportunities for high physical activity at school are more likely to have high levels of physical activity at home. On days when children do not have physical activity at school they are more likely to be sedentary at home (Dale, Corbin, & Dale, 2000).

The impact recess has on children has focused on how recess affects instruction. The longer children have to sit without a recess break the more likely they are to be fidgety during class time. This effect is greater for boys than girls. After recess some children returned to academic work and were more inattentive while other children returned from recess and were more attentive. "Recess is doing different things for different children" (Pellegrini, 1995, p. 83). Children who are sedentary at recess are attentive when they return to class, whereas children who are active at recess are less attentive.

One of the major concerns with playground recess is the potential for playground bullying. The reduced adult supervision on playgrounds can allow for children to physically dominate others. Pellegrini (1995) found that boys tend to engage in rough-and-tumble play on the playground with children of equal dominance levels or equal social status. Popular and rejected children engage in equal amounts of rough and tumble play; however, rejected children's rough-and-tumble play was more likely to lead to aggression due to rejected children's lower ability to distinguish social cues during play. Play specialists generally view rough-and-tumble play as desirable but do not advocate overt aggression with intent to inflict physical or psychological harm on others.

Designing for Accessibility

Playgrounds are increasingly becoming more accessible for children and adults with disabilities. Implementation of accessibility standards for children's playground equipment makes it possible for children and adults with mobility impairments to interact with others on the playground. The guidelines for accessibility emphasize the access to the playground and use of the equipment for children with disabilities. The principle behind designing playgrounds for all people, including people with disabilities, is referred to as "universal design." Universal design, as opposed to developing special facilities only for people with disabilities, allows for integration of all people into the same environments (Moore, Goltsman, & Iacofano, 1997).

The United States Access Board (1994), which is responsible for creating design standards for access to public places issued a rule for playgrounds. This rule for playgrounds recommends detailed guidelines for the following design considerations:

1. a route to the playground (approach)
2. a route to the play equipment inside the playground (enter)
3. accessible play elements (use)

The *Approach* to playgrounds involves an accessible route from the street or parking lot to the playground. *Entering* the playground requires a compromise on surfacing and safety conditions in that the surfacing chosen must meet safety recommendations as well as be firm enough to support a wheel chair or other assistive mobility device. Currently, poured rubber surfacing and maintained engineered wood fibers are the two surfaces that have passed accessibility tests. In addition, an accessible path is required over or through the containment area for the surfacing. *Use* of the playground elements themselves is the final design consideration. Playground elements can be accessed by children either by placing them on ground level or by providing ramps or transfer stations for access to elevated play events.

The playground elements that are accessible to children must contain a variety of play elements which encourage different types of play including slides, swings, overhead equipment and activity panels (Hendy, 2001; Thompson, Hudson, & Bowers, 2002). Currently, adoption of the U.S. Access Boards Guidelines is on a state by state basis for playgrounds. Each individual state must decide whether to update their own accessibility guidelines in order to put them in line with the federal guidelines (Sutterby, 2004).

Designing for Safety

Equipment safety. Outdoor play environments are areas that encourage risk-taking behavior. The apparatus of playgrounds is designed to propel children at speeds that they could not achieve on their own. Apparatus is designed to let children climb heights and challenge themselves physically in ways that are not possible at ground level. Children leap from swings and hang upside-down in order to challenge their environments. Risk-taking is part of a child's growth to maturity, and playgrounds are places where children can develop an understanding of risk under the supervision of adults. Risk is inherent in playground activities and should be managed rather than avoided (Frost, Brown, Sutterby, & Thornton, 2005). Risk-taking can be an educational aspect for children as they challenge individual actions or pieces of equipment often repeating the same actions over and over again in order to master them (Smith, 1998).

Public playgrounds and playground equipment have become increasingly standardized over the last 10–15 years (Frost, Wortham, & Reifel, 2005). For example, outdoor play environments through the 1970s and 1980s emphasized replacing traditional metal playground equipment with community built playgrounds built out of materials such as railroad ties, tires, and loose parts (see Hewes & Beckwith, 1974; Hogan, 1982; Frost, 1992). Playgrounds today are designed under a different set of expectations. Modern play equipment is typically designed by certified play equipment manufacturers, installed by certified playground installers and evaluated by certified playground inspectors.

The influence of guidelines for playground safety created by the Consumer Product Safety Commission (1997) and the American Society for Testing and Materials (1998) led to manufacturing guidelines and standards for playground equipment manufacturers. These standards are often used as protection against litigation but they also often limit innovative design. National safety guidelines and standards are important in preventing serious injury to children. CPSC guidelines and ASTM standards were violated in 94% of 190 cases of serious injuries resulting in litigation (Frost & Sweeney, 1996).

Playground injuries that result in emergency room visits have remained relatively stable throughout the last half of the 1990s and the early 2000s at around 200,000 a year. Falls onto playground equipment or onto hard surfacing are the most common cause of playground injuries, whereas asphyxiation by ropes, cords, or entrapment is the most common cause of death. The types of playground equipment involved in the largest number of playground injuries are climbers at public playgrounds and swings at home playgrounds (Tinsworth & McDonald, 2001). Swings are the most common play equipment at home or backyard playgrounds. Frost and Sweeney (1996) found that falls were associated with 60% of injuries resulting in litigation. Asphyxiation was the cause of 6 out of 13 deaths associated with playground equipment accidents resulting in litigation.

The National Program for Playground Safety (Hudson, Thompson, & Olsen, 2004) has conducted several national playground safety surveys. A report on the most recent survey was released in 2004. This report is based on data from on-site visits to more than 3,000 playgrounds during 2003. The study focused on four major factors: supervision, age appropriate design, fall surfacing, and equipment and surfacing maintenance. In the area of supervision on the report card used by NPPS decreased from an overall B- in the 2000 report to C in the 2004 report. Contributing factors included lack of training for supervisors, lack of visibility because of the large size of play structures, use of completely enclosed crawl spaces, and lack of signs regarding expected playground behavior. Increasingly, lack of supervision was cited in lawsuits over children's injuries.

Grades on the NPPS report card improved from 2000 to 2004 with age appropriate design improving from C to C+. The grade on fall surfacing improving from C to B− and the grade on equipment maintenance was not stated but noted as improved. The NPPS stressed that there should be separate play areas and equipment for younger (aged 2–5) children and older children (aged 5–12) and that signs should be posted to alert users to the age distinctions. They noted that appropriate surfacing per

the Consumer Product Safety Commission (CPSC) guidelines should be installed and maintained and that equipment should be routinely inspected and repaired and that other CPSC guidelines be met. The reader should note that the nation's playgrounds still earn grades on safety that in some respects are quite low.

Litigation and the standardization of playground equipment have resulted in the unintended elimination of play equipment available to children on many American playgrounds (Harrison, 2001). Some schools have removed playground equipment without replacing it because of the high cost of manufactured equipment. The types of materials used for playground equipment are also changing the playground movement of the 1970s and 1980s emphasized homemade playground equipment built from wood and tires. However, this playground equipment frequently does not meet safety standards and is being removed. The standardization of playgrounds also may be making playgrounds less interesting to children as only static heavy duty playground equipment is available in most public playgrounds. Children may not find such playgrounds as interesting as video games and other high excitement activities.

Environmental safety. One safety controversy of special interest is the issue of the effects of playing on wood playground equipment pressure-treated with arsenic and other toxic compounds. In 1990, the U.S. Consumer Product Safety Commission (Tyrrell, 1990) conducted a study of risk of skin cancer from dislodgeable arsenic on pressure-treated wood playground equipment. Their study of seven playground equipment wood samples from major manufacturers concluded that arsenic can be released from pressure-treated wood. In five out of the seven samples, the detection level of dislodgeable arsenic was a negligible risk; in two of the seven samples, there was a small risk. The estimated risk for lumber (not finished equipment) purchased from retail sources was somewhat higher and posed a "possible hazard."

In 2002 the Environmental Protection Agency announced that the use of CCA in lumber would be phased out by the end of 2003 and that manufacturers had agreed to halt uses of wood treated with chromated copper arsenate (CCA). CCA is an insecticide and preservative commonly used in pressure-treated wood to combat rot and insect infestation. The risk to children is primarily due to the transfer of arsenic residue from children's hands to their mouths during and after playing on CCA-treated wood, and the EPA recommended that children's hands be washed immediately after playing on such wood (Eisler, 2002; Dolesh, 2004; Smede, 2004).

The reader should be aware that not all pressure-treated wood is treated with toxic materials and that manufacturers are developing "safe" alternatives. The potential health consequences of playing on or around treated wood have been widely debated. For example, in 1998, Devenzio (1998) concluded; "…science overwhelmingly indicates that, when used as recommended, wood that is pressure-treated with CCA is harmless to people, plants, and animals" (p. 65). However, in 2004, the evidence is accumulating that CCA is harmful to children, and major playground equipment manufacturers are switching to kid-friendly preservatives.

Elements of the Play Environment

Children have preconceived notions about the type of play that should occur in different play spaces. According to Scales (1996), "Children bring predictable sets of expectations for play to various sites" (p. 241). Children's play is often disrupted when play spaces are ambiguous or there is a lack of clarity as to what type of play is expected in a play area. Some of the elements to consider when designing a play environment are the amount of space available for play, the features of the play environment, the loose parts available for play, nature areas and gardening, and of course, playground equipment.

Space and zoning the play environment. Hendricks (2001) suggests that a minimum of 2000 square meters is required for outdoor play spaces. This size area will support natural elements as well as active exploration. Children in play spaces typically organize themselves into small groups, so play yards should have spaces and subspaces, some small for "secretive play" and larger spaces to allow for running and active play. Designers should look at the world from a height of 90 cm to see the view of the child.

Zoning is an important element of play space design (Moore, 1992). The way the equipment is zoned or arranged helps the child to determine the appropriate type of play in a certain location. For example, in Moore's study, the visual boundary of the sand area suggested to children that the sand area should be used in a specific manner as an area for construction play. Equipment itself inspires different types of play and complexity of play structures helps to encourage social interactions. Consequently, a variety of play spaces and equipment should be available to children.

The ability to manipulate the environment is important for helping children to engage in play (Noren-Bjorn, 1982; Moore, 1992). Children prefer play equipment that is multifunctional, with moving parts and areas for encapsulation (Moore, 1992). Loose parts such as sand toys and wheeled toys that children can use to manipulate the environment are popular choices for children when they are available for outdoor play (Frost, Brown et al., 2005).

The creation of space for outdoor play is more than just equipment choices. Armitage (2001) describes the ways children use play spaces from an anthropological perspective. The design of play spaces by adults often leads to conflict as the adult perspective on play may differ from how children view the play space. Organized games played by older players (especially boys) often dominate play areas, which leaves little room for younger players. The game goes where the ball goes even through or over the games of other children. Simple obstructions to mark boundaries or having an L-shaped playground reduce the amount of conflicts between organized game players and others on the playground.

The location of play in outdoor environment can affect the type of play that occurs there. In addition, the age and gender of children influence the type of play and how children engage in playground activities. Children tend to select locations for play by gender. They use the same playground equipment in different ways. A play structure for example, may be the site for both active and passive play as children use it for chase games and then as a base or shelter (Pellegrini, 1995).

Loose parts. Children use portable play materials or loose parts outdoors as well as fixed playground equipment. Play materials for children in outdoor environments can increase the complexity of play through increasing the possible play options of children (Rivkin, 1995). The types of loose parts that children can use outdoors changes as children's play activities change. Infants and toddlers for example, are learning about the world, cause and effect and learning through their senses. They will frequently engage in functional or practice play that will require materials like rattles, grasping toys, push-pull toys, and sound-making materials in the outdoor play environment. Preschoolers, who are learning to pretend engage in construction and dramatic play, require materials such as dramatic play props, wheeled toys, and construction play materials. Schoolage children learning about following rules engage in organized games, requiring such materials as balls, bats, nets, jump ropes, and racquets. Schoolage children also are interested in work-play activities including gardening, hobbies, and collecting (Frost, Wortham, & Reifel, 2001).

In a study of the influence of materials on children's outdoor play, Hartle (1996) investigated four conditions of play environments, minimal, additional housekeeping, additional constructive, and additional combined housekeeping and constructive. The addition of both housekeeping and constructive materials increased the amount of pretense play, whereas functional play activities such as running were more common in the minimal condition. Boys were more likely than girls to pretend during the construction condition. Girls were more likely than boys to pretend during the housekeeping condition. Cross-gender play was most frequently observed in the combined condition. Qualitative observations from this study indicated that the construction materials were used frequently in pretense in addition to their use as construction materials. Girls were involved in more real-life themes, whereas boys were involved in more fantasy themes, leading them to use materials in unintended ways.

Natural areas. Frost, Wortham, and Reifel (2005) and Frost, Brown et al. (2005) maintain that contemporary playgrounds have been "dumbed down" as a result of growing standardization of manufactured equipment and fear of litigation. Entire categories of equipment, especially for preschool age children, are "not recommended." This prevents creative designers from eliminating objectionable elements of equipment, making them reasonably safe, and consequently maintaining a wide variety of play options for children. "Dumbing down," refers not just to reduced opportunities for motor development but also to deemphasis on play-related cognitive, language, and social development, resulting from "high stakes testing." Tree roots for example, a natural element on many playgrounds and all forest areas are viewed as tripping hazards in the Consumer Product Safety Commission Handbook for Public Playground Safety (1997).

Manufactured equipment such as swings, slides, climbers, and rotating equipment, properly designed, installed, and maintained, are very valuable, primarily for motor development.

However, traditional games, gardens, animal habitats, building areas and materials, storage facilities, and sand and water provide much richer and broader developmental benefits than does fixed manufactured structures (Frost, Wortham, & Reifel, 2005; Frost, Brown et al., 2005).

Despite such benefits, nature is a disappearing element on many playgrounds. Natural elements on playgrounds provide important sensory stimulation for children of all ages, and provide for sensations of visual (observing plants or insects), olfactory (smelling flowers), tactile (feeling textures of leaves, rocks, grass), auditory (hearing rustling leaves, birdsong), and gustatory (tasting nontoxic fruits and plants). Natural elements such as trees and shrubs can provide protection from the sun and wind (Jolley, 1995).

Over a period of several years, Moore and Wong (1997) worked with children to transform a concrete covered playground into a lush, naturalized environment. Their rich observations and descriptions provide both practical and scholarly insight into the nature and value of natural learning. Their "Environmental Yard," became a wonderland of ponds, gardens, animals and redwoods and resulted in the disappearance of antisocial behavior and boredom among children. The testimony of the children themselves eliminated misgivings about the social and educational value of natural settings in an urban school context. The complexity, beauty, and ever-changing landscape presented a growing array of opportunities for teaching and learning.

In a remarkably sensitive examination of the meaning of nature to children, two natural historians (Nabhan & Trimble, 1994) describe what wild places offer to children.

... where children make their contacts with the natural world, they often name the same key ingredients: small places, trees, and water (brooks and frog ponds)... children favor small paces close by—with dirt, trees, bushes, and loose parts—to build and dabble in. Trees... can be climbed and hidden behind; they can become forts or bases; with their surrounding vegetation and roots, they become dens and little houses; they provide shelter, landmarks and privacy; fallen they become part of an obstacle course or material for den building. (Nabhan & Trimble, 1994, p. 17)

Gardening. Gardening is an activity related to play environments in that children can participate in the creation of part of their environment. Gardening is a work/play activity, needing direct assistance from adults and popular for both children and adults. Self-activity involving gardening was one of Froebel's essential principles in the development of young children. His garden projects involved both individual and communal plots designed to develop individual responsibility and sense of community. Gardening also allowed children to begin to understand the unity and inner connection that man had with the universe (Brosterman, 1997). Gardens allow children to experience the cycles of nature and develop habits of responsibility and nurturance and allow children to find satisfaction in doing something useful (Rivkin, 1995).

Stimulus shelters or secret spaces. The idea of outdoor "stimulus shelters" (Moore, 1986) or "secret spaces" is the subject of a number of scholars but nowhere better described than in a special issue of the *Michigan Quarterly Review*, edited by Elizabeth Goodenough (2000). How adults create spaces for young children's play and leisure helps determine how they will see reality. Children need space and time every day to reflect, to create, or to do nothing—places where songs creep into being, sandcastles are built, smells of flowers are savored, sand and water trickle through fingers, and memories are stirred.

Stimulus shelters include the creation of a "home base." Having a "home base" is described in Hartle (1996). Play in this study was typically initiated at the base (climber, stoops in doorways) and then would revolve around the base as children would undertake journeys away from the home base. Bases would have agreed on names and would be returned to at the end of the journey. Unique features, such as iron grates and fences, of the playground also serve as dramatic play elements as well as a home base. These unique features can be transformed through play into prison doors or witch's gates (Armitage, 2001).

A sense of enclosure encourages the use of smaller spaces. However, the creation of hidden play spaces is problematic for many playground designers, educators, and parents. In Denmark, hidden play spaces are encouraged because play leaders feel it is not healthy for children to be supervised by adults at all times. American playgrounds do not equal those of Scandinavian countries in providing natural areas, but a gradual movement is transforming a growing number of outdoor American environments. Some of the most notable are described in case studies by Stine (1997). In the United States, playground designers are expected to have all areas of the playground easily supervised (Hendricks, 2001). Thus, the twig is bent to adult's oft-erroneous expectations.

Playground Equipment and Play

Playground equipment is designed to be used in specific, intended ways. However, observations of children's play reveal that children frequently use playground equipment in unintended ways. A more appropriate way for adults to view play on playground equipment is to look at the actions of children on playgrounds and how playground equipment influences these activities. Without oversimplifying the multitude of activities that a child can engage in on the playground, three movement activities are commonly associated with and promoted by playground equipment. These activities are climbing, mechanical motions such as swinging and sliding, and brachiation (swinging by the arms).

Climbing. Children frequently develop the ability to climb before they can walk. Children enjoy climbing for many reasons including the sense of triumph associated with reaching a height, to reach an object or to increase their visual field (Readdick & Park, 1998; Williams, 1994). Children also climb to engage in dramatic play and chase games (Clarke, 1999; Frost, Wortham, & Reifel, 2005). Climbing equipment including fire poles, geodesic domes, and chain link climbers, is the most common type of playground equipment, making up more than 50% of playground equipment (Thompson, 1988). However, children view all parts of the playground as climbable as children use slides, tic-tac-toe panels, and support structures as scalable parts of playground equipment (Frost, Sutterby, Therrell, Brown, & Thornton, 2001; Frost, Brown et al., 2005).

Climbing is a fundamental motor skill that requires perceptual motor skills like hand-eye coordination, balance, and upper body strength (Gallahue, 1990). Climbing is also associated with affective factors such as fear, motivation, and self efficacy. In addition, more complex climbing involves cognitive factors such as visual perceptual memory (Boshker, Bakker, & Michails, 2002).

Frost, Brown, Thornton, and Sutterby (2002) & Frost, Brown et al. (2005), found that children's climbing developed as children develop physically and as a result of their experience with climbing equipment. As children move from beginning to intermediate to advanced climbers, they adjust their hand and foot patterns, speed, visual focus and climbing style. Beginner climbers moved cautiously when climbing with a hand-to-hand and foot-to-foot pattern. They focus on their hands and feet when climbing and were limited to climbing up equipment. Advanced climbers were able to move quickly and confidently, focusing on other aspects of the playground rather than their hands and feet, were also able to use the equipment in novel and challenging ways.

The skill level presented by the child when climbing also was influenced by the type of climber. The child reverted to less sophisticated climbing patterns when engaged with more difficult or novel climbing equipment. Climbing equipment presents different challenge levels to children in that the incline, distance between climbing affordances, size and stability of affordances, and height reached by the equipment. One other factor that influenced the skill level of the children was fitness. Children who were less physically fit or obese were less likely to engage or succeed in climbing on the more advanced climbers (Frost, Brown, Thornton, & Sutterby, 2002; Frost, Brown et al., 2005).

Enhanced motion. Swinging and sliding are among the most popular playground activities, ranking in the top five in most playground use studies (Shin, 1994; Park, 1998; Ihn 1998; Riddel, 1992). Other equipment that provides similar motion-play experiences for children are spring rockers, merry-go-rounds, and see-saws (Thompson, 1988). Swings and similar equipment allow children to mechanically propel their bodies at a faster rate than they can produce through their own physical abilities and are important for the development of the vestibular and proprioceptive systems as well as in sensory integration (Yisreal, 1998; Langendorfer, 1988). The visual connection between vestibular and proprioceptive systems is also developed through swinging as swingers use visual cues to adjust their balance and movement when swinging (Post, Peper, & Beek, 2003).

Swings are available in many types including rope swings, belt swings, tire swings, and chair swings. Chair swings and other types are designed to support children with disabilities and allow them to participate in swinging (Frost, Brown et al., 2005). Motorized swings sooth babies to sleep as the motion stimulates the raphe system that is involved in sleeping and relaxation (Cheng, Ching, Yung, & Tsu, 1997).

Swinging behaviors develop as children gain strength, coordination, and experience. Fox and Tipps (1995) developed an 8-point scale to describe the development of children's swinging behaviors. Swinging typically begins with balance, observation, trial and error, and adaptation, where beginners adapt behaviors observed in others. Stage 4 is timing where children work to coordinate muscle movements. Stages 5 and 6 are demonstrating prowess and refinement as children become increasingly better coordinated. Stages 7 and 8 involve the child becoming secure in his swinging and finally beginning to experiment with different ways of swinging.

Swings are used in many unintended ways by children, including standing on the swings, laying on their stomachs and jumping from swings. Swings also provide a social atmosphere as children engage in competition when swinging and use the swings as a place to socialize. Swings also provide an opportunity for adults and children to interact as in the initial stages of swinging children require adult assistance in order to participate (Frost, Brown, Wisneski, & Sutterby, 2003).

Brachiation. Brachiation is a skill that involves supporting the weight of the body with the hands and arms. Overhead ladders, ring treks, and other overhead equipment develop the skill of brachiation. Overhead equipment is common and consists of about 10–12% of all playground equipment (Bowers & Bruya, 1988). Use of overhead equipment is associated with the development of upper body strength, balance, and perceptual motor coordination.

Children typically develop the grip strength to support their weight around the age of 24–36 months. Obese children at older ages may have difficulty supporting their body weight based solely on their grip strength (Frost & Kim, 2000). The typical developmental pattern for use of overhead equipment begins with hanging from the hands and then dropping to the ground. Children as young as 3 years old supported by adults were able to use modified overhead equipment. As these children develop they begin to be able to traverse the overhead ladder; however, their body movements are basically uncontrolled. As children gain experience, they begin to coordinate their arm and leg movements allowing them to experiment with skipping bars, moving backward, and other challenging activities (Frost, Brown, Thornton, Sutterby, & Therrell, 2002; Frost, Brown et al., 2005).

SUMMARY

The development of high quality play environments indoors and out requires continued research into how the environments of play affect children's development. Play can be viewed from many different lenses or rhetorics, which reflect the importance and value of play for children's development. The lenses on play can view play from educational or anthropological perspectives and look at domains such as social, emotional, cognitive, and language development (Frost, Wortham, & Reifel, 2005; Sutton-Smith, 1997). One lens on play is the importance society places on the elements of the play environment. Increased societal interest in ways to enhance brain development, standardization, and accountability will continue to influence play environments in the coming decade.

Play exists in many different contexts and children from different language and cultural backgrounds have different concepts of play, including differences in activities, settings, materials, and play partners. Enhancing play for children in American schools requires research into materials and outcomes that can be measured. School environments are under increasing scrutiny because of the accountability movement and must compete for space, time, and dollars.

Play environments consist of many elements. Teachers setting up a classroom for play must consider the type of play they want to encourage and the educational objective of the play. The materials available for play such as dramatic play props, manipulatives, and replica toys encourage children to play in specific ways. In addition, the inclusion of content area materials such as literacy and number materials encourages academic type play. Play spaces also can be an important element as visual boundaries and stimulus shelters in the classroom can lead to move involved play.

Research into outdoor environments requires continued scrutiny of how litigation and regulations are affecting play environments, ostensibly to help ensure greater safety, accessibility, and opportunities for physical activity. Creating outdoor environments involves more than playground equipment, it is creating spaces that are attractive to children because they have unique features, natural areas, gardens, and encapsulated spaces. Creating play environments with these elements gives children a variety of ways of engaging with the environment as it allows for quiet and active play as well as solitary and group play, and functional, dramatic, and games with rules play.

Creating safe and engaging outdoor environments is increasingly important as more and more children are becoming obese and unhealthy because of poor diet and lack of exercise. Recess for children is declining in schools, whereas sedentary activities are increasing both at home and at school. In order to reduce this trend, communities will need to place increased emphasis on outdoor play and physical activity.

Research into the types of activities children engage with playground equipment will give playground designers and manufacturers information about better ways to develop equipment for children. Access to equipment allows children to engage in activities that are difficult or impossible indoors. Activities such as climbing, swinging and brachiation are important for the physical, motor, and emotional development of children. These activities allow children to take risks and master challenges.

In conclusion, indoor and outdoor play environments will continue to change due to societal and technological changes. Hopefully these changes will be of benefit for all children. The challenge will remain for communities to ensure that children have access to safe, stimulating and creative play environments, indoors and out.

References

Almqvist, B. (1994). Educational toys, creative toys. In J. Goldstein (Ed.) *Toys, play and child development* (pp. 46-66). Cambridge: Cambridge University Press.

American Society for Testing and Materials (1998). *Standard consumer safety performance specifications for playground equipment and public use.* West Conshohocken, PA: American Society for Testing and Materials.

Armitage, M. (2001). The ins and outs of school playground play: Children's use of "play places." In J. Bishop & M. Curtis (Eds.), *Play today in the primary school playground* (pp. 37-58). London: Open University Press.

Axline, V. (1969). *Play therapy.* New York: Ballantine.

Bagley, D., & Chaille, C. (1996). Transforming play: An analysis of first-, third-, and fifth-graders' play. *Journal of Research in Childhood Education, 10,* 134-142.

Ball, D. L. (1992). Magical hopes: Manipulative and the reform of math education. *American Educator, 16,* 14-18.

Bar-Or, O. (2000). Juvenile obesity, physical activity, and lifestyle changes. *The Physician and Sports Medicine, 28*(11), 51-58.

Barbour, A. (1999). The impact of playground design on the play behaviors of children with differing levels of physical competence. *Early Childhood Research Quarterly, 14*(1), 75-98.

Barnett, L. (1984). Research note: Young children's resolution of distress through play. *Journal of Child Psychology and Psychiatry and Allied Disciplines, 25,* 477-483.

Bedrova, E., & Leong, D. (2004). Chopsticks and counting chips: Do play and foundational skills need to compete for the teacher's attention in an early childhood classroom? In D. Koralek (Ed.), *Spotlight on young children and play* (pp. 4-11). Washington, DC: National Association for the Education of Young Children.

Bishop, K. (2004). Designing sensory play environments for children with special needs. In R. Clements & L. Fiorentino (Eds.), *The child's right to play: A global approach* (pp. 233-242). Westport, CT: Praeger Publishers.

Board of Directors, Association for Play Therapy. (1997). Minutes. *Association for Play Therapy Newsletter, 16,* 14.

Boschker, M., Bakker, F., & Michaels., C. (2002). Memory for the functional characteristics of climbing walls: Perceiving affordances. *Journal of Motor Behavior, 34*(1), 25-36.

Bowers, L., & Bruya, L. (1988). Results of the survey. In L. Bruya & S. Langendorfer (Eds.), *Where our children play: Elementary school playground equipment* (pp. 31-44). Reston, VA: American Alliance for Health, Physical Education, Recreation & Dance.

Bredekamp, S., & Copple, C. (1997). *Developmentally appropriate practice in early childhood programs.* Washington, DC: National Association for the Education of Young Children.

Brosterman, N. (1997). *Inventing kindergarten.* New York: Harry N. Abrams.

Burghardt, G. (2004). Play and the brain in comparative perspective. In R. Clements & L. Fiorentino (Eds.), *The child's right to play: A global approach* (pp. 293-308). Westport, CT: Praeger Publishers.

Burroughs, E., & Murray, S. (1992). The influence of play material on discourse during play. *Journal of Childhood Communication Disorders, 14*(2), 119-128.

Centers for Disease Control and Prevention (1997). Guidelines for school and community programs to promote lifelong physical activity among young people, *Morbidity and Mortality Weekly Report, 46* (No. RR-6).

Cheng, H., Ching, H., Yung, J., & Tsu, F. (1997). An automatic swinging instrument for better neonatal growing development. *Revolutionary Science Instruments, 68*(8), 3192-3196.

Clarke, L. (1999). Development reflected in chase games. In S. Reifel (Ed.), *Play and culture studies, Vol. 2* (pp. 73-82). Stamford, CT: Ablex.

Consumer Product Safety Commission. (1997). *Handbook for public playground safety*. Washington, DC: U.S. Consumer Product Safety Commission.

Cross, D. (1997). *Kidstuff: Toys and the changing world of American childhood*. Cambridge, MA: Harvard University Press.

Dale, D., Corbin, C., & Dale, K. (2000). Restricting opportunities to be active during school time: Do children compensate by increasing physical activity levels after school. *Research Quarterly for Exercise and Sport, 71*(3), 240-248.

deMarrais, K., Nelson, P., & Baker, J. (1994). Meaning in mud: Yup'ik Eskimo girls at play. In J. Roopnarine, J. Johnson, & F. Hooper (Eds.), *Children's play in diverse cultures* (pp. 179-209). Albany: State University of New York Press.

Devenzio, H. (1998). Questioning treated wood on playgrounds. *Parks and Recreation, 33*(4), 64—69.

DeVries, R. (2001). Transforming the "play oriented curriculum" and work in constructivist early education. In A. Göncü & E. Klein (Eds.), *Children in play, story and school* (pp. 72-106). New York: Guilford Press.

Dolesh, R. (2004). Arsenic and your playground. *Parks and Recreation, 39*(4), 61-67.

Eisler, P. (2002, February 13). Industry to phase out arsenic-tainted wood. *USA Today* p. A4.

Epstein, L., Paluch, R., Kalakanis, L., Goldfield, G., Cerny, F., & Roemmich, J. (2001). How much activity do youth get? A quantitative review of heart-measured activity. *Pediatrics, 108*(3). Accessed May 15, 2005 at pediatrics.org/cgi/content/full/108/3/e44

Erikson, E. (1950). *Childhood and society*. New York: Norton.

Escobedo, T. (1998). The canvas of play: A study of children's play behaviors while drawing. In S. Reifel (Ed.), *Play and culture studies, Vol. 2* (pp. 101-122). Stamford, CT: Ablex.

Farver, J. (1999). Activity setting analysis: A model for examining the role of culture in development. In A. Goncu (Ed.), *Children's engagement in the world: Sociocultural perspectives* (pp. 99-127). Cambridge: Cambridge University Press.

Fasoli, L. (1999). Developmentally appropriate play and turtle hunting. In. E. Dau (Ed.), *Child's play: Revisiting play in early childhood setting* (pp. 53-59). Sydney: Maclennan and Petty.

Fein, G. (1995). Toys and stories. In A. Pellegrini (Ed.), *The future of play theory: A multidisciplinary inquiry into the contributions of Brian Sutton-Smith* (pp. 151-164). Albany: State University of New York Press.

Fisher, E. (1992). The impact of play on development. A meta-analysis. *Play & Culture, 5,* 159-181.

Fox, J., & Tipps, R. (1995). Young children's development of swinging behaviors. *Early Childhood Research Quarterly, 10,* 491-504.

Frost, J. (1992). *Play and playscapes*. Albany, NY: Delmar.

Frost, J., Brown, P., Thornton, C., & Sutterby, J. (2002). *The nature and benefits of children's climbing behaviors*. Unpublished manuscript.

Frost, J., Brown, P., Sutterby, J., & Thornton, C. (2005). *The developmental benefits of playgrounds*. Wheaton, MD: Association for Childhood Education International.

Frost, J., Brown, P., Thornton, C., Sutterby, J., & Therrell, J. (2002). *The developmental benefits and use patterns of overhead equipment on playgrounds*. Unpublished manuscript.

Frost, J., & Jacobs, P. (1995). Play deprivation and juvenile violence. *Dimensions, 23,* 14-20, 39.

Frost, J., & Kim, S. (2000). *Developmental progress in preschool age children's using an overhead bar*. Unpublished manuscript.

Frost, J., Sutterby, J., Therrell, J., Brown., & Thornton, C. (2001). *The relevance of height for child development and playground safety*. Unpublished manuscript.

Frost, J., & Sweeney, T. (1996). *Cause and prevention of playground injuries: Case studies*. Wheaton, MD: Association for Childhood Education International.

Frost, J., Wortham, S., & Reifel, S. (2005). *Play and child development*. Upper Saddle River, NJ: Merrill, Prentice Hall.

Gabbard, C. (2000). Physical education: Should it be part of the core curriculum? *Principal, 79*(3), 29-31.

Gallahue, D. (1990). *Understanding motor development: Infants, children, adolescents*. Indianapolis, IN: Benchmark Press.

Goodenough, E. (Ed.). (Summer, 2000). Special Issue: Secret spaces of childhood, Part 2. *Michigan Quarterly Review. 39*(3), 678.

Gordan-Larsen, P., McMurray, R., & Popkin, B. (2000). Determinants of adolescent physical activity and inactivity patterns. *Pediatrics, 105*(6). Accessed May 15, 2005 at pediatrics.org/cgi/content/full/105/6/e83.

Grossman, B. (2004). Play and cognitive development: A Piagetian perspective. In R. Clements & L. Fiorentino (Eds.), *The child's right to play: A global approach* (pp. 89-94). Westport, CT: Praeger Publishers.

Haight, W. (1998). Adult direct and indirect influences on play. In D. Fromberg & D. Bergan (Eds.), *Play from birth to twelve and beyond: Contexts, perspective, and meanings* (pp. 259-265). New York: Garland.

Haight, W., & Miller, P. (1993). *Pretending at home: Early development in a sociocultural context*. Albany: State University of New York Press.

Harrison, L. (2001). Where have all the swing sets gone? *Time Bonus Section Families, 157*(19), 11-12.

Hartle, L. (1996). Effects of additional materials on preschool children's outdoor play behaviors. *Journal of Research in Childhood Education, 11*(1), 68-81.

Hendricks, B. (2001). *Designing for play*. Burlington, VT: Ashgate.

Hendy, T. (2001). The Americans with Disabilities Act insures the right of every child to play. *Parks & Recreation, 36*(4), 108-118.

Hewes, J., & Beckwith, J. (1974). *Build your own playground: A sourcebook of play sculptures*. Boston, MA: Houghton Mifflin Company.

Hogan, P. (1982). *The nuts and bolts of playground construction*. West Point, NY: Leisure Press.

Hogan, C., & Howe, N. (2001). Do props matter in the dramatic play center?: The effects of prop realism on children's play. *Canadian Journal of Research in Childhood Education, 8*(4), 51-66.

Hudson, S., Thompson, D., & Olsen, M. S. (2004). The 2004 safety report card. *Today's Playground. 4*(5), 16-20.

Ihn, H. (1998). *Preschool children's play behaviors and equipment choices in an outdoor environment*. Unpublished research report, University of Texas at Austin.

Isenberg, J., & Quisenberry, N. (2003). *Play: Essential for all children. A position paper of the Association for Childhood Education International*. Olney, MD: Association for Childhood Education International.

James, O. (1997). *Play therapy: A comprehensive guide*. Northvale, NJ: Aronson.

Jarrett, O. S., Maxwell, D. M., Dickerson, C., Hoge, P., Davies, G., & Yetley, A. (1998). The impact of recess on classroom behavior: Group effects and individual differences. *Journal of Educational Research, 92*(2), 121-126.

Jolley, J. (1995). Developmentally appropriate outdoor play environments for infants and toddlers. *Working Papers in Early Childhood Development*. The Hague, Netherlands: Bernard Van Leer Foundation.

Kieff, J., & Casbergue, R. (2000). *Playful learning and teaching: Integrating play into preschool and primary programs*. Boston, MA: Allyn & Bacon.

Kieff, J., & Chaille (2001). The silencing of recess bells. *Childhood Education, Annual Theme*, 77(5), 319-320.

Kline, S. (1993). *Out of the garden: Children's toys in the age of marketing*. London: Verso.

Kline, S. (1995). The promotion and marketing of toys: Time to rethink the paradox? In A. Pellegrini (Ed.), *The future of play theory: A multidisciplinary inquiry into the contributions of Brian Sutton-Smith* (pp. 165-185). Albany: State University of New York Press.

Kluger, J. (2001). Toxic playgrounds. *Time, 158*(2), 48-49. July 16.

Kluger, J., & Park, A. (2001). The quest for a superkid. *Time, 157*(17), 50-55.

Landreth, G. (1991). *Play therapy: The art of the relationship*. Bristol, PA: Accelerated Development.

Langendorfer, S. (1988). Rotating, spring rocking, and see-saw equipment. In L. Bruya & S. Langendorfer (Eds.) *Where our children play: Elementary school playground equipment* (107-131). Reston, VA: American Association for Health, Physical Education, Recreation and Dance.

Leeb-Lundberg, K. (1984). The block builder mathematician. In E. Hirsch (Ed.) *The block book* (pp. 30-51). Washington, DC: National Association for the Education of Young Children.

MacNoughton, G. (1996). Is Barbie to blame?: Reconsidering how children learn gender. *Australian Journal of Early Childhood, 21*(4), 18-24.

Martini, M. (1994). Peer interaction in Polynesia: A view from the Marquesas. In J. Roopnarine, J. Johnson, & F. Hooper, (Eds.), *Children's play in diverse cultures* (73-103). Albany: State University of New York Press.

McKelvie, P., & Low, J. (2002). Listening to Mozart does not improve children's spatial ability: Final curtains for the Mozart effect. *British Journal of Developmental Psychology, 20*, 241-258.

Moore, G. (1987). The physical environment and cognitive development in child care centers. In C. Weinstein & T. Davids (Eds.), *Spaces for children: The built environment and child development* (pp. 117-138). New York: Plenum.

Moore, M. (1992). *An analysis of outdoor play environments and play behaviors*. Unpublished doctoral diss., University of Texas at Austin.

Moore, R. (1986). *Childhood's domain: Play and place in child development*. London: Croom Helm.

Moore, R., Goltsman, S., & Iacofano, D. (1997). *Play for all guidelines: Planning, design and management of outdoor play settings for all children*. Berkeley, CA: MIG Communications.

Moore, R., & Wong, H. (1997). *Natural learning: Creating environments for rediscovering nature's way of teaching*. Berkeley, CA: MIG Communications.

Nabhan, G., & Trimble, S. (1994). *The geography of of childhood: Why children need wild places*. Boston: Beacon Press.

Neuman, S., & Roskos, K. (1992). Literacy Objects as Cultural Tools: Effects on Children's Literacy Behaviors in Play. *Reading Research Quarterly, 27*(3), 202-25.

Noren-Bjorn, E. (1982). *The impossible playground*. West Point, NY: Leisure Press.

O'Brien, J., Boatwright, T., Chaplin, J., Geckler, C., Gosnell, D., Holcombe, J., & Parrish, K. (1998). The impact of positioning equipment on play skills of physically impaired children. In M. Duncan,

G. Chick, & A. Aycock (Eds.), *Play and culture studies: Explorations in the fields of play* (pp. 149-160). Greenwich, CT: Ablex.

Park, Y. (1998). *Preschool children's play behaviors and equipment choices of two playgrounds*. Unpublished master's thesis, University of Texas at Austin.

Parten, M. (1933). Social play among preschool children. *Journal of Abnormal and Social Psychology, 28*, 136-147.

Pellegrini, A. (1995). *School recess and playground behavior: Educational and developmental roles*. Albany: State University of New York Press.

Pellegrini, A. D., Huberty, P. D., & Jones, I. (1995). The effects of recess timing on children's playground and classroom behaviors. *American Educational Research Journal, 32*(4), 845-864.

Pellegrini, A., & Jones, I. (1994). Play, toys and language. In J. Goldstein (Ed.) *Toys, play and child development* (pp. 27-45). Cambridge: Cambridge University Press.

Piaget, J. (1962). *Play, dreams and imitation in childhood*. New York: Norton.

Post, A., Peper, C., & Beek, P. (2003). Effects of visual information and task constraints on intersegmental coordination in playground swinging. *Journal of Motor Behavior, 35*(1), 64-78.

Power, T. (2000). *Play and exploration in children and animals*. Mahwah, NJ: Lawrence Erlbaum Associates.

Rauscher, F., Shaw, G., & Ky, K. (1993). Music and Spatial Task performance. *Nature, 365*, 611.

Readdick, C., & Park, J. (1998). Achieving great heights: The climbing child. *Young Children, 53*(6), 14-19.

Reifel, S., & Yeatman, J. (1991). Action, talk and thought in block play. In B. Scales, M. Almy, A. Nicolopoulou, & S. Ervin-Tripp (Eds.), *The social context of play and development in early care and education* (pp. 156-172). New York: Teachers College Press.

Riddell, C. (1992). *The effects of contrasting playgrounds on the play behaviors of kindergarten children*. Unpublished master's thesis, University of Texas at Austin.

Rivkin, M. S. (1995). *The great outdoors: Restoring children's right to play outside*. Washington, DC: National Association for the Education of Young Children.

Rogers, C. (1951). *Client-centered therapy*. Boston: Houghton-Mifflin.

Roopnarine, J, Johnson, J. & Hooper, F (Eds.). (1994). *Children's play in diverse cultures*. Albany: State University of New York Press.

Roskos, K., & Neuman, S. (1998). Play as an opportunity for literacy. In O. Saracho & B. Spodek (Eds.), *Multiple perspectives on play in early childhood education* (pp. 101-115). Albany: State University of New York Press.

Rost, D., & Hanses, P. (1994). The possession and use of toys in elementary-school boys and girls: Does giftedness make a difference? *Educational Psychology, 14*(2), 181-194.

Rubin, K. (1977). The social and cognitive value of preschool toys and activities. *Canadian Journal of Behavioral Science, 9*, 382-385.

Sallis, J., McKenzie, T., Kolody, B., Lewis, M., Marshall, S., & Rosengard, P. (1999). Effects of health-related physical education on academic achievement: Project Spark. *Research Quarterly for Exercise and Sport, 70*(2), 127-134.

Sandall, S. (2004). Play modifications for children with disabilities. In D. Koralek (Ed.), *Spotlight on young children and play* (pp. 44-45). Washington DC: National Association for the Education of Young Children.

Sawyer, R. (1997). *Pretend play as improvisation: Conversation in the preschool classroom*. Mahwah, NJ: Lawrence Erlbaum Associates.

Scales, B. (1996). Researching the hidden curriculum. In Reifel, S. & Chafel, J. (Eds.), *Advances in Early Education and Day Care: Theory and Practice in Early Childhood Education, Vol. 8*, 237-262. Greenwich, CT: JAI Press.

Schultz, K. (1998). On the elimination of recess. *Education Week, 17*(39), 38.

Shin, D. (1994). *Preschool children's symbolic play indoors and outdoors.* Unpublished doctoral diss., University of Texas at Austin.

Shine, S., & Acosta, T. (1999). The effect of a physical and social environment on parent-child interactions: A qualitative analysis of pretend play in a children's museum. In S. Reifel (Ed.), *Play and culture studies, Vol. 2* (pp. 123–142). Stamford, CT: Ablex.

Shine, S., & Acosta, T. (2000). Parent-child play in a children's museum. *Family Relations, 49*(1), 45–52.

Slaughter, D., & Dombrowski, J. (1989). Cultural continuities and discontinuities: Impact on social and pretend play. In M. Bloch & A. Pellegrini (Eds.), *The ecological context of children's play* (pp. 282–310). Norwood, NJ: Ablex.

Smede, S. (2004). The changing world of wood: Solutions, trends and an industry's future. *Today's Playground, 4*(5), 13–15.

Smilansky, S., & Sheftaya, L. (1990). *Facilitating play: A medium for promoting cognitive, socioemotional, and academic development in young children.* Gathersburg, MD: Psychosocial & Educational Publications.

Smith, S. (1998). *Risk and our pedagogical relation to children: on the playground and beyond.* Albany: State University of New York Press.

Sobel, D. (1993). *Children's special places: Exploring the role of forts, dens and bush houses in middle childhood.* Tucson, AZ: Zephyr Press.

Steinberg, S. (1997). The bitch who has everything. In S. Steinberg & J. Kinchloe (Eds.) *Kinderculture: The corporate construction of childhood* (pp. 207–218). Boulder, CO: Westview Press.

Stine, S. (1997). *Landscapes for learning: Creating outdoor environments for children and youth.* New York: John Wiley and Sons.

Stratton, G., Marsh, I., & Moores, J. (2000). Promoting children's physical activity in primary school: an intervention study using playground markings. *Ergonomics, 43*(10), 1538–1546.

Sutterby, J. (2002). *Todos somos amigos: Cross-cultural and cross-linguistic play interactions in a two-way immersion prekindergarten classroom.* Unpublished doctoral dissertation: University of Texas at Austin.

Sutterby, J. (2004, January). Texas accessibility guidelines for playgrounds. *Newsletter for the Texas Council for Exceptional Children,* 5–8.

Sutterby, J., Brown, P., Thornton, C. & Therrell, J. (2002). *Parents' views on children's toys.* Washington, DC: Consumer Product Safety Commission.

Sutterby, J., Brown, P., & Thornton, C. (2004, April). *Physical activity levels during free play and physical education.* Paper presented at the annual meeting of the American Education Research Association, San Diego, CA.

Sutton-Smith, B. (1997). *The ambiguity of play.* Cambridge, MA: Harvard University Press.

Sutton-Smith, B. (1999). Evolving a consilience of play definitions: Playfully. In S. Reifel (Ed.), *Play and culture studies, Vol. 2* (pp. 239–256). Stamford, CT: Ablex.

Thompson, D. (1988). Swings, slides and climbing equipment. In L. Bruya & S. Langendorfer (Eds.), *Where our children play: Elementary school playground equipment* (pp. 67–105). Reston, VA: American Association for Health, Physical Education, Recreation and Dance.

Thompson, D., Hudson, S., & Bowers, L. (2002). Play areas and the ADA: Providing access and opportunities for all children. *The Journal of Physical Education, Recreation & Dance, 73*(2), 37–42.

Tinsworth, D., & McDonald, J. (2001). *Special study: Injuries and deaths associated with children's playground equipment.* Washington, DC: Consumer Product Safety Commission.

Trawick-Smith, J. (1992). The physical classroom environment: How it affects learning and development. *Dimensions of Early Childhood, 20,* 34–42.

Trawick-Smith, J. (1993, April). *Effects of realistic, non-realistic, and mixed-realism play environments on young children's symbolization, social interaction and language.* Paper presented at the annual meeting of the American Educational Research Association, Atlanta.

Trawick-Smith, J., & Landry-Fitzsimmons, K. (1992). A descriptive study of spatial arrangements in a family child care home. *Child and Youth Care Quarterly, 21,* 97–114.

Troster, H., & Brambring, M. (1994). The play behavior and play materials of blind and sighted infants and preschoolers. *Journal of Visual Impairment & Blindness, 88*(5), 421–432.

Tyrrell, E. A. (1990). *Transmittal of estimate of risk of skin cancer from dislodgeable arsenic on pressure treated wood playground equipment.* Washington, DC: U.S. Consumer Product Safety Commission.

Tudge, J., Lee., S., & Putnam, S. (1998). Children's play in sociocultural context: South Korea and the United States. In M. Duncan, G. Chick, & A. Aycock (Eds.), *Play and culture studies: Explorations in the fields of play, Vol. 1* (pp. 77–90). Greenwich, CT: Ablex.

United States Access Board. (1994). *Recommendations for accessibility guidelines: Recreational facilities and outdoor developed areas.* Washington, DC: U.S. Access Board.

Uttal, D., Marzolf, D., Pierroutsakos, S., Smith, C., Troseth, G., Scudder, K., & DeLoache J. (1998). Seeing through symbols: The development of children's understanding of symbolic relations. In O. Saracho, & B. Spodek (Eds.), *Multiple perspectives on play in early childhood education: SUNY series, early childhood education* (pp. 59–79). Albany: State University of New York Press.

Van Hoorn, J., Nourot, P., Scales, B., & Alward, K. (2003). *Play at the center of the curriculum* (3rd ed.). New York: Merrill.

Vygotsky, L. (1966). Play and its role in the mental development of the child. *Soviet Psychology, 12*(6), 62–76.

Vygotski, L. (1978). *Mind in Society: The Development of Higher Mental Processes.* Cambridge, MA: Harvard University Press.

Watson, M. (1994). The relation between anxiety and pretend play. In A. Slade & D. Wolf (Eds.), *Children at play: Clinical and developmental approaches to meaning and representation* (pp. 33–47). New York: Oxford University Press.

Whitehurst, M., Groo, D., & Brown, L. (1996). Prepubescent heart rate response to indoor play. *Pediatric Exercise Science, 8,* 245–250.

Whiting, B. (1980). Culture and social behavior. *Ethos, 2,* 95–116.

Williams, G. (1994). Talk on the climbing frame. *Early Child Development and Care, 102,* 81–89.

Woods, I. (1996). *Rethinking the Froebelian metaphor: Culture and development in multiple settings.* Unpublished doctoral diss., University of Texas at Austin.

Yisreal, L. (1998). Sensory integration therapy. *Fast Facts On: Developmental Disabilities, 114.* Kansas City, MO: UMKC Institute for Human Development. Accessed May 15, 2005 at www.moddrc.com/Information-Disabilities/FastFacts/SensoryIntegration-htm.

·18·

CHILDHOOD POVERTY: IMPLICATIONS FOR SCHOOL READINESS AND EARLY CHILDHOOD EDUCATION

Rebecca M. Ryan
Rebecca C. Fauth
Jeanne Brooks-Gunn
Columbia University

In 2004, nearly one in five children under age 5 in the United States was living below the poverty line, a level that largely surpasses rates of other industrialized countries. Although rates of child poverty have declined in recent years, from 22% for all children in 1993 to 18% today, children in the United States are still more likely to be poor than any other age group (Proctor & Dalaker, 2003; U.S. Census Bureau, 2004). Proportions are much higher for black and Hispanic children, with 34% of black children and 30% of Hispanic children living in poverty in 2004, compared to 10% of white children (U.S. Census Bureau, 2004). For families, living in poverty means that their before-tax income falls at or below a federally established threshold (i.e., $15,670 for a family of three in 2004). People living in "severe poverty," with incomes below 50% of the poverty threshold, represent 41% of the poverty population in the United States, indicating that many families with children subsist well below the national standard. Children in poverty not only lack basic financial resources, but they also suffer from deficits that often accompany poverty, such as inadequate food, clothing, housing and health care (Haveman & Wolfe, 1994). Not surprisingly, these conditions have serious consequences for children's health and development.

Growing up in poverty can significantly impact a child's readiness to learn upon school entry. Early childhood, typically defined as birth to age 5, is a critical period for infant and toddler development. During this period children are set on developmental trajectories that are mutable but become increasingly difficult to change over time (Carnegie Corporation, 1994; McCormick, Brooks-Gunn, Workman-Daniels, Turner, & Peckham, 1992; Rutter, 1990; Smith, Brooks-Gunn, & Klebanov, 1997). For this reason, young children are particularly vulnerable to the effects of deprivation and the impacts can last through young adulthood (Axinn, Duncan, & Thornton, 1997; Duncan, Yeung, Brooks-Gunn, & Smith, 1998). Research done over the past 20 years has consistently linked childhood poverty with unfavorable early cognitive, verbal, and behavioral outcomes for young children (Dearing, McCartney, & Taylor, 2001; Smith et al., 1997). Differences between children in and out of poverty, particularly in the cognitive domain, tend to appear around 24 months and are of equal or greater size by age 5. These early problems remain when children enter elementary school, where poor children exhibit lower school achievement (Smith et al., 1997). The gap often persists through middle and high school, where children living in poverty have higher rates of special education placement, grade retention, teenage pregnancy, and school dropout (Dawson, 1991; Duncan et al., 1998). Not only are early differences sustained into adolescence, but poverty experienced during the first 5 years is particularly harmful to children's development (Duncan et al., 1998). With 20% of infants (ages 0 to 1 years), toddlers (ages 2 to 3 years) and preschoolers (ages 3 to 5 years) poor in this country (U.S. Census Bureau, 2004), a percentage that exceeds rates for older children, early childhood poverty and its effects on children's outcomes concern all those involved in the field of early childhood education.

In this chapter, we examine associations between poverty and young children's development, up to age 5-years when most children leave early education programs and enter formal schooling.[1] First, we explore the complexities in measuring poverty and studying its effects on young children. In so doing, we review key large-scale, national studies that have been used to examine poverty's effects on child development. Second, findings gleaned from these studies on direct associations between poverty and children's cognitive, verbal, and behavioral outcomes during the first 5 years of life are reviewed. The extent to which depth and persistence of poverty moderate these associations is also addressed in this section. Third, we consider the potential pathways through which poverty may influence child development. Here, two theories frame the discussion, one emphasizing the role of familial relationships and parenting (Conger & Elder, 1994; Elder & Caspi, 1988; McLoyd, 1990) and another stressing the impact of parental investments in resources for children (Becker, 1991; Mayer, 1997). We address links between family poverty and maternal mental health and parent-child interactions as part of the former model. The latter theory encompasses associations between poverty status and factors such as the quality of home environment, neighborhoods, nonmaternal child care, and health and nutrition. Finally, we consider the role of public policy in the lives of children growing up in poverty. Early intervention programs and welfare policy are highlighted as two policy areas that have changed over the past decade and play a significant role in the lives of young children living in poverty. Early intervention programs, particularly those including center-based services beginning in infancy, have shown immediate and strong positive effects on low-income children's IQ scores (Campbell & Ramey, 1994) and sociobehavioral outcomes (Yoshikawa, 1995). The welfare reform bill passed in 1996, which mandated work requirements and time restrictions for recipients, dramatically altered the daily lives of female-headed households with young children. Results from preliminary welfare reform experiments suggest that although the effects of earning supplements for welfare recipients had a positive impact on preschool and young school-age children, work requirements and time limits had mixed impacts (Morris, Huston, Duncan, Crosby, & Bos, 2001). In our discussion of both initiatives, we present early childhood as a time of great vulnerability and great opportunity for children.

METHODOLOGICAL CONSIDERATIONS IN STUDYING POVERTY

In the United States, the official poverty threshold is frequently used to assess families' economic status. This threshold, which was originally developed in 1959, is based on expected food expenditures (i.e., thrifty food basket) for families of varying sizes and adjusted annually for the Consumer Price Index cost of living. In 2004, the poverty threshold for a single mother raising two children was $15,670 (U.S. Census Bureau, 2004). Whereas the use of this threshold allows for annual comparisons to be made, researchers have criticized the poverty threshold on numerous counts, notably that the current poverty measure is dated (Citro & Michael, 1995), does not include alternative transfers such as food stamps, housing subsidies, and tax benefits (e.g., the Earned Income Tax Credit), does not consider regional and urban differences in the cost of living (Betson & Michael, 1997) and potentially underestimates material hardship (e.g., difficulty affording food and paying rent, residing in crowded conditions, experiencing housing problems, etc.) for children (Mayer & Jencks, 1988).

An extension of the poverty threshold that attempts to distinguish various gradients of poverty is the income-to-needs ratio. The ratio is calculated to adjust income for household size according to current poverty thresholds; an income-to-needs ratio of 1.0 indicates the family is living at the poverty threshold, a ratio of 0.5 is indicative of living at half of the poverty threshold and a ratio of 2.0 is defined as living at twice the poverty threshold (Duncan & Brooks-Gunn, 1997). Persistence of poverty, measured via the number of years families live in poverty and whether families cycle in and out poverty, and depth of poverty (how far below the poverty threshold a family's income falls), respectively, also have been considered in research (Duncan & Brooks-Gunn, 1997).

Socioeconomic status (SES) is an alternative to the poverty threshold as an assessment of economic wellbeing. Measures of SES may include household heads' occupational status, class and prestige, years of formal education, labor market earnings, wealth, as well as average neighborhood income, or a composite index of various attributes (Entwisle & Astone, 1994; Hernandez, 1997). The existing research on family SES suggests that the different components of SES, namely occupation, education, and income, are conceptually and empirically distinct, which indicates that index measures may not be the best measurement method and that the impacts of each item on outcomes should be considered independently (Ensminger & Fothergill, 2003; Entwisle & Astone, 1994; Haveman & Wolfe, 1994; Mayer, 1997).

Findings regarding associations between the various indicators of poverty and children's outcomes vary depending on the extent to which SES factors are included in analyses. Although variables such as income, employment, and education are independent of each other to a certain extent, they are also typically correlated, as individuals with higher education and stable employment tend to earn more money than those with less schooling and erratic employment. In the present chapter, we focus on associations between income, specifically, and children's outcomes; however, the unique contributions of poverty to variations in young children's outcomes are highlighted only if statistical controls for potentially confounding demographic and background characteristics are included in analytic models (e.g., if poverty is used as a predictor of outcomes, maternal education is controlled).

---

[1]Although kindergarten can be considered part of early childhood education, we focus on children aged 0 to 5 years who are not yet in kindergarten.

Studies Used to Examine Associations Between Poverty and Young Children's School Readiness

Before the 1990s, much of the research investigating the impact of poverty on children's outcomes suffered from methodological shortcomings such as flawed measures or unrepresentative samples. The use of data from large, longitudinal studies such as the National Longitudinal Survey of Youth (NLSY), the Infant Health and Development Program (IHDP), the Panel Study of Income Dynamics (PSID), and, more recently, the Early Childhood Longitudinal Study—Kindergarten Class of 1998–1999 (ECLS-K) and the National Institute of Child Health and Human Development's Study of Early Child Care (NICHD-SECC) have remedied many of these methodological problems as they include adequate assessments of child development and families' economic status (Brooks-Gunn, Berlin, Leventhal, & Fuligni, 2000).

Although national in scope, the NLSY sample includes an overrepresentation of minority and economically disadvantaged white respondents. The Children and Young Adults substudy of the NLSY sampled all children born to female NLSY participants spanning from 1986 to 1994 to retrieve information on children's health, cognitive and socioemotional development, school experiences, and family and home environment (West, Hauser, & Scanlon, 1998). Extensive information on families' demographic and background characteristics including household composition, income, employment, and education was also gathered. The IHDP is a multisite randomized trial of an early intervention program for premature, low birthweight children. Although all children were born at heightened risk for health and developmental problems, the eight participating sites were heterogeneous in terms of SES and available resources. Although the main focus of the study was on clinical assessments and developmental testing for children, data on families' SES was also collected. The Child Development Supplement of the PSID gathered information on parents and their 0- to 12-year-old children. It aimed to create a nationally representative dataset of families to study the formation of human capital. As such, information pertaining to parental time, money, and psychological resources, sibling characteristics and social capital was collected to assess the linkages between these variables and focal children's cognitive and behavioral development (West et al., 1998). The ECLS-K study was designed to examine the educational experiences of America's children through the use of a nationally representative sample of over 20,000 children enrolled in about 1,000 kindergarten programs during the 1998–1999 school year (West, 1999). The study assesses children's development including physical, cognitive, and socioemotional domains as well as children's home, school, and classroom environments through the use of multiple informants—children, primary caregivers, teachers, and school administrators. Finally, the NICHD study is a national sample of families with full-term healthy infants created to study child care experiences of children in the United

States Questionnaires, interviews and observations were used to assess family demographic, economic, and psychological characteristics, children's cognitive and language development, school readiness, behavioral outcomes, and health (West et al., 1998). Since the 1990s, the use of these studies to examine linkages between family economic status and children's outcomes has greatly expanded the body of work on child poverty. In the following section, we draw largely from these studies in our discussion of associations between poverty and children's outcomes.

ASSOCIATIONS BETWEEN POVERTY AND YOUNG CHILDREN'S SCHOOL READINESS

One of the main goals of early childhood education is to prepare young children for entry into kindergarten and elementary school. This preparedness, often referred to in policy contexts as school readiness, has been conceptualized in different ways since it gained acceptance in the United States in the 1920s (Kagan & Rigby, 2003; May, & Campbell, 1981).[2] Two schools of thought have emerged—readiness to learn and readiness for school; the former emphasizes the developmental level at which a child is ready to grasp certain new material, whereas the latter stresses the more finite accumulation of skills, mostly cognitive and linguistic, needed to succeed in primary school (Gagne, 1970; Good, 1973; Gray, 1927; Kagan & Rigby, 2003). Here we draw from both schools of thought, understanding that maturational readiness involves the ability to understand new material and the possession of specific skills (Gesell, 1925; Kagan & Rigby, 2003). Both notions maintain that school readiness involves the cognitive, social, and physical domains of child development, as well as child health. From this holistic perspective, a child's ability to pay attention in class, form relationships with peers and teachers, and arrive at school in good health is as important to her early and later school success as her cognitive and literacy skills. The following section examines the extent to which growing up in poverty can compromise the cognitive and socioemotional aspects of children's development. Children's physical development and health are covered as part of the following section, on mechanisms through which poverty can affect child outcomes.

Links between family income and children's cognitive and behavioral outcomes have been established in numerous studies over the last half century. Much of the research has examined differential IQ scores between lower and higher SES children (Bradley & Corwyn, 2002; Brooks-Gunn & Duncan, 1997; Duncan & Brooks-Gunn, 1997). Lower verbal ability has also been associated with living in poverty for preschool age children (Smith et al., 1997). Although the links between poverty and children's social development have not been as consistent or strong as those found for cognitive outcomes, there still exists

---

[2]The meaning of "school readiness" is hotly debated, particularly as the phrase relates to early education policy formation. The nuances of these debates are beyond the scope of this chapter. However, the authors take a view of readiness that takes into account the whole of a child's cognitive and language as well as social and physical development; we consider not only the skills a child possesses on school entry but also a childs potential for developing those capacities. For a more thorough description of this view, see Kagan (1990, 1995).

much evidence that children growing up in poverty develop more emotional and behavioral problems than children who live above the poverty line (Duncan & Brooks-Gunn, 1997; Duncan, Brooks-Gunn, & Klebanov, 1994; Korenman, Miller, & Sjaastad, 1995; McLeod & Shanahan, 1993; Sameroff, Seifer, Barocas, Zax, & Greenspan, 1987). Because early cognitive and behavioral outcomes have been shown to predict later school success (Chen, Lee, & Stevenson, 1996; Cunningham & Stanovich, 1997; Luster & McAdoo, 1996; Shonkoff & Phillips, 2000), differences found between children living in and out of poverty are important not only to understanding children's experiences in early education but also how those experiences might presage later ones.

Although research on poverty and child development has a long history, this section focuses on studies that used large, cross-sectional datasets to investigate potential associations (see Children's Defense Fund, 1994; Klerman, 1991). Although earlier research tended to highlight overall differences between poor and nonpoor children on relevant outcomes without controlling for noneconomic variables (e.g., teenage parenthood, low maternal education, unemployment, single parenthood, low birthweight) that might contribute to that variation, the more recent large-scale research initiatives have frequently included or oversampled low-income families as well as included measures of these other known correlates to child development as an attempt to isolate the effects of poverty on children's development (Brooks-Gunn & Duncan, 1997; Dearing et al., 2001; Duncan & Brooks-Gunn, 1997; Smith et al., 1997). With large, nationally representative datasets, researchers also can use more conservative methods of statistical estimation (e.g., modeling fixed effects by comparing siblings, controlling for maternal IQ), which allow them to more precisely delineate the independent contribution of income poverty on children's school readiness (Blau, 1999; Dearing et al., 2001; Duncan et al., 1994; Duncan et al., 1998).

Cognitive Outcomes

Measures of cognitive development include children's IQ scores, verbal skills, and, for schoolaged children, achievement. These domains are measured using full-scale intelligence tests, expressive, and receptive language assessments and tests of learning ability, respectively. Most of the poverty research has compared cognitive and school outcomes for adolescents and older children in and out of poverty, rather than for young children during the first 5 years of life (Brooks-Gunn, Klebanov, & Liaw, 1995). This section draws mostly from research using two notable exceptions to this trend, the Children of the National Longitudinal Survey of Youth (NLSY) and the Infant Health and Development Program (IHDP). Both studies measure child language (using the Peabody Picture Vocabulary Test-Revised [PPVT-R]) during the first 5 years, whereas the IHDP also measures IQ (using the Bayley Scales of Infant Development at age 2 years, Standford-Binet at age 3 years, and the WPPSI at age 5 years) and NLSY measures achievement (using the Peabody Individual Achievement Test [PIAT] at ages 5 to 6 years) through early childhood. Recent research on poverty

and early child development using the ECLS-K, which included in depth assessments of children's competence in language and literacy, mathematics, and knowledge of the social and physical worlds, and the NICHD Study of Early Child Care, which measured children's IQ, school readiness (a composite scale including a wide range of cognitive abilities) and receptive and expressive language at age 3 years, also are discussed.

Negative associations between poverty and children's cognitive outcomes tend to emerge at age 2 years but generally not before (Klebanov, Brooks-Gunn, McCarton, & McCormick, 1998; Korenman & Miller, 1997; Smith et al., 1997). Using the IHDP dataset, Klebanov and colleagues (Klebanov et al., 1998) tested the links between family poverty (defined as family income 150% of the poverty threshold or less) and children's IQ scores measured at ages 1, 2, and 3 years (controlling for child gender, race, and birthweight) and found that family risk factors associated with poverty, such as single parenthood and low maternal education, had negative effects on age 1 year IQ scores, whereas income itself did not. At age 2 years, however, both family risk and income predicted lower scores (i.e., poor children scored 4.4 points lower than nonpoor children). Averaging family income over the first 5 years of life, another study using the IHDP data found even larger associations between poverty status and age 2 years IQ scores (Smith et al., 1997). Scholars debate why income effects only appear after infancy, whereas factors such as family risk level do impact early IQ scores. Some suggest that aspects early environment most effected by income, such as parent's ability to afford toys, books, and trips, become important only at the onset of language (Klebanov et al., 1998). Alternatively, the measures used to assess infant IQ may not tap the domains of cognitive development most correlated with income, such as emergent verbal skills, thus differences between children living in and out of poverty may be present but undetected (Brooks-Gunn, Leventhal, & Duncan, 1999).

It is clear, however, that negative effects of poverty on children's cognitive outcomes detected during toddlerhood tend to increase by 3 years old and are sustained or grow throughout early childhood. For instance, studies have shown that the differences between poor and nonpoor children's IQ and vocabulary scores increased nearly 2 points from age 2 to 3 years (Klebanov et al., 1998). In other studies, variation in IQ, PPVT-R and reading recognition scores by income remained stable at around 4 points or higher at ages 2, 3, and 5 years (Duncan et al., 1994; Smith et al., 1997). Recent findings from the ECLS-K study found that over the course of kindergarten, low-SES children caught up to their peers in terms of basic reading skills (e.g., reciting letters) but became even further behind their classmates on more complex reading skills such as reading words (Denton, West, & Walston, 2003). Taken together, results from these studies suggest that starting around the age of 2 years, children reared in poverty generally scored between 15% and 40% of a standard deviation lower on standardized cognitive assessments compared with their nonpoor peers; effect sizes vary depending on children's place along the income distribution. These effects on test scores are sustained when children reach school age (Brooks-Gunn & Duncan, 1997; Smith et al., 1997), and are accompanied by lower levels of school achievement, higher levels of grade retention and eventual dropout among poor children and adolescents (Axinn et al., 1997).

Although few dispute that poverty negatively impacts children's cognitive development, there exists debate over how large income effects really are. Recent research focusing on the use of more conservative estimation techniques including averaging income over time (rather than using a single point in time estimate), controlling for additional factors correlated with both income and child cognitive scores (e.g., maternal IQ) and comparing siblings (see, e.g., Blau, 1999; Duncan et al., 1998; Taylor, Dearing, & McCartney, 2004). Taylor and colleagues (2004), using data from the NICHD-SECC, reported that a 1 point increase in family income-to-needs, averaged over the child's life, was associated with gains in IQ, school readiness, and language scores of 3% to 5% of a standard deviation measured at age 3 years even after controlling for maternal intelligence and child health outcomes. Although the estimated effects were small, the researchers determined that income effect sizes were equal to and in some cases larger than those for known determinants of child outcomes such as maternal intelligence and participation in early intervention programs. Recent findings using ECLS-K data revealed that SES accounted for more variance in children's cognitive scores than a host of other relevant variables including race/ethnicity, family educational expectations, access to quality child care, and home reading environment (Lee & Burkam, 2001). On the contrary, others have found that the effect of income on child outcomes is *not* as large as that of family background characteristics (Blau, 1999; Klebanov, Brooks-Gunn, Chase-Lansdale, & Gordon, 1997; Smith et al., 1997). Blau (1999) in particular has suggested that income effects alone are not practically important using similar analytic techniques with the NLSY dataset. It is important to note, however, that income remained significant in both studies even when holding correlated family and environmental factors constant, indicating that poverty does independently impact young children's developmental trajectories, to some degree.

Depth of poverty. Although the size of poverty effects vary with the estimation method used, income has been consistently shown to have a greater influence on child cognitive outcomes for those at the lowest end of the income distribution, indicating that family income effects are nonlinear. For example, an additional $10,000 a year in income would have a larger effect on a child in poverty than a nonpoor child, a larger effect on a child living near poverty than a middle-class child and so on along the income continuum. Smith and colleagues (1997) investigated this hypothesis by comparing cognitive scores of children in six different income-to-needs groups: deep poverty (<.5), poverty (.5 to 1), near poor (1 to 1.5), lower middle-class (1.5 to 2), middle-class (2 to 3), and affluent (>3) and found the largest cognitive deficits (8 to 12 points) for 3- to 6-year-old children living in deep poverty (i.e., income-to-needs <.5). Smaller, yet significant income effects also were found across other income group comparisons for IQ, verbal, and math scores. Another study comparing poor and middle-class children 3 years of age and older, controlling for a range of maternal and child characteristics including child health outcomes, found that children

living below the poverty line scored about 10 percentage points lower on the PPVT and nine percentage points lower on the PIAT math and verbal subtests than children living at three times the poverty threshold (Korenman et al., 1995). These differences are quite large from an educational perspective, as a 6- to 12-point disparity might mean, for instance, the difference between being placed in a special education class or not (Brooks-Gunn & Duncan, 1997).

These findings indicate that income matters more at deeper levels of disadvantage, suggesting that the development of children in poverty may be more sensitive to changes in income than development among nonpoor children. A recent study using data from the NICHD-SECC examined the differential impacts of income fluctuations and found that only for children in poverty, increases in income between 1 and 3 years of age were positively associated with cognitive outcomes measured at 3 years (Dearing et al., 2001). Specifically, children living in poverty whose families experienced an increase in income-to-needs of at least 1 standard deviation above the mean (approximately 70%) scored on par with their nonpoor counterparts on all cognitive outcomes measured. These results suggest that although early childhood poverty can disrupt child cognitive development, those effects are somewhat elastic and can be reversed if income increases, at least when children are as young as 3 years of age.

Persistence of poverty. Related to these findings, studies have shown that the length of time children live in poverty also moderated the size of income effects on their development. For example, children in the IDHP who lived in poverty for 4 of their first 5 years scored nine points lower on the WPPSI at age 5 years than children who had never been poor, a large effect by any measure. By contrast, children who had been poor for some but not all of the 4 years had IQ scores that were, on average, only four points lower than those of nonpoor children (Duncan et al., 1994), a small impact at less than a third of a standard deviation. Similarly, children in the IHDP and NLSY datasets who experienced consistent poverty during the first 5 years were doing worse across all outcomes than children who had been poor for transient periods when both groups were compared to nonpoor children (Smith et al., 1997). Thus, the longer a child spends in poverty, the more that child tends to lag behind nonpoor or temporarily poor classmates. When you consider the effects of deep poverty and long-term poverty together, it becomes clear that many children living in poverty in the United States are at a severe disadvantage in terms of their cognitive development during the early education years.

Timing of poverty. The negative effects of poverty are not localized to the first 5 years of life, for deprivation experienced during early childhood is particularly detrimental to later child outcomes. Using the PSID, Duncan and colleagues (1998) examined the association between timing of poverty and older adolescents' (16 to 25 years) high school graduation rates and educational attainment. Although living in poverty at any time during childhood or adolescence was negatively associated with educational achievement, poverty during early childhood was the most important determinant of high school completion and years of education, including college attendance. Using more conservative estimation techniques that compared siblings (thus controlling for potentially confounding family characteristics) they found that poverty experienced during early childhood was the only significant income predictor of high school graduation. So, like deep and persistent poverty, early childhood poverty is especially harmful to children's development over time.

Behavioral Outcomes

Young children's social or emotional development is typically measured using parent report assessments of children's behavior, such as levels of friendliness, cooperation, and engagement, as well as instances of temper tantrums, defiance, and aggression. According to existing research, a higher percentage of children in poverty report emotional or behavioral problems than nonpoor children from early childhood through the teen years (Coiro, Zill, & Bloom, 1994; Pagani, Boulerice, & Tremblay, 1997). Typically, however, more modest income effects are found for children's social development when compared to the larger and more consistent effects found for cognitive outcomes. For example, although past research reported that increases in families' incomes were associated large increases in children's IQ scores, only small concomitant decreases in internalizing (e.g., withdrawal, depression) and externalizing (e.g., fighting, defiance) behavior problems were found (Dearing et al., 2001; Duncan et al., 1994). One study reported the strongest income effects for behavior problems scores, not achievement scores, once mother's intelligence was controlled (Blau, 1999). The author attributed this finding to the relative elasticity of behavioral outcomes when compared to more static, cognitive measures. Although most of the behavioral effects are smaller and less significant than those for cognitive outcomes, there is still evidence that growing up in poverty is harmful to children's emotional development.

Depth of poverty. The association between depth of poverty and behavioral outcomes parallels effects on children's cognitive scores—the deeper the poverty, the stronger the negative impact on outcomes. In the IHDP, 3-year-olds in deep poverty scored two points higher on internalizing symptoms than less poor children (income-to-needs ratios of 1.5 to 2); by the time the children were 5 years of age, this gap had widened to more than a five-point difference (Brooks-Gunn et al., 1999). In NICHD-SECC, an increase in family income-to-needs was associated with positive social behavior only for children in poverty, such that poor children who experience a rise in income equal to one standard deviation above the mean during their first 3 years scored similarly to nonpoor children (Dearing et al., 2001). Another study revealed that a 10% increase in family income meant nearly a 1.5% of a standard deviation decrease in negative behavior for children in poverty; nonpoor children only experienced a .91% decrease (Taylor et al., 2004). These findings reveal how our poorest young children may be at a particular disadvantage on entering school in terms of their ability to attend in class, regulate their behavior, and form relationships with peers and teachers but also how leaving poverty during the early years may help children escape these outcomes.

Persistence of poverty. Resembling trends in cognitive outcomes, stronger effects on behavioral outcomes are found when duration of poverty is considered. In the IHDP, 5-year-olds who were persistently poor exhibited more internalizing and externalizing problems than children who experienced short-term poverty as well as those who had never been poor (Duncan et al., 1994). The children of the NLSY dataset revealed somewhat subtler trends, as short-term poverty was related to externalizing, and long-term poverty was associated with internalizing problems for 4- to 8-year-old children (McLeod & Shanahan, 1993). According to a later study, after experiencing persistent poverty during the early years (e.g., 0 to 5 years of age), children 4- to 5-years-old were more likely to be depressed than those who were never poor. Higher depression levels remained even if poverty subsisted over the next 4 years, although continued poverty did not increase this gap (McLeod & Shanahan, 1996). For antisocial behavior, however, the longer children spend in poverty from ages 4 to 8 years, the higher their scores are relative to those of nonpoor peers. A recent study of American Indian children in rural community found that children in families who were lifted out of poverty by the introduction of a casino experienced a reduction in externalizing symptoms that put them on par with nonpoor children; their internalizing symptoms, however, were unaffected by the income change (Costello, Compton, Keeler, & Angold, 2003). Taken together, these findings suggest that persistent poverty affects internalizing and externalizing symptoms differently, with persistent early poverty having lasting but stable effects on symptoms such as depression and early poverty having ever increasing but changeable effects on symptoms like aggression.

Conclusion

In sum, there exists an abundance of research indicating that poverty experienced during the first 5 years of life can seriously hinder child development in both cognitive and socioemotional domains. Regarding intellectual outcomes, scholars debate the practical significance of income effects on children's scores after other factors correlated with poverty, such as low maternal education, single, or teenage parenthood, and low maternal intelligence are held constant. Still, the preponderance of evidence suggests that as children in poverty leave early childhood, their cognitive performance is lower than that of their nonpoor counterparts, a gap that persists later in school. Increases in income, however, can significantly alter this dynamic, with children who leave the poverty ranks during their first 3 years catching up with never poor children on cognitive tests. The same does not seem to hold true for some socioemotional outcomes. Although income effects on outcomes such as depression and antisocial behavior are smaller than those on IQ, early poverty may put children at a disadvantage that does not abate if families leave poverty and, for externalizing symptoms, can grow worse if poverty continues beyond early childhood. The next two sections describe processes through which poverty may cause these outcomes and the roles public policy can play in moderating those links.

PATHWAYS THROUGH WHICH POVERTY IMPACTS YOUNG CHILDREN'S SCHOOL READINESS

The research reviewed thus far suggests that growing up in poverty can seriously compromise a young child's readiness to enter school and her performance thereafter. It reveals little, however, about the mechanisms through which poverty operates to jeopardize child development and, thus, sheds little light on ways to ameliorate negative child outcomes in early education and beyond. These mechanisms, or "pathways," by definition are factors related to both income and to a least one child outcome such that it causally links the two. Pathways are distinct from correlates of poverty, such as low maternal education and single parenthood, in that they imply a process by which income and child development are related, one that can help us to understand how poverty affects children's lives. Most pathways posited in the poverty literature can be grouped under two overarching theories. The first focuses on the impact of poverty on relationships and interactions within families. In this view, exemplified by the "family stress model" (Conger & Elder, 1994; Elder, 1999; Elder & Caspi, 1988), financial pressure or deprivation undermines parents' psychological and emotional resources, disrupting parenting styles, parent-child interactions and child development as a result (Conger & Conger, 2000; Dodge, Pettit, & Bates, 1994; Sampson & Laub, 1994). Although this model has been connected mostly to socioemotional and behavioral outcomes in children (Conger et al., 1992; Conger, Patterson, & Ge, 1995; Dodge et al., 1994; McLoyd, 1990; Sampson & Laub, 1994), family stress also has been linked to poorer child cognitive development (Guo & Harris, 2000; Jackson, Brooks-Gunn, Huang, & Glassman, 2000; Linver, Brooks-Gunn, & Kohen, 2002; Yeung, Linver, & Brooks-Gunn, 2002). The second theory in question emphasizes the role of income in allowing parents to purchase materials, experiences and services that foster children's skills and abilities. These goods and services include stimulating learning materials, nutritious food, safe living conditions and quality child care. According to this perspective, children in low-income families have fewer opportunities to build their skills because their parents cannot afford to make these investments. This perspective, developed in the field of economics, is sometimes called the investment model (Haveman & Wolfe, 1994; Mayer, 1997). The following section reviews processes implicated in both the family stress and investment models, identifying how these mechanisms affect different domains of child development and may operate in tandem to account for links between poverty and child development.

The Family Stress Model

Economic stress includes poverty, unstable work, income loss, and unemployment. These conditions cause financial strain that

frequently make it necessary for families to cut back on consumption of goods and services, seek public assistance, live in undesirable and unsafe neighborhoods, or assume additional employment to make ends meet (Edin & Lein, 1997; Yeung & Hofferth, 1998). According to the theory of family stress, these financial hardships can lead to emotional distress in parents, such as increased levels of depression and anxiety. Emotional instability may lead to other problems such as marital conflict, which, in turn, may lead to harsher, less supportive, and more detached parenting behavior. Even without marital discord, maternal or paternal emotional instability can hinder a parent's ability to be supportive, sensitive, and consistent with children (McLoyd, 1990). The literature describing the importance of parenting to child development is too extensive to review here (see Bornstein, 1995, for a comprehensive review). In short, however, parenting characterized by high levels of warmth, cognitive stimulation and clear limit-setting has been consistently associated with favorable cognitive, emotional, and behavioral outcomes for children (Baumrind, 1966; Belsky, 1999; Berlin, Brady-Smith, & Brooks-Gunn, 2002; Berlin & Cassidy, 2000; McLoyd, 1998; Thompson, 1999). By contrast, parenting characterized by harsh, arbitrary discipline or emotional detachment has been linked to the development of insecure infant-mother attachments, with possible long lasting effects on socioemotional, behavioral, and cognitive outcomes (Shonkoff & Phillips, 2000). These associations—from financial strain, to parental depression and anxiety, to marital discord and disrupted parenting, and finally to negative child outcomes—represent the crux of the family stress model.

This theory is primarily used to explain how disruption in family relationships because of financial loss impacts the behavior of adolescents (Conger, Rueter, & Conger, 2000; McLoyd, 1989). Research on financial loss is distinct from poverty studies in that it examines how declines in income alter family dynamics, rather than how persistent deprivation shapes lives. In his classic work on the Great Depression, Elder (1999) found that parental emotional distress caused by income loss led to marital conflict and punitive parenting, particularly by fathers. Children in this study, especially boys, who experienced arbitrary treatment at the hands of their fathers tended to have poorer adjustment during adolescence and poorer academic and interpersonal outcomes in later years (Elder, 1999). More recently, Conger and colleagues (1992; 2002) found that among white teenagers in a depressed farming community, economic pressure triggered maternal depression, and, thus, marital conflict, which decreased levels of both maternal and paternal nuturant parenting. In turn, the lack of supportive parenting was positively associated with adjustment problems during the children's teen years. Similar associations between income loss and adolescent socioemotional functioning (e.g., depression, anxiety, low self-esteem) via maternal depression and harsh discipline also have been found in samples of Black, urban youth (McLeod & Nonnemaker, 2000; McLoyd, Jayaratne, Ceballo, & Borquez, 1994). This array of findings suggests that a family's economic loss can affect child development indirectly through its emotional impact on parents.

Researchers have extended the family stress model to explain the effects of poverty on child functioning. McLoyd (1990) hypothesizes that, like income loss, living in poverty imposes extraordinary burdens on parents, such as struggling to afford basic food and clothing, unemployment, living in low-quality housing conditions, and residing in unsafe neighborhoods. These circumstances affect parent mental health and parenting practices through mechanisms similar to those posited in literature on income loss. In many studies, low-income parents have reported higher levels of depression and anxiety than nonpoor parents and, in turn, unfavorable emotional health has been negatively associated with supportive parenting within these families (Alpern & Lyons-Ruth, 1993; Petterson & Albers, 2001; Wasserman, Rauh, Brunelli, Garcia-Castro, & Necos, 1990). Specifically, maternal emotional distress and depression have been repeatedly associated with harsh discipline, low supportiveness and parent emotional detachment, as well as, higher conflict between parents and children (Petterson & Albers, 2001). Some studies suggest that the impact of this dynamic is more pronounced among disadvantaged families (Cicchetti & Toth, 1995; Petterson & Albers, 2001), with maternal depression and negative parenting practices exerting stronger influence over the developmental outcomes of low-income children than nonpoor children.

Although much research has examined this theory in relation to adolescents and older children (McLeod & Nonnemaker, 2000; Sampson & Laub, 1994), fewer studies have applied the family stress model to young children. Because of the strength of the association between poverty and young children's development, this dearth in literature marks a significant oversight (Duncan & Brooks-Gunn, 1997; Korenman et al., 1995). Furthermore, one study using data collected just prior to the onset of the Great Depression revealed that family instability had a larger effect on young children's achievement and emotional outcomes than it did on adolescents', mostly likely because young children require more nurturance and guidance from adults than older children (Elder & Caspi, 1988). This association has been tested more recently, and studies have found that financial stress and poverty impact preschoolers' behavior problem scores via associations between income and parents' emotional health, marital relationships, or parenting practices (Dodge et al., 1994; Duncan et al., 1994; Jackson et al., 2000; Linver et al., 2002; McLeod & Shanahan, 1993; Yeung et al., 2002). When intellectual outcomes are studied, however, the mediating effects of parenting and other factors related to family stress are weaker and less consistent than they are in predicting socioemotional indicators (Hanson, McLanahan, & Thomson, 1997; Miriam R. Linver, Brooks-Gunn, & Kohen, 1999; Linver et al., 2002; Yeung et al., 2002). One recent study documented that although authoritarian, harsh parenting as a result of maternal emotional distress substantially explained the link between income and behavior problems among 3- and 5-year-olds in the IHDP, only 2% of the difference in IQ scores between children in and out of poverty was explained by these processes (Linver et al., 2002). Another study revealed that low parent supportiveness as a result of financial strain had a larger effect on behavior problems among preschool children than it did on cognitive outcomes, but maternal depression and low supportiveness were nonetheless associated with school readiness scores (Jackson et al., 2000).

Similar findings emerge in studies on reading, math and language achievement among children of the NLSY (Guo & Harris, 2000), especially for girls (Smith & Brooks-Gunn, 1997). A study of female youth found that ineffective parenting and financial stress were positively associated with cognitive distress for teens, or the inability to concentrate on and complete cognitive tasks (McLoyd et al., 1994). This finding suggests an interplay between children's socioemotional and cognitive development, which may account for the relevance of the family stress model to understanding poverty's effects on both domains.

It is important to recognize that just as parental emotional distress and punitive parenting can hinder early behavioral and cognitive development, good parenting can buffer young children against the negative effects of growing up in poverty. Literature on economic stress and early child development contains much evidence that parenting behaviors characterized by warmth, supportiveness and clear-limit setting is associated with more positive developmental outcomes for children (Shonkoff & Phillips, 2000). Moreover, parents living in poverty who develop positive relationships with their children can significantly reduce the developmental risks associated with financial deprivation (Apfel & Seitz, 1997; Cowen, Work, & Wyman, 1997; Luthar, 1999; McLoyd, 1990; Werner & Smith, 1992). Some specific findings illuminate these points. Elder and Caspi (1988) found that fathers who were emotionally stable prior to the Great Depression tended not to become unstable after the market crash despite a serious decline in income, and were subsequently less likely to experience marital conflict or parent in arbitrary and inconsistent ways, the main factors associated with low self confidence and achievement among children in the study. Similarly, data from another study revealed that nurturant and involved parenting among families in a depressed rural community significantly compensated for the stressors of economic hardship in terms of children's school performance, peer relationships, self-confidence, antisocial behavior, and emotional distress (Conger & Conger, 2000). These findings indicate that the way parents adapt to economic stress plays a crucial role in how and to what extent poverty can impact young children's developmental trajectories.

Factors that can help foster emotional health and positive parenting for low-income mothers include various forms of social support (Cowen, Wyman, Work, & Parker, 1990). Mothers who have stable emotional support, such as a confidant or some companionship, are less likely than mothers without social ties to report parenting anxiety or parent in coercive and punitive ways (Crnic & Greenberg, 1987; McLoyd, 1997). Similarly, the availability of parenting support, including other adults in the household to help with child care and chores, has been shown to increase mothers' responsiveness and sensitivity to infants (Crockenberg, 1987). Although parents' resources somewhat determine the availability of social support, public policy initiatives such as social services, community-based programs, and early intervention can help to provide this kind of assistance (Shonkoff & Phillips, 2000). The roles of welfare policy and early intervention programs in this regard are addressed in a later section.

The Investment Model

Although the family stress model focuses on the links between economic deprivation and children's socioemotional environment, the investment model emphasizes the links between poverty and children's resources. It posits that without sufficient income, parents cannot buy the materials, experiences, and services that facilitate children's positive development. The theory attributes variation in cognitive and behavioral outcomes between children in and out of poverty to this disparity in parental investments. Although the model stresses purchasing power, economists frame these investments in terms of both money—purchasing of good and services—and time—providing stimulating experiences (Becker, 1991). In this way, parental employment is both positive for child development because it allows for greater monetary investment and negative because parents spend less time teaching and interacting with children. Striking the optimal balance between these competing investments marks a central challenge for all families. For low-income families, this challenge proves even greater, for although slight changes in income matter more for children in poverty than children at higher income levels (Dearing et al., 2001), low-income parents who work still sacrifice time with their children without gaining much buying power in exchange. The following section explores the implications of this double jeopardy. The role of parental investments in home environment, neighborhood and child care, as well as poor health conditions and nutrition are explored. These factors are not an exhaustive list, but illustrate the processes by which low economic resources can shape a child's environment.

Home environment. Many aspects of the home environment are relevant to children's development including the availability of learning materials, interactions between parents and children, and the physical condition of the home (e.g., crowding, cleanliness, etc.). The most commonly used measure of home environment quality among developmental psychologists is the Home Observation for Measurement of the Environment (HOME), developed by Caldwell and Bradley (1984), which includes items assessing availability of learning materials, such as the number of books, magazines, puzzles, and educational toys in the home.[3] The HOME also includes items gauging the physical conditions of the home, such as whether the home is cluttered, cramped, dirty and unsafe, aspects that reflect parents' purchasing power and, in part, how they choose to allocate resources.

In numerous studies of child development, scores on the HOME have been highly associated with a range of child outcomes, including malnutrition, developmental delay, growth stunting and poor school performance (Bradley, 1995; Garrett, Ng'andu, & Ferron, 1994). Early HOME scores are highly predictive of children's later IQ scores, even more so than some early cognitive assessments (Elardo & Bradley, 1981). In light of its emphasis on aspects of the home environment that can (although do not have to be) bought by parents, it makes sense that scores on the HOME scale vary significantly by income. A recent study using data from the NLSY revealed that nonpoor children had greater access to learning materials in the home and were taken on enriching trips and events (e.g., museum visits) more frequently than their poor counterparts (Bradley, Corwyn, McAdoo, & Garcia Coll, 2001). Parents of nonpoor (compared with poor) children were twice as likely to read to their children more than three times a week and more likely to teach their children about letters, colors, shapes, and sizes. The physical environments of families in poverty also were less safe and clean, and darker and more cluttered than those of nonpoor families. These differences were greatest during the early childhood years, when income has the greatest impact on child development, and decreased during later childhood. Moreover, differences in responses between poor and nonpoor parents were larger than differences by race or ethnicity, and effect sizes for the associations between poverty status and HOME scores were proportional across race (Bradley et al., 2001). Thus, according to the HOME scale, children in poverty spend less time in stimulating activities and possess fewer enriching materials than nonpoor children.

Given these disparities, it is not surprising that quality of home environment accounts for a substantial proportion of the associations between family poverty and young children's outcomes, especially those in the cognitive domain. The number of learning materials and stimulating experiences, as measured by the HOME scale, explain a significant percentage of the variation in IQ scores in the preschool years (Brooks-Gunn, Duncan, Klebanov, & Sealand, 1993; Duncan et al., 1994; Linver et al., 2002; Yeung et al., 2002). In fact, HOME scores have been found to reduce the effect of poverty on child cognitive outcomes by up to one half, which means that 50% of the difference in scores between children in and out of poverty can be attributed to differences in the quality of their home environments (Bradley, 1995; Korenman et al., 1995). In some studies, HOME scores are also associated with shifts in family income and the extent to which changes in family income explain child outcomes. Higher HOME scores reduce the deleterious impacts of declines in family income on children's school readiness, achievement and language scores before and during elementary school (Dearing et al., 2001; Korenman et al., 1995; Yeung et al., 2002). Furthermore, HOME scores are highly sensitive to changes in income such that small monetary gains at the lowest level of the income distribution can raise HOME scores more than gains at higher income levels (Garrett et al., 1994). Because of the associations between HOME scores and children's cognitive outcomes, and between HOME scores and family income, the home environment is a potentially powerful instrument of change or intervention for children in low-income families.

---

[3]The scale also taps parenting quality in terms of both teaching (e.g., how often parents read to the child or tell her stories) and emotional warmth (e.g., hugging and kissing, praising and responding to the child). In this way, the HOME scale measures factors associated with the family stress model, although its emphasis on materials and experiences for which parents spend time and money aligns it more closely with the investment model.

In addition to predicting cognitive outcomes, home quality, including the amount of stimulating materials and learning experiences children receive, also may serve as a pathway between poverty status and young children's behavioral development (Dearing et al., 2001; Linver et al., 2002; Yeung et al., 2002). This link may stem, in part, from the above-mentioned associations between poverty and parental mental health. That is, a parent who experiences high levels of depression and anxiety may be less likely to interact positively with her child to provide stimulating experiences than a parent with stable emotional health. Supporting this theory, Yeung and colleagues (2002) found that HOME scores affected children's behavior problem scores via their influence on maternal emotional distress and parenting practices. Thus, although exposure to a stimulating home environment can affect children's behavioral development, that link likely includes processes associated with the family stress model.

Other studies have found that parenting practices (Linver et al., 1999), the availability of learning materials (Duncan et al., 1994), and the physical environment (Dunifon, Duncan, & Brooks-Gunn, 2001) operate independently as pathways through which income can influence children's cognitive and behavioral outcomes. Some studies have sought to distinguish between these factors in accounting for income effects. One study examined the impacts of cognitively stimulating materials, time spent using materials with children and the physical condition of the home separately and found that the cleanliness and safety of the home attenuated the positive association between income and 3- to 5-year-olds' achievement scores the most compared with other facets of the home environment; however, the presence of stimulating toys, books and games also were effective in reducing income effects on children's outcomes (Yeung et al., 2002). Language outcomes, by contrast, were more strongly associated with both materials in the home and time parents spent using them with children. For behavioral outcomes, both the physical environment and presence of materials yielded large associations. Thus, different aspects of the home environment may affect child development in different ways, with physical environment having strong associations with both cognitive and behavioral outcomes and time parents spend with children influencing language development.

Neighborhood-level impacts. The neighborhoods that families live in may serve as an additional investment made by parents that affects child well-being, as financial constraints often force low-income families to live in impoverished communities. There is growing body of research that has examined associations between neighborhood structural variables including census-based (or a similar administrative data source) neighborhood income or SES (e.g., percent poor, on public assistance, unemployed, professionals, college-educated, and female-headed households), and children's outcomes. These associations have been found controlling for individual- and family-level background characteristics such as child sex and age, maternal age and educational attainment, and family race/ethnicity, income, and composition. Thus, findings presented in the following section represent neighborhood effects above and beyond the impacts of family-level economic well-being. Much of the past research in this domain utilized the same national studies used to examine income poverty effects on children's outcomes.

Neighborhood level income/SES has been associated with early child cognitive outcomes over and above family characteristics. A series of studies conducted in the 1990s by Brooks-Gunn and colleagues found that residence in neighborhoods with mean incomes greater than $30,000, compared with less affluent neighborhoods (i.e., mean incomes between $10,000 and $30,000), was positively associated with 3-year-olds' IQ scores (Brooks-Gunn, Duncan et al., 1993; Chase-Lansdale, Gordon, Brooks-Gunn, & Klebanov, 1997). This positive association between residence in a high-SES neighborhood and children's IQ remained when children entered school at 5 to 6 years of age (Duncan et al., 1994). Similar positive effects of neighborhood affluence were found on early school-aged children's reading and verbal ability (Chase-Lansdale & Gordon, 1996; Chase-Lansdale et al., 1997; Kohen, Brooks-Gunn, Leventhal, & Hertzman, 2002); these findings were strongest for boys and white children. Just as neighborhood affluence has been associated with child development, neighborhood poverty also significantly predicts young children's cognitive outcomes. Studies have documented a negative association between neighborhood poverty and early school-aged children's math and verbal achievement (Chase-Lansdale et al., 1997; Kohen et al., 2002; McCulloch & Joshi, 2001).

Although findings are less consistent than those found for achievement outcomes, neighborhood-level SES also may affect children's behavior problems. Researchers found that neighborhood low-SES, male unemployment, and low percentage of managerial or professional workers were positively associated with maternal-reported behavior problems for young children 3 to 4 years of age (Brooks-Gunn, Duncan et al., 1993; Chase-Lansdale et al., 1997). The results were less consistent for kindergarten-aged children. Two studies documented positive associations between male joblessness in the neighborhood and 5- to 6-year-old children's internalizing and externalizing behavior problems (Chase-Lansdale & Gordon, 1996; Chase-Lansdale et al., 1997), whereas other analyses revealed that neighborhood SES was positively associated with behavior problems, particularly internalizing symptoms (Chase-Lansdale & Gordon, 1996; Chase-Lansdale et al., 1997; Duncan et al., 1994).

Reasons given for the associations between neighborhood-level SES and young children's cognitive and behavioral outcomes include the availability, accessibility, affordability, and quality of community resources, including medical care and schools, children's exposure to violence (both experiencing and witnessing), and neighborhood effects on parental mental health and behaviors (see Leventhal & Brooks-Gunn, 2000, for a review of neighborhood effects and relevant pathways of influences). Although neighborhood effects may be stronger for older children and youth, because of their heightened exposure to contexts outside of the home, young children growing up in impoverished environments are still at risk for unfavorable outcomes. It is important to note that children growing up in poverty may experience impoverished home environments in tandem with impoverished neighborhood environments, two contexts that can work in tandem to disrupt optimal children's cognitive and socioemotional development.

Child care. Along with aspects of the home environment and neighborhood, parents make investments in their children by placing them in nonmaternal child care and preschool programs. With the increase in single parenthood and divorce and the decreasing value of men's wages, women's incomes have become essential to meeting many families' needs (Hernandez, 1997). For this reason, parents' investments in child care are often not a choice but a necessity. In the coming years, the need for nonmaternal care among poor families will likely grow because of the 1996 Welfare Reform Bill's work requirements and time limits. Increasingly then, child care is a context in which children develop during their early years and, as such, can mediate income effects on young children's outcomes.

Family factors and the mother-child relationship predict child outcomes with more power than specific child care characteristics (Helburn, 1995; NICHD Early Child Care Research Network, 1997b, 1998b). Specifically, maternal sensitivity and quality of the home environment (as measured by the HOME) are more strongly related to child outcomes than child care quality or time in care (Brooks-Gunn, Han, & Waldfogel, 2002). Most research on child care suggests, however, that children's experience in care can impact their cognitive and social development during the early years. The size and direction of these effects, however, depend on age of entry into care, quality of care, and parents' poverty status. First, links between day care and negative socio-emotional outcomes like aggression and noncompliance have been found mostly for children entering care in the first year of life, who then continue care extensively through their preschool years (Baydar & Brooks-Gunn, 1991; Belsky, 1988; Haskins, 1995; Waldfogel, Han, & Brooks-Gunn, 2002). Additionally, full-time maternal employment (usually a proxy for nonmaternal care) before 9 months is associated with poorer child cognitive outcomes by age 3 for white children, even controlling for home environment and maternal sensitivity (Brooks-Gunn et al., 2002). More recent research suggested that the child care-child development link was linear, with more time in early care predicting more socioemotional adjustment problems in kindergarten (NICHD Early Child Care Research Network, 2003). However, other studies find that quantity of care does not relate linearly to child outcomes (Love et al., 2003). Perhaps it is not day care generally, but day care among young infants for a certain amount of time that predicts negative socioemotional and cognitive outcomes.

More than child age, the effects of child care on cognitive and social development have been shown to depend on the quality of care children receive. In high-quality environments, caregivers engage children in diverse, cognitively stimulating activities, initiate and respond to child verbalizations, have frequent positive interactions with children that include smiling, touching, holding, among many other socially and cognitively enhancing behaviors. Child care studies have shown with great consistency that utilization of high-quality day care predicted more favorable cognitive outcomes for children during infancy, toddlerhood, the preschool years, and perhaps through elementary school (Burchinal et al., 2000; Clarke-Stewart & Fein, 1983;

Helburn, 1995; Howes, 1990; Howes & Smith, 1995; Love et al., 2003; NICHD Early Child Care Research Network, 2002). Most recently, a study of mothers and children in welfare-to-work programs found that children in higher quality care had higher reading readiness scores and fewer social problems (Loeb, Fuller, Kagan, & Carroll, 2004).

Research has documented that high quality child care was positively associated with children's cognitive and language development, communication skills and school readiness. Most compelling is research showing that high quality programs benefited children from disadvantaged families more or exclusively when compared to more affluent or otherwise nondisadvantaged children.[4] Using data from the National Longitudinal Study of Youth (NLSY), Caughy and colleagues (Caughy, DiPietro, & Strobino, 1994) found that for low-income children, amount of time in care—in terms of both age of entry and hours—was positively associated with scores on a reading recognition and mathematics assessment; this association was particularly strong for children in center-based care. Similarly, other studies have found that gains in receptive language and other communication skills because of early care are stronger or are only present in low-income subsamples (Helburn, 1995; Schliecker, White, & Jacobs, 1991). In a recent study, children of mothers on welfare who attended center-based child care were found to have higher school and reading readiness scores than children in kith and kin care by 40% to 60% of a standard deviation (Loeb et al., 2004). These findings point to two related conclusions: (1) low-income children in general benefit cognitively from early and extensive participation in high quality center-based care; and (2) children from impoverished home environments benefit more from early and extensive care than children from less poor homes. Experiencing high quality day care can, in this framework, mitigate the familial and environmental risks children in poverty face during the vulnerable early years by providing opportunities for learning and socialization they may not receive at home.

It is essential to point out, however, that although high quality care can serve as a protective factor, poor quality child care can serve as a risk factor for children in already impoverished or disadvantaged environments. Studies not specifically addressing at-risk children find that low-quality care, particularly if initiated within the first year, can have negative effects on a range of developmental outcomes (Belsky, 1986; Brooks-Gunn et al., 2002; Howes, 1990; NICHD Early Child Care Research Network, 1997a, 1998a). Low-income parents, particularly single parents, who nonetheless work are less likely to be able to afford quality child care and, when they do pay for care, spend a disproportionate amount of their incomes on such fees (U.S. Census Bureau, 1995). A recent study by Han and colleagues (2003) drives home the possible implications of more children in poverty entering nonmaternal care, for early maternal employment had the largest negative effects on children below 200% of poverty when both nonmaternal care and the child's home environment were of low quality. With larger numbers of poor children entering nonmaternal care and preschool as a

---

[4]This relationship has not always been found (Bryant, Burchinal, Lau, & Sparling, 1994).

result of welfare reform, it is unclear what percentage of low-income children will be able to enroll in high quality programs. Thus, depending on the investments both parents and the state and federal governments make in child care, nonmaternal care could serve as a protective factor for children whose parents work in the low wage sector, or it could hinder an already vulnerable child's chances for developing optimally.

Child health and nutrition. Another aspect of parental investment important for children's well-being before birth and throughout their development is the presence of adequate health conditions and prevention including neonatal care, proper nutrition and safety from environmental toxins (Ross & Duff, 1982). Research has shown that poorer children suffer worse health than higher income children all along the income gradient, with children in poverty faring worse than middle income children, who fare worse than the affluent (Case, Lubotsky, & Paxson, 2002). These disparities increase over time, such that disparities during early childhood grow more pronounced by adulthood. This finding holds true for children with similar chronic conditions, such as asthma, and is not explained by maternal education or availability of health insurance (Case et al., 2002). The implications of these effects extend beyond children's physical development. Health problems and nutritional deficits also are important pathways through which poverty affects children's cognitive and school-related outcomes. Past research suggests that the prevalence of health problems accounts for as much as 20% of the differential in IQ scores between poor children and their nonpoor peers during preschool (Goldstein, 1990).

Disparities in child health outcomes by poverty status begin very early in life. Before birth, children in poverty experience more health problems than their nonpoor counterparts, resulting in higher percentages of low birthweight infants (Starfield et al. 1991). Compared to full-term children, low birthweight children are likely to face less favorable outcomes including impairments in arithmetic, motor and spatial skills, language, and memory and poor achievement outcomes such as grade repetition and special education placement (Hack, Klein, & Taylor, 1995; Klebanov, Brooks-Gunn, & McCormick, 1994; McCormick et al., 1992; McCormick, Gortmaker, & Sobol, 1990; Taylor, Klein, Minich, & Hack, 2000). Studies that have examined long-term outcomes of low birthweight children have found that they are still at risk for adverse outcomes as adolescents and possibly into adulthood (Conley & Bennett, 2000; Hack et al., 1995).

Although child malnutrition is not as prevalent in the United States as it is in other countries, poverty is associated with nutrition-related disorders (Lewitt & Kerrebrock, 1997; United Nations Children's Fund, 1998). In one study, chronic malnutrition was negatively associated with cognitive test scores even after controlling for family poverty status and its correlates (Korenman et al., 1995). Findings from a recent study suggest that nutritional supplements taken during children's first 2 years of life were positively associated with their educational attainment as adults (Li, Barnhart, Stein, & Martorell, 2003). Along the same lines, children in poverty experience higher rates of growth stunting (low height-for-age) and wasting (low weight-for-height) than their nonpoor counterparts, which in turn are negatively linked with cognitive test scores (Korenman

et al., 1995; Miller & Korenman, 1994). Unfortunately, common strategies used to reduce the incidences of low birthweight and preterm deliveries (e.g., encouraging women to seek early prenatal care, improving the quality of available prenatal care) have not been extremely effective in reducing problematic births (Klerman et al., 2001).

In terms of exposure to environmental toxins, children from low-income families are four times as likely to experience elevated blood lead levels as their higher-income peers because of their heightened exposure to lead paint (16.3% versus 4.0%, respectively; Brody et al. 1994). At young ages, elevated blood lead levels are associated with stunted growth, lower IQ and various physical impairments (Schwartz 1994; Schwartz, Angle, & Pitcher 1986; Schwartz & Otto 1991). One study of young children 1- to 3-years-old found that although chelation therapy helped reduce children's blood lead levels, IQ scores remained lower and parent-rated behavior problem scores remained higher among children who received a placebo (Rogan et al., 2001). In addition to risk of lead poisoning, poor children have greater exposure to toxic environmental conditions resulting from residential proximity to waste incinerators or air pollution (Evans, 2001).

Conclusion

In conclusion, the family stress and investment models are not mutually exclusive pathways through which poverty impacts child development, but rather act as mechanisms that may operate simultaneously in children's lives. Poverty may be harmful to children through its impacts on parents' mental health and parenting practices and also through the limitations it places on parents' investments in materials and resources for children. The former theory has been more closely linked to children's socioemotional outcomes, perhaps because parenting quality impacts the parent-child relationship, a child's earliest framework for emotional and behavioral development. Furthermore, negative parenting practices and child behavior may reinforce one another, with harsh parenting triggering negative child reactions that then enhance parent emotional distress and negative behavior (Elder & Caspi, 1988). The latter model is more relevant to cognitive outcomes, most likely because the materials and resources in question are intellectually stimulating or relate to physiological maturation. These processes may function separately or may operate concurrently, interacting with one another. That is, emotionally distressed parents may spend less time taking advantage of available resources for their children, while navigating limited resources in terms of time and/or money may cause parents emotional distress. The next section discusses ways that public policy can intervene in these processes to practically improve the lives of children and families in poverty.

POLICY IMPACTS

As summarized in the previous sections, poverty is harmful to children's cognitive and behavioral development at any age, but particularly if deprivation is experienced during the early years. Possible explanations for this link include amplified family stress due to financial hardship leading to marital conflict and less effective parenting techniques. Alternatively, or in addition, poverty limits parents' ability to create stimulating home environments and provide other resources for children. Early intervention and welfare policies can influence these mechanisms in ways that ameliorate the negative effects of poverty on young children's outcomes. Early intervention aims to promote child well-being in a variety of domains including physical health, cognitive development, mental health and relationships. Current welfare policy is primarily concerned with encouraging employment for low-income families through job training, income supplements and time limits, among other strategies. Both policy contexts can affect children through their impacts on components of the family stress and parental investment models. For example, attending an early intervention program may bolster children's cognitive scores by providing children with enriched center-based child care experiences. Parents also may benefit from such programs if the services help reduce parental stress and depression and improve parenting skills, which then indirectly affects their children. Welfare policies can affect children through resulting changes in both time and money investments by parents. On the one hand, increases in family income as a result of earning supplements or higher wages improve parents' ability to purchase goods and services for their children. On the other hand, alterations in parental employment can reduce the amount of time parents have to spend with children. An overview of early intervention programs and relevant research on children's outcomes is provided below, followed by a similar discussion of welfare policy, focusing on the 1996 welfare legislation.

Early Intervention

Early intervention programs offer one way to facilitate favorable outcomes among low-income children (Brooks-Gunn, 2003). Early intervention targets disadvantaged children before they enter elementary school, starting either prenatally with home health visits, from birth or from preschool. Although early intervention is a relatively broad term that encompasses a variety of tactics and programs, it usually involves center-based services that focus on children's development in both cognitive and emotional domains. Theory supporting these programs suggests that experiencing high quality center care can mitigate the familial and environmental risks poor and low-income children face by providing opportunities for learning and socialization they may not receive at home. Although information is somewhat limited on which specific ingredients are key to a successful program, a number of studies have explored short- and long-term impacts of early intervention programs on children's outcomes.

Short-term impacts. Effects of early intervention programs examined at or prior to age 5 years are considered short-term impacts. The findings from experimental studies on early intervention for at-risk children during this time are consistent—"child-focused" early care that provides an enriching learning environment can enhance disadvantaged children's cognitive, communication and language skills (Barnett, 1995; Brooks-Gunn

et al., 1994; Shonkoff & Phillips, 2000). Specifically, such programs have been shown to arrest or reduce declines in poor children's IQ scores relative to nonpoor children during the preschool years (Barnett, 1995; Burchinal, Lee, & Ramey, 1989). The Abecedarian Project, which began in the early 1970s, serves as an exemplar of early intervention programs. All participating children were from low-income families and the educational intervention involved intensive, cognitive, language and socioemotional enhancing curriculum for the first 5 years (Burchinal, Campbell, Bryant, Wasik, & Ramey, 1997; Committee on Ways and Means, 2000; Haskins, 1995). Across time, program children scored higher on IQ tests than those in the control group. When children were in elementary school, following the completion of the intervention, treatment group children's reading and math test scores remained higher than control children's. More recent studies such as Project CARE and IHDP, both of which used high quality center-based care as part of their intervention model, showed substantial short-term increases in IQ and some gains in child language skills and child behavior (Barnett, 1995; Committee on Ways and Means, 2000). Most recently, an experimental study of the Early Head Start program reported positive treatment effects on children's cognitive outcomes at age 3 (Love et al., 2002). Although the tenacity of these early benefits in the absence of continuous and intensive services stand in considerable question, conventional wisdom in the field of child development and early education holds that targeted early intervention programs can enhance the cognitive development of at-risk children, thus serving as a protective factor.

Some variation exists in outcomes depending on the point at which programs intervene. In general, children who entered early childhood programs in the first year of life have exhibited moderately large gains in IQ measured at the end of the program (Andrews et al., 1982; Brooks-Gunn, Klebanov, Liaw, & Spiker, 1993; Campbell & Ramey, 1994; Infant Health and Development Program, 1990; Johnson & Walker, 1991). Significant, but smaller, IQ effects are present when the intervention began slightly later during the preschool years (Royce, Darlington, & Murray, 1983). As few programs have systematically manipulated age of entry into the program, it is difficult to hypothesize the optimal age for children to begin early childhood education programs. Unfortunately, by the time children enter kindergarten, which often coincides with the end of the intervention, the cognitive gains often attenuate (see Brooks-Gunn, 2003). For example, when low birthweight children who participated in the IHDP were assessed at 5 years of age (2 years following the end of the intervention), the program effects on IQ scores declined and were only significant for heavier low birthweight children (Brooks-Gunn et al., 1994). Thus, for the lighter low birthweight children, the most at-risk group, IQ effects were not sustained by the time children entered kindergarten.

As explained previously, children's socioemotional development is increasingly viewed as an important ingredient of school readiness. Few early intervention studies assessed these outcomes for participating children because program goals often focus on cognitive enhancement. Research that does exist, however, suggests that early intervention can reduce the rate of emotional and behavioral problems among disadvantaged children. Studies such as Project CARE and IHDP showed some gains in child behavior, in that children who received intervention services through these programs had fewer behavior problems than nonintervention children, although effects were fairly small (Barnett, 1995; Brooks-Gunn, Klebanov et al., 1993; Committee on Ways and Means, 2000; Infant Health and Development Program, 1990). Data from another intervention in Houston reported similar findings for 4- to 7-year-old children (Andrews et al., 1982). The Early Head Start program also had favorable impacts on children's engagement with their parents, attentiveness during play and aggressive behavior at age 3 (Love et al., 2002). Overall, results from early intervention program evaluations consistently conclude that in the short-term, participation in these programs reduces the gap between poor and nonpoor children's cognitive and socioemotional outcomes.

Long-term impacts. The finding that intervention effects "fade out," particularly in the case of well publicized and researched programs like Head Start, has cast doubt about the overall efficacy of early intervention programs as protective agents (Johnson & Walker, 1991; McCarton et al., 1997) (e.g., Schweinhart, Barnes, Weikart, Barnett, & Epstein, 1993). The Abecedarian Project represents a notable exception to this trend. Assessments of program children at 8 and 12 years of age revealed significant IQ and math and reading achievement effects (Campbell & Ramey, 1994, 1995), the latter of which were still apparent when children were reexamined at 15 years of age (Campbell, Pungello, Miller-Johnson, Burchinal, & Ramey, 2001). These enduring effects were most pronounced for children who received infancy, preschool and primary school intervention, indicating the importance of longer-term interventions (i.e., those that occur following children's entry into formal schooling) for low-income children. Currie and colleagues (Currie & Thomas, 1995; Garces, Duncan, & Currie, 2002) have reported similar long-term gains among Head Start participants, with Head Start children scoring higher on vocabulary tests, repeating grades less often, and attending school for longer. In response to reports of Head Start's "fade out" effects, Currie and Thomas (2000) have shown that children whose test score gains diminish were more likely to attend low quality elementary schools, suggesting that poor schools rather than ineffective intervention drove the decline in scores. By contrast, children who attended higher quality schools, like those who in other studies received consistent and intensive intervention services, exhibited lasting gains. Thus, rather than "fade out," intervention effects more accurately diminish in the face of the poor school and other environmental conditions that children in poverty experience.

Program evaluations that have examined long-term links between early intervention and children's behavior problems have mixed results. Children who participated in the Perry Preschool Program in Michigan, a model preschool program that emerged out of the 1960s' War on Poverty, experienced reductions in delinquent behavior in early adolescence and less involvement with the criminal justice system as young adults up to 27 years of age compared with children who did not participate in the intensive intervention program (Karoly et al., 1998; Schweinhart et al., 1993). Although the program had short-term impacts on

behavioral outcomes, participation in the Houston Parent-Child Development Center was not associated with preadolescents' and adolescents' delinquency (Andrews et al., 1982), nor were long-term behavioral impacts found for Abecedarian children (Campbell et al., 2001). However, results from other studies do show that early education programs can produce sizable long-term benefits on social adjustment and delinquency (Barnett, 1995; Yoshikawa, 1995). Much of this variation may stem from program intensity, duration, quality and characteristics of children and families.

Differential impacts of early intervention. Because the effects of early intervention programs prove inconsistent, especially when examined in the long-term, it is important to examine how program impacts vary for certain subgroups of children and families. Factors that may moderate program efficacy include the dosage or intensity of treatment for individual families, familial risk factors such as low maternal education and female-headed household, as well as program type.

It is difficult to assess dose-related impacts of early intervention because programs have generally not randomly assigned children to varying intensities of the treatment. Studies that have examined impacts on children receiving larger or smaller doses are limited, for families who choose to use the program more frequently may differ from families that seldom use available services; these family-level differences may actually account for any divergent effects found between the groups. Using data from the IHDP, Hill and colleagues (Hill, Brooks-Gunn, & Waldfogel, 2003) created comparable groups of high-dosage treatment children and children in the control group who, based on background characteristics measured before treatment, would have received had high-dosage had they been selected for the treatment. Analyses revealed that these high-dosage children had IQ scores that were seven points higher at age 5 and nearly four points higher at age 8 than their matched controls, impacts that are moderate but significant; effects remained at age 8 when the sample was divided into the heavier and lighter low birthweight groups (see Figure 18.1). Previous analyses that did not factor dosage into analytic models did not find sustained effects for the lighter low birthweight children. These analyses temper the arguments regarding early intervention's "fade out" after preschool, suggesting that at high doses, treatment effects may be sustained after children leave the program.

When treatment impacts are compared for children with different levels of biological, environmental and familial risk factors, there is some evidence that even within programs tailored for disadvantaged families, more vulnerable families experience greater benefits than families who are less at-risk (Brooks-Gunn, Berlin, & Fuligni, 2000; Brooks-Gunn, Fuligni, & Berlin, 2003; Bryant & Maxwell, 1997). Data from the IHDP revealed more pronounced age 3 IQ effects for children in poverty and children whose mothers had low education (Brooks-Gunn, Gross, Kraemer, Spiker, & Shapiro, 1992). In the Abecedarian Project, the subgroup of program children whose mothers had the lowest IQ scores were far less likely to have IQ scores in the mentally retarded or borderline range than similar children in the control group at 3 years of age (Ramey & Ramey, 1999) and

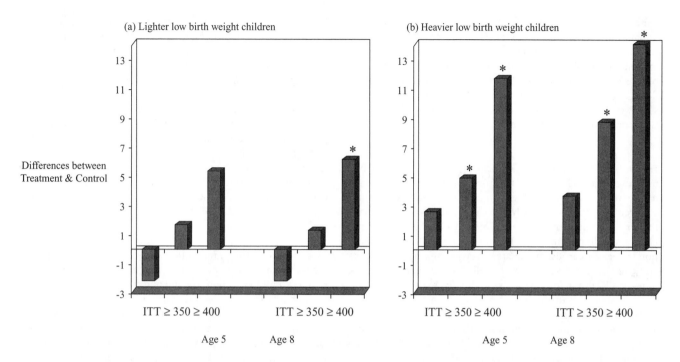

FIGURE 18.1. Dose-related treatment effect on IQ at ages 5 and 8 for the (a) lighter and (b) heavier low birthweight children from the Infant Health and Development Program.
Note: ITT = Intent to treat (Lighter LBW N = 677; Heavier LBW N = 350); 350 = 350 or more days of attendance at the IHDP centers over a 2-year period when children were 12 to 36 months old (Lighter LBW N = 195; Heavier LBW N = 123); 400 = 400 or more days of attendance (Lighter LBW N = 90; Heavier LBW N = 43); Lighter LBW = 1000 to 2000 grams; Heavier LBW = 2001 to 2500 grams. Age 5 IQ from the WPSSI; age 8 IQ from the WISC; propensity score matching (without replacement); estimates based on regression.* $p < .05$
Source: Hill et al., 2003.

showed the largest gains in IQ and school achievement at 12 years of age (Campbell & Ramey, 1994). Other analyses based on the IHDP data revealed that for children in poverty, however, treatment effects are seen regardless of the number of risk factors present including maternal education, employment and verbal ability. Furthermore, Liaw and colleagues (Liaw, Meisels, & Brooks-Gunn, 1995) found that the IHDP's effects decreased overall as family risk factors increased. Results from the EHS program offers a possible explanation for these discordant findings; EHS families with a moderate number of risk factors, as opposed to those with very high or low risks, benefited most from intervention (Love et al., 2002). Perhaps more vulnerable families benefit most from intervention up to the point at which risks become so overwhelming to families that the type of services currently offered cannot help.

The final explanation for discrepancies in findings across studies is the type of program, notably center-based or home-based. Center-based programs provide intervention services for children and parents mostly at community sites and typically include a high-quality child care component. Home-based programs, by contrast, offer treatment through staff who visit families in their homes to provide a range of parent and child-focused services. Most interventions that report positive program effects on children's outcomes have been center-based initiatives

(Barnett, 1995; Brooks-Gunn, 2003; Karoly et al., 1998). Although there are exceptions (Gomby, Culross, & Behrman, 1999), home visiting programs as a whole have not been as successful in promoting positive outcomes for children (Baker, Piotrkowski, & Brooks-Gunn, 1999; Gomby et al., 1999; St. Pierre & Layzer, 1999). Most recently, data from the Early Head Start evaluation revealed that IQ effects were seen only for children in the center-based and mixed-approach (both center- and home-based care) groups; the IQ scores of children attending exclusively home-based programs did not vary according to treatment (Love et al., 2002). It is important to note, however, that no studies have examined the unique role home visiting can play within a program that also offers center-based services. It may be that home visiting, which has been shown to improve parenting skills and parent mental health (Barnard, Magyary, Booth, Mitchell, & Spieker, 1988; Booth, Mitchell, Barnard, & Spieker, 1989; Brooks-Gunn, Berlin, & Fuligni, 2000; Erickson, Korfmacher, & Egeland, 1992; Lyons-Ruth, Connell, Grunebaum, & Botein, 1990), can complement center-based services and enhance its effects.

Collectively, these findings present a portrait of the optimal contexts for early intervention. First, children who attend early intervention programs consistently are more likely than their counterparts to reap the benefits of such attendance. Second, benefits of early intervention are more likely to last if children remain in programs for at-risk families and enter high quality schools. Intervention programs also prove more effective for moderately at-risk subgroups of low-income families, probably because these children have the most to gain from early educational experiences. Finally, center-based services may be better suited to facilitating positive cognitive outcomes than exclusively home-based approaches.

Impacts on parents. As we explained previously, parents' behavior with their children and their time and money investments can serve as important pathways mediating poverty effects on children's outcomes. Not only can early intervention programs moderate the deleterious impacts of early childhood disadvantage on children's outcomes, but these early childhood education endeavors can also moderate poverty's impacts on parents, and children as a result. These benefits include improvements in mental health, parenting skills and home environment.

A number of evaluations have reported treatment effects on maternal mental health, most notably levels of depression and anxiety, although not consistently so (Barnard et al., 1988; Booth et al., 1989; Erickson et al., 1992; Lyons-Ruth et al., 1990). Mothers whose low birthweight children participated in the IHDP intervention reported lower emotional distress than nonintervention mothers one year into the program; findings were most pronounced for mothers experiencing large numbers of negative life events (Klebanov, Brooks-Gunn, & McCormick, 2001). Mothers of children who participated in the Early Head Start program did not differ from non-program families on assessments of their mental health, although parenting stress was lower among mothers in the treatment group compared with controls for families in home-based programs (Love et al., 2001). Home-visiting programs have had more success altering parenting behavior than they have with child outcomes, perhaps because these programs tend to be parent-focused. Home-based programs have been shown to enhance parental mental health as evidenced by the reduction of depressive affect and the increase in positive coping and provision of maternal support (Barnard et al., 1988; Booth et al., 1989; Brooks-Gunn, Berlin, & Fuligni, 2000; Erickson et al., 1992; Lyons-Ruth et al., 1990).

By improving parent well-being, early intervention programs theoretically influence children through their effects on parent behavior. Supporting this theory, the most prominent impacts of early intervention programs on parents' outcomes are found for their interactions with their children. A number of studies have reported more positive parent-child interactions for dyads participating in interventions (Andrews et al., 1982; Brooks-Gunn, Berlin, & Fuligni, 2000; Field, Widmayer, Greenberg, & Stoller, 1982; Love et al., 2002). The National Evaluation of Early Head Start, which videotaped in-home, parent-child interactions, found program effects in terms of parents' increased supportiveness and decreased emotional detachment and harshness (Love et al., 2002). Home-based programs in particular have been shown to enhance parent responsiveness and warmth and reduce parent harshness (Barnard et al., 1988; Booth et al., 1989; Brooks-Gunn, Berlin, & Fuligni, 2000; Erickson et al., 1992; Lyons-Ruth et al., 1990).

Finally, early intervention programs may impact the quality of the home environment. A recent review of early education impacts revealed that a number of home-based and mixed-approach interventions significantly improved HOME scores for participating families (Brooks-Gunn, Berlin, & Fuligni, 2000). Few studies include assessments of the home environment, however, making it difficult to generalize across all interventions. Recent data from the Early Head Start evaluation found parents in the treatment group provided more language and learning experiences in the home compared with families in the control group (Love et al., 2002). Treatment families were also more likely to read to their children daily. As we reviewed earlier, providing a more stimulating home environment in these ways can greatly enhance child cognitive, as well as emotional, development.

Conclusion. Early intervention programs targeted at low-income families can help close the gap between poor and nonpoor children's cognitive and behavioral outcomes through their effects on components of the aforementioned family stress and investment models. Regarding the theory of family stress, participating in early intervention can enhance children's outcomes indirectly by improving parents' mental health and their parenting practices as a result. More directly, parents can improve their parenting skills through early intervention programs, which may, in turn, improve their relationships with their children and children's subsequent development. Early intervention also can influence investments in children in terms of resources, materials and time. Specifically, many programs provide high-quality center-based child care, which not only allows parents to seek or hold jobs, but also offers children enriching experiences. These programs also improve the quality of children's home environments. In sum, high-quality early intervention programs can help children in poverty prepare for school and equip their parents to aid them in that process. However, research suggests that early intervention services cannot achieve long-term success alone; higher quality schools and programs for families in poverty are essential to children's continued success.

Welfare Reform

The Social Security Act of 1962 amended the preexisting welfare policy, Aid to Dependent Children, by expanding the role of the federal government, offering services in addition to cash assistance and extending benefits to families with unemployed fathers. This new policy was entitled, Aid to Families with Dependent Children (AFDC), which, before 1996, was the categorical, means-tested, cash benefit provided to needy children and their caretakers. The Personal Responsibility and Work Opportunity Reconciliation Act of 1996 (PRWORA) marked the repeal of AFDC and the creation of its present substitute, Temporary Assistance for Needy Families (TANF). Unlike its predecessor, TANF is funded through block grants, providing states with greater flexibility in determining eligibility and benefit levels. The purpose of the 1996 legislation was fourfold: (1) to provide assistance to families in poverty so children can remain in their homes, (2) to promote job training, work and marriage, (3) to prevent childbirth outside of marriage and (4) to encourage the formation of two parent families (Greenberg et al., 2002). Under TANF, recipients must work following 2 years of cash assistance and may not remain on the rolls after cashing out their 5-year lifetime limit.

The welfare reform provisions that may have the largest impact on children's outcomes include the work mandates, income supplements, noncompliance sanctions, and time limits (Duncan & Brooks-Gunn, 2000). Studies are beginning to surface that examine impacts of PRWORA on families in poverty. There are a number of extant, pre-PRWORA studies, however, that examine associations between different combinations of welfare, work requirements, income supplements, time limits, and other provisions and child and family outcomes. We review findings from these studies and discuss their relevance to pathways between poverty and child outcomes covered previously.

For younger preschool- and early school-aged children, findings are mixed regarding the impact of welfare receipt and various welfare policies on children's outcomes. One study revealed that welfare receipt at age 1 (compared with no welfare receipt) was negatively associated with 3-year-olds' IQ scores; scores were especially low for the children who left AFDC by age 3 without simultaneously leaving poverty (Smith, Brooks-Gunn, McCarton, & Kohen, 2001). Other studies found that unemployment was negatively associated with children's cognitive test scores (Brooks-Gunn, Klebanov, Smith, & Lee, 2001) and positively associated with children's behavior problems (Smith, Brooks-Gunn, Klebanov, & Lee, 2000) regardless of welfare receipt, indicating that low-income and not welfare status could be driving negative impacts on children. Mandatory employment, however, a facet of many existing welfare programs, has few associations with preschool-aged children's cognitive development, according to more recent research; earnings supplements, however, did yield small but significant positive impacts on children's achievement (Morris, 2002; Morris, Duncan, & Clark-Kauffman, 2003). These findings were most robust for long-term welfare recipients, for whom poverty was most entrenched. Recent research warns, however, that time limits may attenuate positive impacts of earnings supplements on early schoolaged children's achievement (Morris, Gennetian, & Knox, 2002), perhaps because parents cannot maintain the level of income they received when wages were supplemented by cash assistance. Overall, these findings suggests that welfare receipt and maternal employment have inconsistent effects on young children, while increasing parents income benefits children for at least as long as income supplements last.

In terms of outcomes for older children, findings are also mixed. One study documented negative associations between family participation in a welfare program that mandated employment and provided earnings supplements and 10- to 11-year-olds' achievement scores (Morris, Duncan et al., 2003). Another study found that preadolescent boys whose families participated in similar programs exhibited favorable school outcomes according to self- and teacher-reported items that included school performance, classroom behavior and future expectations compared with children whose families did not participate in the program (Mistry, Crosby, Huston, Casey, & Ripke, 2001). These results suggest that the impact of altering parental investments in children in terms of time and money may vary given the context within and population to whom the program is offered.

When specific welfare policies were examined with adolescent samples, it was revealed that youth whose families participated in welfare programs mandating time limits and providing earnings supplements generally exhibited lower school performance, more grade repetition, and special education placements than control children (Gennetian et al., 2002). Additionally, time limits and earnings supplements were associated with increased problematic behavior among youth (Morris, 2002). It is important to note that none of the negative impacts on program children could be traced back to contemporaneous increases in maternal employment, although there was some evidence that maternal employment is positively associated with youths' responsibilities at home (e.g., caring for a younger sibling). These studies suggest that time limits particularly may work against positive effects of earning supplements, at least for adolescent children.

The Three-Cities study is one of the first to examine the impacts of employment and welfare post-PRWORA. Early findings from the study were similar to those found using the older, pre-PRWORA data. Analyses revealed no significant impacts of long- or short-term employment or welfare receipt on a range of preschool children's outcomes including their quantitative and reading skills. For adolescents, however, moves off of welfare, regardless of mothers' work schedule, was positively associated with their reading skills and negatively associated with their substance use, whereas recent moves onto welfare were unfavorably associated with outcomes (Chase-Lansdale et al., 2003), once again documenting the deleterious impact of welfare receipt on youths' outcomes.

In general, children may not benefit from parents' increased employment if it is not accompanied by sufficient increases in income to lift families out of poverty (Morris, Bloom, Kemple, & Hendra, 2003). For young children and preadolescents, the inclusion of earnings supplements in welfare packages appears to bolster their well-being. For example, a recent Michigan-based study reported no associations between maternal employment and parenting behavior; whereas, the wage-welfare combination was favorably associated with positive parenting (Dunifon, Kalil, & Danziger, 2003). These parenting behaviors were then negatively associated with young children's behavior problems. Similarly, a study based on data from the IHDP revealed that transitions off of welfare without subsequent transitions out of poverty was associated with higher observed authoritarian parenting compared with families that left both welfare and poverty (Smith et al., 2001). Moreover, impacts of time-limited cash assistance with concomitant supplemental supports (e.g., child care) on children's outcomes may vary according to families' dependency on cash assistance. One study found that children from families with low welfare dependence experienced less favorable school-related outcomes than children from families receiving non-time-limited cash assistance; findings were especially strong for adolescent children (Morris, Bloom et al., 2003). A recent study found that the hardest to employ adults (e.g., lengthy tenure of unemployment, low maternal education, family health problems) experienced the largest increases in employment rates and subsequent increases in income compared with other low-income families following participation in an experimental welfare program (Yoshikawa, Magnuson, Bos, & Hsueh, 2003). These improved economic circumstances were not, however, positively associated with improved academic and behavioral outcomes for children. Post-hoc analyses revealed that these newly employed, disadvantaged mothers were experiencing increased rates of depression and adhering to fewer family routines following their entry into the workforce.

Each of the welfare policies discussed earlier—mandatory employment, time limits and earnings supplements—could influence components of the family stress and investment models and child outcomes in the process. Existing research, however, does not make it clear how these strategies are likely to function in children's lives. The effect of maternal employment, particularly in the child's first few years, is the least understood. It may yield unfavorable outcomes because it will increase maternal stress and reduce the time families spend together. Conversely, gainful employment may enhance parents' mental health and feelings of efficacy, leading to more positive parenting and child outcomes. Mothers' employment could also raise family income which could greatly improve children's early environments. The extent to which maternal employment fails to move families out of poverty, however, may account for the lack of positive impacts on children's outcomes. Supporting this theory, time limits have not produced favorable results, perhaps because many families do not leave poverty once they leave welfare rolls. Earning supplements, by contrast, are associated with better child outcomes, mostly likely because they increase parents' ability to invest in their children and may reduce factors such as maternal stress and depression.

Conclusion. Taken together, these results suggest that what matters most for children in poverty is raising family income. This finding comes as no surprise when you consider the direct effects of poverty on child development and the benefits associated with even small upward shifts in income, particularly for children living in deep and entrenched deprivation. Combining parental employment with earnings supplements generous enough to lift families out of poverty offers the most direct path to this goal. If more families leave poverty, we can imagine enhanced parent mental health, improved parenting, enriched home environments, and better child care and health conditions as possible results, all of which could go a long way toward narrowing the gap between poor and nonpoor children's school readiness.

CONCLUSION

In this chapter, we address the growing need for researchers, practitioners, and policy makers in the field of early childhood education to understand the implications of poverty in young children's lives. Countless studies have found that, to varying degrees, poverty has negative effects on children's school readiness across cognitive and socioemotional outcomes. Particularly

harmful is deep poverty experienced consistently over time and beginning early in life. This kind of early childhood poverty not only impacts preschool and early school related outcomes, but it is more closely linked with achievement and behavioral problems during late adolescence and early adulthood than poverty experienced at any other time. Although early poverty can be severely detrimental, recent research indicates that alleviating families' economic hardship before children reach preschool can seriously reduce the risks associated with early deprivation (Dearing et al., 2001). These findings relate to the increasing body of research on early development, which suggests that the first 3 years of life is a time of great opportunity and great vulnerability for children developing crucial emotional and physiological capacities (Shonkoff & Phillips, 2000). Intervening at this point, then, proves particularly important to children's success in preschool and beyond.

We stress that intervention and policy surrounding childhood poverty must consider the pathways through which poverty affects child development. Two broad theories of influence are discussed, the family stress model and the investment model. Because the family stress model hinges on parenting and parent-child relationships, it is more closely related to child emotional and behavioral outcomes, although cognitive development is inextricably linked to these processes as well. This theory argues that although emotional stress can lead to negative parenting and poor child outcomes, warm and supportive parenting can significantly protect children against the ravages of early deprivation. The investment model implicates the monetary limitations poor parents face in raising their children; regardless of parenting quality, children in poverty most likely lack the materials, services, and resources that nonpoor children enjoy and this disparity impacts their development.

With these processes in mind, we highlight the role that public policies, particularly those surrounding early intervention and welfare, can play in moderating these pathways. Because of its positive effects on child cognitive and behavioral outcomes, early intervention itself can be considered an investment parents make in their children, similar to participation in high quality child care. Additionally, many early education programs incorporate parents into programs because they view parents as engines of change. By providing support and assistance, programs can alleviate parental stress and thus improve parenting quality. Early intervention programs can also enhance parents' role as teachers of their children, thereby helping to create more enriching home environments. We stress, however, that early intervention is most effective when it is delivered in high doses, begins prenatally or during infancy, and is followed by participation in parent and child services for at-risk families and entrance into high-quality schools.

Welfare policies do not aim to enhance child development as specifically, however, components of the system affect young children's lives. We have illustrated how aspects of welfare reform, namely maternal employment, time limits and earning supplements, can all impact parents' mental health, purchasing power and time with their children. It is clear that families with young children who see their incomes fall or remain below the poverty line once they leave the welfare rolls will experience psychological and financial stress that will no doubt affect their children. Studies of welfare initiatives suggest, however, that programs allowing parents to work and earn incomes above poverty may help young children most of all. Policy makers need to recognize this possible variation in welfare's effects on children and ensure that welfare programs seek to help and not hinder children's healthy development. Because early experiences are so important to child development, without proper supports and intervention, many children in poverty will continue to lag behind their nonpoor peers in early education and beyond. For the same reason, however, through mindful support systems and targeted intervention we can increase the odds of positive outcomes for children in poverty and begin to close that gap.

ACKNOWLEDGMENTS

The authors would like to thank the National Science Foundation, the National Institute of Child Health and Human Development and the Spencer Foundation. Additional support was provided by the MacArthur Foundation Network on Family and the Economy.

References

Alpern, L., & Lyons-Ruth, K. (1993). Preschool children at social risk: Chronicity and timing of maternal depressive symptoms and child behavior problems at school and at home. *Development and Psychopathology, 5*, 371-387.

Andrews, S. R., Blumenthal, J. B., Johnson, D. L., Kahn, A. J., Ferguson, C. J., Lasater, T. M., et al. (1982). The skills of mothering: A study of Parent Child Development Centers (New Orleans, Birmingham, Houston). *Monographs of the Society for Research in Child Development, 47*(6, Serial No. 198).

Apfel, N., & Seitz, V. (1997). The firstborn sons of African American teenage mothers: Perspectives on risk and resilience. In S. S. Luthar, J. A. Burack & et al. (Eds.), *Developmental psychopathology: Perspectives on adjustment, risk, and disorder* (pp. 486-506). New York: Cambridge University Press.

Axinn, W., Duncan, G. J., & Thornton, A. (1997). The effects of parents' income, wealth and attitudes on children's completed schooling and self-esteem. In G. J. Duncan & J. Brooks-Gunn (Eds.), *Consequences of growing up poor* (pp. 518-540). New York: Russell Sage Foundation.

Baker, A., Piotrkowski, C. S., & Brooks-Gunn, J. (1999). The Home Instruction Program for Preschool Youngsters (HIPPY). *The Future of Children, 9*, 116-133.

Barnard, K. E., Magyary, G. S., Booth, C. L., Mitchell, S. K., & Spieker, S. J. (1988). Prevention of parenting altercations for women with low social support. *Psychiatry, 51*, 248-253.

Barnett, W. S. (1995). Long-term effects of early childhood programs on cognitive and school outcomes. *The Future of Children, 5*, 25-50.

Baumrind, D. (1966). Effects of authoritative control on child behavior. *Child Development, 37*, 887-907.

Baydar, N., & Brooks-Gunn, J. (1991). Effects of maternal employment and child-care arrangements on preschoolers' cognitive and behavioral outcomes: Evidence from the Children of the National Longitudinal Survey of Youth. *Developmental Psychology, 27*, 932-945.

Becker, G. S. (1991). *A treatise on the family*. Cambridge, MA: Harvard University Press.

Belsky, J. (1986). Infant day care: A cause for concern? *Zero to Three, 7*(1), 1-7.

Belsky, J. (1988). The "effects" of infant day care reconsidered. *Early Childhood Research Quarterly, 3*, 235-272.

Belsky, J. (1999). Interactional and contextual determinants of attachment security. In J. Cassidy & P. Shaver (Eds.), *Handbook of attachment theory and research* (pp. 249-264). New York: Guilford.

Berlin, L. J., Brady-Smith, C., & Brooks-Gunn, J. (2002). Links between childbearing age and observed maternal behaviors with 14-month-olds in the Early Head Start Research and Evaluation Project. *Infant Mental Health Journal, 23*, 104-129.

Berlin, L. J., & Cassidy, J. (2000). Understanding parenting: Contributions of attachment theory and research. In J. Osofsky & H. E. Fitzgerald (Eds.), *The World Alliance for Infant Mental Health handbook of infant mental health, Vol. 3: Parenting and child care* (pp. 133-170). New York: John Wiley & Sons.

Betson, D. M., & Michael, R. T. (1997). Why so many children are poor. *The Future of Children, 7*(2), 25-39.

Blau, D. M. (1999). The effect of child care characteristics on child development. *Journal of Human Resources, 34*(4), 786-822.

Booth, C. L., Mitchell, S. K., Barnard, K. E., & Spieker, S. J. (1989). Development of maternal social skills in multiproblem families: Effects on the mother-child relationship. *Developmental Psychology, 25*, 403-412.

Bornstein, M. H. (Ed.). (1995). *Handbook of parenting*. Mahwah, NJ: Lawrence Erlbaum.

Bradley, R. H. (1995). Environment and parenting. In M. H. Bornstein (Ed.), *Handbook of Parenting, Vol. 2: Biology and ecology of parenting* (pp. 235-261). Mahwah, NJ: Lawrence Erlbaum Associates.

Bradley, R. H., & Corwyn, R. F. (2002). Socioeconomic status and child development. *Annual Review of Psychology, 53*, 371-399.

Bradley, R. H., Corwyn, R. F., McAdoo, H. P., & Garcia Coll, C. T. (2001). The home environments of children in the United States part I: Variations by age, ethnicity, and poverty status. *Child Development, 72*, 1844-1867.

Brooks-Gunn, J. (2003). Do you believe in magic?: What we can expect from early childhood intervention programs. *Society for Research in Child Development Social Policy Report, VVII*(1).

Brooks-Gunn, J., Berlin, L. J., & Fuligni, A. S. (2000). Early childhood intervention programs: What about the family? In J. P. Shonkoff & S. J. Meisels (Eds.), *Handbook of early childhood intervention* (2nd ed., pp. 549-588). New York: Cambridge University Press.

Brooks-Gunn, J., Berlin, L. J., Leventhal, T., & Fuligni, A. S. (2000). Depending on the kindness of strangers: Current national data initiatives and developmental research. *Child Development, 71*, 257-268.

Brooks-Gunn, J., & Duncan, G. J. (1997). The effects of poverty on children. *The Future of Children, 7*(2), 55-71.

Brooks-Gunn, J., Duncan, G. J., Klebanov, P. K., & Sealand, N. (1993). Do neighborhoods influence child and adolescent development? *American Journal of Sociology, 99*, 353-395.

Brooks-Gunn, J., Fuligni, A. S., & Berlin, L. J. (Eds.). (2003). *Early child development in the 21st century: Profiles of current research initiatives*. New York: Teachers Colllege Pres..

Brooks-Gunn, J., Gross, R. T., Kraemer, H. C., Spiker, D., & Shapiro, S. (1992). Enhancing the cognitive outcomes of low birthweight, premature infants: For whom is the intervention most effective? *Pediatrics, 89*, 1209-1215.

Brooks-Gunn, J., Han, W. J., & Waldfogel, J. (2002). Maternal employment and child cognitive outcomes in the first three years of life: The NICHD Study of Early Child Care. *Child Development, 73*, 1052-1072.

Brooks-Gunn, J., Klebanov, P., Liaw, F. R., & Spiker, D. (1993). Enhancing the development of low birthweight, premature infants: Changes in cognition and behavior over the first three years. *Child Development, 64*, 736-753.

Brooks-Gunn, J., Klebanov, P. K., & Liaw, F. R. (1995). The learning, physical, and emotional environment of the home in the context of poverty: The Infant Health and Development Program. *Children & Youth Services Review, 17*, 251-276.

Brooks-Gunn, J., Klebanov, P. K., Smith, J. R., & Lee, K. (2001). Effects of combining public assistance and employment on mothers and their young children. *Women and Health, 32*, 179-210.

Brooks-Gunn, J., Leventhal, T., & Duncan, G. (1999). Why poverty matters for young children: Implications for policy. In J. D. Osofsky & H. E. Fitzgerald (Eds.), *WAIMH handbook of infant mental health, Volume 3: Parenting and child care* (pp. 92-131). New York: John Wiley & Sons, Inc.

Brooks-Gunn, J., McCarton, C., Casey, P., McCormick, M., Bauer, C., Berenbaum, J., Tyson, J., Swanson, M., Bennett, F., Scott, D., Tonascia, J., & Meinert, C. (1994). Early intervention in low birth weight, premature infants: Results through age 5 years from the Infant Health and Development Program. *Journal of the American Medical Association, 272*, 1257-1262.

Bryant, D. M., Burchinal, M., Lau, L. B., & Sparling, J. J. (1994). Family and classroom correlates of Head Start children's developmental outcomes. *Early Childhood Research Quarterly, 9*, 289-304.

Bryant, D. M., & Maxwell, K. (1997). The effectiveness of early intervention for disadvantaged children. In M. J. Guralnick (Ed.), *The effectiveness of early intervention* (pp. 23-46). Baltimore: Brookes.

Burchinal, M., Lee, M., & Ramey, C. T. (1989). Type of day-care and preschool intellectual development in disadvantaged children. *Child Development, 60*, 128-137.

Burchinal, M. R., Campbell, F. A., Bryant, D. M., Wasik, B. H., & Ramey, C. T. (1997). Early intervention and mediating processes in cognitive performance of children of low-income African American families. *Child Development, 68*, 935-954.

Burchinal, M. R., Roberts, J. E., Riggins, R., Jr., Zeisel, S. A., Neebe, E., & Bryant, D. (2000). Relating quality of center-based child care to early cognitive and language development longitudinally. *Child Development, 71*, 339-357.

Caldwell, B. M., & Bradley, R. H. (1984). *Home Observation for Measurement of the Environment*. Little Rock: University of Arkansas.

Campbell, F. A., Pungello, E. P., Miller-Johnson, S., Burchinal, M., & Ramey, C. T. (2001). The development of cognitive and academic abilities: Growth curves from an early childhood educational experiment. *Developmental Psychology, 37*, 231-242.

Campbell, F. A., & Ramey, C. T. (1994). Effects of early intervention on intellectual and academic achievement: A follow-up study from low-income families. *Child Development, 65*, 684-698.

Campbell, F. A., & Ramey, C. T. (1995). Cognitive and school outcomes for high risk African American students at middle adolescence: Positive effects of early intervention. *American Educational Research Journal, 32*, 743-772.

Carnegie Corporation. (1994). *Starting points: Meeting the needs of our youngest children*. New York: Author.

Case, A., Lubotsky, D., & Paxson, C. (2002, February). *Economic status and health in childhood: The origins of the gradient*. Princeton, NJ: The Center for Health and Wellbeing, Princeton University.

Caughy, M. O., DiPietro, J. A., & Strobino, D. M. (1994). Day-care participation as a protective factor in the cognitive development of low-income children. *Child Development, 65*, 457-471.

Chase-Lansdale, P. L., & Gordon, R. A. (1996). Economic hardship and the development of five- and six-year-olds: Neighborhood and regional perspectives. *Child Development, 67*, 3338-3367.

Chase-Lansdale, P. L., Gordon, R. A., Brooks-Gunn, J., & Klebanov, P. (1997). Neighborhood and family influences on the intellectual and behavioral competence of preschool and early school-age children. In J. Brooks-Gunn, G. J. Duncan & J. L. Aber (Eds.), *Neighborhood poverty: Vol. 1. Context and consequences for children* (pp. 79-118). New York: Russell Sage Foundation Press.

Chase-Lansdale, P. L., Moffitt, R. A., Lohman, B. J., Cherlin, A. J., Coley, R. L., Pittman, L. D., et al. (2003). Mothers' transitions from welfare to work and the well-being of preschoolers and adolescents. *Science, 299*, 1548-1552.

Chen, C., Lee, S., & Stevenson, H. (1996). Long-term prediction of academic achievement of American, Chinese and Japanese adolescents. *Journal of Educational Psychology, 88*, 750-759.

Children's Defense Fund. (1994). *Wasting America's future*. Boston: Beacon Press.

Cicchetti, D., & Toth, S. L. (1995). Child maltreatment and attachment organization: Implications for intervention. In S. Goldberg, R. Muir & e. al. (Eds.), *Attachment theory: Social, developmental, and clinical perspectives*.

Citro, C. F., & Michael, R. T. (Eds.). (1995). *Measuring poverty: A new approach*. Washington, DC: National Academy Press.

Clarke-Stewart, K. A., & Fein, G. G. (1983). Early childhood programs. In P. H. Mussen (Ed.), *Handbook of child psychology*, Vol. 4. *Socialization, personality, and social development* (pp. 918-999). New York: John Wiley & Sons.

Coiro, M. J., Zill, N., & Bloom, B. (1994, December). *Health of our nation's children* (No. Vital Health and Statistics, Series 10, No.191). Hyattsville, MD: U.S. Department of Health and Human Services.

Committee on Ways and Means. (2000). *The 2000 Green Book*. Washington, DC: U.S. Government Accounting Office.

Conger, K. J., Rueter, M. A., & Conger, R. D. (2000). The role of economic pressure in the lives of parents and their adolescents: The Family Stress Model. In L. J. Crockett & R. K. Silbereisen (Eds.), *Negotiating adolescence in times of social change* (pp. 201-223). New York: Cambridge University Press.

Conger, R. D., & Conger, K. J. (2000). Resilience in midwestern families: Selected findings from the first decade of a prospective longitudinal study. *Journal of Marriage & Family, 64*, 361-373.

Conger, R. D., Conger, K. J., Elder, G. H., Lorenz, F. O., Simons, R. L., & Whitbeck, L. B. (1992). A family process model of economic hardship and adjustment of early adolescent boys. *Child Development, 63*, 526-541.

Conger, R. D., & Elder, G. H. (1994). *Families in troubled times: Adapting to change in rural America*. New York: Aldine de Gruyter.

Conger, R. D., Patterson, G. R., & Ge, X. (1995). It takes two to replicate: A mediational model for the impact of parents' stress on adolescent adjustment. *Child Development, 66*, 80-97.

Conger, R. D., Wallace, L. E., Sun, Y., Simons, R. L., McLoyd, V. C. C., & Brody, G. H. (2002). Economic pressure in African American families: A replication and extension of the family stress model. *Developmental Psychology, 38*, 179-193.

Conley, D., & Bennett, N. G. (2000). Is biology destiny? Birth weight and life chances. *American Sociological Review, 65*, 458–467.

Costello, E. J., Compton, S. N., Keeler, G., & Angold, A. (2003). Relationships between poverty and psychopathology: A natural experiment. *Journal of the American Medical Association, 290*, 2023–2029.

Cowen, E. L., Work, W. C., & Wyman, P. A. (1997). The Rochester Child Resilience Project (RCRP): Facts found, lessons learned, future directions divined. In S. S. Luthar, J. A. Burack & e. al. (Eds.), *Developmental psychopathology: Perspectives on adjustment, risk, and disorder*. New York: Cambridge University Press.

Cowen, E. L., Wyman, P. A., Work, W. C., & Parker, G. R. (1990). The Rochester Child Resilience Project: Overview and summary of first year findings. *Development & Psychopathology, 2*, 193–212.

Crnic, K., & Greenberg, M. (1987). Maternal stress, social support, and coping: Influences on the early mother-infant relationship. In C. F. Z. Boukydis (Ed.), *Research on support for parents and infants in the postnatal period* (pp. 25–40). Norwood, NJ: Ablex Publishing.

Crockenberg, S. (1987). Predictors and correlates of anger toward and punitive control of toddlers by adolescent mothers. *Child Development, 58*, 964–975.

Cunningham, A., & Stanovich, K. (1997). Early reading aquisition and its relation to reading experience and ability 10 years later. *Developmental Psychology, 33*, 934–945.

Currie, J. M., & Thomas, D. (1995). Does Head Start make a difference? *The American Economic Review, 85*, 341–364.

Currie, J. M., & Thomas, D. (2000). School quality and the longer-term effects of Head Start. *Journal of Human Resources, 35*, 755–774.

Dawson, D. A. (1991, June). *Family structure and children's health: United States, 1988* (No. Series 10, No.178). Hyattsville, MD: U.S. Department of Health and Human Services, Public Health Service.

Dearing, E., McCartney, K., & Taylor, B. A. (2001). Change in family income-to-needs matters more for children with less. *Child Development, 72*, 1779–1793.

Denton, K., West, J., & Walston, J. (2003). *Reading—Young children's achievement and classroom experiences (NCES 2003–070)*. Washington, DC: U.S. Department of Education, National Center for Education Statistics.

Dodge, K. H., Pettit, G. S., & Bates, J. E. (1994). Socialization mediators of the relation between socioeconomic status and child conduct problems. *Child Development, 65*, 649–665.

Duncan, G. J., & Brooks-Gunn, J. (2000). Family poverty, welfare reform, and child development. *Child Development, 71*, 188–196.

Duncan, G. J., & Brooks-Gunn, J. (Eds.). (1997). *Consequences of growing up poor*. New York: Russell Sage Foundation Press.

Duncan, G. J., Brooks-Gunn, J., & Klebanov, P. (1994). Economic deprivation and early-childhood development. *Child Development, 65*, 296–318.

Duncan, G. J., Yeung, W. J., Brooks-Gunn, J., & Smith, J. R. (1998). How much does childhood poverty affect the life chances of children? *American Sociological Review, 63*, 406–423.

Dunifon, R., Duncan, G. J., & Brooks-Gunn, J. (2001). As ye sweep, so shall ye reap. *American Economic Review, 91*, 150–154.

Dunifon, R., Kalil, A., & Danziger, S. K. (2003). Maternal work behavior under welfare reform: How does the transition from welfare to work affect child development? *Children and Youth Services Review, 25*, 55–82.

Edin, K., & Lein, L. (1997). *Making ends meet: How single mothers survive welfare and low-wage work*. New York: Russell Sage Foundation.

Elardo, R., & Bradley, R. H. (1981). The Home Observation for Measurement of the Environment (HOME) Scale: A review of research. *Developmental Review, 1*, 113–145.

Elder, G. H. (1999). *Children of the great depression: Social change in life experience*. Boulder, CO: Westview Press.

Elder, G. H., & Caspi, A. (1988). Economic stress in lives: Developmental perspectives. *Journal of Social Issues, 44*, 25–45.

Ensminger, M. E., & Fothergill, K. E. (2003). A decade of measuring SES: What it tells us and where to go from here. In M. H. Bornstein & R. H. Bradley (Eds.), *Socioeconomic status, parenting, and child development* (pp. 13–27). Mahway, NJ: Lawrence Erlbaum Associates.

Entwisle, D. R., & Astone, N. M. (1994). Some practical guidelines for measuring youth's race/ethnicity and socioeconomic status. *Child Development, 65*, 1521–1540.

Erickson, M. F., Korfmacher, J., & Egeland, B. R. (1992). Attachments past and present: Implications for therapeutic intervention with mother infant dyads. *Development and Psychopathology, 4*, 495–507.

Evans, G. W. (2001). Environmental stress and health. In A. Baum, T. A. Revenson & J. E. Singer (Eds.), *Handbook of health psychology* (pp. 365–385). Mahwah, NJ: Lawrence Erlbaum Associates.

Federal Interagency on Child and Family Statistics. (2003). *America's children: Key national indicators of well-being*. Washington, DC: U.S. Government Printing Office.

Field, T., Widmayer, S., Greenberg, R., & Stoller, S. (1982). Effects of parent training on teenage mothers and their infants. *Pediatrics, 69*, 245–269.

Gagne, R. M. (1970). *The conditions of learning*. New York: Holt, Rinehart & Winston.

Garces, E., Duncan, T., & Currie, J. M. (2002). Longer term effects of Head Start. *American Economic Review, 92*, 999–1012.

Garrett, P., Ng'andu, N., & Ferron, J. (1994). Poverty experiences of young children and the quality of their home environments. *Child Development, 65*, 331–345.

Gennetian, L. A., Duncan, G. J., Knox, V. W., Vargas, W. G., Clark-Kauffman, E., & London, A. S. (2002).*How welfare and work policies for parents affect adolescents: A synthesis of research*. New York: Manpower Demonstration Research Corporation.

Gesell, A. (1925). *The mental growth of the preschool child: A psychological outline of normal development from birth to the sixth year*. New York: Macmillan.

Goldstein, N. (1990). *Explaining socioeconomic differences in children's cognitive test scores* (No. Working Paper no. H-90-1). Cambridge, MA: Malcolm Weiner Center for Social Policy, John F. Kennedy School of Government, Harvard University.

Gomby, D. S., Culross, P. L., & Behrman, R. E. (1999). Home visiting: Recent program evaluations–analysis and recommendations. *The Future of Children, 9*(1), 4–26.

Good, C. V. (Ed.). (1973). *Dictionary of Education* (3 ed.). New York: McGraw-Hill.

Gray, W. S. (1927). Training and experience that prepare for reading. *Childhood Education*, 210–214.

Greenberg, M. H., Levin-Epstein, J., Hutson, R. Q., Ooms, T. J., Schumacher, R., Turetsky, V., et al. (2002). The 1996 welfare law: Key elements and reauthorization issues affecting children. *The Future of Children, 12*(1), 27–57.

Guo, G., & Harris, K. M. (2000). The mechanisms mediating the effects of poverty on children's intellectual development. *Demography, 37*, 431–448.

Hack, M., Klein, N. K., & Taylor, H. G. (1995). Long-term developmental outcomes of low birth weight infants. *The Future of Children, 5*, 176–196.

Hanson, T. L., McLanahan, S., & Thomson, E. (1997). Economic resources, parental practices, and children's well-being. In G. J. Duncan & J. Brooks-Gunn (Eds.), *Consequences of growing up poor* (pp. 190–238). New York: Russell Sage Foundation.

Haskins, R. (1995). Losing ground or moving ahead? Welfare reform and children. In L. Chase-Lansdale & J. Brooks-Gunn (Eds.), *Escape from poverty: What makes a difference for children?* New York: Cambridge University Press.

Haveman, R., & Wolfe, B. (1994). *Succeeding generations: On the effects of investments in children.* New York: Russell Sage Foundation.

Helburn, S. W. (Ed.). (1995). *Cost, quality, and child outcomes in child care centers: Technical report.* Denver: Department of Economics, Center for Research in Economic and Social Policy, University of Colorado.

Hernandez, D. J. (1997). Child development and the social demography of childhood. *Child Development, 68,* 149–169.

Hill, J., Brooks-Gunn, J., & Waldfogel, J. (2003). Sustained effects of high participation in an early intervention for low-birth-weight premature infants. *Developmental Psychology, 39,* 730–744.

Howes, C. (1990). Can the age of entry into child care and the quality of child care predict adjustment in kindergarten? *Developmental Psychology, 26,* 292–303.

Howes, C., & Smith, E. W. (1995). Relations among child care quality, teacher behavior, children's play activities, emotional security, and cognitive activity in child care. *Early Childhood Research Quarterly, 10,* 381–404.

Infant Health and Development Program. (1990). Enhancing the outcomes of low-birth-weight, premature infants: A multisite, randomized trial. *Journal of the American Medical Association, 263,* 3035–3042.

Jackson, A. P., Brooks-Gunn, J., Huang, C.-C., & Glassman, M. (2000). Single mothers in low-wage jobs: Financial strain, parenting, and preschoolers' outcomes. *Child Development, 71,* 1409–1423.

Johnson, D. L., & Walker, T. (1991). A follow-up evaluation of the Houston Parent-Child Development Center: School performance. *Journal of Early Intervention, 15,* 226–236.

Kagan, S. L. (1990). Readiness 2000: Rethinking rhetoric and responsibility. *Phi Delta Kappan, 72,* 272–279.

Kagan, S. L. (1995). *By the bucket: Achieving results for young children.* Washington, DC: National Governors' Association.

Kagan, S. L., & Rigby, E. (2003, February). *Policy matters: Setting and measuring benchmarks for state policies.* Washington, DC: Center for the Study of Social Policy.

Karoly, L. A., Greenwood, P. W., Everingham, S. S., Hoube, J., Kilburn, M. R., Rydell, C. P., Sanders, M. R., & Chiesa, J. R. (1998). *Investing in our children: What we know and don't know about the cost and benefit of early childhood interventions.* Santa Monica, CA: RAND.

Klebanov, P. K., Brooks-Gunn, J., Chase-Lansdale, L., & Gordon, R. (1997). Are neighborhood effects on young children mediated by features of the home environment? In J. Brooks-Gunn, G. Duncan & J. L. Aber (Eds.), *Neighborhood poverty: Context and consequences for children* (Vol. 1, pp. 119–145). New York: Russell Sage Foundation Press.

Klebanov, P. K., Brooks-Gunn, J., McCarton, C., & McCormick, M. C. (1998). The contribution of neighborhood and family income to developmental test scores over the first three years of life. *Child Development, 69,* 1420–1436.

Klebanov, P. K., Brooks-Gunn, J., & McCormick, M. C. (1994). School achievement and failure in very low birth weight children. *Journal of Developmental and Behavioral Pediatrics, 15,* 248–256.

Klebanov, P. K., Brooks-Gunn, J., & McCormick, M. C. (2001). Maternal coping strategies and emotional distress: Results of an early intervention program for low birth weight young children. *Developmental Psychology, 37,* 654–667.

Klerman, L. V. (1991). *Alive and well?* New York: National Center for Children in Poverty, Columbia University.

Klerman, L. V., Ramey, S. L., Goldenberg, R. L., Marbury, S., Hou, J., & Cliver, S. P. (2001). A randomized trial of augmented prenatal care for multiple-risk, medicaid-eligible African American women. *American Journal of Public Health, 91,* 105–111.

Kohen, D., Brooks-Gunn, J., Leventhal, T., & Hertzman, C. (2002). Neighborhood income and physical and social disorder in Canada: Associations with young children's competencies. *Child Development, 73,* 1844–1860.

Korenman, S., & Miller, J. E. (1997). Effects of long-term poverty on physical health of children in the National Longitudinal Survey of Youth. In G. J. Duncan & J. Brooks-Gunn (Eds.), *Consequences of growing up poor* (pp. 70–99). New York: Russell Sage Foundation.

Korenman, S., Miller, J. E., & Sjaastad, J. E. (1995). Long-term poverty and child development in the United States: Results from the NLSY. *Children and Youth Services Review, 17,* 127–155.

Lee, V. E., & Burkam, D. T. (2001). *Inequality at the starting gate: Social background differences in achievement as children begin school.* Washington, DC: Economic Policy Institute.

Leventhal, T., & Brooks-Gunn, J. (2000). The neighborhoods they live in: Effects of neighborhood residence upon child and adolescent outcomes. *Psychological Bulletin, 126,* 309–337.

Lewitt, E. M., & Kerrebrock, N. (1997). Population-based growth stunting. *The Future of Children, 7,* 149–156.

Li, H., Barnhart, H. X., Stein, A. D., & Martorell, R. (2003). Effects of early childhood supplementation on the educational achievement of women. *Pediatrics, 112,* 1156–1162.

Liaw, F. R., Meisels, S. J., & Brooks-Gunn, J. (1995). The effects of experience of early intervention on low birth weight, premature children: The Infant Health and Development Program. *Early Childhood Research Quarterly, 10,* 405–431.

Linver, M. R., Brooks-Gunn, J., & Kohen, D. E. (1999). Parenting behavior and emotional health as mediators of family poverty effects upon young low-birthweight children's cognitive ability. *Annals of the New York Academy of Sciences, 896,* 376–378.

Linver, M. R., Brooks-Gunn, J., & Kohen, D. E. (2002). Family processes as pathways from income to young children's development. *Developmental Psychology, 38,* 719–734.

Loeb, S., Fuller, B., Kagan, S. L., & Carroll, B. (2004). Child care in poor communities: Early learning effects of type, quality, and stability. *Child Development, 75,* 47–65.

Love, J. M., Harrison, L., Sagi-Schwartz, A., Van IJzendoorn, M. H., Ross, C., Ungerer, J. A., Raikes, H., Brady-Smith, C., Boller, K., Brooks-Gunn, J., Constantine, J., Kisker, E., Paulsell, D., & Chazan-Cohen, R. (2003). Child care quality matters: How conclusions may vary with context. *Child Development, 74,* 1021–1033.

Love, J. M., Kisker, E. E., Ross, C. M., Schochet, P. Z., Brooks-Gunn, J., Boller, K., Paulsell, D., et al. (2001). *Building their futures: How Early Head Start programs are enhancing the lives of infants and toddlers in low-income families.* Washington, DC: U.S. Department of Health and Human Services.

Love, J. M., Kisker, E. E., Ross, C. M., Schochet, P. Z., Brooks-Gunn, J., Paulsell, D., Boller, K., Constantine, J., Vogel, C., Fuligni, A. S., & Brady-Smith, C. (2002). *Making a difference in the lives of infants and toddlers and their families: The impacts of Early Head Start.* Washington, DC: U.S. Department of Health and Human Services.

Luster, T., & McAdoo, H. P. (1996). Family and child influences on educational attainment: A secondary analysis of the High/Scope Perry preschool data. *Developmental Psychology, 32,* 26–29.

Luthar, S. S. (1999). *Poverty and children's adjustment.* Thousand Oaks, CA: Sage Publications.

Lyons-Ruth, K., Connell, D. B., Grunebaum, H., & Botein, S. (1990). Infants at social risk: Maternal depression and family support services as mediators of infant development and security of attachment. *Child Development, 61*, 85-98.

May, C. R., & Campbell, R. M. (1981). Readiness for learning: Assumptions and realities. *Theory into Practice, 20*, 130-134.

Mayer, S. E. (1997). *What money can't buy: Family income and children's life chances*. CaMbridge, MA: Harvard University Press.

Mayer, S. E., & Jencks, C. (1988). Poverty and the distribution of material hardship. *The Journal of Human Resources, 24*, 88-113.

McCarton, C., Brooks-Gunn, J., Wallace, I., Bauer, C., Bennett, F., Bernbaum, J., Broyles, R., Casey, P., McCormick, M., Scott, D., Tyson, J., Tonascia, J., & Meinert, C. (1997). Results at 8 years of intervention for low birthweight premature infants: The Infant Health and Development Program. *Journal of the American Medical Association, 227*, 126-132.

McCormick, M. C., Brooks-Gunn, J., Workman-Daniels, K., Turner, J., & Peckham, G. (1992). The health and developmental status of very low birth weight children at school age. *Journal of the American Medical Association, 267*, 2204-2208.

McCormick, M. C., Gortmaker, S. L., & Sobol, A. M. (1990). Very low birth weight children: Behavior problems and school difficulty in a national sample. *Journal of Pediatrics, 117*, 687-693.

McCulloch, A., & Joshi, H. E. (2001). Neighborhourhood and family influences on the cognitive ability of children in the British National Child Development Study. *Social Science and Medicine, 53*, 579-591.

McLeod, J. D., & Nonnemaker, J. M. (2000). Poverty and child emotional and behavioral problems: Racial/ethnic differences in processes and effects. *Journal of Health and Social Behavior, 41*, 137-161.

McLeod, J. D., & Shanahan, M. J. (1993). Poverty, parenting, and children's mental health. *American Sociological Review, 58*, 351-366.

McLeod, J. D., & Shanahan, M. J. (1996). Trajectories of poverty and children's mental health. *Journal of Health and Social Behavior, 37*, 207-220.

McLoyd, V. C. (1989). Socialization and development in a changing economy: The effects of paternal job and income loss on children. *American Psychologist, 44*, 293-302.

McLoyd, V. C. (1990). The impact of economic hardship on black families and children: Psychological distress, parenting, and socioemotional development. *Child Development, 61*, 311-346.

McLoyd, V. C. (1997). The imact of poverty and low socioeconomic status on the socioemotional functioning of African-American children and adolescents: Mediating effects. In R. D. Taylor & M. C. Wang (Eds.), *Social and emotional adjustment and family relations in ethnic minority families* (pp. 7-34). Mahwah, NJ: Lawrence Erlbaum Associates.

McLoyd, V. C. (1998). Socioeconomic disadvantage and child development. *American Psychologist, 53*, 185-204.

McLoyd, V. C., Jayaratne, T. E., Ceballo, R., & Borquez, J. (1994). Unemployment and work interruption among African American single mothers: Effects on parenting and adolescent socioemotional functioning. Special Issue: *Children and poverty. Child Development, 65*, 562-589.

Miller, J. E., & Korenman, S. (1994). Poverty and children's nutritional status in the United States. *American Journal of Epidemiology, 140*, 233-243.

Mistry, R. S., Crosby, D. A., Huston, A. C., Casey, D. M., & Ripke, M. N. (2001). Lessons from New Hope: The impact on children's well-being of a work-based antipoverty program for parents. In G. J. Duncan & P. L. Chase-Lansdale (Eds.), *For better and for worse: Welfare reform and the well-being of children and families* (pp. 179-200). New York: Russell Sage Foundation.

Morris, P. A. (2002). The effects of welfare reform policies on children. *Social Policy Report, XVI*(1).

Morris, P. A., Bloom, D., Kemple, J., & Hendra, R. (2003). The effects of a time-limited welfare program on children: The moderating role of parents' risk of welfare dependency. *Child Development, 74*, 851-874.

Morris, P. A., Duncan, G. J., & Clark-Kauffman, E. (2003). *Child well-being in an era of welfare reform: The sensitivity of transitions in development to policy change*. New York: MDRC.

Morris, P. A., Gennetian, L. A., & Knox, V. (2002). *Welfare policies matter for children and youth*. New York: MDRC Policy Brief.

Morris, P. A., Huston, A. C., Duncan, G. J., Crosby, D. A., & Bos, J. M. (2001). *How welfare and work policies affect children: A synthesis of research*. New York: The Next Generation, Manpower Demonstration Research Corporation.

NICHD Early Child Care Research Network. (1997a). The effects of infant child care on infant-mother attachment security: Results of the NICHD Study of Early Child Care. *Child Development, 68*, 860-879.

NICHD Early Child Care Research Network. (1997b). Familial factors associated with the characteristics of nonmaternal care for infants. *Journal of Marriage and the Family, 59*, 389-408.

NICHD Early Child Care Research Network. (1998a). Early child care and self-control, compliance, and problem behavior at 24 and 36 months. *Child Development, 69*, 1145-1170.

NICHD Early Child Care Research Network. (1998b). Relations between family predictors and child outcomes: Are they weaker for children in child care? *Developmental Psychology, 34*, 1119-1128.

NICHD Early Child Care Research Network. (2002). Structure, process, outcome: Direct and indirect effects of caregiving quality on young children's development. *Psychological Science, 13*, 199-206.

NICHD Early Child Care Research Network. (2003). Does quality of child care affect child outcomes at age 4 1/2? *Developmental Psychology, 39*, 451-469.

Pagani, L., Boulerice, B., & Tremblay, R. E. (1997). The influence of poverty on children's classroom placement and behavior problems. In G. J. Duncan & J. Brooks-Gunn (Eds.), *Consequences of growing up poor* (pp. 311-339). New York: Russell Sage Foundation.

Petterson, S. M., & Albers, A. B. (2001). Effects of poverty and maternal depression on early child development. *Child Development, 72*, 1794-1813.

Proctor, B. D., & Dalaker, J. (2003). *Poverty in the United States: 2002* (No. U.S. Census Bureau, Current Population Reports, P60-222). Washington, DC: U.S. Government Printing Office.

Ramey, S. L., & Ramey, C. T. (1999). Early experience and early intervention for children "at risk" for developmental delay and mental retardation. *Mental Retardation & Developmental Disabilities Research Reviews, 5*, 1-10.

Ross, C. E., & Duff, R. S. (1982). Medical care, living conditions, and children's well-being. *Social Forces, 61*, 456-474.

Royce, J. M., Darlington, R. B., & Murray, H. W. (1983). Pooled analyses: Findings across studies. In Consortium for Longitudinal Studies (Ed.), *As the twig is bent ... lasting effects of preschool programs* (pp. 411-460). Hillsdale, NJ: Erlbaum.

Rutter, M. (1990). Psychosocial resilience and protective mechanisms. In J. Rolf, Masten, A.S., Cicchetti, D., Nuechterlein, K.H., & Weitraub, S. (Ed.), *Risk and protective factors in the development of psychopathology*. New York: Cambridge University Press.

Sameroff, A. J., Seifer, R., Barocas, B., Zax, M., & Greenspan, S. (1987). IQ scores of 4-year old children: Social environmental risk factors. *Pediatrics, 79*, 343-350.

Sampson, R. J., & Laub, J. H. (1994). Urban poverty and the family context of delinquency: A new look at structure and process in a classic study. *Child Development, 65*, 523-540.

Schliecker, E., White, D. R., & Jacobs, E. (1991). The role of day care quality in the prediction of children's vocabulary. *Canadian Journal of Behavioural Science, 23*, 12-24.

Schweinhart, L. J., Barnes, H. V., Weikart, D. P., Barnett, W. S., & Epstein, A. S. (1993). *Significant benefits: The High/Scope Perry Preschool Study through age 27*. Ypsilanti, MI: High/Scope Press.

Shonkoff, J. P., & Phillips, D. A. (Eds.). (2000). *From neurons to neighborhoods: The science of early child development*. Washington, DC: National Academy of Sciences.

Smith, J. R., & Brooks-Gunn, J. (1997). Correlates and consequences of harsh discipline for young children. *Archives of Pediatric and Adolescent Medicine, 151*, 777-786.

Smith, J. R., Brooks-Gunn, J., & Klebanov, P. (1997). Consequences of living in poverty for young children's cognitive and verbal ability and early school achievement. In G. J. Duncan & J. Brooks-Gunn (Eds.), *Consequences of growing up poor* (pp. 132-189). New York: Russell Sage Foundation.

Smith, J. R., Brooks-Gunn, J., Klebanov, P. K., & Lee, K. (2000). Welfare and work: Complementary strategies for low-income women? *Journal of Marriage and the Family, 62*, 808-821.

Smith, J. R., Brooks-Gunn, J., McCarton, C., & Kohen, D. (2001). Transitions on and off AFDC: Implications for parenting and children's cognitive development. *Child Development, 72*, 1512-1533.

St. Pierre, R. G., & Layzer, J. I. (1999). Using home visits for multiple purposes: The Comprehensive Child Development Program. *The Future of Children, 9*, 134-151.

Taylor, B. A., Dearing, E., & McCartney, K. (2004). Incomes and outcomes in early childhood. *Journal of Human Resources, 39*, 980-1007.

Taylor, H. G., Klein, N., Minich, N. M., & Hack, M. (2000). Verbal memory deficits in children with less than 750 g birth weight. *Child Neuropsychology, 6*, 49-63.

Thompson, R. A. (1999). Early attachment and later development. In J. Cassidy & P. Shaver (Eds.), *Handbook of attachment theory and research* (pp. 265-286). New York: Guilford.

U.S. Census Bureau. (1995, Fall). *Who's Minding the Kids? Child Care Arrangements (1995)*. Washington, DC.

U.S. Census Bureau (2004). Age and sex of all people, family members and unrelated individuals iterated by income-to-poverty ratio and race. Retrieved May 9, 2005, From http://pabdb3.census.gov/macro/032004/pov/new01_100_01.htm

United Nations Children's Fund. (1998). *The state of the world's children 1998*. New York: Oxford University Press.

Waldfogel, J., Han, W., & Brooks-Gunn, J. (2002). The effects of early maternal employment on child cognitive development. *Demography, 39*, 369-392.

Wasserman, G. A., Rauh, V. A., Brunelli, S. A., Garcia-Castro, M., & Necos, B. (1990). Psychosocial attributes and life experiences of disadvantaged minority mothers: Age and ethnic variations. *Child Development, 61*, 566-580.

Werner, E. E., & Smith, R. S. (1992). *Overcoming the odds: High risk children from birth to adulthood*. Ithaca, NY: Cornell University Press.

West, J. (1999). *Early Childhood Longitudinal Study, Kindergarten Class 1998-1999: Project summary*. Retrieved March 16, 2004, from http://www.nces.ed.gov/ecls/pdf/ksum.pdf

West, K. K., Hauser, R. M., & Scanlon, T. M. (Eds.). (1998). *Longitudinal surveys of children*. Washington, DC: National Academy Press.

Yeung, W. J., & Hofferth, S. L. (1998). Family adaptations to income and job loss in the U.S. *Journal of Family and Economic Issues, 19*, 255-283.

Yeung, W. J., Linver, M. R., & Brooks-Gunn, J. (2002). How money matters for young children's development: Parental investment and family processes. *Child Development, 73*, 1861-1879.

Yoshikawa, H. (1995). Long-term effects of early childhood programs on social outcomes and delinquency. *The Future of Children, 5*, 51-75.

Yoshikawa, H., Magnuson, K. A., Bos, J. M., & Hsueh, J. (2003). Effects of earnings-supplement policies on adult economic and middle-childhood outcomes differ for the "hardest to employ". *Child Development, 74*, 1500-1521.

· 19 ·

EFFECTIVE PRESCHOOL PROGRAMS FOR

CHILDREN AT RISK OF SCHOOL FAILURE:

A BEST-EVIDENCE SYNTHESIS

Bette Chambers
Success For All Foundation

Alan C. K. Cheung
The Hong Kong Institute of Education

Robert E. Slavin
Johns Hopkins University

The education of young children who are at risk for school failure is at a crossroads. Most reviews of preschool intervention programs demonstrate that, from an economic perspective, preschool is by and large a worthwhile investment (Barnett, 1995). In addition to short-term effects on academic achievement, long-term effects of several programs include fewer arrests, fewer teen pregnancies, and higher employment (Gilliam & Zigler, 2000). Depending on the study, researchers have found that for each dollar spent on preschool somewhere between $4 and $8 is saved in later social service costs to society (Barnett, 1995; Karoly et al., 1998).

Recent research on brain research and cognitive development is reinforcing this evidence that early education is crucial in getting children off to a good start in life (Bowman, Donovan, & Burns, 2001; Magnuson, Meyers, Ruhm, & Waldfogel, 2003). Based in part on this research, local, state, and national policy makers are establishing new early childhood programs, and trying to improve the quality of the ones that exist. Seven states now have universal preschool and 39 states and the District of Columbia provide learning standards for early childhood

programs (National Center for Early Development and Learning, 2003).

The importance of effective early childhood education is growing as expectations rise for the knowledge and skills children should have at kindergarten entry. A Maryland State Department of Education study reached the conclusion that only 34% of children qualifying for free lunch are "fully ready for kindergarten" (Aizenman, 2002). This is resulting in academic programs that are designed for kindergarten and first grade students being "pushed down" to preschool. The challenge is to find effective ways of preparing children for kindergarten that are appropriate for their level of development and that provide them with the language and cognitive skills that form the basis for success in primary school.

There is now little argument about the effectiveness of preschool itself. Many studies have shown short- and long-term impacts of participation in high-quality preschool programs in comparison to no preschool experience (for example, Barnett, Frede, Mosbasher & Mohr, 1987; Berrueta-Clement, Barnett, Schweinhart, Epstein, & Weikart, 1984). Furthermore, there is evidence that center-based preschool programs are more effective and cost-effective than programs that only intervene with the child's family (Bryant & Ramey, 1987; White, Taylor, & Moss, 1992), although combinations of the two approaches can be particularly effective (see Reynolds, 1994; Yoshikawa, 1995). Today, the important question before researchers and policy makers is what *kind* of preschool is most effective for young children? What particular programs have positive outcomes and what elements of these programs contribute to their effectiveness? That is the focus of this review. This review examines the evidence for the effectiveness of various preschool programs for young children who are at risk of school failure because of poverty, both to assist educators and policy makers in deciding the types of programs to implement and to inform researchers about the current evidence on preschool programs and to guide further research.

An underlying assumption of this chapter is that essentially all children can succeed and that their cognitive, linguistic, and social development is mediated by their caregivers' and teachers' abilities to establish warm, nurturing relationships with them and to offer them stimulating experiences. We begin by outlining some of the challenges that inhibit improvements in the experiences that many children in high poverty settings encounter today.

CHALLENGES FOR EARLY CHILDHOOD EDUCATION FOR AT-RISK CHILDREN

The rapid growth of preschool programs and increasing expectations for their impact, run up against a harsh reality. The low status of early childhood education in our society leads to low salaries, which leads to low staff qualifications and high staff turnover, particularly for children who are at risk of school failure because of poverty. The overall teacher shortage, being felt most acutely in high-poverty areas, means that it is difficult to find qualified teachers even in public schools that require certified teachers. Yet educators working with preschool children often have little more than a high school degree or a 2-year Child Development Associate degree, a minimal credential for a job of such complexity and importance. The six-state study of prekindergarten conducted by the National Center for Early Development and Learning (2003) found that more than 30% of the pre-kindergarten teachers did not have bachelor's degrees and of those that did, more than half majored in something other than early childhood education.

Clearly, the long-term solution to the early education crisis is to find ways to increase the qualifications of preschool teachers, to provide incentives for well-prepared teachers to teach in high-poverty settings, and to expand the availability of high-quality preschool programs (Barnett, Tarr, & Frede, 1999). Although some states are moving to improve the qualifications of the early childhood educators in their jurisdictions, most individuals who work with young children in poverty have low levels of education. So serious questions remain: What kinds of programs are most appropriate for young children today? If the primary goal of preschool is to prepare children for success in elementary school (Karoly et al., 1998), then what types

of preschool practices have the highest likelihood of achieving that goal? What programs have had this effect in the past? What are their characteristics? Using quantitative synthesis (Slavin, 1986), this chapter applies consistent, well-justified standards of evidence to shed light on these questions.

EARLY CHILDHOOD CURRICULUM MODELS

Early childhood curriculum models have been categorized along a continuum according to the nature of the teacher's interaction with the children. At one end of scale, there is the academic, direct instruction model, in which the teacher follows a highly scripted program, with clear expectations of how the children should behave, and consistent ways of responding to the children's behavior. The goal of the academic approach focuses on promoting children's cognitive development. Programs that fall under this approach are referred to as direct instruction (Bereiter & Engelmann, 1966), behaviorist (Schweinhart & Weikart, 1997), or rationalist (Bereiter & Engelmann, 1966). The Demonstration and Research Center for Early Education (DARCEE) program an example of a program that falls into this category (Gray, Klaus, Miller & Forrester, 1966).

At the other end of the continuum is the child-centered, maturational, or developmental interaction approach. The goals of this approach are enhancing children's self-esteem, independence, and social development. In the maturational approach children learn mostly through unstructured free-play activities in an environment rich in resources for them to explore with minimal teacher direction. Many traditional nursery schools take a maturational approach to educating preschoolers. The Bank Street approach to early education is another example of a maturational approach (Roopnarine & Johnson, 1999).

Somewhere between these two extremes lies the cognitive-developmental approach, which is characterized by planned activities that are implemented flexibly in response to the needs and interests of the children. The goals of this approach are the promotion of cognitive and social development through planned activities that the teacher and children initiate and work on together. Programs that include literacy activities such as interactive book reading, phonemic awareness, alphabetic instruction, and opportunities for writing, promote children's emergent literacy (Bowman, Donovan, & Burns, 2001; Neumann, Copple, & Bredekamp, 1999; Whitehurst et al., 1994). Early education programs such as, High/Scope (Weikart, 1998) and Dialogic Reading (Whitehurst & Lonigan, 1998), exemplify the cognitive-developmental approach. Even though it is quite structured and involved a careful sequencing of tasks, we have included Montessori in the cognitive-developmental category because of its emphasis on individual instruction and on children's intrinsic control (Roopnarine & Johnson, 1999).

PREVIOUS REVIEWS

As noted earlier previous reviews of preschool interventions have focused on the question of whether or not preschool attendance influences future school success (e.g., Currie, 2000;

Gilliam & Zigler, 2000; Gorey, 2001; Karweit, 1993). Most reviews, such as Gilliam and Zigler's (2000) meta-analysis of evaluations of state-funded preschool programs, have found modest support for widespread implementation of preschool for low-income children. These studies are not reviewed in this chapter, unless there is a clear description of the program that was implemented in the preschool condition. Two previous reviews have summarized comparisons of different types of interventions (Barnett, 1995; White, Taylor, & Moss, 1992).

White, Taylor, and Moss' (1992) meta-analytic review focused on preschool programs for "handicapped, disadvantaged, and at-risk" children. His definition of at-risk children was those who suffered "trauma surrounding birth," so the only studies relevant for this review were those for disadvantaged children. He concluded that early intervention benefited most children, but could not identify which types of interventions were most effective. His findings call into question widely held beliefs in the importance of parent involvement and in the efficacy of beginning interventions as early as possible.

Barnett (1995) reviewed 36 studies of preschool attendance, Head Start, child care, and home visiting programs. He concluded that early childhood interventions have large short-term effects on intelligence measures and sizable effects on school achievement, grade retention, special education placement, and social adjustment. His review notes that the research usually evaluates model demonstration projects that are implemented in ideal situations, (i.e. with well-educated teachers, who receive ample training and follow-up support), and therefore may not be representative of what the program would look like in a typical implementation. In contrast, most evaluations of large-scale public programs provide so little description of the implementations that they are only comparing preschool attendance versus nonattendance, rather than the effectiveness of a type of preschool program.

METHOD

This review uses "best-evidence synthesis" (Slavin, 1986), a quantitative synthesis method that applies systematic, well-justified inclusion criteria and computes effect sizes as do meta-analyses but discusses the findings of the included studies as do narrative reviews. Because the literature on preschool interventions is small and diverse, this method is particularly appropriate. This review attempts to identify unbiased, meaningful information from experimental studies, discusses each of those studies, computes effect sizes, and describes the contexts, designs, and findings of each study.

Literature Search Strategy

We conducted an exhaustive search for all reviews and empirical investigations of center-based preschool programs for disadvantaged children. We searched ERIC/EDRS, Dissertation Abstracts, PsychINFO, Social Science Abstracts, Education Abstracts, and other education-related indexes. We also conducted a manual search of the major education and early childhood journals.

We found numerous studies of early childhood interventions; however, most were of low quality, without an equivalent comparison group. We also conducted a manual search of early childhood journals and dissertations. We computed effect sizes for the studies that met our criteria for inclusion, described later, but also discuss some other notable studies that did not meet those criteria.

Criteria for Inclusion

This chapter focuses on center-based, replicable educational interventions that are designed to enhance young children's cognitive, educational, and social outcomes. To be included in the quantitative synthesis studies had to meet the following demographic, program, and methodological criteria.

1. *Demographic criteria.* Programs for children aged 3–5 years, who were at-risk for school failure due to poverty, were the focus of the review. Studies that were designed specifically to meet the needs of non-English-speaking or children with special needs were not included in this review. If programs began before infancy and continue through preschool, such as the Carolina Abecedarian Study (Campbell & Ramey, 1995), it is impossible to determine the effects of the preschool intervention alone, so these studies are excluded from the quantitative synthesis.

2. *Program criteria.* Educational programs offered in a group setting with the purpose of preparing children to be successful in primary school were included. If the study compared preschool participation to nonparticipation, it was only included in the quantitative synthesis if there was a specific intervention that was clearly described making the study not just one of preschool attendance but of that particular program.

   The group setting could be prekindergarten classes in elementary schools, child care centers, or Head Start centers. Any early childhood setting that offered a regularly scheduled educational program to a group of preschoolers was eligible. The duration of the intervention needed to be at least 12 weeks, with an intensity of exposure of at least 3 hours per week.

   A reader might wonder why there are no studies in the review of such well-known approaches to early childhood education, such as the Project Approach, Reggio Emilia, or the Creative Curriculum. These programs have been excluded only because there were no studies that fit all of the inclusion criteria.

3. *Methodological criteria.* We intended to review only studies that had been conducted in the past decade; however, so few empirical studies investigating the effectiveness of preschool programs have been conducted that we summarize here all of the experimental and quasi-experimental studies from as early as 1960 up to the present. Studies that were published in refereed journals, technical reports, or dissertations, or were unpublished evaluations, were included. The studies compared children taught in a well-defined educational intervention to those taught in a traditional curriculum or

other well-defined interventions. Studies that only compared preschool attendance to nonattendance, without a clear articulation of the preschool program, were not included. For that reason, a number of well-known studies that appear in previous reviews were excluded from this review, such as the study of Irvine's evaluation of the New York State experimental prekindergarten program (1980).

Studies used either random assignment or other matching criteria to establish comparability of the groups. If experimental and control groups were matched on demographic characteristics a pretest had to have been given before (not after) the interventions began to determine equivalence. If there were pretest differences, analyses were conducted to control for these differences. Studies that were pre-post comparisons with no control group were excluded.

Studies measured the dependent variables that most impact school achievement:

- language/literacy, mathematics, social/emotional outcomes;
- educational outcomes such as special education placement, grade retention, and high school graduation;
- long-term social adjustment outcomes such as delinquency, welfare dependence, or employment.

A few notable studies of preschool interventions have been reported numerous times. Sometimes this is due to the longitudinal nature of the studies as with the Consortium for Longitudinal Studies, which followed the subjects from early interventions to determine the long-term impacts (Lazar & Darlington, 1982). For these redundant reports we were careful to code each outcome only once. Brief interventions, designed only to improve a narrow skill such as phonological awareness, were not included.

Limitations of Quantitative Synthesis

It should be noted that a quantitative synthesis is limited by the evidence provided by studies that meet the inclusion criteria. Qualitative studies, case studies, and pre-post studies were excluded from the review. Although some excluded studies include descriptions and other information that would be useful in guiding policy and practice, these studies do not show how much children would have benefited from one program or type of intervention in comparison to another.

It is important to note that most of the research on effective preschool programs was conducted before 1990. Because of the limited recent research on this topic, many of the studies included in this review were conducted in the 1960s and 1970s. The curricular models that were studied at that time have evolved and the current versions of those models may be different than the programs that were implemented in the initial evaluations. Furthermore, standard practices, social conditions, and such factors as access to television and other media have also changed, meaning that control groups today may be different from control groups 30–40 years ago. For these reasons,

it cannot be assumed that these studies would have the same effects today.

Computation of Effect Sizes

We computed an effect size for each comparison of an experimental intervention with a traditional or no-preschool control. Some studies produced more than one effect size. We calculated the effects sizes by dividing the experimental mean minus the control mean by the standard deviation of the control group (Cooper & Hedges, 1994). When some of this information was missing, we estimated effect sizes using pooled standard deviations, exact t or p values, percentages, or other estimation methods (Cooper, 1998). As the standard deviations for IQ measures varied considerably from study to study, we used 16 to calculate the effect sizes for IQ across all studies, as that is the normal standard deviation for the Stanford Binet.

Generally affect sizes above .20 are considered educationally meaningful, and those above .40 are noteworthy. Effect sizes above .70 demonstrate a very strong relationship.

If we could not compute an effect size, we reported the findings, rather than exclude the study. We grouped these studies into those where the comparison was to a no-preschool group and those where children attended a traditional program.

RESULTS

Only 12 studies met our inclusion criteria, five of which compared some form of preschool to no preschool. Overall, children who attended preschool programs performed better on all outcomes than children who did not attend preschool (see Table 19.1). Our analyses only included studies that had a clear description of the preschool program and all of the studies that met our criteria compared participation in a cognitive-developmental program to no preschool attendance. Because there were no studies comparing participation in an academic preschool to other types of programs, it is unclear whether it was the cognitive-developmental approach or just preschool participation that made the difference.

Studies Comparing Preschool to No Preschool

Perry Preschool. The most often cited study of preschool interventions for at-risk children is the initial evaluation and follow-up studies of the Perry Preschool (Berrueta-Clement et al., 1984; Weikart, Bond, & McNeil, 1978). One hundred twenty-three African-American preschoolers with IQs between 50 to 88, from a high-poverty neighborhood in Ypsilanti, Michigan, participated in the study. Note that these children were not only economically disadvantaged but also had quite low IQs, as well. There were five cohorts, starting in 1962 through 1967. The first group started at age 4 with 1 year of preschool experience and the remaining cohorts started at age 3 with 2 years of preschool experience. Children were randomly assigned to the experimental or the control group. They were comparable on their initial IQ, SES, and gender. Children were followed up through age 27 (Schweinhart, Barnes, & Weikart, 1993).

The experimental program was a precursor to High/Scope, a cognitive-developmental curriculum based on Piagetian principles. It was a half-day program with a balance of teacher-initiated and child-selected activities and weekly home visits.

Effects on cognition at the end of prekindergarten were significant, with an effect size of +1.12 but faded over time to +0.04 at seventh grade. Educational effects varied from an effect size of +0.10 for grade retention to +0.37 for high school graduation. Long-term social adjustment outcomes were stronger. For example, the former Perry Preschool students had less dependence on welfare (ES = +0.46) and had fewer arrests (ES = +0.73) and higher employment (ES = +0.55).

Institute for Developmental Studies (IDS). The IDS developed a program of games and activities to build children's language and general cognitive skills and self-esteem. Teachers worked with individual children and small groups. An active parent component had group and individual meetings to help parents fit into the community. The program began in 1961 in public schools in Harlem. Four-year-olds were randomly assigned to the experimental or control condition. Eight cohorts of children were tested, and after the first four years additional control groups were added: a group that began only in kindergarten, a group that began only in first grade, and two control groups who attended Head Start.

There were significantly higher scores for the experimental group on IQ and receptive language scores after the end of preschool (ES = +0.58 and +0.51, respectively) and kindergarten (ES = +0.55 and +0.39). By the end of third grade, the IQ effects had diminished but the PPVT effect was stronger (ES = +0.27 and +0.55) (Deutsch, Deutsch, Jordan, & Grallo, 1983).

High/Scope. In another retrospective study, Barnett et al. (1987) compared High/Scope to no preschool experience for a group of low-income children in South Carolina. Children were matched on a number of factors: gender, ethnicity, parents in home, mother's education, and Developmental Indicators for the Assessment of Learning (DIAL-R) scores. The control group was a more advantaged group than the intervention group, and had higher DIAL-R scores. The original sample sizes for the experimental control groups were 334 and 194, respectively. On follow-up, the initial ability difference between the two groups still existed. The Cognitive Skills Assessment Battery (CSAB; Boehm & Slater, 1981) was used as the main outcome measure. Age, ethnicity, and initial DIAL-R scores were used as covariates. Preschool was found to have a significant effect on CSAB scores with an effect size of +0.30 at the end of kindergarten.

Chicago Child-Parent Centers. Reynolds and his colleagues (Reynolds, 1994, 1995; Reynolds, Temple, Robertson, & Mann, 2001) conducted one of the most comprehensive longitudinal studies of a large-scale early intervention program. They examined the long-term effects of an early childhood intervention on educational achievement and juvenile arrest. Subjects were 1,539 low SES children, mostly African American. The children in the experimental group (*N* = 989) enrolled

in the Chicago Child-Parent Center (CPC) program. The focus of the CPC program was on acquisition of basic skills in language arts and math through relatively structured but diverse learning experiences in relatively small classes (17 children to 2 adults). Continued educational and family-support services were provided to those children who continued schooling in the affiliated schools. A total of 553 children in the experimental group participated through third grade. The children in the comparison group did not have preschool experience but were enrolled in an alternative full-day kindergarten. One hundred sixty-six children in the comparison group received 0–3 years of schoolage extended services after finishing kindergarten. Effects on reading were significantly higher for CPC participants than for controls for every grade from first (ES = +0.51) to sixth (ES = +0.35), except for third grade (ES = + 0.09). After kindergarten there were no statistically significant differences between children who participated in 1 year versus 2 years of preschool (Reynolds, 1995).

The attrition rate for the two groups was similar by age 20 years. Among the age 20 follow-up sample, the experimental and control groups were similar in a number of demographic and familial characteristics, but there were a few differences. First, children in the experimental group had a higher percentage of parents who had completed high schools. Several covariates were used to adjust for initial group differences. Compared to the control group, the experimental group had significantly higher rates of high school completion (ES = +0.28) and lower rates of grade retention (ES = +.23), juvenile arrest (ES = +0.20).

Preschool Program Comparisons

Eight studies compared an experimental program to a traditional program and/or other another experimental program (see Table 19.2). On short-term cognitive outcomes such as IQ and language achievement, the academic programs produced better outcomes than the cognitive-developmental programs. However, on educational outcomes, such as grade retention and special education placement, effect sizes for the cognitive-development programs were generally higher than for academic programs. For long-term social outcomes such as, lower arrest rates and higher employment, cognitive-developmental programs also performed better than academic programs. The specific studies and their findings are described below.

Studies With Random Assignment

High/Scope curriculum comparison project. In 1967, Weikart (1998) followed up the Perry Preschool study with a comparison of High/Scope, Direct Instruction, and a traditional nursery school. Sixty-eight high poverty 3- and 4-year-olds participated in half-day classes conducted each weekday morning. Teachers made a weekly home visit to each mother and child for an hour and a half. At the end of preschool, the Direct Instruction group significantly outperformed the nursery group on IQ (ES = +0.66). However, the IQ difference among the groups diminished over time. On follow-up, the High/Scope and

TABLE 19.1. Studies Comparing Preschools and No Preschools

Studies Using Random Assignment

Author	Intervention Description	Design	Treatment Duration	Study Duration	N	Subjects Characteristics	Evidence of Initial Equality	Outcome Measure and Effect Sizes
Berrueta-Clement et al. (1984)	Perry Preschool vs. no preschool	Random assignment with pretest	1 to 2 yr PreK	23 years PreK-Age 27	5 Waves W0 = 28 W1 = 17 W2 = 26 W3 = 27 W4 = 25 N = 123	Low SES African-American preschoolers in Ypsilanti, MI	Well matched on pretest IQ and social background characteristics	**Grade / IQ / PPVT:** End of PreK +0.71* +1.20*; Kindergarten +0.31* +0.35*; 1st grade +0.29* +0.26; 2nd grade +0.08 +0.10; 3rd grade +0.06 +0.09; 4th grade +0.03; 8th grade +0.04. **Education / ES:** Yrs in Special Ed +0.29*; Grade Retention +0.10; High School Grad +0.37*. **Social Adjustment / ES:** Had fewer arrests +0.73*; Earned $2,000+ +0.60*; Owned a home +0.55*; Welfare as an adult +0.46*; Delinquency +0.41*; Employment +0.55*
Deutsche et al. (1983)	Institute of Developmental Studies vs. no preschool	Random assignment	5 yrs	5 yrs PreK-3rd grade	n = 400 (Exp and self selected control only)	Low SES students in Harlem, NY	Well matched on parental motivation and desire for the child to participate in an enrichment program	**Grade / IQ / PPVT:** End of Pre-K +0.45* +0.51*; Kindergarten +0.45* +0.39*; 3rd grade +0.24 +0.55*

Studies with Matching

Author	Intervention Description	Design	Treatment Duration	Study Duration	N	Subjects Characteristics	Evidence of Initial Equality	Outcome Measure and Effect Sizes
Barnett et al. (1987)	High/Scope vs. no preschool	Matched control	1 yr PreK	2 yrs PreK-K	n = 389	4-year-old children in 11 schools in South Carolina	Poorly matched on two parents in home, mother's education, and initial DIAL-R scores, C > E	**Cognitive skills Assessment Battery (CSAB) — Grade:** Kindergarten +0.30**. **The effect varied greatly across schools with ES ranging from +1.28 to −0.35

Studies with Matching

Author	Intervention Description	Design	Treatment Duration	Study Duration	N	Subjects Characteristics	Evidence of Initial Equality	Outcome Measure and Effect Sizes
Englemann (1968)	Direct Instruction = DI Head Start = He/St	Matched control	2 yrs PreK & K	2 yrs PreK-K	n = 43	Four-year-old culturally disadvantaged children who were eligible for Head Start	Well matched on initial IQ test scores, SES, and ethnicity	**IQ / DI / ES / He/St:** End of PreK 112.47 +0.66* 102.57; End of K 121.08 +1.34* 99.61
Evans (1985)	Direct Instruction = DI Headstart = He/St	Retrospective Study	1 to 2 yrs PreK	9 yrs PreK-9th grade	n = 64	Subjects were low-income, minority (mostly black) students in urban school districts	Similar preschool WPPSI mean scores between the two surviving groups (DI and HS)	**MAT Reading / DI / ES / He/St / Control:** 6th grade 56.38 ns 47.14 52.28; 8th grade 32.95 ns 29.42 33.52; Competency test I 44.43 ns 45.72 42.80; Competency test II 38.66 ns 38.90 35.78; School sentiment 15.74 ns 15.58 18.50. Insufficient data to compute ES

Chambers et al. (2001) — Curiosity Corner vs. regular preschool — Matched control — Pre-K / 1 yr PreK — $n = 316$ — Three- and 4-year-old children enrolled in child care centers and preschools in four high poverty urban school districts in New Jersey — Matched on demographics. Pretest scores were used as covariates to adjust for initial differences

Measures	ES
Expressive Lang	+0.24
Receptive Lang	+0.06
Visual Reception	−0.06

Whitehurst et al. (1999) — Dialogic Reading vs. regular Head Start — Matched control (classrooms were randomly assigned, not children) — 1 yr PreK / 4 yrs PreK–3rd grade — $n = 280$ — Children with low SES in various Head Start centers in Suffolk County, New York — Ex post facto matching procedure. Pretest scores were used as covariates to adjust for initial differences

Grade	Lang
End of PreK	+0.10
Kindergarten	+0.15

Grade	Word Reading	Word Attack
1st grade	ns	ns
2nd grade	ns	ns

Insufficient data to compute ES

Karnes et al. (1983) — Direct Instruction = DI; DI Ameliorative = Am; Montessori = Mont; Mont Community Integrated = CI; Traditional = Trad — Random assignment — 1 yr PreK / 17 yrs PreK–post high school — $n = 123$ — Low-income children from Champaign/Urbana Illinois — Random assignment with similar family characteristics

IQ/Language	DI	Am	Mont	CI
Short-term IQ	In favor of DI & Am			
Long-term IQ	no difference			
Short-term lang	In favor of DI & Am			
Long-term lang	no difference			

Education	DI	Am	Mont	CI
Special Education	−0.20	+0.04	−0.18	−0.18
Grade Retention	+0.09	+0.16	+0.42	−0.13
High School Grade	−0.45	−0.17	+0.11	−0.55
School Success	−0.34	−0.18	+0.37	−0.42

Miller & Dyer (1975) and Miller & Bizzel (1984) — Direct Instruction = DI; DARCEE = Dar; Montessori = Mont; Traditional = Trad — Random assignment — 1 yr PreK / 12 yrs PreK–10th grade — BE = 64, Dar = 64, Mon = 83, Trad = 53, N = 214 — African American students with low SES in Louisville, KY — Random assignment

IQ	DI	Dar	Mont
End of PreK	+0.11	−0.11	−0.09
Kindergarten	−0.02	−0.11	−0.11
1st grade	−0.13	0.00	+0.02
2nd grade	−0.26	−0.09	+0.11
7th grade	−0.16	−0.05	+0.11
8th grade	0.00	−0.08	+0.14
10th grade	−0.13	−0.14	−0.01

Reading	DI	Dat	Mont
7th grade	−0.05	−0.41	−0.03
8th grade	+0.28	+0.17	+0.56

Van de Riet & Resnick (1973) and Sprigle & Schaefer (1985) — Learning to learn = LTL; LTL Head Start = He/St — Random Assignment — 2 to 3 yrs (PreK to 1st) and 3 yrs 4th–6th grade / 5 yrs PreK–3rd grade — $n = 90$ — 4- and 5-year-old black children from the same neighborhood — Random assignment with similar IQ pretests

Grade	IQ	Achievement	Creativity
Kindergarten	++	++	++
1st grade	++	++	++
2nd grade	++	++	++
3rd grade	++	++	++

Grade	Reading
4th grade	+0.61*
5th grade	+0.83*
6th grade	+0.51

School	LTL	ES	HS
Special Education	4.50%	+0.57*	23.0%
Grade Retention	0.0%	+0.62*	15.3%

TABLE 19.2. Studies Comparing Alternative Preschool Programs

Author	Intervention Categories	Design	Treatment Duration	Study Duration	N	Subjects Characteristics	Evidence of Initial Equality
Schweinhart & Weikart (1997)	Direct Instruction = DI DI High/Scope = Hi/Sc Traditional = Trad	Paired random assignment	1–2 yrs PreK	20 yrs PreK-Age 23	n = 68	3- and 4-year-old children (Black 65% and White 35%) living in Ypsilanti, MI	Random assignment. Well matched on SES, pretest IQ and most family characteristics
Reynolds et al. (1992 & 1995)	CPC vs. no preschool	Matched control	1 to 2 yrs PreK	PreK-Age 20	N = 1539	Four-year-old culturally disadvantaged children who were eligible for Head Start	Well matched on demographics and family background except SES and parents completed high school, C > E. ANCOVA was used.

Outcome Measure and Effect Sizes

Studies Using Random Assignment

Schweinhart & Weikart (1997)

	DI	ES	Hi/Sc	ES	Trad
IQ					
End of PreK	103.20	+0.66*	96.50	+0.24	92.70
K	98.10	+0.37	94.90	+0.17	92.20
1st grade	96.70	+0.07	93.70	-0.12	95.60
4th grade	97.40	+0.36	96.20	+0.29	91.50
CAT					
1st grade	99.60	-0.15	102.10	-0.09	105.90
2nd grade	160.00	+0.15	167.00	+0.33	154.30
4th grade	133.60	-0.39	121.70	-0.58	158.20
Literacy					
Age 15	16.90	-0.28	18.70	+0.05	18.40
Age 23	23.20	-0.27	23.60	-0.21	25.10
Education					
Yrs in Special Ed	1.9	-0.07	2.1	-0.15	1.7
Grade Retention	20%	-0.03	40%	-0.47	19%
High School Grad	58%	-0.27	71%	-0.16	78%
Social Adjustment					
Ever employed during last five years	100%	+0.49	100%	+0.49	94%
Months on welfare in the last 10 yrs	13.3	+0.01	9.3	+0.15	13.7 (29.6)
Monthly income $1001 to $3500	21%	-0.42	56%	+0.32	40%
Lifetime arrests	65%	-0.53*	46%	-0.14	39%
Juvenile arrests	22%	-0.57	9%	+0.20	4%

Reynolds et al. (1992 & 1995)

Grade	Reading	Cognitive Readiness
Kindergarten	—	+0.77*
Grade 1	+0.51*	
Grade 2	+0.35*	
Grade 3	+0.09	
Grade 4	+0.24*	
Grade 5	+0.31*	
Grade 6	+0.36*	

Education	ES
Special Ed	+0.23*
Grade Retention	+0.23*
High School Grad	+0.28*

Social Adjustment	ES
lower juvenile arrest	+0.20*
less violent arrest	+0.19*

nursery groups had a higher high school grade point average than the Direct Instruction group, fewer years in special education, and fewer failed grades. In addition, students who attended High/Scope and nursery programs were more likely to have attended college or vocational training. High/Scope and nursery attendance also had an effect on delinquency, and employment. A higher percentage of High/Scope and nursery participants were employed than the Direct Instruction group (Schweinhart & Weikart, 1997).

Two studies by Karnes, Shwedel, and Williams (1983) and Miller and Dyer (1975) compared multiple programs, representing different curricular approaches. In each case, we computed effect sizes for each experimental group compared to the traditional condition.

Ameliorative Approach. Karnes and her colleagues (1983) compared five different programs: the Direct Instruction (Bereiter & Engelmann, 1966); Montessori; a community integrated program, with a few low-income children integrated into middle-class preschools; a traditional preschool; and the Ameliorative Approach, designed by Karnes. The Ameliorative Approach (later known as GOAL for Games-Oriented Activities for Learning) was a cognitive-developmental program designed to promote language and general cognitive development and enhance school-related motivation, and social, emotional, and motor development. It included structured and unstructured periods that encompassed language, math, science, social studies, art, and music activities.

The short-term cognitive and language results favored the Ameliorative Approach and Direct Instruction but these faded with time. Long-term educational outcomes favored the Montessori program, particularly lower retention rates (ES = +0.42).

The study findings are confounded by unequal duration of treatments. There were two cohorts. Only the 1965 cohort had a traditional condition and only the 1966 cohort had the community-integrated program. The Direct Instruction Program continued through kindergarten and the Ameliorative Approach received an hour daily of additional training in kindergarten. These duration differences make the comparisons difficult to interpret.

The Louisville experiment. Miller and Dyer (1975) compared four different programs: two academic programs (Direct Instruction and DARCEE [Gray, Klaus, Miller & Forrester, 1966]), one cognitive-developmental (Montessori), and one maturational (Traditional). In 1968, 214 4-year-old children were randomly assigned to the four programs in Head Start classes in Louisville. There was a no-preschool control group that was excluded from our analyses because it was a nonequivalent, more advantaged group of children. The DARCEE program was didactic in nature like Direct Instruction but it focused more on association, classification, and sequencing, along with the development of aptitudes such as achievement motivation, task persistence, and delay of gratification. Children attended classes daily from September 1968 to June 1969. About one quarter of the children attended a token economy Follow Through kindergarten program.

The children were tested each spring through second grade on measures of IQ, achievement, curiosity, persistence, inventiveness, and classroom behavior. They were followed up in 7th to 12th grade as part of the Consortium for Longitudinal Studies project. Generally immediate small positive effects for Direct Instruction on cognitive skills faded, whereas the positive effects for Montessori increased over time, particularly for boys (Miller & Bizzell, 1984).

Learning to Learn. Sprigle and Schaefer (1985) followed up on a randomized evaluation of Learning to Learn, a cognitive-developmental program, which compared it to a standard Head Start program (Van de Riet & Resnick, 1973). Ninety 4- and 5-year-old African-American children participated in either 3 years of compensatory education from preschool to first grade, or 2 years from kindergarten to first grade.

Statistically significant short-term effects for intelligence, achievement and creativity favored the Learning to Learn participants. In the follow-up study for Grades 4 through 6, in fourth and fifth grade the Learning to Learn participants scored significantly higher in reading (ES = +0.61 and 0.83), and sixth grade differences were positive but not statistically significant (ES = +0.51). The most striking differences were for special education placement and grade retention (ES = +0.57 and ES = +0.62, respectively). However, these effects were not influenced by the number of years of participation in the program. Children who started the program in kindergarten achieved at the same level as those who began in preschool, calling into question the importance of starting earlier.

Studies With Matching

Direct Instruction: Engelmann. A small matched study involving both disadvantaged and middle class students was conducted by Engelmann (1968) to examine the effectiveness of direct instruction on IQ and achievement in reading and arithmetic. Students were well matched on initial IQ, gender, ethnicity, and SES. The fifteen disadvantaged children in the experimental group attended three 20-minute sessions daily—a language concept class, an arithmetic class, and a reading class, for 2 years beginning at age 4. The main focus of the experimental program was basic academic concepts. In contrast, 28 disadvantaged children in the control group attended a regular preschool program, which emphasized play and traditional nursery school activities. In addition to the disadvantaged children, a comparison group of 18 middle-class children attending a Montessori school were added to the study to demonstrate the differential effects of the experimental program, which we excluded because there were no pretests to determine equivalency.

Children were administered a Stanford Binet IQ test after the first and second year of instruction. At the end of prekindergarten, the experimental group outperformed the control group on the IQ test (112.25 vs 102.57) with an effect size of +0.66. At the end of second year, the experimental group again outscored the control group (121.08 vs 99.61) with an effect size of +1.34.

Direct Instruction: Evans. In a retrospective study, Evans (1985) examined 44 high school students from an original sample of 92 participants who had previously participated in two different preschool programs. Twenty-seven students attended at least 1 year of Direct Instruction (DI) and 17 students received a traditional Head Start for 1 year before kindergarten. In addition, 20 students who had no preschool experience were added to the study for comparison. The control group was matched with the two preschool groups on age, sex, grade, school, free lunch, and ethnic minority status. Subjects were mostly African American and from low-income families in an urban school district. The attrition rate was higher for the Head Start group. By 8th grade, 17 out of the 47 participants in the Head Start group remained in the follow-up study compared to 27 out of 45 in the DI group. To ensure the comparability of the two preschool groups, preschool Wechsler Preschool and Primary Scale of Intelligence (WPPSI) mean scores between the two survival groups were compared. The scores suggested that there was no significant difference among the three groups. The MAT achievement tests in 6th and 8th grade and the high school competency tests were used to measure the performance of the participants in this follow-up study. Overall, no significant differences among the three groups were found in any of these measures. One interesting finding was that males without a history of preschool scored lowest on most of these measures.

Curiosity Corner. Curiosity Corner is a cognitive-developmental program with an integrated thematic curriculum that includes an emphasis on language development, readiness, self-concept, and parent involvement. There is a balance of teacher-directed, whole and small group activities, and child-selected activities. Chambers, Chamberlain, Hurley, and Slavin (2001) evaluated this program in high-poverty communities in New Jersey. Two age groups participated in the study. The first group was 169 3-year-old children enrolled in privately run early childhood centers and the second group was 147 4-year-old children attending publicly run preschool classrooms. Each group was compared to a comparison group matched on demographic characteristics. The majority of the children were African American. PPVT pretests were given to establish a baseline. At the end of the school year, the children were tested on three language subtests of Mullen Scales of Early Learning (MSEL). Children in the 3-year-old Curiosity Corner classes scored significantly higher on expressive language than their counterparts in the control group. The combined 3- and 4-year-old effects size was +0.24. No significant differences were found on children's receptive language or visual reception, and no differences were found among the 4 year olds.

Dialogic Reading. Whitehurst and his colleagues (Whitehurst et al., 1999; Whitehurst & Lonigan, 1998) developed an emergent literacy intervention program (Dialogic Reading) and compared it to a regular Head Start program. Dialogic Reading is an interactive story-reading program designed to enhance children's oral language and listening comprehension abilities. Subjects were 280 preschoolers in two cohorts in Suffolk County, New York. The first cohort of 127 children attended Head Start during the 1992–1993 school year. The second cohort of 153

children started during the 1993–1994 school year. Classes were randomly assigned to experimental and control groups. PPVT and DSC (memory, auditory segmenting, print concepts, and writing) pretests were administered at the beginning of Head Start and were used as covariates in the final analysis. Posttests were given at the end of Head Start, kindergarten, first, and second grade. At the end of Head Start (age 4), the experimental group scored significantly higher than the control group on three of the five measures, with an average effect size of +0.13. At the end of kindergarten, the intervention group scored significantly higher than the control on four of the five measures, with an effect size of +0.13. The intervention group scored significantly higher than the control group on a language measure with an effect size of +0.15. However, in first and second grade, no differences were found between the experimental and the control group in both Word Reading and Word Attack tests.

DISCUSSION

The findings of this quantitative synthesis support previous narrative reviews of the literature on preschool programs for low-income children. Overall, academic programs and cognitive-developmental programs were superior to traditional programs and to control groups of children who did not attend preschool.

When compared to traditional programs, academic programs generally produced better outcomes than cognitive-developmental programs on immediate and short-term cognitive outcomes. However, cognitive-developmental programs produced better outcomes than academic programs on short-term educational and long-term social adjustment outcomes.

Aspects of each of these approaches have benefits that can inform the creation of a comprehensive preschool program. Academic approaches generally have clearly defined specific objectives. It is easier for teachers to monitor the progress of children if they have a clear idea of what they are working toward. They then provide carefully planned experiences designed to move children toward success on cognitive performance and this gives a significant advantage as they enter kindergarten and first grade. At the same time, the cognitive-developmental approach emphasizes the importance of giving children choice and fostering their self-esteem, scaffolding children's development by providing the foundational knowledge in an interactive, constructivist way.

Although the curriculum is one important factor that differentiates early childhood programs, another factor that also differentiates programs is the level of intensity of the program, the degree of support that the teachers are provided in implementing the curriculum. Teachers may receive very little support, perhaps just a teacher's manual with suggested activities; or at the other extreme they may receive a teacher's manual, extensive initial training, follow-up coaching, and many high-quality materials. To create replicable programs that teachers with a broad range of education, experience, and resources can implement effectively, more comprehensive programs are likely necessary. Initial training and a teacher's manual alone are not likely to be enough to help teachers prepare at-risk children for school, especially in areas where the preparation of preschool teachers is very limited.

The curricular approach can be an important factor in determining program effectiveness, particularly in small, well-controlled studies in which each model is likely to be implemented as designed. In larger scale investigations of different curricula, however, what actually gets implemented in the classroom can vary widely. Therefore, as research expands beyond small scale, closely controlled studies to more naturalistic implementations with the variability that is likely in actual implementations, it is important for researchers to observe and describe what actually happens in the both treatment and comparison conditions. This fidelity of implementation data might help explain the difference, or lack thereof, in some studies. Many of the studies that were reviewed for this chapter lacked sufficient description of both conditions, particularly the comparison condition.

Limitations of This Review

It has been close to 30 years since the seminal studies of preschool interventions, such as the Perry Preschool study. It is surprising that since then there have been so few studies of alternate preschool approaches. In 1982, in the conclusion of the report of the Consortium for Longitudinal Studies, Craig Ramey called for an expansion of research on the "educational format, timing, and intensity" of preschool interventions. However, although much has been written about preschool interventions, we found very few recent rigorous studies that could be included in this review. Of the 12 studies that met our inclusion criteria, only 2 (Whitehurst et al., 1999; Chambers et al., 2001) had been conducted since 1990. With only 12 studies, each studying different types of programs over different durations on different outcomes, it is impossible to come to definitive conclusions.

Another limitation is the lack of clear description of the traditional condition in many of the studies. Readers should interpret our results that compared the experimental programs to traditional programs with caution. There was likely considerable variation in what actually took place in the traditional classes. Researchers are encouraged to observe and describe clearly the actual intervention that the children in all conditions in their studies experience.

Some of the programs were continued into elementary school in one form or another. For example, the IDS program (Deutsch et al., 1983) provided enrichment to students through the third grade and the Chicago Child-Parent Centers (Reynolds et al., 2001) continued support for some students up to sixth grade. This made delineating the unique effects for preschool intervention problematic.

Finally, the studies from the 1960s to 1980s may or may not reflect the findings that would be found today. In particular, control groups today are certainly different from those of 20–30 years ago. For example, children from disadvantaged backgrounds today who do not attend preschool are nevertheless more likely to receive experiences (such as child care) that resemble preschool. Children today watch much more television and have access to computers, which could impact cognitive, language and social development.

Implications for Policy and Practice

Longitudinal research on the effects of high quality preschool experiences on the achievement and long-term social adjustment of at-risk children clearly justifies the expansion of such programs. But the evidence on which kinds of programs are most likely to have positive impacts is too limited for confident conclusions. Academically oriented programs produce academically related outcomes, whereas cognitive-developmental programs have their impacts primarily on language and social adjustment.

An implication of these findings is that preschool programs should have a balanced focus both on academic preparation and on broader cognitive and social activities. Although in the past kindergartens mostly focused on children's social and emotional development, they now regularly teach reading (Xue & Meisels, 2004). Preschools need to help prepare children for kindergarten by providing a solid foundation in alphabet knowledge, phonemic awareness, oral language skills, extensive background knowledge, in addition to self-care and social skills (such as taking turns and cooperating with others). Yet long-term studies caution that a sole focus on academics may not be optimal in the long run. There is no reason that exploratory, cognitively challenging activities cannot be combined with academic preparation to give young children the best preparation possible for success in school and in life.

Future Research

The National Research Council's (2000) From Neurons to Neighborhoods suggests that programs that combine child-focused educational activities with explicit attention to parent-child interaction patterns and relationship building have the greatest impact. This report calls for research to address the question of how different types of interventions influence specific outcomes for particular children.

Summarizing effects across studies proved challenging because the studies measured different outcomes. With few effects for each variable, it was impossible to calculate an average effect size for different types of programs. If future studies collect outcome measures that are comparable it would facilitate the study of various program designs (Karoly et al., 1998).

An inherent problem in evaluation of preschool programs is that the impact of these programs may not be obvious until several years after preschool, and short-term impacts can be deceptive. For example, a preschool program could focus on literacy and children would perform better on literacy measures on kindergarten entry. But if they merely learned the literacy skills they would have learned in kindergarten or first grade, then did the early instruction give them a valuable leg up or did it just move forward a process that would have worked just as well starting later? The same could be true of a program that focused on vocabulary or on a narrow subset of cognitive skills. This means that longitudinal studies are essential in this area; however, these are difficult and expensive to carry out.

Although it is clear that compensatory education has both short- and long-term benefits, the optimal length of participation in compensatory education is still unclear (Barnett, 1995). Some programs begin intervention at birth, or before, some at preschool, and others do not start until kindergarten. Sprigle and Schaefer (1985) found that participating for 2 years beginning in kindergarten had the same impact as 3 years beginning in preschool. Although it would seem evident that participating in both preschool and primary-grade interventions would be more effective than participating in either preschool or primary-grade interventions alone, White (1985) found that preschool participation alone was more effective than an elementary intervention and that a combined intervention added little. Clearly there is a need for research that will determine the impact of various preschool programs, with and without follow-up into primary school.

There is a tremendous need for systematic, large-scale, longitudinal, randomized evaluations of the effectiveness of preschool interventions in bringing children from high-risk environments to normative levels of academic achievement. This research could have implications for whole school reform and the coordination of preschool and primary education services for children from high poverty communities. Our children deserve to begin school with the possibility of reaching their potential.

ACKNOWLEDGEMENT

This paper was written under funding from the Institute of Education Sciences, U.S. Department of Education (Grant No. OERI-R-117-4000). However, any opinions expressed do not necessarily reflect IES positions or policies.

We would like to thank Dana Andrews for assistance with the literature search.

References

Aizenman, N. C. (2002, February 27). Many kindergartners unready, report says: Increasing rigors require more skills. *The Washington Post*, p. B1.

Barnett, W. S. (1995). Long-term outcomes of early childhood programs: Analysis and recommendations. *The Future of Children, 5*, 6–24.

Barnett, W. S., Tarr, J. E., & Frede, E. C. (1999). *Children's educational needs and community capacity in the Abbott Districts*. New Brunswick, NJ: Center for Early Education Research, Rutgers University.

Barnett, W. S., Frede, E. C., Mosbasher, H., & Mohr, P. (1987). The efficacy of public preschool programs and their relationship of program quality to efficacy. *Educational Evaluation and Policy Analysis, 10*(1), 37–49.

Bereiter, C., & Engelmann, S. (1966). Teaching disadvantaged children in preschool. Englewood Cliffs, NJ: Prentice Hall.

Berrueta-Clement, J., Barnett, W., Schweinhart, L., Epstein, A., & Weikart, D. (1984). *Changed lives: The effects of the Perry Preschool Program on youths through age 19* (Monograph of the High/Scope Educational Research Foundation No. 8). Ypsilanti, MI: High/Scope Press.

Boehm, A. E., & Slater, B. R. (1981). *Cognitive Skills Assessment Battery*. New York: Teachers College Press.

Bowman, B. T., Donovan, M .S., & Burns, M. (Eds.). (2001). *Eager to learn: Educating our preschoolers*. Washington, DC: National Research Council.

Bryant, D. M., & Ramey, C. T. (1987). An analysis of the effectiveness of early intervention programs for environmentally at-risk children. In M. J. Guralnick & F. C. Bennett (Eds.), *The effectiveness of early intervention for at-risk and handicapped children* (pp 33–78). Chapel Hill, NC: Academic Press.

Campbell, F. A., & Ramey, C. T. (1995). Cognitive and school outcomes for high-risk African American students at middle adolescence: Positive effects of early intervention. *American Education Research Journal, 32*, 743–772.

Chambers, B., Chamberlain, A., Hurley, E., & Slavin, R. (2001, April). *Curiosity Corner: Enhancing preschoolers' language through comprehensive reform*. Paper presented at the annual meeting of the American Educational Research Association, Seattle, WA.

Cooper, H. M. (1998). *Synthesizing research (3rd ed.)*. Thousand Oaks, CA: Sage.

Cooper, H. M., & Hedges, L. V. (Eds.) (1994). *The handbook of research synthesis*. New York: Russell Sage Foundation.

Currie, J. (2000). *Early childhood intervention programs: What do we know?* Chicago: Joint Center for Poverty Research.

Deutsch, M., Deutsch, C. P., Jordan, T. J., & Grallo, R. (1983). The IDS Program: An experiment in early and sustained enrichment. In The Consortium for Longitudinal Studies, *As the twig is bent... lasting effects of preschool programs* (pp. 377–410). Hillsdale, NJ: Lawrence Erlbaum.

Engelmann, S. (1968). The Effectiveness of Direct Instruction on IQ Performance and Achievement in Reading and Arithmetic. In J. Hellmuth (Ed.), *Disadvantaged Child* (Vol. 3). (pp. 461–483). New York: Brunner/Mazel.

Evans, E. D. (1985). Longitudinal follow-up assessment of differential preschool experience for low-income minority group children. *Journal of Educational Research, 78*, 197–202.

Gilliam, W. S., & Zigler, E. F. (2000). A critical meta-analysis of all evaluations of state funded preschool from 1977 to 1998: Implications for policy, service delivery and program evaluations. *Early Childhood Research Quarterly, 15*, 441–473.

Gorey, K. M. (2001). Early childhood education: A meta-analytic affirmation of the short- and long-term benefits of educational opportunity. *School Psychology Quarterly, 16*, 9–30.

Gray, S. W., Klaus, R. A., Miller, J. O., & Forrester, B. J. (1966). *Before first grade*. New York: Teachers College Press.

Irvine, D. J. (1980). Evaluation of the New York State experimental prekindergarten program. Albany: New York State Education Department. (ERIC Document Reproduction Service No. ED 217 980)

Karnes, M. B., Shwedel, A. M., & Williams M. B. (1983). A comparison of five approaches for educating young children from low-income homes. In The Consortium for Longitudinal Studies, *As the twig is bent... lasting effects of preschool programs* (pp. 133–170). Hillsdale, NJ: Lawrence Erlbaum.

Karoly L. A., Greenwood, P. W., Everingham, S. S., Hoube, J., Kilburn, M. R., & Rydell, C. P. (1998). *Investing in our children: What we know and don't know about the costs and benefits of early childhood interventions*. Santa Monica, CA: RAND.

Karweit, N. (1993). Effective preschool and kindergarten programs for students at risk. In B. Spodek (Ed.), *Handbook of Research on the Education of Young Children* (pp. 385–411). New York: Macmillan Publishing Company.

Magnuson, K., Meyers, M., Ruhm, C., & Waldfogel, J. (2003). *Inequality in preschool education and school readiness*. New York: Columbia University.

Lazar, I., & Darlington, R. (1982). Lasting effects of early education: A report from the Consortium for Longitudinal Studies. *Monographs of the Society for Research in Child Development, 47*(2–3), Serial No. 195. Chicago: University Chicago Press.

Miller, L. B., & Bizzell, R. P. (1984). Long-term effects of four preschool programs: Ninth- and tenth-grade results. *Child Development, 55*, 1570–1587.

Miller, L. B., Dyer, J. L. (1975). Four preschool programs: Their dimensions and effects, *Monographs of the Society for Research in Child Development, 40*(5–6, Serial No. 162).

National Center for Early Development and Learning (2003). *Multi-state study of prekindergarten*. Chapel Hill: The University of North Carolina, FPG Child Development Institute, NCEDL.

National Research Council and Institute of Medicine (2000). *From neurons to neighborhoods: The science of early childhood development*. Washington, DC: National Academy Press.

Neuman, S. B., Copple, C., & Bredekamp, S. (1999). *Learning to read and write: Developmentally appropriate practices for young children*. Washington, DC: National Association for the Education of Young Children.

Ramey, C. T., & Ramsey, S. L. (1998). Early intervention and early experience. *American Psychologist, 53*(2), 109–120.

Reynolds, A. J. (1995). One year of preschool intervention or two: Does it matter? *Early Childhood Research Quarterly, 10*, 1–31.

Reynolds, A. J. (1994). Effects of a preschool plus follow-on intervention for children at risk, *Developmental Psychology, 30*(6), 787–804.

Reynolds, A. J., Temple, J. A., Robertson, D. L., & Mann, E. A. (2001). Long-term effects of an early childhood intervention on educational achievement and juvenile arrest: A 15-year follow-up of low-income children in public schools. *Journal of the American Medical Association, 285*(18), 2339–2346.

Rogoff, B. (1990). *Apprenticeship in thinking: Cognitive development in social context*. New York: Oxford University Press.

Roopnarine, J. L., & Johnson, J. E. (1999). *Approaches to Early Childhood Education*. Merrill.

Schweinhart, L. J., Barnes, H. V., & Weikart, D. P. with Barnett, W. S., & Epstein, A. S. (1993). *Significant benefits: The High/Scope Perry Preschool study through age 27* (Monographs of the High/Scope Educational Research Foundation No. 10). Ypsilanti, MI: High/Scope Press.

Schweinhart, L. J., & Weikart, D. P. (1997). *Lasting differences: The High/Scope Preschool curriculum comparison study through age 23* (Monographs of the High/Scope Educational Research Foundation No. 12) Ypsilanti, MI: High/Scope Press.

Slavin, R. E. (1986). Best-evidence synthesis: An alternative to meta-analytic and traditional reviews. *Educational Researcher, 15*(9), 5–11.

Sprigle, J. E., & Schaefer, L. (1985). Longitudinal evaluation of the effects of two compensatory preschool programs on fourth- through sixth-grade students. *Developmental Psychology, 21*(4), 702–708.

Van de Riet, V., Resnick, M. B. (1973). Learning to learn: An effective model for early childhood education. Gainesville: University of Florida.

Weikart, D. P. (1998). Changing early childhood development through educational intervention. *Preventive Medicine, 27*, 233–237.

Weikart, D. P., Bond, J. T., & McNeil, R. (1978). *The Ypsilanti Perry Preschool Project preschool years and longitudinal results through fourth grade* (Monographs of the High/Scope Educational Research Foundation No. 3). Ypsilanti, MI: High/Scope Press.

White, K. R., & Casto, G. (1985). Efficacy of early intervention. *Journal of Special Education, 19*(4) 401–416.

White, K. R., Taylor, M. J., & Moss, V. D. (1992). Does research support claims about the benefits of involving parents in early intervention programs? *Review of Educational Research, 62*, 91–125.

Whitehurst, G. J., Epstein, J. N., Angell, A. C., Payne, A. C., Crone, D. A., & Fischel, J. E. (1994). Outcomes of an emergent literacy intervention in Head Start. *Journal of Educational Psychology, 86*, 542–555.

Whitehurst, G. J., & Lonigan, C. J. (1998). Child development and emergent literacy. *Child Development, 68*, 848–872.

Whitehurst, G. J., Zevenbergen, A. A., Crone, D. A., Schultz, M. D., Velting, O. N., & Fischel, J. E. (1999). Outcomes of an emergent literacy intervention from Head Start through second grade. *Journal of Educational Psychology, 91*(2), 261–272.

Xue, Y., & Meisles, S. J. (2004). Early literacy instruction and learning in kindergarten: Evidence from the early childhood longitudinal study-kindergarten class of 1998–1999. *American Educational Research Journal, 41*, 191–229.

Yoshikawa, H. (1995). Long-term effects of early childhood programs on social outcomes and delinquency. *The Future of Children, 5*(3) 51–75.

EDUCATIONAL POLICY IN THE UNITED STATES REGARDING BILINGUALS IN EARLY CHILDHOOD EDUCATION

Ann-Marie Wiese
WestEd

Eugene E. Garcia
Arizona State University

INTRODUCTION

Educating children from bilingual immigrant and nonimmigrant families is a major concern of school systems throughout the United States, given that the population of students who come to school not speaking English has grown over 60% in the last decade (Garcia, 2002). In addition, education is not a successful experience for many of these students. One third of Hispanics and two thirds of immigrant students drop out of school (National Research Council, 1997). Early education before the schooling years has not drawn significant policy attention. That is not the case for young children from age 5 (kindergarten) and age 10 (grade 3). Although the education of bilingual students in the United States at these age/grade levels is a continuous story of underachievement, it need not be in the future. The current challenge is to improve academic outcomes, and as such, educational policy must focus on providing both equity and fostering excellence. Historically, educational policy regarding bilingual students has been marked by a continuing tension between the ideologies of assimilation and multiculturalism (for a thorough discussion see (Saracho & Spodek, 2004; Wiese & Garcia, 2001). Key policy "players" in the education of bilingual students have included the federal courts, the U.S. Congress, state related agencies and state level initiatives.

At the national level, the aim has been to provide equal educational opportunity to underachieving students. At the federal, state, and local school district levels, policy makers and the public have urged changing teaching methods, adopting new curricula, allocating more funding and holding educational institutions accountable. Such actions have and will continue to affect bilingual students directly. Still, the active track record of policy action has not left a clear path; it is one to be negotiated. It is this complex collage of policy that this chapter addresses with the goal of informing those that are providing direct instructional services to bilingual students.

The present discussion is an attempt to identify and describe key federal, state, and local policy, both litigation and legislation, from approximately the last 50 years, in order to further an understanding of how such declarations either disadvantage or enhance the education of bilingual students during the early years of schooling. The authors begin with an overview of significant federal court cases as they relate to bilingual students, and in particular, the focus is on establishing rights based language minority status.[1] Then, the authors move to a discussion of significant federal legislation centered around the Bilingual Education Act, from its inception in 1968, through its demise in 2001. This is followed by a review of state policy in the United States, with a focus on a shift toward "English Only" policies in key states. The authors conclude the chapter by looking to how the rights of language minority groups are articulated in the international arena, and, at the same time, provide an overview of the legal rights of bilingual students.

THE FEDERAL COURTS: ESTABLISHING LEGAL RIGHTS

Lau v. Nichols: Establishing Ground

The 1974 United States Supreme Court decision of *Lau v. Nichols* is the landmark case that established language minority status as a claim for discrimination and indicated that limited English proficient students (LEP) must be provided support to access the curriculum:

(T)here is no equality of treatment merely by providing students with English instruction. Students without the ability to understand English are effectively foreclosed from any meaningful discourse. Basic English skills are at the very core of what these public schools teach. Imposition of a requirement that, before a child can effectively participate in the education program he must already have acquired those basic skills is to make a mockery of public education. We know that those who do not understand English are certain to find their classroom experiences wholly incomprehensible and in no way meaningful. (p. 18)

This articulation of the rights of language minority students prevails today. The class action lawsuit was filed against the San Francisco Unified School District on March 25, 1970 and involved 12 American-born and foreign-born Chinese students. Before the suit, the district initiated pullout program in 1966, at the request of parents of LEP students. In a 1967 school census, the district identified 2,456 LEP Chinese students. By 1970, the district had identified 2,856 such students. Of this number, more than half (1,790) received no special instruction. In addition, over 2,600 of these students were taught by teachers who could not speak Chinese. Still, the district argued that it had made initial attempts to serve this population of students. The Supreme Court's majority opinion overruled an appeals court that had ruled in favor of the district. Instead, the Court ruled in favor of the students and parents.

The opinion relied on statutory (legislative) grounds, and avoided any reference to constitutional determination, although plaintiffs had argued that the equal protection clause of the Fourteenth Amendment of the U.S. Constitution was relevant to the case. A student's right to special educational services

flowed from the district's obligations under the Title VI of the 1964 Civil Rights Act, which prohibits discrimination on the grounds of race, color, or national origin in programs or activities receiving federal financial assistance. On May 25, 1970, the Department of Health, Education, and Welfare (HEW) issued a memorandum that also justified the requirement of special educational services.[2]

The plaintiffs did not request an explicit remedy, such as a bilingual or ESL program, and the Court did not address this issue. Thus, *Lau* does not articulate that children must receive a *particular* educational service, but instead supports the mandate laid out in the 1970 HEW clarifying guidelines for "affirmative steps to rectify the language deficiency in order to open its instructional program." This explicit avoidance by the court to specify a particular remedy has plagued efforts to identify primary language instruction as an essential ingredient for instruction of bilingual students in subsequent federal litigation and legislation.

After *Lau*, the domain of the language minority education lawsuits belonged almost exclusively to Latino bilingual litigants. Although some cases were litigated to ensure compliance with the *Lau* requirements of "affirmative steps," most subsequent cases involved issues left unanswered by *Lau*: Who are these students? What form of additional educational services must be provided? In *Aspira of New York, Inc. v. Board of Education* (1975), a suit was brought by a community action group on behalf of all Hispanic children in the New York School District. The plaintiff argued that these students could not successfully participate in an English schooling context because of their lack of English proficiency, but that they could successfully participate in a Spanish language curriculum (Roos, 1984). The U.S. district court hearing this case adopted a language dominance procedure to identify those students eligible for non-English, Spanish-language instructional programs.

The procedure called for parallel examinations to obtain language proficiency estimates on Spanish and English standardized achievement tests. All students scoring below the 20th percentile on an English language test were given the same (or a parallel) achievement test in Spanish. Students who scored higher on the Spanish achievement test and Spanish language proficiency test were to be placed in a Spanish-language program. These procedures assumed adequate reliability and validity for the language and achievement tests administered. Such an assumption was, and still is, highly questionable. However, the court argued that it acted in "reasonable manner," admitting that in the absence of better assessment procedures it was forced to follow previous (*Lau*) precedents. A subsequent case, *Otero v. Mesa County School District No. 51* (1975), concluded that a clear relationship between low academic achievement and a lack of English proficiency must be clearly demonstrated before a court could mandate special instructional services. In

---

[1]Although this is a comprehensive review of litigation, the authors recognize that some relevant cases have not been included. For example, the authors have grounded their discussion around *Lau v. Nichols*, and subsequent critical cases that lent weight to Lau such as *Castañeda v. Pickard*, as opposed to *Brown v. Board of Education*, given the chapter's focus on the issue of language minority rights, and not race.

[2]The Equal Educational Opportunity Act of 1974 expanded the reach of Title VI of the Civil Rights Act of 1964 to all educational institutions, not just those receiving federal assistance, but did not prescribe a specific remedy. It was an effort by the U.S. Congress to define what constitutes a denial of constitutionally guaranteed equal educational opportunity. See the following section and Wiese and Garcia (2001) for further discussion.

essence the court refused to direct the Colorado school district to implement bilingual education programs only on the basis of low achievement exemplified in non-English speaking students. While these cases established a requirement for eligibility regarding a special "action," the following section centers on the court case which established a standard for "appropriate action" as required by *Lau*.

Castañeda v. Pickard: Articulating a Standard for "Appropriate Action"

In the key Fifth Circuit decision of *Castaneda v. Pickard* (1981), the court interpreted Section 1703(f) of the Equal Education Opportunity Act of (1974) as substantiating the holding of *Lau* that schools cannot ignore the special language needs of students. The Equal Educational Opportunities Act of 1974 (EEOA) extended Title VI of the Civil Rights Act of 1964 to all educational institutions, not just those receiving federal funding. Section 1703 (f) of the EEOA provides:

No state shall deny equal educational opportunities to an individual on account of his or her race, color, sex, or national origin by—the failure of an educational agency to take appropriate action to overcome language barriers that impede equal participation by its students in its instructional programs. (EEOA, 1974, §1703 (f))

Furthermore, the court then pondered whether the statutory requirement of the EEOA that districts take "appropriate action to overcome language barriers" should be further delineated. The plaintiffs urged on the court a construction of "appropriate action" that would necessitate bilingual programs that incorporated bilingual students' primary language. The court concluded, however, that Section 1703(f) did not embody a congressional mandate that any particular form of remedy be uniformly adopted. If Congress wished to intrude so extraordinarily on the local districts' traditional curricular discretion, it must speak more explicitly. This conclusion, the court argued, was buttressed by the congressional use of "appropriate action" in the statute, instead of "bilingual education" or any other educational terminology.

However, the court did conclude that Congress required districts to adopt an appropriate program, and that by creating a cause of action in federal court to enforce Section 1703(f), it left to federal judges the task of determining whether a given program was appropriate. Although the court noted that Congress had not provided guidance in that statute or in its brief legislative history on what it intended by selecting "appropriateness" as the operative standard, it continued with reluctance and hesitancy and described a mode of analysis for a Section 1703(f) case:

1. The court will determine whether a district's program is "informed by an educational theory recognized as sound by some experts in the field or, at least, deemed a legitimate experimental strategy." The court explicitly declined to be an arbiter among competing theorists. The appropriate question is whether some justification exists, not the relative merits of competing alternatives.

2. The court will determine whether the district is implementing its program in a reasonably effective manner (e.g., adequate funding, qualified staffing).

3. The court will determine whether the program, after operating long enough to be a legitimate trial, produces results that indicate the language barriers are being overcome. A plan that is initially appropriate may have to be revised if expectations are not met or if the district's circumstances significantly change in such a way that the original plan is no longer sufficient. (p. 73)

As a result of *Castaneda*, it became legally possible to substantiate a violation of Section 1703(f), following from *Lau*, on three grounds: (a) the program providing special language services to eligible language minority students is not based on sound educational theory; (b) the program is not being implemented in an effective manner; or (c) the program, after a period of "reasonable implementation," does not produce results that substantiate language barriers are being overcome so as to eliminate achievement gaps between bilingual and English-only speaking students. It is obvious that these criteria allow a local school district to continue to implement a program with some educational theoretical support for a "reasonable" time before it will make judgments upon its "positive" or "negative" effects.

Furthermore, in the *Castaneda* decision, the court again spoke, reluctantly but firmly, to the issue of program implementation. In particular, the court indicated that the district must provide adequate resources, including trained instructional personnel, materials, and other relevant support that would ensure effective program implementation. Therefore, a district that chooses a particular program model for addressing the needs of its bilingual students must demonstrate that its staffing and materials are adequate for such a program. Implicit in these standards is the requirement that districts staff their programs with language minority education specialists, typically defined by state-approved credentials or professional coursework (similar to devices used to judge professional expertise in other areas of professional education).

The *Keyes* court decision speaks directly to the issue of professionally competent personnel serving bilingual students. The case was originally initiated in 1969 by a class of minority parents on behalf of their minor children attending the Denver public schools, to desegregate the public schools and to provide equal educational opportunities for all children. In granting the preliminary injunction the trial court found that during the previous decade the school board had willfully undertaken to maintain and intensify racial segregation (*Keyes v. School District No. 1, Denver, Colorado*, 1969). The Tenth District Court decision ordered a desegregation plan for a particular area of the schools in Denver, and then a Supreme Court decision in 1973 actually expanded the district court's jurisdiction. The Supreme Court determined that the entire Denver public school system required desegregation.

In 1974, during the development of a court-ordered desegregation plan, the Congress of Hispanic Educators (CHE) sought intervention on behalf of themselves as educators and on behalf of their own minor children who attended the Denver schools. The CHE was interested in ensuring that the desegregation plan ordered by the court included that educational treatment of bilingual students to overcome the deficits created by numerous years of attendance in segregated and inferior schools. A sequence of additional proceedings and negotiations followed with final comprehensive court hearings commencing in May 1982.

In December 1983, Judge Richard Matsch issued a 31-page opinion, which is the most lengthy and complete language-programming discussion to date in a judicial decision. Judge Matsch, applying the *Castañeda* standards, found that Denver had failed to direct adequate resources to its language program, the question of teacher qualifications being a major concern. Moreover, this decision made it clear that all school districts in the United States must attend to the requirements laid out in *Castañeda*. A few years later, the Seventh Circuit Court of Appeals, which includes Wisconsin, Illinois, and Indiana, ruled on the obligations of the states under the EEOA (*Gomez v. Illinois*, 1987). The Court applied the tripartite test established in *Castañeda* and extended to state education agencies, as well as to local education agencies, the obligation to ensure that the needs of the students of limited English proficiency be met. In doing so, the *"Castañeda Standard"* with deference to *Lau* has become the most visible legal articulation of educational rights for bilingual students in public schools.[3]

Summarizing the Rights of Language Minority Students

The previous discussion highlighted the increasing number of court initiatives influencing the educational services for language minority students. The court opinions in particular have generated some understanding of a language minority pupil's legal standing as it relates to the educational treatment received. At the national level, this legal standing stems from court opinions specifically interpreting Section 1703(f) of the 1974 U.S. Equal Educational Opportunities Act. The courts have consistently refused to invoke a corollary to the Fourteenth Amendment to the U.S. Constitution with respect to educational treatment. Even so it is evident that litigation has increased (and is likely to continue) and has been an avenue of educational reform that has produced significant changes in educational programs for language minority students. However, like almost all litigation, it has been a long (range of 4–13 years in court prior to an operational decision) and often highly complicated and resource-consuming enterprise.

Although hesitant, U.S. federal courts have played a significant role in shaping educational policy for bilingual students. They have spoken to issues of student identification, program implementation, resource allocation, professional staffing, and program effectiveness. Moreover, they have obligated both local and state educational agencies to language minority education responsibilities. Most significantly, they have offered to language minority students and their families a forum in which minority status is not disadvantageous. It has been a highly ritualized forum, extremely time-and-resource-consuming. Still, the federal courts have been a responsive institution and will likely continue to be used as a mechanism to air and resolve the challenges of educating language minority students.

FEDERAL LEGISLATION: NO CHILD LEFT BEHIND AND THE DEMISE OF THE BILINGUAL EDUCATION ACT

As part of a larger 2001 reauthorization of the Elementary and Secondary Education Act of 1965, a measure known as No Child Left Behind (NCLB), the Bilingual Education Act was eliminated. Under provisions of this new reauthorization, specifically Title III: Language Instruction for Limited English Proficient and Immigrant Students, federal funds will continue to support the education of bilingual students, referred to in the new law as LEP students. However, Title III differs markedly from the initial enactment of Title VII: The Bilingual Education Act (BEA) and any of its five subsequent reauthorizations.

The Bilingual Education Act, 1968–1988

Since its inception in 1968 through its final reauthorization in 1994, Title VII of ESEA: The Bilingual Education Act stood as the United States' primary federal legislative effort to provide equal educational opportunity to language minority students. The legislation was reauthorized on five occasions (1974, 1978, 1984, 1988, 1994).[4] Although the aim of the legislation was never one of establishing language policy, the role of language became a prominent marker as the legislation articulated the goals and nature of education for language minority students.

Like *Lau v. Nichols*, the initial Title VII legislation built on the Civil Rights Act of 1964 and originated as part of the "war on poverty" legislation. The legislation was primarily a "crisis intervention" (Garcia & Gonzalez, 1995), a political strategy to funnel poverty funds to the second largest minority group in the Southwest, Mexican Americans (Casanova, 1991). The BEA was intended as a demonstration program to meet the educational needs of low-income, limited-English-speaking children. The legislation was intended as a remedial effort, aimed at overcoming students' "language deficiencies," and these "compensatory efforts were considered to be a sound educational response to the call for equality of educational opportunity" (Navarro, 1990, p. 291). No particular program of instruction was recommended in fact financial assistance was to be provided to local educational agencies "to develop and carry out new and imaginative ... programs" (BEA, 1968, §702). Among the approved activities were the following programs: bilingual

---

[3]Although the district court freed the school district from court control regarding desegregation in 1995, bilingual education is one program still under federal court supervision.
[4]This overview of the legislation will highlight the major changes in each reauthorization.

education, history and culture, early childhood education, and adult education for parents.

Although the role of native language instruction was not specifically addressed until the 1974 reauthorization, as a practical matter, all of the programs funded under the BEA in its early years featured native language instruction. The 1974 reauthorization even defined bilingual education as, "instruction given in, and study of, English, and, to the extent necessary to allow a child to progress effectively through the educational system, the native language" (§703(a)(4)(A)(i)).[5] Other significant changes in terms of eligibility included the elimination of poverty as a requirement; the inclusion of Native American children as an eligible population; and a provision for English-speaking children to enroll in bilingual education programs to "acquire an understanding of the cultural heritage of the children of limited English-speaking ability" (§703 (a)(4)(B)).

Over the next 15 years the national sentiment shifted to focus on English acquisition as the primary goal of education for language minority students. As such, the 1978 reauthorization added language to the 1974 definition of bilingual education emphasizing the goal of English language proficiency. Bilingual education programs that encouraged native language maintenance would only foster children's allegiance to minority languages and cultures, and this was not an acceptable responsibility for schools. Native language maintenance was the responsibility of families, churches, and other institutions outside the school (Casanova, 1991; Crawford, 1999). So, although bilingualism was viewed as a laudable goal, the ultimate benefit of programs would be judged in terms of English language acquisition and subject matter learning (Birman & Ginsburg, 1983).

The 1984 reauthorization of the BEA targeted funds to transitional bilingual education: 60% of Title VII funds were allocated to the various grant categories, and 75% of these funds were reserved for transitional bilingual education programs. Transitional bilingual education programs were specified as providing "structured English-language instruction, and, to the extent necessary to allow a child to achieve competence in the English language, instruction in the child's native language" (§703 (a)(4)(A)). So, the purpose of native language instruction was to support transition to English instruction. In contrast, developmental bilingual education programs were defined as providing "structured English-language instruction and instruction in a second language. Such programs shall be designed to help children achieve competence in English and a second language, while mastering subject matter skills" (§703 (a)(5)(A)). So, the goal of this program included native language and English language competence, yet no funding allocations were specified.

In addition to delineating these two bilingual education programs, the grant categories included special alternative instructional programs (SAIPS) that did not require the use of native language and four percent of Title VII funds were allocated to SAIPS. These programs were created in recognition "that in some school districts establishment of bilingual education programs may be administratively impractical" (§702 (a)(7)). Although the 1984 grant categories remained the same for the 1988 reauthorization, funds allocated to SAIPS were increased to 25%. Furthermore, the 1998 legislation included a 3-year limit on an individual's participation in transitional bilingual education programs or SAIPS: "No student may be enrolled in a bilingual program ... for a period of more than 3 years" (§7021 (d)(3)(A)).

ESEA Reauthorizations of 1994 and 2001: From Bilingual Education to English Only

With regards to limited English proficient students, the 2001 reauthorization of the Elementary and Secondary Education Act marks a complete reversal from the reauthorization in 1994. Table 20.1 provides a summary of key differences in how the 1994 and the 2001 reauthorizations of the ESEA address the education of LEP students.

As the summary of the legislation demonstrates, areas where significant changes are evident include: purpose, program, allocation of funds, and accountability and assessment. Whereas the 1994 version of the Bilingual Education Act included among its goals "developing the English skills and to the extent possible, the native-language skills" of LEP students, the new law focuses only on attaining "English proficiency." In fact, the word "bilingual" has been completely eliminated from the law and any government office affiliated with the law. A new federal office has been created to replace the Office of Bilingual Education and Minority Languages Affairs (OBEMLA) and oversee the provisions of the new law. It is now the Office of English Language Acquisition, Language Enhancement, and Academic Achievement for Limited-English-Proficient Students (OELALEAALEPS or as it is commonly referred to, OELA). What was formerly known as the National Clearinghouse for Bilingual Education, is now known as the National Clearinghouse for English Language Acquisition and Language Instruction Educational Programs.

In regards to allocation of funds, through Title III of NCLB federal funds to serve bilingual students will no longer be federally administered via competitive grants designed to ensure equity and promote quality programs; programs that served as

---

[5]The inclusion of native language instruction in the definition of bilingual education was influenced by bilingual programs in Dade County, Florida, which were founded to address the needs of the first wave of professional-class Cuban immigrants. These same programs were some of those featured in the congressional hearings for the 1968 law. The Cuban immigrants saw themselves as temporary residents of the United States who would soon return to their country, and therefore, wanted to preserve their culture and language. Thus, the bilingual programs encouraged Spanish language maintenance and English language acquisition (Casanova, 1991). At the same time, the success of the programs gave encouragement to the idea of bilingual education as a method of instruction for students from disadvantaged backgrounds (Hakuta, 1986). Native language instruction could serve as a bridge to English language acquisition, by providing equal access to the curriculum until students were English proficient. Although the BEA acknowledged the role native language could play in supporting a transition to English, it did not promote bilingual education as an enrichment program where the native language was maintained. These very programs were among those described in hearings on the 1968 law.

TABLE 20.1. Significant Differences in the 1994 and 2001 Reauthorizations of the ESEA

Issue	1994 Title VII: Bilingual Education Act	2001 Title III: Language Instruction, Limited English Proficient, and Immigrant Students
Eligible Populations	Limited English proficient students Recent immigrants which: "have not been attending one or more schools in any one or more States for more than three full years." (§7501(7)) Native Americans, Native Alaskans, Native Hawaiians, Native American Pacific Islanders	Limited English proficient students Immigrant children and youth: 3–21 years of age, not born in any state, "have not been attending one or more schools in any one or more states for more than 3 full academic years." §3301(6) Native Americans, Native Alaskans, Native Hawaiians, Native American Pacific Islanders
Purpose	"(A) To help such children and youth develop proficiency in English, and to the extent possible, their native language; and (B) meet the same challenging State content standards and challenging State student performance standards expected of all children." (§7111(2)) "The use of a child or youth's native language and culture in classroom instruction can—(A) promote self-esteem and contribute to academic achievement and learning English by limited English proficient children and youth." §7102(14)) The "unique status of Native American languages" and language enhancement.	"To help ensure that children who are limited English proficient, including immigrant children and youth, attain English proficiency, develop high levels of academic attainment in English, and meet the same challenging State academic content and student academic achievement standards as all children are expected to meet." (§3102(1)) Programs for Native Americans: "develop English proficiency and, to the extent possible, proficiency in their native language." §3211(2)
Programs	Competitive grants to local education agencies (schools, districts). State education agencies approve the grant application before submission but play no official role in the grant's implementation. "Quality bilingual education programs enable children and youth to learn English and meet high academic standards including proficiency in more than one language." (§7102(9)) Priority is given to programs which "provide for development of bilingual proficiency both in English and another language for all participating students." (§7116 (i)(1))	"To streamline language instruction educational programs into a program carried out through formula grants to State educational agencies and local educational agencies." (§3102(7)) "To implement language instruction educational programs, based on scientifically-based research on teaching limited English proficient children." (§3102.(9))
Allocation of Funds	Cap of 25% of funds for SAIPs, can be lifted if an applicant has demonstrated that developing and implementing a bilingual education program is not feasible.	95% of funds must be used for grants at the local level to teach LEP children; each state must spend this percentage to award formula subgrants to districts.
Accountability and Assessment	Local education agency (LEA) is the locus of control and is granted great flexibility on how to best serve students. LEA sets own goals and ways of assessing them.	To hold various educational agencies accountable for "increases in English proficiency and core academic content knowledge ... by requiring—(A) demonstrated improvements in the English proficiency of limited English proficient students each fiscal year; and (B) adequate yearly progress" (§3102(8)).

guiding lights to the larger nation. Instead, resources will be allocated primarily through a state formula program for language instruction educational programs (LIEPs) that are "based on scientifically-based research" (U.S. Department of Education, 2002a). LIEPs are defined as "an instruction course in which LEP students are placed for the purpose of developing and attaining English proficiency, while meeting challenging State and academic content and student academic achievement standards. A LIEP may make use of both English and a child's native language

to enable the child to develop and attain English proficiency" (U.S. Department of Education, 2003, p. 20).

The formula grants will be distributed to each state based on their enrollments of LEP and immigrant students.[6] Each state must then allocate 95% of the funds to individual local education agencies (LEAs). The argument for the formula grants claims that the previous system of competitive grants "benefited a small percentage of LEP students in relatively few schools" (U.S. Department of Education, n.d.). In fact, resources will be

[6]Those programs awarded funds under the 1994 reauthorization will continue to be eligible.

spread more thinly than before—between more states, more programs, and more students. Through competitive grants, Title VII support for instructional programs previously served about 500,000 "eligible" bilingual students out of an estimated 3.5 million nationwide. Under the new law, districts will automatically receive funding based on the enrollments of LEP and immigrant students. However, the impact of federal dollars will be reduced. Last year, for example, about $360 was spent per student in Title VII-supported instructional programs. This year, despite the overall increase in appropriations, Title III will provide less than $135 per student. Funding for all other purposes—including teacher-training, research, and support services—will be restricted to 6.5% of the total budget. That amounts to about $43 million this year. Last year, by contrast, $100 million was spent on professional development alone in order to address the critical shortage of teachers qualified to meet the needs of bilingual students.

Finally, accountability provisions mandate annual assessment in English for any student who has attended school in the United States (excluding Puerto Rico) for 3 or more consecutive years and attainment of "annual measurable achievement objectives" (U.S. Department of Education, 2002a). States are required to hold subgrantees accountable for making adequately yearly progress (AYP).[7] Subgrantees must report every second fiscal year and include a description of the program as well as the progress made by children in learning English, meeting state standards, and attaining English proficiency. States report every second year to the Department of Education, and the Department of Education reports every second year to Congress. Subgrantees failing to meet AYP must develop an improvement plan with sanctions if they continue to fail for 4 years (U.S. Department of Education, 2002b). In fact, failure to meet AYP can eventually result in the loss of Title III funds.

In summary, federal policies have begun to emphasize the teaching and learning of English with little regard for the development of academic bilingual competency for students coming to school speaking a language other than English. It is unclear whether this reflects only a swing in policy direction or if it will "stay the course" in a political climate that is likely to change as the demographic increase in US bilingual populations become a reality. For now, state policies have begun to mirror this shift, and in particularly dramatic ways in three states with significant populations of bilingual children.

STATE POLICY: LEGISLATION AND INITIATIVES

Through state legislation, 12 states mandate special educational services for language minority students, 12 states permit these services and one state prohibits them. Twenty-six states have no legislation that directly addresses language minority students.

State program policy for language minority students can be characterized as follows:

1. implementing instructional programs that allow or require instruction in a language other than English (17 states);
2. establishing special qualifications for the certification of professional instructional staff (15 states);
3. providing school districts supplementary funds to support educational programs (15 states);
4. mandating a cultural component (15 states); and
5. requiring parental consent for enrollment of early grade students in bilingual education (11 states).

Eight states (Arizona, California, Colorado, Illinois, Indiana, Massachusetts, Rhode Island, and Texas) impose all of the above requirements concurrently.

Such a pattern suggests continued attention by states to issues related to language minority students [see Garcia (2001a) for details]. Of particular interest is a subset of states, which when taken together are home to almost two thirds of this nation's language minority students: California, Florida, Illinois, New York, New Jersey, and Texas. In these states, a bilingual, ESL, or some other form of credential/endorsement is available to teachers. However, such a credential is only a requirement in three of the six states. This suggests that even in states with significant proportions of language minority students, there is no direct mandate for teacher professional standards. Valencia (1991) suggests that this may be due to the concentration of language minority students in particular districts; this is particularly true for Chicano students in the Southwest. Even though their academic presence is felt strongly by individual districts, they do not exert this same pressure statewide. The authors of this chapter propose that this will change with time. With ever-increasing numbers, language minority students will surely have an impact statewide. The question is whether the response will be a positive one, such as mandating teacher credential requirements around effective methods for teaching bilingual students, or whether the response will be a negative one. Most recently, the success of "English only" initiatives in three states can be read as a negative response towards the growing populations of language minority students.

"English Only" State Policies

Three state initiatives in California (1998), Arizona (2000), and Massachusetts (2002) are the most recent efforts by states to restrict the use of a language other than English in the delivery of educational services to bilingual children. Although each state differs in the exact process by which such initiatives come before the public for a vote, the general process is similar in nature. In essence, the initiative process allows citizens to place an issue of interest on the ballot for voter approval or rejection.[8]

---

[7]As of February 2004, for AYP calculations states can include in the LEP subgroup, students who have achieved English language proficiency to ensure they receive credit for improving English language proficiency from year to year (2004).

[8]Additional information on the initiative process in each state can be found on-line. For California, visit http://www.ss.ca.gov/elections_initiatives.htm. For Arizona, visit http://www.azsos.gov. For Colorado, visit http://www.sos.state.co.us/pubs/elections. For Massachusetts, visit http://www.sec.ma.us/ele.

In California, the 1998 successful ballot initiative was titled "English Language in Public Schools" and resulted in the following changes to the state education code:

1. Requires all children be placed in "English language classrooms", and that English language learners be educated through a prescribed methodology identified as "Structured English immersion" or "Sheltered English immersion."
2. Prescribes methodology that would be provided as a temporary transition period "not normally intended to exceed one year."

The law allows instruction in the child's native language only in situations in which a waiver is granted, done so in writing and done so yearly by parents requiring a school visit by a parent. A waiver can be granted so that a student can be enrolled in a bilingual education program under three circumstances:

(a) the child already knows English, "as measured by standardized tests of English vocabulary comprehension, reading and writing in which the child scores at or above the state average for his or her grade level or at or above the 5th grade average, whichever is lower";
(b) the "child is age 10 years or older" and such instruction is approved by the principal and the teacher; or
(c) the child has special needs and has been placed for a period of at least 30 days during that school year in and English language classroom and still the principal and teacher feel the child has special physical, emotional, psychological or educational needs.

As it stands, this "English only" policy allows native language instruction only through an exclusionary and complicated process for the 1.6 million students in the state that are identified as limited in their English language proficiency. As such, this state policy extends beyond current federal law which neither requires nor prohibits the use of native language. Moreover, teachers, administrators, and school board members can be held personally liable for fees and damages by the child's parents and guardians for using the native language when waivers have not been pursued or granted.

The Arizona and Massachusetts statutes, which passed in November 2000 and 2002 respectively, are much like California's and require that all public school instruction be conducted in English. Table 20.2 provides a comprehensive comparison of the key features of the statutes in all three states, highlighting both similarities and some differences.

Like California, in Arizona and Massachusetts parents may still request a waiver of the requirements for children who already know English, are 10 years or older, or have special needs best suited to a different educational approach. However, the waiver provision becomes more restrictive in both states. Children who already know English are subject to an oral evaluation in addition to the written standardized measures. For children with special individual needs a written description of no less than 250 words documenting the special individual needs for the specific child must be provided and permanently added to the child's official school records. In addition, the special individual needs are more narrowly defined as physical or psychological only.

The waiver application itself must contain the original authorizing signatures of both the school principal and the local superintendent of schools. Furthermore, any such decision to issue such an individual waiver is to be made subject to the examination and approval of the local school superintendent, under guidelines established by, and subject to, the review of the local governing board and ultimately the state board of education. Teachers and local school districts may reject waiver requests without explanation or legal consequence, the existence of special individual needs does not compel issuance of a waiver, and parents are to be fully informed of their right to refuse to agree to a waiver.

Once Question 2 passed, Massachusetts amended the law to provide students and their families a way to bypass the waiver process and still participate in a particular type of bilingual program. In July 2003, by a slim margin of victory, the legislature made modifications that allowed student enrollment in two-way bilingual programs. The law would now include the following language: "Two-way bilingual programs for students in kindergarten through grade 12 ... shall be unaffected. This means that if a district offers a two-way bilingual program a parent of an English learner may choose to have his or her child participate in such a program without applying for or receiving a waiver" (G. L. c. 71A (§4)). As an article in the Boston Globe described it, the decision would in fact, "water down the state's tough new English immersion law" (Lewis & Kurtz, 2003).

The Defeat of "English Only" in Colorado

It also should be noted that a proposition similar to those in Arizona and Massachusetts was defeated in Colorado in 2002. The defeat of Amendment 31 was the first rejection of such an "English only" state initiative. With a 55% to 44% margin, the defeat has been attributed to a variety of factors, including timing of the initiative and the campaign against it, a clear and concise message for the opposition, and successful fundraising (Escamilla, Shannon, Carlos, & Garcia, 2003). In terms of timing, an attempt to put the initiative on the ballot in 2000 failed because the Colorado Supreme Court determined it was unconstitutional. This provided ample time to build a coordinated opposition. In terms of message, after extensive polling that indicated that the general public did not understand bilingual education, the campaign dropped this as an issue. Instead, the campaign focused on the legal liability of individual teachers and the requirement of parental waivers. Overall, the message broadcast was that Amendment 31 was punitive, would eliminate parental choice, and would be costly. Finally, the opposition to Amendment 31 waited until very late in the campaign to announce a $3 million private donation.

Approximately 4 months before the election, political consultants coordinating the opposition secured the donation from a woman whose daughter attended a two-way bilingual program. Had the amendment passed in Colorado, it would have been even more restrictive than those passed in Arizona,

TABLE 20.2. "English Only" Initiatives in Three States

	California: Proposition 227	Arizona: Proposition 203	Massachusetts: Question 2
Election	General Election June 1998 Passed: 69% to 31%	General Election November 2000 Passed: 63% to 37%	General Election November 2002 Passed: 68% to 32%
Purpose/ Goals	"All children in California public schools shall be taught in English as rapidly and effectively as possible." (§1.300(f))	"All children in Arizona public schools shall be taught in English as rapidly and effectively as possible." (§1.2)	"All children in Massachusetts public schools shall be taught in English as rapidly and effectively as possible." (§1(f))
Educational Program	"All children in California public schools shall be taught English by begin taught in English. In particular, this shall require that all children be placed in English language classrooms. Children who are English learners shall be educated through sheltered English immersion during a temporary transition period not normally intended to exceed one year." (Article 2.305)	"All children in Arizona public schools shall be taught English by being taught in English and all children shall be placed in English language classrooms. Children who are English learners shall be educated through sheltered English immersion during a temporary transition period not normally to exceed one year." (§15–752)	"All children in Massachusetts public schools shall be taught English by English by being taught in English and all children shall be placed in English language classrooms. Children who are English learners shall be educated through sheltered English immersion during a temporary transition period not normally to exceed one year." (§4)
Definition of Terms	"'**English language classroom**' means a classroom in which the language of instruction used by personnel is overwhelmingly the English language, and in which such teaching personnel possess a good knowledge of the English language." Article 2.305)	"'**English language classroom**' means a classroom in which English is the language of instruction used by the teaching personnel, and in which such teaching personnel possess a good knowledge of the English language. English language classrooms encompass both English language mainstream classrooms and sheltered English immersion classrooms." (§15–751)	"'**English language classroom**' means a classroom in which the language of instruction used by the teaching personnel is overwhelmingly the English language, and which such teaching personnel are fluent and literate in English. English language classrooms encompass both English language mainstream classrooms and sheltered English immersion classrooms." (§2(b))
	"'**Sheltered English Immersion**' or '**Structured English Immersion**' means an English language acquisition process for young children in which nearly all classroom instruction is in English but with the curriculum and presentation designed for children who are learning the language." (Article 2.305)	"'**Sheltered English Immersion**' or '**Structured English Immersion**' means an English language acquisition process for young children in which nearly all classroom instruction is in English but with the curriculum and presentation designed for children who are learning the language. Books and instructional materials are in English and all reading, writing and subject matter are taught in English." (§15–751)	"'**Sheltered English immersion**' means an English language acquisition process for young children in which nearly all classroom instruction in English but with the curriculum and presentation designed for children who are learning the language. Book and instructional materials are in English. . . . This educational methodology represents the standard definition of 'sheltered English' or 'structured English' found in educational literature." (§2(e))
Native Language	Not specifically addressed.	"Although teachers may use a minimal amount of the child's native language when necessary, no subject matter shall be taught in any language other than English, and children in this program learn to read and write solely in English." (§15–751)	"Although teachers may use a minimal amount of a child's native language when necessary, no subject matter shall be taught in any language other than English, and children in this program learn to read and write solely in English." (§2 (e))
Assessment	Not specifically addressed.	"Standardized, nationally-normed written test of academic subject matter given in English shall be administered at least once each year to all Arizona public school children in grades 2 and higher." (§15–755) Only students classified as severely learning disabled may be exempted from this test." (§15–755) "The scores for students classified as 'limited-English' shall be separately sub-aggregated . . . although administration of this test is solely required for monitoring educational progress, Arizona public school officials and administrators may utilize these test scores for other purposes as well if they so choose." (§15–755)	"Standardized, nationally-normed written test of academic subject matter given in English shall be administered at least once each year to all Arizona public school children in grades 2 and higher who are English learners." (§7) "A nationally-normed test of English proficiency shall be similarly administered at least once each year to all Massachusetts schoolchildren in grades Kindergarten and higher who are English learners." (§7) "Only English learners classified as severely learning disabled may be exempted from these tests." (§7)

Massachusetts, and California. Schools would have been forced to report a "0" score for students who did not take English language achievement tests. Furthermore, It would have explicitly outlawed bilingual instruction in the Colorado constitution, and prohibited the legislature from appealing or amending the English only mandate. The latter stipulation would have prevented a change similar to the provision made by the Massachusetts legislature regarding two-way bilingual programs.

Implementation of the English Only Statute in California

In recent efforts to document the implementation of Proposition 227 in California, yet another "English Only" policy was reported to be a substantial influence on the organizational environments of bilingual students (Garcia & Curry, 2000; Palmer & Garcia, 2000). That policy is embedded in California's use of an English academic test (Stanford 9) as part of a newly defined academic performance index (API) designed by the state to either reward or sanction schools for measured progress or failure of such progress. In these studies, school district administrators, including principals, as well as classroom teachers indicate that Spanish bilingual students are receiving more instructional emphasis in English, even in school districts and schools that have used the Proposition 227 waiver process to maintain their bilingual education programs.

This new accountability policy, by requiring "high stakes" assessment in English only, has done more than Proposition 227 to move instruction into English for non-English speaking students (for a detailed account, see Garcia & Curry, 2000; Palmer & Garcia, 2000). Overall, the California, Arizona, and Massachusetts policy provisions are the most restrictive measures proposed yet for serving bilingual language minority students, either nationally or within any state, via legislation or the courts. It is anticipated that the results of these policies will have substantive effects on the future on bilingual education and its practice within and beyond these states.

CONVERGENCE OF STATE AND LOCAL POLICIES

In the wake of the contemporary educational "zeitgeist" which embraces excellence and equity for all students, best reflected in *A Nation at Risk* (U.S. Department of Education, 1983), the articulation of national goals in *Goals 2000* (1994), and the more recent initiatives by President Bush in the No Child Left Behind Act of 2001 attention to bilingual and immigrant children and their families has been significant. The major thrust of any such effort aimed at these populations has been centered on identifying why such populations are not thriving, and how institutions serving them can be "reformed" or "restructured" to meet this educational challenge.

Following this theme are recent analyses and recommendations by the California State Department of Education in its efforts to better train infant and toddler caregivers in state-supported programs and the U.S. Department of Education regarding reforms for federally funded education programs

(García & Gonzalez, 1995; U.S. Department of Education, 1997). Other agencies also have addressed this issue, including the following: (1) Roundtable on Head Start Research of the National Research Council, in its efforts to provide an issue analysis of research needed to producing a thriving future for Head Start for a highly diverse population of children and families (Phillips & Cabrera, 1996); (2) National Council of Teachers of English and the International Reading Association, in their treatment of language arts standards (NCTE/IRA, 1996), and (3) National Association for the Education of Young Children's position statement regarding linguistic and cultural diversity (NAEYC, 1996). All these articulations have attended to the "vulnerabilities" of bilingual students and have addressed issues of language and culture given their past treatment and the present conceptual and empirical understanding of how institutions must be more responsive. These reform initiatives have been used to construct new educational initiatives for bilingual students throughout the United States.

Historically, educational reform in California aimed at bilingual students has diverged from many of these reform recommendations. The following discussion will deal with three substantive challenges regarding response to reform for bilingual students in California, and to some degree in Texas. The authors suggest that new "English only" policy initiatives converge with other "reform" policies and in turn, have a profound impact on the schooling of bilingual students at the local level.

As was discussed earlier, California has targeted "language of instruction" through the passage of Proposition 227 in 1998 (García & Curry, 2000), and soon thereafter an "English only" state school accountability program followed (García, 2001b). These two recent state policies, further enhanced by district level policies, dictate the move towards "English Only" reading programs (Stritikus, 2002). What emerges at the local level from the varied perspectives of teachers and principals (Stritikus, 2002) is that these multiple policies are significantly altering the educational landscape for California's student population, especially bilingual students. Teachers are experiencing these policies as top-down reforms. This has in effect reduced teacher autonomy regarding classroom instruction. As teachers suggested, current educational trends posit higher test scores and a school's API ranking as the educational goals of students and teachers. This misplaced focus, argue teachers, leads to the impoverishment of student learning in the classroom (Stritikus, 2002). For bilingual educators, this further means the erosion of primary language instruction and curriculum.

Most disheartening is the recent analysis of the achievement gap between bilingual and nonbilingual student in California. According to Stanford 9 data published in 2002 (California State Department of Education, 2002), the gap between English-fluent and non-English-fluent students has increased. According to this same data, since California's Proposition 227 passed in 1998, 88% of California's non-English fluent students have been placed into English immersion classes that are designed to not normally exceed 1 year. Since 1998, Stanford 9 test scores have shown a widening gap between non-English fluent and English fluent students.

The impact of California's "English Only" reform policies on bilingual students find strong parallels in the research findings of McNeil and Valenzuela (2001) for bilingual students in Texas. Drawing on emerging research on high stakes testing and their individual investigations (McNeil, 1988, 2000; Valenzuela, 1997, 1999), the authors identify a set of alarming educational trends regarding the impact of the Texas Assessment of Academic Skills (TAAS). Some of the critical issues identified by McNeil and Valenzuela mirror the set of concerns raised by teachers in California: TAAS-based teaching and test preparation are usurping a substantive curriculum; TAAS is divorced from children's experience and culture and is widening the educational gap between rich and poor, and between mainstream and language minority students (McNeil & Valenzuela, 2001).

The educational trends in California and Texas are similar.[9] Both states use one test to determine academic outcomes for students. Both have placed a tremendous emphasis on school ranking and are witness to a drastic increase in the implementation of mandated scripted reading programs at the expense of other effective instructional practices for second language learners. California's educational system is growing more and more prescriptive, just as Texas has, discrediting the cultural and linguistic assets students bring to the classroom. McNeil and Valenzuela state that the TAAS system in Texas is "playing out its inherent logic at the expense of our poorest minority children" (2001, p. 63). In sum, in California, and to some degree in other states such as Texas, "English only" policy initiatives continue to have negative effects on bilingual students. They are subtractive in nature, ignoring the linguistic resources bilingual students bring to the classroom, and disregard responsive attributes of programs that work well for these students.

CONCLUSION

As the United States advances educational policy for any of its students in an ever-diversified population, it is even more important to understand the dramatic shifts in technology, globalization, and democratization. For now, policy is almost characterized by a "blind spot" when it comes to the new demographic reality, particularly the growth of bilingual students.

These circumstances pose a particular challenge to educators and those among us who look to educational agencies for help in realizing the moral imperatives of equity and social justice. These agencies are being called on to develop and implement models of culturally competent practices in creating and delivering services to growing numbers of bilingual students. Furthermore, class has become increasingly more important in today's policy context than race, ethnicity, national origin, or English-speaking abilities in determining access to opportunities, power and privilege in American society (Wilson, 1978). Still, West (1993) reminds us that race is still important, and if we conclude that class and race counts, we also conclude that language does so as well. Garcia (2001a, 2001b) indicates that language will continue to be at the forefront of federal and state policy activity. As such, this chapter has attempted to deepen an understanding of the education of bilingual students through

educational policy at the federal and state levels. If we can attend to policy that "counts," then one could predict that as more bilingual students enter the "right" kind of schools, barriers to their academic, social, and economic success and mobility will fall. In that policy arena, language distinctions will blend with other features of our society to create a more "equalitarian" society (Garcia, 2001b), a society in which the negative effects of racial, ethnic, linguistic and class, differences are eliminated. This is, of course, a highly optimistic scenario of the future of bilingual students and American society in general. Still, it is most certainly a preferable prediction to one that argues that America could become another Bosnian nightmare, where racial and ethnic conflicts could escalate into major avenues of social unrest.

Rights of Language Minority Groups in the International Arena

Skutnabb-Kangas (Skutnab-Kangas, 2000; 2002) and Crawford (2002) remind us that the United States is only one of the world's many nation-states that must deal with issues of students coming to public schools not speaking the schooling language. In particular, the United Nations has spoken directly to the rights of a minority group to its language by explicitly indicating:

Prohibiting the use of the language of a group in daily discourse or in schools or the printing and circulation of publications in the language of the group falls within the agreed upon constraints regarding linguistic genocide. (United Nations, 1948)

In 1994, the United Nations Human Rights Committee spoke again to this international issue (United Nations, 1994). It is the most far-reaching human rights articulation of an international body addressing linguistic rights:

In those states in which ethnic, religious or linguistic minorities exist, persons belonging to such minorities shall not be denied the right, in community with other members of their group, to enjoy their own culture, to profess and practice their own religion, or to use their own language.

Skutnabb-Kangas (2002) has summarized this UN position as: (1) protecting all individuals on the State's territory or under its jurisdiction such as immigrants and refugees irrespective of their legal status; (2) recognizing the existence of a linguistic right; and (3) imposing positive obligations on the State to protect that right. Under this interpretation, the United States is in violation of this international standard. Still, throughout this chapter, several important conclusions regarding the responsibilities of educational agencies have been established. Using a question-and-answer format, Table 20.3 sets out some of these responsibilities. These are adapted from Roos (1984) and Garcia (2001b), and are still legally valid today. They represent a practical guide for understanding the legal status of bilingual students and the legal liability of the educational agencies that serve them.

---

[9]It is important to note that Texas accountability policies allow for the use of a Spanish language academic test.

TABLE 20.3. Legal Rights of Bilingual Students and Legal Liabilities of Agencies That Serve Them

Question: Is there a legally acceptable procedure for identifying language minority students in need of special instructional treatment?

Answer: Yes. The legal obligation is to identify all students who have problems speaking, understanding, reading, or writing English because of a home language background other than English. In order to do this, a two-phase approach is common and acceptable. First, the parents are asked, through a home language survey or on a registration form, whether a language other than English is spoken in the child's home. If the answer is affirmative, the second phase is triggered. In the second phase, students identified through the home language survey are given an oral language proficiency test and an assessment of their reading and writing skills.

Question: Once the students are identified, are there any minimal standards for the educational program provided to them?

Answer: Yes. First, a number of courts have recognized that special training is necessary to equip a teacher to provide meaningful assistance to limited-English-proficiency students. The teacher (and it is clear that it must be a teacher, not an aide) must have training in second-language acquisition techniques in order to teach English as a second language.

Second, the time spent on assisting these students must be sufficient to assure that they acquire English skills quickly enough to assure that their disadvantages in the English language classroom does not harden into a permanent educational disadvantage.

Question: Must students be provided with instruction in the student's native language as well as English?

Answer: At the present time, the federal obligation has not been construed to compel such a program. However, the federal mandate is not fully satisfied by an ESL program. The mandate requires English language help plus programs to assure that students not be substantively handicapped by any delay in learning English. To do this may require either (a) a bilingual program that keeps the students up in their course work while learning English or (b) a specially designed compensatory program to address the educational loss suffered by any delay in providing understandable substantive instruction. Finally, it is legally necessary to provide the material resources necessary for the instructional components. The program must be reasonably designed to succeed. Without adequate resources, this requirement cannot be met.

Question: What minimal standards must be met if a bilingual program is to be offered?

Answer: The heart of a basic bilingual program is a teacher who can speak the language of the students as well as address the students' limited English proficiency. Thus, a district offering a bilingual program must take affirmative steps to match teachers with these characteristics. These might include allocating teachers with language skills to bilingual classrooms, and affirmative recruitment of bilingual teachers. Additionally, it requires the district to establish a formal system to assess teachers to insure that they have the prerequisite skills. Finally, where there are insufficient teachers, there must be a system to insure that teachers with most (but not all) of the skills are in bilingual classrooms, that those teachers are on a track to obtain the necessary skills and that bilingual aides are hired whenever the teacher lacks the necessary language skills.

Question: Must there be standards for removal of a student from a program? What might these be?

Answer: There must be definite standards. These generally mirror the standards for determining whether a student is in need of special language services in the first place. Thus, objective evidence that the student can compete with English-speaking peers without a lingering language disability is necessary.

Several common practices are unlawful. First, the establishment of an arbitrary cap on the amount of time a student can remain in a program fails to meet the requirement that all language minority students be assisted. Second, it is common to have programs terminate at a certain grade level, for example, sixth grade. While programs may change to accommodate different realities, it is unlawful to deny a student access to a program merely because of grade level.

Question: Must a district develop a design to monitor the success of its program?

Answer: Yes. The district is obligated to monitor the program and to make reasonable adjustments when the evidence suggests that the program is not successful.

Monitoring is necessarily a two-part process. First, it is necessary to monitor the progress of students in the program to assure (a) that they are making reasonable progress toward learning and (b) that the program is providing the students with substantive instruction comparable to that given to English-proficient pupils. Second, any assessment of the program must include a system to monitor the progress of students after they leave the program. The primary purpose of the program is to assure that the LEP students ultimately are able to compete on an equal footing with their English-speaking peers. This cannot be determined in the absence of such a post-reclassification monitoring system.

Question: May a district deny services to a student because there are few students in the district who speak her or his language?

Answer: No. The 1974 Equal Educational Opportunities Act and subsequent court decisions make it clear that every student is entitled to a program that is reasonably designed to overcome any handicaps occasioned by a language deficit. The number of students who speak a particular language may be considered to determine how to best address the student needs given human and fiscal resources available. Still, some form of special educational services must be provided.

References

Arizona, Proposition 203: English Language Education for Children in Public Schools (2000).

Aspira of New York v. Board of Education of the City of New York, 394 F. Supp. 1161 (1975).

Bilingual Education Act, Pub. L. No. (90-247), 81 Stat. 816 (1968).

Bilingual Education Act, Pub. L. No. (93-380), 88 Stat. 503 (1974).

Bilingual Education Act, Pub. L. No. (95-561), 92 Stat. 2268 (1978).

Bilingual Education Act, Pub. L. No. (98-511), 98 Stat. 2370 (1984).

Bilingual Education Act, Pub. L. No. (100-297), 102 Stat. 279 (1988).

Bilingual Education Act, Pub L. No. (103-382), (1994).

Birman, B. F., & Ginsburg, A. L. (1983). Introduction: Addressing the needs of language minority children. In K. A. Baker & A. A. d. Kanter (Eds.), *Bilingual education: A reappraisal of federal policy* (pp. ix-xxi). Lexington: D.C. Heath and Company.

California State Department of Education. (2002). *Public school accountability act.* Retrieved June 8, 2004, from http//www.cde.ca.gov/psaa/

California, Proposition 227: English Language in Public Schools (1998).

Casanova, U. (1991). Bilingual education: politics or pedagogy. In O. Garcia (Ed.), *Bilingual Education* (Vol. 1, pp. 167-182). Amsterdam: John Benjamins Publishing Company.

Castañeda v. Pickard, 64b F.2d 989 (1981).

Civil Rights Act, Pub. L. No. (88-352), 78 Stat. (1964).

Colorado, Amendment 31: English Language Education (2002).

Crawford, J. (1999). *Bilingual education: History, politics, theory, and practice.* (Fourth ed.). Los Angeles: Bilingual Education Services, Inc.

Department of Health, Education, and Welfare, 35 Fed. Reg. II, 595 (1970).

Escamilla, K., Shannon, S., Carlos, S., & Garcia, J. (2003). Breaking the code: Colorado's defeat of the anti-bilingual education initiative (Amendment 31). *Bilingual Research Journal, 27*(3), 357-382.

Elementary and Secondary Education Act of 1965, Title II, Pub. L. No. (89-10), 27 Stat. (1965).

Equal Educational Opportunities Act of 1974, Pub. L. No. (93-380), 88 Stat. 514 (1974).

Garcia, E. (2001a). *Hispanics Education in the United States: Raices y alas.* Lanham, ML: Rowman and Littfield Publishers Inc.

Garcia, E. (2001b). *Understanding and Meeting the Challenge of Student Diversity* (Third ed.). Boston, MA: Houghton Mifflin Company.

Garcia, E. (2002). Bilingualism and schooling in the United States. *International Journal of the Sociology of Language, 155*(156), 1-92.

Garcia, E., & Curry, J. E. (2000). The education of limited English proficient Students in California schools: An assessment of the influence of Proposition 227 in selected districts and schools. *Bilingual Research Journal, 24*(1-2), 15-36.

Garcia, E. E., & Gonzalez, R. (1995). Issues in systemic reform for culturally and linguistically diverse students. *Teachers College Record, 96*(3), 418-431.

Goals 2000: Educate America Act, H.R. 1804 (1994).

Gomez v. Illinois State Board of Education, 811 F.2d 1030 (1987).

Hakuta, K. (1986). *Mirror of language: The debate on bilingualism.* New York: Basic Books.

Keyes v. School Dist. No. 1., 303 F. Supp. 279 (1969).

Keyes v. School Dist. No. 1, Denver, Colorado, 413 U.S. 189 (1973).

Keyes v. School Dist. No. 1 (Keyes XIII), 576 F. Supp 1503 (1983).

Keyes v. Congress of Hispanic Educators (Keyes XIX), 902 F. Supp. 1274 (1995).

Lau v. Nichols, 414 U.S. 563 (1974).

Lewis, R., & Kurtz, M. (2003, July 15). Legislature loosens law on English immersion. *Boston Globe.* Retrieved June 8, 2004, from http://nl.newsbank.com

Massachusetts, Question 2: English Language Education in Public Schools (2002).

McNeil, L. M. (1988). *Contradictions of control: School structure and school knowledge.*

McNeil, L. M., & Valenzuela, A. (2001). The harmful impact of the TAAS system of testing in Texas: Beneath the accountability rhetoric. In M. Kornhaber, & G. Orfield (Eds.), *Raising standards or raising barriers? Inequity and high-stakes testing in public education* (pp. 138-158). New York: Century Foundation.

National Association for the Education of Young Children. (1996). *NAEYC position paper: Responding to linguistic and cultural diversity—Recommendations for effective early childhood education.* Washington, DC: Author.

National Council of Teachers of English and the International Reading Association (1996). *Standards for the English language arts.* Urbana, IL, Newark, DE: Author.

National Research Council. (1997). *The new Americans: Economic, demographic, and fiscal effects of immigration.* Washington, DC: National Academy Press.

Navarro, R. A. (1990). The problems of language, education, and society: Who decides. In E. E. Garcia & R. V. Padilla (Eds.), *Advances in Bilingual Education Research* (pp. 289-313). Tucson: University of Arizona Press.

No Child Left Behind, Congressional Record, Volume 147 (2001).

Otero v. Mesa County School District No. 51, (408 F. Supp. 162 (1975).

Palmer, D., & Garcia, E. E. (2000). Proposition 227: Bilingual educators speak. *Bilingual Research Journal, 24*, 169-178.

Phillips, D., & Cabrera, N. (1996). *Beyond the blueprint, directions for research on Head Start's families, National Research Council.* Washington, DC: National Academy Press.

Roos, P. (1984, July). *Legal guidelines for bilingual administrators.* Austin, TX: Society of Research in Child Development.

Saracho, O. N., & Spodek, B. (2004). Historical perspectives in language policy and literacy reform. In O. N. Saracho & B. Spodek (Eds.), *Comtemporary perspectives on language policy and literacy instruction in early childhood education.* Greenwich, CT: Information Age Publishers.

Skutnab-Kangas, T. (2000). *Linguistic genocide in education—or worldwide diversity and human rights?* Mahwah, New Jersey: Lawrence Erlbaum Associates.

Skutnabb-Kangas, T. (2002). American ambiguities and paranoias. *International Journal of the Sociology of Language, 155*/156, 179-186.

Stritikus, T. (2002). *Immigrant children and the politics of English-only: Views from the classroom.* New York: LFB Scholarly Publishing.

United Nations. (1948). *The Convention of the Prevention and Punishment of the Crime of Genocide.* New York: Author.

United Nations. (1994). *Convention on the Prevention and Punishment of the Crime of Genocide, e794.*

U.S. Department of Education. (2004). *Press release: Secretary Paige announces new policies to help English language learners.* Washington, DC: Author.

U.S. Department of Education. (n.d.) *Executive summary of the No Child Left Behind Act of 2001.* Retrieved June 8, 2004, from http://www.ed.gov/nclb/overview/intro/execsumm.html

U.S. Department of Education (1997). *National Assessment of Educational Progress, NAEP in 1996 trends in academic progress*. Washington, DC: US Government Printing Office.

U.S. Department of Education, The National Commission on Excellence in Education. (1983, April). *A nation at risk: The imperative for educational reform*. Washington, DC: Author.

U.S. Department of Education, Office of Elementary and Secondary Education. (2002a). *Outline of programs and selected changes in the No Child Left Behind Act of 2001*. Washington, DC: Author.

U.S. Department of Education, Office of Elementary and Secondary Education. (2002b). *Outline of programs and selected changes in the No Child Left Behind Act of 2001*. Washington, DC: Author.

U.S. Department of Education, Office of English Language Acquisition, Language Enhancement, and Academic Achievement for Limited English Proficient Students. (2003). *Non-regulatory guidance on the Title III state formula grant program*. Washington, DC: Author.

Valencia, R. (1991). *Chicano school failure and success: Research and policy agendas for the 1990s*. New York: Falmer Press.

Valenzuela, A. (1997). Mexican American youth and the politics of caring. In E. Long (Ed), *From sociology to cultural studies* (pp. 113-127). Second Volume: Sociology of Culture Annual Series. London: Blackwell.

Valenzuela, A. (1999). *Subtractive schooling: U.S-Mexican youth and the politics of caring*. Albany: State University of New York Press.

West, C. (1993). Learning to talk of race. In R. Gooding-Williams (Ed.), *Reading Rodney King, reading urban uprising* (pp. 23-31). New York: Routledge.

Wiese, A.-M., & Garcia, E. E. (2001). The bilingual education act: Language minority students and us federal educational policy. *International Journal of Bilingual Education and Bilingualism, 4*(4), 229-248.

Wilson, W. J. (1978). *The declining significance of race*. Chicago: University of Chicago Press.

CHILD CARE FOR YOUNG CHILDREN

Carollee Howes
Kay Sanders
University of California at Los Angeles

In the late 1980s, in the first version of this chapter for the handbook of Research on the Education of Young Children, we reviewed the empirical studies on child care from the 1970s and 1980s. By-and-large, the studies reviewed were small single-site studies (Phillips & Howes, 1987). Only two studies that could be considered nationally representative existed, the landmark National Day Care Study (Ruopp, Travers, Glantz, & Coelen, 1979) and the then newly released National Child Care Staffing Study (Howes, Phillips, & Whitebook, 1992; Howes, Sakai, Shinn, Phillips, Galinsky, & Whitebook, 1995; Howes, Whitebook, & Phillips, 1992; Phillips, Howes, & Whitebook, 1992; Phillips, Voran, Kister, Howes, & Whitebook 1994; Whitebook, Howes, & Phillips, 1990; Whitebook, Howes, & Phillips, 1998). We concluded:

We have sufficient research in the area of child care to make several overarching conclusions. Child care quality appears more important than either child care form or age of entry in predicting children's development. Quality in child care is closely linked to the adult providing care. In settings where the adult can effectively perform both nurturing and teaching roles, children are able to develop more social and cognitive competence. Teacher effectiveness is linked to individual characteristics, including formal education and specialized training, and to setting characteristics, particularly salaries and adult-child ratio. Although family and child care influences are difficult to separate, most studies find that the best predictors of children's outcomes are a combination of family and child care influences.

In essence, we now know that good child care can enhance development, we also know how to provide good child care. Despite this impressive knowledge base, child care quality in America is far from optimal. Simultaneously, we are losing our well-educated and well-trained teachers and providers because of poverty-level salaries. If we, as a nation are to provide good quality child care for our children, efforts must

be made to enhance both salaries and the supply of high quality care. (Howes & Hamilton, 1993)

What has changed in the past decade and a half? This is the central question of our review. The most major policy change during this time is the passage of the 1996 federal Personal Responsibilities and Work Opportunities Act. The passage of this law meant that poor women could no longer stay out of the workforce to care for their young children themselves. Therefore, a substantial proportion of women do not have the choice to decide not to work and to receive welfare. Instead, these women are now required to seek work. The funds available to pay for the child care of the children of women required to leave welfare and the restrictions on what kind of care the funds could be used for vary by state regulations and are beyond the scope of this chapter. However, in most states there are now more poor women needing and using child care and more public funds available to pay for care in the home that is exempted from regulation than there were in the last edition of this chapter. This policy change as well as a general shift in applied developmental psychology research to include more poor children and children of color as research participants has changed the landscape of research on child care. As we will explore, the knowledge base of evidence-based research on child care is quite different than it was. But, again as we will explore, do the conclusions about relations between children's experiences in child care and children's development remain the same?

To answer these questions about change in what we know and in how we know what we know, we analyzed research studies on relations between child care attendance and children's development conducted since the last review. To be included in the review the study had to be published in a peer-reviewed journal, had to include a measure of child care quality, and had to have been conducted within the United States.[1] We used quality as a criterion because our previous conclusions suggested that the influence of child care on children's development depended on the quality of the care. We included only reports published since 1993. We tried to include only studies when the data was collected after 1987. In some cases we had to estimate the date of data collection as many published articles did not include this information. The 22 studies and 59 articles from these studies meeting this criterion are in Table 21.1. In the first section of this chapter, we analyze this new database, using it to examine changes in the way we study child care. The concluding sections of this analysis included topics that have emerged as important for further studies in child care. The second section of the chapter uses the same topic headings as the 1993 handbook chapter to describe changes in what we know as a result of the last decade and a half of research in child care.

CHANGES IN THE CHILD CARE RESEARCH LITERATURE BASE

How We Changed Our Way of Studying Child Care in the Last Decade and a Half

The research base for examining the influence of child care on children's development has changed dramatically since its early years of studying children enrolled in demonstration and laboratory programs. The participants in the research studies, the forms of child care studied, the scale of studies, and the scope of the research design have all changed. As well as these changes in features of child care research there have been conceptual changes in how quality is defined and in attention to children's relationships within child care. Although the current studies do reflect more inclusive and diverse sampling, some recent reviews suggest that there are different ways of conceptualizing race and class, which need to be incorporated into future research.

Participants: children and programs. Perhaps the most striking change in the last 10 years in the research studies found in Table 21.1 is a move away from studying the effects of child care in predominately white children with well-educated mothers to using a more diverse set of participants. Nine or half of the 17 studies that included children in the design had at least one third African-American or Latino/a children and their families. Six of the studies included a majority of African-American or Latino/a children and their families. Note as well what is not included. Only rarely are Native American, Asian-American, or Middle Eastern children and families included in these studies and then only in such small numbers to preclude analysis.

There was as well increased diversity in form of care studied. Ten of the 22 studies included home-based care. Five of these 10 studies included licensed exempt care. This is a departure from the previous trend of studies, which focused exclusively on center-based care. In all of the studies, the tendency is towards representative rather than convenience sampling, another aspect of increasing diversity.

Multisite versus single-site studies. Before 1993, all but a very few studies examining relations between child care and children's development were conducted in only one location. As can be seen in Table 21.1, this has dramatically changed. Two very large studies, the NICHD Early Child Care Study (ECCRN, 1996, 1997a, 1997b, 1997c, 1998a, 1998b, 1999, 2000a, 2000b, 2001a, 2001b, 2001c, 2001d, 2002, 2003b), and Early Head Start (Love, Harrison, Sagi-Schwartz, Van IJzendoorn, Ross, Ungerer, Raikes, Brady-Smith, Boller, Brooks-Gunn, Constantine, Kisker, Paulsel, & Chazan-Cohen, 2003), used 10 and 17 sites, respectively. Both of these multisite studies included all forms of child care. The two studies are complementary in that they used similar child care measures, but the NICHD study overrepresented white affluent families and the Early Head Start study low-income families of color. Unfortunately, given the timing of the two studies the NICHD findings are by-and-large published, whereas the bulk of the early Head Start findings are not yet published.

In addition to these studies, several multisite studies strategically sampled based on licensing and form of care. Historically, the first multisite studies to sample strategically targeted different state licensing environments. The Three State Study (McCartney, Scarr, Rocheleau, Phillips, Abbott-Shim, Eisenberg, Keffe, Rosenthal, & Ruh, 1997; Phillips, Mekos, Scarr, McCartney, & Abbott-Shim, 2001) sampled center-based care provided under different auspices in three states with different licensing environments. The Family and Relative Care Study (Howes, Galinsky, & Kontos, 1998; Kontos, Howes, Galinsky, & Shinn, 1997; Kontos, Howes, Shin, & Galinsky, 1995) sampled relative, licensed-exempt, and licensed in-home care in three states. The Cost, Quality, and Outcome study (Burchinal, Peisner-Feinberg, Bryant, & Clifford, 2000a; Helburn & Howes, 1996; Howes, Phillipsen, & Peisner-Feinberg, 2000; Peisner-Feinberg, Burchinal, Clifford, Culkin, Howes, & Kagan, 1999; Peisner-Feinberg & Burchinal, 1997; Peisner-Feinberg, Burchinal, Clifford, Culkin, Howes, Kagan, & Yazejiank, 2001; Phillipsen, Burchinal, Howes, & Cryer, 1997) sampled center-based care in four states with different licensing environments.

The second wave of multisite studies sampled strategically on the basis of family characteristics rather than licensing environments or form of care. The Best Practices study (Howes, James, & Ritchie, 2003; Howes, Shivers, & Ritchie, 2004; Ritchie & Howes, 2003; Wishard, Shivers, Howes, & Ritchie, 2003) sampled four different cultural communities, each community was instrumental in identifying good center-based care. The Child

---

[1]We recognize that by including only studies of child care in the United States we have limited this review. To adequately address studies of child care beyond the United States would lead to a much larger and comprehensive chapter than we could fit within the page limits. Child care is nested within the social-political and economic context of a nation. Therefore, it is impossible to generalize across national boundaries without fully exploring these wider contexts.

TABLE 21.1. Major Child Care Studies 1993—2003

Name of Study	Principal Authors	Year First Data Collection**	Form of Care	Participants	Mothers' Formal Education/ Income	Child Participants Race/Ethnic	Scope of Study	Child Care Quality-Structure	Child Care Quality Process	Child Care Domains of Child Experience	Child Outcomes
Three State Study	(McCartney, Scarr, Rocheleau, Phillips, Abbott-Shim, Eisenberg, Keffe, Rosenthal, & Ruh, 1997; Phillips, Mekos, Scarr, McCartney, & Abbott-Shim, 2001)	1988*	Center care	718 children, their mothers, their teachers	College educated	83% white, 9% African American	One data collection point 3 sites	Ratio, group size, teacher education, training compensation, parent fees, center auspice	ITERS, ECERS, Assessment Profile	Social behavior, relationships, separation and reunions	Social
Indiana	(Hestenes, Kontos, & Bryan, 1993; Kontos, 1994; Kontos & Wilcox-Herzog, 1997)	1990	Center and Family Care all regulated	117 children, mothers, providers	Most some college	Primarily white	One data collection point 1 site	Ratio, group size, teacher education, training	ECERS, FDCERS,	Peer Play Scale, Cognitive play Scale	Cognitive, social
NICHD Study of Early Child Care	More than 40 sites, quality related studies: (ECCRN, 1996, 1997a, 1997b, 1997c, 1998a, 1998b, 1999, 2000a, 2000b, 2001a, 2001b, 2001c, 2001d, 2002, 2003)	1991	All	1364 children, their parents, their child care providers and teachers	30% high school or less; 33% some college; 37% BA or more; more attrition in less well educated	All English speaking; 78% White; 11% African-American; 6% Latino—more attrition in nonwhite	Birth through sixth grade 10 sites	Ratio, Group size, Provider education, Provider specialized training	Observation Ratings of the Caregiving Environment (ORCE)	Interaction with adults, affect, interactions with peers, engagement with materials, academic activity, attachment to mother	Cognitive, language, social
Florida Quality Improvement Project	(Howes, 1997; Howes & Smith, 1995)	1991	Center care	840 children, their teachers, 150 child care centers	Unknown	64% white, 34% African American; 50% low income	Three data collection points over 5 years longitudinal study of classrooms not children, Infants, toddlers, and preschool age 1 site	Ratio, group size, teacher education, training	ITERS ECERS Adult Involvement Scale; Peer Play Scale; Caregiver Sensitivity; Attachment Q Sort	Interaction with adults, affect, interactions with peers, engagement with materials, academic, cognitive play, relationship quality	
	(Ghazvini & Readddick, 1994)	1991	Center care	201 parents			One data collection point, 1 site		Self report ECERS		Parent-caregiver communication
Otitis media	(Creps & Vernon-Feagans, 1999, 2000; Vernon-Feagans, Emanuel, & Blood, 1997; Vernon-Feagans, Hurley, & Yont, 2002; Vernon-Feagans, Manlove, & Volling, 1996; Volling & Feagans, 1995)	1992	Center care	36 children; 16 with chronic otitis media	44% BA degree	All white	Weekly health checks for three years	Ratio, group size	Classroom observations	Observation of interactions with adults and peers	Social, language

TABLE 21.1. (Continued)

Name of Study	Principal Authors	Year First Data Collection**	Form of Care	Participants	Mothers' Formal Education/Income	Child Participants Race/Ethnic	Scope of Study	Child Care Quality-Structure	Child Care Quality Process	Child Care Domains of Child Experience	Child Outcomes
Family and Relative Care	(Howes, Galinsky, & Kontos, 1998; Kontos, Howes, Galinsky, & Shinn, 1997; Kontos, Galinsky, Howes, Shin, & Galinsky, 1995)	1992	In-home: 112 regulated; 54 non regulated, non-relative; 60 relatives	226 mothers and children	40% high school or less; 30% some college; 30% BA or more	English and Spanish speaking; 42% white, 23% African American; 31% Latino	One visit: children M age = 26.3 years (10 to 65 months) 3 sites	Ratio, Group size, Provider education, Provider specialized training, compensation	FDCERS Adult Involvement Scale; Peer Play Scale; Caregiver Sensitivity; Attachment Q Sort	Interaction with adults, affect, interactions with peers, engagement with materials, academic, Cognitive play, relationship quality	
	(Burchinal, Roberts, Nabors, & Bryant 1996; Burchinal, Roberts, Riggins, Zeisel, Neebe, & Bryant, 2000)	1992	Center care	89 children	Almost all high school or less	All African American	10 months through 36 months 1 site	Ratio, group size, teacher education, training	ITERS ECERS		Cognitive, language
Cost Quality and Outcome	(Helburn & Howes, 1996; Howes, 2000; Howes, Phillipsen, & Peisner-Feinberg, 2000; Peisner-Feinberg & Burchinal, 1997; Peisner-Feinberg, Burchinal, Clifford, Culkin, Howes, Kagan, & Yazejiank, 2001; Phillipsen, Burchinal, Howes, & Cryer, 1997)	1993	Center	826 children, child care providers, teachers, parents	20% high school or less; 44% some college; 36% BA or more; more attrition in less well educated	English- and Spanish-speaking; 68% white, 15% African American; 6% Latino more attrition in nonwhite	Age three through sixth grade 4 sites	Ratio, Group size, Provider education, Provider specialized training, compensation	ECERS; Observations Adult Involvement Scale; Peer Play Scale; Caregiver Sensitivity; Student Teacher Relationship	Interaction with adults, affect, interactions with peers, engagement with materials, academic relationship quality	Cognitive, social, language
	(Burchinal, Howes, & Kontos 1999; Howes & Norris, 1997)	1993	Family Child Care all regulated	100 Providers	na	na	Two data collection points 1 site	Ratio, group size, provider education, training	FDCERS, Caregiver sensitivity		
	(Elicker, Fortner-Wood, & Noppe, 1999)	1995	Family Child Care	41 children, their providers, their parents	Middle to high SES	All white	12–19 months, one data collection, 1 site	Group size	ITERS, Attachment Q-Set, social interaction	Attachment relationship quality, provider-child interaction	Social
Best Practices	(Howes, James, & Ritchie, 2003; Ritchie & Howes, 2003; Wishard, Shivers, Howes, & Ritchie, 2003)	1996	Center care	12 programs serving low income children of color; 156 children; their primary caregivers, other teaching staff	Eligible for subsidized care on the basis of income	39% Latino, 32% African American, 16% white; 7% Asian; 6% biracial	3 years; mixed method 2 sites	Ratio, group size, teacher education, training compensation, supervisory structure, motivation to continue teaching	ECERS (with scores of 5 or above), Caregiver sensitivity. Adult Involvement Scale; teacher engagement in pre-academic activity; Peer Play Scale;; Attachment Q Sort	Peer Play Scale, Cognitive play Scale, activities, Relation quality	Cognitive, language, social

Early Head Start	Early Head Start Research Consortium, (Love, Harrison, Sagi-Schwartz, Van Ijzendoorn, Ross, Ungerer, Raikes, Brady-Smith, Boller, Brooks-Gunn, Constantine, Kisker, Paulsel, & Chazan-Cohen, 2003)	1996	All forms	3001 children, families, providers	Head Start income eligible; 48% less than high school	63% Latino or African American	Birth to kindergarten 17 sites	Ratio, Group size, Provider education, Provider specialized training	ITERS, ECERS. Caregiver sensitivity	Observations	Cognitive, Language, social
	(Fuller & Kubuyama, 2000)	1996	center	170 program directors			One data collection, one state	Reported ratio, group size, teacher education			
	(Dettling, Parker, Lane, Sebanc, & Gunnar, 2000; Watamura, Donzella, Alwin, & Gunnar, 2003)	1996	Family child care	21 children			40–69 months, one data collection, 1 site		ORCE		Cortisol production
	(McWilliams, Scarborough, & Kim, 2003; Raspa, McWilliams, & Ridley, 2001)	1996	Center	78 children and their teachers	78% medium or high SES	50% white; 37% African American	12–34 months; one data collection, 1 site	Ratio, group size	ITERS, Caregiver sensitivity	Observations of interaction and enagement	
Child Care in Poor communities	(Loeb, Fuller, Kagan, & Carrol, 2003)	1998	All forms	451 mothers	Welfare recipients	41% African American, 32% Latino, 24% white	Two data collection points 3 sites	Ratio, Group size, Provider education, Provider specialized training	EDCERS, FDCERS, Caregiver Sensitivity		Cognitive, language, social
Partnership	(Howes, Shivers, & Ritchie, 2004)	1999	Center Care	10 programs serving low income children of color; 70 children; their primary caregivers	Eligible for subsidized care on the basis of income	59% Latino, 27% African American; 10% white—new immigrants; 11% Asian; 3% biracial	Two data collection points	Ratio, group size, teacher education, training compensation, supervisory structure, motivation to continue	ECERS (with scores of 4 or above), Caregiver sensitivity. Adult Involvement Scale; teacher engagement in pre-academic activity; Peer Play Scale; Attachment Q Sort	Peer Play Scale, Cognitive play Scale, activities, Relationship quality	None

TABLE 21.1. (*Continued*)

Name of Study	Principal Authors	Year First Data Collection**	Form of Care	Participants	Mothers' Formal Education/Income	Child Participants Race/Ethnic	Scope of Study	Child Care Quality-Structure	Child Care Quality Process	Child Care Domains of Child Experience	Child Outcomes
Welfare, children and families	(Votruba-Drzal, Coley, & Chase-Lansdale, 2004)	1999	All forms	204 children and their families	Eligible for welfare	61% African American, 30% Latino, 9% white	Ages 2–4; one data collection point		ECERS/FDCERS. Caregiver sensitivity	Cognitive, Social	
New Hope	(Huston, Duncan, Granger, Bos, McLoyd, Mistry, Crosby, Gibson, Magnuson, Romich, & Ventura, 2001)	1999	All forms	344 children and their families	Eligible for welfare, 47% high school grad.	55% African American, 29% Latino, 12% white	Ages 3–5 one data collection, 1 site	Parent reported ratio and group size, form of care			Social
	(Wiltz & Klein, 2001)	1999	Centers	122 children, their classrooms	Primarily college educated	61% white, 23% African American, 8% Latino	Age 4, one data collection point	Ratio, auspice, NAEYC accreditation	ECERS, Classroom practices inventory	Teacher-child interaction, children's activities	Children's perceptions of care

*Approximate when not reported in published article.

Care in Poor Communities study (Loeb, Fuller, Kagan, & Carrol, 2003) sampled three different ethnic communities and all forms of care as the new welfare legislation was implemented. The Welfare, Children and Families study (Votruba-Drzal, Coley, & Chase-Lansdale, 2004) sampled low-income families in three cities again after the implementation of new welfare legislation.

Single-site studies published during this period, as can be seen in Table 21.1, tended to focus on relations between child care and children's development. For example, the Florida Quality Improvement Study examined relations between changes in licensing regulation and children's experiences in center care (Burchinal, Howes, & Kontos, 2002; Howes, 1997; Howes & Smith, 1995), whereas another single-site study examined changes in family child care regulation (Howes & Norris, 1997). Two studies focused on a particular chronic condition, otitis media, and child care (Burchinal et al., 1996, 2000; Creps & Vernon-Feagans, 1999, 2000; Vernon-Feagans, Emanuel, & Blood, 1997; Vernon-Feagans, Hurley, & Yont, 2002; Vernon-Feagans, Manlove, & Volling, 1996). Another examined relations between changes in children's cortisol production and child care quality (Dettling, Parker, Lane, Sebanc, & Gunnar, 2000).

Longitudinal design: long-term effects. Another dramatic difference in research is that child care researchers began to follow children as they moved from child care into formal schooling. Longitudinal studies include the NICHD early child care study and the Early Head Start Study (no longitudinal results as yet), and the Cost Quality and Outcome Study. Between these three studies more than 4,000 children are being followed across time. Because of the sampling strategies of these studies they collectively represent a very diverse group of children in terms of family background and child care experiences. Unfortunately for this review, children do take a long time to grow up and the longitudinal results are not yet as comprehensive as they will be and may tend to raise as many questions as they answer. For example, the NICHD study reports some disturbing relations between time in child care and problematic social competence (ECCRN, 2003a) during the children's transition to kindergarten. In this analysis the quality of the child care the children attended had less influence on children's outcomes than the cumulative time in care. By contrast, the Cost, Quality, and Outcome study found that positive relationships between children and teachers and the emotional climate of the classroom at age 3 predicted social competence with peers in second grade (Howes, 2000). Comparisons between these two results are difficult to summarize even though the children in the two studies are similar in class and race backgrounds because the children in the NICHD study were studied from birth to kindergarten, the children in the Cost Quality and Outcome study from age 3 to second grade, and the two studies included forms of child care and different measures of quality (see Table 21.1).

Quality. By the year 2003, advocates, parents, and researchers could generally agree that good child care provides children with warm and positive relationships with child care providers, a safe and healthy environment, and opportunities for children to learn (Hofferth, Shauman, Henke, & West, 1998). And again

by 2003, there is general agreement among researchers that child care quality can be defined and reliably measured (Abbott-Shim, Lambert, & Mc Carty, 2000; Kontos et al., 1995; Lamb, 1998). Most research on child care comes from an ecological theoretical perspective (Bronfenbrenner & Morris, 1998; Sameroff, 1983). Within this theoretical perspective dimensions of the environment are considered to influence each other in a bidirectional manner and in ways that influence children's development. In child care research, these models of influence are conceptualized as structural dimensions of the child care environment influencing process dimensions, that in turn influence children's development (ECCRN, 2002; Network, 2002). These influences, from an ecological perspective, are nested within the cultural and familial contexts of the community. Thus, although there is an implied directionality (structure to process to outcome) there is as well an assumption that child characteristics such as gender or relationship history can influence process. For example, children who enter child care from difficult life circumstances engage in different interactions with providers than children who enter child care with positive and stable relationship histories (Howes & Ritchie, 2002).

There are several implicit assumptions made in modeling the influence of child care quality on children's development. The first set of assumptions has to do with families and child care and the second with relations between structure and process dimensions. Families are assumed to influence children's development independent of child care (ECCRN, 1998b). As well, families are assumed to influence children's development indirectly by their selection of child care. Families with more advantages, more education and income, and mothers with higher vocabularies, less authoritarian childrearing beliefs, and more stimulating home environments, all factors associated with enhanced cognitive, language, and social development, tend to use child care that is higher in quality (ECCRN, 1997c; Johnson, Jaeger, Randolph, Cauce, Ward, & Network, 2003; Punpungello & Kurtz-Costes, 1999). This finding holds true across all ethnic groups (Johnson et al., 2003), although the issue may be one of availability not choice for Latino families .(Buriel & Hurtado, 1998).

For all families who live in poverty, finding affordable child care that is high enough quality to enhance, as opposed to inhibit development, is nearly impossible (Buriel & Hurtado, 1998; Johnson et al., 2003, Phillips et al., 1994). Furthermore, families in particularly difficult life circumstances, where the mother suffers from depression, or family violence, or the children have developmental problems, including early emotional problems, are unlikely to have the social resources to find high quality care and maintain enrollment (Love et al., 2003; Newcombe, 2003).

Finally, these researchers assume that the same processes that enhance development within families are expected to enhance development within child care. Therefore, just as sensitive and responsive parenting is linked to children's construction of secure child-mother attachments at home, sensitive and warm provider behaviors are expected to be associated with secure child-teacher relationships (Howes, 1999). Rich language environments with lots of child-adult talk, positive affect, responsivity to children's vocalizations, and cognitive stimulations at home enhance children's language development (Bloom, 1991; Hart & Risley, 1992; Hoff-Ginsberg, 1991; Tamis-Le Monda, 2002; Tamis-LeMonda, Bornstein, & Baumwell, 2001) and are expected as well to enhance language development at child care. Home environments that have plenty of social and physical resources, where adults interactively read to children, and where connections are made between actions and ideas are homes that foster cognitive development (Bradley et al., 1989; Bradley, Corwyn, Burchinal, McAdoo, & Coll, 2001; Bradley, Corwyn, McAdoo, & Coll, 2001; Storch & Whitehurst, 2002; Whitehurst, Arnold, Epstein, & Angell, 1994; Whitehurst & Lonigan, 2002) and if child care programs are like these homes then they are expected to enhance cognitive development.

To a large extent the assumption that basic processes within families that influence child development are the same processes in child care is warranted. Studies measuring exactly the same behaviors identified at home in child care find similar associations between these interactions and children's development (Caughy, DiPetro, & Strobine, 1994; Dickenson & Smith, 2001; Howes & Ritchie, 1999; Howes & Ritchie 2002; McCartney, 1984; ECCRN, 2000b; Whitehurst et al., 1994). These studies have particular power because they include children from a wide range of class and race.

Some observational measures of process quality in child care, notably the NICHD Early Child Care Research Network's ORCE, Arnett's caregiver sensitivity scale and Howes's adult involvement scale, have built from this developmental research within the family base and find associations between high scores on these measures and children's development (Arnett, 1989; ECCRN, 1996, 2000a, 2002, 2003b; Howes, 1997; Howes et al., 1998; Howes & Hamilton, 1992; Howes & Smith, 1995; Howes & Stewart, 1987; Kontos et al., 1997). (See Table 21.1 for studies using these measures.)

There are, as well, problems with the assumption that replicating what goes on in "good" homes will become "good" child care. Traditionally, "good" has been conceptualized in much psychological research from the white, middle-class perspective (Garcia Coll, 1996; Harrison, 1990), and this conceptualization may not always map onto the perspectives, childrearing practices or experiences of poor families or African-American and Latino families (Johnson et al., 2003; Spencer, 1990).

Home and child care agreement on language use in the program is another area where straightforward assumptions about continuity or "good" may turn out to be more complicated. The status of the home language in the community at large, the verbal and literacy proficiency of the adults (at home and at child care), and the age of the child are probably all important to consider when assessing the literature on home languages in programs and children's development. This topic is better covered elsewhere in this volume, but it is important to keep this in mind when considering the assumptions underlying measurement of child care quality.

The assumption of "good at home good at child care" is also problematic in terms of the roles of motherhood versus the roles of the teacher. Katz in a classic essay warned that teachers are not mothers (Katz, 1980). Mothers mother in larger part from an emotional investment in their children and from their

understandings of how they were mothered (Belsky, Jaffee, Hsieh, & Silva, 2001; Van IJzendoorn, Juffer, & Duyvesteyn, 1995). Caregivers, teachers, and child care providers understand that they must constantly reflect on their knowledge of children's development, their knowledge of the particular children with whom they are engaged, and balancing the needs of the child, the group, and the child within the group (Ahnert & Lamb, 2003; Ahnert, 2000; Howes & Ritchie, 2002).

The second implicit set of assumptions made in modeling the influence of child care quality on children's development has to do with relations between structure and process (Phillips & Howes, 1987). Child care researchers have typically conceptually identified two different dimensions of child care quality: structure and process. Structural dimensions of child care are those features that can be regulated such as the qualifications of teachers who work in care or the number of bathrooms of what size, while process refers to features such as warm, sensitive, and stimulating adult-child interactions that can be observed. This conceptual framework assumes that both structure and process dimensions of child care can be measured but the measurement of process quality requires close observation and measuring instruments based, as discussed earlier, on what developmental psychological research has defined as warm, sensitive, and stimulating. It further assumed that structural dimensions predict process dimensions, not children's development. That is, a fit was expected between a structure that supported good caregiving, and furthermore good caregiving would enhance development. These assumptions have now been tested in the NICHD study and in the Cost Quality and Outcome Study. In both studies, pathways were found linking structural dimensions to process dimensions to children's outcomes (ECCRN, 2002; Peisner-Feinberg et al., 2001; Phillipsen et al., 1997).

In all but one study presented in Table 21.1 structural quality was assessed. Adult:child ratios, group size, and educational and specialized training were the most common features. In almost all of the studies in Table 21.1, process quality of care was observed rather than reported by parents or program directors. Fifteen of the studies in Table 21.1 used a version of the Environmental Rating Scales (Early Childhood Environmental Rating Scale ECERS) (Harms & Clifford, 1980; Harms, 1998); Infant and Toddler Environmental Rating Scale ITERS (Harms, Cryer, & Clifford, 1990); the Family Day Care Environmental Rating Scale FDERS (Harms & Clifford, 1989). Nine studies used the Arnett's caregiver sensitivity rating. This means that the structural and process quality sampled can be compared across studies.

Unresolved and Emerging Issues in the Study of Child Care

Contested definitions of quality. During the last decade, the definition of quality described above and followed by the studies in Table 21.1 has been contested both within the research community and from the outside. Parents do not necessarily agree that structural features of quality identified through research such as that reviewed in Table 21.1 are highest priority for them (Holloway, Rambaud, Fuller, & Eggers-Pierola, 1995; Johnson et al., 2003; Liang, Fuller, & Singer, 2000; Singer, Fuller, Keiley, & Wolf, 1998), although few parents disagree that they want their children to be safely cared for by someone who will treat them well. A small-scale study, based on qualitative interviews of parents, indicate aspects of quality that are based on an emic understanding of childrearing and the perceived role of child care in that community (Fuller, 1996). When parents articulate how a child care program meets their child's needs, they articulate concerns similar to process quality constructs: how attentive the teacher is to their children, how their children react to the provider, how nice a teacher is or whether the teacher liked their children (Fuller, 1996; Ispa, 1998; Cryer, 1997). Parents view quality in child care programs as "How do I want to raie my child, and how will day care providers advance my preferred form of socialization and early learning?" (Fuller, 1996, p. 84). This understanding may not always map onto the constructs of quality as defined by the research community because researchers might be sampling behaviors quite different from how these particular parents wish to raise their children. For example, there is often disagreement between parents and experts on styles of physical punishment and the learning of letters.

Furthermore, early childhood educators disagreed over whether quality should be defined by attention to children's individual needs or their collective experiences (Maccoby & Lewis, 2003), whether children learned best with child initiated or didactic learning (Kessler & Swadener, 1992) and whether quality was nested within ethnicity (Johnson et al., 2003; Delpit, 1988). In response to these issues, Burchinal (Burchinal et al., 2000a) reanalyzed data from several major studies examining whether relations between quality assessments and children's outcomes were similar across ethnicity. She reports very similar associations, at least for white, African-American, and Latino children. However, future researchers may need to elaborate their definitions of quality to address these concerns.

Adult relationships seen as more important, but what about peers? In 1993 a significant portion of the Handbook chapter covered children's relationships with teachers and peers. In the intervening years, the notion that children form attachment relationships with their child care providers has become well accepted in the research community (Howes, 1999; Thompson, 1999; Thompson, 2000). We have as well, come to understand that child-child care caregiver attachments form in similar ways to child-mother attachments, although the context of the relationship formation requires attention to caregiving behaviors for groups of children as well as individual children (Ahnert & Lamb, 2003; Ahnert, 2000). We now have long-term data that suggests that the quality of children's relationships with their child care caregivers influences the quality of their relationships with other adults, particularly teachers into adolescence (Howes & Aikins, 2002; Howes , Hamilton, & Phillipsen, 1998; Howes et al., 2000; Howes & Tonyan, 2000). We have come to understand as well that the attachment relationships children form with their child care providers help to organize not only their relationships with their teachers but their approach to learning in school (Howes & Ritchie 2002; Peisner-Feinberg et al., 2001).

Peer relationships and child care continue as well to be important topics for researchers. The NICHD study reported that at ages 2 and 3 children who had experienced positive and responsive caregivers and the opportunity to engage with other children in child care were observed to be more positive and skillful in their peer play in child care but not in play with a friend in a laboratory (ECCRN, 2001b). But, as discussed earlier, when the children were 4.5 and in kindergarten, teachers, caregivers, and mothers rated children with more time in child care as having more problematic relationships and behaviors with others (ECCRN, 2003a). When *Child Development* published this article, they invited commentary. In their commentary, Fabes and colleagues (Fabes, Hanish, & Martin, 2003) argued that peers must be considered as socialization agents within child care as well as adults. Almost all children in child care are cared for in conjunction with other children, same age or younger or older. Whatever the age distribution, children in child care pass through one of the most well established stages in development, that of forming same-sex peer groups within the larger group (Maccoby, 1998). Recent research on same-sex peer play suggests that boys and girls in child care may have very different developmental trajectories in the development of social competence, with girls more influenced by adult's than boys (Fabes et al., 2003). These provocative findings, we hope, will lead to more descriptive as well as analytic research on the socialization of social competence within peer interactions in child care.

Issues of race. As we discussed earlier, there is a dramatic increase in researchers including children and families of color in child care research. However, the issue is not only whom you study, but also how you study children of color in child care. The lead article in the September/October 2003 issue of *Child Development*, the research leading journal in our field suggests that up until now much of the research on the effects of child care on normative development does not include children of color (Johnson et al., 2003). The authors argue that, although it is important to include more children of color, simply using existing research paradigms may not be enough. Research that includes children of color often include children of color who are poor, and the contexts of culture/ethnicity and race versus poverty cannot be disentangled easily (Johnson et al., 2003). The cultural and contextual features that influence development in children of color are different than those for white children (Coll, Lamberty, Jenkins, McAdoo, Cunic, Wasik, & Garcia, 1996; Harrison, Wilson, Pine, Chan, & Buriel, 1990). For example explicit and implicit socialization of children around issues of race and culture within child care have different meanings for white children and children of color (Caughy et al., 1994; Caughy, O'Campo, Randolph, & Nickerson, 2001; Johnson et al., 2003).

Poor women, often poor women of color, have always been the child care providers for white affluent children, Children of color have less often been cared for by white caregivers. But recent data suggests that same ethnic child-caregiver matches are declining for children of color (Chang, 1993). Beyond issues of continuity of caregiving practices between home and child care (Johnson et al., 2003) when the children and the caregivers have different experiences of race and racism, there are unexplored issues of status imbalance implicit in these relationships. We look forward to more research examining these issues.

Issues of poverty, particularly welfare reform. Research in child care reflecting the issue of child care itself, can take the point of view of the mother or the point of view of the child. For example, a child care center at the bus stop may be optimal for the mother's work-family stress, and horrid for the child's development if it is not a safe and secure place for the child. The advent of a growing literature on mothers and children following changes in welfare policy reflects these competing foci. In our search of the literature it was difficult to find published studies of children's development following welfare changes that included observations of the quality of care used by the parent moving off welfare. Part of this is a timing issue. There has been relatively little time to conduct and publish these studies. Another part of this is the particular circumstances of child care and welfare. Most states permit child care transition monies to be used in license exempt as well as licensed care. Because the amount of money is minimal, as it makes more economic sense to keep the money within the social network of the recipient, and as most women moving off welfare have little time or resources to search for care between the time that they find employment and they must start, much of the child care is informal care. Also, parental selection of child care includes a parent's cultural models (taken-for-granted beliefs) and some parents may prefer informal care because of a belief that relatives and home-based child care are best for the needs of their child, especially the very young child (Fuller, 1996). As Table 21.1 illustrates, child care researchers have been slow to move toward studies of quality in license exempt child care. Again, we expect to see changes in this research base.

CHANGES IN WHAT WE KNOW FROM THE LAST DECADE AND A HALF OF RESEARCH ON CHILD CARE

Changes in the Definition of What Is Child Care

As this chapter is being written, there is an increasing public perception that preschool and child care are distinct. This perception contributes to discontinuity in care, and to care in license exempt settings for the most affluent and most poor children. A historical point of view on child care suggests that there has been always a tension between child care as a service to working mothers and child care as a developmental or educational service to children. By the 1993 chapter, most of the reviewed literature was not making a distinction between these two functions. Child care was a term that included full- and part-day care of children in a variety of settings (Howes & Hamilton, 1993).

This has changed. As we were finishing this article Kay attended a parent meeting at a program we considered a model child care program. At the meeting the director spent several minutes distinguishing between child care and preschool to emphasize that the program was a "preschool," an educational

program, and places that were "child care" were just baby-sitting. Beyond parental and lay person's perceptions, more and more policy and research reports appear to be distinguishing between child care and preschool. At least two states have court rulings requiring educational prekindergarten programs for portions of the population of 4-year-olds in their states (Committee for Economic Development, 2002). Current trends are for states to fund early childhood education as a preschool program, often covering only half or less of a working mother's day as opposed to funding whole day programs that provide both safe care and a developmental program. Although many of these state funded programs are need-based rather than universal, poor working families, particularly when the parents work nontraditional hours, find it difficult to enroll their children if there is no full day care or transportation. Meanwhile, media emphasis on early brain development (see Shonkoff, 2000, for a balanced view of this literature) has contributed to families who can make choices independent of affordability, selecting part-day early childhood programs, most often called preschools, that promise early enrichment and learning. When these are working parents many hours of child care for the children need to be provided in another setting, often by license exempt providers working in the child's home.

An increase in attention to basic academics at younger ages has as well contributed to confusion around the role of setting and caregivers in child care. Are these (predominantly) women teachers or not? If so what are their qualifications? Do only teachers in center-based child care prepare children for school or are family child care providers also preparing children for school?

Changes in Who Uses Child Care and What Forms of Child Care

By 1987, over half of the mothers with children under 1 year old were in the workforce (Hayes, Palmer, & Zaslow, 1990). Although by 1996 55% of mothers with children under three and 74% of mothers of schoolage children were in the work force (Early & Burchinal, 2001), it is clear that this period was less one of dramatic increases and more one of consolidation of trends toward working mothers. Age correlates with forms of child care used by parents also have not changed. Infants and toddlers tend to be cared in home-based care, preschoolers in center based care (Early & Burchinal, 2001; ECCRN, 1997a, 2000a). In addition to age correlates, more educated mothers continue to use child care more often than less well-educated mothers (Singer et al., 1998).

There is increasing sophistication in distinguishing between use of child care, preference for child care form, and availability of child care form. Early and Burchinal (2001) used 1995 National Household Economics Survey to make some of these distinctions. In this data set, children from families that are at least twice the poverty threshold were more likely than poor children to be in nonparental care and to spend more hours in nonparental care. Among families using child care,

African-American infants and toddlers were more likely to be in relative care than white or Latino infants and toddlers regardless of family income. Thus, the usage data is highly associated with class and race. However, there were few income, ethnic, or age differences in the care forms that parents preferred to use.

Traditionally, African-American families have preferred and used center-based care for preschool age children and this trend has continued (Fuller, Holloway, & Liang, 1996). Understanding Latino families' use and preference patterns regarding child care has been more problematic. A recent California analysis suggests that part of the problem in understanding use and preference in Latino families has been child care supply: the proportion of public child care relative to the proportion of Latino children is much smaller than the relative proportions for African-American and white children (Fuller et al., 2003).

A second issue in untangling child care use and preference for Latino families has been the failure to account for social and cultural characteristics related to migration that also may influence the preferences, perceptions, and choices that Latino families make when it comes to choosing care for their children. The child care preferences of native (U.S.)-born Latina mothers are somewhat distinct from those of foreign-born Latina mothers (Buriel, 1993; Buriel & Hurtado-Ortiz, 2000). Although both groups (and a comparison group of Anglo-American mothers) preferred relatives as their first choice for child care, foreign-born Latina mothers were more likely to express a preference for licensed child care centers as a second choice than either U.S.-born Latina or Anglo mothers. This is a significant finding in two respects: (1) it shows that the preference for relative care is not a specifically Latino value related to a cultural emphasis on the family, as this also was the first preference of Anglo mothers; and (2) It demonstrates the importance of distinguishing between different immigrant generations of Latino families, as U.S.-born Latinas preferred family child care homes, whereas mothers born abroad expressed a preference for center-based care. It should not be assumed that Latino families, *as a group*, will not use child care centers if they are available. This research found that the need for child care was most evident among first generation immigrant Latina mothers, who reported significantly less satisfaction with their current child care arrangement than native-born Latina and Anglo mothers. Although more foreign born mothers would increase their use of licensed child care (both centers and family child care homes) if they could, U.S.-born Latina mothers reported overall satisfaction with their current child care arrangements. Researchers concerned with the experiences of children and families from Central and South American countries contend that immigration status, country of origin and the acculturation processes experienced by immigrant families are significant factors to consider when examining socialization processes (Knight, 1993; Garcia Coll, 2002). Although the research described above did not include all of the recommended features that specifically pertain to immigrant families, studies, such as the ones described earlier, indicate that these aspects of the immigrant experience should be included in child care research that examines child care use and preference among families of Central and South American descent.

Changes Regarding Quality of Child Care in Different Forms of Care

In 1993 we concluded that process quality in family child care homes was somewhat lower than in center-based care. We qualified this statement by saying that there was relatively little data to use for this conclusion. We now have both more data and more sophisticated ways of examining quality. The large multi-site studies examining representative child care using the environmental quality rating scales found quality to vary widely within both child care centers and licensed family child care homes. The average and range of environmental quality scores in the centers of the Cost Quality and Outcome study and the licensed family child care homes in the Family and Relative Care study was almost identical (Kontos et al., 1995; Peisner-Feinberg & Burchinal, 1997). In both forms of care, the majority of the scores fell into a range considered mediocre and a small proportion into categories considered either unsafe and dangerous or good and enhancing of development. In the one published study comparing nonparental, license-exempt care (referred to as license-exempt) and the more regulated licensed family child care homes, license-exempt care environmental quality scores were significantly lower than environmental quality scores in licensed family child care (Kontos et al., 1995). This same study found that the lower environmental quality scores of license-exempt care were not offset by increased emotional quality. However, relationship quality, in terms of children constructing positive relationships with caregivers, were similar to children in other home-based care settings (Kontos et al., 1995).

Comparisons of these findings with the NICHD early child care research network data are problematic because both quality and relative care were measured differently. In the NICHD study fathers were included in relative care and the environmental rating scales were not used. Instead, the ORCE (see Table 21.1) provides an indication of positive caregiving. Using this measure the location of the highest level of positive caregiving changed over development. Initially children cared for by in home caregivers, including fathers and grandparents, who cared for only one child received the most positive caregiving. Children cared for in home based arrangements with relatively few children per adult also received the most positive caregiving (ECCRN, 2000a). The least positive caregiving was found in center based care with higher ratios of children to adults. However, when the children were 36 months of age, the significance of child adult ratio decreased, and in home arrangements became less positive. Observed positive caregiving was a fairly uncommon feature, because it was determined as "very uncharacteristic" for 6% of the children in the NICHD sample, "somewhat uncharacteristic" for 51%, "somewhat characteristic" for 32%, and "highly characteristic" for 12% (ECCRN, 2000a).

Changes Concerning the Influence of Quality Care on Children's Development

Differences in children's development in different quality care. In 1993, we concluded that child care quality was linked to children's concurrent development in child care. Since that time, two panels of the National Academy of Sciences have reviewed the evidence validated this conclusion on concurrent development and suggested that there are as well positive influences on long-term development (Bowman, Donovan, & Burns, 2000; Shonkoff & Phillips, 2000).

One of the most consistent and ubiquitous findings in this literature links the quality of child care children experience to virtually every measure of development that has been examined. (Shonkoff & Phillips, 2000)

The extent of influence child care quality has on children's development tends to depend on domain of development with cognitive, language, and academic skill development being more influenced than social and emotional development (Burchinal et al., 1996; ECCRN, 2000a, 2000b, 2003a, 2003b; Kontos et al., 1995; Peisner-Feinberg & Burchinal, 1997; Peisner-Feinberg et al., 2001). The extent of influence child care quality has on children's development also tends to depend on how family factors that are confounded with child care are controlled (Burchinal & Nelson, 2000; ECCRN & Duncan, 2003; Newcombe, 2003).

And how much child care quality matters may depend on the range of child care quality studied. There may be contexts in which the highest quality child care sampled in the study is not sufficiently high to positively influence children's development and may instead be at a neutral or negative level (Love et al., 2003). Because child care quality tends to be lower in license exempt home-based care (Kontos et al., 1995) and in center-based care for infants and toddlers as opposed to preschoolers (Phillipsen et al., 1997), children who begin child care as younger children are less likely to receive care of high enough quality to influence development. It is extremely difficult to examine the age of entry versus the quality of care in the lives of real children. Again, how family influences are controlled is critical in this analysis. The reasons why a family uses infant care may be as important in understanding long term development as age of entry per se, and if these reasons are controlled, age of entry out of context may have no meaning (Newcombe, 2003).

Changes in Predicting Child Care Quality From Structural Features

In 1993, we concluded, "Teacher (caregiver) effectiveness is linked to individual characteristics, including formal education and specialized training, and to setting characteristics, particularly salaries and adult-child ratio." This conclusion has held up well over time.

We are fortunate to have had two very comprehensive reviews of the evidence-based literature linking child care quality and caregiver characteristics published in 2000: *Eager to Learn: Educating our preschoolers* (Bowman et al., 2000) and *From Neurons to Neighborhoods: The Science of Early Childhood Development* (Shonkoff & Phillips, 2000). Bowman et al. (2000) concludes, "A college degree with specialized education in child development and the education of young children ought to be required for teachers of young children" (p. 271).

Shonkoff and Phillips (2000) has a similar conclusion, with the reservations that "staff-child ratio may be relatively more important for infants and toddlers and that the educational level of the provider may become more important as children move beyond the infant years into toddlerhood." This age-related reservation was based on early findings of the NICHD Early Child Care Study (ECCRN, 1996; Network, 1996). Subsequent analysis of this data set has demonstrated that, for center-based child care for all ages, caregivers with more formal education provide higher quality care (ECCRN, 2000a, 2002; Network, 2000a, 2002).

Direct evidence for the advantage of a B.A. degree in early childhood can be found in a recent article by Howes and colleagues (Howes et al., 2003). In three studies, two large and representative, one from small and selected primarily high-quality center-based programs, teachers with B.A. degrees were the most effective teachers. Effective teaching was measured within classrooms and was based on stimulation, responsivity, and engagement of children in meaningful activities. In an earlier analysis based on the two large and representative studies (Howes, 1997), B.A. in early childhood teachers were directly compared to A.A. in early childhood teachers, with similar results favoring the B.A. level teachers.

As in 1987, the current early childhood workforce is so poorly compensated that qualified caregivers cannot afford to enter or remain in the field (Bowman et al., 2000; Lamb., 1998). Increasingly, the child care workforce is composed of poor women of color for whom access to B.A. level education is problematic, even if compensation levels for their work were raised to a sustainable level (McDonough, 1997). As the population of children in the United States becomes increasingly ethnically diverse and as changes in welfare move more poor children of color into the child care system, there is an increasing need for an ethnically diverse, well-educated teaching force.

This dilemma leads us to the issue of alternative pathways to quality. There is a long history in the child care field of in-service education or training of teachers. Bowman et al. (2000) reviews the literature linking training to effective teaching and concludes that most training has not been intensive, continuous, and individualized and therefore can not be recommended as an alternative pathway to quality (p. 276).

There are some relevant qualifications to this finding. First, providers with CDA credentials are more effective teachers than providers with no training (Abbott-Shim et al. 2000; Howes, 1997). Second, a reanalysis of the Cost Quality and Outcome study data set with particular emphasis on caregiver training suggests that although caregivers with B.A. degrees provide the highest quality care, caregivers who report that they attend training workshops do benefit from them (Burchinal, Cryer, Clifford, & Howes, 2002). That is, caregivers with B.A. degrees who also attended workshops provided the highest level of care, but caregivers without degrees who report attending workshops provide higher quality care than those who do not attend. Two similar analysis of family child care providers yielded similar results (Burchinal et al., 1999; Vandell, Burchinal, O'Brien, & McCartney, 2002).

Third, in a small study of high-quality center-based programs serving low-income children of color, a small number of teachers were equally effective to teachers with B.A. degrees in early childhood (Howes et al., 2003). An analysis of the pathways to teaching of these teachers suggested that motivation for staying in the field, being mentored, and being supervised could predict their effective teaching practices.

Adult:child ratio has received less research attention than caregiver qualifications. Adult:child ratio was endorsed by both National Academy of Sciences reports (Bowman et al., 2000; Shonkoff & Phillips, 2000). The majority of the literature on adult:child ratios has used a linear approach. That is, smaller numbers of children per adult are associated with more positive outcomes. NAEYC and other professional groups have pointed out that the number of children per adult may vary with the developmental age of the children cared for and have set standards. Few published studies have used these thresholds as a basis for investigation. One study using two large and representative data sets of center based care (Florida Quality Improvement Study and Cost Quality and Outcome Study) not only found that providers engaged in more effective teaching when classrooms met the NAEYC ratios but that having a more highly educated provider did not compensate for poorer ratios (Howes, 1997) This finding is relevant because the practices of grouping and regrouping of children across the day and of having a well-educated teacher supervise several classrooms taught by less well-educated teachers are not consistent with what we know concerning effective teaching and teacher-child ratios. The second new study supporting professionally recommended adult:child ratios comes from the NICHD early child care study. It also supports the NAEYC adult:child ratios (ECCRN, 2002).

Although having relatively few children per adult predicts quality in family child care as well as in center based child care (ECCRN, 2002), there is some indication that very small (less than two children) home-based settings where the provider does not intend to provide child care but is instead helping out a family member or friends may not provide as high quality care as home-based settings with four to six children (Kontos et al., 1995). Unlike the NAEYC guidelines for adult: child ratios in center-based care, professional organizations' guidelines for the mix of age and numbers of children in family child care do not readily map on to process quality indicators of child care (Burchinal et al., 1999; Vandell et al., 2002).

CONCLUSIONS

The introduction asked whether the conclusions about the relations between children's experiences in child care and children's development remained the same since the late 1980s. We conclude that children growing up in child care are developing within a web of social relationships—with the adults and peers they encounter in child care settings. In many cases, children construct these relationships independent of their experiences within their families with people they encounter outside of their family. Their parents, as well, may construct peer relationships with the adults who care for their child in child care and sometimes construct relationships with other parents in child care.

For the most fortunate of these children, this means that the child is firmly and securely held in a safety web of connected and positive relationships. These fortunate children are growing up trusting that adults will keep them safe, organize their learning, and be people worth trusting. They are learning that peers are a source of social support and companionship, and that there are bridges between home and child care. In order for these fortunate circumstances to be true for all children, there needs to be a major increase in child care quality across all forms of care and for all children and families.

The context of race, culture, and the impact of poverty cannot be discounted from the discussions of quality and the accompanying practices associated with child care programs. Children who are poor and children who are of color are least likely to experience the kind of high-quality child care that leads to trusting and positive relationships. The policy push of welfare reform and lack of available child care for women who are affected by these reforms may hinder the establishment of an optimal web of trusting relationships for their children. Many poor children and children of color are in poor quality child care that, by its negative adult-child and child-child interactions and lack of support for exploration and learning, disrupts development and makes problematic home–child care continuity. Others are in license-exempt care, which may or may not be more continuous with home practices but of such poor quality to interfere with positive development.

There are significant and important changes in the research literature base for these conclusions. We are beginning to establish significant long-term effects of child care through multistate, longitudinal designs, although the findings from longitudinal studies are presently conflicting and incompatible measures, as well as different types of child care under study make comparisons difficult.

There is not an exclusive focus on white, middle-class children anymore, which has called into question some basic assumptions regarding our definitions of quality child care. By including children other than those from white, middle-class families, researchers must challenge themselves to include the cultural, racial, and ethnic contexts in which all children experience development in child care.

There is an increased research base on differing types of care, such as, comparisons between licensed types of care like centers and homes or unlicensed non-parental child care. There are distinctions regarding the definition of child care and the usage of child care by different racial/ethnic and income groups. In the public and some advocates' eyes, care of children from affluent families by license exempt caregivers appears to have different salience and meaning than the care of poor children by license exempt caregivers. Because of the policy implications that assumptions like these can have, it is imperative that research into varying forms of care and child care usage couch the findings within the social and cultural context of the participants.

Although much has changed since the writing of the first handbook chapter on child care, in essence the conclusion from a decade ago still stands. Children, all children, can benefit from high-quality child care as researchers have defined this care. Unfortunately, there is still insufficient child care available that is high quality and affordable for all children.

References

Abbott-Shim, M., Lambert, R. & Mc Carty, F. (2000). Structural model of Head Start Classroom Quality. *Early Childhood Research Quarterly, 15*, 115–134.

Ahnert, L., & Lamb, M. E. (2003). Shared care: Establishing a balance between home and child care settings. *Child Development, 74*, 1044–1050.

Ahnert, L., Rickert, H. & Lamb, M. E. (2000). Shared caregiving: Comparisons between home and child-care setting. *Developmental Psychology, 36*, 339–351.

Arnett, J. (1989). Caregivers in daycare centers Does training matter? *Applied Developmental Psychology, 10*, 514–552.

Belsky, J., Jaffee, S., Hsieh, K.-H., & Silva, P. (2001). Child rearing antecedents of intergenerational relations in young adulthood: A prospective study. *Developmental Psychology, 37*, 801–813.

Bloom, L. (1991). *Language development form two to three.* Cambridge: Cambridge University Press.

Bowman, B., Donovan, M. S., & Burns, S. (Eds.). (2000). *Eager to learn: Educating our preschoolers.* Washington, DC: National Research Council.

Bradley, R. H., Caldwell, B. M., Rock, S. L., Ramey, C. T., Barnard, K. E., Gray, C., Hammond, M. A., Mitchell, S., Gottfried, A. W., Siegel, L., & Johnson, D. L. (1989). Home environments and cognitive development in the first 3 years of life. A collaborative study involving six sites and three ethnic groups in North America. *Developmental Psychology, 25*, 217–235.

Bradley, R. H., Corwyn, R. F., Burchinal, M., McAdoo, H. P., & Coll, C. G. (2001). The Home Environments of children in the United States Part II: Relations with behavioral development through age thirteen. *Child Development, 72*, 1868–1886.

Bradley, R. H., Corwyn, R. F., McAdoo, H. P., & Coll, C. G. (2001). The home environments of children in the United States Part I: Variations by age, ethnicity, and poverty status. *Child Development, 72*, 1844–1867.

Bronfenbrenner, U., & Morris, P. A. (1998). The ecology of developmental processes. In W. D. R. M. Lerner (Ed.), *Handbook of Child Psychology: Vol. 1 Theoretical models of human development* (5th ed., Vol. 1, pp. 993–1028). New York: John Wiley & Sons.

Burchinal, M. R., Roberts, J. E., Riggins, R., Zeisel, S., Neebe, E., & Bryant, D. (2000). Relating quality of center-based child care to early cognitive and language development longitudinally. *Child Development, 71*, 339–357.

Burchinal, M. R., Cryer, D., Clifford, R. M., & Howes, C. (2002). Caregiver training and classroom quality in child care centers. *Applied Developmental Science, 6*, 2–11.

Burchinal, M. R., Howes, C., & Kontos, S. (2002). Structural predictors of child care quality in child care homes. *Early Childhood Research Quarterly, 17*, 87–105.

Burchinal, M. R., & Nelson, L. (2000). Family selection and child care experiences: implications for studies of child outcome. *Early Childhood Research Quarterly, 15*, 385–341.

Burchinal, M. R., Peisner-Feinberg, E., Bryant, D. M., & Clifford, R. (2000). Children's social and cognitive development and child care equality: Testing for differential associations related to poverty, gender, or ethnicity. *Applied Developmental Science, 4*, 149–165.

Burchinal, M. R., Roberts, J. E., Nabors, L. A., & Bryant, D. (1996). Quality of center child care and infant cognition and language development. *Child Development, 67*, 606–620.

Burchinal, M. R., Howes, C., & Kontos, S. (1999). Recommended Child Adult Ratio Guidelines and Child Care Quality in Child Care Homes.

Buriel, R. (1993). Childrearing Orientations in Mexican American Families: The Influence of Generation and Sociocultural Factors. *Journal of Marriage and the Family, 55*(November), 987–1000.

Buriel, R., & Hurtado, M. T. (1998). *Child Care in the Latino Community: Needs, Preferences, and Access.* Claremont: The Tomas Rivera Policy Institute.

Buriel, R., & Hurtado-Ortiz, M. T. (2000). Child Care Practices and Preferences of Native- and Foreign-Born Latina Mothers and Euro-American Mothers. *Hispanic Journal of Behavioral Sciences, 22*, 314–331.

Caughy, M. O., DiPetro, J., & Strobine, D. M. (1994). Day care participation as a protective factor in the cognitive development of low income children. *Child Development, 65*, 457–471.

Caughy, M. O., O'Campo, P., Randolph, S. M., & Nickerson, K. (2001). *The influence of racial socialization practices on the cognitive and behavioral competence of young African-American children.* Unpublished manuscript, University of Houston.

Chang, H. (1993). *Affirming Children's Roots.* San Francisco: California Tomorrow.

Coll, C. G., Lamberty, G., Jenkins, R., McAdoo, H. P., Cunic, K., Wasik, B., et al. (1996). An integrative model for the study of developmental competencies in minority children. *Child Development, 67*, 1891–1914.

Creps, C. L., & Vernon-Feagans, L. (1999). Preschoolers' social behavior in daycare :Links with entering day care in the first year. *Journal of Applied Developmental Psychology, 20*, 461–479.

Creps, C. L., & Vernon-Feagans, L. (2000). Infant dayare and otitis media: Multiple influences on children's later development. *Journal of Applied Developmental Psychology, 21*, 357–378.

Cryer, D., & Burchinal, M. (1997). Parents as Child Care Consumers. *Early Childhood Research Quarterly, 12*(1), 35–58.

Delpit, L. (1988). The silenced dialogue: Power and pedagogy in educating other people's children. *Harvard Education Review, 58*, 280–298.

Dettling, A. C., Parker, S. W., Lane, S., Sebanc, A. M., & Gunnar, M. (2000). Quality of care and temperament determine change in cortisol concentrations over the day for young children. *Psychoneuroendocrinology, 25*, 819–836.

Dickenson, D., & Smith, M. W. (2001). Supporting language and literacy development in the preschool classroom. In D. Dickinson & P. O. Tabors (Eds.), *Beginning literacy with language: Young children learning at home and at school.* Baltimore: Brooks.

Early, D. M., & Burchinal, M. R. (2001). Early childhood care: relations with family characteristics and preferred care characteristics. *16*, 475–497.

ECCRN. (1996). Characteristics of infant child care; Factors contributing to positive caregiving. *Early Childhood Research Quarterly, 11*, 269–306.

ECCRN. (1997a). Child care in the first year of life. *Merrill Palmer Quarterly, 43*, 340–361.

ECCRN. (1997b). The effects of infant child care on infant-mother attachment security Results of the NICHD Study of Early Child Care. *Child Development, 68*, 860–879.

ECCRN. (1997c). Familial factors associated with characteristics of nonmaternal care for infants. *Journal of Marriage and the Family, 59*, 389–408.

ECCRN. (1998a). Early child care and self control, compliance, and problem behavior at 24 and 36 months. *Child Development, 69*, 1145–1170.

ECCRN. (1998b). Relations between family predictors and child outcomes Are they weaker for children in child care? *Developmental Psychology, 34*, 1119-1128.

ECCRN. (1999). Child care and mother-child interaction in the first year of life. *Developmental Psychology, 35*, 1399-1413.

ECCRN. (2000a). Characteristics and quality of child care for toddlers and preschoolers. *Applied Developmental Science, 4*, 116-135.

ECCRN. (2000b). The relation of child care to cognitive and language development. *Child Development, 71*, 960-980.

ECCRN. (2001a). Before Head Start: Income and ethnicity, family characteristics, child care experiences, and child development. *Early Education and Development, 12*, 545-576.

ECCRN. (2001b). Child Care and children's peer interaction at 24 and 36 months: The NICHD Study of Early ChildCare. *Child Development, 72*, 1478-1500.

ECCRN. (2001c). Child-care and family predictors of preschool attachment and stability from infancy. *Developmental Psychology, 37*, 847-862.

ECCRN. (2001d). Nonmaternal care and family factors in early development: An overview of the NICHD study of early child care. *Journal of Applied Developmental Psychology, 22*, 457-492.

ECCRN. (2002). Structure>Process>Outcome: Direct and indirect effects of caregiving quality on young children's development. *Psychological Science, 13*, 199-206.

ECCRN. (2003a). Does amount of spent in child care predict socioemotional adjustment during the transition to kindergarten? *Child Development, 74*, 976-1005.

ECCRN. (2003b). Does quality of child care affect child outcomes at age 4 1/2? *Developmental Psychology, 39*, 451-469.

ECCRN, & Duncan, G. J. (2003). Modeling the impacts of child care quality on children's preschool cognitive development. *Child Development, 74*, 1454-1475.

Elicker, J., Fortner-wood, C., & Noppe, I. C. (1999). The context of infant attachment in family child care. *journal of Applied Developmental Psychology, 20*, 319-336.

Fabes, R. A., Hanish, L. D., & Martin, C. L. (2003). Children at play: The role of peers in understanding the effects of child care. *Child Development, 74*, 1039-1043.

Fuller, B., Holloway, S., Rambaud, M., & Eggers-Pierola, C. (1996). How do mothers choose child care? Alternative cultural models in poor neighborhoods. *Sociology of Education 69*(2), 83-104.

Fuller, B., Holloway, S., & Liang, X. (1996). Family Selection of Child-Care Centers: The Influence of Household Support, Ethnicity, and Parental Practices. *Child Development, 67*, 3320-3337.

Fuller, B., Holloway, S. D., Bozzi, L., Burr, E., Cohen, N., & Suzuki, S. (2003). Explaining local variability in childcare quality state funding and regulation in California. *Early Education and Development, 14*, 47-66.

Fuller, B., & Kubuyama, E. (2000). *Child Care and Early Education: Policy Problems and Options* (PACE Policy Memo). Berkeley: University of California.

Garcia Coll, C., Crinic, K., Lamberty, G., Wasik, B., Jenkins, R., Garcia Vazquez, H., & McAdoo, H. P. (1996). An integrative model for the study of developmental competencies in minority children. *Child Development, 67*, 1891-1914.

Garcia Coll, C., & Pachter, L. M. (2002). Ethnic and minority parenting. In M. H. Bornstein (Ed.), *Handbook of Parenting: Social conditions and applied parenting* (2nd ed., Vol. 4, pp. 1-20). Mahwah, NJ: Lawrence Erlbaum Associates.

Ghazvini, A. S., & Readddick, C. A. (1994). Parent-Caregiver communication and quality of care in diverse child care setting. *Early Childhood Rearch Quarterly, 9*, 207-222.

Harms, T., & Clifford, R. (1989). *The Family Day Care Rating Scale*. New York: Teacher's College Press.

Harms, T., & Clifford, R. M. (1980). Early childhood environmental rating scale. New York: Teacher's College Press.

Harms, T., Clifford, R. M., & Cryer, D. (1998). *Early Childhood Environment Rating Scale: Revised Edition*. New York: Teachers College Press.

Harms, T., Cryer, D., & Clifford, R. (1990). *Infant/toddler Environmental Rating Scale*. New York: Teachers College Press.

Harrison, A. O., Wilson, M. N., Pine, C. J., Chan, S. Q., & Buriel, R. (1990). Family ecologies of ethnic minority children. *Child Development, 61*, 347-362.

Hart, B., & Risley, T. R. (1992). American parenting of language-learning children: Persisting differences in family-child interactions observed in natural home environments. *Developmental Psychology, 28*, 1096-1105.

Hayes, C. D., Palmer, J. L., & Zaslow, M. J. (1990). *Who cares for America's children ? Child care policy for the 1990's*. Washington, DC: National Academy Press.

Helburn, S. W., & Howes, C. (1996). Child care cost and quality. In *The Future of Children* (Vol. 6, pp. 62-81). Los Altos, CA: David and Locitle Packard Foundation.

Hestenes, L., Kontos, S., & Bryan, Y. (1993). Children's emotional expression in child care centers varying in quality. *Early Childhood Research Quarterly, 8*, 295-307.

Hoff-Ginsberg, E. (1991). Mother-child conversation in different social classes and communicative settings. *Child Development, 62*, 782-796.

Hofferth, S. L., Shauman, K. A., Henke, R. R., & West, J. (1998). *Characteristics of children's early care and education programs Data form the 1995 National Household Education Survey, National Center for Education Statistic*.

Holloway, S. D., Rambaud, M. F., Fuller, B., & Eggers-Pierola, C. (1995). What is appropriate practice at home and in child care? Low income mothers' views on preparing their children for school. *Early Childhood Research Quarterly, 10*, 451-473.

Howes, C. (1997). Children's Experiences in Center Based Child Care as a Function of Teacher Background and Adult Child Ratio. *Merrill Palmer Quarterly, 43*, 404-426.

Howes, C. (1999). Attachment Relationships in the Context of Multiple Caregivers. In J. Cassidy & P. R. Shaver (Eds.), *Handbook of Attachment Theory and Research* (pp. 671-687). New York: Guilford.

Howes, C. (2000). Social-emotional classroom climate in child care, child-teacher relationships, and children's second grade peer relations. *Social Development, 9*, 191-204.

Howes, C., & Aikins, J. W. (Eds.). (2002). *Peer relations in the transition to adolescence*. New York: Academic.

Howes, C., Galinsky, E., & Kontos, S. (1998). Child care caregiver sensitivity and attachment. *Social Development, 7*, 25-36.

Howes, C., & Hamilton, C. E. (1993). Child Care for Young Children. In B. Spodek (Ed.), *Handbook of Research on the Education of Young Children* (pp. 322-336.). New York: Macmillan.

Howes, C., & Hamilton, C. E. (1992). Children's relationships with teachers Mothers and child care teachers. *Child Development, 63*, 859-878.

Howes, C., Hamilton, C. E., & Phillipsen, L. (1998). Stability and continuity of child-caregiver and child-peer relationships, *69*, 418-426.

Howes, C., James, J., & Ritchie, S. (2003). Pathways to effective teaching. *Early Childhood Research Quarterly, 18*, 104-120.

Howes, C., & Norris, D. (1997). Adding School Age Children Does it Change Quality in Family Child Care? *Early Childhood Research Quarterly, 12*, 327-342.

Howes, C., Phillips, D. A., & Whitebook, M. (1992). Thresholds of quality in child care centers and children's social and emotional development. *Child Development, 63*, 449-460.

Howes, C., Phillipsen, L., & Peisner-Feinberg, E. (2000). The consistency and predictability of teacher-child relationships during the transition to kindergarten. *Journal of School Psychology, 38*, 113-132.

Howes, C., & Ritchie, S. (1999). Attachment organizations in children with difficult life circumstances. *Developmental and Psychopathology, 11*, 254-268.

Howes, C., & Ritchie, S. (2002). *A Matter of Trust: Connecting Teachers and Learners in the Early Childhood Classroom*. New York: Teachers College Press.

Howes, C., Sakai, L., Shinn, M., Phillips, D., Galinsky, E., & Whitebook, M. (1995). Race social class and maternal working conditions as influences on children's behavior in child care. *Applied Developmental Psychology, 16*, 107-124.

Howes, C., Shivers, E. M., & Ritchie, S. (2004). Improving social relationships in child are through a researcher-program partnership. *Early Education and Development, 15*, 57-78.

Howes, C., & Smith, E. (1995). Child care quality, teacher behavior, children's play activities, emotional security and cognitive activity in child care. *Early Childhood Research Quarterly, 10*, 381-404.

Howes, C., & Stewart, P. (1987). Child's play with adults, toys, and peers: An examination of family and child-care influences. *Developmental Psychology, 23*, 423-430.

Howes, C., & Tonyan, H. (2000). Links between adult and peer relationship across four developmental periods. In K. A. Kerns & A. M. Neal-Barnett (Eds.), *Examining associations between parent-child and peer relationships* (pp. 85-114). New York: Greenwood/Praeger.

Howes, C., Whitebook, M., & Phillips, D. A. (1992). Teacher characteristics and effective teaching in child care Findings from the National Child Care Staff Study. *Child and Youth Care Forum, 21*, 309-414.

Huston, A. C., Duncan, G. J., Granger, R., Bos, J., McLoyd, V., Mistry, R., et al. (2001). Work-based antipoverty programs for parents can enhance the school performance and the social behaviours of children. *Child Development, 72*, 318-336.

Ispa, J., Thornburg, K., & Venter-Barkley, J. (1998). Parental child care selection criteria and program quality in metropolitan and non-metropolitan communities. *Journal of Research in Rural Education, 14*, 3-14.

Johnson, D. J., Jaeger, E., Randolph, S. M., Cauce, A. M., Ward, J., & Network, N. E. C. C. (2003). Studying the effects of early child care experiences on the development of children of color in the United States: Towards a more inclusive research agenda. *Child Development, 74*, 1227-1244.

Katz, L. (1980). Mothering and teaching—some significant distinctions. In L. Katz (Ed.), *Current topics in Early Childhood Education* (Vol. 1, pp. 20-29). Norwood, NJ: Ablex.

Kessler, S., & Swadener, B. B. E. (1992). *Reconceptualizing the early childhood curriculum: Beginning the dialogue*. New York: Teacher's College Press.

Knight, G., Bernal, M., Cota, M., Garza, C., & Ocampo, K. (1993). Family socialization and Mexican-American identity and behavior. In M. Bernal & G. Knight (Eds.), *Ethnic Identity: Formation and transmission among Hispanics and other minorities* (pp. 105-129). Albany: State University of New York Press.

Kontos, C., Howes, C., Galinsky, E., & Shinn, M. B. (1997). Children's experiences in family child care and relative care as a function of family income and ethnicity. *Merrill Palmer Quarterly, 43*, 386-403.

Kontos, S., (1994). The ecology pf family child care. *Early childhood Research Quarterly, 9*, 87-110.

Kontos, S., Howes, C., Shin, M., & Galinsky, E. (1995). *Quality in family child care and relative care*. New York: Teachers College Press.

Kontos, S., Howes, C., & Galinsky, E. (1997). Does training make a difference to quality in family child care. *Early childhood Research Quarterly, 12*, 1-372.

Kontos, S., & Wilcox-Herzog, A. (1997). Influence of children's competence in early childhood classroom. *Early Childhood Research Quarterly, 12*, 247-262.

Lamb., M. E. (1998). Nonparental child care: Context quality and correlates. In I. E. Siegel & K. A. Renninger (Eds.), *Handbook of Child Psychology* (Vol. 4, pp. 39-55). New York: Wiley.

Liang, X., Fuller, B., & Singer, J. D. (2000). Ethnic differences in child care selection: The influence of family structure, parental practices, and home language. *Early Childhood Research Quarterly, 15*, 357-384.

Loeb, S., Fuller, B., Kagan, S. L., & Carrol, B. (2004). Child care in poor communities: Early learning effects of type, quality, and stability. *Child Development, 75*, 47-65.

Loeb, S., Fuller, B., Kagan, S. L., & Carrol, B. (2004). Child care in poor communities: Early learning effects of type, quality, and stability. *Child Development, 75*, 47-65.

Love, J., Harrison, L. J., Sagi-Schwartz, A., Van IJzendoorn, M., Ross, C., Ungerer, J. A., et al. (2003). Child care quality matters: How conclusions may vary with context. *Child Development, 74*, 1021-1033.

Maccoby, E., & Lewis, C. (2003). Less Day care or different day care. *Child Development, 74*, 1069-1075.

Maccoby, E. E. (1998). *The two sexes: Growing up apart; Coming together*. Cambridge, MA: Harvard University Press.

McCartney, K. (1984). Effect of quality of day-care environment on children's language development, *Developmental Psychology, 22*, 436-454.

McCartney, K., Scarr, S., Rocheleau, A., Phillips, D., Abbott-Shim, M., Eisenberg, M. et al. (1997). Teacher-child interaction and child-care auspices as predictors of social outcomes in infants, toddlers, and preschoolers. *Merrill Palmer Quarterly, 43*, 426-450.

McDonough, P. M. (1997). Choosing colleges: *how social class and schools structure opportunity*. Albany: State University of New York Press.

McWilliams, R. A., Scarborough, A. A., & Kim, H. (2003). Adults interactions and child engagement. *Early Education and Development, 14*, 7-27.

Newcombe, N. (2003). Some controls control too much. *Child Development, 74*, 1050-1052.

Peisner-Feinberg, E. S., & Burchinal, M. R. (1997). Relations between preschool children's child-care experiences and concurrent development: The cost, quality and outcome study. *Merrill Palmer Quarterly, 43*, 451-478.

Peisner-Feinberg, E. S., Burchinal, M. R., Clifford, R. M., Culkin, M. L., Howes, C., Kagan, S. L., et al. (2001). The relation of preschool child care quality to children's cognitive and social developmental trajectories through second grade. *Child Development, 72*, 1534-1553.

Phillips, D., Mekos, D., Scarr, S., McCartney, K., & Abbott-Shim, M. (2001). Within and beyond the classroom door: Assessing quality in child care centers. *Early Childhood Research Quarterly, 15*, 475-496.

Phillips, D. A., & Howes, C. (1987). Indicators of quality in child care Review of Research. In D. Phillips (Ed.), *Predictors of quality child care* (pp. 1-20). Washington, DC: National Association for the Education of Young Children.

Phillips, D. A., Howes, C., & Whitebook, M. (1992). The effects of regulation and auspice on child care quality. *American Journal of Community Psychology, 20*, 25-51.

Phillips, D. A., Voran, M., Kister, E., Howes, C., & Whitebook, M. (1994). Child care for children in poverty Opportunity or inequity. *Child Development, 65*, 472-492.

Phillipsen, L. C., Burchinal, M. R., Howes, C., & Cryer, D. (1997). The prediction of process quality from structural features of child care. *Early Childhood Research Quarterly, 12*, 281-303.

Punpungello, E., & Kurtz-Costes, B. (1999). Why and how working women choose child care A review with a focus on infancy. *Developmental Review, 19*, 31-96.

Raspa, M., McWilams, R. A., & Ridley, S. (2001). Child care quality and children's engagement. *Early Education and Development, 12*, 209-224.

Ritchie, S., & Howes, C. (2003). Program practices and child-caregiver relationships. *Journal of Applied Developmental Psychology, 24*, 497-516.

Ruopp, R., Travers, J., Glantz, F., & Coelen, C. (1979). *Children at the center Final results of the national day care study*. Cambridge MA: Abt Associates.

Sameroff, A. (1983). Developmental Systems. In W. Kessen (Ed.), *Handbook of Child Psychology: Vol 1. History, theories, and methods* (4th ed., pp. 237-294). New York: John Wiley & Sons, Inc.

Shonkoff, J. P., & Phillips, D. A. (Eds.). (2000). *From Neurons to Neighborhoods*. Washington, DC: National Academy Press.

Shonkoff, J. P. P., Deborah A. (2000). *From Neurons to Neighborhoods: The Science of Early Childhood Development*. Washington, DC: National Academy Press.

Singer, J. D., Fuller, B., Keiley, M. K., & Wolf, A. (1998). Early child care selection variation by geographic location, maternal characteristics, and family structure. *Developmental Psychology, 34*, 1129-1144.

Spencer, M. B. (1990). Development of minority children: An introduction. *Child Development, 61*, 267-269.

Storch, S. A., & Whitehurst, G. J. (2002). Oral language and code-related precursors to reading; Evidence from a longitudinal structural model. *Developmental Psychology, 38*, 934-947.

Tamis-Le Monda, C. S. B. M. H. (2002). Maternal responsiveness and early language acquisition. *Advances in Child Development, 29*, 89-127.

Tamis-LeMonda, C., Bornstein, M. H., & Baumwell, L. (2001). *Maternal responsiveness and children's achievement of language milestones. 72*, 748-767.

Thompson, R. A. (1999). Early attachment and later development. In J. Cassidy & P. R. Shaver (Eds.), *Handbook of attachment* (pp. 265-287). New York: Guilford Press.

Thompson, R. A. (2000). The legacy of early attachments. *Child Development, 71*, 145-152.

Van IJzendoorn, M. H., Juffer, F., & Duyvesteyn, M. (1995). Breaking the intergenerational cycle of insecure attachments: A review of attachment-based interventions on maternal sensitivity and infant security. *Journal of Child Psychology and Psychiatry, 36*, 225-248.

Vandell, D. L., Burchinal, M., O'Brien, M., & McCartney, K. (2002). Do regulatable features of child-care homes affect children's development. *Early Childhood Research Quarterly, 17*, 52-86.

Vernon-Feagans, L., Emanuel, D., & Blood, I. (1997). The effects of Otitus Media and the quality of daycare on children's language development. *Journal of Applied Developmental Psychology, 18*, 395-409.

Vernon-Feagans, L., Hurley, M., & Yont, K. (2002). The effect of otitis media and day care quality on mother/child book reading and language use at 48 months. *Journal of Applied Developmental Psychology, 23*, 113-133.

Vernon-Feagans, L., Manlove, E. E., & Volling, B. (1996). Otitis Media and the social behavior of day care attending children. *Child Development, 67*, 1528-1539.

Volling, B., & Feagans, L. (1995). Infant day care and children's social competence. *Infant Behavior and Development, 18*, 177-188.

Votruba-Drzal, E., Coley, R., & Chase-Lansdale, L. (2004). Child care and low-income children's development: Direct and moderated effects. *Child Development, 75*, 296-312.

Watamura, S. E., Donzella, B., Alwin, J., & Gunner, M. (2003). Morning-to-afternoon increases in cortisol concentrations for infants and toddlers at child care: Difference and behavioral correlates. *Child Development, 74*, 1006-1020.

Whitebook, M. H., Howes, C., & Phillips, D. (1990). Who cares? *Child care teachers and the quality of care in America: National Child Care Staffing Study*. Oakland, CA: Center for the Child Care Workforce.

Whitebook, M. H., Howes, C., & Phillips, D. A. (1998). *A decade following the National Child Care Staffing Study*. Washington, DC: Center for the Child Care Workforce.

Whitehurst, G. J., Arnold, D. S., Epstein, J. N., & Angell, A., L. (1994). A picture book reading intervention in day care and home for children from low income families. *Developmental Psychology, 30*, 679-689.

Whitehurst, G. J., & Lonigan, C. J. (2002). Emergent literacy: Development from prereaders to readers. In S. Newman & D. Dickinson (Eds.), *Handbook of Early Literacy Research* (pp. 11-29). New York: Guilford.

Wiltz, N. W., & Klein, E. L. (2001). "What do you do in child care?" Children's perceptions of high and low quality classrooms. *Early Childhood Research Quarterly, 16*, 209-236.

Wishard, A. G., Shivers, E., Howes, C., & Ritchie, S. (2003). Child care program and teacher practices: Associations with quality and children's experiences. *Early Childhood Research Quarterly, 18*, 65-103.

· 22 ·

FAMILY CONTEXT IN EARLY CHILDHOOD:
A LOOK AT PRACTICES AND BELIEFS
THAT PROMOTE EARLY LEARNING

Barbara H. Fiese
Tanya Eckert
Mary Spagnola
Syracuse University

A family is a place where minds come in contact with one another. If these minds love one another the home will be as beautiful as a flower garden. But if these minds get out of harmony with one another it is like a storm that plays havoc with the garden.

—Buddha

It is virtually impossible not to be a member of a family. Yet, how families influence and are influenced by children is as numerous as the species of plants in a flourishing garden. In this chapter, we aim to describe how families are dynamic systems with shared practices and beliefs that contribute to child well-being and preparedness to learn. In some cases, and at some times, families function in such a way that children's growth is fostered and there is optimal development. In other cases, however, individual and socioeconomic forces compromise the family's ability to provide a supportive environment for their children. Thus, we focus on how being raised under high-risk conditions such as poverty and parental psychopathology may derail positive family process and make the child vulnerable to behavioral and learning problems. There is reason for optimism, however, as we discuss protective factors that may promote positive development through responsive parent-child interactions and structured home environments.

Family life is often marked by transitions. Marriage, the birth of a child, going to school, leaving home, marriage of children, becoming grandparents are just a few of the transitions that members experience as part of normative changes (Walsh, 2003). Several transitions are apparent during early childhood; gaining autonomy through learning to walk, asserting opinions in learning to talk, and being poised to learn when transitioning from home to school. We also address in this chapter how families may connect with schools to ease transitions, an area frequently ignored. We think it is important to consider not only how families affect children but how educators can better understand and interact with families. We conclude with recommendations for partnerships between educators and parents and future research directions.

TRANSACTIONAL FAMILY MODEL

Family Ecologies

There are several ways to consider how family dynamics affect child outcome. Generally, theoretical models differ in regards to the extent to which family functioning is proposed to directly affect child development or is considered ancillary to other social processes. At one end of the spectrum, are models that propose that families directly affect children and that problematic behaviors are the logical and crucial result of poor family functioning. For example, theories developed during the 1950s emphasized the role of the mother-child relationship in developing psychopathology. Overcontrolling and domineering mothers were portrayed as the progenitors of their child's mental problems (Lidz, Cornelison, Fleck, & Terry, 1957). The child's symptoms were recast as predictable responses to tensions in the family, giving rise to such concepts as the family scapegoat (Vogel & Bell, 1960). These depictions of a direct link between family (primarily mother) process and child harm were not limited to explanations of child psychopathology. Dr. Benjamin Spock was a strong proponent of the central role of parents (primarily mothers) in directly shaping their child's development (Spock, 1955).

At the other end of the spectrum, are models that propose that families actually have relatively little influence on child behavior outside of their genetic contributions (Scarr & Kidd, 1983) and choice of neighborhood that contains an influential peer group (Harris, 1995). These approaches, too, have come under scrutiny with the realization that genes and even peer groups do not operate in isolation but are embedded in broader environments such as families, communities, schools, and culture (O'Connor & Plomin, 2000). These two extreme perspectives are similarly limited in that they do not consider the broader ecology of child development nor the process by which children and parents mutually influence each other.

Bronfenbrenner (1979) has most clearly outlined the multiple ecologies embedded within each other that contribute to child development. At the core is the child herself, possessing her own temperament, style of engaging with others, and personality. These characteristics are expressed within the context of the family who reside within a neighborhood influenced by community standards. The community itself is regulated by a legal system that is consistent with and affected by cultural norms and practices. Most proximal to the child's experience are interactions within the family context. However, this is not to say that other aspects of the child's ecology do not affect her development. For example, schools are an integral part of neighborhoods and are dependent on community resources. The child's educational experiences are positively related to the amount of resources available to the community and schools.

Bronfenbrenner's model reminds us that any aspect of development or learning cannot be viewed in isolation. Take, for example, the practice of bedtime stories. During early childhood, reading bedtime stories has been found to be associated with better academic performance in the early school years (Serpell, Sonnenschein, Baker, & Ganapathy, 2002; Whitehurst et al., 1988). But the way in which this activity is structured is influenced by culture, family dynamics, and child characteristics. In Eastern cultures, the stories themselves may include messages focusing on responsibility to family and respect for elders. Fung, Miller, and Lin (2004) report that Taiwanese parents of preschoolers often rely on the confucian text, *The Rules of the Disciples,* originally written by a Chinese scholar, Yu-xiu Li (1662–1722). The book is considered a primer in how a young person should act and behave in daily life with particular attention to obedience at home, being a good listener, with individual desires taking a back seat to family obligations. As the United States becomes increasingly multiethnic, expectations for what is considered "normative" behavior is embedded in cultural values. Tales of strong family unity and solidarity, may be reinforced in Mexican-American families (Zinn & Wells, 2000) and bedtime

stories that revolve around parental authority may be told to children of Caribbean immigrant families (Roopnarine, Bynoe, & Singh, 2004).

In addition to cultural variations in thematic content of bedtime stories, there are neighborhood influences on accessibility to books. Poorer communities, both urban and rural, may provide fewer resources for families who do not have ready access to reading materials. Even where libraries exist, there are barriers to parent use for fear of damaging books and transportation problems (Nespeca, 1995).

At the level of parent-child interaction, parents' beliefs about the importance of early book reading may influence their likelihood to read a bedtime story (DeBaryshe, 1995). As these brief examples serve to illustrate, any set of behaviors observed in early childhood is but one slice of the broader context of family, neighborhood, and culture. Whereas Bronfenbrenner's model provides an appreciation of interlinking clusters of influence, it does not address the process of change inherent in families and child development. To address this aspect we turn to the transactional model.

Transactions in Development

The transactional model as proposed by Sameroff and colleagues (Sameroff, 1995; Sameroff & Chandler, 1975; Sameroff & Fiese, 2000) emphasizes the mutual effects between parent and caregiver, embedded and regulated by cultural codes. In this model, child outcome is neither predictable by the state of the child alone nor the environment in which he or she is being raised. Rather, it is a result of a series of transactions that evolve over time with the child responding to and altering the environment. Thus, to be able to predict how families influence children one must also ask how children influence families.

Let us return to bedtime stories and their connection to early literacy skills as an example. Consider a situation in which there are birth complications and the caregiver has relatively few economic resources. Once the caregiver brings the infant home from the hospital, there may be residues of worry and anxiety about the child's health and concern about how to pay for continued care. The worry and concern may lead to inconsistent parenting patterns such that at times the child is responded to sensitively and at other times the caregivers' preoccupations prevent responsive parenting. In an attempt to get the caregiver's attention, the child may develop some behaviors that can be interpreted as a difficult temperament (e.g., whining, difficulty in soothing, persistence). When bedtime arrives, the caregiver may be exhausted by strained interactions throughout the day and prefer to leave the child with a bottle rather than reading a story. Over time, the child is not exposed to joint book reading and family routines are carried out in a perfunctory way rather than as an opportunity to set aside time to be together. When the child arrives at school he or she is ill-equipped to read and may not meet normative expectations for language development. The process is outlined in Figure 22.1.

What was the cause of this outcome? Did the mother's reasonable worry about a potentially medically vulnerable child lead to poor language skills? Did the child's difficult

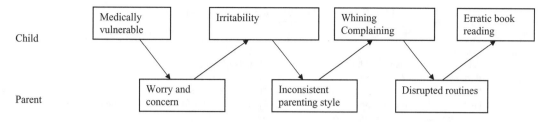

FIGURE 22.1. Transactional model between parent and child.

temperament cause him or her not to read? Did the disruption of bedtime routines directly result in delays in language development? From a transactional perspective, poor literacy skills are not the result of any one factor but develop over time through a series of exchanges between child and caregiver in a given environment. For early childhood educators, the significance of this model resides both in understanding dynamic change processes as well as opportunities for intervention. If child outcome is the product of multiple influences then there are multiple avenues for implementing change. In this case, it may be possible to redefine the relationship between caregiver and child through interaction coaching and encouraging responsive parenting styles (McDonough, 1993). It also may be possible to educate caregivers about the significance of joint book reading and create a bedtime routine that involves caregiver and child. (For further discussion on planning interventions based on the transactional model see Fiese & Wamboldt, 2001; Sameroff & Fiese, 2000). The transactional model also highlights the importance of how parent-child interactions become part of parent belief systems that regulate child behavior over time. In order to better elucidate this process, it is important to consider how families, as a group, regulate behavior and how children contribute to family process.

FAMILY PRACTICES AND REPRESENTATIONS

In light of our discussion about developmental ecologies and transactions, we should consider the essential tasks of the family and how families organize themselves as a group to fulfill these tasks. Families are complex, and at times confusing, entities as any family member can attest. Landesman, Jaccard, and Gunderson (1991) have proposed that families are responsible for providing structure and care in six domains: (1) physical development and health, (2) emotional development and well-being, (3) social development, (4) cognitive development, (5) moral and spiritual development, and (6) cultural and aesthetic development. How do families go about organizing their busy lives in order to fulfill all these demands? Within the multiple domains of responsibility tasks are carried out in a changing developmental landscape where expectations for competence in any one domain will be tempered and regulated by age. One way to tackle the complexity of the issue is to consider processes that are developmentally sensitive and reflect overall family organization.

Family life is organized around beliefs and practices that extend across generations and are altered with time. Parent belief systems have been found to be important in understanding cultural and family influences on child development (Harkness & Super, 1996). Rather than duplicate this work, we aim to place how families represent their collective activities as part of the transactional process evident in families with young children. Reiss (1989) has made the distinction between the practicing and representing family. Family practices are directly observable patterns of interaction that serve to stabilize family life through their predictability and repetitiveness over time. These interactions tend to be fairly consistent but are often altered when the child undergoes a developmental transition. For example, warmth and responsiveness may be detectable during infancy by parent and child maintaining close physical proximity and back and forth eye contact. Once the child is a toddler, however, interaction patterns shift to encourage autonomy and a smile across the room replaces direct physical contact. During the preschool years, interactions through language and the expression of support and reinforcement shifts from physical to verbal displays.

Family representations, by contrast, are detected indirectly and refer to the belief systems that families create that in turn regulate behavior. Internal working models of relationships develop within the context of the family and guide individual behavior over time. In contrast to family practices that are reportable and observable, family representations must be detected indirectly and rely on interpretations of personal events (Fiese & Sameroff, 1999). Family practices and representations are embedded in transactional process whereby family practices become the subject of representations, which in turn affect how family members interact with each other. We have found two aspects of family life capture these processes, both of which have practicing and representing elements. We now turn our attention to the study of family routines and stories as illustrations of the practicing and representing family and their influences during early childhood.

Family Routines and Rituals

In previous work, we have made a distinction between routines of daily living and rituals in family life that parallel aspects of the practicing and representing family (Fiese et al., 2002). Routines and rituals can be considered in terms of how they are communicated, time commitment, and continuity. In the case of routines, communication tends to be fairly instrumental with a focus on "this is what needs to be done." Routines typically involve a momentary commitment with little afterthought to

TABLE 22.1. Definitions of Routines and Rituals

Characteristic	Routines of daily living	Rituals in family life
Communication	Instrumental "This is what needs to be done."	Symbolic "This is who we are."
Commitment	Perfunctory and momentary Little conscious thought given after the act.	Enduring and affective "This is right." The experience may be repeated in memory.
Continuity	Directly observable and detectable by outsiders. Behavior is repeated over time.	Meaning extends across Generations and is interpreted by insiders. "This is what we look forward to and who we will continue to be across generations."

Reprinted from Fiese et al. (2002). A review of 50 years of research in naturally occurring family routines and rituals: Cause for celebration? *Journal of Family Psychology, 16*, 381–390.

the activity once it is completed. Routines tend to be repeated over time in a similar manner. Rituals, on the other hand, are communicated through symbols and convey "this is who we are" as a group. There is an emotional commitment to rituals and they often evoke strong affect. Once the activity is over, there is a tendency to replay it in memory with particular attention to feelings of belonging and connection with others. Rituals provide continuity over time and are frequently passed down across generations. When routines are disrupted, it is a hassle. When rituals are disrupted, there is a threat to group identity. The distinguishing features are outlined in Table 22.1.

Routines are most closely associated with family practices and can be part of daily and weekly activities such as mealtime, bedtime, and getting ready for school. Rituals also can occur in these settings if there is a symbolic and emotional investment in the activity and also may extend to settings such as annual celebrations (e.g., birthdays) and religious observances. During the child-raising years, maintaining routines and rituals is one way in which family tasks are carried out (Bennett, Wolin, & McAvity, 1988). Indeed, there is reason to believe that the practice of family routines is sensitive to developmental transitions within the family. In a cross-sectional study of parents whose oldest child was either an infant or of preschool age, the practice of regular routines was found to be different according to different stages of parenthood (Fiese, Hooker, Kotary, & Schwagler, 1993). Families whose lives were centered on the caregiving demands of raising an infant reported fewer predictable routines than parents whose oldest child was of preschool age. Mothers of young infants report more satisfaction in their parenting role and feel more competent when there are regular routines in the household (Sprunger, Boyce, & Gaines, 1985). During the preschool and early school years, parents and children begin to negotiate and make compromises around routine activities such as bedtime (Nucci & Smetana, 1996). Across the elementary school years, children are assigned increasing levels of responsibility in carrying out family based routines (Grusec, Goodnow, & Cohen, 1996). There is preliminary evidence to suggest that children raised in households with predictable routines are more likely to achieve and perform well in the early school years when compared to children with less predictable home based routines (Brody & Flor, 1997; Fiese, 2000).

The routines of daily living begin to shape children's behavior and expectations very early on. Infants and toddlers learn to sooth themselves during bedtime routines, expand their vocabulary during playtime routines, and become part of the social group during family mealtimes. What may appear on the surface to be mundane daily activities is in fact the child's early learning playground. The daily routines of early childhood prepare the child for more formalized learning on several levels. The repetition of routine activities may reinforce newly learned skills. The predictability of routines may aid in regulating behavior, providing a guide for what is acceptable and what is not. Routines that are flexible encourage children to become more active participants in family life, which in turn may lead to feelings of competence when approaching new and novel tasks.

The affective component of family rituals may have an indirect effect on children during the early childhood years. Parents who report more meaning in their family rituals also report more satisfaction in their marriages (Fiese et al., 1993). Previous research has demonstrated that marital satisfaction is related to parenting style, which in turn is related to child outcome (Cowan, Cowan, Heming, & Miller, 1991). Thus, the emotional investment in family activities may indirectly influence child outcome through providing an overall atmosphere of rewarding relationships that benefit multiple members.

Daily routines will also be regulated by cultural expectations. For example, Caribbean immigrant families expect young children (prekindergarten and kindergarten age) to have homework and will organize approximately 5 hours per week in the family's routine to attend to the child's homework (Roopnarine et al., 2004). Less frequent, but equally important in developing a sense of personal identity are cultural celebrations that remind family members of their origins and often involve opportunities for storytelling and cementing relationships through the preparation of different ethnic dishes (Falicov, 2003).

To summarize, routines are directly observable and provide predictability and order to family life. During early childhood families are faced with the task of creating schedules around feeding, sleeping, and increasingly over time activities outside the home. There is the potential for these family-based practices to set the stage for the child's responsiveness to structure and order in the classroom. Children who have experienced regular routines in the home may have expectations for environmental orderliness that eases their transition to school where key educational tasks are embedded in structured and sequenced activities (Norton, 1993).

Whereas the routines of daily living may prepare children to respond to order, rituals in family life reflect the affective and emotional climate of relationships. Children who are raised in homes where collective gatherings are deliberately planned, eagerly anticipated, and hold symbolic significance are likely to feel that they belong to a valued group and in turn create a stronger sense of self (Fiese, 1992).

There is preliminary evidence to suggest that families who maintain meaningful family rituals across the transition from kindergarten to elementary school have children who perform better academically. In a longitudinal study of 70 families who were originally interviewed when their child was 4 and then again when their child was 9 years of age we found different patterns of family ritual stability. For some families, the meaning associated with family rituals remained relatively high over the 5-year period, for others it remained relatively low. There were some families in which the affective component declined over time. It was this latter group in which children experienced the most difficulty in the early school years and performed less well on tests of academic achievement (Fiese, 2002). We speculate that in instances where meaningful rituals are disrupted there are likely other stresses within the family. Children may be keenly aware of changes in routines and ritual involvement. Whereas young children may not be able to articulate the amount of stress present in the family environment they certainly notice when eagerly anticipated events are canceled or altered in a significant way. Rituals may signify to the child the relative health of family relationships. Thus, children who feel emotionally connected to their families may be less likely to develop internalizing and externalizing symptoms that can affect engaging in classroom activities (Brody & Flor, 1997; Fiese, 2000).

Family routines and rituals are one way to access family practices and representations relevant to early child development. Whereas these practices and beliefs may provide templates for regular patterned interactions on a daily basis, families also face the task of dealing with events that may be out of the ordinary and are cause for comment. In these instances, it is helpful to consider how family stories may be part of the practicing and representing family.

Family Stories

Family stories can be rich accounts of how the family makes sense of its social world, expressions of rules of conduct, and beliefs about the trustworthiness of relationships. When families are called up to recount a personal experience they set an interpretive frame that reflects how individuals understand events, how family members work together (or not), and expectations for reward or disappointment when interacting with others. It is possible to distinguish between the *act* of storytelling and the *content* of family tales. The act is closely linked to the practicing family and includes how parents and children engage each other in recounting personal experiences. The content, or coherence, of family narratives reflects beliefs and hold messages for conduct. We discuss each aspect in turn.

There are notable developmental and individual differences associated with the act of storytelling during early childhood. As a family event, parents report telling stories about their own growing up experiences with increasing regularity from infancy throughout the preschool years (Fiese, Hooker, Kotary, Schwagler, & Rimmer, 1995). Around approximately 2 years of age, children develop the capacity to create personalized autobiographical memory (Howe & Courage, 1997). During early childhood, parents and children routinely engage in recounting tales of personal experience with some estimates of up to eight times per hour (Miller & Moore, 1989). Parents aid children in the process of talking about past personal events in a scaffolding process, providing support for elaboration of details and reflection on how to behave. There are important individual differences in these interactions that have significant connections to the child's language development and later literacy skills. Simply put, some parents encourage their children to elaborate on past events with particular attention to how the child felt, how others responded, and connections across time and setting. Other parents, however, focus on just getting the facts and tend to repeat details rather than elaborate (Fivush & Fromhoff, 1988). These stylistic differences are related to children's narrative competence. Children whose parents use elaborative and topic extending styles when reminiscing are more likely to develop complex narrative productions, develop narrative competence at a quicker pace, and perform better on standardized measures of vocabulary (McCabe & Peterson, 1991; Peterson & McCabe, 2004).

These differences extend to the school settings as children who more competently construct narratives are more likely to develop early literacy skills (Snow, 1983) and less likely to be labeled learning disabled (Roth, 1986). Furthermore, children who engage in elaborative storytelling may develop a more differentiated sense of self and felt security through the emotional connections reinforced during joint storytelling (Fivush, Bohanke, Robertson, & Duke, 2004). Thus, the act of storytelling not only sets the stage for being a competent narrator but also provides a stage for affective bonds in the family context, an aspect of the representing family.

The content of family stories, in contrast to the act, revolves around themes associated with socialization and trustworthiness of relationships. Through routine talk about trips to the park, personal transgressions when growing up, and lessons learned during challenging times families create a scrapbook of experiences that serve to represent family identity and provide roadmaps for behavior (Pratt & Fiese, 2004).

There is a developmental course to and individual differences in the thematic content of these stories. During early childhood, many of these tales include metaphors for how to behave. Many of the personal accounts and reminisces between parent and child during the early school years focus around such themes as "How did you feel?" and "What would you do next time?" (Fivush & Fromhoff, 1988; Miller & Moore, 1989; Peterson & McCabe, 2004). These exchanges provide opportunities for parents to reinforce expectations for conduct as well as opportunities for the child to bring to the conversation their own concerns and dilemmas.

Interestingly, the types of stories told to boys and girls may differ in their emphasis on emotion versus practical advice. Boys are more likely to hear stories that involve elements of striving for success and how things work (Fiese & Bickham, 2004) whereas girls are more likely to hear stories that include themes of personal relationships and emotional significance (Fivush et al., 2004; Peterson & McCabe, 2004).

Thematic content also varies by culture with Eastern cultures more likely to emphasize themes of family responsibility and Western culture more likely to emphasize themes of personal independence (Miller, Wiley, Fung, & Liang, 1997; Wang, 2004). Early childhood educators will recognize that many children in American schools today move between two languages. It is not clear whether children exposed to family narratives in one language and schooled in another language presents challenges in developing literacy skills. It is apparent, however, that common phrases heard at home or in the course of telling family stories may become incorporated into school time conversations, presenting additional challenges for educators.

In addition to providing messages consistent with cultural values and codes of conduct, family stories also provide access to representations of relationships. Generally speaking, family stories differ in the degree to which relationships are depicted as sources of support and reward or are considered threatening and potentially sources of harm (Fiese et al., 1999). Families whose stories include expectations for rewarding and fulfilling relationships are more likely to engage in positive and warm interactions and report that their children have fewer behavior problems in the preschool years (Dickstein, St. Andre, Sameroff, Seifer, & Schiller, 1999; Fiese & Marjinsky, 1999). The depiction of responsive and secure relationships in narratives is also related to how the child creates images of family life. Oppenheim and colleagues have demonstrated that children whose parents create coherent and positive accounts of family life are more likely to be securely attached and to create more emotionally positive narratives when talking about family events (Oppenheim, Emde, & Warren, 1997; Oppenheim, Nir, Warren, & Emde, 1997).

Although family stories can be sources of entertainment, we are interested in them as markers of family functioning and illustrative of how personal meaning is transmitted across generations. There is a transactional process evident between the act of storytelling and the beliefs that are created over time. Children who engage in elaborative storytelling and reminiscence during preschool years are exposed to narratives rich in vocabulary and explanation. As an act, the child develops narrative competence that is associated with emerging literacy skills. The ways in which relationships are depicted in these stories provide a template for relationship expectations and guide behavior. Children who are exposed to personal accounts that depict social relationships as sources of support and reward are more likely to view others as trustworthy and may ultimately become more socially competent. No doubt, educators can detect differences in children who come to school with a story to tell that revolves around excitement about learning and engaging in new experiences in contrast to children who are wary to share family secrets and shy away from interacting with others.

Integrating Family Practices and Representations

From a transactional perspective, both the practicing and representing family code behavior across time and affect one another. Repetitive family practices come to have meaning over time and become the subject of representations. Representations, in turn, affect how the family interacts. We return to bedtime stories to illustrate this process. Consider a situation in which parents have been brought up in the tradition of telling bedtime stories. Around the time that the child begins to talk, the parents implement a routine where they settle the child to sleep with a story. Initially, the stories may be short and take the form of nursery tales. As the child begins to expect the routine event, they may ask for particular stories, some of which may be experiences that the parent had when he or she was a child. These stories are told over and over again in an interactional context where the child is exposed not only to the content of the event but is a conversational partner. If the parent recounts tales of personal success or connectedness with others the child creates images of relationships as rewarding and sources of support in times of need. As the child begins to tell their own stories at bedtime, parents and child have the opportunity to problem solve about personal challenges that may encourage feelings of competence. At the point that the child transitions to school, he or she is a competent narrator paving the way for early literacy skills and socially ready to engage with others. We represent this process in Figure 22.2.

To summarize, family affects on child development are multiply determined and evolve over time. The child contributes to this process through his or her own personal style and experiences that are part of family life. Through repetitive interaction patterns and reinforcement of beliefs, family identity is created. These interactions and beliefs serve to stabilize family life, ease transitions, and regulate child behavior. When there are environmental risks, however, different aspects of family functioning can be compromised making the child vulnerable to develop behavioral and learning problems. We now turn to

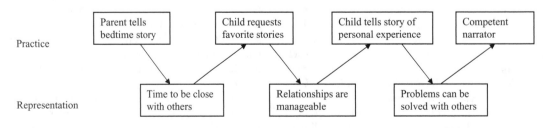

FIGURE 22.2. Transactions between family practices and representations.

two risk factors, poverty and parental psychopathology, and examine the potential for family practices and representations to protect children from the known risks associated with these conditions.

FAMILY RISK AND PROTECTIVE FACTORS

We have emphasized the multiply determined nature of family process in relation to child development. Family process is not a unidimensional variable but one that operates in the realm of behavior and beliefs that are subject to stresses and conditions in the environment. Risk conditions do not operate in isolation either and are likely to cluster together and have cumulative rather than singular effects (Sameroff, 1995). Two notable risk conditions are poverty and parental psychopathology.

Poverty and the Family

Poverty is a wide-reaching problem, with current estimates placing 38% of children in the United States being raised in low-income or poverty conditions. Children who are of an ethnic or racial minority are at greater risk for being raised in low-income or poverty conditions with 57% of African American, 64% of Latino, and 34% of Caucasian children meeting such criteria (National Center for Children in Poverty NCCP, 1993). These statistics are even more alarming when we consider that income levels are at their worst for families during their children's preschool and early years (Brooks-Gunn, Duncan, & Aber, 1997).

Children raised in poverty often are ill-equipped to make the transition from home to school (Rimm-Kaufmann, Pianta, & Cox, 2000) and oftentimes perform poorer on standardized tests (Haveman & Wolfe, 1995). By the time they reach school age, children raised in low-income or poverty conditions are more likely than middle-class or upper-middle-class children to experience multiple stressors in their immediate environment; overcrowding, poor quality of housing, and neighborhood violence, to name a few. Factors such as these have been linked to greater psychological distress in both urban and rural children (Duncan, 1997; Evans, & English, 2002; McLoyd, 1990) and arguably have a negative impact on children's ability to explore new learning experiences and develop intellectually. Children who are more challenged psychologically by experiencing multiple stressors are in a less positive position to acquire new skills.

There are anecdotal examples of children who have succeeded despite any one of these stressors. One may call to mind a child who has thrived in school despite a background of poverty. If this child "made it," why can't another? Despite similarities in one or a few risk factors, it is important to consider that it is not the presence of any particular stressor or a specific combination of risk factors that is uniquely detrimental for children. Rather, it is the cumulative value of any combination of them (Sameroff & Fiese, 2000). Sameroff and colleagues have demonstrated that when parental education, employment status, parental psychopathology, parent-child interaction patterns, child temperament, and neighborhood conditions are

considered simultaneously child intelligence levels can be predicted both concurrently and prospectively (Gutman, Sameroff, & Cole, 2003). What is of interest for our discussion is that neither a single risk variable or even clusters of risk predicted child performance. Multiple risk factors acting in concert predict less optimal outcomes. For this reason, it is not possible to devise a simple formula identifying exactly which factors determine a negative outcome. Thus, it is not sufficient to state that being raised in poverty leads to poor outcomes for children. Rather, it is essential to consider "which aspects of poverty, when, for whom, and under what conditions" lead to compromised functioning. We consider how neighborhood factors, parental psychopathology, and family process may contribute to child outcome in these high-risk conditions.

Neighborhood factors. Families live in neighborhoods. Neighborhood factors, particularly high concentration of poverty within relatively small geographic areas, have been associated with poorer child performance on measures of mental health, verbal ability, IQ scores, and school achievement (Leventhal, 2000, 2003). Findings such as these are not exclusive to children in urban neighborhoods. Low-income and poverty status in children and families living in rural communities have been identified as a risk factor as well (Evans, 2003; Evans, & English, 2002).

Leventhal and Brooks-Gunn (2003) consider neighborhoods indexes of larger social environments that provide institutional resources, relationships and ties among community members, and reinforce norms and a sense of collective efficacy. In poorer neighborhoods institutional resources can be limited such that there are fewer libraries, schools are in disrepair, and the streets may be poorly lit and dangerous (Brooks-Gunn et al., 1997). Opportunities to form relationships with neighbors and develop sources of support can be compromised when there is a need to keep doors locked and transience is common. Faced with increasing rates of violence, families may feel powerless in protecting their children from gangs and illegal activities (Sampson, Raudenbusl, & Earls, 1997). What may be considered adaptive and supportive behavior in middle class neighborhoods may actually place children at greater risk in poorer neighborhoods. For example, maintaining distance from some neighbors and sacrificing employment to be able to monitor childrens' behavior more closely may be adaptive for some high risk families (Burton & Jarrett, 2000).

There are several differences in early literacy skills and the home environments of children raised in poverty compared to those who are not. In a large study of nearly 30,000 children and their families using NLSY data files, Bradley and colleagues (Bradley, Corwyn, McAdoo, & Garcia-Coll, 2001) employed the HOME inventory to assess different aspects of children's experiences in their homes, targeting specific comparisons between nonpoor and poor families, further broken down by race/ethnicity, comparing poor and nonpoor European-American, African-American and Latino American families. For European American, African American and Latino American families, it was observed that nonpoor parents were more likely to spontaneously speak to their children (excluding scolding) than poor parents. In addition, it was found that regardless of racial/ethnic group, poor families were more likely to have no books in the household and that regardless of race/ethnicity, poor parents were more likely than nonpoor parents to endorse that they never read to their children or only read to them a few times per year.

Poverty status had a greater impact on the availability of learning materials than did ethnicity. Generally, poor children were much less likely to have three or more children's books during infancy and early childhood than were nonpoor children. In addition, poor children were less likely to visit enriching places and events in the community. These differences were found across all ethnic groups and all age groups. During infancy and childhood, and across all racial/ethnic groups, nonpoor mothers were twice as likely to read to their children three or more times per week than were poor mothers.

The results of the Bradley and colleagues study suggest that children raised in poorer environments are less likely to be exposed to routine book reading and that their verbal environment, overall, may be relatively impoverished. However, this is not true for all children raised in low-income homes. There is some preliminary evidence to suggest that the practice of regular book reading routines may protect children from developing inadequate literacy and language skills. Keltner (1990) examined the routine practices of families whose child was enrolled in Head Start. She found that families who practiced regular and predictable routines had children who were more engaged, cooperative, and socially competent as rated by their teachers than children whose family life was less regularized.

Kubicek (2002) interviewed 80 mothers who met the income criteria for eligibility in Early Head Start. The mothers reported to the investigators that they were able to develop at least three caretaking routines (e.g., getting dressed, playtime, mealtime, bedtime) and that these routines provided an efficient way to accomplish the tasks of raising a young child. Furthermore, the mothers often remarked that these were the times that they set aside to be together as a family. Although the findings are preliminary and the Kubicek sample includes only women who had completed high school, these results point to potential protective function of routines under conditions of poverty. It is interesting to note that Kubicek found that over half of her sample reported that they read to their child everyday. These findings are in contrast to those reported by Bradley and colleagues (Bradley, Corwyn, McAdoo, & Garcia Coll, 2001). The discrepancy may be the limited sample size and higher education level of the Kubicek sample. Educational status of parents is associated with reading and literacy activities in the home (Hart & Risley, 1992; Klebanov, Brooks-Gunn, & Duncan 1994). However, on close examination of the Bradley and colleague study it is interesting to note that whereas close to one third of poor parents of infants and toddlers reported that they never or rarely read to their children, a greater percentage of poor parents of preschool age children reported that they read to their child on at least a weekly basis if not more frequently. This shift in reading patterns suggests that even under poverty conditions a transactional process may be in place whereby the child's growing interest in stories may prompt parents to read more routinely. It is not clear, however, whether limited exposure to book reading during infancy and toddler years may place the

child at additional risk such that engaging in joint book reading may be a necessary precursor to early literacy skills. With these limitations in mind, there is the prospect that when family caretaking routines are more predictable, there is more opportunity for joint book reading.

Serpell and colleagues (2002) have examined both the routine practices of book reading as well as parents' beliefs about the importance of joint book reading. Serpell and colleagues found that regardless of income, the more time a family spent reading aloud with their children (practice) and the way that they thought of it as an important routine (belief) was associated with the frequency with which the child engaged in joint-book reading at home. Parents endorsed the importance of joint book reading as important either for its entertainment value or for skill promotion. Lower income families were more likely to endorse the importance of joint book reading in terms of the child's developing reading skills. Children's literacy competencies were related to both factors as well as investment in homework routines, even when controlling for income level.

These preliminary studies suggest that there is the potential for routine practices and beliefs to promote early literacy and learning skills under low income and poverty conditions. Certainly, these are not the only protective factors as parent warmth, responsivity, and investment in home based learning activities have been found to be strong predictors of child outcome in poverty conditions (Linver, Brooks-Gunn, & Kohen, 2002). We suggest that routines may provide predictable settings and cues for learning that allow parents to be close with their children and foster literacy skills.

Parental Psychopathology and Family Process

Parent mental health has been associated with compromised child-rearing behavior. Economic hardship, in turn, increases the likelihood that parents will experience mental health problems (McLoyd, 1990). The symptoms of depression, including loss of interest, thoughts of death, sleep and appetite changes have negative implications for the family environment (Dickstein, Seifer, & Magee, 2000) and are often associated with disruptions in mother-child interaction (Downey & Coyne, 1990). Parent mental health appears to directly influence how parents interact with their children. Parents experiencing depression are more likely to be irritable, erratic in discipline strategies, and less likely to provide learning opportunities in the home (Bradley, 1995). Several models have been proposed to explain the link between parental depression and child outcome. For the purposes of our discussion, two considerations seem relevant.

First, parental depression and emotional distress is closely associated with poverty and low-income status. One potential pathway between emotional distress and child outcome under these high-risk conditions is the mediating role of parent-child interaction and family practices. In a compelling study using longitudinal data from the Infant Health and Development Project, Linver, Brooks-Gunn and Kohen (2002) tested two models whereby income level and emotional distress affected child cognitive and behavioral development. They conclude that income level and provision of learning materials were strong predictors of child cognitive development and maternal emotional distress was associated with child behavioral problems. When considering the multidetermined nature of child development, it makes sense that different aspects of the family environment are predictive of different child outcomes. In the case of poverty, availability of resources and investment in learning activities may place strains on the practicing family and predictability of routines. Depressed caregivers have less frequent verbal exchanges with their children, perhaps contributing to lower vocabulary and early literacy skills (Rush, 1999). In the case of emotional distress, parent representations and beliefs concerning relationships may increase the likelihood that child behavior problems develop.

Dickstein and colleagues examined the family stories told by parents of toddlers (1999). A portion of the sample currently met criteria for depression, another portion had a history of depression but was not currently experiencing symptoms, and the third group had no psychiatric history. Parents were interviewed about their family of origin experiences, current family traditions, and perceptions of their child's development. The authors report that mothers who were currently experiencing depression created a less coherent account of family relationships and depicted relationships as less rewarding overall. Furthermore, these dimensions were related to how the family interacted at the dinner table with more negative affect associated with less coherent stories. Interestingly, coherence was not directly related to child behavior problems. We report on these findings to illustrate that parent beliefs may be affected by emotional distress and serve to mediate the relation between parent psychopathology and child outcome.

Summary

During early childhood, family factors contribute to emerging literacy skills, child behavioral regulation, and the child's ability to make the transition from home to school settings. Rich verbal environments with regular routines appear to contribute to the child's ability to be an active learner. Parent-child interaction patterns characterized by warm and responsive interactions are related to the child behavior regulation. We examined how family practices and representations may be affected by poverty and parental psychopathology. Emerging literacy skills are multi-determined (Whitehurst et al., 1988). Family process affects the likelihood that children are prepared to learn through verbal exchanges, support of learning materials in the home, and the social and emotional climate (Britto & Brooks-bunn, 2001). Rates of verbal exchange (Rush, 1999) as well as emotional support and investment in learning have been found to be part of how families practice and prepare their children for school. Opportunities for one-to-one conversations often occur in such routine settings as trips to the grocery store, during mealtime, and when preparing for bed. Thus, family practices are not necessarily carefully constructed lesson plans but promote learning through the natural stream of family activities. For early childhood educators, the challenge then becomes how to connect with the busy lives of families to best prepare their children for school?

CONNECTING SCHOOLS AND FAMILIES

The crucial issue in successful learning is not home or school—teacher or student—but the relationship between them. Learning takes place where there is a productive learning relationship. (Seeley, 1985, p. 11)

The importance of connecting families and schools has been discussed for many years. Bronfenbrenner's (1979, 1992) ecological systems theory has provided a conceptual framework that emphasizes the interface of home and school as an important context for understanding children's development. As Bronfenbrenner (1991) stated, "The informal education that takes place in the family is not merely a pleasant prelude, but rather a powerful prerequisite for success in formal education from the primary grades onward" (p. 5). Recent theoretical work in the area of family and school partnerships, such as Epstein's (1987) theory of overlapping spheres of influence, Comer's (1995) school development process, and Pianta and Walsh's (1996) contextual-systems model, draw heavily on Bronfenbrenner's early work. For the purposes of connecting families and schools, it is not necessary to expand on the details of each of these recent theories. The collective point these theories stress is that children develop in the context of the family and that awareness must develop between the child-family system and the school-schooling system. In addition, these theories provide a conceptual framework that are compatible with the changing demographic characteristics of our population and cultivate home-school connections across culture, race, and ethnicity (Huang & Gibbs, 1992).

Connecting schools and families does not necessarily rely on a specific model or approach (Christenson & Sheridan, 2001). Rather, connecting schools and families means building a relationship between school and families that is intended to improve children's learning and tackle barriers that obstruct children's learning (Wynn, Meyer, & Richards-Schuster, 1999). Over 120 research studies have documented that strong, positive connections between families and schools have an affirmative impact on children's learning as well as protect children from high-risk circumstances (Weissberg & Greenberg, 1998). As a result of these factors, the connection between families and schools has been conceptualized as "a safety net" (Christenson, 1999), which can support and promote children's learning and development (Christenson & Sheridan, 2001).

In addition to improving children's outcomes, connecting families and school can be mutually beneficial to families and educators (Kagan, 1987; Lombana, 1983). Bronfenbrenner (1979) stressed the value of families and schools exchanging ideas and information in order in order for both groups to develop positive attitudes about educating children. For example, when educators develop strong connections with parents, it is likely that educators will increase their attention toward factors related to their students' home life, such as improving self-confidence or encouraging extracurricular interests (Epstein, 1992). When parents develop strong connections with educators, it is likely that parents will increase their attention toward factors related to their children's school education, such as learning progress or academic accomplishments (Epstein, 1992). The mutually beneficial overlap between home and school results in "school-like families" and "family-like schools" (Epstein, 1992).

Recent national and federal initiatives have emerged to further encourage the connection of families and schools. For example, components of the National Education Goals (National Education Goals Panel, 1999), the Individuals with Disabilities Education Act (IDEA; U.S. Congress, 1999), and Title 1 (U.S. Department of Education, 1997) included mandates for family involvement in school issues. In addition, a national position statement on home-school collaboration was adopted by the National Association of School Psychologists (NASP; 1999), which underscored the importance of developing meaningful connections between families and schools. In another example, the *National Standards for Parent/Family Involvement Programs* (National PTA, 1998) identified fundamental aspects that schools should address when promoting family involvement in school issues. These aspects, based on work developed by Epstein (1995), include (a) ensuring regular, two-way, meaningful communication between families and schools; (b) promoting and supporting parenting skills that occur in families; (c) acknowledging that parents play an essential role in assisting children to learn; (d) encouraging parents to assist and support their schools; (e) affirming that parents are full partners in decision making; and (f) providing resources to strengthen schools, families, and student learning. Furthermore, the Partnership for Reading, authorized by the No Child Left Behind Act of 2001, represents a collaborative effort by the U.S. Department of Education, the National Institute for Literacy, and the National Institute of Child Health and Human Development, attempts to build the connection between evidence-based reading research and family literacy programs.

In early childhood programs, home visitation has been used as a means to connect families with schools. Programs such as the *Infant Health and Development Program* for low birth weight infants systematically engaged families in their homes with the aim of reducing risks associated with low birth weight and poverty (Ramey et al., 1992). Although elements of the home visitation programs proved to be effective in improving child outcomes, many of these effects were short-lived once the child was enrolled in school programs that did not include home visitations. The successful elements of the home visitation programs could well inform early childhood educators as they connect with families (Liaw & Brooks-Gunn, 1994).

Despite the agreement regarding the importance of family and school connections, applied practices have been delayed (Christenson & Sheridan, 2001; Rimm-Kaufmann & Pianta, 1999). In many cases, the connections established between family and school can be described as incidental, infrequent, and uncoordinated with children, family, or school needs (Epstein, 1992). Barriers impacting the development of effective family-school partnerships include (a) inadequate school personnel training; (b) unseemly interpersonal skills of school personnel or family members; (c) narrow conceptualizations of family roles in education; (d) underdeveloped communication systems; and (e) restricted opportunities for families and schools to interact (Christenson, 1999). In addition, the changing demographic characteristics of American school children, particularly with respect to culture, language, and family background, have direct implications for families, teachers, schools and communities (Pianta & Cox, 1999). For example, the U.S. Department of Commerce, Bureau of the Census (2002) reports that the number of schoolage children who spoke a language other than English doubled between 1979 and 1999 (U.S. Department of Education, 2003). As a result, there is a greater potential for misunderstanding and miscommunication between school personnel and language minority families (Huang & Gibbs, 1992; Zill, 1999). These findings are further compounded by research suggesting that school personnel often adhere to cultural characteristics of the Caucasian middle class (Pianta & Cox, 1999; Skinner, Bryant, Coffman, & Campbell, 1998). Therefore, it is important to recognize that effective family-school connections can only be made when school personnel recognize and understand the differences and similarities of children from various socioeconomic and cultural backgrounds (Bowman, 1992; Huang & Gibbs, 1992).

In those instances in which strong family and school connections have been made (e.g., Comer, 1980, 1988; Paths to Partnership, 1991), it often has been related to individual characteristics displayed by educators or community members. These characteristics include individuals displaying (a) strong leadership skills, (b) a foundation in child development and factors related to healthy development, (c) appreciation of how children can benefit from coordinated school and family partnerships, (d) experience with systems approaches to preventing and solving problems, and (e) knowledge of the differences between prevention and treatment (Epstein, 1992). Given the education, training, and responsibilities of early childhood educators, this group of professionals is in a unique leadership position to forge school and family connections. The remaining section of this chapter will focus on strategies early childhood educators can utilize to promote family and school connections.

Rethinking School and Family Roles

It has been argued that reconceptualizing and redefining school and family roles may facilitate the development of connections between schools and families (Comer, Haynes, Joyner, & Ben-Avie, 1996; Harry, 1992; Seeley, 1985; Weiss & Edwards, 1992). Educators have traditionally defined family roles within the context of parents serving as volunteers, homework helpers, and fund-raisers (Davies, 1991; Henderson & Berla, 1994). Christenson and Sheridan (2001) stress the importance of broadening school and family roles in order to emphasize the complementary efforts that families and schools provide toward educating children. The U.S. Department of Education (Moles, 1993) advocated building "family-school roles" that encourage shared responsibility and shared roles, in which families and educators would work together as co-communicators, co-supporters, co-learners, co-teachers, and co-decision makers. For example, displaying academic work in the school and community or publicizing children's achievements in school and community publications illustrates school and family as "co-communicators" (Moles, 1993). Organizing success teams composed of educators and family members to assist students who need additional support establishes school and family as "co-supporters" (Moles, 1993). Addressing the needs of language minority families within a home-school instructional success that consists of bilingual or intercultural members may provide a more meaningful bridge between home and school (Huang & Gibbs, 1992). In addition, providing families the opportunity to inform educators of family customs and cultures as well as providing educators the opportunity to inform parents regarding important child development issues exemplifies school and family as "co-learners" and "co-teachers" (Harry, 1992). Other activities that can facilitate "co-teaching" are linking instructional strategies employed at school with themes experienced at home, such as using family stories in written assignments. Finally, involving parents and educators in establishing school policies and practices allows school and family to serve as "co-decision makers" (Harry, 1992; Moles, 1993). Rethinking school and family roles along these lines may be one step in connecting schools and families.

Developing a Climate for Partnership

In order to promote school and family connections, it has been reasoned that a positive climate must be established between school and family that conveys the message that "mutual respect and interdependence of home, school, and community are essential to children's development" (McAfee, 1993, p. 21). However, creating this type of a climate cannot be accomplished overnight. Significant time, effort, and resources need to be invested on the part of schools and families to establish a climate for partnership. Establishing trust between families and schools, slowly introducing a framework for developing family and school connections, and developing successful communication patterns are contributing factors that will be discussed in further detail.

Building and establishing trust. Trust between the family and school is an essential component in developing connections (Haynes et al., 1996). Research examining trust between home and school environments suggests that parent trust of teachers was significantly greater than teacher trust of parents (Adams & Christenson, 1998; 2000). These results may come as no surprise, but suggest the importance of schools building and establishing trust among families. One approach to building trust is fostering welcoming school environment to children and families. Schools that present warm, friendly, and open settings are viewed by parents and community members as "family-friendly" communities (Finders & Lewis, 1993). Additional actions that can promote trust include (a) acceptance of parents; (b) sharing information and resources; and (c) focusing on parents' aspirations, concerns, and needs (Margolis & Brannigan, 1990).

Developing the framework for partnership. Family-school partnerships could learn from research studies

examining the characteristics of effective family-centered mental health services have been helpful in identifying important components necessary for establishing a framework for partnership. Six components have been identified by McWilliam, Tocci, and Harbin (1998) and include family orientation, positiveness, sensitivity, responsiveness, friendliness, and child and community skills. These components are largely the responsibility of the school to create and instill among its' educators. Schools need to lay this foundation in order to begin creating an initial partnership framework with families. Once this foundation has been established, a belief system needs to be created that reflects the connection between families and schools. Liontos (1992) identified five beliefs that can encourage healthy connections between families and schools: (a) all families have strengths; (b) parents can learn ways to help their children if provided with opportunity and support; (c) parents have important information and perspectives about their children; (d) schools and families influence each other; and (e) blame is not attributed to the family or school. The final stage in creating a framework for partnership is to adopt a helping style that permits families and schools to work together effectively. Successful features of this helping style have been identified and include (a) understanding and empathy; (b) accessibility and responsiveness; (c) mutual contributions and agreed-on roles; (d) desire to work together in pursuit of agreed-on goals; (e) shared responsibility in taking actions to achieve such goals; (f) loyalty, trust, and honesty in dealings involving the partnership; (g) full disclosure of pertinent information about partners; and (h) parental locus of decision making (Dunst & Paget, 1991; Vosler-Hunter, 1988).

Developing Early Connections

It has been maintained that family and school connections should develop early and extend over time (Rimm-Kaufmann & Pianta, 1999). This assumption is consistent with models of family involvement supported by early childhood educators, because of recognition that family input is extremely important (Bagnato & Neisworth, 1991). For example, family strengths and needs are often made explicit in early childhood programs and early childhood educators often emphasize family support when conceptualizing and implementing these programs. In addition, early intervention and education of young children mandates assessing and intervening within a family context (Bagnato & Neisworth, 1991; Erickson, 1992). The Preschool Program of Public Law 99-457 (U.S. Department of Education, 1986) emphasizes "parental partnership" (House of Representatives Report 99-860, 1986) by providing more financial coverage of costs related to parent involvement programs and supplying flexible programs that combine home and school options. As noted by Silverstein (1989), "Congress was trying to say 'Do not have professionals come into a family situation and assume that the mom and dad don't know anything" (pp. A-3 and A-4). The philosophical underpinnings of early childhood educators, combined with the legal mandates influencing practice have resulted in parents actively participating in assessment and goal-setting procedures.

In this context, early childhood educators view their clients as "children and families."

One initiative that has direct implications for early childhood educators interested in developing early connections between families is family literature programs. These programs integrate literacy instruction of young children with the development of parents' skill and knowledge in supporting the learning process of their children at home (Dickinson & Tabors, 2001). The Family Partnership in Reading Initiative and the National Research Council have developed research-based methods to promote literacy and language activities for parents and their young children (Armbruster, Lehr, & Osborn, 2003; Burns, Griffin, & Snow, 1999). Publications have been developed for parents, caregivers, and early childhood educators that illustrate how to develop early connections between families and schools. For example, the Family Partnership in Reading recommends that families establish communication mechanisms with early childhood educators so that families understand what is occurring at school or in early childcare education programs and support these activities at home (Armbruster et al., 2003). In addition, the Family Partnership in Reading highlights learning activities that are important for young children, including (a) talking often to young children; (b) showing young children how books and print are used; (c) focusing young children's attention on the sounds of spoken language; (d) identifying and recognizing letters of the alphabet; (e) encouraging young children to spell and write; and (f) building vocabulary (Armbruster et al., 2003). Practical examples of family activities that parents can use to promote their young children's learning at home include engaging in family story telling or imaginary story telling that focuses on recent events (Armbruster et al., 2003, Burns et al., 1999). As children begin to develop more advanced skills, families can make storybooks that highlight school or family events (Armbruster et al., 2003, Burns et al., 1999).

Although early family and school connections may develop, it is possible that these connections may change as young children enter more structured educational settings, such as prekindergarten or kindergarten. In these settings, the conceptualization of education and the view of family may be consistent with elementary school programs that have not traditionally fostered family and school connections (Duff, 1990). Recent efforts have been directed at changing the relationships among schools and families during young children's transition to more structured educational settings (Rimm-Kaufman & Pianta, 1999). For example, children's competence in kindergarten has been traditionally viewed as an indicator of a successful school transition. However, if early childhood educators are committed to developing early school and family connections, then positive school and family connections in kindergarten should be considered a primary indicator of a successful school transition (Rimm-Kaufman & Pianta, 1999).

Strategies for Developing Early Connections

A number of strategies can be employed by early childhood educators to develop early family and school connections. These strategies are based on the work of Christenson and Sheridan (2001), Epstein (1992), Erickson (1992), and Rimm-Kaufman and Pianta (1999), focusing on five key areas: (1) developing a shared vision of family and school connections; (2) creating opportunities for the family, child, and school to connect; (3) developing communication channels to encourage family and school connections; (4) creating opportunities for families and schools to work together on shared goals; and (5) engaging in planning to continue family and school connections as young children transition to new educational settings. Across all strategies, the importance of increasing cultural sensitivity among school personnel and developing communication channels that respect the diversity of spoken languages will promote communication and cooperation across schools and families (Pianta & Cox, 1999).

Establishing a vision of family and school connections. In order to develop a shared vision of family and school connections, a planning committee of members from the school and members of families should be organized. The planning committee should work together to create a shared vision of what constitutes appropriate and meaningful family and school connections. Early childhood educators can play a leadership role in this process, by organizing the planning committee, assisting in brainstorming activities, and ensuring that parents play an active role in the process. After a shared vision has been created and accepted by the planning committee, a vision statement should be developed and publicized. This vision statement should be provided to all educators and families involved with the school setting.

Creating opportunities for connection. Opportunities for the family, school, and child to develop connections should be created. The vision planning committee should identify activities that allow families to connect with educators in school and nonschool settings. For example, schools can sponsor educational (e.g., check in with teacher) and noneducational (e.g., game night) activities that focus on creating family and school connections. The vision planning committee should also identify activities for educators to connect with families in community and family settings. For example, a school-family picnic can be sponsored at a local park or a family-school night can be scheduled at a public library. In many of these instances, community or corporate sponsorship can be obtained in order to defray the costs of these activities. All events should be posted on a family-school calendar that is displayed at school and copied for all families to take home.

Developing communication channels to support connections. Nontraditional communication options should be created to support easy contacts between school and family. The vision planning committee should identify alternative mechanisms for families and schools to communicate. For example, schools and families can co-sponsor and co-develop family-school newsletters that discuss pertinent issues related to children, home, and school. Weekly family-school "check-in" notes or phone calls can be used to increase communication regarding children's progress in both settings. Additional opportunities for family and educators to meet and discuss relevant issues following extended school breaks or during emergency situations should be identified and attempts should be made to accommodate diverse family schedules.

Creating goal-sharing opportunities for connections. Creating opportunities for families and schools to work together on shared goals should be identified by the vision planning committee. In some cases, early childhood educators may need to develop and direct these opportunities, such as providing brief workshops or information sessions on child development. In other cases, families may be responsible for organizing and implementing these opportunities, such as organizing a panel of parents to discuss child-raising issues. Opportunities for families to assist educators (e.g., assisting with classroom activities) and opportunities for educators to assist families (e.g., identifying interesting educational resources for parents) should be identified and promoted.

Transitioning connections. As children transition from one classroom to another or one school setting to another, it becomes necessary to plan for the evolution of new family and school connections. The vision planning committee should identify activities that can support the transitioning of home and school connections. For example, as children transition from prekindergarten to kindergarten, activities for family and educators in both settings can be planned. In many cases, these activities may be similar to those described for creating initial opportunities for connection (e.g., library night in community; game night at school). Activities specific to the classroom transition process can also be created. For example, as children are introduced to the new classroom setting, parents also can be invited and given the opportunity to meet with the new educator.

INTEGRATING FAMILY CONTEXT AND EARLY CHILDHOOD EDUCATION: SUMMARY AND CONCLUSIONS

In this chapter, we have outlined how families are complex and dynamic systems. Families practice regular routines that organize daily life and can provide a sense of order and predictability for young children. Over time, families create beliefs about relationships based, in part, on repetitive interactions occurring in routine settings such as mealtime, bedtime, and preparing for school. Child functioning at any given point in time is the result of a series of transactions between parenting practices and beliefs about relationships. Children may be placed at risk for less than optimal outcomes when family life is disrupted either because of poverty and lack of resources or parental psychopathology. For early childhood educators, the take-home message is that families come to create definitions of who they are as a group. This family identity will shape how the child responds to classroom structure, his or her preparedness to engage in educational activities, and potentially academic success. We want to emphasize that there are multiple ways in which

families create their identity. For some families, there are high expectations for child success and daily life is organized around supporting enriching activities. For other families, protecting children from harm is a priority and family level efforts must be directed toward keeping the family safe. In either case, families typically work hard to insure optimal development for their children given the context in which they live.

There are four lessons to consider when linking families and early childhood educators. First, it may be beneficial to capitalize on routines as a way to connect families and educators. Setting aside regular times to review newly learned skills at home and perhaps creating family night activities that support learning can become part of routine communications between parents and early childhood educators. Parents should be assured that what appears as a mundane task may afford opportunities for learning. Routine conversations at the dinner table, counting the silverware when putting away the dishes, learning about bacteria when taking a walk to the pond are examples where daily practices are rich learning opportunities. Indeed, folding learning into these routine interactions will likely result in more sustained interest than presenting children with additional drill sheets during homework time. Second, storytelling provides a rich opportunity to develop early literacy skills, problem solve, and gain valuable insight to the world of children. These stories need not be complicated, or even revealing of family secrets. Rather they can set the stage for linking personal events experienced in home and school. Third, families are diverse. With the changing nature of family structure, it is important to remember that a child's family is not necessarily restricted to a mother and/or father. Extended family members, neighbors, and kinship ties outside the local area can be sources of support. Each family will create their own unique routines and have their own stories to tell that can aid educators in better understanding the children under their charge. Fourth, by their very nature families change. Not only are there changes in membership through births, deaths, and dissolution of relationships but also there are developmental changes that foster the child's growth. By being sensitive to the ways in which families negotiate transitions between developmental stages as well as prepare their children to transition from home to school settings, educators may become a valuable resource for families during these vulnerable periods.

Families and early childhood educators bear the responsibility of preparing future generations to become productive citizens and lifelong learners. Recognizing the complexity of family life is not an impossible challenge but one worthy of respect. Through an appreciation of the diversity of family practices and beliefs, early childhood educators can be active tenders of the young child's garden of learning.

ACKNOWLEDGMENTS

Preparation of this chapter was supported, in part, by grants from the National Institute of Mental Helth (R01 MH51771-01) to the first author and the National Science Foundation to the first and second authors.

References

Adams, K. S., & Christenson, S. L (1998). Differences in parent and teacher trust levels: Implications for creating collaborative family-school relationships. *Special Services in the Schools, 14,* 1–22.

Adams, K. S., & Christenson, S. L (2000). Trust and the family-school relationship: Examination of parent-teacher differences in elementary and secondary grades. *Journal of School Psychology, 38,* 477–497.

Armbruster, B. B., Lehr, F., & Osborn, J. (2003). *A child becomes a reader: Birth through preschool.* Washington, DC: National Institute for Literacy.

Bagnato, S. J., & Neisworth, J. T. (1991). *Assessment for early intervention: Best practices for professionals.* New York: Guilford Press.

Bennett, L. A., Wolin, S. J., & McAvity, K. J. (1988). Family identity, ritual, and myth: A cultural perspective on life cycle transition. In C. J. Falicov (Ed.), *Family transitions: Continuity and change over the life cycle* (pp. 211–234). New York: Guilford Press.

Bowman, B. T. (1999). Kindergarten practices with children from low-income families. In R. C. Pianta & M. J. Cox (Eds.), *The transition to kindergarten* (pp. 281–304). Baltimore, MD: Paul H. Brookes Publishing Co.

Bradley, R. H. (1995). Home environment and parenting. In M. Bornstein (Ed.), *Handbook of Parenting.* Hillsdale, NJ: Erlbaum.

Bradley, R. H., Corwyn, R. F., McAdoo, H. P., & Garcia-Coll, C. (2001). The home environments of children in the United States Part 1: Variations by age, ethnicity, and poverty status. *Child Development, 72*(6), 1844–1867.

Britto, P. R., & Brooks-Gunn, J. (2001). Beyond shared book reading: Dimensions of home literacy and low-income African-American preschooler's skills. In P. R. Rebello & J. Brooks-Gunn (Eds.), *The role of family literacy environments in promoting young children's emerging literacy skills* (pp.73–89). San Francisco, CA: Jossey-Bass.

Brody, G. H., & Flor, D. L. (1997). Maternal psychological functioning, family processes, and child adjustment in rural, single-parent, African American families. *Developmental Psychology, 33,* 1000–1011.

Bronfenbrenner, U. (1979). *The ecology of human development.* Cambridge, MA: Harvard University Press.

Bronfenbrenner, U. (1991). What do families do?: Part 1. *Teaching Thinking and Problem Solving, 13,* 3–5.

Bronfenbrenner, U. (1992). Ecological systems theory. In R. Vasta (Ed.), *Annals of child development: Six theories of child development: Revised formulations and current issues* (pp. 187–249). London: Jessica Kingsley.

Brooks-Gunn, J., Duncan, G. J., & Aber, J. L. (1997). *Neighborhood poverty: Vol. 1. Context and consequences for children.* New York: Russell Sage Foundation.

Burns, M. S., Griffin, P., & Snow, C. E. (1999). *Starting out right: A guide to promoting children's reading success.* Washington, DC: National Academy Press.

Burton, L. M., & Jarrett, R. L. (2000). In the mix, yet on the margins: the place of families in urban neighborhood and child development research. *Journal of marriage and the family, 62,* 1114–1135.

Christenson, S. L. (1999). Families and schools: Rights, responsibilities, resources, and relationships. In R. C. Pianta & M. J. Cox (Eds.), *The transition to kindergarten* (pp. 143–178). Baltimore, MD: Paul H. Brookes Publishing Co.

Christenson, S. L., & Sheridan, S. M. (2001). *Schools and families: Creating essential connections for learning.* New York: Guilford Press.

Comer, J. (1980). *School power.* New York: Free Press.

Comer, J. (1988). *Maggie's American dream.* New York: New American Library.

Comer, J. (1995). *School power: Implications of an intervention project.* New York: Free Press.

Comer, J. P., Haynes, N. M., Joyner, E. T., & Ben-Avie, M. (1996). *Rallying the whole village: The Comer process for reforming education.* New York: Teachers College Press.

Cowan, P. A., Cowan, C. P., Heming, G., & Miller, N. B. (1991). Becoming a family: Marriage, parenting, and child development. In P. A. Cowan & M. Hetherington (Eds.), *Family transitions* (pp. 79–110). Hillsdale, NJ: LEA.

Davies, D. (1991). Schools reaching out: Family, school, and community partnerships for student success. *Phi Delta Kappan, 72,* 376–382.

DeBaryshe, B. D. (1995). Maternal belief systems: Linchpin in the home reading process. *Journal of Applied Developmental Psychology, 16,* 1–20.

Dickinson, D. K., & Tabors, P. O. (2001). *Beginning literacy with language: Young children learning at home and school.* Baltimore, MD: Paul H. Brookes Publishing Co.

Dickstein, S., Seifer, R., & Magee, K. D. (2000, June). *Mental health promotion in early Head Start: Lessons from research on postpartum depression.* Paper presented at the Fifth Head Start National Research Conference, Washington, DC.

Dickstein, S., St. Andre, M., Sameroff, A. J., Seifer, R., & Schiller, M. (1999). Maternal depression, family functioning, and child outcomes: A narrative assessment. *Monographs of the Society for Research in Child Development, 64*(2, Serial No. 257).

Downey, G., & Coyne, J. C. (1990). Children of depressed parents: An integrative review. *Psychological Bulletin, 108*(1), 50–76.

Duncan, G. J., & Brooks-Gunn, J. (1997). The effects of poverty on children. *Future of Children, 7*(2), 55–71.

Dunst, C. J., & Paget, K. (1991). Parent-professional partnerships and family empowerment. In M. Fine (Ed.), *Collaboration with parents of exceptional children* (pp. 25–44). Brandon, VT: Clinical Psychology Publishing.

Epstein, J. L. (1987). Toward a theory of family-school connections: Teacher practices and parent involvement. In K. Hurrelmann, F. Kaufmann, & F. Losel (Eds.), *Social interaction: Potential and constraints* (pp. 121–136). New York: deGruyter.

Epstein, J. L. (1992). School and family partnerships: Leadership roles for school psychologists. In S. L. Christenson & J. C. Conoley (Eds.), *Home-school collaboration* (pp. 499–516). Silver Spring, MD: The National Association of School Psychologists.

Erickson, M. F. (1992). School-based interventions for infants and toddlers in a family setting. In S. L. Christenson & J. C. Conoley (Eds.), *Home-school collaboration* (pp. 245–263). Silver Spring, MD: The National Association of School Psychologists.

Evans, G. (2003). A multimethod analysis of cumulative risk and allostatic loading among rural children. *Developmental Psychology, 39*(5), 924–933.

Evans, G., & English, K. (2002). The environment of poverty: Multiple stressor exposure, psychophysiological stress, and socioemotional adjustment. *Child Development, 73*(4), 1238–1248.

Falicov, C. J. (2003). Immigrant family processes. In F. Walsh (Ed.), *Normal Family Processes* (3rd ed., pp. 280–300). New York: Guilford.

Fiese, B. H. (1992). Dimensions of family rituals across two generations: Relation to adolescent identity. *Family Process, 31,* 151–162.

Fiese, B. H. (2000). Family matters: A systems view of family effects on children's cognitive health. In R. J. Sternberg & E. L. Grigorenko (Eds.), *Environmental effects on cognitive abilities* (pp. 39–57). Mahwah, NJ: LEA.

Fiese, B. H. (2002). Routines of daily living and rituals in family life: A glimpse at stability and change during the early school yeras. *Zero to Three, 22*, 10-13.

Fiese, B. H., & Bickham, N. L. (2004). Pincurling grandpa's hair in the comfy chair: Parents' stories of growing up and potential links to socialization in the preschool years. In M. W. Pratt & B. H. Fiese (Eds.), *Family stories across time and generations* (pp. 259-277). Mahwah, NJ: Erlbaum.

Fiese, B. H., Hooker, K. A., Kotary, L., & Schwagler, J. (1993). Family rituals in the early stages of parenthood. *Journal of Marriage and the Family, 57*, 633-642.

Fiese, B. H., Hooker, K. A., Kotary, L., Schwagler, J., & Rimmer, M. (1995). Family stories in the early stages of parenthood. *Journal of Marriage and the Family, 57*, 763-770.

Fiese, B. H., & Marjinsky, K. A. T. (1999). Dinnertime stories: Connecting relationship beliefs and child behavior. *Monographs of the Society for Research in Child Development, 64*(2, Serial No. 257).

Fiese, B. H., & Sameroff, A. J. (1999). The family narrative consortium: A multidimensional approach to narratives. *Monographs of the Society for Research in Child Development, 64*(2, Serial No. 257).

Fiese, B. H., Sameroff, A. J., Grotevant, H. D., Wamboldt, F. S., Dickstein, S., & Fravel, D. L. (1999). The stories that families tell: Narrative coherence, narrative interaction, and relationship beliefs. *Monographs of the Society for Research in Child Development, 64*(2, Serial No. 257).

Fiese, B. H., Tomcho, T., Douglas, M., Josephs, K., Poltrock, S., & Baker, T. (2002). Fifty years of research on naturally occurring rituals: Cause for celebration? *Journal of Family Psychology, 16*, 381-390.

Fiese, B. H., & Wamboldt, F. S. (2001). Family routines, rituals, and asthma management: A proposal for family based strategies to increase treatment adherence. *Family, Systems, and Health, 18*, 405-418.

Finders, M., & Lewis, C. (1993). Why some parents don't come to school. *Educational Leadership, 51*, 50-54.

Fivush, R., Bohanke, J., Robertson, R., & Duke, M. (2004). Family narratives and the development of children's emotional well-being. In M. W. Pratt & B. H. Fiese (Eds.), *Family narratives across time and generations* (pp. 55-76). Mahwah, NJ: Erlbaum.

Fivush, R., & Fromhoff, F. A. (1988). Style and structure in mother-child conversations about the past. *Discourse Processes, 11*, 337-355.

Fung, H., Miller, P. J., & Lin, L. (2004). Listening is Active: Lessons from the narrative practices of Taiwanese familiesl. In M. W. Pratt & B. H. Fiese (Eds.), *Family stories and the life course: Across time and generations* (pp. 303-323). Mahwah, NJ: Erlbaum.

Grusec, J. E., Goodnow, J. J., & Cohen, L. (1996). Household work and the development of concern for others. *Developmental Psychology, 32*, 999-1007.

Gutman, L. M., Sameroff, A. J., & Cole, R. (2003). Academic growth curve trajectoiries from 1st grade to 12th grade: Effects of multiple social risk factors and preschool child factors. *Developmental Psychology, 39*, 777-790.

Harkness, S., & Super, S. (Eds.). (1996). *Parental cultural beliefs systems: Their origins, expressions, and consequences.* New York: Guilford.

Harris, J. R. (1995). Where is the child's environment? A group socialization theory of development. *Psychological Review, 102*, 458-489.

Harry, B. (1992). *Cultural diversity, families, and the special education system: Communication and empowerment.* New York: Teachers College Press.

Hart, B., & Risley, T. R. (1992). American parenting of language-learning children: Persisting differences in family-child interactions observed in natural home environments. *Developmental Psychology, 28*(6), 1096-1105.

Haveman, R., & Wolfe, B. (1995). The determinants of children's attainments: A review of methods and findings. *Journal of Economic Literature, 33*, 1829-1878.

Haynes, N. M., Ben-Avie, M., Squires, D. A., Howley, J. P., Negron, E. N., & Corbin, J. N. (1996). It takes a village: The SDP school. In J. P. Comer, N. M. Haynes, E. T. Joyner, & M. Ben-Avie (Eds.), *Rallying the whole village: The Comer process for reforming education* (pp. 42-71). New York: Teachers College Press.

Henderson, A. T., & Berla, N. (Eds.). (1994). *A new generation of evidence: The family is critical to student achievement.* Washington, DC: National Committee for Citizens in Education.

House of Representatives Report 99-860. (1986, September). *Education of the Handicapped Act Amendments of 1986.* Washington, DC. Author.

Howe, M., & Courage, M. (1997). The emergence and early development of autobiographical memory. *Psychological Review, 104*, 499-523.

Huang, L. N., & Gibbs, J. T. (1992). Partners or adverseries? Home-school collaboration across culture, race, and ethnicity. In S. L. Christenson & J. C. Conoley (Eds.), *Home-school collaboration* (pp. 81-109). Silver Spring, MD: The National Association of School Psychologists.

Kagan, S. (1987). Home-school linkages: History's legacy and the family resource movement. In S. Kagan, D. Powell, B. Weissbourd, & E. Zigler (Eds.), *America's family support programs* (pp. 161-181). New Haven: Yale University Press.

Keltner, B. (1990). Family characteristics of preschool social competence among Black children in a Head Start program. *Child Psychiatry and Human Development, 21*, 95-108.

Klebanov, P. K., Brooks-Gunn, J., & Duncan, G. J. (1994). Does neighborhood and family poverty affect mothers' parenting, mental health, and social support? *Journal of Marriage and the Family, 56*(2), 441-455.

Kubicek, L. F. (2002). Fresh perspectives on young children and family routines, *Zero to Three, 22*, 4-9.

Landesman, S., Jaccard, J., & Gunderson, V. (1991). The family environment: The combined influence of family behavior, goals, strategies, resources, and individual experiences. In M. Lewis & S. Feinman (Eds.), *Social influences and socialization in infancy* (pp. 63-96). New York: Plenum.

Leventhal, T., & Brooks-Gunn, J. (2000). The neighborhoods they live in: The effects of neighborhood residence on child and adolescent outcomes. *Psychological Bulletin, 126*(2), 309-337.

Leventhal, T., & Brooks-Gunn, J. (2003). Children and youth in neighborhood contexts. *Current Directions in Psychological Science, 12*(1), 27-31.

Liaw, F., & Brooks-Gunn, J. (1994). Cumulative familial risks and low birthweight children's cognitive and behavioral development. *Journal of Clinical Child Psychology, 23*, 360-372.

Lidz, T., Cornelison, A., Fleck, S., & Terry, D. (1957). The intrafamilial environment of schizophrenic patients: II. Marital schism and marital skew. *American Journal of Psychiatry, 114*, 241-248.

Linver, M. R., Brooks-Gunn, J., & Kohen, D. E. (2002). Family processes as pathways from income to young children's development. *Developmental Psychology, 38*, 719-734.

Liontos, L. B. (1992). *At-risk families and schools: Becoming partners.* Euguene, OR: ERIC Clearinghouse on Educational Management, College of Education, University of Oregon.

Lombana, J. (1983). *Home-school partnerships.* New York: Grune & Stratton.

Margolis, H., & Brannigan, G. G. (1990). Strategies for resolving parent-school conflict. *Reading, Writing, and Learning Disabilities, 6*, 1-23.

McAfee, O. (1993). Communication: The key to effective partnerships. In R. C. Burns (Eds.), *Parents and schools: From visitors to partners* (pp. 21–34). Washington, DC: National Education Association.

McCabe, A., & Peterson, C. (1991). Getting the story: A longitudinal study of parental styles in eliciting narratives and developing narrative skill. In A. McCabe & C. Peterson (Eds.), *Developing narrative structure* (pp. 217–253). Hillsdale, NJ: Erlbaum.

McDonough, S. C. (1993). Interaction guidance: Understanding and treating early infant-caregiver relationship disturbances. In C. H. Zeenah (Ed.), *Handbook of infant mental health* (pp. 414–426). New York: Guilford.

McLoyd, V. C., & Wilson, L. (1990). Maternal behavior, social support, and economic conditions as predictors of distress in children. *New Directions for Child Development, 46,* 49–69.

McWilliam, R. A., Tocci, L., & Harbin, G. L. (1998). Family-centered services: Service providers' discourse and behavior. *Topics in Early Childhood Special Education, 18,* 206–221.

Miller, P. J., & Moore, B. B. (1989). Narrative conjunctions of caregiver and child: A comparative perspective on socialization through stories. *Ethos, 17,* 43–64.

Miller, P. J., Wiley, A. R., Fung, H., & Liang, C. (1997). Personal storytelling as a medium of socialization in Chinese and American families. *Child Development, 68,* 557–568.

Moles, O. (1993). *Building school-family partnerships for learning: Workshops for urban educators.* Washington, DC: Office of Research, Office of Education Research Improvement, U.S. Department of Education, 20208.

National Association of School Psychologists (1999). *Position statement on home-school collaboration: Establishing partnerships to enhance outcomes.* Bethesda, MD: Author.

National PTA (1998). *National standards for parent/family involvement programs.* Chicago: Author.

Nespeca, S. M. (1995). Parental involvement in emergent literacy skills of urban Head Start children. *Early Child Development & Care, 111,* 153–180.

Norton, D. (1993). Diversity, early socialization, and temporal development: The dual perspective revisited. *Social Work, 38,* 82–90.

Nucci, L., & Smetana, J. G. (1996). Mothers' concepts of young children's areas of personal freedom. *Child Development, 67,* 1870–1886.

O'Connor, T. G., & Plomin, R. (2000). Developmental behavioral genetics. In A. J. Sameroff, M. Lewis & S. M. Miller (Eds.), *Handbook Developmental Psychopathology* (pp. 218–236). New York: Kluwer.

Oppenheim, D., Emde, R., & Warren, S. (1997). Children's narrative representations of mothers: Their development and associations with child and mother adaptation. *Child Development, 68,* 127–138.

Oppenheim, D., Nir, A., Warren, S., & Emde, R. N. (1997). Emotion regulation in mother-child narrative co-construction: Associations with children's narratives and adaptation. *Developmental Psychology, 33,* 284–294.

Peterson, C., & McCabe, A. (2004). Echoing our parents. In M. W. Pratt & B. H. Fiese (Eds.), *Family stories across time and generations* (pp. 27–54). Mahwah, NJ: Erlbaum.

Pianta, R., & Walsh, D. B. (1996). *High-risk children in schools: Constructing and sustaining relationships.* New York: Routledge.

Pianta, R. C., & Cox, M. J. (1999). The changing nation of the transition to school: Trends for the next decade. In R. C. Pianta & M. J. Cox (Eds.), *The transition to kindergarten* (pp. 363–380). Baltimore, MD: Paul H. Brookes Publishing Co.

Pratt, M. W., & Fiese, B. H. (2004). Families, stories and the life course: An ecological context. In M. W. Pratt & B. H. Fiese (Eds.), *Family stories across time and generations.* Mahwah, NJ: Erlbaum.

Ramey, C., Bryant, D., Waskik, B., Sparling, J., Fendt, K., & LaVange, L. (1992). Infant Health and Development Program for low birth weight, premature infants: Program elements, family participation, and child intelligence. *Pediatrics, 3,* 454–465.

Reiss, D. (1989). The practicing and representing family. In A. J. Sameroff & R. Emde (Eds.), *Relationship disturbances in early childhood.* (pp. 191–220). New York: Basic Books.

Rimm-Kaufmann, S. E., & Pianta, R. C. (1999). Patterns of family-school contact in preschool and kindergarten. *School Psychology Review, 28,* 426–438.

Rimm-Kaufmann, S. E., Pianta, R. C., & Cox, M. J. (2000). Teachers' judgments of problems in the transition to kindergarten. *Early Childhood Research Quarterly, 15,* 147–166.

Roopnarine, J., Bynoe, P. F., & Singh, R. (2004). Factors tied to the schooling of children of English-speaking and Caribbean immigrants in the United States. In U. P. Gielen & J. Roopnarine (Eds.), *Childhood and adolescence: Cross-cultural perspectives and applications* (pp. 319–349). Westport, CT: Praeger.

Roth, F. P. (1986). Oral narrative abilities of learning-disabled children. *Topics in Language Disorders, 7,* 21–30.

Rush, K. (1999). Caregiver-chid interactions and early literacy development of preschool children from low-income families. *Topics in Early Childhood Special Education, 62*(1), 3–14.

Sameroff, A. J. (1995). General systems theories and developmental psychopathology. In D. Cicchetti & D. Cohen (Eds.), *Handbook of developmental psychopathology* (Vol. 1, pp. 659–695). New York: Wiley.

Sameroff, A. J., & Chandler, M. J. (1975). Reproductive risk and the continuum of caretaking causality. In F. D. Horowitz, M. Hetherington, S. Scarr-Salapetek & G. Siegel (Eds.), *Review of child development research* (Vol. 4, pp. 187–244). Chicago: Chicago University Press.

Sameroff, A. J., & Fiese, B. H. (2000). Transactional regulation: The developmental ecology of early intervention. In S. J. Meisels & J. P. Shonkoff (Eds.), *Early intervention: A handbook of theory, practice, and analysis* (pp. 3–19). New York: Cambridge University Press.

Sampson, R. J., Raudenbush, S. W., & Earls, F. (1997). Neighborhoods and violent crime: A multilevel study study of collective efficacy. *Science, 277,* 918–924.

Scarr, S., & Kidd, K. K. (1983). Developmental behavior genetics. In *Handbook of child psychology: Vol 2 Paul H. Mussen, editor* (pp. 345–433). New York: Wiley.

Seeley, D. S. (1985). *Education through partnership.* Washington, DC: American Enterprise Institute for Policy Research.

Serpell, R., Sonnenschein, S., Baker, L., & Ganapathy, H. (2002). Intimate culture of families in the early socialization of literacy. *Journal of Family Psychology, 16,* 391–405.

Silverstein, R. (1989). *The intent and spirit of P. L. 99-457: A sourcebook.* Washington, DC: National Center for Clinical Infant Programs.

Skinner, D., Bryant, D., Coffman, J., & Campbell, F. (1998). Creating risk and promise: Children's and teachers' co-constructions in the cultural world of kindergarten. *Elementary School Journal, 98,* 297–310.

Snow, C. E. (1983). Literacy and language: Relationships during the preschool years. *Harvard Educational Review, 53,* 165–189.

Spock, B. (1955). *Baby and child care.* London: Bodley Head.

Sprunger, L. W., Boyce, W. T., & Gaines, J. A. (1985). Family-infant congruence: Routines and rhythmicity in family adaptations to a young infant. *Child Development, 56,* 564–572.

U.S. Department of Education (1986). *Education of the Handicapped Amendments.* Washington, DC: Author.

U.S. Department of Education, National Center for Education Statistics (2003). *The Condition of Education 2003.* Washington, DC: U.S. Government Printing Office.

Vogel, E. F., & Bell, N. W. (1960). The emotionally disturbed child as the family scapegoat. In N. W. B. E. F. Vogel (Ed.), *The family*. Glencoe, IL: Free Press.

Vosler-Hunter, R. W. (1989). *Changing roles, changing relationships: Parent-professional collaboration on behalf of children with emotional disabilities*. Portland, OR: Portland State University, Research and Training Center on Family Support and Children's Mental Health.

Walsh, F. (2003). *Normal family processes* (3rd ed.). New York: Guilford.

Wang, Q. (2004). The cultural context of parent-child reminiscing: A functional analysis. In M. W. Pratt & B. H. Fiese (Eds.), *Family stories and the life course: Across time and generations*. Mahwah, NJ: Erlbaum.

Weiss, H. M., & Edwards, M. E. (1992). The family-school collaboration project: Systemic interventions for school improvement. In S. L. Christenson & J. C. Conoley (Eds.), *Home-school collaboration* (pp. 215–243). Silver Spring, MD: The National Association of School Psychologists.

Whitehurst, G. J., Falco, F., Lonigan, C. J., Fischel, J. E., DeBaryshe, B. D., Valdez-Menchaca, M. C. et al. (1988). Accelerating language development through picture-book reading. *Developmental Psychology, 24*, 552–558.

Wynn, J., Meyer, S., & Richards-Schuster, K. (1999). Furthering education: The relationship of schools and other organizations. *The CEIC Review, 8*, 8–9, 17–19.

Zill, N. (1999). Promoting educational equity and excellence in kindergarten. In R. C. Pianta & M. J. Cox (Eds.), *The transition to kindergarten* (pp. 67–108). Baltimore, MD: Paul H. Brookes Publishing Co.

Zinn, M. B., & Wells, B. (2000). Diversity within Latino families: New lessons for family social science. In D. H. Demo, K. R. Allen & M. A. Fine (Eds.), *Handbook of family diversity* (pp. 252–273). Oxford: Oxford University Press.

· 23 ·

EARLY CHILDHOOD TEACHERS' BELIEFS AND ATTITUDES ABOUT INCLUSION: WHAT DOES THE RESEARCH TELL US?

Michaelene M. Ostrosky
Bernadette M. Laumann
Wu-Ying Hsieh
University of Illinois at Urbana-Champaign

Although research on inclusion in early education settings has appeared in the empirical literature since the 1970s, the inclusion of preschoolers with disabilities with their typically developing peers in early childhood settings emerged as a major service alternative in the 1990s. In 1986 Public Law 99-457 mandated the free and appropriate public education of preschoolers (ages 3–5) with disabilities, thus expanding opportunities for younger children with special needs to receive a free education aimed at enhancing their skills and development. Increasingly, young children with special needs are included in typical early childhood settings such as Head Start, child care, and public and private preschools (Guralnick, 2001; Odom, 2000).

Definitions of inclusion vary across stakeholder groups and the individuals within these groups, such as teachers, administrators, and family members. For example, Allen and Schwartz (2001) define inclusion as "belonging to a community—a group of friends, a school community, or a neighborhood" (p. 2), whereas the Council for Exceptional Children, Division for Early Childhood Education's (DEC) position statement on inclusion (2000) notes "Inclusion as a value supports the right of all children regardless of their diverse abilities to participate actively in natural settings within their communities. A natural setting is one in which the child would spend time if he or she had not had a disability" (see Box 23.1 for the full text of the DEC position statement). In its mission statement the National Association for the Education of Young Children (NAEYC) (1996) encourages its members to "promote inclusion, access, and nondiscrimination in the full range of programs serving young children, their families, and adults preparing to work in the early childhood education profession."

In an attempt to synthesize key findings from the Early Childhood Research Institute on Inclusion, Odom (2002) and his colleagues describe eight major points learned through their focused research agenda on this topic. These points are: (a) inclusion is about belonging and participating in a diverse society; (b) individuals define inclusion differently; (c) beliefs about inclusion influence its implementation; (d) programs, not children, have to be prepared for inclusion; (e) collaboration is the cornerstone of effective inclusive programs; (f) specialized instruction is an important component of inclusion; (g) adequate support is necessary to make inclusive environments work; and (h) inclusion can benefit children with and without disabilities (p. 156).

Despite the strong research base on preschool inclusion and the increased availability of inclusive programs and services, a number of issues still remain. Bricker (2000) notes that barriers to successful inclusion are complex and the quality of instruction, such as the provision of individualized and specialized training, often fails to adhere to recommended practices in early

---

Box 23.1 DEC Position Statement on Inclusion

Inclusion, as a value, supports the right of all children, regardless of abilities, to participate actively in natural settings within their communities. Natural settings are those in which the child would spend time had he or she not had a disability. These settings include, but are not limited to home, preschool, nursery schools, Head Start programs, kindergartens, neighborhood school classrooms, child care, places of worship, recreational (such as community playgrounds and community events) and other settings that all children and families enjoy.

DEC supports and advocates that young children and their families have full and successful access to health, social, educational, and other support services that promote full participation in family and community life. DEC values the cultural, economic, and educational diversity of families and supports a family-guided process for identifying a program of service.

As young children participate in group settings (such as preschool, play groups, child care, kindergarten) their active participation should be guided by developmentally and individually appropriate curriculum. Access to and participation in the age appropriate general curriculum becomes central to the identification and provision of specialized support services.

To implement inclusive practices DEC supports: (a) the continued development, implementation, evaluation, and dissemination of full inclusion supports, services, and systems that are of high quality for all children; (b) the development of preservice and inservice training programs that prepare families, service providers, and administrators to develop and work within inclusive settings; (c) collaboration among key stakeholders to implement flexible fiscal and administrative procedures in support of inclusion; (d) research that contributes to our knowledge of recommended practice; and (e) the restructuring and unification of social, educational, health, and intervention supports and services to make them more responsive to the needs of all children and families. Ultimately, the implementation of inclusive practice must lead to optimal developmental benefit for each individual child and family.

Note: Adopted: December 1993; Reaffirmed: December 1996; Revised: June 2000

---

education. DEC and NAEYC have developed recommended practices that lay the foundation for providing early childhood education in inclusive settings (see Bredekamp & Copple, 1997; Sandall, Hemmeter, Smith, & McLean, 2005), yet observations in early education settings often reveal inappropriate practices being implemented. For example, Bricker (2000) discusses the inadequate social interactions that frequently occur in inclusive early childhood settings, with children with disabilities being treated differently by their peers, and children with disabilities spending large portions of their time in isolation. It appears that many of the problems related to preschool inclusion have to do with the definition of inclusion, the quality of services, the intensity and specificity of services, the creation of meaningful social experiences for children, and the infrastructure needed to ensure effective and sustainable inclusive services for children (Odom, 2000). Also, changing demographics of the population of preschoolers with disabilities and the need to provide culturally appropriate and responsive services complicates the development and delivery of inclusive programs (Barrera & Corso, 2003; Lynch & Hanson, 2004).

A variety of factors can influence the successful implementation of inclusive education. One significant factor is the attitudes that general education teachers have toward students with disabilities. Whether general educators' attitudes are positive or negative has a tremendous impact on the outcomes of inclusion (D'Alonzo, Giordano, & Vanleeuwen, 1997; Smith & Smith, 2000). Indeed, adult behavior influences children's ideas about and interactions with other children (Bricker, 1995; Lieber et al., 1998). Consequently, teachers' attitudes play an important part in educating students with disabilities in general education classrooms (Eichinger, Rizzo, & Sirotnik, 1991).

In this chapter, we highlight what the research has taught us regarding early childhood inclusion, with particular emphasis on teachers' attitudes and beliefs (see Fig. 23.1). We conclude the chapter with ideas for future research and suggestions for supporting teachers in inclusive efforts.

THE IMPORTANCE OF TEACHERS' BELIEFS AND ATTITUDES

Attitudes and beliefs are "a subset of a group of constructs that name, define, and describe the structure and content of mental states that drive a person's actions" (Richardson, 1996, p. 102). Allport (1967) defined attitude as "a mental and neural state of readiness which is organized through experience that exerts influence upon the individual's response to all objects and situations with which it is related" (p. 8). In turn, Richardson (1996) defines beliefs as "psychologically held understandings, premises, or propositions about the world that are felt to be true" (p. 103). Because teachers' perceptions influence their behaviors (e.g., classroom management, instructional strategies) (Brownell & Pajares, 1999), how they perceive inclusion has the potential to strongly impact their classroom practices.

Unfortunately, not all public school teachers have positive attitudes toward students with disabilities. Many teachers have not received adequate training or education in including students with disabilities into the general education curriculum (D'Alonzo et al., 1997). For example, general education teachers reported feelings of incompetence in handling children's challenging behaviors such as outbursts or noncompliance due to insufficient training in special education (Monahan, Marino, & Miller, 1996). Because of this tension, teachers may develop negative attitudes toward inclusive education (D'Alonzo et al., 1997).

In inclusive settings, both general and special educators are challenged to create innovative programs to serve a variety of students from diverse backgrounds and cultures, with a full range of abilities (York & Reynolds, 1996). Inclusion requires both general and special educators to define new roles for themselves, examine long-held beliefs about themselves as teachers, and assume responsibilities for which they may not have been prepared. Given the impact that teachers' beliefs and attitudes have on the daily decisions they make in the classroom, it is important to attend to what the literature reports about early childhood (ECE) and early childhood special education (ECSE) teachers' beliefs and attitudes about inclusion especially in light of the variety of disciplines involved and environments within which early childhood professionals work. Early education programs throughout the United States operate in a wide variety of settings (e.g., Head Start, child care, public school prekindergarten programs) by various personnel (e.g., therapists, psychologists, administrators, child care teachers, etc.). Early childhood professionals hold a wide range of views concerning philosophy, teaching practices, appropriate curriculum, and knowledge about teaching young children with disabilities.

According to Richardson (1996), teachers' beliefs come from three sources: personal experience, experience with schooling and instruction, and formal knowledge about teaching. From the empirical literature six variables emerge that confirm and extend Richardson's three sources of teachers' beliefs. These variables influence the formation of professionals' beliefs and attitudes about inclusion: (a) type of preservice training and level of educational attainment, (b) quality and amount of inservice training for inclusion, (c) adequate time for planning and collaboration, (d) "hands-on" experiences with inclusion, (e) type and severity of a child's disability, and (f) perceived outcomes for children with or without disabilities. These variables are some of the same factors that researchers found to influence elementary and secondary teachers' beliefs and attitudes about inclusion (see Baker & Zigmond, 1995; Monahan et al., 1996; Olson, Chalmers, & Hoover, 1997; Pearman, Huang, & Mellblom, 1997; Scruggs & Mastropieri, 1996; Smith & Smith, 2000; Villa, Thousand, Meyers, & Nevin, 1996; Wood, 1995; York & Reynolds, 1996). Early childhood research that addresses each of the six variables is discussed in the following sections.

Type of Preservice Training and Level of Educational Attainment

Stoiber, Gettinger, and Goetz (1998) designed the *My Thinking About Inclusion Scale (MTAI)* to assess early childhood practitioners' (i.e., early childhood special educators, early childhood general educators, paraprofessionals, speech therapists, administrators, and psychologists) and parents' beliefs about inclusion. Respondents with more formal education (e.g., bachelor's or master's degrees in education or a related field) held more positive beliefs about inclusion than those with less education (e.g., paraprofessionals). Stoiber et al. surmised that this difference may be because respondents with more education were exposed to the concept of inclusion in college courses. These researchers also found that practitioners preferred the use of field-based approaches where they could participate in direct, "hands-on" experiences to improve their understanding of effective inclusive practices.

Marchant (1995) interviewed 10 teachers who had been teaching in public-sponsored preschools for at least 2 years. All 10 teachers had masters degrees and had chosen to work in inclusive settings. All of the teachers held positive beliefs and

attitudes about the benefits of an integrated model for children with and without disabilities and their families. Although many of these teachers had ECSE training and held graduate degrees, they felt frustrated by administrative and systems-level issues that arose in their programs. Marchant concluded that preservice training should prepare teachers not only for classroom level issues surrounding inclusion but also prepare them to address complex administrative issues that arise in inclusive programs (e.g., system procedures and politics, budget constraints, and problems with space and facilities). Harbin and Salisbury (2000) note that "The interdependent relationships between structure, services, supports, and outcomes are consistent with ecological theories of development. These theories suggest that the child's development is influenced not only by the family, neighborhood, subculture, and community, but by the systems of services and supports that serve them as well" (p. 65).

Lieber and her colleagues (1998) discovered that although classroom teachers may use similar phrases to describe inclusive practices, they may actually use them to mean different things. These researchers also found that teachers who team-taught in the same classroom did not always hold similar beliefs about inclusion and that teachers' beliefs often reflected their initial training (ECE or ECSE) as well as the type of classroom setting in which they were employed. Lieber and her colleagues also found that regardless of their preservice or inservice training, a number of preschool teachers were not observed engaging in strategies that are believed to be recommended practices in early childhood inclusion. Level of educational attainment (master's degree vs. bachelor's degree) did not impact whether a teacher was more capable of individualizing curriculum for a child with disabilities.

Two recent studies have reported preservice early childhood teachers' beliefs and attitudes about inclusion. Baum and McMurray-Schwarz (2001) conducted focus groups with 19 undergraduate early childhood preservice teachers to discuss their beliefs about several issues (e.g., teacher role, inclusion, parent involvement). Students were divided into focus groups based on their year in college and follow-up interviews were conducted with six participants. An interesting finding in this study was that the students in their intermediate (junior) and advanced (senior) years of college stated that when they first decided to major in ECE, they did not believe in inclusion but had changed their views during the course of their preservice training. When asked why they had a difficult time accepting the concept of inclusion as beginning students, students indicated that their prior opinions were based on their previous experiences with children with special needs (outside of the teacher preparation program) and that they had not been positively exposed to inclusion during their own elementary and high school experiences.

Proctor and Niemeyer (2001) interviewed six ECE undergraduates and completed a document review of their reflective journals during their student teaching semester to examine the development of preservice teachers' beliefs about inclusion. Findings included seven major student teacher beliefs about inclusion: (1) appropriate resources are essential; (2) an academically focused (as opposed to child centered philosophy) does not support inclusion; (3) inclusion is best and valuable for all children except if instruction is continually disrupted by children with special needs; (4) children with special needs are children and are not defined by their disability; (5) children with special needs are competent; (6) part of the role of teaching young children with special needs is being their advocate; and (7) families of children with special needs may not feel as if other families share or understand their concerns (p. 60). In addition to addressing the formation of positive beliefs about inclusion, attention must also focus on training practitioners and preservice teachers to use recommended practices, including individualized instructional methods, for young children with disabilities who are enrolled in inclusive settings.

Recommended practice in ECSE advocates designing early childhood environments to promote children's safety, active engagement, learning, participation, and membership (Sandall, et al., 2005). Instruction should be individualized with educational goals and objectives established to address the learning and developmental needs of children with disabilities. Unfortunately, parents often express concerns about the adequacy of instruction for their children in inclusive settings (Bennett, Lee, & Lueke, 1998; Guralnick, 1994; Hanson et al., 2001). Mlawer (1993) has called for professionals to assume stronger advocacy roles in implementing recommended practices so that families are not in the position of trying to hold professionals accountable for providing an appropriate and individualized education for their children.

Specialized instruction is a necessary component of successful inclusive preschool programs. This requires an understanding of how all young children learn, as well as how teaching strategies can be adapted and fine-tuned to meet the needs of children with disabilities. Evidence-based practices exist for teaching targeted skills in adult- and child-initiated activities and within naturally occurring routines and activities (McWilliam, Wolery, & Odom, 2001; Wolery, 2005). One of the most frequently noted findings in the preschool inclusion literature is that children with disabilities engage in social interaction with peers less often than typically developing children (e.g., Guralnick, 1980; Guralnick, Connor, Hammond, Gottman, & Kinnish, 1996) and children with disabilities are at risk for rejection from their typically developing peers (Odom, 2002). Several naturalistic interventions have been identified in the literature to support young children's development (Rule, Losardo, Dinnebeil, Kaiser, & Rowland, 1998), including activity-based instruction (Bricker, Pretti-Frontczak, & McComas, 1998), enhanced milieu teaching (Kaiser & Hester, 1994), and embedded learning opportunities (Horn, Leiber, Sandall, Schwartz & Li, 2000). Interventions such as these require teachers to identify opportunities that occur in the natural setting, and provide support for practicing the skills to be learned in such settings. Rather than setting aside specific times to work on children's learning objectives, teaching opportunities are included within daily activities or routines (e.g., teaching requesting skills during snack time, addressing social skills during center times, supporting the development of self-care skills as children arrive and depart from school). Kohler, Anthony, Steighner, and Hoyson (1998) examined the social skill development (e.g., initiating, responding) of four preschoolers with autism using a naturalistic teaching approach, while Malmskog and McDonnell (1999) used naturalistic teacher-mediated intervention strategies (e.g.,

gain child's attention, time delay, access to reinforcers, expansion, and feedback) to demonstrate increased engagement by Head Start preschoolers during play sessions. Finally, Horn and her colleagues (2000) described the need for early educators to use embedded learning opportunities to incorporate teaching strategies related to specific individualized outcomes into the daily activities in typical early childhood environments.

Although the relationship between preservice training and teachers' beliefs about inclusion is not always clear cut and is at times even puzzling, research does speak to the need for knowledge and skill in providing specialized instruction as a necessary component of successful inclusive preschool programs. Preservice training that includes positive experiences in inclusive environments appears to be an important contributor to teachers' positive beliefs and attitudes about inclusion.

Quality and Amount of Inservice Training for Inclusion

A frequently cited issue with regard to inclusive education is a lack of training and support for teachers in inclusive settings (Scruggs & Mastropieri, 1996). Gemmell-Crosby and Hanzlik (1994) analyzed questionnaire data from 71 preschool teachers who worked in privately funded programs, to assess their attitudes toward inclusion. The sample was highly educated, with all teachers holding undergraduate or graduate degrees. All participants were currently teaching or had previously taught young children with disabilities. Findings indicated that the teachers' feelings of competency in working with young children with special needs were correlated with a positive attitude toward inclusion, and the level of support services and training they received regarding inclusion.

In another study, Buysse, Wesley, Keyes, and Bailey (1996) worked with ECSE consultants to recruit general early childhood teachers from child care classrooms that enrolled young children with disabilities for whom they were the consultant. The special education consultants met with the child care teachers and had them complete two scales. One scale assessed the child care teachers' comfort-level teaching children with different types of disabilities. The second scale assessed the child care teachers' global attitudes toward inclusion. The drawback to inclusion that was most frequently selected by these child care teachers was the lack of specialized training in serving children with special needs. This is not surprising given that community early childhood programs rarely employ teachers with formal special education or early intervention training (Wolery, Martin et al., 1994). Additionally, the lack of therapists providing support to community EC programs (Wolery, Venn et al., 1994), even on a consultant basis (Dinnebeil, McInerney, Fox, & Juchartz-Pendry, 1998), impacts teachers' comfort level in serving young children with special needs.

Dinnebeil and colleagues (1998) surveyed 400 community-based preschool teachers and child care providers concerning their attitudes and perceptions toward inclusion. The majority of participants indicated positive beliefs and attitudes about inclusion, with only 4% believing that children with special needs should not be cared for in the same setting as typical children. However, 70% of the respondents indicated that a lack of knowledge about teaching young children with disabilities

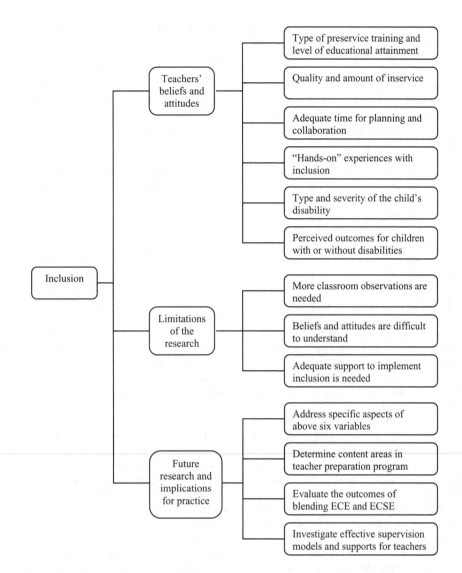

FIGURE 23.1. Overview of early childhood teachers' beliefs and attitudes about inclusion.

was a major barrier to inclusion. The questionnaire included 20 inservice topics that respondents could identify as areas of interest. The topics of interest identified by most respondents were *creating learning activities for children with physical disabilities* (80%) followed by *controlling children's problem behaviors* (73%) and *obtaining information about the child's condition* (69%). Providing focused training and additional support is clearly needed for teachers to feel competent in serving young children with special needs in inclusive settings.

Adequate Time for Planning and Collaboration

Early childhood teachers in inclusive classrooms are concerned about having enough time for planning and collaboration with special education support staff and/or families of the children with special needs. All children are best understood within the context of their families, and establishing partnerships with

families of children with disabilities is vitally important to understanding young children's strengths and needs as well as families' goals, priorities, and dreams for their children. Unfortunately, it is not uncommon to find relationships among parents of children with special needs and administrators characterized by a lack of trust, respect, and shared values (Dinnebeil, Hale, & Rule, 1996; Dinnebeil & Rule, 1994; Erwin & Soodak, 1995; Soodak & Erwin, 2000). The burden of gaining entry into inclusive programs has often fallen on families (Erwin & Soodak, 1995; Soodak & Erwin, 2000), requiring them to assume advocacy roles throughout the process. Skills in collaborating with families and other professionals, as well as time for planning and collaborating, have emerged as influencing factors related to inclusion.

Although the 10 teachers in the Marchant (1995) study described previously all shared generally positive beliefs about inclusion, concerns were noted related to: administration (e.g., system level procedures and politics, budget constraints, problems with space or facilities), time, and the classroom (e.g., meeting the individual needs of all children, integrating therapies, teaming /communicating with families and specialists). Despite the fact that some teachers had specific training in working with students with disabilities, they described concerns about the lack of time provided for planning and collaborating with special education support staff. Research has shown repeatedly that simply placing children with and without special needs in the same settings does not accomplish the goals of inclusion and may not be sufficient for addressing individual educational objectives (Bricker, 2000; Carta, Schwartz, Atwater, & McConnell, 1991; Wolery, Strain, & Bailey, 1992). Adequate training and time for planning and collaborating can help make inclusion a positive experience for all.

Gallagher (1997) met with preschool special education personnel (i.e., ECSE teachers, teacher assistants, speech therapist) during their first year working as inclusion consultants in private preschools and community-based child care centers. Although they voiced predominantly positive beliefs about inclusion, participants were concerned that finding enough time for planning and collaborating with community-based preschool and child care teachers made their new role as inclusion consultants difficult. They felt that the lack of planning time with ECE teachers impacted their effectiveness as consultants for the children on their case loads. This finding was echoed by Stoiber et al. (1998), who found that limited time and limited opportunities for collaboration with other professionals were the most frequently noted barriers to successful inclusion.

These three research teams (Gallagher, 1997; Marchant, 1995; Stoiber et al., 1998) all found that early childhood teachers and other related special education personnel shared the concern that inadequate time for collaboration and planning impacts teachers' beliefs and attitudes about inclusion. These studies were conducted in different regions of the United States and with teachers of varying professional backgrounds, yet similar system-level concerns emerged in each study regardless of the discipline or type of preschool setting.

It appears that some of the greatest barriers to inclusion are the interactions that occur among adults for the lack of collaboration is a frequently mentioned obstacle to inclusion in both the early childhood research and applied literature. Additionally, an important issue to consider that emerges in some inclusive programs is the potential power differential created between early childhood teachers' training and expertise related to serving children with special needs and the specialists' training and expertise (Wolery, Brashers, & Neitzel, 2002). This power differential might result in a lack of collaboration and joint problem solving if specialists assume a more direct style of interaction. In discussing how important collaboration is to the success of preschool inclusion, Sandall and Schwartz (2002) note that "Collaboration is the cornerstone of effective inclusion. Collaborative teams hold shared beliefs, work toward common goals, have varying areas of expertise, use collaborative skills, and share the work" (p. 13).

"Hands-On" Experiences With Inclusion

The themes of "hands-on" experiences with inclusion and preschool providers' attitudes have been studied by several researchers. Eiserman, Shisler, and Healey (1995) surveyed preschool teachers and administrators ($n = 220$) and found that these participants held moderately positive attitudes about inclusion. At the time of this study, most respondents (86%) reported having modest or no exposure to serving children with disabilities. However, of those teachers who had served a child with disabilities ($n = 106$), 82% characterized their experience as being very or somewhat positive. Eiserman and colleagues found that preschool providers in this area of the United States knew little about federal legislation concerning serving children with disabilities (e.g., the American with Disabilities Act), had limited direct experience with children with disabilities, and provided services within a community where few options for preschool inclusion were available.

Stoiber and her colleagues (1998) concluded that the "context in which inclusion takes place plays an important role in the development of practitioners' beliefs about inclusion" (p. 121). These researchers found that early childhood practitioners who had the most "hands on" experiences with inclusion held the most positive beliefs. This outcome may be attributed to feelings of professional competency, for successful experiences with inclusion might cause one to believe more passionately in inclusion as a value and a process. Results from these two studies indicate that teachers' positive beliefs are shaped by direct experiences with inclusion. What these results do not describe is the context in detail.

Type and Severity of the Child's Disability

Assessing the "comfort zone" of ECE educators (Buysee et al., 1996) regarding inclusion is based on findings from the elementary and secondary school literature that indicated the severity of the child's disability may impact teachers' attitudes toward including a particular child in their classroom. Children with mild or moderate disabilities are most likely to be included in early childhood settings such as child care, community-based preschools, and Head Start (Odom & Diamond, 1998), and several researchers have studied ECE teachers' feelings of comfort based on type and severity of disability.

Buysse and her colleagues (1996) reported that the comfort zone for serving young children with disabilities was lowest when a hypothetical child was described as having severe-to-profound disabilities in the areas of leg functioning, tonicity, and appropriate behavior. Gallagher (1997) reported that inclusion facilitators were concerned about the individual needs of children with more intense disabilities being served in community-based preschools that lacked special equipment or staff who were adequately trained to provide assistance to these children. Similarly, Eiserman et al. (1995) found that public and private preschool providers perceived themselves as least able to serve children with multiple disabilities and autism. Finally, Stoiber and her colleagues (1998) reported that practitioners indicated that preschoolers with challenging behavior, neurological problems, or autism need the most accommodations to be successfully included in early childhood classrooms.

It is clear that these teachers' beliefs about inclusion and their sense of efficacy about teaching children with disabilities may be related to the severity of the child's disability. The complexity of accommodating children with severe physical disabilities or autism is a very practical concern for teachers who have limited experiences teaching children with these types of disabilities or who work in settings with few resources for specialized equipment and training.

Perceived Outcomes for Children With or Without Disabilities

Research has shown that numerous benefits result from inclusive education. At the federal, state and local levels, early childhood and ECSE standards and the need for accountability are pushing early educators to pay increased attention to child outcomes and factors that support child growth and development. Young children with and without disabilities and society reap positive results when inclusive education is implemented. Typically developing children benefit in numerous ways from inclusive experiences (Diamond & Innes, 2000), including increased knowledge about disabilities (Diamond, Hestenes, Carpenter, & Innes, 1997) and a willingness to interact with children with disabilities (Okagaki, Diamond, Kontos, & Hestenes, 1998). Typically developing children have shown a greater understanding of individual differences, and greater opportunities to have friendships with students with disabilities as a result of inclusion (Salend & Duhaney, 1999).

Research suggests that children's attitudes toward people with disabilities develop during the preschool and early elementary years (Innes & Diamond, 1999). Children are more accepting toward their peers with disabilities and they develop friendships with children with disabilities more easily during the early years because children are less likely to notice differences and compare themselves to their classmates (Cook, Tessier, & Klein, 1996). As a result, discrimination toward children with disabilities is reduced, and children tend to have more positive attitudes toward their peers with disabilities (Favazza & Odom, 1997). Children learn to value differences and treat others in an empathic manner. These positive attitudes developed in the early years might lead toward a greater awareness and acceptance of disabilities in adulthood (Stainback & Stainback, 1996).

The literature shows that children with disabilities make at least as much progress in inclusive programs as they do in programs that do not include typically developing peers (Buysse & Bailey, 1993; Lamorey & Bricker, 1993). Research indicates that children with and without disabilities benefit in terms of their social, cognitive, moral, language, and motor development as a result of inclusive education (Baker, Wang, & Walberg, 1995). Children with disabilities observe, imitate, and learn age-appropriate skills when interacting and playing with their typically developing peers. They also learn social skills and show improvement in their academic performance through interactions with their typically developing peers in natural environments (Slavin, 1990).

In three studies involving interviews with early childhood practitioners, respondents indicated that they believe inclusive settings provide positive outcomes for young children with and without disabilities (Gallagher, 1997; Lieber et al., 1998; Marchant, 1995). They also reported that one of the most rewarding aspects of inclusion is observing children with and without disabilities learn from one another and progress in their development.

Research Design

The majority of researchers who have studied practicing and pre-service early childhood teachers' beliefs and attitudes about inclusion used quantitative research methodologies. Attitudes about inclusion were typically assessed using surveys or questionnaires (Buysse et al., 1998; Dinnebeil et al., 1998; Eiserman et al., 1995; Stoiber et al., 1998). Some studies employed qualitative designs that included interviews and focus groups (Gallagher, 1997; Marchant, 1995; Proctor & Niemeyer, 2001). One study (Lieber et al., 1998) employed a mixed methods design, combining classroom observations and interviews. Clearly, the field is in need of additional research that involves the use of classroom observations to learn more about how early childhood teachers' beliefs and attitudes influence their daily practices with young children with disabilities in inclusive settings.

LIMITATIONS OF THE RESEARCH

The six themes that emerge from the studies discussed provide an initial glimpse into understanding early childhood teachers' beliefs and attitudes about inclusion. There are however, several limitations to these studies. First, assessing the construct of early childhood educators' beliefs and attitudes about inclusion and how those beliefs and attitudes inform practice is an area in need of additional observational research in inclusive settings. A more careful, systematic examination of teachers' actual practice is needed. As Lieber and her colleagues (1998) note, there is a need to conduct further research that more specifically describes the links between preservice teacher education, early childhood program quality, and child outcomes for children with disabilities.

Second, it is difficult to truly understand teachers' beliefs and attitudes about inclusion because of the variety of disciplines and settings represented in the research literature. In several studies, the participants represented many different roles and professional backgrounds found in inclusive early childhood settings (Eiserman et al., 1995; Gallagher, 1997; Lieber et al., 1998; Marchant, 1995; Stoiber et al., 1998). Thus, findings reported in these studies not only reflect teachers' beliefs and attitudes about inclusion but also include the beliefs and attitudes of persons who hold positions other than that of the classroom teacher in the inclusion setting (e.g., paraprofessionals, administrators).

Third, whereas the inclusion of young children with disabilities is occurring more frequently than ever in child care and other community-based early childhood settings (McDonnell, Brownell, & Wolery, 1997; Salisbury, 1991; Wolery et al., 1993), staff may or may not receive adequate support to implement inclusion. Given the variety of service delivery models for young children with special needs and their families (Odom et al., 1999), teachers, caregivers, and administrators working in early childhood settings may or may not have access to training, technical assistance, and other resources necessary to provide high quality inclusive programs for young children (Bricker, 1995; Gallagher, 1997). It is difficult for teachers to retain positive attitudes or feel competent working with young children with special needs if they do not have administrative supports or adequate training in systems-level advocacy skills (e.g., advocating for additional support staff, technical assistance, adaptive equipment) (Gallagher, 1997; Marchant, 1995; Mitchell & Philibert, 2002).

Participants in several studies expressed positive attitudes about the benefits of inclusion for children with and without disabilities (Baum & McMurray-Schwartz, 2001; Buysse et al., 1998; Gallagher, 1997; Gemmell-Crosby & Hanzlik, 1994; Lieber et al., 1998; Marchant, 1995; Proctor & Niemeyer, 2001, Stoiber et al., 1998). This is a critical finding in the sense that early childhood practitioners and preservice teachers in these studies seem to hold positive beliefs and attitudes about inclusion itself; however, they are concerned with the practical aspects of working with young children with disabilities. This makes intuitive sense because early childhood teachers carry the major responsibility for ensuring positive outcomes for all the children in their care, especially with the increased emphasis on accountability. It is critical for early childhood practitioners to have access to meaningful preservice and inservice activities that promote the implementation of recommended practices in inclusion. Specific information about these practices needs to be disseminated to early childhood practitioners and future educators using a variety of formats such as coursework, practitioner-oriented journals, on-site technical assistance, inservices, conferences, and Internet-based courses.

FUTURE RESEARCH AND IMPLICATIONS FOR PRACTICE

Providing adequate time for planning and collaboration, "hands-on" experiences with children with a variety of disabilities, and meaningful preservice and in-service education are variables that research has shown are necessary to support inclusion. The next stage of research in this area should address specific aspects of these variables that assist early childhood educators in expanding their knowledge about teaching young children with disabilities thereby developing feelings of competency as teachers of *all* children in inclusive settings.

In a review of the literature on the effects of attitudes concerning preschool inclusion Stoneman (1993) notes that "across studies the most salient concern about preschool integration is the inadequate preparation and training of teachers" (p. 242). Results from several studies indicate that early childhood educators want more training and better preparation for working with young children with disabilities. The next decade of research should determine which specific content areas and experiences in teacher preparation programs successfully prepare new teachers for inclusive classrooms. Additionally, research needs to be conducted to determine which "hands-on" experiences are most salient in assisting early childhood teachers to feel competent and successful teaching in inclusive settings. In-depth comparisons of preservice versus inservice preparation

programs as well as approved certification versus alternate licensure might provide additional insight into training and preparing the next generation of early childhood educators.

As a result of inclusion, the fields of ECE and ECSE are collaborating more than ever before. As more colleges and universities develop blended or unified early childhood teacher certification programs (Miller & Stayton, 1998), there is a need to critically evaluate how well these programs are preparing teachers for inclusive preschool settings. It is extremely probable that students entering college today have had very different school experiences from many practitioners who are currently working in inclusive classrooms. For example, many undergraduate education majors enter college having experienced being a student in an inclusive school setting, in addition to taking required courses in special education. These experiences have the potential to positively impact the way inclusive education is conceptualized and implemented in the future.

University faculty involved in both ECE and ECSE need to create ongoing opportunities for students to work in collaboration in order to prepare them for the realities of inclusion. Institutions that prepare future ECE and ECSE teachers need to support the development of collaborative preservice programs and opportunities for faculty to co-teach and collaborate on supervision and placement issues (Miller & Stayton, 1999). Future research needs to address which specific preservice experiences most positively influence teachers' feelings of competency in working with young children with disabilities in inclusive settings. Discovering specific factors that mediate teacher beliefs and attitudes about inclusion and their day-to-day practice is clearly needed. Just as inclusion has reshaped our views of service delivery for young children with disabilities, inclusion continues to influence methods of personnel preparation and professional development for both ECE and ECSE professionals.

In order to prepare early childhood professionals to be competent facilitators of inclusion, preservice programs must provide students with "hands-on" experiences with young children with a variety of disabilities through field experiences and related coursework (Miller et al., 2003). These field-based experiences and courses should include opportunities for ECSE and ECE preservice students to collaborate with one another to implement joint activities and complete assignments. Activities such as these help build a predisposition in preservice teachers toward collaboration and teaming among professionals in the implementation of inclusion for young children in early childhood settings.

Training for practitioners and preservice teachers also should include instruction in adult learning strategies and opportunities to engage in supervised collaborative consultation (Dinnebeil, McInerney, Roth, & Ramaswamy, 2001). The literature includes many approaches to training based on the principles of adult learning. Some examples include clinical supervision (Fenichel, 1992), peer collaboration (Pugach & Johnson, 1995), coaching (Finerty, 1996; Miller, Harris, & Watanbe, 1991), and mentoring (Fenichel & Eggbeer, 1993; Gallacher, 1997). Long-term, more intensive training, which allows time for teachers to become involved in their own learning, is more likely to produce positive outcomes with respect to changing teacher behavior (Miller et al., 1991). Gaining expertise in these approaches to working with adults should be embedded within preservice ECSE teacher preparation programs.

More research also needs to be conducted on effective supervision models and supports for teachers currently employed in inclusive preschool settings. Findings by Lieber et al. (1998) and others point out that although early childhood teachers may have positive beliefs and attitudes about inclusion, many are not implementing recommended practices in their daily interactions with children. A teacher's skills at implementing meaningful inclusive opportunities for children with disabilities are critical to young children's achievement (Bricker, 1995). More classroom-based research involving early childhood teachers who implement recommended practices in inclusion should be conducted. Such studies may identify barriers to using recommended practices as well as strategies to encourage teachers to use these practices. For example, the formation of local communities of practice (Buysse et al., 2001; Buysee, Sparkman, & Wesley, 2003; Hutchinson & Martin, 1999; Palinscar, Magnusson, Marano, Ford, & Brown, 1998; Wesley & Buysee, 2001) may offer opportunities for key stakeholders (e.g., researchers, teachers, paraprofessionals, and parents) to share knowledge and skills with one another: "... a community of practice can be defined as a group of professionals and other stakeholders in pursuit of a shared learning enterprise, commonly focused on a particular topic (e.g., methods to promote early literacy learning, strategies for increasing parent participation)" (Buysee et al., 2003, p. 266). In communities of practice, *all* the members learn from one another rather than a single individual acting as the "expert", whereas the others act as passive recipients of the expert's knowledge. The entire group meets to discuss their experiences, what worked and did not work, and then shares this information with the larger educational community (Buysee et al., 2001, p. 183). Consistent opportunities for university faculty, practicing ECE and ECSE professionals, and preservice teachers to meet regularly to share information and ideas is necessary in order for professionals to better understand their own beliefs and practices and to be challenged by new beliefs and practices (Richardson, 1996). Additional research on collaborative processes such as these might provide insight on some of the intricacies of successful inclusion.

The gap between recommended practices and the reality of inclusive education is astonishing for many children, families, and professionals (Erwin, Soodak, Winton, & Turnbull, 2001). Many scholars have written about the limited use of research in affecting practices (Fuchs & Fuchs, 1998; Hoshman & Polkinghorne, 1992; Kaestle, 1993; Malouf & Schiller, 1995; Turnbull & Turnbull, 2001). Yet translating research into practice continues to be an elusive goal across many areas of educational research. Certainly inclusive education is no exception. Continued research on teachers' attitudes, beliefs, and practices about inclusion has the potential to shape future preservice and inservice programs and improve the quality of inclusive education provided to young children with and without disabilities and their families.

References

Allen, K. E., & Schwartz, I. S. (2001). *The exceptional child: Inclusion in early childhood education.* Albany, NY: Delmar.

Allport, G. (1967). Attitudes. In M. Fishbein (Ed.), *Readings in attitude theory and measurement* (pp. 1–13). New York: John Wiley & Sons.

Baker, J. M., & Zigmond, N. (1995). The meaning and practice of inclusion for students with learning disabilities: Themes and implications from the five cases. *Journal of Special Education, 29,* 163–180.

Baker, W. T., Wang, M. C., & Walberg, H. J. (1995). The effects of inclusion on learning. *Educational Leadership, 52*(4), 33–35.

Barrera, I., & Corso, R. M. (2003). *Skilled dialogue: Strategies for responding to cultural diversity in early childhood.* Baltimore, MD: Brookes.

Baum, A. C., & McMurray-Schwarz, P. (2001, April). *Exploring the beliefs of early childhood preservice teachers.* Paper presented at the annual meeting of the American Educational Research Association. Seattle, WA.

Bennett, T., Lee, H., & Lueke, B. (1998). Expectations and concerns: What mothers and fathers say about inclusion. *Education and Training in Mental Retardation and Developmental Disabilities, 33,* 108–122.

Bredecamp, S., & Copple, C. (Eds.). (1997). *Developmentally appropriate practice in early childhood programs* (revised edition). Washington, DC: National Association for the Education of Young Children (NAEYC).

Bricker, D. (1995). The challenge of inclusion. *Journal of Early Intervention, 19,* 179–194.

Bricker, D. (2000). Inclusion: How the scene has changed. *Topics in Early Childhood Special Education, 20,* 14–19.

Bricker, D., Pretti-Frontczak, K., & McComas, N. (1998). *An activity-based approach to early intervention.* Baltimore, MD: Brookes.

Brownell, M. T., & Pajares, F. (1999). Teacher efficacy and perceived success in main-streaming students with learning and behavior problems. *Teacher Education and Special Education, 22,* 154–164.

Buysee, V., & Bailey, D. B. (1993). Behavioral and developmental outcomes in young children with disabilities in integrated and segregated settings: A review of comparative studies. *Journal of Special Education, 26,* 434–461.

Buysee, V., Sparkman, K. L., & Wesley, P. W. (2003). Communities of practice: Connecting what we know with what we do. *Exceptional Children, 69,* 263–277.

Buysee, V., Wesley, P. W., & Able-Boone, H. (2001). Innovations in professional development: Creating communities of practice to support inclusion. In M. J. Guralnick (Ed.), *Early childhood inclusion: Focus on change* (pp. 179–200). Baltimore, MD: Brookes.

Buysse, V., Wesley, P. W., & Keyes, L. (1998). Implementing early childhood inclusion: Barrier and support factors. *Early Childhood Research Quarterly, 13,* 169–184.

Buysse, V., Wesley, P. W., Keyes, L., & Bailey, D. B. (1996). Assessing the comfort zone of child care teachers in serving young children with disabilities. *Journal of Early Intervention, 20,* 189–203.

Carta, J. J., Schwartz, I. S., Atwater, J. B., & McConnell, S. R. (1991). Developmentally appropriate practice: Appraising its usefulness for young children with disabilities. *Topics in Early Childhood Special Education, 11,* 1–20.

Cook, R. E., Tessier, A., & Klein, M. D. (1996). *Adapting early childhood curricula for children in inclusive settings.* Englewood Cliffs, NJ: Merrill.

D'Alonzo, B. J., Giordano, G., & Vanleeuwen, D. M. (1997). Perceptions by teachers about the benefits and liabilities of inclusion. *Preventing School Failure, 42*(1), 4-11.

Diamond, K. E., Hestenes, L., Carpenter, E., & Innes, F. K. (1997). Relationships between enrollment in an inclusive class and preschool children's ideas about people with disabilities. *Topics in Early Childhood Special Education, 17*, 520-537.

Diamond, K. E., & Innes, F. K. (2000). The origins of young children's attitudes toward peers with disabilities. In M. J. Guralnick (Ed.), *Early childhood inclusion: Focus on change* (pp. 159-177). Baltimore, MD: Brookes.

Dinnebeil, L. A. , Hale, H., & Rule, S. (1996). A qualitative analysis of parents' and service coordinators' descriptions of variables that influence collaborative relationships. *Topics in Early Childhood Special Education, 16*, 322-347.

Dinnebeil, L. A., McInerney, W., Fox, C., & Juchartz-Pendry, K. (1998). An analysis of the perceptions and characteristics of child care personnel regarding inclusion of young children with special needs in community-based programs. *Topics in Early Childhood Special Education, 18*, 118-128.

Dinnebeil, L. A., McInerney, W. F., Roth, J., & Ramaswamy, V. (2001). Itinerant early childhood special education services: Service delivery in one state. *Journal of Early Intervention, 24*(1), 35-44.

Dinnebeil, L. A., & Rule, S. (1994). Variables that influence collaboration between parents and service coordinators. *Journal of Early Intervention, 18*, 349-361.

Division for Early Childhood (2000). *Position statement on inclusion.* Retrieved September 14, 2004, from http://www.dec-sped.org/pdf/positionpapers/Position%20Inclusion.pdf

Eichinger, J., Rizzo, T., & Sirotnik, B. (1991). Changing attitudes toward people with disabilities. *Teacher Education and Special Education, 14*, 121-126.

Eiserman, W. D., Shisler, L., & Healey, S. (1995). A community assessment of preschool providers' attitudes toward inclusion. *Journal of Early Intervention, 19*(2), 149-167.

Erwin, E. J., & Soodak, L. C. (1995). I never knew I could stand up to the system: Families' perspectives on pursuing inclusive education. *The Journal of the Association for Persons with Severe Handicaps, 20*, 136-146.

Erwin, E. J., Soodak, L. C., Winton, P., & Turnbull, A. (2001). "I wish it wouldn't all depend on me": Research on families and early childhood inclusion. In M. J. Guralnick (Ed.), *Early childhood inclusion: Focus on change* (pp. 127-158). Baltimore, MD: Brookes.

Favazza, P. C., & Odom, S. L. (1997). Promoting positive attitudes of kindergarten-age children toward individuals with disabilities. *Exceptional Children, 63*, 405-418.

Fenichel, E. (Ed.). (1992). *Learning through supervision and mentorship to support the development of infants, toddlers, and their families: A source book.* Arlington, VA: ZERO TO THREE/National Center for Clinical Infant Programs.

Fenichel, E., & Eggbeer, L. (1993). Zero to Three's TOTIS (training of trainers intensive Seminar) and city TOTS (training of teams) initiatives. *ZERO TO THREE, 14*(1), 3.

Finerty, M. F. (1996). Coaching for growth and development. In R. L. Craig (Ed.), *The ASTD training & development handbook: A guide to human resource development* (4th ed., pp. 415-436). New York: McGraw-Hill.

Fuchs, D., & Fuchs, L. S. (1998). Researchers and teachers working together to improve instruction for diverse earners. *Learning Disabilities Research & Practice, 13*, 126-137.

Gallacher, K. K. (1997). Supervision, mentoring, and coaching: Methods for supporting personnel development. In P. J. Winton, J. A. McCollum, & C. Catlett (Eds.), *Reforming personnel preparation in early intervention: Issues, models, and practical strategies* (pp. 191-214). Baltimore, MD: Brookes.

Gallagher, P. A. (1997). Teachers and inclusion: Perspectives on changing roles. *Topics in Early Childhood Special Education, 17*, 363-386.

Gemmell-Crosby, S., & Hanzlik, J. R. (1994). Preschool teachers' perceptions of including children with disabilities. *Education and Training in Mental Retardation and Developmental Disabilities, 29*, 279-290.

Guralnick, M. J. (1980). Social interaction among preschool handicapped children. *Exceptional Children, 46*, 248-253.

Guralnick, M. J. (1994). Mothers' perceptions of the benefits and drawbacks of early childhood mainstreaming. *Journal of Early Intervention, 18*, 168-183.

Guralnick, M. J. (Ed.). (2001). *Early childhood inclusion: Focus on change.* Baltimore, MD: Brookes.

Guralnick, M. J., Connor, R. T., Hammond, M. A., Gottman, J. M., & Kinnish, K. (1996). Immediate effects of mainstreamed settings on the social interactions and social integration of preschool children. *American Journal of Mental Retardation, 100*, 359-377.

Hanson, M. J., Horn, E., Sandall, S., Beckman, P., Morgan, M., Marquart, J., et al. (2001). After preschool inclusion: Children's educational pathways over the early school years. *Exceptional Children, 68*, 65-83.

Harbin, G., & Salisbury, C. (2000). Recommended practices in policies, procedures, and systems change. In S. Sandall, M. E. McLean, & B. J. Smith (Eds.), *DEC recommended practices in early intervention/early childhood special education* (pp. 65-75). Longmont, CO: Sopris West.

Horn, E., Lieber, J., Sandall, S., Schwartz, I., & Li, S. (2000). Supporting young children's IEP goals in inclusive settings through embedded learning opportunities. *Topics in Early Childhood Special Education, 20*, 208-223.

Hoshman, L. T., & Polkinghorne, D. E. (1992). Refining the science-practice relationship and Professional training. *Education and Training in Psychology, 47*, 55-66.

Hutchinson, N. L., & Martin, A. (1999). Fostering inclusive beliefs and practices during pre-service teacher education through communities of practice. *Teacher Education and Special Education, 22*, 234-250.

Innes, F. K., & Diamond, K. E. (1999). Typically developing children's interactions with peers with disabilities: Relationships between mothers' comments and children's ideas about disabilities. *Topics in Early Childhood Special Education, 19*, 103-111.

Kaestle, C. F. (1993). The awful reputation of educational research. *Educational Researcher, 22*, 23-31.

Kaiser, A. P., & Hester, P. (1994). Generalized effects of enhanced milieu training. *Journal of Speech and Hearing Research, 17*, 1320-1340.

Kohler, F. W., Anthony, L. J., Steighner, S. A., & Hoyson, M. (1998). Teaching social Interaction skills in integrated preschool: An examination of naturalistic tactics. *Topics in Early Childhood Special Education, 21*, 93-103.

Lamorey, S., & Bricker, D. D. (1993). Integrated programs: Effects on young children and their Parents. In C. Peck, S. Odom, & D. Bricker (Eds.), *Integrating children with disabilities into community-based programs: Ecological perspectives on research and implementation* (pp. 249-269). Baltimore, MD: Brookes.

Lieber, J., Capell, K., Sandall, S. R., Wolfberg, P., Horn, E., & Beckman, P. (1998). Inclusive preschool programs: Teachers' beliefs and practices. *Early Childhood Research Quarterly, 13*(1), 87-105.

Lynch, E. W., & Hanson, M. J. (2004). *Developing cross-cultural competence: A guide for working with children and their families.* Baltimore, MD: Brookes.

Malmskog, S., & McDonell, A. P. (1999). Teacher-mediated facilitation of engagement by Children with developmental delays in inclusive preschools. *Topics in Early Childhood Special Education, 19*, 203-216.

Malouf, D. B., & Schiller, E. P. (1995). Practice and research in special education. *Exceptional Children, 61*, 414-424.

Marchant, C. (1995). Teachers' views of integrated preschools. *Journal of Early Intervention, 19*, 61-67.

McDonnell, A. P., Brownell, K., & Wolery, M. (1997). Teaching experience and specialist support: A survey of preschool teachers employed in programs accredited by NAEYC. *Topics in Early Childhood Special Education, 17*, 263-285.

McWilliam, R. A., Wolery, M., & Odom, S. L. (2001). Instructional perspectives in inclusive Preschool classrooms. In M. J. Guralnick (Ed.), *Early childhood inclusion: Focus on change* (pp. 503-527). Baltimore, MD: Brookes.

Mitchell, L. M., & Philibert, D. B. (2002). Family, professional, and political advocacy: Rights and responsibilities. *Young Exceptional Children, 5*(4), 11-18.

Mlawer, M. A. (1993). Who should fight?: Parents and the advocacy expectation. *Journal of Disability Policy Studies, 4*, 105-115.

Miller, P. S., Harris, C., & Watanbe, A. (1991). Professional coaching: A method for increasing Effective and decreasing ineffective teacher behaviors. *Teacher Education and Special Education, 14*(3), 183-191.

Miller, P. S., Ostrosky, M. M., Laumann, B., Thorpe, E., Sanchez, S., & Fader-Dunne, L. (2003). Quality field experiences underlying performance mastery. In V. D. Stayton, P. S. Miller, & L. A. Dinnebeil (Eds.), *DEC personnel preparation in early childhood special education: Implementing the DEC recommended practices* (pp. 113-138). Longmont, CO: Sopris West.

Miller, P. S., & Stayton, V. D. (1998). Blended interdisciplinary teacher preparation in early education and intervention: A national study. *Topics in Early Childhood Special Education, 18*, 49-58.

Miller, P. S., & Stayton, V. D. (1999). Higher education culture—A fit or misfit with reform in teacher education? *Journal of Teacher Education, 50*, 290-302.

Monahan, R. G., Marino, S. B., & Miller, R. (1996). Teacher attitudes toward inclusion: Implications for teacher education in School 2000. *Education, 117*(2), 316-320.

National Association for the Education of Young Children. (1996). *Mission, philosophy, and goals.* Retrieved September 14, 2004, from http://www.naeyc.org/about/mission_statement.asp

Odom, S. L. (2000). Preschool inclusion: What we now and where we go from here. *Topics in Early Childhood Special Education, 20*, 20-27.

Odom, S. L. (Ed.). (2002). *Widening the circle: Including children with disabilities in preschool programs.* New York: Teachers College Press.

Odom, S. L., & Diamond, K. E. (1998). Inclusion of young children with special needs in early childhood education: The research base. *Early Childhood Research Quarterly, 13*, 3-25.

Odom, S. L., Horn, E. M., Marquart, J. M., Hanson, M. J., Wolfberg, P., Beckman, P., et al. (1999). On the forms of inclusion: Organizational context and individualized service models. *Journal of Early Intervention, 22*, 185-199.

Okagaki, L, Diamond, K. E., Kontos, S. J., & Hestenes, L. L. (1998). Correlates of young children's interactions with classmates with disabilities. *Early Childhood Research Quarterly, 13*, 67-86.

Olson, M. R., Chalmers, L., & Hoover, J. H. (1997). Attitudes and attributes of general Education teachers identified as effective inclusionists. *Remedial and Special Education, 18*, 28-35.

Palincsar, A. S., Magnusson, S. J., Marano, N., Ford, D., & Brown, N. (1998). Designing a community of practice: Principles and practices of the GisML community. *Teaching and Teacher Education, 14*, 5-19.

Proctor, R., & Niemeyer, J. A. (2001). Preservice teacher beliefs about inclusion: Implications for early intervention educators. *Journal of Early Intervention, 24*, 55-66.

Pearman, E. L., Huang, A. M., & Mellblom, C. I. (1997). The inclusion of all students: Concerns and incentives of educators. *Education & Training in Mental Retardation, 32*(1), 11-20.

Pugach, M. C., & Johnson, L. J. (1995). Unlocking expertise among classroom teachers through Structured dialogue: Extending research on peer collaboration. *Exceptional Children, 62*, 101-110.

Richardson, V. (1996). The role of attitudes and beliefs in learning to teach. In J. Sikula (Ed.), *Handbook of research on teacher education* (pp. 102-119). New York: Macmillan.

Rule, S., Losardo, A., Dinnebeil, L., Kaiser, A., & Rowland, C. (1998). Translating research on naturalistic instruction into practice. *Journal of Early Intervention, 21*, 283-293.

Salend, S. J., & Duheney, L. M. G. (1999). The impact of inclusion on students with and without disabilities and their educators. *Remedial and Special Education, 20*, 114-126.

Salisbury, C. (1991). Mainstreaming during the early childhood years. *Exceptional Children, 58*, 146-155.

Sandall, S., Hemmeter, M. L., Smith, B. J., & McLean, M. E. (2005). *DEC recommended practices: A comprehensive guide for practical application in early intervention/early childhood special education.*

Sandall, S., & Schwartz, I. (2002). *Building blocks for teaching preschoolers with special needs.* Baltimore, MD: Brookes.

Scruggs, T. E., & Mastropieri, M. A. (1996). Teacher perceptions of mainstreaming/inclusion, 1958-1995: A research synthesis. *Exceptional Children, 63*, 59-74.

Slavin, R. E. (1990). General education under the regular education initiative: How must it change? *Remedial and Special Education, 11*, 40-50.

Smith, M. K., & Smith, K., E. (2000). "I believe in inclusion, but...": Regular education early childhood teachers' perceptions of successful inclusion. *Journal of Research in Childhood Education, 14*, 161-180.

Soodak, L. C., & Erwin, E. J. (2000). Valued member or tolerated participant: Parents' experiences in inclusive early childhood settings. *Journal of The Association for Persons with Severe Handicaps, 25*, 29-41.

Stainback, W., & Stainback, S. (1996). *Controversial issues confronting special education: Divergent perspectives.* Needham Heights, MA: Allyn and Bacon.

Stoiber, K. C., Gettinger, M., & Goetz, D. (1998). Exploring factors influencing parents' and early childhood practitioners' beliefs about inclusion. *Early Childhood Research Quarterly, 13*, 107-124.

Stoneman, Z. (1993). The effects of attitude on preschool integration. In C. A. Peck, S. L. Odom, & D. D. Bricker (Eds.), *Integrating young children with disabilities into community programs* (pp. 223-248). Baltimore, MD: Brookes.

Turnbull, A. P., & Turnbull, H. R. (2001). *Families, professionals, and exceptionality: Collaborating for empowerment* (4th ed). Upper Saddle River, NJ: Merrill/Prentice Hall.

Villa, R. A., Thousand, J. S., Meyers, H., & Nevin, A. (1996). Teacher and administrator perceptions of heterogeneous education. *Exceptional Children, 63*(1), 29-45.

Wesley, P. W., & Buysee, V. (2001). Communities of practice: Expanding professional roles to promote reflection and shared inquiry. *Topics in Early Childhood Special Education, 21*(2), 114-123.

Wolery, M. (2005). DEC recommended practices: Child-focused practices. In S. Sandall, M. L. Hemmeter, B. J. Smith, & M. E. McLean (Eds.), *DEC recommended practices: A comprehensive guide for practical application in early intervention/early childhood special education* (pp. 71–106). Longmont, CO: Sopris West.

Wolery, M., Brashers, M. S., & Neitzel, J. C. (2002). Ecological congruence assessment for Classroom activities and routines: Identifying goals and intervention practices in childcare. *Topics in Early Childhood Special Education, 22*(3), 131–142.

Wolery, M., Holcombe-Ligon, A., Brookfield, J., Huffman, K., Schroeder, C., Martin, C. G., et al. (1993). The extent and nature of preschool mainstreaming: A survey of general early educators. *Journal of Special Education, 27*, 222–234.

Wolery, M., Martin, C. G., Schroeder, C., Huffman, K., Venn, M. L., Holcombe, A., et al. (1994). Employment of educators in preschool mainstreaming: A survey of general early educators. *Journal of Early Intervention, 18*, 64–77.

Wolery, M., Strain, P. S., & Bailey, D. B. (1992). Reaching potentials for children with special needs. In S. Bredekamp & T. Rosegrant (Eds.), *Reaching potentials: Appropriate curriculum and assessment for young children* (Vol. 1, pp. 92–112). Washington, DC: National Association for the Education of Young Children.

Wolery, M., Venn, M. L., Holcombe, A., Brookfield, J., Martin, C. G., Huffman, K., et al. (1994). Employment of related service personnel in preschool programs: A survey of general early educators. *Exceptional Children, 61*, 25–39.

Wood, M. (1995). Whose job is it anyway? Educational roles in inclusion. *Exceptional Children, 64*, 181–195.

York, J. L., & Reynolds, M. C. (1996). Special education and inclusion. In J. Sikula (Ed.), *Handbook of research on teacher education* (pp. 820–836). New York: Macmillan.

·24·

PRESCHOOL TEACHERS' PROFESSIONAL DEVELOPMENT

Olivia N. Saracho
University of Maryland

Bernard Spodek
University of Illinois

Early childhood education has been defined as the education of children from birth through age eight. While this is seen as a single developmental stage, it includes children in a number of different institutions under a number of different auspices serving a number of different purposes, and including both care and education. In the United States, early childhood education as so defined, includes the education of children in infant-toddler programs, in child care homes, in center-based child care programs, in preschools or nursery schools, in public school kindergartens and prekindergartens, and in the lower primary grades (Grades 1–3) of elementary schools. These may be public school programs, private not-for-profit programs, and private for-profit programs. Each type of program and each kind of institutional sponsoring arrangement may have different requirements for teaching staff.

The teaching staffs in these various early childhood settings vary from well-educated individuals with graduate degrees to those with little more than a high school education. All early childhood education personnel in institutional settings in America are called "teachers," although their qualifications may vary greatly. Teachers in public school in all the states must have at least a Bachelor's degree and a state teachers' certificate, license, or endorsement. In other settings the requirements vary greatly. Although no one challenges the requirements for public school teachers—in fact, there are often calls to increase their qualifications—questions often have been raised about the necessary qualifications of early childhood teachers in other settings, including child care centers, private preschools, and Head Start programs. Because of this concern, teacher education

researchers have focused their investigations on the relationship of early childhood teachers' preparation to the quality of the program being provided to young children, especially those below public school age. In addition, recent national policy discussions have focused on issues of teacher quality. In meeting its goals, the *No Child Left Behind Act* (NCLB) expects a "highly qualified teacher" and better-prepared paraprofessionals in all classrooms as well as a public report on staff qualifications (NCLB, 2001).

Researchers, educators, and policy makers have been searching for ways to ensure that classrooms are staffed with high quality, well-prepared teachers. This has become a major concern as research has shown the educational effects of teachers' qualifications. An increased demand for new teachers is expected as a result of increased enrollments and expected teacher retirements (Goldhaber & Brewer, 2000). According to the National Commission for Teaching and America's Future (NCTAF), "more new teachers will be hired in the next decade than in any previous decade in our history" (NCTAF, 1996, p. 76), and many recently hired teachers are inadequately prepared for the profession. The foremost fear is hiring teachers with temporary, provisional, or emergency licenses, or no license at all (Saracho & Spodek, 2003).

Research studies on the importance of the teachers' professional development on the students' learning have drawn attention to the issue of teacher quality in an unprecedented way. It is suggested that the quality of teachers in U.S. classrooms at many levels needs to be improved if educational outcomes are to be substantially improved (Darling-Hammond & Sykes, 2003).

Teachers' education determines "teacher quality," because it describes the teachers' characteristics in relation to content knowledge, classroom behavior, academic ability, advanced education degree work, and teacher education experiences. The teachers' college degree and certification are important characteristics that identify teacher quality. Such a degree and certificate are important in other fields and should be just as important in early childhood education. For example, lawyers, cosmetologists, and physicians are among the many professions that require a practitioner to have a license (the equivalent of a teaching certificate) in order to practice in their profession. The license or certificate does not guarantee high-quality performance. It does, however, establish a minimum standard for performance in a field. Unfortunately, this type of legal protection does not exist for young children when it comes to education. Teacher certification indicates that teachers have a degree and have gone through a rigorous screening, training, and assessment to be qualified to teach. This process protects the client, in this case children. Unfortunately, teachers who do not have a degree or are not certified are permitted to teach young children in a variety of settings, including child care centers and preschools outside the public school system. They also may provisionally be allowed to teach in the public schools. Advocates of the teaching profession believe that a college degree and certification are essential in developing and maintaining the teaching profession and serve to guarantee that only those who are qualified are allowed to join that profession (Laczko-Kerr & Berliner, 2002). Unfortunately, this does not happen in early childhood education.

A demand for an increase in the number of early childhood teachers has developed because of changes in work and family patterns, in the creation of national early childhood initiatives, and in the increased number of mothers of preschool children joining the paid workforce (Early & Winton, 2001). This has led to more than 60% of American preschoolers being cared for during most of the work week by adults other than their parents (Bureau of Labor Statistics, 1999). Thus, children's enrollment in early childhood education programs has increased dramatically. In 2001, 66% of all 4-year-olds attended an early childhood education program, which is a 23% increase from 30 years ago (National Center for Education Statistics, 2003, United States Bureau of the Census, 1970). Hirschman (2002) estimated that by the year 2005 all 4-year-olds will be eligible for a free education in state sponsored prekindergartens, thus increasing the demand for early childhood teachers even further. The purpose of this chapter is to review and analyze studies that relate to the preparation of early childhood education teachers, the quality of educational programs for young children, and the relationship between the two.

TEACHERS' PREPARATION AND QUALITY OF CHILDREN'S PROGRAMS

Research suggests that the early childhood teacher's professional development affects the quality of early childhood programs in which they are employed and predicts the developmental outcomes of the children in their classes. Research further suggests that the quality of early childhood programs is related to outcomes for children (Cost, Quality and Outcomes Study Team, 1995; Dunn, 1993; Peisner-Feinberg et al., 1999) and that the level of education attained by early childhood education teachers is positively related to the quality of their programs (Cost, Quality and Outcomes Study Team, 1995; National Institute of Child Health and Human Development (NICHD) Early Child Care Research Network, 1996; Whitebook, Howes, & Phillips, 1990). The strongest relationship exists between the number of years of a teacher's education and the appropriateness of that teacher's classroom behavior. Reviews of research concluded that better outcomes for young children are related to the teachers' educational background and quality of education (Barnett, 2003, 2004; Bowman, Donovan & Burns, 2000; Howes, & Brown, 2000), including whether the teacher has a Bachelor's degree in early childhood education. Thus, teachers' qualifications make a difference in the students' achievement outcomes (Darling-Hammond, 2000).

Although early childhood teachers have a major role in caring for America's young children (Early & Winton, 2001), and educational outcomes are positively related to the quality of programs (Cost, Quality and Outcomes Study Team, 1995; National Institute of Child Health and Human Development (NICHD) Early Child Care Research Network, 1996; Whitebook, Howes, & Phillips, 1990), studies have revealed the mediocre quality of many educational settings for young children (Cost, Quality, and Child Outcomes Study Team, 1995). This is due to structural variables, especially the teachers' education and experience (Abbott-Shim, Lambert, & McCarty, 2000; Cryer, Teitze, Burchinal, Leal, & Palacios, 1999; Howes & Brown, 2000; Saluja, Early, & Clifford, 2002); caregiving behaviors; access to various types of activities; and interactions with children, other teachers, and other children (Bowman et al., 2000; Holloway, Kagan, Fuller, Tsou, & Carroll, 2001; Phillips, Mekos, Scarr, McCartney, & Abbott-Shim, 2000; Shonkoff & Phillips, 2000).

Bachelors' Degree Versus Less Education

Several studies support the contributions of a Bachelor's degree and specialized early childhood training to teacher behavior and program quality. Whitebook (2003a, 2003b) identified a number of important studies of teachers of 3- to 5-year-olds, including (1) *the Bermuda College Training Program Study* (Arnett, 1989); (2) *the National Child Care Staffing Study* (Howes, Phillips, & Whitebook, 1992; Whitebook et al., 1990); (3) *the Cost, Quality and Child Outcomes Study* (Blau, 2000; Helburn, 1995; Howes, 1995; Howes, 1997; Phillipsen, Burchinal, Howes, & Cryer, 1997); (4) *the Florida Quality Improvement Study* (Howes, 1997; Howes, Galinsky, Shinn, Gulcur, Clements, Sibley, Abbott-Shim, & McCarthy, 1998); (5) *the Three-State Study: Massachusetts, Georgia and Virginia* (Phillips, Mekos, Scarr, McCartney, & Abbott-Shim, 2000; Scarr, Eisenberg & Deater-Deckard, 1994); (6) *the Then and Now: Changes in Child Care Staffing* (Whitebook, Sakai, Gerber, & Howes, 2001; Whitebook, & Sakai, 2003, 2004); (7) *the Head Start FACES Study* (Zill, Resnick, Kim, Hubbell-McKey, Clark,

TABLE 24.1. Contributions of a Bachelor's Degree and Specialized Early Childhood Training
to Teacher Behavior and Program Quality

Study & Researchers	Teachers	Results	Conclusion
Bermuda College Training Program Study (Arnett, 1989)	• no early childhood preparation • 2 or 4 hour course credit • ECE degree	• Teachers with a Bachelors' degree in early childhood education were less authoritarian, had more positive interactions, and were not as punitive and detached as the other teachers. • Teachers who had taken two or four years of training at Bermuda College Training were less authoritarian in their child rearing attitudes than those with no training, had more positive interactions, and were less detached than those with no training.	Teachers with a Bachelor's degree in early childhood education were the most skilled in working with young children and the next skilled teachers were those who received college level training without completing a degree.
National Child Care Staffing Study (Howes, Phillips & Whitebook, 1992; Whitebook et al., 1990)	• Bachelor's and college-level course work in early childhood education, • Bachelor's in a non early childhood education field, • some college course work in early childhood education, • high school or vocational school level training in early childhood education, • no Bachelor's degree or specialized training.	• Teachers who had some college level training or a Bachelor's degree in early childhood education provided more appropriate caregiving and were more sensitive, less harsh, and less detached than those teachers who had vocational school level training or lower • Teachers of preschool children who had some college level training or a Bachelor's degree with or without specialized training or who had college level specialized training but not a Bachelors' degree provided more appropriate caregiving. • Teachers of infants and toddlers who had either a Bachelor's degree and some college level training or who had some college level specialized training but no Bachelors degree provided more appropriate caregiving. • Teachers who were more sensitive teachers and more responsive caregivers had children who achieved higher language scores, spent less time in aimless wandering, and displayed higher levels of peer play.	Teachers with more formal education provided "better" and both appropriate caregiving at the classroom level and individual teacher sensitivity.
Cost, Quality and Child Outcomes Study (Blau, 2000; Helburn, 1995; Howes, 1995; Howes, 1997; Phillipsen, Burchinal, Howes & Cryer, 1997)	• high school and some early childhood education workshops, • some early childhood education college courses, • two year early childhood education degree, • Bachelor's degree or more advanced degree in early childhood education.	Teachers who had an AA degree in early childhood education were • more sensitive and less harsh than teachers with other backgrounds • more effective than teachers with some college or just high school plus workshops. • more responsive than teachers with other backgrounds, provided that they were in compliance with regulations governing adult-child ratios. • those teachers whose children achieved higher scores on the Peabody Picture Vocabulary Test (Dunn, 1984) than did children in classrooms with teachers who only had a high school background.	• Supported the important role of teacher education and specialized training in early childhood education. • Teachers with the most advanced education were the most effective in sensitivity, responsiveness, and constructiveness.

(Continued)

TABLE 24.1. (Continued)

Study & Researchers	Teachers	Results	Conclusion
Florida Quality Improvement Study (Howes, 1997; Howes et al., 1998)	• high school and some early childhood education workshops, • CDA credential, • some early childhood education college courses, • Bachelor's degree or more advanced degree in early childhood education.	• Teachers who had at least a Bachelor's degree in early childhood education were more sensitive than the rest of the teachers. • Teachers who had CDA training had more positive initiation with their children than did the teachers in other classrooms. • Teachers who had at least a Bachelor's degree in early childhood education or CDA training encouraged more language play and had more positive management with their children than those teachers who only had a high school education. • Teachers who had at least a Bachelor's degree in early childhood education were moreresponsive than did the teachers in other classrooms. • Teachers who had at least a Bachelor's degree in early childhood education had children who engaged in more creative activities than children in all other classrooms.	• Teachers with a higher professional preparation and in-service education improved the overall quality of the classroom. • Teachers' higher education (a) increased the teachers' sensitivity and responsiveness; (b) promoted positive peer interaction; (c) encouraged positive initiations; and (d) decreased the teachers' harshness, negative management, and detachment. • Coherent teacher education programs are more successful than those programs where teachers only take courses or informal workshops.
The *Three-State Study: Massachusetts, Georgia and Virginia* (Whitebook, Sakai, Gerber and Howes (2001)	• no specialized training; • workshops or in-service training; • a child development associate certificate; • vocational school or high school training; and • college- or graduate-level early childhood courses. • Education was captured in nine categories, ranging from none to an Ed.D. or Ph.D.	Teacher education and teacher training showed modest significance with relationships quality measures, such as adult-child interactions and developmentally appropriate activities, teacher wages was the variable most highly correlated with process quality.	• The wide range of quality among teachers' educational level may have affected the results. • Wages and child-teacher ratios predicted classroom quality.
Then and Now: Changes in Child Care Staffing (Whitebook, Sakai, Gerber & Howes, 2001; Whitebook & Sakai, 2004)	• some college and some specialized college training at the college level and • a Bachelor's degree or higher and specialized early childhood education or child development training.	• The Bachelor's degree was important. It accounted for higher quality. • Teachers who had a Bachelor's degree or higher and specialized training usually left their jobs when they earned lower wages, worked with fewer highly-trained teachers, and worked in a climate with less stability. • Teachers who were highly trained usually left the center when they earned lower wages, worked with fewer teachers with a four-year degree or higher, worked in centers with high turnover, and did not belong to a professional organization. • Teachers who had a Bachelor's degree or more were the ones who maintained a high level of classroom quality.	• Teacher education and training contributed to classroom processes. • Teachers do not work in solitude • Teacher attributes need to be understood in the context of the educational composition and stability of the staff as a whole. • The Bachelors' degree plays a prominent role in program quality.

TABLE 24.1. (Continued)

Study & Researchers	Teachers	Results	Conclusion
Head Start FACES Study (Zill, Resnick, Kim, Hubbell McKey, Clark, Pai-Samant, Connell, Vaden-Kiernan, O'Brien, & D'Elio, 2001)	• one-third of the teachers had a Bachelor's degree or higher while • one-third had some college-level experience.	• Classrooms with higher levels of quality had teachers with higher levels of education, experience, and positive attitudes and knowledge about early childhood education. • Higher levels of teacher education (e.g., four-year degrees or higher) influence teacher attitudes and knowledge, translating into higher levels of classroom quality. • Teachers who had higher education levels rated higher in sensitivity. • Children in classrooms of teachers with more education scored slightly higher on vocabulary knowledge and story and print concepts	• Teachers with a higher professional preparation improved the overall quality of the classroom. • A four year degree is important in enhancing program quality
New Jersey Studies (Barnett, Tarr, Lamy & Frede, 1999, 2001).	Teachers were grouped in two educational levels: • whether or not they had a Bachelor's degree and • whether their degree was in early childhood education or in another field. (Many teachers had a degree in elementary education with a concentration in early childhood education).	• The highest quality programs in the school districts were those who had teachers with a Bachelor's degree.	• Teachers with a Bachelor's degree, regardless of major, provided quality programs in the school districts.

Pai-Samant, Connell, Vaden-Kiernan, O'Brien, & D'Elio, 2001); and (8) *the New Jersey Studies* (Barnett, Tarr, Lamy, & Frede, 1999, 2001). These studies are summarized in Table 24.1. These studies distinguish the impact of the teachers' Bachelor's degree from other levels of education and training. In addition, these studies were selected from articles in peer-reviewed journals or peer-reviewed advisory reports from agencies. They support the results of other studies and suggest that early childhood teachers with at least a Bachelor's degree and specialized training in early childhood education or child development are most effective and provide better quality of early childhood education programs.

Bermuda College Training Program Study

The *Bermuda College Training Program Study* (Arnett, 1989) supported the importance of a Bachelor's degree and college level training in early childhood education in securing child care quality. The study, however, had a rather small and mixed sample of 50 child care teachers in Bermuda. The mixed sample consisted of teachers who (1) had no early childhood training, (2) had received credit for two or four courses at the Bermuda College Training Program, or (3) had a four-year degree in early childhood education. Teachers with a Bachelors' degree in early childhood education were less authoritarian, had more positive interactions, and were not as punitive or detached as the teachers who had a lower educational level. Teachers who have

taken 2 to 4 years of training at the Bermuda College Training Program were less authoritarian in their childrearing attitudes, had more positive interactions, and were less detached than those teachers with no training. The outcomes suggested that teachers with a Bachelor's degree in early childhood education were the most skilled in working with young children; the next skilled teachers were those who received college level training at less than a Bachelor's degree. Because of the small number of subjects who differed in their early childhood background, it is difficult to generalize from this study in relation to the specific effects of training. The study did specify that the teachers' training included a focus on child development theories, play, or curriculum development. This suggests that information about the teachers' formal education and the content of their training should be collected in future studies.

Cost, Quality and Child Outcomes Study

The *Cost, Quality and Child Outcomes Study* (CQCO) (Blau, 2000; Helburn, 1995; Howes, 1995; Howes, 1997; Phillipsen, Burchinal, Howes & Cryer, 1997) replicated the NCCSS study to test the importance of teacher education and specialized training in 370 preschool and 122 infant/toddler classrooms. It specifically focused on the lead teachers' educational background to determine if the teachers' education and training affected the program quality and teachers' behavior. Adult-child ratios rather than individual teacher characteristics contributed to higher levels of teacher responsiveness. High correlations with teacher education and training directed the researchers to categorize lead teachers based on their education, that is, if they had a Bachelor's degree, some college, or a high school diploma (Helburn, 1995; Howes, 1995). Mean scores per class were computed when more than one lead teacher was in the classroom. The results showed that the preschool teachers' education was important. In addition, teachers with more education and a moderate amount of experience, and who earned higher wages, provided higher quality in classrooms. Teachers who had less than 37 months of experience were better than the other teachers. In relation to sensitivity, lead teachers who had a Bachelor's degree and some college education had a higher sensitivity; while lower sensitivity was found among teachers with only extensive experience. Most of the results supported a negative relationship between years of experience and teacher behavior and classroom practice. Perhaps it is worth investigating if teachers' perseverance in their professional development or educational requirements might modify these results.

A relationship was found between the teachers' formal education and specialized training (Helburn, 1995; Howes, 1995). Howes (1997) computed subsequent analyses to refine the contingent impact of training and education. She categorized lead teachers based on a combination of their formal education and specialized training: (1) high school and some early childhood education workshops, (2) CDA credential, (3) some early childhood education college courses, (4) 2-year early childhood education degree, and (5) Bachelor's degree or more advanced degree in early childhood education. Because only a small number of teachers were identified who had a CDA credential, this group was omitted from the analysis. The results indicated that the most effective teachers were those who had the most advanced education. Teachers who had a Bachelor's or a more advanced degree in early childhood education were more sensitive than those teachers who had an associate degree in early childhood education. However, teachers who had an associate degree in early childhood education were:

1. more sensitive and less harsh than teachers with other backgrounds.
2. more effective than teachers with some college or just high school plus workshops.
3. more responsive than teachers with other backgrounds, provided that they were in compliance with regulations governing adult-child ratios.
4. those teachers whose children achieved higher scores on the Peabody Picture Vocabulary Test (Dunn, 1984) than did children in classrooms with teachers who only had a high school education.

In the CQCO study and other similar studies, Blau (2000) doubted whether unnoticed attributes in the centers might be mistook with the results of structural inputs, such as teacher education. Blau (2000) reanalyzed the CQCO data employing two new techniques to control for bogus relationships. The results of these analyses indicated significant effects for teacher education and training, but the effects were generally less vigorous.

Several factors relating to education and training continued to be statistically significant, although some were contradictory. For example, workshop training and lower levels of formal education had more effects. Additional analyses indicated that workshop based training and an early childhood education college degree offered the most effective kind of teacher preparation. Blau's reanalysis of the data supported the continuous result of the Bachelor's degree and proposed that the specific convention of specialized training for staff in various positions may be more complicated. Blau, an economist, recommended that this new technique of analyzing the data be used in the future when replicating similar studies.

Florida Child Care Improvement Study

The *Florida Child Care Improvement Study* (Howes, Smith, & Galinsky, 1995; Howes, Galinsky et al., 1998) examined whether teachers who had a Bachelor's degree or higher in early childhood education provided better quality experiences that would help 3- to 5-year-olds achieve better outcomes. This study showed that child care teachers with a higher professional preparation and in-service education improved the overall quality of the classroom. This kind of education (a) increased the teachers' sensitivity and responsiveness; (b) promoted positive peer interaction; (c) encouraged positive initiations; and (d) decreased the teachers' harshness, negative management, and detachment. The study showed that the teachers' effectiveness as evidenced in increased sensitivity, responsiveness, positive initiations, and decreased negative management, promotion of positive peer interaction) would improve when teachers had at least a Child Development Associate credential (or the equivalent), although teachers with a Bachelor's and advanced education were the most effective. Apparently, teachers with a Bachelor's degree in early childhood education (or higher) provided 3- to 5-year-olds with better quality preschool experiences that leads to the children achieving better outcomes. Teachers who had at least a CDA credential or the equivalent were better than those with less education, although teachers who had a Bachelor's degree or an advanced education were the best teachers. Thus, this study supported the results that an increase in professional preparation and in-service education in teachers would improve the overall quality of the early childhood education program and teacher effectiveness.

To further examine this complicated interrelationship, Howes (1997) then reanalyzed the data from the Florida Quality Improvement Study by separating the teachers according to the same educational level categories that were used in the CQCO study: (1) high school and some early childhood education workshops, (2) CDA credential, (3) some early childhood education college courses, (4) 2-year early childhood education degree, and (5) Bachelor's degree or more advanced degree in early childhood education. Because a small number of teachers had an Associate of Arts degree in early childhood education, this group was omitted from the analysis. However, as enough teachers had a CDA credential, the CDA group was included.

The results were that:

- Teachers who had at least a Bachelor's degree in early childhood education were more sensitive than the rest of the teachers.
- Teachers who had a CDA credential had more positive initiation with their children than did the teachers in other classrooms.
- Teachers who had at least a Bachelor's degree in early childhood education or CDA credential encouraged more language play and had more positive management with their children than those teachers who only had a high school education.
- Teachers who had at least a Bachelor's degree in early childhood education were more responsive than did the teachers who had a lower educational level.
- Teachers who had at least a Bachelor's degree in early childhood education had children who engaged in more creative activities than children who were with teachers who had a lower educational level.

Howes (1997) concluded that, in preparing teachers to be more effective in their teaching and in providing children with effective educational experiences, "coherent" teacher education programs are more successful than simply enrolling in college courses or attending informal workshops. She concluded that teachers with the most advanced education and training seemed to be the most effective, but teachers with an Associate of Arts degree and CDA credential were more effective than teachers with some college or just a high school education plus workshops. The Florida study supports the position that although a Bachelor's degree in early childhood education is the most effective for good program quality and child outcomes, other combinations of training and formal education also can lead to more effective teaching behaviors.

Cost, Quality and Child Outcomes Study (CQCO) and Florida Child Care Improvement Study

To further examine if formal education in early childhood education is most effective for improving program quality and child outcomes, Howes (1997) reanalyzed sample data sets from the *Cost Quality and Outcome Study* (Helburn, 1995) and the *Florida Quality Improvement Study* (Howes, Smith, & Galinsky, 1995) and classified the data into five categories of integrated specialized training and formal education: (1) high school education and no specialized training; (2) early childhood education and some specialized training in postsecondary institutions; (3) Associate of Arts degree in Child Development or a related field; (4) CDA credential; and (5) Bachelor's or higher degree in Child Development or a related field. Because the samples of teachers who had a Bachelor's degree in a related field and teachers who did not have any specialized training were small, they were removed from the analysis. The results showed that teachers with a Bachelor's degree were the ones associated with high quality classrooms. Teachers who had an Associate of Arts degree and CDA credential were more effective than those

teachers who had some specialized training in postsecondary institutions or only had a high school diploma and some workshops. However, these teachers did not offer the same high level of care as did the teachers who had a Bachelor's degree.

Three-State Study: Massachusetts, Georgia, and Virginia

The *Three-State Study: Massachusetts, Georgia and Virginia* (Phillips, Mekos, Scarr, McCartney & Abbott-Shim, 2000; Scarr, Eisenberg & Deater-Deckard, 1994) examined child care quality in infant, toddler, and preschool classrooms for Massachusetts, Georgia, and Virginia, which are three states that have across-the-board range of child care regulations. Scarr and her colleagues (1994) studied the process quality as well as the teachers' education and training. The teachers' educational background was categorized into five educational levels (1) no specialized training; (2) workshops or in-service training; (3) CDA credential; (4) vocational school or high school training; and (5) college or graduate courses in early childhood education. The teachers' education ranged from none to an Ed.D. or a Ph.D. teacher education and teacher training indicated a modest relationship to the process of quality measures. These results may be attributed to the wide range of quality among classrooms. Later, Phillips and associates (2000) analyzed this data set and found that teacher education and training contributed to classroom processes. However, they suggested that future studies should factor the number of teachers with different educational and training backgrounds within centers and classrooms. Studies also should consider the effects teachers have on teacher behavior and program quality.

Recent Studies

Recently, Marshall, Creps, Burstein, Glantz, Robeson, and Barnett (2001) examined the quality and features of programs for children between 2.9 and 5 years of age. More than one half of the classrooms in the sample did not meet the benchmark of good care. Only 10% of classroom staff in centers serving predominantly low-income families had a 2-year college degree or more, compared to 28% for centers that were serving low- to moderate-income families. Thus, along with other studies shows that better program quality depends on better-educated teachers. The analysis did not distinguish between teachers who had an Associate of Arts degree or higher and less than an Associate of Arts degree; therefore, it is difficult to assess the relative contribution of the Bachelor's degree over and above a 2-year degree. In a later study, Howes, James, and Ritchie (2003) found that a Bachelor's degree is important. The teachers in their sample who had a Bachelor's degree were more effective teachers (especially in their responsive involvement and participation with children in activities that promote language development and emergent literacy) than most teachers who did not have a Bachelor's degree. They also found important alternative pathways for obtaining effective teaching behaviors, which included being mentored, being supervised in a reflective fashion, and the teachers' reasons for staying in the field. The 12 teachers without Bachelor's degrees in the alternative pathway to teaching were no different in responsive involvement and engaging children in emergent literacy than those teachers who had a Bachelor's degree. It is important to keep in mind that 12 is a small number of teachers in any analysis; therefore, caution needs to be used before generalizing from this study.

Granger and Marx (1988) found that Head Start teachers in New York City had a low (50%) level of teacher certification. There also was a relationship found between teacher training, teacher stability, and program quality. In a further analysis, Granger (1989) found a relationship among teacher training, teacher stability, and program quality. Honig and Hirallal (1998) studied 81 teachers of 3- to 5-year-old children that they classified into two groups:

1. Teachers low in education, experience, and training whose education ranged from having a high school education through an Associate of Arts degree, one to four training courses, and one to three years of experience.
2. Teachers high in education, experience, and training group who had a Bachelor's degree or higher, 5 or more training courses, and 4 or more years of experience.

Their results showed that neither the teachers' years of experience nor stability in their child care position increased the teachers' enrichment of children's learning or socioemotional development in any way. They also found that a high degree of formal education did not ensure positive teacher support for young children if training and experience were low. Although Honig and Hirallal (1998) considered the teachers' education, training and experience, there were other variables that were studied that might have had an impact on their conclusions, such as the content of the different types of early childhood education courses and where the teachers received training credit for these courses. In addition, teachers may have been grouped into broad set of categories. Nevertheless, the study supported the importance of specialized preparation in child development or early childhood education to determine if formal education influences the teachers' behaviors and that to appropriately care for young children requires education and training rather than just experience working with young children (Helburn, 1995; Whitebook, Howes, & Phillips, 1990).

McCarty, Lambert, and Abbott-Shim (1998) investigated Head Start teachers' beliefs and practices in relation to the quality of the teachers' classrooms (e.g., high, moderate, low). They showed that teachers in low-quality classrooms had shown more inappropriate practices than did teachers in either high or moderate quality classrooms. Later, Abbott-Shim, Lambert, and McCarty (2000) explored classroom quality in Head Start classrooms and found that the teachers' educational level influenced their beliefs relating to instructional activities and attitudes toward families. Their study suggested that improving the teachers' educational level may improve their beliefs about instructional practices and that program administrators need to assess the teachers' training, education, and supervision to guide their beliefs in a developmentally appropriate mode. Better-educated early childhood teachers provided children with easy to follow

directions and presented uninvolved children with new activities that were not repetitive or low-level activities (de Kruif, McWilliam, Ridley, & Wakely, 2000). Children in these qualified teachers' classrooms were more sociable, exhibited a more developed use of language, and performed at a higher level on cognitive tasks (Bowman, Donovan, & Burns, 2000; Dwyer, Chait, & McKee, 2000; Howes, 1997). It can be concluded that the professional development of early childhood teachers is important (Bowman, Donovan, & Burns, 2000).

Teachers' Education and Quality of Programs

Teachers who are considered to be qualified teachers are those with a Bachelor's degree and some specialized content in child development or early childhood education (Barnett, 2003, 2004; Whitebook, 2003a, 2003b). The Association for Childhood Education International (ACEI, 1998) advocated that all early childhood settings (child care centers, home care, Head Start programs, nursery schools, kindergartens, public or private primary schools) should have qualified early childhood teachers that are recognized as professionals. This requires having qualified teachers in early childhood education with a license and/or professional certification. Early childhood teachers need to be educated within teacher education programs that (a) are explicitly linked to early childhood education; (b) offer a strong knowledge base in appropriate teaching practices and child development (Bowman et al., 2000); and (c) teach them to use developmentally appropriate practices that help children to build on their emerging understandings and skills (Helburn, 1995; Howes, Whitebook, & Phillips, 1992; Kontos & Wilcox-Herzog, 1997).

Early childhood teachers need to have the knowledge, skills, and sensitivity to interact successfully with young children, parents, guardians, paraprofessionals, community organizations, and others whose actions affect their classroom children to be able to provide them with an effective learning and developmental environment that focuses on the young children's interests and needs in a diverse society (ACEI, 1998). Initiatives to improve the quality of young children's learning require that states and communities plan and implement campaigns to guarantee a high-quality education by acquiring information about the programmatic factors that lead to best practices and best outcomes in early childhood education, especially regarding the professional preparation of teachers (Whitebook, 2003a,b).

Effective Teacher Education Programs

One of the requirements for teacher preparation programs, institutions, and organizations is that they provide evidence that support their effectiveness at promoting teachers' learning, improving professional practice, and boosting the students' learning. Many debates have emerged on what it would mean to do so (see Cochran-Smith [2001a]), although most teacher educators believe and indeed, adopt the position that research evidence shows that teacher education has positive effects on the teachers' instruction and K–12 students' learning (Cochran-Smith, 2001b). Laczko-Kerr and Berliner (2002) found that certified teachers were more effective than uncertified teachers to the point that those who were highly qualified could be easily distinguished from those teachers who were less qualified.

An effective early childhood teacher can only achieve a high level of professional sophistication through a formal education (Bowman, Donovan, & Burns, 2000; Lamb, 1998). According to the recent National Research Council Report on Early Childhood Pedagogy, "... each group of children in an early childhood education and care program should be assigned a teacher who has a bachelor's degree with specialized education related to early childhood" (Bowman et al., 2000, p. 239).

STATE REQUIREMENT FOR TEACHER QUALIFICATIONS

In the United States, no state or national standards or certificates for teachers of young children exist outside the requirements of the public schools. State child care regulations establish minimal standards within the licensing regulations needed to operate an early childhood center. Early childhood teachers in these centers have minimal educational requirements (Saluja et al., 2002; Burton, Whitebook, Young, Bellm, Wayne, Brandon, & Maher, 2002). These standards represent a level below which harm might be caused to children rather than a level of program quality.

Requirements for State-Financed Prekindergarten Programs

Minimum qualifications for teachers in state financed prekindergarten programs range from requiring teachers to have completed 24 credit hours in one state, a Child Development Associate (CDA) credential in 11 states, and a Bachelor's degree in 20 states and the District of Columbia, to a Master's degree (after 5 years of employment) in New York State (Barnett, 2003, 2004). These requirements are presented in Table 24.2.

Requirements for Private Early Childhood Programs

The requirements for teachers in state financed early childhood education programs are higher than the requirements for teachers in private early childhood classrooms. In many states, teachers in private early childhood programs only need to pass a criminal records or child abuse registry check. Teachers may not need to complete any college courses. Some may have not even be required to graduate from high school (Iowa Early Care and Education Professional Development Project, 2000). Only 21 states require that early childhood teachers attend *any* preservice training, much less hold even an associate degree in early childhood education (Azer, LeMoine, Morgan, Clifford, & Crawford, 2002; Mitchell, 2001). Table 24.3 presents these requirements.

Requirements for Head Start Programs

Most Head Start preschool teachers are less qualified than those teachers in public school d programs. Head Start has attempted to improve teacher qualifications by requiring that 50% of its teachers have at least an associate degree by the year 2003. The 2001–2002 Head Start Program Information Report estimated that approximately 30% of the Head Start teachers had at least a Bachelor's degree at that time. A national average of 29% of the Head Start teachers had a Bachelor's degree or higher, 23% had an Associate of Arts degree, 35% had a CDA credential, and 13% with no degree or CDA credential. The Head Start teachers' qualifications differed across states, with 64% having a Bachelor's degree or higher in New York state as compared with 12% having a Bachelor's degree in Alaska and Alabama (National Institute for Early Education Research, 2003). The Georgia State University Research Center found in its study of three classrooms on Head Start Quality that 13% of the teachers had a high school or GED diploma. Most of the teachers (66%) had attended either a technical school or some college. Only 14% of the teachers had a Bachelor's degree, and 6% had attended graduate school or received a graduate degree. Most of them (73%) had a CDA credential and 17% had either not enrolled in CDA training or had not achieved a higher level of formal education (Zill, Resnick, Kim, Hubbell-McKey, Clark,

TABLE 24.2. Pre-Service Requirements for Teachers in State-Financed PreKs

Child Development Associate (CDA)	Arizona, Colorado, Connecticut, Delaware, Florida, Iowa (in private ECE setting), Massachusetts (if in private ECE setting), Missouri, Oregon, Vermont (if in private ECE setting), Virginia
Associate's degree (AA)	Ohio (by 2008)
AA in Early Childhood or equivalent	Alabama, Georgia, North Carolina, Washington
College Credits in Early Childhood	California (24 credits)
Bachelor's (BA) degree without specific Early Childhood endorsement or equivalent	District of Columbia, Louisiana, Maine, Michigan, Minnesota, Nebraska, Nevada, New Jersey, New York, West Virginia, Wisconsin
Bachelor's (BA) degree with specific Early Childhood endorsement or equivalent	Arkansas, Illinois, Iowa (if in public school setting), Kansas, Kentucky, Maryland, Massachusetts (if in public school setting), Oklahoma, Pennsylvania, Rhode Island, South Carolina, Tennessee, Texas, Vermont (if in public school setting)

Source: National Center for Early Development & Learning (NCEDL). (2001). *Public school pre-K programs: National survey of states.* National Center for Early Development & Learning (NCEDL), 2001.

From: Ackerman, D. J. (2003). *States' efforts in improving the qualifications of early care and education teachers,* p. 6.

Author's note: Alaska, Hawaii, Idaho, Indiana, Mississippi, Montana, New Hampshire, North Dakota, South Dakota, Utah, and Wyoming do not have state-financed preKs

TABLE 24.3. Pre-Service Requirements for Teachers in Private ECE Centers

No requirements	Alaska, Arizona, Arkansas, Colorado, Connecticut, Idaho, Indiana, Iowa, Kentucky, Louisiana, Maine, Michigan, Mississippi, Missouri, Nebraska, New Mexico, New York, North Carolina, North Dakota, Ohio, Oklahoma, Oregon, Pennsylvania, South Carolina, South Dakota, Tennessee, Utah, Virginia, West Virginia, Wyoming
10 clock hours or less of training	Georgia (10 hours within 1st year of working), Montana (8 hours within 1st year of working), Nevada (3 hours within 1st year of working), Texas (8 hours)
11–20 hours of training	Alabama (12 hours), Washington (20 hours)
More than 20 hours of training	Delaware (60 hours plus 1 year experience), Florida (40 hours), Maryland (90 hours plus 1 year experience), Wisconsin (2 non-credit ECE courses plus 80 days experience)
Child Development Associate (CDA)/ Certified Child Care Professional (CCP)	District of Columbia, Hawaii (plus 1 year experience), Illinois, Kansas (plus 1 year experience), Minnesota (plus 1,560 hours of experience), New Jersey (plus 6 credits in Early Childhood or related field)
College coursework in Early Childhood or equivalent	California (6 semesters), Massachusetts (2 year vocational child care course), Vermont (12 credits plus 3 years Experience)
Associate's degree (AA) in Early Childhood or equivalent	New Hampshire (2 year vocational child care course)
Bachelor's (BA) degree	Rhode Island (but must meet standards for state Early Childhood certificate, with 24 Early Childhood Education credits and 6 credits in student teaching

Source: Azer, et al., 2002; LeMoine, 2002.

From: Ackerman, D. J. (2003). *States' efforts in improving the qualifications of early care and education teachers*, p. 7.

Author's note: Of the states that have no requirements for teachers in private ECE centers, Alaska, Idaho, Indiana, Mississippi, North Dakota, South Dakota, Utah, and Wyoming also do not have any state-financed preKs.

Pai-Samant, Connell, Vaden-Kiernan, O'Brien, & D'Elio, 2001). Similar statistics can be found for other states, such as Texas and Illinois. In New York City, Granger and Marx (1988) found that half of the Head Start teachers were certified.

Requirements for Public School Early Childhood Programs

Typically, educational requirements for teachers in public school early childhood education programs are similar to those of teachers in Grades K–12. Teachers are required to have at least a Bachelor's degree and a teaching certificate. A teaching certificate is an indication of the teachers' qualifications. Although certification requirements differ among states, a standard certificate normally means that the teachers have been awarded an undergraduate or graduate degree after completing a program at a state-approved teacher education program. For graduation, teachers are required to complete a major in a field of education—often from 18 to 40 education credits—and 8 to18 weeks of student teaching. They also are required to complete a significant number of courses in general education and possibly a minor in a field other than education.

The quality of teacher education programs is ensured in two ways. To receive an initial certificate, the candidate must graduate from a program of teacher education that is approved by a state department of education. This approval insures a minimum level of program quality. Programs may also be accredited by the National Council on Accreditation of Teacher Education (NCATE). The National Association for the Education of Young Children works with NCATE to review early childhood teacher education programs. This accreditation is voluntary and builds upon current knowledge in the field of early childhood education. In addition, many states require that teacher candidates pass one or more tests, providing another measure of teacher

quality. These may be tests of basic skills, subject matter knowledge, or teaching knowledge or skills as the basis for the initial certification, continuing license, or admission to the teacher education program (Darling-Hammond & Sykes, 2003).

Differences in Requirements Among Early Childhood Education Programs

Teacher qualifications have generally been an issue in all early childhood programs. The qualities of the teachers in these programs is not much different from the essential qualifications that are needed to work in an early childhood classroom that provides young children with the kind of "real" education that begins in kindergarten (Bowman et al., 2000; Hinkle, 2000; Laverty, Burton, Whitebook, & Bellm, 2001). It differs essentially from the "folk belief" (Genishi, Ryan, Ochsner, & Yarnall, 2001, pp. 1175–1210) that early childhood teachers only need to have maternal attributes to be a "suitable" early childhood teacher (Nelson, 2001). Early childhood teachers need a broad range of educational background and experience.

The teachers' qualifications in Head Start, state-financed prekindergartens and private early childhood education centers differ from those of the public school kindergarten teachers (see Table 24.4).

Barnett (2003b) indicated that states have established a minimum of postsecondary degree standards for teachers in state-financed prekindergarten programs. This was discussed earlier. Kindergarten teachers in all 50 states are required to have at least a Bachelor's degree, although several states also require a kindergarten endorsement on an elementary education teaching certificate or an early childhood education certificate (Ackerman, 2003; Bureau of Labor Statistics, 2002, Kaye, 2001). In Head Start programs, only half of their teachers are required to improve their qualifications from a Child Development Associate

TABLE 24.4. Minimum Post-Secondary Degree Requirements for Preschool Teachers, By State[8]

State	Kindergarten	State Financed Pre-K	Child Care[2]
ALABAMA	BA[1]	BA[1]	None
ALASKA	BA	CDA[5]	None
ARIZONA	BA	CDA	None
ARKANSAS	BA	BA[1]	None
CALIFORNIA	BA	40 credits[6]	6 credits[3]
COLORADO	BA	CDA	None
CONNECTICUT	BA[1]	CDA	None
DELAWARE	BA[1]	CDA	CDA
DISTRICT OF COLOMBIA	BA[1]	BA	CDA
FLORIDA	BA	None	None
GEORGIA	BA	AA[1]	None
HAWAII	BA	CDA	CDA
IDAHO	BA	N/A	None
ILLINOIS	BA	BA[1]	CDA or CCP
INDIANA	BA	N/A	None
IOWA	BA[1]	None	None
KANSAS	BA	BA	CDA
KENTUCKY	BA[1]	CDA	None
LOUISIANA	BA[1]	BA[1]	None
MAINE	BA	BA[1]	None
MARYLAND	BA[1]	BA[1]	None
MASSACHUSETTS	BA[1]	3 credits[4]	3 credits[4]
MICHIGAN	BA	AA	None
MINNESOTA	BA	CDA	CDA
MISSISSIPPI	BA	N/A	None
MISSOURI	BA[1]	CDA	None
MONTANA	BA	N/A	None
NEBRASKA	BA	BA[1]	None
NEVADA	BA[1]	BA[1]	None
NEW HAMPSHIRE	BA	CDA[5]	12 credits[7]
NEW JERSEY	BA	BA[1]	CDA
NEW MEXICO	BA	None	None
NEW YORK	BA	BA	None
NORTH CAROLINA	BA[1]	AA[1]	None
NORTH DAKOTA	BA	N/A	None
OHIO	BA[1]	AA[1]	None
OKLAHOMA	BA	BA[1]	None
OREGON	BA	CDA	None
PENNSYLVANIA	BA	BA	None
RHODE ISLAND	BA[1]	BA[1]	BA[1]
SOUTH CAROLINA	BA	BA[1]	None
SOUTH DAKOTA	BA	N/A	None
TENNESSEE	BA	BA[1]	None
TEXAS	BA	BA[1]	None
UTAH	BA[1]	N/A	None
VERMONT	BA	BA[1]	12 credits[4]
VIRGINIA	BA[1]	CDA	None
WASHINGTON	BA	AA[1]	None
WEST VIRGINIA	BA	BA	None
WISCONSIN	BA[1]	BA[1]	None
WYOMING	BA	N/A	None

AA—Associate Degree; BA—Bachelor's Degree; CDA—Child Development Associate Credential; Pre-K—Pre-kindergarten; CCP—Certified Childcare Professional. N/A—state does not provide finances for pre-k; None—no post-secondary degree requirements.

[1] with courses or certification in early childhood.

[2] many states require professional training or ongoing development.

[3] 2 year vocational child care course or 6 credits in early childhood education.

[4] in topics related to early childhood education or child development.

[5] Head Start requirements used because all state pre-k funds supplement Head Start program.

[6] 24 credits in early childhood education and 16 credits more in general education.

[7] in early childhood education, 6 of which may be non-credit courses.

[8] update June, 2003.

Source: Barnett, W. S. (2003b). Better teachers, better preschools: Student achievement linked to teacher qualifications. *NIEER Policy Facts*.

From: Whitebook, M. (2003a). *Bachelor's degrees are best: Higher qualifications for pre-kindergarten teachers led to better learning environments*. Washington, D.C.: The Trust for Early Education.

Also Whitebook, M. (2003b). Early Education Quality: Higher Teacher Qualifications for Better Learning Environments—A Review of the Literature. Berkeley, CA: Center for the Study of Child Care Employment.

TABLE 24.5. A Professional Continuum for Teacher Development

Recruitment to a teacher education program based on academic background and ability to work with children	Preservice preparation in an NCATE accredited school of education	Initial intern license based on INTASC tests of subject matter & teaching knowledge	New teacher induction: 1–2 years of early career mentoring & evaluation	Continuing license based on performance assessments, evaluations, and student work	Ongoing professional development in and out of the classroom	Advanced certification based on NBPTS performance assessments & exams

NCATE = National Council for Accreditation of Teacher Education
INTASC = Interstate New Teacher Assessment and Support Consortium
NBPTS = National Board for Professional Teaching Standards
Source: National Commission on Teaching and America's Future (1996). *What matters most: Teaching for America's future.* New York: Author., p. 67.

Credential to an Associate of Arts, Bachelor's, or advance degree in early childhood education according to the pending bill by the year 2008 (Whitebook, 2003a,b).

Ryan and Ackerman (2004) recommended that states require that teachers of 3- and 4-year-olds improve their qualifications and develop plans of professional preparation to build their professional expertise. The National Commission on Teaching and America's Future (1996) suggested a plan to help the teachers to continue with their professional development, as noted in Table 24.5.

RECONCEPTUALIZING TEACHERS' PROFESSIONAL DEVELOPMENT

Statistics show that less than 50% of lead teachers in early childhood programs for 3- and 4-year-olds, including child care, school-based prekindergarten, and Head Start programs, have a 4-year college degree (Saluja, Early, & Clifford, 2002). Yet, as noted earlier, a broad disparity is found between the effects of qualified early childhood teachers and those hired according to existing policies and practices found in these programs. Much is at stake for young children and their families as states and communities struggle with the issues of the early childhood teachers' qualifications.

A national trend has emerged to improve the level of teacher qualifications, focusing on college degrees in early childhood education, child development, or a related field. The federal *No Child Left Behind Act of 2001* (HR1) requires schools to hire "highly qualified" teachers in every classroom by the academic year of 2005–2006. Recent policy developments have drawn unprecedented attention to issues of teacher quality (Darling-Hammond, & Sykes, 2003). On May 21, 1998, New Jersey's Supreme Court mandated that New Jersey's Abbott districts (the 30 highest poverty districts in the state) provide children above age 3 with a high-quality preschool education to teach them skills and abilities that they would need to succeed in kindergarten. The Supreme Court established a few basic standards for quality preschool education, including a requirement to have a certified teacher in these classrooms (Barnett, Tarr, Lamy, & Frede, 2001).

A recent congressional reauthorization of Head Start established performance standards for programs that require a Bachelor's degree for qualified classroom staff (Bowman et al 2000). *The Head Start Act* (1998) asserted that by September 30, 2003, at least 50% of its teachers be required to advance

their education from their CDA credential, which consists of 120 clock hours of instruction in children's health, safety, and development (Council for Professional Recognition, 2000) to acquiring an Associate (AA/AS), a Bachelor's (BA/BS), or advanced degree in early childhood education or a related subject. It was assumed that by Fall 2003, Head Start would elevate its standards to where all teachers would have an associate degree (Head Start Act, 1998). As this goal was not achieved, it was established that, by 2008, pending a reauthorization bill, 50% of Head Start teachers would have a Bachelor's degree (BA/BS). In addition, the government attempted to upgrade the early childhood education teachers' qualifications and credentials by increasing the minimum preservice requirements for teachers in private early childhood education settings (Ackerman, 2003; Azer, 1999; Azer & Bowie, 2000; Azer, LeMoine, Morgan, Clifford, & Crawford, 2002; LeMoine, 2002). For example:

- in 1999 Alabama increased their preservice training requirement from no hours to 12 hours of training in child care and development
- Florida increased the minimum preservice early childhood education training from 30 to 40 clock hours
- Massachusetts increased their teacher preparation requirements from requiring a high school vocational program in child care to requiring entry-level teachers to complete at least a 2-year postsecondary vocational child care course
- Washington increased the minimum preservice early childhood education training from no preservice qualifications necessary to begin teaching in a private early childhood education setting to requiring a minimum of 20 hours of approved training

Since 1999, four states have increased their entry-level requirements for teachers, whereas 10 states (Alabama, Colorado, Kentucky, Montana, Nevada, New Hampshire, North Dakota, South Carolina, Vermont, and Wyoming) have acted to extend the number of continuing staff development hours that early childhood education teachers need to attain on an annual basis (Azer, 1999; Azer & Bowie, 2000; Azer et al., 2002; LeMoine, 2002). The attempts to increase the teachers' annual early childhood education from 9 to 15 hours each year seems impressive, but the training of early childhood education teachers in private settings throughout the United States ranges between 3 to 24 hours with an annual average of 10 hours. Furthermore, five of the states (Colorado, Kentucky, North Dakota, South Carolina, and Wyoming) required that the early childhood education teachers' training increase their annual training. Presently, they do not have a minimum preservice requirement for the early childhood education teachers nor are they required to have a strong knowledge base in child development or appropriate teaching practices (Ackerman, 2003). Furthermore, the National Commission on Teaching and America's Future (1996) contended that *all* teachers need to have an experienced teacher supervise a 1-year internship and continuing professional development based on current research related to their present classroom teaching and learning activities and provided them with opportunities for continued learning through "ongoing conversations and coaching" (p. 43) (see Table 24.5). In 2002, Dr. Jack Shonkoff, chair of the National Research Council's Committee on Integrating the Science of Early Childhood Development, submitted the inquiry to Congress concerning the incongruity relating to child development, public policies, and teachers:

> How can the recently enacted *No Child Left Behind Act* emphasize the need for stronger performance standards and financial incentives to attract bright and highly motivated teachers, while we simultaneously tolerate large percentages of inadequately trained and poorly compensated providers of early child care and education who have an important influence on the foundations of school readiness? (Testimony to the U.S. Senate Committee on Health, Education, Labor and Pensions, February 12, 2002, p. 3, cited in Whitebook, 2003b)

Ryan and Ackerman (2004) believed that it is conceivable to develop a certified preschool teaching workforce within a brief span of time. The Abbott district in New Jersey assured that early childhood programs will have qualified teachers who are suitably credentialed preschool teachers by September 2006. In order to meet these deadlines, early childhood administrators need to generate a monitoring system that helps them to monitor the teachers' progress toward meeting the certification deadline (Ryan & Ackerman, 2004).

Challenges in Meeting the Mandate

To date, many states have difficulty meeting the standards of the *No Child Left Behind Act*, especially in private early childhood programs (Bellm, Burton, Whitebook, Broatch, & Young, 2002). Early and Winton (2001) described the challenges that early childhood teacher preparation programs encounter in their attempt to meet the challenge of early childhood teachers professional development. Teachers find that their academic studies compete with their jobs and their family related responsibilities. They are further challenged by poor working conditions and low wages in private preschools and child care centers (Early & Winton, 2001). They are confronted with other challenges as well. Teachers also experience different staffing patterns in programs as well as different training issues. Teachers vary in their literacy skills, their English proficiency, their ability to communicate (especially in other languages), their economic background, their current family status, and a range of personal characteristics (e.g., social support levels, depression) that may limit their access to education and their ability to learn as adults (Phillips, Crowell, Whitebook, & Jo, 2003; Whitebook & Sakai, 2003).

Teacher preparation programs also make it difficult for the early childhood teachers to be able to meet the mandate. Early and Winton (2001) found that many 4-year institutions lack of expertise in early childhood education have difficulty attracting and retaining ethnically and racially diverse faculty. These challenges are greater in 4-year institutions than those found in 2-year institutions, where prerequisites for employment may include having a doctorate and contributing to the research literature of the field. In addition, early childhood teachers encounter problems with transfer of credits. Courses in community college child care or child development programs may have the same titles as those in 4-year teacher education programs. However, the content may not be the same and the criteria for successfully completing the course also may not be the same. Although community colleges often complain that 4-year institutions refuse to accept their courses for credit, they too often are unwilling to provide the same course content or have the same course requirements as the 4-year institutions. They argue that to do so would limit the students they could accept in the program. This lack of a "career ladder" in early childhood education makes it difficult for existing teachers in child care centers and preschools to meet the increased requirements that are being suggested. This is a dilemma that the field has yet to resolve.

Teachers reported to Ryan and Ackerman (2004) two reasons for not wanting to meet this mandate: (1) they believe that they already have all the education they need for the job and (2) they do not get the time off from their work duties to undertake further study. These results suggested that the states, the early childhood education programs' administration, the leaders in the different early childhood schools, and the early childhood education teachers need to share this responsibility. Ryan and Ackerman (2004) found that some teachers in the Abbott district had a Bachelor's degree, but they have difficulty obtaining a preschool to third grade certification.

In meeting the deadline, each district could identify these teachers and design a plan of action to meet the Abbott deadline. For example, for those teachers who indicated that time restrictions interfered with their capacity to improve their qualifications, district administrators could provide them with the types of support that can help them to achieve their goal. Because they found differences between districts in terms of teachers' attempts and capacities to meet the mandate, they believe that some districts have been more successful in recruiting certified teachers and/or supporting preschool teachers in obtaining their certification. The variety of strategies used by these school districts may be useful in aiding teachers to meet the deadline for the mandate. Ryan and Ackerman (2004) supported the court mandate that required early childhood teachers to obtain a Bachelor's degree and teaching credential in a short period of time. The early childhood teachers' qualifications can lead to establishing a cadre of knowledgeable professionals whose expertise can facilitate ongoing improvement in the schools.

SUMMARY

Early childhood teachers are being required to increase their level of sophistication in early childhood education, knowledge, developmentally appropriate practices, and teaching strategies that provide quality care and education to young children. This suggests that early childhood educators become increasingly professional. They need a knowledge base that includes child development knowledge, pedagogical knowledge, knowledge of learning and teaching styles, and knowledge of how to promote creativity. Teachers of young children must also know how to nurture the relationship between the home and the school. They must know about the informal learning and teaching processes that occur in the home and how to nurture them. They need to know about ways to build a close relationship between home and school (Saracho & Spodek, 2003). We can learn from the experience of early childhood educators in other countries as well as our own. In many countries, early childhood education teachers are prepared in 4-year Bachelor's degree programs. Other countries require that early childhood teachers either graduate from 4-year or 2-year programs. In many cases, the standards of preparation are increasing, however (Spodek & Saracho, 1993, 1996).

The studies reviewed here on program quality and children's outcomes in child care, public preschools, and Head Start programs support the importance of a college education and specialized training at least a Bachelor's degree in early childhood education to generate teacher behaviors that will promote high-quality programs and learning for young children. The teacher's behavior has a major impact on child development (Shonkoff & Phillips, 2000).

The teacher's advanced education helps them to become more sensitive, appropriate, and able to create responsive learning environments. The studies support the conclusion that optimum teacher behavior, skills, and knowledge are best achieved through a 4-year college degree in early childhood education or child development. However, future studies need to consider the thresholds of education and training: the content, format, and quality of specialized early childhood training; variations in strategies for teachers with varying characteristics and needs; and the factors that scaffold teachers' knowledge, enabling them to engage in effective teaching strategies with children. An emerging body of evidence has suggested alternative pathways to effective teaching to increase the quality of teachers for young children. Howes, James, and Ritchie (2003) reported that alternative pathways to effective teaching included factors such as staying in the field for the sake of benefiting one's community, being mentored early in their careers, and receiving ongoing supervision.

References

Abbott-Shim, M., Lambert, R., & McCarty, F. (2000). Structural model of Head Start classroom quality. *Early Childhood Research Quarterly, 15,* 115–134.

Ackerman, D. J. (2003). *States' efforts in improving the qualifications of early care and education teachers.* Retrieved on July 22, 2004, from http://circ.web.ca/research/complete/USqualifications.html and http://nieer.org/resources/research/Ackerman.pdf and http://www.ccw.org/pubs/ccw_pre-k_10.4.02.pdf

Arnett, J. (1989). Caregivers in day-care centers: Does training matter? *Journal of Applied Developmental Psychology, 10*(4), 541–552.

Association for Childhood Education International (ACEI, 1998). Preparation of Early Childhood Education Teachers ACEI position paper. Olney, MD: Author. Retrieved on May 27, 2004, from http://www.udel.edu/bateman/acei/prepec.htm

Azer, S. L. (1999). *Child care licensing: Training requirements for roles in child care centers and family child care.* Boston: The Center for Career Development in Early Care and Education. Retrieved on July 22, 2004, from http://ericps.crc.uiuc.edu/nccic.cctopics/cclicensing.pdf

Azer, S. L., & Bowie, P. (2000). *Training requirements in child care licensing regulations: 2000.* Boston: The Center for Career Development in Early Care and Education.

Azer, S. L., LeMoine, S., Morgan, G., Clifford, R. M., & Crawford, G. M. (2002). Regulation of child care. *Early Childhood Research & Policy Briefs, 2*(1). Also available at http://www.fpg.unc.edu/~ncedl/PDFs/RegBrief.pdf

Barnett, W. S. (2003). Better teachers, better preschools: Student achievement linked to teacher qualifications. *Preschool Policy Matters, 2.* New Brunswick, NJ: National Institute for Early Education Research.

Barnett, W. S. (2004). Better teachers, better preschools: Student achievement linked to teacher qualifications. NIEER *Policy Facts.* New Brunswick, NJ: National Institute for Early Education Research.

Barnett, W. S., Tarr, J., Lamy, C., & Frede, E. (1999). *Children's educational needs and community capacity in the Abbott Districts.* New Brunswick, NJ: Center for Early Education, Rutgers University.

Barnett, W. S., Tarr, J., Lamy, C., & Frede, E. (2001). *Fragile lives, shattered dreams: A report on implementation of preschool education in New Jersey's Abbott districts.* New Brunswick, NJ: National Institute for Early Education Research, Rutgers University. Retrieved on July 24, 2004, from http://nieer.org/resources/research/FragileLives.pdf

Bellm, D., Burton, A., Whitebook, M., Broatch, L. & Young, M. (2002). *Inside the pre-K classroom: A study of staffing and stability in state-funded prekindergarten programs.* Washington, DC: Center for the Child Care Workforce. Retrieved on July 20, 2004 from http://www.ccw.org/pubs/ccw_pre-k_10.4.02.pdf and http://nieer.org/docs/index.php?DocID=55

Blau, D. M. (2000). The production of quality in child care centers: Another look. *Applied Developmental Science, 4*(3), 136–148.

Bryant, D., Clifford, R. M., Saluja, G., Pianta, R., Early, D., Barbarin, O., Howes, C., & Burchinal, M. (2004). *Diversity and directions in state pre-kindergarten programs.* Chapel Hill, NC: FPG Child Development Institute.

Bryant, D., Maxwell, K., Taylor, K., Poe, M., Peisner-Feinberg, E., & Bernier, K. (2003). *Smart start and preschool child care quality in North Carolina: Change over time and relation to children's readiness.* Chapel Hill, NC: FPG Child Development Institute.

Bowman, B., Donovan, M. S., & Burns, S. (Eds.). (2000). *Eager to learn: Educating our preschoolers.* Washington, DC: National Research Council. Retrieved on July 20, 2004, from http://books.nap.edu/books/0309068363/html/261.html

Brown, J., Burr, E., Johnson, L. R., Krieger, M., & Mihaly, J. (2001). *Inventory of early childhood education training in California.* Berkeley: Policy Analysis for California Education.

Bryant, D., Clifford, R. M., Saluja, G., Pianta, R., Early, D., Barbarin, O., Howes, C., & Burchinal, M. (2004). *Diversity and directions in state pre-kindergarten programs.* Chapel Hill, NC: FPG Child Development Institute.

Bureau of Labor Statistics, U. S. Department of Labor. (1999). *Labor force participation of fathers and mothers varies with children's ages.* Retrieved on July 2, 2004, from http://www.bls.gov/opub/ted/1999/Jun/wk1/art03.htm

Bureau of Labor Statistics, U. S. Department of Labor. (2002) *Occupational outlook handbook, 2002-03 edition, Bulletin 2540.* Retrieved on July 18, 2004, from http://www.bls.gov/oco/

Burton, A., Laverty, K., & Duff, B. (2002). *A profile of the Alameda County child care center workforce 1995-2001: Continuing evidence of a staffing crisis.* Washington, DC: Center for the Child Care Workforce. Retrieved on July 22, 2004, from http://www.co.alameda.ca.us/childcare/alameda_cccw_2002.pdf

Burton, A., Whitebook, M., Young, M., Bellm, D., Wayne, C., Brandon, R. N., & Maher, E. (2002). *Estimating the size and components of the U.S. child care workforce and caregiving population: Key findings from the child care workforce estimate* (Preliminary report). Washington, DC: Center for the Child Care Workforce. Retrieved on July 2, 2004, from http://www.hspc.org/publications/early_ed/ccw_May_2002.pdf

Cochran-Smith, M. (2001a). Reforming teacher education: Competing agendas. *Journal of Teacher Education, 52,* 263-265.

Cochran-Smith, M. (2001b). Teacher Quality & Student Achievement. *Education Policy Analysis Archives, 8*(1). Retrieved on July 21, 2004, from http://epaa.asu.edu/epaa/v8n1/

Cost, Quality and Child Outcomes Study Team. (1995). *Cost, quality and child outcomes in childcare centers* (Executive summary). Denver: University of Colorado at Denver. Retrieved on July 22, 2004, from http://www.fpg.unc.edu/~ncedl/pages/cq.cfm

Council for Professional Recognition (2000). *The Child Development Associate national credentialing program: Making a difference in the early care and education of young children.* Washington, DC: Author.

Cryer, D., Tietze, W., Burchinal, M., Leal, T., & Palacios, J. (1999). Predicting process quality from structural quality in preschool programs: A cross-country comparison. *Early Childhood Research Quarterly, 14*(3), 339-361.

Darling-Hammond, L. (2000). Teacher Quality & Student Achievement. *Education Policy Analysis Archives, 8*(1). Retrieved on July 20, 2004, from http://epaa.asu.edu/epaa/v8n1/

Darling-Hammond, L., & Sykes, G. (2003, September 17). Wanted: A national teacher supply policy for education: The right way to meet the "Highly Qualified Teacher" challenge. *Education Policy Analysis Archives, 11*(33). Retrieved on July 21, 2004, from http://epaa.asu.edu/epaa/v11n33/

de Kruif, R. E. L., McWilliam, R. A., Ridley, S. M., & Wakely, M. B. (2000). Classification of teachers' interaction behaviors in early childhood classrooms. *Early Childhood Research Quarterly, 15,* 247-268.

Dwyer, M. C., Chait, R., & McKee, P. (2000). *Building strong foundations for early learning: Guide to high-quality early childhood education programs.* Washington, DC: U.S. Department of Education, Planning and Evaluation Service. Retrieved from http://www.ed.gov/offices/OUS/PES/early_learning/Foundations.doc

Dunn, L. S. (1984). Peabody picture vocabulary Test (revised). Circle Pines, MN: American guidance service.

Dunn, L. S. (1993). Proximal and distal features of day care quality and children's development. *Early Childhood Research Quarterly, 8,* 167-192.

Early, D. M., & Winton, P. J. (2001). Preparing the workforce: Early childhood teacher preparation at 2- and 4-year institutions of higher education. *Early Childhood Research Quarterly, 16,* 285-306

Genishi, C., Ryan, S., Ochsner, M., & Yarnall, M. M. (2001). Teaching in early childhood education: Understanding practices through research and theory. In V. Richardson (Ed.), *Handbook of research on teaching* (4th ed., pp. 1175-1210). Washington, DC: American Educational Research Association.

Goldhaber, D. D., & Brewer, D. I. (2000). Does teacher certification Matter? High School Teacher Certification Status and Student Achievement. *Education Evaluation and Policy Analysis, 22*(2), 129-145.

Granger, R. (1989). The staffing crisis in early childhood education. *Phi Delta Kappan, 71,* 130-134.

Granger, R., & Marx, E. (1988). *Who is teaching? Early childhood education in New York.* New York: Bank Street College of Education.

Head Start Act. (1998). *Community Opportunities, Accountability, and Training and Education Services Act of 1998,* Public Law 105-285ùOct. 27, 1998.

Helburn, S. W. (Ed.). (1995). *Cost, quality and child outcomes in child care centers: Technical report.* Denver: University of Colorado at Denver, Department of Economics, Center for Research in Economic and Social Policy.

Hinkle, D. (2000). *School involvement in early childhood.* Washington, DC: National Institute on Early Childhood Development and Education, U.S. Department of Education, Office of Educational Research and Improvement. Retrieved on July 2, 2004, from http://www.ed.gov/pubs/schoolinvolvement/

Hirschman, B. (2002). *Floridians set limits on class size, approve pre-K for all 4-year-olds. South Florida Sun-Sentinel.* Retrieved on July 2, 2004, from http://nieer.og/news/print.php?NewsID=166

Holloway, S. D., Kagan, S. L., Fuller, B., Tsou, L., & Carroll, J. (2001). Assessing child-care quality with a telephone interview. *Early Childhood Research Quarterly, 16*(1), 165-189.

Honig, A. S., & Hirallal, A. (1998). Which counts more for excellence in childcare staff-years in service, education level or ECE coursework? *Early Child Development & Care, 145,* 31-46.

Howes, C. (1995). Reconceptualizing the early childhood work force. In S. W. Helburn (Ed.), *Cost, quality, and child outcomes in child care centers.* Technical report. Denver: University of Colorado at Denver, Department of Economics, Center for Research in Economic and Social Policy, 159-170. Retrieved on July 20, 2004, from http://ist-socrates.berkeley.edu/~iir/cscce/pdf/teacher_summary.pdf

Howes, C. (1997). Children's experiences in center-based child care as a function of teacher background and adult-child ratio. *Merrill-Palmer Quarterly, 43,* 404-425.

Howes, C., & Brown, J. (2000). Improving child care quality: A guide for proposition 10 commissions. In N. Halfon, E. Shulman, M. Shannon, & M. Hochstein (Eds.), *Building community systems for young children* (pp. 1-24). Los Angeles: UCLA Center for Healthier Children, Families and Communities. Retrieved on July 22, 2004, from http:// www.healthychild.ucla.edu/Publications/Documents/Improving%20child%20care1200.pdf

Howes, C., Smith, E., & Galinsky, E. (1995). *The Florida child care quality improvement study: Interim Report.* New York: Families and Work Institute.

Howes, C., Galinsky, E., Shinn, M., Gulcur, L., Clements, M., Sibley, A., Abbott-Shim, M., & McCarthy, J. (1998). *The Florida child care quality improvement study: 1996 report.* New York: Families and Work Institute. Retrieved on July 20, 2004, from http://www.familiesandwork.org/index.asp?PageAction=VIEWPROD&ProdID=86

Howes, C., James, J., & Ritchie, S. (2003). Pathways to effective teaching. *Early Childhood Research Quarterly, 18*(1), 104-120.

Howes, C. Phillips, D. A., & Whitebook, M. (1992). Teacher characteristics and effective teaching in child care: Findings from the

National Child Care Staffing Study. *Child and Youth Care Forum, 21*, pp. 399–414.

Howes, C., Whitebook, M., & Phillips, D. (1992). Thresholds of quality: Implications for the social development of children in center-based child care. *Child Development, 63*, 449–460.

Iowa Early Care and Education Professional Development Project. (2000). *Iowa early care and education practitioner qualifications*. Des Moines: Iowa Department of Education.

Kaye, E. A. (2001). *Requirements for certification of teachers, counselors, librarians, administrators of elementary and secondary schools*. Chicago: University of Chicago Press.

Kontos, S., & Wilcox-Herzog, A. (1997). Teachers' interactions with children: Why are they so important? *Young Children, 52*(2), 4–12.

Laczko-Kerr, I., & Berliner, D.C. (2002, September 6). The effectiveness of "Teach for America" and other under-certified teachers on student academic achievement: A case of harmful public policy. *Education Policy Analysis Archives, 10*(37). Retrieved on July 20, 2004, from http://epaa.asu.edu/epaa/v10n37/

Lamb, M. E. (1998). Nonparental child care: Context, quality, correlates, and consequences. In W. Damon, I. E. Siegel & K. A. Renninger (Eds.), *Handbook of Child Psychology, 4*, pp. 73–133. New York: Wiley.

Laverty, K., Burton, A., Whitebook, M., & Bellm, D. (2001). *Current data on child care salaries and benefits in the United States: March 2001*. Washington, DC: Center for the Child Care Workforce. Retrieved on July 22, 2004, from http://www.ccw.org/tpp/pubs/2001%20Compendium.pdf

LeMoine, S. (2002). *Center Child Care Licensing Requirements: Minimum Pre-service Qualifications and Annual Ongoing Training Hours for Teachers and Master Teachers*. Retrieved on July 22, 2004, from http://nccic.org/pubs/cclr-teachers2002.html

Marshall, N. L., Creps, C. L., Burstein, N. R., Glantz, F. B., Robeson, W. W., & Barnett, W. S. (2001). *The cost and quality of full day, year-round early care and education in Massachusetts preschool classrooms*. Cambridge, MA: Wellesley Center for Women and Abt Associates.

McCarty, F., Lambert, R., & Abbott-Shim, M. (1998, April). *The relationship between teacher belief and practices, and Head Start classroom quality*. Paper presented at the annual meeting of the American Educational Research Association, San Diego, CA.

Mitchell, A. W. (2001). *Education for all young children: The role of states and the federal government in promoting prekindergarten and kindergarten*. New York: Foundation for Child Development. Retrieved on July 2, 2004, from http://www.ffcd.org/ourwork.htm

National Center for Early Development & Learning (NCEDL). (2001). *Public school pre-K programs: National survey of states*. Chapel Hill, NC: Author. Retrieved on July 28, 2004, from http://www.fpg.unc.edu/~ncedl/pre-kprograms/index.cfm

National Center for Education Statistics. (2003). *The condition of education*. Washington, DC: United States Government Printing Office.

National Commission on Teaching & America's Future. (1996). *What matters most: Teaching for America's future*. New York: Author. Retrieved on July 12, 2004, from http://www.nctaf.org/article/?c=4&sc=42 or http://www.nctaf.org/publications/WhatMattersMost.pdf

National Institute for Early Education Research. (2003). Head Start Investment. *Preschool Policy Matters, 4*. Retrieved on July 21, 2004, from http://nieer.org/resources/policybriefs/4.pdf

National Institute of Child Health and Human Development (NICHD) Early Child Care Research Network. (1996). Characteristics of infant child care: Factors contributing to positive caregiving. *Early Childhood Research Quarterly, 11*, 269–306.

National Institute of Child Health and Human Development (NICHD) Early Child Care Research Network. (2000). Characteristics and quality of child care for toddlers and preschoolers. *Applied Developmental Science, 4*(3), 116–135.

Nelson, J. A. (2001). *Why are early care and education wages so low? New York: Foundation for Child Development*. Retrieved on July 26, 2004, from http://ffcd.org/nelson/pdf

No Child Left Behind (NCLB). (2001). *No Child Left Behind*. Conference report to accompany H. R. Rep. No. 107-334, 107th Congress, 1st session (2001).

Peisner-Feinberg, E. S., Burchinal, M. R., Clifford, R. M., Culkin, M. L., Howes, C., Kagan, S. L., Yazejian, N., Byler, P., Rustici, J., & Zelazo, J. (1999). *The children of the cost, quality, and outcomes study go to school: Executive summary*. Chapel Hill: University of North Carolina at Chapel Hill, Frank Porter Graham Child Development Center. Retrieved on July 20, 2004, from http://www.abtassoc.com/reports/ccqual.PDF

Phillips, D., Crowell, N., Whitebook, M. & Jo, J. Y. (2003). Child care workers in the aftermath of September 11th. Berkeley, CA: Center for the Study of Child Care Employment.

Phillips, D., Mekos, D., Scarr, S., McCartney, K., & Abbott-Shim, M. (2000). Within and beyond the classroom door: Assessing quality in child care centers. *Early Childhood Research Quarterly, 15*, 475–496.

Phillipsen, L. C., Burchinal, M. R., Howes, C., & Cryer, D. (1997). The prediction of process quality from structural features of child care. *Early Childhood Research Quarterly, 12*, 281–303.

Reynolds, A. J., Temple, J. A.; Robertson, D. L., & Mann, E. A. (2001). Long-term effects of an early childhood intervention on educational achievement and juvenile arrest. *Journal of the American Medical Association, 285*, 2339–2346.

Ryan, S., & Ackerman, D. J. (2004). *Creating a qualified preschool teaching workforce Part I getting qualified: A report on the efforts of preschool teachers in New Jersey's Abbott Districts to improve their qualifications*. New Brunswick NJ: National Institute for Early Education Research. Retrieved on July 12, 2004, from http://nieer.org/docs/index.php?DocID=91 http://nieer.org/resources/research/GettingQualified.pdf www.nieer.org

Saluja, G., Early, D. M., & Clifford, R. M. (2002, Spring). Demographic characteristics of early childhood teachers and structural elements of early care and education in the United States. *Early Childhood Research and Practice 4*(1). Retrieved on July 2, 2004, from http://ecrp.uiuc.edu/v4n1/saluja.html

Saracho, O. N., & Spodek, B. (2003). Improving teacher quality. In O. N. Saracho & B. Spodek (Eds.). *Studying teachers in early childhood settings* (pp. 209–221). Greenwich, CT. Information Age Publishers.

Saracho, O. N., & Spodek, B. (1993). Professionalism and the preparation of early childhood practitioners. *Early Child Development and Care, 89*, 1–17.

Scarr, S., Eisenberg, M., & Deater-Deckard, K. (1994) Measurement of quality in child care centers. *Early Childhood Research Quarterly, 9*, 131–151.

Shonkoff, J. P. & Phillips, D.A., eds. (2000). *From neurons to neighborhoods: The science of early childhood development*. Washington, DC: National Academy Press. Retrieved on July 20, 2004, from http://stills.books.nap.edu/books/0309069882/html/261.html

Spodek, B. & Saracho, O. N. (1996). Preparation of early childhood personnel. In T. Husen & T. N. Postlewaite (Eds.), *International encyclopedia of education* (2nd ed., pp. 1629–1636). Oxford: Pergamon.

The Business Roundtable/Corporate Voices for Working Families. (2004). *Early Childhood Education: A call to action from the business community*. Retrieved on July 26, 2004, from http://www.businessroundtable.org/pdf/901.pdf

United States Bureau of the Census. (1970). *School enrollment: Social and economic characteristics of student, October 1969* (Current Population Reports, P-20 Series). Washington, DC: Author.

Whitebook, M. (2003a). *Bachelor's degrees are best: Highr qualifications for pre-kindergarten teachers led to better learning environments*. Washington, DC: The Trust for Early Education. Retrieved on July 22, 2004, from http://www.trustforearlyed.org/docs/WhitebookFinal.pdf

Whitebook, M. (2003b). *Early education quality: Higher teacher qualifications for better learning environments—a review of the literature*. Berkeley, CA: Center for the Study of Child Care Employment. Retrieved on July 22, 2004, from http://iir.berkeley.edu/cscce/pdf/teacher.pdf

Whitebook, M., & Sakai, L. (2004). *By a thread: How centers hold on to teachers, how teachers build lasting careers*. Kalamazoo, MI: Upjohn Institute for Employment Research. Retrieved on July 22, 2004, from http://www.upjohninstitute.org/publications/titles/bat.html

Whitebook, M., Howes, C., & Phillips, D. (1990). *The national child care staffing study. Final report: Who cares? Child care teachers and the quality of care in America*. Washington, DC: Center for the Child Care Workforce.

Whitebook, M., & Sakai, L. (2003). Turnover begets turnover: An examination of job and occupational instability among child care center staff. *Early Childhood Research Quarterly, 18*, 273–293.

Whitebook, M., Sakai, L., Gerber, E., & Howes, C. (2001). *Then & now: Changes in child care staffing, 1994–2000, Technical Report*. Washington, DC: Center for the Child Care Workforce.

Zill, N., Resnick, G., Kim, K., Hubbell McKey, R., Clark, C., Pai-Samant, S., Connell, D., Vaden-Kiernan, M., O'Brien, R., & D'Elio, M. (2001). *Head Start FACES: Longitudinal findings on program performance, Third progress report*. Washington, DC: Research, Demonstration, and Evaluation Branch & Head Start Bureau, Administration on Children, Youth and Families, U.S. Department of Health and Human Services. Retrieved on July 20, 2004, from http://www.acf.dhhs.gov/programs/core/pubs_reports/faces/meas_99_intro.html

Part

·IV·

RESEARCH AND EVALUATION STRATEGIES FOR EARLY CHILDHOOD EDUCATION

· 25 ·

ALTERNATIVE MEANS OF ASSESSING CHILDREN'S LEARNING IN EARLY CHILDHOOD CLASSROOMS

Dominic F. Gullo
Queens College, City University of New York

The significance and importance of assessment in early childhood education has never been as integral to the accountability of the field as it is today. With the passing of P.L 107-110 (the *No Child Left Behind Act of 2001*), assessment of children's learning is in the forefront of the minds of school administrators, teachers, policy makers, and parents. According to the U.S. Department of Education (2002), the passing of the *No Child Left Behind Act of 2001* will result in "the creation of assessments in each state that measure what children know and learn in reading and math. . . . Student progress and achievement will be measured according to tests that will be given to every child, every year."

According to the National Association for the Education of Young Children (NAEYC, 2003), on going assessment of children's learning in early childhood education should occur primarily to determine children's curricular needs. The early childhood curriculum should be modified to match the strengths and needs of each child based on the information gleaned from the assessment data. This assessment goal may be in conflict with the stated goal of P.L. 107-110.

When one thinks of assessment, one often thinks of the paper and pencil tests that were pervasive in their own schooling. Although this type of assessment practice may provide valid information about older children's learning, these methods are often problematic in assessing younger children's current performance status or progress (Gullo, 1997). According to Gullo, the problem stems from the mismatch between the young child's developmental capabilities and the performance expected in various paper-and-pencil assessment formats as well as the mismatch between the content and strategies assessed and the content and strategies emphasized in the early childhood curriculum.

In its policy statement, NAEYC states that early childhood assessment practices should reflect and take into account children's level of developmental capabilities and performance (2003). Early childhood professionals agree that the developmental characteristics of young children may affect their behavior in response to assessment procedures and outcomes (Gullo, 1997, 2005; Meisels, 1987; NAEYC, 2003). These include developmental limitations in areas such as language, cognitive, and physical responses (Gullo, 1997, 2005), motivational differences (Gullo, 1997, 2005), children's perceptions of their performance (Gullo & Ambrose, 1987; Stipek, 1981), and their ability to generalize knowledge from one context to another (Hills, 1993; Meisels, 1993).

With regard to the curriculum, the process of assessment should be consistent with the manner in which the curriculum is viewed by the early childhood education profession (Meisels, 1992; National Commission on Testing and Public Policy, 1990). Two implications are suggested related to the relationship between curriculum and assessment. First, children should be assessed within the context of the classroom as they are engaged in meaningful curriculum activities. Second, the primary purpose of assessment is to inform practice. Assessment findings should suggest to teachers how the curriculum is working for individual children (Gullo, 1997).

Given the relationship between the child's development and assessment and between curriculum practice and assessment, conventional paper-and-pencil assessment procedures are contraindicated for children within the early childhood age span. The results of these types of assessments often do not yield the kinds of information that will inform practice and often the results are unreliable, because of the developmental nature of the child during the early years. What is suggested are alternative means of assessing children's learning within the context of the early childhood curriculum.

ALTERNATIVE ASSESSMENT STRATEGIES

According to the North Central Regional Educational Laboratory (NCREL), alternative assessment is defined as "any form of assessment that requires students to produce a response rather than select from a list of possible responses ... (alternative assessment) ... measures more complex learning goals that ... supports the instruction needed to help students achieve these goals" (2003). When considering alternative forms of assessment, there are a number of principles that should be kept in mind when making assessment decisions.

First, the alternative assessment practices should be developmentally and culturally appropriate and should capitalize on the actual work taking place in the classroom. Meaningful context is important for both curriculum considerations (Bredekamp & Copple, 1997; Gullo, 1992) as well as in considering appropriate alternative assessment practices and strategies (Gullo, 1997, 2005; Hills, 1993).

Second, alternative assessment practices should enhance both the teacher's and the child's involvement in the process of assessment (Gullo, 1997, 2005). Both teachers and children should be actively involved in the assessment process. This will inform both the teacher and the learner in ways that should ultimately enhance both instruction and learning.

Third, alternative assessment practices should be informative to others, such as parents and school administrators, as well as teachers (Gullo, 1997). The information obtained from alternative assessment practices should provide a clear and concrete basis for presenting information about the child's progress (Gullo, 2005; Hills, 1993).

Fourth, alternative assessment practices should provide a close match between the assessment and curriculum goals. When schools make decisions about assessment with little regard to how the assessment fits curriculum goals and objectives, they run the risk of collecting information about the child that will have little relevance to curriculum planning and modification (Gullo, 2005; Bergan & Field, 1993). A greater risk ensues when curriculum decisions are made based on assessment information that has little relevance to curriculum content or instructional strategies (Meisels, 1989; Meisels & Atkins-Burnett, 2004). Each of these four principles will be discussed more fully throughout the chapter. Research to substantiate these principles also will be presented.

According to Gullo (1997), it is important to consider the following when making decisions regarding alternative assessment procedures:

- What will the assessment procedures reveal about the child's level of academic progress?
- How will the information from the alternative assessment procedures assist in making decisions about curriculum development and/or modifications?
- How will the alternative assessment process aid children's understanding of their own accomplishments and progress?

According to Mindes (2003), there are numerous reasons why professionals in early childhood education should consider alternative assessment strategies when assessing young children. The first reason lies in the fact that there is little overlap between what is measured in norm referenced assessments and what actually goes on in the classroom with children.

Second, the purpose of norm-referenced assessments is to compare the relative performance of one child in comparisons to other children of similar age or grade characteristics. Norm-referenced assessments do not assess the manner in which a child changes over time, developmentally or academically. In other words, it is difficult to compare the child to him or herself during the course of the year, using norm-referenced assessments as they do not measure the process of learning.

Third, there is a lack of consistency in how children perform from one norm-referenced test to another. This may result in wide variability on children's performance from one assessment instrument to another.

Finally, the results of norm-referenced assessments are not very useful in helping early childhood teachers individualize instruction. This is important in that there is a wide variety of developmental levels represented among children in early childhood classrooms. In addition, because children with special needs are often mainstreamed into the regular classroom, the need for individualization is paramount.

CRITICISMS OF NORM-REFERENCED ASSESSMENTS

Although there is an appropriate place for using norm-referenced assessments, they should not be the sole means of assessing children in the early childhood classroom. As long as one is aware of the limitations of norm-referenced assessment, their results can be used in proper perspective and in conjunction with other types of assessments. Some of the limitations of norm-referenced assessments are discussed later.

Standardized Test Administration

As has been discussed previously, children in the early childhood classroom represent vast differences in developmental levels, approaches to learning, and individual needs. Because of the nature of norm-referenced assessments, one must strictly adhere to the instructions for test administration. The same procedures are utilized for all children and there is little room for modification of those procedures to meet the needs and/or learning styles of individual or specific groups of children (Gullo, 2005; Mindes, 2003; Wortham, 2001).

Prior Learning Experiences Are Not Reflected

Norm-referenced assessments do not reflect how test performance is affected by prior experiences. In addition, they do not take into account how children actually learn the material that is being assessed (Meyers, Pfeffer, & Erlbaum, 1985;

NAEYC, 2003). It is more usual than not that norm-referenced assessments do not closely match the goals and objectives of the curriculum that is being taught in the classroom. Therefore, curriculum goals and objectives are inadequately represented in test items.

Bias

One should be cognizant of the composition of the sample on which the norm-referenced assessment was standardized. "Children's backgrounds have a profound influence on their knowledge, vocabulary, and skills" (McAfee & Leong, 2002, p. 19). Often assessments are biased against children of different cultural or linguistic backgrounds (Gullo, 2005; Neisworth & Bagnato, 1996; McLean, 1998; 2000; Mindes, 2003), as well as biased against children with developmental delays or special needs (Cohen & Spenciner, 2003). One of the greatest challenges facing early childhood educators today is the ability to identify appropriate assessment instruments and procedures that are bias-free. Valencia and Suzuki (2001) argue for a judicious use of a variety of assessments and strategies.

Influence on the Curriculum

Norm-referenced assessments do not reflect curriculum sensitivity (Gullo, 2005; Mindes, 2003). Many published norm-referenced assessments do not take into account contemporary approaches to curriculum and instruction in early childhood education. They often are based on skill development approaches alone and reflect a theoretical perspective that is more behavioral than one that reflets multiple theoretical approaches. They assess specific skills or knowledge learned rather than the assessing the process of learning. This often times leads to teachers teaching to the test; thus, the norm-referenced assessment has the effect of narrowing the curriculum. This is of particular concern given the passing of the *No Child Left Behind Act of 2001* (U.S. Department of Education, 2002). Additionally, norm-referenced assessments may not reflect the characteristics of individual children such as motivation, level of cognitive or language development, or educational settings (Gullo, 1997).

ALTERNATIVE ASSESSMENT: LINKING CURRICULUM AND ASSESSMENT

There are a number of distinct advantages of using alternative assessment procedures in the early childhood classroom. These advantages include the usefulness of the information resulting from the assessment process, the recognition of the different developmental characteristics among individual children, as well as the link between assessment, the child as learner, and curriculum goals, content and instructional strategies (Gullo, 2005). Specifically, some of the advantages in using alternative assessment procedures include the following:

- Alternative assessment focuses on the developmental and achievement changes in children over time. Teachers are able to identify and document a child's progress in the classroom and use this information to make modifications in the curriculum to meet the individual needs of the child.

- When used appropriately, alternative assessment focuses on the individual child rather than on groups of children. The progress that a child makes is benchmarked against him or herself, rather than using the information to compare one child to another.

- By assessing children frequently and in many educational settings, the procedures used in alternative assessment don't rely on the "one chance" opportunity for the child to demonstrate competence. Teachers will gain insights into the settings, contexts, and types of activities that best facilitate learning and development for individual children.

- Alternative assessment provides a close match between the curriculum and assessment, a stated criticism of the relationship between norm-referenced assessments and curriculum. When used in this manner, assessment provides information for further curriculum development and modification.

- It is estimated that classroom teachers spend about 14 hours per year preparing the children in their classroom to take norm-referenced achievement assessments, 26 hours for reading assessments, and about 18 hours for teacher prepared assessment procedures (Maness, 1992). Therefore, alternative assessment procedures don't interrupt the process of curriculum implementation.

- Alternative assessment procedures help children better understand their own learning. When assessment is done within the context of the learning environment, children have opportunities to reflect on their own learning in conjunction with the teacher or other children.

- Finally, alternative assessment provides concrete information to share with the families of children (Culbertson & Jalongo, 1999; Shepard & Bleim, 1995). In this manner, alternative assessment helps parents understand the progress that their children are making and how they learn. It also helps parents understand the curriculum and instruction that is being implemented in the classroom.

According to Cohen and Spenciner (1994), the role of the teacher changes when alternative assessment procedures are used. The teacher has a direct influence on the assessment process, and the link between assessment and curriculum is closed. When there is a close relationship between curriculum content, instructional strategies, and assessment, the goals for instruction, views of teaching, and theories of how children learn and develop are articulated and aligned (Herman, Aschbacher, & Winters (1992).

Although there is a range of alternative assessment approaches, generally speaking, these approaches are characterized by tasks requiring:

- children to demonstrate, construct, or generate knowledge or skills;

- children to use critical thinking and problem-solving skills; or

- children to be engaged in meaningful tasks within a meaningful context (Herman et al., 1992).

In this chapter, five approaches to alternative assessment will be described and discussed. In addition, research examining the efficacy of each of these approaches will be presented. The five approaches that will be discussed include: curriculum-based assessment; play-based assessment; dynamic assessment; project assessment; and portfolio assessment. The alternative assessment approaches described in this chapter share some common traits, but at the same time, are unique in their specific approach to assessing children in the context of the classroom. In addition, although there may be similarities in the ways in which teachers use the data collected from these approaches, there are also some distinct differences.

It should be noted that there are other forms of alternative assessment approaches used in early childhood education classrooms, such as task analysis and responsive assessment. However, those that are the focus of this chapter are those that are most widely used in typical early childhood classrooms. In many instances, the approaches described in this chapter include characteristics of both task analysis and responsive assessment.

CURRICULUM-BASED ASSESSMENT

Curriculum-based assessment describes a wide-ranging approach for alternative assessment that directly links the assessment process to the curriculum content and instructional strategies used within the early childhood classroom (Cohen & Spenciner, 1994). According to Bergen (1997), assessing a child within the learning context is extremely useful and informative. Specifically, assessing a child with the learning context makes it possible to assess the child/context variables that may affect the learning capacity and the demonstration of learning for that child (Bergen & Mosley-Howard, 1994). This proves useful for curriculum planning and modification. With young children, it may be observed that learning within a specific context may be different from day to day, and all of these factors must be taken into account when assessing the child's learning.

According to Cohen and Spenciner (1994), curriculum-based assessment has three distinct purposes:

* to determine eligibility of a child for participating in specific curriculum and learning experiences;
* to develop the specific curriculum and instruction goals for that child based on their performance within the classroom context; and
* to assess the child's progress as they proceed through the curriculum.

Within a curriculum-based assessment procedure, the child's behavior in developmental, social, preacademic, or academic areas are used as the basis for assessing the child. The information gleaned from this process is then used to make modifications to the curriculum that are more suited to the child and his or her level of development or academic capacity.

Curriculum-based assessment is a process that involves a number of distinct yet interrelated steps. The primary assumption of this process is that the teacher knows the curriculum, what is being taught, and how what is being taught is presented to the children. The process involves the following:

* the teacher-developed system for utilizing curriculum-based assessment provides a direct connection between it and the curriculum and instruction practices used within the classroom context;
* the teacher uses the results of the curriculum-based assessment to modify the curriculum and instructional practices, insuring that the child's developmental and academic needs are being met;
* after modifications are instituted the child is assessed again within the modified curricular context;
* the teacher determines whether the modifications have benefited the child in the intended manner; and
* the process repeats itself in a dynamic fashion.

A special application of curriculum-based assessment is curriculum-based language assessment (Mindes, 2003). This particular application is used when the teacher is not sure that the child has the linguistic capacity to function adequately within the curriculum that is being used in the classroom. It is particularly useful in helping the teacher bridge the gap between the linguistic capacity of the child and the kinds of demands that are being placed on the child by the curriculum.

Another specialized application, albeit comprehensive application of curriculum-based assessment is the Work Sampling System (Meisels, Jablon, Dichtelmiller, Dorfman & Mardsen, 2001). This system is a standards-based approach and can be modified to meet all state and local needs, including requirements for children with special educational needs. The Work Sampling System is comprised of three distinct components which are developmental checklists, developmental portfolios, and a summary report. According to Wortham (2001), the Work Sampling System is based on a philosophy that the assessment of children's within the context of the curriculum is appropriate in that this approach:

* documents the child's daily activity
* reflects an individualized approach to assessment
* integrates assessment with curriculum and instruction
* assesses many elements of learning
* allows teachers to learn how children reconstruct knowledge through interacting with materials and peers (p. 252).

Research has demonstrated that the use of curriculum-based assessment is effective in a number of ways in early childhood classrooms. One of the primary findings is that curriculum-based assessment, when applied appropriately, leads to educators being able to amend and align their instruction to meet the individual needs of students in their classrooms (Meisels, Bickel, Nicholson, Xue, & Atkins-Burnett, 2001; Phillips, Fuchs, & Fuchs, 1994). The result of this is that curriculum-based assessment improves teaching practice.

In one study, it was found that curriculum-based assessment could be used to establish academic growth benchmarks for young children with learning disabilities in the area of literacy (Deno, Fuchs, Marston, & Shin, 2001). The authors found that young children who had curriculum-based assessment as compared to children who did not, had growth rates on grade level reading performance of 1.39 words gained per week as compared to .5 words gained per week. The authors of the study concluded that it is possible for young children who were identified as learning disabled could attain similar academic achievement in the area of reading as compared to their non-learning-disabled counterparts. They state that in their analysis of effective intervention research, children with learning disabilities could achieve rates of growth that were comparable to their classroom peers who were not identified as learning disabled. According to the authors, this was achieved expressly due to the curriculum-based assessment approach. Curriculum-based assessment revealed specific interventions that were sufficiently efficient to individual children.

In another study (VanDerHeyden, Witt, Naquin, & Noell, 2001), it was found that curriculum-based assessment was effective in identifying kindergarten children with deficiencies in readiness skills. They suggest using curriculum-based assessment as a screening device within the context of the classroom. They found that curriculum-based assessment was both a reliable and valid assessment procedure to scrutinize readiness in kindergarten children.

PLAY-BASED ASSESSMENT

It is often said that play is at the heart of the early childhood curriculum, especially for children at the younger age ranges. Play, for young children, is voluntary and intrinsically motivating. When teachers systematically observe children at play, they can gain valuable insights into developmental and academic competencies.

According to Mindes (2003), it is the teacher as assessor role that makes this approach to assessment work. As the assessor, the early childhood educator makes numerous decisions during the assessment process:

- when to change the play props;
- what kinds of props to use;
- when to add stimulation to the play theme;
- when to mediate;
- when to actively engage in the play process; and
- when to end the play process.

According to Van Hoorn, Nourot, Scales, and Alward (1999), one of the easiest ways for early childhood educators to begin assessing children utilizing a play-based approach is to make a list of the critical skills and applications of knowledge and use this list by matching it to the curriculum goals and objectives. They offer the following as examples of curriculum/assessment matches:

- prepare a play-based assessment observation log that is keyed to various learning areas and social contexts within the classroom.

- keep track of where the child plays in the classroom.
- document whether the child plays alone, with one other child, or with more than one child.
- stages of play with various objects and in various activities are listed for each child in the class. The teacher then keeps track of how the child is progressing through these stages.
- keep track of the role of play for each child. How does the child use props? How does the child engage in make-believe activities? How does the child engage in social interaction during play? What role does language/communication play?

Using play activities as a means of assessing the child's knowledge and skills is not entirely a new phenomenon. Teachers have long been observing children during play and making decisions about the child based on those observations. Much of the research on play-based assessment however has been done on young children with special needs.

Bricker, Pretti-Frontczak, and McComas (1998) suggest making a chart with specific categories to use with young children who have special needs. They suggest using the following categories:

- fine and gross motor abilities;
- cognitive skills;
- social interaction;
- interactive communication; and
- self-help and self-care skills.

They also suggest that this approach be integrated into the planned curriculum activities which are designed to meet the individual goals for the child. The information from this particular type of approach can then be used for further intervention, curriculum modification, and individualized planning.

Calhoon (1997) studied young children with language delays in order to determine the effectiveness of a play-based assessment approach in analyzing children's language capabilities. The author concluded that a play-based assessment approach provided a much broader picture of children's linguistic capabilities as compared to other assessment approaches. In addition, it was found that the play-based approach also yielded more helpful information in planning curricular modifications and interventions.

In a similar study, Farmer-Dougan and Kaszuba (1999) compared a play-based assessment model to standardized assessment of cognition and social skills in preschool children. The authors found that the findings gleaned from the play-based assessment accurately reflected the children's level of cognitive and social functioning.

It also has been shown that the play context may affect the assessment outcome. Malone (1994) conducted a study with preschool children having cognitive delays. The children in the study were observed at home during independent play and at school during group free play. It was found that the children's assessed developmental age was more predictive of the behaviors during the independent play episodes at home than in the group free play episodes at school. The author suggests that these findings highlight the need to consider the variations in behavior may be associated with the specific play context.

Finally, Myers (1996) conducted a study to ascertain the relative efficacy of play-based assessment as compared to other forms of assessment. In this study, preschool children who were referred for special education were randomly assigned to either a multidisciplinary, standardized assessment or a play-based assessment group. The results of the study found that play-based assessments took less time to complete and had a high congruence with other forms of developmental ratings. In addition, the play-based assessment group also resulted in more favorable parent and staff perceptions and provided more useful reports.

DYNAMIC ASSESSMENT

Dynamic assessment is a form of alternative assessment that can be combined with other forms of assessments. In this type of assessment, the learner is directly engaged in the learning process by using mediated learning experiences. Mediated learning experiences are the foci of dynamic assessment (Cohen & Spenciner, 1994).

This approach utilizes a test-intervene-retest design. A mediated learning experience can be described as in interaction that takes place between the assessor and the child. The assessor mediates the environment to the child though appropriate framing, selecting, focusing, and feeding back to the child the experiences that the child is having. The purpose in doing this is to produce in the child-appropriate learning systems and routines. Actual curriculum activities comprise the assessment tasks that are presented to the child. Thus, the approach combines both assessment and teaching. Dynamic assessment is a procedure that was designed by Reuven Feuerstein (1979, 1980), and based on the theoretical work of Vygotsky (1978, 1986).

Lidz (1991) describes three components comprising the dynamic assessment approach. These include:

- the assessor actively facilitates learning in the child while engaging the child in active participation in the learning task.
- evaluation of the process is the primary emphasis of the assessment procedure. A major focus is on metacognitive processes that the child uses in learning. The teacher/assessor uses questions, suggestions and prompts to help the child better understand, on a conscious level, what he/she is learning and how he/she is learning.
- the results of the assessment yields information on how change can be produced in the child and how malleable the child is within the learning context.

According to Mindes (2003), the dynamic assessment approach is particularly useful for early childhood teachers who are interested in linking classroom instruction to specific learner outcomes. Mindes states that "... the approach links test results to task analysis to teaching to individualization of instruction. It is an opportunity for making the learning process apparent to those children who may need special assistance in linking thinking to academic requirements . . . " (p. 159).

A number of studies have been conducted examining the efficacy of dynamic assessment as compared to other forms of assessment or how it added to the information yielded from different assessment systems. In one study, Jacobs (2001) found that by incorporating dynamic assessment components to a computerized preschool language-screening test, the computerized assessment was enhanced and continued investigation of its validity was possible.

In another study (Bolig & Day, 1993), it was found that dynamic assessment could be used to respond to the criticism of traditional intelligence tests. The researchers found that dynamic assessment could be used to identify children's learning ability, to determine how or what to teach to children, to assess giftedness in culturally diverse children and children who come from homes of economic poverty. In addition, they found that through the use of dynamic assessment, individual differences could be controlled and different domains of giftedness could be identified and explored.

In one study, examining the effects of dynamic assessment on content specific material, Jitendra and Kameenui (1993) found that children at different levels of mathematical performance could be identified. In their study of third graders, they found that dynamic assessment indicated important and significant differences between novices and experts in their ability to use specific mathematical strategies for solving problems.

In another study, Spector (1992) found that dynamic assessment was able to measure phonemic awareness to predict progress in beginning reading. This study, conducted with kindergarteners, supported the utility of the developed measures and was able to demonstrate the applicability of the principles of dynamic assessment to the measurement in kindergarten-aged children.

There also have been studies utilizing dynamic assessment procedures that were conducted with young children with special needs. Findings from these studies have implications for both teachers and children. Delclos (1987) found that after teachers viewed dynamic assessment situations, their academic expectations for cognitively delayed children were raised. Lidz and Pena (1996) compared dynamic assessment to traditional assessment for determining language delays among Latino preschool children. They found that there was increased accuracy among teachers in their ability to assess children's language abilities using dynamic assessment.

PROJECT ASSESSMENT

Project assessment is another type of alternative assessment that is used to assess children's academic progress through the assessment of their knowledge and problem-solving skills by observing them in actual problem-solving situations. These problem solving problems are actual activities that are being done in curricular activities. One example of a project assessment procedure is "Project Spectrum" (Gardner, Feldman, & Krechevsky, 1998; Krechevsky, 1991). The strategy put forth in "Project Spectrum" is to recognize that there is potential variation in all children and in all curriculum activities. The goal of assessment in "Project Spectrum" is to identify children's domain-specific strengths in area not necessarily addressed in more traditional assessment systems.

"Project Spectrum" is based on the theoretical foundation of Gardner's (1983) multiple intelligences theory. Gardner (1999) suggests to teachers that they should provide to children various avenues to become engaged in curriculum content and multiple opportunities for developing and demonstrating understanding and competence. In addition, teachers should utilize varied products and processes for assessing children and documenting their work.

Gardner (1999) offers suggestions to teachers describing how a multiple intelligences perspective could enhance their teaching. This can be accomplished by:

- providing powerful points of entry to student learning—catching multiple ways to introduce and begin the study of a topic.
- offering apt analogies derived from different dimensions and appealing to various intelligences.
- providing multiple representations of the central or core ideas of a topic of study (pp. 186–187).

Krechevsky (1991) states that "It is the responsibility of the educational system to discover and nurture proclivities. Rather than building around a test, the Spectrum approach is centered on a wide range of rich activities; assessment comes about as part-and-parcel of the child's involvement over time in these activities" (p. 44).

According to Gullo (2005), there are a number of "Project Spectrum" characteristics that are consistent with the features of developmentally and culturally appropriate practice. These include:

- The curriculum and assessment procedures become integrated. Early childhood practices that are developmentally appropriate view the relationship between curriculum and evaluation as transactional, that is, each simultaneously affects the other. By using activities embedded within the curriculum as a means to evaluate, and using the outcome of the evaluation as a method to modify the curriculum, this relationship becomes actualized.
- The procedure embeds assessment into real-word activities that are meaningful to children. By putting the problem solving activity into a context for which children have referents in reality, one is more likely to maintain the interest and motivation necessary to obtain valid and reliable results.
- The procedures used are intelligence-fair—they do not rely solely or primarily on language and logical thinking. Also, children's styles of performance are identified. Just as children do not develop in compartmentalized way, they also do not learn or demonstrate competence in this manner. And just as the curriculum must be sensitive to the multiple modes of learning that children use to acquire and construct knowledge, evaluation must be similarly sensitive.
- The procedures used identify and emphasize children's strengths. Rather than focus on what children don't know and can't do, they focus on what they can do and do know,

and this allows one to approach evaluation and subsequent curriculum development from a positive vantage point. The modus operandi is that all children can learn (pp. 84–85).

The utilization of this assessment approach has been studied to determine its efficacy as compared to other forms of assessment. Importantly, Chen (1998) found that the core method for assessing child progress on curriculum activities is teacher observation. Hatch and Gardner (1996) have demonstrated that this approach to assessment was useful and valid in assessing the pluralistic abilities of each individual child as compared to more standardized forms of assessment.

Another study (Wexler-Sherman, Gardner, & Feldman, 1988) showed that the project approach to assessment was successful in fusing assessment with curriculum within a preschool setting. They compared the project assessment approach to other more standard forms of assessment in this pilot project. Hebert (1992) examined the utilitarian characteristics of this approach as compared to more standardized assessment modes. It was found that by using a project assessment approach, the assessment process became more meaningful through using learning experiences.

Finally, Vialle (1994) conducted a study with childcare centers for children who came from homes of economic poverty. It was found that this framework for assessment is productive for all children, and is especially appropriate for children who reflect atypical profiles of intelligence.

PORTFOLIO ASSESSMENT

The National Association for the Education of Young Children (Bredekamp & Rosegrant, 1992) defines assessment as "the process of observing, recording, and otherwise documenting the work that children do and how they do it, as a basis for a variety of educational decisions that affect the child" (p. 10).

As has been stated previously, one way in which early childhood professionals have responded to the need for an assessment process that fits within the paradigm of developmentally appropriate practice, and to respond to the need to view assessment data as useful information for educational decision making, has been to use the actual work done by students within the context of the curriculum as the basis for assessing children's knowledge and skills. The need for a tool that would enable the teacher to methodically collect and organize those materials that were deemed useful in describing the progress that children were making, both developmentally and academically, grew out of this movement. Portfolios became the solution.

According to Vavrus (1990), portfolios are a systematic and organized collection of the work that children do as they are engaged in classroom activities. The child's work that is represented in the portfolio are those that reflect curriculum goals, content, and strategies. It should be noted that portfolios are not, in and of themselves, an assessment tool. Rather, they provide a convenient way to organize and store the information that is gathered about children (Gullo, 2005).

According to Sewell, Marczak, and Horn (2003), portfolio assessment is widely used in educational settings as a means for examining and measuring children's progress. This is accomplished by documenting the learning process as it occurs naturally within the classroom context. Portfolio assessment is based on the principle that children should demonstrate what they know and what they do (Cole, Ryan, and Kick, 1995). Demonstrating what they know and can do can be contrasted with *telling* what they know, which is more typical in a more standardized form of assessments such as teacher-made tests or standardized tests.

Sewell et al. (2003) cite instances in which portfolio assessment is most useful and instances in which portfolio assessment may not be particularly useful. As will be seen, how useful portfolio assessment is will depend on how one plans on using the information as well as the characteristics of the programs that the children who are being assessed attend.

Portfolio assessment is most useful:

1. for evaluation program goals and outcomes that are flexible and/or individualized for children;
2. for programs that value the individuals involved being part of program change or in making decisions related to personal change;
3. for providing meaningful information related to the process of behavioral change over time;
4. for providing a means of communicating with a wide range of audiences regarding program accountability or child progress; and
5. for providing a possible means of assessing more complex aspects of behavioral change, rather than simply measuring those behavioral changes that are most easily measured.

There also are instances where portfolio assessment may not be the most efficacious means of documentation. These include:

1. assessing children's behavior in programs where the goals are very concrete and are uniform for all children who participate in the program;
2. assessing children where the purpose is to rank them quantitatively or in a standardized manner; and
3. assessing children for the purpose of comparing them to each other using standardized norms.

Purposes of a Portfolio

Portfolios provide a useful and practical means for early childhood educators to examine children's strengths, both in their developmental and learning processes and progress. Portfolios also provide a means for targeting those areas of development and achievement where there is a need for support. Shanklin and Conrad (1991) describe portfolios as a means by which educational professionals become empowered as decision makers. By developing a portfolio system for collecting information about children, teachers are able to determine what information is important to collect, what type of analysis protocol is appropriate, how the information resulting from the analyses will be used for decision making and curriculum modification, and how the information will be shared with others.

The information about children's developmental status and educational achievement found in portfolios has many uses for the early childhood educator (Nall, 1994; Shepard, 1989). In addition, there are also many benefits for teachers, children, and families that result from this method of assessment. It is difficult to differentiate the uses from the benefits. Often times, the way in which the information contained in the portfolio is used becomes the benefit. A number of these uses/benefits are discussed below.

Focus on change. The information gathered for the portfolio, mainly in the form of documentation of children's learning processes or the actual products that children produce as a result of engaging in curriculum activities, allows the teacher to focus on the changes in development and achievement that occur in children over time. By examining these processes and products, teachers are able to chart children's progress throughout the curriculum and over time. In this manner, the information gathered as part of the portfolio permits teachers to focus both on children's developmental and educational processes as well as products.

Focus on individualized instruction. The records of children's leaning processes and curriculum products contained in portfolios, when used properly, permit early childhood educators to compare children's progress. The progress that is charted is compared is not compared to how other children are progressing, but rather, the comparative measure is the child, him or herself. As such, portfolio assessment focuses on the individual child, rather than on groups of children. Children's progress is measured against their own rate of acquisition and development of knowledge and skills. This information can be used to then make the appropriate modifications in the curriculum in response to children's strengths and needs. Because the focus is on the individual child, collecting assessment data based on actual performance in curriculum activities as a means of documenting developmental and academic progress doesn't rely on the "one chance" opportunity for children to demonstrate competence. Information is collected on a regular basis, and often. In this manner, teachers have several opportunities to observe and record children's behaviors in various contexts. This improves both the reliably and validity of the assessment and better insures that what is being observed accurately reflects that which the child is capable.

Focus on the curriculum. As was stated previously, it is important that assessment closely reflects the content and the instructional strategies that are part of the everyday classroom teaching. Using activities that reflect what the child actually does in the curriculum as assessment tools provides such a match. The resulting assessment data are, therefore, germane for subsequent curriculum development and adjustment. When used appropriately, the materials contained in the portfolio provide a concrete and systematic means for modification of the curriculum. The purposes of this are twofold. It not only supports the individual needs of the child, but helps teachers recognize in a more general manner, "what works" and "what doesn't work" in the curriculum as it is being implemented—both in terms of content and instruction. Additionally, when curriculum-based activities and products are collected for assessment purposes, this form of assessment does not interrupt the process of curriculum implementation. According to Maness (1992), teachers spend approximately 14 hours per year in preparing their students to take standardized tests, 26 hours in reading tests, and 18 hours in preparing teacher-made assessment measures. If collected and used appropriately, the information collected for portfolios do not require time out from "teaching" the curriculum.

Focus on teacher and child reflection. Both teachers and children participate in the process of collecting information that is to be included in portfolios. In this manner, teachers and children increase their opportunities to reflect on those things that are part of the teaching-learning process. Teachers should encourage children to select their "best" work to include in the portfolio. By doing this, children become aware of their own accomplishments. Through this process, teachers gain valuable insights into how children view their own competencies and accomplishments. Teachers can reflect on the ways in which the curriculum serves the needs of the children by discussing portfolio entries with them. When both teachers and children become full participants in the process of collecting materials for inclusion in portfolios, they increase the number of opportunities for learning about themselves in the process of teaching and learning.

Focus on sharing information with others. When curriculum activities and materials are used as the basis of evidence used to assess children, they provide concrete and meaningful information to present to parents, other teachers, administrators, and other pertinent members of the public sector. These types of materials allow the teacher to focus on what progress children have made by presenting actual examples of their actual work. In this manner, others will gain a better understanding of the developmental progression of where children started, to where they have progressed, and where they will go next in the curricular process. This process also gives others not directly involved, a better understanding of the curriculum—what are the goals and outcomes expected as well as why particular teaching strategies, materials and activities are utilized.

Variation in Portfolio Types

There are three variations of portfolios that are most used in the field of early childhood education (Mills, 1989; Vermont Department of Education, 1988, 1989). The first variation is called the "works in progress" portfolio. The "works in progress" portfolio contains stories, artwork, problem-solving examples, and the like, on which children are currently working. Depending on the types of work collected and the frequency with which it's collected, this type of portfolio can become unmanageable within a short amount of time. The "works in progress" portfolio potentially can contain all of the work that the child is doing. Because of its "richness," can soon lose its potential for assessment.

The second portfolio variation is called the "current year" portfolio. The "current year" portfolio contains particular selections of work that are mutually agreed on for inclusion by the teacher and the child. The work contained in the "current year" portfolio must meet certain criteria. These are the curriculum products that are then scrutinized by teachers in order to elucidate for them children's levels of accomplishments. This particular type of portfolio also gives teachers a better understanding of how to structure or restructure the curriculum for the child's next step.

The third variation is called the "permanent portfolio." Contained in the "permanent portfolio are examples of child produced curriculum products that are highly selective. The "permanent portfolio" will accompany the child to his or her next class. Whereas the number of examples of children's work that are contained in the "permanent portfolio" needs to be limited, they should, at the same time, provide the receiving teacher with a clear understanding of the child developmental and academic accomplishments from the previous year.

Contents of a Portfolio

Information included in portfolios as documentation of behavioral changes in children should be collected from various sources, through multiple methods, and over multiple points in time (Shaklee, Barbour, Ambrose, & Hansford, 1997). Although there are many types of items that can be selected to be included in a child's portfolio, the items should reflect that work that the child does spontaneously as a part of the curriculum. It should be noted that at times it is not possible to include the "authentic" product. A case in point would be examples of block construction. In particular cases, such as this, other appropriate means should be used that characterize the child's work.

Samples of children's work. According to Dichtelmiller, Jablon, Marsden, Dorfman, & Meisels, 2001), actual samples of children's work should comprise the major contents of a portfolio. These samples may take different forms and include such things as writing examples, artwork, mathematical calculations, photographs of children's projects, and so on. Importantly, the work samples should be dated so that progress can be documented. Attempts should be made to include samples from all parts of the school year—the beginning, middle, and end. Teachers also should take great care to insure that the samples are representative of the many types of opportunities that are available to the child in the classroom. Additionally, efforts should be made to include examples that represent efforts that take place in multiple curriculum and classroom contexts. Work representing all areas of the curriculum should be included in the portfolio. It should be cautioned that it is easy to over represent those areas that are paper-and-pencil type tasks. The teacher should choose some of the work that is included in the portfolio, and the child should select some of the work.

There are both advantages and disadvantages in using examples of children's actual work. According to Cryan (1986) and Gullo (1997, 2005), the actual work of children provides the early childhood professional with real and direct, rather than contrived or extrapolated evidence of children's progress. In addition, if the samples are collected and dated, as suggested earlier, they can be interpreted and used at a later date by individuals other than the teacher who collected the work.

According to Decker and Decker (1990), there also may be some prospective disadvantages in using children's actual classroom work as assessment. One potential disadvantage is storage. This particular issue was briefly addressed earlier in this chapter. Given the number of children in a classroom, multiplied by the number of samples of work collected as representative, the amount of material that is to be stored could become unmanageable. A potential resolution to this problem would be to use advanced, but existing technology, such as computer scanners (Gullo, 2005). By using this technology, pictures, writing samples, and examples of problems can be scanned and kept on a disk until a printed copy is needed.

A second potential disadvantage to using the actual work of children is that it is difficult to know how many samples, or which samples, are accurately representative of the child and his or her capabilities and potential. Although there are potential disadvantages, the advantages of using children's work outweigh them.

Anecdotal records. As was mentioned earlier, there are times when it is not suitable to include the "actual" work of the child. At these times, it becomes necessary to incorporate a description of the work into the portfolio. This is especially true if the work is deemed significant in documenting developmental or academic progress. One appropriate method would be to use an anecdotal record to detail this information. An anecdotal record is a brief, narrative description of an event. Anecdotal records should be used especially if no other means are available to document and understand an event (Cohen, Stern, & Balaban, 1997; Cook, Tessier, & Klein, 2000). Events such as a problem solving processes or social interactions that takes place during an activity would be appropriately documented using anecdotal records. As with other examples of children's work, anecdotal records should be dated so that developmental progress or advances in academic accomplishments can be noted.

Curriculum checklists. Checklists can be used to document a sequenced series of behaviors or skills that are often linked directly to the educational or developmental goals that are curriculum based (Gullo, 2005). There are a variety of descriptive characteristics that can be included on checklists (Cryan, 1986; Mindes, 2003; Wortham, 2001). Some of these include: behavioral categories such as social/emotional behavior; interests; specific academic skills; specific knowledge; or specific concepts. Checklists can either describe behaviors of a general nature, such as problem-solving skills, social skills, critical thinking skills, or attitudinal characteristics, or describe specific skills such as word attack skills, steps in performing a science experiment, or concepts required in order to perform mathematical operations. Designed and used appropriately, checklists can be used as a guide for understanding children's development, academic progress, as well as for the development and modification of the curriculum.

Other portfolio items. There also are other means of representing the actual work that children do. These also are appropriate for inclusion in children's portfolios. These include, but are not limited to, audiotapes, videotapes, reading logs, conference records, and test results. These items will add to the richness of the information that can be obtained from the previous examples of children's work described.

Criteria for Including Children's Work in Portfolios

When making decisions about which examples of children's work to include in the child's portfolio, a number of criteria should be considered (Shanklin & Conrad, 1991). Teachers should ask themselves the following three questions when deciding what to place into a child's portfolio:

1. What will the samples of children's work tell me about their level of development or academic progress?
2. How will the information obtained from the samples of children's work help me make decisions about curriculum development, individualization, and modification?
3. How does the actual process of collecting the samples of children's work assist children in the understanding of their own developmental and /or academic accomplishments?

Finally, much has been written regarding quality standards for portfolios. Paulson, Paulson, and Meyer (1991) suggest a number of principles to consider when developing a portfolio system that includes the systematic collecting of children's work.

First, the process of selection of work examples should provide both children and teachers with the opportunity to learn something about the learning process. Through the process of selecting what will be included in the portfolio, both teachers and children are required to reflect about how the included samples demonstrate what has been learned, developed or achieved.

Second, children should be encouraged to become active participants in the process of their own leaning. Portfolios should be done by children, rather than done for children. Through the participation process, children are taught to value their work and themselves.

Third, portfolios should reflect the manner in which children's development and academic accomplishments progresses over time. The portfolio should contain a wide array of work samples that reflect the progress that is being made by the child as opposed to merely containing lists or collections of children's work and tests.

Fourth, portfolios must have some type of common structure across all children. It is through this structure that they become effective and useful for instruction and curriculum development. A rationale, goals, standards, and a systematized procedure for selecting and collecting work samples should be considered an integral part of that structure.

Finally, the function of the portfolio may change from the beginning of the academic experience to the end of the academic experience. The work collected over that time span, measuring developmental change and academic progress may differ from the work that is passed on to the next teacher as the best evidence of change over time.

Research has shown that portfolio assessment is effective and useful in a number of ways. Benson and Smith (1998), in an in-depth qualitative study, found that first grade teachers who utilized a portfolio approach to assessment realized a number of benefits. The study demonstrated that teachers:

- found portfolios were beneficial as a means of communicating more effectively with children's families about the kinds of progress their child was making in the class. This finding also was demonstrated in a study with kindergarten teacher (Diffily & Fleege, 1994). They found that kindergarten teachers found portfolios helpful in reporting children's progress to parents;

- viewed portfolios as an effective tool to motivate, encourage, and instruct children in their classrooms in the skills of self-assessment; and

- saw portfolios as a mechanism to monitor and improve on their own instructional skills and curriculum modification.

In another study with teachers of exceptional learners, Shaklee and Viechnicki (1995) found that portfolio assessment was an effective model of assessment for assessing children as exceptional learners, as well as assessing their ability to use, generate, and pursue knowledge. They also noted that the portfolio model of assessment was efficacious in terms of credibility, transferability, dependability, and confirmability.

CONCLUSIONS

What should be evident from the information, ideas, and research presented in this chapter is that assessment in early childhood education should ideally flow out of, if not become integrated within curriculum and instructional practices. Assessment should serve the teacher as well as the learner by being sensitive to the individual manner in which children learn and develop and the manner in which each child negotiates the challenges of the curriculum requirements. In addition, assessment should be sensitive to the cultural and linguistic diversity of the children that are present in early childhood programs today. Assessment also should be the driving force for modification of the curriculum in order to meet children's individual needs.

Although a stated goal of alternative assessment procedures as discussed and described in this chapter is to be sensitive to individual differences in children, a parallel to this is that an alternative assessment system also should be sensitive to the unique characteristics of the curriculum being implemented in the classroom. It should be noted that there should be a link between the curriculum content and teaching strategies and the assessment procedures. As described, one of the advantages of using an alternative assessment approach is that it doesn't disrupt the process of curriculum implementation, and in fact, reflects the goals of the curriculum. The many developmental and learning activity areas in the early childhood classroom afford teachers countless opportunities to engage in the assessment of children within contexts that are meaningful and diverse.

References

Allinder, R. M., Bolling, R. M., Oats, R. G., & Gagnon, W. A. (2000). Effects of teacher self-minitoring on implementation of curriculum-based measurement and mathematics computation achievement of students with disabilities. *Remedial and Special Education, 21*(4), 219-226.

Benson, T. R., & Smith, L. J. (1998). Portfolios in first grade: Four teachers learn to use alternative assessment. *Early Childhood Education, 25*(3), 173-180.

Bergan, J., & Field, J. K. (1993). Developmental assessment: New directions. *Young Children, 48*(5), 41-47.

Bergen, D. (Ed.). (1994). *Assessment methods for infants and toddlers: Transdisciplinary team approaches.* New York: Teachers College Press.

Bergen, D. (1997). Usinjg Observational techniques for evaluating young children's learning. In Saracho, O. & Spodek, B. (Eds.). *Issues in early childhood educational assessment and evaluation* (pp. 108-128). New York: Teachers College Press.

Bergen, D., & Mosley-Howard, S. (1994). Assessment methods for culturally diverse young children. In D. Bergen (Ed.), *Assessment methods for infants and toddlers: Transdisciplinary team approaches.* New York: Teachers College Press, 190-206.

Bolig, E. E., & Day, J. D. (1993). Dynamic assessment and giftedness: The promise of assessing training responsiveness. *Roeper Review, 16*(2), 110-113.

Bredekamp, S., & Copple, C. (1997). *Developmentally Appropriate Practice in Early Childhood Programs—Revised Edition.* Washington, DC: National Association for the Education of Young Children.

Bradekamp, S., & Rosegrant, T. (1992). *Reaching potentials: Appropriate curriculum and assessment for young children* (Vol. 1). Washington, DC: National Association for the Education of Young Children.

Bricker, D., Pretti-Frontczak, K., & McComas, N. (1998). *An activity-based approach to erly intervention.* Balimore: Paul H. Brookes.

Calhoon, J. M. (1997). Comparison of assessment results between a formal standardized measure and a play-based format. *Infant-Toddler Intervention: The Transdisciplinary Journal, 7*(3), 201-204.

Chen, J. (1998). *Project spectrum: Early learning activities.* New York: Teachers College Press.

Cohen, L. G., & Spenciner, L. J. (1994). *Assessment of young children.* New York: Longman Press.

Cohen, L. G., & Spenciner, L. J. (2003). *Assessment of children and youth with special needs.* New York: Longman Press.

Cohen, R., Stern, V., & Balaban, N. (1997). *Observing and recording the behavior of young children* (4th ed.). New York: Teachers College Press.

Cole, D. J., Ryan, C. W., & Kick, F. (1995). *Portfolios across the curriculum and beyond.* Thousand Oaks, CA: Corwin Press.

Cook, R. E., Gandini, L., & Foremen, G. (2000). *Adapting early child-hood curriculum for children with special needs* (5th ed.). Upper Saddle River, NJ: Merrill/Prentice Hall.

Cook, R. E., Tessier, A., & Klein, M. D. (2000). *Adapting early childhood curricula for children in inclusive settings.* (5th ed). Englewood Cliffs, NJ: Merrill.

Culbertson, L., & Jalongo, M. (1999). But what's wrong with letter grades? Responding to parents' questions about alternative assessment. *Childhood Education, 75*(3), 130-135.

Cryan, J. R. (1986). Evaluation: Plague or promise? *Childhood Education, 62,* 344-350.

Decker, C. A., & Decker, J. R. (1990). *Planning and administering early childhood programs.* Columbus, OH: Merrill Publishing Co.

Delclos, V. R. (1987). Effects of dynamic assessment on teachers' expecations of handicapped children. *American Educational Research Journal, 24*(3), 325-336.

Deno, S. L., Fuchs, L. S., Marston, D., & Shin, J. (2001). Using curriculum-based measurement to establish growth standards for students with learning disabilities. *School Psychology Review, 30*(4), 507-524.

Dichtelmiller, M. L., Jablon, J. R., Marsden, D. B., Dorfman, A. B., & Meisels, S. J. (2001). *Work sampling in the classroom.* New York: Pearson Early Learning.

Diffily, D., & Fleege, P. O. (1994). The power of portfolios for communicating with families. *Dimensions of Early Childhood, 22*(2), 40-41.

Farmer-Dougan, V. & Kaszuba, T. (1999). Reliability and validity of play-based observations: Relationship between the PLAY Behaviour Observation System and the standardized measures of cognitive and social skills. *Educational Psychology: An International Journal of Experimental Educational Psychology, 19*(4), 429-440.

Feuerstein, R. (1979). *Dynamic assessment of retarded performers.* Baltimore: University Park Press.

Feuerstein, R. (1980). *Instrumental enrichment.* Baltimore: University Park Press.

Galagan, J. E. (1985). Psychoeducational testing: Turn out the lights, the party's over. *Exceptional Children, 52*(3), 288-299.

Gardner, H. (1983). *Frames of mind: The theory of multiple intelligences.* New York: Basic Books.

Gardner, H. (1999). *The disciplined mind: What all students should understand.* New York: Simon and Schuster.

Gardner, H., Feldman, D. H., & Krechevsky, M. (1998). *Project spectrum: Preschool assessment handbook.* New York: Teachers College Press.

Gullo, D. F. (1992). *Understanding appropriate teaching in early childhood education: Curriculum, implementation, evaluation.* Washington, DC: National Education Association.

Gullo, D. F. (1997). Assessing student learning through the analysis of pupil products. In Saracho, O. & Spodek, B. (Eds.). *Issues in early childhood educational assessment and evaluation.* New York: Teachers College Press, 129-148.

Gullo, D. F. (2005). *Understanding assessment and evaluation in early childhood education* (2nd ed.). New York: Teachers College Press.

Gullo, D. F., & Ambrose, R. P. (1987). Perceived competence and social acceptance in kindergarten: Its relationship to academic performance. *Educational Research, 8*(1), 28-32.

Hatch, T., & Gardner, H. (1996). If Binet had looked beyond the classroom: The assessment of multiple intelligences. *NAMTA Journal, 21*(2), 5-28.

Hebert, E. A. (1992). Portfolios invite reflection—from students and staff. *Educational Leadership, 49*(8), 58-61.

Herman, J. L., Aschbacher, P. R., & Winters, L. (1992). *A practical guide to alternative assessment.* Alexandria, VA: Association for Supervision and Curriculum Development.

Hills, T. W. (1993). Assessment in context: Teachers and children at work. *Young Children, 48*(5), 20-28.

Jacobs, E. L. (2001). The effects of dynamic assessment components to a computerized preschool language screening test. *Communication Disorders Quarterly, 22*(4), 217-226.

Jitendra, A. K., & Kameenui, E. J. (1993). An exploratory study of dynamic assessment involving two instructional strategies on experts and Novices' performance in solving part-whole mathematical word problems. *Diagnostique, 18*(4), 305-325

Krechevsky, M. (1991). Project spectrum: An innovative assessment alternative. *Educational Leadership, 49*(6), 43-48.

Lidz, C. (1991). *Practitioner's guide to dynamic assessment.* New York: Guilford.

Lidz, C., & Pena, E. (1996). Dynamic assessment: The model, its relevance as a nonbiased approach, and its application to Latino American preschool children. *Language, Speech, and Hearing Services in the Schools, 27*(4), 367-372.

Malone, D. M. (1994). Contextual variation of correspondences among measures of play and developmental level of preschool children. *Journal of Early Intervention, 18*(2), 199-215.

Maness, B. J. (1992). Assessment in early childhood education. *Kappa Delta Pi Record, 28*(3), 77-79.

McAfee, O., & Leong, D. J. (2002). *Assessing and guiding young children's development and learning* (3rd ed.). Boston: Allyn and Bacon.

McLean, M. (1998). Assessing children for whom English is a second language. *Young Exceptional Children, 1*(3), 20-25.

McLean, M. (2000). *Conducting child assessments* (CLAS Technical report No. 2.). Champaign: University of Illinois at Urbana-Champaign, Early Childhood Research Institute on Culturally and Linguistically Appropriate Services.

Meisels, S. J. (1987). Uses and abuses of developmental screening and school readiness testing. *Young Children, 42*(4-6), 68-73.

Meisels, S. J. (1989). High stakes testing in kindergarten. *Educational Leadership, 46*(7), 16-22.

Meisels, S. J. (1992). *The work sampling system: An overview.* Ann Arbor: University of Michigan.

Meisels, S. J. (1993). Remaking classroom assessment with the work sampling system. *Young Children, 48*(5), 34-40.

Meisels, S. J., & Atkins-Burnett, S. (2004). The Head Start National Reporting System, *Young Children, 59*(1), 64-66.

Meisels, S. J., Bickel, D. D., Nicholson, J., Xue, Y., & Atkins-Burnett, S. (2001). Trusting teachers' judgments: A validity study of curriculum-embedded performance assessment in kindergarten—grade 3. *American Educational Research Journal, 38*(1), 73-95.

Meisels, S. J., Jablon, F. R., Dichtelmiller, M. L. Dorfman, A. B., & Marsden, D. B. (2001). *The Work Sampling System* (4th ed.). New York: Pearson Early Learning.

Meyers, J., Pfeffer, J., & Erlbaum, V. (1985). Process assessment: A model for broadening assessment. *Journal of Special Education, 18*(2), 1-84.

Mills, R. (1989). Portfolios capture rich array of student performance. *The School Administrator, 47*(10), 8-11.

Mindes, G. (2003). *Assessing young children.* Upper Saddle River, NJ: Merrill/Prentice Hall.

Myers, C. L. (1996). Play-based assessment in early childhood special education: An examination of social validity. *Topics in Early Childhood Special Education, 16*(1), 102-126.

Nall, S. (1994). Assessment through portfolios in the all-day kindergarten. *National All-Day Kindergarten Network Newsletter, 4*(1), 1,3.

National Association for the Education of Young Children. (1988). NAEYC position statement on standardized testing of young children 3 through 8 years of age. *Young Children, 49,* 60-63.

National Association for the Education of Young Children. (2003). *Early Childhood Curriculum, Assessment, and Program Evaluation: Building an Effective, Accountable System in Programs for Children Birth through Age 8.* (Position Statement). Washington, DC: National Association for the Education of Young Children.

National Commission on Testing and Public Policy. (1990). *From gatekeeper to gateway: Transforming testing in America.* Chestnut Hill, MA: Author.

Neisworth, J., & Bagnato, S. (1996). Assessment. In S. Odom & M. McLean (Eds.), *Early intervention/early childhood special education: Recommended practices.* Austin, TX: Pro-Ed.

North Central Regional Educational Laboratory. (2003). Student assessment. http://www.ncrel.org/sdrs/areas/issues/methods/assment/as7stud.htm

Paulson, F. L., Paulson, P., & Meyer, C. (1991). What makes a portfolio? *Educational Leadership, 49,* 60–63.

Phillips, N., Fuchs, L. S., & Fuchs, D. (1994). Effects of classwide curriculum-based measurement and Peer tutoring: A collaborative researcher-practioner Interview study. *Journal of Learning Disabilities, 27*(7), 420–434.

Saracho, O., & Spodek, B. (Eds.), (1997). *Issues in early childhood educational assessment and evaluation.* New York: Teachers College Press.

Sewell, M., Marczak, M. & Horn, M. (2003). The use of portfolio assessment in evaluation. Retrieved on September 18, 2003, from http://ag.arizona.edu/fcr/fs/cyfar/Portfo~3htm

Shaklee, B. D., Barbour, N. E., Ambrose, R., & Hansford, S. J. (1997). *Designing and using portfolios.* Boston: Allyn and Bacon.

Shaklee, B. D., & Viechnicki, K. J. (1995). A qualitative approach to portfolios: The early assessment for exceptional children. *Journal for the Education of the Gifted, 18*(2), 156–170.

Shanklin, N., & Conrad, L. (1991). *Portfolios: A new way to assess student growth.* Denver: Colorado Council of the International Reading Association.

Shepard, L., (1989). Why we need better assessment. *Educational Leadership, 46*(7), 4–9.

Shepard, L., & Bleim, C. (1995). Parents' thinking about standardized tests and performance assessment. *Educational Researcher, 24*(8), 25–32.

Spector, J. E. (1992). Predicting progress in beginning reading: Dynamic assessment of phonemic awareness. *Journal of Educational Psychology, 84*(3), 553–563.

Stipek, D. J. (1981). Childrens perceptions of their own and their classmates' ability. *Journal of Educational Psychology, 73,* 404–410.

U.S. Department of Education. (2002). Inside No Child Left Behind. Retrieved on September 18, 2003, from http://www.ed.gov/offices/OESE/esea/factsheet.html

Valencial, R. R., & Suzuki, L. A. (2001). *Intelligence testing and minority students: Foundations, performance factors, and assessment.* Thousand Oaks, CA: Sage.

VanDerHeyden, A. M., Witt, J. C., Naquin, G., & Noell, G. (2001). The reliability and validity of curriculum-based measurement readiness probes for kindergarten students. *School Psychology Review, 79,* 59–65.

Van Hoorn, J., Nourot, P., Scales, B., & Alward, K. (1999). *Play at the center of the curriculum.* Upper Saddle, NJ: Merrill/Prentice Hall.

Vavrus. L. (1990). Putting portfolios to the test. *Instructor* (August), 48–51.

Vermont Department of Education. (1988). *Working together to show results: An approach to school accountability.* Montpelier, VT: Author.

Vermont Department of Education. (1989). *Vermont writing assessment: The portfolio.* Montpelier, VT: Author.

Vialle, W. (1994). Profiles of intelligence. *Australian Journal of Early Childhood Education, 19*(4), 30–34.

Vygotsky, L. (1978). *Mind and society: The development of higher psychological processes* (M. Cole, V. Jonh-Steiner, S. Scribner, & E. Souberman, Eds.). Cambridge, MA: Harvard University Press.

Vygotsky, L. (1986). *Thought and language* (A. Kosulin, Trans.). Cambridge, MA: Harvard University Press.

Webster, R., McInnis, E. & Carver, L. (1986). Curriculum biasing effects in standardized and criterion-referenced reading achievement tests. *Psychology in the Schools, 23*(2), 205–213.

Wortham, S. C. (2001). *Tests and measurements in early childhood education.* Columbus, OH: Merrill.

Wexler-Sherman, C, Gardner, H, & Feldman, D. (1998). A pluralistic view of early assessment: The project spectrum approach. *Theory into Practice, 27*(1), 77–83.

· 26 ·

EVALUATING THE QUALITY OF EARLY CHILDHOOD EDUCATIONAL SETTINGS

Richard Lambert
University of North Carolina at Charlotte

Martha Abbott-Shim
Quality Counts, Inc.

Annette Sibley
Quality Assist, Inc.

INTRODUCTION

Since the late 1980s, the majority of American mothers with young children have worked outside the home (Phillips & Adams, 2001; Public Agenda, 2003). Therefore, most young children spend some part of their day in out-of-home care. To meet this demand, child care, family child care, and preschool education are evolving into essential components of the economic infrastructure for our society and indispensable support systems for the families that rely on their services. They also are becoming educational programs that are increasingly linked to our public education system.

The settings or contexts for early childhood education differ greatly. Within the home context, children are cared for by their parents or by other relatives and caregivers in their own home. Children attend family child care homes that are either licensed or registered by the state (typically three to seven children) or unregulated (typically fewer than three children). Within the center or classroom context, children are cared for in part-day and full-day programs. Part-day programs include private preschools that are typically not regulated by the state, Head Start, which is federally monitored, and prekindergarten programs, which are usually monitored by the state. Full-day programs include child care centers that operate under various auspices: nonprofit, church-related, independent private for-profit, and private for-profit chains. Often there are Head Start classrooms and prekindergarten classrooms within child care centers.

CRITICAL REFLECTIONS ON ASSESSMENT

As the role that child care and early childhood education plays in our society continues to evolve, researchers have begun to more fully understand the complex interchanges between the development of young children and the quality of various contexts in which they develop (Phillips, 1996). Our understanding of what young children can learn and do, and how supportive contexts can strengthen learning is expanding (Bowman, Donovan, & Burns, 2000). Parents and policy makers also are becoming increasingly aware of the importance of early learning, including an increased understanding of how children develop, which is leading to more public demand for quality.

Whereas the public is demanding more out-of-home care and economic realities make it a part of the typical American family with young children, the cost of high quality care and education is beyond the reach of most American families. Therefore, the public is not only demanding higher quality, but more public investment in the care delivery system. Policy makers are generally convinced of the public necessity and economic value of early childhood programs, and they expect a return for the investment of public funds and a measure of accountability. Although public policy is increasingly addressing educational reform, accountability, and achievement gaps, attention is also focused on the role of early education in fostering school readiness. Public schools expect children to enter kindergarten ready to learn (Kagan, Moore, & Bredekamp, 1997).

In response to state and federal mandates, such as the No Child Left Behind legislation (U.S. Department of Education, 2001), state accountability programs at the elementary and secondary levels, are directly equating aggregated child outcomes with quality. Few measures of classroom quality exist at the elementary and secondary levels. The measures that do exist are not supported by sufficient validity evidence to justify their use for high stakes decision making. Public policy makers have turned to aggregated test scores and high-stakes testing programs as the definitive measures of the quality of elementary and secondary schools, and classrooms.

For the first time, accountability systems using aggregated test scores are being imposed on early childhood programs. This is happening with the federally funded Head Start program. President Bush's *Good Start, Grow Smart* initiative places great importance on the National Reporting System, which requires local programs to provide child test score data to a centralized database. These data are subsequently reviewed by federal program administrators as an indicator of program effectiveness (Horn, 2003). However, early childhood experts have reported that the assessment measures are not linguistically and culturally appropriate for the Head Start population (Moore & Yzaquirre, 2004).

As this culture of accountability reaches down into early childhood education and attempts to redefine quality as indicated solely by aggregated child outcomes, why should early childhood programs measure quality? Measuring quality is essential because self-evaluation, along with more formal program evaluation methods, are important strategies that early childhood programs can use to understand the processes involved in meeting the needs of the children and families they serve. It is also essential for empirical research purposes.

Educators in general welcome accountability. They both enjoy the rewards that come with knowing and understanding the progress that children are making and recognize the need to understand more about how children are developing in order to better plan instructional activities. However, focusing accountability systems solely on aggregated child outcomes falls short of providing educators with the information they need to improve and maintain quality programming. In a sense, this focus is exclusively summative in nature, and ignores the formative evaluation strategies by which teachers understand how they are helping children grow and develop.

Program evaluation is most useful and leads directly to program improvement when it is comprehensive in nature, relying on multiple methods and data sources of the highest technical quality available. Child assessments aligned with program goals and curricular strategies, feedback from parents and other stakeholders, evaluations of the classroom environment, and an examination of the overall program climate, systems, and connection to community resources are all potential data sources. Evaluation of early childhood programs cannot substantially rely on aggregated child assessments. Reliability and validity of the information provided by assessments is hard to achieve when assessing young children. The reliability and validity of assessment information increases with the age of the children being assessed (National Education Goals Panel, 1998). Caution should be exercised when using standardized, norm-referenced testing with young children (National Research Council, 2000). Multiple indicators are always better for decision-making purposes, and it is important to keep in mind the purpose for which the measures were designed and validated.

Furthermore, when assessing young children it is difficult to rely on assessments that involve paper-and-pencil techniques, focused and extended periods of cooperation and attention, or that require highly developed verbal abilities. Academic achievement is not a concept that generalizes down from the middle grades to elementary and to early childhood. Developmentally appropriate curricula for young children are not simply a scaled back version of elementary curricula. The purpose of assessments with young children is more effective as formative tools for planning instruction, understanding the variability and level of development of individual children, and identifying those children who need further referral for more targeted assessment, rather than as a measure of instructional quality. Formative assessments are a part of quality instruction and they play a central role for teachers of young children. Although child assessments are an important component of a system of ongoing evaluation of quality, careful examination of the classroom context, program resources and climate, and community resources are central elements in a comprehensive evaluation system.

Measures of contextual quality, in contrast to child outcome measures, can be used to demonstrate the efforts that teachers make to shape the environmental conditions and teaching practices that they control: the quality of their own classrooms as effective contexts for learning. Research has demonstrated that the quality of the early childhood education is associated with children's developmental outcomes (National Research Council, 2000). Although child assessments may provide teachers with an understanding of what children can and cannot do, child assessments do not offer any feedback concerning the processes necessary to improve the quality of the early learning experiences, and thereby impacting developmental progress. The combination of child assessments and formative evaluation of early learning experiences for young children leads to a culture of continuous quality improvement and enhanced child outcomes (Lambert & Abbott-Shim, 2003).

The measurement of quality in early childhood settings has begun to lag behind the relatively recent developments in child development research (National Research Council & Institute of Medicine, 2000). For example, Dickinson (2002) has critiqued widely accepted early childhood measures, including the Early Childhood Environment Rating Scale (Harms & Clifford, 1980), the Assessment Profile for Early Childhood Programs: Research Edition II (Abbott-Shim & Sibley, 1998), and the National

Association for the Education of Young Children Accreditation instrument (NAEYC, 1998), in regard to literacy and the processes by which children acquire emergent literacy skills. He concludes that the instrumentation has not kept up with research regarding how children learn, and therefore, are not adequately assessing the quality of early literacy environments. This argument can be extended to the measurement of other dimensions of quality. Theory concerning effective teaching practices and early learning environments continues to evolve and similarly, the measurement of teacher beliefs and attitudes has not kept abreast of these developments.

The measurement of quality also has become rather entrenched in the field of early childhood education. The persistent use of measures allows them to gain acceptance and "incremental validity" merely because everyone uses them (National Research Council, 2000). The measurement strategies used to assess quality run the risk of becoming institutionalized within the early childhood research culture.

DEFINING QUALITY

Quality is an elusive concept. Definitions of quality in early childhood education will differ from varying perspectives—parents, teachers, administrators, and researchers. Different ethnic and cultural backgrounds also bring unique perspectives to the definition of quality (Phillips, 1996). The prevailing definitions of quality focus primarily on features of classrooms and programs and need to be expanded (Phillips, 1996). Love, Meckstroth, and Sprachman (1997) suggest that the quality of early childhood settings can be examined along five dimensions of classroom and program environments, including: (1) classroom dynamics, (2) classroom structural variables, (3) classroom staff characteristics, (4) administration and support services, and (5) parent involvement. Within this chapter, the last dimension will be broadened to include community resources and involvement. Classroom dynamics, often called process dimensions of quality, include interactions between children, between adults and children, and the range of intentional teacher strategies that characterize the classroom environment. Classroom structural variables include the physical setting and furnishings, group size, and adult-child ratio. Classroom staff characteristics include demographic descriptors, including education level, training in early childhood education, and teacher beliefs. Education includes formal education at both secondary and higher education levels, and is a proxy for knowledge. Training encompasses both specialized training programs for professional credentials, such as the Child Development Associate Credential, and individual workshops and conference presentations. Teacher beliefs and attitudes, in most instances, are an indicator of the degree to which teachers value and report that they implement developmentally appropriate practices. Administration and support services include the overall climate and working conditions of the program, as well as the mentoring, technical assistance, and supervision given to teachers. Administration also encompasses the program's support for teachers' reflective practices, professional development, salary levels, and turnover. The parent and community involvement dimension not only includes

the quantity and quality of parental support for and interaction within the program but also extends to the attitude and approach the program takes toward parents including communication and training in child development, parenting practices, and home-learning activities that support program goals. Community involvement includes the availability of and program's access to community resources and services. Important information about connections between the program, the parents and the community can be explored through several questions, including: What are the most salient features of the community context? To what extent does the community contain resources that are helpful to families with young children? To what extent does the program assist families in taking advantage of the existing community resources? How well does the program recruit families and children? Has the program made meaningful connections to other community agencies and funding sources? These five dimensions of quality will provide an organizational framework for discussing the research literature for both the predictors of quality and the correlates of quality.

HISTORICAL PERSPECTIVE OF QUALITY

Historically, the evaluation of quality has been conducted for different reasons. The focus of the initial child care research after World War II was designed to examine the effects of child care on maternal attachment. This research was based on cultural attitudes, influenced by such early researchers as Bowlby (1951) and Spitz (1945), which contended that parental full-time childrearing, particularly in the early years, was essential to healthy psychological development. Subsequently, a significant body of research has shown that children demonstrate typical development in "high-quality" settings (Belsky & Steinberg, 1978).

Because of the increased use of child care and the realization that child care was not a temporary phenomenon but, rather, represented a change in childrearing practices (Hofferth & Phillips, 1987), a second phase of child care research was conducted. This research was designed to define and measure the critical components of quality. Starting with the Abt Study in the 1970s (Ruopp, Travers, Glantz, & Coelen, 1979) and continuing through the 1990s with the NICHD Study of Early Child Care (National Institute of Child Health and Human Development, 1998), large-scale, federally funded research has established new paradigms that focus on the structural and process variables using complex research designs based on theoretical models (Bronfenbrenner, 1979).

At the turn of the century, the focus has shifted again, placing emphasis on child outcomes and school readiness. As we enter the 21st century, the social, economic, and political climate calls for answers about how well early childhood programs prepare children to succeed in school. School readiness is becoming the marker for quality in early childhood education. This shift has been influenced by the increased public investment in Head Start and child care to support family self-sufficiency.

The U.S. General Accounting Office (GAO) reviewed the increased public investment in child care and reported that in fiscal year 2000, states spent $5.3 billion in federal Child Care and

Development Funds for subsidized child care for low income families while earmarking just 4% of the funds for quality improvements (U.S. General Accounting Office, September 2002). States have had wide latitude in deciding how to allocate funds for quality improvements and have funded initiatives to increase teacher compensation, provide teacher training, improve professional credentials, support compliance with state standards, achieve accreditation, provide incentives for programs to exceed state standards, and provide higher reimbursement rates for subsidized children served in accredited programs. The GAO also reported that state officials based their funding decisions on existing child care quality research findings.

The National Research Council and two other teams of reviewers examined the research on child care quality and concluded: "These studies have shown relationships between structural attributes, child-caregiver interactions and children's developmental progress that suggest many state initiatives are targeted on aspects of child care settings that have the potential for enhancing developmental outcomes. However, this is not sufficient to conclude that states' initiatives are necessarily effective in enhancing child care quality" (U.S. General Accounting Office, 2002, p. 29).

Few states have evaluated the effectiveness of their state initiatives to increase the quality of early childhood programs. Only three states—Massachusetts, Washington, and Florida—implemented research designs and methodological approaches that isolated an initiative's effects and produced conclusive findings (U.S. General Accounting Office, September 2002). Florida's study found that reduced child-to-teacher ratios and increased teacher education contributed to higher program quality and gains in children's development. The state of Washington found no effect of compensation on teacher retention. Massachusetts confirmed that low compensation was related to low retention. Although current research provides promising directions in which to target quality improvement funds and initiatives, it offers little specific guidance on how to modify ongoing initiatives or the most cost effective investments to improve quality.

The GAO also concluded that "to represent the diversity of the 50 states and their quality improvement approaches, more research that employs experimental or quasi-experimental designs will be needed to determine the effectiveness of states' quality improvement initiatives" (U.S. General Accounting Office, 2002, p. 29). The states might use the research agenda of the U.S. Department of Health and Human Services (HHS) as a model for their work. The HHS research agenda addresses three goals: improve the capacity to respond to policy questions; strengthen data collection and analysis systems for child care research; and increase knowledge about the effectiveness of child care policies and programs on child development and in helping low-income families obtain and retain work. HHS proposes to achieve these goals through state research partnerships, field-initiated research, and demonstration, evaluation, and analysis systems for child care research (U.S. General Accounting Office, 2002).

As social, economic, and political conditions place increased pressure on early care and education programs to produce child outcomes and justify public and private investments, program evaluation becomes essential. Additional rigorous evaluation and research is needed to guide policy makers', administrators,' and practitioners' efforts to measure child care quality and its variation.

MEASUREMENT OF QUALITY

Early childhood education researchers have the opportunity to develop and refine a variety of methods and strategies for documenting the quality of early childhood programs (Lambert, 2003). The development of measures necessitates an on-going commitment to establish and reestablish strong reliability and validity. *The Standards for Educational and Psychological Measurement* (AERA, APA, & NCME, 1999) provide critically important criteria for the measurement of quality.

These standards make it clear that an understanding of the intended use of an instrument is fundamental to the proper interpretation of the information it provides. Although it has become an unfortunately common early childhood evaluation practice to use an instrument for multiple purposes, no measure can successfully sustain multiple demands on the information it provides without specific attention to multiple purposes during development and validation (Standard 15.1) (AERA, APA, & NCME, 1999). When a research measure is used for program improvement purposes, there is a tendency to "teach to the test" and quality can be artificially and momentarily raised by executing discrete, identified items instead of understanding the construct represented by those items.

With the growing importance and application of multilevel modeling to educational policy analysis, there is also a need for measures of the broader contextual quality of early childhood educational settings (Lambert, 2003; Phillips, 1996). The contextual conceptions of quality rely primarily on ecological models (Bronfenbrenner, 1979) and have been applied to the support of quality in early childhood education (Gormley, Kagan, & Cohen, 1995; Kagan, 1993). This includes the sensitivity to the cultural and linguistic aspects of teachers' behaviors and the families and children they serve. The challenge for the field of early childhood education is to capture the breadth and depth of this context through valid and reliable measurement.

When seeking to meet this challenge, a battery of measures provides more useful information than a single indicator of quality. The most informative and comprehensive evaluation systems are built on program goals that have been translated into measurable objectives and specific indicators. However, in the absence of such a system early childhood programs often let commonly used measurement tools define quality practice rather than selecting batteries that are comprised of measures chosen to match program needs. Researchers and program administrators can work together to select the most useful combination of tools and resources necessary for measuring quality, while carefully considering the burden that any measurement process places on children, families, and teachers. The decision to use internal or external observers and assessors also can be considered while weighing the advantages and disadvantages of each against the purpose of the measurements. The remainder of this section will review measurement tools addressing first, global quality measures and then, instruments evaluating specific aspects of quality. The purpose of each measure and available technical information will be discussed.

MEASURES OF GLOBAL QUALITY

The most widely used measure of environmental quality, the Early Childhood Environment Rating Scale (ECERS), (Harms & Clifford, 1980), has become a quality standard itself in the field of early childhood education. When statements in the early childhood research literature are made about attributes correlating with "quality" or predicting "quality," the referent for "quality" is usually the ECERS measure. This is also true for the companion instruments, Infant Toddler Environment Rating Scale (ITERS) (Harms, Cryer, & Clifford, 1990) and the Family Day Care Rating Scale (FDCRS; Harms & Clifford, 1984). The purpose of these measures is to evaluate the quality of the environments in the respective settings. Each instrument includes items that are rated on a 7-point scale ranging from inadequate to excellent with four descriptive anchors provided for the 1, 3, 5, and 7 ratings.

The ECERS was revised, now known as ECERS-R (Harms, Clifford, & Cryer, 1998), to broaden the measurement of quality to include cultural diversity, family concerns, and individual children's needs. The authors field-tested the revised instrument in 45 classrooms but do not report validity information. They state that the predictive validity of the original ECERS (Peisner-Feinberg & Burchinal, 1997; Whitebook, Howes, & Phillips, 1990) and its construct validity (Rossbach, Clifford, & Harms, 1991; Whitebook et al., 1990) should hold true for the revised measure also (Harms et al., 1998). In her review of the revised measure, Paget (2001) indicates that more empirical evidence for the validity of the revised measure is needed. The authors report interrater reliability at 86% of agreement across all indicators, and item level agreement within a score of 1 point on each 7-point scale was 71%. Weighted Kappa interrater reliability scores for each item range from .28 to .90. The authors recognize the need for further research to extend the psychometric properties of the ECERS-R (Harms et al., 1998).

Harms and her colleagues report strong content validity for the ITERS and a weaker justification for criterion validity (Clifford et al., 1989). The Spearman's correlation coefficient for interrater reliability for the overall ITERS was .84 and the subscales ranged from .58 to .89. The Cronbach alpha coefficient for internal consistency for the overall ITERS was .83, however subscale coefficients varied substantially (Clifford et al., 1989). The test-retest reliability with a 3- to 4-week interval was reported as a Spearman correlation coefficient of .79 for the overall scale and subscales ranged from .58 to .76. The reviewers (Constantine & Iverson, 1995) recommend cautious use of the ITERS as a research tool until stronger psychometric properties and construct validity are established.

For the FDCRS the authors report that individual item median interrater reliabilities were .90 or greater (Harms & Clifford, 1984). Internal consistency coefficients (Cronbach alpha) for all subscales were .83 or greater, except the Adult Needs subscale of .70. The authors established content validity through the instrument's link to ECERS and ITERS and a match to the

Child Development Associate credential standards. In addition, Howes and Stewart (1987) found the FDCRS scores correlated positively with children's observed behaviors and regulable dimensions of family day care homes. Iverson (1992) recommends additional research to establish test-retest reliability and construct validity for this instrument.

Another global quality measure, the Assessment Profile for Early Childhood Programs: Research Version (Abbott-Shim & Sibley, 1992), was originally standardized using 401 preschool classrooms. In 1998 the authors revised the instrument, Assessment Profile for Early Childhood Programs: Research Edition II (Abbott-Shim & Sibley, 1998), using a national standardization sample of 2,820 classrooms: 190 Head Start classrooms in two southern states, and 933 kindergarten, 935 first grade and 762 second grade classrooms across 31 states and the Navajo Nation. The purpose of this tool is to evaluate the learning environment and teaching practices in classrooms for young children. It is an observation checklist with dichotomous items and includes five scales: Learning Environment, Scheduling, Curriculum Methodology, Interacting, and Individualizing. These five scales have met the unidimensionality criteria for Information Response Theory (IRT) creation of scales and have shown a strong fit to a three-parameter IRT model (Abbott-Shim, Neel, & Sibley, 2001). Content validity was documented through a review of the instrument by a wide range of early childhood professionals and a cross-reference of the items with the initial NAEYC Accreditation Criteria (National Association for the Education of Young Children, 1998). Criterion related validity was established by examining the relationship of the Assessment Profile for Early Childhood Programs: Research Version to the ECERS (Harms & Clifford, 1980). In these criterion related validity studies, Wilkes (1989) found a significant correlation ($r = .64$, $p < .001$), and Abbott-Shim (1991) found a significant correlation ($r = .74$, $p < .001$). The reliability coefficients for the five scales (Learning Environment, Scheduling, Curriculum, Interacting, and Individualizing) range from .79 to .98 for the Kuder-Richardson 20 and from .81 to .98 for the Spearman-Brown corrected split-half. The IRT based reliability coefficients for the five scales range form .83 to .91 (Abbott-Shim, Neel & Sibley, 1992). Interrater reliabilities between a trainer and 14 observers was reported as a mean of 93% agreement with a range of 83 to 97% agreement, and for 16 observers as a mean of 95% agreement with a range of 85 to 98% agreement (Abbott-Shim, Lambert, & McCarty, 2000).

The Assessment Profile for Early Childhood Programs: Preschool, Toddler, Infant, School-Age, and Administration instruments (Abbott-Shim & Sibley, 1987) are formative evaluation measures used for program improvement purposes. These measures are much more comprehensive than the research tool and provide user-friendly procedures for self-evaluation of early childhood settings. As formative measures, they are supported by software that provides extensive analyses and detailed program improvement recommendations. The Assessment Profile for Family Child Care Homes (Sibley & Abbott-Shim, 1987) is a companion tool for formative evaluation purposes in the family child care setting. From 1988 to 1999 the National Association of Family Child Care Homes had exclusive rights for use of this instrument in their accreditation process.

The Assessment Profile for Homes with Young Children: Research Version (Abbott-Shim & Sibley, 1993) was developed using the items on the Assessment Profile for Early Childhood Programs: Research Version (Abbott-Shim & Sibley, 1992) as the basis for selection of similar items from the Family Child Care Homes measure. The Assessment Profile for Homes with Young Children: Research Version has only been used in the NICHD Early Child Care Research Project and the authors have never established any psychometric properties.

The Observational Record of the Caregiving Environment (ORCE) (NICHD Early Child Care Research Network, 1996) was developed by the research team to observe children birth through 5 years of age and caregiver behaviors in any setting. Two composite scores were derived: (1) caregiver sensitivity including fostering exploration, sensitivity to non-distress, positive regard, detachment (reverse coded); flatness of affect (reverse coded), and intrusiveness (reverse coded); and (2) stimulation of development. Criterion-related validity has been examined as the research team has shown a relationship between ORCE variables and the HOME and the Assessment Profile for Homes with Young Children. Predictive validity has been demonstrated as the ORCE variables relate to child outcomes (NICHD Early Child Care Research Network, 1998).

The Home Observation of the Measurement of the Environment (HOME) (Bradley & Caldwell, 1984) was originally developed to assess the home environment. The HOME was revised to assess the child's experience in home-like informal child care settings and now includes two companion measures, the Infant-Toddler Child Care HOME (IT-CC-HOME) and the Early Childhood Child Care HOME (EC-CC-HOME) (Bradley, Caldwell & Corwyn, 2003). The authors (2003) report that content validity for the CC-HOME is based on careful reviews of the literature. Criterion validity is established through studies linking the original HOME scores to various aspects of child well-being (Bradley, 1994; Bradley, Corwyn, & Whiteside-Mansell, 1996). In a more recent study, the CC-HOME scores were linked to child outcomes on the Bayley at 24 months and school readiness and language comprehension at 36 months of age (Clarke-Stewart, Vandell, Burchinal, O'Brien, & McCartney, 2002). Convergent validity is reported as significant correlations ranging from .16 to .61 with subscales on the ORCE and significant correlations ranging from .21 to .69 with the Assessment Profile for Homes with Young Children: Research Version. The reliability alpha coefficient was .81 (NICHD Early Child Care Research Network, 1996). Reliability also was reported for interobserver agreements as Pearson correlations of .94 and .98 and Winer correlations of .97 and .99 during two data collection periods (Bradley et al., 2003).

The High/Scope Program Quality Assessment (PQA): Preschool Version (High/ Scope Educational Research Foundation, 1998) is designed to evaluate the quality of early childhood programs and identify staff training needs. Interrater reliability between the trainer and 18 observers was an average of 79% for exact agreement and 97% for agreement within one point of each other. The Cronbach's alpha coefficient was .95 for 49 independent observers and .96 for 642 teacher self-assessments. Validity for an earlier version of the PQA was reported as a significant overall correlation (.86) with the ECERS and a significant correlation (.48) with the Caregiver Interaction Scale (Arnett, 1989). High/Scope researchers report that studies have shown that PQA scores are positively and significantly associated with child outcomes (High/Scope Educational Research Foundation, 1997; Mardell-Czudnowski & Goldenberg, 1990).

MEASURES OF SPECIFIC ASPECTS OF QUALITY

Several measures focusing on specific aspects of quality have been used in the early childhood research literature. The Caregiver Interaction Scale (Arnett, 1989) was designed to evaluate a caregiver's interactions within a classroom. Four scales were derived through a principal components analysis: positive interaction, punitiveness, permissiveness, and detachment. Items are rated on a 4-point scale. Observers achieved a criterion of 80% agreement in the original validation study.

The Literacy Environment Checklist, the Classroom Observation tool, and the Literacy Activities Rating Scale (Smith, Dickinson, & Sangeorge, 2002) are companion instruments in the Early Language Literacy Classroom Observation (ELLCO) Toolkit. The Literacy Environment Checklist has been used in preschool classrooms to assess the impact of a literacy intervention. The authors report Cronbach's alpha reliability coefficients for the Total score as .84, for the Books composite .73, and for the Writing composite .75. The Classroom Observation tool has been used in research to evaluate the quality of early literacy environments in preschool through Grade 5 settings. This measure includes two composites: General Classroom Environment, and Language, Literacy and Curriculum. The Cronbach's alpha reliability coefficient for the Total score was .90, for the General Classroom Environment was .83, and for the Language, Literacy and Curriculum was .86. Validity is reported as moderate correlations between the two Classroom Observation composite scores and total score and the Learning Environment scale of the Assessment Profile for Early Childhood Programs: Research Edition II (Abbott-Shim & Sibley, 1998). Smith et al. (2002) report that the Classroom Observation measure predicts children's early literacy development in receptive vocabulary and early literacy abilities. The Literacy Activities Rating Scale has only been used in preschool classrooms. The Cronbach's alpha reliability coefficients for the Total score were .66, for the Full-Group Book Reading composite .92, and for the Writing composite .73.

The Early Childhood Work Environment Survey (Jorde Bloom, 1993) is a measure designed to capture teacher attitudes about the early childhood center where they work. It asks teachers to rate the working conditions, practices, staff relations, and physical setting. The results help program administrators understand the teacher attitudes toward their working conditions and the organizational climate of the center. The measure is based on Jorde Bloom's theoretical and empirical work on program management strategies, congruence between administrator and teacher perceptions, and program improvement (Jorde Bloom, 1986a, 1986b).

The Policy and Program Management Inventory (PMI) (Lambert, Abbott-Shim, Oxford-Wright, 1997) was designed to measure management climate in Head Start programs. Particular attention was paid to the voice of Head Start teachers and their perceptions of administrators in the development of the items. Three validation studies have been completed that offer evidence for the reliability, construct validity, and predictive validity of the PMI (Lambert, 2002). The measure yields five scale scores: Communication, Hiring and Retention, Policy Clarity, Support, and Management Climate. Coefficient alpha reliabilities ranged from .87 for Policy Clarity to .98 for Management Climate. It also has been shown to be a useful indicator of teacher and administrator perceptual congruence as well as a correlate of teacher job satisfaction. All five of the PMI scale scores were correlated (.65–.74) with teacher job satisfaction.

MEASURES UNDER DEVELOPMENT OR IN EARLY STAGES OF USE

The development of measures of quality has lagged because it is a time-consuming and costly process, particularly when researchers apply the rigorous procedures of test construction. Although we have the benefits of advances in technology and sophisticated statistical analyses, gathering sufficiently large data sets over time remains cost prohibitive. Several measures, from among many currently under development, are highlighted here for the promise they have begun to show. The Program Administration Scale (Talan & Jorde Bloom, 2004) is an observational tool designed to measure the quality of early childhood leadership and management with a particular focus on the management systems in place within programs. The Classroom Assessment Scoring System (La Para, Pianta & Stuhlman, 2004) is an observational instrument that addresses classroom quality as measured by three major components: emotional support, classroom management, and instructional support. The instrument is being developed for observations in preschool through third grade classrooms. The CIRCLE Teacher Behavior Rating Scale (Landry, Gumnewig, Assel, Crawford, & Swank, 2004) is an observational tool that examines specific behaviors teachers can use to stimulate the cognitive and emergent literacy richness of the classroom environment. It shows promise as a tool that can fill a void in the current set of quality measures as it guides the observer to a wide range of intentional instructional activities that teachers can incorporate into their interactions with children. The Use of Center Time measure (Lambert & Mynhier, 2004) is an observational tool designed to capture whether a teacher makes use of the child-directed activities as instructional opportunities. The items outline a range of behaviors that teachers can use to extend, enhance, and guide the choices and interactions children display during center time and free play.

This chapter focuses primarily on standardized measures of quality. However, it is worth noting there are other valuable approaches to measuring quality and indicators of quality. Qualitative methods including key informant interviews and documents review are useful strategies. Secondary data sources also can provide invaluable contextual information, such as financial structures within the community, professional development opportunities, regulatory structures at the state level, and other political, economic, and social conditions that produce variation in the quality of early childhood settings (Phillips, 1996).

PURPOSES FOR MEASURING QUALITY

Scarr, Eisenberg, and Deater-Deckard (1994) identified three major purposes for measuring quality in early childhood settings. First, the measurement of quality for the regulation of child care evaluates a program against mandatory standards. Similarly, measuring quality for accreditation is a form of voluntary accountability to high standards. Both systems represent the application of summative evaluation in early childhood settings. Second, the evaluation of programs for quality improvement and development is formative in nature. In early childhood education formative evaluation strategies typically take place as programs prepare for accreditation and monitoring visits. Finally, the measurement of quality in early childhood settings takes place in empirical research. There is a wealth of literature in the field of early childhood education that tests hypotheses about both the predictors of quality and the child outcome correlates of quality. The following sections of this chapter will explore these three perspectives with the measurement of quality in the empirical literature reviewed for predictors and correlates of quality.

SUMMATIVE EVALUATION OF EARLY CHILDHOOD QUALITY

Chelimsky (1997) suggests that the purpose of summative evaluation is "evaluation for accountability." At the state and national level, external, summative evaluations are most commonly conducted by state licensing departments, Head Start, and NAEYC. These evaluations have significant practical applications and important implications for assessing program quality. Increasingly, summative evaluation is being used for high-stakes decision making about a program's eligibility for additional resources, continuation funding, or replication in other settings.

The mandatory, minimum quality standards of state licensing departments are designed to protect the health and safety of children and to enforce thresholds for minimum quality. These standards tend to focus on structural characteristics versus educational processes and both standards and assessment procedures vary considerably across states. Numerous studies have revealed that the quality of child care is higher in those states with more stringent child care regulations than in states with less stringent regulations (Helburn, Culkin, Morris, Howes, Phillipsen, Bryant, Clifford, Cryer, Peisner-Feinberg, Burchinal, Kagan, & Rustici, 1995, Howes, Smith, & Galinsky, 1995; Phillips, Mekos, Scarr, McCartney, & Abbott-Shim, 2000; Phillips & Zigler, 1987; Phillipsen, Burchinal, Howes, & Cryer, 1997; Whitebook, Howes, & Phillips, 1990; Zigler & Ennis, 1989; Zigler & Gilman,1993). Nevertheless, Taaffee-Young, White-Marsland, and Zigler (1997) contend that state licensing standards are inadequate measures of quality. Taaffee-Young and colleagues devised a 5-point rating system based on structural and programmatic dimensions of quality. This rating system provided "fine-grained" analyses of state regulations and allowed for within and across state analyses to determine the interrelatedness of the individual regulatory indices that affected quality. Based on this refined, uniform rating system, Taaffee-Young and colleagues reported that none of the state licensing standards met the criteria for "optimal" or "good" standards of developmentally appropriate practices, 33% of the state standards were minimally acceptable, 59% were poor, and 8% were very poor. In principle, state licensing standards are mandatory and protective. Yet, state monitoring agencies are routinely challenged by inadequate funding, excessive caseloads, and inconsistent interpretation of standards among monitoring staff. In an effort to streamline its monitoring system, Georgia reduced its evaluation tool to highly discriminating critical variables (Feine, 1988). This modified tool is used with programs with a history of compliance. No empirical evidence is available to determine if the change in the comprehensiveness of the evaluation process and accountability system impacted program quality.

Head Start mandates and evaluates quality against national performance standards. Program compliance is mandatory for continuation of funding. Head Start has developed its own comprehensive tool, Program Review Instrument for Systems Monitoring (PRISM), for self-evaluation and program improvement (Head Start Bureau, 2003). Using the PRISM, the Head Start Bureau conducts comprehensive, weeklong evaluations of Head Start programs to determine if the program is in compliance and effectively implementing the federally mandated Head Start Performance Standards.

In contrast, NAEYC standards are voluntary rather than mandatory and indicative of high quality professional standards. The current NAEYC Accreditation standards include interactions among teachers and children, curriculum, relationships among teachers and families, staff qualifications and professional development, administration, staffing, physical environment, health and safety, nutrition and food service, and evaluation (National Association for the Education of Young Children, 1998). Revised NAEYC standards, performance criteria, and assessment instruments are in the final stages of development and will be fully implemented in 2006 (National Association for the Education of Young Children, 2004). When a program's internal assessment is validated by an external agent, the program receives a professional accreditation designation.

NAEYC and Head Start program reviews are predicated on an assumption that the program meets state licensing standards. Because of the wide variation in standards among these three systems, each assessment of quality is distinctively different and one system cannot be used as proxy for another. Although all three evaluation systems are summative in character, each also provides an opportunity for programs to develop a plan of correction and therefore, to some degree, also serves a formative purpose.

In recent years, high-stakes, summative evaluation systems are emerging and are associated with differential reimbursement, or tiered reimbursement programs. Tiered reimbursement systems have been developed by states to provide a higher rate of reimbursement for subsidized children served in higher quality child care settings. The GAO reported that 38 states used differential reimbursement rates for subsidized child care to encourage administrators to improve the quality of their programs, including increased staff education or training, general quality improvements, facility improvements to promote health and safety, and accreditation (U.S. General Accounting Office, 2002).

Differential reimbursement systems require reliable and valid measurement of quality that distinguishes increments of quality. Some states, such as Maryland and Georgia, have relied upon national accreditation for the highest level of reimbursement (Gormley & Lucas, 2000). Many states have used correlates of quality such as staff education, ECERS ratings, staff compensation, and parent involvement. However there is insufficient empirical data that validates the incremental measurement of quality, particularly for high-stakes summative purposes. In addition, GAO reports that few states have evaluated the effects of their differential reimbursement programs as an incentive to improve quality.

FORMATIVE EVALUATION OF EARLY CHILDHOOD QUALITY

Although summative evaluation is focused on "accountability," formative evaluation is a "self-correcting" system and is generally situation specific. What applies in one situation is not necessarily expected to generalize to all situations but, rather, to address the specific circumstances of the conditions assessed; it is anticipated that the results are "point-in-time" findings and subject to change. Therefore, findings generally remain internal and are less likely to be reported in the empirical literature (Bella & Jorde Bloom, 2003; Sibley, VandeWiele, & Herrington, 1996). Despite increasing political and economic pressures, high-level stakeholders are less likely to be consumers of formative evaluation, preferring, instead, the concise "outcome-oriented" results of summative evaluation.

Formative evaluation assumes that a well-formulated theoretical foundation has been identified with clearly defined objectives for classroom practices and instructional approaches in order to achieve the desired outcomes. Ongoing assessment validates the fidelity of the implementation of a comprehensive curriculum, checks the practical application of theoretical assumptions, and measures progress toward realizing predefined objectives and outcomes. Formative evaluation is essentially a strategy for "self-correcting." Formative evaluation has the greatest potential to positively influence quality when the criteria, the measures, and the methodologies are expansive and contribute additional information to practitioners about their effectiveness in implementing their program. Formative evaluation measures are most informative when they are comprehensive and exploratory. In contrast, the ideal summative measures will possess the technical quality necessary to rely on highly discriminating, critical criteria.

Typically, programs that incorporate formative evaluation strategies have been programs with funding mandates, such as Head Start. The intent of the Head Start monitoring system is to ensure that grantees not only adhere to the mandated Head Start Performance Standards but also to the philosophy and goals of Head Start. Self-evaluation is central to the monitoring process and produces specific program improvement plans. As the public investment in Head Start has significantly increased, so has the pressure to report on outcomes for children and families. The combined approaches of formative and summative evaluation are critical to Head Start's ability to self-monitor and to respond to the public demands for accountability.

The Head Start experience forecasts the importance of formative and summative evaluation for subsidized, large-scale early childhood programs such as military child care programs, state-funded Pre-K programs, child care programs serving publicly subsidized children, and corporate child care chains. As the financial investment increases so does accountability. "The higher the stakes for programs and public investments, the more critical and rigorous are the standards for design, instrumentation, and analysis" (NAEYC & NAECS/SDE Joint Position Statement, 2003, p. 19).

Before the launch of the NAEYC accreditation system in 1985, formative evaluation or self-evaluation was largely unknown to early childhood practitioners. NAEYC was instrumental in bringing formative evaluation to the forefront for early childhood programs. National accreditation standards were established in response to the lack of uniform standards across the country and the lack of consensus in defining quality. Although the NAEYC accreditation system is a summative evaluation of quality, it has also incorporated the self-study process and therefore, formative evaluation. Ongoing evaluation is one of the accreditation standards and focuses on staff, program, and children.

When NAEYC established standards of quality and the first national accreditation system for early childhood programs, it also asserted that "achieving accreditation should not be viewed as an end-product, but rather as part of an on-going process of continuous quality improvement" (National Association for the Education of Young Children, 1998, p. 66). Although the self-study process documents that a program meets national accreditation standards, the intent of the accreditation system also was to utilize self-study as an ongoing "teaching and learning tool."

The approach to merging formative and summative evaluation systems is efficient and purposeful. At the same time, this duality of purpose is vulnerable to false positives. Because the formative and summative evaluation tools and methods are the same, program improvement efforts are susceptible to "teaching-to-the-test," which may produce short-term performance that lacks stability over time and overlooks the underlying concepts, spirit, and intent of the standards.

In addition, unlike Head Start, independently operated child care programs have generally lacked a well-defined theoretical approach, clearly defined educational goals, and a consensus about best practices for early education. The establishment of national accreditation standards was a landmark effort to articulate a theoretical approach based on developmentally appropriate practices for children birth to age 5 and to establish goals for best practices. In this context, accreditation has framed the theoretical foundation, identified goals, and developed the tools and process of both formative and summative evaluation. It is noteworthy that NAEYC reports that fewer than 10% of eligible early childhood programs participate in the accreditation system.

Researchers play an important role when they are able to work closely and collaboratively with practitioners to conduct formative evaluation. Researchers bring to the practitioner objectivity, knowledge of measurement, and expertise in scientific methodology. At the same time, to effectively design and implement a formative evaluation approach, researchers must work closely with the practitioners to reflect the philosophy, goals, implementation strategies, and context of their programs. Posavac and Carey (2003) suggest that "the evaluator's role falls somewhere between the role of the social scientist concerned about theory, the design of research, and the analysis of data" and that of "evaluators sensitive to the concerns and style of the service delivery staff" (p. 19). The degree to which researchers and practitioners are able to establish an open and genuinely collaborative relationship directly influences the richness and effectiveness of the formative evaluation process to document and influence the quality of practices.

PREDICTORS OF QUALITY

Researchers continue to examine the predictors of quality in early childhood settings and several reliable indices of child care quality have been documented and others are emerging from more recent studies. Classroom dynamics, or process quality, can be examined in regard to the development of instruments that measure overall quality. The factors or components of classroom quality and degree to which they are indicators of overall quality provide insights into the underlying constructs of classroom dynamics. The ECERS, ITERS, and FDCRS are the most well-known measures of process quality in early childhood settings. Factor analyses of the ECERS measure have consistently yielded two factors: interactions within the classroom environment, and the materials and physical features of that environment (Clifford, Rossbach, Burchinal, Lera, & Harms, 2002; Lamy & Frede, 2002).

In a second-order factor analysis, Abbott-Shim, Lambert and McCarty (2000) showed that the five scales on the Assessment Profile for Early Childhood Programs: Research Version (Abbott-Shim & Sibley, 1992) are observable representations of a single underlying construct of quality. It was found that the Curriculum scale had the highest path coefficients (.69 and .59) with the quality latent variable in two different data sets, each including approximately 175 classrooms. The Individualizing (.45 and .59) and Interacting (.59 and .52) scales had slightly lower path coefficients and the Learning Environment (.41 and .37) and Scheduling (.31 and .34) scales had the lowest coefficients.

In regard to the classroom structure dimension of quality, adult-child ratio and group size, there are somewhat inconsistent findings for the prediction of quality. The National Day Care Study (Ruopp et al. 1979) reported class size to be the single most important determinant of preschool children's learning experience and staff-child ratio was found to be a less important structural feature. Ruopp et al. (1979) found that an increase in the percentage of children not receiving appropriate caregiving actually accompanies the increase in number of children per adult. Whitebook et al. (1989) reported that a lower adult-child ratio was found to be associated with higher quality. This same finding held true for group size in that, as the group size increased, there was a general increase in the percentage of children receiving inappropriate caregiving and engaged in developmentally inappropriate activities. In additional analyses,

Howes, Phillips, and Whitebook (1992) found a modest negative relationship between adult-child ratio and appropriate caregiving as well as a similar relationship between group size and developmentally appropriate activities. The Cost, Quality, and Outcomes Study (Helburn et al., 1995) reported that the number of children per adult and staff wages were the most important factors in predicting classroom quality. In examining classroom structure within the Head Start setting, Abbott-Shim and her colleagues (2000) found that both class size and child-adult ratio had direct effects on classroom quality.

The adult-child ratio has not been a consistent predictor of quality in family child care homes either. The NICHD Study of Early Care (NICHD Early Child Care Research Network, 1996, 2000a, 2000b), the National Day Care Home Study (Fosburg, 1981), and several smaller studies (Clarke-Stewart, Gruber, & Fitzgerald, 1994) found that fewer children in the family child care home setting predicted higher quality care, whereas both the Family Child Care and Relative Study (Kontos, Howes, Shinn, & Galinski, 1995) and the Vancouver Day Care Project (Goelman & Pence, 1987) found the child care homes with more children but not large group sizes provided higher quality services.

The child care research indicates the importance of the relationship between staff characteristics and classroom quality. In regard to staff education, neither the definition of teacher qualifications (Doherty, 1991) nor the strength of the relationship with quality has been consistent across studies. Child-related education/training, but not formal education, was related to preschool classroom quality in the National Day Care Study (Ruopp et al., 1979). In another child care study, Berk (1985) dichotomized the teacher education variable into teachers with only a high school education and those with at least 2 years of college. Based on this distinction, it was found that the teacher's education was the most important predictor of the teachers' communicative behavior with children in the classroom. The National Child Care Staffing Study (Whitebook et al., 1989) found that teachers with more formal education and early childhood training at the college level demonstrated more sensitive and appropriate caregiving behaviors in the classroom. However, this study also found that teachers with postsecondary school training in early childhood education provided more appropriate caregiving. Furthermore, the Cost, Quality, and Outcomes Study (Helburn et al., 1995) found that the education level of the teaching staff was positively related to child care quality; higher quality centers had a higher proportion of their staff with at least a baccalaureate degree. Helburn et al. also found a modest correlation between quality and the teachers' early childhood training. In another child care study, Phillipsen et al. (1997) report that process quality, including overall quality, teacher sensitivity, and teacher-child interactions, was higher in classrooms with teachers with more formal education. Another important educational characteristic, adult literacy, as it predicts quality as measured by ITERS, ECERS, and FCDRS has been explored (Phillips, Crowell, & Whitebook, 2002). Child care teachers with higher English literacy provided higher quality language learning environments and these associations were sustained when the influence of the teachers' educational backgrounds were taken into account.

The findings on specialized training and formal education in family child care settings are more consistent. In the largest study of family child care homes (Kontos et al., 1995), caregivers with more education and training provided higher quality care in homes with more children than caregivers with less education and training in homes with fewer children. Burchinal, Howes, and Kontos (2002) also found that caregiver training most consistently predicted global quality in the family child care setting.

A limited body of literature has examined the relationship between Head Start quality and teachers' beliefs and attitudes, in describing staff characteristics. Granger and Marx (1988) used a randomly selected sample of Head Start teachers in New York City to report a relatively low level of teacher certification (50%) and a low level of teacher satisfaction with salary, benefits, and professional prestige. Granger (1989), in further analysis of these data, found correlations between teacher training, teacher stability, and program quality. Chafel (1992) presented a comprehensive argument that teachers' education, training, salaries, class size, and ratio are related to the funding level and quality of the Head Start program. Abbott-Shim et al. (2000) found that Head Start teachers' level of formal education directly affected their inappropriate beliefs about developmental teaching practices. Their inappropriate beliefs were associated with their inappropriate perceptions about developmental instructional activities, which in turn had a direct effect on classroom quality. Both teachers' educational level and teachers' beliefs had indirect effects on classroom quality through perceptions of instructional activities.

Turning to the broader early childhood research, Isenburg (1990) reviewed the research on teachers' beliefs and classroom practices, and suggested teachers' beliefs as well as behaviors may lead to an increased understanding of variation in practice. Although numerous researchers have focused primarily on the assessment of kindergarten teachers' beliefs and practices in relation to program characteristics, they have not specifically addressed the relationship to classroom quality (Burts, Hart, Charlesworth, DeWolf, Ray, Mannal, & Fleege, 1993; Rusher, McGrevin, & Lambiotte, 1992; Stipek, Daniels, Galuzzo, & Milburn, 1992). When Bryant, Clifford, and Peisner (1991) assessed kindergarten teachers' knowledge and attitudes about developmental appropriate practices, they found that the teachers' developmental appropriateness score along with the principals' score accounted for 18% of the variance in the total ECERS (Harms & Clifford, 1980) classroom quality score. In the development of the Classroom Practices Inventory (CPI), Hyson, Hirsh-Pasek, and Rescorla (1990) found a relationship between preschool teachers' educational attitudes and the CPI classroom quality score.

In a more recent study, the differences in Head Start teachers' beliefs and practices between those teaching in high, moderate and low quality classrooms have been examined (McCarty, Lambert, & Abbott-Shim, 1998). It was found that the teachers in lowquality classrooms had significantly higher scores on measures of inappropriate beliefs and inappropriate activities than teachers in moderate and high quality classrooms. Therefore, the teachers in low-quality classrooms tended to embrace statements about inappropriate beliefs and practices more than those teachers in either high or moderate quality classrooms.

The ability of administrators to employ, train, retain, and monitor quality teachers is crucial to a program's success in delivering high quality services to children and families. The stability of the teaching staff as shown through program efforts to hire and retain qualified teachers has been recognized as a component of program quality in child care (Doherty, 1995; Helburn et al., 1995; Howes & Olenick, 1986; Whitebook et al., 2001) and Head Start settings (Chafel, 1992; Granger, 1989; Granger & Marx, 1988). Child care research has shown that low pay, minimal benefits, and stressful work conditions are the major reasons for teachers leaving their jobs (Jorde-Bloom, 1987; Kontos & Stremmel, 1988; Whitebook et al., 2001).

Administrators also play a critical role in budgeting for staff salaries and benefits. Teachers' wages in child care have been linked to classroom quality. The National Child Care Staffing Study (Whitebook et al., 1989) reported that staff wages were the most important predictors of the quality of care that children receive. The Cost, Quality, and Outcomes Study (Helburn et al., 1995) reported that staff wages were one of the most important factors in predicting classroom quality. Other child care studies also have found that teachers' wages strongly predict quality (Howes et al., 1992; Phillipsen et al., 1997; Scarr et al., 1994). Phillips, Mekos, Scarr, McCartney, and Abbott-Shim (2000) found that teacher wages significantly predicted quality in infant, toddler and preschool classrooms, even after the variance attributable to regulatory and structural indicators of quality was removed.

Researchers have begun to explore the relationship between accreditation and other measures of quality. Smith and Endsley (1996) found that accredited family child care providers scored statistically significantly higher on five of the seven subscales of the Assessment Profile for Family Day Care Homes (Sibley & Abbott-Shim, 1987) than the nonaccredited family child care providers. Similarly, the National Association for the Education of Young Children (NAEYC) Accreditation predicted higher quality child care centers (Whitebook, Sakai, Gerber, & Howes, 2001). These researchers found higher overall quality for centers completing the self-study process and achieving accreditation than centers initiating the self-study process but not advancing to the validation phase and accreditation. Whitebook and her colleagues caution that nearly 40% of those centers achieving accreditation were rated as mediocre on the ECERS-R measure (Harms, Clifford, & Cryer, 1998). It is possible that the study by Whitebook et al., failed to establish concurrent validity because the purpose, data collection procedures, and scoring protocol for the two measures differ substantially. The accreditation process and instrument for measuring quality engages internal and external observers and involves consideration of all observed criteria. Because interrater reliability is not controlled and complex decision rules are not standardized, the probability of false positives increases. In contrast, the ECERS involves an external observer's rating of a series of criteria arranged in hierarchical and prerequisite order. If a lower-level, prerequisite criterion is not observed, then quality ratings are lowered even though higher-level criteria may have been observed. As a result higher performance indicators are dismissed and the probability of false negatives increases when measuring quality. This research signifies the need for further validation of measurement instruments and the significance of self-study, formative processes.

Turning to the parent and community involvement dimension, parent-caregiver communication systems have been explored. Ghazvini and Readdick (1994) have found that all three communication patterns (one-way, two-way, and three-way communication among parents, caregivers, and community resource staff) were positively correlated with the quality of care. Other researchers have examined both caregiver and parent attitudes regarding communication (Endsley & Minish, 1991; Hughes, 1985; Powell, 1977) but have not considered this variable in relation to quality. Wishard, Shivers, Howes, and Ritchie (2003) found modest associations between teacher articulated and program practices related to community involvement and classroom quality. Their findings suggest that the practices are related to quality yet based within ethnic communities. As Phillips (1996) advocates, there is a need to contextualize concepts of quality in early childhood research and further explore community-level constructs in relation to quality.

In summary, the GAO report (U.S. General Accounting Office, 2002) highlighted three major research reviews of predictors that contribute to child care quality and children's developmental progress. The three research teams concluded that the following specific structural components contribute to caregivers' ability to create developmentally supportive environments or children's developmental progress: the Science of Early Childhood Development Committee (Shonkoff & Phillips, 2000) researchers identified staff wages, lower staff turnover, caregiver education, and caregiver training; Vandell and Wolfe (2000) found smaller group size, lower child-to-staff ratios, caregiver education, and caregiver training; and Love, Schochet, and Meckstroth (1996) identified smaller group size, lower child-to-staff ratios, and safer equipment and space. The same research teams concluded that the following aspects of child-caregiver interactions contribute to children's developmental progress: caregiver continuity fosters attachment and social development, and the classrooms' verbal environment contributes to children's cognitive and language development (Shonkoff & Phillips, 2000); emotionally supportive and cognitively enriching settings contribute to children's development (Vandell & Wolfe, 2000); and Love and his colleagues (1996) identified appropriate caregiving, developmentally appropriate practice, and caregiver responsiveness as contributing to children's development. Further exploration of these same child outcome correlates of quality and others is provided in this next section.

OUTCOME CORRELATES OF QUALITY

Young children enter kindergarten with a wide range of developmental levels across the various domains. Although much of these differences can be associated with demographic and socioeconomic factors, attendance in preschool education has been associated with developmental advantages, particularly for children from lower income homes (Barnett, 1995, 1998; Frede, 1998). Most of this research was conducted by evaluating the impact of high-quality preschool programs. However, the quality of out-of-home care for American children varies greatly (Helburn et al., 1995; Howes et al., 1992; NICHD Early

Child Care Research Network, 2000b, 2003; Scarr, McCartney, Phillips, & Abbott-Shim, 1993). Therefore, researchers have focused on the connection between the quality of the classroom and child developmental outcomes, approaching quality both as a composite or global factor and as measuring specific dimensions of the environment. Although much of the research literature focuses on global measures of quality, it is also important to recognize that classroom practice is a multidimensional construct that is both influenced by and interacts with characteristics of the program, community and cultural context, and family (Wishard et al., 2003).

The relationship between child care quality and children's social development has been studied extensively over the last few decades (Bryant, Peisner-Feinberg, & Clifford, 1993; Howes, 2000; Howes & Hamilton, 1993; Howes & Olenick, 1986; Howes et al., 1992; McCartney, 1984; NICHD Early Child Care Research Network, 2000, 2003; Phillips & Howes, 1987; Phillips, McCartney, & Scarr, 1987; Ruopp et al., 1979; Scarr & Eisenberg, 1993; Vandell, Henderson & Wilson, 1988; Vandell & Powers, 1983; Whitebook et al., 1989). In general, children who experience high-quality child care demonstrate more positive social outcomes than children who experience low-quality child care (Shonkoff & Phillips, 2000).

Classroom quality in child care settings also has been connected with cognitive development (Doherty, 1991; Scarr & Eisenberg, 1993; Shonkoff & Phillips, 2000). Specifically, attendance in high quality child care has been linked to enhanced cognitive development for low-income children (Campbell & Ramey, 1994; Lazar & Darlington, 1982; McCartney, Scarr, Phillips, & Grajek, 1985; Wasik, Ramey, Bryant, & Sparling, 1990). The cognitive advantage of high-quality child care for young children has been shown to persist into the elementary schools years (Campbell & Ramey, 1994; Lazar & Darlington, 1982; Peisner-Feinberg, Clifford, Yazejian, Culkin, Howes, & Kagan, 1998).

In addition, the association between child care quality and the language development of toddlers and preschool-aged children has been studied for the last several decades and moderately strong positive associations have been demonstrated (Burchinal, Roberts, Riggins, Zeisel, Neebe, & Bryant, 2000; Goelman & Pence, 1987; McCartney, 1984; NICHD Early Child Care Research Network, 2000, 2003, Peterson & Peterson, 1986; Phillips et al., 1987; Schliecker, White, & Jacobs, 1991).

A substantial body of literature also has demonstrated the importance of quality child care to language development in infants (Burchinal, Roberts, Nabors, & Bryant, 1996; Melhuish, Lloyd, Martin, & Monney, 1990; O'Connell & Farran, 1982). The association between quality child care during infancy and cognitive and language development has been found to persist into the preschool (Burchinal, Lee, & Ramey, 1989; Roberts, Rabibowitch, Bryant, Burchinal, Koch, & Ramey, 1989) and elementary years (Vandell & Corasaniti, 1990).

Much of the child care literature employs global ratings of the quality of the classroom environment such as the ECERS (Harms & Clifford, 1980) in relation to social skills. For example, in child care settings that were higher in overall quality children were found to display more smiling and laughing, to show a greater intensity of positive affect, and to display less intense negative affect than children in lower quality settings (Hestenes, Kontos,

& Bryan, 1993). Although type of care children receive (home, center, or family setting) has not shown a relationship to their social skills, the quality of the care has been associated with their social functioning (Lamb, Hwang, Broberg, & Bookstein, 1988). Higher overall quality was associated with fewer internalizing and social withdrawal problems and more positive social behaviors. In addition, 4-year-old boys who attended high quality care were described as having lower levels of fearfulness and unhappiness, and better social skills, as compared to boys in lower quality care (Hagekull & Bohlin, 1995).

Classroom quality in child care settings also has been conceptualized in a very comprehensive way, using multiple indicators of both process and structural features. Using this strategy, classroom quality has been associated with the quality of children's experiences in child care, their competent peer behaviors, and their participation in learning activities (Wishard et al., 2003). Many research studies have identified specific features of the quality of the classroom. Both structural features of the classroom, such as group size, and process dimensions, such as the warmth, safety, stimulation, nurturance, and richness of interactions, have been associated with developmental outcomes for young children (Shonkoff & Phillips, 2000). The remainder of this section will focus on studies of particular aspects of quality and their relationship to child outcomes.

Relatively few studies exist that have explored the relationship between classroom quality and child social functioning in preschool settings such as Head Start which serve predominantly low income children. In one study, the overall quality of Head Start classroom environments was not related to teachers' ratings of children's social behaviors (Bryant, Lau, Burchinal, & Sparling, 1994). However, when specific instructional strategies of the teacher were examined in Head Start settings, several associations between quality and child outcomes were found. For example, children tended to generalize the positive social behaviors they learn in Head Start to other settings when classrooms had a balanced and varied schedule. This scheduling dimension of quality also moderated the influence of maternal depression on child disruptive behaviors in the classroom (Lambert, Abbott-Shim, & McCarty, 1999).

The Head Start teacher's ability to recognize individual differences in children and individualize instruction based on these differences was found to moderate the relationship between the child's age and teacher ratings on a developmental checklist. The individualizing scale score from the Assessment Profile for Early Childhood Programs: Research Version (Abbott-Shim & Sibley, 1992) was negatively associated with the age-postassessment slope, indicating that age mattered less to a child's progress on the checklist in classrooms in which the teacher was able to tailor classroom activities to the unique needs of children who are younger than their peers (Lambert, Abbott-Shim, & McCarty, 1998).

Higher quality Head Start classrooms tended to have lower mean scores on a parent-reported measure of children's problem behaviors. In addition, the teacher's ability to individualize instruction tended to moderate the association between the child's age and prosocial behaviors while also moderating the association between maternal depression and parents' reports of their children's problem behaviors (Lambert, Abbott-Shim, & McCarty, 2002).

With regard to classroom dynamics, Howes et al. (1992) showed that children in child care settings who are more secure in their relationships with their caregivers tended to also exhibit more positive peer interactions in the classroom. This security has been associated with teachers who exhibited more appropriate caregiving behaviors, whereas lower quality teachers tended to engender more avoidant and ambivalent responses from children. Low classroom quality also has been associated with more solitary and purposeless behavior in children (Vandell & Powers, 1983). The acquisition of social competence in young children does not, therefore, appear to be simply related to extended contact with peers but, rather, to the positive classroom dynamics that generate from teachers who are able to create the appropriate context for positive peer interactions.

Several studies have attempted to establish a connection between caregivers' ability to interact with children in a positive and nurturing manner and the development of children. Children who form secure attachments to their caregivers tend to exhibit more social competence when interacting with peers (Howes, 1987; Howes, Matheson, & Hamilton, 1994; Pianta & Nimetz, 1991). A teaching style characterized by respectful, engaging, responsive, and democratic interactions with children was associated with more child knowledge of social problem solving (Holloway & Reichhart-Erickson, 1988).

Love (1993) found that when caregivers were attentive and encouraging in their interactions with children, the children exhibited fewer negative social behaviors, such as fighting and crying, and were more likely to be involved in classroom activities. The quality of caregiver-child interactions was associated with children's social adjustment and behavior problems (Scarr, McCartney, Abbott-Shim, Phillips, & Eisenberg, 1995). Children's affect was also associated with the quality of the caregiving behaviors exhibited by teachers (Hestenes et al., 1993).

Child care and preschool research has examined the relationships between structural features and the developmental progress of children. Small group sizes and children to adult ratios have been associated with positive outcomes for children (Bowman et al., 2001). Specifically, children in classes with more favorable group sizes and ratios have been shown to engage in more social interaction and complex play, as well as more complex language and cognitive gains (Howes, 1997; Howes et al., 1992; Kontos, Howes, & Galinsky, 1997; Layzer, Goodson, & Moss, 1993; McGurk, Mooney, Moss, & Poland, 1995; Phillipsen et al., 1997; Smith, 1999). Given a low student-teacher ratio and adequate classroom space as opposed to more crowded conditions, Holloway and Reichhart-Erickson (1988) found that children spent more time engaging in focused, solitary play.

The wages that a program pays have been linked to staff turnover, classroom quality, and child social development (Whitebook et al., 1989). Children who experience a series of caregivers and who lack a stable caregiving arrangement have been shown to be at risk for poor peer relationships and a poor ability to maintain interest in engaging in social interactions (Cummings, 1980; Rubenstein & Howes, 1979). Preschool children who transfer classes or schools tend to show increased negative affect, activity level, physical aggression, and sleep disturbance (Howes, 1987).

Teacher turnover has been associated with children's social behaviors in child care settings. Children who maintained secure relationships with their caregivers had a higher frequency of complex play when they did not change teachers than when they did. High turnover rates in child care centers also were associated with more aggressive behaviors in 4-year-old children (Howes & Hamilton, 1993). Teacher turnover also has been associated with lower parental satisfaction with child care services, higher parental anxiety about leaving the child in care, and lower parental confidence that child care would bring about benefits for the child (Shinn, Phillips, Howes, Galinsky, & Whitebook, 1991).

Not all of the child care research has reported positive benefits for children. Recent child care research has demonstrated associations between time spent in out-of-home care and increases in the stress response (Watamura, Donzella, Alwin, & Gunnar, 2003). Problem behaviors, including aggressive and defiant behaviors, also have been associated with time spent in care (NICHD Early Child Care Research Network, 2003). However, these findings may not contraindicate child care itself, as much as they demonstrate the risks presented to children by low quality care (Greenspan, 2003).

CONCLUSION

This chapter has attempted to describe the current climate of early childhood education as it strives to measure, understand, and improve the quality of the services provided to children and families. This chapter has examined the history of research on the quality of early childhood programs, discussed the purposes of quality assessment, reviewed several of the more widely used instruments, and summarized some of the literature focusing on the predictors and correlates of quality.

Research evidence has demonstrated that high quality care helps children develop foundational skills for later success in school. It helps children development cognitively and socially by preparing them for the emergent academic skills of kindergarten, and by helping them transition to the social role of student. In summary, high-quality settings prepare children for lifelong learning by helping them engage with learning, and develop problem-solving skills, a healthy curiosity and optimism about the world around them, and a sense of security and attachment to caregivers. When care is available, affordable, and of high quality, it enables parents to work outside the home with less stress about their children's experiences in care settings.

However, most American children who receive care outside the home are still served by settings of poor to moderate quality. Future research on the quality of these settings can contribute to the theoretical knowledge base of the field and to the ongoing policy debates regarding funding, governance, accountability, and quality improvement strategies for early childhood and education programs. As more public funding enters the child care marketplace, the demand for quality teachers and caregivers continues to rise. Further research is needed to determine the most optimal strategies for educating, training, and retaining qualified teachers.

The current policy climate for early childhood settings includes a strong focus on quantitative indicators of the success of educational and social programs. The public demand for early childhood childhood education has extended to include the majority of American young children. This demand is growing and reaches early childhood practitioners accompanied by a host of regulatory demands, a web of funding intricacies, and high expectations from parents and policy makers about the quality of the services and the impact of public investments in their delivery. These challenges embody an opportunity for the field to grow and evolve.

More evidence is needed to demonstrate the effectiveness of specific instructional strategies that teachers can use to guide children's learning and development. As more focus is placed on child outcomes and aggregated test scores as the mark of quality, research is addressing the evaluation of instructional strategies designed to enhance scores on specific child outcome measures (U.S. Department of Education, 2004). In order to be most useful to practitioners and researchers alike, such studies will need to highlight the overall impact of targeted instructional strategies on both the quality of the classroom environment and overall child development across all domains, while offering the processes needed to adopt and implement those instructional strategies that show promise.

The next phases of research on the quality of care for young children can expand the current horizons by continuing to take a broader view of quality. The use of comprehensive batteries of measurement strategies including multiple informants and data sources beyond the child and classroom, such as the family and community contexts, can enrich the description of quality. A broader view of quality requires expanded theoretical models that attempt to describe and explain the quality of early childhood settings along with strategies for quality improvement. Corresponding advances in analytical strategies are also necessary to test broader models of quality.

Given that the field of research and evaluation in early childhood education has been developing and using a range of measures of the classroom quality for many years, it is uniquely situated to impact the broader arena of educational research. Although there is a need to continue to both improve the technical properties of the measurement tools used to measure quality and revise and update them as the knowledge base and theory expand, such a broad foundation of research and measurement tools, for the most part, does not exist at the elementary and secondary levels in American education (for a notable exception, see the Assessment of Practices in Early Elementary Classrooms [APEEC]; Hemmeter, Maxwell, Ault, & Schuster, 2001). The next phase of early childhood research could focus on models of the successful use of data from quality measurements as the centerpieces in systems of reflection and quality improvement. Early childhood research is poised to demonstrate that child developmental progress is most successfully enhanced when sound theoretically and empirically based care and instructional strategies are realized in the classroom by practitioners who are capable of their complete and proper implementation, reflective about their own practice, and equipped with quality feedback about their successive attempts at quality improvement. This process assumes a link between formative and summative assessment and evaluation, program administrators who understand how to nurture and develop teachers and caregivers, and a policy climate that permits reward structures sufficient to retain these key players as they develop. It does not assume that quality improvement is the singular arena of off-the-shelf instructional strategies that only have meaning and value in their ability to quickly impact test scores.

If early childhood research and evaluation is to provide the models for the processes that lead from innovations to enhanced child outcomes, then there are several new directions for instrument development work as it relates to quality. First, the field needs to continue to augment the existing battery of measures designed to capture global features of the classroom environment, with reliable, valid, and culturally sensitive measures that focus on specific intentional instructional strategies which teachers and caregivers can understand and implement. This effort can take the form of both implementation checklists associated with specific curricular and instructional strategies and observational measures that focus on fine grained aspects of teacher-child interactions. In addition, teacher performance appraisal instruments used in public school settings with early childhood teachers are often the same measures used with teachers who work in the elementary and secondary levels, or loose adaptations thereof. If early childhood teachers are encouraged to reflect about and improve their practice as the concepts of best practice continue to evolve, then the feedback they receive about their performance and growth as professionals will be most helpful if it is specific to quality early childhood settings.

Therefore, the challenge for early childhood researchers is to adequately reflect the breadth and depth of the contexts that influence child development and do so through reliable, valid, and culturally sensitive measurements that provide meaningful feedback to practitioners. This challenge entails developing and testing both formative and summative systems of evaluation that draw upon the information provided by our best measurement tools. These systems can provide guidance to administrators and teachers who strive to provide quality services about the processes through which practice can change and improve, while offering actionable information to policy makers.

References

Abbott-Shim, M. (1991). *Quality care: A global assessment.* Unpublished manuscript. Georgia State University.

Abbott-Shim, M., Lambert, R., & McCarty, F. (2000). Structural model of Head Start classroom quality, *Early Childhood Research Quarterly, 15*(1), 115–134.

Abbott-Shim, M., Neel, J., & Sibley, A. (2001). *Assessment profile for early childhood programs: Research edition II: Technical manual.* Atlanta, GA: Quality Counts, Inc.

Abbott-Shim, M., & Sibley, A. (1992). *Assessment profile for early childhood programs: Research version.* Atlanta, GA: Quality Assist, Inc.

Abbott-Shim, M., & Sibley, A. (1998). *Assessment profile for early childhood programs: Research edition II.* Atlanta, GA: Quality Counts, Inc.

Abbott-Shim, M., & Sibley, A. (1987). *Assessment profile for early childhood programs: Preschool, toddler, infant, school age and administration.* Atlanta, GA: Quality Assist, Inc.

Abbott-Shim, M., & Sibley, A. (1993). *Assessment profile for homes with young children: Research version.* Atlanta, GA: Quality Assist, Inc.

American Educational Research Association (AERA), American Psychological Association (APA) and National Council on Measurement in Education (NCME). (1999). *Standards for educational and psychological testing.* Washington, DC: AERA Publications.

Arnett, J. (1989). Caregivers in day care centers: Does training matter? *Developmental Psychology, 10,* 541–552.

Barnett, W. S. (1995). Long-term effects of early childhood programs on cognitive and school outcomes. *The Future of Children, 4,* 25–50.

Barnett, W. S. (1998). Long-term effects on cognitive and school success. In W. S. Barnett and S. S. Boocock (Eds.), *Early care and education for children in poverty: Promises, programs and long-term outcomes* (pp. 11–44). Albany, NY: State University of New York Press.

Bella, J., & Jorde Bloom, P. (2003). *ZOOM: The impact of early childhood leadership training on role perceptions, job performance, and career decisions.* Wheeling, IL: The Center for Early Childhood Leadership.

Belsky, J., & Steinberg, L. D. (1978). The effects of daycare: A critical review. *Child Development, 49*(4), 92–949.

Berk, L. (1985). Relationships of educational attainment, child-oriented attitudes, job satisfaction, and career commitment to care giver behavior toward children. *Child Care Quarterly, 14,* 103–129.

Bloom, P. J. (1986a). Teacher job satisfaction: A framework for analysis. *Early Childhood Research Quarterly, 15,* 182–197.

Bloom, P. J. (1986b). *A model for improving the quality of work life in the early childhood setting.* Paper presented at the annual meeting of the Midwest Educational Research Association, Chicago, IL.

Bowlby, J. (1951). *Childcare and the growth of love.* Harmondsworth: Penguin.

Bowman, B., Donovan, S. M., & Burns, S. (2000). *Eager to Learn: National Research Council, Commission on Behavioral and Social Sciences and Education.* Washington DC: National Academy Press.

Bradley, R. (1994). The HOME Inventory: Review and reflections. In H. W. Reese (Ed.), *Advances in child development and behavior* (Vol. 25, pp. 241–288). Orlando, FL: Academic Press.

Bradley, R. H., & Caldwell, B. M. (1984). The HOME Inventory and family demographics. *Developmental Psychology, 20*(2), 315–320.

Bradley, R., Caldwell, B., & Corwyn, R. (2003). The child care HOME inventories: Assessing the quality of child care homes. *Early Childhood Research Quarterly, 18*(3), 294–309.

Bradley, R., Corwyn, R., & Whiteside-Mansell, L. (1996). Life at home: Same time, different places—An examination of the HOME Inventory in different cultures. *Early Development and Parenting, 6,* 1–19.

Bronfenbrenner, U. (1979). *The ecology of human development: Experiences by nature and design.* Cambridge, MA: Harvard University Press.

Bryant, D. M., Clifford, R. M., & Peisner, E. S. (1991). Best practices for beginners: Developmental appropriateness in the kindergarten. *American Educational Research Journal 28*(4), 783–803.

Bryant, D. M., Clifford, R. M., & Peisner-Feinberg, E. (1993). *Evaluation of public preschool programs in North Carolina: Final report.* Chapel Hill, NC: Frank Porter Graham Child Development Center.

Bryant, D., Lau, L., Burchinal, M., & Sparling, J. (1994). Family and classroom correlates of Head Start children's developmental outcomes. *Early Childhood Research Quarterly, 9,* 289–310.

Burchinal, M., Lee, M., & Ramey, C. (1989). Type of day-care and preschool intellectual development in disadvantaged children. *Child Development, 60,* 128–137.

Burchinal, M., Roberts, J., Nabors, L., & Bryant, D. (1996). Quality of center child care and infant cognitive and language development. *Child Development, 67,* 606–620.

Burchinal, M., Roberts, J., Riggins, R., Zeisel, S., Neebe, E., & Bryant, D. (2000). Relating quality of center-based child care to early cognitive and language development longitudinally. *Child Development, 71*(2), 339–357.

Burchinal, M. R., Howes, C., & Kontos, S. (2002). Structural predictors of child care quality in child care homes. *Early Childhood Research Quarterly, 17,* 87–105.

Burts, D., Hart, C., Charlesworth, R., De Wolf, M., Ray, J., Mannal, K., & Fleege, P. (1993). Developmental appropriateness of kindergarten programs, and academic outcomes in first grade. *Journal of Research in Childhood Education, 8*(1), 23–31.

Campbell, F., & Ramey, C. (1994). Effects of early intervention on intellectual and academic achievement: A follow-up study of children from low-income families. *Child Development, 65,* 684–698.

Chafel, J. (1992). Funding Head Start: What are the issues? *American Journal of Orthopsychiatry, 62*(1), 9–21.

Chelimsky, E. (1997). *The* coming transformations in evaluation. In E. Chelimsky and W. Shadish (Eds.), *Evaluation for the 21st century: A handbook* (pp. 1–26). Thousand Oaks, CA: Sage Publications.

Clarke-Stewart, K. A., Gruber, C. P., & Fitzgerald, L. M. (1994). *Children at home and in day care.* Mahwah, NJ: Lawrence Erlbaum Associates.

Clarke-Stewart, K. A., Vandell, D. L., Burchinal, M., O'Brien, M., & McCartney, K. (2002). Do regulable features of child-care homes affect children's development? *Early Childhood Research Quarterly, 17*(1), 52–86.

Clifford, R., Rossbach, H., Burchinal, M., Lera, M., & Harms, T. (2002). *Factor structure of the Early Childhood Environment Rating Scale (ECERS): An international comparison.* Manuscript in preparation.

Clifford, R., Russell, S., Fleming, J., Peisner, E., Harms, T., & Cryer, D. (1989). *Infant Toddler Environment Rating Scale (ITERS), Reliability and Validity Studies.* Chapel Hill: Frank Porter Graham Child Development Center, University of North Carolina.

Constantine, N., & Iverson, A. (1995). Review of the Infant Toddler Rating Scale (ITERS). In Conoley, J., & Impara J. (Eds.), *The Twelfth Mental Measurements Yearbook* (pp. 483–48). Lincoln, NE: Buros Institute of Mental Measurements.

Cummings, E. (1980). Caregiver stability and daycare. *Developmental Psychology, 16,* 31–37.

Dickinson, D. K. (2002). Shifting Images of Developmentally Appropriate Practice As Seen Through Different Lenses. *Educational Researcher, 31*(1), 26–32.

Doherty, G. (1991). *Quality matters in child care.* Huntsville: The Jesmond Publications.

Doherty, G. (1995). *Quality matters: Excellence in early childhood programs.* Reading, MA: Addison-Wesley Publishers.

Endsley, R., & P. Minish. 1991. "Parent-Staff Communication in Day Care Centers during Morning and Afternoon Transitions," *Early Childhood Research Quarterly, 6*(2), 119–135.

Feine, R. J. (1988). Human Services Instrument Based Program Monitoring and Indicated Systems. In S. LaMendola (Ed.), *Information Technology and Human Services.* Thousand Oaks, CA: Sage Publishing.

Fosburg, S. (1981). *Family day care in the United States: National day care home study, Vol. I, summary of findings.* (Office of Human Development Services, DHHS Publication No. (OHDS) 80-30282). Washington, DC: U.S. Department of Health and Human Services.

Frede, E. C. (1998). Preschool program quality in programs for children in poverty. In W. S. Barnett & S. S. Boocock (Eds.), *Early care and education for children in poverty, promises, programs and long-term outcomes* (pp. 11-44). Buffalo: SUNY.

Ghazvini, A. S., & Readdick, C. A. (1994). Parent-caregiver communication and quality of care in diverse child care settings. *Early Childhood Research Quarterly, 9*(2), 207-222.

Goelman, H., & Pence, A. (1987). Effects of child care, family, and individual characteristics on children's language development: The Victoria day care research project. In D. Phillips (Ed.), *Quality in child care: What does the research tell us?* (pp. 89-104). Washington, DC: National Association for the Education of Young Children.

Gormley, W. T., Kagan, S. L., & Cohen, N. E. (1995). Options for government and business roles in early care and education: Targeted entitlements and universal supports. New Haven, Conn: Quality 2000, Yale University.

Gormley, W., & Lucas, J. (2000, August). *Money, Accreditation, and Child Care Center Quality.* Paper prepared for the Foundation for Child Development. New York, NY.

Granger, R. (1989). The staffing crisis in early childhood education. *Phi Delta Kappan, 71*(2), 130-134.

Granger, R., & Marx, E. (1988). *Who is teaching? Early childhood teachers in New York City's publicly funded programs.* New York: Bank Street College of Education.

Greenspan, S. (2003). Child care research: A clinical perspective. *Child Development, 74,* 1064-1068.

Hagekull, B., & Bohlin, G. (1995). Child care Quality, Family and Child Characteristics and Socioemotional Development. *Early Childhood Research Quarterly, 10,* 505-526.

Harms, T., Cryer, D., & Clifford, R. (1990). *Infant Toddler Environment Rating Scale (ITERS).* New York: Teachers College Press.

Harms, T., Cryer, D., & Clifford, R. (2003). *Infant Toddler Environment Rating Scale-Revised (ITERS-R).* New York: Teachers College Press.

Harms, T., & Clifford, R. (1980). *Early Childhood Environment Rating Scale (ECERS).* New York: Teachers College Press.

Harms, T., Clifford, R., & Cryer, D. (1998). *Early Childhood Environment Rating Scale-Revised (ECERS-R).* New York: Teachers College Press.

Harms, T., & Clifford, R. (1984). *Family Day Care Rating Scale (FDCRS).* New York: Teachers College Press.

Head Start Bureau. (2003). *Program Review Instrument for Systems Monitoring of Head Start and Early Head Start Grantees (PRISM).* Washington, DC: Head Start Information and Publication Center.

Helburn, S., Culkin, M., Morris, J., Mocan, N., Howes, C., Phillipsen, L., Bryant, D., Clifford, R., Cryer, D., Peisner-Feinberg, E., Burchinal, M., Kagan, S., & Rustici, J. (1995). *Cost, quality, and child outcomes in child care centers.* Denver: University of Colorado at Denver.

Hestenes, L., Kontos, S., & Bryan, Y. (1993). Children's emotional expression in child care centers varying in quality. *Early Childhood Research Quarterly, 8,* 295-307.

High Scope Educational Research Foundation, (1998). *Program Quality Assessment (PQA)- Preschool Version.* Ypsilanti, MI: High Scope Press.

Hofferth, S., & Phillips, D. A. (1987). Childcare in the United States, 1970-1995. *Journal of Marriage and Family, 49,* 559-571.

Holloway, S. D., & Reichhart-Erickson, M. (1988). The relationship of child care quality to children's free-play behavior and social problem-solving skills. *Early Childhood Research Quarterly, 3,* 39-53.

Horn, W. (2003). *Head Start Bulletin: Improving Head Start: A Common Cause.* (Issue 76).

Howes, C. (2000). Social-emotional classroom climate in child care, child-teacher relationships, and children's second grade peer relations. *Social Development, 9,* 191-204.

Howes, C. (1997). Children's experiences in center-based child care as a function of teacher background and adult-child ratio. *Merrill-Palmer Quarterly 43*(3), 404-425.

Howes, C. (1987). Social competency with peers: contributions from child care. *Early Childhood Research Quarterly, 2,* 155-167.

Howes, C., & Hamilton, C. E. (1993). The changing experience of child care: changes in teachers and in teacher-child relationships and children's social competence with peers. *Early Childhood Research Quarterly, 8,* 15-32.

Howes, C., Matheson, C., & Hamilton, C. (1994). Maternal, teacher, and child care history correlates of children's relationships with peers. *Child Development, 65,* 264-273.

Howes, C., & Olenick, M. (1986). Child care & family influences on toddlers' compliance. *Child Development, 57,* 202-216.

Howes, C., Phillips, D., & Whitebook, M. (1992). Thresholds of quality: Implications for the social development of children in center-based care. *Child Development, 63,* 449-460.

Howes, C., Smith, E., & Galinsky, E. (1995). *The Florida child care quality improvement study: Interim report.* New York: Families and Work Institute.

Howes, C., & Stewart, P. (1987). Child's play with adults, toys and peers: An examination of family and child care influences. *Developmental Psychology 23,* 423-430.

Hughes, R. (1985). The informal help-giving of home and center child care providers. *Family Relations, 34,* 359-366.

Hyson, M., Hirsh-Pasek, K., & Rescorla, L. (1990). Classroom Practices Inventory (CPI): An observation instrument based on NAEYC's guidelines for developmentally appropriate practices for 4- and 5-year-old children. *Early Childhood Research Quarterly, 5*(4), 475-494.

Isenberg, J. P. (1990). Reviews of research, Teachers thinking and beliefs about classroom practices. *Childhood Education, 66,* 5, 322-327.

Iverson, A. (1992). Review of the Family Day Care Rating Scale (FDCRS). In J. Kramer & J. Conoley (Eds.), *The Eleventh Mental Measurements Yearbook* (pp. 339-340). Lincoln, NE: Buros Institute of Mental Health.

Jorde Bloom, P. (1993). *Early Childhood Work Environment Survey.* Evanston, IL: Early Childhood Professional Development Project, National-Louis University.

Jorde Bloom, P. (1987). Training for Early Childhood Leadership and Advocacy: A Field-based Model, *Illinois School Research and Development 24*(1), 29-33.

Jorde Bloom, P. (1986a). Teacher job satisfaction: A framework for analysis. *Early Childhood Research Quarterly, 15,* 182-197.

Jorde Bloom, P. (1986b). *A model for improving the quality of work life in the early childhood setting.* Paper presented at the annual meeting of the Midwest Educational Research Association, Chicago, IL.

Kagan, S. L. (1993). *The essential functions of the early care and education system: Rationale and definition.* (Essential Functions and Change Strategies Task Force). New Haven, CT: Quality 2000, Yale University.

Kagan, S. L., Moore, E., & Bredekamp, S. (Eds.) (1997). *Getting a good start in school.* Washington, DC: National Education Goals Panel.

Kontos, S., Howes, C., & Galinsky, E. (1997). Does training make a difference to quality in family child care. *Early Childhood Research Quarterly, 12,* 351-372.

Kontos, S., Howes, C., Shinn, M., & Galinsky, E. (1995). *Quality in Family Child Care and Relative Care.* New York: Teachers College Press, Columbia University.

Kontos, S., & Stremmel, A. J. (1988). Caregivers' perceptions of working conditions in a child care environment. *Early Childhood Research Quarterly, 3,* 77-90.

Lamb, M. E., Hwang, C., Broberg, A., & Bookstein, F. L. (1988). The effects of out-of-home care on the development of social competence in Sweden: A longitudinal study. *Early Childhood Research Quarterly, 3*, 379-402.

Lambert, R. (2003). Considering purpose and intended use when making evaluations of assessments: A response to Dickinson. *Educational Researcher, 32(4)*, 1-4.

Lambert, R. (2002). Evaluating management climate in Head Start programs: The measurement properties of the Policy and Program Management Inventory. *NHSA Dialog: A Research-to-Practice Journal for the Early Intervention Field, 6*, 37-52.

Lambert, R., & Abbott-Shim, M. (2003, March). *An evaluation of a structured mentoring program for early childhood teachers: The Individualized Learning Intervention.* Paper presented at the annual meeting of the North Carolina Association for Research in Education, Holly Springs.

Lambert, R., Abbott-Shim, M., & Oxford-Wright, C. (1997). *Policy and Program Management Inventory (PMI).* Atlanta: Center for the Study of Adult Literacy, Georgia State University.

Lambert, R., Abbott-Shim, M., & McCarty, F. (2002). The relationship between classroom quality and ratings of the social functioning of Head Start children. *Early Child Development and Care, 172(3)*, 231-245.

Lambert, R., Abbott-Shim, M., & McCarty, F. (1999, April). *Social functioning of Head Start children in classrooms of varying quality.* Paper presented at the biennial meeting of the Society for Research in Child Development, Albuquerque, NM.

Lambert, R., Abbott-Shim, M., & McCarty, F. (1998). The influence of teacher individualizing practices on child developmental progress. *NHSA Dialog: A Research-to-Practice Journal for the Early Intervention Field, 2(1)*, 75-88.

Lambert, R., & Mynhier, A. (2004). *Use of center time.* Charlotte: Department of Educational Leadership, UNC Charlotte.

Lamy, C., & Frede, E. (2002, April). *Measuring classroom quality in urban preschool settings.* Paper presented at the annual meeting of the American research Association, New Orleans, LA.

Landry, S. H., Gumnewig, S., Assel, M., Crawford, A., & Swank, P. (2004). *The CIRCLE Teacher Observation Rating Scale.* Unpublished manuscript.

La Paro, K. M., Pianta, R. C., & Stuhlman, M. (2004). Classroom Assessment Scoring System (CLASS); Findings from the Pre-K Year. *The Elementary School Journal, 104(5)*, 409-426.

Layzer, J., Goodson, B., & Moss, M. (1993). *Life in preschool, Vol. I of an observational study of early childhood programs for disadvantaged four year olds: Final report.* Cambridge, MA: Abt Associates.

Lazar, I., & Darlington, R. (1982). Lasting effects of early education: A report from the Consortium for Longitudinal Studies. *Monographs of the Society for Research in Child Development, 47(2-3), Serial No. 195*.

Love, J. (1993). *Does children's behavior reflect child care classroom quality?* (ERIC Document Reproduction Service No. 356085).

Love, J., Meckstroth, A., & Sprachman, S. (1997). *Measuring the quality of program environments in Head Start and other early childhood programs: A review and recommendations for future research.* Washington, DC: National Center for Education Statistics. (Report No. NCES-9736).

Love, J. M., Schochet, P. Z., & Meckstroth, A. (1996). *Are they in any real danger? What research does—and doesn't—tell us about child care quality and children's well-being.* Plainsboro, NJ: Mathematica Policy Research.

Mardell-Czudnowski, C., & Goldenberg, D. (1990). *Developmental Indicators for the Assessment of Learning-Revised.* Circle Pines, MN: American Guidance Services, Inc.

McCarty, F., Lambert, R., & Abbott-Shim, M. (1998). An examination of teacher beliefs and practices, and their relationship to Head Start classroom quality. *NHSA Dialog: A Research-to-Practice Journal for the Early Intervention Field, 2(1)*, 91-94.

McCartney, K. (1984). Effects of quality of day care environment on children's language development. *Developmental Psychology, 20*, 244-260.

McCartney, K., Scarr, S., Phillips, D., & Grajek, S. (1985). Day care as intervention: Comparisons of varying quality programs. *Journal of Applied Developmental Psychology, 6*, 247-260.

McGurk, H., Mooney, A., Moss, P., & Poland, G. (1995). *Staff-child ratios in care and education services for young children.* London: HMSO.

Melhuish, E., Lloyd, E., Martin, S., & Monney, A. (1990). Type of child care at 18 months: Relations with cognitive and language development. *Journal of Child Psychology and Psychiatry and Allied Disciplines, 31(6)*, 861-870.

Moore, E., & Yzaguirre, R. (2004, June 9). Head Start's National Reporting System Fails Our Children. *Education Week*.

National Association for the Education of Young Children (NAEYC) and National Association of Early Childhood Specialists in State Departments of Education (NAECS/SDE). (2003). *Joint Position Statement: Early childhood curriculum, child assessment, and program evaluation—Building and accountable and effective system for children birth through age eight.* Washington, DC: NAEYC Publications.

National Association for the Education of Young Children (NAEYC). (1998). *NAEYC accreditation criteria and procedures of the National Association for the Education of Young Children.* Washington, DC: NAEYC Publications.

National Association for the Education of Young Children (NAEYC). (2004). Retrieved November 13, 2003, from http://www.naeyc.org/accreditation

National Institute of Child Health and Human Development Early Child Care Research Network. (2003). Does amount of time spent in child care predict socio-emotional adjustment during the transition to kindergarten? *Child Development, 74*, 976-1005.

National Institute of Child Health and Human Development Early Child Care Research Network. (2000a). Characteristics and quality of child care for toddlers and preschoolers. *Applied Developmental Science, 4*, 116-135.

National Institute of Child Health and Human Development Early Child Care Research Network. (2000b). The relation of child care to cognitive and language development. *Child Development, 71*, 960-980.

National Institute of Child Health and Human Development Early Child Care Research Network (1996). *Observational Record of the Caregiving Environment (ORCE)*. Retrieved November 13, 2003, from http://www.isisweb.org/ICIS2000Program/web_pages/group422

National Research Council. (2000). Preschool program quality and children's learning and development. In B. Bowman, M. Donovan, & M. Burns (Eds.), *Eager to learn: Educating our preschools* (pp. 128-181). Washington, DC: National Academy Press.

National Research Council and Institute of Medicine. (2000). In J. P. Shonkoff and D. Phillips (Eds.), *From neurons to neighborhoods: The science of early childhood development committee on integrity the science on early childhood development.* Washington, DC: National Academy Press.

O'Connell, J., & Farran, D. (1982). Effects of day care experience on the use of intentional communicative behaviors in a sample of socioeconomically depressed infants. *Developmental Psychology, 18*, 22-29.

Paget, K. (2001). Review of the Early Childhood Rating Scale-Revised (ECERS-R). In B. Plake and J. Impura (Eds.), *The Fourteenth Mental*

Measurements Yearbook. Lincoln, NE: Buros Institute of Mental Measurements.

Peisner-Feinberg, E., & Burchinal, M. (1997). Relationships between preschool children's child care experiences and concurrent development: The Cost, Quality and Outcome Study. *Merrill-Palmer Quarterly, 43*(3), 451–477.

Peisner-Feinberg, E., Clifford, R., Yazejian, N., Culkin, M., Howes, C., & Kagan, S. L. (1998, April). *The longitudinal effects of child care quality: Implications for kindergarten success.* Paper presented at the Annual Meeting of the American Educational Research Association. San Diego, CA.

Peterson, C., & Peterson, R. (1986). Parent-child interaction and day care: Does quality of day care matter? *Journal of Applied Developmental Psychology, 7,* 1–15.

Peth, P. (1998). The NICHD Study of early child care (Report No. NIH-Pub-98-4318). Bethosda, MD: National Institute of Child Health and Human Development. (ERIC Document Reproduction Service No. ED427882).

Phillips, D. (1996). Reframing the quality issue. In S. L. Kagan & N. Cohen (Eds.), *Reinventing early care and education: A vision for a quality system* (pp. 43–64). San Francisco, CA: Jossey-Bass Publishers.

Phillips, D., & Adams, G. (2001). Child care and our youngest children. *The Future of Children,* 11, 35–51.

Phillips, D., Crowell, N., & Whitebook, M. (2002). *Literacy levels of child care providers: Cause for concern.* Unpublished manuscript.

Phillips, D. and Howes, C. (1987). Indicators of quality in child care: Review of research. In D. Phillips (Ed.), *Quality in child care: What does the research tell us?* (pp. 43–56). Washington, DC: National Association for the Education of Young Children.

Phillips, D., McCartney, K., & Scarr, S. (1987). Child-care quality and children's social development. *Developmental Psychology, 23,* 537–543.

Phillips, D., Mekos, D., Scarr, S., McCartney, K. & Abbott-Shim, M. (2000). Within and beyond the classroom door: Assessing quality in child care centers. *Early Childhood Research Quarterly. 15*(4), 475–496.

Phillips, D., & Zigler, E. (1987). The checkered history of federal child care regulation. In E. Z. Routhkopf (Ed.), *Review of research in education.* Washington, DC: American Educational Research Association.

Phillipsen, L., Burchinal, M., Howes, C., & Cryer, D. (1997). The prediction of process quality from structural features of child care. *Early Childhood Research Quarterly 12,* 281–304.

Phillipsen, L. C., Burchinal, M. R., Howes, C., & Cryer, D. (1997). The prediction of process quality from structural features of child care. *Early Childhood Research Quarterly, 12*(3), 281–303.

Pianta, C., & Nimetz, S. (1991). Relationship between children and teachers. Associations with behavior at home and in the classroom. *Journal of Applied Developmental Psychology, 12,* 379–393.

Posavac, E. J., & Carey, R. G. (2003). *Program evaluation: Methods and case studies.* Englewood Cliffs: Prentice Hall.

Powell, D. (1977). Day care and the family: *A study of interactions and congruency. Final research report of the parent caregiver project.* Detroit, MI: Merrill Palmer Institute.

Public Agenda. (2003). *The Family: Overview.* Retrieved November 19, 2003, from http://www.publicagenda.org/issues

Roberts, J., Rabinowitch, S., Bryant, D., Burchinal, M., Koch, M., & Ramey, C. (1989). Language skills of children with different preschool experiences. *Journal of Speech and Hearing Research, 32,* 773–786.

Rossbach, C., C., & Harms, T. (1991). *The Early Childhood Environment Rating Scale (ECERS).* New York: Teachers College Press.

Rubenstein, J., & Howes, C. (1979). Caregiving and infant behavior in day care and homes. *Developmental Psychology, 15,* 1–24.

Rusher, A., McGrevin, C., & Lambiotte, J. (1992). Belief systems of early childhood teachers and their principals regarding early childhood education. *Early Childhood Research Quarterly, 7,* 277–296.

Ruopp, R., Travers, J., Glantz, F., & Coelen, C. (1979). *Children at the center: Final results of the national child care study.* Cambridge, MA: Abt Associates.

Scarr, S., & Eisenberg, M. (1993). Child care research: Issues, perspectives, and results. *Annual Review of Psychology, 44,* 613–644.

Scarr, S., Eisenberg, M., & Deater-Deckard, K. (1994). Measurement of quality in child care centers. *Early Childhood Research Quarterly, 9,* 131–151.

Scarr, S., McCartney, K., Abbott-Shim, M., Phillips, D., & Eisenberg, M. (1995). *Small effects of large quality differences in child care centers on children's behaviors and adjustment.* Unpublished manuscript.

Scarr, S., McCartney, K., Phillips, D., & Abbott-Shim, M. (1993). Quality of child care as an aspect of family and child care policy in the United States. *Pediatrics, 91,* 182–188.

Schliecker, E., White, D., & Jacobs, E. (1991). The role of day care quality in the prediction of children's vocabulary. *Canadian Journal of Behavioral Science, 23,* 12–24.

Shepard, L., Kagan, S. L., & Wurtz, E. (Eds.). (1998). *Principles and recommendations for early childhood assessments.* Washington, DC: National Educational Goals Panel.

Shinn, M., Phillips, D., Howes, C., Galinsky, E., & Whitebook, M. (1991). *Correspondence between mothers' perceptions and observer ratings of quality in child care centers.* Unpublished manuscript.

Shonkoff, J. P., & Phillips, D. (Eds.) (2000). *From neurons to neighborhoods: The science of early childhood development.* Washington, DC: National Academy Press.

Sibley, A., & Abbott-Shim, M., (1987). *Assessment Profile for Family Day Care Homes.* Atlanta, GA: Quality Assist.

Sibley, A., Vande Wiele, L., & Herrington, S. (1996). *Georgia Head Start Quality Initiative: First year report of findings.* Atlanta, Georgia: Quality Assist, Inc.

Smith, A. B. (1999). Quality child care and joint attention. *International Journal of Early Years Education, 7*(1), 85–98.

Smith, M., Dickinson, D., & Sangeorge, A. (2002). *The Early Language and Literacy Classroom Observation.* Baltimore, MD: Brookes Publishing.

Smith, A., & Endsley, R. (1996). Comparison of accredited and non-accredited family child care programs on program quality, and provider professionalism, and family support. *Child and Youth Care Forum, 25,* 6.

Spitz, R. A. (1945). Hopitalism: An inquiry into the genesis of psychiatric conditions in early childhood. *Psychoanalytical Study Child, 1,* 55–74.

Stipek, D., Daniels, D., Galuzzo, D., & Milburn, S. (1992). Characterizing early childhood education programs for poor and middle-class children. *Early Childhood Research Quarterly, 7,* 1–19.

Tafafe-Young, K., White-Marsland, K. & Zigler, E. (1997). The Regulatory Status of Center-Based Infant and Toddler Child Care. *American Journal of Orthopsychiatry, 67,* 4.

Talan, T., & Jorde Bloom, P. (2004). Program Administration Scale. Center for Early Childhood Leadership, Wheeling, IL.

U.S. Department of Education. (2001). *No Child Left Behind Act of 2001.* Retrieved October 25, 2000, from http://www.ed.gov/nclb.

U.S. Department of Education (2004). The preschool Curriculum Evaluation Research (PCER) Program. Retrieved November 12, 2003, from http:/www.ed.gov/offices/OERI/ pcer-materials/index.html.

U.S. General Accounting Office. (2002). *Child Care Quality Improvement Initiatives*. Washington, DC: U.S. GAO.

Vandell, D., & Corasaniti, M. (1990). Child care and the family: Complex contributions to child development. In K. McCartney (Ed.), *New directions in child development*. San Francisco: Jossey-Bass.

Vandell, D., Henderson, V. K., & Wilson, K. S. (1988). A longitudinal study of children with varying quality day care experiences. *Child Development, 59,* 1286-1292.

Vandell, D., & Powers, C. (1983). Child care quality and children's free play activities. *American Journal of Orthopsychiatry, 53,* 489-500.

Vandell, D. L., & Wolfe, B. (2000). *Child care quality: Does it matter and does it need to be improved?* Washington, DC: US Department of Health and Human Services.

Wasik, B., Ramey, C., Bryant, D., & Sparling, J. (1990). A longitudinal study of two early intervention strategies: Project CARE. *Child Development, 61,* 1682-1696.

Watamura, S., Donzella, B., Alwin, J., & Gunnar, M. (2003). Morning-to-afternoon increases in cortisol concentrations for infants and toddlers at child care: Age differences and behavioral correlates. *Child Development, 74,* 1006-1020.

Whitebook, M., Howes, C., & Phillips, D. (1990). *Who cares? Child care teachers and the quality of care in America. Final Report of the National Child Care Staffing Study.* Oakland, CA: Child Care Employee Project.

Whitebook, M., Howes, C., Phillips, D., & Pemberton, C. (1989). *Who cares? child care teachers and the quality of care in America. Final report of the National Child Care Staffing Study.* Oakland, CA: Child Care Employee Project.

Whitebook, M., Sakai, L., Gerber, E., & Howes, C. (2001). *Then and now, changes in childcare staffing: 1994-2000. Technical Report.* Center for Childcare Workforce.

Wilkes, D. (1989). Administration, classroom program, sponsorship: Are these indices of quality care in day care centers. (Doctoral dissertation, Georgia State University, 1989). *Dissertation Abstracts International 50,* AAI8922912.

Wishard, A., Shivers, E., Howes, C., & Ritchie, S. (2003). Child care program and teacher practices: Associations with quality and children's experiences. *Early Childhood Research Quarterly, 18,* 65-103.

Zigler, E., & Ennis, P. (1989). Child care: Science and social policy. The child care crisis in America. *Canadian Psychology, 30(2),* 116-125.

Zigler, E., & Gilman, E. (1993). The National Head Start Program for disadvantaged preschoolers. In E. Zigler and S. Styfco (Eds.), *Head Start and beyond* (pp. 1-41). New Haven, CT: Yale University Press.

· 27 ·

INTEGRATION, INNOVATION, AND EVALUATION IN SCHOOL-BASED EARLY CHILDHOOD SERVICES

Janette Pelletier
Carl Corter
University of Toronto

OVERVIEW

This chapter examines evaluation of integrated, innovative services for young children and families in elementary schools. Services are integrated in two ways: by providing combined services such as parenting support, childcare, and kindergarten education; and by providing service that integrates parents and community through various forms of involvement. These integrative initiatives may foster innovation when they are adapted or designed in local context through learning communities that bring all parties into service delivery change and design. We emphasize approaches that may be universal and thus inclusive of all children, not targeted solely to children at risk. We note the ideas and social forces behind these approaches and the methodological challenges in understanding how they are designed and implemented and how well they work in different contexts. We address the challenges of developing an evidence base that informs program improvement, professional practice, and policy in these complex approaches to early childhood supports. We illustrate the issues by describing a series of four studies we have carried out on schools as community hubs serving young children and their families.

SOCIETAL CONTEXT FOR INTEGRATED EARLY CHILDHOOD SERVICES IN SCHOOLS

Interest in Early Childhood

Public and political interest in early childhood development has reached unprecedented levels over the last decade in many countries around the globe. Integrated and comprehensive services for early childhood have been part of this tide (e.g., Organization for Economic Cooperation and Development [OECD], 2001), along with related waves of recent interest in readiness for school (e.g., Saluja, Scott-Little, & Clifford, 2000), school reform (e.g., Fullan, 2000), and parent/community involvement in children's services (e.g., Corter & Pelletier, 2004). The depth of interest reflects multiple social and economic forces and societal goals, as well as advances in scholarly understanding of early foundations for optimal human development (Keating & Hertzman, 1999). Throughout the 1990s, social forces relating to economic restructuring and competition eroded many traditional supports for children, while simultaneously elevating goals related to training children for academic and eventual economic success.

Preparing children for success in the "Information Age" brings a closely related set of ideas; in fact, the computer metaphor may have whetted public appetite for new research on the neural basis for the importance of early learning and experience (Pelletier & Corter, 2002). In the context of a global knowledge economy, investing in the early years is seen as sound economics. Investment in school–community collaborations is also seen as good value in terms of boosting academic achievement (Kirst & Kelley, 1995) and global competitiveness. International agencies, including the development banks and UNICEF, have identified early childhood development as important, partly as a country development strategy. The investment in young children also appears to make sense from the standpoint of other long-standing goals of developed countries: the prevention of societal ills associated with poverty and reducing the burden of social and mental health costs (e.g., Garbarino & Ganzel, 2000; Tremblay, Masse, Pagani, & Vitaro, 1996).

Integrated Services

Interest in integrated and comprehensive early childhood supports has been strong for more than a decade (Kagan, 1991), but such approaches have not been widely adopted in North America. Some impressive efforts exist, but approaches remain "spotty and fragmented" (Schorr, 1997). There are a few state- or provincewide efforts in North Carolina, California, Quebec, and Ontario. In contrast, the Organization for Economic Co-operation and Development's (OECD) *Starting Strong* report (2001) shows that a number of European OECD members have countrywide policies that appear to be achieving what is only a patchwork promise in North America. For example, Sweden balances local initiative with national pressures, such as regulation and supports for integrated services. *Starting Strong* asserts a number of holistic principles including the inseparability of early care and education, and universality rather than targeted provision. Although Sweden's integrative approach is based on broad social policies that have been in place for decades, other OECD countries have had more fragmented services for young children. In the Netherlands, for example, the push for integration is much more recent, with new federal funding just coming online (vanVeen, 2003, personal communication). The push was partly fuelled by demonstration projects and dissemination of results which in turn created demand by parents for this approach to services. The United Kingdom launched a series of Sure Start initiatives that include comprehensive services and systematic data collection for evaluation and accountability (Glass, 1999).

In the United States, promising school-based initiatives have included Edward Zigler's Schools for the 21st Century (Zigler, Finn-Stevenson, & Stern, 1997), James Comer's school community approach (Comer, Haynes, Joyner, & Ben-Avie, 1996), and full-service schools (Dryfoos, 1994). These models of schools as community hubs have broad supports for children and families, with Zigler's model highlighting childcare and other preschool services. Although these models are widely acclaimed, resources and the radical changes required for schools and other agencies to implement the models has limited their replication. The Carnegie Corporation's (1994) strategy has provided supports and advocacy for broad-based programs of support for early childhood in order to achieve multiple societal goals, with service integration and community connections as keys. Some successful state level programs triggered by this initiative continue, but they struggle to survive in the face of ongoing challenges, such as changes in state governments (Levine & Smith, 2001). Other U.S. initiatives in comprehensive community services for early childhood (Regional Educational Laboratories' Early Childhood Collaboration Network, 1995) have included scattered success stories based on limited evidence and generally limited prospects for sustainability or scaling up. Of course, Head Start has provided comprehensive, targeted support to many young children and families in the United States (Ripple & Zigler, 2003); in some cases, the support may be integrated through "wrap-around" integration with childcare and other services (Brush, Deich, Traylor, & Pindus, 1995). Early Head Start is also a comprehensive approach with multiple services of care, education, maternal health and home visiting but is less widely available. In some U.S. jurisdictions, school districts and state departments of educations are active partners in increasing early childhood opportunities using the school base as a platform (Halfron et al., 2001). However, these efforts often involve modest efforts at integration and limited evaluation. A similar patchwork picture applies to Canada (Pelletier & Corter, 2002) and other parts of the world. Nevertheless, integrated initiatives for early childhood at the local or state/provincial level continue to spring up in a number of countries. For example, the province of Quebec now provides universal integrated full-time care and education for children from 1 year through school age (Tougas, 2002). Many of these initiatives remain under-evaluated, limiting the chances for improvement and redesign and for wider application of successful approaches.

Why Now?

In North America, locally based efforts to improve poor neighborhoods with comprehensive programs date back to settlement houses in the 19th century (Kubisch, Weiss, Schorr, & Connell, 1995). What is new that might make it time for lasting changes in their application to early childhood? Two notable developments seen around the world are the spikes of interest in early childhood and educational reform. These developments provide public attention and the public will to consider action. The two spikes are connected, too, in that most visions of educational reform include early childhood and school readiness as important components (e.g., Leithwood, Fullan, & Watson, 2003). School reform also may open up the education system to new approaches, which may include mutually beneficial collaborations with community agencies and services (e.g., Lawson, 1999a; Novella, 1996).

A final answer to the question of "Why now?" relates to research and local evaluations. The potential to make all this work will be greatly enhanced if the new "knowledge society" spawns local realities of "learning communities" supporting young children and families (Torjman, Leviten-Reid, Camp, & Makhoul, 2001). These learning communities could include integrated service programs combining roles, relationships, and learning. Part of the learning is about each other as partners, including professionals, parents, and children. Another part of the learning is analysis of the program with continuous processing of child, parent, and community needs, scans of best practice for ideas, not recipes, social construction of local plans, and evaluations of outcomes. The learning community extends beyond the program, as ideas and findings are shared with others and local knowledge is used to leverage policy and funding support from government and other sources.

MODELS AND CONCEPTUAL PERSPECTIVES

The Meaning of Integration

What does integration mean and why do it? Services may be integrated at a number of levels: from government policy and the organization of ministries or departments of government, down to the direct interactions in the day-to-day lives of children, parents, and professionals and their community agencies (Knapp, 1995). Local integration efforts often are challenged by lack of integration at higher levels. For example, putting together childcare and elementary education in schools is made more difficult when care and education are managed by separate ministries and policies and are staffed by professionals with separate training and regulation (Mathien & Johnson, 1998). Local efforts at integration also vary in the way in which services are integrated (Ingram, Bloomberg, & Seppannen, 1996). Integration may involve a networked approach across different locations, but more often involves a central location, or hub, with links out into service at other community locations.

There are differences in degree of integration, as well as type (Mattessich & Monsey, 1992). In some cases, loose integration means little more than co-location of services with some degree of coordination among participating agencies. In other cases, it may mean coordination of service and referrals through case management across otherwise disconnected services (Gilliam, Zigler, & Leiter, 2000). Collaborative and "seamless" programs represent higher levels of integration. Deeply integrated programs may develop common curriculum approaches to both child and parent support, integrated staffing, common governance, protocols, and funding sources for the integrated work. Often these differences are described along a "continuum of change," with initial levels involving co-location or coordination and higher levels being collaboration, deep integration or even transformation of the organizations themselves (Melaville & Blank, 1996). Interorganizational and interprofessional collaboration is challenging. The institutional and professional barriers to integration are considerable, given the different organizational cultures and "political economies" of different service sectors and agencies (Crowson & Boyd, 1995). Lists of barriers abound: power imbalances among participants, professional identity and turf issues, inflexible funding packets for traditional services, statutory and regulatory barriers, limited funding and technical support, and so on (Ingram, Bloomberg, & Seppannen, 1996).

Why Do It?

Of course integration is not an end in itself. Among policy analysts and organizations advocating it (e.g., National Association for the Education of Young Children [NAEYC], 1994), integration is seen as a means to improve supports to young children and their families and to enhance outcomes for them. Some conceptual arguments for integration are related to principles of child development. Thus, we know that children's development is holistic, so if children are integrated, why shouldn't services be? For example, school readiness requires more than cognitive and language skills; it also requires emotional regulation and social skill with neurobiological underpinnings (Blair, 2002). The kindergarten teacher who provides breakfast for hungry students out of his own pocket and provision, understands the link between the development of mind and body, but services for children usually do not match the theoretical or practical understanding (Lerner, Rothbaum, Boulos, &

Castellino, 2002). Integration is also seen as building community as well as child and family outcomes (e.g., Hyman, 2002), and stronger communities and families are necessary for better child outcomes. Community improvement includes improving community agencies themselves. Integration may bring about practical improvements in organizations by fostering learning and new ideas through collaborative change. Kagan and Neuman (2003) extend this idea by pointing out that combining forces may multiply the avenues for resources and for advocacy and policy influence.

The Social Ecology of Integration

Improving community, family, and child outcomes are often intertwined in integrated programs. Community outcomes may be linked in two-way connections to parent supports. Outcomes for parents may be processes affecting child outcomes. The conceptual framework of social ecology helps to map this complexity (Bronfenbrenner, 1979, 1989; Lerner et al., 2002). In fact, it has become a key part of the argument for working on integration in policy and practice. Evidence on the impacts of social ecological factors on child development and the dynamic interplay across systems in the life of the child is accumulating, from micro systems in which the child participates directly, all the way up to the macro level of government policies and economies and their ripple-down effects.

As one concrete example, starting at a macro level, we know that countries differ in socioeconomic gradients, or the degree of difference between the "haves" and "have-nots." In turn, these differences are related to outcomes for children; steeper gradients relate to poorer outcomes for all children (Keating & Hertzman, 1999). Closer to home, neighborhood is a strong predictor of child health, well-being, and cognitive achievement. Children who live in poorer neighborhoods with few community supports fare worse than children whose communities are cohesive and thriving (Bacon & Brinksults, 2003; Kohen, Brooks-Gunn, Leventhal, & Hertzman, 2002). Furthermore, local neighborhood ecologies and strengths may alter the straight prediction from demographics (Yancey & Saporito, 1995). At the family level, work/welfare, poverty, and service access affect children's outcomes over time. For example, a "bundled" program of family supports (wage supplements, childcare, and health services) for parents in poverty, begun in the preschool years, can improve parents' functioning and children's later adaptation in school (Huston et al., 2001).

Understanding the importance of social ecology, family, and neighborhood points to supporting children and their parents in community sites with due regard for the dynamic interplay of intersecting strands of culture, government policy, public and private services, the parents' world of work, neighborhood, the child's immediate interactions in the family, school, and so on. This interplay is challenging enough for academics trying to examine it. For parents trying to negotiate the maze of home, work, or welfare, and disconnected services, it can be a nightmare of trying to patch childcare, education, and other supports together. When those parents are recent immigrants, are operating in a new language, or have children with special needs, they, and their children, are particularly likely to be left dangling.

In a helpful academic analysis of this complexity Lerner (Lerner et al., 2002) merges ideas on developmental systems theory with Bronfenbrenner's (1989) social ecological theory to produce a process–person–context–time model for understanding the integrated nature of interacting/dynamic systems in the development of children. In a simplified version, the person is a child, a holistic being made up herself of integrated systems. The process is the fused interactions of the child with the context (e.g., environment/parent/teacher), and the context is nested levels of influence from the immediate micro level of direct interaction between the child and others (e.g., home, early childhood program), up to the macro level of cultural and societal influences (e.g., cultural values, government policies and sponsored programs). Time includes ontogenetic change in the child and cultural–social change in the context. After reviewing the value of this approach to interpreting basic research on parenting and child development, Lerner applies it to social policy and programs as both a rationale for service integration and as a model to understand how it works: "Given the integrative scholarship associated with developmental systems theory, it would seem logical that social programs and public policies would use this model as a framework for the creation of comprehensive child and family services" (p. 334).

Integration and the Ecology of Continuity

Aside from charting complex influences in children's lives and lending support to integrate service approaches, the ecological perspective also sharpens the meaning of the principle of continuity in early childhood programming. Continuity works both horizontally as the child and parent move across settings at one point in time and vertically as the child moves through developmental transitions in time (Saracho & Spodek, 2003). Continuity may be fostered by home–school partnerships and service integration (Regional Educational Laboratories' Early Childhood Collaboration Network, 1995). Service integration can work horizontally or vertically. For example, childcare integrated with parent education is horizontal integration; childcare in schools for preschoolers, and before and after school care for older children, has the potential to provide vertical as well as horizontal integration. Continuity can mean a more secure environment for the child, more recognition of the child's individual needs, better programming, and more consistent expectations, and mutual support from adults. Working for continuity can also be the basis for common goals and working partnership between parents and professionals.

Evidence on Benefits

As indicated earlier, some of the arguments for integration are practical and some are conceptual. A range of benefits is assumed in policy positions emphasizing integration (e.g., NAEYC, 1994; Beach & Bertrand, 2000). Most focus is on the child or family, but other potential benefits also are noted, such as positive impact on the participating organizations, increased efficiencies or economies in delivering services, or broader community impact. Generally, however, the evidence base for judging the arguments is sparse. For example, in a review, St. Pierre and colleagues found little evidence that effective services for families needed to be coordinated (St. Pierre & Layzer, 1998; St. Pierre, Layzer, Goodson, & Bernstein, 1999).

In one exception, Mathien and Johnson (1998) conducted a study of integrated care and school programs for kindergarten children in several provinces in Canada. Their study found some evidence of benefit. An economic analysis showed that the costs of running an integrated childcare and kindergarten program were marginally less per child than the combined costs of running separate care and kindergarten programs for the same length of time. At the same time, program quality ratings showed that the integrated programs achieved higher ratings. In addition, the study surveyed general attitudes toward the desirability of integrated care and education among parents and professionals. Interestingly, parents were very supportive, but both childcare and kindergarten professionals were less enthusiastic about integration.

The School as the Hub of Integration

Pros and cons. There are a number of arguments for basing integrated early childhood services in schools (Zigler, Finn-Stevenson, & Stern, 1997; Lawson, 1999a). Recognition and development of the educational value of a range of early childhood services may be enhanced by connection to the formal education system. Schooling is universal and it is normative—a service almost every parent expects to connect to, whatever the diversity of their backgrounds and their child's special needs. Furthermore, there is a school in almost every community. A window of opportunity is open as schools around the world are being reformed; the intersection of growing worldwide interest in early childhood and in school reform represents a unique opportunity for community-building among services and between parents and services (Lawson, 1999a). Childcare and early education can play a pivotal part in these synergies. For example, caring for the whole child and building a seamless day with integrated "before- and after-school care" are important roles with primary school age children. Another important role is that early childcare and preprimary education represent points of contact for parents with unique potential to bridge them into other service connections. Early care and education is not only normative but usually entails regular and natural contact between parents and professionals with frequent face-to-face meetings and daily dropoffs and pickups. All this contributes to generally high parent satisfaction with early childhood care (Cryer & Burchinal, 1997), and this comfort can help in connecting parents to schools and integrated services. Thus the "culture" of the school may benefit from "multicultural" collaboration with other services.

Are there reasons for not choosing schools as the base? Of course. In some communities—rural settings, for example—service integration may work better as a network than as a hub (Chaskin & Richman, 1992). In addition, schools have particular ways of working that often do not match other service sectors (Crowson & Boyd, 1995). In some cases, they are embedded in conservative organizational structures and restrictive regulations from districts and government ministries (Corter & Pelletier, 2004). In other cases, educational reform may rain down from above and change may be dictated from higher levels with little appreciation of what is needed for success at the school level. An example is the recent mandating of parents' roles in governance in many jurisdictions around the world, often with little real success (Corter & Pelletier, 2004). To successfully integrate parents and community in schools or to integrate services in schools, initiatives must take into account parents' needs and include local chemistry and scope for flexibility at both the school and community level. This is seen in research on many fronts: for example, school level factors such as climate and leadership are crucial to promoting parent participation (Parker & Leithwood, 2000; Griffith, 1998). Top-down models alone cannot produce the needed changes.

Models of school-based services. There are models of school-based services that pull together the many levels of program design and implementation, process and outcomes, along with the need for evaluation. One of the best examples is Lawson's Caring School Communities (1999a). The need for local evaluation within communities of practice is a theme; designers and frontline staff need to reflect together on evidence of how they are doing. Lawson's material includes extensive guides for directing projects in a journey of overcoming predictable barriers and finding new ways to deliver effective service and schooling in local context. Again, there is limited empirical research on these models.

Findings on school–community initiatives. In a general survey, Melaville (1998) studied 20 "well-regarded" school–community initiatives in the United States to describe their outlines in terms of underlying models and design/implementation issues (initiation, staffing, governance, funding, programs, participation, and technical assistance). Some of these initiatives are statewide (e.g., Caring Communities in Missouri and Healthy Start in California), some are city-based (e.g., Family Resource Schools in Denver; Beacon Schools in New York City), and one is based on partnerships growing out of the ideas of Comer and Zigler at Yale University (CoZi Project). With respect to models, Melaville (1998) characterizes initiatives as generally beginning in one of four advocacy and reform approaches: school reform, services reform, child/youth development, and community reform. Interestingly, however, most initiatives report being influenced by all of these approaches. All include strong roles for parental involvement.

On issues of design and implementation, Melaville (1998) presents some common findings across programs. For example, analysis of staffing shows the importance of clearly defined roles for frontline staff with overall coordination between the school and other participating services with the connection between the school principal and the project coordinator being key (see also Sanders & Harvey, 2002). The findings emphasize the need for ongoing technical assistance (see also Wandersman & Florin,

2003). For example, 80% of program respondents wanted more help in developing parent participation and in professional development. Most initiatives do not have data on the process of design and implementation across levels of policy, program, organization, child and family, and community. Most initiatives do not have data on impact on the child or parent. There are limits on the resources of the funders in providing technical assistance, and there is always more to do.

The need for deeper investigation in this area is also seen in a survey of school-linked early childhood initiatives in the United States (Halfon et al., 2001). The investigators considered sites that met criteria of comprehensiveness, integration, and sustainability. They reviewed an exhaustive list of possible initiatives through Web searches, contact with all state departments of education, key informant interviews, and a review of relevant literature. The investigators reviewed 112 sites; found 45 potential sites that met the criteria, and finally selected 6 sites to be case studies. The case studies include some pieces of deep integration and collaboration (seamless program, common staff, and blended funding) but overall seem to be examples of more modest coordination among early childhood services with the school as a key partner. One of the findings from the survey is that reform or system change at the school district reduces fragmentation and improves the chances for program integration. A key finding from the survey is that most of the programs would like to conduct more rigorous evaluations but lack the funds to do so. Outcome/Process evaluation data are seen as important to sustainability.

Parent and Community Involvement

Models of involvement and a role for relationships. School-based models of parent–community involvement (PCI) and suggested practices have flourished over the last decade (see Epstein & Conners, 2002); many models of school reform include parent–community involvement (e.g., Borman, Hewes, Overman, & Brown, 2003). Often there are accountability or learning effectiveness reasons for this interest. Parents want to have a say in what goes into the curriculum, they want to support learning, they want to know how their children are doing, and they want a civil school society for their children (e.g., Corter, Harris, & Pelletier, 1998; Melaville & Blank, 2000; Olmsted & Lockard, 1995). Schools need parent/community perspectives if they are going to serve young children, particularly in the face of push-down curriculum and standardized test regimes. This means input from parents and other services, particularly early childhood professionals who are sometimes more oriented to the whole child and her or his family. Positive experiences of parents in integrated early childhood programs may build parents' capacities to relate to schools and other services (Davies, 1995). For example, Peters and his colleagues (Peters et al., 2000) found that participation in integrative, community-based preschool programs led to more positive reports of relationships with teachers by parents of low socioeconomic status (SES). This positive outcome, in turn, may be a process effecting positive outcomes for children (Pelletier, 2002; Pelletier & Brent, 2002).

Involvement and service equity. PCI has other potential roles in service integration efforts. It has the potential to build community support for the initiative. It may empower families to provide more effective environments (Seefeldt, Denton, Coalper, & Younoszal, 1999). PCI also may figure into the redress of service inequities. Often children and families who are the most poorly connected to services have the greatest need. A PCI orientation may help deal with this problem. By contrast, parent involvement/education initiatives may widen gaps between "haves" and "have-nots" unless there are serious outreach efforts to underserved groups (Corter & Pelletier, 2004). For example, Cunningham et al., (2000) found that a universally available parenting course in elementary schools was less likely to be taken up if parents had less education, if they were immigrants, or were single parents. Other barriers to parent connections to schools and services are parental depression, workfare and scheduling conflicts (Lamb-Parker et al., 2001), and language barriers (e.g., Delgado-Gaitan & Trueba, 1991). Thus, active attention needs to be paid to barriers to involvement, particularly those that further marginalize underserved groups. Service integration can help if it combines the separate outreach capabilities of individual organizations into more powerful networks (Corter, 2001). For example, in cities where immigrant parents speak many languages, and where professional competence in those languages is scattered across individual service agencies, pooling of outreach in different languages in an integrated network can bring in a more diverse range of parents.

Involvement beyond education. Interest in PCI is not limited to the education sector. Parent involvement also may improve service impact on children in various service sectors from pediatric hospital care to childcare, to preschool intervention, to school reform (Crowson & Boyd, 1995). Parent involvement can have a darker side, if downloading and service cuts mean that parents are being used inappropriately to take on service roles better left to professionals. Parent involvement can shade into family responsibility positions that are political and not taken with the best interests of children and families in mind. Thus, political philosophies of governments can affect the nature of PCI. For example, Ferguson and Prentice (2000) studied government regulations and policies on childcare across Canadian provinces and found that polices ranged from "silence" on the issue of parental involvement to "full control." Silence reflected government philosophies of parents as "consumers/purchasers," whereas control by parents reflected "citizenship" philosophies of collaboration.

Designing and critiquing parent community involvement. Although PCI is inevitably included as part of integrative services initiative for young children, it is important to keep in mind that there are many different forms of PCI and different forms may be more or less effective as mediators of child outcomes depending on the characteristics of local communities and local aims of integrative services (Corter & Pelletier, 2004). Of course, PCI may be an end in itself if democratic participation is one of the goals of the project, with successful outcomes being parent participation in planning or governance. As an integration strategy PCI, like service integration itself, needs to be planned and evaluated in terms of the project aims and the potential processes linking programs to outcomes. Assuming that global parent involvement automatically flows into child outcomes is not borne out by meta-analyses (White, Taylor, & Moss, 1992; Mattingly, Prislin, McKenzie, Rodriguez, & Kayzar, 2002). Bridging the difficulties in moving PCI from principles to practice is documented by a number of studies showing the challenges of parents taking up roles in planning or formal governance bodies. For example, Blank and colleagues (Blank et al., 2001) found that parents who serve on advisory groups along with professionals and administrators generally "come as individuals without the power of organizational affiliation and support" (p. 23) and are often overpowered by other members. Alternative approaches to giving parents input into planning include school or agency-level action research strategies such as surveys and focus groups (Barrett, 1999; Corter, Harris, & Pelletier, 1998; Ontario Ministry of Education, 2001).

EVALUATIONS AND INNOVATIONS

Complexities of Researching Comprehensive Community Initiatives

Integration of services on school sites simplifies the lives of children and families and may improve service quality and access and child and family outcomes. However, it is enormously complex in terms of personal, professional, and organizational change. It is also an enormously complex topic for study. Community service integration projects belong to a category of complex change initiatives called Comprehensive Community Initiatives (CCIs), which present particular challenges for evaluation (Connell, Kubisch, Schorr, & Weiss, 1995; Connell & Kubisch, 1995; Weiss, 1995; see also Knapp, 1995). They are underevaluated and underconceptualized. They rarely describe how the programs are developed or implemented. If they assess child and family outcomes at all, measures are limited in many cases to client satisfaction, and they almost never explore processes that mediate between programs and outcomes. The limits on available evidence concerning integrated early childhood initiatives in schools were pointed out earlier.

A major problem in studying these initiatives is that they do not fit traditional evaluation methods. Connell and Kubisch (1995) put the problem this way: "Up to this point, CCIs have had three general options to follow: (1) retreat to process documentation of the initiatives and greatly reduce expectations about obtaining credible evidence of their impacts; (2) try to "force fit" the initiatives themselves into the procrustean bed of existing and accepted evaluation methods in order to estimate their impacts; and (3) put off evaluating CCIs until the initiatives are more "mature" and "ready" to be evaluated using existing strategies" (p. 1). In terms of conceptualization, they also argue for a "theory of change" to guide both the development of the project and the research to evaluate it. The theory of change has to be broad enough to include organizational/program/professional change and individual change for children and families. Conceptualization of organizational, program, and professional change, should guide the description and analysis of the development and implementation process (Kellogg Foundation, 1998). According to Connell and Kubisch (1995), "...at their most general level, CCI theories are quite similar to many program theories: the initiative plans to do X in order to accomplish Y and Z. But this similarity vanishes quickly when one realizes that, unlike most programs, CCI theories have multiple strands (economic, political, and social), which operate at many levels (community, institutional, personal network, family, and individual), are co-constructed in a collaborative process by diverse stakeholders, and evolve over the course of the initiative" (p. 1).

Given the complexity and amount of effort required in collaboration and service integration, better understanding of process and accounting of outcomes are both crucial. Process includes interactions and changes at the level of children and families (Lerner et al., 2002) and for programs and organizations. Integration itself is not the goal. Successful initiatives must "focus on results," while "consciously attending to process on an ongoing basis" (Fullan, 2001; Weiss, 1995; Lawson, 1999b).

Is an evidence base possible and must it be exclusively experimental? Despite the calls for more systematic research extending back more than a decade (e.g., Kagan, 1991; Knapp, 1995) in-depth studies of integrative, school-linked services for early childhood are sparse (Halfon et al., 2001). The current calls for evidence-based approaches across all service sectors provide strong motivation for research but have sometimes been interpreted as limiting evidence to the experimental method. However, in fields such as education, there are strong arguments for systematic qualitative alternatives and a range of approaches (Eisenhart & Towne, 2003; Reynolds, 2004); the case for broad, complementary strategies is even more compelling in complex, community initiatives (Knapp, 1995). Of course, the impact on public and policy awareness that comes from randomized experimental demonstration approaches like the comprehensive, integrative Abecedarian Early Childhood Intervention (Campbell, Ramey, Pungello, Sparling, & Miller-Johnson, 2002) or quasi-experimental evaluations such as that of the Chicago parenting centers (Reynolds, Temple, Robertson, & Mann, 2001) is indisputable. The economic analysis of benefits and costs of these projects has provided a bottom-line mantra ("dollars saved for dollar invested") that reaches the hearts of politicians of all stripes and meets tests for "science-based" evidence. Notwithstanding the limits of the widely cited demonstration projects—in terms of program elements selected, populations served, and even era of implementation—these projects have helped set the stage for trying and evaluating other types of approaches with other populations. Local contexts require local adaptations. There will not be a single "one size-fits-all" approach to integrated programming. Replication of programs with demonstrated success requires flexibility and evaluation in the new setting (Schorr, Sylvester, & Dunkle, 1999) and it requires attention to the implementation process and how it works, as well as to processes that mediate and moderate the import of programs (Reynolds, 2004). The capacity for further innovation in

local settings requires more than the flexible replication of best practices.

In the case of service integration projects, the programming and implementation need to be co-constructed in local communities and evaluated at multiple levels (Connell & Kubisch, 1995). What are the aims of service integration in particular communities? How do agencies and different professional staff come together to work in new ways? How do organizations come to collaborate with shared purpose, programming, and perhaps even funding and governance? What are the different ways that parents and communities can be involved? How do any of these dimensions translate into the immediate environments of children and families in ways that might affect development and learning or that would support other social goals? Is there evidence that child development or other societal goals are being met?

Qualitative methodological approaches such as ethnographies and action research help answer these questions and fill out the possible processes (mediators) connecting programs and outcomes. They can also contribute to the picture of how context (moderators) affect the processes linking programs and outcomes in particular settings and across different levels of analysis within a setting. Action research also has the potential advantage of directly engaging practitioners and of producing more comprehensible findings.

Design research approaches. Design research is a hybrid approach that may help to improve local initiatives and to go beyond replication toward innovation. Design research combines some of the descriptive richness of ethnography and the collaborative ideas of action research with more iterative and quantitative measurement of programs, processes, outcomes, and contexts (Bereiter, 2002; Design-Based Research Collective, 2003; Cobb, Confrey, diSiessa, Lehrer, & Schauble, 2003). Although design research is typically applied to relatively simple initiatives such as curriculum development at a classroom level, the concepts may be applied to more complex undertakings. Cobb et al. (2003) describe a number of variants, including school district restructuring "experiments" involving organizational change. Design research teams working in local contexts keep an eye on what works, and what does not, with feedback to program design and redesign. Design researchers may develop modest theories about mediators of success, as well as contextual moderators. Design research is pragmatic and eclectic.

The Design-Based Research Collective (2003) defines the paradigm in terms of certain characteristics:

1. Goals of designing better programs are interwoven with goals of developing theory or prototheory about what works.
2. Development of program and research take place through continual cycles of design, enactment, analysis, and redesign.
3. Research must lead to sharable theories that help practitioners and other designers to understand the implications.
4. Research must account for how designs work in real settings, focusing on interactions that illuminate the learning issues or processes leading to program outcomes.
5. Research methods must "document and connect processes of enactment to outcomes of interest."

Cobb et al. (2003) describe the examination of ecology and process as follows:

Design experiments ideally result in greater understanding of learning ecology—a complex, interacting system involving multiple elements of different types and levels—by designing its elements and by anticipating how these elements function together. . . . a design theory explains why designs work and suggests how they may be adapted to new circumstances. (p. 9)

A primary purpose of design research is to develop theories about effective process and the means to support it. Process can mean constructs as varied as "knowledge building," "learning relevant social practices," "interest," and "identity." Means may be "affordances, materials, teaching practices, policy levers" and so on.

Bereiter (2002) argues that design research is not defined by a particular method but by its purpose: that of sustained innovation. It is also defined as being carried out in "communities of practice" having particular characteristics of innovativeness, responsiveness to evidence, and dedication to continual improvement. Communities of practice include researchers, designers, and practitioners working together to solve problems, test new ideas, and address negative results. Inclusion of practitioners in the research process helps insure that practice change accompanies design change and that practitioners are empowered to act and learn along with the design team (Wenger, 2001).

Application to integrated initiatives. Cobb et al. (2003) describe a number of variants, including school district restructuring "experiments" involving organizational change. Does the "Design Research" approach really apply to the case of integrated service initiatives in schools? Or are organizational designs for integration too complex for the approach? Do larger-scale initiatives across multiple sites eliminate possibilities for iterative design and reduce the scope for innovation? In our own research, as described later, we find design research ideas to be helpful, although the approach does not match our approach exactly. Some overlapping features are:

• Our aims are both pragmatic and conceptual/theoretical.
• Theories are humble and contextualized.
• How designs work (or fail) is described in multilevel process and context.
• Programs are designed or improved with collaboration among community agencies, practitioners, and researchers.
• Communities of practice work together and reflect on evidence to improve and innovate.
• Research contributes ideas and findings that foster a "learning organization" approach to the entire program.

However, the designs we employ are varied and could also be described in other ways. They take some of the lessons learned from the evaluation of CCIs. Our "theories of change" include organizational change as "process," in addition to "process" at the level of the child's and parent's microsystems. In more general terms, the evaluations we conduct are contextualized case studies with multiple levels of measurement and analysis across levels from program to process to child outcomes. Several of the projects involve quasi-experimental community comparison groups. One design also includes pre- and posttests. Although these designs do not yield the same definitive statements about causality as randomized experimentation, they are rich enough to provide converging evidence on processes and related ideas that improve local programs and contribute to an "evolving data base about what works and what is promising" (Schorr, Sylvester, & Dunkle, 1999).

CASE STUDY SUMMARIES

Local Context

Integrative supports for young children and families have a long history in the city of Toronto and the province of Ontario, as well as elsewhere. In 1887 Hester How, the first female school principal in Ontario, combined elementary schooling and preschool care by allowing pupils to bring their preschool siblings to school to play at the back of the classroom (Stapleford, 1989). Before her innovation, many children in the less privileged school neighborhood were truants because their mothers had to work and the children stayed home to care for younger sibs. A century later, in the 1980s and into the early 1990s, Ontario provincial policy supported the provision of childcare in schools and center space was part of the design in newly constructed schools. However, this approach was not sustained and its full potential was explored only in some pilot sites. Colocation did not lead to widespread integration and program continuity even for kindergarten children who might spend half a day in "school" and half a day in "care" in the same site. Furthermore, in 1994 the provincial government at the time put an end to expanding this form of integration as well as to other directions for even more ambitious early childhood supports. Promising initiatives such as parenting centers in Toronto schools (Gordon, 1987) were left without provincial support. Nevertheless, The Early Years Study (McCain & Mustard, 1999), commissioned by the same government, set out an ambitious plan for the integration of all early child development programs into a network of community-based early child development and parenting programs, which would be available to all young children and their families. The report documented the need for a system of early child development supports with an extensive research rationale, including evidence on the biological embedding of early experience. The provincial government subsequently took steps to implement the recommendations, but without involving core programs of kindergarten and childcare. As an example, a centerpiece was the establishment of a limited number of early years parenting centers, which initially were geared toward information dissemination and providing sites for existing parenting programs; these were not generally sited in school communities with childcare and other services. In the meantime, local integrated projects described below were developing at the community-school (Corter, 2001), school board (Pelletier & Brent, 2002) and city–school board levels (Corter et al., 2002) with participation and evaluation by a university team in collaboration with the community partners.

Project 1: Havenwood Place

Background. In 1997, the grassroots story of Havenwood Place began in one elementary school that served many recent immigrant families and faced issues of minority languages, unfamiliarity with a new culture and new school system, lack of resources in families, children seen as unprepared for schools and the school and teachers unprepared for the growing diversity (Corter, Harris, & Pelletier, 1998). For example, teachers tended to describe children of immigrants as "not ready" and to attribute sole responsibility to the parents. Not surprisingly, given the demographic profile, the school suffered from low scores on provincial standardized tests. However, the principal had a vision of "leveling the playing field." He believed that involving parents was key to more educational opportunities for all children and had begun outreach efforts through community ethnocultural groups. In the same community a variety of service agencies working with families and young children were facing the same challenges of serving the rapidly diversifying community, and they also were involved in discussions around service alliances to serve children under 6 years of age. One visionary agency head pushed the proposition that by pooling limited resources, outreach would be more successful with underserved groups and floated the idea of putting a one-stop shopping approach to service into the school. Within a few months the school found space, one agency found provincial funds for a coordinator, and the project was up and running.

Development and implementation. With relatively little external infrastructure support and little reference to existing models or literature, local community service agencies began to meet with parents and members of the school staff to bring in programs for families. A variety of community sectors donated staff time and relocated existing service delivery to Havenwood Place. Educational services included the local school board, public library, and a university partner. Health services included infant development, community health, and child and adolescent mental health. Social service agencies included a family education center and family services and parenting programs. The core of the idea was to use a community center's preschool parent–child program as a foundation for integrating other services and to site the program in a place accessible to the community. Once underway, the program resembled a kindergarten with spaces for parents and additional furniture. Parents joined in the "teaching" with modeled book reading and constructive play ("parent" is used generically in this and subsequent project reports, and the term includes some grandparents and guardians). Parent education circles were held in parallel with center-based activities. Although the general program was offered on a drop-in basis, more specialized programming was embedded in regularly scheduled blocks during the week. On some days, a translator or community worker from a service agency was present so that a particular language group could be targeted for attention. Parent and community volunteers participated on a weekly basis. Teacher education (early childhood and elementary) and social work students carried out their practicum placements and internships in the center under the supervision of cooperating teachers and social workers. The coordinator was a social worker with experience in family-community work. The program evolved through management meeting planning and systematic parent input and support by participant researchers.

Research role. As Havenwood Place mushroomed up in a matter of months and grew in scope, we were already conducting research on parent involvement in the school. We were invited to extend our research by evaluating the project and we joined the steering committee as participant observers and as contributors to the ideas and design. As the project developed, the research team fed findings back to the steering committee. The case study analysis described the organizational development via interviews with key players and meeting notes and reports. The school context was assessed with kindergarten parent surveys and a teacher focus group on readiness. The program was assessed through a narrative descriptive framework of people, space, time, materials, and activities (Pelletier, Power, & Park, 1993) and the Early Childhood Environment Rating Scale-Revised (ECERS-R). Graduate education students working on placements logged observations of program–child interactions. Professional perspectives came from interviews. Parent satisfaction with services and suggestions for the program were gauged by surveys. Demographic data on the surveys supported the service providers' perceptions that outreach was going well; clients matched the demographics of the neighborhood. Client satisfaction was predictably high, but parents had ideas for improvement that were taken up for discussion with the steering committee. From the ground-level of professionals, parents, and children, the program appeared to be working, as suggested by the following observations from a graduate education student:

A student teacher log on one child's first weeks at Havenwood Place:

When Jamal arrived, I said "Hello." He said, "No, get away from me." Jamal then hid in the coat area. When he joined his Mom in the play area, he played with toys but did not want anyone else near him. . . . When he attended on a subsequent day, Jamal screamed that he wanted to leave. His mother said she was leaving because the people attending a workshop in another area of the room could not hear. She put on her coat and Jamal ran outside. I asked the mother to be patient and said that everyone had kids here and that the parents could probably understand the noise. She said, "It's easier to stay at home, because he is just like this. I just stay home and never leave." She was obviously upset. I went outside and asked Jamal to please come inside; he initially refused. I mentioned that snack time was in ten minutes and he was welcome to leave after that. Jamal stomped his feet as he entered the classroom. He sat down for snack and proceeded to take the snack by the handful. I mentioned he could have as many as he liked but they were to be taken one at a time and that the plate was in the center of the table where other children could reach. I eventually removed the plate because Jamal would not follow the rules, but kept a close eye on him. Every time he finished a snack I asked if he wanted another. During a school break day, Jamal's older brother, Jorum, attended and I played house with both children. Jorum stayed with me all morning, and gave me a hug at the end and said, "Thank you." Mother also mentioned Jorum spoke about me at home. Over the next two weeks Jamal's behavior changed; although he tried to grab snacks. Jamal listened when asked to stop and waited for seconds; he began to play with other children with little fighting; he listened to stories and participated in the literacy program. Mother commented how he liked the program and asked to attend every day.

Observations on program development and design. The researchers' participant observation in the Steering Committee, along with the documentation of notes and reports, provided a rich picture of the development and early implementation of a complex program with more than a dozen participating agencies. In addition to the challenges of coordinating the multiple agencies with different organizational cultures, there were additional tasks of connecting the program to the community of potential users and to the culture of the host school and to the Board. Among the issues with which providers needed to contend was how much of the program should be focused on the child and how much on the parent? With time, the core program developed to be a child-driven curriculum in which parents participated; additional parent workshops were held on a "parent-withdrawal" basis. Teachers and facilitators explicitly modeled talk and demonstrated how to facilitate concept development. Another struggle was a professional one: To what extent should specialists from the service sectors run aspects of the program and to what extent should a generalist teacher/facilitator run the program? Ultimately, the program began with parents and children together; specialists came in to provide a "parent-only" time to discuss issues such as parenting, discipline, nutrition, and other topics. Issues of treatment versus prevention were examined. Given its prevention focus, should the center be a place where families could be treated for problems or a place where referrals would be made? In time, the space was able to house areas where parents could have access to necessities such as clothing, food, immunizations, and supplies, but also a place where parents could receive referrals or find out about other community services available to them. Translators and parent volunteers who spoke the many languages of the families were there to provide assistance with language. This became another issue, that is, in order to make this work, translators were needed. There were not enough professionals who spoke the languages of the families; volunteer lay workers assisted. Because of the many language and cultural groups of the families at the center, another struggle concerned degree of ethnospecificity versus cross-cultural programming. As time went on, feedback from surveys and direct contacts showed that parents enjoyed the cross-cultural blend. They learned as much about other languages and cultures as they did about English. Documentation such as pamphlets and information letters were provided in most of the target language groups. For the most part, parents and children wanted to learn about English schooling and about North American culture. They preferred to borrow children's books in English rather than in their own language although program staff strongly encouraged literacy in the home languages. None of this was anticipated and could only be known from working through the struggles and systematically attending to process.

Keys to success in getting integration underway. In the face of these complexities and challenges, the clear successes in quickly establishing the center and continuously improving it were remarkable. Two factors emerging as key to this grassroots success in the case study material were the role of inspired leaders and a cohesive steering committee, in which the goals of serving young children and families often outweighed agency interests and professional boundaries. Because the steering committee was "socially constructing" the program rather than implementing an existing one, there was continuous receptivity to formative evaluation information and exploration of new ideas. This stance helped to energize the organization to engage in continuing struggles around funding, integration of various services within the program, maintaining school board support for use of space, and the need to provide excellent educational content for preschoolers and their parents. With respect to the program content, a variety of co-located and co-ordinated services ranging from health to library were being delivered effectively and in an environment which rated in the good to excellent range on the ECERS-R scale. However, it took nearly a year before collaborative programming began to take hold. A program subcommittee worked on a tracking system for particular children/families identified as being at clinical risk for follow up within the program and its multiple elements or for outside referrals. A coherent approach to family literacy was also being developed to bring together previously disconnected elements (e.g., library programming, informal parent education, ECE programming).

A learning organization. The findings of the Havenwood Place project were process-oriented. We learned how to provide service delivery for those who were traditionally underserved. We learned that engaging parents early provided a growing capacity for parent–school engagement; parents reported that the school felt like a second home. We learned that innovative grassroots programs can be established with little external infrastructure support as long as there is strong leadership and a coherence of vision on the part of the key players—the school administration, the community service agencies, the front line staff working with children and parents and the families themselves. The commitment to work together meant tough organization-building, but this targeted work bridged cultural differences among the professional groups. Another key to success was the openness to ideas. Descriptive case study material, fed back in formative fashion, contributed to the improving design. A graduate student from our team and staff from the project presented the emerging case study at an NAEYC convention. As the project continued to unfold in succeeding years, the project coordinator and partner agency staff reported on the project in a local professional journal and framed the lessons in a theory of change (Cantwell, Bodolai, & Shariff, 2001). Success was thus built on a common mission to work together in a learning community. Finally, we learned that sustainability and scaling up require major external infrastructure support. In that light, another outcome of the Havenwood project was the school board's decision to provide the funding to scale up to 10 Parent Readiness Centers across the board. This became the focus for Project 2, described later.

TABLE 27.1. Follow-up Grade 3 Tests (percentage of students meeting expectations)

	Reading		Writing		Math	
	01	02	01	02	01	02
Havenwood School	32	40	40	60	57	70
District Average	57	56	58	60	70	67

Epilogue. Interestingly, we did not have systematic measures of how these changes affected children's readiness or how they might ripple through the school. Nevertheless, in following up the outcomes at Havenwood School over several years, it was possible to track the school's performance on the annual provincewide standardized tests. In 2002, the first cohort of children who had come through Havenwood Place and the Readiness Center participated in the Grade 3 standardized tests. The school's scores in reading, writing and mathematics increased substantially from the 2001 results. Across 125 elementary schools, Havenwood School was in the top 25% of positive change scores in all three areas of reading, writing and mathematics (see Table 27.1). This is not experimental evidence for effects of Havenwood Place, but it is a finding consistent with beneficial effects of the program.

Project 2: Parent Readiness Centers

Development and implementation. Sustainability and scaling up of Project 1 required major support, which was given by the school board: 10 new school-based centers inspired by Havenwood Place were opened, generally in neighborhoods with large immigrant populations and lower socioeconomic status. The model for the center was loosely based on bringing parents to preschool programs with their children but with more of a focus on school readiness and looking ahead to the provincial kindergarten curriculum (Pelletier & Corter, 2005). Details of how to define the model and implement it were left to the teachers, a board consultant, and the research team. Each school provided a large kindergarten classroom for the program. The Readiness Centers were led by trained kindergarten teachers who developed the program based on the provincial kindergarten curriculum with particular attention to goals for children's literacy and numeracy development. The Ontario Kindergarten Program (Ontario Ministry of Education, 1998) includes learning expectations for 4- and 5-year-olds, and these expectations are modified to suit the developmental levels of the children. The Parent Readiness Center program was designed for 4-year-olds and their families; that is, teachers taught classes of approximately 10 to 12 children and accompanying parents, bringing the "class size" to approximately 24. Families participated in this unique "junior kindergarten" program for approximately 12 weeks, 3 times a week. Teachers used instructional time to model teaching strategies and questioning techniques. Parents then accompanied their children to activity time to participate in play, craft, science, mathematics and language activities with their child. In addition, based on the Havenwood collaborative model, there were special parent-only times facilitated by various community service representatives. Topics for the parent-only sessions included behavior management, health and nutrition, library services, computer software workshops, educational television, music, literacy workshops, make and take learning workshops, and others.

Research approach and multiple measures. Systematic measures were collected on the process, programs, interactions, and child outcomes. The design research began with focus group interviews with kindergarten teachers. Swick and McKnight's (1989) research had shown that kindergarten teachers were more supportive of parent involvement than teachers with experience at other grade levels, and we wanted to assess these teachers' openness to this type of program. As the project got underway, the research team participated in regular meetings with a board consultant and the teachers who were running the 10 readiness center programs. This routine became the forum for sharing ongoing measurement, feedback to sites, and plans for improvement. Teachers were eager to hear regular observational reports as well as occasional summary reports that showed trends in the findings, for example, differences among parent groups depending on home language. For example, there were differences in parents' goals for children in attending the programs, depending on whether the parents had English as a first language or as a Second Language (ESL). ESL parents more often mentioned academic goals (e.g., literacy, numbers, language) whereas majority language parents mentioned more social adaptive goals (e.g., cooperation with peers, play, share with others).

Individual teachers were interviewed weekly about their impressions of the previous week, their celebrations and challenges, as well as about their goals for the following week. The ongoing feedback from the researchers and from the other teachers helped them to modify their plans for the week. This process fostered an emerging parent curriculum with parent and researcher input. Parents were interviewed at the beginning of the program about their goals for themselves and their child, about their feelings of being their child's teacher at home, and about their views of parent involvement. Before the sessions ended, all parents were interviewed about their feelings of being involved and about changes in their approaches to parenting and teaching. More than half the participating families were recent immigrants to Canada and spoke a language other than English. The ESL groups were predominantly Chinese, Eastern European, East Indian, Tamil, and Vietnamese. Researchers also participated in the centers by observing and recording the processes of the programs.

Scaling up in Year 2 continued as the 10 half-day centers became full-day programs and 4 new full-day centers were added. This support came hand in hand with the ongoing research. As reports of the success became known in the school board, the additional funds were found. Interviews with parents and staff captured the impact on families and schools and how it changed over time. Researchers continued to participate in the program as observers and facilitators; field notes were used to describe what occurred among people, how the space was used, how time was differentially directed to children, parents and combined families, and how materials supported families in their own cultures and in the new culture of English schooling. The ECERS-Revised was used as a standardized measure of program quality.

Child outcome follow-up. The following year, when the children were in senior kindergarten, a battery of readiness measures was administered to children who had participated in the Readiness Center program and to children who had not participated. The children who had not participated fell into two groups—those who had other preschool experience and those who had no preschool experience outside the home. The readiness measures included a standardized vocabulary test (Stanford-Binet Vocabulary subtest), a standardized early reading measure (Test of Early Reading Ability–II), a newly developed number knowledge task (Case, 2000), child interviews about kindergarten (children's school scripts—Pelletier, 1998, 1999), and teacher ratings of readiness in five areas as assessed by the Early Developmental Instrument (Offord & Janus, 1999). Readiness also was assessed through the reports of parents in social as well as academic realms.

Findings. The multiple measures collected over time permitted ongoing formative and summative evaluation of the family involvement program. Initial focus group interviews with kindergarten teachers prior to the program had shown that they believed that children's readiness for school was the responsibility of parents with teachers being responsible for academic learning once the children came to school. As they moved into their Readiness Center roles, these teachers saw one-way responsibilities to directly prepare children with assistance from the parents. However, teachers' views of readiness changed dramatically over the course of their participation—gradually, their goals for meeting curriculum expectations through teaching children changed to meeting broader goals through working with parents. Increasingly teachers' goals became parent- and child-focused rather than child-focused, and their views of parents became increasingly positive. Parents revealed goals that helped teachers to understand their situations—their fears about not understanding a new culture or school system, their goals for their children to have a better life and good education, and hopes that they themselves would learn English or would learn about the school system. There were notable group differences between families who spoke a language other than English and those who spoke English as a first language. ESL parents' goals for themselves and their children were significantly more academic in nature; English first language parents' goals for themselves and their children were somewhat more social. An important finding from this research that held for all parents, was that parents who participated in the program felt significantly more efficacious as parents and as teachers of their children than at the outset of the program (Pelletier & Brent, 2002), a finding consistent with Hoover-Dempsey's work (Reed, Jones, Walker, & Hoover-Dempsey, 2000).

The following year, when the children were in senior kindergarten, readiness measures showed a significant effect of family participation in the Readiness Center program. ESL children had significantly higher vocabulary, early reading, and number knowledge scores than a matched group of children who had

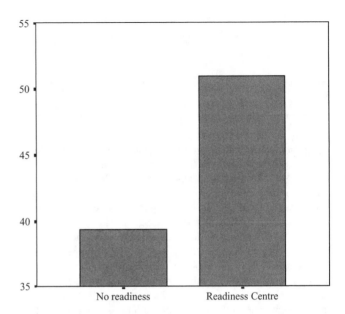

FIGURE 27.1. Comparison of readiness scores for ESL children with and without Readiness Center experience.

no other preschool experience (see Figure 27.1). Another set of important findings were parents' reports of improved feelings of efficacy, about the importance of involvement, and about teachers' changing understanding of the true meaning of partnership in education. The process thus appears to include building relationships among schools and families. Of course, parents' personal development may be an outcome in itself, a process leading to child outcomes.

The experimental critique and rejoinders. In spite of what looked like positive outcomes, the research is open to "experimental" critique. The Parent Readiness Center research suffered from nonrandom assignment of families to conditions because it was a naturally occurring intervention in the school board. Thus competing causal interpretations are possible, including the possibility of selection bias—more motivated and competent parents would be more likely to bring their children to the centers (cf., Gilliam, Ripple, Zigler, & Leiter, 2000). Nevertheless, the richness of the database allowed us to address this possibility and questions of process and cause. For example, demographic surveys were available for subgroups of families in the kindergarten classes in Year 2 (including those who had Readiness Center experience, and those who did not). An analysis showed that there were no demographic differences between groups, that is, of parents who had Readiness Center experience, who had another form of preschool experience or who had no preschool experience whatsoever. Furthermore, there was active program outreach on the part of the Readiness Center teachers; for example, they took books to the nearby apartment complex and encouraged mothers to bring their children for story time while the laundry was in the machines in the adjacent room. Interviews with participating parents suggested that many came only because of these extraordinary efforts.

Perhaps most tellingly, "program effects" varied across centers and were positively associated with program quality. Specifically, child outcomes in Year 2 were significantly related to two environment subscales on the ECERS-R in Year 1: interaction quality and program structure. The association of the program structure subscale with outcome mirrors previous findings on the importance of explicit programming for children in successful comprehensive preschool programs (Ramey & Ramey, 1998; Peters et al., 2000). The association of outcome with the interaction subscale and the triangulation of this subscale with the qualitative reports of teachers and parents is strongly suggestive of a process pathway from program to outcome through enhanced relationships and self esteem (Pelletier & Brent, 2002).

In support of this process story, we found that strong relationships developed among professionals, researchers, and parents. The qualitative measures showed that teachers moved from "instrumental" to "respectful" relationships with parents, with some teachers reporting that it was the most humbling and important work they had ever done. Effects on parents were equally positive. The "teacher" was the highest rated part of the program and parental self-efficacy improved as a result of participation (Pelletier & Brent, 2002). Finally, the ECERS-R evidence strongly suggests that program quality and interaction effects make a difference for children. In spite of these rejoinders, the issue of nonexperimental design remained. Thus, Project 3 addressed the issues of selection bias by employing a pre-/postdesign evaluating a different version of bringing parents to school.

Project 3: Parents in Kindergarten

Ecology change and program design change. The positive findings from Study 2 made a compelling story with the qualitative documentation of positive interaction processes leading to client and professional satisfaction and hard data on child outcomes. However, in the meantime a provincewide push for junior kindergarten programs in all boards meant that money which has supported the Readiness Centers would now go to junior kindergarten programs for 4-year-olds. Nevertheless, based on the trends shown in the previous project, research funding was subsequently obtained to transform the program and move it directly into the kindergarten classroom. The research brought parents to kindergarten with their child one day a week for 12 weeks. Thus, the research was carried out with 4- and 5-year-old children and their families in 17 kindergarten classrooms mainly in high-risk neighborhoods in the original school board and in a middle-class, predominantly white, school in another board. The program moved the Readiness Center model into the kindergarten classroom with the addition of teacher assistance for the kindergarten teacher on the day of the program. This allowed the kindergarten teacher to participate more freely in the parent program. Children from all kindergarten classes in the participating schools were given consent forms to take home. Classes were randomly assigned to the control group or to the intervention group. Demographic characteristics of the control and intervention groups were identical. All control and intervention group children were pretested on a battery of academic and social measures in the fall term of the kindergarten year and were posttested on alternate versions of the same measures during the last month of kindergarten. Additional interviews were held with parents and teachers.

Preliminary results and partial replication. First year results partially replicated the Readiness Center project results. Children whose families were ESL showed significantly greater gains when their parents participated in the program; however, the difference for English first language children was not significant. Parental participation was linked to mother's occupational status; lower occupational and stay-at-home status were linked to greater participation. Qualitative data also revealed some similar patterns to the Readiness Center study; that is, parents enjoyed the program and believed they became better parents as a result of participation. Teachers, likewise, noted that their instructional strategies changed when parents were involved; specifically, teachers targeted their teaching to parents, who in turn could facilitate their own child's learning in the class and at home. Research has continued into a second year of the project with additional analyses and an additional cohort of children and parents contributing data. The first year evaluation of Project 3 allowed us to draw tentative conclusions about process and outcome. For example, the more tightly controlled experimental design of Project 3, with pre-/ postcontrol for selection bias, yielded the same child outcome results as the quasi-experimental design of Project 2. There have been quixotic findings about what works best for whom and these relate to factors of parent education and occupation level.

In spite of the controls added to Project 3 and promising outcomes, we are still analyzing "what" processes or factors may have jointly contributed to the findings. Furthermore, in both Projects 2 and 3, the levels of analysis are limited to the participants, their interactions, and to the programs. In order to enhance the impact on early childhood development and programming, we need to move beyond the school to examine widescale community and ecological context. Project 4 aims to do just that in an ambitious multilevel program and evaluation.

Project 4: Toronto First Duty

Aims. In Projects 2 and 3 the focus was on school readiness via integration between parents and schools; community services were invited into the projects but were not integral in the way they were in Project 1, Havenwood Place. In Project 4, the Toronto First Duty initiative set out with broad child development and parenting support goals and a vision of core integrated services to achieve the goals. Funding and support for the project came from multiple sources including the municipal government, a foundation, and the school board. The project is currently in the implementation stage, so the research picture to date is limited to program design and process with most of the outcome story still to come.

Project development. The "...first duty of a state is to see that every child born therein shall be well-housed, clothed, fed and educated, till it attain years of discretion," according to the

19th-century British social reformer John Ruskin. This quote provided the title for the 1997 City of Toronto First Duty report recommending a municipal strategy for supporting young children. The Toronto First Duty project (TFD) grew from the City strategy and from the leadership of the Atkinson Charitable Foundation, the Toronto District School Board, and other community partners. Integrating services to provide better support for the development of young children through 6 years of age, along with support for their parents, is at the heart of TFD. Part of integration is breaking down service "silos" marked by professional and jurisdictional barriers in order to optimize service. The project intends to do this at the level of local collaborative work among different professional groups and different agencies. It is also aimed at informing higher-level policies, at the municipal and provincial levels, and bringing about changes that will enable effective practices. Integration also includes various forms of outreach and parent involvement with services to support child development and to support parent education and employment.

The role of research. Research and evaluation is a crucial part of the project with support from city, foundation, and federal sources for a university research team (Corter et al., 2002). The data gathering and analysis extends across four years and across multiple levels of analysis from the children's experiences in the program to costs and benefits of the initiative. In its design, the research includes traditional program evaluation components with a final report on the pilot project in 2005. However, the evaluation is also working collaboratively with sites to provide formative feedback that honors some of the design research tenets of systematically feeding back findings to sites for improvement and redesign. The evaluation also works to build theoretical understanding, which goes beyond describing the program and its impacts, to describing and analyzing the process of developing and implementing a complex, innovative program across multiple sites, as well as the resulting micro-level processes that affect the lives of children and the adults who nurture and teach them.

The evaluation is designed to support change beyond the five sites in several ways. One will be to develop narrative guides that are evidence-based stories, not cookbooks, that support scaling up the project on a citywide basis, and beyond. These guides can support local exploration and social construction of effective professional and organizational changes necessary to overcome barriers and integrate efforts for improved outcomes. Another way is to contribute to policy via "evidence-based storytelling" that makes the findings accessible to the general public and to policy makers at various governmental levels. Of course, impact on policy making will require hard data on outcomes of new and expanded services offered, but it will also require hard and soft data to report on potential processes representing likely casual pathways leading to impacts on children and parents.

Levels of analysis and measurement. The TFD evaluation aims to analyze the development, implementation, and impacts of the pilot sites within three general levels of analysis across the implementation of the project:

- program, policy, and services;
- children and parents; and,
- community and public awareness.

To track these levels, a variety of techniques for data gathering is being used, including document collection of meeting notes and other records from site agencies, participant observation in organizational meetings at the site and projectwide levels, focus groups and interviews with program staff, parents, and children, surveys with parents and staff. As in our previous projects described earlier, direct observation of programs and direct observations and assessment of children are also being carried out. A new client information system is being implemented that includes detailed demographic information on participants and detailed intake and tracking information on individual use of each element of the integrated services.

Key questions. In this research, several key questions focus on the design and understanding of integration and knowledge-building research:

1. What does service integration and innovation mean in practice at each of the sites? Can these practices be characterized along a continuum of integration, from coordination to transformation, with new forms of programming, joint planning, pooling of funding, management etc.? What's new, what's been done before, and how long does it take to change? What are the beliefs of service providers about the effects of these practices in achieving their own aims and those of the funders? How do sites develop shared beliefs and practice plans—for example, concrete curriculum for children and programming for parents? How do they implement their plans and monitor outcomes? How do site partners overcome barriers, act flexibly, communicate, and learn together?
2. How are parents and communities involved in the planning, implementation, and ongoing development of the pilots? How are they and their children affected? How are underserved groups brought into the process and into the services? What are the experiences of children and parents in the pilot programs? What is the level of community awareness of needs to support young children and the pilot projects? Are there links to other community services and supports that are not a formal part of the pilot? Is there evidence that the pilot increases community capacity (knowledge, collaboration) to meet changing community needs?
3. How does the evaluation process work in relation to the goals of the funders and sites? Are the aims of collaborative design and formative feedback achieved? Can the evaluation process support the development of integration and innovation and learning (self-evaluation) by organizations? Can it support community and public awareness of early childhood education, development, and care successes?

Findings to date. Information and measures collected during the first 2 years of implementation are being analyzed and provide preliminary answers to these questions. Some examples follow.

1. Professional and organizational change has been charted through meeting notes, site documents, interviews and surveys with staff. Detailed case studies of each of the five sites were produced at the beginning of the project (e.g., Corter et al., 2002) and are updated in subsequent, semiannual progress reports. These reports are fed back to the sites and to the overall project steering committee and form the basis for focus group discussions of progress. Professional change and challenges have been areas of particular focus; a number of strategies have been developed at both the site and project levels to overcome the inevitable challenges to merging professional cultures and work. These range from creating more opportunities for shared meetings among frontline staff within sites—allowing for time to build trust and understanding—to projectwide knowledge sharing in workshops and interactive Web sites. In iterative fashion, each of these strategies is then evaluated to determine the degree of success and need for redesign or alternative steps.

2. Parent involvement and impacts on children and family. Focus groups and interviews with parents and children show that client satisfaction is high for the program participants. Nevertheless, the information being fed back to the project shows room for improvement and reflection. For example, despite some efforts to include parent input through focus groups and representation on site committees, parents at large do not feel that they have had input into program design ("nobody asked us")—even though they like the result. Parent outreach efforts are underway, but sites are not satisfied with the results to date. The intake and tracking system is beginning to provide hard data on how well sites are doing in reaching the underserved. Client postal codes and corresponding demographic data from the census will permit literal mapping of the footprint of participation in service across the community and across variations in demographic factors.

The question of whether the evaluation serves the aims of the project by contributing to knowledge building is answered positively by some of the formative feedback activity described in reporting these findings. Another interesting example, is the attempt to operationalize what integration means for purposes of clarifying the funder's vision and giving sites the opportunities to reflect on and plan their own progress. This example is the development of an R&D tool consisting of indicators of change in moving toward integration.

Toronto First Duty indicators of change. Progress reports from the research team raised questions about how much integrative change was taking place. The sites and the projectwide steering committee wanted more detail and description on the core elements of integration. And they wanted benchmarks to monitor progress toward goals of the overall project and goals of each site. The Indicators of Change tool was developed to meet these needs. It operationally defines the funders' visions and expectations but is not meant to be used summatively. Instead it is meant to give formative support to planning and priority setting and to feed discussion at the site and projectwide levels. The sites have used the tool to review progress to date in meetings with members of the research team. They also have identified

where they began as the project got underway and the goals that they expect to achieve by the end of the project. An outline of the TFD Indicators tool and a graphic representation of one site's self assessment are presented in Figure 27.2.

The Indicators of Change tool is designed partly to clarify the meaning of integration and the TFD funders' model. Tensions between funders and grantees in top-down initiatives are often a "flashpoint" for conflict (Kubisch et al., 2002), particularly when there is lack of clarity around the funders' intentions. The TFD Indicators provide some of this clarity. The exercise of using the tool also builds bottom-up capacity in the sites to reflect systematically and periodically on organizational and practice change and integration.

CONCLUSION

The focus in this chapter is on ways of thinking about school-based programs of integrated early childhood services and evaluating how these programs work in local contexts. The case studies of projects we have evaluated include attempts at knowledge building for the benefit of the individual projects and for external audiences ranging from local policy makers and analysts to other scholars interested in integrative programming for early childhood. Our "evidence-based storytelling" about program–process–outcome is meant to be complementary to other approaches including stricter "science" approaches. Our use of rich measurement allows us to explore program design and implementation, different types of outcomes, and potential causal processes linking programs and outcomes.

In Project 1, a multiservice, preschool parent–child center, we saw grassroots program development and design that led to better community outreach and both empowerment and satisfaction among parents and participating agencies and professionals. However, we did not have systematic evidence on other important outcomes such as school readiness. In Project 2, a unique parent–child kindergarten readiness program, child outcomes were rigorously assessed. Differences were found between program participants and a comparison group, but selection bias was not ruled out by the quasi-experimental design. Nevertheless, we were able to rule out confounding by demographic factors. We also traced potential process pathways though other measurement points, including parents' goals in participating in the program, changed relationships between parents and teachers, and quality of interactions in the program. The evidence for causal pathways is not definitive but points to the strong possibility that the relationships and interactions between the adults helped minority language parents to achieve their academic goals for their children. In Project 3, a program for parents embedded in regular kindergarten classrooms, the causal link between parenting support and academic outcomes for children was replicated in a pre-post treatment and comparison group design.

Project 4 is a multisite, integrated services pilot built around a core of kindergarten, childcare, and parenting programs. It was specifically designed to test a model that could be scaled up but adapted to local circumstances. The project is still in the process of implementation, and our evidence concerns process more

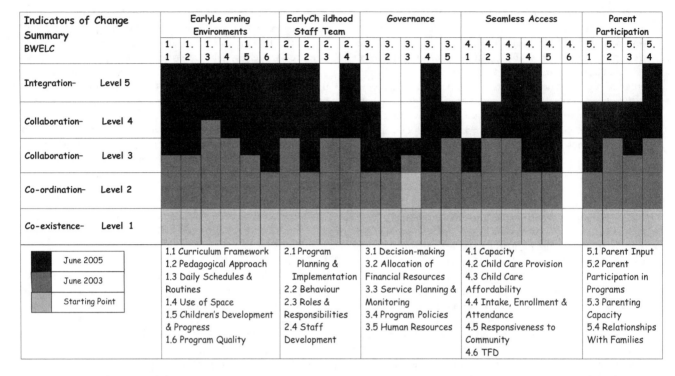

FIGURE 27.2. Indicators of change.

Outline of Toronto First Duty Indicators

The Toronto First Duty incorporates five core integrative elements: early learning environments, early childhood staff teams, local governance, seamless access, and parent involvement. The elements are broad categories that work together to create an integrated service delivery model that is available to all young children and their families in a community. Taken together, the elements represent the building blocks of the Toronto First Duty.

A unique set of program indicators define specific activities and practice for each core element. Indicators are used to track the progress that Toronto First Duty sites are making towards implementing the five core elements. Each program indicator is ranked on a scale from 1 to 5.

- Level 1 describes practices in early childhood and family programs that are co-located in the same building or neighbourhood but they operate as separate and distinct services.
- Level 2 rating describes individual programs that are sharing information with each other and perhaps coordinating specific activities.
- Level 3 indicates some specific joint TFD activities that merge human resources, space, or materials to offer new program opportunities.
- Level 4 describes an expansion of joint TFD activities and a clear influence on the operation of the original core programs.
- A rating of 5 describes full integration of existing and expanded programs into a blended service delivery system within a defined neighbourhood or community.

than outcomes, with descriptions focusing on organizational and professional change. The professional change in learning to work and think together across professional lines is another story of relationship building. The process of organization change is enormously complex, but one story line is how integration happens. The struggles and successes to date in implementing the integrated service model are documented in a variety of sources of data from meeting notes to interviews. A particularly interesting window into the integration process is a self-study tool designed by the project research team. It allows sites to assess their progress and goals for integrated early learning environments, staff teams, local governance, seamless access, and parent involvement. This exemplifies the approach of building capacity for self-assessment into the project teams at the community level, along with providing formative feedback.

In fact, our knowledge-building approach assumes that we can join project developers and practitioners in a "learning community" approach to evaluating and improving. This approach has much in common with design research approaches featuring collaboration among designers, practitioners, and researchers and evidence-based feedback to improve results (Cobb et al., 2003). Part of the approach is developing accessible "prototheory" about processes linking programs and outcomes or "theories of change." These aren't meant as take-away lessons, they are contextualized and meant to be used by project developers and practitioners.Contextualization means paying attention to the ecology of program–process–outcome links. For example, relationship-building between professionals and parents doesn't automatically flow into academic readiness for children. However, if it is connected to goals of minority language parents, and if it is supported by quality program environments, it may contribute.

The research approach illustrated here is also akin to particular suggestions about non-traditional research approaches needed to understand complex community initiatives, as building community capacity for accountability (Wandersman & Florin, 2003) or as an "ongoing developmental learning process" (Knapp, 1995). We hope that the research we are doing can help bridge the separate cultures of research, practice, and policy (Shonkoff, 2000) by generating "reasonable working hypotheses" that guide actions aimed at outcomes and that can be tested in new contexts.

ACKNOWLEDGMENTS

We are grateful to the parents, children, professionals, and others who have participated in and collaborated with the research described in this chapter. We are indebted to the graduate students and colleagues who have helped us think about service integration for young children and families and who helped carry out the research projects. The other members of the Toronto First Duty Research Team contributed substantially to the evaluation and ideas surrounding that initiative. Special thanks also go to our research partners in the Peel District School Board and Toronto District School Board. We would also like to thank the sponsors of the research and development projects described in this chapter: Atkinson Charitable Foundation, City of Toronto, Deutsche Bank, Ontario Ministry of Education, and Social Sciences and Humanities Council of Canada (grant file 410-2002-1625, awarded to JP). Preparation of this chapter and many other aspects of the work was supported by the Dr. R. G. N. Laidlaw Centre at the Institute of Child Study, part of the Ontario Institute for Studies in Education at the University of Toronto; thanks especially to Christine Davidson.

References

Bacon, J., & Brink, S. (2003). Understanding the early years: Research results for five pilot communities. *Education Canada, 43*, 16–17.

Barrett, M. (1999). Local evaluation of Program Without Walls: Lessons learned. *Imprint, 25*, 11–12.

Beach, J., & Bertrand, J. (2000). *More than the sum of the parts: An early childhood development system for Canada.* (Occasional Paper No. 12): Childcare Resource and Research Unit, University of Toronto Retrieved August 16, 2004, from http://www.childcarecanada.org/resources/CRRUpubs/op12/index.html

Bereiter, C. (2002). Design research for sustained innovation. Cognitive studies. *Bulletin of the Japanese Cognitive Science Society, 9*, 321–327.

Blair, C. (2002). School readiness: Integrating cognition and emotion in a neurobiological conceptualization of children's functioning at school entry. *American Psychologist, 57*, 111–127.

Blank, M., Hale, E., Housman, N., Kaufmann, B. I., Martinez, M., McCloud, B., et al. (2001). *School-community partnerships in support of student learning: Taking a second look at the governance of the 21st Century Community Learning Centers Program.* Washington, DC: Institute for Educational Leadership.

Borman, G. D., Hewes, G. M., Overman, L. T., & Brown, S. (2003). Comprehensive school reform and achievement: A meta-analysis. *Review of Educational Research, 73*(2), 125–230.

Bronfenbrenner, U. (1989). Ecological systems theory. In R. Vasta (Ed.), *Six theories of child development: Revised formulations and current issues.* Greenwich, CT: JAI.

Bronfenbrenner, U. (1979). *The ecology of human development.* Cambridge, MA: Harvard University Press.

Brush, L., Deich, S., Traylor, K. T. Pindus, N. (1995). Options for Full-Day Services for Children Participating in Head. Retrieved May 10, 2005 from http://www.eric.ed.gov ERIC ED 394738.

Campbell, F. A., Ramey, C. T., Pungello, E. P., Sparling, J., & Miller-Johnson, S. (2002). Early childhood education: Young adult outcomes from the Abecedarian Project. *Applied Developmental Science, 6*, 42–57.

Cantwell, J., Bodolai, P., & Shariff, A. (2001). Partners in prevention. *Imprint, 30*, 1–3.

Carnegie Corporation of New York. (1994). *Starting points: Meeting the needs of our youngest children.* New York: Author.

Case, R. (2000, April). *Measuring number sense from a developmental perspective.* Unpublished manuscript, Toronto, Ontario, Canada: Institute of Child Study, University of Toronto.

Chaskin, R. J., & Richman, H. A. (1992). Concerns about school-linked services: Institution-based versus community-based models. School-linked Services: *The Future of Children, 2.* Retrieved August 16, 2004, from http://www.futureofchildren.org/homepage2824/archive.htm.

Cobb, P., Confrey, J., DiSessa, A., Lehrer, R., & Schauble, L. (2003). Design experiments in educational research. *Educational Researcher, 32*(1), 9–13.

Comer, J. P., Haynes, N. M., Joyner, E. T., & Ben-Avie, M. (1996). *Rallying the whole village: The Comer process for reforming education.* New York: Teachers College Press.

Connell, J., & Kubisch, A. (1995). Applying a theory of change approach to the evaluation of comprehensive community initiatives: Progress, prospects, and problems. In A. C. Kubisch, K. Fulbright-Anderson, J. P. Connell (Eds.), *New approaches to evaluating community initiatives. Vol. 2. Theory, measurement and analysis.* Washington, DC: Aspen Institute. Retrieved May 6, 2005, from http://www.aspenroundtable.org/vol2/connell.htm

Connell, J., Kubisch, A., Schorr, L., & Weiss, C. H. (1995). *New approaches to evaluating community initiatives: Concepts, methods, and contexts.* Washington, DC: Aspen Institute. Retrieved May 6, 2005, from http://www.aspenroundtable.org.

Corter, C. (2001). Integrating early childhood services and communities: A role for schools. *Every Child, 7*(3), 10–11.

Corter, C., Bertrand, J., Griffin, T., Endler, M., Pelletier, J., & McKay, D. (2002). *Toronto First Duty Starting Gate Report: Implementing integrated foundations for early childhood.* Toronto, Ontario, Canada: City of Toronto.

Corter, C., Harris, P., & Pelletier, J. (1998). *Parent participation in Elementary schools: The role of school councils in development and diversity:* Transfer Grant Report to the Ministry of Education and Training of Ontario, including case study of Havenwood Place, an integrated services, preschool parent centre. Unpublished Report.

Corter, C., & Pelletier, J. (2005). Parent and community and involvement in schools: Policy panacea or pandemic? In N. Bascia, A. Cumming, A. Datnow, K. Leithwood and D. Livingstone (Eds.), *International handbook of educational policy*. (pp. 295–327). Dordrecht, The Netherlands: Kluwer.

Crowson, R. L., & Boyd, W. L. (1995). Integration of services for children. In L. Rigsby, M. Reynolds & M. Wang (Eds.), *School-Community Connections*. (pp. 121–142). San Francisco: Jossey-Bass.

Cryer, D., & Burchinal, M. (1997). Parents as child care consumers. *Early Childhood Research Quarterly, 12*, 35–58.

Cunningham, C., Boyle, M., Offord, D., Racine, Y., Hundert, J., Secord, M., et al. (2000). Triministry study: Correlates of school-based parenting course utilization. *Journal of Consulting and Clinical Psychology, 68*, 928–933.

Davies, D. (1995). Collaboration and family empowerment as strategies to achieve comprehensive services. In L. Rigsby, M. Reynolds & M. Wang (Eds.), *School Community Connections*. San Francisco: Jossey-Bass.

Delgado-Gaitan, C., & Trueba, H. (1991). *Crossing cultural borders: Education for immigrant families in America*. New York: Falmer Press.

Design-Based Research Collective. (2003). Design-based research: An emerging paradigm for educational inquiry. *Educational Researcher, 32*, 5–8.

Dryfoos, J. G. (1994). Under one roof. *American School Board Journal, 181*, 28–31.

Eisenhart, M., & Towne, L. (2003). Contestation and change in national policy on "scientifically based" education research. *Educational Researcher, 32*, 31–38.

Epstein, J., & Conners, L. (2002). Family, school, community partnerships. In M. Bornstein (Ed.), *Handbook of parenting* 2nd ed., Vol. 5, pp. 407–437. Englewood, NJ: Erlbaum.

Ferguson, E. B., & Prentice, S. L. (2000). Exploring parental involvement in Canada: An ideological maze. In J. Hayden (Ed.), *Landscapes in early education: cross-national perspectives on empowerment, a guide for the new millennium*. (pp. 219–238). New York: Peter Lang.

Fullan, M. (2000). The three stories of education reform. *Phi Delta Kappan, 81*, 581–584.

Fullan, M. (2001). *Leading in a culture of change*. San Francisco, CA: Jossey-Bass.

Garbarino, J. & Ganzel, B. (2000). The human ecology of early risk. In J. P., Shonkoff, & S. T. Meisels, . (Eds.). *Handbook of early childhood intervention*. (pp. 78–96). New York: Cambridge University Press.

Gilliam, W. S., & Zigler, E. & Leiter, V. (2000). A critical meta-analysis of all evaluations of state-funded preschool from 1997 to 1998: Implications for policy, service delivery and program evaluation. *Early Childhood Research Quarterly, 15*, 441–473.

Gilliam, W. S., Ripple, C. H., Zigler, E. F., & Leiter, V. (2000). Evaluating child and family demonstration initiatives: Lessons from the comprehensive child development program. *Early Childhood Research Quarterly, 15*, 41–59.

Glass, N. (1999). Sure Start: The development of an early intervention programme for young children in the United Kingdom. *Children & Society, 13*, 257–264.

Gordon, M. (1987). Toronto Board of Education Parenting Centres. *Journal of the Canadian Association for Young Children,* (Fall), 41–61.

Griffith, J. (1998). The relation of school structure and social environment to parent involvement in elementary schools. *The Elementary School Journal, 99*, 53–79.

Halfon, N., Sutherland, C., View-Sneider, M., Kloppenburg, A., Wright, R., Uyeda, J., et al. (2001). *Reaching Back to Create a Brighter Future: The Role of Schools in Promoting School Readiness*. Los Angeles: UCLA Centre for Healthier Children, Families and Communities.

Huston, A. C., Duncan, G. J., Granger, R., Bos, J., McLoyd, V., Mistry, R., et al. (2001). Work-based antipoverty programs for parents can enhance the school performance and social behavior of children. *Child Development, 72*, 318–336.

Hyman, J. (2002). *Not quite chaos: Toward a more disciplined approach to community building*. Baltimore, MD: Anne E. Casey Foundation.

Ingram, D., Bloomberg, L., & Seppannen, P. (1996). *Collaborative initiatives to develop integrated services for children and families*. Minneapolis, Minnesota: Center for Applied Research and Educational Improvement, College of Education and Human Development, University of Minnesota.

Kagan, S. (1991). *United we stand: Collaboration for child care and early education services*. New York: Teacher's College Press.

Kagan, S., & Neuman, M. (2003). Integrating early care and education. *Educational Leadership, 60*, 58–63.

Keating, D. P., & Hertzman, C. (1999). *Developmental health and the wealth of nations: Social, biological, and educational dynamics*. New York: Guilford Press.

Kirst, M. W., & Kelley, C. (1995). Collaboration to improve education and children's services: Politics and policy making. In L. Rigsby, M. Reynolds & M. Wang (Eds.), *School community connections*. (pp. 21–44). San Francisco: Jossey-Bass.

Knapp, M. S. (1995). How shall we study comprehensive, collaborative services for children and families? *Educational Researcher, 24*, 5–16.

Kohen, D., Brooks-Gunn, J., Leventhal, T., & Hertzman, C. (2002). Neighbourhood income and physical and social disorder in Canada: Associations with young children's competencies. *Child Development, 73*(6), 1844–1860.

Kubisch, A. C., Auspos, P., Brown, P., Chaskin, R., Fulbright-Anderson, K., & Hamilton, R. (2002). *Voices from the field II: Reflections on comprehensive community change*. Washington, DC: The Aspen Institute.

Kubisch, A., Weiss, C. H., Schorr, L., & Connell, J. (1995). Introduction. In J. P. Connell, A. Kubisch, L. Schorr, & C. H. Weiss (Eds.), *New approaches to evaluating community initiatives: Concepts, methods and contexts, Vol. 1*. Washington, DC: Aspen Institute. Retrieved May 6, 2005, from http://www.aspeninstitute.org

Lamb-Parker, F., Piotrkowski, C. S., Baker, A., Kessler-Sklar, S., Clark, B., & Peay, L. (2001). Understanding barriers to parent involvement in Head Start: a research-community partnership. *Early Childhood Research Quarterly, 16*, 35–51.

Lawson, H. (1999a). *Developing caring communities for children and youth: Unity of purpose for strong families, schools, community health and social service agencies, and neighbourhood organizations*. A training curriculum prepared for the Department of Elementary and Secondary Education, Missouri Department of Education. St. Louis, MO: Missouri Department of Education.

Lawson, H. (1999b). Journey analysis: A framework for integrating consultation and evaluation in complex change initiatives. *Journal of Educational and Psychological Consultation, 10*, 145–172.

Leithwood, K., Fullan, M., & Watson, N. (2003) What should be the boundaries of the schools we need? *Education Canada, 43*, 12–15

Lerner, R., Rothbaum, F., Boulos, S., & Castellino, D. (2002). Developmental systems perspective on parenting. In M. Bornstein (Ed.), *Handbook of parenting* (2nd ed. Vol. 2, pp. 407–437). Englewood, NJ: Erlbaum.

Levine, M., & Smith, S. (2001). Starting points: State and community partnerships for young children. *The Future of Children,*

11. Retrieved May 5, 2005, from http://www.futureofchildren.org/information2826/information_show.htm?doc_id79416

Mathien, J., & Johnson, L. (1998). *Early childhood services for kindergarten-age children in four Canadian provinces: Scope, nature and models for the future.* Caledon Institute of Social Policy. Ottawa: ON.

Mattessich, P., & Monsey, B. (1992). Collaboration: *What makes it work. A review of research literature on factors influencing successful collaboration.* St. Paul, MN: Amherst H. Wilder Foundation.

Mattingly, D., Prislin, R., McKenzie, S. L., Rodriguez, J. L., & Kayzar, B. (2002). Evaluating evaluations: The case of parent involvement programs. *Review of Educational Research, 72,* 549-576.

McCain, N., & Mustard, F. (1999). *Reversing the real brain drain: Early years study.* Toronto, ON: Ontario Children's Secretariat.

Melaville, A. I. (1998). *Learning together: The developing field of school community initiatives.* Flint, MI: Mott Foundation.

Melaville, A. I., & Blank, M. J. (1996) *Together We Can: A Guide for Crafting a Profamily System of Education and Human Services. Special Report.* [Rev. ed.]. Office of Educational Research and Improvement, U.S. Department of Education and the U.S. Department of Health and Human Services. Washington, DC

Melaville, A. I., & Blank, M. J. (2000). It takes a whole community. *Principal, 80,*18-20.

NAEYC. (1994). Principles to link by: Integrated service systems that are community-based and school-linked: NAEYC position statement. Retrieved August 16, 2004, from http://www.naeyc.org/resources/position_statements/pslink98.htm.

Novella, K. (1996). Can urban school reform and community development be joined? *Education and Urban Society, 28,* 237-257.

Offord, D., & Janus, M. (1999). *The readiness to learn tool, version 5a (now known as the Early Development Instrument-EDI).* Hamilton: McMaster University.

Olmsted, P., & Lockard, S. (1995). Do parents and teachers agree? *High Scope Resource, 14,* 1-9.

Ontario Ministry of Education. (1998). *The kindergarten program.* Toronto, ON: Author.

Ontario Ministry of Education. (2001). *School councils: A guide for members.* Toronto, ON: Author.

Organization for Economic Cooperation and Development. (2001). *Starting strong: Early childhood education and care.* Paris: Author.

Parker, K., & Leithwood, K. (2000). School councils' influence on school and classroom practice. *Peabody Journal of Education, 75,* 37-65.

Pelletier, J. (1998). Children's understanding of school in English first language and French immersion kindergartens. *The Canadian Modern Language Review, 55,* 239-259.

Pelletier, J. (1999). "Tell me what you do at school" . . . A comparison of children's school scripts in English first language and French immersion second language kindergarten programs. *Language and Education, 13,* 1-15.

Pelletier, J. (2002). Parents come to kindergarten: A unique junior kindergarten program for four year olds and their families. FINE Harvard Family Research Project. Retrieved May 6, 2005, from www.gse.harvard.edu~hfrp/projects/fine/resources/digest/parents.html.

Pelletier, J., & Brent, J. (2002). Parent participation and children's school readiness: The effects of parental self-efficacy, cultural diversity and teacher strategies. *International Journal of Early Childhood, 34,* 45-60.

Pelletier, J., & Corter, C. (2002). Competing worldviews on early childhood care, education, and development in the Canadian context. In L. Chan & E. Mellor (Eds.), *International Developments in Early Childhood Services* (pp. 29-52). New York: Peter Lang.

Pelletier, J., & Corter, C. (2005). *Design, implementation and outcomes of a school readiness program for diverse families.* To appear in The School Community Journal.

Pelletier, J., Power, R., & Park, N. (1993). Research on excellence. In C. Corter & N. Park (Eds.), *What makes exemplary kindergarten programs effective?* Toronto: Ontario Ministry of Education.

Peters, R. DeV., Arnold, R., Petrunka, K., Angus, D. E., Brophy, K., et al. (2000). Developing Capacity and Competence in the Better Beginnings, Better Futures Communities: Short Term Findings Report. Kingston, Ontario: Better Beginnings, Better Futures Research Coordination Unit Technical Report. Retrieved May 6, 2005, from http://bbbf.queensu.ca/pub.html#sterm.

Ramey, C. T., & Ramey, S. L. (1998). Early Intervention and Early Experience. *American Psychologist, 53*(2), 109-120.

Reed, R., Jones, K. P., Walker, J. M. & Hoover-Dempsey, K. V. (2000, April). *Parents' motivations for involvement in children's education: Testing a theoretical model.* Paper presented at the Annual Conference of the American Educational Research Association, New Orleans, LA.

Regional Educational Laboratories' Early Childhood Collaboration Network. (1995). A Framework for Home, School, and Community Linkages. Retrieved May 10, 2005, from http://www.sedl.org/prep/hscklinkages.pdf.

Reynolds, A. J. (2004). Research on early childhood interventions in the confirmatory mode. *Children and Youth Services Review, 26,* 15-38.

Reynolds, M., Temple, J. A., Robertson, D. L., & Mann, E. A. (2001, June). *Age 21 cost-benefit analysis of the Title I Chicago child-parent centers.* Paper presented at the Annual Meeting of the Society for Prevention Research, Washington, DC.

Ripple, C. H., & Zigler, E. (2003). Research, policy, and the federal role in prevention initiatives for children. *American Psychologist, 58,* 482-490.

Saluja, G., Scott-Little, C., & Clifford, R. (2000). Readiness for school: A survey of state policies and definitions. *Early Childhood Research and Practice, 2.*

Sanders, M. G., & Harvey, A. (2002). Beyond the school walls: A case study of principal leadership for school-community collaboration. *The Teachers College Record, 104,* 1345-1368.

Saracho, O., & Spodek, B. (2003). Recent trends and innovations in the early childhood education curriculum. *Early Child Development and Care, 173,* 175-183.

Schorr, L. (1997). *Common purpose: Strengthening families and neighbourhood to rebuild America.* New York: Doubleday.

Schorr, L., Sylvester, K., & Dunkle, M. (1999). *Strategies to achieve a common purpose: Tools for turning good ideas into good policies, special report.* Washington, DC: Institute for Educational Leadership.

Seefeldt, C., Denton, K., Calper, A., & Younoszal, T. (1999). The relation between Head Start parents' participation in a transition demonstration, education, efficacy and their children's academic abilities. *Early Childhood Research Quarterly, 14,* 99-109.

Shonkoff, J. (2000). Science, policy, and practice: Three cultures in search of a shared mission. *Child Development, 71,* 181-187.

St. Pierre, R., & Layzer, J. (1998). Improving the life chances of children living in poverty: Assumptions and what we have learned. *Society for Research in Child Development, Social Policy Report, 12,* 1-25.

St. Pierre, R., Layzer, J., Goodson, B., & Bernstein, L. (1999). The effectiveness of comprehensive, case management interventions: Evidence from the National Evaluation of the Comprehensive Child Development Program. *American Journal of Evaluation, 20*(1), 15-34.

Stapleford, E. (1989, June). *Day care: An historical perspective as a basis for policy issues*. Paper presented at the annual meetings of the Canadian Psychological Association, Halifax, June.

Swick, K., & McKnight, S. (1989). Characteristics of kindergarten teachers who promote parent involvement. *Early Childhood Research Quarterly, 4*, 19–29.

Torjman, S., Leviten-Reid, E., Camp, C., & Makhoul, A. (2001). From information to application: How communities learn. The Caledon Institute of Social Policy. Retrieved May 10, 2005, from http://www.caledoninst.org

Tougas, J. (2002). *Reforming Quebec's early childhood care and education: The first five years*. Childcare Resource and Research Unit, University of Toronto, Occasional Paper #17.

Tremblay, R. E., Masse, L., Pagani, L., & Vitaro, F. (1996). From childhood physical aggression to adolescent maladjustment: The Montreal prevention experiment. In R. D. Peters, & R. J. McMahon (Eds.), *Childhood disorders, substance abuse, and delinquency: Prevention and early intervention approaches* (pp. 268–298). Thousand Oaks, CA: Sage.

W. K. Kellogg Foundation (1988). *W. K. Kellogg Foundation Evaluation Handbook*. Battle Creek, MI: W. K. Kellogg Foundation.

Wandersman, A., & Florin, P. (2003). Community Interventions and Effective Prevention. *American Psychologist, 58*(6/7), 441–448.

Weiss, C. H. (1995). Nothing as practical as good theory: Exploring theory-based evaluation for comprehensive community initiatives for children and families. In J. Connell, A. Kubisch, L. Schorr, & C. H. Weiss (Eds.), *New approaches to evaluating community initiatives: Concepts, methods, and contexts*. (pp. 65–92). Washington, DC: Aspen Institute.

Wenger, E. (2001). *Communities of practice: Learning as a social system*. Retrieved May 10, 2005, from http://www.co-i-l.com/coil/knowledge-garden/cop/lss.shtml

White, K. R., Taylor, J. J., & Moss, V. D. (1992). Does research support claims about the benefits of involving parents in early intervention programs? *Review of Educational Research, 62*, 91–125.

Yancey, W. L., & Saporito, S. (1995). Ecological embededness of educational process and outcomes. In L. Rigsby, M. Reynolds & M. Wang (Eds.), *School community connections*. (pp. 193–228). San Francisco: Jossey-Bass.

Zigler, E., Finn-Stevenson, M., & Stern, B. (1997). Supporting children and families in the schools: The school of the 21st century. *American Journal of Orthopsychiatry, 6*, 396–407.

QUALITATIVE RESEARCH: PARADIGMS AND POSSIBILITIES

J. Amos Hatch
University of Tennessee

Gina Barclay-McLaughlin
University of Tennessee

Qualitative research approaches have contributed substantial understanding to the field of early childhood education over the past decade, and this review seeks to capture some of the breadth and depth of those contributions. Qualitative research has not, however, ascended to the status of what Kuhn (1970, p. 10) called "normal science" as many researchers predicted it might. Our view is that although qualitative approaches to studying the education of young children have increased in number and sophistication, they have not fulfilled their promise. One of our goals is to utilize the qualitative studies reviewed in this chapter to make the case that the possibilities for qualitative research in our field are underrealized. We plan to accomplish this goal by discussing qualitative approaches in terms of alternative research paradigms that offer unique opportunities to add to the knowledge base in early childhood education.

The logic of our attempt is straightforward. The promise of qualitative research in early childhood will be more fully realized if researchers and consumers of research have a better understanding of what qualitative research is and is not, what it can and cannot do, and where it fits and does not fit with traditional conceptions of science. A first step is to begin to make distinctions among sets of alternative assumptions at the core of different qualitative research paradigms. Once it can be seen that different paradigms lead to different research questions, different research approaches, and different research findings, then different possibilities will become apparent.

In this chapter, we begin with a brief overview of characteristics that make qualitative research unique. We next provide an introduction to four qualitative research paradigms, contrasting these to the positivist paradigm that continues to dominate empirical work in early childhood and other education contexts. Then, using the qualitative paradigm framework as an organizer, we present a review of selected qualitative studies published since the 1993 *Handbook of Research on the Education of Young Children* (Spodek, 1993). We conclude by using the exemplary work done over the past decade to emphasize possibilities for qualitative research in the future.

CHARACTERISTICS OF QUALITATIVE RESEARCH APPROACHES

Qualitative research is not a unitary, static concept. Many kinds of qualitative inquiry are being utilized today, and new approaches are being developed all the time. As will be seen in the paradigm discussion that follows, different approaches operating on different ontological and epistemological assumptions emphasize certain characteristics, deemphasize others, and offer alternatives to still others. The descriptions below are necessarily brief and based on an earlier synthesis of characteristics identified by scholars from a variety of disciplines (Hatch, 1998, pp. 51–55). What follows is a list of overarching characteristics that help define the borders of a complex, changing field of inquiry.

- Natural Settings—Qualitative researchers study social phenomena as they occur naturally in everyday life because they believe human behavior cannot be understood outside the contexts of its natural occurrence.
- Participants' Perspectives—Capturing the insider perspectives of actors in specific social settings is a primary concern of qualitative researchers.
- Researcher as Instrument—The principal data of qualitative studies (field notes from participant observation, interview transcriptions, and artifacts) are gathered directly by the researchers themselves.
- Extended Engagement—As understanding social phenomena from participant perspectives is the goal, spending long periods of direct engagement in the contexts in which those phenomena are enacted is important.
- Centrality of Meaning—Understanding the meanings that individuals use to make sense of their social surroundings is an essential element of qualitative work.
- Complexity—Qualitative researchers assume that social settings are unique, dynamic, and complex; they resist quantitative approaches that reduce complex settings to isolated and disconnected variables.
- Subjectivity—Qualitative work is as interested in inner states at the core of human activity as the overt activity itself, and bringing these inner states to light requires the application of subjective judgment on the part of researchers.
- Flexible Design—Because the act of doing qualitative research often leads researchers in directions they did not anticipate as studies are planned, research questions, methods, and analysis procedures are often altered as studies are implemented.
- Reflexivity—Qualitative researchers acknowledge that they are part of the worlds they study, and systematically monitoring their influence, bracketing their biases, and recognizing their emotional responses is part of their research responsibility.

QUALITATIVE RESEARCH PARADIGMS

Hatch (2002) identified four qualitative research paradigms based on Kuhn's (1970) argument that schools of scientific thought reach paradigm status when they have generated firm answers to the following questions: What are the fundamental entities of which the universe is composed? How do these interact with each other and the senses? What questions can legitimately be asked about such entities and what techniques employed in seeking solutions? Hatch described four qualitative paradigms that meet these criteria: postpositivist, constructivist, critical/feminist, and poststructuralist (see Fig. 28.1 for a summary of ontological and epistemological assumptions, methodologies, and products for these and the positivist paradigm). To establish a framework for organizing the review to follow, we briefly describe the positivist paradigm that undergirds traditional quantitative research. We then outline the assumptions that make each qualitative paradigm distinct from other worldviews and offer a prominent example of early childhood research done in that paradigm. For these examples, we selected studies that were published before the time period of the review in this chapter (i.e., before 1993), that were reported in book-length publications, and that we believe have had a significant impact on the field.

The positivist research paradigm is assumed by many to define "scientific" inquiry. Traditional quantitative research in early childhood and other fields is based on the positivist assumption that reality exists and is driven by universal, natural laws.

	Ontology (Nature of reality)	Epistemology (What can be known; Relationship of knower & known)	Methodology (How knowledge is gained)	Products (Forms of knowledge produced)
Positivist	Reality is out there to be studied, captured, and understood	How the world is really ordered; Knower is distinct from known	Experiments, quasi-experiments, surveys, correlational studies	Facts, theories, laws, predictions
Postpositivist	Reality exists but is never fully apprehended, only approximated	Approximations of reality; Researcher is data collection instrument	Rigorously defined qualitative methods, frequency counts, low-level statistics	Generalizations, descriptions, patterns, grounded theory
Constructivist	Multiple realities are constructed	Knowledge as a human construction; Researcher and participant co-construct understandings	Naturalistic qualitative methods	Case studies, narratives, interpretations, reconstructions
Critical/Feminist	The apprehended world makes a material difference in terms of race, gender, and class	Knowledge as subjective and political; Researchers' values frame inquiry	Transformative inquiry	Value mediated critiques that challenge existing power structures and promote resistance
Poststructuralist	Order is created within individual minds to ascribe meaning to a meaningless universe.	There is no "Truth" to be known; Researchers examine the world through textual representations of it.	Deconstruction; Genealogy; Data-based, multivoiced studies	Deconstructions; Genealogies; Reflexive, polyvocal texts

FIGURE 28.1. Research Paradigms.
Source: From Hatch, J. Amos. (2002). *Doing qualitative research in education settings* (p. 13). Albany: State University of New York Press.

Positivists treat reality as being componential, that is, consisting of components that can be taken apart for study, separately verified, and put back together. They assume an objective universe that has order independent of human perceptions. Researchers and the objects of their research are assumed to be mutually independent. The product of positivist research is verifiable knowledge in the form of facts, theories, and laws. Prediction is the ultimate aim of positivist science—if conditions are controlled, positivist researchers can predict what will happen when certain changes are introduced.

Postpositivism is the first qualitative paradigm identified by Hatch (2002) as an alternative to traditional positivist science. Postpositivists believe that although there is inherent order in the universe, that order can never be known completely. Reality can be approximated but never fully apprehended, and researchers use disciplined research techniques to ensure that empirical data drive their findings. Products of postpositivist qualitative research are generalizations, descriptions, patterns, and grounded theory. William Corsaro's (1985) sociological analysis of the creation and maintenance of peer culture in a preschool is a prominent example of an early childhood postpositivist study. Corsaro acted as an active participant observer and described patterns of social behavior that raised the notion of children's peer culture to new levels of awareness and understanding.

The constructivist paradigm is a second qualitative research domain. Constructivists assume that absolute realities are unknowable, and the objects of inquiry ought to be individual perspectives that are taken to be constructions of reality. Researchers are often joined with participants in a process of co-constructing reality through mutual engagement in the research act. Knowledge produced within the constructivist paradigm is often presented in the form of case studies or rich descriptions of interpretations generated as part of the research process. Accounts include enough contextual detail and sufficient representation of participant voices that readers can place themselves in the shoes of the participants. An apt example is Elizabeth Graue's (1993) study of the social construction of kindergarten readiness in three demographically different communities. Graue interviewed children, teachers, and parents, observed in kindergarten classes, and collected relevant documents. Her findings were descriptions of three sets of locally constructed meanings that revealed contextualized differences in how kindergarten readiness was understood and acted upon.

A third qualitative paradigm, the critical/feminist perspective, is based on the assumption that the material world is made up of historically situated structures that have a real impact on the life chances of individuals. These structures are perceived to be real, and their perceived realness leads to differential treatment based on race, gender, and social class. Critical scholars are most interested in exposing inequalities based on race, social class, and other forms of difference; and feminist researchers focus on issues related to the ways women are oppressed. In this worldview, it is assumed that knowledge is always mediated through the political positionings of the researcher and that researchers have an obligation to attempt to bring about social change as a part of the research process. The products of critical/feminist work are critiques that seek to expose structures that ensure the maintenance of control by those in power. These critiques reveal the kinds and extent of oppression being experienced by participants and call for awareness, resistance, solidarity, and transformation. A notable critical study in early childhood education is Sally Lubeck's (1985) comparison of a Head Start program serving African-American children and a preschool for European-American children. Lubeck observed and interviewed in both settings, describing different processes through which preschool teachers transmitted values, life experiences, and cultures, summarizing that "individuals are not 'right' or 'wrong', that people are not 'culturally deprived', and that social groups do not stretch out along a line from 'primitive' to 'advanced'" (p. 146).

Within a fourth qualitative paradigm, poststructuralists argue that order is created in the minds of individuals in an attempt to give meaning to an inherently meaningless existence. Thus, there are multiple realities, each with its own claims to coherence, and none can be logically privileged over another. These claims take form in the discourses that people use to make sense of their lives. Poststructuralists reject the notion of Truth with a capital T. They believe that multiple truths exist and that these are always local, subjective, and in flux. Researchers do not have direct access to the truths experienced by those they study, and they often produce multivocal texts. These texts include multiple voices that attempt to represent the specific, situational, partial, and temporary nature of the stories being told. One such multivocal text is *Preschool in Three Cultures* by Joseph Tobin, David Wu, and Dana Davidson (1989). In this study, the researchers showed videotaped segments of classroom life in preschools in China, Japan, and the United States to administrators, teachers, parents, and students across the cultural groups, recording their explanations for what was shown on the tapes. The findings are descriptions and comparisons of preschools in three cultures told through the multiple voices of the participants and researchers.

QUALITATIVE RESEARCH ON THE EDUCATION OF YOUNG CHILDREN

Based on the qualitative research paradigms described earlier, we have divided the review to follow into four sections: Postpositivist Studies, Constructivist Studies, Critical/Feminist Studies, and Poststructuralist Studies. We have tried to include enough information about the methodology and findings of each study to demonstrate the efficacy of applying assumptions from each paradigm to the study of early childhood contexts. Each study reviewed was published in a refereed journal, as a freestanding book, or as a chapter in an edited book. To give some structure to the presentation of the studies within each paradigm, we ordered them from those that deal most directly with children, to those focused on families, through those that deal with teachers and administrators. Following the review, we present a section on the promises of qualitative research. In this concluding section, we select key examples from findings in each paradigm to make a case for extending the presence and influence of qualitative research in early childhood education.

We utilized the usual personal, library, and electronic resources available to identify studies for inclusion in this review. We realize that we have not included all of the important qualitative work done over the past decade, but we believe we have collected studies that provide useful examples of research across the four qualitative paradigms. Readers will note that a higher number of postpositivist studies are included in the review than constructivist, critical/feminist, or poststructuralist projects. That makes sense because our search revealed that the majority of studies identified were based on postpositivist assumptions. Careful readers will notice that, as they move through the review from postpositivist to poststructuralist paradigms, increasingly more of the studies are published in books than refereed journals. Again, this makes sense given the conservative nature of mainstream refereed journals and the necessity of publishing alternative work in edited collections and freestanding books.

The most difficult part of organizing this review was categorizing individual qualitative studies into one of the four paradigms. Making absolute classifications was made more difficult because qualitative researchers, like other scholars, do not share a common language for talking about their work. In addition, as a group, they do not share our belief that exploring and revealing paradigmatic assumptions ought to be a part of any qualitative research report. Although some studies were easy to classify because authors' metaphysical assumptions were evident in their descriptions of methods and/or in the organization of their findings, others were more illusive because evidence for placing studies in one paradigm over another was not clear-cut.

As we completed the analysis required to place studies into paradigms, we used the paradigmatic framework summarized in Fig. 28.1 as a guide. We read each research report searching for evidence related to each element in the framework: ontology, epistemology, methodology, and products. We kept track of patterns of evidence and made summary judgments based on that evidence. To give readers a sense of how this process played out, we have summarized our analysis of the four studies introduced above as historically prominent examples of work done within each qualitative paradigm. The same processes that we used to classify these studies were followed as each study in the review was categorized as postpositivist, constructivist, critical/feminist, or poststructuralist.

William Corsaro's (1985) *Friendship and Peer Culture in the Early Years* is a self-proclaimed ethnography of peer culture in a preschool. Although Corsaro never overtly explicates his ontological or epistemological assumptions, he locates his work inside research traditions (ethnography and sociolinguistics) that are historically postpositivist in nature. Corsaro sees himself as the primary data collection instrument in his research. This is evident in his careful description of "reactive field entry strategies" (pp. 28–31) and his detailed rationale for personally organizing and transcribing all audiovisual data associated with the study (pp. 40–47). In terms of methods, it is clear that Corsaro's approach was rigorous and systematic in the postpositivist tradition. For example, he discusses research elements such as "sampling units" (pp. 23–24), "generation of hypotheses" (p. 27), "validity estimation" (p. 48), and "indefinite triangulation" (pp. 48–49), all of which indicate attempts to bring systematic rigor to qualitative work. In addition, the findings are supplemented with tables and charts that summarize Corsaro's efforts to document the "consistency, frequency, and distribution" (p. 39) of patterns across participants and settings. Finally, the products of the research fit the profile for postpositivist work. They are descriptions of patterns and themes that characterize peer culture in preschool. This study's categorization in the postpositivist qualitative paradigm is straightforward.

The subtitle of Elizabeth Graue's (1993) *Ready for What? Constructing Meanings of Readiness for Kindergarten* clearly marks her study as fitting in the constructivist qualitative research paradigm. Graue includes a discussion of "social construction" as part of a theoretical framework chapter in which she identifies her ontological and epistemological assumptions as they relate to this study (pp. 20–26). In this section, she explains her metaphysical perspective as follows: "Instead of assuming that the nature of objects and categories exist in physical reality, the social constructivist focuses attention on the meanings constructed in interactions of people in settings" (p. 20). Her overarching research question is a direct expression of her ontological and epistemological assumptions: "How was the meaning of readiness constructed in a given community?" (p. 38). Her study design includes co-constructing meaning through giving participants opportunities to study and respond to observation and interview data and to provide feedback on researcher vignettes and interpretations. Graue participated in the role of teacher aide in each of the classrooms she observed, and she did everything she could to keep her presence as researcher as unobtrusive as possible so that classroom interactions would be "relatively typical" (p. 46). The products of the study fit the constructivist paradigm as well. They are organized into three "cases," (p. 270) within which the stories of how readiness was constructed in each school setting are told. Quotes from the participant interviews and field-note records are woven into a rich narrative description that takes the reader inside the settings of the research and allows the voices of the participants to make the case for the researcher's interpretations.

Unlike the other three prominent examples in this section, Sally Lubeck's (1985) *Sandbox Society: Early Education in Black and White America* was not easy to classify. If fact, it was difficult to locate a book-length qualitative research report done before 1993 that neatly fit the criteria for the critical-feminist paradigm. But Lubeck's book provides a good example of the processes we used to determine the placement of studies that were difficult to categorize. Plenty of evidence exists that *Sandbox Society* is a report of research that fits the critical/feminist paradigm. The problem for classification purposes was that the text also includes indications that it is a postpositivist study. Ontologically, the prologue of the book spells out Lubeck's critical perspective in clear terms. Here she notes how the processes of cultural transmission in our society "recreate the social order" (p. xi) and limit the life chances of certain individuals and groups. She also challenges the common belief that racial and social class differences cause inequality, arguing instead that "inequality causes differences" (p. x). Lubeck also includes "social structural" explanations within her discussion of the causes and consequences of difference. In this section, she explains that "institutions are stratified and serve to maintain those in power"

(p. 5). Lubeck's research approach includes some of the transformative qualities of the critical-feminist paradigm. She details how the focus of the study and data collection procedures changed as her perspective on the Head Start program shifted during the study. Also, Lubeck's conclusions include a challenge to policy makers to acknowledge that "differences among peoples within American society are deeply grounded in a social system that is premised on an unequal distribution of resources" (p. 146). All these indicators make it reasonable to classify Lubeck's study within the critical-feminist paradigm, and we are comfortable doing so. However, the organization of the findings of the report and Lubeck's description of her data collection and analysis include elements that fit with postpositivist assumptions. The findings are presented in sections that look more like the products of a postpositivist analysis than a value-mediated critique. In addition, Lubeck names her work "ethnography" in her description of methods. Although in the early 1980s ethnography was often used as a synonym for qualitative research, the methods themselves seem more descriptive than transformative. To conclude, Lubeck's study was difficult to classify because it included elements of two qualitative paradigms. As with other studies in the review to follow, we processed the information we had and made the best judgment we could.

Preschool in Three Cultures by Joseph Tobin, David Wu, and Dana Davidson (1989) is a prominent example of the application of poststructuralist assumptions to early childhood research. The authors' explicit aim was to produce a multivocal text that included the voices of Japanese, Chinese, and American preschool teachers, administrators, parents, children, and child-development experts. Their research methods were designed to elicit multiple stories, "a telling and retelling of the same event from different perspectives" (p. 4). The researchers videotaped in selected preschools in three cultures, then gathered more data as edited versions of these tapes were shown to the participants in the original settings, to teachers, administrators, and parents in other cities in the same country, and to similar groups in the other two nations. The videos were intentionally "subjective, idiosyncratic, and culture-bound, . . . (projecting) images that were ambiguous, that opened up rather than closed down possibilities for discussion and interpretation" (p. 7). The authors' epistemological assumption of multiple truths as opposed to absolute Truth is clear. Their poststructuralist understanding that the world can only be examined through textual representations of it is also clear. Their expressed aim is to present the voices of participants "who tell their own stories, creating their own texts that discuss, deconstruct, and criticize our account of their schools. Each of these texts reacts to earlier texts while never entirely replacing, subsuming, or negating them" (pp. 4-5). The products of the study are indeed polyvocal texts that take the reader on a complex journey that challenges the usual linear, cause-and-effect thinking that characterizes quantitative (and most qualitative) research done in early childhood education.

The point of the review to follow is not to justify our classification scheme, so the paradigmatic details in the discussion of prominent examples here are abbreviated in favor of more description of research methods and findings. Our intent is to review selected qualitative studies done over the past 10 years and make the case that even more and even better qualitative work ought to be done. One of our reasons for using the notion of paradigms to organize this review is to encourage more consistency in the ways researchers think and talk about their work. It is our hope that the organization of this review and the examples within it will encourage such consistency in the future.

We also hope it is clear that we are not promoting one paradigm as better or worse than another. It is illogical to point out strengths and weaknesses of individual paradigms because such an analysis would require applying a set of values from outside the assumptions of the paradigm in question. Kuhn (1970) himself pointed out that the logic of paradigmatic thinking is necessarily circular, so the ontological and epistemological assumptions of one paradigm fit only that paradigm. The internal logic of each paradigm will make sense only to those individuals who are standing inside that worldview. So, for example, the metaphysical assumptions of the poststructuralist paradigm would seem alien to the thinking of a postpositivist, and vice versa. Any discussion of strengths and weaknesses across paradigms would require the valuation of one set of paradigmatic assumptions over another—a position we are not willing to take. It is possible to assess the unique contributions of work done within each paradigm, and we will do that in the concluding section of this chapter.

One other caveat may help readers process the review below. The basic data collection strategies of all qualitative approaches are observation, interviewing, and artifact collection. No single paradigm has exclusive ownership of any one of these basic data collection tools. Our review includes examples of research projects within each paradigm that utilize observation, interviewing, or artifact collection as data gathering strategies. How these are applied will be different across paradigms. For example, interviews have an important place in the data collection alternatives of each qualitative paradigm. Because of differences among how postpositivists, constructivists, critical/feminists, and poststructuralists think about researcher-participant interactions and the relationship between data and "reality," interviews will take on a different form and feel depending on the paradigm. But, as a general rule, it is impossible to say that interviewing (or any data collection strategy) fits best in one paradigm but not another.

Postpositivist Studies

Researchers operating within the postpositivist paradigm produce findings that reveal the patterned ways groups of individuals operate in different social situations. For early childhood researchers, this means providing a rigorous analysis and description of participants' apprehended reality of schools, classrooms, playgrounds, homes, and other early education and care settings. Postpositivist researchers help practitioners and policy makers by revealing the understandings that players in early childhood settings use to organize and make sense of what is going on around them. In the studies reviewed below, complex elements of children's literacy learning are described in classroom and home settings, classroom processes in settings that include children who are English language learners or children with disabilities are analyzed, young children's understandings of race and ethnicity are detailed, an analysis of metaplay in early childhood classrooms is presented, the perspectives of family day care providers are documented, and teachers' uses of child observation in two countries are described.

Anne Haas Dyson (1997, 2003) conducted a series of studies examining the interplay of children's actions as writers, peers, community members, and consumers of popular culture. The data for her studies were collected through participant observation in classrooms and on playgrounds; formal and informal interviews with children, teachers, parents, and community members; artifact collection, especially samples of children's writing; audio recording of children's talk, especially during peer discussion sessions; and analyses of commercial media referred to by children. Dyson's research projects focused on children's literacy development in the contexts of child and school cultures and the broader influences of popular media. Dyson's mode was to select particular children in particular primary school settings and carefully document their writing accomplishments within the complexities of their everyday worlds. She took the role of a nonparticipant observer, preferring to be quiet and unobtrusive rather than active and involved in classroom interactions. In *Writing Superheroes* (1997), Dyson focused on how stories composed by children in a school characterized by socioeconomic and racial diversity were shaped by children's need for belonging, their ideological positionings, their familiarity with and attraction to popular media, and their need to define a place for themselves in a diverse world. In *The Brothers and Sisters Learn to Write* (2003), Dyson explored literacy development imbedded in the complex social worlds of two 6-year-old girls and a small circle of friends (the "brothers and sisters") in an urban K–5 school. In the latter study, Dyson explored the ways popular culture was expressed in children's communicative practices, the ways nonacademic practices and materials were utilized by children in school literacy activities (and vice versa), and the consequences of reconceptualizing nonacademic material for individual and classroom learning. Dyson's work has sought to challenge traditional, linear, cause-and-effect studies of literacy learning and to place childhoods themselves and children's localized symbols and practices at the center of literacy research.

Mona Matthews and John Kesner (2003) examined the interactions of sixteen first graders during literacy events with their classmates over an academic school year. A subset of six students was selected for more in-depth observations. Participating children represented diverse levels of reading achievement and varying levels of acceptance from their classmates. During the study, children were observed in the classroom for a total of 138 hours, including mornings and early afternoons when literacy events typically occurred. Participant observation sessions were video- or audiotaped in an effort to capture a range of interactions among the children. The intent was to examine how children with different levels of acceptance from their classmates and different levels of reading ability experienced peer-only literacy events. Data analysis was guided by the constant comparative method. Results suggested that children enjoyed involvement with peers during peer-only literacy events. Some children seemed to participate in the events with a level of awareness of how to proceed. For others, just knowing what was required was insufficient. More salient to their success was the notion of status within a group. This kind of within group positioning appeared to be vital to successful participation and ultimately to literacy achievement. Unfortunately, some children lacked crucial social skills and insight for navigating the social terrain. Insights from the study point to the crucial role of the teacher in considering the social dimensions of literacy development and learning.

Rebekah Fassler (1998) served as a participant observer for the first six months of a school year in order to explore the complexities of peer interactions and peer support in an English as a Second Language (ESL) kindergarten classroom. The classroom, located in a large urban public elementary school, had 31 students representing eight different languages. None of the students was proficient in English or spoke it as a primary language. The study captured the ways children interacted during a range of classroom events, activities, and contexts as they attempted to learn English. Classroom observations and an in-depth focus on selected children offered insights on choices individual children made, as well as how, when, and with whom they interacted as they engaged in experiences involving English. Data were collected through observational field notes, informal conversations with the teacher, audiotaping, and gathering a range of program-related artifacts. Observations were designed to capture and document teacher and student efforts to communicate and negotiate shared meaning in English throughout a variety of classroom events, activities, social situations, and contexts. Findings from Fassler's analysis suggested that the teacher of this ESL classroom gave children many opportunities to have informal peer interactions. This kind of freedom to interact informally made possible a range of ways children worked to achieve conversation and share meaning as they collectively sought to accomplish social goals. It was evident that children's enthusiasm about communication was linked to their desire to create friendships. Their interest in engaging each other spontaneously led to language practice. Fassler concluded that when children are free to interact in natural ways, they will support each other in learning a new language. Teachers should provide these opportunities for peer interaction and support in addition to more structured forms of instruction and learning activities.

Carol Beaumont (1999) served as a participant observer to examine unstructured peer assistance in a full inclusion, bilingual second grade classroom in a large, urban elementary school. Participants in this 1-year ethnographic study included 11 special education students and 22 regular education students in a program designed to serve students with a "severe disorder of oral language" or a "specific learning disability" (p. 236). Of the 33 participating students, 30 were Mexican Americans and the same number of students qualified for free or reduced lunch. Particular focus was given to three students who reflected a variety of learning characteristics, ranging from mild to moderate disabilities, distinct personalities, diverse styles of interacting, and a variety of developmental and educational histories. Data were collected in three phases and included 150 hours of field notes based on 9 months of classroom observations. Additional data included interviews with all students and teachers, audio- and videotape recordings, and samples of student work products. Data were analyzed using a constant-comparative method to generate themes and categories. Results revealed the complexities of giving and receiving help among students. Findings suggested that helping interactions were frequently used to accomplish social goals or work out social agendas. Consequently, access to peer assistance was not always contingent on cognitive or linguistic skills. Interviews, as well as field notes, suggested ambivalence about giving and receiving peer support, indicating the complexity of social and academic dimensions of helping interchanges. Beaumont concluded that the teacher can play a pivotal role in facilitating social interactions and maximizing peer assistance and support to enhance learning.

Robyn Holmes (1995) completed a 6-year study of kindergartners' perceptions of race and ethnic identity. She conducted informal interviews with children and collected their artwork, but participant observation was her primary data collection tool. She asked teachers to introduce her and treat her as a new student when she first entered the five kindergarten settings of her study. Her goal was to come to understand race from children's perspectives, and she made a concerted effort to participate as a student and relate to her informants as a peer. Holmes used a tape recorder and took field notes during observation periods, and data from these sources were transcribed and filled in at the end of each data collection session. Her analyses revealed that children's view of their universe is dualistic in nature—that is, they see the world in terms of antithetical pairs: boy/girl, black/white, are friends/aren't friends, big/little, grown-ups/kids, good/bad. The children's classification schemes for groups of people relied on color words and ethnic terms (e.g., black, white, Japanese, Spanish). Because the children thought about race and ethnicity in absolute terms, groups were perceived to be internally homogeneous and membership considered unconditional. African-American children included references to skin color in their self-descriptions, whereas European Americans rarely did so. However, even when children held negative perceptions of other groups, they did not apply the generalizations on which those perceptions were based when they selected friends in the classroom. Holmes concluded that giving young children opportunities to interact with peers from cultural groups different from their own is essential for acquiring knowledge about matters of racial identity and social cognition.

Jeffrey Trawick-Smith (1998) described and classified metaplay behaviors of preschoolers. Metaplay is a process where children suspend their pretend play roles to talk and think about play. The study involved 12 preschool children enrolled in a community-based child care center. Participating children were Euro-Americans ranging in age from 2 to 5 years from middle- or working-class families. Pairs of children were videotaped as they engaged in spontaneous play. The designated play area had a supply of traditional play props, play materials not predesigned for any particular use, and blocks. Videotapes were reviewed, transcribed, and analyzed to identify metaplay behaviors. The primary researcher and a secondary observer then independently categorized transcripts representing metaplay. The process of negotiating, categorizing, combining,

dividing, renaming, constructing rules, and refinement led to the development of a typology of metaplay behaviors. The analysis generated three distinct categories of metaplay behaviors: initiations, responses, and constructions. These categories were further classified based on their symbolic or social functions. Findings revealed that significant social and symbolic interactions took place beyond the actual make-believe play scene. Children, especially 5-year olds, demonstrated tremendous ability to initiate conversations and negotiations beyond the direct role play scene. Older children performed more metaplay behaviors than younger study participants, suggesting that with increased age, there is not only more frequency of play, but older preschoolers are more able to cognitively shift beyond the play itself. Although younger children demonstrated symbolic play abilities and engaged in simple make-believe play, they were less likely to engage in metaplay.

Janice Stewart (1995) selected four kindergarten students from a larger 3-year longitudinal study to examine home literacy environments and children's perceptions of literacy events at home. Two participating children (one African American and one biracial) lived in an urban neighborhood. Two others were Caucasian children living in a rural community. Children were observed in their homes eight times during 3-hour blocks. Field notes were taken during each observation and a story-reading session was recorded during one of the home visits. Data were based on videotapes of classroom instructions, tapes of reading interactions between the mothers and children of the four participants, and interview sessions with their parents. Data were organized and coded based on six domains of literacy events: deliberate, communication, religious, media related, daily, and school. Although all case study children were involved in a range of literacy events, they were involved in varying ways, frequency, and time. For example, parents demonstrated different styles of interacting during story reading. Questions and comments during the story took different forms. Some parents were more inclined to initiate interactions, while others supported child-initiated interactions. Literacy related materials observed in the home, engagements observed between parents and children, and interview comments from parents and children suggested that parents valued and promoted positive literacy experiences for their children despite categorical labels (i.e., socioeconomic status, neighborhood context, race/ethnicity). Stewart concluded that the home environment was strategic for literacy development for children of the study. Although observations suggested that substantive differences existed between home and school contexts, literacy events in the home appeared to play an important role as children begin to learn to read.

Margaret K. Nelson (1995) studied family day care providers' perspectives on their work, contrasting providers' definitions of quality with those of early childhood experts. Following the collection of demographic data via questionnaires, Nelson conducted semistructured interviews with 30 registered and 40 unregistered family day care providers. Providers in the study believed that family day settings offered a unique and valuable experience to young children because the care received there closely approximated care provided by mothers in their own homes. Providers were proud that they were able to supply parents and children with an atmosphere of mothering that did not include the rigid schedules, curriculum, and educational activities of center-based child care facilities. Many of the participants in the study started providing family day care because they wanted to ensure that their own children could remain at home. When asked about how they learned to care for children, providers pointed to the importance of experience over training, often mentioning their own mothers' care of them. They referred to the experience of raising their own children as their most important qualification. Nelson's analysis included an exploration of the limits of mothering as the central feature of family day care provision. Although providers perceived mothering to be the most desirable style, because the children in their care were not their own and were being cared for for a fee, providers were caught in contradictions that made them vulnerable. By becoming too attached to children, providers were vulnerable to emotional disappointment when children left or when parents did not seem to care for their children in ways approved of by providers. If providers did not set limits on the amount of time and resources they devoted to the children they cared for, they would be vulnerable to being taken advantage of by parents. Furthermore, when failures occurred, providers who equated mothering with child care were vulnerable to feeling self-doubt—as if they had failed not just as workers, but as mothers. Nelson concluded that definitions of quality that permeate the early childhood field ought to acknowledge the perspectives of those working directly with children, including those working in family day care.

Amos Hatch, Susan Grieshaber, and colleagues reported findings from a long-term study of early childhood teachers' perspectives on child observation and accountability in Australia and the United States (Grieshaber, Halliwell, Hatch, & Walsh, 2000; Hatch, Grieshaber, Halliwell, & Walsh, 2001; Hatch & Grieshaber, 2002). Systematically observing and recording children's classroom behaviors, then using that information to make classroom decisions, has a long history in early childhood pedagogy. This study was designed to describe teachers' uses of and thinking about classroom observation in contemporary classrooms in both countries. The complete data set for the study included open-ended questionnaires sent to over 200 teachers, written critical incident descriptions from a subset of 24 volunteers, and transcriptions from taped interviews with 25 teachers and from two teleconference focus group interviews with 7 participants. Inductive data analysis procedures were utilized to identify patterned uses of child observation in both countries and to describe teachers' perspectives on the place of child observation in their respective countries. A cross-national analysis was completed to compare responses. U.S. uses for child observation included: assessing academic progress, adjusting curriculum/teaching, diagnosing instructional needs, gathering information for reports to parents, dealing with behavior problems, assessing social adjustment, and collecting documentation for special education placement. Australian uses were: identifying individual strengths and weaknesses, understanding children to guide their behavior, informing work with parents and other professionals, extending shared interests within a group, noting individual interests that can extend group learning, reflecting on the flow of the day, and evaluating your own teaching. Hatch and colleagues summarized that traditional uses of

child observation to inform teaching are being threatened in both countries. Teachers reported that concerns for meeting the expectations of the accountability movement are making it difficult to avoid changing child observation into a tool for measuring children's academic progress. Early childhood educators in Australia had more balance in their approach to utilizing child observation in traditional ways, but teachers in both countries believed the nature of child observation is changing because of accountability concerns.

Constructivist Studies

Constructivist researchers assume that individually constructed realities are legitimate objects of investigation. They believe that the voices of individuals give depth and breadth to understandings of experience. They co-construct their participants' stories and bring a human face to the early childhood knowledge base. Our review of constructivist early childhood studies includes research that reveals individual teachers' experiences of working with children whose first language is other than English. These detailed narratives of what is like to guide the development of English language learners are examples of the value of constructivist work to get insider perspectives on important aspects of early education. They allow readers to step inside diverse settings and share teachers' reflective accounts of what they learned about themselves, their students, and their important work. In addition, our review demonstrates the power of constructivist research to capture local meanings in relation to educational improvement initiatives (in these cases, in Head Start settings), and to illuminate different teachers' applications of early education pedagogical approaches (in this case, developmentally appropriate practices).

Celia Genishi, Susan Stires, and Donna Yung-Chan (2001) conducted a collaborative study over two academic school years to investigate the processes involved in children learning English as a second language. The context for the study was a prekindergarten classroom in New York City. Most of the 16 participating children lived adjacent to the Chinatown community and were from families with limited income. Many of the families had recently immigrated to the United States, and the primary languages spoken among them included Cantonese, Mandarin, and Fujianese. The teacher spoke Cantonese. Data sources included field notes, anecdotal notes from the teacher, audio- and videotapes, and materials and records from the teachers' portfolio. The study was designed to focus carefully on four children. The teacher, who was a co-researcher on the project, included children in planning daily activities and facilitated the process of implementing the plans. This routine was designed to promote English language development and to guide children through the multiple symbolic systems they encountered in their world. A number of themes emerged from a four-phased data analysis process. Among these themes was the suggestion that a core vocabulary evolves through student participation in classroom routines (i.e., morning greetings, calendar and weather activities, and social response like excuse me or thank you). Another theme was that spontaneity with the language or responses made by children demonstrated the strength of the core vocabulary. Interactions children had among each other, another theme, were valuable; nonetheless, the interactions between children and teacher offered a clearer sense of the language learning process. Observations revealed individual differences in motivation to learn English and in children's facility with and use of the English language. Concluding comments from the researchers emphasized the variety of experiences children need for understanding a world of multiple and complex symbols. They recommended a balanced, child-centered curriculum with a variety of activities that children help plan, along with a predictable schedule of activities and learning events that support language development, peer interactions, and effective communication.

Jill Fitzgerald and George Noblit (1999) examined the complex process of reading and writing development for students in a first grade class. They focused on the literacy learning experiences of two students (Carlos and Roberto), who were English language learners. The data collection process included extensive field notes, daily teacher reflections, work samples from the children, weekly videotapes, and information from informal and formal assessments. In this study, Fitzgerald acted as both teacher and researcher, co-constructing meaning from data that both she and Noblit, her research colleague, gathered independently. Fitzgerald spent a year teaching first grade when on leave from her university teacher education professorship. Part of her objective was to determine if what she had been teaching on campus could be put into practice in a real classroom. Throughout the narrative report, Fitzgerald reflected on her own feelings and involvement as she described the process of working with Carlos and Roberto. A complex narrative of a year's progress organized the substantive findings of the study. The narrative documented the uneven progress of the two boys toward developing reading and writing competence in English. Descriptions of differences in the two boys' progress were utilized to demonstrate the unique needs of individual learners and the difficulties associated with expecting the same outcomes from the same instructional strategies when different children are involved. Overall, the authors summarized that both children made progress in learning to read in English within a classroom that was carried out from a first language perspective (like Fitzgerald promoted in her university teaching). Fitzgerald's candid reflections on her teaching efforts reveal moments of overwhelming success as well as periods of self-doubt and uncertainty. Fitzgerald recommended similar processes to others, describing how learning and new understandings were generated through reflective teaching and thoughtful, systematic data collection and analysis.

Maike Philipsen and Jo Agnew (1995) tell the story of a Head Start program in a rural, poor, mostly African-American community in the southeastern United States. Philipsen and Agnew were part of a research team that was invited by the mayor to examine the long-term effects of school closings on the local community. Team members participated in the social events of the community, visited schools, churches, businesses, and homes, conducted approximately 50 interviews, and collected artifact data in order to construct a history reflecting the changes that resulted from school consolidation efforts. Philipsen and Agnew's analysis focused on the local Head Start's continuing importance in the life of the community, contrasted with the educational experiences of older children bussed to predominantly white schools in neighboring communities. Interviews were treated as conversations. Although the researchers came in with broad, open-ended questions, they allowed the participants to choose the direction of their answers. The story of the Head Start program under investigation revealed close connections between the community and the program. Teachers and parents shared educational values, commitment to children, and racial backgrounds. Parents felt a sense of ownership in the program, and teachers felt supported. The Head Start program was constructed as a collective, with an orientation toward meeting the needs of the group as opposed to stressing individuality. In contrast, when children were forced to attend schools outside their community, they experienced a loss of cultural identity, and they and their families felt disconnected from the schools to which they were bussed. From the parents' perspective, the new schools lacked the discipline, structure, and commitment that parents believed African-American students needed. Philipsen and Agnew concluded that major losses are incurred when community institutions that meet the needs of children and families are replaced by institutions without commitments to local values and social norms.

Sally Lubeck and Jackie Post (2000) described an alternative approach to thinking about research and program improvement in Head Start. Based on their belief that the emphasis on accountability and measuring improvement in terms of children's individual performance distorts local meanings and ignores the social nature of human intelligence, Lubeck and Post designed a collaborative research and program improvement project with Head Start teachers. The researchers made careful records of the evolvement of a community of practice in a Head Start program over a 2-year period. Meetings were recorded and tapes transcribed, observers acted as active participants in classrooms, and formal and informal interviews were conducted with teachers and administrators. Lubeck and Post documented how the program improvement efforts of a Head Start took shape in the light of community needs and resources, local cultural understandings, and established institutional practices. Researchers and teachers developed a "mutual mentoring project" (p. 41) that involved collaboration between university and Head Start educators and among the teachers themselves. University personnel worked in classrooms as assistants to assistants, teachers visited each other's classrooms, and university and Head Start educators met together to share practical teaching approaches. Lubeck and Post's analysis revealed the processes through which teachers construct knowledge together— "to think in conjunction with others, to play off, add, invert, transform, and link information" (p. 53). They contrasted this approach with the usual top-down training approaches that assume knowledge to be in the heads of experts then transferred to passive teachers in need of new ways of thinking. They presented their study as an example of what's possible when subjective experiences in real settings, group learning dynamics and an emphasis on local, contextualized meanings are brought to the foreground.

Mary Hauser (1995) used a life history approach in her study of a first grade teacher working in a multiethnic school. Giving voice to a teacher of young children was one of Hauser's explicit purposes, as was constructing the story of how one teacher provides classroom experiences that embody sensitivity to cultural differences. In order to capture the teacher's story, Hauser interviewed the teacher several times over a year's period, acted as participant-observer in her classroom, and interviewed the teacher's brother and several of her teaching colleagues. Interviews with the first grade teacher were based on broad questions such as "What is it like for you to teach?" and "What is the meaning of what you do for you?" (p. 67). The teacher's life history included experiences as the daughter of immigrant parents with limited educational opportunities, as a student who was culturally different than her high school peers, as a teacher's assistant in an urban elementary school when attending college, and as a Peace Corps volunteer in South America after college. The teacher made clear connections between her own life experiences and the kind of program she was providing for students from cultures represented by six different languages. She had come to recognize the power of cultural difference in the learning process, and this led her to learn about the cultural experiences of her students so she could adjust to their needs. Hauser concluded that valuable insights into understanding early childhood practice are available when researchers search out connections between life stories and teaching philosophies.

Carol Ann Wien (1995) studied five Canadian early childhood teachers working in five urban day care centers. She was interested in examining teaching practice as it was found in real classroom settings. She visited each center five or six times over several months, observing in classrooms, interviewing teachers after observations, and videotaping portions of each observation. Videotaped events were reviewed by the teachers as part of postobservation interviews. From these data, Wien wrote feedback papers, synthesizing the practical teaching knowledge discovered for each teacher. The feedback papers then became devices for engaging teachers in the final construction of their portrayals in the report. Teachers gave feedback that shaped the final description, and one disagreed with Wien's analysis, sending the researcher back to her data for further analysis. Wien presented five stories of teachers' development and implementation of practical knowledge. Each story represented an example of how individual teachers negotiated their way between conflicting forms of practice that dominate contemporary early childhood thinking: developmentally appropriate practice and teacher dominion. For Wien, developmentally appropriate practice means shared power between adults and children, recognition of a variety of modes by which children come to understand their worlds, and perceiving teachers as co-inquirers with children. Teacher dominion locates power in the teacher, utilizes teacher direction as the primary form of instruction, and sees teachers as dispensers and children as receivers of knowledge. The stories in the final report provided five examples of different adjustments to these conflicting forces. One teacher seemed balanced between the two frameworks; another wanted to be more child-centered but was highly programmatic; a third shifted her balance from one perspective to the other; a fourth claimed allegiance to a single framework while the researcher saw her favoring another; and a fifth had clear preference for one set of practices and worked hard to match her ideal. Although

acknowledging her own bias in favor of developmentally appropriate practice, Wien called for more balanced thinking in our conceptualizations of effective practice—to see teaching as a "dialogic relation" (p. xiv) in which teachers negotiate their way among complex conflicting demands and processes.

Critical/Feminist Studies

Working to transform a world that reduces the life chances of oppressed people is an explicit goal of research undertaken within the critical/feminist paradigm. Researchers take an openly political stance and work to expose the inequities, injustices, and oppressive practices that keep powerful groups in power and insure that those on the bottom of the social, economic, and political ladder stay there. In early childhood, they shine a light on the dark side of our field, raising our consciousness of the oppressive consequences of unjust systems and practices. Studies in our review provide examples of areas in which critical and feminist research assumptions can be usefully applied. The review includes examples of feminist work that looks at gendering processes and the outcomes of masculine hegemony from the earliest stages of life through adulthood. And, the review contains studies that range from an application of critical theory to the exploration of children's play, to an examination of how adults exercise power over the bodies and emotions of young children, to critical analyses of the effects of poverty, difference, and disempowerment on adults and communities.

Shirley Kessler and Mary Hauser (2000) studied children's play in classrooms for 3-, 4-, and 5-year-olds. Their goal was to explore ways in which concepts from critical theory and critical pedagogy could be applied to understanding children's play in early childhood settings. Kessler and Hauser acted as passive participant observers in a variety of preschool and Head Start settings. They recorded children's behavior during free play sessions that were scheduled as part of normal classroom activity, then analyzed data from these observations in an effort to identify opportunities to "foster a form of pedagogy aimed at the liberation of human potential and the fostering of democratic communities in the classroom" (p. 61). The researchers' analyses yielded descriptions of play behaviors in the following areas: challenges to received social identities, power and authority, exercise of agency, resistance, and developing classroom culture and communal social relations. Among the findings of the study were that sociodramatic play offered few opportunities for children to challenge their received identities (e.g., boys played with boys' toys and girls with girls' toys), free play did provide children with opportunities to construct and play out interactions related to power and authority as well as resist directives from teachers and other children, and play did contribute to children's opportunities to create classroom culture and develop communal relations. Kessler and Hauser concluded that critical pedagogy does have a place in early childhood curriculum, especially during children's play. They called for observant teachers who demonstrate alternative possibilities for gendered role-play and create environments that provide opportunities for children to exercise agency, resist expectations, and create patterns of relationship that enhance a democratic classroom.

Robin Leavitt (1994) applied what she called a "multitheoretical" (p. 25) approach to the study of everyday experiences of young children in infant-toddler day care settings. Leavitt utilized critical and feminist theoretical frameworks (among others) to establish the philosophical bases for her work. The study treated knowledge as subjective and inherently political, and Leavitt took an openly transformative stance as a researcher, seeking to challenge existing structures and promote resistance. The data on which Leavitt based her critique consisted of her own participant observation field notes and those of practicum students under her supervision in twelve classrooms in six licensed day care centers. Data collection took place over a 7-year period and included records of informal interviews with caregivers. Leavitt's report described "problematic lived experiences related to power and emotion of infants, toddlers, and their caregivers" (p. 91). In terms of power, children's actions, choices, and freedom were severely constrained by caregivers' command over children's bodies and the use of space and time in the classroom. Descriptions of the rigid management of daily routines such as feeding, sleeping, and diapering and the ways caregivers controlled children's behavior and play showed how power is used to socialize young children to be docile and accept adult authority. The problematics of emotional socialization were detailed in descriptions of situations in which caregivers were disengaged from children's emotional needs. Children were treated as objects of work, and their emotions, usually expressed through crying, were often ignored, treated as a nuisance, or even punished. Leavitt characterized child care work as "alienated emotional labor" (p. 64). The problematic caregiving revealed in the study was more understandable within the context of the caregivers' own lack of positive social identity, individual autonomy, community respect, and sufficient pay. Leavitt called for a shift toward emotionally responsive, empowering caregiving based on reciprocity and empathy. She argued for a reorganization of caregiver work and for caregiving to become a more reflective activity.

Susan Grieshaber (1998) interviewed 20 first-time Australian parents in a study of the processes of gendering from the earliest stages of life. She sought to examine the micro relations within father-mother-infant relationships and the macro links between family relationships and social structure. She solicited parent-participants through newspaper and radio advertisements and conducted unstructured interviews with volunteers three times—once before the birth of the baby, once at 2-3 months, and again at 5-7 months. Interview data were recorded, transcribed, and participants had the chance to review and edit/change their interviews. Grieshaber's analysis started from the premise that "everyday life is understood as an arena for gender politics" (p. 21). Her goal was to reveal cultural meaning systems that are saturated with hegemonic forms of masculinity. Her findings were organized into discussions of three issues discovered in parent responses: whether to learn the sex of the infant before birth, parental preferences for a boy or girl, and imagined or actual interactions with infants. Twelve couples opted not to learn the sex of their unborn child, whereas eight wanted to know. Of those not wanting to know, fathers usually made the decision and wives went along. Those choosing to know wanted to be prepared with appropriately gendered names, clothing, and furnishings before the baby's birth. Many more mothers and fathers who had a preference preferred their firstborn children to be sons. Reasons for wanting boys were connected to understandings that boys should be dominant, more responsible, and in charge. Thirteen of 20 infants turned out to be girls, and fathers who wanted boys openly admitted their disappointment, while their wives rationalized their preferences in some way. Fathers had a difficult time imagining the care of their infants. They frequently talked about interactions that involved activities that children would not be capable of for several years (e.g., playing sports and camping). Although they did participate in nurturing activities to some extent once their infants were born, fathers continued to take a future orientation to having relationships with their children. Grieshaber concluded that the processes of gendering observed confirmed the pervasive power of hegemonic masculinity operating in the daily domesticity of the families studied.

Elizabeth Quintero (1999) posited that global societies are becoming increasingly connected and programs should offer opportunities, through participation, that help children and families that are marginalized transform their circumstances. In support of this perspective, two family literacy projects with a critical, participatory focus were selected for examination. The primary role of a critical, participatory family literacy project is to offer families information about literacy and codes of power in the United States in order to understand the influence this information has on their lives. One of the participating programs provided services to Mexican and Mexican-American families, and the other served Hmong women and their infants. Participants of the projects were from marginalized groups and linked to Head Start programs. The data collection process included field notes, formal parent interviews twice during the year, informal conversations, video segments of classes in progress, and reactions to class activities. Data were organized into three categories: culture (family and school expectations, needs, and strengths), cognitive development, and language development. Preliminary findings revealed the complex nature of interactions, tensions between diverse values and beliefs, and need for greater depth in understanding differences. For example, practices that might appear to be "developmentally inappropriate" from mainstream early childhood education perspectives should be understood within a broader view that takes into account such factors as context, history, values, and customs. Although Quintero believes that Head Start programs demonstrated successful models of culturally sensitive programming for children and families, the changing needs of families require continuous changes in understanding and programming. Quintero contended that collaboration between families and educators offers opportunities for "multidirectional participatory learning" (p. 476). That is, teachers and parents can learn from each other, teachers can learn from students, and students can learn from other students. Quintero concluded that the goal in early childhood education should be to explore ways to increase understandings of cultural groups in order to support families from diverse cultures as they care for and address the needs of their children.

Gina Barclay-McLaughlin (2000) conducted a study in one of the largest public housing developments in the United States.

The research was an attempt to increase understandings of poverty and its influence on child development and parenting. Data from this study were collected primarily through interviews in the homes of 25 residents of this urban neighborhood. Participants in the study were parents recruited from an early intervention program serving children from the prenatal stage of development through age 5 and their families. Each informant was interviewed at least twice for approximately 90 min per session using a set of guiding questions. Themes were identified during the analysis to increase understandings about the experience of poverty and other contextual contributions. Barclay-McLaughlin's history of working in the community and with the community-based early intervention program helped her understand the value of establishing rapport, respect, and trust for obtaining information that would be useful to the project. Analysis revealed what participants described as a growing deterioration of the neighborhood, a pattern of decline of a communal system of support that no longer served as a resource for sustaining children and their families. Residents who once shared so much in common began to withdraw from each other and from opportunities to provide traditional support, guidance, direction, and tangible resources for children. Increasingly, children were left alone to face challenging periods and situations and to form and pursue their goals without adequate guidance. The stories shared showed how families once created a viable community of neighbors who socialized together, parented each other's children, and provided role models, resources, and support for each other's aspirations. But their stories also showed how the community support residents once cherished may never be revived, given the pervasive influences of contemporary urban poverty.

Lynda Ames and Jeanne Ellsworth (1997) spent 3 years collecting observation, interview, and unobtrusive data in a study of the empowerment and disempowerment of Head Start mothers. They interviewed Head Start administrators and staff, attended meetings and events, and examined documents related to Head Start, but the focus of their study was on collecting the stories of participating Head Start mothers who were poor, mostly white, undereducated women living in a rural area of New York state. The researchers argued that the services provided to Head Start mothers were aimed largely at correcting presumed deficiencies found in parents. Head Start parent involvement practices were based on the assumption that reforming deficient parents was a way to improve their children's chances in school and life. Ames and Ellsworth analyzed how the mothers in their study actually made use of the services provided and their participation in the activities of Head Start, examining the mothers' own views of how their Head Start experiences made their lives better or worse. In areas of emphasis in Head Start parent programs such as parenting and nutrition, the researchers showed how mothers transformed potentially disempowering, patronizing experiences into opportunities to take control and exercise their own power. For example, Head Start expectations that mothers come to centers to participate in children's learning environments were transformed by mothers into mechanisms for community building; and classes on cooking were used as opportunities for isolated mothers to connect and share ideas with others. Although these outcomes were essentially side-effects, the researchers made the case that the ways Head Start is structured (e.g., centers are in local communities and parents are given space, responsibility, and a small budget) and the basic culture of respect in the centers they observed were key to making possible the unintended empowerment of mothers. They concluded by lamenting current Head Start emphases on administrative control and accountability, worrying that these changes may reduce mothers' chances for participation and empowerment.

Deborah Ceglowski (1994) investigated Head Start salary policies from a feminist perspective. She conducted individual interviews with three administrators and focus group interviews with 10 teachers over a year's time. Focus groups sessions were held with groups of two or three teachers; all interviews were taped, transcribed, and returned to participants for feedback. The analysis revealed two distinct groups among the teachers, and Ceglowski described composites of "low-income" and "middle-income" teachers to represent these groups. Both low- and middle-income teachers agreed that their salaries were low, that their work was important, and that they cared for their students and the students' families. However, the low-income teachers, who depended on their salaries for economic survival, held different views of the value of their work to themselves and society than did middle-income teachers whose salaries served to supplement those of their husbands. Low-income teachers argued that society devalues Head Start teaching and that their administrators were not committed to improving salaries. Middle-income teachers valued the positive identity associated with working with others and were more likely to see increases in their salaries as detrimental to the overall structure of the social agency in which their Head Start program was situated. Ceglowski discusses her findings in terms of "women's work." As in other gender-segregated fields, caring for children is "natural" for women, requiring no special knowledge or expertise and, therefore, is devalued by society. Women's commitment to children and the program works against them when it comes to salary considerations. The study foregrounds the human side of salary discussions in early childhood; and the feminist analysis reveals some of the complex relationships among women's work, socio-economic status, caring, and early childhood teaching.

Poststructuralist Studies

Poststructuralists live in a paradoxical world. They attempt to organize meaningful descriptions of what they take to be essentially meaningless existences, they refuse to acknowledge truth claims that go beyond the moments of their creation, they believe it is impossible for them to represent the experiences of others, and they assume that lives are created as texts are written (see Hatch & Wisniewski, 1995). Some poststructuralists embrace these paradoxes and produce data-based studies that attempt to capture multiple truths that are assumed to be local, subjective, and temporary. In this review, we have included research projects that provide new ways of thinking and talking about topics related to concepts such as civilizing bodies, panopticism, surveillance, bodily pleasures, performance, discourses, and counterdiscourses.

Robin Leavitt and Martha Power (1997) analyzed field note data from a 6-year study in 14 child care programs for infants through 5-year-olds. Their analysis was framed within a poststructuralist theoretical perspective on how children's embodied selves are managed in early childhood settings. The researchers asked what the child's experience was when the teacher turned her gaze on the child-body. Their report described processes through which teachers and caregivers in preschool and child care centers civilized the uncivilized bodies of children in their charge. Dimensions of Leavitt and Power's analysis included: *body time* (temporal regimes were established by teachers and children were expected to conform to the schedule regardless of their natural physical needs related to eating, sleeping, and using the bathroom); *body rules* (children had to learn appropriate body uses to accommodate teacher rules—for example, walk quietly, keep your hands to yourself, sit cross-legged, and raise your hand); *body transgressions* (children learned that negative consequences resulted from not meeting teacher expectations for body control); *resisting bodies* (children were not always passive recipients of classroom body rules); *body play* (pleasure that children experienced through physical play in the classroom was regulated by teachers); and *isolated bodies* (children were discouraged from touching each other as well as their adult caregivers). The researchers concluded that the extent of surveillance of children's bodies seemed excessive to the point of trading children's sense of autonomy and spontaneous pleasure for adults' sense of power and control. They proposed alternative ways of conceptualizing "body care" (pp. 69–71) in which teachers can become more comfortable with their own embodiedness, learn to restrain their need to control everything that goes on in the classroom, and respect children's rights to their own bodies and desires.

Donna Grace and Joseph Tobin (1997) studied children's video production in Grades 1, 2, and 3 in a Hawaiian elementary school. The 3-year study was part of a joint project among teachers and university educators to provide children with opportunities to write and produce their own videos in an effort to develop a form of literacy that integrated art, language arts, problem solving, technology skills, and performance. The researchers acted as participant observers throughout the process, participating more as children learned the skills necessary to make videos, then observing more as children took increased responsibility for the production of their own work. The researchers viewed their student-participants as part of an interpretive community with shared interests, experiences, and understandings related to their age, generation, and mutual contexts. Grace and Tobin analyzed their data within a framework adapted from Bakhtin's (1984) description of carnivals popular during the Middle Ages. The researchers linked "carnivalesque" elements from Bakhtin (e.g., laughter, bodily pleasures, bad taste, and hierarchical inversion) to the activities and motives of children as they made videos. They provided examples from their data of children exploring the boundaries between rules and freedom, in much the same ways that peasants explored similar boundaries centuries ago. Student productions included such themes as laughter and parody (using humor to ridicule television shows, movies, books, classrooms, and field trips), the fantastic and horrific (creating scripts that included superheroes and/or terrible monsters), the grotesque body (generating shock and surprise by referring to body parts and body functions that are not considered appropriate in polite company), and the forbidden (including mock-violence that transgressed the official expectations of the school). Grace and Tobin concluded that producing videos gave children the chance to experience pleasure in their own way and on their own terms. They argued that so-called child-centered curricular approaches rarely involve freedom of the type that leads to this kind of pleasure and that providing such freedom is a worthy goal for early childhood teachers.

Joseph Tobin's (2000) study of how children think and talk about media representations of violence, gender, race, and class was conducted in an elementary school in Hawaii. In an effort to get beyond the "effects paradigm" (p. 3) that dominates most research on children and media, Tobin and his research associates utilized focus group data collection strategies to generate children's talk about movies. Tobin argued that typical media studies are linear, decontextualized, adversarial, and unidirectional. His approach was to show film clips to groups of children, then record their conversations, thus producing multivocal texts from which an analysis of how children understand popular media could be made. Thirty-two focus groups were conducted, during which a video clip of the Disney movie, *Swiss Family Robinson*, was shown. Children were videotaped while they viewed the clip and throughout the group interviews that followed. Utilizing analysis frameworks adapted from literary and poststructural critique, Tobin revealed children's ways of thinking about how gender, race, colonialism, and class were represented in media. Instead of focusing on data excerpts that made sense, Tobin's approach was to look closely at moments in transcripts that were most "odd, incoherent, and uncanny" (p. 138). His interpretive readings of these "richly ambiguous texts" (p. 139) led him to conclude that children are not the unwitting victims of media effects that they are usually portrayed to be. Children are capable of making insightful, sometimes resistant, interpretations. Researchers cannot know the effects of media by studying the media themselves; they must talk with children about the sense the children themselves bring to the experience. Tobin noted that different children bring different understandings to their interpretations of media messages and concluded that those differences are connected to local meanings that are produced in local community discourses and counterdiscourses.

Tobin (1997) also utilized focus group data collection methods in a study of early childhood teachers' perspectives on sex play in early childhood classrooms in the United States and Ireland. In 20 focus group interviews with teachers from a variety of early childhood settings in both countries, Tobin recorded teachers' discussions around eight stories he constructed from real events he or his students had observed. The stories were meant to be evocative in the sense that they portrayed problematic issues involving young children, their teachers, and sex. For example, one story described a group of preschool children playing a childbirth game, during which one little girl's panties were pulled down; and another portrayed a male teaching assistant reading to a female child while she relaxed on his lap. Tobin presented data excerpts within a narrative that built the case that teachers from the United States were generally more concerned about sex in early childhood classrooms than their Irish counterparts, many of whom were surprised that the scenarios described were considered controversial at all. U.S. focus group responses suggested that preoccupation with sexuality in preschool reflects the projection of larger social problems onto the field of early childhood education, a vulnerable segment of society that lacks the power and voice to resist. Tobin's analysis of U.S. perspectives was organized into five categories under the heading of societal "dangers" projected onto early childhood settings: sexually transmitted disease, gynecological maladies, excessive female desire, dangerous sexual knowledge, and homophobia/androphobia (p. 126). He also identified three categories of solutions or reactions to the perceived dangers: panopticism (hypervigilant surveillance), litigation, and nostalgia for simpler times. Tobin concluded that U.S. concerns are gradually influencing Irish early childhood educators, especially in urban settings, and that teachers in both Ireland and the United States long for simpler times when sexuality in preschools was a less dangerous topic.

Karen Gallas (1998) is a teacher-researcher who studied her classes of first and second grade students over a 4-year period. Gallas observed, audiotaped, and interviewed children as well as collected classroom artifacts such as children's art and writing samples. Because she was a participant her own research, she also recorded her own reflective responses to the events and actions in her data. The object of her research was to examine how primary students worked to understand the social terrain of the classroom and how Gallas, as their teacher, made sense of their work. Gallas adopted performance as a theoretical lens for interpreting children's social interactions. She rejected the application of sociological, psychological, or other categories which adults might use to make sense of children's social encounters. Instead, she reconceptualized children's ongoing social relations as a series of performances that were continually reinvented. Through the creation of these performances, children took on certain characters or personae, some short lived and others more permanent. Her research findings described what Gallas called the "subtextual dynamics of classroom life" (p. 22). For example, Gallas detailed the social acts that "bad boys" used to push the boundaries of social discourse in order to intimidate others and maintain power in the classroom. She described how some boys experiment with the bad boy personae to see how it fits, whereas others find the role so stimulating and the social rewards so enticing that they take on the bad boy image as a permanent identity. Gallas utilized the performance perspective to describe other elements of classroom social dramatics such as gender, silence, posing, and difference. She concluded by emphasizing the complexity of classroom life, reminding teachers and researchers that the social worlds of the primary classrooms she described were unique to the place, time, and actors involved, and encouraging other teacher-researchers to bring their own insights to discussions of charged issues such as gender and race.

POSSIBILITIES

The initial years of the 21st century have been marked by a shift away from the acceptance of alternative perspectives on what constitutes legitimate research. This change signals a turnabout from the prevailing research ethos of the late twentieth century when multiple forms of inquiry, including several genres of qualitative work, were recognized as valuable contributors to the knowledge base in education. The political conservatism of the new century has extended its influence into the world of academic research, essentially redefining positivism as the one and only valid research paradigm. The legislation and official rhetoric associated with No Child Left Behind (NCLB) educational reform efforts specifically define "scientifically based research" as the only form of inquiry to be utilized to inform government policy making—and scientifically based means solidly rooted in the traditional positivist mode (see Jacob & White, 2002).

Although the full impact of this politicization of educational research cannot be known at this writing, it is clear that the status of qualitative research approaches has been challenged, government funding for qualitative projects has been curtailed, and qualitative researchers and their advocates have been left out of the mix as power and influence have been distributed by conservative government leaders. Secondary effects that may be expected include a decrease in space for qualitative research reports in mainstream journals, fewer advanced graduate students selecting qualitative approaches for their doctoral research, and fewer private funding sources being willing to support qualitative research projects. In short, the gains that qualitative researchers fought so hard to achieve during the 1980s and 1990s have been threatened in the early 21st century.

Although we worry about the consequences of the conservative redefinition of research in the short run, we are confident that those who happen to be politically powerful will not be allowed to dictate what constitutes legitimate research for long. The unique contributions of qualitative research approaches that brought them to respectability earlier are still needed and continue to be valued by those who are able to conceive of research models that go beyond the assumptions of positivism. In order to demonstrate the efficacy of alternative research approaches, qualitative researchers need to produce work that has self-evident value. It needs to be done so well that its contribution cannot be ignored. In the body of this chapter, we reviewed several recent qualitative studies that have made significant contributions to the early childhood research literature. The studies demonstrate the promise of early childhood qualitative research for the new century. They exemplify the possibilities for making a contribution across the four qualitative paradigms described. In the following sections, we highlight contributions from the past and project possibilities for future work in each paradigm.

Postpositivist Studies

In this review of postpositivist studies, important areas of concern are addressed in ways that produce understandings that are missing from studies based on positivist assumptions. For example, No Child Left Behind (NCLB) reform efforts have been heavily concentrated on early literacy learning and have utilized a narrow band of "scientifically based" (i.e., positivist) studies to justify isolating specific skills and teaching those directly, thereby raising scores on outcome measures associated with learning to read. The research synthesis of the National Reading Panel (2000) is held up as the model for defining "scientifically based" and setting criteria for selecting studies that are worthy of inclusion in the officially sanctioned knowledge base. By way of example, one study included in the National Reading Panel synthesis measured students' word recognition performance on three different tests at the end of second grade. Half of the students tested had received instruction in a whole-language classroom and half in a phonics/skill-based classroom. One measure showed significant difference that favored the whole language classroom, whereas no significant differences were found on the other two measures. The authors concluded that instructional approach had little effect on word recognition.

Positivist science assumes that the world can be broken down into components that can be studied independently and put back together into a meaningful whole. The logic of the National Reading Panel and NCLB is that information from studies like this can be put together to form a comprehensive picture of the essential elements of effective instruction. As with all research paradigms, if you are standing inside the ontological and epistemological assumptions of the positivist paradigm, this approach makes sense. But what is missing when what counts as science is limited to studies done in the positivist tradition? The postpositivist studies that focused on literacy learning in our review reveal part of the answer.

Research projects like the word recognition study above leave out understandings of the complex social processes the surround literacy development in classroom, home, and community contexts—understandings like those provided in the postpositivist work of Dyson (1997, 2003), Matthews and Kesner (2003), and Stewart (1995). Dyson's studies reveal the richness and complexity that everyone knows characterize real classroom and community contexts. Her analyses of connections among school literacy activities, popular culture, and children's social relationships provide insights that can help teachers who work in similar settings set up classrooms and plan activities that improve children's chances for literacy learning. Matthews and Kesner described patterned relationships between children's social acceptance among first grade peers and their successful participation in peer-only literacy events. Their study is an example of how postpositivist analyses can inform teachers and program planners by systematically examining the day-to-day unfolding of classroom practices. Stewart's study of literacy events kindergartners experienced at home shows teachers and policy makers the importance children's literacy experiences away from school contexts. It also challenges some widely held stereotypes about how parents from certain socioeconomic, neighborhood, or ethnic/racial groups value and promote literacy learning. Postpositivist work in the area of literacy provides an example of the power of this kind of research to describe the patterned ways that complex processes play out in real settings.

In addition to revealing information about how literacy development actually unfolds in real settings, the postpositivist research in our review contributes understandings in the important areas of English language learning, peer interaction, play, classroom diversity, special education, teaching as work,

child assessment, and accountability. These examples point to the promise that postpositivist approaches have for illuminating the ways young children and their teachers and parents work together to make sense in their complex worlds. Eliminating such contextualized understandings leaves a knowledge base that may explicate relationships among variables but tell us nothing about the social phenomena that surround teaching, learning, and living in early childhood contexts.

Constructivist Studies

Constructivists are directly focused on the constructed realities of participants in social settings. They build their work on the assumption that as an objective reality separate from the perceptions of those participating in social settings is impossible to capture, then the perceptions of the participants themselves ought to be the substance of interest. In our review of constructivist early childhood studies, we included three different approaches to applying constructivist paradigmatic principles to the study of classrooms in which English language learners were students. The power in these studies is their capacity to take readers inside the thinking and actions of teachers working in the kinds of settings that have come to define classroom life for more and more early childhood educators.

In the Genishi, Stires, and Yung-Chang (2001) study, Yung-Chang was the teacher in the classroom under examination, and she was a full partner in the design, execution, analysis, and publication of the research. Including her in the co-construction of the story of the research provides insights into the workings of her classroom that would not be available in studies framed by other paradigms. Similarly, Fitzgerald taught in a public school for a year to see if the methods she was teaching to pre-service teachers were actually doable in a real first grade of English language learners (Fitzgerald & Noblit, 1999). She and Noblit designed a study that relied heavily on Fitzgerald's reflective accounts of her experiences working in a diverse setting, and their report is a complex narrative describing the positive and negative dimensions of those experiences. Again, research done within none of the other paradigms would generate these kinds of data or findings. Hauser's (1995) life history of a first grade teacher working in a school setting characterized by diversity is another example of constructivist work that takes the reader inside the constructed realities of an early childhood context. In this study, a careful analysis of how the teacher and others close to her describe her thinking and actions reveals connections between her life story and the stories of caring and learning that she creates in her classroom. And, again, the narratives generated in this study would not be fore-grounded in other paradigmatic approaches.

Other studies in our review capture the perspectives of early childhood professionals involved in reform efforts. In an era of early childhood reform based on narrow definitions of what constitutes scientifically based research, it is instructive to remember the centrality of human experience in all change activity. The richness of insights available through constructivist-based research point up the shortsightedness of positivist approaches to assessing the effects of one-size-fits-all approaches to reform in Head Start and other early childhood settings. Constructivist studies provide possibilities for bringing voices of direct experience to discussions of educational change and to the myriad other issues facing early childhood education in the 21st century.

Critical/Feminist Studies

Critical/feminist researchers work within a paradigm that assumes all knowledge to be subjective and political. They believe that the lifeworlds experienced by individuals and groups who are oppressed are defined by the differential ways they are treated by those in power. Exposing the structures that keep oppressed people at the bottom of the social hierarchy is not just a byproduct of critical/feminist research; it is the central reason to engage is such work. In this paradigm, the research act is a tool for actively transforming the life chances of those who struggle to get a fair shake in our society.

In the review of early childhood studies done within the assumptions of the critical/feminist paradigm, we included studies that provide three examples of critical/feminist critiques of Head Start programs and practices. Although these studies are different in setting, participants, and focus, they are each a strong example of the effectiveness of this kind of research to reveal elements of early childhood programs (in this case, Head Start programs) that would be taken for granted or ignored in other paradigmatic approaches.

Quintero's (1999) settings were two critical, participatory family literacy projects associated with Head Start programs for Mexican and Mexican-American families and Hmong women and their children. Participants were the marginalized adults in the family literacy projects, and Quintero's focus was a critical analysis of differences between the cultural belief systems of the parents and the values and beliefs enacted in the Head Start programs. She concluded that "multidirectional participatory learning" (p. 476) is needed so that parent perspectives are taken into account as programs develop and change. Ames and Ellsworth (1997) conducted their feminist analysis of Head Start parent involvement practices in rural sections of upstate New York. These researchers revealed the ways Head Start mothers took advantage of parent involvement activities that were disempowering because they were based on mothers' assumed deficiencies as parents. They showed how the mothers turned the Head Start activities into opportunities for taking control and exercising their own autonomy. Ames and Ellsworth called for more, not less, chances for Head Start mothers to be empowered as decision makers and active participants in parent education programs. Ceglowski (1994) studied Head Start salary policies in a feminist analysis of a center that included low- and middle-income teachers. Her study exposed the difference in teachers' perspectives on low salaries based on whether the teachers were working to supplement family incomes supported largely by husbands' paychecks or were the primary breadwinners in their families and dependent of their Head Start pay for survival. Ceglowski summarizes by pointing out the irony that women's commitment to children and Head Start philosophies actually works to keep their salaries low.

In an era in which Head Start research seems obsessed with using standardized (positivist) test to evaluate children's progress, scholarship like the critical/feminist studies reviewed is especially important. In fact, our field loses something vital when critical/feminist work is devalued or ignored. Studies done in Head Start and other early childhood settings (like those included in this review) provide a balance to the "mainstream" (i.e., positivist) research that is currently officially sanctioned by the federal government. In an even bigger sense, critical/feminist work offers the promise of keeping us honest as a field. Leaving out this perspective opens the door for blindly following courses of action that perpetuate the inequalities that characterize our society and pervade our field.

Poststructuralist Studies

Poststructuralist qualitative researchers provide intellectual tools for exploring the boundaries of early childhood. The search for Truth that drives empirical work in the positivist, postpositivist, constructivist, and critical/feminist paradigms is seen as misplaced or misguided by poststructuralists. The grand narratives that are the stock and trade of researchers in the other paradigms are dismissed or deconstructed by poststructuralists. In place of Truth claims and grand theories, poststructuralist researchers seek multiple truths that are self-consciously local, idiosyncratic, and in flux. In the place of traditional early childhood theory, they are likely to approach the substantive analysis of their data using theoretical understandings from scholars who have effectively deconstructed the modern discourses on which traditional work is based. In place of traditional quantitative and qualitative paradigmatic assumptions, poststructuralist researchers are likely to design polyvocal approaches to data collection and analysis, generating research outcomes that look and feel different from those generated in the other paradigms. It is our view that there is great value in challenging the taken for granted norms of quantitative and qualitative research and trying out uncharted ways of gathering and processing empirical representations of experience and understanding. The poststructuralist studies in our review offer examples of the contributions these kinds of studies can make to the ways we think and talk about our field.

Grace and Tobin's (1997) study of children's media productions and Tobin's (2000) examination of how children understand media representations of race, culture, and violence are specific examples of how poststructuralist studies bring new ways of thinking to research on media and children. Both studies challenge the grand narratives associated with traditional research on the effects of media on young children (i.e., exposure to certain types of media produces negative outcomes for children), and both apply postmodern theoretical constructs to the analysis and interpretation of textual representations of children's perspectives. In the Grace and Tobin project, primary age students were seen as members of an interpretive community who were capable of generating their own media based on local values and understandings. The researchers analyzed their data within a framework adapted from Bakhtin's (1968) descriptions of the medieval carnival, providing postmodern understandings and insights that interrupt the usual ways early childhood researchers and educators conceptualize young children's relations with media. Similarly, Tobin's (2000) study of children's understandings of how race, gender, and violence are represented in the popular media challenges taken for granted assumptions by positioning young children as active agents in critiquing and resisting cultural stereotypes that characterize much of popular culture. Tobin uses layered focus group data gathering techniques to generate multivocal text from which an analysis can be made. But Tobin's analysis intentionally seeks out the ambiguous, the odd, and the incoherent in the textual data, thus applying postmodern techniques from literary criticism and other fields to the analysis of children's perspectives on media effects. Both studies highlight the power of poststructuralist approaches to enrich the discourses related to media and young children.

Tobin and other researchers included in the review bring conceptual perspectives from poststructuralist scholarship to their analyses of data collected in early childhood settings. These concepts and the poststructuralist assumptions at the base of their inquiries lead to findings that look very different from the outcomes of positivist research or the descriptions, analyses, or interpretations of work done within the other qualitative paradigms. Poststructuralist studies represent the frontiers of inquiry in our field and beyond. Although many may be uncomfortable with assumptions that are so different from traditional conceptualizations of science, the possibilities for opening up new ways of understanding cannot be ignored.

In summary, we have tried to make the case that, despite the trend to resurrect positivist approaches as the only way to do science, the contributions of qualitative work done in the past and the possibilities for qualitative research in the future are vital to the field of early childhood education. We believe that understanding and acknowledging ontological and epistemological assumptions at the base of any research paradigm are essential to high quality research efforts. By organizing this chapter around postpositivist, constructivist, critical/feminist, and poststructuralist qualitative paradigms, we hope we have demonstrated the usefulness of paying attention to paradigmatic differences and the efficacy of continuing and expanding early childhood qualitative research across these paradigms.

As reflective social scientists and thoughtful professional practitioners, we do not have to adopt the assumptions of an alternative paradigm to appreciate and learn from that paradigm's contributions. Neither should we feel trapped into disavowing our beliefs about what constitutes rigorous scientific inquiry because of shifting political circumstances. It seems much healthier for early childhood educators and researchers to try to understand the elements that make paradigms distinct and to celebrate the unique contributions that carefully done research can make, whatever the paradigmatic framework.

References

Ames, L. J., & Ellsworth, J. (1997). *Women reformed, women empowered: Poor mothers and the endangered promise of Head Start.* Philadelphia, PA: Temple University Press.

Bakhtin, M. (1984). *Rabelais and his world.* Bloomington: Indiana University Press.

Barclay-McLaughlin, G. (2000). Communal isolation: Narrowing the pathways to goal attainment and work. In S. Danziger, & A. C. Lin (Eds.). *Coping with poverty: The social contexts of neighborhood, work, and family in the African-American Community* (pp. 52–75). Ann Arbor: University of Michigan Press.

Beaumont, C. J. (1999). Dilemmas of peer assistance in a bilingual full inclusion classroom. *Elementary School Journal, 99,* 233–254.

Ceglowski, D. (1994). Conversations about Head Start salaries: A feminist analysis. *Early Childhood Research Quarterly, 9,* 367–386.

Corsaro, W. A. (1985). *Friendship and peer culture in the early years.* Norwood, NJ: Ablex.

Dyson, A. H. (1997). *Writing superheroes: Contemporary childhood, popular culture, and classroom literacy.* New York: Teachers College Press.

Dyson, A. H. (2003). *The brothers and sisters learn to write: Popular literacies in childhood and school cultures.* New York: Teachers College Press.

Fassler, R. (1998). Room for talk: Peer support for getting into English in an ESL kindergarten. *Early Childhood Research Quarterly, 13,* 379–409.

Fitzgerald, J., & Noblit, G. W. (1999). About hope, aspiration, and uncertainty: First-grade English-language learners' emergent reading. *Journal of Literacy Research, 6,* 133–182.

Gallas, K. (1998). *Sometimes I can be anything: Power, gender, and identity in a primary classroom.* New York: Teachers College Press.

Genishi, C., Stires, S. E., & Yung-Chan, D. (2001). Writing in an integrated curriculum: Prekindergarten English language learners as symbol makers. *The Elementary School Journal, 101,* 399–416.

Grace, D. J., & Tobin, J. (1997). Carnival in the classroom: Elementary students making videos. In J. Tobin (Ed.), *Making a place for pleasure in early childhood education* (pp. 159–187). New Haven, CT: Yale University Press.

Graue, M. E. (1993). *Ready for what? Constructing meanings of readiness for kindergarten.* Albany: State University of New York Press.

Grieshaber, S. (1998). Constructing the gendered infant. In N. Yelland (Ed.), *Gender in early childhood* (pp. 15–35). New York: Routledge.

Grieshaber, S., Halliwell, G., Hatch, J. A., & Walsh, K. (2000). Child observation as teachers' work in contemporary Australian early childhood programmes. *International Journal of Early Years Education, 8,* 41–55.

Hatch, J. A. (1998). Qualitative research in early childhood education. In B. Spodek, O. Sarancho, & A. Pelligrini (Eds.), *Yearbook in early childhood education: Issues in early childhood educational research* (pp. 49–75). New York: Teachers College Press.

Hatch, J. A. (2002). *Doing qualitative research in education settings.* Albany: State University of New York Press.

Hatch, J. A., & Grieshaber, S. (2002). Child observation and accountability in early childhood education: Perspectives from Australia and the United States. *Early Childhood Education Journal, 29,* 227–231.

Hatch, J. A., Grieshaber, S., Halliwell, G., & Walsh, K. (2001). Child observation in Australia and the USA: A cross-national analysis. *Early Child Development and Care, 169,* 39–56.

Hatch, J. A., & Wisniewski, R. (1995). Life history and narrative: Questions, issues, and exemplary works. In J. A. Hatch & R. Wisniewski (Eds.), *Life history and narrative* (pp. 113-136). London: Falmer.

Hauser, M. E. (1995). Life history of a first grade teacher: A narrative of culturally sensitive teacher practice. In J. A. Hatch (Ed.), *Qualitative research in early childhood settings* (pp. 63-78). Westport, CT: Praeger.

Holmes, R. M. (1995). *How young children perceive race*. Thousand Oaks, CA: Sage.

Jacob, E., & White, C. S. (2002). Theme issue on scientific research in education. *Educational Researcher, 31,* 3-29.

Kessler, S. A., & Hauser, M. (2000). Critical pedagogy and the politics of play. In L. D. Soto (Ed.), *The politics of early childhood education* (pp. 59-71). New York: Peter Lang.

Kuhn, T. S. (1970). *The structure of scientific revolutions*. Chicago: University of Chicago Press.

Leavitt, R. L. (1994). *Power and emotion in infant day care*. Albany: State University of New York Press.

Leavitt, R. L., & Power, M. B. (1997). Civilizing bodies: Children in day care. In J. Tobin (Ed.), *Making a place for pleasure in early childhood education* (pp. 40-75). New Haven, CT: Yale University Press.

Lubeck, S. (1985). *Sandbox society: Early education in black and white America*. London: Falmer.

Lubeck, S., & Post, J. (2000). Creating a Head Start community of practice. In L. D. Soto (Ed.), *The politics of early childhood education* (pp. 33-57). New York: Peter Lang.

Matthews, M. W., & Kesner, J. (2003). Children learning with peers: The confluence of peer status and literacy competence within small-group literacy events. *Reading Research Quarterly, 38,* 208-234.

National Reading Panel. (2000). *Report of the National Reading Panel: Teaching children to read*. Washington, DC: National Institute of Child Health and Human Development.

Nelson, M. K. (1995). Family day care as mothering: A study of providers' perspectives. In J. A. Hatch (Ed.), *Qualitative research in early childhood settings* (pp. 23-43). Westport, CT: Praeger.

Philipsen, M., & Agnew, J. (1995). Heart, mind, and soul: Head Start as a reminder of the powerful function of schools for their communities. In J. A. Hatch (Ed.), *Qualitative research in early childhood settings* (pp. 45-62). Westport, CT: Praeger.

Quintero, E. (1999). The new faces of Head Start: Learning from culturally diverse families. *Early Education & Development, 10,* 475-497.

Spodek, B. (Ed.). (1993). *Handbook of research on the education of young children*. New York: Macmillan.

Stewart, J. P. (1995). Home environments and parental support for literacy: Children's perceptions and school literacy achievement. *Early Education and Development, 6,* 97-126.

Tobin, J. (1997). Playing doctor in two cultures: The United States and Ireland. In J. Tobin (Ed.), *Making a place for pleasure in early childhood education* (pp. 119-158). New Haven, CT: Yale University Press.

Tobin, J. (2000). *Good guys don't wear hats: Children's talk about the media*. New York: Teachers College Press.

Tobin, J. J., Wu, D. Y., & Davidson, D. H. (1989). *Preschool in three cultures: Japan, China, and the United States*. New Haven, CT: Yale University Press.

Trawick-Smith, J. (1998). A qualitative analysis of metaplay in the preschool years. *Early Childhood Research Quarterly, 13,* 433-452.

Wein, C. A. (1995). *Developmentally appropriate practice in real life: Stories of teacher practical knowledge*. New York: Teachers College Press.

·29·

FEMINIST ISSUES IN EARLY CHILDHOOD SCHOLARSHIP

Candra D. Thornton
Auburn University

Lisa S. Goldstein
The University of Texas at Austin

Feminism places at its center the experiences, responsibilities, worldviews, and lives of women and girls. Because of women's predominance in our field and because of the long-standing and multiple associations of women and young children, early childhood education easily lends itself to feminist analysis and interpretation. However, feminist perspectives have only recently taken hold in early childhood theorizing and research. When the previous edition of the *Handbook of Research on the Education of Young Children* (Spodek, 1993) was complied and published, there wasn't enough early childhood educational work grounded in feminism to fill a chapter. Clearly, things have changed.

In the early 1990s, feminist perspectives were just gaining a toehold in early childhood as the traditional boundaries of the field were opening up and beginning to incorporate a new range of theoretical viewpoints. Over the past decade, however, feminist perspectives on early childhood education have grown increasingly common and have made significant contributions to our knowledge base. For example, the original version of the National Association for the Education of Young Children's guidelines for developmentally appropriate practices (Bredekamp, 1986) made no mention of any feminist theorists or of any ideas commonly associated with feminist thought; the revised version, published in 1997, evokes and reflects feminist theory in its call for the creation of caring communities as the cornerstone of developmentally appropriate practices (Bredekamp & Copple, 1997).

Feminist scholarship grounds its focus on women and women's experiences in "an ideology of social transformation" (Humm, 1992, p. 406). In the case of research and practice in early childhood education, feminist perspectives have indeed begun to transform the thinking in our field. As this chapter will demonstrate, feminist forms of early childhood scholarship enact this ideology of social transformation in a range of ways. What ties these varying feminist perspectives together is a commitment to foregrounding the voices, questions, interests, and concerns of women, the group of people most knowledgeable about, most committed to, and most closely involved in the lives and the education of young children.

CHAPTER OVERVIEW

In writing this chapter we reviewed close to 300 conceptual, theoretical, and empirical articles, research syntheses, and books. As a result of this review, we feel confident saying that the connections between feminist thought and early childhood education have grown strong and plentiful in the past decade.

Our review uncovered a very diverse body of literature. It became clear to us that there isn't one monolithic feminist perspective on early education nor is there one specific way to do feminist research in the field; instead there is a complex and multilayered web of perspectives that coexist and inform each other. The variety that characterizes the feminist writing on early childhood education presented us with a dilemma as we structured and organized this chapter; we did not feel comfortable taking on the responsibility of making decisions about which researchers can be called feminists and which cannot, nor did we want to put ourselves in the position of making judgments or determinations about which research paradigms and methodologies "count" as feminist.

Rather than labeling certain researchers or certain pieces of scholarship as feminist, we looked to the literature and identified the topics that emerge as central to feminist thinking in early childhood education: gender; young children and their families; teachers, teaching, and teacher education; the influence of societal forces on young children's lives; and research methodologies. We elected to label these topics feminist and we considered all early childhood education research focused on these topics to be part of the body of literature reviewed here. Although this decision creates a broader and more inclusive representation of the relationship between feminism and early childhood than might be expected, we feel it allows us to portray the contributions that feminist scholarship has made to our field as fully and richly as possible.

The topics most prominent in feminist research in early childhood are topics that have always been central to our inquiry in the field. Throughout the first *Handbook of Research on the Education of Young Children* (Spodek, 1993) there are mentions of gender (Baroody, 1993; Howe, A., 1993; Pellegrini & Boyd, 1993); young children and their families (Howes & Hamilton, 1993; Stevens, Hough & Nurss, 1993); teachers, teaching, and teacher education (Saracho, 1993); the influence of societal forces on young children's lives (Banks, 1993; Clements & Nastasi, 1993; Meisels, Steele & Quinn-Leering, 1993); and methodological issues in early childhood research (Goodwin & Goodwin, 1993; Harms & Clifford, 1993; Peters, 1993; Walsh, Tobin & Graue, 1993). What makes these topics feminist now?

Although these topics are fundamental to early childhood education, there is much that has changed in the past decade as feminist scholars have brought their viewpoints and their ideology of transformation to the consideration of these topics. The specific areas of focus within each topic, the kinds of questions asked about each topic, the research techniques used and the interpretations constructed, and the knowledge bases and theoretical frameworks drawn on have been shaped and influenced by the inclusion of feminist perspectives. Furthermore, the ability to group all of these interrelated topics together under the umbrella of feminism allows new kinds of analysis and interpretation to occur and new connections to be made within the field.

CHAPTER FRAMEWORK

Because the five feminist topics that we have placed at the heart of this chapter—gender; young children and their families; teachers, teaching and teacher education; the influence of societal forces on young children's lives; and research methodologies—are the focus of scholars working from a wide range of theoretical orientations, we organized the research studies we reviewed in a manner that would highlight both the

similarities and differences among them. To that end we elected to group the studies along the lines of their relationship to the long-standing beliefs and assumptions that have shaped the field of early childhood education, and have created three loosely defined bodies of work: traditionally oriented scholarship, critically informed scholarship, and postmodern scholarship. We derived these categories through analysis of the current theoretical landscape of early childhood education and reflection upon the changes that have taken place in the field since the publication of the first *Handbook of Research on the Education of Young Children* (Spodek, 1993).

Scholarship in early childhood education has had a long and deep association with the foundational beliefs and practices of the fields of child development and psychology; for close to a century research and theorizing in early childhood education were dominated by this view. The scholarship we will refer to as "traditionally oriented" is grounded in this perspective and aims to contribute to the conversations and viewpoints that have been a part of the field since its inception. For example, we consider research that is informed by and builds on psychological, developmental, Piagetian, constructivist, behaviorist, maturationist, and Deweyan theories to be traditionally oriented scholarship.

In the early 1990s, a small group of scholars began to challenge the dominance of the traditional, developmentalist view of early childhood and to engage publicly in the process of reconceptualizing early childhood educational theories, practices, and research (Genishi, Ryan, Ochsner, & Yarnall, 2001). These reconceptualist scholars asked different kinds of questions, sought different kinds of answers, and drew on different theoretical foundations in an effort to critique, problematize, augment, and enrich our understandings of children, childhood, and education. In the past decade, the field has witnessed the construction of a reconceptualist orientation to early childhood grounded not in psychology but in a broad range of theoretical perspectives including (but not limited to) critical theory, Marxist theory, feminist theory, queer theory, postcolonial theory, and postmodern and poststructuralist theories.

In this chapter, the body of research grounded in reconceptualist perspectives has been divided into two categories: critically informed scholarship and postmodern scholarship. Although there is a great deal of theoretical fluidity between these categories, we drew a distinction in order to show more clearly the range of approaches to early childhood theorizing represented in reconceptualist research.

Critically informed scholarship works to redraw the boundaries of the field and to redescribe the acceptable sources of theoretical support for research in early childhood. Furthermore, critically informed scholars engage in research that intends both to shed light on the sociocultural, political, and historical forces impacting the field of early childhood education and to foster social justice and equity within early childhood and its institutions (J. Jipson, personal communication, March 2004). For the purposes of this chapter, scholarship is also considered to be critically informed if it draws on more typical early childhood theoretical frames but uses them in new ways, such as Goldstein's (1999) reinterpretation of Vygotsky's theories through a feminist lens.

Postmodern scholarship takes a very different stance in relation to the traditional contours of the field. Rather than working within the boundaries of early childhood education as traditionally oriented scholarship does, or redrawing the boundaries of the field as critically informed scholarship does, postmodern scholarship strives to interrogate and interrupt the assumptions and beliefs upon which early childhood education rests. As a result, scholars researching from postmodern vantage points understand, interpret, and represent early childhood in new ways.

As the traditional boundaries of the field of early childhood education began to relax over the past decade, critically informed and postmodern scholarly perspectives emerged, took hold, and joined traditionally oriented scholarship in the early childhood research literature. At the present time, these perspectives coexist, each informing the field in significant—but different—ways. Taken together, the traditionally oriented, critically informed, and postmodern perspectives allow us to develop a more complex and more comprehensive understanding of gender, young children and their families, teachers, teaching and teacher education, the influence of societal forces on young children's lives, and research methodologies in childhood education.

We have organized this chapter by topic and perspective. Recent research on each of the five feminist topics we have identified will be addressed in turn from the perspective of traditionally oriented, critically informed, and postmodern scholarship. Our intent is both to allow readers to develop a thorough understanding of the range of literature on each topic and to provide a means for readers to explore the important similarities, the significant differences, and the overlapping and conflicting goals and purposes of these three scholarly perspectives. We conclude the chapter by posing questions that emerge from this multiperspectival view of early childhood education and by considering the implications of this work for early childhood policy and practice.

GENERAL

Within the traditionally oriented perspective, research on gender predominantly focuses on the developmental stages in the construction of gender knowledge. The effects on children's development of early gender-based experiences, particularly those encountered at school, are frequently researched. The critically informed literature also links school and gender, but it moves past the developmental questions raised in traditionally oriented scholarship, focusing instead on the social perceptions of gender differences. Postmodern scholarship, on the other hand, moves in a much different direction. Within this perspective, gender is positioned as a form of fantasy play, a game in which the behaviors of "girls" and "boys" are acted out.

Traditionally Oriented Scholarship

The traditionally oriented view of gender is grounded in research focused on universal ages and stages of gender-knowledge construction, where gender is defined as a cognitive construct

created by children's experiences with behaviors commonly associated with men and women (Ruble & Martin, 1998). Within this scope, normalized measures suggest that the initial onset of gender role awareness may begin as early as 10- to 12-months of age (Leinbach & Fagot, 1993; Levy & Haaf, 1994) and that by age 3, own- and other-sex gender schemas are in place, are being organized into sex role scripts (Bauer, 1993; Levy & Boston, 1994), and are influencing gender-based playmate separation (Chick, Heilman-Houser, & Hunter, 2003). These and similarly framed research studies supporting the notion that gender schemes are constructed through individual experiences are influenced by Derman-Sparks's (1989) work on the antibias curriculum, which suggests that young children's educational environments should be free from all forms of sexism and gender bias.

Strong support for this antibias stance came from Butterworth's (1991) study in which the effectiveness of three nonsexist pedagogy strategies was tested. Her study found that female teachers' modeling of nonsexist behaviors, reinforcement of children's nonsexist play behaviors, and institution of girls-only block play times were "very effective . . . in countering sexist involvement and behavior" (Butterworth, 1991, p. 6). Support also came from Paley (1992), who shares vignettes of her experiences implementing non-sexist pedagogy and curriculum in her kindergarten classroom. Butterworth's and Paley's testimonies, and others like them, gave the antibias curriculum credibility in the field and positioned an antibias approach to gender as the most desirable stance.

The revised edition of the developmentally appropriate practice (DAP) guidelines (Bredekamp & Copple, 1997) reflects the influence of the antibias curriculum. Whereas the original guidelines mention only that "multicultural and non-sexist experiences, materials, and equipment should be provided for children of all ages" (Bredekamp, 1986, p. 7), the revised guidelines state with much more specificity that in developmentally appropriate early childhood educational settings:

Non-sexist activities and materials are provided to help individual children develop positive self-identity. . . . Books and pictures include people of different races, ages, and abilities, and of both genders in various roles. (Bredekamp & Copple, 1997, p. 131)

Overall, traditionally oriented scholarship consists largely of research regarding the developmental stages of gender cognition. The dominant research finding, that stereotypic gender schemes begin forming at very young ages, has a strong presence in early childhood education, and has led to the use of antibias curricular materials and the gender-neutral definition of developmentally appropriate practice.

Critically Informed Scholarship

In order to understand the critically informed perspective on gender in early childhood, it is essential to look outside the field: Gilligan's (1982) work in feminist moral theory forms the foundation on which this aspect of reconceptualist scholarship has been built. In pointing out that Kohlberg's stages of moral development (Kohlberg, 1969) were based solely on the examination of male experience, Gilligan foregrounded the ways in which female moral development took its own unique shape. In Kohlberg's view, females' moral development was understood to be less sophisticated than males'; through Gilligan's work, female moral development was seen instead as distinctly different from male moral development. The goals of acknowledging and affirming gender difference and allowing girls' experiences to be examined and understood in their own right have been hallmarks of critically informed scholarship on gender in early childhood education.

For example, Thorne (1993) presents vignettes that reveal girls experiencing relationships in ways qualitatively different from those of boys. Thorne characterizes girls as having intimate social interactions, such as combing friends' hair and complementing others' appearances. Also, girls tend to pair with each other in best friend dyads and, because each girl generally participates in multiple pairs at the same time, they create complicated social networks. These, Thorne says, are social relationships that almost never occur between boys: "... boys stress position and hierarchy, whereas girls emphasize the construction of intimacy and connection" (Thorne, 1993, p. 95). Along similar lines, Porath (2001) explored gender differences with regard to children's interpersonal understanding; her findings suggest that girls possess higher levels of social interest and awareness than boys of the same age, as well as higher conceptualizations of interpersonal situations. Porath argues that girls' capacity for social cognition be accepted as a "form of intelligence and as a legitimate domain of inquiry..." (p. 113) by the educational community.

Porath's work (2001) is a strong example of a critically informed perspective in that the purpose of the research is to challenge the gender neutralization present in nonsexist, antibias early childhood curriculum. Based upon her findings, she recommends that schools ensure that "girls'[social] interests and strengths are nurtured" (p. 122) This idea is echoed in Pellegrini, Kato, Blatchford and Baines's (2002) study of first grade children's playground social games. According to their data, girls consistently engaged in verbal games and other types of social play, whereas boys engaged in less personal, physical play.

Critically informed scholarship on gender in early childhood acknowledges and affirms the differences between boys' and girls' social worlds, and argues for girls' social nature to be valued in schools. The critically informed perspective builds on the traditionally oriented scholarship that seeks to identify gender differences by presenting research that focuses on the significance and value of these differences. Most important, critically informed scholarship on gender gives attention and affirmation to the perceptions and experiences of girls.

Postmodern Scholarship

Postmodern scholarship does not position gender as experientially developed cognition as traditionally oriented scholarship does, nor does it position gender as a collection of experiential differences as critically informed scholarship does. Rather, postmodern scholarship positions gender as a form of continuous participation with the ideas that define masculinity and

femininity. These ideas, or discourses, are socially and culturally created realities that are central to our ways of thinking and producing meaning (Davies, 2001; Ryan, Ochsner, & Genishi, 2001). According to Burman (1994), discourses define "who we are, why we are the way we are, and where we are going" (p. 48).

Postmodern scholarship positions gender as a thing to *do*, not as a thing to *be*. Davies (1989, 1993) uses children's writing and literature to illustrate that male and female are discursive categories, and to support the notion that our actions are shaped by the discourses of each category. She says: "When I talk about the experience of being "a woman," I refer to the experience of being assigned to the category female, of being discursively, interactively, and structurally *positioned* as such...." (Davies, 2001, p. 69–70, author's emphasis). In other words, we do the behaviors characteristically done by those in our gender category. Grieshaber (1998) and Walkerdine (1994) report similar research and theoretical positions on the performative act of gender; West and Fenstermaker (1993) present gender as a "situated accomplishment" (p. 156) and socially mandated behavior management plan.

Gallas (1998) highlights the power held by culture in gender discourse, stressing that children's understanding of what it means to be a girl and what it means to be a boy affects their views of behaviors, social roles, and gender-based expectations. MacNaughton (1997) contends that young children's knowledge of masculinity and femininity is revealed in their play, which "provides a window on what they see as the norms for girls and boys, women and men, and how the culture in which they live understands this" (p. 63). Children play out the struggles they are facing as they wrestle with learning gender, and in the process have opportunities either to accept or to refuse socially required gender characteristics (Alloway, 1995; MacNaughton, 1996).

As two cases in point, MacNaughton (1997) and Danby (1998) each present data depicting preschool children's interactions with gender discourse during typical daily classroom play activities. MacNaughton's case study on gender power struggles during preschool block play showed girls moving back and forth between masculine and feminine discourses, situating themselves within whichever gender's stereotypical behavior—sweet and polite or aggressive and dominating—they believed would allow them to overpower their male classmates and gain them access to the blocks. Danby (1998) described a similar episode in which girls moved seamlessly between feminine domestic play and masculine aggressive play after being bullied by boy classmates. Other work also found this type of gender fluidity: MacNaughton's (1996) and Hughes and MacNaughton's (2000) investigations of young children's stereotypical gender play with Barbie dolls and action figures depicted children shifting easily from pretending to be female characters to pretending to be male characters.

For postmodern scholars, gender is a social construction. Ideas of gender performance and the dominant voice of culture within gender discourse represent the central focus of their research on gender. Seeing children's behaviors as discursive acts provides us with opportunities to discuss and question children's evolving understandings of gender differences in new ways. Postmodern scholarship encourages early childhood educators to focus curricular and pedagogical energy on gender as a discourse defined by cultural values because, as Gallas (1998) explains, as long as the male/female dichotomy exists, the non-sexist education promoted in the traditionally oriented literature will not have an impact on children's lives.

The most recent scholarship on gender from the traditionally oriented, critically informed, and postmodern perspectives collectively considers questions concerning origins of gender knowledge, manifestations of gender differences, and the social discourse of gender. The varied scholarly approaches offer unique perspectives on and interpretations of this central feminist topic, thereby simultaneously enriching and complicating our understandings of gender and young children.

YOUNG CHILDREN AND THEIR FAMILIES

Early childhood educators and researchers from each of the three perspectives highlighted in this chapter are committed to the investigation of issues that affect children and families, knowing that research findings provide information that builds awareness and knowledge, expands existing ways of thinking, and questions social assumptions. Traditionally oriented research largely focuses on causal relationships between family/home environments and child outcomes; critically informed literature broadens the research scope by including social issues that are overlooked by traditionally oriented scholarship, such as the experiences of mothers in poverty, diverse family structures, and gay/lesbian parents. Taking a different stance in relation to this topic, postmodern scholarship challenges the very idea of family, positioning it as a hegemonic discourse dominant in Western society.

Traditionally Oriented Scholarship

Academics working from a traditional, developmentalist perspective have invested great effort in measuring the causal affects of nuclear family issues and the influence of family members—especially parents—on young children's development. Exploring the negative impact of factors like abuse, divorce, and day care has been of particular interest to traditionally oriented scholars. The following examples represent a sample of findings from research in this vein: physically abused children typically have delayed development of play skills, show low levels of playful energy, and frequently interrupt their own play with behavior outbursts (Cooper, 2000); physically abused children are generally more depressed, have lower self-esteem, and demonstrate more hopelessness than their non-abused peers (Cerezo & Frias, 1994); children who spent longer periods of time in child care or those whose care was not of high quality commonly demonstrate behaviors such as physical aggression and acting out (Belesky, 1999; Egeland & Heister, 1995), have a poor tolerance for frustration (Han, Waldfogel & Brooks-Gunn, 2001), rebel against authority (Belesky, 2001), and are socially rejected by peers (Bates, Marvinney, Kelly, Dodge, Bennett & Pettit, 1994). Overall, traditionally oriented research highlights

the ways in which familial matters can have significant negative affects on young children's emotional, social, and cognitive development.

Critically Informed Scholarship

The revised DAP guidelines (Bredekamp & Copple, 1997) emphasize the importance of developing and maintaining healthy school-home partnerships, yet offer no elaboration on the terms "parents" or "families." Critically informed scholars argue that this omission perpetuates traditional assumptions about families and family structures. As Burman (1994) points out, the term family carries with it the implicit image of a "normal," intact, and nuclear structure; variations are correspondingly defined in relation to this norm, as seen in terms such as "nontraditional" and "broken." Critically informed scholarship strives to expand the field's working understanding of family. Moving beyond implicit assumptions, beliefs, and definitions, critically informed research explores a wider and more diverse conception of family life.

For example, Polakow (1993) explored the experiences of families living in poverty. She used the testimonies and "narratives of endurance and survival" (p. 41) of young single mothers whose income was below the poverty line to reveal the social forces that keep financially struggling women in oppressed conditions: limited access to jobs that pay wages high enough to afford daycare, shortage of shelters for homeless mothers with hungry children, and lack of health insurance for medical needs. By focusing scholarly attention on mothers and children in poverty, Polakow's work makes central a population typically marginalized or overlooked in the early childhood literature on families.

Critically informed scholarship also broadens conversations about families by challenging traditional assumptions and interpretations of family structure. This includes research on the experiences of adoptive families (Greenberg, 2001); foster families (Wozniak, 2002); single father families (Winters, 2001); grandparents-as-parents families (Smith, Dannison & Vach-Hasse, 1998); and gay/lesbian parented families (Ciano-Boyce & Shelley-Sireci, 2002; Golombok, Perry, Burston et al., 2003).

Critically informed efforts to reconceptualize the social boundaries of family composition to include same-sex parent families require teachers and schools to reexamine their conceptions of homosexuality. Corbett's work on teacher homophobia (1993) and M. Carter's (1998) discussion of antihomosexual bias hidden within curriculum and school policies provide valuable research on this issue. Kroeger (2001) shares a personal experience as a bisexual teacher working with a lesbian couple family as a way of challenging teachers' homophobia; Casper, Cuffaro, Schultz, Silin, and Wickens (1996) and Lakey (1997) discuss the process of including gay and lesbian perspectives in schools; Frieman (1996) and Meadows (2001) offer research-based advice and resource references for teachers working with sexual diversity in the classroom.

Critically informed scholarship encourages early childhood educators to expand traditional definitions of family diversity to include consideration of issues like poverty, alternative guardianship, and sexual orientation. Here again, critically informed scholarship builds on and broadens the traditional boundaries of the field.

Postmodern Scholarship

A fundamental assumption of traditionally oriented research on children and families is that children's emotional, social, and cognitive developments are affected by family circumstances and parental behaviors. Critically informed scholarship claims that traditional definitions and conceptions of family life need to be diversified by including consideration of arrangements and social circumstances beyond the boundaries of the nuclear family. Postmodern research pushes this issue even further, seeking to deconstruct the hegemonic nature of the discourse of family and to illuminate the embedded power structures that define families and that directly affect the lives of young children.

Burman (1994) asserts that Western society comfortably holds the notion that the nuclear family is a social unit necessary for human survival. She points out that traditional discussions about families within developmental psychology contexts tend to "treat the family as a universal, common, and unchanging structure without any reference to cultural or historical specificity" (p. 66); this is in spite of the fact that historical analysis traces the construction of the current notion of family throughout history, government, and culture (Cannella, 1997).

A focus on power—its acquisition, use, and denial—is a central feature of postmodern research on families. One example of this is the examination of the influence of governmental power on the experiences of families living in poverty. Swadner (1995) names child advocacy programs such as the Children's Defense Fund and Women, Infants, and Children (WIC) as places in which the government has a strong influence on the discourse of family. Head Start, a federally funded educational program designed specifically for low-income preschool children between the ages of 3- to 5-years and their families is also an example of government involvement in family life, as is the federal prosecution of parents who fail to pay child support (Burman, 1994).

Another type of power circulating within the discourse of family involves the relationships between adult and child family members. Investigating this notion, Grieshaber (2001b) looked at conversation transcripts between a mother, Bev, and her 5-year-old son, Robert, as they played a computer game together. The study revealed that rather than Bev having greater power than Robert, it was the son who exercised techniques of power over his mother. Grieshaber explains that Bev's nurturant femininity and permissive mothering strategies allowed Robert to use masculine power behaviors to gain increasingly dominant positions in their interpersonal transactions. Furthermore, Robert participates in the dominant discourse of masculinity as a means of "occupying a position that is institutionally more powerful than that of his mother" (Grieshaber, 2001b, p. 231), suggesting that power lies in gender discourse—specifically, patriarchy—rather than in adult-child or family discourse.

To summarize the postmodern scholarship reviewed here, the overarching objective is to interrupt the early childhood community's dominant way of thinking about families by investigating the various power relationships that exist within the discourse of family. The point argued is that Western culture's conceptualizations and beliefs about young children and families are based on research grounded in longstanding hegemonic assumptions.

Scholarship on young children and their families from the traditionally oriented, critically informed, and postmodern perspectives collectively addresses a wide gamut of issues pertinent to early childhood education. Working with families is one of teachers' most important responsibilities; the diversity among research objectives, analyses, and findings created by the multiple perspectives coexisting in the field provides invaluable support for our work with children.

TEACHING, TEACHERS, AND TEACHER EDUCATION

The teacher plays a pivotal role in early childhood education and thus is the focus of a large amount of research in our field. Much of the recent work done on teaching, teachers, and teacher education has focused on the various facets of what being both a woman and a teacher of young children means within Western society. Traditionally oriented scholarship highlights the parallels between mothering and teaching responsibilities, positioning them both as natural female roles. Critically informed scholarship encourages the expansion of the boundaries surrounding the mother/teacher relationship to include new sources of knowledge and new definitions of good teaching. A key goal of postmodern scholarship on teaching, teachers, and teacher education is to deconstruct the mother/teacher discourse and to dismantle the equation of teaching with women.

Traditionally Oriented Scholarship

Traditionally-oriented scholarship largely focuses on the close alignment between the duties of teaching and mothering: teacher-mother dualities, teacher as caregiver, and teacher-child relationships. Researchers explored the issues facing women who simultaneously participate in the roles of teacher and mother, such as physical exhaustion (MacDonald, 1994), and separation, child care, or nursing arrangements (Claffey, 1995). MacDonald (1999) questioned dual role preservice teachers about the interplay between the two roles. She found that for most of her participants, being a mother was the inspiration for the choice to become a teacher; furthermore, she discovered that these preservice teachers believed their mothering experience would make them better teachers. Whitaker (2001) explored how dual role preservice teachers and single role preservice teachers made the transition from university classroom student to field experience student, finding that the mothers had a harder time adjusting because only their university knowledge, not their maternal knowledge, was valued.

Traditionally oriented research also explored the mother/teacher role alignment by looking at ways in which teachers, like mothers, serve as children's caregivers (Bradley & Caldwell, 1995). Early childhood teachers fill the role of caregiver in that they protect children, offer affection, comfort hurts, appreciate accomplishments, meet children's physical needs like food, sleep, exercise, and toileting (Jalongo, 2002; Murphy & Leeper, 2003). Teachers also offer stimulation, understand young children's unique needs (Gable, 2002), facilitate children's spiritual growth (Turner, 2000), and strengthen their moral development (Johansson, 2002).

The image of teachers as caregivers establishes a strong teacher-child bond; it can even be seen in the structure and names of Reggio Emilia programs which not only reflect an emphasis on teacher-child relationships but also explicitly connect them to mother and child relationships: *asilo nido*, which means nest, is the concept of infant/toddler environments and *scuola maternal*, the maternal school, is the place for children between the ages of 3 and 6 years (Finegan, 2001; see also Edwards & Raikes, 2002).

In general, traditionally oriented scholarship has focused on the parallels and overlaps between teaching and mothering young children. Both in the physical sense, such as being both a teacher and a mother, as well as in the implied sense, such as the Reggio program names, women and early childhood education are seen as interwoven.

Critically Informed Scholarship

Redrawing the boundaries around what it means to teach and to be a teacher of young children has been a central theme of critically informed research. For instance, researchers examined early childhood education practices in non-Western cultures. Jalongo, Hoot, Pattnaik, Cai and Park (1997) explain that by engaging in this type of research, educators are able to discover common challenges, broaden understandings of what is best for children, and examine ways to become global advocates for young children.

Escobedo's (1993) work is an example of research meant to broaden teachers' understandings of appropriate practice. Escobedo found that culturally, economically, linguistically, or racially diverse children experienced academic success when their cultural identity was reinforced and when they engaged in instructional experiences that were relevant and meaningful. Ladson-Billings and Gomez (2001) found that when white teachers who worked with diverse populations shifted their attention from children's perceived cultural deficits to their capabilities, the scholastic performance of the children improved.

Similarly, Swadener (1995) promoted "at promise" as a model for white teachers to use when thinking about children with racial, ethnic, and linguistic backgrounds different from their own. Thinking of these children in nondeficit ways created opportunities for them to be repositioned in their relationship to society. Ladson-Billings's (1994, 1995) culturally relevant pedagogy likewise encouraged this type of paradigm shift (see also Blasi, 2002).

Researchers working to reconceptualize the field of early childhood education also explored women teachers' knowledge, decision making, and experience. Critically informed

scholars questioned some of the fundamental assumptions about women's "natural" feelings for children. Unlike traditionally oriented work, which describes caring teachers as patient, affectionate, nurturing, and devoted (Nowak-Fabrykowski & Caldwell, 2002; Teven, 2001; Vogt, 2002), critically informed theorizing on the relationship between caring and teaching focuses on the ways in which caring can serve as a foundation for teacher decision making (Goldstein, 1998) and classroom management (Dalton & Watson, 1997). Along similar lines, Jipson (1995) used her personal experiences as a daughter, mother, teacher, and professor to interrupt the romantic "teacher as mother" metaphor. Her writing highlights the mismatch between teacher authority and maternal nurture and shows how that mismatch creates problems and tensions for students and for teachers (see also Anijar, 1998).

Other critically informed early childhood researchers approach the feminist topic of teaching, teachers, and teacher education with a different focus. Coffey and Delamont (2000) question existing "malestream" perspectives and practices in education, and argue for a revisioning of teaching that would disrupt traditional classroom processes through new pedagogies, inquiry into curriculum content, and the establishment of management strategies encouraging collaboration and democratic values. Likewise, Brady (1995) asserts that "developing one's role as a feminist educator involves asking oneself questions about the nature of every theory and practice which determines the conditions of our environment" (p. 2), and calls for a feminist pedagogy of multiculturalism "aimed at restructuring the relations of power" (p. 4) in schools and in society in ways that benefit all children.

Critically informed research also seeks to expand the realm of teacher education pedagogy. Of recent interest is the biographical exploration of the relationship between women's life histories and the formation of their teacher identities (M. Marsh, 2003). Other critically informed scholarship looks at preservice teachers' identities as stories (K. Carter, 1993) and at the impact of personal history on shaping the thoughts and beliefs of preservice teachers (Knowles & Holt-Reynolds, 1994; Short & Burke, 1996; Thornton, 2002). Although this way of thinking about teacher education is not new (see Bruner, 1987), critically informed research built on the theoretical work of the past and brought it to new levels of application and understanding. For example, Munby, Russell, and Martin (2001) utilized Bruner's narrative and paradigmatic modes of thought to explore teachers' knowledge and teacher education through the metaphor of a hitchhiker's guide; Zeichner and Liston (1996) built on Dewey's *How We Think* (1933) to create a reflective teaching pedagogy.

The central point of critically informed scholarship on this topic has been to expand and improve the ways in which early childhood educators approached teaching and teacher preparation. Multicultural perspectives, reflective teaching, and biographical inquiry were incorporated into the traditional maternal portrait of teaching, and new models of teaching emerged from this reconceptualist work. In these models, critical thinking, reflection, and attention to lived experience were seen as integral parts of women's work as early childhood teachers.

Postmodern Scholarship

A significant objective of postmodern research on teaching, teachers, and teacher education has been to deconstruct discourses of sexism within the field of early childhood education (Coffey & Delamont, 2000). Sexism exists within the socially constructed beliefs that women hold intuitive and innate knowledge about how to teach young children (Miller, 1996) and that teaching is something "women do instinctively and are instinctively good at because they 'love children" (Maher, 1999, p. 47). Moving beyond critically informed scholarship's focus on women's lived experiences, research from the postmodern perspective looks more broadly at the societal structures presently reproducing and reinscribing sexist beliefs and practices.

Leavitt (1994) challenges this sexist discourse with vignettes from infant-toddler day care settings that reveal the social power structures that keep female early childhood teachers marginalized. Leavitt explains that regardless of how instinctive or innate teaching/mothering/loving children may appear to be for women, the emotional investment that is required of teachers is not natural. Rather, she says, it is bought and sold labor:

The emotional labor of the caregivers is complex, as they are expected to develop a sense of investment in each child that enables them to sustain caring throughout the day and over time, but also each day release children to their parents. In short, caregivers are expected to emotionally engage intensely, and disengage gracefully, and do both upon demand. (Leavitt, 1994, p. 61)

Maher (1999), drawing on the work of Walkerdine (1992), explains that women were originally placed in classrooms because of their maternal nature and because they provided a loving and supportive mother image as opposed to the harsh, authoritative father image provided by men. It is this type of maternal image that researchers working with a postmodern perspective challenge (Burgess & Carter, 1992). By juxtaposing female early childhood teachers as maternal and nurturing against males who are harsh and authoritative, women are positioned as the weaker sex (Maher, 1999) and relegated to lower social status.

Researchers using a postmodern lens argue instead that "for women who teach, there need be no conflict between nurturance and authority" (Miller, 1992, p. 107). Grieshaber discusses early childhood teachers making conscious decisions to change their "subjectivity from being positioned through discourse as a caring teacher, the accepted or taken-for-granted position for a female teacher" (2001a, p. 68), to being positioned in ways that are more authoritative (see Weedon, 1997, for a full explanation of subjectivity). MacNaughton (1997) tells of an early childhood teacher who, when faced with new insights on implicit sexist discourse in children's free play, consciously decides to move from a position of hands-off pedagogy to one that includes critical questioning and active involvement. In what MacNaughton terms a "feminist reconstruction of the developmentalist pedagogic gaze" (p. 324), social activism was added to this teacher's understanding of appropriate early childhood practices.

Although many scholars working from a postmodern perspective argue for the deconstruction of the social understanding of what it means to be a female early childhood teacher, others use postmodern research to examine early childhood educational practices and discourses in new ways. Ryan and Campbell (2001) brought postmodern perspectives to bear on issues of "equity, identity, and the politics of classroom life" (p. 57); Ochsner (2001) used postmodern theories to examine the nature and role of heterosexuality, masculinities, and femininities in a preschool classroom; whereas J. Marsh (2000) engaged in a postmodern inquiry into assumptions about gender roles and superhero play in the lives of young children. Scholarship along these lines makes space for us to consider new possibilities and new conceptions of early childhood teaching.

Traditionally oriented, critically informed, and postmodern scholars build on different theoretical foundations, ask different questions, and focus on different facets of early childhood teaching and teacher education. However, these researchers all share a focus on the roles and the nature of women's work as early childhood teachers and teacher educators, and all ground their scholarship in a commitment to understanding and improving our practices in the field.

SOCIETAL FORCES AND CONTEXTS

The social milieu is an element of concern for academics from all three schools of thought represented in this chapter. For those working with a traditionally oriented perspective, research efforts attempt to show that although children's internal development progresses in universal and independent ways, the quality of that development is dependent on their environment. Critically informed work, by contrast, offers a different understanding of the relationship between children's development and their environment: children are not positioned as passive victims but, rather, as active participants who are able to engage with their environment and shape their own experiences. Postmodern scholarship interrupts both viewpoints by providing research indicating that there is no relationship between children and social forces or contexts; rather, children participate in the discourses that make up their social milieu.

Traditionally Oriented Scholarship

The ways in which popular culture, media, and economic circumstances affect young children's development has held the attention of researchers working within the traditionally-oriented perspective over the past decade. Concerns regarding the ways in which various social environments influence young girls are well represented in the scholarship. Gilbert (1998), in a study that investigated the relationship between popular culture and children's perception of their bodies, found that television, movies, pulp fiction media, and the sports and fashion industries influenced the ways in which young children perceived themselves as well as how they wanted to be perceived by others. Pipher (1994) agrees with Gilbert's position, positing a correlation between media-related early childhood experiences and later adolescent behaviors: young children exposed to glamorous teen and adult images in the media become adolescents who imitate the images they perceive to be the most sexually striking and financially impressive.

Looking at the issue from a different angle, Farrell posits that "[o]ne of the strongest early influences on gender is the mass toy market.... The universal Barbie doll is a case in point" (Farrell, 1998, p. 105). Other research explores the notion that toys and movies are meant to play a role in the psyche and gender identity of those who use and watch them. Brown, Thornton, and Sutterby (2004) raise questions regarding the movie, television, toy, fashion, and magazine industries' targeting of children as a consumer demographic, perceiving them not as playing children, but as sophisticated consumers (see also John, 1999; Kirn & Cole, 2001).

Henry Giroux (1998, 1999) raises similar arguments about the socialization affects of media. Although generally considered to be a critically informed theorist, Giroux's work on this topic is included here as traditionally oriented scholarship because the concerns he expresses about the impact of media on young children are in alignment with developmental psychology socialization theories. Giroux proposes that Walt Disney movies such as *The Little Mermaid* and *The Lion King* utilize "narrowly defined gender roles" (1998, p. 58), reinforce negative female stereotypes, and tell stories in which female characters are subordinate to male characters. He goes on to say that these movies are full of messages that children absorb passively and then play out in their own lives. Steinberg and Kincheloe (1998) coined the term "kinderculture" to describe this powerful influence that popular culture has on young children, representing it as a form of corporate pedagogy. In their discussion, Steinberg and Kincheloe accuse corporations and commercial industries of taking advantage of and profiting from young children's vulnerability.

In addition to examining the social forces of media and popular culture on children, traditionally oriented researchers worked to add correlations between children's socioeconomic status and academic achievement to the existing body of scholarship. Researchers such as Bowey (1995), Corcoran (1995), Smith and Dixon (1995), and Walker, Greenwood, Hart, and Carta (1994) all found statistical correlations suggesting that economically poor children are also at risk of being academically poor students, particularly compared to their higher income peers. Research efforts to find explanations for the correlation produced these results: according to Duncan and Brooks-Gunn (1997, 2000), children who live in poverty have less healthy physical and cognitive development, which subsequently interferes with intellectual and academic achievement; Ripke and Crosby's research (2002) indicates that children in poverty have limited access to "safe, nurturing learning environments" and "opportunities to engage in warm and responsive interactions with adults" (p. 214); Smith, Brooks-Gunn, and Klebanov (1997) posit that economically poor children are at a high risk of exposure to living conditions and illnesses that are harmful to their immediate development as well as to their future academic and employment performances.

Societal forces such as popular culture and poverty are considered to be significant by researchers utilizing traditional theories. Traditionally oriented scholarship suggests that the quality of young children's development is dependent upon the nature of the experiences they have with their environment. This keystone belief is the departure point for the critically informed and postmodern perspectives on the relationship between children and social forces.

Critically Informed Scholarship

Critically informed research seeks to move the field beyond drawing simple causal connections about children and social forces. Instead, the relationship between children and their environment is described with children as active participants in their environment, shaping their own context in important ways. Jipson and Reynolds (1998) recognize the multiple factors involved in determining the ways in which children interact with societal forces and contexts, and argue that media's influence on children is shaped by elements such as economics, culture, history, age, gender, and the particular situations in which exposure occurs.

Other critically informed research explores the role of popular culture in the early childhood curriculum. For example, J. Marsh looked at the effects of Teletubbies television shows (1999a) and Batman/Batwoman comic book cartoons (1999b) on children's literacy and oral communication efforts. Findings from these studies suggest that academic activities grounded in popular culture are successful because of the children's increased motivation to participate in activities related to their social interests. Along similar lines, Belton (2001) explored how young children actively use popular culture to shape their experiences in school. She found that the media has positive effects on children's story writing, particularly in its ability to stimulate the imagination.

In a further exploration of the role of popular culture on children's experiences at school, J. Marsh (2000) investigated connections between kindergarten and first grade literacy curriculum and girls' superhero role play. Whereas previous research on superhero play focused on boys or suggested that girls take on masculine character roles in order to engage in this type of play, J. Marsh's research indicated that superhero play is strongly attractive to girls. Furthermore, J. Marsh found that this type of participation with popular culture provided girls with contexts and stories in which they could actively position themselves as heroic females.

Critically informed scholarship has not only focused on extending the field's understanding of the impact of popular culture on children's experience; it also included investigations of students at risk of academic failure. Research on this matter has been addressed in similar fashion to that within the traditionally oriented perspective, but, like all critically informed scholarship in early childhood education, has worked to broaden the traditional conversation to include new areas of inquiry. For example, Lubeck (1995) took the "at-risk" label used to describe children whose low socioeconomic status was mirrored in low academic performance and applied it to the children's mothers. She argued that financially poor mothers were at risk of failure because of the Western tradition of blame: "[i]f a child does not fare well, emotionally, socially, or academically, it is the family— but the mother specifically—who is implicated" (Lubeck, 1995,

p. 54). Furthermore, she explained, mothers at risk are those who, because of their economic situation, are not able to be and to do what is expected of "good" mothers.

Lubeck (1995) goes on to point out that economically challenged mothers' options for change are essentially nonexistent because of the oppressive economic and social forces surrounding them, and as a result their children's hope for change is also limited. Similar ideas were expressed by Polakow (1994), who described the scarcity of support services for poor mothers with young children and argued that the public policy on welfare reform contributes directly to the destruction of families.

Overall, critically informed scholarship on the relationship between societal forces and young children reflects the perspective's viewpoint regarding the shortfalls of universal statements intended as descriptions of children's experiences. Critically informed research posits instead that children are active agents in their interaction with social contexts and that their interactions are positioned within the social, cultural, and historical variables unique to each individual child. Research on this topic also reflects the ongoing critically informed effort to foreground the voices of populations not represented in traditionally oriented scholarship.

Postmodern Scholarship

The starting point for postmodern researchers' consideration of the influence of societal forces on children's lives is the process of challenging and questioning the discourse of socialization that is prevalent in early childhood education (Burman, 1994; Grieshaber & Cannella, 2001). The socialization theories that resonate throughout traditionally oriented scholarship describe children as being influenced and shaped by external forces like television and video games to a degree that is both "considerable" and "profound" (Kawecki, 1994, p. 489). Scholars with a postmodern viewpoint disagree with this because it positions children as sponges passively and uncritically absorbing experiences and information (Davies, 2001). Instead, postmodern scholarship advocates that young children be regarded as agentic beings, recognizing that through daily participation in language systems and discourses, children actively decide for themselves which characteristics to incorporate into their identities (Davies, 2001).

Case study research conducted by Hughes and MacNaughton (2001) targets gender socialization ideas associated with Barbie dolls. The premise of their research is that when children play, they actively recreate the discourses to which they have been exposed. Hughes and MacNaughton stress that children live in a social world in which some discourses, such as gender stereotypes, are "more available, more desirable, more recognizable, more pleasurable, and therefore more powerful than others" (2001, p. 123; see also Cannella, 2001). They further assert that children do not absorb gender messages by playing with Barbie dolls as has been argued in traditionally oriented scholarship (e.g., Farrell, 1998); rather, Barbie dolls serve as props with which children can act out their understandings of gender discourse (Alloway, 1995; Kellner, 1998; MacNaughton, 1994).

Hughes and MacNaughton's (2001) research, as well as that by MacNaughton (1996), challenges the proposed social benefits of shielding children from popular culture and other forms of media. They explain that societal problems such as sexism are not caused by Barbie dolls but rather by the discourse of patriarchy that saturates Western society. Furthermore, researchers using a postmodern perspective argue that the common adult practice of making censorship decisions about toys and movies positions children, especially females, as a population without agency who can be easily manipulated and influenced (Craven, 2002). Alloway (1995) theorizes that situating young girls within a discourse of manipulation forces them deeper into the female stereotype of dependence.

Postmodern scholarship on the influence of social forces on children's experiences calls into question some of the bedrock notions of early childhood education. Interrogating our unexamined assumptions and challenging our long-standing beliefs about children and society are central features of postmodern research in our field.

The considerations of the relationship between children and their social contexts presented here differ dramatically in their fundamental assumptions about children. In traditionally oriented research, children are passive, vulnerable, and require adult protection. In critically informed scholarship, children are active meaning-makers—resilient, resourceful, and able to engage with adults and the adult world in productive ways. For postmodern scholars, children have agency and power as great as that of adults: children resist, reinterpret, and establish fluid relationships with their surroundings. When taken together, these three perspectives provide a rich and complex picture that challenges us to think deeply about our own beliefs and assumptions about children, about our curricular and pedagogical decisions, and about our scholarly inquiries in early childhood education.

RESEARCHING EARLY CHILDHOOD EDUCATION

In addition to exploring various dimensions of gender, young children and their families, teachers, teaching and teacher education, and the influence of societal forces on young children's lives, early childhood researchers have also looked at the topic of research itself. As presented here, the central objective of traditionally oriented scholarship on research is to provide information about the purposes and methods for conducting research in early childhood education; critically informed scholarship reflects the introduction of qualitative research to early childhood contexts and the emergence of considerations of reflexivity; and the postmodern scholarship focuses on the power dynamics inherent in research relationships.

Traditionally Oriented Scholarship

Traditionally oriented scholarship regarding research practices in early childhood generally includes explanations of quantitative data collection methods and measurement strategies that can be used to study children and their environments. Goodwin and Goodwin (1996) provide an overview of research fundamentals and explain various styles of quantitative research design: survey and developmental research, correlative research, causal-comparative research, experimental research, and single-subject research. Lerner, Hauser-Cram and Miller (1998) offer explanations of longitudinal and cross-sectional research designs, pointing out that these are among the most commonly used and powerful research designs in early childhood education.

Because of the long-standing interest in the use of psychometrics and other tests informed by educational psychology, issues of measurement are a central consideration in traditionally oriented discussions of research in early childhood education. Goodwin and Goodwin (1993), for example, review the aspects of children's development and skill that can be measured effectively and explore the purposes and goals of measurement. They also provide information regarding standards for validity and reliability in educational testing and measurement.

We conducted literature searches in various databases seeking traditionally oriented considerations and examinations of the process of doing research in early childhood education. We found research texts and articles written to describe techniques and methods and to offer instruction and guidance. Meta-level analyses and reflective theorizing about the research endeavor do not appear to be a feature of traditionally oriented scholarship. This serves to illustrate traditionally oriented scholars' comfort with and acceptance of the research techniques that have long been used in early childhood education (Bloch, 1992).

Critically Informed Scholarship

Critically informed scholarship does not demonstrate the same complacency toward traditional forms of early childhood educational research. Just as critically informed scholars have worked to encourage the early childhood field to reposition ideas about gender, families, teaching, and society, they also have worked to realign the boundaries around research. Most notably, critically informed researchers pioneered the use of qualitative methodologies. Hatch (1998) explains that although qualitative methods have been a part of educational research since the mid-1950s, qualitative research conducted in early childhood settings by early childhood researchers is still in its earliest stages.

Early childhood scholars engaging in qualitative inquiry have explored the full range of methodologies employed by qualitative researchers in the other social sciences, such as ethnography, teacher research and other forms of action research, case study, naturalistic inquiry, observational studies, linguistic analysis, and arts-based research. Similarly, early childhood educational researchers cited throughout this chapter have published studies built on the data gathering techniques familiar to qualitative researchers in other areas of education: participant observation, interviews, dialogue journals, email correspondence, analysis of curriculum materials and other documents, self-study, and so on.

In addition to discussions of research methodologies, method, strategies, and techniques, critically informed scholarship offers reflections on ethical issues embedded in qualitative research, particularly the challenges arising from the differences of power and privilege between researchers and study participants. For example, Hatch (1998) accused researchers of violating ethics of privilege when they use children and teachers as study participants for their own personal gain. He expressed particular concern about researchers' motives when conducting research for the purpose of paper publication or conference presentation.

In effort to address these issues, Goldstein (2000) built ethical safeguards meant to minimize power differentials into the data collection procedure of a collaborative study in a primary grade classroom. Despite these precautions, Goldstein concluded that "... collaboration is fraught with ethical and relational complexities. ... No clear definitions or reviews of the literature could purge research relationships of power and status inequities ..." (Goldstein, 2000, p. 528). Qualitative research by definition involves interpersonal relationships; Goldstein and Hatch bring the reality of the ethics of power and privilege to the forefront of critically informed conversations on researching early childhood education.

Embracing qualitative research did not cause these ethical dilemmas to arise in early childhood education; unequal distribution of power and privilege is a feature of all research with human participants. However, the reflexivity that is a hallmark of qualitative research made these issues explicit and demanded that we think carefully about our relationships with our research participants. In broadening the methodological boundaries of early childhood education to include qualitative research, critically informed scholars have brought new techniques, new perspectives, and new concerns to the field.

Postmodern Scholarship

In order to shed light on the ways in which postmodern perspectives inform our thinking about research issues in early childhood education, we needed to draw on scholars writing about research in other educational settings and contexts. Most of the postmodern literature focusing on methodological and ethical concerns in educational research concentrates on the field of education in general rather than on early childhood education in particular. However, in the instances in which early childhood researchers have written about research in our field from a postmodern viewpoint (e.g., Tobin, 1995), the issues raised and the perspectives offered are identical to those found in the more general postmodern literature on research issues such as the nature of social research, reflexivity, and the place of the researcher in the research (Coffey, 1999). As a result, we feel comfortable casting our net broadly when seeking insight into this topic.

Tobin (1995) highlights the differences between early childhood research informed by an interpretivist, reconceptualist perspective and research positioned within a postmodern viewpoint:

Most qualitative research in early childhood education reflects the belief that people pretty much mean what they say, that texts have stable meaning, and that the reality of a classroom can be captured by a careful ethnographer. Post-structural research, in contrast, is characterized by a suspicion of the meaning of words and actions, a lack of belief in the stability of textual meaning, and a cynicism about the claims of ethnography and other naturalistic methods. (p. 226)

Tobin's words demonstrate that postmodern scholarship on research issues often involves raising questions rather than answering them.

The multiple forms of power held by educational researchers are examined critically in postmodern writings on research. In a broad sense, qualitative researchers strive to gain an emic perspective, or insider's view, of a given situation through collaborative and ethnographic research. The objective in discovering and presenting the view of the participants rather than that of the researcher (Manning, 1997) is to shift the privileged and powered position of "knower" from the researcher to the participants (Lather, 1995). Those whose research is informed by the postmodern perspective concur with Manning's and Lather's vision, but argue that this goal is impossible to achieve. Rather, postmodern scholars assert that every story has a researcher/narrator who ultimately holds the power of telling the string of events (K. Carter, 1993); regardless of how invisible the narrator attempts to be, a "superior, more knowing attitude" is assumed toward the research participants because "it is the narrator ... who provides the interpretations, and who modulates the [participants'] voices" (K. Carter, 1993, p. 9). To counteract the problem of the researcher/narrator shaping the meaning of the research findings, Emihovich (1995) asserts that researchers should create narratives where the purpose is not to relate the truth, but to come to a sense of shared understanding as to what is known.

In addition to the power of narration, postmodern scholarship interrogates researchers' role in representing participants' voices (Munro, 1995). As discussed throughout this chapter, the postmodern perspective recognizes identity as something fluid and situational; thus, the act of 'voicing' marginalized groups in research is interpreted as being in itself an oppressive social act (K. Howe, 1998).

Applying these issues and concerns to research in early childhood education, we argue that postmodern research serves to disrupt the field's easy acceptance of qualitative research. As the use of qualitative research methodologies has become increasingly common in early childhood education, the postmodern literature serves the crucial function of complicating and challenging beliefs and understandings and by raising questions about researchers' power in the construction of data representation as well as in the privileging and marginalizing of participant voices.

Researching early childhood education is included in this chapter as a central feminist topic because of the significant effect research methodology has on the direction of our field. The relatively recent emergence of qualitative methodology in early childhood has created dramatic changes not only in the way research is conducted, but also in the way research findings influence daily classroom life. The integration of ethnography, narrative inquiry, and observational methods with the more traditional quantitative research strategies has provided early childhood education with rich data from which better pedagogical and curricular decisions can be made.

QUESTIONS AND CHALLENGES

The ideology of social transformation that is the core of feminist thought has begun to reshape the field of early childhood education. In the past decade, the wide range of perspectives brought to bear on investigations and interpretations of the topics central to feminist research in early childhood—gender, young children and their families, teachers, teaching and teacher education, social contexts, and research—have served to broaden the field considerably. Drawing on philosophical sources and theoretical knowledge bases not previously used in early childhood education, this scholarship has created new possibilities. The multiple perspectives informing feminist inquiry have also raised questions and presented challenges for our field.

Early childhood education has long been grounded in a particular set of certainties. These certainties—that children develop along paths shaped by the realities of human biology, by the vicissitudes of individual variation, and by the influences of the environment, or that children benefit from stable and loving relationships with adult caregivers, for example—will be familiar to everyone with training in our field. These certainties are the product of the pervasive and robust association of early childhood education with the science of developmental psychology. Much of the research cited in this chapter, however, is not grounded in developmental psychology, science, or any other theoretical perspective commonly applied in the field of early childhood education. Philosophy, cultural studies, feminist moral theory, critical media studies, literary criticism, feminist and queer theories, and historical studies are some of the academic disciplines informing the critically informed and postmodern work in this review. In fact, some of the scholarship we have presented here explicitly and directly questions or contradicts many of the certainties early childhood education holds dear: in these works, developmental psychology is rigorously critiqued, science is held in suspicion, and the possibility of achieving certainty is actively rejected.

Broadening the foundation of our field in order to explore feminist topics more deeply has created new kinds of instability and ambiguity. Can our field cope with the challenge of embracing not only traditionally oriented research but also critically informed and postmodern research on young children? Rather than the certainty and clarity that have characterized our field for many years, we would have dissonance and discord. What would happen if child development were no longer the stable center of the field?

In our view, the challenge facing our field at this point in time is not deciding whether or not early childhood education can change and grow and embrace new theoretical perspectives. As the research presented in this chapter clearly illustrates, change and growth are already taking place. It is too late to turn back. Even as you read these words there is early childhood scholarship in progress that is grounded in perspectives that we cannot foresee, scholarship that will further broaden and enhance our work with young children.

The real challenge facing us now relates to our field's response to this new theoretical diversity. We do not think it wise to ignore, resist, marginalize, minimize, discount, discredit, or flee from new lines of inquiry or new knowledge sources. As society changes, childhood changes. And as childhood changes, early childhood education must change. As our review of the recent research on the central feminist topics in early childhood education—gender; young children and their families; teachers, teaching and teacher education; the influence of societal forces on young children's lives; and research methodologies—has demonstrated, new theoretical perspectives offer us the means through which to ask and answer new questions, and serve as tools for deepening our understanding of the needs of young people.

As a field we must work to develop the flexibility necessary to entertain conflicting, competing, or even mutually exclusive interpretations of a given issue. We must strive to forge new visions of early childhood teaching and early childhood teacher education in which theoretical diversity is seen as a strength. We must welcome new perspectives, even those that challenge prevailing views, and celebrate the richness they bring to our field. We believe this invitation to accept discomfort and uncertainty and to expect and to seek new sources of knowledge is the most significant contribution feminism has made to early childhood education.

Broadening the boundaries of the field and embracing theoretical diversity opens new spaces and creates new possibilities for practice and policy. When the traditional developmentalist views of early childhood are no longer positioned as the only legitimate knowledge base from which to make informed decisions about early childhood education, the value ascribed to the many other sources of knowledge in our field is increased and

the sharp dividing lines between practitioners, scholars, teacher educators, parents, administrators, researchers, and children become blurred. Eliminating the old hierarchies of theoretical power, prestige, and privilege that have operated in the field will allow alternate forms of knowledge and information to receive serious consideration.

This shift has the potential to change the professional terrain of early childhood education. When the individuals most involved in the lives and the education of young children can work together within professional relationships grounded in mutual respect, new lines of communication can be established, new connections can be made, new forms of inquiry can be developed, and new theorizing can occur.

This commitment to embracing theoretical diversity within the field of early childhood education can have a wider impact as well. Building partnerships with scholars and practitioners working with and for young children in the context of other fields of study will allow us to transcend the typical borders of our field. Intellectual coalitions forged with pediatricians, with poets and authors and musicians and artists, with policy makers and lawyers, lobbyists and legislators would provide us with new kinds of insight, influence, and perspective on children and childhood, and would serve to enrich the understandings of early childhood education that inform those other fields.

Most important, though, these cross-disciplinary intellectual partnerships would lead to the generation of ideas and knowledge that would have been impossible otherwise. In seeking theoretical diversity, we have the ability to transform not only the field of early childhood education but also the world in which early childhood education takes place.

References

Alloway, N. (1995). *Foundation stones: The construction of gender in early childhood*. Carleton, Victoria: The Curriculum Corporation.

Anijar, K. (1998). Childhood and caring: A capitalist taxonomy of the mar(x)ket place. In M. E. Hauser & J. A. Jipson (Eds.), *Intersections: Feminisms/early childhoods* (pp. 283–299). New York: Peter Lang.

Banks, J. A. (1993). Multicultural education for young children: Racial and ethnic attitudes and their modification. In B. Spodek (Ed.), *Handbook of research on the education of young children* (pp. 236–250). New York: Macmillan.

Baroody, A. J. (1993). Fostering the mathematical learning of young children. In B. Spodek (Ed.), *Handbook of research on the education of young children* (pp. 151–175). New York: Macmillan.

Bates, J., Marvinney, D., Kelly, T., Dodge, K., Bennett, R., & Pettit, G. (1994). Child-care history and kindergarten adjustment. *Developmental Psychology, 30*(5), 690–700.

Bauer, P. (1993). Memory for gender-consistent and gender-inconsistent event sequences by twenty-five-month-old children. *Child Development, 64*, 285–297.

Belesky, J. (2001). Developmental risks (still) associated with early child care. *Journal of Child Psychology and Psychiatry, 42*(7), 845–859.

Belton, T. (2001). Television and imagination: An investigation of the influence on children's story-making. *Media, Culture & Society, 23*(6), 799–821.

Blasi, M. (2002). An asset model: Preparing preservice teachers to work with children and families "of promise." *Journal of Research in Childhood Education, 17*(1), 106–121.

Bloch, M. (1992). Critical perspectives on the historical relationship between child development and early childhood education research. In S. Kessler & B. B. Swadner (Eds.), *Reconceptualizing the early childhood curriculum: Beginning the dialogue* (pp. 3–21). New York: Teachers College Press.

Bowey, J. (1995). Socioeconomic status differences in preschool phonological sensitivity and first grade reading achievements. *Journal of Educational Psychology, 87*, 476–487.

Bradley, R., & Caldwell, B. (1995). Caregiving and the regulation of child growth and development: Describing proximal aspects of caregiving systems. *Developmental Review, 15*(1), 38–85.

Brady, J. (1995). *Schooling young children: A feminist pedagogy for liberatory learning*. Albany: SUNY Press.

Bredekamp, S. (Ed.). (1986). *Developmentally appropriate practice in early childhood programs*. Washington, DC: National Association for the Education of Young Children.

Bredekamp, S., & Copple, C. (Eds.). (1997). *Developmentally appropriate practice in early childhood programs*. (Rev. ed.). Washington, DC: National Association for the Education of Young Children.

Brown, P., Thornton, C. D., & Sutterby, J. (2004). Kids getting older younger: The adultification of children's play. In R. Clements & L. Fiorentino (Eds.), *The child's right to play: A global approach* (pp. 177–183). Westport, CT: Greenwood Press.

Bruner, J. (1987). Life as narrative. *Social Research, 54*(1), 11–32.

Burgess, H. & Carter, B. (1992). "Bringing out the best in people:" Teacher training and the "real" teacher. *British Journal of Sociology of Education 12*, (3), 349–359.

Burman, E. (1994). *Deconstructing developmental psychology*. London: Routledge Publications.

Butterworth, D. (1991). Gender equity in early childhood: The state of play. *Australian Journal of Early Childhood, 16*(4), 3–9.

Cannella, G. S. (1997). *Deconstructing early childhood education*. New York: Peter Lang.

Cannella, G. S. (2001). Natural born curriculum: Popular culture and the representation of childhood. In J. Jipson & R. Johnson (Eds.), *Resistance and Representation: Rethinking childhood education* (pp. 15–22). New York: Peter Lang.

Carter, K. (1993). The place of story in research on teaching and teacher education. *Educational Researcher, 22*(1), 5–12.

Carter, M. (1998). Strategies to strengthen our anti-bias practices. *Child Care Information Exchange, 121*, 85–87.

Casper, V., Cuffaro, H., Schultz, S., Silin, J., & Wickens, E. (1996). Toward a most thorough understanding of the world: Sexual orientation and early childhood education. *Harvard Educational Review, 66*(2), 271–293.

Cerezo, M. A., & Frias, D. (1994). Emotional and cognitive adjustment in abused children. *Child Abuse & Neglect, 18*, 923–932.

Chick, K., Heilman-Houser, R., & Hunter, M. (2003). The impact of child care on gender role development and gender stereotypes. *Early Childhood Education Journal, 29*(3), 149–154.

Ciano-Boyce, C., & Shelley-Sireci, L. (2002). Who is mommy tonight? Lesbian parenting issues. *Journal of Homosexuality, 43*(2), 1–14.

Claffey, A. (1995). When child care teachers become parents. *Day Care and Early Education, 22*(3), 4–7.

Clements, D., & Nastasi, B. K. (1993). Electronic media and early childhood education. In B. Spodek (Ed.), *Handbook of research on the education of young children* (pp. 251–276). New York: Macmillan.

Coffey, A. (1999). *The ethnographic self: Fieldwork and the representation of identity*. Thousand Oaks, CA: Sage.

Coffey, A., & Delamont, S. (2000). *Feminism and the classroom teacher*. London: Routledge Falmer.

Collinson, V., Killeavy, & Stephenson, H. (1999). Exemplary teachers: Practicing in ethics of care in England, Ireland, and the United States. *Journal for a Just and Caring Education, 5*(4), 349–366.

Cooper, R. (2000). The impact of child abuse on children's play: A conceptual model. *Occupational Therapy, 7*(4), 259–277.

Corbett, S. (1993). A complicated bias. *Young Children, 48*(3), 29–31.

Corcoran, M. (1995). Rags to rags: Poverty and mobility in the United States. *Annual Review of Sociology, 21*, 237–267.

Craven, A. (2002). Beauty and the belles: Discourses on feminism and femininity in Disneyland. *European Journal of Women's Studies, 9*(2), 123–142.

Dalton, J., & Watson, M. (1997). *Among friends: Classrooms where caring and learning prevail*. Oakland, CA: Developmental Studies Center.

Danby, S. (1998). The serious and playful work of gender: Talk and social order in a preschool classroom. In N. Yelland (Ed.), *Gender in early childhood* (pp. 175–205). New York: Routledge.

Davies, B. (1989). *Frogs and snails and feminist tales: Preschool children and gender*. Sydney: Allen & Unwin.

Davies, B. (1993). *Shards of glass*. Syndey: Allen & Unwin.

Davies, B. (2001). *A body of writing: 1990–1999*. Walnut Creek, CA: AltaMira Press.

Derman-Sparks, L. (1989). *Anti-bias curriculum: Tools for empowering young children*. Washington, DC: National Association for the Education of Young Children.

Dewey, J. (1933). *How we think: A restatement of the relation of reflective thinking to the educative process*. Boston: D. C. Heath & Co.

Duncan, G., & Brooks-Gunn, J. (Eds.). (1997). *Consequences of growing up poor*. New York: Russell Sage Foundation.

Duncan, G., & Brooks-Gunn, J. (2000). Family poverty, welfare reform, and child development. *Child Development, 71*(1), 188–196.

Edwards, C. P., & Raikes, H. (2002). Extending the dance: Relationship-based approaches to infant/toddler care and education. *Young Children, 57*(4), 10–17.

Egeland, B., & Heister, M. (1995). The long-term consequences of infant care and mother-infant attachment. *Child Development, 66*, 74–85.

Emihovich, C. (1995). Distancing passion: Narratives in social science. *Qualitative Studies in Education, 8*(1), 37–48.

Escobedo, T. (1993). Curricular issues in early education for culturally and linguistically diverse populations. In S. Reifel (Ed.), *Advances in early education and day care: Vol. 5. Perspectives in developmentally appropriate practice* (pp. 213–246). Greenwich, CT: JAI Press.

Fagot, B., & Levy, L. (1998). Gender identity and play. In D. P. Fromberg & D. Bergen (Eds.), *Play from birth to twelve and beyond* (pp. 187–192). New York: Garland.

Farrell, A. (1998). Gendered settings and human rights in early childhood. In N. Yelland (Ed.), *Gender in early childhood* (pp. 98–112). New York: Routledge.

Finegan, C. (2001, Winter). Alternative early childhood education: Reggio Emilia. *Kappa Delta Pi Record*, 82–84.

Frieman, B. (1996). Issues in education: What heterosexual teachers need to know about homosexuality. *Childhood Education, 73*(1), 40–42.

Gable, S. (2002). Teacher-child relationships throughout the day. *Young Children, 57*(4), 42–6.

Gallas, K. (1998). *"Sometimes I can be anything." Power, gender, and identity in a primary classroom*. New York: Teachers College Press.

Genishi, C., Ryan, S., Ochsner, M., & Yarnall, M. (2001). Teaching in early childhood education: Understanding practices through research and theory. In V. Richardson (Ed.) *Handbook of research on teaching* (pp. 1175–1210). Washington, DC: American Educational Research Association.

Gilbert, K. (1998). The body, young children, and popular culture. In N. Yelland (Ed.), *Gender in early childhood* (pp. 55–71). New York: Routledge.

Gilligan, C. (1982). *In a different voice: Psychological theory and women's development*. Cambridge, MA: Harvard University Press.

Giroux, H. (1998). Are Disney movies good for your kids? In S. Steinberg & J. Kincheloe (Eds.), *Kinderculture: The corporate construction of childhood* (pp. 53–67). Boulder, CO: Westview Press.

Giroux, H. (1999). *The mouse that roared: Disney and the end of innocence*. Lanham, MD: Rowman & Littlefield.

Goldstein, L. S. (1998). More than gentle smiles and warm hugs: Applying the ethic of care to early childhood education. *The Journal of Research in Childhood Education, 12*(2), 244–261.

Goldstein, L. S. (1999). The relational zone: The role of caring relationships in the co-construction of mind. *American Educational Research Journal, 36*(3), 647–673.

Goldstein, L. S. (2000). Ethical dilemmas in designing collaborative research: Lessons learned the hard way. *Qualitative Studies in Education, 13*(3), 517–530.

Golombok, S., Perry, B., Burston, A., Murray, C., Mooney-Somers, J., Stevens, M., & Golding, J. (2003). Children with lesbian parents: A community study. *Developmental Psychology, 39*(1), 20-34.

Goodwin, W. L., & Goodwin, L. D. (1993). Young children and measurement: Standardized and nonstandardized instruments in early childhood education. In B. Spodek (Ed.), *Handbook of research on the education of young children* (pp. 441-463). New York: Macmillan.

Goodwin, W. L., & Goodwin, L. D. (1996) *Understanding quantitative and qualitative research in early childhood education.* New York: Teachers College Press.

Greenberg, J. (2001). "She is so my real mom!" Helping children understand adoption as one form of family diversity. *Young Children, 56*(2), 90-91.

Grieshaber, S. (1998). Constructing the gendered infant. In N. Yelland (Ed.), *Gender in early childhood* (pp. 16-35). New York: Routledge.

Grieshaber, S. (2001a). Advocacy and early childhood educators: Identity and cultural conflicts. In S. Grieshaber & G. Cannella (Eds.), *Embracing identities in early childhood education: Diversity and possibilities* (pp. 60-72). New York: Teachers College Press.

Grieshaber, S. (2001b). Beating mum: How to win the power game. In J. Jipson & R. Johnson, *Resistance and representation: Rethinking childhood education* (pp. 223-237). New York: Peter Lang.

Grieshaber, S., & Cannella, G. (2001). From identity to identities: Increasing possibilities in early childhood education. In S. Grieshaber & G. Cannella (Eds.), *Embracing identities in early childhood education: Diversity and possibilities* (pp. 3-22). New York: Teachers College Press.

Han, W., Waldfogel, J., & Brooks-Gunn, J. (2001). The effects of early employment on later cognitive and behavioral outcomes. *Journal of Marriage and the Family, 63*, 336-54.

Harms, T., & Clifford, R. M. (1993). Studying educational settings. In B. Spodek (Ed.), *Handbook of research on the education of young children* (pp. 477-492). New York: Macmillan.

Hatch, J. A. (1998). Qualitative research in early childhood education. In B. Spodek, O. Saracho, & A. Pellegrini (Eds.), *Issues in early childhood educational research: Yearbook in early childhood education: Vol. 8* (pp. 49-75). New York: Teachers College Press.

Howe, A. C. (1993). Science in early childhood education. In B. Spodek (Ed.), *Handbook of research on the education of young children* (pp. 225-235). New York: Macmillan.

Howe, K. (1998). The interpretive turn and the new debate in education. *Educational Researcher, 27*(8), 13-20.

Howes, C., & Hamilton, C. E. (1993). Child care for young children. In B. Spodek (Ed.), *Handbook of research on the education of young children* (pp. 322-336). New York: Macmillan.

Hughes, P., & MacNaughton, G. (2000). Identity-formation and popular culture: Learning lessons from Barbie. *Journal of Curriculum Theorizing, 16*(3), 57-68.

Hughes, P., & MacNaughton, G. (2001). Fractured or manufactured: Gendered identities and culture in the early years. In S. Grieshaber & G. Cannella (Eds.), *Embracing identities in early childhood education: Diversity and possibilities* (pp. 114-130). New York: Teachers College Press.

Humm, M. (Ed.). (1992). *Modern feminisms: Political, literary, cultural.* New York: Columbia University Press.

Jalongo, M. R. (2002). "Who is fit to teach young children?" Editorial: On behalf of children. *Early Childhood Education Journal, 29*(3), 141-2.

Jalongo, M. R., Hoot, J., Pattnaik, J., Cai, W., & Park, S. (1997). Early childhood programs: International perspectives. In J. Isenberg & M. R. Jalongo (Eds.), *Major trends and issues in early childhood education: Challenges, controversies, and insights* (pp. 172-187). New York: Teachers College Press.

Jipson, J. (1995). Teacher-mother: An imposition of identity. In J. Jipson, P. Munro, S. Victor, K. F. Jones & G. Freed-Rowland (Eds.), *Repositioning feminism and education: Perspectives on educating for social change* (pp. 20-35). Westport, CT: Bergin & Garvey.

Jipson, J., & Reynolds, U. (1998). Anything you want: Women and children in popular culture. In S. Steinberg & J. Kincheloe (Eds.), *Kinderculture: The corporate construction of childhood* (pp. 227-247). Boulder, CO: Westview Press.

Johansson, E. (2002). Morality in preschool interaction: Teachers' strategies for working with children's morality. *Early Child Development and Care, 172*(2), 203-221.

John, D. R. (1999). Through the eyes of a child: Children's knowledge and understanding of advertising. In M. C. Macklin and L. Carlson (Eds.), *Advertising to children: Concepts and controversies* (pp. 3-26). Thousand Oaks, CA: Sage Publications.

Katz, L. (1993). What can we learn from Reggio Emilia? In C. Edwards, L. Gandini, & G. Forman (Eds.), *The hundred languages of children: The Reggio Emilia approach to early childhood education* (pp. 19-37). Norwood, NJ: Ablex Publishing.

Kawecki, I. (1994). Gender differences in young children's artwork. *British Educational Research Journal, 20*(4), 485-491.

Kellner, D. (1998). Beavis and Butt-head: No future for postmodern youth. In S. Steinberg & J. Kincheloe (Eds.), *Kinderculture: The corporate construction of childhood* (pp. 85-102). Boulder, CO: Westview Press.

Kirn, W., & Cole, W. (2001, April 30). What ever happened to play? *Time, 157*(17), 56-58.

Knowles, G., & Holt-Reynolds, D. (1994). An introduction: Personal histories as medium, method, and milieu for gaining insight into teacher development. *Teacher Education Quarterly, 22*(1), 5-12.

Kohlberg, L. (1969). Stage and sequence: The cognitive developmental approach to socialization. In D. Goslin (Ed.), *Handbook of socialization theory and research* (pp. 118-140). Chicago: Rand McNally.

Kroeger, J. (2001). A reconstructed tale of inclusion for a lesbian family in an early childhood classroom. In S. Grieshaber & G. Cannella (Eds.), *Embracing identities in early childhood education: Diversity and possibilities* (pp. 73-86). New York: Teachers College Press.

Ladson-Billings, G. (1994). *The dreamkeepers: Successful teachers of African American children.* San Francisco: Jossey-Bass.

Ladson-Billings, G. (1995). Toward a theory of culturally relevant pedagogy. *American Educational Research Journal, 32*(3), 465-491.

Ladson-Billings, G., & Gomez, M. (2001). Just showing up: Supporting early literacy through teachers' professional communities. *Phi Delta Kappan, 82*(9), 675-80.

Lakey, J. (1997). Teachers and parents define diversity in an Oregon preschool cooperative—Democracy at work. *Young Children, 52*, 20-28.

Lather, P. (1995). The validity of angels: Interpretive and textual strategies in researching the lives of women with HIV/AIDS. *Qualitative Inquiry, 1*, 41-68.

Leavitt, R. (1994). *Power and emotion in infant-toddler day care.* Albany: SUNY Press.

Leinbach, M., & Fagot, F. (1993). Categorical habituation to male and female faces: Gender schematic processing in infancy. *Infant Behavior and Development, 16*, 317-332.

Lerner, R., Hauser-Cram, P., & Miller, E. (1998). Assumptions and features of longitudinal designs: Implications for early childhood education. In B. Spodek, O. Saracho, & A. Pellegrini (Eds.), *Issues in early childhood educational research* (pp. 113-138). New York: Teachers College Press.

Levy, G. (1999). Gender-typed and non-gender typed category awareness in toddlers. *Sex Roles: A Journal of Research, 41*(11-12), 851-73.

Levy, G., & Boston, M. (1994). Preschoolers' recall of own-sex and other-sex gender scripts. *Journal of Genetic Psychology, 155*, 369-371.

Levy, G., & Haaf, R. (1994). Detection of gender-related categories by 10-month-old infants. *Infant Behavior and Development, 17*, 449-451.

Lubeck, S. (1995). Mothers "at risk." In B. B. Swadener & S. Lubeck (Eds.), *Children and families "at promise:" Deconstructing the discourse of risk* (pp. 50-75). Albany: State University of New York Press.

MacDonald, J. (1994, April). *Teaching and parenting: Effects of the dual role.* Paper presented at the Annual Meeting of the American Educational Research Association, New Orleans, LA.

MacDonald, J. (1999, April). *When mothers become teachers: Effects of the mothering experience on prospective teachers.* Paper presented at the Annual Meeting of the American Educational Research Association, Montreal, Quebec, Canada.

MacNaughton, G. (1994). "You can be dad:" Gender and power in domestic discourses and fantasy play within early childhood. *Australian Research in Early Childhood Education* (1), 93-101.

MacNaughton, G. (1996). Is Barbie to blame?: Reconsidering how children learn gender. *Australian Journal of Early Childhood, 21*(4), 18-24.

MacNaughton, G. (1997). Who's got the power? Rethinking gender equity strategies in early childhood. *International Journal of Early Years Education, 5*(1), 57-66.

Maher, F. (1999). Progressive education and feminist pedagogies: Issues in gender, power, and authority. *Teachers College Record, 101*(1), 35-59.

Manning, K. (1997). Authenticity in constructivist inquiry: Methodological considerations without prescription. *Qualitative Inquiry, 3*(1), 93-115.

Marsh, J. (1999a, April). Teletubby tales: Popular culture in the early years language and literacy curriculum. Paper presented at the Annual Meeting of the American Educational Research Association, Montreal, Quebec, Canada.

Marsh, J. (1999b). Batman and Batwoman go to school: Popular culture in the literacy curriculum. *International Journal of Early Years Education, 7*(2), 117-132.

Marsh, J. (2000). "But I want to fly too!" Girls and superhero play in the infant classroom. *Gender & Education, 12*(2), 209-221.

Marsh, M. (2003). *The social fashioning of teacher identities.* New York: Peter Lang.

Meadows, M. (2001). Gay, lesbian, transgendered and bisexual families: The teacher or caregiver's role in the development of positive relationships. Rural, urban and minority education. *Journal of Early Education and Family Review, 8*(3), 24-29.

Meisels, S. J., Steele, D. M., & Quinn-Leering, K. (1993). Testing, tracking, and retaining young children: An analysis of research and social policy. In B. Spodek (Ed.), *Handbook of research on the education of young children* (pp. 279-292). New York: Macmillan.

Miller, J. (1992). Teachers, autobiography, and curriculum: Critical and feminist perspectives. In S. Kessler & B. B. Swadener (Eds.), *Reconceptualizing the early childhood curriculum: Beginning the dialogue* (pp. 102-122). New York: Teachers College Press.

Miller, J. (1996). *School for women.* London: Virago.

Munby, H., Russell, T., & Martin, A. (2001). Teachers' knowledge and how it develops. In V. Richardson (Ed.), *Handbook of research on teaching* (pp. 877-904). New York: Macmillan.

Munro, P. (1995). Multiple "I's": Dilemmas of life-history research. In J. Jipson, P. Munro, S. Victor, K. F. Jones & G. Freed-Rowlan (Eds.), *Repositioning feminism and education: Perspectives on educating for social change* (pp. 140-152). Westport, CT: Bergin & Garvey.

Murphy, L., & Leeper, E. (2003). *More than a teacher: Caring for children, number two.* Washington, DC: Child Development Services Bureau. ED082401.

Nowak-Fabrykowski, K., & Caldwell, P. (2002). Developing a caring attitude in the early childhood pre-service teachers. *Education, 123*(2), 358-365.

Ochsner, M. B. (2001). Developing reciprocity in a multi-method small-scale research study. In G. MacNaughton, S. A. Rolfe, & I. Siraj-Blatchford (Eds.), *Doing early childhood research: International perspectives on theory and practice* (pp. 254-63). Buckingham, UK: Open University Press.

Paley, V. G. (1992). *You can't say you can't play.* Cambridge, MA: Harvard University Press.

Pellegrini, A. D., & Boyd, B. (1993). The role of play in early childhood development and education: Issues in definition and function. In B. Spodek (Ed.), *Handbook of research on the education of young children* (pp. 105-121). New York: Macmillan.

Pellegrini, A. D., Kato, K., Blatchford, P., & Baines, E. (2002). A short-term longitudinal study of children's playground games across the first year of school: Implications for social competence and adjustment to school. *American Educational Research Journal, 39*(4), 991-1015.

Peters, D. (1993). Trends in demographic and behavioral research on teaching in early childhood settings. In B. Spodek (Ed.), *Handbook of research on the education of young children* (pp. 493-505). New York: Macmillan.

Pipher, M. (1994). *Reviving Ophelia: Saving the selves of adolescent girls.* New York: Putnam.

Polakow, V. (1993). *Lives on the edge: Single mothers and their children in the other America.* Chicago: University of Chicago Press.

Polakow, V. (1994). Welfare reform and the assault on daily life: Targeting single mothers and their children. *Social Justice, 21*(1), 27-33.

Porath, M. (2001). Young girls' social understanding: Emergent interpersonal expertise. *High Ability Studies, 12*(1), 113-127.

Ripke, M., & Crosby, D. (2002). The effects of welfare reform on the educational outcomes of parents and their children. In W. G. Secada (Ed.), *Review of research in education* (Vol. 26, pp. 181-261). Washington, DC: American Educational Research Association.

Ruble, D., & Martin, C. (1998). Gender development: Social, emotional, and personality development. In W. Damon & N. Eisenberg (Eds.), *Handbook of child psychology* (Vol. 4, 5th ed., pp. 933-1016). New York: John Wiley & Sons.

Ryan, S., & Campbell, S. (2001). Doing research for the first time. In G. MacNaughton, S. A. Rolfe, & I. Siraj-Blatchford (Eds.), *Doing early childhood research: International perspectives on theory and practice* (pp. 56-63). Buckingham, UK: Open University Press.

Ryan, S., Ochsner, M., & Genishi, C. (2001). Miss Nelson is missing! Teacher sightings in research on teaching. In S. Grieshaber & G. Cannella (Eds.), *Embracing identities in early childhood education: Diversity & possibilities* (pp. 45-59). New York: Teachers College Press.

Saracho, O. N. (1993). Preparing teachers for early childhood programs in the United States. In B. Spodek (Ed.), *Handbook of research on the education of young children* (pp. 412-426). New York: Macmillan.

Short, K., & Burke, C. (1996). Examining our beliefs and practices through inquiry. *Language Arts, 73*(2), 97-104.

Smith, A., Dannison, L., & Vach-Hasse, T. (1998). When "grandma" is "mom": What today's teachers need to know. *Childhood Education, 75*(1), 12-16.

Smith, J. R., Brooks-Gunn, J., & Klebanov, P. (1997). Consequences of living in poverty for young children's cognitive and verbal ability and early school achievement. In G. J. Duncan & J. Brooks-Gunn (Eds.), *Consequences of growing up poor* (pp. 132-189). New York: Russell Sage Foundation.

Smith, S., & Dixon, R. (1995). Literacy concepts of low- and middle-class four-year-olds entering preschool. *Journal of Educational Research, 88,* 243–253.

Spodek, B. (Ed.). (1993). *Handbook of research on the education of young children.* New York: Macmillan.

Staudt, M. M. (2001). Psychopathology, peer relations, and school functioning of maltreated children: A literature review. *Children & Schools, 23*(2), 85–101.

Steinberg, S., & Kincheloe, J. (1998). Introduction: No more secrets—kinderculture, information saturation, and the postmodern childhood. In S. Steinberg & J. Kincheloe (Eds.), *Kinderculture: The corporate construction of childhood* (pp. 1–30). Boulder, CO: Westview Press.

Stevens, J., Hough, R., & Nurss, J. (1993). The influence of parents on children's development and education. In B. Spodek (Ed.), *Handbook of research on the education of young children* (pp. 337–351). New York: Macmillan.

Swadener, B. B. (1995). Children and families "at promise:" Deconstructing the discourse of risk. In B. B. Swadener & S. Lubeck (Eds.), *Children and families "at promise:" Deconstructing the discourse of risk* (pp. 17–49). Albany: SUNY Press.

Teven, J. (2001). The relationship among teacher characteristics and perceived caring. *Communication Education, 50*(2), 159–170.

Thorne, B. (1993). *Gender play: Girls and boys in school.* New Brunswick, NJ: Rutgers University Press.

Thornton, C. D. (2002). *Ambiguity with/in early childhood pre-service teachers' beliefs.* Unpublished doctoral dissertation, University of Texas at Austin.

Tobin, J. (1995). Post-structural research in early childhood education. In J. A. Hatch (Ed.), *Qualitative research in early childhood settings* (pp. 223–243). Westport, CT: Praeger.

Turner, S. (2000). Caretaking of children's souls. Teaching the deep song. *Young Children, 55*(1), 31–33.

Veltman, M., & Browne, K. (2001). Three decades of child maltreatment research: Implications for the school years. *Trauma, Violence & Abuse, 2*(3), 215–240.

Vogt, F. (2002). A caring teacher: Explorations into primary school teachers' professional identity and ethic of care. *Gender and Education, 14*(3), 251–264.

Walker, D., Greenwood, C., Hart, B., & Carta, J. (1994). Prediction of school outcomes based on early language production and socioeconomic factors. *Child Development, 65,* 606–621.

Walkerdine, V. (1992). Progressive pedagogy and political struggle. In C. Luke & J. Gore (Eds.), *Feminisms and critical pedagogy* (pp. 15–24). New York: Routledge.

Walkerdine, V. (1994). Femininity as performance. In L. Stone (Ed.), *The education feminism reader* (pp. 57–69). New York: Routledge.

Walsh, D. J., Tobin, J., & Graue, M. E. (1993). The interpretive voice: Qualitative research in early childhood education. In B. Spodek (Ed.), *Handbook of research on the education of young children* (pp. 151–175). New York: Macmillan.

Weedon, C. (1997). *Feminist practice and poststructuralist theory* (2nd ed.). Oxford: Basil Blackwell.

West, C., & Fenstermaker, S. (1993). Power, inequality, and the accomplishment of gender: An ethnomethodological view. In P. England (Ed.), *Theory on gender/Feminism on theory.* (pp. 151–174). New York: Aldine de Gruyter.

Whitaker, M. (2001). Doin' what comes naturally: When mothers become teachers. *Educational Foundations, 15*(3), 27–45.

Winters, J. (2001). The daddy track. *Psychology Today, 34*(5), 18–23.

Wozniak, D. F. (2002). *They're all my children: Foster mothering in America.* New York: New York University Press.

Zeichner, K. (1993). Traditions of practice in U. S. pre-service teacher education programs. *Teaching and Teacher Education, 9*(1), 1–13.

Zeichner, K., & Liston, D. (1996). *Reflective teaching: An introduction.* Mahwah, NJ: Lawrence Erlbaum Associates.

BEYOND CERTAINTIES: POSTMODERN PERSPECTIVES, RESEARCH, AND THE EDUCATION OF YOUNG CHILDREN

Susan Grieshaber
Queensland University of Technology

Sharon Ryan
Rutgers, The State University of New Jersey

INTRODUCTION

The "Western" world currently exists in a condition of postmodernity (Harvey, 1990), which, literally speaking, means after the "modern" era. The late 1960s is associated with the beginning of the postmodern era and the condition of postmodernity exemplifies the changes that have occurred in contemporary society since that time. These changes include a multitude of transformations such as global economic processes in which trade and capital now flow freely around the world (Burbules & Torres, 2000); a move from organized to "disorganized capitalism" (Lash & Urry, 1987); new global forms of media and communications technologies that result in changes to identity and interaction in both local and global contexts (Burbules & Torres, 2000); a new capitalist work order where importance is placed on "knowledge and flexible learning needed to design, market, perfect and vary goods and services as symbols of identity, not the actual product itself as a material good" (Gee, Hull, & Lankshear, 1996, p. 26); and the corporatization of schooling and childhood through consumer culture (Kenway & Bullen, 2001). There also have been significant alterations in architecture, cultural activities such as the arts and music, and ways in which time and space are conceptualized and subsequently used (Harvey, 1990). In sum, Best and Kellner (1991) distinguish postmodernity in terms of time, as "a sociohistorical epoch" (p. 164); in regard to art and modernism, as a "configuration of art after/against modernism" (p. 164), and postmodern knowledge as a "critique of modern epistemology" (p. 164).

Although many of these changes have occurred since the late 1960s, contemporary society also retains many features of modern society, of which schooling and education are one example. Schools are creations of modernist industrial society, and have experienced changes in postmodern times. Educational institutions now talk about concepts associated with postmodernity such as lifelong learning, learners who are able to work as collaborative members of teams, and who can use a range of information and communication technologies. Despite these examples of how educational rhetoric (and not necessarily practice) has changed in an attempt to accommodate postmodern conditions, practices such as assessment tend to rest on modernist notions of measurement such as testing, in which individual performance is calculated against a set of established standards that can be applied to all students (such as a particular year cohort across a country or state).

Similar to assessment practices in schools, the contradiction between the postmodern and the modern is reflected in the complexity of contemporary life. Attempts to explain such complexity tend to reject modernist theories on the basis that they purport to tell "the truth" (as opposed to there being many "truths"); accept certainty (rather than entertain the idea of uncertainty), and because they are based on universal assumptions of a "one size fits all" approach. As suggested by Best and Kellner (1991), theoretical positions associated with postmodernity engage in critiques of modern epistemology. They also attempt to understand the conditions of postmodernity and the changes to society that have occurred as a result of the condition of postmodernity. An important part of this critique involves action, offering both practical and theoretical alternatives as a result of critiquing modern epistemology. Postmodern perspectives therefore, are political because they challenge the modernist focus on the macro and universal to the exclusion of the micro; they embrace ambiguity and uncertainty, and provide hope for the marginalized, dispossessed and disempowered as they refuse modernist discourses that classify, control, and measure against what is considered the "norm." As such, they often address modernist constructions such as issues of social justice, diversity, and equity (cf. Cannella & Bailey, 1999).

Marginalization, dispossession and disempowerment are the very things with which "one size fits all" approaches are unable to deal, but this back and forth between modernism and postmodernism signals the frequent interplay between the two in everyday life. There are similarities and differences among postmodern theories and it is possible for several different theories to be brought to bear on similar issues. For example, poststructuralism (e.g., Foucault, 1980) is concerned with issues of power, as is postcolonial theory (e.g., Gandhi, 1998). Some of the boundaries between the different postmodern theories can be fuzzy and difficult to identify. As a consequence, several postmodern theories may be drawn on to address particular matters. For instance, gender can be viewed from the theoretical perspectives of feminist poststructuralism and queer theory.

This chapter serves as a reference for early childhood educators seeking explanations of ways in which alternative and diverse (postmodern) theoretical perspectives have contributed to research about the education of young children since the first edition of this Handbook (Spodek, 1993). Explanations of what postmodernism is and the theories used to explain it have been adequately covered elsewhere in relation to society generally (Best & Kellner, 1991; Harvey, 1990) and education specifically (Cherryholmes, 1988; Usher & Edwards, 1994). Similarly, the account by Cannella and Bailey (1999) of postmodern research in early childhood education has provided understandings about postmodernism, and constructions of research, theories, theorists and methodologies associated with the postmodern. The intent of this chapter is to build on the work of Cannella and Bailey by presenting an overview of how the field has begun to think about the condition of postmodernity and the issues associated with it.

Why Postmodernism?

For most of the 20th century, child development theory and research has been the main informant for early childhood practices. One catalyst for the use of postmodern perspectives in early education was a questioning of the field's reliance on child development knowledge. Egan (1983), Fein and Schwartz (1982), Silin (1987), and Spodek (1977) challenged the relevance of child development knowledge for curriculum-making in early childhood education on the basis that educational goals have political and moral concerns as their origins. Although psychological theories can offer guidance about the appropriate time to present knowledge and when it will more likely be meaningful to students, they are unable to inform questions of what to teach. The critiques of child development (e.g., Bloch, 1992; Burman, 1994; Cannella, 1997; Silin, 1995), child-centered pedagogy (Walkerdine, 1984), and developmentally appropriate practice (Bernhard et al., 1998; Cannella, 1997; Lubeck, 1998a, 1998b; Mallory & New, 1994) represent a search for options beyond what is available in child development about what to teach, to whom, when, where, and why. More specifically, Burman's (1994) deconstruction of developmental psychology critiqued the moral-political themes in developmental psychology and took on the giants of the paradigm including Piaget, behaviorism, social and cognitive development, and child centeredness.

Burman (1994) argued that developmental psychology has become such a taken-for-granted aspect of our everyday lives as parents, children, and families that its presence is almost imperceptible. She named five ways in which this has occurred: an obsession with techniques of measuring that is devoid of context; a focus on the (in)adequacy of mothers and the regulation (normalization) of their actions and behaviors according to the prescriptions of developmental psychology that make them seem natural parts of life; the perpetuation of race, class, and gender domination through the normalization and naturalization of cultural practices adopted by the Anglo middle class; the inability to use psychoanalysis as a platform for questioning the dominance of objectivity and control that pervade developmental psychology in matters concerning children and their care; and the failure to theorize context in any shape or form in regard to the focus on the individual child (mother, family) and the deficits associated with poor mothering, class, and cultural membership.

The attempts of Burman (1994) and others to respond to the conditions of postmodernity can be likened to the ways in which early childhood education has responded to changing circumstances in the past. History has shown that early childhood education has been permeable to a wide range of social and intellectual influences including Rousseau's romanticism (Weber, 1984), John Locke's environmentalism (Cleverley & Phillips, 1987), Darwin's theory of evolution (Crain, 2000), the "scientific" approach to child study (Baker, 2001; Kliebard, 1986), behaviorism (Burman, 1994; Crain, 2000), Dewey's reconstruction of experience (Weber, 1984), Freudian psychoanalysis (Cleverley & Phillips, 1987), Erikson's stages of affective growth (Weber, 1984), Piaget's cognitive approach (Cannella, 1997; Silin, 1995), not to mention the vigorous application of teaching, learning and curriculum approaches that draw on combinations of these and other perspectives (see Weber, 1984). However, as Bloch (1992) has noted, there was little room for theory or methods outside psychological or biological perspectives: "The terms 'critical theory', 'interpretivist or symbolic research', or 'postmodern' are rarely heard in seminar rooms, publications, or conferences focusing on early childhood education" (p. 3).

Although early childhood education has been permeable to the influence of various psychological theories and research, Tobin (1995) has said that those who research in early childhood education "are stuck in time, too often failing to engage with emerging theory in the humanities and social sciences" (p. 224). Several years later, this sentiment was echoed by Soto and Swadener (2002) in their statement "early childhood literature was rarely informed by feminist, critical, postmodern, or post-structural theory" (p. 49). This may be the case, but Prochner (2001) cites "transcendentalism, the child study movement, behaviorism, and psychoanalysis" (p. 205) as examples of old ideas coupled with new theories that produced a "profound effect on the development of the infant school, kindergarten and nursery school" (p. 205). However, as these ideas did not replace existing thinking, Prochner (2001) suggests that early childhood education is "stuck in a reconstruction of the past that reflects present needs. . . . ECE lacks both a critical historical awareness and a futures orientation" (p. 205). The advantage of theoretical positions associated with the postmodern is that they engage with emerging theory in the humanities and social sciences, they hold the potential to produce a critical historical awareness, and they can be proactive toward the future. Nevertheless, theoretical positions associated with the postmodern certainly do not have all the answers, nor are they infallible and beyond critique. What they do offer those undertaking research about the education of young children is a greater repertoire of theoretical and methodological tools.

The fundamental argument of this chapter is that research informed by postmodern theories has an important place when considering the education of young children. Postmodern approaches open a plethora of theoretical positions that can provide insight into issues and circumstances that go beyond the scope of developmental psychology and in doing so, offer sources of information and perspectives that are untapped by developmental psychology.

Our Positioning

As in any writing associated with postmodern approaches, we make our position clear. We are both early childhood teachers who have been using postmodern theories in our research and teaching. This chapter is representative of our current standpoint and perceptions on early childhood education, children and childhood, research with and about children, educational and family institutions, and, ultimately, life. It is explicitly political and in no way purports to depict a value free process or product, or a discovery of "truths." Instead, it provides another set of perspectives and discourses for looking at children, childhood, and early childhood education, which we hope are challenging and engaging. As such, this chapter favors empirical research that uses postmodern theoretical perspectives. By empirical research, we mean studies of early childhood education that use data collected with teachers, children, and families. We choose to foreground empirical research rather than conceptual or theoretical critiques (these are not ignored) because of the way in which empirical research integrates theory and practice, and because it provides a powerful way to show what

such research means in the everyday worlds of early childhood education.

Research With/In the Postmodern

Because research is a "cultural invention of the white western (male) academic world," all research is political and "represents a privileged position" (Grieshaber, 2001, p. 136). Research is a modernist construct, therefore research in the postmodern presents another set of contradictions as it represents "the very embodiment of the enlightenment focus on reason and truth combined with the modern belief in science and the scientific method as our path to truth, reason and liberation" (Cannella & Bailey, 1999, p. 9). Although we live with the contradiction of modernist bureaucracies in conditions of postmodernity, given the postmodern critique of epistemology, the task of postmodern research is to reinvent what it means to do research, and the way relationships involved in research are construed and constructed.

Research involves a triad of researchers; of those who fund it and/or are policy makers, and those who are the objects of research, the "researched" (Mayall, Hood, & Oliver, 1999). The researched can be anyone, but are often those who are marginalized, disempowered or dispossessed in some way, including children, the elderly, and those belonging to minority groups. Mayall et al. (1999) name the objects of research interest as those who

. . . are predominantly members of socially disadvantaged groups . . . [who] come in for designation as problems, as threats to the social order, so warranting intervention to restore harmony; or they are variously identified as socially, economically or politically disadvantaged and in need of help and redress. (p. 1)

What is apparent from this quote is the way in which socially disadvantaged groups are seen as problematic and in need of attention to remedy perceived deficits. Mayall et al. (1999) make the point that governments are finding larger sections of the population increasingly problematic, which means that governments perceive the social order as progressively more threatened. Even though it would be easy to associate these "objects of research interest" with modernity, the fact is that socially, economically, and politically disadvantaged groups are also connected with research that uses postmodern perspectives. Feminist perspectives, for example, have shown that women and children have often been "lumped together" (Thorne, 2002, p. 251) for research purposes and that qualitative and quantitative methodological approaches reveal a gendered history, having been allied with minority and majority groups respectively (Oakley, 1999).

Even though research that takes account of gender and children has increased, and other aspects of diversity such as culture, race, ethnicity, sexuality, and socioeconomic status are being considered in research design, there are still calls for culturally sensitive research approaches (Tillman, 2002); arguments against assuming that "general traits of individuals are attributable categorically to ethnic group membership" (Gutiérrez & Rogoff, 2003, p. 19); and appeals for rethinking race and ethnicity in educational research (Lee, 2003). In the

United States, the 2000 census data included the option for people to identify themselves and their children by more than one race (Lopez, 2003). Given the growth of the mixed race population, Lopez (2003) has pointed out the importance of collecting accurate data about mixed heritage, and that for educational research the "potential impact of allowing for mixed heritage identifications is presently undetermined" (p. 35).

Postmodern researchers are attempting to grapple with this cultural hybridity in their research designs by ensuring that those who are "researched" are an integral part of the research process and that their voices are heard. In an effort to recreate research that is more equitable and emancipatory, postmodern research involves taking account of whose interests are being served by the research being undertaken; for whom the research is being carried out; and whether the research methods being used are suitable for those involved in the research. As a consequence, a range of methods have been developed that enable marginalized groups like children to represent their own views. Researchers also employ dialogic and self-reflexive designs (Lather, 1991) that enable the researchers' perspective to be presented as one of several ways of making sense of data, and drawing conclusions about particular phenomena.

EARLY CHILDHOOD RESEARCH USING POSTMODERN PERSPECTIVES

In the following sections, we describe research using postmodern perspectives that examines various aspects of early childhood education. Although categorizing studies always involves making arbitrary decisions, we have chosen to group this research as it pertains to some of the main topics of the field. Reflecting the focus of our field, we begin with a discussion of research about children and childhood before moving to teaching and learning, families, policy and governance, and teacher education. Within each of these broad topics, we show some of the differing theoretical perspectives being used, and the kinds of studies that have been conducted.

THE POLITICS OF CHILDREN AND CHILDHOOD

In this section, we consider changing understandings of children and childhood, investigating approaches to studying children and childhood that are based on sociology, and research that contests the positioning of children as Other. The sociology of childhood has some characteristics that link it to the postmodern in that it critiques modern views of the relationship between children and society, but it also retains some vestiges of modernist approaches by encouraging the use of "traditional" qualitative research approaches such as ethnography (Prout & James, 1997). To us, the sociology of childhood is one of those theoretical positions that can be located somewhere between modern epistemology and postmodern theorizing. We outline this perspective because it offers new insights into how educators might conceptualize and enact pedagogy that acknowledges the way children and childhood are constantly changing.

The Sociology of Childhood

For the duration of the 20th century, children were studied mostly through the modernist paradigm of developmental psychology (Burman, 1994). Toward the end of the 20th century and in line with other changes to society came alternative ways of understanding childhood and researching with children, mostly from sociologists and anthropologists working in an emerging theoretical perspective called the sociology of childhood (Corsaro, 1997; James, Jenks & Prout, 1998; Jenks, 1982, 1996; Mayall, 1994; Prout & James, 1997).

Prout and James (1997) have identified six key characteristics of the sociology of childhood (p. 8), including understanding children and childhood as cultural and historical constructions rather than as biological commodities. Children are seen to operate as competent and active members of their own cultural and social worlds, constructing and determining their social worlds as well as those of adults. Thus children have social agency, something that was not recognised in the "orderly, meaningful, coherent narratives" (Tobin, 1995, p. 234) of Piaget and Erikson. Instead of "uncovering meaning that was already there, or imposing adult meanings onto children's conversation" (Tobin, 1995, p. 234), Prout and James (1997) state that children's "social relationships and cultures" are "worthy of study in their own right, independent of the perspective and concerns of adults" (p. 8).

James et al. (1998) differentiate between the presociological child and the sociological child, associating the former with biological notions of development (such as the evil, innocent, immanent, naturally developing and unconscious child), and the latter with versions of childhood that have been constructed within the social contexts of children's lives and that include the socially constructed, the tribal, minority group, and social structural child. Challenges from the sociology of childhood to the ways in which children have been understood, positioned, and researched within developmental psychology have resulted in concern that childhood is in "crisis" (see Wyness, 2000) and that childhood has been lost (see Foley, Roche, & Tucker, 2001). Wyness (2000) argued that explanations of childhood being in crisis are associated with the perceived decline in the nuclear family and the waning of opportunities for play in childhood. He suggested reframing the ways in which childhood is understood. For Foley et al. (2001), arguments about "childhood lost" amount to "nostalgia for a 'golden age" (p. 1), in which such lamentation centers on a perceived universal experience of childhood. Robb (2001) prompts us to remember that the experience of childhood is changing and that there is no evidence that such change is straightforward and linear, as in the modernist understanding: "It [the changing experience of childhood] also reminds us of the sheer diversity of children's experience and the danger of making sweeping generalizations" (p. 25).

Researchers and scholars associated with the sociology of childhood have generated much literature about the politics of researching with children. Christensen and James (2000a) align questions about methodological representation and reflexivity raised during the latter part of the 20th century with the problematic positioning of children in the social and cultural sciences. They argue for research with, rather than on, children, reflecting a change from positioning children as objects to subjects of research activities, and recommend paying attention to "the wider discourses of childhood, to the power relations, organizational structures and social inequalities which, in large part, shape children's everyday lives" (p. 7).

Recent attempts to ensure that the voices of the researched are heard have included Qvortrup's (1997) argument that children are an "unjustified exclusion" (p. 87) from statistics and social accounting, Alderson's (1995) emphasis on listening to children, Roberts's (2000) idea about not just listening to children but hearing them, and Punch's (2002) account of dilemmas posed for adult researchers working with children who accept that aspects of the research process are the same for children and adults. Drawing on her work in classrooms in rural Bolivia, Punch noted that the implications of using different data collection techniques with children such as task based methods of drawing, photographs, diaries, spider diagrams, activity tables, and worksheets, have been discussed only recently. Punch (2002) advocates a critical and reflexive approach to ensure that the use of particular methods goes beyond mere fun, that useful data are generated and that such methods are aimed at helping children "feel comfortable with an adult as researcher" (p. 330).

Adopting a technique used with adults in research settings, Alderson (2000) explored the idea of children as researchers in a similar way to how adult participants in research can be involved as "a co-researcher or co-producer of data" (p. 241). She and others (Alderson & Goodey, 1996; Davis, Watson, & Cunningham-Burley, 2000) also have considered issues associated with research undertaken with disabled children. These examples demonstrate the significant contribution that the sociology of childhood has made to moving the agenda from studying children as objects, to involving them as integral parts of research processes.

Children as Other

Postcolonial studies investigate how colonization has subjugated those who have been colonized, not only by physical force, but also by imposing specific administrative and management systems to civilize, regulate, reform, and provide cultural "enlightenment" (Gandhi, 1998). Those colonized are seen as primitive and needing to be "civilized" by the imperial powers. Using the notion of colonialism/postcolonialism, Cannella and Viruru (2004) and Viruru and Cannella (2001) have challenged constructions of children and childhood on which developmental psychology is founded. They do this by bringing attention to the ways in which children have been positioned by developmental psychology and their voices marginalized. Arguing that the universal child of developmental psychology is also the "colonized Other" (Viruru & Cannella, 2001, p. 162), they show that children have been "created as a group of people who must be observed and who are in opposition to, at least in intellectual ability, agency, and behavior, to adults" (p. 162). From a postcolonial view, locating children as primitive and naïve means that they are subjected to continual control, administration and surveillance, thereby supporting the ultimate

aim of developmental psychology, which is the "development" of children into correctly socialized and mature adults.

Leavitt (1994) and Leavitt and Power (1997) disturb our thinking about the way in which children's bodies are "othered" or civilized by staff in day care settings. A plethora of anecdotes enlightens readers about how children were required to adapt their bodies to the routines set by the teachers, and how, when this did not occur, children were admonished and punished (Leavitt, 1994; Leavitt & Power, 1997). Children also were required to move their bodies in certain ways (e.g., raising hands if wanting to speak), control bodily functions (e.g., not wetting themselves during nap time), engage in rituals set by the teachers (such as waiting to be told when they could drink their juice), and were actively discouraged from touching other children and the teachers. Enthusiastic bodily expression and pleasure was curtailed, and transgressions and resistant behavior dealt with by using rewards and privileges, the threat of punishment, and comparison with others who were performing correctly. Leavitt and Power (1997) concluded:

Teachers in day care centers *overcivilize* the young children in their care—that the expectations, restraint, manipulation, and isolation of children's physical bodies and emotional selves is excessive and objectifying. To these teachers, children's bodily well being is secondary to their management. (p. 44)

In her research in India, Viruru (2001a) applied the postcolonial concept of children as colonized "Other" to show that dominant discourses of early childhood education and care are written from positions of privilege and affluence, and are far removed from the daily reality of many non-"Western" children's lives. In coming to understand how she had been positioned by these same dominant discourses to see only what was lacking, Viruru's ethnography of a small urban school showed that not all successful learning in early childhood education rests on principles of developmentally appropriate practice. In particular, Viruru challenged "Western" notions of giving children classroom choices and the necessity of learning to "use their words" in times of conflict with others, given the local belief that such deep emotions are conveyed more effectively through indirect means and not language.

These empirical works are instructive because readers are provoked to go beyond surveillance and control of children's bodies, and see them as more than objects to be managed, and as part of tasks to complete within a set timeframe.

THE POLITICS OF TEACHING AND LEARNING

The pivotal role of early childhood practitioners was emphasized by Ryan and Ochsner (1999) in their proposal that confronting inequity in early childhood curricula means shifting the "pedagogical focus from children's development to the politics of children's learning" (p. 19). To achieve this, Ryan and Ochsner advocated an expansion of our understandings of "what constitutes good teaching" (p. 14). Admittedly, this may take some time given that research about teaching in early childhood education is a young field of study (Genishi, Ryan,

Ochsner, & Yarnall, 2001). In this section, we discuss research about teaching and learning that is informed by several different perspectives and in so doing raise issues about equity, pedagogy, curriculum, and policy in early childhood education. Research considered here discusses teaching and learning and how it intersects with gender, race, sexuality, sexual identity, and popular culture. We also reflect on research about teaching and learning in culturally and linguistically diverse early childhood classrooms.

Gender

Given that women dominate early childhood education (Goldstein, 1998), it follows that feminist approaches are a likely source of alternative theorizing and research about teaching young children. Researchers have used an array of feminist theories and queer theory to examine gender equity in regard to both the workforce and young children. The topics we examine here are the feminization of the profession, the place of men in early childhood education, and gender equity in teaching and learning.

A feminized profession. The fact that early childhood education is a feminized field has raised concerns about the education of boys (Alloway & Gilbert, 2002). It is also a reason that men avoid teaching in the early years, and when combined with the low status and poor levels of remuneration, acts as a deterrent to males (King, 1998). According to Titus (2004), a powerful socially constructed discourse in the United States has driven a moral panic about "underachieving boys" (p. 145), resulting in complaints that "boys are victims of female teachers who allegedly dominate the profession, create a feminized culture in the school, design curriculum for female's learning style, and cater to and reward female patterns of behaviour" (p. 152). Furthermore, as Alloway and Gilbert (2002) report, the feminized early childhood profession is one reason that has been suggested for the problems that boys are experiencing with literacy. Another critic, Somers (2000), has blamed boys' underachievement on "progressive" and "child-centered" educational theories in schools in the United States: these are philosophies that are associated explicitly with early childhood education. Other biologically inspired reasons implicated in the moral panic about underachieving boys in the United States include differences in brain structuring between males and females, pop psychology that focuses on innate gender differences, and workshops for teachers that reinforce differences between how males and females learn (Titus, 2004).

These concerns are consistent with the "crisis" of masculinity (Gardiner, 2002), calls for new versions of masculinity (Buchbinder, 1994), and claims that boys have lower levels of literacy skills than girls. The media have responded passionately to claims that boys have lower levels of literacy than girls, but more in-depth investigation through disaggregating data on school performance reveals there is much more to be considered than gender (Titus, 2004). Achievement is affected in significant ways by the intersection of social class, race and gender (Gilbert & Gilbert, 1998) and it is misleading to imply that boys and girls are

homogeneous populations with standardized achievements (Titus, 2004). According to Alloway and Gilbert (2002), the problem with literacy in the early years concerns the invisibility of men's literacy practices, the social construction of masculinity that dissociates it from literacy practices such as reading and writing, and that boys' early experiences with literacy are associated with feminine practices (p. 11). Although one of the remedies proposed to address the underachievement of boys has been to increase the numbers of male early childhood practitioners, Alloway and Gilbert (2002) suggest that the connection between technologies and masculinity may prove a fruitful avenue for providing positive literacy experiences for boys, but note that increasing the number of males in early childhood education is a simplistic solution that misrepresents the complexity of the relationship between gender and early literacy. Proposals made on the basis that increasing the number of males in early childhood education will improve boys' achievement generally, and literacy levels specifically, simply because of the presence of men, are not only founded on biology but also fail to acknowledge that there are groups of girls who also experience difficulty with literacy learning (Alloway, 2000; Gorard, Rees, & Salisbury, 1999).

Gilbert and Gilbert (1998) recommended specific practices for teachers to help boys understand their masculinity and create new versions of it, and Alloway and Gilbert (2002) have put forward explicit pedagogies for early childhood practitioners that challenge perceptions of literacy as feminized. However, recent highly influential publications that focus on reading and writing in developmentally appropriate ways (e.g., the joint statement by the International Reading Association (IRA) and the National Association for the Education of Young Children (NAEYC), IRA & NAEYC, 1998), do not engage with gender and literacy.

Men in early childhood education. The obvious imbalance of men to women teachers in the profession has been a consistent focus of research in a number of countries and signals that this is not just an isolated issue, but one that has concerned the field increasingly over the past 30 years (see, for example, Cameron, Moss, & Owen, 1999; Clyde, 1996; Goodman, 1987; Jensen, 1996; Jones, 2003; King, 1998; Murray, 1996; Powderly & Westlake, 1998; Pringle, 1998; Robb, 2001; Ruxton, 1992, 1994; Siefert, 1973; Silin, 1997; Sumsion, 1999, 2000a, 2000b, 2000c). Although earlier examinations of this issue attributed lower numbers of male teachers to inadequate remuneration, working conditions and status of early childhood work, postmodern researchers have conceptualized this problem differently by examining the politics of knowledge circulating around male early childhood educators. The concerns raised over the years have been discussed by Sumsion (2000a), who has named five competing discourses that are evident in the literature: (1) male as victim; (2) noncritical advocacy for an increased male presence in early childhood education; (3) critiques of interpretive research; (4) feminist perspectives; and (5) the "traditional" early childhood stance (p. 263).

The "male as victim" discourse is exemplified by the association of male employment in early childhood education with pedophile tendencies (see Cameron, Moss & Owen, 1999; King,

1998; Murray, 1996; Silin, 1997; Skelton, 1991). This is what Cameron et al. (1999) refer to as a polarization between the discourses of risk and equality: "The contradictions are plain: on the one hand, valuing and encouraging men workers so as to improve gender equality, and on the other suspecting their involvement in something damaging to children" (p. 17). Sumsion (2000a) maintains that such assumptions are evidence of moral panic and are "compounded by a potent blend of (i) misconceptions that men who elect to work with young children are necessarily homosexual; (ii) homophobia; and (iii) the common tendency to conflate homosexuality with paedophilia" (p. 263).

Several scholars have used queer theory to analyze these issues and others associated with the employment of men in early childhood education, including linking male early childhood practitioners with child sexual abuse (Johnson, 2000) and increased surveillance of all of those who work in early childhood education (Johnson, 1997, 2000; Silin, 1997). Queer theory works to depict the power relations operating in society through questioning normative understandings of heterosexuality. It emerged during the 1990s as a reworking of gay and lesbian theory that was combined with political action (Tobin, 1997b) and challenges all understandings of normativity and its related privileges that flourish in heterosexual culture (Britzman, 1995; Warner, 1993).

James King (1998) tackled the matter of men teaching in early childhood and elementary classrooms, acknowledging (as noted previously) that most men avoid teaching young children because of the feminization of early childhood education and the related lower status and remuneration that accompanies it. Examining teaching as female culture and using queer theory, King showed that the dominant discourse associated with teaching young children is care, and that when men enact care they cross gender borders and so threaten patriarchal work relations. As a result they are marginalized or treated with suspicion, particularly if they use physical touch as part of their teaching.

The male teachers in King's study saw themselves as different from the women with whom they worked: "They systematically devalued women's teaching and nonteaching behaviors to establish themselves as different, and women as other" (p. 105). Their resistance was evident in how they refused requests to discipline children sent to them from their female colleagues' classrooms, which King understood as removing themselves from perpetuating patriarchal relations and roles. But at the same time these males, both gay and straight, carried the burden of being constructed as sexual predators within a homophobic stereotype and therefore as threats to young children. King argued that these teachers bear the brunt of society's discomfort and unwillingness to confront "the sensual attachments we all have to children" (p. 123), by projecting these feelings "onto the figure of the homosexual" (p. 123). Silin (1997) also paired childhood innocence and ignorance about sexuality with the stereotype of the homosexual male early childhood teacher as a predatory pedophile, which he says works to silence our own enjoyment of touching children and locates our fears with the dangers posed to children from perverts and pedophiles. According to Silin (1997), these cultural constructions or moral panics are created to divert attention from "more pervasive forms of physical and social violence perpetrated against children in our country" (p. 215).

The connection between moral panics associated with male early childhood workers touching young children as part of their work, increased surveillance of those who work with young children, and child abuse, has been taken up by Johnson (2000a). Building on his earlier work (Johnson, 1997), Johnson (2000a) logged the disappearance of touch in the care of young children by situating "no touch" as an historical construct and locating it as a "truth effect" rather than a truth. As Johnson (2000a) shows, the discourse of child abuse has itself been constructed, along with other psychological concepts such as self esteem, in the past 50 years. "No touch" policies have been fashioned from the moral panic associated with child abuse and are measures of social control that attempt to stem the tide of panic and reassure; but, at the same time, they regulate and police behavior, and reinforce stereotypical assumptions about the assumed relationships among homosexuality, pedophilia, and child abuse (Johnson, 2000a).

Gender equity, teaching and learning. Whether it is from the perspective of children or teachers, by far the largest amount of research examining gender in early education is concerned with equity strategies in the classroom. Research reviewed here is drawn from cultural feminist and feminist poststructuralist positions, as well as combinations of other theories that might include critical theory and Bourdieu's philosophical anthropology.

The application of cultural feminism to education was responsible for a move from the equal opportunity approach of liberal feminism to a gender inclusive model. Based on the work of Belenky, Clinchy, Goldberger, and Tarule (1986), Gilligan (1982), and Noddings (1984), recognition of the value of female experiences and ways of knowing were included in education initiatives through the use of curriculum and teaching strategies that documented, valued and protected feminine contributions and qualities. Changes in early childhood education incorporated efforts to ensure that girls engaged in "masculine" activities such as block play and construction by making these areas more appealing to them. This was done by placing home corner equipment in the block area, that is, feminizing a male dominated area. Stories that valued female experiences were added to curriculum materials in an endeavor to make curricula more girl friendly.

The block area in early childhood settings is a masculine province and it is unusual for girls to play there (Paley, 1984). Epstein's (1995) cultural feminist case study illustrated how girls had opportunities to experience alternative ways of being beside those allied with stereotypical understandings by providing them with block play time without boys. The girls used domestic narratives in their block building that "reinscribed conventional (hetero) sexist gendered relations" (p. 66). Their confidence in their abilities to build with blocks grew and a change was noted in the ways boys viewed what girls could do.

Cultural feminism has been used in combination with critical theory to research issues such as teaching students in graduate early childhood classes in more relational and caring ways (Jipson, 1992). It also has been used to critically appraise the purposes of compensatory education programs for children, resulting in allegations that compensatory education is "fundamentally racist, sexist, and classist . . . [and has been] developed to change the cultures of women and minorities so that their values and beliefs will be similar to those of the while middle class" (Kessler, 1998, p. 198). Another study that documented the combined efforts of a researcher and first grade teacher (Hauser & Marrero, 1998) to investigate how equity operated in a first grade classroom revealed unresolved differences between researcher and teacher in their understandings of feminism, gender and equity.

Goldstein's (1997) study depicted what a cultural feminist approach looked like in a multiage K-1-2 classroom, as well as her own experiences of teaching a feminist early childhood curriculum as a second grade teacher. Basing the enactment of teaching on an ethic of care, Goldstein described the idea of teaching with love as the domain of women, as something that women teachers can claim because of the historical involvement of women in teaching and the ways in which it has been undertaken by women. Although Goldstein recognized the general ambivalence about "love's role in classroom life" (p. 160), she remains a strong advocate for making love, care and concern the heart of early childhood curricula.

In contrast to cultural feminists, feminist poststructuralists oppose an essentialized gendered way of knowing and argue instead that gender is discursively produced. Rather than one gender identity, individuals including teachers and children perform a number of gendered ways of knowing and being that depend on the social context and the meanings circulating within a set of social relationships. The classic studies of Walkerdine (1981) and Davies (1989) prompted further research about being identifiably young and male, and to a lesser extent, young and female. These and other work in early childhood settings such as teacher accounts (e.g, Gallas, 1994, 1998) have shown that boys enter early childhood settings performing masculinity in a variety of ways such as dominating the use of computers (Alloway, 1995); engaging in physical and aggressive activities in the block area (Danby & Baker, 1998; MacNaughton, 2000), the dress up and outdoor playing areas (Davies, 1989; MacNaughton, 1995), and general classroom spaces (Davies, 1993; Dyson, 1994; Gallas, 1994, 1998; Jordan, 1995; Jordan & Cowan, 1995; Kamler, Maclean, Reid, & Simpson (1994). Danby and Baker (1998) showed how older boys aged 5 provided lessons to younger boys about how to be masculine in the block area that included threats, conflict, and aggression. Gallas (1994) related stories about "bad" boys in her classroom, describing how they are "very interested in power of all sorts and usually are not nice boys. In school, they control classrooms in very subtle ways" (p. 52). Her later work (Gallas, 1998) depicted other aspects of "bad" boy behavior that also contradicted the label of "bad" by being "good".

From their feminist poststructuralist study of how children are initiated into the culture of elementary schooling, Kamler et al. (1994) found that girls were noticed and commended for behaving well and received more comments about their personal appearance than boys, while boys attracted attention for their aggressive and intrusive behaviour. Correspondingly, a study by Reid (1999) that used a combination of Foucauldian discourse analysis and Bourdieu's notion of *habitus* demonstrated that male aggression was comprehended by the first grade teacher as normal and acceptable in school settings (p. 188), whereas classroom aggression by girls was seen as deviant, and naughty girls were disciplined to be good and thoughtful (p. 188).

On the playground, Thorne's (1993) ethnography of two North American elementary schools found that girls were more likely to call for assistance from teachers than boys. The cost of such action for boys was higher as they were ridiculed more by their peers than girls who sought teacher support. Similarly, the Kamler et al. (1994) study revealed that the playground behavior and unsupervised classroom activities of all children were notable for their gendered peer conversations. In a scenario that depicted masculinity and its relationship to femininity, Mac Naughton (1995) analyzed the actions of a boy aged 5 engrossed in digging in a mud patch while a girl waited patiently nearby for over 20 minutes for him to finish, hoping to play a game of her choosing with him.

The pivotal role of the teacher was illustrated by Wilson Keenan, Solsken, and Willett (1999) in a study aimed at changing gendered language practices in a first/second grade urban classroom. By the third year of the study, it was apparent that teacher absence in small group interactions enabled the production of stereotypical language, whereas teacher presence in whole class discussions ensured the performance of language practices consistent with those that were officially sanctioned. What was notable besides the teacher effect associated with the use of officially sanctioned language was the struggle children experienced participating in multiple discourses, and the revelation that girls in this class shouldered a greater responsibility for reconstituting gender identities through changed use of language and relations than did boys.

An action research project in which fourteen early childhood teachers participated encouraged them to rethink gender in early childhood education through interrogating nine myths (MacNaughton, 2000). The myths included ideas such as gender being natural and normal, that children are too young to know and understand about gender, that gender is not an issue at "my center," and that gender equity is "just good practice, isn't it"? MacNaughton (2000) systematically debunked all myths using a combination of theoretical explanations supported by practical examples. She recommended that children be provided with alternative ways of being masculine and feminine and made practical suggestions about how to reconceptualize traditional early childhood pedagogies so that they are aimed at achieving more equitable outcomes.

The limitations of teachers observing children from a developmental perspective are exposed by Campbell and Smith (2001). In their attempts to understand how fairness operates in children's lives, they analysed a vignette from a child development perspective and then juxtaposed it against a feminist poststructuralist reading. What was obscured by the child development observation was the silencing and marginalization of one girl by another girl and a boy; physical threats made by the boy against the silenced girl; and the intervention of the teacher, who inadvertently supported the way in which the girl was being silenced and marginalized. This example is a stark reminder of how particular theoretical perspectives can restrict what is seen and heard, and how subsequent teacher action is also constrained by the developmental lens of the observer.

Although these studies are informed by different theoretical perspectives, most conclude by recommending that early childhood teachers need to introduce alternative and oppositional discourses into classrooms so that children can experience and therefore expand their understandings of what it can mean to be boys and girls. However, such action is notoriously difficult and challenging (MacNaughton, 2000; Wilson Keenan et al., 1999), and there is little recognition of the enormous struggle or emotional cost involved in reconstituting subjectivities and institutional practices in ways that diminish the binaries between femininity and masculinity (Wilson Keenan et al., 1999, is an exception). Similarly, there is a dearth of alternative conceptions of masculinity and femininity, possibly because of the limited ways we have of thinking about these binaries. Those that do exist seem to consist of expanding the repertoire of stereotypical practices of masculinity by incorporating aspects of femininity and vice versa.

In education research about gender, feminist poststructuralism has been used frequently enough to prompt McLeod (2001) to ask whether its application to education is becoming/has become another dominant discourse. McLeod (2001) contends that a discourse of redemption grounds ideas about both gender construction and suggestions of ways in which gender can be remade more equitably. As such, this discourse of redemption is itself normative and regulatory, promising to rescue educational research "from innocent, old-fashioned "theories [of gender]"", and to "free children from the confines of gender binaries and lead them to embrace an enriched, self-aware, and more authentic gender identity" (p. 277).

Children's Sex Play and Sexual Identity

The silence in child development texts about children's sexuality has been noted by Johnson (2000a) and Theilheimer and Cahill (2001), with the latter advocating that the lack of recognition about sexuality and specifically homosexuality, needs to be addressed by early childhood educators by opening the door to the early childhood closet to "take myths, beliefs and norms off the shelves, examine them, and discard damaging ones" (p. 111). As the work of Boldt (1997), Johnson (1997, 2000a), King (1997, 1998), Kroeger (2001), Silin (1995, 1997), and Tobin (1997a, 1997b) demonstrates, sexuality, sex play, and homosexuality are curriculum rather than developmental concerns and go well beyond the child development frame of "sex roles, Freudian identity theories, sexual abuse, and talking to children about reproduction" (Theilheimer & Cahill, 2001, p. 108). Sexuality, sex play and sexual identity interact closely with gender, which is evident in some of the literature reviewed.

Although social justice issues have been on the professional agenda for many years, advice to early childhood staff about how to deal with sexual identity issues (such as homosexuality) for both parents and children has been slow to emerge (see Clay, 1990; Corbett, 1993; Casper & Schultz, 1999; Wickens, 1993, for examples). Research by Robinson (2002) illustrated that early childhood settings espousing strong social justice values tended not to challenge homophobic discourses and therefore conveyed contradictory messages about social justice. That is, some aspects of diversity and difference were "considered more worthy of attention and respect than others" (Robinson, 2002, p. 431). This hierarchical aspect of social justice is perhaps reflective of personal and practitioner experience, as well as the difference in comfort levels between confronting gendered behavior and discussing homophobia.

Another reason that teachers may be reluctant to include sexuality issues as part of a social justice curriculum could be cultural norms. Using a range of explicit scenarios about kissing games, children playing doctor, and male teachers Tobin (1997a), found very distinct responses from teachers located in the United States in comparison to their counterparts in Ireland. Those from the United States expressed fear and moral panic over displays of children's sexuality, especially when the prospect of litigation was considered. These teachers felt that surveillance of children's play and regulation of it according to parental expectations would ensure their protection from threats of litigation. The Irish teachers were not as concerned about the children's play or about litigation, but did indicate that they were moving toward where the teachers from the United States were already located and would have to consider parental expectations and responses to games such as "kiss and strip" and birthing of babies.

Queer theory has been used to consider how teachers handle children's gender bending and sexuality within the classroom. Boldt's (1997) stories and dialogue from children in her third grade classroom tell of her struggle to realize that her own gendered and heteronormative assumptions, as well as those of many of the children, were part of the fabric of the classroom and the reason that the children were both restricted and empowered in their performance and enactment of gender and heteronormativity. Boldt resolved that demonstrations of particular behavior such as gender bending and its subsequent heteronormative responses do not necessarily predict future behaviour ("tom" boys do not necessarily grow up to be lesbians and effeminate boys do not automatically become gay men). Thorne (1993) too, illustrated that children move in and out of established gender patterns, and that they set up their own gender "rules" to subsequently break them. Boldt also might be reassured by Dunne's (1997) study of the childhoods of women who are not heterosexual, which noted not only the multiplicity of childhood experiences of these women but also their agency in responding to their experiences and the intractable gender boundaries with which they had to deal.

Another way in which queer theory has been used empirically is illustrated by Kroeger's (2001) reworking of personal and professional ideas about including a lesbian family in an early childhood program. The challenges and personal struggles encountered by Kroeger show how developmentally appropriate curriculum guidelines for early childhood educators that profess to support teaching for social justice, can be limiting and restrict options available for contextually sensitive and relevant teacher responses. Kroeger's story exemplifies the multifaceted approaches that can be developed by teachers, depending on their specific contexts and in this case, the personal investment by the teacher and her motivation to resolve the dilemma of inclusion in the most effective way for the family. The message that activism can take many forms, which may sometimes be different from those prescribed in manuals and come from teacher initiative, is a constructive and optimistic development.

Cultural, Racial, Class and Linguistic Diversity

In the education literature generally, much recent work has raised issues relating to culture, race, class and language. Pollock (2001) for instance, has asked of schools in the United States, "how and why do different race groups achieve differently" (p. 2), and Lee (2002) noted that racial and ethnic gaps that were narrowed in the 1970s and 1980s widened again in the 1990s, causing concern about racial and ethnic equity (p. 3). In early childhood education, research inspired by postmodern perspectives has brought new understandings about children, teaching, and learning from practitioners working in settings that are not only culturally, racially, and linguistically diverse but also that differ in terms of children's class or socioeconomic status (SES).

In the United States, racial and ethnic diversity is particularly significant because of increasing demands of the standardization and accountability movement. One teacher's response to the constraints of recent *No Child Left Behind* policies has been documented by Larson and Gatto (2004) in two ethnographic studies. In her third grade urban classroom (69% African American, 26% white (one had recently immigrated from Bosnia), and 5% Latino children), Gatto (Larson & Gatto, 2004) constructed "a new space for learning we call tactical underlife that builds on . . . [the] concept of a pedagogy of tactics to resist standardization" (p. 37). As part of her tactics, Gatto "does not follow the mandated lesson plan format . . . does not use the text-books . . . and the spelling, grammar, phonics, and math workbooks are sent back to the book room" (p. 19). Instead, Gatto capitalized on her students wanting to have fun and together they constructed a "tactical space within the prescriptive space of school in which traditional power relations are transformed and all languages, literacies, and knowledges count" (p. 37). Her curriculum strategies are based on inquiry as a social practice; multiliteracies are privileged and what transpires is "a fluid, non-linear interaction among the class members, including her . . . which in turn transforms the social relations" (p. 21). In addition to sociocritical perspectives of literacy, and sociocultural and sociohistorical learning theory, Larson and Gatto (2004) drew on New Literacy Studies (e.g., Gee, 2001) to argue that literacy is much more complex than one-dimensional mandated curricula and assessment. They propose that teachers facing demands of standardization and accountability similar to Gatto can use the space of "tactical underlife" to create their own areas of resistance and at the same time enable students to learn in meaningful and engaging ways.

Maintaining the focus on urban schools, an action research longitudinal study framed investigations of how practitioners in two Canadian schools responded to the cultural, racial, and linguistic diversity of children in their classes (kindergarten to grade five) (Pacini-Ketchabaw & Schecter, 2002). The explicit goal was to foster equity and inclusion for minority students, with researchers working collaboratively with small groups of

practitioners in each school over a 3-year period. They concluded that there were four discourses operating in the schools about how teachers dealt with diversity: (1) the discourse of difference as deficit (two teachers); (2) the preparation of minority students and families to facilitate the school's agenda' (21 teachers); (3) intercultural sensitivity as a pedagogic tool (11 teachers); and (4) diversity as curriculum (five teachers). Teachers' different levels of understanding about diversity governed much of what happened in classrooms and a small number of teachers changed their views about how to assist children pedagogically during the period of the research. Of concern to the researchers was the clustering of practitioners into deficit discourses, particularly the second category, where teachers privileged "a focus on preparing minority families to facilitate the school's agenda and position[ed] minority children and families as 'others'" (Pacini-Ketchabaw & Schecter, 2002, p. 412). Although the authors indicated that the research produced many positive effects, it also showed the difficulty of challenging pedagogically, dominant discourses about cultural, racial and linguistic diversity.

There are few studies that look closely at the intersections between race and gender. One that does is Scott's (2002) ethnography of first grade African-American girls' social relations on the playgrounds of two racially mixed elementary schools in the northeast region of the United States. Scott's analysis drew on black feminist theory, illustrating that in a game played regularly at Rosemount school (40% of children were African American; 30% white; 20% Hispanic; and 10% Asian), "any White girl had more social agency to initiate the game than did her non-White counterparts" (p. 410). However, by adhering to the rules to gain admission to the group, the African-American girls then "developed and maintained a game within a game" (p. 411) by reclaiming "their voice and divergent opinions of boys" (p. 411). At this same school, African-American boys preferred to be linked romantically with high-status girls, who were invariably white. Although her focus was African-American girls, Scott raised concerns about how the Hispanic and Asian-American girls were positioned in the milieu of high and low status rankings. The second school had a population of 84% African American and 16% Latino children, with different group dynamics operating. Here assertiveness and "female group interdependence" (p. 411) were valued and boys "did not possess the social agency to dominate girls" (p. 412). Boys thought that the girls were "interested in romantic relationships with them" (p. 412), but, paradoxically, the girls suggested that the boys were the "sexually precocious ones" (p. 412).

Indigenous teachers such as Hewett (2001) have remained marginalized because of colonization and associated lingering assumptions that Native Hawaiian people engage primarily in tourist oriented occupations rather than professional roles such as teaching. Hewett says that when "most *haole* [white people] . . . meet native (brown) people like me, they don't expect us to be in professional roles" (p. 120). Such troubling notions sit alongside the predicaments encountered by Kaomea (2001a, 2001b, 2003), an indigenous academic working and researching in Native Hawaiian early childhood and elementary educational communities. Kaomea (2003) used defamiliarizing analytical tools to investigate the Hawaiian studies *kapuna*

(Hawaiian grandparent, ancestor, relative, or close friend of the grandparent's generation, p. 24) program. She used techniques such as making the familiar "Lei Day" strange, to expose the complex interaction of a multitude of factors that work together to perpetuate the program's "colonialist and capitalist dynamics" (p. 23). Although showing that the *kapuna* were unknowingly complicit in their own oppression, Kaomea struggled with the reaction of the local Hawaiian community to her revelations.

Using the postcolonial perspective of children as colonized Other, Viruru (2001b) took the issue of language further, arguing that language is a privileged form of communication in dominant "Western" ways of seeing the world. Her work in India showed that many people "seemed to communicate through what was not said rather than what was" (Viruru, 2001b, p. 40). In "Western" ways of thinking, silence is seen as a lack, but as Viruru (2001b) illustrated, silence is also a way of knowing. This perceived "lack" was situated alongside "Western" child development views of thinking about children and their construction as needy, without voice (silent) and as "underdeveloped" (p. 40).

Turning to children and issues of race, MacNaughton and Davis (2001) examined the understandings of indigenous Australians and their cultures held by 37 Anglo-Australian children aged 4 and 5 years. The children consistently defined indigenous Australians as Other, emphasizing the differences between "them" and "us" and highlighting the differences as "exotic" (p. 87). Despite this, there were some emerging understandings about colonization and its lasting effects, and the commodification of cultural artefacts of indigenous Australians (p. 90). MacNaughton and Davis (2001) also surveyed and interviewed 25 early childhood practitioners to find out "what they thought and taught about indigenous Australians and their cultures" (p. 85). Children attending centers where the research was undertaken were mostly from Anglo-Australian families. Recommendations identified that practitioners needed support to develop teaching strategies that do not rely on the white/black binary.

Popular Culture

Popular culture has been an area of discussion in early childhood education for some time, with recent postmodern conversations converging on notions of children as informed and sophisticated consumers (Kincheloe, 2002; Luke & Luke, 2001) as opposed to children being portrayed as innocent and as market victims. Debate about young children and popular culture has concentrated on superhero play, in particular around the polarized issue of whether or not it should be allowed in early childhood settings (e.g., Boyd, 2002; Bergen, 1994; Greenberg, 1995; Gronlund, 1992; Hampton, 2002; Kostelnick, Whiren, & Stein, 1986; Paley, 1984). Recent explorations of popular culture using postmodern approaches have been made by Dyson (1994, 1996, 1997), Jones (2002), Marsh (1999, 2000, 2002a, 2002b), Orellana (1994), and Tobin (2000). Here we discuss a small number of research studies undertaken in early childhood settings that attempt to understand children's responses to media and that use aspects of popular culture as a pedagogical tool.

Investigating young boys' dependency on superhero play in a nursery school setting in the United Kingdom, Jones (2002) combined Derrida's concept of deconstruction with practitioner research in what appears to be the first application of deconstructive thinking to center based play of this type. Jones offered a reading that disrupted binary ways of thinking about masculinity and femininity in children's superhero play, thus suggesting an alternative conception of how superhero play can create spaces for children to think differently. Marsh's (2002a) study concentrated on girls and superhero play in an infant classroom in the United Kingdom, concluding that girls found superhero play very attractive and were able to "explore agency and autonomy through such play and actively position themselves as females within a heroic discourse" (p. 209).

Other studies of children and their interaction with popular culture also indicate that we need to rethink assumptions that locate children as unsophisticated consumers of these media and that they have no place in early childhood classrooms. For example, Marsh (2000b) demonstrated the utility of capitalizing on young children's interest in *Teletubbies* to enhance oral language and literacy by including Teletubby texts in the curriculum and Tobin (2000) used several theoretical perspectives to analyze children's talk about short excerpts from two movies and two television commercials to show that children had gone well beyond facile conceptions of what was being portrayed. Dyson's (1994, 1996, 1997, 1998) ongoing work continues to illustrate the links between popular culture and literacy practices and how children's interest in popular culture can be a persuasive stimulus for them to explore issues of power and identity in early childhood classrooms. Although the superhero storylines and children's use of these identities depicted in Dyson's (1997) research with children aged 7 to 9 years provides powerful ways for them to experience the triumph of good over evil, Dyson noted that these storylines are limiting in their often stereotypical rendering of race, class, gender, culture, and ethnicity. With the support of their teacher, the children worked through the limitations and challenges of commercial media culture to learn about participating in the classroom as a community of difference, not only in their peer relations but also in their writing.

THE POLITICS OF FAMILIES

Although there has been much discussion about the decline of the family, postmodernists are more concerned with charting transformations in family forms and structures that are often a consequence of social and economic change. How to do this without sliding into nostalgia or deficit models of the family is the challenge for researchers using postmodern approaches. Carrington (2002) provides a compelling argument about the need to change our ways of looking at families through new theoretical framings and the necessity of new vocabulary to accompany these innovative approaches. She says, that it is "No longer appropriate to draw on narratives of oedipalized gender, sexual and role stereotypes. Nor is it possible to assume any type of practical homogeneity" (p. 135). In this section, we consider research that has been undertaken with families based on gender, race and ethnicity (and combinations of these factors) that moves beyond the pervasive narratives noted by Carrington (2002), as well as projects that make links between parents and early childhood curriculum.

Race, Ethnicity and Gender

In the postmodern globalized world, families are complex and multifaceted entities, often reflecting diversity through hybridity and multilingualism, where two or more languages are learnt at the same time. Racial and ethnic identity formation of Asian-American children in the Midwest of the United States was the focal point of a study by Adler (2001), which drew on postmodern-feminism, feminist interview techniques, and racial identity development theory. Adler surveyed 20 families (Japanese, Chinese, Korean, Filipino, and Hmong), and interviewed 12 parents in depth to conclude that parents were generally more aware of their own racial identity development than that of their children. She also found that parents believed it was the school's responsibility to "provide a multicultural and anti-bias environment" (p. 285), but that they were unsure of whether this was happening in their children's classrooms. Furthermore, Adler established that parents responded positively to their children's experiences of "ethnic teasing, discrimination, and racism . . . by modelling ethnic pride as well as helping them ignore or find a way to cope with such incidents" (p. 285). Parents were concerned about color blindness and the invisibility of Asian-American children, as well as the homogenization of teacher assumptions about these children, specifically in relation to the stereotype of the "model minority" (p. 289). Adler raised the importance of teachers recognizing and understanding the difference between ethnicity and culture. Parents also expressed the need for teachers to understand about intragroup differences relating to cultural orientations and knowledge, political and historical information, and family histories (p. 289).

A small number of studies investigating gender have used feminist poststructuralism when researching with families in their homes. For instance, Simpson (1999) video taped her 4-year-old son building with a construction set and her subsequent analysis showed that she unknowingly used her authority as mother to position her son more powerfully than her 6-year-old daughter. As a result, the female child was required to be patient and put her own desires aside while waiting for those of her brother to be realized. Simpson (1999) explained how she did not realize that in the process of videotaping her son she was setting up what would become a situation of conflict that all three family members found distressing. Similar experiences of dominant masculinity and the way it is constructed and enacted have also been depicted by Grieshaber (2004), in which female children are required to prepare and serve food to the males in the family and clean up afterward. In these instances, dominant masculinity has enabled young boys aged 5 and 6 to take no responsibility for preparing and cleaning after meals, and for one son to yell and scream profanities at his mother when she failed to serve his meal as he demanded (Grieshaber, 2004). In these cases, the mothers were unknowingly complicit in constructing and perpetuating dominant masculinity and its opposite position of passive femininity.

Dominant masculinity also was a factor in a study involving 40 first-time parents (20 mothers and 20 fathers) (Grieshaber, 1998), as mothers deferred to fathers' preferences about knowing the sex of the baby before its arrival. Fathers were generally silent on the issue of nurturing the newborn babies, talking much more about what they would do with the children when they were older (such as fishing, and playing golf and cricket). In contrast, interviews after the birth found that fathers were involved in a variety of caring activities with their babies, thus substantiating the idea that masculinity does not encompass talking about nurturing activities.

Located in the United States, Orellana's (1999) study used a combination of sociocultural, critical, and feminist poststructuralist theories to analyze observations of two young children and interviews with their parents. The observations were made while the children were playing in their bilingual home and preschool school environments. Although both parents in each family spoke Spanish and English, both children had one parent who was a native speaker of Spanish and one parent who was a native speaker of English. Before attending preschool, the children spoke very little English because both families placed a greater emphasis on Spanish. The analysis revealed that when children had opportunities to cross gender borders in their play, they moved to the binary associated with the more powerful position and were more reluctant to adopt vulnerable positions (p. 113). More powerful positions were associated with masculinity and the ability to speak English, whereas more vulnerable positions were connected with speaking Spanish and femininity.

Families and Early Childhood Curriculum

Parental involvement in early childhood education has always been highly valued because it is believed to improve child outcomes (Hoover-Dempsey & Sandler, 1997) and to be of educational benefit to the nation (National Education Goals Panel, 1998). As part of the critique of developmentally appropriate practice (DAP) (Bredekamp, 1987), Powell (1994) observed that parents are situated by the NAEYC position statement about DAP as both consumers in selecting early childhood programs and as contributors to early childhood programs. However, it is only recently that the nature of parental involvement and the way that parents are positioned by early childhood staff has been studied using postmodern perspectives.

The comprehensive study of cultural, linguistic, and racial diversity in Canadian early childhood education (Bernhard, Lefebvre, Chud, & Lange, 1995) included 199 teachers from centers in three cities (Toronto, Vancouver, and Montréal), family studies in these same cities and a study of 78 faculty from three provinces. Bernhard et al. (1995) found that administrators and teachers were positioned as "experts" and transmitted a standard model of early childhood education or "dominant culture and language to the children and families" (p. 67). Teachers also were expected to make difficult decisions for which Bernhard et al. stated that they were "not adequately prepared" (p. 67). Being positioned as expert belies a spirit of collaboration between teachers and families and this is problematic given the rhetoric associated with early childhood programs about working with parents for the educational betterment of their children. Adopting a standard model of ECE resulted in teachers making "judgements of children based on universal patterns of development described in North American textbooks and journals" (p. 67). Thus parents and teachers had "different focuses for their children and different expectations of each other" (p. 67). Bernhard et al. (1995) predicted that the situation would worsen because of the increasing number of families from different cultural, linguistic, and racial backgrounds using early childhood educational services. The researchers concluded that with continued use of the standard model, dissatisfaction from parents and teachers would intensify.

A recent study undertaken in a large Midwestern public university in the United States investigated how home-school relations are built into the curriculum of an elementary education program, and correspondingly, the perspectives that preservice teachers developed as they moved through the program (Graue, Oen, & Shirley, 2004). The 107 participants were "typical of the elementary teaching force" (Graue et al., 2004, p. 7) in that they were "overwhelmingly female, white, from middle class and upper middle class families ... they did not have children ... and they hoped to teach younger rather than older children" (Graue et al., 2004, pp. 7–8). Similarly to what Powell (1994) described, Graue et al. (2004) indicated that most students positioned families as "supporters of teacher work" (p. 2). Students entering the program held views about families and education that reflected their own experience, explained by Graue et al. (2004) as the way in which "personal narrative is normatively constructed as the standard for teaching practice" (p. 2). Most disturbing but hardly surprising was the finding that these preservice teachers were content with professional relationships with families that retained their power and kept "families in place" (p. 19). Furthermore, despite the program being described as "critical, multicultural, and social reconstructivist" (p. 19), Graue et al. (2004) state that there "was nothing critical, multicultural or social reconstructivist about their thinking about families" (p. 19). Cultural differences were approached as tokenistic tourist oriented affairs, reflecting the ability of students to use what they knew from their own experiences but unfortunately missing the mark of authentic engagement with families.

In their assessment of "162 early childhood texts and policy documents published in the 1990s that had parent involvement as their key concern", Hughes and MacNaughton (2000, p. 242) found that parents were positioned as "'others', preventing the creation of equitable parent-staff relationships" (p. 241). More specifically, discourses in the texts and policy documents placed parents as clients, and practitioners as professional experts, thus subordinating or "othering" parental knowledge to that of early childhood professionals. Hughes and MacNaughton argued that attempts to revision parental involvement with the aim of creating equitable relationships are difficult because of the way that parents are Othered. They used Habermas's modernist understanding of communicative consensus and Lyotard's postmodern notion of emancipatory dissensus to provoke debate about how to establish relationships with parents that are more inclusive and respectful (p. 256). They also recommend "redefining

the benefits of parent involvement in early childhood education" (p. 256) and recognizing the substantial knowledge base that parents have about their children.

Revisioning of parental involvement in early childhood education is the basis of Smith's (2000) justification for including parents as observers of children. To Smith, excluding parents from observing children reinforces ideas about parents as clients and teachers as professionals. She advocates the inclusion of parental observations as one of a set of multiple views about children that can facilitate more responsive curriculum practices and enhance relationships between teachers and parents.

Linked to the idea of too few male early childhood practitioners is concern about the increase in families headed by single females and the consequent reduction of male role models in boys' lives (Titus, 2004), and the argument that there are too few male role models in homes to support boys' literacy learning (see Alloway & Gilbert, 2002). In these examples, the problem is attributed to biological rather than cultural roles and is more complex than the provision of more male role models. Overall, families without fathers do experience less favorable outcomes for children (Titus, 2004), but there is no definitive evidence about specific causes. For instance in regard to literacy learning, where single parenthood "correlates with poverty, boys and girls in these families are likely to find themselves at risk [in terms of literacy learning] whether the parent is a mother or father" (Alloway & Gilbert, 2002, p. 9). Furthermore, it is women who do the literacy work at home, and even when fathers are present in the home, they engage minimally with literacy whether it is with sons or daughters (Alloway & Gilbert, 2002, p. 9).

These studies highlight the diversity of families that enter and participate in early childhood services and suggest that traditional views of the parent-teacher partnership are not always helpful as often teachers cannot be experts when it comes to considerations of culture and language, among other things.

THE POLITICS OF TEACHER EDUCATION

There has been little research and application of postmodern perspectives to teacher education, despite the work by Bernhard et al. (1995) and Minaya-Rowe (2002); the case made by Saracho and Spodek (1995) to prepare teachers to teach for cultural, linguistic and racial diversity, and the comments by García and McLaughlin (1995) that many early childhood educators "do not have the knowledge base and related skills to address the challenge of diversity" (p. xxii). Recent research in the United States has found that two- and four-year early childhood preservice teacher education courses provide little course work about educating children from diverse linguistic and cultural backgrounds (Early & Winton, 2001), and national policy documents simultaneously call for the addition of this content in programs of preparation. Thus, it is very difficult for teachers to begin to know how to make connections with children whose backgrounds and experiences are different from their own.

The Canadian study by Bernhard et al. (1995) involved interviews with 78 faculty whose job it was to prepare early childhood educators in colleges and universities. Most of those interviewed were responsible for designing multicultural and diversity courses in their workplaces and most were not from minority groups (p. 60). Bernhard et al. (1995) found that the "large majority of the ECE programs . . . had no specific courses dealing with diversity. . . . About one third (32%) of the institutions had diversity policies and another 12 percent were developing them" (p. 65). There were 16 courses offered at various institutions, and for 12 of these it was compulsory that students completed them. Courses named as having the least content related to diversity were "Human Development, Administration, Practicum, and Health and Safety" (p. 65). In metropolitan areas, the student body reflected the faculty composition in that it was comparatively homogeneous and contained few students from minority groups. Faculty were not sure about how to "address family language issues" (p. 64) and believed that more content related to issues of diversity should be included in courses. Given this, it is not surprising that half of the faculty interviewed thought that graduates were not adequately prepared to work with children and families from a diverse range of backgrounds. Respondents expressed this more strongly when they were outside metropolitan areas.

The relation between child development knowledge and early childhood teacher preparation was a topic of debate during the mid-1990s, with Goffin (1996) calling for a more meaningful relationship between the two, and Lubeck (1996), recognizing the challenges of a postmodern era, questioning the "passing on of a codified body of knowledge in teacher education" (p. 147). Lubeck suggested that a vital part of teacher education is learning to think critically, and "to interrogate the assumptions that underlie any and all knowledge claims, in particular regarding their usefulness in the creation of a more equitable society" (p. 149). To move beyond the traditional approach to early childhood teacher preparation (passing on a codified body of knowledge), Lubeck recommended a dialogic model of teaching and teacher education. She recognized that there are "many ways of understanding how children develop and learn, many ways to teach, and a range of curricular options" (p. 147). This array of options provides opportunities for teachers to ensure that they use reflective practices and that they attend to the diverse range of needs of children in postmodern society.

Although we have documented research about the education of young children, families, and teachers that is based on postmodern approaches, we know little about how postmodern perspectives are being used in early childhood teacher education programs. Bernhard et al. (1995), Hatch (2000), and Ryan and Grieshaber (2005) are exceptions. This is pertinent given the points made by Bernhard et al. (1995) and Lubeck (1996) about the diversity of contemporary society and when considered with other conditions of postmodernity, makes a strong case for proactive teacher education approaches rather than reactive or habitual responses.

POLICY AND GOVERNANCE

The creation and implementation of policy in early childhood education is not value free or neutral. Postmodern theories enable questions to be asked about who makes policy decisions, what their interests and values are, and who is constrained and enabled by particular policies (Bloch, Holmlund, Moqvist, & Popkewitz, 2003). At the same time, while permitting an understanding of whose interests are served by particular laws and mandates, the conditions of postmodernity also contribute to the policies that govern teaching, parenting, and learning.

In their analysis of the discourse of children and families "at promise," Swadener and Lubeck (1995) stated that the label "at risk" that has been attached to children and families is

highly problematic and implicitly racist, classist, sexist, and ableist, and a 1990s version of the cultural deficit model which locates problems or "pathologies" in individuals, families and communities rather than in institutional structures that create and maintain inequality. (p. 3)

The early years of the 21st century are little different from the situation to which Swadener and Lubeck referred. It is simply that along with changes in social conditions have come changes in the nature of needs, dependencies and pathologies, how they are conceptualized and how they can be prevented. Needs, dependencies, and pathologies are now expressly connected with the conditions of postmodernity. For example, in the United States the discourse of dependency/independency now requires families to be self sufficient and not depend on state and corporate welfare except in "uncertain times" (Bloch, 2003, p. 220). Accordingly, the "new needy" (p. 220) are those who are unable to be self sufficient, whereas those who are categorized as the most needy resist "state and private help" (p. 221). Bloch is critical of policies (not only in the United States) that attach blame to single mothers and see "marriage and employment as the way to normalize family" (p. 225). This theme is part of Cannella's (2003) analysis of child welfare in the United States as gendered, and her conclusion that women and children, particularly those who are poor and lack resources, "have been reconstituted as the morally deficient who corrupt society" (p. 188). Cannella argues that marriage is privileged and that teen and single motherhood are constructed as oppositional discourses and blamed for "all society's ills" (p. 187). Thus, while postmodern conditions of globalization and immigration are contributing to hybridity in family forms, many current political forces are attempting to restrict or limit for the diversity of family forms.

The condition of postmodernity means that childhood is also under reformation. As Luke and Luke (2001) put it, the Nintendo generation, those who came of age in the 1990s and were the first to transit through an electronically mediated childhood created concern because print traditions and practices were being ignored:

This group had grown up with electronic toys and games, post-MTV media fare, VCRs and home computers, and the first generation of CD games and internet "dungeons and dragons" gaming rooms. Symptoms of addiction shifted from joystick arthritis to "playstation thumb". Variously labelled Generation-X, web surfies, screenagers, digi-kids, techno-kids or cyberpunks, by the end of the millennium, computer savvy cybernauts had left parents and teachers behind in the emerging generational-digital divide. (p. 103)

Luke and Luke (2001) go on to argue that a moral panic has been created "over the emergence of an uncivil, unruly techno-subject" (p. 99). This panic is based on adolescent and child "technical competence, practice and engagement [that is seen] as a sign of deficit" (p. 103). The idea is that adolescence is too late to fix the problems of youth (Luke & Luke, 2001), so prevention and intervention programs must be moved to a more malleable section of the population where success is deemed more likely—those under the age of 5.

This view of the early childhood years as a means of preventing later educational and social problems such as chronic unemployment and criminal activity (Vandell & Wolfe, 2000) is reflected in the titles of United States policy documents such as the *No Child Left Behind Act, A Noble Bet in Early Care Education,* and *Universal Preschool: Much to Gain.* These arguments are supported by the demonstrated cost savings associated with model preschool programs like the High Scope/Perry Preschool Program and the Abercedarian Early Childhood Intervention project (Barnett, 1996; Masse, 2002). Not surprisingly these arguments are compelling to policy makers around the world as well as in the United States. However, to ensure that public dollars are not wasted but return their investment, along with this public commitment, is increasing standardization and regulation of early education. This standardization pervades all aspects of the field but especially classroom practice where teachers of young children are being told increasingly to use externally imposed curricula, and demonstrate learning outcomes or competencies.

One example of this regulation can be seen in the mandating of particular forms of early literacy practices. Children's competence (and adult lack of competence) with information and communication technologies has provoked alarm about the lack of attention to print traditions and produced a litany of policies (*No Child Left Behind*; California's Proposition 227; the United Kingdom National Literacy Strategy) promoting a resurgence of traditional literacy practices. Manyak's (2004) qualitative case study of a reading group in a first grade class is an example of how the monolingual mandate in California (Proposition 227) is working to ensure not only the dominance of written and spoken English but also the operation of a "reductive set of classroom literacy practices" (p. 136).

The case study described the experiences of Spanish-speaking Latina/o children learning to read and write with the aid of a bilingual reading support teacher who spoke only English during instruction. Lessons were "highly structured" (p. 134) and focused on "segmenting and blending letter sounds of simple words that she [the reading support teacher] had been trained to implement by the district the previous summer" (p. 134). Manyak detailed how literacy practices focused specifically on children's individual performances such as prescribed body movements and vocalizations, the correct timing of responses and continual correction of "students when their letter sounds were tinged with Spanish" (p. 143). Although children resisted these "disciplinary literacy pedagogies" (p. 146), their actions identified them as experiencing difficulties and as a result they were subjected to "more intensive training" (p. 146). Here, the problem is framed as preventing print and speech

deficient adolescents by concentrating on traditional literary practices with young children. The fact that many young children are more proficient than their parents and teachers with information and communication technologies is ignored in the quest to demonstrate competency in traditional literary modes.

Another application of this standardization can be seen in the way quality is being defined and applied to early childhood services as part of these policies. Research over the past 20 years has concentrated on defining quality in all of its dimensions such as staff qualifications, staff-child ratios, resources, educational backgrounds of teachers, curricula approaches, and the like. These are important issues for early childhood education but naming best practice in a plethora of minute descriptions that seek to delimit its very essence also can lead to programs that are not responsive to local circumstances. Drawing on a range of postmodern theories, but predominantly Foucault's poststructuralism, Dahlberg, Moss, and Pence (1999), argue that the discourse of quality in early childhood education is a socially constructed concept aligned with notions of modernism that position children as empty vessels to be prepared for learning and school, who need assistance in their development, and who are placed in early childhood institutions that produce prespecified outcomes. In the modernist sense, quality encompasses the standards and accountability movements and is therefore concerned with making judgments that are universal, (believed to be) objective, efficient, consistent, reliable, and reducible to numbers. Dahlberg et al. (1999) propose a discourse of meaning making that is contextual, putting judgments made in relationship with others at the center:

> [The discourse of meaning making] speaks of personal agency and responsibility to produce or construct meaning and deepen understanding about pedagogical work and other projects, foregrounding practice and context, always in relationship with others and following rigorous procedures. It assumes multiple perspectives and voices and the possibility of finding some agreement with others, while being wary of total agreement or consensus; uncertainty and indeterminacy are viewed as unavoidable. (p. 113)

The discourse of meaning making is not value-free, neutral, or objective because it involves studying actual practices, and making moral and political choices and ethical judgements as part of an ongoing process of dialogue and critical reflection. To Dahlberg et al. (1999), the modernist notion of quality cannot be reconceptualized to account for the conditions of postmodern society such as uncertainty, complexity, diversity, values, and multiple perspectives.

CONCLUSIONS

The central arguments of this chapter have been first, to show that research motivated by postmodern perspectives has an important place in any research agenda about the education of young children, and second, that the theoretical tools available through postmodern conceptualizations can provide insight into issues about diversity and other conditions of postmodernity that are not possible within developmental frameworks (e.g., the power relations involved in colonialism, gendering, and normativity of all types; and "othering" of children).

The research reviewed here highlights that postmodern theories have been used in early childhood education to pose alternative ways of viewing children and childhood, and to show how facets of diversity (e.g., gender, class, culture, race, language, sexuality) have implications for teaching, learning, families, teacher education, policies, and governance. This review has revealed that much of the research has been undertaken in regard to the sociology of childhood, gender, popular culture and issues related to children's sex play and sexual identity. Significant gaps remain and under-researched areas include teacher education, policy, families, and cultural, racial, class, and linguistic diversity as well as the intersection of aspects of these areas of diversity.

In our appraisal, future research using postmodern perspectives should try to build on the work that has been done by examining further the issue of men practitioners in early childhood education and the way which children have been "othered" by developmental approaches. These are issues and concerns that require extended exploration using alternative theories as they have the potential to offer different ways of conceptualizing both teaching and those who are to be taught. In addition, the research base needs to be expanded to include accounts of how educators in the many differing sectors of early childhood education are using postmodern concepts in their daily work.

Research using postmodern approaches has shown that practitioners are often at the forefront of dealing with conditions of postmodernity (such as diversity in all its forms) and that when faced with specific situations are able to respond creatively with ideas and resources that extend what is currently available. A case in point is Kroeger's (2001) experience of working with a lesbian family, which shows that when practitioners face issues that are characteristic of postmodern society, postmodern approaches are useful tools for investigation. Second, Genishi (1992) has shown the value of researching with teachers, and Genishi et al. (2001) have made it clear that in comparison with other research in early childhood education (both postmodern and traditional), there is a dearth of research about early childhood teachers. If we are to access practitioners' cutting edge responses to the conditions of postmodernity, we need ways of working with those in the field as we have a great deal to learn from them.

Much of the literature that uses postmodern perspectives is concerned with issues of power in relation to domination, resistance and privilege. Postmodern theories have certainly been influential in enhancing understandings of how domination, resistance, and privilege work in concert (Schutz, 2004), and the relationships of power that are involved in the interplay of these concepts in daily life. However, Eisner (in Schutz, 2004) has noted "theory not only reveals, it conceals..." (p. 21), leading Schutz (2004) to argue for "more *strategic* deployments of postmodern ideas, and of theory more broadly, in education" (p. 21). Schutz wants a more finely tuned analysis and exchange of ideas about the relationships among oppression, resistance, and privilege in education because of the tendency

of postmodern approaches to focus on the "relatively nurturing forms of "pastoral" control generally experienced by the privileged" (p. 15). This is in contrast to the marginalized who often experience "brutal discipline" (p. 15). Such a dialogue is imperative as it has the potential to show how the privileged "dominate others and are themselves enmeshed (often through pastoral processes) in systems of domination" (Schutz, 2004, p. 21). This idea lends itself to investigating the Reggio Emilia "fascination" in the United States, which Johnson (2000b) says is symbolic of the latest cargo cult (curriculum) being presented to early childhood educators and just another in the long list of influences on the field that have included multiculturalism, whole language, Vygotsky, DAP, and constructivism (p. 74). To Johnson (2000b), the euphoria associated with Reggio Emilia:

illustrates our fixation with out-dated, limited theoretical traditions (e.g. developmental psychology and child development), our atheoretical and anti-intellectual approach to conceptualizing the field (we seem to like safety and normative practices), and our ready identification of what is the truth (e.g. child-centered, play-based, individualistic curricula) and what is not the truth (i.e. phonics, worksheets, rote memory curricula). (p. 75)

Schutz (2004) leads us to ask how is it that the field has been colonized and dominated by outdated, atheoretical, and anti-intellectual approaches, and who is enmeshed in perpetuating these approaches and priming the field to wait for the next developmental, safe, child-centered, play-based "cult" to embrace? Furthermore, as a field we need to know how resistance is handled by the privileged and the dominated; and to identify the processes are that are integral to these systems of domination for the privileged, for those who resist, and for those who are dominated. And what of those who embody more than one of these categories, for instance, those who are both privileged and dominated, and who resist?

Finally, we reiterate that the fundamental argument of this chapter has been that research informed by postmodern theories has an important place when considering the education of young children. Because it offers opportunities for understanding beyond the reach of developmental psychology, research that is based on postmodern theories has begun to make distinctive contributions to the education of young children specifically in regard to pedagogy, curricula, policy, families, early childhood teacher education, and to how young children and childhood are understood. Moreover, theoretical tools such as poststructural deconstruction have the capacity to invert the unidirectional and hierarchical relationship of the theory-practice binary (where practice has always been positioned subordinately to theory), thus providing openings for the intermingling of theory and practice (and vice versa), and for the actions of children, parents, and practitioners to make theoretical contributions to the education of young children. The potential of research grounded in theories of the postmodern can be realized in exploring alternative understandings about the agency and positioning of children, families and practitioners, and the dimensions of power that are possible within such frames.

References

Adler, S. M. (2001). Racial and ethnic identity formation of Midwestern Asian-American children. *Contemporary Issues in Early Childhood, 2*(3), 265–294.

Alderson, P. (1995). *Listening to children: Children, ethics and social research*. Ilford: Barnardo's.

Alderson, P. (2000). Children as researchers: the Effects of participation rights on research methodology. In P. Christensen & A. James (Eds.), *Research with children: Perspectives and practices* (pp. 241–257). London: Falmer.

Alderson, P., & Goodney, C. (1996). Research with disabled children: How useful is child centred ethics? *Children and Society 10*, 106–116.

Alloway, N. (1995). *Foundation stones: The construction of gender in early childhood*. Carlton, Victoria: Curriculum Corporation.

Alloway, N. (2000). Exploring boys' literacy performance at school: Incorporating and transcending gender. *Contemporary Issues in Early Childhood, 1*(3), 333–337.

Alloway, N., & Gilbert, P. (Eds.). (1997a). *Boys and literacy: Professional development units*. Carlton, Victoria: Curriculum Corporation.

Alloway, N., & Gilbert, P. (Eds.). (1997b). *Boys and literacy: Teaching units*. Carlton, Victoria: Curriculum Corporation.

Alloway, N., & Gilbert, P. (2002). *Boys and literacy learning: Changing perspectives*. Watson, ACT: Australian Early Childhood Association.

Baker, B. M. (2001). *In perpetual motion: Theories of power, educational history, and the child*. New York: Peter Lang.

Barnett, W. S. (1996). Lives in the balance: Age 27 cost-benefit analysis of the High/Scope Perry preschool program. Ypsilanti, MI: High/Scope Press.

Belenky, M. F., Clinchy, B. M., Goldberger, N. R., & Tarule, J. M. (1986). *Women's ways of knowing: The development of self, voice, and mind*. New York: Basic Books.

Bergen, D. (1994). Should teachers permit or discourage violent play themes? *Childhood Education, 70*(5), 300–301.

Bernhard, J., Gonzalez-Mena, J., Chang, H., O'Loughlin, N., Eggers-Pierola, C., Fiati, G., & Corson, P. (1998). Recognizing the centrality of cultural diversity and racial equality: Beginning a discussion and critical reflection on developmentally appropriate practice. *Canadian Journal of Research in Early Childhood Education, 7*, 81–90.

Bernhard, J. K., Lefebvre, M. L., Chud, G., & Lange, R. (1995). *Paths to equity: Cultural, linguistic and racial diversity in Canadian early childhood education*. North York, ON: York Lanes Press.

Best, S., & Kellner, D. (1991). *Postmodern theory: Critical interrogations*. London: Macmillan.

Bloch, M. (1992). Critical perspectives in the historical relationship between child development and early childhood education research. In S. A. Kessler & B. B. Swadener (Eds.), *Reconceptualizing the early childhood curriculum: Beginning the dialogue* (pp. 3–20). New York: Teachers College Press.

Bloch, M. N. (2003). Global/local analyses of the construction of "Family-Child Welfare". In M. N. Bloch, K. Holmlund, I. Moqvist, I., & T. S. Popkewitz (Eds.), *Governing children, families and education: Restructuring the welfare state* (pp. 195–230). New York: Palgrave.

Bloch, M. N., Holmlund, K., Moqvist, I., & Popkewitz, T. S. (Eds.). (2003). *Governing children, families and education: Restructuring the welfare state*. New York: Palgrave.

Boldt, G. (1997). Sexist and heterosexist responses to gender bending. In J. Tobin (Ed.), *Making a place for pleasure in early childhood education* (pp. 188–213). New Haven: Yale University Press.

Boyd, B. J. (2002). Teacher response to superhero play: To ban or not to ban? In K. M. Paciorek (Ed.), *Taking sides: Clashing views on controversial issues in early childhood education* (pp. 96–103). Guilford, CA: McGraw-Hill/Dushkin.

Bredekamp, S. (Ed.). (1987). *Developmentally appropriate practice in early childhood programs serving children from birth through age 8* (Exp. ed.). Washington, DC: National Association for the Education of Young Children.

Bredekamp, S., & Copple, C. (Eds.). (1997). *Developmentally appropriate practice in early childhood programs* (Rev. ed.). Washington, DC: National Association for the Education of Young Children.

Britzman, D. P. (1995). Is there a queer pedagogy or, stop reading straight. *Educational Theory, 45*(2), 151–165.

Buchbinder, D. (1994). *Masculinities and identities*. Melbourne: Melbourne University Press.

Burbules, N. C., & Torres, C. A. (2000). Globalization and education: An introduction. In N.C. Burbules & C. A. Torres (Eds.), *Globalization and education: Critical perspectives* (pp. 1–26). New York: Routledge.

Burman, E. (1994). *Deconstructing developmental psychology*. London: Routledge.

Cameron, C., Moss., P., & Owen, C. (1999). *Men in the nursery: Gender and caring work*. London: Paul Chapman.

Campbell, S. & Smith, K. (2001). Equity observation and images if fairness in childhood. In S. Grieshaber & G. S. Cannella (Eds.), *Embracing identities in early childhood education: Diversity and possibilities* (pp. 89–102). New York: Teachers College Press.

Cannella, G. S. (1997). *Deconstructing early childhood education: Social justice and revolution*. New York: Peter Lang.

Cannella, G. S. (2003). Child welfare in the Unites States: The construction of gendered, oppositional discourse(s). In M. N. Bloch, K. Holmlund, I. Moqvist, I., & T. S. Popkewitz (Eds.), *Governing children, families and education: Restructuring the welfare state* (pp. 173–193). New York: Palgrave.

Cannella, G. S., & Bailey, C. (1999). Postmodern research in early childhood education. In S. Reifel (Ed.), *Advances in Early Education and Day Care* (Vol. 10, pp. 3–39). Greenwich, CI: JAI Press.

Cannella, G. S., & Viruru, R. (2004). *Childhood and postcolonialization: Power, education, and contemporary practice*. New York: RoutledgeFalmer.

Carrington, V. (2002). *New times: New families*. Dordrecht, The Netherlands: Kluwer.

Casper, V., & Schultz, S. B. (1999). *Gay parents/straight schools: Building communication and trust*. New York: Teachers College Press.

Cherryholmes, C. H. (1988). *Power and criticism: Poststructural investigations in education*. New York: Teachers College Press.

Christensen, P., & James, A. (2000a). Introduction: Researching children and childhood: Cultures of communication. In P. Christensen & A. James (Eds.), *Research with children: Perspectives and practices* (pp. 1–8). London: Falmer.

Christensen, P., & James, A. (Eds.). (2000b). *Research with children: Perspectives and practices*. London: Falmer.

Clay, J. (1990). Working with lesbian and gay parents and their children. *Young Children, 45*(2), 31–35.

Cleverley, J., & Phillips, C. (1987). *Visions of Childhood*. Sydney: Allen & Unwin.

Clyde, M. (1996). "Men should not be asked to pay nursemaid to young children": Bias in the workplace. In B. Creaser & E. Dau (Eds.), *The anti-bias approach in early childhood* (pp. 147-160). Sydney: Harper Educational.

Corbett, S. (1993). A complicated bias. *Young Children, 48*(3), 29-31.

Corsaro, W. (1997) *The Sociology of Childhood*. Thousand Oaks, CA: Pine Forge Press.

Crain, W. (2000). *Theories of development: Concepts and applications* (4th ed.). Upper Saddle River, NJ: Prentice Hall.

Dahlberg, G. Moss, P. & Pence, A. (1999). *Beyond quality in early childhood education and care: Postmodern perspectives*. London: Falmer.

Danby, S., & Baker, C. (1998). How to be masculine in the block area. *Childhood, 5*(12), 151-175.

Davies, B. (1989). *Frogs and snails and feminist tales: Preschool children and gender*. North Sydney, NSW: Allen & Unwin.

Davies, B. (1993). *Shards of glass*. Sydney: Allen and Unwin.

Davis, J., Watson, N., & Cunningham-Burley, S. (2000). Learning the lives of disabled children: Developing a reflexive approach. In P. Christensen & A. James (Eds.), *Research with children: Perspectives and practices* (pp. 201-224). London: Falmer.

Dunne, G. A. (1997). *Lesbian lifestyles: Women's work and the politics of sexuality*. Basingstoke: Macmillan.

Dyson, A. H. (1994). The Ninjas, the X-Men, and the ladies: Playing with power and identity in an urban primary school. *Teachers College Record, 96*, 219-239.

Dyson, A. H. (1996). Cultural constellations and childhood identities: On Greek gods, cartoon heroes, and the social lives of school children. *Harvard Educational Review, 66*, 471-495.

Dyson, A. H. (1997). *Writing superheroes: Contemporary childhood, popular culture, and classroom literacy*. New York: Teachers College Press.

Dyson, A. H. (1998). Folk processes and media creatures: Reflections on popular culture for literacy educators. *The Reading Teacher, 51*, 392-402.

Early, D. M., & Winton, P. J. (2001). Preparing the workforce: Early childhood teacher preparation at 2-and 4-year institutions of higher education. *Early Childhood Research Quarterly, 16*, 285-306.

Egan, K. (1983). *Education and psychology: Plato, Piaget, and scientific psychology*. New York: Teachers College Press.

Epstein, D. (1995). Girls don't do bricks. In J. & I. Siraj-Blatchford (Eds.), *Educating the whole child: Cross curricula skills, themes and dimensions* (pp. 56-69) Milton Keynes: The Open University Press.

Fein, G., & Schwartz, P. M. (1982). Developmental theories in early education. In B. Spodek (Ed.), *Handbook of research in education* (pp. 82-104). New York: The Free Press.

Foley, P., Roche, J., & Tucker, S. (2001). Foreword: Children in society: Contemporary theory, policy and practice. In P. Foley, J. Roche, & S. Tucker (Eds.), *Children in society: Contemporary theory, policy and practice* (pp. 1-6). Basingstoke: Palgrave.

Foucault, M. (1980). *Power/knowledge Selected interviews and other writings 1972-1977* (C. Gordon, L. Marshall, J. Mepham & K. Soper, Trans.). Brighton: Harvester.

Gallas, K. (1994). *The languages of learning: How children talk, write, dance, draw, and sing their understanding of the world*. New York: Teachers College Press.

Gallas, K. (1998). *"Sometimes I can be anything": Power, gender, and identity in a primary classroom*. New York, Teachers College Press.

García, E. E., & McLaughlin, B. (1995). Introduction. In E. E. García & B. McLaughlin (Eds.), *Meeting the challenge of linguistic and cultural diversity in early childhood education* (pp. vii–xxiii). New York: Teachers College Press.

Gandhi, L. (1998). *Postcolonial theory: A critical introduction*. St Leonards, NSW: Allen & Unwin.

Gee, J. P. (2001). Reading, language abilities, and semiotic resources: Beyond limited perspectives in reading. In J. Larson (Ed.), *Literacy as snake oil: Beyond the quick fix* (pp. 7-26). New York: Peter Lang.

Gee, J. P., Hull, G., & Lankshear, C. (1996). *The new work order: Behind the language of the new capitalism*. St Leonards, N. S. W.: Allen and Unwin.

Genishi, C. (Ed.). (1992). *Ways of assessing children and curriculum: Stories of early childhood practice*. New York: Teachers College Press.

Genishi, C., Ryan, S., Ochsner, M., & Yarnall, M. (2001). Teaching in early childhood education: Understanding practices through research and theory. In V. Richardson (Ed.), *Handbook of research on teaching* (4th ed., pp. 1175-1210). Washington, DC: American Educational Research Association.

Gilbert, R., & Gilbert, P. (1998). *Masculinity goes to school*. St. Leonards, N. S. W.: Allen & Unwin.

Gilligan, C. (1982). *In a different voice*. Cambridge, MA: Harvard University Press.

Goffin, S. (1996). Child development knowledge and early childhood teacher preparation: Assessing the relationship—A special collection. *Early Childhood Research Quarterly, 11*(2), 117-133.

Goldstein, L. (1997). *Teaching with love: A feminist approach to early childhood education*. New York: Peter Lang.

Goldstein, L. (1998). The distance between feminism and early childhood education: An historical perspective. In M. E. Hauser & J. A. Jipson (Eds.), *Intersections: Feminisms/early childhoods* (pp. 51-66). New York: Peter Lang.

Goodman, J. (1987). Masculinity, feminism, and the male elementary school teacher: A case study of preservice teachers'perspectives. *Journal of Curriculum Theorizing, 7*, 30-59.

Gorard, S., Rees, S., & Salisbury, J. (1999). Reappraising the apparent underachievement of boys at school. *Gender and Education, 11*(4), 441-454.

Graue, E., & Brown, C. P. (2003). Preservice teachers' notions of families and schooling. *Teaching and Teacher Education, 19*, 719-735.

Graue, E., Oen, D., & Shirley, V. (2004, April). *The immutability of preservive teachers ideas about home-school relations*. Paper presented at the Annual Meeting of the American Educational Research Association, San Diego, CA.

Greenberg, J. (1995). Making friends with the Power Rangers. *Young Children, 50*(5), 60-61.

Gronlund, G. (1992). Coping with Ninja Turtle play in my kindergarten classroom. *Young Children, 48*(1), 21-25.

Grieshaber, S. (1998). Constructing the gendered infant. In N. Yelland (Ed.), *Gender in early childhood* (pp. 15-35). London: Routledge.

Grieshaber, S. (2001) Equity issues in research design. In G. Mac Naughton, S. Rocco & I. Siraj-Blatchford (Eds.), *Researching early childhood* (pp. 136-146). Crows Nest, Australia: Allen & Unwin.

Grieshaber, S. (2004). *Rethinking parent and child conflict*. New York: RoutledgeFalmer.

Gutiérrez, K. D., & Rogoff, B. (2003). Cultural ways of learning: Individual traits or repertoires of practice. *Educational Researcher, 32*(5), 19-25.

Hampton, M. (2002). Limiting superhero play in classrooms: A philosophy statement. In K. M. Paciorek (Ed.), *Taking sides: Clashing views on controversial issues in early childhood education* (pp. 86-95). Guilford, CA: McGraw-Hill/Dushkin.

Harvey, D. (1990). *The condition of postmodernity: An enquiry into the origins of cultural change*. Oxford: Basil Blackwell.

Hatch, J. A. (2000). Introducing postmodern thought in a thoroughly modern university. In L. Diaz Soto (Ed.), *The politics of early childhood education* (pp. 179–193). New York: Peter Lang.

Hauser, M. E., & Marrero, E. (1998). Challenging curricular conventions: It is feminist pedagogy if you don't call it that? In M. E. Hauser & J. A. Jipson (Eds.), *Intersections: Feminisms/early childhoods* (pp. 161–176). New York: Peter Lang.

Hewett, K. A. (2001). Eh, No Act!: The power of being on the margin. In J. A. Jipson & R. T. Johnson (Eds.), *Resistance and representation: Rethinking childhood education* (pp. 117–123). New York: Peter Lang.

Hoover-Dempsey, K. M., & Sandler, H. M., (1997). Why do parents become involved in their children's education? *Review of Educational Research, 67*(1), 3–42.

Hughes, P., & MacNaughton, G. (2000). Consensus, dissensus or community: The politics of parent involvement in early childhood education. *Contemporary Issues in Early Childhood, 1*(3), 241–258.

International Reading Association (IRA) and the National Association for the Education of Young Children (NAEYC). (1998). *Learning to read and write: Developmentally appropriate practices for young children.* Retrieved 16 May, 2004, from http://www.naeyc.org/resources/position_statements/position_statement1.htm

James, A., Jenks, C. & Prout, A. (1998). *Theorizing childhood.* New York: Teachers College Press.

Jensen, J. J. (1996). *Men as workers in childcare services: A discussion paper.* London: European Commission Network on Childcare.

Jenks, C. (1982). Introduction: Constituting the child. In C. Jenks (Ed.), *The sociology of childhood: Essential readings* (pp. 9–24). London: Batsford Academic.

Jenks, C. (1996). *Childhood.* London: Routledge.

Jipson, J. (1992). The emergent curriculum: Contextualizing a feminist perspective. In S. Kessler & B. Swadener (Eds.), *Reconceptualizing the early childhood curriculum: Beginning the dialogue* (pp. 149–164). New York: Teachers College Press.

Johnson, R. T. (1997). The "no touch" policy. In J. Tobin (Ed.), *Making a place for pleasure in early childhood education* (pp. 101–118). New Haven, CT: Yale University Press.

Johnson, R. T. (2000a). *Hands off! The disappearance of touch in the care of children.* New York: Peter Lang.

Johnson, R. T. (2000b). Colonialism and cargo cults in early childhood education: Does Reggio Emilia really exist? *Contemporary Issues in Early Childhood, 1*(1), 61–78.

Jones, A. (2003). The monster in the room: Safety, pleasure and early childhood education. *Contemporary Issues in Early Childhood 4*(3), 235–250.

Jones, L. (2002). Derrida goes to nursery school: Deconstructing young children's stories. *Contemporary Issues in Early Childhood, 3*(1), 139–145.

Jordan, E. (1995). Fighting boys and fantasy play: The construction of masculinity in the early years of school. *Gender and Education, 7*(1), 69–86.

Jordan, E., & Cowan, A. (1995). Warrior narratives in the kindergarten classroom. *Gender and Society 9*(6), 727–743.

Kamler, B., Maclean, R., Reid, J., & Simpson, A. (1994). *Shaping up nicely: The formation of schoolgirls and schoolboys in the first month of school.* Canberra, ACT: Department of Employment, Education and Training.

Kaomea, J. (2001a). Dilemmas of an indigenous academic: A Native Hawaiian story. *Contemporary Issues in Early Childhood 2*(1), 67–82.

Kaomea, J. (2001b). Pointed noses and yellow hair: Deconstructing children's writing on race and ethnicity in Hawai'i. In J. A. Jipson & R. T. Johnson (Eds.), *Resistance and representation: Rethinking childhood education* (pp. 151–180). New York: Peter Lang.

Kaomea, J. (2003). Reading erasures and making the familiar strange: Defamiliarizing methods for research in formerly colonized and historically oppressed communities. *Educational Researcher, 32*(2), 14–26.

Kenway, J., & Bullen, E. (2001). *Consuming children: Education-entertainment-advertising.* Buckingham, UK: Open University Press.

Kessler, S. (1998). How does theorizing about feminisms help poor children? In M. E. Hauser & J. A. Jipson (Eds.), *Intersections: Feminisms/early childhoods* (pp. 177–204). New York: Peter Lang.

Kincheloe, J. L. (2002). The complex politics of McDonald's and the new childhood: Colonizing kidworld. In G. S. Cannella & J. L. Kincheloe (Eds.), *Kidworld: Childhood studies, global perspectives, and education* (pp. 75–121). New York: Peter Lang.

King, J. R. (1997). Keeping it quiet: Gay teachers in the primary grades. In J. Tobin (Ed.), *Making a place for pleasure in early childhood education* (pp. 235–250). New Haven, CT: Yale University Press.

King, J. R. (1998). *Uncommon caring: Learning from men who teach young children.* New York: Teachers College Press.

Kliebard, H. M. (1986). *The struggle for the American curriculum 1893–1958.* New York: Routledge.

Kostelnick, M. J., Whiren, A. P., & Stein, L. C. (1986). Living with He-man: Managing superhero fantasy play. *Young Children, 41*(4), 3–9.

Kroeger, J. (2001). A reconstructed tale of inclusion for a lesbian family in an early childhood classroom. In S. Grieshaber & G. S. Cannella (Eds.), *Embracing identities in early childhood education: Diversity and possibilities* (pp. 73–86). New York: Teachers College Press.

Larson, J., & Gatto, L. A. (2004). Tactical underlife: Understanding students' perceptions. *Journal of Early Childhood Literacy 4*(1), 11–42.

Lash, S., & Urry, J. (1987). *The end of organised capitalism.* Oxford: Basil Blackwell.

Lather, P. (1991). *Getting smart: Feminist research and pedagogy with/in the postmodern.* New York: Routledge.

Leavitt, R. L. (1994). *Power and emotion in infant-toddler day care.* Albany: SUNY.

Leavitt, R. L., & Power, M. B. (1997). Civilizing bodies: Children in day care. In J. Tobin (Ed.), *Making a place for pleasure in early childhood education* (pp. 39–75). New Haven: Yale University Press.

Lee, C. D. (2003). Why we need to re-think race and ethnicity in educational research. *Educational Researcher, 32*(5), 3–5.

Lee, J. (2002). Racial and ethnic achievement gap trends: Reversing the progress toward equity? *Educational Researcher, 31*(1), 3–12.

Lopez, A. M. (2003). Mixed-race school-age children: A summary of sensus 2000 data. *Educational Researcher, 32*(6), 25–37.

Lubeck, S. (1996). Deconstructing "child development knowledge" and "teacher preparation." *Early Childhood Research Quarterly, 11*(2), 147–167.

Lubeck, S. (1998a). Is developmentally appropriate practice for everyone? *Childhood Education, 74*(5), 283–292.

Lubeck, S. (1998b). Is DAP for everyone? A response. *Childhood Education, 74*(5), 299–301.

Luke, A., & Luke, C. (2001). Adolescence lost/childhood regained: On early intervention and the emergence of the techno-subject. *Journal of Early Childhood Literacy, 1*(1), 91–120.

MacNaughton, G. (1995). A post-structuralist analysis of learning in early childhood settings. In M. Fleer (Ed.), *DAPcentrism: Challenging developmentally appropriate practice* (pp. 25–54). Watson, ACT: Australian Early Childhood Association.

MacNaughton, G. (2000). *Rethinking gender in early childhood education*. St. Leonards, NSW: Allen & Unwin.

MacNaughton, G., & Davis, K. (2001). Beyond 'Othering': Rethinking approaches to teaching young Anglo-Australian children about indigenous Australians. *Contemporary Issues in Early Childhood, 2*(1), 83–93.

Mallory, B., & New, R. (Eds.). (1994). *Diversity and developmentally appropriate practices: Challenges for early childhood education*. New York: Teachers College Press.

McLeod, J. (2001). When poststructuralism meets gender. In K. Hultqvist & G. Dahlberg (Eds.), *Governing the child in the new millennium* (pp. 259–289). New York: RoutledgeFalmer.

Manyak, P. C. (2004). Literacy instruction, disciplinary practice, and diverse learners: A case study. *Journal of Early Childhood Literacy, 4*(1), 129–149.

Marsh, J. (1999). Batman and Batwoman go to school: Popular culture in the literacy curriculum. *International Journal of Early Years Education, 7*, 117–131.

Marsh, J. (2000a). 'But I want to fly too!': Girls and superhero play in the infant classroom. *Gender and Education, 12*(2), 209–220.

Marsh, J. (2000b). Teletubby tales: Popular culture in the early years language and literacy curriculum. *Contemporary Issues in Early Childhood, 1*(2), 119–133.

Masse, L. (2002). *A benefit-cost analysis of the Carolina Abercedarian preschool program*. Unpublished doctoral dissertation, Rutgers University, NJ.

Mayall, B. (1994) Introduction. In B. Mayall (Ed.) *Children's childhoods: Observed and experienced* (pp. 1–12). London; Washington, DC: Falmer Press.

Mayall, B., Hood, S., & Oliver, S. (1999). Introduction. In S. Hood, B. Mayall, & S. Oliver (Eds.), *Critical issues in social research: Power and prejudice* (pp. 1–9). Buckingham: Open University Press.

Minaya-Rowe, L. (Ed.) (2002). *Teacher training and effective pedagogy in the context of student diversity*. Greenwich, CT: Information Age Publishing.

Murray, S. B. (1996). 'We all love Charles': Men in child care and the social construction of gender. *Gender and Society, 10*(4), 368–385.

National Education Goals Panel. (1998). *The national educational education goals report. Building a nation of learners*. Washington, DC: National Education Goals Panel.

Noddings, N. (1984). *Caring*. Berkeley: University of California Press.

Oakley, A. (1999). People's ways of knowing: Gender and methodology. In S. Hood, B. Mayall, & S. Oliver (Eds.), *Critical issues in social research: Power and prejudice* (pp. 154–170). Buckingham: Open University Press.

O'Brien, P. (1999). New minds for new times: Education and the new work order. In D. Meadmore, B. Burnett, & P. O'Brien (Eds.), *Understanding education: Contexts and agendas for the new millennium* (pp. 106–115). Frenchs Forest, Australia: Prentice Hall—SprintPrint.

Orellana, M. F. (1994). Appropriating the Voice of the Superheroes: Three preschoolers bilingual language uses in play. *Early Childhood Research Quarterly, 9*(2), 171–193.

Orellana, M. F. (1999). Language, play, and identity formation: Framing data analyses. In B. Kamler (Ed.), *Constructing gender and difference: Critical research perspectives on early childhood* (pp. 97–117). Creskill, NJ: Hampton Press.

Pacini-Ketchabaw, V., & Schecter, S. (2002). Engaging the discourse of diversity: Educators' frameworks for working with linguistic and cultural difference. *Contemporary Issues in Early Childhood, 3*(3), 400–414.

Paley, V. G. (1984). *Boys and girls: Superheroes in the doll corner*. Chicago: University of Chicago Press.

Pollock, M. (2001). How the question we ask most about race in education is the very question we most suppress. *Educational Researcher 30*(9), 2–12.

Powderly, K., & Westlake, K. (1998). Men in child care. *Every Child, 4,* 9.

Pringle, K. (1998). Men and childcare: Policy and practice. In J. Popay, J. Hearn, & J. Edwards (Eds.), *Men, gender divisions and welfare* (pp. 312–336). London: Routledge.

Prochner, L. (2001). "The proof of the home is in the nursery": An American proverb revisited. In J. A. Jipson & R. T. Johnson (Eds.), *Resistance and representation: Rethinking childhood education* (pp. 205–221). New York: Peter Lang.

Prout, A., & James, A. (1997). A new paradigm for the sociology of childhood? Provenance, promise and problems. In A. James & A. Prout (Eds.), *Constructing and reconstructing childhood: Contemporary issues in the sociological study of childhood* (pp. 7–33). London: Falmer.

Punch, S. (2002). Research with children: The same or different from research with adults? *Childhood 9*(3), 321–341.

Qvortrup, J. (1997). A voice for children in statistical and social accounting: A plea for children's right to be heard. In A. James & A. Prout (Eds.), *Constructing and reconstructing childhood: Contemporary issues in the sociological study of childhood* (pp. 85–106). London: Falmer.

Reid, J. (1999). Little women/little men: Gender, violence and embodiment in an early childhood classroom. In B. Kamler (Ed.), *Constructing gender and difference: Critical perspectives on early childhood* (pp. 167–189). Creskill, NJ: Hampton Press.

Robb, M. (2001). Men working in childcare. In P. Foley, J. Roche, & S. Tucker (Eds.), *Children in society: Contemporary theory, policy and practice* (pp. 230–238). Basingstoke, UK: Palgrave.

Roberts, H. (2000). Listening to children: and Hearing them. In P. Christensen & A. James (Eds.), *Research with children: Perspectives and practices* (pp. 225–240). London: Falmer.

Robinson, K. H. (2002). Making the invisible visible: Gay and lesbian issues in early childhood education. *Contemporary Issues in Early Childhood, 3*(3), 415–434.

Ruxton, S. (1992). *"What's he doing at the family centre?" The dilemmas of men who care for children: A research report*. London: National Children's Home.

Ruxton, S. (1994). Men: Too dangerous to work with children? *Working with Men, 1*, 16–20.

Ryan, S. K., & Grieshaber, S. (2005). Shifting from developmental to postmodern practices in early childhood teacher education. *Journal of Teacher Education, 56*(1), 34–45.

Ryan, S. K., & Grieshaber, S. (2004, April). *Early Childhood in the Spotlight: Critically Appraising the Current Policy Interest in Educating Young Children*. Paper presented at the Annual Meeting, American Educational Research Association, San Diego.

Ryan, S., & Ochsner, M. (1999). Traditional practices, new possibilities: Transforming dominant images of early childhood teachers. *Australian Journal of Early Childhood, 24*(4), 14–20).

Ryan, S., Ochsner, M., & Genishi, C. (2001). Miss Nelson is missing! Teacher sightings in research and teaching. In S. Grieshaber & G. S. Cannella (Eds.), *Embracing identities in early childhood education: Diversity and possibilities* (pp. 45–59). New York: Teachers College Press.

Saracho, O. N., & Spodek, B. (1995). Preparing teachers for early childhood programs of linguistic and cultural diversity. In E. E. García & B. McLaughlin (Eds.), *Meeting the challenge of linguistic and cultural diversity in early childhood education* (pp. 154–169). New York: Teachers College Press.

Schutz, A. (2004). Rethinking domination and resistance: Challenging postmodernism. *Educational Researcher, 33*(1), 15-23.

Schweinhart, L. (2002). Making validated educational models central in preschool standards. Retrieved June 7, 2004, from http://nieer.org/resources/research/schweinhart.pdf

Scott, K. A. (2002). "You want to be a girl and not my friend": African-American/Black girls' play activities with and without boys. *Childhood, 9*(4), 397-414.

Siefert, K. (1973). Some problems of men in child care center work. *Child Welfare, 102*(3), 167-171.

Silin, J. G. (1987). The early educator's knowledge base: A reconsideration. In L. G. Katz (Ed.), *Current topics in early childhood educations* (pp. 17-31). Norwood, NJ: Ablex.

Silin, J. G. (1995). *Sex death and the education of children: Our passion for ignorance in the age of aids.* New York: Teachers College Press.

Silin, J. G. (1997). The pervert in the classroom. In J. Tobin (Ed.), *Making a place for pleasure in early childhood education* (pp. 214-234). New Haven, CT: Yale University Press.

Simpson, A. (1999). I had it first! Children and power. In B. Kamler (Ed.), *Constructing gender and difference: Critical research perspectives on early childhood* (pp. 119-151). Cresskill, NJ: Hampton Press.

Skelton, C. (1991). A study of the career perspectives of male teachers of young children. *Gender and Education, 3*, 279-289.

Smith, K. (2000). Reconceptualising the role of parents in observation. *Australian Journal of Early Childhood, 25*(2), 18-21.

Soto, L. D., & Swadener, B. B. (2002). Toward liberatory early childhood theory, research and praxis: Decolonizing a field. *Contemporary Issues in Early Childhood, 3*(1), 38-66.

Spodek, B. (1977). What constitutes worthwhile educational experiences for young children? In B. Spodek (Ed.), *Teaching practices: Reexamining assumptions* (pp. 5-20). Washington, DC: National Association for the Education of Young Children.

Spodek, B. (Ed.). (1993). *Handbook of research on the education of young children.* New York: Macmillan.

Sumsion, J. (1999). Critical reflections on the experiences of a male early childhood worker. *Gender and Education, 11*, 455-468.

Sumsion, J. (2000a). Oppositional discourses: Deconstructing responses to investigations of male early childhood educators. *Contemporary Issues in Early Childhood, 1*(3), 259-275.

Sumsion, J. (2000b). Rewards and risks: Tensions experienced by men enrolled in an early childhood teacher education program. *Asia Pacific Journal of Teacher Education, 28*, 87-100.

Sumsion, J. (2000c). Negotiating otherness: A male early childhood educator's gender positioning. *International Journal of Early Years Education, 8*, 129-140.

Swadener, B. B., & Lubeck, S. (1995). The social construction of children and families "at risk": An introduction. In B. B. Swadener & S. Lubeck (Eds.), *Children and families "at promise": Deconstructing the discourse of risk* (pp. 1-14). Albany: State University of New York Press.

Theilheimer, R., & Cahill, B. (2001). A messy closet in the early childhood classroom. In S. Grieshaber & G. S. Cannella (Eds.), *Embracing identities in early childhood education: Diversity and possibilities* (pp. 103-113). New York: Teachers College Press.

Thorne, B. (1993). *Gender play: Boys and girls in school.* Buckingham: Open University Press.

Thorne, B. (2002). Editorial. From silence to voice: Bringing children more fully into knowledge. *Childhood, 9*(3), 251-254.

Tillman, L. C. (2002). Culturally sensitive research approaches: An African-American perspective. *Educational Researcher 31*(9), 3-12.

Titus, J. J. (2004). Boy trouble: Rhetorical framing of boys' underachievement. *Discourse: Studies in the cultural politics of education, 25*(2), 145-169.

Tobin, J. (1995). Post-structural research in early childhood education. In J. A. Hatch (Ed.), *Qualitative research in early childhood settings* (pp. 223-243). Westport, CT: Praeger.

Tobin, J. (1997a). Playing doctor in two cultures. In J. Tobin (Ed.), *Making a place for pleasure in early childhood education* (pp. 119-158). New Haven, CT: Yale University Press.

Tobin, J. (1997b). The missing discourse of pleasure and desire. In J. Tobin (Ed.), *Making a place for pleasure in early childhood education* (pp. 1-37). New Haven, CT: Yale University Press.

Tobin, J. (2000). *Good guys don't wear hats: Children's talk about the media.* New York: Teachers College Press.

Usher, R., & Edwards, R. (1994). *Postmodernism and education.* London: Routledge.

Vandell, D. L., & Wolfe, B. (2000). *Child care quality: Does it matter and does it need to be improved?* Madison: Institute for research on Poverty, University of Wisconsin.

Viruru, R. (2001a). *Early childhood education: Postcolonial perspectives from India.* New Delhi: Sage.

Viruru, R. (2001b). Colonized through language: The case of early childhood education. *Contemporary Issues in Early Childhood 2*(1), 31-47.

Viruru, R., & Cannella, G. S. (2001). Postcolonial ethnography, young children, and voice. In S. Grieshaber & G. S. Cannella (Eds.), *Embracing identities in early childhood education: Diversity and possibilities* (pp. 158-172). New York: Teachers College Press.

Walkerdine, V. (1981). Sex power and pedagogy. *Screen Education, 38*, 14-21.

Walkerdine, V. (1984). Developmental psychology and the child-centred pedagogy: The insertion of Piaget into early education. In J. Henriques, W. Hollway, C. Urwin, C. Venn, & V. Walkerdine (Eds.), *Changing the subject: Psychology, social regulation and subjectivity* (pp. 153-202). London: Methuen.

Warner, M. (1993). *Fear of a queer planet: Queer politics and social theory.* Minneapolis: University of Minnesota Press.

Weber, E. (1984). *Ideas influencing early childhood education: A theoretical analysis.* New York: Teachers College Press.

Wickens, E. (1993). Penny's question: 'I will have a child in my class with two mums—what do you know about this?' *Young Children, 48*(3), 25-28.

Wilson Keenan, J. Solsken, J., & Willett, J. (1999). "Only boys can jump high": Reconstructing gender relations in a first/second-grade classroom. In B. Kamler (Ed.), *Constructing gender and difference: Critical perspectives on early childhood* (pp. 33-70). Creskill, NJ: Hampton Press.

Wyness, M. G. (2000). *Contesting childhood.* London and New York: Falmer.

EARLY CHILDHOOD EDUCATION RESEARCH
IN CROSS-NATIONAL PERSPECTIVE

Jaipaul L. Roopnarine
Aysegul Metindogan
Syracuse University

The title of this chapter is somewhat of a misnomer, given that early childhood educators have devoted considerably more energy toward studying within culture rather than cross-national similarities and differences in early childhood education practices and outcomes (see volumes by Feeney, 1992; Hayden, 2000). With a shorter history, cross-national early childhood education research is more limited in its focus and scope (e.g., Lamb, Sternberg, Hwang, & Broberg, 1992; Olmsted & Weikart, 1995; Tietze, Cryer, Bairrao, Palacios, & Wetzel, 1996; Tobin, Wu, & Davidson, 1989). Noting this, we shape our chapter in more general terms around research that has been conducted within and across cultures. Coalescing hard data on different early childhood education models across cultures remains cumbersome, if not daunting. Despite the richness evident in the quantitative and qualitative accounts of early childhood education research in different cultures, there is tremendous variability in terms of the quality and rigor of the studies that contribute to this thin but growing literature.

Early childhood education today is guided by diverse disciplines (e.g., child development, psychological anthropology and cross-cultural psychology, history and folklore, pediatrics) (see Jahoda & Krewer, 1997; Super & Harkness, 1997) and an expanding knowledge base on childhood development across cultural and ethnic groups (Comunian & Gielen, 2000; Gielen & Roopnarine, 2004; Laosa, 1999; LeVine, 2004; Shweder et al., 1998). At the same time, academic discourses on intracultural and intercultural variations in early childhood education have grown steadily (Katz, 1989, 2003; Lubeck, Jessup, & Jewekes, 2003). The latter has been aided, in part, by the formation of international and regional early childhood organizations (e.g., Association of Childhood Education International-ACEI;

International Association for Children's Right to Play; World Congress for Toys, Games, and Media; European Early Childhood Educational Research Association; Pacific Early Childhood Educational Research Association; Caribbean Early Childhood Association; Council for Early Childhood Association and Services-Hong Kong; The Consultative Group on Early Childhood Care and Development) and specific academic outlets for research publications on culture and development (e.g., *International Journal of Early Childhood; Early Childhood Research Quarterly; International Journal of Psychology; International Journal of Behavioral Development; Journal of Cross-Cultural Psychology; European Journal of Research in Early Childhood Education,* to name a few).

It is safe to say that more than ever before, people across cultures are sharing common information about what we know about childhood development and learning (e.g., acquisition of basic cognitive and social skills), diverse methods of childrearing (e.g., individualistic-collectivistic, transnational parenting, or parenting across geographic borders), and how to educate young children in an increasingly global community (e.g., culturally and developmentally appropriate practices and academically oriented programs; Bredekamp & Copple, 1997; Gielen & Chumachenko, 2004; Jipson, 1991; Lillemyr, Fagerli, & Sobstad, 2001; Robinson, 2003; Tobin, 1998).

A major goal of this chapter is to provide an overview of two common types of early childhood education research in different regions of the world: cultural and cross-national. In line with the suggestions of researchers of culture and childhood development (e.g., Greenfield, 1997), we find the cultural and cross-cultural frameworks more appropriate and complementary in interpreting early childhood education research compared with other formulations on multicultural education (e.g., cultural competence; skilled dialogue; Barrera, Corso, & Macpherson, 2003). Besides, the cultural approach meshes well with contextually appropriate practice (CAP; Woodhead, 1997).

As can be deduced from the various chapters in this volume, early childhood education research covers a vast terrain: curriculum philosophies, contents and goals, parental ethnotheories about early education, policies, staffing, private and public regulations, parental involvement, parental leave, administration, and assessments of cognitive and social outcomes, among others. Obviously, it would be impossible to summarize every aspect of the vast early childhood international literature in a single chapter. Thus, we target parental beliefs about early education and care, early childhood curricula, the efficacy of early childhood education practices, and process quality in day care. Our emphasis is on preschool and kindergarten-age children, including those in day care, with occasional reference to grade school children. Most early childhood programs worldwide serve children between 3 and 6 years of age. Compulsory education for most societies begins between 6 and 7 years of age (UNESCO, 2003).

Before proceeding, a few qualifications are necessary. There are projects conducted within particular regions and reports published in different languages that we were unable to access. Thus, our review is far from complete because of its overreliance on materials published in English. In addition to journal articles and UNESCO reports, there are several volumes that aided our current mission: *Preschool in Three Cultures: Japan, China, and the United States* (Tobin, Wu, & Davidson, 1989), *Early Childhood Education in Asia and the Pacific* (Feeney & Naroll, 1992), *Child Care in Context* (Lamb et al., 1993), *International Handbook of Early Childhood Education* (Wodill, Bernhard, & Prochner, 1992), *Early Childhood Services: Theory, Policy, and Practice* (Woodhead, 2000), *International Handbook of Childcare Policies and Programs* (Cochran, 1993), *Globalization and Education: Critical Perspectives* (Burbules & Torres (2000), *The IEA Preprimary Study: Early Childhood Education and Care in 11 Countries* (Olmsted & Weikart, 1995), *The First Five Years: A Critical Perspective on Early Childhood Care and Education in India* (Swaminathan, 1998), *Bambini* (Gandini & Edwards, 2001), *Contested Childhood: Diversity and Change in Japanese Preschools* (Holloway, 2000), *Kindergartens and Culture: The Global Diffusion of an Idea* (Wollons, 2000), and other publications on the changing nature of early childhood education and care in Russia (Ispa, 1994), Australia (Brennan, 1998) and New Zealand (May, 2001).

There is a sizable body of work on intervention for infants and toddlers with developmental disabilities and neurological impairments (Guralnick, 2003) and on providing educational and other services for children with disabilities in different parts of the world (Odom, Hanson, & Kaul, 2003). We eschew much of the research on children with disabilities. Attempts to provide "thick description" (Geertz, 1973) of early childhood education can lead to oversimplification of key issues of importance to the field. Hence, we stick to phenomena that are germane to early childhood education for children without disabilities. The struggle to determine what information to include in a review of the literature is not uncommon in the social sciences and education (see D'Andrade, 2004).

Because most children live in the developing societies, and good descriptions of the education and care of children in postindustrialized countries already exist (e.g., Bertram & Pascal, 1999; Feeney, 2001; Gandini & Edwards, 2001; Klein, 1996; Lamb, 1998; Lee, 2001; Lubeck, Jessup, & Jewkes, 2001; Nager & Shapiro, 2000; Olmstead & Weikart, 1995; Reynolds, 2000; Roopnarine & Johnson, 2005; Weis, Altbach, Kelly, & Petrie, 1991), we attempt to devote a little more attention to early childhood education in other regions of the world. For the purpose of this chapter, developing societies include the less economically endowed and the economically emerging nations of Asia, Latin America and the Caribbean, Africa, and Eastern Europe. A number of countries in these regions are undergoing significant transformations demographically, politically, socially, and economically (see World by Income, World Bank 2002), whereas others are mired in the throes of perpetual poverty.

CONTRASTING REALITIES IN THE LIVES OF CHILDREN GLOBALLY

Of the estimated 2.175 billion children under 18 in the postindustrialized and the developing societies of the world, about 800 million are between 0 and 6 years of age (Lillemyr et al., 2001). A majority of young children are nonwhite, non-European, and live in Africa, Asia, and the Caribbean and Latin America (World Data Bank, 2002). Only about a third are affected by early childhood education (Lillemyr et al., 2001). The everyday lives of young children in the post industrialized and developing societies are governed by contrasting realities grounded in diverse economic, health, and political systems, familial arrangements, religious traditions and customs, gendered ideologies, educational opportunities, and family socialization beliefs, goals, and practices (see volumes by Gielen & Roopnarine, 2004; Roopnarine & Gielen, 2005). Not surprisingly, among childhood experiences and difficulties, psychological and educational risks associated with wars, ethnic conflicts, living in the street, child abuse and neglect, pediatric AIDS, and poverty have raised the most anxieties among professionals and lay persons alike (Aptekar, 2004; Melton, 1992). Paradoxically, in the face of such dramatic differences in children's daily lives, there are convergences in childhood and educational experiences across societies that are driven, in part, by increased globalization (Arnett, 2001; Lee, 2001). A few scholars (see Arnett, 2001; Gielen & Roopnarine, 2004) point to changes in childrearing beliefs and practices as consequences of stepped-up globalization (see Adler & Gielen, 2003).

Rates of enrollment in early childhood education programs constitute one barometer of the commitment by nations to assist children in improving their life chances economically, socially, and educationally. In developing nations, lower educational attainment is associated with the increased likelihood of economic and social exploitation, poor family planning, and a life condemned to physical labor (Gielen & Chumachenko, 2004). Behind this realization are continued population growth, the changing demographics of family structural configurations (e.g., single parents; dual-earner couples; trial families), challenges to traditional masculine-feminine roles in childrearing (see Roopnarine & Gielen, 2005), emphasis on educating children who live in poverty, and a growing awareness of the need for high-quality early childhood education and care in most countries (e.g., Guyana's Educational Plan for revising preprimary education; Ministry of Education Document: Sukhdeo, 2004; Morrison & Milner, 1999). The early childhood years have long been recognized as a period during which children acquire a number of social and cognitive skills that place them on a solid foundation toward building positive attitudes about school and schooling later on—the great multiplier effect, if you will (see Gilliam & Zigler, 2000; Goldbeck, 1999; Marcon, 1999; Myers, 1992; Reynolds, 2000; Weikart & Schweinhart, 2005; Zigler, Taussig, & Black, 1992). Still, there are gaping disparities in preschool enrollments between the developed and developing societies.

Undoubtedly, economic and other resources (e.g., trained teachers, materials, physical environment) and public will and commitment are at the heart of each nation's desire and ability to implement education programs and childcare services for young children. According to Kamerman (1999), in the OECD countries, national policies, public commitment and pressures, and the establishment and enforcement of regulations have influenced early childhood enrollments during the latter half of the last century. As a result, early childhood enrollment (3-5 years) became pervasive in Italy and France and in the Nordic countries (0-6 years) (Kamerman & Kahn, 1996). In the United States, day care and early education continue to exist side by side but somewhat autonomously. In short, the OECD countries have entrenched early childhood education and childcare programs that are well subsidized and geared towards preparing children for life in the information age (see Gandini & Edwards, 2001; Lamb et al., 1992; Olmsted & Weikart, 1995). Additionally, the postindustrialized countries have the ability to expend more resources on compensatory education for economically disadvantaged children and children with disabilities (see Kamerman, 1999; Reynolds, 2000; Powell, 2005; Zigler & Styfco, 2004).

By contrast, developing countries struggle to meet the basic educational, medical, and nutritional needs of young children. In some regions, early childhood enrollment patterns are closer to those in postindustrialized countries. But patterns of enrollment fluctuate dramatically and are not always tied to a country's economic status (e.g., Guyana, a poor nation, has a 98% preschool enrollment rate). Bangladesh, Egypt, Ethiopia, Nepal, Saudi Arabia, Senegal, and certain Eastern European countries have some of the lowest preprimary enrollments in the world (Range = 2-25%; Digest of Education Statistics, 2003).

CONCEPTUAL AND METHODOLOGICAL ISSUES: CULTURAL AND CROSS-CULTURAL RESEARCH

In view of the content covered in this chapter, we would be remiss in not pursuing a discussion on conceptual and methodological issues that are central to the organization and

interpretation of research on culture and childhood development. Cultural and cross-cultural studies are grounded in different albeit related ancestral traditions. They speak to within and between group variations and their respective meanings for understanding pancultural and local principles of human development and education (the classic *etic* and *emic* views in interpreting educational and psychological phenomena; see Berry, 1989; Gielen, 2004; Greenfield, 1997; Shweder et al., 1998; Super & Harkness, 1997). Furthermore, increased sophistication in the design of instruments for collecting data and analytical strategies for reducing data have enabled us to more capably address issues such as cultural equivalence (e.g., mean differences and similarities and slope differences and similarities together) and within culture variations (see Krishnakumar, Buehler, & Barber, 2004; Van De Vijver & Leung, 1997).

Conceptual Issues

Accepting that an omnicultural portrait of early childhood education research across the world would be virtually impossible at this time, we turn to the two fairly well established conceptual approaches referred to above to assist us in organizing and interpreting some of what we know about early childhood education across cultures. The first, cultural, has its roots in psychological anthropology—bridging anthropological and psychological principles—whereas the second, cross-cultural, is more in step with logical positivism, which has governed much of the work in its parent discipline, the psychological sciences (Greenfield, 1997; Jahoda & Krewer, 1997). Although both paradigms have as their core mission to "unpack" the role of culture in human development, they are set apart by important demarcations (see Greenfield, 1997).

In a way, early childhood education researchers (e.g., Gandini & Edwards, 2001; Kagan, 2003; Ladson-Billings, 2000; Roopnarine et al., 2003; Tobin et al., 1989; Tobin, 1998) are keenly aware of the need to examine culture as process. In line with the tenets of cultural psychology, early childhood researchers see cultural beliefs and practices as key to understanding educational and childcare processes in the home and school environments. There is wide acceptance that the young child shapes and is shaped by its developmental niche and microniche (Super & Harkness, 1997; Weisner, 1998). Emphasis is on within-ethnic group or within-country variations. This is not to say that between-group and cross-indigenous differences are ignored (Kim & Berry, 1993; Morelli, Rogoff, Oppenheim, & Goldsmith, 1992). However, early childhood researchers also utilize culture as an independent or antecedent variable for comparative purposes (e.g., Chen & He, 2005; Farver & Shin, 1997). Phenomena (e.g., levels of cooperation, aggression, shyness, and social inhibition) present in one culture are explored in others with the goal of finding common ground in shared meaning or universal trends (see Greenfield, 1997, for a more detailed discussion). Note that a distinction has been made between Type I universals tied to phylogenetic inheritance (e.g., language, perception) and Type II universals that are more prone to environmental influences over longer durations (Horowitz, 1987). Despite the logic of their empirical bent, the cultural and cross-cultural frameworks have had a crucial role in guiding early childhood education research within and across cultures.

The conceptual question for early childhood education researchers in the 21st century is this: Will the cultural and cross-cultural paradigms maintain their adequacy for framing the educational needs of young children in a period of rapid change? The two-way flow of professional, cultural, and personal knowledge about childrearing and early education between the postindustrialized (e.g., developmentally appropriate practices; child-centered training, democracy in the classroom) and developing societies through digital communities, cultural exchanges, and contemporary global consumerism (McWorld syndrome; Robinson, 2003) have forced us to reflect and modify firmly established goals and practices in raising and educating young children. As an example, societies that were once steeped in collectivistic childrearing ideologies must contend with children who defy long-held customs in childrearing because they increasingly come face to face with conflicting information and ideas stemming from outside their own culture (Arnett, 2001). A form of childhood transnationalism is emerging where children come to identify with multiple cultural mores. Young children in some immigrant groups in the developed world already forge multiple cultural alliances through their parents' insistence that natal culture values be maintained alongside those present in their new communities. These children are likely to develop hybrid or self-selected identities (Roopnarine, Bynoe, & Singh, 2004). These are but a few of the changes that present contradictions between traditional ways of educating children and modern efforts to design early childhood programs that consider the local and global culture in the context of delocalization and global consciousness (Arnett, 2001; Tomlinson, 1999). Will early childhood education practices change the culture or will the culture change early childhood education practices?

Methodological and Analytical Issues

As indicated, quantitative and qualitative methodological and analytical procedures (Greenfield, 1997; Krishnakumar et al., 2004; Poortinga, 1997; Van De Vijver & Leung, 1997) have been adequately applied to early childhood education research. However, simply employing "culture as an explanatory variable is not satisfactory, and culture must be deconstructed into a set of psychologically meaningful constructs, which are then used to explain the cultural differences observed" (Van De Vijver & Leung, 1997, p. 260). In other words, using culture as an independent variable to determine group differences without appropriate sampling and determination of cultural equivalence of observational/assessment instruments prior to data analysis would provide a false picture as to the culture's role in human and educational development. Mean group comparisons alone may not tell us what specifically in the culture is responsible for potential differences on dependent measures (Van De Vijver & Leung, 1997).

In the main, both ethnographic and quantitatively oriented research in the early childhood education area has assessed social and cognitive competence with related instruments and procedures presumed to have identical or shared meaning across cultural groups. As will become clear, cultures not only define growth and competence differently, beliefs about early childhood education practices vary markedly (Roopnarine et al., 2003; Super & Harkness, 1997) and could possibly confound shared meaning of findings specific to cross-national comparisons. Of relevance here are determinations of cross-cultural equivalence in constructs and research findings in more quantitatively based research—although qualitative approaches are not entirely immune to this problem. A few seminal questions cut to the core of the issue. Do indicators of psychological adjustment, social skills, and cognitive competence among young children have the same basic conceptual and iterative meaning across cultures? Are mean group differences in young children's social and cognitive skills across cultures accurately depicting cultural differences? What is the meaning of quality early childhood education as defined by class size, teacher-child ratios, per pupil spending, appropriate/inappropriate behaviors, and so on across cultures? Answers to these questions are critical in evaluating the merit of cross-cultural early childhood research.

There are two points we wish to make here. First of all, indicators of social and cognitive functioning must have the same meaning across cultures on a conceptual and psychometric plane in order to make meaningful inferences about cultural differences. Concern is with structural, scalar, and measurement unit equivalence (Van De Vijver & Leung, 1997). The psychometric properties of a wide number of cognitive and social scales of measurement developed and standardized in North America and Europe have not been sufficiently assessed either through confirmatory or exploratory factor analysis on cross-cultural or cross-ethnic samples. How items on scales of measurement load on the same constructs and the strength of coefficients on individual items for different cultural groups lay the foundation for more meaningful group comparisons of children's cognitive and social functioning. Furthermore, as item response theory suggests, there needs to be a test of differential item functioning (Holland & Thayer, 1988). Simply assessing the internal consistency of measurement instruments, a common practice, may convey little about the relevance of each item for different cultures. Individuals in some cultures may find certain items or questions more appealing and others repugnant, and can more readily determine degrees of differences in responses on some items and not others. As a result, their responses to items or questions could be swayed. Through appropriate statistical techniques (i.e., item characteristic curves and Chi-Square), biased items must be discarded until identical items that eventually form a scale show the same statistical properties for each group under study (see Van De Vijver & Leung, 1997).

EARLY CHILDHOOD EDUCATION RESEARCH GLOBALLY

For all the focus on the rights and welfare of young children globally, with rare exceptions (e.g., Rao, Koong, Kwong, & Wong, 1999; Soderman, Chhikara, Hsiu-Ching, & Kuo, 1999), most of the within and cross-national empirical work on the efficacy and meaning of early childhood education is confined to the postindustrialized societies. Moreover, educational accounts of early childhood education in the developing societies tend to be less data-based and largely descriptive in nature, detailing the evolution of early childhood education, government expenditures, demographic characteristics, the needs of young children and their rights, teacher/caregiver training, and tensions between teaching children to read and write and respecting children's individual needs. For example, considerations of early education in Jamaica, Ghana, Fiji, Nigeria, South Africa, India, Singapore, Bahrain, Turkey, Nepal, Eritrea, Kenya, Laos, Malaysia, Chile, Mexico, and Hong Kong all outline the state of early childhood education with little attention given to systematic assessments of cognitive and social outcomes (Agrawal & Kanta, 1990; Ahuja, Sharma, & Tiwari, 2000; Andreoni, 1997; Bekman, 1993; Cisneros-Cohernour, Moreno, & Cisneros, 2000; Crane, 1998; Eckstein, 1994; Emblen, 1998; Hadeed, 1993; Joshi, 1996; Lijadu, 1993; Mathisen, Herrera, Merino, Villalon, & Suzuky, 2000; Miller, 1999; Morrison, 2000; Morrison & Milner, 1997; Njideka, 1999; Oktay & Zembat, 1995; Rao & Koong, 2000; Swadener, Kabiru, & Njenja, 1997; Raban & Ure, 1999; Swaminathan, 1998b). This is understandable due to concerted efforts by developing nations to establish different health and educational programs for young children amid competition for resources. Accordingly, following the cultural perspective, when cross-national comparisons are not inherent in accounts of early childhood education, differences/similarities are made from within culture descriptions of early childhood education research.

"DESIRED" CHARACTERISTICS OF YOUNG CHILDREN AND BELIEFS ABOUT EARLY EDUCATION ACROSS CULTURES

Acknowledging that the impact of contemporary globalization on childhood development and education is now being studied (see Arnett, 2001; Burbules & Torres, 2000) and that worldwide cultures are witnessing remarkable transitions in terms of (re)defining childrearing goals and the educational needs of young children (e.g., childcare; methods of discipline; technological versus social intelligence; family-centered versus child-centered training; developmentally appropriate/inappropriate practices), we provide a synopsis of parental beliefs about "desired" childhood behaviors and early childhood education practices across cultures. The findings from the different studies were gathered using questionnaires, structured and semistructured interviews, and observations. Most studies used small, nonrandom middle-class samples and employed qualitative and quantitative methodologies.

The underlying significance of childrearing beliefs or internal working models for childhood development and the structuring of everyday social and educational experiences for children have been discussed in other publications (Goodnow & Collins, 1991; Roopnarine et al., 2002; Sigel & McGillicuddy-De Lisi, 2002; Super & Harkness, 1997). Associations have been established between parental beliefs about children's competencies

and children's perceptions of their own competencies on academic subjects and between parental beliefs and later academic performance (Hortacsu, 1995; Jacobs, 1991; McGillicuddy-De Lisi & Subramanian, 1994), aggression (Hastings & Rubin, 1999), and health and physical well-being (Engle, Zeitlin, Medrano & Garcia, 1996). Understanding ideas about what is valued in childhood behavioral and cognitive development and what is expected of early childhood education programs may shed light on what drives early childhood education practices in different cultures. In addition, we may be better able to discern the responsibilities of schools and parents in children's academic and emotional development (Stevenson, Lee, & Schweingruber, 1999).

In a recent paper, LeVine (2004) convincingly argues against making population level generalizations when it comes to designating what are appropriate and inappropriate childhood behaviors. Evaluative criteria for an "intelligent child" and "a competent child" vary within (e.g., social class, family structure, gender) (Ogbu, 1981) and between cultural and ethnic groups (see Holloway et al., 1995; Holloway, 2000; Okagaki & Sternberg, 1993). Ostensibly, applying a universal metric to common early childhood behaviors such as good manners, obedience, cooperation, autonomy, interdependence, emotional connection to others, assertiveness, and academic prowess is elusive at best. Often class and culture/ethnicity are confounded. Similarly, within culture variations receive far less attention than between culture variations.

Furthermore, depending on economic and environmental conditions, parental goals for the health, education, and overall well-being of children are arranged hierarchically across cultures (LeVine, 1974). Parents and teachers, consciously and subconsciously, put cultural scripts to work to help children achieve a definition of the self and to acquire the moral and social values that are required of life within given cultural communities (Super & Harkness, 1997). It is highly unlikely that these scripts remain static. Some of the goals and expectations for young children within and across cultures are reframed over time, whereas others succumb to the pressures of global changes (Arnett, 2001; Dubrow, 1999).

Beginning with English-speaking Caribbean countries (e.g., Barbados, Guyana, Trinidad and Tobago, Jamaica, Antigua, Grenada, St. Kitts, St. Lucia, and Belize), when asked about their beliefs about childhood competence and their behavioral expectations of young children, low-income, African- and Indo-Caribbean parents see "good children" as academically competent, cooperative, respectful, compliant, and obedient (Dubrow, 1999; Roopnarine & Brown, 1997; Wilson, Wilson, & Berkeley-Caines, 2003). Broadly speaking, some of these same characteristics are desired of children among East Indian (Kakar, 1991), Turkish (Sunar & Fisek, 2005), and Egyptian parents (Ahmed, 2005), although intergenerational differences have been found in encouragement of independence and open expression of ideas by children in Turkey (Sever, 1989).

Other attempts have been made to understand what contributes to the development of "a moral" or "a good" child. Middle-class, suburban Japanese parents, teachers, professors, and children who are between $6\frac{1}{2}$ and 7 years and enrolled in a traditional kindergarten were asked about their views on *Sunao*. Japanese children suggested that *Sunao* means being gentle, mild, kind, and helping parents at home (a good child-iiko), whereas adults saw *Sunao* as a part of the child's personality development that involves displaying one's thoughts honestly, being able to maintain interpersonal harmony, and the ability to work with others in expressing and building the self (Lewis, 1986; White & LeVine, 1986; Taylor, Lichtman, & Ogawa, 2000). But Japanese parents stress the emotional connection between children and others as an overriding feature of childhood socialization as well (Lebra, 1994; Tobin et al., 1989). In the same vein, middle-class, urban South Korean parents embrace emotional closeness and interdependence as a significant part of childrearing. *Chong* (affection, oneness, sacrifice, empathy, caring, sincerity, shared experiences) and *Uri* (we) are instilled through *Eung-Seok*—indulgence and flexibility in caregiving routines. In the confines of interdependent practices, South Korean children are expected to be self-reliant but not selfish (Shin, 2001). The Chinese, too, strongly encourage the development of cooperative behavior and group harmony among children (Chen & Ye, 2004), and use storytelling to convey moral and social standards (Miller, Wiley, Fung, & Liang, 1997). These beliefs and practices depart from the definition of self-other relationships and highly organized routines in childrearing observed in most Western industrialized societies. To gain a sense of agency, demonstrations of assertiveness and autonomy are highly encouraged during care and education in Western postindustrialized societies (Super, Harkness, & Keefer, 1992). But even here, we must be careful in making sweeping generalizations amid intercultural variations in childrearing values and practices in the range of postindustrialized societies.

Cultural differences in belief systems extend to other constructs also, namely, "developmental timetables" and how children learn. That is, the timing and importance attributed to different social and educational activities differ across cultures and social class levels. Among the least industrialized societies (e.g., Nepal), there is the suggestion that children are expected to acquire societal norms of behaviors on their own without direct input from adults (Levy, 1996), and in some cultures (e.g., English-speaking Caribbean) unrealistic levels of maturity are demanded of very young children (e.g., ability to sit still for long periods of time, intellectual precocity) (Leo-Rhynie, 1997; Roopnarine, Bynoe, Singh, & Simon, 2005). In the developed societies, earlier expectations of cognitive competence were found among Israeli mothers of European compared to African or Asian background (Nino, 1979), and American mothers had earlier expectations of achievement and social skills with peers, whereas Japanese mothers had earlier expectations of courtesy, emotional control, and compliance with authority figures (Hess, Kasigawa, Azuma, Price, & Dickson, 1980). On questions such as when would you expect a child to amuse herself, disagree with others without fighting, count from 1 to 10, speak on the telephone, know her surname, feed self, and assist with chores around the house, Lebanese-Australian mothers expected most of these skills to develop at a later age than Anglo-Australian mothers (Goodnow, Cashmore, Cotton, & Knight, 1984). When Greek parents were asked to express their views about the appropriate age for young children to learn prewriting skills, they responded as follows: 15.5% suggested 2 years of age, 37.3% suggested 3 years, 34.7% suggested 4 years, and 12.5% suggested

5 years or over (Laloumi-Vidali, 2000). Generally, there are more relaxed attitudes toward child training and early developmental expectations in a number of developing societies in Asia (see Laungani, 2005) and preindustrial societies in Africa (see Fouts, 2004) compared to North America and Europe.

The asymmetry in ideas just laid out is not limited to desired childhood behaviors and developmental expectations only. Parents in different ethnic and cultural groups in the developed and developing societies hold different views on what children should learn, and about the content of early childhood education. Put differently, parents across cultures place different emphases on less-structured play-based early childhood curricula and more structured, academically laced instructional approaches. The disadvantages of early academic training during the preschool years and, conversely, the benefits of culturally developmentally appropriate practices have dominated academic exchanges in postindustrialized societies (see Burts et al., 1992; Elkind, 1983; Roopnarine & Metindogan, in press). However, the prevalence and meaning of play-based, developmentally appropriate practices for educating children in the developing societies are less clear. As can be deduced later, parents and educators in several developing societies prefer more academically oriented programs for young children and some cultural groups view play as frivolous or cursory to early childhood development (Roopnarine et al., 2003).

In a review of the literature regarding parental beliefs and ratings about the benefits of play, Roopnarine and his colleagues (Roopnarine et al., 2003) concluded that parents from different cultural and socioeconomic groups were far from uniform in the value attributed to play in early childhood development and its role in the early childhood curriculum. The general trend was that among middle-income European Americans and Europeans, play was viewed more favorably (Bishop & Chase, 1971; Farver, Kim, & Lee, 1995; Haight, Parke, & Black, 1997; Johnson, 1986; van der Kooj & Slatts-van den Hurk, 1991) than among parents from other ethnic groups within developed and developing societies (Gaskins, 2001; Holmes, 2001; Pan, 1994; Roopnarine, 1999). However, interpreting the findings from these and other studies on parental beliefs about the importance of play is far from straightforward. Italian parents from middle-income backgrounds saw play as a naturally occurring event that children engaged in (New, 1994), Mayan parents viewed it as a sign of health among children (Gaskins, 2001), and Latina, black, and white low-income mothers in Boston preferred more academic rather than play-based activities in order to enhance their children's literacy and numeracy skills (Holloway et al., 1995). Middle-class Asian and middle- to lower-class Caribbean immigrants acknowledged the value of play for social development but preferred academically based activities for their preschool-aged children (Parmer & Harkness, 2004; Roopnarine, Bynoe, & Singh, 2004). Thai parents with high educational attainment had positive attitudes about play (Bloch & Waichadit, 1981) but engaged in low rates of higher-order play such as pretend and games with rules (Tulananda & Roopnarine, 2001).

Cross-national and within culture perspectives on early childhood education practices lend credence to variations in the receptiveness of more self-discovery play-based curricula that consider the child's level of social and cognitive development.

Teachers in the United States indicated concerns about the lack of the role of culture, caretaking, interconnectedness, and multiple ways of knowing in early childhood education and noted that developmentally appropriate practices may be culturally biased (Jipson, 1991). In several cultural groups, there is a strong push for early academic achievement. Mothers in Zimbabwe (Hampton, 1989), Laos (Emblen, 2000), in Asian and Caribbean immigrant groups in the United States, and in Greece (Lalouni-Vidali, 2000) show a preference for academic subjects and homework for young children (Farver & Shin, 1997; Parmar & Harkness, 2004; Roopnarine et al., 2004). Japanese and Chinese parents, children, and teachers had more positive attitudes toward homework than American parents, teachers, and children, respectively (Stevenson & Lee, 1990), and Chinese parents in Hong Kong were more likely to rate socialization for academic achievement as an individual goal of parenting than British parents (Pearson & Rao, 2003). By comparison, British and American mothers' and fathers' perspectives about hurrying children in academic, sports and other activities, responsibility taking, and overscheduling were very similar in spite of the competitive pressures in American society. There were no gender of parent differences and parents had concerns about "hurrying behaviors" across the two countries (Moore & Klass, 2000).

An extensive survey of administrators', teachers' and parents' knowledge and beliefs about developmentally appropriate practices (patterned after the NAEYC guidelines) for children 3–5 years of age enrolled in "representative programs" was conducted in Finland, Ecuador, China, and the United States. Educators and parents in Ecuador and China emphasized pushing academic skills earlier and deemphasizing aesthetic skills more than parents in Finland and the United States. Teachers in Ecuador and China believed that children should listen and learn from demonstrations. Administrators in China regarded the enforcement of rules and punishing misbehaviors as more important than their counterparts in the other three countries. There was greater agreement in educational goals between parents and administrators in Finland, Ecuador, and China than in the United States, and more parents in the United States advocated teaching children in a straightforward manner (see also Carlson & Stenmalm, 1989). Of the four groups, administrators in the United States voiced the strongest support for developmentally appropriate practices (Hoot, Parmar, Hujala-Huttunen, Cao, & Chacon, 1996). Findings from a cross-national study by Tobin et al. (1989) provide additional support for the preference for academics and strict treatment of children in the classroom in Chinese preschools.

Often overshadowed by the need to focus on early academic training, early childhood program goals are becoming more flexible in a number of societies. A shift in curricular content from teacher-centered pedagogy toward play-based education is being advocated in Malaysia (Miller, 1999) and Hong Kong (Rao & Koong, 2000); and in a survey of attitudes toward the child's right to play, 67.6% of teachers in Japan, 78.5% in Korea, and, 56.7% in China gave affirmative responses to play being a part of the curriculum. Korean teachers had more positive attitudes about integrating play in the curriculum than either the Chinese or Japanese teachers (Ishigaki & Lin, 1999). Flexibility in

approach may be as much a function of context as of degree of acceptance of developmental appropriateness. In Taiwan, "experimental or exploratory programs," as compared to "efficient schools," where academic subjects are taught in a structured manner, are more inclined to be play-based (Chang, 2002; Johnson & Chang, 2003). The same is true for child-oriented rather than role-oriented preschools in Japan (Holloway, 1999). In Jamaica (Morrison & Milner, 1997) Turkey (Gol-Guven & Krishnakumar, 2002), and Singapore (see the volume by Honig, 1998; Raban & Ure, 1999) "progressive" programs are interspersed amid more structured programs.

EARLY CHILDHOOD CURRICULA ACROSS CULTURES

How early childhood education programs are implemented and how their intended goals are accomplished across cultures will depend in good part on the societal and parental goals for young children enumerated above. The objectives of early childhood education around the world are captured in two deceptively simple questions: What should we teach young children? and How do we teach them? (Bruner, 1999). In the postindustrialized world, early childhood education is supposedly driven by a vast knowledge base on how children develop and learn (Bredekamp & Copple, 1997). Corresponding data on childhood development in most of the world's cultures are now being amassed. Having said that, the early childhood field is rife with disagreements on curricula for different cultural groups in both the developed and developing world (Roopnarine & Metindogan, 2005). Nevertheless, it is worth repeating that early childhood education provides opportunities for socialization, prepares children for school readiness and, in the case of intervention, serves to ameliorate behavioral and cognitive difficulties later on (Shonkoff & Meisels, 2002; Reynolds, 2000; ECLS, 1998–1999). Within cultures and cross-nationally, there are basic factors that impinge on early childhood curricula and care: locus of policy making agency, parental involvement, administrative oversight, age groups served, criteria for enrollment, funding sources, location of education or care, teachers/caregivers, and program philosophy and quality (Kamerman, 1999; Lubeck et al., 2002).

Competing philosophical approaches to early childhood education are normative in North America, Europe, Australia, and other developed nations. In North America, there are such diverse models and approaches as High Scope, Portage Home-Based Program, Mixed-Age, Montessori, Spectrum, Steiner, Project Approach, Reggio Emilia, Inclusive Education Models, Behavioral, an assortment of early stimulation Programs for Infants and Toddlers, Developmental Interaction, Sociomoral, Head Start, Pyramid among others (see Reynolds, 2000; Nager & Shapiro, 2000; Roopnarine & Johnson, 2005 for detailed descriptions of these programs). A few of the approaches such as Portage, Montessori, Reggio Emilia, and High Scope have had strong global appeal. For instance, the Portage Home-Based Model for children with developmental delays has been implemented in Japan, Turkey, India, England, Jamaica, Netherlands,

Cyprus, Latvia, Gaza Strip, Saudi Arabia, Ireland, and Pakistan (Shearer & Shearer, 2005), the proliferation of the Reggio philosophy in the United States is duly recorded (New, 2005), and the Montessori approach has been in existence in other societies (e.g., India, Japan and Thailand) for decades (Feeney, 1992).

Quite a few of the above-mentioned programs are play-based and less academically inclined, whereas others are more structured and stress the learning of basic skills. As stated already, some ethnic/cultural groups have serious reservations about the lack of academic focus of play-based curricula (Roopnarine et al., 2003, Roopnarine et al., 2004). Observations of Taiwanese kindergartens revealed that play objects were used as a "bait" to invite children's participation in structured lessons and for relaxation after long seat work (Lin, Johnson, & Johnson, 2003), and a number of teachers use a blend of academic and play-based philosophical approaches in early childhood classrooms in the United States (Stipek et al., 1992, 1995). Generally, early childhood programs in the developed world stress the development of the "whole child." In other words, teachers emphasize the physical, social, emotional, and intellectual growth of children, and accept play as a central component of curricula (see Germeten, 1999; Jones, Dockett, Perry & Westcott, 2002; Lillemyr et al., 2001).

By and large, the plurality of educational programs present in the post-industrialized world may not exist in most developing countries. Often economic pressures and parents' and teachers' beliefs about the rigors of early childhood development and schooling (see Roopnarine et al., 2003; Super & Harkness, 1997) have led to more teacher-centered pedagogy. Nonetheless, it would be a mistake to assume that variability in early childhood education practices does not exist in the developing countries. In some countries, the language of play-based practices has seeped into the early childhood curricula (e.g., Jamaica) and, in principle, administrators and teachers embrace the virtues of child-centeredness and extol the benefits of play and creative activities in engaging children's minds (Hoon & Lazar, 1992). In others, it is difficult to gauge to what extent early childhood teachers are abandoning adult-centered pedagogy because elements (e.g., arithmetic and reading requirements) of the primary school curricula are seen in the preprimary classrooms, there is the expectation that children come prepared to learn once they enter primary schools, and upper-class parents solicit the assistance of early childhood programs to prepare their children to pass competitive entrance examinations to enter elite schools (see Feeney, 1992; Roopnarine et al., 2003; Johnson & Johnson, 2003; Swadener, Kabiru, & Njenga, 1997; Tobin et al., 1989).

Keeping in mind within-culture variations due to social class and educational attainment, and type of program (private vs. public; full- vs. part-day; state-run), an examination of early childhood curricula in several developing countries (e.g., Guyana, Jamaica, Fiji, Bahrain) indicates that children are given few choices within very structured educational settings. Parents may relinquish authority over children to teachers, who in turn, exercise almost total control over their young charges. Take the case of Chinese kindergartens (*youeryan*). Teachers exercise full control over children and both parents and teachers place great value on learning academic skills through rote memory and recitation (Lin, Johnson, & Johnson, 2003; Tobin, Wu, & Davidson, 1989; Wu, 1992). Similar emphases on didactic teaching, academics and "mimetic instruction" (reinforced imitation with repetition) were apparent in curricula in Bahrain, India, Thailand, Singapore, Korea, Taiwan, Ecuador, and Hong Kong (Hadeed, 1994; Hoon & Lazar, 1992; Hoot, Parmar, Hujala-Huttunen, Cao, & Chacon, 1996; Karikalan, 1998; Lee, 1992; Lim, 1998; Lin, Johnson & Johnson, 2003; Opper, 1992; Suvannathat & Passornsiri, 1992), and the school readiness function was echoed by parents of kindergartners in Kenya (Swadener et al., 1997) and Turkey (Gol-Guven & Krishnakumar, 2003), and displayed in the graduation ceremonies of rural Malaysian children (Miller, 1999).

Parenthetically, Singapore, Korea, Malaysia, and Hong Kong are closer to the postindustrialized societies in standard of living. In these societies, "flexibility" or a blend of the academic and play-based methods is encouraged among teachers. A similar pattern exists for Mexican kindergarten programs—social skills and creativity combined with oral and written communication and mathematical skills are foci of the kindergarten curriculum (Cisneros-Cohernour et al., 2000). Kenyan parents articulated the role of early childhood programs in providing nutritional supplements, safety, healthcare, custodial care, and in the transmission and maintenance of cultural values, languages, stories, and traditions (Swadener, et al., 1997). In Indonesia, children are taught to become national-minded citizens and to acquire the skills necessary for primary education and beyond (Thomas, 1992), whereas in the Philippines a great diversity of programs all seem to have the collective purpose of encouraging the child's emotional, mental, social, physical, and aesthetic development (Chattergy, 1992).

It may be argued that definitions of early childhood education are now emerging in some societies as familial roles change and societal demands for school-related skills peak. Arguably, early childhood education and care have multiple definitions in the developing societies (see Cleghorn & Prochner, 1997). Increases in the training of teachers and childcare workers (including parents) and kinship and nonkinship members, and participation in community efforts to develop early childhood programs to meet the needs of children in the 21st century will no doubt stretch the limits to which attempts are made to modify local belief systems and customs about the care and education of children (Swadener et al., 1997). At the moment, the degree to which competing principles of early childhood education help define the boundaries and success of educating children in the poorer nations of the world will depend on how seriously local cultural knowledge is considered.

CHILD CARE ACROSS CULTURES

The childcare literature on North American and European families is vast (Ahnert, Gunnar, Lamb, & Barthel, 2004; Essa & Burnham, 2001; Lamb et al., 1992, Lamb, 1998; National Institute of Child Health and Human Development (NICHD) Early Child Care Research Network, 2001, 2003). Research investigations have ascertained the effects of day care on children's intellectual and social development (see Lamb, 1998; NICHD

Early Child Care Research Network, 2001, 2002, 2003) by considering child characteristics, family characteristics, center characteristics, and childcare quality—both structural and process variables (e.g., child-teacher ratio, well-educated and trained caregivers, healthy and safe environment and positive caregiving that involves sensitivity and responsivity). All of these factors have been associated with or implicated in influencing child development outcomes (see Essa & Burnham, 2001; Lamb, 1998).

Findings from the different waves of studies conducted in the United States over three decades on the effects of day care on children's socioemotional and cognitive development have been controversial (see Lamb, 1998). Overall, high quality day care experiences have no discernible negative consequences on children's attachment and cognitive development. Recent results from one of the most comprehensive research studies conducted on the effects of day care among children in several cities in the United States have shown that childcare quality measured from 6 months onward was positively linked to cognitive and language development at 2, 3, and 4½ years (NICHD Early Child Care Research Network, 2002, 2003). In another study (Loeb, Fuller, Kagan, Carrol, 2004), cognitive benefits were evidenced in poor children in center care whose mothers entered the welfare-to-work programs. However, quantity of day care over the first 4.5 years of life was linked to externalizing problems and conflicts with adults at age 54 months (NICHD Early Child Care Research Network, 2003) and there are concerns over elevated cortisol, an indicator of stress, in young children in day care (Ahnert et al., 2004).

Our aim is not to discuss the effects of day care across cultures but to highlight cross-national attempts at defining issues critical to providing quality childcare for young children in different contexts. Unlike the postindustrialized societies, maternal employment, though on the rise, remains low in the developing societies (see Roopnarine & Gielen, 2005). Moreover, the cultural context of non-maternal care may involve siblings, grandparents, and other nonkinship members (see Swadener et al., 1997; Flinn, 1992; Ahmed, 2005), and process quality may be laden with culture-specific meanings (see Ahnert & Lamb, 2003). Consider for a moment what Australian families expect of day care for their children: care and education, professionalism, and qualified staff (Liu, Yeung, & Farmer, 2001). Such expectations, although highly desired, may not be realistic in poorer nations where economic, physical, and sociopolitical resources most likely determine the nature of care young children receive. Concerted efforts are under way in several societies (e.g., India, Kenya) to develop crèches, community programs, and on-site centers where women work, and to train local staff and educate teenagers to care for young children (Swadner et al., 1997; Swaminathan, 2000). Some researchers have articulated the differing but complementary roles of familial members and childcare workers: childcare workers focus more on cognitive stimulation and behavioral guidance whereas familial members may focus more on the child's emotional needs (Ahnert & Lamb, 2003).

In countries such as Singapore, Hong Kong, and Korea, where high-quality day care centers are on the increase, there are attempts to define process quality and to improve existing

standards. In Hong Kong, formal assessments of 60 preschools serving 4-year-olds revealed that process quality varied considerably, with more predictable quality evident in schools that surpass government requirements for staff qualifications, teacher-child ratios, and space and equipment (Rao, Koong, Kwong, & Wong, 2003). Using somewhat similar measures (Early Childhood Environment Rating Scale, ECERS; Caregiver Interaction Scale), two studies (Tietze, Cryer, Bairrao, Palacios, & Wetzel, 1996; Cryer, Tetze, Burchinal, Leal, & Palacios, 1999) examined process quality in Germany, Spain, Portugal, and the United States. The ECERS assesses quality care along seven dimensions: personal care routines, furnishings and displays for children, language-reasoning experiences, fine and gross motor activities, creative activities, social development, and adult needs (Harms & Clifford, 1980). Although the earlier study indicated country differences in terms of personalized care and availability and use of space and play materials, the second suggested that despite differences among the childcare systems in the five countries, no single measure stood above the others in predicting process quality in the early childhood settings across countries. In other words, process quality appears to be a multifaceted construct with the possibility that each structural feature may have unique effects on specific aspects of childhood development, and on teacher-child and parent-child relationships in different cultures (see Sheridan & Schuster, 2001). Furthermore, the reasons why different ethnic groups in the developed world choose different forms of childcare may have more to do with family structure, familial practices, and home language than the multitude of variables tied to the caregiving environment (Dahlberg, Moss, & Pence, 1999; Liang, Fuller, & Singer, 2000).

Taken together, indices of process quality (teacher-child ratios; formal caregiver training; space and equipment) deemed important in the postindustrialized societies may have less applicability to the developing world. Just as they hierarchically arrange socialization goals, in the developing societies parents may have little choice other than to accept the limited possibilities available to them. Process quality as defined in the post-industrialized societies becomes a luxury that may not be within reach in the developing countries. As a survey of Portuguese mothers suggested, in a number of countries parents may choose childcare primarily out of convenience and cost (Folque, Ulrich, & Siraj-Blatchford, 2000). There is a dire need to explore alternative ways of assessing and improving childcare quality in most of the world's societies (Dahlberg et al., 1999).

EFFICACY OF EARLY EDUCATION AND INTERVENTION ACROSS CULTURES

Ultimately, early childhood researchers, practitioners/teachers, policy makers, and governments need to know whether early childhood education and intervention models make a difference in children's later intellectual and social functioning. Like so many other areas of early childhood research, scientific inquires that have examined the efficacy of early childhood programs are largely based on samples of children and families in the developed societies. After presenting a brief summary of the data from the United States, we discuss the results of a few studies from other regions of the world. Rather than repeat in detail the findings on the vast array of studies on early intervention and early childhood education in the United States, we direct the reader to several excellent reviews on the impact of different programs for economically disadvantaged families (Gilliam & Zigler, 2000; Goldbeck, 2001; Haskins, 1992; Levenstein, Levenstein, & Oliver, 2002; Levenstein, Levenstein, Shiminski, & Stoltzberg, 1998; Reynolds, 2000; Zigler et al., 1992; Zigler & Styfco, 2004), to descriptions of the cognitive skills and knowledge of kindergartners (ECLS study, West et al., 1998), and screening for school readiness (Pianta & McCoy, 1997).

In a nutshell, the hundreds of studies conducted on a variety of programs with different educational philosophies, structure, and location suggest that good quality early childhood intervention programs have short-term benefits for children's cognitive functioning (Gilliam & Zigler, 2001; Baker, Piotrkowski, & Brooks-Gunn, 1998; Tzuriel, Kaniel, Kanner, & Haywood, 1999; Zigler & Styfco, 2004). There is consensus, moreover, that a number of programs (e.g., Head Start, High/Scope, Mother-Child Home Program, Chicago Child-Parent Center Program, Home Instruction for Preschool Youngster-HIPPY) may have sustained effects on school achievement, psychosocial variables (Levenstein, et al., 1998; Reynolds, 2000; Schweinhart & Weikart, 1997; Weikart & Schweinhart, 2005), and school placements (Spiess, Buchel, & Wagner, 2003).

Regrettably, we know comparatively less about the impact of center-based and home-based early childhood programs on childhood and family development in other cultures. There are a number of home-based programs aimed at teaching mothers how to communicate, interact, and work with their young children (e.g., Portage, MISC, TEEP), and a few center-based programs that involve varying amounts of cognitive and social stimulation (Shearer & Shearer, 2005; Kuyk, 2005). No doubt, the emphasis on the home environment is due to the large body of work on the links between the role of parental aspirations, encouragement, and cognitive stimulation and children's intellectual and social development (Collins et al., 2000). We take a closer look at a few programs that attempt to improve the lives of young children in different parts of the world.

The Portage home-based model rooted in behavioral principles of learning has three major components: parental involvement, home-based programming, and the use of the precision teaching method. With the assistance of a home teacher, the program aims to assist the caregiver to become a more effective teacher/nurturer of his/her child within the context of the home environment. The Portage procedures use precise definitions, task analysis, direct teaching methods, and daily assessments. Home visits include direct intervention, informal interaction and play, and family support efforts, each lasting about 30 minutes (see Shearer & Shearer, 2005, for more details). Although the Portage home-based method has been used extensively across cultures, the data on its effectiveness are rather sparse. Shearer and Shearer (2005) claim that gains of between 1.2 and 1.8 months mental age found in U.S. samples were replicated in Finland, India, Jamaica, Japan, Netherlands, and the United Kingdom. A more in-depth study of 268 children in the Gaza Strip showed that after 3 years of exposure to the Portage Model

of instruction, experimental group children exceeded controls on personal, social, adaptive, motor, and language development as measured by the Developmental Profile II and the Batelle Developmental inventory (Ghazaleh, Ghazaleh, & Oakland, 1990).

Relatedly, mediational intervention for sensitizing parents as caregivers (e.g., focusing, verbal and nonverbal communication, broadening cognitive awareness, rewarding) was conducted among Ethiopian and Israeli mothers. Assessments conducted 1 to 3 years after Israeli mothers were trained on how to respond to their children revealed significantly higher PPVT IQ (mean = 101) than control group children (mean = 84), and that maternal requests for expansion of ideas and rewarding with explanation were related to cognitive performance at age 4. Among the Ethiopian mothers, there were noticeable increases in all maternal strategies (focusing, expanding, etc.) even after working with children for brief periods (Klein, 1996). Somewhat similar gains have been found for rural Jamaican families and children (Powell, 2005).

One of the most impressive intervention projects established outside the United States was conducted in Turkey (Kagitcibasi, 1999). The Turkish Early Enrichment Project (TEEP) lasted ten years and involved 255 families and their 3- to 5-year-old children from five low-income districts of Istanbul. Initially the families were followed for 4 years and were assessed again 6 years later. In the second and third years, 90 mothers received training in the Home Instruction Program for Preschool Youngsters (HIPPY) method that focuses on childhood stimulation in the areas of language, problem solving, perceptual, and numeracy skills in preparation for school. In addition, mothers were offered social support (to support the socioemotional development of child and empower the mother to deal with problems). Not only did program mothers' literacy skills improve, they were less punitive and more verbal and cognitively stimulating toward their children post intervention. Experimental group children had higher Stanford-Binet IQ scores, school grades, achievement and Wechsler scores, and fared better on several measures of socioemotional development (e.g., dependency, self-concept, school adjustment) than control group children. By the 6-year follow-up, mothers who received training had children who were more likely to be in school (86% vs. 67% in control group), performed better in school throughout the primary school years, had higher WISC-R scores, more positive attitudes toward school, and better self-concepts. Parent-child, spousal relationships, and the status of the mother improved, and children received more support for schooling as educational expectations increased. In sum, both parents and children benefited from the intervention (Kagitcibasi, 1999).

A program that has experienced more moderate success was implemented in Holland. The Pyramid method (van Kuyk, 2001, 2005) serves children between $2^{1}/_{2}$ and 6 years of age and provides support to those who need assistance. It has four broad concepts—nearness, distance, child initiative, teacher initiative—and is grounded in principles of constructivism, building trusting relationships, and scaffolding (see Kuyk, 2005). The effectiveness of the model was tested among children from disadvantaged backgrounds enrolled in preschools, prekindergartens, and kindergartens. Comparisons were made among children enrolled in Pyramid, those enrolled in the High Scope (Kaleidscope) method adapted for use in the Netherlands, and control children. The Pyramid and the Kaleidscope methods produced weak to strong positive effects (Cohen effect) in the areas of language development and the development of reading compared with controls. Assessments made subsequently, after adjustments were made in language components of the Pyramid curriculum, indicated that the Pyramid method had a strong effect on language development and the development of thinking, whereas the Kaleidscope method had moderate to weak effects on the development of thinking (Kuyk, 2005). Other work in European countries (e.g., Portugal) showed that the High/Scope program led to significant short-terms gains in children's educational achievement, self-esteem, and in lowering anxiety (Sylva & Nabuco, 2000).

Finally, an intervention study carried out in Austria over a 4-year period successfully implemented play in the Viennese elementary school curriculum without negative consequences for academic achievement (Hartmann & Rollett, 1994). Children in the play-based program appeared more content with school, had more positive attitudes toward learning and were more motivated than controls. Teachers reported that children in play-based classrooms were more companionable, less aggressive, and displayed fewer behavioral disorders than their counterparts in control classrooms. Apparently, opportunities for play made school more attractive and may have relieved some of the strain inherent in predominantly academic programs. However, child-centered programs in cultures in which traditional academics are emphasized may not produce identical results. For example, among children in Trinidad, neither teacher-centered nor child-centered programs influenced academic achievement in core subjects through the primary school years (Kutnick, 1994).

In all, the findings from across societies provide strong to moderate support for investment in the early educational stimulation of young disadvantaged children in particular. The demonstrated lasting cognitive and social benefits of early intervention programs in the developed and developing societies have implications for the large number of young children around the world who live in poverty and have limited access to early education. In these societies, home-based early childhood programs may have more promise for improving the life chances of children and parents given the dynamic systemic effects observed in the Turkish study. As we use these findings as a guide to improve the educational lives of young children, it is necessary to consider indigenous goals, beliefs, and practices regarding early childhood education and the stage of economic development of different societies.

RECOMMENDATIONS FOR FUTURE RESEARCH

To recap, societies around the world are witnessing unprecedented changes in familial living arrangements and childhood experiences within the context of globalization. These changes or "transitions" necessitate new visions for early childcare and education practices and research agendas. Broadening our focus to include frameworks that assist us to calibrate developmental change in families and children in a contemporary global community would be a good start. In this regard, cultural paradigms that balance local practices and global influences may be better able to steer early childhood education research in the future. It is no secret that the needs of young children are the same worldwide: health, safety, happiness and rewarding life, education, and so on. It should not be presumed that meeting the early childhood education needs of young children across cultures requires the same approaches. Within and across societies, there is a need to investigate more fully: (a) paternal involvement in childrearing and in the early childhood education process; (b) how early childhood education changes parent-child relationships vis-à-vis the local culture—parental discipline, authority, and control of children, investment in children's and parents' own education; (c) transnational and hybrid identity formation as children become more immersed in the global culture; (d) what quality early childhood education means to parents and children in cultures in transitions; and (e) the efficacy of different culturally defined models and approaches (hybrid) of home-based and center-based education.

References

Adler, L. L., & Gielen, U., P. (Eds.) (2003) *Migration: Immigration and emigration in international perspective.* Westport, CT: Praeger Publishers/Greenwood Publishing Group.

Ahmed, R. A. (2005). Egyptian families. In J. L. Roopnarine, & U. Gielen (Eds.), *Families in global perspectives* (pp. 151–168). Boston, MA: Allyn & Bacon.

Andreoni, H. (1997). Early childhood education in Eritrea proceeding as we would finish. *International Journal of Early Childhood, 29,* 1, 42–49.

Agrawal, S. P., & Kanta, N. (1990). *Child Education in India.* New Delhi: Concept Publishing Company.

Ahnert, L., Gunnar, M. R., Lamb, M. E., & Barthel, M. (2004). Transition to child care: Associations with infant mother attachment, infant negative emotion, and cortisol elevations. *Child Development, 75,* 639–650.

Ahnert, L., & Lamb, M. E. (2003). Shared care: Establishing a balance between home and child care settings. *Child Development, 74,* 1044–1049.

Ahuja, A., Sharma, N., & Tiwari, S. (2000) Alternate child care options: Preferences of the Hill Community. *International Journal of Early Childhood, 32,* 2, 91–96.

Aptekar, L. (2004). The changing developmental dynamics of "children in particularly difficult circumstances": Examples of street and war traumatized children. In U. Gielen, U. & J. L. Roopnarine (Eds.), *Childhood and adolescence: Cross-cultural and practical applications* (pp. 377–410). Westport, CT: Praeger.

Arnett, J. J. (2002). The psychology of globalization. *American Psychologist, 57*, 774–783.

Barrera, I., Corso, R. M., & Macpherson, D. (2003). *Skilled dialogue: Strategies for responding to cultural diversity in early childhood.* Baltimore, MD: Brookes Publishing.

Baker, A. J. L., Piotrkowski, C. S., & Brooks-Gunn, J. (1998). The effects of the Home Instruction Program for Preschool Youngsters (HIPPY) on children's school performance at the end of the program one year later. *Early Childhood Research Quarterly, 13*, 571–588.

Bekman, S. (1993). Preschool education system in Turkey revisited. *OMEP International Journal of Early Childhood, 25*, 1, 13–19.

Berry, J. W. (1989). Imposed etics—emics—derived etics: the operationalization of a compelling idea. *International Journal of Psychology, 24*, 721–735.

Bertram, T., & Pascal, C. (1999). *The Effective Early Learning Project: The Quality of Adult Engagement in Early Childhood Settings in the UK.* Paper presented at the Annual EECERA (European Early Childhood Education Research Association) Conference Helsinki, Finland.

Bishop, D. W., & Chase, C. A. (1971). Parental conceptual systems, home play environment, and potential creativity in children. *Journal of Experimental Child Psychology, 12*, 318–338.

Bloch, M. (2005). Making progress? Conceptualizing and reconceptualizing approaches to early childhood education and child care in the twenty-first century. J. L. Roopnarine & J. E. Johnson (Eds.), *Approaches to early childhood education* (4th ed., pp. 423–435). Columbus, OH: Merrill/Prentice Hall.

Bloch, M., & Wichaidat, W. (1986). Play and school work in the kindergarten curriculum: Attitudes of parents and teachers in Thailand. *Early Child Development and Care, 24*, 197–218.

Bredekamp, S., & Copple, C. (1997). (Eds.). *Developmentally appropriate practice in early childhood programs.* (Rev. ed.). Washington, DC: NAEYC.

Brennan, D. (1998). *The politics of Australian child care.* Cambridge University Press

Bruner, J. (1999, April). *Global perspectives on early childhood education: Keynote address.* Paper presented at The Committee on Early Childhood Pedagogy, National Academy of Sciences and National Research Council workshop on Global perspectives on early childhood education, Washington, DC.

Burbules, N. C., & Torres, C. A. (2000). Globalization and education: An introduction. In N. C. Burbules & C. A. Torres (Eds.), *Globalization and education: Critical Perspectives* (pp. 1–26). New York: Routledge.

Burts, D., Hart, C., Charlesworth, R., Fleege, P., Mosley, J., & Thomasson, R. (1992). Observed activities and stress behaviors in classrooms with developmentally appropriate versus developmentally inappropriate kindergarten classrooms. *Early Childhood Research Quarterly, 7*, 297–318.

Carlson, H., & Stenmalm, L. (1989). Professional and parent views of early childhood programs: A cross-cultural study. *Early Child Development and Care, 50*, 51–66.

Chang, P. (2003) Contextual understanding of children's play in Taiwaneese kindergartens. In D. E. Lytle (Ed.), *Play and educational theory and practice. Play & Culture studies* (pp. 19–32). Westport, CT: Praeger.

Chattergy, V. O. (1992). Early childhood education in the Philippines. In S. Feeney & F. Naroll (Eds.), *Early childhood education in Asia and Pacific: A source book* (pp. 135–164). New York: Peter Lang Publishing.

Chen, X., & He, Y. (2005). The family in Mainland China: Structure, organization, and significance for child development. In J. L. Roopnarine & U. Gielen (Eds.), *Families in global perspectives* (pp. 51–62) Boston, MA: Allyn & Bacon.

Cisneros-Cohernour, E. J., Moreno, R. P., & Cisneros, A. A. (2000). Curriculum reform in Mexico: Kindergarten teachers' challenges and dilemmas. Proceedings of the Lilian Katz Symposium. In D. Rothenberg (Ed.), *Issues in early childhood education: Curriculum reform, teacher education, and dissemination of information* (pp. 139–148). Urbana-Champaign: University of Illinois.

Cleghorn, A., & Prochner, L. (1997). Early childhood education in Zimbabwe: Recent trends and prospects. *Early Education & Development, 8*, 339–352.

Cochran, M. (Ed.). (1993). *International handbook of child-care policies and programs.* Westport, CT: Greenwood Press.

Collins, W. A., Maccoby, E., Steinberg, L., Hetherington, E. M., & Bornstein, M. H. (2000). Contemporary research on parenting: The case of nature versus nurture. *American Psychologist, 55*, 218–232.

Comunian, A., & Gielen, U. (Eds.). (2000). *International perspectives on human development.* Lengerich, Germany: Pabst.

Crane, J. (1998). The Pacific world of early childhood education. *International Journal of Early Childhood, 30*, 2, 8–18.

Cryer, D., Tietze, W., Burchinal, M., Leal, T., & Palacios, J. (1999). Predicting process quality from structural quality in preschool programs: A cross-country comparison. *Early Childhood Research Quarterly, 14*, 3, 339–361.

D'Andrade, R. G. (2004). The search for simplicity. *Cross-Cultural Research, 38*, 220–235.

Dahlberg, G., Moss, P., & Pence, A. (1999). *Beyond quality in early childhood education and care: Postmoden perspectives.* London: Falmer Press.

Davies, R. (1997a, April). *A historical review of the evolution of early childhood care and education in the Caribbean.* Paper presented at the second Caribbean Conference on Early Childhood Education, Barbados.

Davies, R. (1997b). *Striving for quality in early childhood development programmes: The Caribbean experience.* (ERIC Document ED 413077). Kingston, Jamaica: University of the West Indies.

Durbrow, E. H. (1999). Cultural processes in child competence: How rural Caribbean parents evaluate their children. In A. S. Masten (Ed.), *The Minnesota Symposia on Child Development* (pp. 97–122). Mahwah, NJ: Lawrence Erlbaum.

Early Childhood Longitudinal Study. (1998-1999). *America's kindergartners.* National Center for Education Statistics. U.S. Department of Education, Office of Educational Research and Improvement. Washington, DC: U.S. Government Printing Office.

Eckstein (1994). South Africa's young children: Winning or losing? *International Journal of Early Childhood, 48*–54.

Elkind, D. (1981). *The hurried child.* Reading, MA: Addison-Wesley.

Emblen, V. (1998). Providers and families: Do they have the same views of early childhood programmes? Some questions raised by working on early childhood education in the Lao people's democratic republic. *International Journal of Early Childhood, 30*, 2, 31–37.

Engle, P. L., Zeitlin, M., Medrano, Y., & Garcia, L. (1996). Growth consequences of low-income Nicaraguan mothers' theories about feeding 1-year olds. In S. Harkness & C. Super (Eds.), *Parents' cultural belief systems: Their origins, expressions, and consequences* (pp. 428–446). New York: Guildford Press.

Essa, E., & Burnham, M. M. (2001). Child care quality: A model for examining relevant variables. In S. Reifel & M. Brown (Eds.), *Early education and care, and reconceptualizing play* (pp. 59–113). Amsterdam: Jai-Elsevier.

Farver, J. A. M., Kim, Y. K., & Lee, Y. (1995). Cultural difference in Korean- and Anglo-American preschoolers' social interaction and play behaviors. *Child Development, 66*, 1088–1099.

Farver, J. A. M., & Shin, Y. L. (1997). Social pretend play in Korean- and Anglo-American preschoolers. *Child Development, 68,* 3, 544–556

Feeney, S. (1992). Issues and implications. In S. Feeney & F. Naroll (Eds.), *Early childhood education in Asia and Pacific: A source book* (pp. 299–314). New York: Peter Lang Publishing.

Feeney, S., & Naroll, F. (Eds). (1992). *Early childhood education in Asia and Pacific: A source book.* New York: Peter Lang Publishing.

Folque, M. A., Ulrich, E. S., & Siraj-Blatchford, I. (2000). Parents' view of quality in early childhood services in Portugal. *International Journal of Early Childhood, 32,* 37–48.

Fouts, H. N. (2005). Families in Central Africa: A Comparison of Bofi Farmer and Forager families. In J. L. Roopnarine, & U. Gielen (Eds.), *Families in global perspectives* (pp. 347–362). Boston, MA: Allyn & Bacon.

Gandini, L., & Edwards, C. P. (Eds.). (2001). *Bambini: The Italian approach to infant/toddler care.* New York: Teachers College Press.

Gaskins, S. (2001, February). *Ignoring play—Will it survive?: A Mayan case study of beliefs and behaviors.* Presented at the annual meetings of the Association for the Study of Play, San Diego, California.

Geertz, C. (1973). *The interpretation of cultures.* New York: Basic Books.

Germeten, S. (1999). *Early childhood education in Norway after reform 97: Starting school, end of play?* Paper presented at the 21st ICCP, World Play Conference in Oslo, Norway.

Ghazaleh, H., Ghazaleh, K. A., & Oakland, T. (1990) Primary and secondary prevention services provided to mentally handicapped infants, children and youth in the Gaza Strip. *International Journal of Special Education, 5,* 21–27.

Gielen, U. (2004). The cross-cultural study of human development: An opinionated historical introduction. In U. P. Gielen & J. L. Roopnarine (Eds.), *Childhood and adolescence: Cross-cultural and practical applications* (pp. 3–45). Westport, CT: Praeger.

Gielen, U., & Roopnarine, J. L. (Eds.). (2004). *Childhood and adolescence: Cross-cultural and practical applications.* Westport, CT: Praeger.

Gielen, U. P., & Chumachenko, O. (2004). All the world's children: Global demographic trends and economic disparities. In U. Gielen, U. & J. L. Roopnarine (Eds.), *Childhood and adolescence: Cross-cultural and practical applications* (pp. 81–109). Westport, CT: Praeger.

Gilliam, W. S., & Zigler, E. F. (2000). A critical meta-analysis of all evaluations of state-funded preschool from 1977 to 1998: Implications for policy, service delivery and program evaluation. *Early Childhood Research Quarterly, 15,* 4, 441–473.

Gol-Guven, M., & Krishnakumar, A. (2002, November). *Evaluation of early childhood classrooms in Turkey.* Paper presented at National Association for the Education of Young Children, New York City.

Golbeck, S. (Ed.). (2001). *Psychological perspectives on early childhood education: Reframing dilemmas in research and practice.* Mahwah, NJ: Erlbaum.

Goodnow, J. J., Cashmore, J. A., Cotton, S., & Knight, R. (1984). Mothers' developmental timetables in two cultural groups. *International Journal of Psychology, 19,* 193–205.

Goodnow, J. J., & Collins, W. A. (1990). *Development according to parents: The nature, sources, and consequences of parents' ideas.* Hillsdale, NJ: Lawrence Erlbaum Associates.

Greenfield, P. M. (1997). Culture as process: Empirical methods for cultural psychology. In J. W. Berry, Y. P. Poortinga, & J. Pandey (Eds.), *Handbook of cross-cultural psychology* (Vol. 1, 2nd ed., pp. 301–346). Boston: Allyn & Bacon.

Guralnick, M. J. (Ed.). (2003). *The effectiveness of early intervention.* Baltimore, MD: Brookes Publishing.

Hadeed, J. (1994). Preschool teacher training in Bahrain. *International Journal of Early Childhood, 26,* 2, 21–26.

Haight, W. L., Parke, R. D., & Black, J. E. (1997). Mothers' and fathers' beliefs about and spontaneous participation in their toddlers' pretend play. *Merrill-Palmer Quarterly, 43,* 271–290.

Hampton, J. (1989). Play and development in rural Zimbabwean children. *Early Child Development and Care, 47,* 1–61.

Harkness, S., Super, C. M., & Keefer, C. H. (1992). Culture and ethnicity. In M. D. Levine, W. B. Carey, & A. C. Crocker (Eds.), *Developmental-behavioral pediatrics* (2nd ed., pp. 103–108). New York: W. B. Saunders Corp.

Harms, T., & Clifford, R. M. (1980). *Early childhood environment rating scale.* New York: Teachers College Press.

Hartman, W., & Rollett, B. (1994). Play: Positive intervention in the elementary school curriculum. In J. Hellendoorn, R. van der Kooj, & Sutton-Smith, B. (Eds.), *Play and intervention* Albany, NY: SUNY Press.

Haskins, R. (1992). Similar history, similar markets, similar policies yield. In M. E. Lamb, K. J. Sternberg, C. P. Hwang, & A. G. Broberg (Eds.), *Child care in context: Cross-cultural perspectives* (pp. 267–280). Hillsdale, NJ: Lawrence Erlbaum Associates.

Hastings, P., & Rubin, K. H. (1999). Predicting mothers' beliefs about preschool-aged children's social behavior: Evidence for maternal attitudes moderating child effects. *Child Development, 70,* 722–741.

Hayden, J. (Ed.). (2000). *Landscapes in early childhood education. Cross national perspectives on empowerment—a guide for the new millennium.* New York: Peter Lang.

Hess, R. D., Kasigawa, K., Azuma, H., Price, G. G., & Dickson, W. P. (1980). Maternal expectations for mastery of developmental tasks in Japan and the United States. *International Journal of Psychology, 15,* 259–271.

Holland, P. W., & Thayer, D. T. (1988). Differential item performance and the Mantel-Haenszel procedure. In H. Wainer & H. I. Braun (Eds.), *Test validity* (pp. 129–145). Hillsdale, NJ: Lawrence Erlbaum Associates.

Holloway, S. (2000). *Contested childhood: Diversity and change in Japanese preschools.* New York: Routledge Press.

Holloway, S., Rambaud, M. F., Fuller, B., & Eggers-Pieorla, C. (1995). What is "appropriate practice" at home and in child care? Low-income mothers' view on preparing their children for school. *Early Childhood Research Quarterly, 10,* 451–473.

Holmes, R. (2001). Parental notions about their children's playfulness and children's notions of play in the United States and Hong Kong. In S. Reifel (Ed.), *Theory in context and out: Play and Culture Studies* (Vol. 3, pp. 291–314). Westport, CT: Ablex.

Honig, A. (1998). Singapore childcare and early education. (Special Issue). *Early Child Development and Care, 144.*

Hoon, S. S., & Lazar, I. (1992). Early childhood education in Singapore. In S. Feeney, & F. Naroll (Eds.), *Early childhood education in Asia and Pacific: A source book* (pp. 165–174). New York: Peter Lang.

Hoot, J. L., Parmar, E. H., Hujala-Huttunen, E., Cao, Q., & Chacon, A. M. (1996). Cross-national perspectives on developmentally appropriate practices for early childhood programs. *Journal of Research in Childhood Education, 10,* 2, 160–169.

Horowitz, F. D. (1987). *Exploring developmental theories: Toward a structural behavioral model of development.* Hillsdale, NJ: Erlbaum.

Hortacsu, N. (1995). Parents' education levels, parents' beliefs, and child outcomes. *Journal of Genetic Psychology, 156,* 373–383.

Ishigaki, E. H., & Lin, J. (1999). A comparative study of preschool teachers' attitudes towards "Children's Right to Play" in Japan, China, and Korea. *International Journal of Early Childhood, 31,* 1, 40–47.

Ispa, J. (1994). *Child care in Russia in transition*. Westport, CT: Bergin & Garvey.

Jacobs, J. E. (1991). Influence of gender stereotypes on parent and child mathematics attitudes. *Journal of Educational Psychology, 83*, 518-527.

Jahoda, G., & Krewer, B. (1997). History of cross-cultural and cultural psychology. In J. W. Berry, Y. P. Poortinga, & J. Pandey (Eds.), *Handbook of cross-cultural psychology* (Vol. 1, 2nd ed., pp. 1-42). Boston: Allyn & Bacon.

Jipson, J. (1991). Developmentally appropriate practice: Culture, curriculum, connections. *Early Education and Development, 2*, 2, 120-136.

Johnson, J. (2001, February). *Taiwanese teacher educators,' teachers,' and parents,' views about play*. Paper presented at the Association for the Study of Play meetings, San Diego, CA.

Johnson, J. E. (1986). Attitudes toward play and beliefs about development. In B. Mergen (Ed.), *Cultural dimensions of play, games, and sports. The Association for the Study of Play* (Vol. 10, pp. 98-102). Champaign, IL: Human Kinetic Publishers.

Johnson, J. E., & Chang, P. (2003). *Teachers' and parents' attitudes about play and learning in Taiwanese kindergartens*. Unpublished manuscript.

Jones, K., Dockett, S., Perry, B., & Westcott, K. (2002). Play in the first years of school. *Journal of Australian Research in Early Childhood Education, 9*, 1, 11-25.

Joshi, R. K. (1996). Status of early childhood education in Nepal. *International Journal of Early Childhood*, 57-61.

Joshi, V. (1998). Little school on the hill: Child education in community development. In M. Swaminathan (Ed). *The first five years: A critical perspective on early childhood care and education in India* (pp. 60-72). London: Sage Publications.

Kagan, S. L. (2003). Children's readiness for school: Issues in assessment. *International Journal of Early Childhood, 35*, (1,2), 114-120

Kakar, S. (1981). *The Inner World: A psycho-analytic study of childhood and society in India*. (2nd ed.). Delhi: Oxford University Press.

Kamerman, S. (1999, April). *Early childhood education and care (ECEC): Preschool policies and programs in the OECD countries*. Paper presented at The Committee on Early Childhood Education Pedagogy, National Academy of Sciences, National Research Council Meetings on Global Perspectives on Early Childhood Education, Washington, DC.

Kamerman, S. B., & Kahn, A. J. (1995). Innovations in toddler day care and family support services: An international overview. *Child welfare, 74*, 6, 1281-1300.

Karikalan, S. J. P. (1998). Moving up to school: Community preschools for the rural poor. M. Swaminathan (Ed.), *The first five years: A critical perspective on early childhood care and education in India* (pp. 100-110). London: Sage Publications.

Katz, L. (1989). Afterword: Young children in international perspective. In P. Olmstead & D. Weikart (Eds.), *How nations serve young children: profiles of child care and education in 14 countries* (pp. 401-406). Ypsilanti, MI: High Scope Press.

Katz, L. (2003). The right of the child to learn in a quality environment. *International Journal of Early Childhood, 35*, (1,2), 13-22.

Kagitcibasi, C. (1999, April). Early learning and human development: The Turkish early enrichment program. Paper presented at The Committee on Early Childhood Pedagogy, National Academy of Sciences, National Research Council Meetings on Global Perspectives on Early Childhood Education, Washington, DC.

Kim, U., & Berry, J. W. (Eds.). (1993). *Indigenous psychologies: Research and experience in cultural context*. Newbury Park, CA: Sage.

Klein, P. S. (1996). *Early intervention: Cross-cultural experiences with a mediational approach*. New York: Garland Publishing.

Krishnakumar, A., Buehler, C., & Barber, B. (2004). Cross-ethnic equivalence of socialization measures in European American and African American families. *Journal of Marriage and the Family, 66*, 809-820.

Kutnick, P. (1994). Does preschool curriculum make a difference in primary school performance: Insights into the variety of preschool activities and their effects on school achievement and behavior in the Caribbean island of Trinidad; Cross sectional and longitudinal evidence. *Early Child Development and Care, 103*, 27-42.

Kuyk, J. J. van. (2003). *Pyramid. The method for young children*. (English version). Arnhem, The Netherlands: Citogroep.

Kuyk, J. J. van. (2005). The Pyramid method. In J. L. Roopnarine & J. E. Johnson (Eds.), *Approaches to early childhood education* (4th ed., 395-422). Columbus, OH: Merrill/Prentice Hall.

Ladson-Billings, G. (2000). *Crossing over to Canaan: The journey of new teachers in diverse classrooms*. San Francisco: Jossey-Bass.

Laloumi-Vidali, E. (2000). Professional views on parents' involvement at the partnership level in preschool education. *International Journal of Early Childhood*, 19-25.

Lamb, M. E. (1998). Nonparental child care: Context, quality, correlates, and consequences. In I. E. Sigel & K. A. Renninger (Eds.), *Handbook of child psychology: Vol. 4. Child psychology in practice* (5th ed., pp. 73-133). New York: Wiley.

Lamb, M. E., Sternberg, K. J., Hwang, C. P., & Broberg, A. G. (Eds). (1992). *Child care in context: Cross-cultural perspectives*. Hillsdale, NJ: Lawrence Erlbaum Associates.

Laosa, L. M. (1999). Intercultural transitions in human development and education. *Journal of Applied Developmental Psychology, 20*, 355-406.

Laungani, P. (2005). Changing patterns of family life in India. In J. L. Roopnarine & U. Gielen (Eds.). *Families in global perspectives* (pp. 85-103). Boston, MA: Allyn & Bacon.

Lebra, T. S. (1994). Mother and child in Japanese socialization: A Japan-U.S. comparison. In P. M. Greenfield & R. R. Cocking (Eds.), *Cross-cultural roots of minority child development* (pp. 259-274). Hillsdale, NJ: Erlbaum.

Leo-Rhynie, E. (1997). Class, race, and gender issues in childrearing in the Caribbean. In J. L. Roopnarine & J. Brown (Eds.), *Caribbean families: Diversity among ethnic groups* (pp. 25-55). Norwood, NJ: Ablex.

Lee, J. (1997). The characteristics of early childhood education in Korea. *International Journal of Early Childhood, 29*, 2, 44-50.

Lee, J. (2001). School reform initiatives as balancing acts: Policy variation and educational convergence among Japan, Korea, England and the United States. *Education Policy Analysis Archives, 9*, 13.

Levenstein, P., Levenstein, S., & Oliver, D. (2002). First grade school readiness of former child participants in a South Carolina replication of the parent-child home program. *Journal of Applied Developmental Psychology, 23*, 3, 331-354.

Levenstein, P. Levenstein, S., Shiminski, A., & Stolzberg, J. E. (1998). Long-term impact of a verbal interaction program for at-risk toddlers: An exploratory study of high school outcomes in a replication of the mother-child home program. *Journal of Applied Developmental Psychology, 19*, 2, 267-286.

LeVine, R. (1974). Parental goals: A cross-cultural view. *Teachers College Record, 76*, 226-239.

LeVine, R. (2004). Challenging expert knowledge: Findings from an African study of infant care and development. In U. P. Gielen, & J. L. Roopnarine (Eds.), *Childhood and adolescence: Cross-cultural and practical applications* (pp. 149-165). Westport, CT: Praeger.

Levy, R. I. (1996). Essential contrasts: Differences in parental ideas about learners and teaching in Tahiti and Nepal. In S. Harkness & C. M.

Super (Eds.). *Parents' cultural belief systems: Their origins, expressions, and consequences.* New York: Guilford Press.

Liang, X., Fuller, B., & Singer, J. (2000). Ethnic differences in child care selection: The influence of family structure, parental practices, and home language. *Early Childhood Research Quarterly, 15,* 357-384,

Lijadu, M. O. (1993). *Family and community education: A Nigerian perspective. Africa; Nigeria.* Paper presented at the World Congress of the Organisation Mondiale pour l'Education Prescholaire, World Organization for Early Childhood Education. (ERIC Document Reproduction Service No. ED353047)

Lillemyr, O. F., Fagerli, O, & Sobstad, F. (2001). *A global perspective on early childhood care and education: A proposed model.* Paris: Unesco. (Action Research in Family and Early Childhood, Monograph No. 17/2001)

Lin, M., Johnson, J. E., & Johnson, K. M., (2003). Dramatic play in Montessori kindergartens in Taiwan and Mainland China. Unpublished manuscript.

Liu, P. W., Yeung, A. S., & Farmer, S. (2001). What do parents want from day care services? Perspectives from Australia. *Early Childhood Research Quarterly, 16,* 385-393.

Loeb, S., Fuller, B., Kagan, S. L., & Carrol, B. (2004). Child care in poor communities: Early learning effects of type, quality, and stability. *Child Development, 75,* 47-65.

Logie, C. (1997, April). *The status of ECCE provision in Trinidad and Tobago.* Paper presented at the Caribbean Conference on Early Childhood Education. Barbados.

Lubeck, S., Jessup, P. A., & Jewkes, A. M. (2001). Globalization and its discontents: Early childhood education in a new world order. In S. Reifel & M. H. Brown (Eds.), *Early education and care, and reconceptualizing play: Advances in early education and day care, 11,* pp. 3-57. Amsterdam: Jai/Elsevier Science.

Marcon, R. A. (1999). Differential impact of preschool models on development and early learning of inner-city children. *Developmental Psychology, 35*(1), 358-375.

Mathiesen, M. E., Herrera, M. O., Merino, J. M., Villalon, B. M., & Suzuky, S. E. (2000) Evaluation of adult-child interaction in preschool classrooms of Concepcion, Chile. *International Journal of Early Childhood, 32,* 14-19.

May, H. (2001). *Politics in the playground: The world of early childhood in postwar New Zealand.* New Zealand: Bridget Williams Books.

McGillicuddy-De Lisi, A. V., & Subramanian, S. (1994). Tanzanian and United States mothers' beliefs about parents' and teachers' roles in children's knowledge acquisition. *International Journal of Behavioral Development, 17,* 209-237.

Melton, G. B. (1993). Is there a place for children in the new world order? *Journal of Law, Ethics & Public Policy, 7,* 2, 491-532.

Miller, L (1997). A Vision for the Early Years Curriculum in the United Kingdom. *International Journal of Early Childhood, 29,* 1, 34-41.

Miller, L. (1999). Teaching and learning about play, language, and literacy with preschool educators in Malaysia. *International Journal of Early Childhood, 31,* 2, 55-64.

Miller, P. J., Wiley, A., Fung, H., & Liang, C. (1997). Personal story-telling as a medium of socialization in Chinese and American families. *Child Development, 68,* 557-568.

Moore, M. K., & Klass, P. H. (2000). Understanding parents' expectations on hurrying: United States and England, *International Journal of Early Childhood, 30*-46

Morelli, G. A., Rogoff, B., Oppenheim, D., & Goldsmith, D. (1992). Cultural variation in infants' sleeping arrangements: Questions of independence. *Developmental Psychology, 28,* 604-613.

Morrison, J. W. (2000). Under colonialism to democratization: Early childhood development in Ghana. *International Journal of Early Childhood, 32*(2), 24-31.

Morrison, J. W. (2001). Early care and education in Ghana. *Childhood Education, 77,* 4, 214-218.

Morrison, J. W., & Milner, V. (1997) Early education and care in Jamaica: A grassroots effort. *International Journal of Early Childhood, 29*(2), 51-68.

Myers, R. (1992). *The twelve who survive: Strengthening programmes of early childhood development in the Third World.* London: Routledge.

Nager, N., & Shapiro, E. K. (Eds.). (2000). *Revisiting a progressive pedagogy.* New York: State University of New York Press.

New, R. (1987). Children's play-una cosa naturale: An Italian perspective. In J. L. Roopnarine & J. E. Johnson, & F. H. Hooper (Eds.), *Children's play in diverse cultures* (pp. 123-147). Albany: State University of New York Press.

New, R. (2005). The Reggio Emilia approach: Provocations and partnerships with U.S. early childhood educators. In J. l. Roopnarine & J. E. Johnson (Eds.), *Approaches to early childhood education* (4th ed., pp. 313-335). Columbus, OH: Merrill/Prentice Hall.

NICHD Early Child Care Research Network. (2001). Nonmaternal care and family factors in early development: An overview of the NICHD study of early child care. *Journal of Applied Developmental Psychology, 22,* 5, 457-492.

NICHD Early Child Care Research Network. (2002). Direct and indirect effects of caregiving quality on young children's development. *Psychological Science, 13,* 199-206.

NICHD Early Child Care Research Network. (2003). Does amount of time spent in child care predict socioemotional adjustment during the transition to kindergarten? *Child Development, 74,* 976-1005.

Nino, A. (1979). The naïve theory of the infant and other maternal attitudes in two subgroups in Israel. *Child Development, 50,* 976-980.

Njideka, E. C. (1999) Literacy in early childhood education: The right of every child. *International Journal of Early Childhood, 31,* 2, 1-5.

Odom, S. L., Hanson, M. J., Blackman, J. A., & Koul, S. (2003). *Early intervention practices around the world.* Baltimore, MD: Paul H. Brookes.

Ogbu, J. (1991). Immigrant and involuntary minorities in comparative perspective. In M. Gibson & J. Ogbu (Eds.), *Minority status and schooling: A comparative study of immigrant and involuntary minorities* (pp. 3-33). New York: Garland Publishing.

Okagaki, L., & Sternberg, R. J. (1993). Parental beliefs and children's school performance. *Child Development, 64,* 36-56.

Oktay, A., & Zembat, R. (1995). Development of preschool education and training of teachers in Turkey . *International Journal of Early Childhood, 27,* 1, 62-67

Olmsted, P., & Weikart, D. P. (1989). *How nations serve young children: Profiles of child care and education in 14 countries.* Ypsilanti, MI: The High/Scope Press.

Olmsted, P., & Weikart, D. P. (1995). *The IEA preprimary study: Early childhood care and education in 11 countries.* Oxford: Pergamon.

Opper, S. (1992). *Hong Kong's young children: Their preschools and families.* Hong Kong: Hong Kong University Press.

Paguio, L. P. (1989) Differences in perceptions of the ideal child among American and Filipino parents. *Early Child Development and Care, 50,* 67-74.

Pan, H. W. (1994) Children's play in Taiwan. In J. L. Roopnarine, J. E. Johnson, Hooper, F. H. (Eds.), *Children's play in diverse cultures* (pp. 31-50). New York: State University of New York Press

Parmar, P. & Harkness, S. (2004). Asian and European American parents' ethnotheories of play and learning: Effects on home routines and children's behavior. *International Journal of Behavioral Development, 28*, 97–104.

Pascal, C., & Bertram, T. (1999), Accounting early for lifelong learning, In L. Abbott & H. Moylett (Eds.), *Early education transformed*. London: Falmer Press.

Pearson, E., & Rao, N. (2003). Socialization goals, parenting practices, and peer competence in Chinese and English preschoolers. *Early Child Development and Care, 173*, 131-146.

Petrogiannis, K., & Melhuish, E. C. (1996). Aspects of quality in Greek day care centers. *European Journal of Psychology of Education, XI*, 2, 177-191.

Pianta, R. C., & McCoy, S. J. (1997). The first day of school: The predictive validity. *Journal of Applied Developmental Psychology, 18*, 1, 1-22.

Poortinga, Y. P. (1997). Towards convergence. In J. W. Berry, Y. P. Poortinga, & J. Pandey (Eds.), *Handbook of cross-cultural psychology* (Vol. 1, 2nd ed., pp. 247-387). Boston: Allyn & Bacon.

Powell, C. (2005). Evaluation of the Roving Caregivers Programme: Rural Family Support Organization. Tropical Medicine Research Unit, University of the West Indies, Mona, Jamaica.

Raban, B., & Ure, C. (1999). Literacy in the preschool: An Australian case study, Landscapes in early childhood education. In J. Hayden (Ed.), *Landscapes in early childhood education: Cross national perspectives* (pp. 316-329). New York: Peter Lang.

Raban, B., & Ure, C. (2000). Literacy in three languages: A challenge for Singapore preschools. *International Journal of Early Childhood, 31*, 45-54.

Rao, N., & Koong, M. (2000). Enhancing preschool education in Hong Kong. *International Journal of Early Childhood, 32*(2), 1-11.

Rao, N., Koong, M., Kwong, M., & Wong, M. (1999, November). *Indicators of high quality preschool programs in Chinese cultural context*. Paper presented at the National Association for the Education of Young Children, New Orleans.

Rescorla, M. L., Hyson, M., & Hirsh-Pasek, K. (Eds.). (1991). Instruction in early childhood: Challenge or pressure. *New Directions in Child Development, 53*. San Francisco: Jossey-Bass.

Reynolds, A. J. (2000) *Success in early intervention: The Chicago child-parent centers*. Lincoln: University of Nebraska Press.

Robinson, J. (2003). Contemporary globalization and education. In S. Bartlett & D. Burton (Eds.), *Education studies: Essential issues* (pp. 239-264). London: Sage.

Roopnarine, J. L. (1999, February). *Parental involvement, ethnotheories about development, parenting styles, and early academic achievement in Caribbean-American children*. Paper presented in the Department of Applied Psychology, New York University.

Roopnarine, J. L., & Brown, J. (Eds.). (1997). *Caribbean families: Diversity among ethnic groups*. Greenwich, CT: Ablex.

Roopnarine, J. L., Bynoe, P. B., & Singh, R. (2004). Factors tied to the schooling of English-speaking immigrants in the United States. In U. Gielen & J. L. Roopnarine (Eds.), *Childhood and adolescence: Cross-cultural and practical applications* (pp. 317-349). Westport, CT: Praeger.

Roopnarine, J. L., Bynoe, P. F., Singh, R., & Simon, R. (2005). Caribbean family in English-speaking Countries: A rather complex mosaic. In J. L. Roopnarine & U. Gielen (Eds.), *Families in global perspective* (pp. 311-329). Boston: Allyn & Bacon.

Roopnarine, J. L., & Gielen, U. (Eds.). (2005). *Families in global perspectives*. Boston, MA: Allyn & Bacon.

Roopnarine, J. L., & Johnson, J. E. (Eds.). (2005). *Approaches to early childhood education* (4th ed.). Columbus, OH: Merrill/Prentice Hall.

Roopnarine, J. L., Johnson, J. E., & Hooper, F. H. (1994) (Eds.). *Children's play in diverse cultures*. Albany: State University of New York Press.

Roopnarine, J. L., & Metindogan, A. (2005). Cultural beliefs about childrearing and schooling in immigrant families and "developmentally appropriate practices": Yawning gaps! In O. N. Saracho & B. Spodek (Eds.), *Contemporary perspectives on families, communities, and schools for young children* (pp. 181-202). Westport, CT: Information Age.

Roopnarine, J. L., Shin, M., Jung, K., & Hossain, Z. (2003). Play and early education and development: The instantiation of parental belief systems. In O. Saracho & B. Spodek (Eds.), *Contemporary perspectives on families, communities, and Schools for young children* (pp. 181-202). Westport, CT: New Age Publishers.

Schweinhart, L. J., & Weikart, D. P. (1997). The high/scope preschool curriculum comparison study through age 23. *Early Childhood Research Quarterly, 12*, 2, 117-144.

Scott-McDonald, K. (1997). The status of child care supports for Jamaican families. In: J. L. Roopnarine, & J. Brown (Eds.), *Caribbean families: Diversity among ethnic groups* (pp. 147-176). Westport, CT: Ablex Publishing.

Sever, L. (1989). Change in women's perceptions of parental child rearing attitudes in Turkey: A three generation comparison. *Early Child Development and Care, 50*, 131-140.

Shearer, D., & Shearer, D. (2005). The Portage Model: An international home approach to early intervention of young children and their families. In J. L. Roopnarine & J. E. Johnson (Eds.), *Approaches to early childhood education* (4th ed., pp. 83-103). Columbus, OH: Merrill/Prentice Hall.

Sheridan, S., & Schuster, K. (2001). Evaluation of pedagogical quality in early childhood education: A cross-national perspective. *Journal of Research In Childhood Education, 16*, 109-124.

Shin, M. (2001). Beyond independent children and authoritative parenting: Korean mothers' perspective. Unpublished doctoral dissertation, Syracuse University.

Shonkoff, J., & Meisels, S. J. (Eds.). (2000). *Handbook of early childhood intervention*. New York: Cambridge University Press.

Shonkoff, J., & Phillips, D. (2000). *From neurons to neighborhoods: The science of early childhood development*. Washington, DC: National Academy Press.

Shweder, R., Goodnow, J., Hatano, G., LeVine, R., Markus, H., & Miller, P. (1998). The cultural psychology of development: One mind, many mentalities. In R. Lerner (Vol. Ed.), *Theoretical models of human development, Vol 1: Handbook of child psychology* (pp. 865-937). New York: Wiley.

Sigel, I., & McGillicuddy-De Lisi, A. (2002). Parental beliefs as cognitions: The dynamic belief systems model. In M. Bornstein (Ed.), *Handbook of parenting* (Vol. 3, 2nd ed., pp. 485-508). Mahwah, NJ: Erlbaum.

Soderman, A. K., Chhikara, S., Hsiu-Ching, C., & Kuo, E. (1999). Gender differences that affect emerging literacy in first grade children: The U.S., India, and Taiwan. *International Journal of Early Childhood, 31*, 2, 9-16.

Soto, L. D., & Negron, L. (1994). Mainland Puerto Rican children. In J. L. Roopnarine, J. E. Johnson, & F. H. Hooper (Eds.), *Children's play in diverse cultures*. Albany: State University of New York Press.

Spiess, C. K., Buchel, S. F., & Wagner, G. G. (2003). Children's school placement in Germany: Does kindergarten attendance matter? *Early Childhood Research Quarterly, 18*, 255-270.

Stevenson, H., & Lee, S. Y. (1990). Contexts of achievement: A study of American, Chinese, and Japanese children. *Monographs of the Society for Research in Child Development, 55*(1-2, Serial No. 221).

Stevenson, H. W., Lee, S., & Schweingruber, H. (1999). Home influences on early literacy. In D. Wagner, R. L. Venezky, & B. V. Street (Eds.), *Literacy: An international handbook* (pp. 251-257). Boulder, CO: Westview Press.

Stipek, D., Feiler, R., Daniels, D., & Millburn, S. (1995). Effects of different instructional approaches on young children's achievement and motivation. *Child Development, 66*(1), 209-223.

Stipek, D., Milburn, S., Clements, D., & Daniels, D. H. (1992). Parents' beliefs about appropriate education for young children. *Journal of Applied Developmental Psychology, 13*, 193-210.

Sukhdeo, F. (2004). *Historical review of nursery education in Guyana.* Turkeyen: Guyana.

Sunar, D., & Fisek, G. O. (2005). Contemporary Turkish families. In J. L. Roopnarine, & U. Gielen (Ed.), *Families in global perspectives.* Boston, MA: Allyn & Bacon.

Super, C., & Harkness, S. (1997). The cultural structuring of child development. In J. Berry, P. Dasen, & T. S. Saraswathi (Eds.), *Handbook of cross-cultural psychology: Basic processes and human development* (pp. 1-39). Needham, MA: Allyn & Bacon.

Suvannathat, C., & Passornsiri, N. (1992). Early childhood education in Thailand. In S. Feeney, & F. Naroll (Eds), *Early childhood education in Asia and Pacific: A source book* (pp. 175-196). New York: Peter Lang Publishing.

Swaminathan, M. (1998a). *The first five years: A critical perspective on early childhood care and education in India.* London: Sage Publications.

Swaminathan, M. (1998b). Learning from experience: An overview of the Suraksha studies. In M. Swaminathan (Ed.), *The first five years: A critical perspective on early childhood care and education in India* (pp. 136-151). London: Sage Publications.

Swadener, E. B., Kabiru, M., & Njenga, A. (1997). Does the village still raise the child? A collaborative study of changing child-rearing and community mobilization in Kenya. *Early Education & Development, 8,* 2, 285-306.

Sylva, K., & Nabuco, M. E. (1996). Research on quality in the curriculum. *International Journal of Early Childhood, 32,* 1-6.

Taylor, S. I., Lichtman, M., & Ogawa, T. (1998). Sunao (Cooperative) children: The development of autonomy in Japanese preschoolers. *International Journal of Early Childhood, 30,* 2, 38-46.

Thomas, R. M. (1992). Early childhood education in Japan. In S. Feeney & F. Naroll (Eds.), *Early childhood education in Asia and Pacific: A source book* (pp. 95-134). New York: Peter Lang Publishing.

Tietze, W., Cryer, D., Bairrao, J., Palacios, J., & Wetzel, G. (1996). Comparisons of observed process quality in early child care and education in five countries. *Early Childhood Research Quarterly, 11,* 447-475.

Tobin, J. (1998). An American Otaku: Or this boy's virtual life. In J. Sefton- Green (Ed.), *Digital Diversions, Youth Culture in the Age of Multimedia.* London: UCL Press.

Tobin, J. J., Wu, D. Y. H., & Davidson, D. H. (1989). *Preschool in three cultures.* New Haven, CT: Yale University Press.

Tomlinson, J. B. (1999). *Globalization and culture.* Chicago: University of Chicago Press.

Tulananda, O., & Roopnarine, J. L. (2001). Mothers' and fathers' interactions with preschoolers in the home in Northern Thailand: Relationships to teachers' assessments of children's social skills. *Journal of Family Psychology, 14,* 676-687.

Tzuriel, D., Kaniel, S., Kanner, E., & Haywood, H. C. (1999). The effectiveness of Bright Start program in kindergarten on transfer abilities and academic achievements. *Early Childhood Research Quarterly, 114,* 111-141.

UNESCO. (1998). Culture Entrance et education prescolaire Culture, childhood and preschool education. In G. Brougère & S. Rayna (Eds.), *Report of the Seminar organized by Université Paris-Nord and MRP with the help of UNESCO* (1-255) Paris: Université Paris-Nord & INRP.

UNESCO. (2003). Digest of Education statistics. Author. Retrieved from World Wide Web. http://nces.ed.gov/programs/do3/ch_2.asp.

van der Kooj, R., & Slaats-van den Hurk, W. (1991). Relations between parental opinions and attitudes about play and childrearing. *Play and Culture, 4,* 108-123.

Van De Vijver, F., & Leung, K. (1997). Methods and data analysis of comparative research. In J. W. Berry, Y. P. Poortinga, & J. Pandey (Eds.), *Handbook of cross-cultural psychology* (Vol. 1, 2nd ed., pp. 257-300). Boston: Allyn & Bacon.

Weikart, D., & Schweinhart, L. J. (2005). The High Scope Curriculum for early child care and education. J. L. Roopnarine & J. E. Johnson (Eds.), *Approaches to early childhood education* (4th ed., pp. 235-250). Columbus, OH: Merrill/Prentice Hall.

Weis, L., Altbach, P. G., Kelly, G. P., & Petrie, H. G. (Eds.). (1991). *Critical perspectives on early childhood education.* Albany: The State University of New York Press.

Weisner, T. (1998). Human development, child well-being, and the cultural project of development. In D. Sharma & K. Fischer (Eds.), *Socioemotional development across cultures: New directions in child development* (pp. 69-85). San Francisco, CA: Jossey-Bass Publishers.

West, J., Denton, K., & Germino-Hausken, E. (2000). *America's kindergartners.* (NCES No. 2000-070). Washington, DC: U.S. Department of Education.

White, M., & Levine, R. (1986). What is an Iiko (good child)? In H. Stevenson, H. Azuma, & K. Hakuta (Eds.), *Child development and education in Japan.* New York: Freeman Press.

Wilson, L. C., Wilson, C. M., Berkeley-Caines, L. (2003). Age, gender, and socioeconomic differences in parental socialization preferences in Guyana. *Journal of Comparative Family Studies, 34,* 213-227.

Woodhead, M. (2000). Towards a global paradigm for research into early childhood education. In H. Penn (Ed.), *Early childhood services: Theory, policy and practice* (pp. 15-35). Buckingham, UK: Open University Press.

Wollons, R. E. (2000). *Kindergarten and cultures: The global diffusion of an idea.* New Haven, CT: Yale University Press.

Woodill, G. Behnhard, J., & Prochner, L. (Eds.). (1992). *International handbook of early childhood education.* New York: Garland Publishing.

World Bank (2002). *World development indicators.* Washington, DC: The World Bank.

Wu, D. Y. H. (1992). Early childhood education in China. In S. Feeney & F. Naroll (Eds.), *Early childhood education in Asia and Pacific: A source book* (pp. 299-314). New York: Peter Lang Publishing.

Wu, D. Y. H. (1996). Chinese childhood socialization. In M. H. Bond (Ed.), *The handbook of Chinese psychology* (pp. 143-154). London : Oxford University Press.

Zigler, E., & Styfco, S. J. (Eds.). (2004). *The Head Start debates.* Baltimore, MD: Brookes Publishing.

Zigler, E., Taussig, C., & Black, K. (1992). Early childhood intervention: A promising preventative for juvenile delinquency. *American Psychologist, 47,* 8, 997-1006.

·32·

HISTORICAL RESEARCH IN EARLY

CHILDHOOD EDUCATION

Blythe S. F. Hinitz
The College of New Jersey

INTRODUCTION

It is well accepted in all disciplines that future endeavors rest on the "learnings" from the past. Historical research is the process that reveals the lessons from the past and opens windows to the future. The purposes of this chapter are twofold: (1) to share the methodologies effective in doing historical research in ECE and provide examples to illustrate the effectiveness of various strategies and (2) to share some of the aspects of ECE history that demonstrate how the primary and secondary sources support theories and positions taken based upon historical data. These purposes are presented through discussion of the following topics: (1) primary and secondary sources, (2) selected controversies as examples of the use of sources, (3) parenting and adult-child relations, (4) violence against children, (5) kindergartens, day nurseries, and preschool programs, (6) models of early education, (7) government-funded programs, (8) professional preparation, (9) archives, print, and online resources, (10) diversity and multicultural perspectives, (11) organizations, and (12) resources.

PRIMARY AND SECONDARY SOURCES

Specific tools are utilized in historical research to give life to the past, so that direct and implied lessons can be acquired. Two such tools are the use of primary and secondary sources as data. Primary and secondary source materials provide a basis for historical study. Primary sources are those created during the time period under consideration or obtained from persons who participated in or were responsible for events,

programs, or occurrences. These sources include, but are not limited to:

- Diaries and journals
- Letters and other correspondence
- Government reports and legislative records
- Birth, death, and census documents and other demographic records
- Statistical files
- Church and court records and other legal documents
- Social service case records, those that document orphanages, "baby farms," and day nurseries
- Autobiographies
- Records of formal and informal oral history interviews and first-person accounts of events
- Medical reports
- Observational research studies
- Board meeting minutes and notes
- Archival materials
- Photographs
- Audio- and videotapes, compact discs, and DVDs
- Newspaper clipping files
- Memorial tributes
- Books and periodical articles written during the time period under review
- Archeological artifacts
- Papers of prominent figures and ordinary people
- Organizational records, including conference programs and proceedings

Secondary sources are derived from primary sources and their interpretation. They include:

- Histories of a time period
- Stories and legends
- Literature and mythology
- Reports of psychoanalysis
- Works of visual art
- Nonphotographic records of dress and architecture

Knowledge of early childhood education history provides the practitioner with a foundation on which to build. Historical research analyzes the contributions of key leaders and the equally important contributions of the thousands of teachers and caregivers who have made our field what it is today. Historical research details the programs and institutions that have been provided for young children in the United States through the decades, utilizing information from a wide variety of fields and subjects. These are not limited to history, but include psychology, home economics, sociology, economics, political science, women's studies, civil and human rights, multicultural and linguistic studies, immigration studies, pediatric medicine, and education. The impact of government actions and legislation on young children and their "significant others" is also the purview of the educational historian. The methodology used draws upon the foundational worldwide historical knowledge base on childhood, parenthood and programs for children. The historian of ECE must consider the diversity of populations served by early education programs, including the impact of racism, sexism, and classism, areas that are just beginning to be explored.

Historical research dealing with young children in the United States has had two main emphases. One is the history of early childhood education (ECE) programs and practices, including those who devised the group models, trained the staff, and those who brought out-of-home programs to fruition. A second focus is the history of parent education and the related views of parenthood espoused during the 19th and 20th centuries.

EXAMPLES OF THE USE OF PRIMARY SOURCES

Building a Theory From Evidence: Controversy

The history of childhood and early education is not immune to the controversies surrounding other areas of historical investigation. A major dispute focuses on research relating to the role and view of children from antiquity through the medieval period. For example, a debate between traditional historians and psychohistorians centers on the principle of *argumentum ex silenito*. In the "argument from silence" traditional historians have stated, in the absence of evidence, that they were convinced that further research would turn up good parenting. Research from primary sources disputes this, demonstrating that widespread child abuse was considered normal during these time periods. The practice of infanticide in Greece and Rome is

described by Celia Lascarides, who read some of the sources in their original languages (Lascarides & Hinitz, 2000, pp. 4–5, 7, 17). Lloyd deMause found supporting evidence for infanticide and child sacrifice in the ancient and medieval world in diaries, letters, autobiographies, and medical reports (1988, pp. 5 of 18, 14 of 18). Reports by ancient authorities such as Tertullian and Plutarch, and archeological discoveries, including children's charred bones, remation urns, and religious paraphernalia, attest to the child sacrifice practiced in Carthage. In *Family Planning in Antiquity,* Eyben details primary sources on routine infanticide from Greek until well into medieval times. Langer used church and court records and medical reports to support statements regarding the excessive violence inflicted on children. Trexler cited census records and reports from foundling hospitals to reveal the differentiated treatment to which female children were subjected in 15th-century Florence.

Other controversies deal with the practice of swaddling and the amount and types of violent behavior inflicted on children. For example, parental attitudes in 18th-century Europe reflected either indifference or intrusiveness. The practices followed by Colonial-era parents in the United States included infanticide and physical abuse (Lascarides in Lascarides & Hinitz, 2000, pp. 174–175, 179–180). Taylor's investigation of 19th-century medical records found that venereal disease organisms that do not survive long outside the body, were regularly detected on children's "private parts" when parents had the disease (cited in deMause, 1988, p. 12 of 18).

Even with overwhelming evidence to support alternative statements, historians sometimes cling to their original theories and formulations. The message for historians of childhood and education is to rely on primary sources first but also to learn as much as possible about the geographic area and the time period from a variety of sources. Avoid the pitfall of relying on any specific theory, which might tempt one to try to make the evidence fit the theory rather than using scientific principles.

CONCEPTS OF CHILDHOOD AND ADULTHOOD

The origin of the concept of "childhood" is another example of historical controversy. In *Centuries of Childhood,* Phillipe Aries uses representations of children in art, records of children's dress and the absence of differences in adult and child activities to determine that the concept of childhood did not exist in the medieval world. However, Shahar's examination of original source documents (1992, reported in Lascarides & Hinitz, 2000, p. 30) found that not only did a concept of childhood exist in the central and late Middle Ages; it was perceived as a distinct stage in the life cycle. Kennedy (2000) says that Aries's analysis focuses on the time in Western history that great shifts were taking place in "emergent middle-class culture." Kennedy (p. 523) characterizes this period as a time of the emergence of the adult's "self-contained, boundaried self." The child, "relatively undersocialized, instinctually unrestrained," was "separated off and increasingly understood as a person whose most salient characteristic is that she is *not* an adult." Hewes (2003), in a letter to *The New Yorker*, states that it was the concept of adulthood rather than childhood that emerged in the late 16th century.

Uses of Historical Evidence

Our knowledge of the reality of children's lives and education in any given time period is derived mainly from what historians of that time and later have written. Few people have access to the primary sources, therefore the information and commentary provided by historians forms the foundation for further work. The omission of evidence in books and reports is just as problematic as the inclusion of incomplete or skewed data. For example, a scholar's published account of a Renaissance Italian father's diary omitted the pledge made to his unborn child for better treatment than he had as a child. The diary entries show that the baby boy was sent out to a wet nurse, and later died from the plague. The scholar included the father's written recriminations after the fact. The omission of the original pledge from the published work slanted the evidence to depict the father in a more favorable light (deMause, 1988, p. 6 of 18).

Kennedy (2000) suggested that any study of adult-child relations should draw on journals, legal and demographic records, tracts, stories, and legends. He cites a negative view of childhood that led to rigid, punitive forms of schooling in the early modern period. Kennedy (522) cites Freud's synthesis of the child as symbolizing both deficit and wholeness for adults, as an influence on early childhood education. He contends that it has led to our appreciation of the significance of play for psychological, social and cognitive development. Kennedy further believes that that a positive view of childhood as a time with its own characteristics, and a genuine adult interest in the child's construction of the world became prevalent in the twentieth century. This corresponds to deMause's Socializing (19th to mid-20th century) and Helping (mid-20th century on) adult modes. The adult in the Helping mode is characterized by responding to and playing with children, and assisting them in reaching their daily goals. (Kennedy, 2000, p. 529) Art, literature, mythology, and psychoanalysis are examined for corroboration. Kennedy (p. 535) concludes that adults construct childhood on the basis of "prevailing cultural images" and the "residues of their own childhoods." He states that the more adults recognize their own childlike aspects, the more they are able to relate to children as persons. He posits a historical progression in adult-child relations that affects the way adults construct the world for children, and increases the extent to which they "seek the good" in them. In his view this leads to adults paying more attention to children, giving the child more care and a greater voice in the adult-child dialogue. The result is projected to be both children and adults who have a greater capacity to "grow." This historical and philosophical formulation, drawing on the arts, literature and psychology, surely has implications for the care and education of young children today.

Finkelstein's work demonstrates the intertwining of social justice and historical research documentation. One paper describes the evolution of American education in school and at home since Colonial times as a transition from an intrusive to a socializing mode. Her presidential address to the History of Education Society (U.S.) provides an overview of the historical roots of violence against children in the United States that has meaning for practitioners in the field today (Finkelstein, 1979, 2000). According to Finkelstein, religious doctrine has led to corporal punishment in homes and schools; and the doctrine of family privacy has limited governmental responsibility and support for children. For example, the home visits that were part of the early kindergarten program were not institutionalized when it moved into the public school system. Teachers traditionally did not mingle socially with children and their families. Finkelstein believes that these limits on the teacher's role indirectly contributed to enduring violence against children (2000, p. 13).

Historical Research on Maternal Employment and Corresponding Group Child Care Programs—Traditional Research Methods

In our socioeconomic tradition, childrearing is conceived of as a moral rather than an economic enterprise. Opposition to maternal employment has led to limited public investment in children. Documented problems with infant schools, orphanages, "baby farms," and day nurseries for poor and orphaned children fueled opposition to the construction of community-based child care facilities. In many instances, there was "class-biased child-saving," (Finkelstein, 2000, p. 16) in which women of wealth provided group programs for the children of the poor and "lower classes" (Grant, 1998, pp. 115–119; Lascarides & Hinitz, 2000, pp. 257–258, 361–367, 337–339). Elizabeth Rose's (1999) study of the evolution of Philadelphia day nurseries utilizing 70 years of case records, as well as board meeting notes, photographs, newspaper clipping files, and books, provides a close look at custodial care programs for the young children of poor working women. Primary source documents provided details about the women who founded and managed the day nurseries, those who utilized them, and those who worked there. The book includes a comprehensive view of the diversity of the charitable day nursery system. One segment was organized by white Protestant elite socialites, another by the Young Women's Union for Jewish immigrant children, a third segment was founded by African-American members of the Women's Union Missionary Society, a fourth by Catholic Charities, and a fifth by the Salvation Army. Documents reveal that home inspections were conducted by members of the National Federation of Day Nurseries (NFDN) to insure that only children whose homes reflected "hard times, scarcity of work for men, illness, insanity [or] desertion" were admitted (Beatty in DeVita & R. Mosher-Williams, 2001, pp. 167–168).

Rose chronicles the addition of a nursery school component, the blurring of the boundary between education and custodial care, and the attitude change that took place in the day nurseries after World War II. The women who used Philadelphia's day nurseries in the 1950s saw working for wages as a way of bettering their family's quality of life, and they demonstrated for the child care they needed to support them (Rose, 1999, pp. 211–213, photograph 8 following p. 84).

CONTEMPORARY METHODS

In their comparative study of three types of home-community visits, Navaz Bhavnagri and Sue Krolikowski (2000) utilized several historical research sources and provided a replicable plan that is available to colleagues and practitioners through the use of technology. A companion case study, also available via the Internet, draws on other specific resources (Bhavnagri, Krolikowski, & Vaswani, 2000). *Home-Community Visits During an Era of Reform (1870–1920)* compares the purposes, procedures, and outcomes of home visits by kindergarten teachers, settlement house workers and public school visiting teachers. For purposes of this chapter, the section on charity kindergarten teachers' visits will be highlighted. The authors drew on books, periodicals, and newspaper articles written during the time period under study to obtain information about practices during that time period. The use of these publications provided the authors with a sense of the way in which the kindergarteners' (teachers') contemporaries viewed their work. It is critically important for historians of education to utilize these types of materials if they are available, because they provide insights that modern authors cannot duplicate. Special education and early childhood publications were consulted, as were statistical and philanthropic volumes. The authors effectively utilized archival photographs from the Jane Addams Collection at the University of Illinois at Chicago and the Visiting Nurse Service of New York to set the scene for an enumeration of the kindergartners' purposes for making frequent home visits. These included:

- educating the parents about kindergarten education
- getting to know children as individuals by knowing their families and communities
- facilitating the "Americanization" of the children and their families
- teaching parents about nutrition, hygiene, child development and alternative methods of discipline and conflict resolution
- utilization of community businesses, services and resources to optimize children's development and promote kindergarten (Bhavnagri, Krolikowski, & Vaswani, Table 1)

The authors then demonstrate the positive outcomes of the kindergarteners' visits that have meaning for today's practitioners, including:

- parents valuing play as education
- families transforming their childrearing practices
- families receiving welfare and other support services
- neighborhood hygiene and ambience transformed
- parents becoming local advocates and leaders
- kindergartens becoming a part of the public schools (Bhavnagri, Krolikowski, & Vaswani, Table 3)

This article appears in an online journal, which makes the text and photographs available to anyone with computer Internet access. The authors demonstrate that a clear presentation of comparative historical data can be a meaningful contribution to the professional literature. Their ability to relate the historical information to current conditions makes it even more valuable.[1] The companion case study on the International Institute of Metropolitan Detroit draws on archival records housed at Wayne State University, literature on interprofessional collaboration and numerous ERIC documents.[2] Students and practitioners can utilize the information presented in these articles in current practical situations that they may encounter.

DOCUMENTING A MOVEMENT

The parent cooperative preschool movement was developed by middle-class college-educated women beginning in the early 1900s. The cooperatives drew on the resources of local universities, medical professionals and educators for support. Parent cooperatives were designed as educational experiences for young children *and* their parents. Many early childhood education leaders began their careers as cooperative preschool parents. In an early chapter of her comprehensive history of parent cooperative preschools, Hewes describes the formative years of this "folk movement" as lacking rational planning or a structural network. The common philosophy she ascribes to the pioneering schools, "that young children learn best through self-initiated activities in a supportive environment," would become the "glue" that held the movement together until the present day (1998, p. 36). Hewes's capsule description of the early cooperative preschools provides a window into some ways that historical research can both inform us and provide a foundation for current practice. For example, the account of the Northside Cooperative in Pasadena, which she deems the first cooperative in America, includes articles from 1914 newspapers found in the William Hailmann papers at the University of California Los Angeles (UCLA) and the Pasadena Public Library. Hewes assembled data from divergent sources to formulate a cohesive description of the background of the school, its community and its philosophy. In her book, Hewes makes extensive use of primary source documents and photographs, formal and informal interviews, and conference papers from diverse organizations. She provides a "roadmap" for finding hidden resources, often in unlikely places.

The limited access of women to higher paying jobs, and the low wages afforded child care workers, are corollaries of the widely held belief that the mother's place is in the home. As Grant documents in her recent study *Raising Baby By the Book*, education for motherhood was supported, as long as it kept the mother and child in the home. Grant seamlessly integrates and synthesizes such primary archival sources as letters, government and organizational documents and reports, and oral interviews in her work. She incorporates secondary sources from the fields

---

[1] For further elucidation of the role of the kindergarten as a bridge between home and school, see Beatty in Wollons, 2000, pp. 47, 54–55.
[2] ERIC documents are still available on microfiche in university libraries.

of psychology, child study, home economics, sociology, education, history, and economics to provide a clear picture of motherhood in the United States from the Colonial period through the 1950s. One example of the way in which the primary source material in the book can inform us and assist in planning for future parent education work is the set of descriptions relating to punishment. Grant reveals that many mothers spanked, scolded, humiliated, screamed at, shamed, frightened or used excessive force with their children (1994, pp. 446-448; 1998, pp. 150-152). A number of the quotes describe changes in mothers' behavior toward their children as a result of study group readings and discussion participation. However, this does not necessarily mean a change in the mother's behavior as a result of acquiescence to prescriptive advice. The study group mothers often disagreed with the experts and modified the edicts when they incorporated new ideas into their personal behavior patterns. According to Grant, many study group mothers rejected the popular literature's claims that they had "tyrannical devotion" to their children, and increased their "therapeutic understanding of the interactions between themselves and their children" as a result of their participation. The group and individual study reported in the literature led to a lessening of parental physical abuse and a greater awareness on the part of the mother of the necessity to foster affective (social and emotional) as well as physical and spiritual good health. This lead to an increasing cognizance of children's developmental needs over time (Hewes, 1998, pp. 70-77).

Using Archives and Oral Histories to Research 20th-Century Federal Early Education Programs

Primary source documents and the transcripts of oral history interviews chronicle U.S. federal government involvement with early education programs. A number of primary source documents relating to the WPA and Lanham Act programs can be found in the ACEI archives at the University of Maryland College Park Libraries. These include the papers of 250 early childhood leaders, a number of whom were involved with the programs. For example, the collection includes the papers of Mary Dabney Davis, who directed the Emergency Nursery Schools for the federal government (Beatty in DeVita & R. Mosher-Williams, p. 177). The National Archives in Washington, DC, is the repository for the papers of other relevant leaders, including Grace Langdon, co-director of the Lanham Act nursery schools. James L. Hymes, Jr. contributed firsthand accounts of both programs in the transcripts of his interviews with Christine Henig and Lois Hayden Meek Stolz (Henig in Hymes, 1979; Stolz in Hymes, 1978). Nourot (in Roopnarine & Johnson, 2000, pp. 18-19) included a brief synopsis of the programs in her overview of early education history. Beatty (1995, pp. 177-192; in DeVita & R. Mosher-Williams, pp. 176-178), utilizing multiple primary and secondary sources, provides a reasoned and critical appraisal of both programs.

Most sources on federal government involvement with programs for young children skip from the 1940s to the 1960s, ignoring the intervening years. Ranck's investigation of federal policies from 1953 to 1961 provides another view. She

determined that the Eisenhower administration did produce "a few tangible policies operating at a very limited level of involvement, along with the expectation that private sector and state governments would carry the weight of most government interventions" (Ranck, 1991, 1992). It was not until the 1960s advent of the "War on Poverty," however, that federal interest in and funding for young children's programs increased to a substantial extent. Programs such as Head Start, Project Follow Through, Parent and Child Centers, and professional development initiatives, such as the Child Development Associate credential, made the 1960s and early 1970s a time of progress for young children and their families. Although these programs were originally intended to benefit primarily low-income children and adults, their ramifications and research have reached into every corner of the early education profession over the past four decades (see Lascarides & Hinitz, 2000/2005, pp. 401-459; Beatty, 1995, pp. 192-200; Morgan in Cryer & Clifford, 2003, pp. 91-92; Goffin & Wilson, 2001, pp. 16-27; Nourot in J. L. Roopnarine & J. E. Johnson, 2000/2005, pp. 22-26, Powell in J. L. Roopnarine & J. E. Johnson, 2000/2005, pp. 55-75).

During the 1980s, a federal government "social safety net" was established. Although Head Start was included as one of its seven programs, the erosion of support for other community agencies damaged its ability to provide a full range of services. The progress that had been made during the 30-year period beginning with the 1962 amendments to the Social Security Act provisions for child care slowed considerably toward the end of that time period. In 1996, the Personal Responsibility and Work Opportunity Act placed restrictions on women and families living in poverty. A review of the child-related federal legislation of these four decades reveals a shift from support for families and children to regulation of their lives.

EARLY CHILDHOOD CURRICULUM HISTORY

The historical study of the three major branches of early childhood education that existed before 1965 (kindergarten, day nurseries/child care, and nursery schools) has been widely documented. This is not enough. In order for the work of the historian of early education to have meaning for the practitioner who interacts with children and families on a daily basis, the impact of the political, scientific, social context, and knowledge base issues surrounding early childhood curriculum should be acknowledged and addressed. A brief overview, with particular emphasis on events occurring during the past 40 years follows. As previously discussed, the "War on Poverty" of the mid-1960s was designed to minimize social inequality and help poor people become actively involved in advocating for their own needs. Deficit models developed during the 1960s assumed the need for compensatory enrichment for these "culturally deprived" children. In addition to the "traditional" Developmental-Interaction Model from Bank Street College of Education, Planned Variation Head Start and Follow Through Models included Montessori, Behaviorist (Direct Instruction), and Piagetian (High/Scope and Kamii-DeVries) curriculum models. All of these models were based on development or learning theories and had a cognitive focus. Twenty years later, reports of longitudinal studies demonstrated positive findings. However, the effectiveness of different curriculum models varied. Professionals and participants questioned which program approaches were effective for which populations, under what circumstances. By the 1990s, there was growing concern for low-income children's "academic underachievement." Increasing demands for public accountability and improved results ensued. Reformulated research questions led to studies on the impact of program components in conjunction with parents and other significant contributors. There was a shift away from developmental psychology and toward cognitive psychology, with the incorporation of new brain research into program planning. The professional literature and the public press implied that early childhood education is essential to school reform efforts and business productivity. State-based prekindergarten programs expanded, funded on the basis of their utilization of research-based curricula. Newly developed criteria for program quality addressed the structural and programmatic characteristics associated with quality, rather than the differential effectiveness of program models.

Professional development and training were affected by the changes that took place during this 40-year period. Practitioners who had participated in the curriculum models of the 1960s and 1970s or had learned about them during the course of their professional preparation found it necessary to return to a higher education institution, or to engage in a professional education program. (This is also known as a professional improvement program or PIP.) Many states implemented new standards for early childhood education programs and curricula that incorporated criteria for personnel working in the field. National credentials (Child Development Associate—CDA, Certified Childcare Professional—CCP), certifications (National Board for Professional Teaching Standards—NBPTS) and accreditation (NAEYC and others) mandated both knowledge and understanding of theory and practice, and the ability to implement programs that meet the needs of children, families, the state, and the country. Thus a rationale for having a working knowledge and understanding of the history of early childhood education is the foundational underpinning it provides for selecting and critiquing the programs of today.

DIVERSITY IN EARLY CHILDHOOD EDUCATION HISTORY

One of the areas of historical inquiry that is just beginning to be addressed by the fields of early childhood education and child development is diversity of population. Beatty (1998, p. 23) suggests that further analysis of cultural, linguistic, racial, economic, and gender issues is needed. Grant (1998, p. 275) in a footnote to her chapter on race, class, and ethnicity in the parent education movement states that, "more research on the National Congress of Colored Parents and Teachers is sorely needed."

Tamura (2001) has addressed the paucity of historical studies about the education of Asian Americans. None of the citations from either the educational or social science literature appears to address the areas of childhood, family or early education. Nor do the suggestions for further work include topics relating to these fields. Finkelstein (2000) points out that many of those who supported group out-of-home programs for children over the last century themselves came from the marginalized populations of African-American women and "feminists." Although much historical research has been published about the impact of Anglo-European philosophies, theories and programs on early education in the United States, very little research on diverse or multicultural populations is available (Stomfay-Stitz, 2001).

The study of the history of diversity in early education begins with a review of multicultural education in the kindergarten. According to Beatty (1995, p. 51), American kindergartens introduced diversity in a controlled way, through exposure to songs, games, and stories from many countries. Although some kindergarten proponents believed that the kindergarten had the potential to unify the races when teaching American values, the curricular multiculturalism was superficial. However, by forging strong connections between the home and the school, American kindergartens incorporated multiple cultures and traditions into their programs from the late 1800s through the 1900s. During the past three decades, a plethora of books on multicultural early childhood education programs and curricula have been published. Most of these volumes focus on practical methods and strategies. However, they provide an accurate picture of the sources available to support practitioners' integration of multicultural aspects into their curricula. There are also a few sources that enrich the knowledge base on early childhood populations that are underrepresented in educational history research literature.[3]

Another aspect of the study of diversity deals with the issues of racial and cultural identity and the impact of racism on young children. Comer (1989, p. 352) says that, "racism interferes with the normal development of those children subjected to it." He states that American society has "avoided, denied, and rationalized the more difficult and more troublesome outcomes of our historical racial experience with blacks, Native Americans, and Hispanics" (p. 356). Comer describes the differentiated effects of immigration with and without continuity, citing the disruption of the organized culture of victimized groups as a major difference between blacks and other immigrant groups. Drawing on accounts of the slavery system and the black church as examples, he demonstrates the effect negative identification as a racial group has on child development, family structure and institutional life. He provides statistical evidence of differentiated educational funding due to historical exclusion from mainstream political, economic and social power structures. He attributes the underachievement and "troublesome behavior" of children from "victimized black families" to "exclusion from the societal mainstream" (p. 359). Comer states that many poor

---

[3]See for example: Baker, 1983; de Gaetano, Williams, & Volk, 1998; de Melendez & Ostertag, 1997; Derman-Sparks, 1989; Gay, 2000; Grieshaber & Cannella, 2001; Hildebrand, Phenice, Gray, & Hines, 2000; King, Chipman, & Cruz-Janzen, 1994; Kendall, 1996; Ramsey, 1987; Sapon-Shevin, 1999; Swinarski, Breitborde, & Murphy, 2003.

children "grow up in primary social networks that are marginal to mainstream institutions" and therefore fail to transmit the experiences and expectations needed to prepare the children for success in the mainstream institution of the school. Accordingly, using "knowledge of history, child development, and human–system interactions to understand the behavior of parents, staff and students" (p. 359) can lead to gains in academic achievement and outstanding social outcomes. The Yale Child Study Center's School Development Program (SDP) exemplifies this problem solving, collaboration, and family involvement model (OERI Consumer Guide, 1993, p. 1 of 3). According to Comer, coherent education policies coupled with equitable funding can overcome obstacles and provide a foundation for a supportive school.

Comer suggests that, "many schools of education give little attention to the way in which minority students have been disadvantaged, and what to do about it" (p. 356). He indicates that teachers should be prepared by training in applied, rather than traditional child development, to facilitate the growth of all children. They should be able to construct environments conducive to overcoming racial, ethnic, gender, and economic barriers, and be fully prepared in the teaching of reading. They should have the "knowledge, skills and sensitivity to protect children from racial attitudes and conditions that interfere with development" (p. 360). He also calls on schools of education to become involved with other departments and schools in mutually enriching ways, in order to benefit the institution and the surrounding community.

The volume *History of Early Childhood Education*, "a multicultural anthology that has focused on little-known women and other key contributors to early childhood education" (Lee, 2001, p. 121), begins to address the expressed need for historical data on diverse populations. It includes chapters on Native Americans, black Americans, Asian-Americans, Hispanic-Americans, bilingualism, and 20th-century influences from countries outside the United States. Anthropological, historical, artifact, interview, artistic, photographic, Internet, newspaper, educational journal, and autobiographical sources were utilized, as well as materials from the journals and archives of historically Black institutions of higher education. The authors included documentation collected by those for whom it had relevance, but rarely published or made available to the profession. A few African-American early childhood leaders are profiled in the chapter sections on the Child Development Associate credential and the OMEP United States National Committee (USNC) (see pp. 421–422, 609–610). Significant readings concerning specific activities designed to honor Mexican-American heritage and accomplishments are referenced in the chapter on Hispanic Americans, as are guidelines for multicultural teacher education (Saracho & Martinez Hancock and Saracho & Spodek in Saracho & Spodek, 1983, pp. 3–5, 125–126). Some of the research and resulting teaching modules that preceded publication of the book were shared in conference presentations (Lascarides & Hinitz, 1987, 1988; Hinitz, 1990, 1993; Hinitz & Lascarides, 1991; Lascarides, 1993).

In recent years, Simpson (1981, 2003a, 2003b, 2003c) has presented the results of her doctoral research and interviews with black early childhood educators in national forums. The recipient of the Region III OMEP-USNC award in 2003, she has produced posters and PowerPoint presentations demonstrating the contributions of past and present female and male black early education leaders in the United States. There is a great need for similar oral histories and historical research studies of Native American, Hispanic-American, and Asian-American early education leaders.

Recent scholarship on progressive education ("new education") and understanding development in the context of culture, gender, race and ethnicity focuses on revisiting central principles to examine embedded assumptions. In their historical overview of the Developmental-Interaction Approach (DIA), Nager and Shapiro (2000) describe the modification of the approach's long-standing focus on individual development by balancing it with "elaboration of the contexts of development, which were implicit but underemphasized in earlier statements" (p. 33). The greater amount of attention paid to culturally responsive pedagogy, and "context-bound" practice recognizes that previous formulations "privileged certain kinds of knowledge" and assumed "that there are preferred ways of acting" (p. 32). Like Comer, Shapiro and her colleagues at Bank Street College of Education recognize that "knowledge of the children's culture and community can help teachers to link students affectively and cognitively to school learning" (p. 31). The children, their families, and their community, become resources for teachers, children and families alike. Nager and Shapiro draw on Bowman and Stott's (1994) investigation of teachers' reflective practice. Citing the roots of teacher beliefs and behaviors in their own past experiences, Bowman and Stott suggest that teachers must restructure their personal knowledge systems (p. 129). It is suggested that unless teachers reorganize their personal, developmental, and pedagogical knowledge, they will have a low level of understanding of themselves and their students.

What is the meaning of this discussion in a chapter on methodology of education history? It has an important and deep meaning. It reminds us that we must engage in reflection, individually and in professional groups of various sizes. We can use events from the recent past or long ago to assist us in our reflection. The discussion demonstrates that recent scholarship can be integrated with existing philosophies, theories, and past research and practice to form new and better programs. The results of reflection may be modifications in thinking and in actions. Some of the changes will be personal and internal, but many of them will impact learning, teaching, and interactions with children, families, and colleagues.

HISTORY OF EARLY CHILDHOOD TEACHER EDUCATION

The recent scholarship on the history of early childhood teacher education at Bank Street College of Education is also germane to this investigation. Grinberg (2002) describes portions of the professional education curriculum designed to assist the student teachers in knowing the context and community in which their children lived. He provides a detailed account and analysis of two of the inquiry-oriented courses offered by Lucy Sprague

Mitchell from the 1930s through the mid-1950s, "Environment" and "Language." The "Environment" course was a "human geography" course that required each student to study the school and local community in which they were doing practice teaching. The requirements included investigation, observation, interviews, and utilization of such information sources as journal and magazine articles and statistical files. Following their individual in-depth investigation of the community, the student teachers formed study groups to discuss and analyze cultural patterns, and then chose a relevant contemporary social issue. "Historical, geographical, cultural-ethnic and economic" data were examined. At the conclusion of the initial learning phase, the student teachers shifted their discussion to the topic of how their new knowledge could be used in teaching the children in their class. They then developed social studies curriculum to be used in their own classrooms.

Mitchell required her students to "experiment with writing in systematic and critical ways" (Grinberg, 2002, p. 5 of 8). In 1937, she set up The Writer's Laboratory to assist children's book authors to "understand the developmental needs and interests of children." Mitchell was concerned with the lack of racial and ethnic diversity among children's writers. She provided scholarships to encourage a more varied racial and class mix in the workshop. Among the authors who participated were Irma Simonton Black, Margaret Wise Brown, William Hooks, Ruth Kraus, Eve Merriam, and Marguerita Rudolph (Wolfe, 2002, pp. 371–374, 385–387).

Lucy Sprague Mitchell created a "safe, caring, respectful, and above all, trusting environment" in her teacher education classes and on trips (Grinberg, 2002, 6 of 8). She challenged her students to think critically, and to engage with ideas, each other, and their professor. A detailed review of the methods and sources employed by Mitchell in her courses is valuable for today's early childhood teacher educator because she demonstrated scholarship, modeled critical pedagogy, was passionate about teaching, and provided leadership as a respected woman educator.[4]

PREPARATION, PLANNING, AND LUCK

Doing historical research takes planning, preparation, assistance from knowledgeable friends and colleagues, and luck. Preparation includes reviewing secondary sources about the time period from both education and other fields, such as psychology, sociology, economics, and history. Anderson (in Boyd & Anderson, 2002) suggests that prior to conducting an oral history interview the interviewer should "master the secondary literature . . . so that you will recognize primary material." Planning involves researching the libraries and archives you expect to visit and reviewing their collections online or from a hard-copy document, before leaving home. A list of important boxes and folders gleaned from this research will prove helpful in maximizing time spent on-site with the primary documents. Preparing a set list of questions in advance will assist you in gathering the

most information in the shortest time period during meetings with significant individuals. As the song says, it is always useful to "get a little help from your friends." Proficient archivists and historians of early childhood education around the world are infinitely supportive of novices and professional colleagues via email, telephone and postal mail.

Luck plays a role in the historical research equation. For example, it is fortunate that the authors Waldo Frank and Jean Toomer saved all of Margaret Naumburg's handwritten letters. These primary source documents have helped to fill in many gaps in information gathered from Naumburg's published work and interviews with her family. It is most unfortunate that Polly Greenberg was unable to dissuade her mother, Margaret Pollitzer Hoben, from discarding most of her original papers from the early years of Walden School and the "new education," prior to her demise. The few remaining papers are in the manuscript division of the Teachers College library in New York City. The profession is richer for having Naumburg's letters available in two different archives, but poorer for lack of the insights Hoben's papers might have provided. This example serves as a reminder that personal papers, documents, and photographs are the property of the owner until they donate them to an archive or library. At that time, the donor may make any stipulation they wish regarding their use, including sealing them until after the person's demise, or limiting access to specific categories of researchers. Often permission in writing from the donor, their family or representative, must be sought by an author who wishes to cite something from a collection. For example, in the case of Abigail Adams Eliot's papers housed at Schlesinger Library, she retained complete control of dissemination while she was alive. The family of Margaret Naumburg retains the final say in the reproduction of materials from her papers. The interviewee must give permission for the use of oral history interviews in hard copy or technologically reproduced formats.

This author's knowledge of the history of education came into play when reviewing the Naumburg letters in the Waldo Frank Papers at the University of Pennsylvania. One document bore a hotel letterhead from Gary, Indiana. A glimpse of the letterhead inspired a search for it's meaning in Naumburg's life. It was discovered that Naumburg had been employed by a New York newspaper to write a series of articles about the "Gary Plan," because of her practical and theoretical knowledge of the "new education," and her standing in the progressive education community. The original typescripts of the articles are in the Margaret Naumburg Papers at the same university library. In this way, archival knowledge from primary source documents was used to provide a more in-depth picture of the life and work of a woman important in the history of early education.

ARCHIVAL RESEARCH SOURCES

Accurate historical research is based mainly on work with primary sources, viewed from the perspective of that time, rather

[4]For further information about Lucy Sprague Mitchell and her work, see Antler, 1995, and Wolfe, 2002.

than through "current lenses." These primary documents may be obtained or reviewed in a variety of ways. The papers of many of the people, programs, schools, institutions of higher education (training schools, normal schools, colleges, and universities), professional organizations, and government entities important to the study of early childhood history are found in archives. A large percentage of the relevant archives are housed at college and university libraries. (For example: University of Pennsylvania [Waldo Frank, Margaret Naumburg]; Indiana State University [NAEYC, OMEP, oral histories]; University of Maryland–College Park [ACEI], Teachers College, Columbia University [Patty Smith Hill, Progressive Education Association, American Montessori Society], Yale [Jean Toomer], Pacific Oaks [James L. Hymes, Jr.]. Others may be found at local and state historical societies (The Filson Club, Louisville, Kentucky [Patty Smith Hill]; Missouri Historical Society, St. Louis—[Jennie Wahlert Papers, William Torrey Harris Papers, Susan Blow Papers]), the Froebel Foundation, Grand Rapids, Michigan; and some schools (City and Country School—NY—Caroline Pratt, Associated Experimental Schools group) and child care agencies (Graham-Windham Services) that continue to serve children and families today. Many materials about the work of the Federal government relating to young children can be found in branches of the National Archives in Maryland (Lois Hayden Meek Stolz Papers and Lawrence Frank oral history interviews—National Institute of Health, National Library of Medicine, History of Medicine Division, Bethesda, MD; WPA, OEO—National Archives II on Adelphi Road, College Park, MD). In some cases, the papers of an early childhood educator, school, or organization have been acquired by the rare books and manuscripts collection along with or as a result of other relatives' papers being donated to that particular library. To the author's knowledge, only Pacific Oaks' library has made a concerted effort to acquire the papers of early childhood educators and teacher educators in the United States. At the 1988 NAEYC History Seminar, Margaret Witt, at that time librarian and archivist at Pacific Oaks, presented *Where are the primary documents for the history of early childhood? A proposal for a national survey.* Attendees participated in the survey by distributing postcards to early childhood professionals aged 50 years or older at the time. The respondents were asked to provide basic contact data and to consider giving their papers to Pacific Oaks on their retirement or at a time they felt was appropriate (such as moving to a smaller home or changing job locations). The official project ended with Witt's retirement from Pacific Oaks; however, some early childhood educators have donated their papers to the archives there.[5]

The purpose of university library special collections is to house and preserve manuscripts and printed books whose age, fragility, or "uncommonness" requires special care, and to provide primary source materials for study. They serve as centers for research by a diverse constituency of students, "serious readers," and scholars from their region, the country, and around the world. Their strong commitment to active public assistance is demonstrated by their efforts towards "optimizing readers' ability conveniently to use and work with the *primary* materials

for studies at all levels" (Penn Special Collections Guide, Yale Beinecke Library Guide).

The majority of college and university libraries have both hard copy and online "finding aids" to enable researchers to access information regarding their collections. Some of the rare and special items can be found online through such electronic bibliographic utilities as RLIUN/Eureka, the database of the Research Libraries Group or the Philadelphia Area Consortium of Special Collections Libraries - PACSCL (that includes the University of Pennsylvania and Rutgers—The State University of New Jersey), or by accessing a specific library's Web site. It is a good idea to visit the special collections website prior to traveling to an archive. One is able to review, download, and print what each collection contains, subdivided by person or entity, and then by box and folder number. This saves precious time in accessing materials when one is at the library, because these collections often have use restrictions and limited hours. When employing online databases, it is helpful to know the correct spelling of names and places about which information is being sought, because the computer usually cannot identify a collection if input data is misspelled. If the correct spelling is not known, try multiple spellings, because as soon as the correct spelling is received by the system, a wonderful world of information is unlocked for the researcher. Researchers may need to make requests in advance of a visit because archival materials could be in storage facilities at a different location.

Each library has its own guide to use of the collections that details its mission, states the regulations in place at that institution and offers guidance to the user. Some collections of papers have biographies or other written materials that offer insight into the collection, the person, or the program. For example, the Margaret Naumburg Papers at the University of Pennsylvania have a Register and Biography written with the support of a grant to aid in the cataloguing of papers by prominent women. Many of the manuscripts in Penn's collection are listed in published guides, such as the *Catalogue of Manuscripts*, edited by N. Zacour and R. Hirsch, and its supplements.

REFERENCE WORKS

There are several reference books that are excellent starting points for investigations into the history of early education. The *Marquis Who's Who* volumes profile leaders in a great variety of fields. Early education leaders may be found in such titles as *Who Was Who in Education; Who's Who Among Women, Who's Who in the East* (or some other section of the United States), *Who's Who in Education, Who's Who in America*, or *Who's Who in the World.* Harvard University Press publishes *Notable American Women.* Each volume contains the in-depth profiles for a 25-year interval. Many female early education leaders are included in these volumes. The *Historical Dictionary of Women's Education in the United States* (Eisenman, 1998) includes entries on early childhood education, early childhood teacher education, early childhood education managers, and a

---

[5]For further information regarding primary archival and library sources see Beatty, 1998, pp. 10-11, 16-17, 20-22.

select group of early childhood educators. The appendices include a compendium of research resources about diverse populations and a timeline of women's education.

PRESERVING CHILD CARE CENTER HISTORY

Child care programs and schools should start archives to maintain records of their progress and achievements. According to Ranck (1995), queries may come to a director internally from parents, staff members, and members of the board. These records may be used in writing grant proposals for funding. Outside entities such as research organizations, colleges and universities, and media sources (newspapers, magazines, television, and radio stations) may request information for projects, political purposes or in celebration of community milestones. Societies of archivists (for example, the Society of American Archivists and the Australian Society of Archivists) have published guides to starting and maintaining an archive, for those programs, organizations, and individuals who are interested in the process (Ranck, 1994, 1995). Participation in this type of project might be assigned to early childhood teacher preparation candidates, in collaboration with their field placement site. Often the students glean nuggets of valuable information from interviews and oral histories, or by reading and organizing center records. They learn about the inside workings of a child care center, and whether the philosophy, curriculum, materials, and program have changed or remained consistent over a period of time (Copeland, 1986; Wineberg, Juzenas, & Trent, 2000). Attention to a school's important documents, long-term personnel, and history may help it avoid the fate of some of the primary documents from John Dewey's Laboratory School at the University of Chicago. Laurel Tanner found the teacher reports from the school's early years stored in a forgotten closet in Judd Hall. She rescued them, oversaw their installation in the University's Regenstein Library, then wrote a masterful volume describing their "lessons for today." (Tanner, 1997, pp. x, xv)

USING THE INTERNET FOR EARLY EDUCATION HISTORICAL RESEARCH

Unfortunately, the History of Education website so lovingly tended by Henk van Setten of the Netherlands was withdrawn in 2002, because of his illness. Its loss has left a void in the online community of educational historians, particularly those whose work centers on children, families, and early childhood education. H-Net, the online address for historians of all persuasions, headquartered in the United States has two moderated list-servs with corresponding Web sites that provide current support for researchers. H-Education (H-Ed) sometimes includes discussions, queries and information related to early childhood education, and H-Childhood includes material relating to children, families, and the impact of external forces upon them. This discussion aptly illustrates the growing importance of the Internet as a resource for historians of early childhood education. Although the History of Education Web site no longer serves as a portal for historians of education, H-Net and the Prentice Hall

Publisher's Foundations of Early Childhood Education Web site are attempting to fill the void. There are several points that are important to remember when utilizing the Web as a historical resource. First, be as specific as possible in choosing a search term. The quality of responses returned by a "search engine" is directly related to the exactness of the search term. This is true for both generalized searches from any computer and for use of library search capabilities. One must be quite cautious in using and citing Web sites. All sites are not equal. One cannot be sure that the information a site offers about the person or program is accurate, fair, or true. It is necessary to research the source of the site. Academic sites and those of professional organizations usually check the content of items before posting them. Detailed information about sources as well as a link to the webmaster or creator of the Web page is usually displayed prominently. There are many sites that post student research papers or dissertations, as well as class Web sites that provide relevant basic information. When using these types of Internet sources, it is wise to check a print source for verification, if possible. However, there are some sites that are placed on the Internet to disparage individuals or theories. They may appear at first glance to be factual, but when examined more closely they show evidence of bias or other difficulties. Some sites are just plain nasty. As with any other type of research source, Internet sources must meet professional standards for both veracity and presentation. A brief look at some of the codes is illustrative. Sites emanating from institutions of higher education (IHEs) around the world often end in the suffix "ac" followed by a country designation (except for many IHEs in the United States). In the United States, Web sites and e-mail address from IHEs end in "edu." Some illustrative examples follow: the College of New Jersey is "tcnj.edu," whereas OISE at the University of Toronto is "oise.utoronto.ca" and "ac.uk" is the ending for the University of Warwick in England. If a URL ends in .net, that usually means a private entity, whether individual or institution. Commercial sites have URLs ending in .com, which signifies an entity that is selling a product or service. The suffix .gov represents federal government Internet sites. Organization Web sites utilizing the .org suffix, such as "Froebelfoundation.org," offer many interesting possibilities. Scholarly resources may be found at all of these types of sites. However, one should proceed with greater caution when using a .com site, because commercial entities sometimes have advertising messages or slanted data embedded in the information provided. When referencing materials obtained from the Internet, it is important to list the date on which the site was accessed. Many Internet sites are unstable and Internet addresses are continually changing, because of updates, simplification, or sometimes because the owner of a page decides to go to a new Internet carrier. Often a link to the new URL will be provided, or a message will appear on the screen stating that you will be taken to the new site in ten seconds. In summary, the online availability of information from libraries, research institutions, schools, government sources and individual entities worldwide makes the educational historian's search for information easier. One can gain access to information bases across the globe. Assuming that one's computer is equipped with up-to-date firewall and anti-virus programs, and one is careful about the sites one enters, the Internet can prove to be a valuable research tool.

DOCTORAL DISSERTATIONS RECENTLY COMPLETED

Two recently completed doctoral dissertations have added significant content to the early childhood education historical knowledge base. Catherine Grubb (2003) has written stirringly of the life and work of Dorothy W. Hewes. Charlotte Garrison (2003) penned a scholarly treatise on James L. Hymes, Jr. Her use of archival sources and numerous in-depth interviews provides us not only with a detailed overview of Hymes's own myriad contributions to our field but also those of his colleagues and friends. Garrison also was fortunate to have probably among the last interviews with Millie Almy and Laura Dittmann.

A major factor that directly impacts the execution of historical research is the presence or absence of funding. Sometimes early childhood historical research is a corollary of funded research in another field. For example, Margaret Naumburg's papers were catalogued with grant funds designated for archival holdings in women's history. Many of the papers and materials in the City and Country School archives came from Bureau of Educational Experiments (BEE) research and the work of the Associated Experimental Schools (AES) organization. Government-sponsored research sometimes has a historical component. The National Archives and the Library of Congress are the repositories of many cubic feet of early education historical materials. Certain holdings in the ACEI collection at the University of Maryland were originally developed with federal funding from the Works Progress Administration or the Lanham Act. The Laura Spelman Rockefeller Memorial Papers at the Rockefeller Archives in North Tarrytown, New York, provide an abundance of information gathered from the Child Study Institutes and other programs coordinated by Lawrence K. Frank. The meticulous records kept by both the grant recipients and the funders are a treasure trove for historians.

Thesis and dissertation research may be funded or unfunded. University scholarships and fellowships sometimes support masters' and doctoral candidates. Assistance through an application process may come from entities such as archive centers, foundations, and organizations that have an interest in the research topic. Faculty members at IHEs often have access to a grants office that will assist them in seeking research funding. Money also may be available from university sources for alternate activity time arrangements, reproduction of sources, secretarial support, "mini-grants," or graduate student assistance. It is beneficial to take advantage of any available support services.

ORGANIZATIONS AND CONFERENCES

The major national venues where historians of ECE in the United States share their work include the History Seminar of the National Association for the Education of Young Children (NAEYC), and the annual meetings of the American Educational Research Association (AERA), the History of Education Society (U.S.) (HES-US), and the Association for Childhood Education International (ACEI). Historical papers of interest are also presented at the annual meeting of the Eastern Educational Research Association. In the international arena, the meetings of the International Standing Conference on the History of Education (ISCHE) have sometimes included papers by members of the Standing Working Group on ECE. At other times the ECE Working Group met separately, as for example, in Copenhagen, Denmark in conjunction with the 1998 World Congress of the World Organization for Early Childhood Education (OMEP).

THE NAEYC HISTORY SEMINAR

The History Seminar of NAEYC began with a 1973 slide presentation by Dorothy W. Hewes, entitled *Where Have We Been, Where are We Going?* By 1982, a "History Buffs" group had been formed within the organization, and its members sought recognition by organizational officers and headquarters staff. The name changed to "History Seminar" in 1987, with the appropriate listing in the annual conference program. By 1995, "History" was listed as a separate conference track. The presentations at the NAEYC History Seminar over more than 20 years mirror historical interests in the early childhood field as a whole. Some papers have been conceptual, addressing such topics as: the concept of the child (DuCharme), what has been learned about child development in two thousand years (Oekerman), the child's encounter with nature (Bartow), historical attitudes that undermine quality care (Young), why kindergartens were universalized and nursery schools were not (Beatty), and why the infant school movement was rejected (A. Pence). Papers concerning specifics of organizational history (NAEYC and Montessori) (Miller, Hewes, Povell, McMath), as well as papers about doing organizational history (Ranck, Prochner) have been presented. Several papers reviewed publications, curricula, materials and equipment in historical context (Lane & Malone; Cline; Cuffaro; Griffin et al.). Some papers addressed such broad topics as: kindergarten philosophy (Bennett & Bultman), an overview of day and residential child care services (P. Pence), the relationship of Kondratieff's economic wave theory to parent cooperative preschools (Hewes), Romanticism (Cantor), or the roots of the "project approach" (DuCharme). Numerous presentations provided new insights into specific programs, schools, models and venues, based on careful study of primary sources, oral history interviews and site visits (School/Center list, p. 3). Most of the descriptions centered on programs in the United States, but, programs from England, Australia, Canada, New Zealand and the People's Republic of China have been represented. Topics relating to families and immigration were discussed by several authors (Diener; Hewes; Cantor; Bhavnagri et. al.). Gender issues have been the subject of papers by Canella, Hinitz, Povell, Ranck, and Sinex and Nelms. Cultural issues were addressed by Ashelman and Gaines, Fenimore and Lascarides. DuCharme; Malone, Lane and Rhoten have discussed aspects of the history of early childhood teacher education.

One of the most helpful aspects of the NAEYC History Seminar is the insights offered by papers on sources for and techniques of "doing" early education history. Numerous authors have shared their expertise on techniques in oral history (Copeland; Boyd and Anderson), archival research (Hewes and Hudson; Brown, Hinitz), composing an organizational history (Ranck), interdisciplinary collaboration (Smith), surveying historical knowledge (Hinitz and Lascarides), and teaching techniques (Hewes, Hinitz and Lascarides). Some of the contributions were entered into the ERIC document system in the year they were presented. Those papers (through the year 2002) should be available on microfiche in libraries. The NAEYC History Seminar enables historians of ECE to make their work accessible to practitioners who can use it for the benefit of children, families and programs.

The History Seminar and the NAEYC History and Archives Committee have supported the dissemination of historical work done by undergraduate and graduate students. Lenore Wineberg and two undergraduate students shared the history of a Wisconsin country school that was closing at the 2000 History Seminar (Wineberg et al.). In honor of its 75th anniversary, NAEYC invited five students, ranging from undergraduates to doctoral students to share their historical research in a special session at the 2001 conference in Anaheim. Four graduate students of Blythe Hinitz presented their history projects at the 2002 History Seminar in New York City (see later for a description of their work).

Recent meetings of the History of Education Society (U.S.) have included papers describing research on early education programs and figures of note, early childhood teacher education, as well as the history of childhood and motherhood by Beatty, Grant, Hinitz, and Domkowski-Nawrotzki, among others. Recent early childhood history presentations at American Educational Research Association (AERA) annual meetings have included a panel of selected authors from the volume *Founding Mothers and Others*, a Readers Theatre presentation coordinated by Mary Hauser (2001), and a historical presentation on female leadership in early education settings (Hinitz, 2003).

BOOKS FOR TEACHER EDUCATION

Several recent books are particularly useful to early childhood teacher educators who plan to include a historical component in their courses. *Sources: Notable Selections in Early Childhood Education* (Paciorek & Munro, 1999), *Educational Foundations: An Anthology* (Chartok, 2000), *Women's Philosophies of Education: Thinking Through Our Mothers* (Titone & Maloney, 1999), *Learning from the Past: Historical Voices in Early Childhood Education* (Wolfe, 2002), and *History of Early Childhood Education* (Lascarides & Hinitz, 2000), each have specific merits that make them useful to practitioners as well as researchers in the field. *Pioneers of Early Childhood Education: A Bio-Bibliographical Guide* (Peltzman, 1998), and *W. N. Hailmann: Defender of Froebel* (Hewes, 2001) provide resources for research on specific individuals. All of these volumes are based on careful historical research. Although it is often difficult to determine the precise sources or dates of historical information, these authors have taken the time to review both primary and secondary information, to compare sources, and to make a reasoned determination in resolving controversies. Each author acknowledges the existence of possible errors in her work, and requests the assistance of colleagues in rectifying them.

Sources: Notable Selections in Early Childhood Education (Paciorek & Munro) provides a starting point for developing historical literacy. It includes selected writings of significance to the early childhood field on child development, programs and practices, pedagogy, crisis management, policy issues and research. Each section consists of excerpts from several time periods, thus providing an overview of the work of classic and contemporary authors, as well as differing philosophies and points-of-view. A biographical note on the author and a short statement establishing relevance precedes each selection. A few suggested Internet links (URLs) are provided at the beginning of each section. However, rapid changes in the availability of Internet sites (see discussion under use of technology) would suggest that instructors consult current texts and journals, and online "search engines," for up-to-date URLs (see for example, Morrison, 2004, 108–109; http://www.google.com; http://www.prenhall.com/goffin; or http://wps.prenhall.com/chet_childhood_cluster_1).

Roselle Chartock's (2000) educational foundations anthology emphasizes the aesthetic, the artistic and the philosophical. Many of the selections provide useful background for educators of young children. Among those that are particularly relevant are: Elizabeth Peabody's *Aesthetic Papers*, the *Reminiscences of Friedrich Froebel*, Maria Montessori's *The Discovery of the Child*, the *Narrative of the Life of Fredrick Douglass, An American Slave*, *Rudolph Steiner in the Waldorf School*, Norman Rockwell's *The Problem We All Live With*, Sylvia Ashton-Warner's *Teacher*, and Maya Angelou's *I Know Why the Caged Bird Sings*. Titone and Maloney (1999) provide a different view of women's educational philosophies. The in-depth biographical sketches and excerpts from the writings of Charlotte Perkins Gilman (on societal parentage and social motherhood), and Anna Julia Cooper (on the education of Black students), showcase the diverse lives and contributions of women to the field of education. The strength of Wolfe's (2002) publication is its extensive compendium of graphic images. The rare photographs, engravings, diagrams, sheet music, and maps provide a striking and compelling view inside programs based on the theoretical and philosophical work of European early educators, and Froebelians and Progressive educators in North America. In writing *History of Early Childhood Education*, Lascarides and Hinitz (2000, p. xix) sought to "bring the history of childhood education and child development closer to our lives. . . . The work examines the impact of history on current practice by focusing on the history of early childhood education within the historical context of each time period" from the 6th century Before the Common Era (B.C.E.) through the 1990s of the Common Era (C.E.). This volume could serve as a resource for both faculty and students, and has provided the basis for the development of upward of 50 creative graduate and undergraduate projects (see for example, Courtney, Phillips, Raslowsky, and Rohrback).

HISTORY OF EDUCATION METHODS FOR TERTIARY PROGRAMS

Doing history of education work with college students can be a productive and fruitful experience. In the author's classes and those of a handful of colleagues, students are encouraged to share their knowledge of the history of early education in creative ways. During the spring of 2003, graduate students at The

College of New Jersey (TCNJ) were challenged to relate reading in *History of Early Childhood Education* to Gardner's Multiple Intelligences. They were then to devise methods of sharing the concepts through activity sequences related to any seven of the Intelligences with the exception of the frequently used Verbal-Linguistic and Mathematical Intelligences. Four students shared their ideas at an interactive workshop during the annual conference of the New Jersey Association for the Education of Young Children (Galen, H. [instructor], Querec Beauchemin, S., Day, C., Lacey, C. & Smith, S., 2003). Examples included a unit-block simulation with construction paper cutouts to demonstrate the work of Caroline Pratt, trade books shared during a discussion of Harriet Johnson, and a challenge to generate ideas for parent involvement in honor of James L. Hymes, Jr. Attendees were assisted in utilizing the Musical Intelligence (with rhythm band instruments) in a sequence devoted to Maria Montessori and Arnold Gesell.

In November 2002 four TCNJ graduate students gave presentations at the NAEYC History Seminar held in New York City. Self-designed and executed "big books" were shared. Rohrbach illustrated her nursery school history "big book" with watercolors. When asked by an audience member whether she had shared the book with her own 4-year-old students, in addition to her college classmates, she gave a negative response. When she returned to her classroom the following week, she decided to share the book at the storytime circle. Thse children had such an enthusiastic response that she used the lesson for a project in a graduate curriculum course. Raslowsky utilized the Internet to obtain unusual photographs of Maria Montessori and integrated them into an illustrated "big book." Courtney (with narration coauthored by Williams Foote) "rocked" the room with his musical presentation of the history of African-American early childhood education. Phillips, a student presenter during the previous year's 75th anniversary conference in California, did a reprise of his poem, *A Slave Named History*. Its stirring stanzas again moved the audience to rapt attention to the literary expression of the deep feelings of a group of people caring for their children under the worst possible conditions. The examples cited above are those that met the highest assessment levels for the project undertaken by all graduate students in the course "Teaching Young Children" at The College of New Jersey. Over the past 4 years, self-selected groups of students have presented:

- simulated game and quiz shows (including the actual computer program from "The Millionaire" television show)
- plays, skits, and puppet shows (live and on videotape)
- "The View"
- a Native American dancer who performed and taught the class a dance
- PowerPoint slide shows
- narrated photographs and sketches of Native Americans from the New Jersey State Museum in Trenton
- hands-on activity lessons

- edited videotapes (for example, one on the Japanese-American internment camps during World War II that represented intensive Internet research) in order to meet the mandate of sharing early education history creatively with their peers and the professor (Hinitz).

Graduate and undergraduate students view historical videotapes, including ACEI's 200th anniversary tape. The course instructor (Hinitz) made a video tape using actual historic books (for example Susan Blow's English translation of Froebel's *Mother Plays and Games*), materials (including original Milton Bradley Froebelian Gifts), historic photographs, and sketches from relevant books. Lists of relevant web site URLs are available on the professor's home page (at http://www.tcnj.edu/~hinitz) and the Merrill Early Childhood Supersite (at http://wps.prenhell.com/chet_childhood_cluster_1/0,6413,497738-.00.html).

An undergraduate class has utilized Morrison (2004) as one of the texts. Several chapters in this volume query why the past is important, and highlight significant Eurocentric figures, their programs, and their theories. "Programs in Action," for example, "The City and Country School Today," and "Diversity Tie-Ins," for example, "Then and Now: The Evolution of American Indian Education" are included in the volume. Embedded in some chapters are "Voices from the Field," for example that of Scott Bultman of the Froebel Foundation USA, who recently opened a Froebelian kindergarten in Grand Rapids, Michigan Bultman has an extensive library and archive of historic and current books and graphics on the kindergarten. These he reprints in small editions. He is also the publisher of such volumes as Hewes (2001) *W. N. Hailmann: Defender of Froebel*, including "The personalized sequel." Bultman is also the purveyor of reproductions of the Froebel Gifts and Occupations, as well as new games designed to support Froebelian kindergarten practice.[6]

RESPONSES TO HISTORICAL QUERIES

In 1998 Barbara Beatty suggested a number of areas in early education history that needed more work, along with questions that needed to be answered. During the ensuing years, other authors, and Beatty herself, have addressed a number of the issues. Since the beginning of the 21st-century, new publications have expanded the early childhood history knowledge base. *History of Early Childhood Education* (Lascarides and Hinitz, 2000) includes a comprehensive treatment of the history of the American nursery school, as well as a general history of early childhood education since the 1960s. Goffin and Wilson (2001) present the history of curriculum development in early childhood education as a basis for the further study of curriculum development. Nager and Shapiro (2000) and their chapter authors, demonstrate that the Developmental Interaction approach has evolved through a process of transformation that increased its relevancy for current practice. In the revised edition, Wolfe (2002) elaborates on selected programs, curricula, methods,

---

[6]See htpp://www.froebelfoundation.org or www.unclegoose.com for further information.

and individuals' work, and succinctly presents them in a pleasing graphic format. Grant (1998) and Rose (1999) have demonstrated that a doctoral dissertation based on intensive archival study can become an erudite yet practical book. Grant provides an in-depth look at advice books and mothers clubs, adeptly interweaving the history of the Rockefeller-funded Child Study Institutes and other group programs for children. Both books offer a wealth of possibilities for future work in the archival resources that they reference.

Recent book chapters and articles have provided an in-depth look at the following topics:

- Americanization and multicultural education in kindergartens in the United States (Beatty in Wollons, 2000)
- Margaret Naumburg and the Walden School (Hinitz in Sadovnik & Semel, 2002)
- Caroline Pratt and the City and Country School (Hauser in Sadovnik & Semel, 2002)
- The politics of preschool advocacy (Beatty in DeVita & Mosher-Williams, 2001)
- The historical roots of violence against children in the United States (Finkelstein, in *History of Education Quarterly,* 2000)

Some sources provide specific responses to Beatty's research questions. One of these is Lascarides's (Lascarides' & Hinitz, Ch.7) discussion of children and families in Colonial America. A few NAEYC History Seminar papers have reviewed the development of infant schools in North America. Bhavnagri and her colleagues (2000) provided information regarding the lessons kindergartens' mobilization of mothers' support have for parent involvement in education. Beatty (2000c) has documented ways in which different groups of Americans were convinced to add an additional year of nonacademic education (kindergarten) to their local public schools. Grant, and Lascarides and Hinitz have looked at the relationships between the kindergarten and other movements and organizations. Goffin and Wilson (2001) describe the effects of competing psychological constructions of child development on nursery schools and child care programs. In 1995 Phyllis Povell presented a paper entitled *Nancy McCormick Rambusch and the Montessori Revival in America* at the NAEYC History Seminar. Goffin and Wilson (2001) and Morrison (2004) present additional rationales for the recent resurgence of interest in Maria Montessori's methods. Grant (1998) and Hewes (1998) describe the intertwining relationships between early childhood education and other fields, including home economics, pediatrics, child welfare, feminism, and political advocacy. During the past 35 years, numerous research studies have been conducted on the *Sesame Street* television program by Children's Television Workshop and by "disinterested third party" researchers. However, a study from the vantage point of the historian of early childhood education still remains to be done.

The following research questions suggested by Beatty in 1998 remain open today:

1. What were the cultural and regional differences in the spread of kindergartens and in kindergarten pedagogy?
2. How did kindergarten directors and teachers interact with mothers, children and families from different class, ethnic, and racial backgrounds?
3. How did kindergartens change or were they changed by the public schools?
4. How have kindergarten programs and curricula changed in the past 50 years?
5. What can a more detailed examination of the relationships and tensions between day nurseries and nursery schools tell us?
6. What were the relationships (or lack of relationships) between child care and nursery school personnel?
7. What new understandings could an analysis of the social class, cultural, and religious associations of the Montessori movement provide?
8. What deeper insights can be provided to the field from further historical analyses of cultural, linguistic, racial, gender, and economic issues?

Early childhood educators and historians of education have added significantly to the knowledge base on early education history during the past 5 years, through their work with primary and secondary sources. Their publications and presentations have implications for bridging the past with the future. New resources and methodologies, and newly discovered aspects of existing resources, strategies and techniques will pave the way for exciting original work in the field of early childhood education historical research during the coming decade. Our challenge is to take the historical knowledge and give it life for today. We have just begun the exploration.

ACKNOWLEDGMENTS

The author would like to thank Barbara Beatty, Julia Grant, Dorothy W. Hewes, and the late Marjorie W. Lee for their assistance with this chapter. The author would like to express appreciation to Mary Hauser, John Powell, Edna Ranck, and Jennifer Wolfe.

References

Almon, J. (1999). *Children at play the Waldorf way.* Paper presented at the annual conference of the National Association for the Education of Young Children, History Seminar, New Orleans, LA.

Anderson, C., Arboleda, M. Q., Phillips, B., Kensey S., Wolf, D. (2001, November). *Lessons from the past for the future.* Papers presented at the annual conference of the National Association for the Education of Young Children, Anaheim, CA.

Anderson, C. J. (2003). *Contributions of James Lee Hymes, Jr., to the field of early childhood education.* Unpublished doctoral dissertation, The University of Texas at Austin.

Antler, J. (1995). *Lucy Sprague Mitchell: The making of a modern woman.* New Haven, CT: Yale University Press.

Aries, P. (1962). *Centuries of childhood: A social history of family life.* Trans. R. Baldick. New York: Vtage Books.

Ashelman, P. and Gaines, C. (1997). *The contributions of African Americans to early childhood education in New Jersey.* Paper presented at the annual conference of the National Association for the Education of Young Children, History Seminar, Anaheim, CA.

Ashby, L. (1997). *Endangered children: Dependency, neglect, and abuse in American history.* New York: Twayne Publishers.

Baker, G. (1983). *Planning and organizing for multicultural instruction.* Reading, MA: Addison-Wesley Publishing Company.

Bartow, M. (2003, November). *The child's encounter with nature: Historical perspectives.* Paper presented at the annual conference of the National Association for the Education of Young Children, History Seminar, Chicago, IL.

Beatty, B. (1995). *Preschool education in America: The culture of young children from the colonial era to the present.* New Haven, CT: Yale University Press.

Beatty, B. (1997, November). *Lessons from the past: Why kindergartens were universalized and nursery schools were not.* Paper presented at the annual conference of the National Association for the Education of Young Children, History Seminar, Anaheim, CA.

Beatty, B. (1998). From infant schools to Project Head Start: Doing historical research in early childhood education. In B. Spodek, O. N. Saracho & A. D. Pellegrini (Eds.). *Yearbook in early childhood education: Issues in early childhood educational research* (Vol. 8, pp. 1–29). New York: Teachers College Press.

Beatty, B. (2000a). Children in different and difficult times: The history of American childhood: Part one. *History of Education Quarterly. 40*(1), 71–84.

Beatty, B. (2000b). The complex historiography of childhood: Categorizing different, dependent, and ideal children. Essay review part two. *History of Education Quarterly. 40*(2), 201–209.

Beatty, B. (2000c). "The letter killeth": Americanization and multicultural education in kindergartens in the United States. In R. Wollons (Ed.), *Kindergartens and cultures: The global diffusion of an idea* (pp. 42–58). New Haven, CT: Yale University Press.

Beatty, B. (2001). The politics of preschool advocacy: Lessons from three pioneering organizations. In C. J. DeVita & R. Mosher-Williams (Eds.). *Who speaks for America's children? The role of child advocates in public policy* (pp. 165–190). Washington, DC: The Urban Institute Press.

Bennett, J. L., & Bultman, K. (2002, November). *Back to the garden: What kindergarten once was and should be again.* Paper presented at the annual conference of the National Association for the Education of Young Children, History Seminar, New York City, NY.

Berger, E. H. (2004). *Parents as partners in education: Families and schools working together* (6th ed.). Upper Saddle River, NJ: Merrill/Prentice Hall.

Berrol, S. C. (1995). *Growing up American: Immigrant children in America then and now.* New York: Twayne Publishers.

Bhavnagri, N. and Korlikowski, S. (1999). *Home-community visits during the era of reform: 1870-1920.* Paper presented at the annual conference of the National Association for the Education of Young Children, History Seminar, New Orleans, LA.

Bhavnagri, N. P., & Krolikowski, S. (2000). Home-community visits during an era of reform (1870-1920). *Early Childhood Research & Practice 2*(1). Retrieved December 2003 from http://ecrp.uiuc.edu/v2n1/bhavnagri.html

Bhavnagri, N. P., Krolikowski, S., & Vaswani, T. G. (2000). A historical case study on interagency collaboration for culturally diverse immigrant children and families. *Proceedings of the Lilian Katz Symposium, Issues in Early Childhood Education: Curriculum, Teacher Education and Dissemination of Information.* Retrieved December 2003 from http://ecap.crc.uiuc.edu/pubs/katzsym/bhavnagri.html

Bhavnagri, N., Korlikowski, S. and Vaswani, T. (2001). *Interagency collaboration for immigrant children and families: A case study of the International Institute of Metropolitan Detroit.* Paper presented at the annual conference of the National Association for the Education of Young Children, History Seminar, Anaheim, CA.

Boyd, S., & Anderson, C. J. (2002, November). *Using oral histories of NAEYC past presidents to gather our history.* Paper presented at the annual meeting of the National Association for the Education of Young Children, New York.

Brosterman, N. (1997). *Inventing kindergarten.* New York: Harry N. Abrams.

Brown, L. (1990). *Association for Childhood Education International (ACEI) historical manuscripts and archives at the University of Maryland-College Park.* Paper presented at the annual conference of the National Association for the Education of Young Children, History Seminar, Washington, DC.

Browning, D. S., & Rodriguez, G. C. (2002). *Reweaving the social tapestry: Toward a public philosophy and policy for families.* An American Assembly book. New York: W. W. Norton & Company.

Bowman, B. T., & Stott, F. M. (1994). Understanding development in a cultural context: The challenge for teachers. In B. L. Mallory & R. S. New (Eds.), *Diversity & developmentally appropriate practices: Challenges for early childhood education* (pp. 119-133). New York: Teachers College Press.

Cannella, G. S. (1996, November). *Early childhood education as a gendered profession.* Paper presented at the annual conference of the National Association for the Education of Young Children, History Seminar, Dallas, TX.

Cantor, P. (1999, November). *Parents and early childhood programs: A historical review.* Paper presented at the annual conference of the National Association for the Education of Young Children, History Seminar, New Orleans, LA.

Cantor, P. (2001, November). *"The Child is Father of the Man": Romanticism and early childhood education.* Paper presented at the annual conference of the National Association for the Education of Young Children, History Seminar, Anaheim, CA.

Carlson, H. (1990). *Change and continuity in child care provision for pauper and working class families in Great Britain-1800, 1900 and 1990.* Paper presented at the annual conference of the National Association for the Education of Young Children, History Seminar, Washington, DC.

Carlson, H. (1992). *Children in Settlement Houses and Orphanages, 1880-1920.* Paper presented at the annual conference of the National Association for the Education of Young Children, History Seminar, New Orleans, LA.

Castle, K. and Lane, M. (2002). *A comparison of Froebel and Piaget's ideas and their impact on early childhood practices today and in the future.* Paper presented at the annual conference of the National Association for the Education of Young Children, History Seminar, New York City, NY.

Chartok, R. K. (Ed.). (2000). *Educational foundations: An anthology.* Upper Saddle River, NJ: Merrill/Prentice Hall.

Clement, P. F. (1997). *Growing pains: Children in the industrial age, 1850-1890.* New York: Twayne Publishers.

Cline, M. B. (1992, November). *Tugboats, apple butter and hammers: Wonderful curricula from America's past.* Paper presented at the annual conference of the National Association for the Education of Young Children, History Seminar, New Orleans, LA.

Comer, J. P. (1989). Racism and the education of young children. *Teachers College Record 90*(3), 352–361. Retrieved December 2003 from http://www.tcrecord.org/Content.asp?ContentII)=478.

Comer, J. P. (2001, April 23). Schools that develop children. *The American Prospect 12*(7). Retrieved December 2003 from http://www.prospect.org/print-friendly/print/V12/7/comer-j.html.

Copeland, M. L. (1986, November). *Saving our past through oral history.* Paper presented at the annual meeting of the National Association for the Education of Young Children, Washington, DC.

Copeland, M. (1986). *Saving our past through oral history.* Paper presented at the annual conference of the National Association for the Education of Young Children, History Seminar, Washington, DC.

Courtney, E. (with narration coauthored by Maisah Williams Foote). (2002, November). *African-American early childhood history through music.* Presentation at the annual conference of the National Association for the Education of Young Children, History Seminar, New York City.

Cuffaro, H. (1987, November). *The role of blocks in the early childhood curriculum from the Froebelian kindergarten to the present.* Paper presented at the annual conference of the National Association for the Education of Young Children, History Seminar, Chicago, IL.

Cuffaro, H. K. (1995). *Experimenting with the world: John Dewey and the early childhood classroom.* New York: Teachers College Press.

Cuffaro, H. Nager, N. & Shapiro, E. K. (2000). The developmental-interaction approach at Bank Street College of Education. In J. L. Roopnarine & J. E. Johnson (Eds.), *Approaches to early childhood education* 3rd ed., (pp. 263–276). Upper Saddle River, NJ: Merrill/Prentice Hall.

de Gaetano, Y., Williams, L. R., & Volk, D. (1998). *Kaleidoscope: A multicultural approach for the primary school classroom.* Upper Saddle River, NJ: Merrill/Prentice Hall.

de Melendez, W. R., & Ostertag, V. (1997). *Teaching young children in multicultural classrooms: Issues, concepts and strategies.* Albany, NY: Delmar.

deMause, L. (1988, Fall). On Writing Childhood History. *Journal of Psychohistory 16*(2). Retrieved December 2003 from http://www.psychohistory.com/childhood/writech1.htm.

Derman-Sparks, L. (1989). *Anti-bias curriculum: Tools for empowering young children.* Washington, DC: National Association for the Education of Young Children.

Diener, C. S. (1990, November). *Stages of childhood and family life as depicted in art.* Paper presented at the annual conference of the National Association for the Education of Young Children, History Seminar, Washington, DC.

DuCharme, C. (1992). *Margaret McMillan and Maria Montessori.* Paper presented at the annual conference of the National Association for the Education of Young Children, History Seminar, New Orleans, LA.

DuCharme, C. (1993, November). *Historical roots of the Project Approach, 1850–1930.* Paper presented at the annual conference of the National Association for the Education of Young Children, History Seminar, Anaheim, CA.

DuCharme, C. (1994). *A review of early kindergarten publications in the U.S., 1850–1930.* Paper presented at the annual conference of the National Association for the Education of Young Children, History Seminar, Atlanta, GA.

DuCharme, C. (1995, November). *The concept of the child: 1890–1940.* Paper presented at the annual conference of the National Association for the Education of Young Children, History Seminar, Washington, DC.

DuCharme, C. (1997). *The Wheelock School: 1888–1938.* Paper presented at the annual conference of the National Association

for the Education of Young Children, History Seminar, Anaheim, CA.

DuCharme, C. (1998). *The Silver Street Kindergarten and the California Kindergarten Training School.* Paper presented at the annual conference of the National Association for the Education of Young Children, History Seminar, Toronto, Ontario, Canada.

DuCharme, C. (1999). *Angels of Tar Flat: Public kindergarten and teacher training in San Francisco, 1870–1906.* Paper presented at the annual conference of the National Association for the Education of Young Children, History Seminar, New Orleans, LA.

DuCharme, C. (2001). *Early kindergarten training schools, 1880–1920: Reclaiming the ideal in teacher education.* Paper presented at the annual conference of the National Association for the Education of Young Children, History Seminar, Anaheim, CA.

Eastman, W. (1996). *Early childhood education in Canada.* Paper presented at the annual conference of the National Association for the Education of Young Children, History Seminar, Dallas, TX.

Eisenmann, L. (Ed.). (1998). *Historical Dictionary of Women's Education in the United States.* Westport, CT: Greenwood Press.

Elkind, D. (1986). *Education of the young child - past, present and future 1986.* Keynote presented at the annual conference of the National Association for the Education of Young Children, History Seminar, Washington, DC.

Falk, J. M. (1994). *Clara Conron: Kansas pioneer teacher.* Paper presented at the annual conference of the National Association for the Education of Young Children, History Seminar, Atlanta, GA.

Falk, J. M. (1992). *105 Years of service to children: The Memorial Day Nursery of Paterson, NJ.* Paper presented at the annual conference of the National Association for the Education of Young Children, History Seminar, New Orleans, LA.

Falk, J. L. M. (1995). *Kindergarten in Kansas: A view from the beginning.* Paper presented at the annual conference of the National Association for the Education of Young Children, History Seminar, Washington, DC.

Finkelstein, B. (2000). A crucible of contradictions: Historical roots of violence against children in the United States. *History of Education Quarterly. 40*(1), 1–21.

Finkelstein, B. (Ed.). (1979). *Regulated children/Liberated children: Education in psychohistorical perspective.* New York: Psychohistory Press.

Fenimore, B. (1999). *Historical foundations of deficit-based descriptions of young children: From "Cultural Deficiency" to "At Risk".* Paper presented at the annual conference of the National Association for the Education of Young Children, History Seminar, New Orleans, LA.

Feussner, J. (1989). *The observations of Anna Freud.* Paper presented at the annual conference of the National Association for the Education of Young Children, History Seminar, Atlanta, GA.

Firestone, C., Dworken, A. and Frew, M. (1989). *Detroit captures its history of early childhood education.* Paper presented at the annual conference of the National Association for the Education of Young Children, History Seminar, Atlanta, GA.

Fisch, S. M., & Truglio, R. T. (Eds.). (2000). *"G" is for "growing": Thirty years of research on children and Sesame Street.* Mahwah, NJ: Lawrence Erlbaum Associates, Inc.

Fowlkes, M. A. (1987). *Celebrating 100 years of kindergartens in Kentucky.* Paper presented at the annual conference of the National Association for the Education of Young Children, History Seminar, Chicago, IL.

Fowlkes, M. A. (1992, October). *Patty Smith Hill: Pivotal figure in childhood education.* Paper presented at the anniversary meeting of the Association for Childhood Education International: One Hundred Years of Kindergarten, Saratoga Springs, New York.

Fowlkes, M. A. (1986, November). *Kentucky kindergartens: Voices from the past*. Paper presented at the Filson Club, Louisville, KY.

Fowlkes, M. A. (1987, November). *Patty Smith Hill of Louisville: Her role in the Americanization of the kindergarten*. Paper presented at the annual meeting of the National Association for the Education of Young Children, Chicago, IL.

Galen, H., Querec Beauchemin, S., Day, C., Lacey, C. & Smith, S. (2003, October). *The nursery school movement: Its relevance for today!* Workshop presented at the annual meeting of the New Jersey Association for the Education of Young Children, New Brunswick, NJ.

Goffin, S. G., & Wilson, C. S. (2001). *Curriculum models and early childhood education: Appraising the relationship* (2nd ed.). Upper Saddle River, NJ: Merrill/Prentice Hall.

Gordon, J. (2001). *A modern history of childhood through art and literature: How they shaped our present*. Paper presented at the annual conference of the National Association for the Education of Young Children, History Seminar, Anaheim, CA.

Grant, J. (1994). Caught between common sense and science: The Cornell child study clubs, 1925–45. *History of Education Quarterly, 34*(4), 433–452.

Grant, J. (1998). *Raising baby by the book: The education of American mothers*. New Haven, CT: Yale University Press.

Greenberg, P. (1969, 1990). *The devil has slippery shoes: A biased biography of the Child Development Group of Mississippi (CDGM): A story of maximum feasible poor parent participation*. [New intro. Sheldon White.] Washington, DC: Youth Policy Institute.

Greenberg, P. (2000). What wisdom should we take with us as we enter the new century? An interview with Millie Almy. *Young Children 55*(1), 6–10.

Grieshaber, S., & Cannella, G. S. (Eds.). (2001). *Embracing identities in early childhood education: Diversity and possibilities*. New York: Teachers College Press.

Griffin, B., Jephson, L., & Van Lue, E. (1997, November). *Bringing the toys of the past into the present by linking the theory of multiple intelligences in the classroom for children from 3–5 years old*. Paper presented at the annual conference of the National Association for the Education of Young Children, History Seminar, Anaheim, CA.

Grinberg, J. (2002). "I had never been exposed to teaching like that": Progressive teacher education at Bank Street during the 1930s. *Teachers College Record 104*(7), 1422–1460. Retrieved December 2003, from http://www.tcrecord.org/ExecSummary.asp?ContentII)=10976.

Grossman, S. and Williston, J. (2002). *A look at English Village Schools in the past: The legacy of Miss Reed*. Paper presented at the annual conference of the National Association for the Education of Young Children, History Seminar, New York City, NY.

Grossman, S. and Williston, J. (2003). *Scattered families: English children evacuated during WWII*. Paper presented at the annual conference of the National Association for the Education of Young Children, History Seminar, Chicago, IL.

Grubb, C. A. (2003). *The lifework of D. W. Hewes: A phenomenological study of pedagogy*. Unpublished doctoral dissertation, The University of Alabama at Birmingham.

Gay, G. (2000). *Culturally responsive teaching: Theory, research, & practice*. New York: Teachers College Press.

Hauser, M. (2002). Caroline Pratt and the City and Country School. In A. R. Sadovnik & S. F. Semel (Eds.), *Founding mothers and others: Women educational leaders during the Progressive era* (pp. 61–76). New York: Palgrave.

Hauser, M., et al. (2001, April). *A Passion Play: Voices from the Early Kindergarten in Teacher Identities: Voices from the Nineteenth and Twentieth Centuries*. Annual Conference of the American Educational Research Association, Division F (History and Historiography), Seattle, WA.

Hawes, J. M. (1997). *Children between the wars: American childhood, 1902–1940*. New York: Twayne Publishers.

Henig, C. (1979). The Emergency Nursery Schools and the Wartime Child Care Centers 1933–1946. In J. L. Hymes, Jr. (Ed.), *Early childhood education living history interviews* (Vol. 3, pp. 4–27). Carmel, CA: Hacienda Press.

Hewes, D. W. (1973). *Where have we been, where are we going?* Paper presented at the annual conference of the National Association for the Education of Young Children, History Seminar, Seattle, WA.

Hewes, D. (1976). *Two centuries of American childhood*. Paper presented at the annual conference of the National Association for the Education of Young Children, History, Anaheim, CA.

Hewes, D. W. (1991). *Discipline in the Victorian-era kindergarten*. Paper presented at the annual conference of the National Association for the Education of Young Children, History Seminar, Denver, CO.

Hewes, D. (1981). *Froebel, Dewey and Piaget*. Paper presented at the annual conference of the National Association for the Education of Young Children, History Seminar, Detroit, MI.

Hewes, D. (1982). *Doing history as a teaching technique*. Paper presented at the annual conference of the National Association for the Education of Young Children, History Seminar, Washington, DC.

Hewes, D. (1984). *Will the real Montessori please stand up?*. Paper presented at the annual conference of the National Association for the Education of Young Children, History Seminar, Los Angeles, CA.

Hewes, D. W. (1985). *Historical issues*. Paper presented at the annual conference of the National Association for the Education of Young Children, History Seminar, New Orleans, LA.

Hewes, D. W. (1987). *Young children in public schools: Lessons from the 1890s*. Paper presented at the annual conference of the National Association for the Education of Young Children, History Seminar, Chicago, IL.

Hewes, D. (1988). *Nisei Nursery: Preschool at Manzanar Relocation Camp, 1942–1945*. Paper presented at the annual conference of the National Association for the Education of Young Children, History Seminar, Anaheim, CA.

Hewes, D. W. (1989). *Public funds vs. private charity: America's puritan heritage*. Paper presented at the annual conference of the National Association for the Education of Young Children, History Seminar, Atlanta, GA.

Hewes, D. W. (1990). *Early childhood commercial exhibit controversies, 1890 to 1990*. Paper presented at the annual conference of the National Association for the Education of Young Children, History Seminar, Washington, DC.

Hewes, D. (1992). *Pestalozzi-Foster father of early childhood education*. Paper presented at the annual conference of the National Association for the Education of Young Children, History Seminar, New Orleans, LA.

Hewes, D. W. (1993). *Children in Utopia: Theosophists at Point Loma, 1896–1942*. Paper presented at the annual conference of the National Association for the Education of Young Children, History Seminar, Anaheim, CA.

Hewes, D. (1994, November). *Do parent co-op preschools float on Kondratieff's economic waves?* Paper presented at the annual conference of the National Association for the Education of Young Children, History Seminar, Atlanta, GA.

Hewes, D. (1995). *The changing role of fathers in parent co-op schools*. Paper presented at the annual conference of the National Association for the Education of Young Children, History Seminar, Washington, DC.

Hewes. D. W. (1995). Sisterhood and sentimentality-America's earliest preschool centers. *Child Care Information Exchange. 106*, 24-29.

Hewes, D. W. (1996, November). *A genealogy of early childhood associations, 1872-1972*. Paper presented at the annual conference of the National Association for the Education of Young Children, History Seminar, Dallas, TX.

Hewes, D. W. (1997). *Fallacies, phantasies, and egregious prevarications in early childhood education history*. Paper presented at the annual conference of the National Association for the Education of Young Children, History Seminar, Anaheim, CA.

Hewes, D. W. (1998). *"It's the camaraderie": A history of parent cooperative preschools*. Davis: Center for Cooperatives, University of California.

Hewes, D. W. (1998). *Toronto's first United States-Canadian early childhood conference*. Paper presented at the annual conference of the National Association for the Education of Young Children, History Seminar, Toronto, Ontario, Canada.

Hewes, D. W. (2000). *A visual retrospective of early childhood education over the past millennium*. Paper presented at the annual conference of the National Association for the Education of Young Children, History Seminar, Atlanta, GA.

Hewes, D. W. (2000). Looking back: How the role of director has been understood, studied, and utilized in ECE programs, policy, and practice. In M. L. Culkin (Ed.), *Managing quality in young children's programs: The leader's role* (pp. 23-39). New York: Teachers College Press.

Hewes, D. (2001). *The egalitarian marriages of six Froebelian leaders in late 19th-century America*. Paper presented at the annual conference of the National Association for the Education of Young Children, History Seminar, Anaheim, CA.

Hewes, D. W. (2001). *W. N. Hailmann: Defender of Froebel*. Grand Rapids, MI: The Froebel Foundation.

Hewes, D. W. (2003, September 15). Inventing grownups. Letter to the editor. *The New Yorker*, 11.

Hewes, D. W., & Ranck, E. R. (2003, January). *Historical chronology of the NAEYC history seminar*. E-mail WORD document sent to Hinitz.

Hewes, D. and Hudson, D. (1986). *Historical archives: How to establish, find, use and maintain them*. Paper presented at the annual conference of the National Association for the Education of Young Children, History Seminar, Washington, DC.

Hildebrand, V., Phenice, L. A., Gray, M., & Hines, R. P. (2000). *Knowing and serving diverse families*. (2nd ed.). Upper Saddle River, NJ: Merrill/Prentice Hall.

Hinitz, B. F. (1977). *The development of creative movement within early childhood education, 1920 to 1970*. Unpublished Ed.D. dissertation. Temple University, Philadelphia.

Hinitz, B. (1983). *Selected pioneers of early childhood education: Their relevance for today*. Paper presented at the annual conference of the National Association for the Education of Young Children, History Seminar, Atlanta, GA.

Hinitz, B. (1985). *Historical research and application in teaching early childhood education*. Paper presented at the annual conference of the National Association for the Education of Young Children, History Seminar, New Orleans, LA.

Hinitz, B. (1990, November). *Teaching historical data to students of early childhood education—Sample module and instructional materials*. Paper presented at the annual conference of the National Association for the Education of Young Children, History Seminar, Washington, DC.

Hinitz, B., & Lascarides, V. C. (1991). *Teaching historical knowledge to students of early childhood education*. Paper presented at the annual conference of the National Association for the Education of Young Children, History Seminar, Denver, CO.

Hinitz, B. (1993, November). *Teaching early childhood education history: Special populations/children with special needs*. Paper presented at the annual conference of the National Association for the Education of Young Children, History Seminar, Anaheim, CA.

Hinitz, B. (1996, November). *Short history of gender issues in ECE and teacher education*. Paper presented at the annual conference of the National Association for the Education of Young Children, History Seminar, Dallas, TX.

Hinitz, B. (1997). *Sharing early education history through media and technology: How do we communicate our past?*. Paper presented at the annual conference of the National Association for the Education of Young Children, History Seminar, Anaheim, CA.

Hinitz, B. (1998). *Sharing early childhood history through media and technology: Helpful hints from the field*. Paper presented at the annual conference of the National Association for the Education of Young Children, History Seminar, Toronto, Ontario, Canada.

Hinitz, B. F. (1998a). Credentialing early childhood paraprofessionals in the United States: The Child Development Associate and other frameworks. *International Journal of Early Years Education. 6*(1), 87-103.

Hinitz, B. F. (1998b). Early childhood education managers. Early childhood teacher education. In L. Eisenmann, L. (Ed.), *Historical dictionary of women's education in the United States* (pp. 139-141, & 141-144). Westport, CT: Greenwood Press.

Hinitz, B. (1999). *Sharing early education history through media and technology: Helpful hints from the field 2*. Paper presented at the annual conference of the National Association for the Education of Young Children, History Seminar, New Orleans, LA.

Hinitz, B. (2000). *Margaret Naumburg and Florence Cane: Sisters in early childhood creative arts*. Paper presented at the annual conference of the National Association for the Education of Young Children, History Seminar, Atlanta, GA.

Hinitz, B. (2001). *Margaret Naumberg and a large urban Board of Education*. Paper presented at the annual conference of the National Association for the Education of Young Children, History Seminar, Anaheim, CA.

Hinitz, B. F. (2001, October 5). *One hundred years later—What's relevant? A letter from Margaret Naumburg*. 2001 Reconceptualizing Early Childhood Education: Research, Theory and Practice Ten Years Later: What's Relevant? (National Conference). Teachers College, Columbia University, New York.

Hinitz, B. (2002). *New York City nursery schools of the early 1900s: Cutting-edge yesterday, relevant today*. Paper presented at the annual conference of the National Association for the Education of Young Children, History Seminar, New York City, NY.

Hinitz, B. (2002). Margaret Naumburg and the Walden School. In A. R. Sadovnik & S. F. Semel (Eds.), *Founding mothers and others: Women educational leaders during the Progressive era* (pp. 37-59). New York: Palgrave.

Hinitz, B. F. (2003, April 22). *Leadership for the new age: The case of Margaret Naumburg* on panel Teacher Leadership: Exploring Dimensions of Teacher Professional Development and Practice for School Renewal. Annual Conference of the American Educational Research Association, Chicago, IL.

Hinitz, B. (2003). *The "aha" experience: How archival research informs current practice*. Paper presented at the annual conference of the National Association for the Education of Young Children, History Seminar, Chicago, IL.

Hinitz, B. F. (2004). Margaret Naumburg. In S. Ware. (Ed.), *Notable American Women* (Vol. 5, pp. 462-464). Cambridge, MA: Harvard University Press.

Horwich, F. R. (1979). Ding Dong School. In J. L. Hymes, Jr. *Early childhood education: Living history interviews* (Vol. 3). (pp. 56–72). Carmel, CA: Hacienda Press.

Hymes, J. L., Jr. (Ed.). (1978–1979). *Early childhood education: Living history interviews* (Vols. 1–3). Carmel, CA: Hacienda Press.

Hymes, J. L., Jr. (1991). *Early childhood education twenty years in review: A look at 1971–1990.* Washington, DC: National Association for the Education of Young Children.

Illick, J. E. (2002). *American Childhoods.* Philadelphia: University of Pennsylvania Press.

International Kindergarten Union (IKU). (1913). *The Kindergarten: Reports of the Committee of Nineteen on the Theory and Practice of the Kindergarten.* (Lucy Wheelock, Ed.). Boston, MA: Houghton Mifflin Company.

Jensen, M. A., & Goffin, S. G. (Eds.). (1993). *Visions of entitlement: The care and education of America's children.* Albany: State University of New York Press.

Kaye, C. (2001). *Young children in the Middle Kingdom: A 50-year historical perspective of early education in the People's Republic of China.* Paper presented at the annual conference of the National Association for the Education of Young Children, History Seminar, Anaheim, CA.

Kendall, F. E. (1996). *Diversity in the classroom: New approaches to the education of young children* (2nd ed.). New York: Teachers College Press.

Kennedy, D. (2000). The roots of child study: Philosophy, history and religion. *Teachers College Record 102*(3), 514–538. Retrieved December 2003, from http://www.tcrecord.org/Content.asp?ContentII=10532.

King, E. W., Chipman, M., & Cruz-Janzen, M. (1994). *Educating young children in a diverse society.* Boston: Allyn & Bacon.

Kliger, S. (1970). Fog over Sesame Street. *Teachers College Record 72*(1), 41–56. Retrieved December 2003, from http://www.tcrecord.org/Content.asp?ContentII=1652.

Kudela, E. (1999). *A history of child care advocates in action at the state level.* Paper presented at the annual conference of the National Association for the Education of Young Children, History Seminar, New Orleans, LA.

Kuschner, D. (1999). *A 'dangerously radical' idea: The historical origins of free play in kindergarten.* Paper presented at the annual conference of the National Association for the Education of Young Children, History Seminar, New Orleans, LA.

Lane, M., & Malone, J. (1990, November). *The goals of early childhood teacher preparation reflected in early textbooks.* Paper presented at the annual conference of the National Association for the Education of Young Children, History Seminar, Washington, DC.

Lane, M., & Malone, J. (1994). *Long-standing manufacturers of commercial early childhood materials and their development.* Paper presented at the annual conference of the National Association for the Education of Young Children, History Seminar, Atlanta, GA.

Lane, M., & Malone, J. (1995). *A look at Frobelian gifts and their contribution to today's early childhood programs.* Paper presented at the annual conference of the National Association for the Education of Young Children, History Seminar, Washington, DC.

Lane, M., & Malone, J. (1998). *Voices of children: 1947–1950.* Paper presented at the annual conference of the National Association for the Education of Young Children, History Seminar, Toronto, Ontario, Canada.

Lane, M., & Rhoten, L. (1999). *A comparison of ABC books, past and present.* Paper presented at the annual conference of the National Association for the Education of Young Children, History Seminar, New Orleans, LA.

Lascarides, V. C. (1993, November). *Teaching early childhood education history: Young Native American children.* Paper presented at the annual conference of the National Association for the Education of Young Children, History Seminar, Anaheim, CA.

Lascarides, V. C., & Hinitz, B. (1987, November). *Survey of historical knowledge: Preliminary report.* Paper presented at the annual conference of the National Association for the Education of Young Children, History Seminar, Chicago, IL.

Lascarides, V. C. & Hinitz, B. (1988, November). *Survey of historical knowledge: Final report.* Paper presented at the annual conference of the National Association for the Education of Young Children, History Seminar, Anaheim, CA.

Lascarides, V. C., & Hinitz, B. F. (1993). Survey of important historical and current figures in early childhood education. In K. Salimova & E. V. Johanningmeier (Eds.), *Why should we teach history of education?* (pp. 264–277). Moscow, Russia: The Library of the International Academy of Self-Improvement.

Lascarides, V. C., & Hinitz, B. F. (2000). *History of early childhood education.* New York: Falmer Press.

Lascarides, V. C. (2000). *Sarah Winnemucca and her school for Northern Piute children: 1844–1891.* Paper presented at the annual conference of the National Association for the Education of Young Children, History Seminar, Atlanta, GA.

Lascarides, V. C. (2001). *Child rearing in the Muslim Middle East: An overview of practices and influences that shape the Arab family,* Paper read by D. Hewes at the annual conference of the National Association for the Education of Young Children, History Seminar, Anaheim, CA.

Lee, M. W. (2001). Review of *History of Early Childhood Education* by V. Celia Lascarides and Blythe F. Hinitz. *Journal of Early Childhood Teacher Education, 22*(2), 121–122.

Leonard, A. M. (1999). *Final recorded reflections of Dr. James L. Hymes, Jr., November 1997.* Paper presented at the annual conference of the National Association for the Education of Young Children, History Seminar, New Orleans, LA.

Lesser, G. S. (1975). *Children and television: Lessons from Sesame Street.* New York: John Wiley.

Levin, R. A., & Hines, L. M. (2003). Educational television, Fred Rogers, and the history of education. *History of Education Quarterly 43*(2), 262–275.

Levy, J., & Johnson, A. (1990). *The first 50 years-Lady Gowrie Child Care Centres in Australia.* Paper presented at the annual conference of the National Association for the Education of Young Children, History Seminar, Washington, DC.

Macleod, D. I. (1998). *The age of the child: Children in America, 1890–1920.* New York: Twayne Publishers.

Malone, J., & Lane, M. (1992). *Arnold Gesell: The boy and the youth.* Paper presented at the annual conference of the National Association for the Education of Young Children, History Seminar, New Orleans, LA.

Malone, J., & Lane, M. (1993). *Arnold Gesell and early childhood education, 1919–1946.* Paper presented at the annual conference of the National Association for the Education of Young Children, History Seminar, Anaheim, CA.

Malone, J., & Lane, M. (1991). *Arnold Gesell: The man behind the norms.* Paper presented at the annual conference of the National Association for the Education of Young Children, History Seminar, Denver, CO.

Malone, J., Lane, M., & Rhoten, L. (1989). *Home-school relations in home economics programs.* Paper presented at the annual conference of the National Association for the Education of Young Children, History Seminar, Atlanta, GA.

Malone, J., & Lane, M. (1997). *One hundred years of childhood as depicted in the popular press*. Paper presented at the annual conference of the National Association for the Education of Young Children, History Seminar, Anaheim, CA.

Maloney, K. E. (1999). Charlotte Perkins Gilman: The origin of education is maternal. In C. Titone & K. E. Maloney (Eds.), *Women's philosophies of education: Thinking through our mothers* (pp. 97–129). Upper Saddle River, NJ: Merrill/Prentice Hall.

Mander, J. (1981). *Four arguments for the elimination of television*. New York: John Wiley.

May, C., & Conner, J. (1993). *Fact or fiction: Kirkpatrick's perceptions and influence on the Montessori Movement*. Paper presented at the annual conference of the National Association for the Education of Young Children, History Seminar, Anaheim, CA.

Maylan Dunn, M. (2002). *Making the outrageous seem ordinary: How Alice Temple helped save the kindergarten*. Paper presented at the annual conference of the National Association for the Education of Young Children, History Seminar, New York City, NY.

McConnell, J. L. (1997). *1954 Brown v. the Topeka Board of Education, reflections of a child: Linda Brown Thompson*. Paper presented at the annual conference of the National Association for the Education of Young Children, History Seminar, Anaheim, CA.

McConnell, J. L. (1998). *1954 Brown v. Topeka Board of Education*. Paper presented at the annual conference of the National Association for the Education of Young Children, History Seminar, Toronto, Ontario, Canada.

McConnell, J. L. (1999). *My reflections as a plaintiff in the Brown v. Topeka Board of Education Decision: Mrs. Vivian Scales*. Paper presented at the annual conference of the National Association for the Education of Young Children, History Seminar, New Orleans, LA.

McMath, J. S. (2001). *Minding the Past: 75 years of books: Events that have shaped NAEYC since its birth in 1926*. Paper presented at the annual conference of the National Association for the Education of Young Children, History Seminar, Anaheim, CA.

Meyer, J. (1999). *Marie Duclos Fretageot: Early childhood Pestalozzian educator of Philadelphia and New Harmony, 1821–1834*. Paper presented at the annual conference of the National Association for the Education of Young Children, History Seminar, New Orleans, LA.

Meyer, J., & Wasson, D. (1997). *The Utopian children of New Harmony: 1824 to 1827*. Paper presented at the annual conference of the National Association for the Education of Young Children, History Seminar, Anaheim, CA.

Meyer, J., & Wasson, D. (1998). *The efforts of Pestalozzian educators to 'teach children what is necessary for them to know'*. Paper presented at the annual conference of the National Association for the Education of Young Children, History Seminar, Toronto, Ontario, Canada.

Miller, K. M. (1989, November). *Before Young Children: NANE Bulletin/Journal*. Paper presented at the annual conference of the National Association for the Education of Young Children, History Seminar, Atlanta, GA.

Miller, K. M. (1986). *Do you remember radio? Edith Sunderlin: A pioneer in radio and NANE*. Paper presented at the annual conference of the National Association for the Education of Young Children, History Seminar, Washington, DC.

Miller, K. M. (1995). *Iowa State University Child Development Laboratories, 1924–1994*. Paper presented at the annual conference of the National Association for the Education of Young Children, History Seminar, Washington, DC.

Miller, K. M. (1999). *Lois Lenski and the writing of Corn Farm Boy*. Paper presented at the annual conference of the National Association for the Education of Young Children, History Seminar, New Orleans, LA.

Miller, K. M. (1997). *Lois Lenski and the writing of Prairie School*. Paper presented at the annual conference of the National Association for the Education of Young Children, History Seminar, Anaheim, CA.

Miller, K. M. (1980). *Write no early epitaph*. Paper presented at the annual conference of the National Association for the Education of Young Children, History Seminar, San Francisco, CA.

Miller, S. H., Replogle, E., & Weiss, H. B. (1995). *Family support in early education and child care settings: Making the case for both principles and practices*. Cambridge, MA: Harvard Family Research Project. (ERIC Document Reproduction Service ED381293)

Moore, M. R. (2002). *Journey to Froebel's birthplace: The story of Friedrich Froebel, kindergarten's founder*. Paper presented at the annual conference of the National Association for the Education of Young Children, History Seminar, New York City, NY.

Morrison, G. S. (2004). *Early childhood education today*. (9th ed.). Upper Saddle River, NJ: Merrill/Prentice Hall.

Murray, G. S. (1998). *American children's literature and the construction of childhood*. New York: Twayne Publishers.

Morgan, G. (2003). Staff roles, education and compensation. In D. Cryer & R. M. Clifford (Eds.). *Early childhood education & care in the USA*. pp. 65–85. Baltimore, MD: Paul H. Brookes Publishing Co.

Nager, N., & Shapiro, E. K. (Eds.). (2000). *Revisiting a progressive pedagogy: The developmental interaction approach*. Albany: State University of New York Press.

Neugebauer, R. (1995). The movers and shapers of early childhood education. *Child Care Information Exchange 106*, 9–13.

Nourot, P. M (2000). Historical perspectives on early childhood education. In J. L. Roopnarine & J. E. Johnson (Eds.), *Approaches to early childhood education*. (3rd ed., pp. 3–37). Upper Saddle River, NJ: Merrill/Prentice Hall.

Oekerman, R. (2000, November). *What have we learned about child development in 2000 years?*. Paper presented at the annual conference of the National Association for the Education of Young Children, History Seminar, Atlanta, GA.

Office of Educational Research and Improvement (OERI). (1993). *Education Consumer Guide: The Comer School Development Program*. Washington, DC: U.S. Department of Education, OERI, Office of Research.

Osborn, D. K. (1991). *Early childhood education in historical perspective*. (3rd ed.). Athens, GA: Education Associates: A division of The Daye Press, Inc.

Paciorek, K. M., & Munro, J. H. (1999). *Sources: Notable selections in early childhood education* (2nd ed.). Guilford, CT: Dushkin/McGraw-Hill.

Peltzman, B. R. (1998). *Pioneers of early childhood education: A bio-bibliographical guide*. Westport, CT: Greenwood Press.

Pence, A. (1982, November). *A fall from grace: Public rejection of the Infant School movement, 1825–1840*. Paper presented at the annual conference of the National Association for the Education of Young Children, History Seminar, Washington, DC.

Pence, P. (1984, November). *All in the family: Toward a unifying history of day and residential child care services*. Paper presented at the annual conference of the National Association for the Education of Young Children, History Seminar, Los Angeles, CA.

Phillips, B. (2002, November). *Poem: A slave named History*. Presentation at the annual conference of the National Association for the Education of Young Children, History Seminar, New York City.

Pitts, N. D. (1999). Anna Julia Cooper: Not the boys less, but the girls more. In C. Titone & K. E. Maloney (Eds.), *Women's philosophies of education: Thinking through our mothers*. (pp. 73–96). Upper Saddle River, NJ: Merrill/Prentice Hall.

Povell, P. (1993). *Maria Montessori, A woman ahead of her time*. Paper presented at the annual conference of the National Association for the Education of Young Children, History Seminar, Anaheim, CA.

Povell, P. (1994). *Mary McLeod Bethune: Race relations leader-at-large*. Paper presented at the annual conference of the National Association for the Education of Young Children, History Seminar, Atlanta, GA.

Povell, P. (1995). *Nancy McCormick Rambusch and the Montessori revival in America*. Paper presented at the annual conference of the National Association for the Education of Young Children, History Seminar, Washington, DC.

Povell, P. (1996, November). *Montessori and Mussolini: A question of gender?* Paper presented at the annual conference of the National Association for the Education of Young Children, History Seminar, Dallas, TX.

Povell, P. (1997). *Standing v. Kramer: A look at the myths and misinterpretations about Maria Montessori*. Paper presented at the annual conference of the National Association for the Education of Young Children, History Seminar, Anaheim, CA.

Povell, P. (1999, November). *Montessori is here to stay: The history of an early childhood organization*. Paper presented at the annual conference of the National Association for the Education of Young Children, History Seminar, New Orleans, LA.

Powell, D. R. (2000). The Head Start Program. In J. I. Roopnarine & J. E. Johnson (Eds.) *Approaches to early childhood education* (3rd ed., pp. 62-82).

Prochner, L. (1996). *Composing a history: The representation of the history of early childhood education in textbooks*. Paper presented at the annual conference of the National Association for the Education of Young Children, History Seminar, Dallas, TX.

Prochner, L. (1998). *A history of early childhood care and education in Canada*. Paper presented at the annual conference of the National Association for the Education of Young Children, History Seminar, Toronto, Ontario, Canada.

Prochner, L. (2000, November). *ECCE in Australia, Canada and New Zealand: A comparative historical study*. Paper presented at the annual conference of the National Association for the Education of Young Children, History Seminar, Atlanta, GA.

Prochner, L. (2001). *A history of kindergarten in Australia, Canada, and New Zealand from 1889-1937*. Paper presented at the annual conference of the National Association for the Education of Young Children, History Seminar, Anaheim, CA.

Ramsey, P. G. (1987). *Teaching and learning in a diverse world: Multicultural education for young children*. New York: Teachers College Press.

Ranck, E. R. (1987). *From Canon Law to Congress: 800 Years of childhood legislation*. Paper presented at the annual conference of the National Association for the Education of Young Children, History Seminar, Chicago, IL.

Ranck, E. R. (1989). *Five fortuitous events in the development of early childhood education*. Paper presented at the annual conference of the National Association for the Education of Young Children, History Seminar, Atlanta, GA.

Ranck, E. R. (1990). *There is no such thing as a free lunch: Following up on fortuitous events*. Paper presented at the annual conference of the National Association for the Education of Young Children, History Seminar, Washington, DC.

Ranck, E. R. (1991, November). *U.S. early childhood policies in the 1950s: A surprising Eisenhower legacy*. Paper presented at the annual conference of the National Association for the Education of Young Children, History Seminar, Denver, CO.

Ranck, E. R. (1992, November). *The Eisenhower legacy for early childhood: The vital links between the Lanham Act and Head Start.* Paper presented at the annual conference of the National Association for the Education of Young Children, History Seminar, New Orleans, LA.

Ranck, E. R. (1993). *We are where we are: 50 years of care and education advocacy*. Paper presented at the annual conference of the National Association for the Education of Young Children, History Seminar, Anaheim, CA.

Ranck, E. R. (1995). Do/will you remember? Taking a child care program's past into the future. *Child Care Information Exchange, 106*, 91-95.

Ranck, E. R. (1995). *Of origins and odometers: The search for early childhood historical paradigms*. Paper presented at the annual conference of the National Association for the Education of Young Children, History Seminar, Washington, DC.

Ranck, E. R. (1996, November). *"When I was a little girl"—Selected memories of leaders*. Paper presented at the annual conference of the National Association for the Education of Young Children, History Seminar, Dallas, TX.

Ranck, E. R. (1997). *Early childhoods: Comparing memories of past and current leaders and pioneers in early care and education*. Paper presented at the annual conference of the National Association for the Education of Young Children, History Seminar, Anaheim, CA.

Ranck, E. R. (1998, November). *Ten years in the life: Writing a history of a national early childhood organization*. Paper presented at the annual conference of the National Association for the Education of Young Children, Toronto, Ontario, Canada.

Ranck, E. R. (1999, November). *"Who were we?" How national early care and education organizations remember their past*. Paper presented at the annual conference of the National Association for the Education of Young Children, History Seminar, New Orleans, LA.

Ranck, E. R. (2000). *Why we care about the past: How early childhood professionals make meaning out of long-ago events*. Paper presented at the annual conference of the National Association for the Education of Young Children, History Seminar, Atlanta, GA.

Ranck, E. R. (2001). *Hail to the Chief and children: How Presidential inaugural addresses have viewed child and family issues, 1789-2001*. Paper presented at the annual conference of the National Association for the Education of Young Children, History Seminar, Anaheim, CA.

Ranck, E. R. (2002). *Connections between First Ladies and American children: A how-to look at growing a nation*. Paper presented at the annual conference of the National Association for the Education of Young Children, History Seminar, New York City, NY.

Ranck, E. R. (2003). *American First Ladies that put children first*. Paper presented at the annual conference of the National Association for the Education of Young Children, History Seminar, Chicago, IL.

Reese, W. J. (2001). The origins of progressive education. *History of Education Quarterly. 41*(1), 1-24.

Reinier, J. S. (1996). *From virtue to character: American childhood, 1775-1850*. New York: Twayne Publishers.

Roderick, T. (2002). *The East Harlem Block Schools and the campaign for community-controlled day care*. Paper presented at the annual conference of the National Association for the Education of Young Children, History Seminar, New York City, NY.

Rohrback, M., & Raslowsky, K. (2002, November). *Big books on history: A student-generated method of presenting the history of early childhood education*. Paper presented at the annual conference of the National Association for the Education of Young Children, History Seminar, New York City.

Roopnarine, J. I., & Johnson, J. E. Eds) (2005). *Approaches to early childhood education* (4th ed). Upper Saddle River, NJ: Pearson/Merrill.

Rose, E. (1999). *A mother's job: The history of day care, 1890–1960.* New York: Oxford University Press.

Sapon-Shevin, M. (1999). *Because we can change the world: A practical guide to building cooperative, inclusive classroom communities.* Boston: Allyn and Bacon, Inc.

Schindler, P. (1991). *Tree house, stone soup and candle making.* Paper presented at the annual conference of the National Association for the Education of Young Children, History Seminar, Denver, CO.

Semel, S. F., & Sadovnik, A. R. (Eds.). (1999). *"Schools of tomorrow," schools of today: What happened to progressive education.* New York: Peter Lang.

Shahar, S. (1992). *Childhood in the Middle Ages.* Trans. C. Galai. London: Routledge.

Simpson, J. (2003a, June). *Early childhood education trailblazers of the 20th century.* PowerPoint presentation by author.

Simpson, J. (2003b, November). *Early childhood educators of the 20th century: Legendary men.* Paper presented at the annual conference of the National Association for the Education of Young Children, Chicago, IL.

Simpson, J. (2003c, November). *Early childhood educators of the 20th century: Those who have gone before us.* Poster presented at the annual meeting of the World Organization for Early Childhood Education, United States National Committee, Chicago, IL.

Simpson, W. J. (1981). *A biographical study of black educators in early childhood education.* Unpublished doctoral dissertation, Fielding Institute, Santa Barbara, CA.

Sinex, A., & Nelms, L. (1996, November). *"You'll never know where you're going if you don't know where you've been" (Emphasis on the Women's Movement).* Paper presented at the annual conference of the National Association for the Education of Young Children, History Seminar, Dallas, TX.

Snyder, A. (Ed.). (1972). *Dauntless women in childhood education 1856–1931.* Washington, DC: Association for Childhood Education International.

Smith, M. (1986). *NAEYC-yesterday and tomorrow.* Keynote presented at the annual conference of the National Association for the Education of Young Children, History Seminar, Washington, DC.

Smith, D. J. (1996). *Old dogs teach new tricks: Interdisciplinary collaboration.* Paper presented at the annual conference of the National Association for the Education of Young Children, History Seminar, Dallas, TX.

Spodek, B., & Saracho, O. N. (1998a). Research in early childhood education: A look to the future. *Yearbook in early childhood education: Issues in early childhood educational research* (Vol. 8, pp. 177–186). New York: Teachers College Press.

Spodek, B., Saracho, O. N., & Pellegrini, A. D. (Eds.). (1998b). *Yearbook in early childhood education: Issues in early childhood educational research.* (Vol. 8). New York: Teachers College Press.

Stolz, L. M. (1978). The Kaiser Child Service Centers. In J. L. Hymes, Jr. *Early childhood education living history interviews* (Vol. 2, pp. 27–56). Carmel, CA: Hacienda Press.

Stomfay-Stitz, A. M. (2001). Editor's Note. *Journal of Early Childhood Teacher Education, 22*(2), 122.

Stone, M. K. (2001). *The progressive legacy: Chicago's Francis W. Parker School (1901–2001).* New York: Peter Lang.

Swinarski, L. A., Breitborde, M., & Murphy, J. (2003). *Educating the global village: Including the child in the world.* (2nd ed.). Upper Saddle River, NJ: Merrill/Prentice Hall.

Willmott, K. E., de Menendez, W. R. & Taglauer, A. E. (2000). *Readiness is now a national and state priority, but hardly a new concept! An overview of readiness in three time periods within the last 115 years of U.S. history.* Paper presented at the annual conference of the National Association for the Education of Young Children, History Seminar, Atlanta, GA.

Wineberg, L. P. Juzenas, L. & Trent, K. (2000). *An oral history of a country school in Wisconsin: 1961–2000.* Paper presented at the annual conference of the National Association for the Education of Young Children, History Seminar, Atlanta, GA.

Wineberg, L., Ranck, E. R., O'Neill, A., and Hinitz, B. (2003). *USNC - OMEP leaders.* Paper presented at the annual conference of the National Association for the Education of Young Children, History Seminar, Chicago, IL.

Wolfe, J. (2000). *The voices of early childhood: Examining the teaching and contributions of Patty Smith Hill to the field of early childhood development and education.* Paper presented at the annual conference of the National Association for the Education of Young Children, History Seminar, Atlanta, GA.

Tamura, E. H. (2001, Spring). Asian Americans in the history of education: An historiographical essay. *History of Education Quarterly, 41*(1), 58–71.

Tanner, L. N. (1997). *Dewey's laboratory school: Lessons for today.* New York: Teachers College Press.

University of Pennsylvania Libraries. (n.d.). *A guide to the Department of Special Collections.* Philadelphia, PA: Author.

URLs for online access to historical information via the Internet Childhood in Urban America Project=http://academic.mu.edu/cuap/H-Childhood History of Childhood and Youth [Society for the History of Children & Youth & H-Net] = http://www.h-net.org/~child H-Education = http://www.h-net.org/~educ H-Net = http://www.h-net.msu.edu

Weikart, D. P., & Schweinhart, L. J. (2000). The High/Scope curriculum for early childhood care and education. In J. L. Roopnarine & J. E. Johnson (Eds.). *Approaches to early childhood education.* 3rd ed. Upper Saddle River, NJ: Merrill, an imprint of Prentice Hall, 277–293.

Weston, P. (1998). *Friedrich Froebel: His life, times & significance.* London: Roehampton Institute.

Wineberg, L. P., Juzenas, L., & Trent, K. (2000, November). *An oral history of a country school in Wisconsin.* Paper and video presented at the annual meeting of the National Association for the Education of Young Children, Atlanta, GA.

Wolfe, J. (2002). *Learning from the past: Historical voices in early childhood education* (Rev. 2nd ed.). Mayerthorpe, Alberta, Canada: Piney Branch Press.

Wortham, S. C. (2003). *Childhood 1892–2002* (2nd ed.). Washington, DC: Association for Childhood Education International.

Yale University. (2002) Beinecke Rare Book and Manuscript Library *Public Services guide.* This is a pamphlet from Beinecke Library at Yale.

Young, A. (1996, November). *Historical attitudes and issues that undermine the provision of quality child care.* Paper presented at the annual conference of the National Association for the Education of Young Children, History Seminar, Dallas, TX.

AUTHOR INDEX

A

Abbott-Shim, M., 376, 377, 381, 386, 424, 429, 430, 466
Aboud, F. E., 31, 284, 286, 288, 290, 291, 292
Adams, M., 14, 16, 17, 18
Alain, M., 33
Alloway, N., 518, 545
Almon, J., 582
Alqvist, F., 35, 39
Altenmuller, E., 253
Amsterdamer, P., 17
Anderson, A., 143
Anderson, J., 143
Andrews, R. K., 37
Angelillo, C., 14
Anning, A., 251
Ariel, S., 13
Arsenio, W., 64, 66, 67
Asarnow, J. R., 29
Asplund, M., 56
Asher, S. R., 24, 25, 31, 33, 37, 38, 39, 41
Astington, J., 18
Atkinson, L., 26
Aumiller, K., 33

B

Bagwell, C. L., 36, 39
Baradaren, L. P., 33
Barber, B. K., 27
Baroody, A. J., 188
Barrett-Pugh, C., 16
Barron, F., 123
Bates, J. A., 27
Bates, J. E., 27, 35, 36, 38, 44
Bateson, G., 12
Battistich, V., 58, 70
Baumrind, D., 26
Beitel, A., 26
Belsky, J., 43
Bengtsson, J., 56
Berger, P. L., 59
Berndt, T. J., 23, 24, 25, 36, 37, 39
Berk, L., 59
Bhavnagri, N., 26, 28, 39, 43, 576
Biemiller, A., 14, 15
Bierman, K. L., 33, 41
Birch, S. H., 30, 31, 39, 40, 44
Bijou, S. W., 3
Bissex, G., 17, 143
Bjorkqvist, K., 34, 35

Black, B., 25, 26, 35, 42
Blau, D. M., 427
Blum, L. A., 66
Blumer, H., 72
Bohlin, G., 30
Boivin, M., 25, 33
Bolin, T., 24
Boller, K., 29
Boney-McCoy, S., 37
Booth, C. L., 31
Booth, F., 56
Boran, S., 15
Borden, M. G., 38
Borja-Alvarez, T., 33
Bornstein, M. H., 27
Borwick, D., 38
Boulton, M. J., 37, 39
Bourchier, A., 11
Bowlby, J. 23, 26
Bowman, B. T., 347
Bradbard, M. R., 26
Bradley, R. H., 28, 41
Brady-Smith, C., 29
Braungart, J. M., 26
Bredekamp, S., 13, 16
Broberg, A., 29
Brody, G. H., 27, 30
Brooks, M. G., 27
Brooks-Gunn, J., 28, 29, 326, 335
Brown, E. G., 26, 40
Brown, J. R., 66, 73
Bruner, J., 18, 72
Bryant, B., 29
Buckley, S., 28
Buckner, J. C., 27
Buhrmester, D., 24
Buhs, E., 31, 36, 38, 40, 44
Bukovsky, L., 26
Bukowski, W. M., 24, 25, 37, 38
Bullock, J., 37
Burchinal M., 29
Burge, D., 26
Burgess, K. B., 40, 44
Burgy, L., 39
Burgess, K. B., 31, 35, 37, 38, 43
Burks, V. M., 26
Burns, M. 347
Byrne, B., 16

C

Cairns, B. D., 34, 35, 38, 43
Cairns, R. B., 34, 38, 45

Calkins, S. A., 38
Campbell, S. N., 29
Campos, J., 11
Carlton, M P., 86
Carson, J., 26
Case, R., 13, 15
Cassidy, J., 26
Chambers, M., 39
Chapman, M., 57
Charlesworth, R., 33
Chazan-Cohen, R., 29
Chen, X., 30, 557
Chien, H., 35
Cicchetti, D., 30
Cielinski, K. L., 26
Chittenden, G. F., 42
Cillessen, E., 31
Circourel, A., 73
Clark, C., 11
Clark, K. E., 26, 27
Clarke, S., 171
Cohen, E., 14
Cohen, R., 31
Coie, J. D., 25, 29, 31, 33, 34, 35, 37, 38
Cole, A. K., 26
Coleman, C. C., 25, 41
Colnerud, G., 58, 70, 77
Comber, B., 15, 153
Conger, R. D., 30
Connolly, K. J., 29
Constintine, J., 29
Cooper, D. H., 33
Copley, J. 189
Coplan, R. J., 31, 38
Copple, C., 13, 16
Coppotelli, H., 25, 34
Correa-Chavez, M., 14
Corsaro, W. A., 30, 32, 73
Costin, S. E., 36
Cotlin, L., 29
Cox, M., 225
Craig, W., 37
Crick, N. R., 33, 34, 35, 38, 39
Crnic, K. A., 27
Cross, W. E., 283
Cummings, J. S., 26
Cummings, M. E., 26
Curtner. M. E., 27

D

Dalton, J., 521
Damon, W., 55

595

SUBJECT INDEX